Writers' *& Artists'* YEARBOOK *2004*

Ninety-seventh Edition

A directory for writers, artists, playwrights, writers for film, radio and television, designers, illustrators and photographers

A & C Black · London

© 2004 A & C Black Publishers Ltd
37 Soho Square, London W1F 0BJ

The publishers make no representation, express or
implied, with regard to the accuracy of the
information contained in this book and cannot
accept any legal responsibility for any errors or
omissions that may take place.

A & C Black uses paper produced with elemental
chlorine-free pulp, harvested from managed
sustainable forests.

A CIP catalogue record for this book is available
from the British Library.

ISBN 0-7136-6659-5

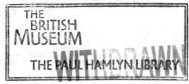
Printed and bound in Great Britain by
William Clowes, Beccles

Contents

Foreword

Eoin Colfer has written several bestselling children's novels, including the *Artemis Fowl* series. The books have been translated into 35 languages and have won awards including British Children's Book of the Year, WHSmith Children's Book of the Year, Bisto Merit Awards and the South African Book Club Book of the Year. The first *Artemis Fowl* film is currently in production due for cinema release in 2004.

I have in my time purchased several copies of the *Writers' & Artists' Yearbook*, yet there is only one copy on my bookshelf. This, I suspect, is a condition common to most authors. When other writers visit my bat-cave – sorry, office – they don't bother asking for a signed first edition of my book, instead they make off with my *Yearbook* secreted up their jumpers. This inevitably happens shortly after I have completed the laborious task of attaching colour-coded paperclips to pages of interest. I know what you're thinking. Colour-coded paperclips. That explains a lot.

My obsession with the *Yearbook* began in the dark era of glitter eye shadow and ozone-puncturing hairdos known as the Eighties. I had recently finished college, and like all males in their twenties, knew all there was to know about the world. The population in general, I decided with humble altruism, deserved the benefit of my wisdom. And the best way to reach my prospective public was through literature.

So I wrote a book. Not content with that, I designed the cover. Multi-tasking even before the phrase was coined. This book qualified as a book because it had many words and quite a few pages. Secure in my sublime self-delusion, I got hold of an industrial stapler, bound the whole lot together and crammed a copy into the nearest postbox. One copy would be sufficient, to the country's foremost publishers. I settled back on the family chaise longue and waited for the publisher's helicopter to land in the garden.

Seasons passed and the helicopter never materialised. Not so much as a postcard from the honoured house. Sighing mightily I widened my net, sending copies of my book to several other publishers. I got some replies this time. Would that I had not. Most were civil enough. We regret to inform you, etc … the opening phrase that haunts every writer's dreams. Still, at least they were polite. But a few less generic replies dropped onto my doormat. There was one note in which the handwriting deteriorated in spots, as the editor suffered from sporadic fits of laughter. A pattern was beginning to emerge. Could it be possible that my manuscript was flawed? Was there a chance that my presentation was not all that it could be? Did genius have to be packaged?

Help arrived in the form of an editor's response. "We regret to inform you …" it began. Nothing new there. I was becoming inured. But there was an addendum pencilled below the type. Get the *Writers' & Artists' Yearbook*. It's worth the investment.

Reluctant as any Irish man in his twenties is to take advice from anyone besides his mother, I decided to act on this particular recommendation. The

Yearbook paid for itself almost immediately. The mere act of purchasing the fat volume made me feel like a legitimate writer. I left the shop, making certain that my grip did not obscure the book title.

At home, I was amazed to discover that the *Yearbook* was not just a list of publishers. Every possible scrap of information needed by the upcoming or established writer was included (for more details buy the book. And if there are paperclips on this book, it is mine: please return it!) but what I needed to know was detailed under the heading 'Submitting material'. Next time, I vowed. Next time.

Next time turned out to be nearly a decade later. My self-esteem had recovered sufficiently to brave the sae trail once more. So I wrote an introductory letter and an interesting summary of the book, and included the first 50 pages – double-spaced.

It worked. Two weeks later I had a publisher. Now I can't put the entire thing down to the *Yearbook*, but it certainly played its part. In public of course, I take all the credit myself. I am a writer after all. But packaging and presentation in my opinion made the difference between desktop and trash, to use a computer analogy.

A few years later my brothers advised me that I needed an agent, as they were running short on beer money. Once again the *Yearbook* was consulted. Not only were the agents listed but they were categorised. These *Yearbook* people were cut from the same cloth as myself. I could almost imagine their desks stacked with coloured paperclips.

My research paid off, and within weeks I was sitting in a top-class hotel treating my new agent to a flute of champagne. Although she insists it was a glass of Guinness in a Dublin pub and she paid.

Since then, I haven't looked back. Things are going well enough for me to be invited to write this Foreword. If you are published and reading this book, hide it away and beware those with baggy jumpers. If you are as yet unpublished, then keep the faith and make sure that all around you can see the title.

Eoin Colfer, April 2003

Newspapers and magazines

Submitting material

Of the titles included in the newspapers and magazines section of the *Yearbook*, almost all offer opportunities to the writer. Many publications do not appear in our lists because the market they offer for the freelance writer is either too small or too specialised, or both. We give here some guidelines to bear in mind when submitting material to a newspaper or magazine.

Before submitting material to any newspaper or magazine it is advisable first to contact the relevant editor. The listings beginning on page 3 give the names of editors for each section of the national newspapers while a quick telephone call or email to a magazine will establish the name of the relevant commissioning editor.

Magazine editors frequently complain to us about the unsuitability of many submissions. When submitting by post writers are advised, in their own interests, to enclose postage for the return of unsuitable material.

Study the market

Before submitting articles or features, always study carefully the editorial requirements of a magazine, not only for the subjects dealt with but for the approach, treatment, style and length. These comments will be obvious to the practised writer but the beginner can be spared much disappointment by buying copies of magazines and studying the market in depth.

The importance of studying the market cannot be overemphasised. It is an editor's job to know what readers want, and to see that they get it. Thus, freelance contributions must be tailored to fit a specific market; subject, theme, treatment, length, etc, must meet the editor's requirements. This is discussed further in *Writing for newspapers* on page 110 and *Writing for magazines* on page 114. For additional information on markets, see the UK volume of *Willings Press Guide*, which is usually available at local reference libraries.

Most newspapers and many magazines these days expect copy to be sent by email. Editors who accept postal submissions expect them to be well presented: neatly typed, double spaced, with good margins, on A4 paper is the standard to aim at. If submitting articles on disk always verify with the editor that your system and theirs are compatible before sending. Most editors also require a hard copy (printout) in addition to the disk.

Illustrations

It is not advisable to send illustrations 'on spec'; check with the editor first. See *Digital imaging for writers* on page 548; listings of *Picture agencies and libraries* start on page 407. For a list of publications willing to pay for cartoons see page 693.

Payment

It has always been our aim to obtain and publish the rates of payment offered for contributions by newspapers and magazines. Many publications, however, are reluctant to state a standard rate, since the value of a contribution may be dependent not upon length but upon the standing of the writer or of the information given. Many other periodicals, in spite of efforts to extract more precise information from them, prefer to state 'by negotiation' or 'by arrangement'.

A number of magazines will accept and pay for letters to the editor, brief fillers and gossip paragraphs, as well as puzzles and quizzes. *Magazines by subject area* starting on page 677 provides a rough guide to these markets.

Overseas contributions

The lists of overseas newspapers and magazines in the *Yearbook* contain only a selection of those journals which offer a market for the freelance writer. For fuller listings, refer to *Willings Press Guide Volume 2 Overseas*. The overseas market for stories and articles is small and editors often prefer their fiction to have a local setting. Some editors require their contributors to be residents of that country.

Some overseas magazine titles have little space for freelance contributions but many of them will consider outstanding work. Potential contributors should check whether it is acceptable to send material by email. Proposals or finished articles mailed from the UK overseas (including the Republic of Ireland) should always be accompanied by return postage in the form of International Reply Coupons (IRCs). IRCs can be exchanged in any foreign country for stamps representing the minimum postage payable on a letter sent from one country to another. For further information *tel* (08457) 223344.

Using an agent to syndicate material written from overseas is worth considering. Most agents operate on an international basis and are more aware of current market requirements. Again, return postage should always be included.

Newspapers and syndicates

The larger newspapers and magazines buy many of their stories, and the smaller papers buy general articles, through one or other of the well-known syndicates. Another avenue for writers is to send printed copies of their stories published at home to an agent for syndication overseas. Listings for *Syndicates, news and press agencies* start on page 119. Listings of *National newspapers UK and Ireland* start on page 3, and the names of editors are included in each.

Most of the larger UK and overseas newspapers depend for news on their own staffs and press agencies. The most important overseas newspapers have permanent representatives in Britain who keep them supplied, not only with news of especial interest to the country concerned, but also with regular summaries of British news and with articles on events of particular importance. While many overseas newspapers and magazines have a London office, it is usual for manuscripts from freelance contributors to be submitted to the headquarters' editorial office overseas.

See also...
- *Regional newspapers UK and Ireland,* page 11
- Newspapers are listed together with magazines for *Australia* (page 97), *Canada* (page 102), *New Zealand* (page 105), *South Africa* (page 107) and *USA* (page 109)

National newspapers UK and Ireland

The Business

292 Vauxhall Bridge Road, London SW1V 1DE
tel 020-7961 0000 *fax* 020-7961 0101
Sun 50p

Standalone Sunday newspaper for the business and financial community. All aspects of business news with in-depth features ranging from captains of industry to the entrepreneurial and small business sector. Wide economic coverage, IT news, and personal finance features. Length: from 200-word news stories to 2500-word features. Payment: by arrangement.

City Editor Rob Bailhache
Deputy Editor Ian Watson
Editor-in-Chief Andrew Neil
Political Editor Andrew Porter
World Business Editor Sylvia Pfeifer

Daily Express

Ludgate House, 245 Blackfriars Road,
London SE1 9UX
tel 0161-228 0789 *fax* 020-7620 1654
Albert House, 17 Bloom Street, Manchester M1 3HZ
tel 0161-228 0789
Editor Chris Williams
Daily Mon–Fri 35p, Sat 50p
Supplements **Saturday, The Sport**

Exclusive news; striking photos. Leader page articles (600 words); facts preferred to opinions. Payment: according to value.

City Editor Stephen Kahn
Diary Editor Kathryn Spencer
Environment Editor John Ingham
Features Editor Yvonne Illsley
Foreign Editor Gabriel Milland
Health Editor Michael Day
Literary Editor Graham Ball
News Editor David Leigh
Political Editor Patrick O'Flynn
Sports Editor Bill Bradshaw
Women's Editor Lorna Frame

Saturday
fax 020-7922 2753
Editor Martin Smith

Daily Mail

Northcliffe House, 2 Derry Street, London W8 5TT
tel 020-7938 6000 *fax* 020-7937 3251
Editor Paul Dacre
Daily Mon–Fri 35p, Sat 50p
Supplements **Weekend**

Highest payment for good, exclusive news. Ideas welcomed for leader page articles (500–800 words). Exclusive news photos always wanted. Founded 1896.

City Editor Alex Brummer
Diary Editor Nigel Dempster
Education Editor Tony Halpin
Features Editor Leaf Kalfayan
Deputy Foreign Editor Gerry Hunt
Health Editor Victoria Lambert
Industrial Editor Darren Behar
Literary Editor Jane Mays
Money Editor Tony Hazell
News Editor Tony Gallagher
Picture Editor Paul Silva
Political Editor David Hughes
Showbiz Editor Nicole Lampert
Sports Editor Colin Gibson
Travel Editor Mark Edmonds
Weekend Editor Heather McGlone

Daily Mirror

1 Canada Square, Canary Wharf, London E14 5AP
tel 020-7293 3000 *fax* 020-7293 3409
Editor Piers Morgan
Daily Mon–Sat 32p
Supplements **The Look, Mirror Football Mania, The Ticket**

Top payment for exclusive news and news pictures. Freelance articles used, and ideas bought: send synopsis only. 'Unusual' pictures and those giving a new angle on the news are welcomed; also cartoons. Founded 1903.

Business Editor Clinton Manning
Features Editor Matt Kelly
Health Editor Jill Palmer
Letters Editor Geraldine Esau
News Editor Connor Hanna
Picture Editor Ian Down
Political Editor James Hardy
Sports Editor Dean Morse

Daily Record

1 Central Quay, Glasgow G3 8DA
tel 0141-309 3000 *fax* 0141-309 3340
website www.record-mail.co.uk/rm
London office 1 Canada Square, Canary Wharf, London E14 5AP
tel 020-7293 3000
Editor Bruce Waddell
Daily Mon–Fri 32p, Sat 35p
Supplements **Saturday**

Topical articles, from 300–700 words; exclusive stories of Scottish interest and exclusive colour photos.

Features Editor Trevor Ward
Health & Science Correspondent Judith Duffy
News Editor Tom Hamilton
Picture Editor Stuart Nicol
Political Editor Paul Sinclair
Sports Editor Alan Thomson
Women's Page Editor Kay Cox

Saturday
Editor Angela Dewar

Lifestyle magazine and entertainment guide. Reviews, travel features, shopping, personalities. Payment: by arrangement. Illustrations: colour.

Daily Sport

19 Great Ancoats Street, Manchester M60 4BT
tel 0161-236 4466 *fax* 0161-236 4535
Editor David Beevers, *Editor-in-Chief* Tony Livesey
Daily Mon–Fri 35p

Factual stories and series. Length: up to 1000 words. Illustrations: b&w and colour photos, cartoons. Payment: £30–£5000. Founded 1988.

Features and News Editor Justin Dunn
Sports Editor Mark Smith

Daily Star

Ludgate House, 245 Blackfriars Road, London SE1 9UX
tel 020-7928 8000 *fax* 020-7922 7960
Editor Peter Hill
Daily Mon–Sat 30p

Hard news exclusives, commanding substantial payment. Major interviews with big-star personalities; short features; series based on people rather than things; picture features. Payment: short features £75–£100; full page £250–£300; double page £400–£600, otherwise by negotiation. Illustrations: line, half-tone. Founded 1978.

Deputy & Political Editor Hugh Whittow
Entertainment Editor Gareth Morgan
Features Editor Dawn Neesom
News Editor Kieron Saunders
Sports Editor Jim Mansell

Daily Star Sunday

Express Newspapers, Ludgate House, 245 Blackfriars Road, London SE1 9UX
tel 020-7928 8000 *fax* 020-7922 7960
Editor Hugh Whittow
Sun 35p

Opportunities for freelances.

The Daily Telegraph

1 Canada Square, Canary Wharf, London E14 5DT
tel 020-7538 5000 *fax* 020-7538 6242
websites www.telegraph.co.uk
www.sport.telegraph.co.uk
www.travel.telegraph.co.uk

www.money.telegraph.co.uk
Editor Charles Moore
Daily Mon–Fri 45p, Sat 75p
Supplements **Appointments, Arts & Books, dotcom.telegraph, Money-Go-Round, Motoring, Property, Telegraph Magazine, Television & Radio, T2, Weekend**

Articles on a wide range of subjects of topical interest considered. Preliminary letter and synopsis required. Length: 700–1000 words. Payment: by arrangement. Founded 1855.

Arts Editor Sarah Crompton
City Editor Neil Collins
Education Editor John Clare
Environment Editor Charles Clover
Fashion Editor Hilary Alexander
Features Editor Richard Preston
Foreign Editor Alec Russell
Health Features Editor Christine Doyle
Health News Editor Celia Hall
Literary Editor Kate Summerscale
Media Correspondent Tom Leonard
News Editor Richard Spencer
Picture Editor Bob Bodman
Political Editor George Jones
Sports Editor David Welch

Electronic Telegraph
email et@telegraph.co.uk
website www.telegraph.co.uk/
Editor Derek Bishton
Daily Free to internet subscribers

Based on *The Daily Telegraph*. Founded 1994.

Juiced
website www.juiced.com
Weekly Free to internet subscribers

Student magazine.

Planet
website www.the-planet.co.uk
Free to internet subscribers

Travel writing from the *Daily Telegraph* and the *Sunday Telegraph*.

Telegraph Magazine
Editor Michelle Lavery
Free with Sat paper

Short profiles (about 1600 words); articles of topical interest. Preliminary study of the magazine essential. Illustrations: all types. Payment: by arrangement. Founded 1964.

Financial Times

1 Southwark Bridge, London SE1 9HL
tel 020-7873 3000 *fax* 020-7873 3076
website www.ft.com
Editor Andrew Gowers
Daily Mon–Sat £1
Supplements **Business Books, Companies & Markets, Creative Business, FT Fund Management,**

FT-IT, How To Spend It, Surveys, Weekend FT, Weekend Money

Articles of financial, commercial, industrial and economic interest. Length: 800–1000 words. Payment: by arrangement. Founded 1888.

Arts Editor Peter Aspden
Banking Editor Charles Pretzlik
City Editor Martin Dickson
Deputy Editor Chrystia Freeland
Features Editor John Gapper
Food & Travel Editor Jill James
Growing Business Correspondent Katherine Campbell
International Affairs Editor Quentin Peel
Investment Editor Philip Coggan
Lex Editor George Graham
Observer Editor Sunny Tucker
Political Editor Brian Groom
Surveys Editor Rhys David
US edition Editor Lionel Barber
Weekend FT Editor Richard Addis
World News Editor Edward Carr

The Guardian

119 Farringdon Road, London EC1R 3ER
tel 020-7278 2332 *fax* 020-7837 2114
164 Deansgate, Manchester M60 2RR
tel 0161-832 7200 *fax* 0161-832 5351
Editor Alan Rusbridger
Daily Mon–Fri 55p, Sat £1
Supplements Education, Friday Review, G2, G3, The Guide, Jobs & Money, Life, Literary Review, Media Guardian, Office Hours, Online, Society, Weekend

Few articles are taken from outside contributors except on its feature and specialist pages. Illustrations: news and features photos. Payment: from £234.14 per 1000 words; from £75 for illustrations. Founded 1821.

Arts Editor Dan Glaister
Business Editor Paul Murphy
Deputy Editor Georgina Henry
Deputy Editor (News) Paul Johnson
Economics Editor Larry Elliott
Education Editor Will Woodward
Fashion Editor Jess Cartner-Morley
Features Editor Ian Katz
Foreign Editor Harriet Sherwood
Home Editor Ed Pilkington
Literary Editor Claire Armitstead
Media Editor Charlie Burgess
News Editor Andrew Culf
Political Editor Michael White
Religious Editor Stephen Bates
Review Editor Annalena McAfee
Science Editor Tim Radford
Sports Editor Ben Clissitt
Travel Editor Andy Pietrasick
Women's Editor Clare Margetson

Guardian Unlimited
website www.guardian.co.uk
Editor-in-Chief Emily Bell
Weekend
Editor Katherine Viner
Free with Sat paper

Features on world affairs, major profiles, food and drink, home life, the arts, travel, leisure, etc. Also good reportage on social and political subjects. Illustrations: b&w photos and line, cartoons. Payment: apply for rates.

The Herald

Scottish Media Newspapers Ltd, 200 Renfield Street, Glasgow G2 3PR
tel 0141-302 7000 *fax* 0141-333 1147
website www.theherald.co.uk
London office 3 Waterhouse Square, 138-142 Holborn, London EC1N 2NY
tel 020-7882 1060
Editor Mark Douglas-Home
Daily Mon–Fri 50p, Sat 55p

Articles up to 1000 words. Founded 1783.

Arts Editor Keith Bruce
Assistant Editor Melanie Reid
Business Editor Ian McConnell
Deputy Editors Joan McAlpine, Kevin McKenna
Diary Editor Ken Smith
Executive Editor Colin McDiarmid
Features Editor Mark Smith
News Editor Magnus Llewellin
Sports Editor Donald Cowey

The Independent

Independent House, 191 Marsh Wall, London E14 9RS
tel 020-7005 2000 *fax* 020-7005 2999
Editor-in-Chief Simon Kelner
Daily Mon–Fri 55p, Sat £1
Supplements Business Review, Education, The Information, Property Supplement, Review, Traveller, Weekend Review, Your Money

Occasional freelance contributions; preliminary letter advisable. Payment: by arrangement. Founded 1986.

Arts Editor David Lister
Business & City Editor Jeremy Warner
Education Editor Richard Garner
Environment Editor Mike McCarthy
Features Editor Lisa Markwell
Foreign Editor Leonard Doyle
Health Editor Jeremy Laurance
Literary Editor Boyd Tonkin
Media Editor Vincent Graff
News Editor Adam Leigh
Picture Editor Lynn Cullen
Political Editor Andrew Grice
Sports Editor Paul Newman

The Independent Magazine
Editor Laurence Earle
Free with Sat paper

Profiles and illustrated articles of topical interest; all material commissioned. Preliminary study of the magazine essential. Length: 500–3000 words. Illustrations: cartoons; commissioned colour and b&w photos. Payment: by arrangement. Founded 1988.

Independent on Sunday

Independent House, 191 Marsh Wall, London E14 9RS
tel 020-7005 2000 *fax* 020-7005 2999

Tristan Davies, *Editor-at-Large* Janet Street-Porter
Sun £1.10
Supplements **Business, Life Etc, The Sunday Review, Sportsweek, Talk of the Town Magazine, Time Off**

News, features and articles. Illustrated, including cartoons. Payment: by negotiation. Founded 1990.
>*Arts Editor, Life Etc* Marcus Field
>*Assistant Editor* David Randall
>*Business Editor* Jason Nissé
>*Comment Executive Editor* Catherine Pepinster
>*Deputy Editor* Michael Williams
>*Environment Editor* Geoffrey Lean
>*Features Editor, Life Etc* Nick Coleman
>*Foreign Editor* Ray Whitaker
>*News Editor* Robert Mendick
>*Picture Editor* Sophie Batterbury
>*Political Editor* Andy McSmith
>*Sports Editor* Neil Morton

The Sunday Review
tel 020-7293 2000 *fax* 020-7293 2027
Editor Andrew Tuck

Original features of general interest with potential for photographic illustration. Material mostly commissioned. Length: 1000–5000 words. Illustrations: transparencies. Payment: £150 per 1000 words.

Ireland on Sunday

Associated Newspapers Ireland Ltd, Embassy House, Ballsbridge, Dublin 4, Republic of Ireland
tel (01) 6375800 *fax* (01) 6375880
email news@irelandonsunday.com
website www.irelandonsunday.com
Editor Paul Drury
Sun €1.50

Mid-market tabloid. Considers unsolicited material. Length: 2500 words (articles/features), 800 words (news). Illustrations: cartoons. Payment: by negotiation. Founded 1997.
>*Features Editor* Philip Nolan
>*News Editor* Ciarán Byrne
>*Sports Editor* Jack White

Irish Examiner

1-6 Academy Street, Cork, Republic of Ireland
tel (021) 4272722, 4802153 (newsroom)
fax (021) 4275477

email (department)@examiner.ie
website www.examiner.ie
Editor Tim Vaughan
Daily Mon–Sat IR90p

Features; mostly commissioned. Length: 1000 words. Payment: by arrangement. Founded 1841.
>*Features Editor* Dan Buckley
>*News Editor* Brian Carroll
>*Picture Editor* John Donovan
>*Sports Editor* Tony Leen

Irish Independent

Independent House, 90 Middle Abbey Street, Dublin 1, Republic of Ireland
tel (01) 7055333 *fax* (01) 8720304/8731787
Editor Vincent Doyle
Daily Mon–Sat €1.30

Special articles on topical or general subjects. Length: 700–1000 words. Payment: editor's estimate of value.
>*Business Editor* Richard Curran
>*Deputy Editor* Michael Wolsey
>*Diary Editor* Angela Phelan
>*Features Editor* Peter Carvosso
>*News Editor* Philip Molloy
>*Picture Editor* Danny Thornton
>*Political Editor* Chris Glennon
>*Sports Editor* Patrick J. Cunningham

Irish Times

11-15 D'Olier Street, Dublin 2, Republic of Ireland
tel (01) 6792022 *fax* (01) 6719407
Editor Geraldine Kennedy
Daily Mon–Sat €1.27

Mainly staff-written. Specialist contributions (800–2000 words) by commission on basis of ideas submitted. Payment: at editor's valuation. Illustrations: photos and line drawings.
>*Arts Editor* Deirdre Falvey
>*Features Editor* Sheila Wayman
>*Finance Editor* Barry O'Keeffe
>*Foreign Editor* Peter Murtagh
>*Literary Editor* Caroline Walsh
>*News Editor* John Maher
>*Picture Editor* Peter Thursfield
>*Sports Editor* Malachy Logan

The Irish Times on the Web
website www.ireland.com

Mail on Sunday

Northcliffe House, 2 Derry Street, London W8 5TS
tel 020-7938 6000 *fax* 020-7937 3829
Editor Peter Wright
Sun £1.20
Supplements **Financial Mail on Sunday, Night & Day, Review, You**

Articles. Payment: by arrangement. Illustrations: line, half-tone; cartoons. Founded 1982.
>*City Editor* Lisa Buckingham

Diary Editor Nigel Dempster
Features Editor Sian James
Literary Editor Marilyn Warnick
News Editor Sebastian Hamilton
Picture Editor Liz Cocks
Political Editor Simon Walters
Sports Editor Malcolm Vallerius

Financial Mail on Sunday
tel 020-7938 6984
email fmos@mailonsunday.co.uk
website www.financialmail.co.uk
Editor Lisa Buckingham, *Personal Finance Editor* Jeff Prestridge

City, industry, business, and personal finance. News stories up to 1500 words. Payment by arrangement. Full colour illustrations/photography commissioned.

Night & Day
tel 020-7938 7051 *fax* 020-7937 7488
Editor Christena Appleyard

Interviews, entertainment-related features and TV listings. Length: 1000–3000 words. Illustrations: colour photos. Founded 1993.

Review
Editor Jim Gillespie

Investigative journalism, reportage, features, and film, TV, book and theatre reviews.

You
Editor Sue Peart, *Deputy Editor* Catherine Fenton

Women's interest features. Length: 500–2500 words. Payment: by arrangement. Illustrations: full colour and b&w drawings commissioned; colour photos.

Morning Star
(formerly Daily Worker)
People's Press Printing Society Ltd, William Rust House, 52 Beachy Road, London E3 2NS
tel 020-8510 0815 *fax* 020-8986 5694
email morsta@geo2.poptel.org.uk
Editor John Haylett
Daily Mon–Sat 60p

Newspaper for the labour movement. Articles of general interest. Illustrations: photos, cartoons, drawings. Founded 1930.
Arts, Media & Features Editor Katie Gilmore
Diary Editor Mike Ambrose
Financial Editor Bill Benfield
Foreign Editor Brian Denny
Health Editor Vicky Bryce
Industrial & News Editor Dan Coysh
Political Editor Adrian Roberts
Sports Editor Mark Barber

News of the World
1 Virginia Street, London E1 9XR
tel 020-7782 1000 *fax* 020-7583 9504
Editor Andy Coulson
Sun 60p

Uses freelance material. Payment: by negotiation. Founded 1843.
Assistant Editor (Features) Gary Thompson
Deputy Editor Neil Wallis
Money Editor Peter Prendergast
News Editor Greg Miskia
Political Editor Ian Kirby
Royal Editor Clive Goodman
Sports Editor Mike Dunn
Travel Editor Jon Barnsley

Sunday Magazine
Phase 2, 5th Floor, 1 Virginia Street, London E1 9BD
tel 020-7782 7900 *fax* 020-7782 7474
Editor Judy McGuire

The Observer
119 Farringdon Road, London EC1R 3ER
tel 020-7278 2332 *fax* 020-7713 4250
Editor Roger Alton
Sun £1.30
Supplements **Business, Cash, Escape, Observer Magazine, Observer Sport Monthly, Observer Food Monthly, Observer Music Monthly, Observer Review, The Observer TV, Sport**

Some articles and illustrations commissioned. Payment: by arrangement. Founded 1791.
Arts Editor Jane Ferguson
Business Editor Frank Kane
City Editor Richard Wachman
Economics Editor William Keegan
Fashion Editor Jo Adams
Foreign News Editor Tracy McVeigh
Literary Editor Robert McCrum
News Editor Andy Malone
OFM Editor Nicola Jeal
OSM Editor Matt Tench
Picture Editor Greg Whitmore
Political Editor Kamal Ahmed
Review Editor Louise France
Screen Editor Akin Ojomu
Sports Editor Brian Oliver
Travel Editor Jeannette Hyde

Observer Magazine
tel 020-7713 4175 *fax* 020-7239 9837
Editor Allan Jenkins

Commissioned features. Length: 2000–3000 words. Illustrations: first-class colour and b&w photos. Payment: NUJ rates; £150 per illustration.

The Observer Online
website www.observer.co.uk

The People
(formerly Sunday People)
1 Canada Square, Canary Wharf, London E14 5AP
tel 020-7293 3000 *fax* 020-7293 3517
website www.thepeople.co.uk
Editor Mark Thomas

Sun 70p
Supplements **People Magazine**

Exclusive news and news-feature stories needed. Investigative features, single articles and series considered. Features should be of deep human interest, whether the subject is serious or light-hearted. Very strong sports following. Payment: rates high, even for tips that lead to published news stories.

Assistant Features Editor Rosie Dunn
Assistant News Editor Ian Edmondson
Features Editor Dawn Alford
Investigations Editor Nyra Mamhood
Picture Editor Paula Derry
Political Editor Nigel Nelson
Sports Editor Lee Clayton

People Magazine
Editor Kerry Parnell

Scotland on Sunday

108 Holyrood Road, Edinburgh EH8 8AS
tel 0131-620 8620 *fax* 0131-620 8491
tel 0141-332 6163
Editor John McLellan
Sun 90p

Features on all subjects, not necessarily Scottish. Payment: varies. Founded 1988.

News Editor Peter Laing
Political Editor Jason Allardyce

Spectrum Magazine
Editor Lee Randall

The Scotsman

Barclay House, 108 Holyrood Road, Edinburgh EH8 8AS
tel 0131-620 8620 *fax* 0131-620 8615
Editor Iain Martin
Daily Mon–Fri 40p, Sat 50p
Supplements **S2, Saturday Magazine**

Considers articles on political, economic and general themes which add substantially to current information. Prepared to commission topical and controversial series from proved authorities. Length: 800–1000 words. Illustrations: outstanding news pictures, cartoons. Payment: by arrangement. Founded 1817.

Arts Editor Andrew Eaton
Business Editor Ian Watson
Education Editor Seonag MacKinnon
Features Editor Charlotte Ross
Foreign Editor Andrew McLeod
Literary Editor David Robinson
News Editor Gordon Hay
Political Editor (Westminster) Fraser Nelson
Assistant Editor (Politics) Hamish Macdonell
Saturday Magazine Editor Sandra Colamartino
Sports Editor Donald Walker
S2 Editor Charlotte Ross

The Star

Independent Star Ltd, Star House, 62A Terenure Road North, Dublin 6w, Republic of Ireland
tel (01) 4901228 *fax* (01) 4902193
Editor Gerard Colleran
Daily Mon–Sat €1.10

General articles relating to news and sport, and features. Length: 1000 words. Illustrations: colour photos. Payment: by negotiation. Founded 1989.

Deputy Editor Danny Smyth
News Editor Michael O'Kane
Picture Editor Bernard Phelan
Political Editor John Downing
Sports Editor Eoin Brannigan

The Sun

News Group Newspapers Ltd, Virginia Street, London E1 9XP
tel 020-7782 4000 *fax* 020-7488 3253
Editor Rebekah Wade
Daily Mon–Fri 28p, Sat 30p
Supplements **Super Goals, The TV Mag**

Takes freelance material, including cartoons. Payment: by negotiation. Founded 1969.

Associate Editor Geoff Webster
Business Editor Ian King
Features Editor Sam Carlisle
Health Editor Jacqui Thornton
Letters Editor Sue Cook
News Editor Sue Thompson
Picture Editor John Edwards
Political Editor Trevor Kavanagh
Showbiz Editor Dominic Mohan
Sports Editor Ted Chadwick
Travel Editor Lisa Bielfeld
Women's Editor Sharon Hendry

The Sunday Business Post

80 Harcourt Street, Dublin 2, Republic of Ireland
tel (01) 6026000 *fax* (01) 6796496/6796498
Editor Ted Harding
Sun €1.75

Features on financial, economic and political topics; also lifestyle, media and science articles. Illustrations: colour and b&w photos, graphics, cartoons. Payment: by negotiation. Founded 1989.

Assistant Editor Kieron Wood
Assistant Editor/Agenda Editor Jennifer O'Connell
Assistant Editor/Crime Correspondent Barry O'Kelly
Assistant Editor/Political Correspondent Sean MacCarthaigh
Assistant Editor/Property Editor Gillian Nelis
Business Editor Eamon Quinn
IT Editor Gavin Daly
Markets Editor Michael Murray
Media Editor Catherine O'Mahony
News Director Fiona Ness
Political Reporter Pat Leahy

Sunday Express
Ludgate House, 245 Blackfriars Road,
London SE1 9UX
tel 020-7928 8000 *fax* 020-7620 1653
Editor Martin Townsend
Sun £1
Supplements **Sunday Express 'S' Magazine, S:2 Magazine**

Exclusive news stories, photos, personality profiles and features of controversial or lively interest. Length: 800–1000 words. Payment: top rates. Founded 1918.

> *City Editor* David Parsley
> *Features Editor* Giulia Rhodes
> *Literary Editor* Graham Ball
> *News Editor* James Murray
> *Political Editor* Tim Shipman
> *Sports Editor* Mike Scott

Sunday Express 'S' Magazine
tel 020-7922 7297
Editor Louise Robinson

S:2 Magazine
tel 020-7922 7025
Editor Margaret Hussey

Sunday Herald
Scottish Media Publishing Ltd, 200 Renfield Street, Glasgow G2 3PR
tel 0141-302 7800 *fax* 0141-302 7815
website www.sundayherald.com
Editor Andrew Jaspan
Sun 90p
Supplements **Review, Seven Days, Sport, Sunday Herald Magazine**

News and stories about Scotland, its characteristics and people. Opportunities for freelances with quality contacts. Founded 1999.

> *Business Editor* Kenny Kemp
> *Deputy Editor* Richard Walker
> *Features Editor* Charlene Sweeney
> *Magazine Editor* Jane Wright
> *News Editor* David Milne
> *Political Editor* Douglas Fraser
> *Sports Editor* David Dick

Sunday Independent
Independent House, 90 Middle Abbey Street, Dublin 1, Republic of Ireland
tel (01) 7055333 *fax* (01) 7055779
Editor Aengus Fanning
Sun £1.20

Special articles. Length: according to subject. Illustrations: topical or general interest, cartoons. Payment: at editor's valuation.

> *Business Editor* Shane Ross
> *Deputy Editors* Anne Harris, Willie Kealy
> *Political Editor* Jody Corcoran
> *Sports Editor* Adhamhnan O'Sullivan

Sunday Life
124 Royal Avenue, Belfast BT1 1EB
tel 028-9026 4300 *fax* 028-9055 4507
email betty.arnold@belfasttelegraph.co.uk
Editor Martin Lindsay
Sun £1

Items of interest to Northern Ireland Sunday tabloid readers. Payment: by arrangement. Illustrations: colour and b&w pictures and graphics. Founded 1988.

> *Features Editor* Stephanie Bell
> *Deputy Editor and News Editor* Martin Hill
> *Photographic Editor* Darren Kidd
> *Sports Editor* Jim Gracey

Sunday Mail
1 Central Quay, Glasgow G3 8DA
tel 0141-309 3000 *fax* 0141-309 3582
website www.record-mail.co.uk/rm
London office 1 Canada Square, Canary Wharf, London E14 5AP
Editor Allan Rennie
Sun 70p
Supplements **Entertainment, MailSport Monthly, 7-Days**

Exclusive stories and pictures of national and Scottish interest; also cartoons. Payment: above average.

> *Assistant Editor* Andrew Sannholm
> *Chief Writer* Donna White
> *Deputy Editor* Bob Caldwell
> *Features Editor* Susie Cormack
> *Health Editor* Dr Gareth Smith
> *News Editor* Jim Wilson
> *Picture Editor* Andrew Hosie
> *7-Days Editor* Liz Steele
> *Showbiz Editor* Billy Sloan
> *Sports Editor* George Cheyne

Sunday Mirror
1 Canada Square, Canary Wharf, London E14 5AP
tel 020-7293 3000 *fax* 020-7293 3939
website www.mirror.co.uk
Editor Mark Thomas
Sun 65p
Supplements **M Celebs**

Concentrates on human interest news features, social documentaries, dramatic news and feature photos. Ideas, as well as articles, bought. Payment: high, especially for exclusives. Founded 1963.

> *Associate Editor* Mike Small
> *Deputy Editor* Richard Wallace
> *Executive Editor (Pictures)* Ivor Game
> *Editor (Sport)* Steve McKenlay
> *Executive Editor (Features)* Jane Johnson
> *News Editor* Euan Stretch

Sunday Post

D.C. Thomson & Co. Ltd, 144 Port Dundas Road,
Glasgow G4 0HZ
tel 0141-332 9933 *fax* 0141-331 1595
Albert Square, Dundee DD1 9QJ
tel (01382) 223131 *fax* (01382) 201064
Editor David Pollington
Sun 65p

Human interest, topical, domestic and humorous
articles, and exclusive news. Payment: on
acceptance.

The Sunday Post Magazine
tel (01382) 223131 *fax* (01382) 201064
Editor Maggie Dun
Monthly Free with paper

General interest articles. Length: 1000–2000 words.
Illustrations: colour transparencies. Payment: varies.
Founded 1988.

Sunday Sport

19 Great Ancoats Street, Manchester M60 4BT
tel 0161-236 4466 *fax* 0161-236 4535
email paul.carter@sportnewspapers.co.uk
Editor Paul Carter
Sun 60p

Founded 1986.
   Assistant Editor Feargal Sharbey
   News Editor Paul Carter
   Picture Editor Mick Applejuice
   Sports Editor Marc Fester

Sunday Telegraph

1 Canada Square, Canary Wharf, London E14 5DT
tel 020-7538 5000 *fax* 020-7513 2504
Editor Dominic Lawson
Sun £1
Supplements **Appointments, City, House and Home,
Review, Sport, Sunday Telegraph Magazine, Travel**

Occasional freelance material accepted.
   Arts Editor Suzannah Herbert
   City Editor Robert Peston
   Comment Editor Mark Law
   Deputy Editor Matthew d'Ancona
   Diary Editor Adam Helliker
   Executive Editor Con Coughlin
   Foreign Editor Topaz Amoore
   Literary Editor Miriam Gross
   News Editor Richard Ellis
   Picture Editor Nigel Skelsey
   Review Editor Anna Murphy
   Sports Editor John Ryan
   Travel Editor Graham Boynton

Sunday Telegraph Magazine
tel 020-7538 7590 *fax* 020-7538 7074
email sunmag@telegraph.co.uk
Editor Lucy Tuck, *Executive Editor* Rebecca Tyrrel
All material is commissioned. Founded 1995.

The Sunday Times

1 Pennington Street, London E98 1ST
tel 020-7782 5000 *fax* 020-7782 5658
website www.sunday-times.co.uk
Editor John Witherow
Sun £1.10
Supplements **Appointments, Doors, Business,
Culture, Funday Times, Money, News Review, Rich
List, Sport, Style, The Sunday Times Magazine, Travel**

Special articles by authoritative writers on politics,
literature, art, drama, music, finance and science,
and topical matters. Payment: top rate for exclusive
features. Founded 1822.
   Culture Editor Helen Hawkins
   Economics Editor David Smith
   Education Correspondent Judith O'Reilly
   Literary Editor Caroline Gascoigne
   News Editor Charles Hymas
   News Review Sarah Baxter
   Chief Political Correspondent Eben Black
   Sports Editor Alex Butler
   Travel Editor Christine Walker

The Sunday Times Magazine
tel 020-7782 7000
Editor Robin Morgan

Articles and pictures. Illustrations: colour and b&w
photos. Payment: by negotiation.

The Sunday Times Scotland

Times Newspapers Ltd, 124 Portman Street,
Kinning Park, Glasgow G41 1EJ
tel 0141-420 5100 *fax* 0141-420 5262
Editor Les Snowdon
Free with *The Sunday Times*

News, features and sport. Illustrations: colour
photos, cartoons and graphics. Payment: £100 per
feature; £50 for illustrations. Founded 1988.

The Sunday Tribune

Tribune Publications plc, 15 Lower Baggot Street,
Dublin 2, Republic of Ireland
tel (01) 661 5555 *fax* (01) 661 5302
email editorial@tribune.ie
Editor Matt Cooper
Sun £1
Supplements **People, Review**

Newspaper containing news (inc. foreign), articles,
features and photo features. Length: 600–2800
words. Illustrations: colour and b&w photos and
cartoons. Payment: £100 per 1000 words; £100 for
illustrations. Founded 1980.
   Arts Editor Lise Hand
   Business Editor Brian Carey
   Deputy Editor Paddy Murray
   News Editor Martin Wall
   Photo Desk Bea McMunn
   Sports Editor Mark Jones
   Supplements Editor Ros Dee

The Times
1 Pennington Street, London E98 1TT
tel 020-7782 5000 *fax* 020-7488 3242
website www.thetimes.co.uk
Editor Robert Thomson
Daily Mon–Fri 45p, Sat 75p
Supplements **Bricks & Mortar, Crème, Football Handbook, The Game, London List, Money, Play, Times 2, Times Law, The Times Magazine, Times Sport, Travel, Weekend**

Outside contributions considered from: experts in subjects of current interest and writers who can make first-hand experience or reflection come readably alive. Phone appropriate section editor. Length: up to 1200 words. Founded 1785.

Arts Editor Sarah Vine
Business/City Editor Patience Wheatcroft
Deputy Editor Ben Preston
Education Editor Tony Halpin
Features Editor Anne Barrowclough
Foreign Editor Bronwen Maddox
Health Editor Nigel Hawkes
Industrial Correspondent Christine Buckley
Literary Editor Erica Wagner
Media Editor Ray Snoddy
News Editor John Wellman
Political Editor Philip Webster
Science Correspondent Mark Henderson
Sports Editor David Chappell
Weekend Times Editor Jane Wheatley

The Times Magazine
Editor Gill Morgan
Free with Sat paper
Features. Illustrated.

Wales on Sunday
Thomson House, Havelock Street,
Cardiff CF10 1XR
tel 029-2058 3583 *fax* 029-2058 3725
Editor Tim Gordon
Sun 60p

National Sunday newspaper of Wales offering comprehensive news, features and entertainments coverage at the weekend, with a particular focus on events in Wales. Accepts general interest articles, preferably with a Welsh connection. Founded 1989.

News Editor Laura Kemp
Senior Assistant Editor Wayne Davies
Sports Editor Nick Rippington

Regional newspapers UK and Ireland

Regional newspapers are listed in alphabetical order under region. Some will accept and pay for letters to the editor, brief fillers, and gossip paragraphs, as well as puzzles and quizzes. See also *Writing for newspapers* on page 110.

BELFAST

Belfast Telegraph
124-144 Royal Avenue, Belfast BT1 1EB
tel 028-9026 4000 *fax* 028-9033 1332 (also photographic), 9055 4540 (news only), 9055 4517 (features), 9055 4508 (sport)
email editor@belfasttelegraph.co.uk
website www.belfasttelegraph.co.uk
Editor Edmund Curran
Daily Mon–Sat 50p
Features Editor John Caruth
News Editor Paul Connolly
Picture Editor Gerry Fitzgerald
Sports Editor John Laverty

Any material relating to Northern Ireland. Payment: by negotiation. Founded 1870.

Irish News
113-117 Donegall Street, Belfast BT1 2GE
tel 028-9032 2226 *fax* 028-9033 7505
website www.irishnews.com
Editor Noel Doran
Daily Mon–Sat 45p
Business Editor Gary McDonald
Features Editor Joanna Braniff
News Editor Stephen McCaffery
Picture Editor Ann McManus
Sports Editor Thomas Hawkins

Articles of historical and topical interest. Payment: by arrangement. Founded 1855.

News Letter
46-56 Boucher Crescent, Boucher Road,
Belfast BT12 6QY
tel 028-9068 0000 *fax* 028-9066 4412
email newsletter@mgn.co.uk
website www.newsletter.co.uk
Editor Nigel Wareing
Daily Mon–Sat 35p
Features Editor Geoff Hill
Picture Editor tba
Sports Editor Brian Millar

Pro-Union. Founded 1737.

CHANNEL ISLANDS

Guernsey Press and Star
Braye Road, Vale, Guernsey GY1 3BW
tel (01481) 240240 *fax* (01481) 240235
Editor Richard Digard
Daily Mon–Sat 37p
  Features Editor Suzanne Heneghan
  News Editor James Falla
  Sports Editor Rob Batiste

News and feature articles. Length: 500–700 words.
Illustrations: colour and b&w photos. Payment: by
negotiation. Founded 1897.

Jersey Evening Post
PO Box 582, Five Oaks, St Saviour, Jersey JE4 8XQ
tel (01534) 611611 *fax* (01534) 611622
email editorial@jerseyeveningpost.com
Editor Chris Bright
Daily Mon–Sat 40p
  Features Editor Elaine Hanning
  News Editor Sue le Ruez
  Picture Editor Peter Mourant
  Sports Editor Ron Felton

News and features with a Channel Islands angle.
Length: 1000 words (articles/features), 300 words
(news). Illustrations: colour and b&w. Payment: £98
per 1000 words. Founded 1890.

CORK

Evening Echo (Cork)
Evening Echo Publications Ltd, 1-6 Academy Street,
Cork, Republic of Ireland
tel (021) 4272722 *fax* (021) 4802135
Editor Maurice Gubbins
Daily Mon–Sat €1.27
  Deputy Editor Vincent Kelly
  News Editor Emma Connolly
  Picture Editor Brian Lougheed

Articles, features and news for the area.
Illustrations: colour prints.

DUBLIN

Evening Herald
90 Middle Abbey Street, Dublin 1,
Republic of Ireland
tel (01) 7055333
email eveningherald@unison.independent.ie
Editor Gerard O'Regan
Daily Mon–Sat €1
  Deputy Editor Noirin Hegarty
  Assistant Editors Dave Kenny, Ronan Price,
  Mark Evans
  Associate Editors Frank Coghlan, Stephen Rae
  Features Editor Dave Lawlor
  News Editor Martin Brennan

  Assistant News Editor Bairbre Power
  Picture Editor Declan Cahill
  Sports Editor David Courtney

Articles. Payment: by arrangement. Illustrations:
line, half-tone, cartoons.

EAST ANGLIA

Cambridge Evening News
Winship Road, Milton, Cambs. CB4 6PP
tel (01223) 434434 *fax* (01223) 434415
email colingrant@cambridge-news.co.uk
Editor Colin Grant
Daily Mon–Sat 36p
  News Editor John Deex
  Sports Editor Chris Gill

The voice of Mid-Anglia – news, views and sport.
Illustrations: colour prints, b&w and colour
graphics. Payment: by negotiation. Founded 1888.

East Anglian Daily Times
30 Lower Brook Street, Ipswich, Suffolk IP4 1AN
tel (01473) 230023 *fax* (01473) 324871
Editor Terry Hunt
Daily Mon–Fri 45p, Sat 50p
  Features Editor Julian Ford
  News Editor Aynsley Davidson
  Picture Editor Paul Nixon
  Sports Editor Nick Garnham

Features of East Anglian interest, preferably with
pictures. Length: 500 words. Illustrations: colour,
b&w. Payment: negotiable; illustrations NUJ rates.
Founded 1874.

Eastern Daily Press
Prospect House, Rouen Road, Norwich NR1 1RE
tel (01603) 628311 *fax* (01603) 612930
website www.ecn.co.uk
London office House of Commons Press Gallery,
House of Commons, London SW1A 0AA
tel 020-7219 3384 *fax* 020-7222 3830
Editor Peter Franzen
Daily Mon–Wed 40p, Thur & Fri 45p, Sat 50p

Limited market for articles of East Anglian interest
not exceeding 900 words. Founded 1870.

Evening News
Prospect House, Rouen Road, Norwich NR1 1RE
tel (01603) 628311 *fax* (01603) 219060
Editor David Bourn
Daily Mon–Sat 32p
  Features Editor Derek James
  News Editor Amanda Patterson
  Picture Editor Nolan Lincoln
  Sports Editor David Cuffley

Interested in local news-based features. Length: up
to 500 words. Payment: NUJ or agreed rates.
Founded 1882.

EAST MIDLANDS

Burton Mail
Burton Daily Mail Ltd, 65-68 High Street,
Burton on Trent DE14 1LE
tel (01283) 512345 *fax* (01283) 515351
Editor Paul Hazeldine
Daily Mon–Sat 32p
  Deputy Editor Killoran Wills
  Features Editor Bill Pritchard
  News and Picture Editor Andy Parker
  Sports Editor Rex Page

Features, news and articles of interest to Burton and
south Derbyshire readers. Length: 400–500 words.
Illustrations: colour and b&w. Payment: by
negotiation. Founded 1898.

Chronicle & Echo, Northampton
Northamptonshire Newspapers Ltd, Upper Mounts,
Northampton NN1 3HR
tel (01604) 467000 *fax* (01604) 467190
Editor Mark Edwards
Daily Mon–Sat 32p

Articles, features and news – mostly commissioned
– of interest to the Northampton area.
Length/illustrations: varies. Payment: by
negotiation. Founded 1931.

Derby Evening Telegraph
Northcliffe House, Meadow Road, Derby DE1 2DW
tel (01332) 291111 *fax* (01322) 253027
website www.thisisderbyshire.co.uk
Editor Mike Norton
Daily Mon–Sat 30p
  News Editor Cheryl Hague
  News Features Editor Sarah Newton
  Picture Editor Steve Mitchell
  Sports Editor David Parkinson

Articles and news of local interest. Payment: by
negotiation.

The Leicester Mercury
St George Street, Leicester LE1 9FQ
tel 0116-251 2512 *fax* 0116-253 0645
Editor Nick Carter
Daily Mon–Sat 28p

Occasional articles, features and news; submit ideas
to editor first. Length/payment: by negotiation.
Founded 1874.

Nottingham Evening Post
Castle Wharf House, Nottingham NG1 7EU
tel 0115-948 2000 *fax* 0115-964 4049
email newsdesk@nottinghameveningpost.co.uk
website www.thisisnottingham.co.uk
Editor Graham Glen
Daily Mon–Sat 30p

Material on local issues considered. Founded 1878.

LONDON

Evening Standard
Northcliffe House, 2 Derry Street, London W8 5EE
tel 020-7938 6000
website www.thisislondon.com
Editor Veronica Wadley
Daily Mon–Fri 35p
  Features Editor Guy Eaton
  News Editor Ian Walker
  Picture Editor David Ofield
  Sports Editor Simon Greenberg

Articles of general interest considered, 1500 words
or shorter; also news, pictures and ideas. Founded
1827.

ES Magazine
Editor Catherine Ostler
Weekly Free with paper

Feature ideas, exclusively about London. Payment:
by negotiation. Illustrations: all types.

NORTH

Evening Chronicle
Newcastle Chronicle and Journal Ltd, Groat Market,
Newcastle upon Tyne NE1 1ED
tel 0191-232 7500 *fax* 0191-232 2256
Editor Paul Robertson
Daily Mon–Sat 30p
  Features Editor Richard Ord
  News Editor Mick Smith
  Picture Editor Rod Wilson
  Sports Editor Paul New

News, photos and features covering almost every
subject of interest to readers in Tyne and Wear,
Northumberland and Durham. Payment: by
arrangement.

Evening Gazette
Gazette Media Company Ltd, Borough Road,
Middlesbrough TS1 3AZ
tel (01642) 245401 *fax* (01642) 232014
email editor@eveninggazette.co.uk
Editor Steve Dyson
Daily Mon–Sat 29p

News, and topical and lifestyle features. Length:
600–800 words. Illustrations: line, half-tone, colour,
graphics, cartoons. Payment: £75 per 1000 words;
scale rate or by agreement for illustrations. Founded
1869.

Hartlepool Mail
Northeast Press Ltd, New Clarence House, Wesley
Square, Hartlepool TS24 8BX
tel (01429) 274441 *fax* (01429) 869024
email mail.news@northeast-press.co.uk
Editor Paul Napier
Daily Mon–Sat 32p

Deputy Editor Neil Hunter
News Editor Gavin Ledwith
Picture Editor Dirk van der Werff
Sports Editor Roy Kelly

Features of local interest. Length: 500 words. Illustrations: colour, b&w photos, line. Payment: by negotiation. Founded 1877.

The Journal

Groat Market, Newcastle upon Tyne NE1 1ED
tel 0191-232 7500 *fax* 0191-261 8869
email jnl.newsdesk@ncjmedia.co.uk
Editor Gerard Henderson
Daily Mon–Sat 35p
  Features Editor Jane Hall
  News Editor Stephen Rouse
  Picture Editor Simon Greener
  Sports Editor Kevin Dinsdale

News, sport items and features of topical interest considered. Payment: by arrangement.

North-West Evening Mail

Newspaper House, Abbey Road, Barrow-in-Furness, Cumbria LA14 5QS
tel (01229) 840150 *fax* (01229) 840164/832141
Editor Steve Brauner
Daily Mon–Sat 34p
  News Editor Steve Hartley
  Sports Editor Leo Clarke

'The Voice of Furness and West Cumbria.' Articles, features and news. Length: 500 words. Illustrations: b&w photos and occasional artwork. Payment: £30 (minimum); £10 for illustrations. Founded 1898.

The Northern Echo

Priestgate, Darlington, Co. Durham DL1 1NF
tel (01325) 381313 *fax* (01325) 380539
Editor Peter Barron
Daily Mon–Sat 32p
  Features Editor Jenny Needham
  News Editor Nigel Burton
  Picture Editor Mike Gibb
  Sports Editor Nick Loughlin

Articles of interest to North-East and North Yorkshire; all material commissioned. Preliminary study of newspaper advisable. Length: 800–1000 words. Illustrations: line, half-tone, colour – mostly commissioned. Payment: by negotiation. Founded 1870.

The Sunday Sun

Groat Market, Newcastle upon Tyne NE1 1ED
tel 0191-201 6251 *fax* 0191-230 0238
email scoop.sundaysun@ncjmedia.co.uk
Editor Peter Montellier
Sun 60p

Key requirements: immediate topicality and human sidelights on current problems. Particularly welcomed are special features of family appeal and news stories of special interest to the North of England. Length: 200–700 words. Payment: normal lineage rates, or by arrangement. Illustrations: photos. Founded 1919.

Sunderland Echo

Echo House, Pennywell, Sunderland, Tyne & Wear SR4 9ER
tel 0191-501 5800 *fax* 0191-534 5975
website www.sunderlandtoday.co.uk
Editor Rob Lawson
Daily Mon–Sat 32p

Local news, features and articles. Length: 500 words. Illustrations: colour and b&w photos, line, cartoons. Payment: negotiable. Founded 1875.

NORTH WEST

Bolton Evening News

Newspaper House, Churchgate, Bolton, Lancs. BL1 1DE
tel (01204) 522345 *fax* (01204) 365068
email ben_editorial@boltoneveningnews.co.uk
website www.thisisbolton.co.uk
tel (01204) 522345 *fax* (01204) 365068
email ben_editorial@newsquest.co.uk
Daily Mon–Sat 30p

Founded 1867.

Daily Post

PO Box 48, Old Hall Street, Liverpool L69 3EB
tel 0151-227 2000 *fax* 0151-472 2474
Editor Jane Wolstenholme
Daily Mon–Sat 32p
Supplement **Day Six**
  Features Editor Louise Douglas
  News Editor Mike Hill
  Picture Editor Steve Shakeshaft
  Sports Editor Richard Williamson

Articles of general and topical interest to North West England. No verse or fiction. Payment: according to value. News and feature illustrations. Founded 1855.

The Gazette, Blackpool

Blackpool Gazette & Herald Ltd, Avroe House, Avroe Crescent, Blackpool Business Park, Squires Gate, Blackpool FY4 2DP
tel (01253) 400888 *fax* (01253) 361870
email bpl.editor.al@blackpoolgazette.co.uk
website www.blackpoolgazette.co.uk
Editor David Helliwell
Daily Mon–Sat 32p

Local news and articles of general interest, with photos if appropriate. Length: varies. Payment: on merit. Founded 1929.

Lancashire Evening Post

Oliver's Place, Fulwood, Preston PR2 9ZA
tel (01772) 254841 *fax* (01772) 880173
Editor Simon Reynolds
Daily Mon–Sat 30p

Topical articles on all subjects. Area of interest
Wigan to Lake District, Lancs, and coast. Length:
600–900 words. Illustrations: colour and b&w
photos, cartoons. Payment: by arrangement.

Lancashire Evening Telegraph

Newspaper House, High Street, Blackburn BB1 1HT
tel (01254) 678678
website www.thisislancashire.co.uk
Editor Kevin Young
Daily Mon–Sat 26p
  News Editor Nick Nunn
  Picture Editor John Napier
  Sports Editor Neil Bramwell

Will consider general interest articles, such as
property, motoring, finance, etc. Payment: by
arrangement. Founded 1886.

Liverpool Echo

PO Box 48, Old Hall Street, Liverpool L69 3EB
tel 0151-227 2000 *fax* 0151-236 4682
website www.liverpool.com
Editor Mark Dickinson
Daily Mon–Sat 32p
  Head of News Andrew Edwards
  Picture Editor Stephen Shakeshaft
  Sports Editor John Thompson

Articles of up to 600–800 words of local or topical
interest; also cartoons. Payment: according to merit;
special rates for exceptional material. Connected
with, but independent of, the *Liverpool Daily Post*.
Articles not interchangeable.

Manchester Evening News

164 Deansgate, Manchester M60 2RD
tel 0161-832 7200 *editorial fax* 0161-834 3814
features fax 0161-839 0968
Editor Paul Horrocks
Daily Mon–Thurs & Sat 30p, Fri 10p
  Features Editor Maggie Henfield
  News Editor Ian Wood
  Picture Editor John Jeffay
  Sports Editor Peter Spencer

Feature articles of up to 1000 words, topical or
general interest and illustrated where appropriate,
should be addressed to the Features Editor.
Payment: on acceptance.

Oldham Chronicle

PO Box 47, Union Street, Oldham, Lancs. OL1 1EQ
tel 0161-633 2121 *fax* 0161-627 0905
email news@oldham-chronicle.co.uk
website www.oldham-chronicle.co.uk

Editor Jim Williams
Daily Mon–Fri 30p

News and features on current topics and local
history. Length: 1000 words. Illustrations: colour
and b&w photos and line. Payment: £20–£25 per
1000 words; £16.32–£21.90 for illustrations.
Founded 1854.

NORTHERN IRELAND – see BELFAST

SCOTLAND

Aberdeen Evening Express

Aberdeen Journals Ltd, PO Box 43, Lang Stracht,
Mastrick, Aberdeen AB15 6DF
tel (01224) 690222 *fax* (01224) 699575
Editor Donald Martin
Daily Mon–Sat 35p
  Features Editor Scott Begbie
  News Editor Richard Prest
  Sports Editor Jim Strachan

Lively evening paper. Illustrations: colour and b&w.
Payment: by arrangement.

The Courier and Advertiser

D.C. Thomson & Co. Ltd, 80 Kingsway East,
Dundee DD4 8SL
tel (01382) 223131 *fax* (01382) 454590
email courier@dcthomson.co.uk
website www.thecourier.co.uk
London office 185 Fleet Street, London EC4A 2HS
tel 020-7400 1030 *fax* 020-7400 1089
Daily Mon–Sat 32p
Founded 1816 and 1801.

Dundee Evening Telegraph and Post

D.C. Thomson & Co. Ltd, 80 Kingsway East,
Dundee DD4 8SL
tel (01382) 223131 *fax* (01382) 454590
email general@eveningtelegraph.co.uk
website www.eveningtelegraph.co.uk
London office 185 Fleet Street, London EC4A 2HS
tel 020-7400 1030 *fax* 020-7400 1089
Daily Mon–Fri 28p

Edinburgh Evening News

108 Holyrood Road, Edinburgh EH8 8AS
tel 0131-620 8620 *fax* 0131-620 8696
Editor Ian Stewart
Daily Mon–Sat 30p
  Features Editor Gina Davidson
  News Editor Jim G. Morrison
  Picture Editor Roger Jonathan
  Sports Editor Martin Dempster

Features on current affairs, preferably in relation to
our circulation area. Women's talking points, local
historical articles; subjects of general interest; health
and beauty, fashion.

Glasgow Evening Times

200 Renfield Street, Glasgow G2 3PR
tel 0141-302 7000 *fax* 0141-302 6600
website www.eveningtimes.co.uk
Editor Charles McGhee
Daily Mon–Sat 30p
Founded 1876.

Inverness Courier

PO Box 13, 9-11 Bank Lane, Inverness IV1 1QW
tel (01463) 233059 *fax* (01463) 243439
email editorial@inverness-courier.co.uk
Editor Jim Love
2 p.w. Tue 42p, Fri 50p
    News Editor Jack Gemmell
    Sports Editor David Beck

Articles of Highland interest only. Unsolicited material accepted. Illustrations: colour and b&w photos. Payment: by arrangement. Founded 1817.

Paisley Daily Express

Scottish and Universal Newspapers Ltd,
14 New Street, Paisley, Renfrewshire PA1 1YA
tel 0141-887 7911 *fax* 0141-889 7148
website www.insidescotland.co.uk
Acting Editor Anne Dalrymple
Daily Mon–Sat 25p
    News Editor Anne Dalrymple
    Sports Editor Matthew Vallance

Articles of Paisley interest only. Considers unsolicited material.

The Press and Journal

Lang Stracht, Aberdeen AB15 6DF
tel (01224) 690222
email pj.editor@ajl.co.uk
website www.thisisnorthscotland.co.uk
Editor Derek Tucker
Daily Mon–Sat 40p
    Deputy Editor Kay Drummond
    News Editor Fiona McWhirr
    Picture Desk Joanna Fraser
    Sports Editor Alex Martin

Contributions of Scottish interest. Payment: by arrangement. Illustrations: half-tone. Founded 1748.

The Sun

News International Newspapers, Scotland,
124 Portman Street, Kinning Park,
Glasgow G41 1EJ
tel 0141-420 5200 *fax* 0141-420 5248
email thescottish-sun@the-sun.co.uk
Editor tba
Daily Mon–Sat 28p
    Features Editor David Reynolds
    News Editor Alan Muir
    Picture Editor Mark Sweeney
    Sports Editor Steve Wolstencroft

Scottish edition of *The Sun*. Illustrations: transparencies, colour and b&w prints, colour cartoons. Payment: by arrangement. Founded 1985.

SOUTH EAST

Evening Echo

Newspaper House, Chester Hall Lane, Basildon, Essex SS14 3BL
tel (01268) 522792 *fax* (01268) 469281
Editor Martin McNeill
Daily Mon–Fri 32p
    Features Editor Sally King
    News Editor Chris Hatton
    Picture Editor Nick Ansell
    Sports Editor Paul Alton

Mostly staff-written. Only interested in local material. Payment: by arrangement. Founded 1969.

Medway Messenger

395 High Street, Chatham, Kent ME4 4PQ
tel (01634) 830600 *fax* (01634) 829484
Daily Mon–Fri 45p
    News Editor Nicky White
    Picture Editor Barry Hollis
    Sports Editor Mike Rees

Paper with emphasis on local news and sport, plus regular feature pages. National news; with editions covering the Medway Towns, Gravesend and Dartford, Swale. Illustrations: line, half-tone.

The News, Portsmouth

The News Centre, Hilsea, Portsmouth PO2 9SX
tel 023-9266 4488 *fax* 023-92673363
email newsdesk@thenews.co.uk
website www.thenews.co.uk
Editor Mike Gilson
Daily Mon–Sat 32p
    Features Editor John Millard
    News Editor Colin McNeill
    Picture Editor Steve Cutner
    Sports Editor Colin Channon

Articles of relevance to southeast Hampshire and West Sussex. Payment by arrangement. Founded 1877.

Reading Evening Post

8 Tessa Road, Reading, Berks. RG1 8NS
tel 0118-918 3000 *fax* 0118-959 9363
Editor Andy Murrill
Daily Mon–Fri 25p
    Features Editor Kate Magee
    News Editor Lucy Rimmer
    Picture Editor Steve Templeman
    Sports Editor Dave Wright

Topical articles based on current local news. Length: 800–1200 words. Payment: based on lineage rates. Illustrations: half-tone. Founded 1965.

The Southern Daily Echo

Newspaper House, Test Lane, Redbridge,
Southampton SO16 9JX
tel 023-8042 4777 *fax* 023-8042 4770
Editor Ian Murray
Daily Mon–Sat 30p
    News Editor Gordon Sutter
    Picture Editor Paul Collins
    Sports Editor Simon Carter
    Supplements Editor Emma Green

News, articles, features, sport. Length: varies.
Illustrations: line, half-tone, colour, cartoons.
Payment: NUJ rates. Founded 1888.

Swindon Evening Advertiser

100 Victoria Road, Old Town, Swindon SN1 3BE
tel (01793) 528144 *fax* (01793) 542434
email editor@newswilts.co.uk
website www.thisiswiltshire.co.uk
Editor Simon O'Neill
Mon–Sat 32p

News and information relating to Swindon and
Wiltshire only. Considers unsolicited material.
Founded 1854.

SOUTH WEST

The Bath Chronicle

Bath Newspapers, Windsor House, Windsor Bridge,
Bath BA2 3AU
tel (01225) 322322 *fax* (01225) 322291
Editor David Gledhill
Daily Mon–Sat 33p
    Features Editor Georgette McCready
    News Editor Paul Wiltshire
    Picture Editor Kevin Bates
    Sports Editor Tony Harrison

Welcomes local news and features. Length: 200–500
words. Illustrations: colour photos. Payment:
10p–13p per printed line; £5 per photo. Founded
1760.

Bristol Evening Post

Temple Way, Bristol BS99 7HD
tel 0117-934 3000
Editor Mike Lowe
Daily Mon–Sat 35p
    Features Editor Bill Davis
    News Editor Kevan Blackadder
    Picture Editor Shaun Thompson
    Sports Editor Chris Bartlett

Takes freelance news and articles. Payment: by
arrangement. Founded 1932.

The Citizen

Gloucestershire Newspapers Ltd, St John's Lane,
Gloucester GL1 2AY
tel (01452) 424442 *fax* (01452) 420664

Editor Ian Mean
Daily Mon–Sat 30p

Local news and features for Gloucester and its
districts. Length: 1000 words (articles/features),
300 words (news). Illustrations: colour. Payment:
negotiable.

Dorset Echo

Newscom, Fleet House, Hampshire Road,
Weymouth, Dorset DT4 9XD
tel (01305) 830930 *fax* (01305) 830956
email newsdesk@dorsetecho.co.uk
Editor David Murdock
Daily Mon–Sat 28p
    Features Editor Mike Clarke
    News Editor Paul Thomas
    Picture Editor Jim Tampin
    Sports Editor Paul Baker

News and occasional features (1000–2000 words).
Illustrations: b&w photos. Payment: by negotiation.
Founded 1921.

Evening Herald

17 Brest Road, Derriford Business Park, Plymouth,
Devon PL6 5AA
tel (01752) 765529 *fax* (01752) 765527
email news@eveningherald.co.uk
website www.thisisplymouth.co.uk
Editor Alan Qualtrough
Daily Mon–Sat 30p

Local news, articles and features. Will consider
unsolicited material. Welcomes ideas for articles and
features. Illustrations: colour and b&w prints.

Express & Echo

Express & Echo Publications Ltd, Heron Road,
Sowton, Exeter, Devon EX2 7NF
tel (01392) 442211 *fax* (01392) 442294/442287
Editor Steve Hall
Daily Mon–Sat 27p
    Head of Content Sue Kemp
    Picture Editor James Millar
    Sports Editor Richard Davies

Features and news of local interest. Length: 500–800
words (features), up to 400 words (news). Illustrations: colour. Payment: lineage rates; illustrations
negotiable. Founded 1904.

Gloucestershire Echo

Cheltenham Newspaper Co. Ltd, 1 Clarence Parade,
Cheltenham, Glos. GL50 3NY
tel (01242) 271900 *fax* (01242) 271803
Editor Anita Syvret
Daily Mon–Fri 32p, Sat 35p

Specialist articles with Gloucestershire connections;
no fiction. Material mostly commissioned. Length:
350 words. Payment: £30 per article, negotiable.
Founded 1873.

Sunday Independent (West of England)

Southern Newspapers plc, Burrington Way,
Plymouth PL5 3LN
tel (01752) 206600 *fax* (01752) 206164
Editor Nikki Rowlands
Sun 65p

News features on West Country topics;
features/articles with a nostalgic theme; short
quirky news briefs (must be original). Length: 600
words (features/articles), 300 words (news).
Illustrations: colour, b&w. Payment: by
arrangement. Founded 1808.

Western Daily Press

Bristol Evening Post and Press Ltd, Temple Way,
Bristol BS99 7HD
tel 0117-934 3000 *fax* 0117-934 3574
website www.westpress.co.uk
Editor Terry Manners
Daily Mon–Sat 34p

National, international or West Country topics for
features or news items, from established journalists,
with or without illustrations. Payment: by
negotiation. Founded 1858.

The Western Morning News

Brest Road, Derriford, Plymouth PL6 5AA
tel (01752) 765500 *fax* (01752) 765535
Editor Barrie Williams
Daily Mon–Sat 34p
   News Editor Laura Snook
   Picture Editor Michael Cranmer
   Sports Editor Mark Stevens

Articles plus illustrations considered on West
Country subjects. Founded 1860.

WALES

South Wales Argus

South Wales Argus Ltd, Cardiff Road, Maesglas,
Newport, Gwent NP20 3QN
tel (01633) 777219 *fax* (01633) 777202
Editor Gerry Keighley
Daily Mon–Sat 32p

News and features of relevance to Gwent. Length:
500–600 words (features); 350 words (news).
Illustrations: colour prints and transparencies.
Payment: £30 (features), £20 (news) per item;
£20–£25 (photos). Founded 1892.

South Wales Echo

Thomson House, Havelock Street,
Cardiff CF10 1XR
tel 029-2058 3622/20223333 *fax* 029-2058 3624
email echo.newsdesk@wme.co.uk
Editor Alastair Milburn
Daily Mon–Sat 32p

Evening paper: news, sport, features, showbiz, news

features, personality interviews. Length: up to 700
words. Illustrations: photos, cartoons. Payment: by
negotiation. Founded 1884.

The Western Mail

Thomson House, Havelock Street,
Cardiff CF10 1XR
tel 029-2058 3583 *fax* 029-2058 3652
Editor Alan Edmunds
Daily Mon–Fri 35p, Sat 40p

Articles of political, industrial, literary or general
and Welsh interest are considered. Illustrations:
topical general news and feature pictures, cartoons.
Payment: according to value; special fees for
exclusive news. Founded 1869.

WEST MIDLANDS

Birmingham Evening Mail

PO Box 78, Weaman Street,
Birmingham B4 6AY
tel 0121-236 3366 *fax* 0121-233 0271
London office 1 Canada Square, Canary Wharf,
London E14 5AP
tel 020-7293 3000 *fax* 020-7293 3793
Editor Roger Borrell
Daily Mon–Sat 32p

Features of topical Midland interest considered.
Length: 400–800 words. Payment: by arrangement.
Founded 1870.

The Birmingham Post

PO Box 18, 28 Colmore Circus,
Birmingham B4 6AX
tel 0121-236 3366 *fax* 0121-625 1105
London office 22nd Floor, 1 Canada Square,
Canary Wharf, London E14 5AP
tel 020-7293 3455 *fax* 020-7293 3400
Acting Editor Roger Borrell
Daily Mon–Sat 40p
   Deputy Editor Peter Bacon
   Head of News Phil Brown
   Picture Editor Paul Vokes
   Head of Sport Fraser Thomson

Authoritative and well-written articles of industrial,
political or general interest are considered,
especially if they have relevance to the Midlands.
Length: up to 1000 words. Payment: by
arrangement.

Coventry Evening Telegraph

Corporation Street, Coventry CV1 1FP
tel 024-7663 3633 *fax* 024-7655 0869
Editor Alan Kirby
Daily Mon–Sat 32p

Topical, illustrated articles with a Coventry or
Warwickshire interest. Length: up to 600 words.
Payment: by arrangement.

Express & Star

Queen Street, Wolverhampton WV1 1ES
tel (01902) 313131 *fax* (01902) 319721
email general@expressandstar.co.uk
website www.westmidlands.com
London office Room 110, Temple Chambers,
Temple Avenue, London EC4Y 0DT
Editor Warren Wilson
Daily Mon–Sat 30p
    Head of Features Jim Walsh
    Head of News John Bray
    Head of Pictures Tony Adams
    Sports Editor Steve Gordos
Founded 1874.

The Sentinel

Staffordshire Sentinel Newspapers Ltd,
Sentinel House, Etruria, Stoke-on-Trent ST1 5SS
tel (01782) 602525 *fax* (01782) 602616
email editor@thesentinel.co.uk
website www.thisisstaffordshire.co.uk
Editor Sean Dooley
Daily Mon–Sat 28p, Sun 35p
    Features Editor Julie Stickels
    Business Correspondent Stephen Houghton
    Managing Editor Roy Coates
    News Editor Martin Tideswell
    Picture Editor Trevor Slater
    Sports Editor Alex Martin

Articles and features of topical interest to the north
Staffordshire/south Cheshire area. Illustrations: colour
and b&w. Payment: by arrangement. Founded 1873.

Shropshire Star

Ketley, Telford TF1 5HU
tel (01952) 242424 *fax* (01952) 254605
Editor Sarah Jane Smith
Daily Mon–Sat 32p
    News Editor John Simcock
    Picture Editor Paul Morstatt-Higgs
    Sports Editor Keith Harrison
    Supplements Dept Sharon Walters

Evening paper: news and features. No unsolicited
material; write to features editor with outline of
ideas. Payment: by arrangement. Founded 1964.

Sunday Mercury

Colmore Circus, Birmingham B4 6AZ
tel 0121-234 5567 *fax* 0121-233 0271
Editor David Brookes
Sun 60p
    Deputy Editor Paul Cole
    Assistant Editor Tony Larner
    Picture Editor Adam Fradgley
    Sports Editor Lee Gibson

News specials or features of Midland interest.
Illustrations: colour, b&w, cartoons. Payment:
special rates for special matter.

Worcester Evening News

Berrows House, Hylton Road, Worcester WR2 5JX
tel (01905) 748200 *fax* (01905) 748009
email sg@newsquestmidlands.co.uk
website www.thisisworcester
Editor Stewart Gilbert
Daily Mon–Sat 25p

Local and national news, sport and features. Will
consider unsolicited material. Welcomes ideas for
articles and features. Length: 800 words (features),
300 words (news). Payment: £50 (features), £35
(news). Illustrations: colour prints.

YORKSHIRE/HUMBERSIDE

Evening Courier

PO Box 19, King Cross Street,
Halifax HX1 2SF
tel (01422) 260200 *fax* (01422) 260341
email editor@halifaxcourier.co.uk
website www.halifaxcourier.co.uk
Editor John Furbisher
Mon–Sat 30p
    Features Editor William Marshall
    News Editor John Kenealy
    Sports Editor Ian Rushworth

Articles of local interest and background to news
events. Length: up to 500 words. Illustrations:
colour photos. Payment: £25–£40 per article; photos
per quality/size used. Founded 1832.

Evening Press

York and County Press, PO Box 29,
76-86 Walmgate, York YO1 9YN
tel (01904) 653051 *fax* (01904) 612853
email newsdesk@ycp.co.uk
website www.thisisyork.co.uk
Editor tba
Daily Mon–Sat 35p
    Assistant Editors Chris Buxton, Bill Hearld
    News Editor Francine Clee
    Picture Editor Martin Oates
    Sports Editor Martin Jarred

Articles of North and East Yorkshire interest,
humour, personal experience of current affairs.
Length: 500–1000 words. Payment: by arrangement.
Illustrations: line, half-tone. Founded 1882.

Grimsby Telegraph

80 Cleethorpe Road, Grimsby,
North East Lincolnshire DN31 3EH
tel (01472) 360360 *fax* (01472) 372257
email newsdesk@grimsbytelegraph.co.uk
website www.thisisgrimsby.co.uk
Editor Peter Moore
Daily Mon–Sat 28p
    Features Editor Barrie Farnsworth
    News Editor David Atkin

Picture Editor David Moss
Sports Editor Geoff Ford

Considers general interest articles. Illustrations: line, half-tone, colour, cartoons. Payment: by arrangement. Founded 1897.

The Huddersfield Daily Examiner

Examiner News & Information Services Ltd,
PO Box A26, Queen Street South,
Huddersfield HD1 2TD
tel (01484) 430000 *fax* (01484) 437789
email editor@examiner.co.uk
website www.examiner.co.uk
Editor Roy Wright
Daily Mon–Fri 32p
  Features editor Andrew Flynn
  Picture editor Neil Atkinson

No contributions required at present. Payment: £10–£15 (short features). Founded 1871.

The Star

York Street, Sheffield S1 1PU
tel 0114-276 7676 *fax* 0114-272 5978
website www.sheffweb.co.uk
Editor Peter Charlton
Daily Mon–Sat 27p
  Features Editor Paul License
  News Editor Bob Westerdale
  Picture Editor Dennis Lound
  Sports Editor Martin Smith

Well-written articles of local character. Length: about 500 words. Payment: by negotiation. Illustrations: topical photos, line drawings, graphics, cartoons. Founded 1887.

Telegraph & Argus

Hall Ings, Bradford, West Yorkshire BD1 1JR
tel (01274) 729511 *fax* (01274) 723634
email bradford.editorial@bradford.newsquest.co.uk
website www.thisisbradford.co.uk
Editor Perry Austin-Clarke
Daily Mon–Sat 32p

Assistant Editor (news) Damian Bates
Assistant Editor (sport & pictures) Simon Waites
Features Editor David Barnett
Sports Editor Blake Richardson

Evening paper: news, articles and features relevant to or about the people of West Yorkshire. Length: up to 1000 words. Illustrations: line, half-tone, colour. Payment: features from £15; line from £5, b&w and colour photos by negotiation. Founded 1868.

Yorkshire Evening Post

PO Box 168, Wellington Street, Leeds LS1 1RF
tel 0113-2432701 *fax* 0113-2388535
Editor N.R. Hodgkinson
Daily Mon–Sat 32p
  Features Editor Anne Pickles
  News Editor Gillian Haworth
  Picture Editor Andy Manning
  Sports Editor Phil Rostron

News stories and feature articles. Illustrations: colour and b&w, cartoons. Payment: by negotiation. Founded 1890.

Yorkshire Post

Wellington Street, Leeds LS1 1RF
tel 0113-243 2701 *fax* 0113-238 8537
website www.yorkshireposttoday.co.uk
London office St Martin's House,
16 St Martin's le Grand, London EC1A 4EN
tel 020-7397 8723
Editor Rachel Campey
Daily Mon–Sat 38p
  Supplement **Yorkshire Post Magazine**
    Deputy Editor John Furbisher
    Features Editor Michael Hickling
    Picture Editor Ian Day
    Sports Editor Bill Bridge

Authoritative and well-written articles on topical subjects of general, literary or industrial interests. Length: max. 1200 words. Payment: by arrangement. Founded 1754.

Magazines UK and Ireland

Listings for regional newspapers start on page 11 and listings for national newspapers start on page 3. For quick reference, magazines are listed by subject area starting on page 677.

Accountancy
40 Bernard Street, London WC1N 1LD
tel 020-7833 3291 *fax* 020-7833 2085
email postmaster@theabg.demon.co.uk
website www.accountancymagazine.com
Editor Chris Quick
Monthly £57.50 p.a.

Articles on accounting, taxation, financial, legal and other subjects likely to be of professional interest to accountants in practice or industry, and to top management generally; cartoons. Payment: £140 per page. Founded 1889.

Accountancy Age
VNU Business Publications, VNU House, 32-34 Broadwick Street, London W1A 2HG
tel 020-7316 9236 *fax* 020-7316 9250
email accountancy_age@vnu.co.uk
website www.accountancyage.com
Editor Damian Wild
Weekly £2 (£100 p.a.)

Articles of accounting, financial and business interest. Illustrations: colour photos; freelance assignments commissioned. Payment: by arrangement. Founded 1969.

Accounting & Business
Association of Chartered Certified Accountants, 10-11 Lincolns Inn Fields, London WC2A 3BP
tel 020-7396 5966 *fax* 020-7396 5958
email john.prosser@accaglobal.com
website www.accaglobal.com
Editor John Rogers Prosser
10 p.a. £85 p.a.

Journal of the Association of Chartered Certified Accountants. Accountancy, finance and business topics of relevance to accountants and finance directors. Length: 1300 words. Payment: £150 per 1000 words. Illustrated. Founded 1998.

Ace Tennis Magazine
Tennis GB, 9-11 North End Road, London W14 8ST
tel 020-7605 8000 *fax* 020-7602 2323
email nigel.billen@acemag.co.uk
Editor Nigel Billen
11 p.a. £2.85

International high profile tennis, including interviews with top players, coaching articles, big tournament reports, health and fitness. Submit synopsis in first instance. Payment: 20p per word. Founded 1996.

Active Life
Computer Publishing, 221-223 High Street, Berkhamstead, Herts. HP4 1AD
tel (01442) 289600 *fax* (01442) 879903
email activelife@computer-publishing.net
Editor Paul Jacques
Monthly £1

Lifestyle advice for the over 50s, including holidays and health, fashion and food, finance and fiction, hobbies and home, personality profiles. Submit ideas in writing. Length: 600–1200 words. Illustrations: colour. Payment: £100 per 1000 words; photos by negotiation. Founded 1989.

Acumen
6 The Mount, Higher Furzeham, Brixham, South Devon TQ5 8QY
tel (01803) 851098
Editor Patricia Oxley
3 p.a. (Jan/May/Sept) £4.50, £12.50 p.a.

Poetry, literary and critical articles, reviews, literary memoirs, etc. Send sae with submissions. Payment: small. Founded 1985.

Aeroplane Monthly
IPC Magazines Ltd, King's Reach Tower, Stamford Street, London SE1 9LS
tel 020-7261 5849 *fax* 020-7261 5269
email aeroplane_monthly@ipcmedia.com
website www.aeroplanemonthly.com
Editor Michael Oakey
Monthly £3.40

Articles and photos relating to historical aviation. Length: up to 3000 words. Illustrations: line, half-tone, colour, cartoons. Payment: £60 per 1000 words, payable on publication; photos £10–£40; colour £80 per page. Founded 1973.

Africa Confidential
Blackwell Publishers Ltd, 73 Farringdon Road, London EC1M 3JQ
tel 020-7831 3511 *fax* 020-7831 6778
website www.africa-confidential.com
Editor Patrick Smith
Fortnightly £91 p.a. students, £385 p.a. institutions

News and analysis of political and economic

developments in Africa. Unsolicited contributions welcomed, but must be exclusive and not published elsewhere. Length: 1200-word features, 200-word pointers. Payment: from £200 per 1000 words. No illustrations.Founded 1960.

Africa: St Patrick's Missions

St Patrick's, Kiltegan, Co. Wicklow,
Republic of Ireland
tel (059) 6473600 *fax* (059) 6473622
email africa@spms.org
website www.spms.org
Editor Rev. Gary Howley
9 p.a. £5 p.a. (€9)

Articles of missionary and topical religious interest. Length: up to 1000 words. Illustrations: line, half-tone, colour.

African Business

IC Publications Ltd, 7 Coldbath Square,
London EC1R 4LQ
tel 020-7713 7711 *fax* 020-7713 7970
email icpubs@africasia.com a.versi@africasia.com
Editor Anver Versi
Monthly £2.50

Articles on business, economic and financial topics of interest to businessmen, ministers, officials concerned with African affairs. Length: 400–750 words; shorter coverage 100–400 words. Illustrations: line, half-tone, cartoons. Payment: £80 per 1000 words; £1 per column cm for illustrations. Founded 1978.

Agenda

The Wheelwrights, Fletching Street, Mayfield,
East Sussex TN20 6TL
tel/fax (01435) 872165
email agendapoetry@lycos.co.uk
Editor Patricia McCarthy, *Assistant Editor* W.S. Milne
Quarterly £26 p.a. (libraries, institutions and overseas: rates on application); £20 OAPs/students

Poetry and criticism. Study the journal before submitting MSS with an sae. Illustrations: half-tone. Payment: variable.

Air International

Key Publishing Ltd, PO Box 100, Stamford,
Lincs. PE9 1XQ
tel (01780) 755131 *fax* (01780) 757261
email malcolm.english@keypublishing.com
Editor Malcolm English
Monthly £3.30

Technical articles on aircraft; features on topical aviation subjects – civil and military. Length: up to 5000 words. Illustrations: colour transparencies/prints, b&w prints/line drawings. Payment: £50 per 1000 words or by negotiation; £20 colour, £10 b&w. Founded 1971.

Air Pictorial International

HPC Publishing, Drury Lane, St Leonards-on-Sea,
East Sussex TN38 9BJ
tel (01424) 720477 *fax* (01424) 443693/434086
Editor Barry C. Wheeler
Monthly £2.95

Covers all aspects of aviation. Many articles commissioned; will consider competent articles exploring fresh ground or presenting an individual point of view on technical matters. Illustrated, mainly with photos. Payment: by arrangement.

Amateur Gardening

IPC Media Ltd, Westover House,
West Quay Road, Poole,
Dorset BH15 1JG
tel (01202) 440840 *fax* (01202) 440860
email amateurgardening@ipcmedia.com
Editor Tim Rumball
Weekly £1.40

Topical, practical or newsy articles up to 1200 words of interest to keen gardeners. Payment: by arrangement. Illustrations: colour. Founded 1884.

Amateur Photographer

(incorporating Photo Technique)
IPC Magazines Ltd, King's Reach Tower,
Stamford Street, London SE1 9LS
tel 020-7261 5100 *fax* 020-7261 5404
email amateurphotographer@ipcmedia.com
Editor Garry Coward-Williams
Weekly £1.95

Editorial submissions are not encouraged. Founded 1884.

Amateur Stage

Platform Publications Ltd, Hampden House,
2 Weymouth Street, London W1W 5BT
tel 020-7636 4343 *fax* 020-7636 2323
email cvtheatre@aol.com
website www.amdram.org.uk/amstagel.htm
Editor Charles Vance
Monthly £2.40

Articles on all aspects of the amateur theatre, preferably practical and factual. Length: 600–2000 words. Illustrations: photos, line drawings. Payment: none. Founded 1946.

Ambit

17 Priory Gardens, London N6 5QY
tel 020-8340 3566
website www.ambitmag.co.uk
Editor Martin Bax, *Poetry Editors* Henry Graham,
Carol-Ann Duffy, *Prose Editors* J.G. Ballard, Geoff
Nicholson, *Art Editor* Mike Foreman
Quarterly £6 inc. p&p (£24 p.a. UK, £26/$52 p.a. overseas; £35 p.a., £37/$74 p.a. institutions)

Poetry, short fiction, art, poetry reviews. New and

established writers and artists. Payment: by arrangement. Illustrations: line, half-tone, colour. Founded 1959.

American Markets Newsletter

175 Westland Drive, Glasgow G14 9JQ
email sheila.oconnor@juno.com
Editor Sheila O'Connor
6 p.a. £34 p.a. (£63 for 2 years)

Editorial guidelines for US, Canadian and other overseas markets, plus information on press trips, non-fiction/fiction markets and writers' tips. Free syndication for all subscribers. Sample issue £5.95 (payable to S. O'Connor).

AN Magazine

AN: The Artists Information Company,
1st Floor, 7-15 Pink Lane,
Newcastle upon Tyne NE1 5DW
tel 0191-241 8000 *fax* 0191-241 8001
email edit@anpubs.demon.co.uk
website www.a-n.co.uk
Contact Editorial Team
Monthly £3.50 (£28 p.a.)

Articles, news and features for visual and applied artists. Illustrations: transparencies, colour and b&w photos. Payment: £130 per 1000 words. Founded as *Artists Newsletter* in 1980.

Angler's Mail

IPC Media Ltd, King's Reach Tower,
Stamford Street, London SE1 9LS
tel 020-7261 5778 *fax* 020-7261 6016
Editor Roy Westwood
Weekly £1

News items about coarse and sea fishing. Payment: by agreement.

Angling Times

EMAP Active, Bushfield House, Orton Centre,
Peterborough PE2 5UW
tel (01733) 232600 *fax* (01733) 465844
email richard.lee@emap.com
Editor Richard Lee
Weekly £1.20

Articles, pictures, news stories, on all forms of angling. Illustrations: line, half-tone, colour. Payment: by arrangement. Founded 1953.

Animals and You

D.C. Thomson & Co Ltd, Albert Square,
Dundee DD1 9QJ
tel (01382) 223131 *fax* (01382) 225511
185 Fleet Street, London EC4A 2HS
tel 020-7400 1030 *fax* 020-7400 1089
Monthly (Fri) £1.75

Features, stories and pin-ups for girls who love animals. Founded 1998.

Antiques & Art Independent

PO Box 1945, Comely Bank, Edinburgh EH4 1AB
tel (07000) 268478
email antiquesnews@hotmail.com
website www.antiquesnews.co.uk
Publisher/Editor Tony Keniston
Quarterly £2

Newspaper for the British antiques and art trade. News, gossip and controversial personal views on all aspects of the antiques world welcome. People stories only. Approach in writing with ideas. Length: 600 words (articles), 200 words (news). Illustrations: b&w prints. Payment: by negotiation. Founded 1997.

Antiques and Collectables

Merricks Media Ltd, Charlotte House,
12 Charlotte Street, Bath BA1 2NE
tel (01225) 786800 *fax* (01225) 786801
email info@antiques.collectables.co.uk
website www.antiques-collectables.co.uk
Editor Diana Cambridge
Monthly £2.60

Features on ceramics, furniture, glass, memorabilia, ephemera, etc aimed at the antiques trade and general collectors. Includes price guide and news. Write with idea in first instance. Length: 1500–2000 (features). Illustrations: transparencies and colour prints. Payment £100–£150. Founded 1998.

Apollo

1-2 Castle Lane, London SW1E 6DR
tel 020-7233 6640 *fax* 020-7630 7791
Editor David Ekserdjian
Monthly £7.80

Scholarly articles of about 3000 words on art, architecture, ceramics, furniture, armour, glass, sculpture, and any subject connected with art and collecting. Payment: by arrangement. Illustrations: half-tone, colour. Founded 1925.

Aquila

New Leaf Publishing Ltd, PO Box 2518, Eastbourne,
East Sussex BN21 2BB
tel (01323) 431313 *fax* (01323) 731136
email info@aquila.co.uk
website www.aquila.co.uk
Editor Jackie Berry
Monthly £31.50 p.a. (£19.95 6 months)

Dedicated to encouraging children aged 8–13 to reason and create, and to develop a caring nature. Short stories and serials of up to 4 parts. Occasional features commissioned from writers with specialist knowledge. Approach in writing with ideas and sample of writing style, with sae. Length: 700–800 words (features), 1000–1100 words (stories or per episode of a serial). Illustrations: colour and b&w, cartoons. Payment: £75 (features); £90 (stories), £80 (per episode). Founded 1993.

The Architects' Journal

EMAP Business Communications,
151 Rosebery Avenue, London EC1R 4GB
tel 020-7505 6700 *fax* 020-7505 6701
Editor Isabel Allen
Weekly £1.80 (£78 p.a.)

Articles (mainly technical) on architecture, planning
and building accepted only with prior agreement of
synopsis. Illustrations: photos and drawings.
Payment: by arrangement. Founded 1895.

Architectural Design

John Wiley & Sons Ltd, 4th Floor, International
House, Ealing Broadway Centre, London W5 5DB
tel 020-8326 3800 *fax* 020-8326 3801
website www.wiley.co.uk/ad/
Editor Helen Castle
6 double issues p.a., £22.50 single issue, £99 p.a.
(£70 p.a. students)

International architectural publication comprising
an extensively illustrated thematic profile and
magazine back section, *AD Plus*. Uncommissioned
articles not accepted. Illustrations: drawings and
photos, line (colour preferred). Payment: by
arrangement. Founded 1930.

The Architectural Review

EMAP Construct, 151 Rosebery Avenue,
London EC1R 4GB
tel 020-7505 6725 *fax* 020-7505 6701
email peter.davey@ebc.emap.com
website www.arplus.com/
Editor Peter Davey
Monthly £6.75

Articles on architecture and the allied arts. Writers
must be thoroughly qualified. Length: up to 3000
words. Payment: by arrangement. Illustrations:
photos, drawings, etc. Founded 1896.

Architecture Today

161 Rosebery Avenue, London EC1R 4QX
tel 020-7837 0143 *fax* 020-7837 0155
Editors Ian Latham, Mark Swenarton
10 p.a. £4 Free to architects

Mostly commissioned articles and features on
today's European architecture. Length: 200–800
words. Illustrations: colour. Payment: by
negotiation. Founded 1989.

Arena

EMAP East, Endeavour House,
189 Shaftesbury Avenue, London WC2H 8JG
tel 020-7437 9011
email arenamag@emap.com
Editor Anthony Noguera
Monthly £3.20

Profiles, articles on a wide range of subjects
intelligently treated; art, architecture, politics, sport,
business, music, film, design, media, fashion.
Length: up to 3000 words. Illustrations: b&w and
colour photos. Payment: £300 per 1000 words;
varies for illustrations. Founded 1986.

Art Business Today

The Fine Art Trade Guild, 16-18 Empress Place,
London SW6 1TT
tel 020-7381 6616 *fax* 020-7381 2596
email abt@fineart.co.uk
website www.fineart.co.uk/Abtonline/abt.htm
Editor Mike Sims
5 p.a. £22 p.a.

Distributed to the fine art and framing industry.
Covers essential information on new products and
technology, market trends and business analysis.
Length: 800–1600 words. Illustrations: colour photos,
cartoons. Payment: by arrangement. Founded 1905.

Art Monthly

4th Floor, 28 Charing Cross Road,
London WC2H 0DB
tel 020-7240 0389 *fax* 020-7497 0726
email info@artmonthly.co.uk
website www.artmonthly.co.uk
Editor Patricia Bickers
10 p.a. £3.50

Features on modern and contemporary visual
artists and art history, art theory and art-related
issues; exhibition and book reviews. All material
commissioned. Length: 750–1500 words.
Illustrations: b&w photos. Payment: features
£100–£200; none for photos. Founded 1976.

The Art Newspaper

70 South Lambeth Road, London SW8 1RL
tel 020-7735 3331 *fax* 020-7735 3332
email contact@theartnewspaper.com
website www.theartnewspaper.com
Editor Anna Somers Cocks
11 p.a. £4.95 (£49 p.a.)

International coverage of visual art, news, politics,
law, exhibitions with some feature pages. Length:
200–1000 words. Illustrations: b&w photos.
Payment: £120 per 1000 words. Founded 1990.

Art Review

Art Review Ltd, Hereford House,
23-24 Smithfield Street, London EC1A 9LB
tel 020-7236 4880 *fax* 020-7246 3351
email info@art-review.co.uk
website www.art-review.com
Editor Meredith Etherington-Smith, *Send material
to* Charlotte Edwards, Associate Editor
Monthly £4.25

Modern and contemporary art features and reviews.
Proposals welcome. Payment: from £400 per 1000
words. Illustrations: colour. Founded 1949.

The Artist
The Artists' Publishing Co. Ltd, Caxton House,
63-65 High Street, Tenterden, Kent TN30 6BD
tel (01580) 763673
Editor Sally Bulgin
Monthly £2.60

Practical, instructional articles on painting for all
amateur and professional artists. Payment: by
arrangement. Illustrations: line, half-tone, colour.
Founded 1931.

Artists and Illustrators
The Fitzpatrick Building, 188-194 York Way,
London N7 9QR
tel 020-7700 8500 *fax* 020-7700 4985
email aim@quarto.com
Editor James Hobbs
Monthly £2.60

Practical and business articles for amateur and
professional artists. Length: 1000–1500 words.
Illustrations: colour transparencies. Payment:
variable. Founded 1986.

Asian Times
Ethnic Media Group, Unit 2.01,
Technology Centre, 65 Whitechapel Road,
London E1 1DU
tel 020-7650 2000 *fax* 020-7560 2001
Editor Emenike Pio
Weekly 50p

News stories, articles and features of interest to
Britain's Asian community. Founded 1983.

Astronomy Now
Pole Star Publications, PO Box 175, Tonbridge,
Kent TN10 4ZY
tel (01903) 266165 *fax* (01732) 356230
email editorial@astronow.cix.co.uk
Managing Editor Steven Young
Monthly £2.85

Aimed at amateur and professional astronomers.
Interested in news items and longer features on
astronomy and some space-related activities.
Writers' guidelines available (send sae). Length:
600–3000 words. Illustrations: line, half-tone,
colour. Payment: 5p per word; from £10 per photo.
Founded 1987.

Athletics Weekly
Descartes Publishing Ltd, 83 Park Road,
Peterborough PE1 2TN
tel (01733) 898440 *fax* (01733) 898441
email jasan.henderson@athletics-weekly.co.uk
Editor Jasan Henderson
Weekly £2.25

News and features on track and field athletics, road
running, cross country, fell and race walking.
Material mostly commissioned. Length: 300–1500

words. Illustrations: colour and b&w action and
head/shoulder photos, line. Payment: varies.
Founded 1945.

Attitude
Northern & Shell Tower, City Harbour,
London E14 9GL
tel 020-7308 5090 *fax* 020-7308 5384
email attitude@nasnet.co.uk
Editor Adam Mattera
Monthly £2.75

Men's style magazine aimed primarily but not
exclusively at gay men. Covers style/fashion,
interviews, reviews, celebrities, humour.
Illustrations: colour transparencies, b&w prints.
Payment: £150 per 1000 words; £100 per full page
illustration. Founded 1994.

The Author
84 Drayton Gardens, London SW10 9SB
tel 020-7373 6642
Editor Fanny Blake
Quarterly £9

Organ of the Society of Authors. Commissioned
articles from 1000–2000 words on any subject
connected with the legal, commercial or technical
side of authorship. Little scope for the freelance
writer: preliminary letter advisable. Illustrations:
line, occasional cartoons. Payment: by arrangement.
Founded 1890.

Auto Express
Dennis Publishing Ltd, 30 Cleveland Street,
London W1T 4JD
tel 020-7907 6200 *fax* 020-7907 6234
email editorial@autoexpress.co.uk
website www.autoexpress.co.uk
Editor David Johns
Weekly £1.50

News stories, and general interest features about
drivers as well as cars. Illustrations: colour photos.
Payment: features £350 per 1000 words; photos,
varies. Founded 1988.

Autocar
Haymarket Publishing Ltd,
60 Waldegrave Road, Teddington,
Middlesex TW11 8LG
tel 020-8267 5630 *fax* 020-8267 5759
email autocar@haynet.com
Editor Steve Fowler
Weekly £2.10

Articles on all aspects of cars, motoring and the
motor industry: general, practical, competition and
technical. Illustrations: line (litho), colour and
electronic (Illustrator). Press day news: Thursday.
Payment: varies; mid-month following publication.
Founded 1895.

B

Attic Futura (UK) Ltd, 16-17 Berners Street,
London W1T 3LN
tel 020-7664 6470 *fax* 020-7070 3401
email letters@bmagazine.co.uk
Editor Gina Johnson
Monthly £2.50

Magazine with international flavour for young
women aged 18–25. Fashion, beauty, real life stories,
topical issues, celebrity features. Contact Catherine
McDonnoll in first instance with ideas for articles.
Founded 1997.

Back Street Heroes

Isis Building, 193 Marsh Wall, Thames Quay,
London E14 9SG
tel 020-7772 8300 *fax* 020-7772 8585
Editor Stu Garland
Monthly £2.99

Custom motorcycle features plus informed lifestyle
pieces. Illustrations: colour, cartoons. Payment: by
arrangement. Founded 1983.

Balance

Diabetes UK, 10 Parkway, London NW1 7AA
tel 020-7424 1000 *fax* 020-7424 1081
email balance@diabetes.org.uk
website www.diabetes.org.uk
Editor Martin Cullen
Bi-monthly £2.95

Articles on diabetes and related health and
lifestyle issues. Length: 1000–1500 words. Payment:
by arrangement. Illustrations: colour. Founded
1935.

The Banker

Tabernacle Court, 16-28 Tabernacle Street,
London EC2 4DD
tel 020-7382 8000 *fax* 020-7382 8568
email stephen.timewell@ft.com
Editor-in-Chief Stephen Timewell
Monthly £215 p.a.

Articles on investment banking and finance, retail
banking, banking technology, banking services and
systems; bank analysis and top 1000 listings.
Illustrations: half-tones and full colour of people,
charts, tables, maps, etc. Founded 1926.

Baptist Times

PO Box 54, 129 Broadway, Didcot,
Oxon OX11 8XB
tel (01235) 517670 *fax* (01235) 517678
Editor Hazel Southam
Weekly 55p

Religious or social affairs, news, features and
reviews. Payment: by arrangement. Founded 1855.

BBC magazines – see page 294

The Beano

D.C. Thomson & Co. Ltd, Albert Square,
Dundee DD1 9QJ
tel (01382) 223131 *fax* (01382) 322214
185 Fleet Street, London EC4A 2HS
tel 020-7400 1030 *fax* 020-7400 1089
Weekly 65p

Comic strips for children. Series, 11–22 pictures.
Payment: on acceptance.

Fun Size Beano
2 p.m. 90p

Founded 1997.

Bella

H. Bauer Publishing, Academic House,
24-28 Oval Road, London NW1 7DT
tel 020-7241 8000 *fax* 020-7241 8056
Editor Rebecca Fleming, *Assistant Editor/Features
Editor* Sue Ricketts
Weekly 62p

General interest magazine for women: practical
articles on fashion and beauty, health, cooking,
home, travel; real life stories, plus fiction up to 1800
words. Payment: by arrangement. Illustrations: line
including cartoons, half-tone, colour. Founded 1987.

Best

The National Magazine Company,
33 Broadwick Street, London W1F 0DQ
tel 020-7439 5000 *fax* 020-7312 4176
Editor Louise Court, *Fiction Editor* Pat Richardson,
Features Editor Charlotte Seligman
Weekly 68p

Short stories. No other uncommissioned work
accepted, but always willing to look at ideas/outlines.
Length: 1000 words for short stories, variable for
other work. Illustrations: line, half-tone, colour,
cartoons. Payment: by agreement. Founded 1987.

Best of British

Ian Beacham Publishing, Bank Chambers,
27A Market Place, Market Deeping, Lincs. PE6 8EA
tel/fax (01778) 342814
email mail@british.fsbusiness.co.uk
website www.bestofbritishmag.co.uk
Editor-in-Chief Ian Beacham
Monthly £2.95

Nostalgic features about life in the 1930s, 1940s,
1950s and 1960 together with stories celebrating
interesting aspects of Britain today. Length: max.
1500 words. Illustrations: colour and b&w.
Payment: from £30 (words); £20 (pictures).
Founded 1994.

The Big Issue

1-5 Wandsworth Road, London SW8 2LN
tel 020-7526 3200

Editor Matt Ford
Weekly £1.20

Features, current affairs, reviews, interviews – of general interest and on social issues. Length: 1000 words (features). No short stories or poetry. Illustrations: colour and b&w photos and line. Payment: £160 per 1000 words. Founded 1991.

The Big Issue Cymru

55 Charles Street, Cardiff CF10 2GD
tel 029-2025 5670 *fax* 029-2025 5673
email edit@bigissuecymru.fsnet.co.uk
Editor Sue West, *Send material to* Cathryn Scott, Deputy Editor
Weekly £1.20

The Welsh edition of the *Big Issue*. Content is relevant to Wales: some articles are taken from the main edition but some news features, arts and music coverage is specially written. Considers unsolicited material. Welcomes ideas for articles and features. Length: 1000–1500 words (articles/features), 200–400 words (news). Illustrations: colour and b&w prints and artwork. Payment: 4p per word (articles/features), 6p per word (news); £40 (cover photo), £20 for first photo (features) and £10 for all others used from that commission; £30 (illustrations). Founded 1994.

The Big Issue in the North

The Big Issue in the North Ltd,
135-141 Oldham Street, Manchester M4 1LL
tel 0161-834 6300 *fax* 0161-819 5000
Editor Kate Markey
Weekly £1.20

Articles of general interest and on social issues; arts features and news covering the north of England. No fiction or poetry, except by the homeless. Contact the news, arts or deputy editor to discuss ideas. Length: 1500 words (features/articles), 300–500 (news), 700 (arts features), 350 words (comment). Payment: £90 per 1000 words. Colour transparencies, puzzles and quizzes. Founded 1992.

The Big Issue in Scotland

The Big Issue in Scotland Ltd, 71 Oxford Street, Glasgow G5 9EP
tel 0141-418 7000 *fax* 0141-418 7061
email editorial@bigissuescotland.com
Editor-in-Chief Mel Young, *Send material to* Claire Black, Deputy Editor
Weekly £1

Features on human rights, animal issues, green issues, injustices, Scotland, medical, scientific, the paranormal, health and crime, plus news and reviews. Also international features/news. Length: 1000–2000 words (articles); 500–800 words (news). Illustrations: colour and b&w. Payment: £100 per 1000 words; £60 per photo/illustration. Founded 1993.

The Big Issue South West

5 Brunswick Court, Brunswick Square, Bristol BS2 8PE
tel 0117-908 0091 *fax* 0117-908 0093
email editorial@bigissuesouthwest.co.uk
website www.bigissuesouthwest.co.uk
Editor Tim Lezard
Weekly £1.20

Social news, general interest features and arts information for the South West. Considers unsolicited material. Length: 1200 words (articles/features), 100–1200 words (news). Payment: negotiable. Illustrations: colour, payment negotiable. Founded 1991.

Bike

EMAP Automotive Ltd, Media House, Lynchwood, Peterborough PE2 6EA
tel (01733) 468000 *fax* (01733) 468196
email bike@emap.com
Editor Tim Thompson
Monthly £3.50

Motorcycle magazine: interested in articles, features, news. Length: articles/features 1000–3000 words. Illustrations: colour and b&w photos. Payment: £150 per 1000 words; photos per size/position. Founded 1971.

Bird Watching

EMAP Active Ltd, Bretton Court, Bretton, Peterborough PE3 8DZ
tel (01733) 264666 *fax* (01773) 465376
email david.cromack@emap.com
Editor David Cromack
Monthly £3.20

Broad range of bird-related features and photography, particularly looking at bird behaviour, bird news, reviews and UK birdwatching sites. Limited amount of overseas features. Emphasis on providing accurate information in entertaining ways. Send synopsis first. Length: 1200 words. Illustrations: colour transparencies, bird identification artwork. Payment: by negotiation. Founded 1986.

Birding World

Sea Lawn, Coast Road, Cley next the Sea, Holt, Norfolk NR25 7RZ
tel (01263) 740913 *fax* (01263) 741014
email steve@birdingworld.co.uk
website www.birdingworld.co.uk
Editor Steve Gantlett
Monthly £43 p.a. (£50 p.a. Europe; £54 p.a. rest of the world, airmail)

Magazine for keen birdwatchers. Articles and news stories about mainly European ornithology, with the emphasis on ground-breaking new material and identification. Length: up to 3000 words (articles);

up to 1500 words (news). Illustrations: good quality colour photos of birds. Payment: up to £25 per 500 words; £10–£40 (illustrations). Founded 1987.

Birdwatch

Solo Publishing Ltd, 3rd Floor, Leroy House, 436 Essex Road, London N1 3QP
tel 020-7704 9495 *fax* 020-7704 2767
website www.birdwatch.co.uk
Editor Dominic Mitchell
Monthly £3.20

Topical articles on all aspects of birds and birding, including conservation, identification, sites and habitats, equipment, overseas expeditions. Length: 700–1500 words. Illustrations: colour slides, b&w photos, colour and b&w line. Payment: from £40 per 1000 words; colour: photos £15–£40, cover £75, line by negotiation; b&w: photos £10, line £10–£40. Founded 1991.

Bizarre

IFG, 9 Dallington Street, London EC1V 0BQ
tel 020-7687 7000 *fax* 020-77687 7096
email bizarre@ifgmags.com
website www.bizarremag.com
Editor Ben Raworth
Monthly £2.95

Features on strange events, adventure, cults, weird people, celebrities, etc. Study the magazine for style before submitting ideas by post or fax. No fiction. Length: 800–2000 words. Payment: £80 per 1000 words. Colour transparencies and prints: £200 per dps, £125 per page. Founded 1997.

Black Beauty & Hair

Hawker Publications, 2nd Floor, Culvert House, Culvert Road, London SW11 5DH
tel 020-7720 2108 *fax* 020-7498 3023
email info@blackbeautyandhair.com
website www.blackbeautyandhair.com
Editor Irene Shelley
Bi-monthly £2.30

Beauty and style articles relating specifically to the black woman; celebrity features. True-life stories and salon features. Length: approx. 1000 words. Illustrations: colour and b&w photos. Payment: £100 per 1000 words; photos £25–£75. Founded 1982.

Bliss!

EMAP Élan Ltd, Endeavour House, 189 Shaftesbury Avenue, London WC2H 8JG
tel 020-7437 9011 *fax* 020-7208 3591
website www.blissmag.co.uk
Editor Helen Johnston
Monthly £1.90

Glamorous young women's glossy magazine. Bright intimate American-style format, with real life stories and reports, beauty, fashion, talent, advice, quizzes. Payment: by arrangement. Founded 1995.

Blueprint

ETP Ltd, Rosebery House, 41 Springfield Road, Chelmsford CM2 6JJ
tel (01245) 491717 *fax* (01245) 499110
email ggibson@wilmington.co.uk
Editor Grant Gibson
12 p.a. £3.75

The magazine of modern architecture, design and culture. Interested in articles, features and reviews. Length: up to 2500 words. Illustrations: colour and b&w photos and line. Payment: negotiable. Founded 1983.

BMA News

British Medical Association, BMA House, Tavistock Square, London WC1H 9JP
tel 020-7383 6122 *fax* 020-7383 6566
Joint Editors Julia Bell, Caroline Jones
51 p.a. £68 p.a.

News and features. Length: 700–2000 words (features), 100–300 words (news). Illustrations: transparencies, colour and b&w artwork and cartoons. Payment: by negotiation. Founded 1966.

Boards

Yachting Press Ltd, 196 Eastern Esplanade, Southend-on-Sea, Essex SS1 3AB
tel (01702) 582245 *fax* (01702) 588434
email editorial@boards.co.uk
website www.boards.co.uk
Editor Bill Dawes
Monthly during summer, Bi-monthly during winter £3.20 (10 p.a.)

Articles, photos and reports on all aspects of windsurfing and boardsailing. Payment: by arrangement. Illustrations: line, half-tone, colour, cartoons. Founded 1982.

The Book Collector

(incorporating Bibliographical Notes and Queries)
The Collector Ltd, PO Box 12426, London W11 3GW
tel/fax 020-7792 3492
email nicolasb@nixnet.clara.co.uk
Editorial Board Nicolas Barker (Editor), A. Bell, A. Edwards, J. Fergusson, T. Hofmann, D. McKitterick, Joan Winterkorn
Quarterly £40 p.a. (£43/$68 overseas)

Articles, biographical and bibliographical, on the collection and study of printed books and MSS. Payment: for reviews only. Founded 1952.

Book and Magazine Collector

Diamond Publishing Ltd, 45 St Mary's Road, London W5 5RQ
tel 020-8579 1082 *fax* 020-8566 2024

Editor Crispin Jackson
Monthly £3.20

Articles about collectable authors/publications/
subjects. Articles must be bibliographical and
include a full bibliography and price guide (no
purely biographical features). Approach in writing
with ideas. Length: 2000–4000 words. Illustrations:
colour and b&w artwork. Payment: £35 per 1000
words. Founded 1984.

Books Ireland
11 Newgrove Avenue, Dublin 4,
Republic of Ireland
tel (01) 2692185 *fax* (01) 260 4927
email booksi@eircom.net
Editor Jeremy Addis, *Features Editor* Shirley Kelly
Monthly (exc. Jan, Jul, Aug) €3.50 (€32 p.a.)

Reviews of Irish-interest and Irish-author books,
articles of interest to librarians, booksellers and
readers. Length: 800–1400 words. Payment: £80 per
1000 words. Founded 1976.

Books Magazine
39 Store Street, London WC1E 7DB
tel 020-7629 2900 *fax* 020-7419 2111
Editor Liz Thomson
Quarterly £1.50

Reviews, features, interviews with authors. No
unsolicited MSS. Payment: negotiable but little
bought in. Founded 1987.

The Bookseller
VNU Entertainment Media Ltd, 5th Floor,
Endeavour House, 189 Shaftesbury Avenue,
London WC2H 8TJ
tel 020-7420 6006 *fax* 020-7420 6103
email letters.to.editor@bookseller.co.uk
website www.thebookseller.com
Editor Nicholas Clee
Weekly £170 p.a.

Journal of the UK publishing and bookselling
trades. While outside contributions are welcomed,
most of the journal's contents are commissioned.
Length: about 1000–1500 words. Payment: by
arrangement. Founded 1858.

Bowls International
Key Publishing Ltd, PO Box 100, Stamford,
Lincs. PE9 1XQ
tel (01780) 755131 *fax* (01780) 757261
Editor Melvyn Beck
Monthly £2.70

Sport and news items and features; occasional,
bowls-oriented short stories. Illustrations: colour
transparencies, b&w photos, occasional line,
cartoons. Payment: sport/news approx. 25p per line,
features approx. £50 per page; colour £25, b&w £10.
Founded 1981.

British Birds
The Banks, Mountfield, Robertsbridge,
East Sussex TN32 5JY
tel (01580) 882039
email editor@britishbirds.co.uk
Editor Dr Roger Riddington
Monthly £58 p.a. (concessionary rates available)

Publishes major papers on identification, behaviour,
conservation, distribution, ecology, movements,
status and taxonomy with official reports on: rare
breeding birds, scarce migrants and rare birds in
Britain. Payment: token. Founded 1907.

British Deaf News
7 Empire Court, Albert Street, Redditch,
Worcs. B97 4DA
tel (01527) 592034, 592044 (text)
fax (01527) 592083 *videophone* (01527) 595318
email editorial@britishdeafness.com
website www.britishdeafnews.com
Editor Catya Wheatley
Monthly £1.95, £20 p.a. non-members (£15 p.a.
BDA members)

Interviews, features, reviews, articles, news items,
letters dealing with deafness. Payment: by arrangement. Illustrations: line, half-tone. Founded 1872.

The British Journal of Photography
Timothy Benn Publishing, 39 Earlham Street,
London WC2H 9LT
tel 020-7306 7000 *fax* 020-7306 7017
email bjp.editor@bjphoto.co.uk
website www.bjphoto.co.uk
Editor Jon Tarrant
Weekly £1.95

Articles on professional, commercial and press
photography, and on the more advanced aspects of
amateur, technical, industrial, medical, scientific
and colour photography. Illustrations: line, half-
tone, colour. Payment: by arrangement. Founded
1854.

British Journalism Review
BJR Publishing Ltd, c/o Sage Publications,
6 Bonhill Street, London EC2A 4PU
tel 020-7374 0645 *fax* 020-7374 8741
email info@sagepub.co.uk
Editor Bill Hagerty
Quarterly £35 p.a. (overseas rates on application)

Comment/criticism/review of matters published by,
or of interest to, the media. Length: 1000–3000
words. Illustrations: b&w photos. Payment: by
arrangement. Founded 1989.

British Medical Journal
BMA House, Tavistock Square, London WC1H 9JR
tel 020-7387 4499 *fax* 020-7383 6418
email editor@bmj.com

website www.bmj.com
Editor Richard Smith BSc, NB, ChBEDd, MFPHM, FRCPE
Weekly £7.90

Medical and related articles. Payment: by arrangement. Founded 1840.

British Philatelic Bulletin

Royal Mail, 148 Old Street, London EC1V 9HQ
fax 020-7250 2389
Editor J.R. Holman
Monthly £1.10

Articles on any aspect of British philately – stamps, postmarks, postal history; also stamp collecting in general. Length: up to 1500 words (articles); 250 words (news). Payment: £60 per 1000 words. Illustrations: colour. Founded 1963.

British Postmark Bulletin
Fortnightly £12.25 p.a. (£24.95 p.a. overseas)

Articles on British postmarks – past and present. Founded 1971.

Broadcast

EMAP Media, 33-39 Bowling Green Lane, London EC1R 0DA
tel 020-7505 8014 *fax* 020-7505 8050
Editor Conor Dignam
Weekly £2.60

News and authoritative articles designed for all concerned with the UK and international TV and radio industry, and with programmes and advertising on TV, radio, video, cable, satellite, digital. Illustrations: colour, b&w, line, cartoons. Payment: by arrangement.

Brownie

The Guide Association, 17-19 Buckingham Palace Road, London SW1W 0PT
tel 020-7834 6242
email MarionT@guides.org.uk chq@guides.org.uk
website www.guides.org.uk
Editor Marion Thompson
Monthly £1.35

Official Magazine of The Guide Association. Short articles for Brownies (girls 7–10 years); fiction with Brownie background (700–800 words); puzzles; 'things to make', etc. Illustrations: colour. Payment: £50 per 1000 words; varies for illustrations.

Buckinghamshire Countryside

Beaumonde Publications Ltd, PO Box 5, Hitchin, Herts. SG5 1GJ
tel (01462) 431237 *fax* (01462) 422015
email info@hertscountryside.co.uk
Editor Sandra Small
Bi-monthly £1.25

Articles relating to Buckinghamshire. No poetry, puzzles or crosswords. Length: approx. 1000 words.

Illustrations: colour transparencies and b&w prints, artwork. Payment: £30 per article. Founded 1995.

Building

The Builder Group plc, 7th Floor, Anchorage House, 2 Clove Crescent, London E14 2BE
tel 020-7560 4000 *fax* 020-7560 4014
email adrian_barrick@buildersgroup.co.uk
Editor Adrian Barrick
Weekly £2.40

Covers the entire professional, industrial and manufacturing aspects of the building industry. Articles on architecture and techniques at home and abroad considered, also news and photos. Payment: by arrangement. Founded 1842.

Building Design

CMP Information Ltd, Ludgate House, 245 Blackfriars Road, London SE1 9UY
tel 020-7861 6467 *fax* 020-7861 6261
email bd@cmpinformation.com
Editor Robert Booth
Weekly Controlled circulation

News and features on all aspects of building design. All material commissioned. Length: up to 1500 words. Illustrations: colour and b&w photos, line, cartoons. Payment: £150 per 1000 words; illustrations by negotiation. Founded 1970.

Built Environment

Alexandrine Press, 1 The Farthings, Marcham, Oxon OX13 6QD
tel (01865) 391518 *fax* (01865) 391687
email alexandrine@rudkinassociates.co.uk
Editors Prof Sir Peter Hall, Prof David Banister
Quarterly £85 p.a.

Articles about architecture, planning and the environment. Preliminary letter advisable. Length: 1000–5000 words. Payment: by arrangement. Illustrations: photos and line.

Burlington Magazine

14-16 Duke's Road, London WC1H 9SZ
tel 020-7388 1228 *fax* 020-7388 1230
email editorial@burlington.org.uk
Editor Richard Shone
Monthly £12.75

Deals with the history and criticism of art; book and exhibition reviews; illustrated monthly Calendar section. Potential contributors must have special knowledge of the subjects treated; MSS compiled from works of reference are unacceptable. Length: 500–5000 words. Payment: up to £140. Illustrations: b&w and colour photos. Founded 1903.

Buses

Ian Allan Publishing Ltd, Riverdene Business Park, Molesey Road, Hersham, Surrey KT12 4RG

tel (01932) 266600 *fax* (01932) 266601
email alan@millar1.demon.co.uk
website www.busesmag.com
Editor Alan Millar, PO Box 3759, Glasgow G41 5YN
tel 0141-427 6294 *fax* 0141-427 9594
Monthly £3.25

Articles of interest to both road passenger transport operators and bus enthusiasts. Preliminary enquiry essential. Illustrations: colour transparencies, half-tone, line maps. Payment: on application. Founded 1949.

Business Life

Cedar Communications, Haymarket House,
1 Oxenden Street, London SW1Y 4EE
tel 020-7925 2544 *fax* 020-7839 4508
website www.cedarcom.co.uk
Editor Alex Finer
Monthly Free

Inflight magazine for British Airways. Articles and features of interest to the European business traveller. All material commissioned; approach in writing with ideas. Length: 850–2500 words. Illustrations: colour photos and line. Payment: £250 per 1000 words; £100–£400 for illustrations. Founded 1985.

Business Scotland

Peebles Media Group, Bergius House, Clifton Street, Glasgow G3 7LA
tel 0141-567 6000 *fax* 0141-331 1395
Editor Graham Lironi
Monthly Controlled circulation

Features, profiles and news items of interest to business and finance in Scotland. Payment: by arrangement. Founded 1947.

Business Traveller

Perry Publications Ltd, Nestor House,
Playhouse Yard, London EC4V 5EX
tel 020-7778 0000 *fax* 020-7778 0011
email editorial@businesstraveller.com
website www.btonline.co.uk
Editor Julia Brookes
Monthly £2.90

Articles, features and news on consumer travel aimed at individual frequent international business travellers. Submit ideas with recent clippings and a CV. Length: varies. Illustrations: colour for destinations features; send lists to Deborah Miller, Picture Editor. Payment: on application. Founded 1976.

Cable Guide

Scorpio Multimedia, 1st Floor, 40 Bernard Street, London WC1N 1LE
tel 020-7419 8419 *fax* 020-7419 8400
website www.cableguide.co.uk

Editor Robin Jarossi
Monthly £3.25 (£30 p.a.)

Features and interviews about programmes featured on cable TV, together with programme listings for cable channels. All material commissioned. Length: up to 1000 words. Illustrations: colour transparencies. Payment: £550 per 1000 words, photo fees negotiable. Founded 1986.

Caledonia

Scott House Publishing Ltd, 28 Melville Street, Edinburgh EH3 7HA
tel 0131-476 4670 *fax* 0131-476 4671
email dcurrie@scotthouse.co.uk
website www.caledonia-magazine.com
Editor Don Currie
Monthly £3

Contemporary features of Scottish interest on personalities, interiors, lifestyle. Send proposal to the Editor. Length: variable. Payment: negotiable. Founded 1999.

Cambridgeshire Journal

The Old County School, Northgate Street, Bury St Edmunds, Suffolk IP33 1HP
email pippa@acornmagazines.co.uk
Editor Pippa Bastin, *Send material to* Pippa Bastin or Alexandra Edoruk
Monthly £2.30

Articles, features and news of interest to Cambridgeshire: history, people, events, natural history and other issues. Also regional lifestyle, i.e. gardens, homes and fashion. Specially commissions most material. Welcomes ideas for articles and features. Length: 1500 words (articles/features), 250 words (news). Payment: £125 (articles/features), none (news). Illustrations: colour transparencies and prints. Founded 1994.

Camcorder User

(incorporating Video Editing and Desktop Video)
WVIP, 53-79 Highgate Road, London NW5 1TW
tel 020-7331 1000 *fax* 020-7331 1242
email rob.hull@wvip.co.uk
Editor Robert Hull
Monthly £3.25

Features on film/video-making techniques, specifically tailored to the amateur enthusiast. Material mostly commissioned. Length: 1000–2500 words. Illustrations: colour and b&w; contact Editor for details. Payment: by arrangement. Founded 1988.

Campaign

Haymarket Business Publications Ltd,
22 Bute Gardens, London W6 7HN
tel 020-8267 4656 *fax* 020-8267 4915
email campaign@haynet.com

Editor Caroline Marshall
Weekly £2.50

News and articles covering the whole of the mass communications field, particularly advertising in all its forms, marketing and the media. Features should not exceed 2000 words. News items also welcome. Press day, Wednesday. Payment: by arrangement.

Camping Magazine
Warner Group Publications, The Maltings, West Street, Bourne, Lincs. PE10 9PH
tel/fax (01778) 391116
Editor John Lloyd
Monthly £2.80

Covers the spectrum of camping and related activities in all shapes and forms – camping is more than a tent on a site! Lively, anecdotal articles written to guidelines and photos are welcome. Talk to the Editor first. Length: 500–1500 words on average. Illustrations: colour. Payment: by arrangement. Founded 1961.

Canal & Riverboat
PO Box 618, Norwich NR7 0QT
tel (01603) 708930 *fax* (01603) 708934
email bluefoxfilms@themag.fsnet.co.uk
website www.canalandriverboat.com
Editor Chris Cattrall
Monthly £2.70

News, views and articles on UK inland waterways and cruising features, DIY articles and historical features. Length: 1500 words (articles/features), 300 words (news). Payment: £100; £25 (news). Illustrations: colour, plus b&w cartoons. Founded 1978.

Car
EMAP Automotive Ltd, 3rd Floor, Media House, Lynchwood, Peterborough PE2 6EA
tel (01733) 468000 *fax* (01733) 468001
email car@emap.com
Editor Greg Fountain
Monthly £3.50

Top-grade journalistic features on car driving, car people and cars. Length: 1000–2500 words. Payment: minimum £250 per 1000 words. Illustrations: b&w and colour photos to professional standards. Founded 1962.

Car Mechanics
Cudham Tithe Barn, Berrys Hill, Cudham, Kent TW16 3AG
tel (01959) 541444, (01733) 203749
fax (01959) 541400
email info@kelsey.co.uk
Editor Phil Weeden
Monthly £2.80

Practical articles on maintaining, repairing and uprating modern cars for DIY plus the motor trade.

Always interested in finding new talent for our rather specialised market but please study a recent copy before submitting ideas or features. Preliminary letter or phone call outlining feature recommended. Payment: by arrangement. Illustrations: line drawings, colour prints or transparencies. Rarely use words only; please supply text and pictures.

Caravan Magazine
IPC Country & Leisure Media Ltd, Focus House, Dingwall Avenue, Croydon CR9 2TA
tel 020-8774 0600 *fax* 020-8774 0939
website www.caravanmagazine.co.uk
Editor Steve Rowe
Monthly £2.99

Lively articles based on real experience of touring caravanning, especially if well illustrated by photos. General countryside or motoring material not wanted. Payment: by arrangement. Founded 1933.

Caribbean Times
(incorporating African Times)
Ethnic Media Group, Unit 2.01, Technology Centre, 65 Whitehchapel Road, London E1 1DU
tel 020-7650 2000 *fax* 020-7650 2001
email caribbeantimes@hotmail.com
Editor Ron Shillingford
Weekly 50p

News stories, articles and features of interest to Britain's African–Caribbean community. Founded 1981.

Carousel – The Guide to Children's Books
The Saturn Centre, 54-76 Bissell Street, Birmingham B5 7HX
tel 0121-622 7458 *fax* 0121-666 7526
email carousel.guide@virgin.net
website www.carouselguide.co.uk
Editor Jenny Blanch
3 p.a. £9.75 p.a. (£13 p.a. Europe; £16 p.a. rest of world)

Reviews of fiction, non-fiction and poetry books for children, plus in-depth articles; profiles of authors and illustrators. Length: 1200 words (articles); 150 words (reviews). Illustrations: colour and b&w. Payment: by arrangement. Founded 1995.

Cat World
Ashdown Publishing, Avalon Court, Star Road, Partridge Green, West Sussex RH13 8RY
tel (01403) 711511 *fax* (01403) 711521
email editor@catworld.co.uk
website www.catworld.co.uk
Editor Jo Rothery
Monthly £2.75

Bright, lively articles on any aspect of cat ownership. Articles on breeds of cats and veterinary articles by acknowledged experts only. No unsolicited fiction. All submissions by email or on disk. Illustrations: colour prints, transparencies, TIFFs. Payment: by arrangement. Founded 1981.

Caterer & Hotelkeeper

Reed Business Information Ltd, Quadrant House, The Quadrant, Sutton, Surrey SM2 5AS
tel 020-8652 8680 *fax* 020-8652 8973/8947
Editor Forbes Mutch
Weekly £2

Articles on all aspects of the hotel and catering industries. Length: up to 1500 words. Illustrations: line, half-tone, colour. Payment: by arrangement. Founded 1893.

The Catholic Herald

Herald House, Lambs Passage, Bunhill Row, London EC1Y 8TQ
tel 020-7588 3101 *fax* 020-7256 9728
email editorial@catholicherald.co.uk
website www.catholicherald.co.uk
Editor Dr William Oddie
Weekly 80p

Independent newspaper covering national and international affairs from a Catholic/Christian viewpoint as well as church news. Length: articles 600–1200 words. Illustrations: photos of Catholic and Christian interest, cartoons. Payment: by arrangement.

Catholic Pictorial

Media House, Mann Island, Pier Head, Liverpool L3 1DQ
tel 0151-236 2191 *fax* 0151-236 2216
Editor David Mahon
Weekly 60p

News and photo features (maximum 800 words plus illustration) of Merseyside, regional and national Catholic interest only; also cartoons. Has a strongly social editorial and is a trenchant tabloid. Payment: by arrangement. Founded 1961.

Catholic Times

1st Floor, St James's Buildings, Oxford Street, Manchester M1 6FP
tel 0161-236 8856 *fax* 0161-237 5590
Editor Stefano Hatfield
Weekly 70p

News (400 words) and news features (800 words) of Catholic interest. Illustrations: colour and b&w photos. Payment: £30–£80; photos £50. Relaunched 1993.

Cencrastus: Scottish & International Literature, Arts and Affairs

Unit One, Abbeymount Techbase, 2 Easter Road, Edinburgh EH8 8EJ

tel/fax 0131-661 5687
email cencrastus1@hotmail.com
Editor Raymond Ross, *Managing Editor* Zsvzsanna Varga
Quarterly £2.95 (back copies £2.50); £12 p.a.

Articles, short stories, poetry, reviews. Payment: by arrangement. Illustrations: line, half-tone. Founded 1979.

Chapman

4 Broughton Place, Edinburgh EH1 3RX
tel 0131-557 2207 *fax* 0131-556 9565
email chapman-pub@blueyonder.co.uk
website www.chapman-pub.co.uk
Editor Joy Hendry
3 p.a. £18 p.a.

'Scotland's Quality Literary Magazine.' Poetry, short stories, reviews, criticism, articles on Scottish culture. Illustrations: line, half-tone, cartoons. Payment: £8.00 per page; illustrations by negotiation. Founded 1969.

Chartered Secretary

16 Park Crescent, London W1B 1AH
tel 020-7612 7045 *fax* 020-7612 7034
email chartsec@icsa.co.uk
website www.charteredsecretary.net
Editor Will Booth
Monthly £5 (£50 p.a. post free UK)

Official magazine of The Institute of Chartered Secretaries and Administrators. Practical and topical articles (2000+ words) on law, finance and management affecting company secretaries and other senior administrators in business, not-for-profit sector, local and central government and other institutions in Britain and overseas. Payment: by arrangement.

Chat

IPC Connect Ltd, King's Reach Tower, Stamford Street, London SE1 9LS
tel 020-7261 6565 *fax* 020-7261 6534
website www.ipcmedia.com
Editor Paul Merrill
Weekly 70p

Tabloid weekly for women: 60 word stories, true life features. Payment: by arrangement. Founded 1986.

Child Education

Scholastic Ltd, Villiers House, Clarendon Avenue, Leamington Spa, Warks. CV32 5PR
tel (01926) 887799 *fax* (01926) 883331
website www.scholastic.co.uk
Editor Jeremy Sugden
Monthly £3.75

For teachers concerned with the education of children aged 4–8. Articles by specialists on practical teaching ideas and methods. Length:

600–1200 words. Payment: by arrangement. Profusely illustrated with photos and artwork; also large full colour picture posters. Founded 1924.

The China Quarterly
School of Oriental and African Studies, Thornhaugh Street, Russell Square, London WC1H 0XG
tel 020-7898 4063 fax 020-7898 4849
email chinaq@soas.ac.uk
Editor Dr Julia Strauss
Quarterly £39/$68 p.a. (£80/$135 institutions, £20/$35 students)

Articles on contemporary China. Length: 8000 words approx.

Choice
1st Floor, 2 King Street, Peterborough PE1 1LT
tel (01733) 555123 fax (01733) 427500
Editor Norman Wright
Monthly £2.50

Pre- and retirement magazine for 50+ readership. Positive attitude to life – experiences, hobbies, holidays, finance, relationships. Most of the magazine commissioned. If suggesting feature material, include selection of cuttings of previously published work. Payment: by agreement, on publication. Founded 1974.

Christian Herald
Christian Media, 96 Dominion Road, Worthing, West Sussex BN14 8JP
tel (01903) 821082 fax (01903) 821081
email news@christianherald.org.uk
features@christianherald.org.uk
website www.christianherald.org.uk
Weekly 65p

Evangelical Christian paper with strong emphasis on news and current affairs. Features up to 800 words – profiles, the changing church, Christians, and contemporary culture (e.g. media, TV, music); cartoons. No short stories. Payment: £20–£60, depending on length/pictures used.

Church of England Newspaper
20-26 Brunswick Place, London N1 6DZ
tel 020-7417 5800 fax 020-7216 6410
email cen@parlicom.com
website www.churchnewspaper.com
Weekly 70p

Anglican news and articles relating the Christian faith to everyday life. Evangelical basis; almost exclusively commissioned articles. Study of paper desirable. Length: up to 1000 words. Illustrations: photos, line drawings, cartoons. Payment: c. £40 per1000 words; photos £22, line by arrangement. Founded 1828.

Church Times
33 Upper Street, London N1 0PN
tel 020-7359 4570 fax 020-7226 3073
email editor@churchtimes.co.uk
website www.churchtimes.co.uk
Editor Paul Handley
Weekly 80p

Articles on religious topics are considered. No verse or fiction. Length: up to 1000 words. Illustrations: news photos, sent promptly. Payment: £100 per 1000 words; Periodical Publishers' Association negotiated rates for illustrations. Founded 1863.

Classic & Sports Car
Haymarket Specialist Motoring Publications Ltd, Somerset House, Somerset Road, Teddington, Middlesex TW11 8RT
tel 020-8267 5399 fax 020-8267 5318
Editor James Elliott
Monthly £3.60

Features on classic cars and sportscars; shows, news and reviews, features and stories. Illustrations: half-tone, colour. Payment: £250 per 1000 words; varies for illustrations. Founded 1982.

Classic Boat & The Boatman
Focus House, Dingwall Avenue, Croydon CR9 2TA
tel 020-8774 0603 fax 020-8774 0943
email cb@ipcmedia.com
website www.classicboat.co.uk
Editor Dan Houston
Monthly £3.60

Cruising and technical features, restorations, events, new boat reviews, practical, maritime history; news. Study of magazine essential: read 3–4 back issues and send for contributors' guidelines. Length: 500–2000 words. Illustrations: colour and b&w photos; line drawings of hulls. Payment: £75–£100 per published page. Founded 1987.

Classic Cars
EMAP Automotive Ltd, Media House, Lynchwood, Peterborough Business Park, Peterborough PE2 6EA
tel (01733) 468219 fax (01733) 468888
email classic.cars@emap.com
Editor Martyn Moore
Monthly £3.50

Specialist articles on older cars. Length: from 500–4000 words (subject to prior contract). Illustrations: half-tone, colour, cartoons. Payment: by negotiation.

Classic Stitches
D.C. Thomson & Co. Ltd, 80 Kingsway East, Dundee DD4 8SL
tel (01382) 462276 fax (01382) 452491
email editorial@classicstitches.com
website www.classicstitches.com

Editor Mrs Bea Neilson
Bi-monthly £3.95

Creative needlework ideas and projects; needlework-based features on designers, collections, work-in-progress and exhibitions. Submissions also welcome for e-mag on website. Length: 1000–2000 words. Illustrations: colour photos, preferably not 35mm. Payment: negotiable. Founded 1994.

Classical Music

Rhinegold Publishing Ltd, 241 Shaftesbury Avenue, London WC2H 8TF
tel 020-7333 1742 *fax* 020-7333 1769
email classical.music@rhinegold.co.uk
website www.rhinegold.co.uk
Editor Keith Clarke
Fortnightly £3.25

News, opinion, features on the classical music business. All material commissioned. Illustrations: colour photos and line; colour covers. Payment: minimum £100 per 1000 words; from £50 for illustrations. Founded 1976.

Classics

SPL, Berwick House, 8-10 Knoll Rise, Orpington, Kent BR6 0PS
tel (01689) 887200 *fax* (01689) 876438
email classics@splpublishing.co.uk
Editor Tim Morgan
Monthly £3.70

News photos and stories of classic car interest and illustrated features on classic car history, repairs, maintenance and restoration. Study magazine before submitting material. Features must have high level of subject knowledge and technical accuracy. Length: up to 2000 words (features); 200 words (news). Illustrations: colour and b&w. Payment: £120 per 1000 words plus £100 per set of supporting photos (features); £120 per 1000 words plus photos based on £100 per page (news). Founded 1997.

Climber

Warners Group Publications plc, West Street, Bourne, Lincs. PE10 9PH
tel (01778) 391117
Editor Bernard Newman
Monthly £2.99

Articles on all aspects of rock climbing/ mountaineering in Great Britain and abroad, and on related subjects. Study of magazine essential. Length: 1500–2000 words. Illustrations: colour transparencies. Payment: according to merit. Founded 1962.

Coin News

Token Publishing Ltd, Orchard House, Duchy Road, Heathpark, Honiton, Devon EX14 1YD
tel (01404) 46972 *fax* (01404) 44788

Editor John W. Mussell
Monthly £2.95

Articles of high standard on coins, tokens, paper money. Length: up to 2000 words. Payment: by arrangement. Founded 1964.

Commando

D.C. Thomson & Co. Ltd, Albert Square, Dundee DD1 9QJ
tel (01382) 223131 *fax* (01382) 322214
8 p.m. 90p

Fictional war stories told in pictures. Scripts: about 135 pictures. Synopsis required as an opener. New writers encouraged; send for details. Payment: on acceptance.

Commercial Motor

Reed Business Information Ltd, Quadrant House, The Quadrant, Sutton, Surrey SM2 5AS
tel 020-8652 3302/3303 *fax* 020-8652 8969
Editor-in-Chief Brian Weatherley
Weekly £1.70

Technical and road transport articles only. Length: up to 1500 words. Payment: varies. Illustrations: drawings and photos. Founded 1905.

Communicate

DMG World Media (UK) Ltd, Queensway House, 2 Queensway, Redhill, Surrey RH1 1QS
tel (01737) 768611 *fax* (01737) 855470
Editor Neil Tyler
Monthly Controlled circulation

Covers all aspects of telecommunications management: analysis pieces (200–700 words), features (1000–2000 words), case studies (300 words). Some material commissioned. Illustrations: colour photos, line, diagrams. Payment: by arrangement. Founded 1980.

Company

National Magazine House, 72 Broadwick Street, London W1V 2BP
tel 020-7439 5000
email company.mail@natmags.co.uk
Editor Sam Baker
Monthly £1.50

Articles on a wide variety of subjects, relevant to young, independent women. Most articles are commissioned. Payment: usual magazine rate. Illustrated. Founded 1978.

Computer Weekly

Reed Business Information Ltd, Quadrant House, The Quadrant, Sutton, Surrey SM2 5AS
tel 020-8652 3122 *fax* 020-8652 8979
website www.computerweekly.com
Editor Karl Schneider, *News Editor* Lindsay Clark
Weekly £2.30

Feature articles on IT-related topics for business/industry users. Length: 1200 words. Illustrations: b&w photos, line, cartoons. Payment: £250 per 1000 words; negotiable for illustrations. Founded 1966.

Computing
VNU Business Publications, VNU House, 32-34 Broadwick Street, London W1A 2HG
tel 020-7316 9158 *fax* 020-7316 9160
website www.computingnet.co.uk
Editor Colin Barker
Weekly £1.70, £100 p.a.

Features and news items on corporate procurement and deployment of IT infrastructure, and on applications and implications of computers and telecommunications. Particular sections address the IT professional career development, and the desktop computing environment. Length: 1600–2200 words. Payment: by negotiation. Illustrations: colour photos, line drawings, cartoons. Founded 1973.

Condé Nast Traveller
Vogue House, Hanover Square, London W1S 1JU
tel 020-7499 9080 *fax* 020-7493 3758
email cntraveller@condenast.co.uk
website www.cntraveller.co.uk
Editor Sarah Miller
Monthly £3.20

Highly illustrated features on travel, style, food and wine, beauty and health. Illustrations: colour. Payment: by arrangement. Founded 1997.

Contemporary
Suite K101, Tower Bridge Business Complex, 100 Clements Road, London SE16 4DG
tel 020-7740 1704 *fax* 020-7252 3510
email info@contemporary-magazine.com
website www.contemporary-magazine.com
Editor Keith Patrick
Monthly £4.95

International magazine with extensive coverage of visual arts, architecture, fashion, film, photography, books, music, dance and sport. Also includes interviews, profiles and art news from around the world. Length: varies. Illustrations: colour transparencies, hi-res scans. Payment: £100 per 1000 words; none for photos. Founded 1997; relaunched 2002.

Contemporary Review
(incorporating the Fortnightly)
Contemporary Review Co. Ltd, PO Box 1242, Oxford OX1 4FJ
tel/fax (01865) 201529
email editorial@contemporaryreview.co.uk
Editor Dr Richard Mullen, *Send material to* Dr Alex Kerr, Managing Editor

Monthly £3.50

Independent review dealing with questions of the day, chiefly politics, international affairs, religion, literature, the arts. Mostly commissioned, but with limited scope for freelance authors with authoritative knowledge. TS returned only if sae enclosed. Intending contributors should study journal first. Length: 2000–3000 words. No illustrations. Payment: £5 per page (500 words), 2 complimentary copies. Founded 1866.

Cosmetic World News
9 Onslow Square, London SW7 3NJ
tel 020-7589 0589 *fax* 020-7838 0908
email mamp@cosmeticworldnews.com
website www.cosmeticworldnews.com
Editor M.A. Murray-Pearce
Bi-monthly £96 p.a.

International news magazine of perfumery, cosmetics and toiletries industry. Worldwide reports, photo-news stories, articles (500–1000 words) on essential oils and new cosmetic raw materials, and exclusive information on industry's companies and personalities welcomed. Payment: by arrangement. Illustrations: b&w and colour photos or colour separations. Founded 1949.

Cosmogirl
National Magazine House, 72 Broadwick Street, London W1F 9EP
tel 020-7439 5081 *fax* 020-7439 5400
email cosmogirl.mail@natmags.co.uk
website www.cosmogirl.co.uk
Editor Celia Duncan, *Send material to* Miranda Eason
Monthly £1.99

Little sister to *Cosmopolitan*. Features 'to inspire teenage girls to be the best they can be'. Specially commissions most material. Welcomes ideas for articles and features. Length: 600 words. All illustrations commissioned. Founded 2001.

Cosmopolitan
National Magazine House, 72 Broadwick Street, London W1V 2BP
tel 020-7439 5000 *fax* 020-7439 5016
Editor-in-Chief Lorraine Candy
Monthly £2.70

Articles. Commissioned material only. Payment: by arrangement. Illustrated. Founded 1972.

Country
A & D Media Ltd, Jesses Farm, Snow Hill, Dinton, Nr Salisbury, Wilts. SP3 5HN
tel (01722) 716996 *fax* (01722) 716926
Editor Geoff Mowday
6 p.a. £2.95 (members only)

Magazine of the Country Gentlemen's Association.

News and features covering rural events, countryside, leisure, heritage, homes and gardens. Some outside contributors used. Payment: by arrangement. Founded 1893.

Country Homes and Interiors

IPC Magazines Ltd, King's Reach Tower, Stamford Street, London SE1 9LS
tel 020-7261 6451 *fax* 020-7261 6895
Editor Deborah Barker
Monthly £2.80

Articles on property, country homes, interior designs. Illustrations: colour. Payment: from £250 per 1000 words. Founded 1986.

Country Life

IPC Media Ltd, King's Reach Tower, Stamford Street, London SE1 9LS
tel 020-7261 7058 *fax* 020-7261 5139
Editor Clive Aslet
Weekly £2.80

Illustrated journal chiefly concerned with British country life, social history, architecture and the fine arts, natural history, agriculture, gardening and sport. Length: about 1000 or 1300 words (articles). Illustrations: mainly colour photos. Payment: according to merit. Founded 1897.

Country Living

National Magazine House, 72 Broadwick Street, London W1F 9EP
tel 020-7439 5000 *fax* 020-7439 5093
website www.countryliving.co.uk
Editor Susy Smith
Monthly £3

Up-market home-interest magazine with a country lifestyle theme, covering interiors, gardens, crafts, food, wildlife, rural and green issues. Do not send unsolicited material or valuable transparencies. Illustrations: line, half-tone, colour. Payment: by arrangement. Founded 1985.

Country Quest

7 Aberystwyth Science Park, Aberystwyth, Ceredigion SY23 3AH
tel (01970) 615000 *fax* (01970) 624699
Editor Beverly Davies, *Send material to* Erica Jones
Monthly £2

Illustrated articles on matters relating to countryside, history and personalities of Wales and border counties. No fiction. Illustrated work preferred. Length: 1000–2500 words. Payment: by arrangement.

Country Smallholding

Archant Regional Ltd, Fair Oak Close, Exeter Airport Business Park, Clyst Honiton, Exeter EX5 2UL

tel (01392) 888475 *fax* (01392) 888550
email editorial@countrysmallholding.com
website www.countrysmallholding.com
Editor Diane Cowgill
Monthly £2.75

The magazine for smallholders. Practical, how-to articles, and seasonal features, on organic gardening, small-scale poultry and livestock keeping, country crafts, cookery and smallholdings. Approach the Editor in writing with ideas. Length: up to 2000 words. Payment: £40 per 1000 words; photos £10, £50 cover. Founded 1975 as *Home Farm*.

Country Walking

EMAP Active Ltd, Bretton Court, Bretton, Peterborough PE3 8DZ
tel (01733) 264666 *fax* (01733) 282653
Editor Jonathon Manning
Monthly £3.10

Features. Length: 1200 words on average. Illustrations: colour transparencies. Payment: by arrangement. Founded 1987.

The Countryman

Countryman Publishing Ltd, 23 Sheep Street, Burford, Oxon OX18 4LS
tel (01993) 824424
email burford@countrymanmagazine.co.uk
Editor David Horan
Monthly £1.95

Every department of rural life except field sports. Copy must be trustworthy, well-written, brisk, cogent and light in hand. Articles up to 1200 words. Skilful sketches of life and character from personal knowledge and experience. Dependable natural history based on writer's own observation. Really good matter from old unpublished letters and MSS. Study magazine before submitting material. Illustrations: b&w and colour photos and drawings, but all must be exclusive and out of the ordinary. Payment: min. £70 per 1000 words, usually more, according to merit. Founded 1927.

Critical Quarterly

Contributions Ollie Garrett, School of English, Queen's Building, The Queen's Drive, Exeter EX4 4QH
website www.criticalquarterly.co.uk
Quarterly £21 p.a. (£88 p.a. institutions)

Fiction, poems, literary criticism. Length: 2000–5000 words. Study magazine before submitting MSS. Payment: by arrangement. Founded 1959.

Cumbria and Lake District Magazine

Dalesman Publishing Company Ltd, Stable Courtyard, Broughton Hall, Skipton, North Yorkshire BD23 3AE

tel (01756) 701381 *fax* (01756) 701326
email editorial@dalesman.co.uk
Editor Terry Fletcher
Monthly £1.50

Articles of genuine rural interest concerning Lakeland and Cumbria. Short length preferred. Illustrations: first-class photos. Payment: according to merit. Founded 1951.

Custom Car

Kelsey Publishing Ltd, Cudham Tithe Barn, Berry's Hill, Cudham, Kent TN16 3AG
tel (01959) 541444 *fax* (01959) 541400
email cc.mag@kelsey.co.uk
website www.kelsey.co.uk/custom
Editor Kev Elliott
Monthly £2.95

Customising, drag racing and hot rods. Length: by arrangement. Payment: by arrangement. Founded 1970.

Cycle Sport

IPC Leisure & Media Ltd, 5th Floor, Focus House, 9 Dingwall Avenue, Croydon CR9 2TA
tel 020-8774 0889 *fax* 020-8774 0952
email cycling@ipcmedia.com
Managing Editor Robert Garbutt, *Deputy Editor* Marguirite Lazel
Monthly £3.50

Articles and features on European professional racing. Specially commissions most material but will consider unsolicited material. Welcomes ideas for articles and features. Length: 1500–2500 words. Illustrations: transparencies, colour and b&w artwork and cartoons, digital images. Payment: £120 per 1000 words; £50–£150 illustrations. Founded 1991.

Cycling Weekly

IPC Music and Sport Ltd, 5th Floor, Focus House, 9 Dingwall Avenue, Croydon CR9 2TA
tel 020-8774 0811 *fax* 020-8774 0952
email cycling@ipcmedia.com
Editor Robert Garbutt
Weekly £2

Racing and technical articles. Illustrations: topical photos with a cycling interest considered; cartoons. Length: not exceeding 2000 words. Payment: by arrangement. Founded 1891.

Cyphers

3 Selskar Terrace, Ravelagh, Dublin 6, Republic of Ireland
tel/fax (01) 4978866
€12/$25 for 3 issues

Poems, fiction, reviews, translations. Payment: €15 per page. Founded 1975.

Dairy Farmer

CMP Information Ltd, Sovereign House, Sovereign Way, Tonbridge, Kent TN9 1RW
tel (01732) 377273 *fax* (01732) 377644
email phollinshead@cmpinformation.com
Editor Peter Hollinshead
Monthly Controlled circulation

In-depth, technical articles on all aspects of dairy farm management and milk marketing. Length: normally 800–1400 words with colour photos. Payment: by arrangement.

Dalesman

Dalesman Publishing Company Ltd, Stable Courtyard, Broughton Hall, Skipton, North Yorkshire BD23 3AE
tel (01756) 701381 *fax* (01756) 701326
email editorial@dalesman.co.uk
Editor Terry Fletcher
Monthly £1.60

Articles and stories of genuine rural interest concerning Yorkshire (1000–1500 words). Payment: according to merit. Illustrations: line drawings and first-class photos preferably featuring people. Founded 1939.

Dance Today!

The Dancing Times Ltd, 45-47 Clerkenwell Green, London EC1R 0EB
tel 020-7250 3006 *fax* 020-7253 6679
email dancetoday!@dancing-times.co.uk
website www.dancing-times.co.uk
Editor Sylvia Boerner, *Editorial Adviser* Mary Clarke
Monthly £1.20

Ballroom and social dancing from every aspect, ranging from competition reports to dance holiday features and musical reviews. Well-informed freelance articles are occasionally used, but only after preliminary arrangements. Payment: by arrangement. Illustrations: action photos preferred, b&w or colour. Founded 1956.

Dancing Times

The Dancing Times Ltd, 45-47 Clerkenwell Green, London EC1R 0EB
tel 020-7250 3006 *fax* 020-7253 6679
email dt@dancing-times.co.uk
website www.dancing-times.co.uk
Editor Mary Clarke, *Editorial Adviser* Ivor Guest
Monthly £2.50

Ballet, contemporary dance and all forms of stage dancing from general, historical, critical and technical angles. Well-informed freelance articles used occasionally, but only after preliminary arrangements. Payment: by arrangement. Illustrations: occasional line, action photos preferred; colour welcome. Founded 1910.

The Dandy

D.C. Thomson & Co. Ltd, Albert Square,
Dundee DD1 9QJ
tel (01382) 223131 *fax* (01382) 322214
185 Fleet Street, London EC4A 2HS
tel 020-7400 1030 *fax* 020-7400 1089
Weekly 65p

Comic strips for children. 10–12 pictures per single
page story, 18–20 pictures per 2-page story.
Promising artists are encouraged. Payment: on
acceptance.

Funsize Dandy
2 p.m. 90p
Founded 1997.

Darts World

World Magazines Ltd, 28 Arrol Road, Beckenham,
Kent BR3 4PA
tel 020-8650 6580 *fax* 020-8654 4343
Editor Tony Wood
Monthly £2.50

Articles and stories with darts theme. Illustrations:
half-tone, cartoons. Payment: £40–£50 per 1000
words; illustrations by arrangement. Founded 1972.

Day by Day

Woolacombe House, 141 Woolacombe Road,
London SE3 8QP
tel 020-8856 6249
Editor Patrick Richards
Monthly £1

Articles and news on non-violence and social
justice. Reviews of art, books, films, plays, musicals
and opera. Cricket reports. Short poems and very
occasional short stories in keeping with editorial
viewpoint. Payment: £2 per 1000 words. No illustrations required. Founded 1963.

Decanter

IPC Country & Leisure Media Ltd, 1st Floor,
Broadway House, 2-6 Fulham Broadway,
London SW6 1AA
tel 020-7610 3929 *fax* 020-7381 5282
email editorial@decantermagazine.com
website www.decanter.com
Editor Amy Wislocki
Monthly £3.40

Articles and features on wines, wine travel and
food-related topics. Welcomes ideas for articles and
features. Length: 1000–1800 words. Illustrations:
colour. Payment: £230 per 1000 words. Founded
1975.

Derbyshire Life and Countryside

Heritage House, Lodge Lane, Derby DE1 3HE
tel (01332) 347087/8/9 *fax* (01332) 290688
email editorials@hhgroup.co.uk

Monthly £1.75

Articles, preferably illustrated, about Derbyshire life,
people and history. Length: up to 800 words. Some
short stories set in Derbyshire accepted; no verse.
Payment: according to nature and quality of
contribution. Illustrations: photos of Derbyshire
subjects. Founded 1931.

Descent

Wild Places Publishing, 51 Timbers Square,
Cardiff CF24 3SH
tel/fax 029-2048 6557
email descent@wildplaces.co.uk
website www.caving.uk.com
Editor Chris Howes
Bi-monthly £3.25

Articles, features and news on all aspects of cave
and mine sport exploration. Submissions must
match magazine style. Length: up to 2000 words
(articles/features), up to 1000 words (news).
Illustrations: colour and b&w. Payment: on
consideration of material. Founded 1969.

The Dickensian

The Dickens Fellowship, Dickens House,
48 Doughty Street, London WC1N 2LX
Editor Dr Malcolm Andrews, School of English,
Rutherford College, University of Kent, Canterbury,
Kent CT2 7NX *fax* (01227) 827001
email M.Y.Andrews@ukc.ac.uk
3 p.a. £9.50 p.a. (£12 p.a. institutions; overseas rates
on application)

Welcomes articles on all aspects of Dickens' life,
works and character. Payment: none. Send
contributions (enclose sae if return required) and
editorial correspondence to the Editor.

Director

116 Pall Mall, London SW1Y 5ED
tel 020-7766 8950 *fax* 020-7766 8840
Editor Joanna Higgins
Monthly £3.25

Authoritative business-related articles. Send
synopsis of proposed article and examples of
printed work. Length: 500–3000 words. Payment: by
arrangement. Illustrations: colour. Founded 1947.

Dirt Bike Rider

Lancaster & Morecambe Newspapers Ltd,
Victoria Street, Morecambe, Lancs. LA4 4AG
tel (01524) 32525 *fax* (01524) 842157
email sean.lawless@rim.co.uk
Editor Sean Lawless
Monthly £2.80

Features, track tests, coverage on all aspects of off-
road motor-cycling. Length: up to 2000 words.
Illustrations: half-tone, colour, cartoons. Founded
1981.

Disability Now

(published by Scope)
6 Market Road, London N7 9PW
tel 020-7619 7323 *fax* 020-7619 7331
minicom 020-7619 733
email editor@disabilitynow.org.uk
website www.disabilitynow.org.uk
Editor Mary Wilkinson
Monthly £18 p.a., free to people on income support;
tape version free to people with visual impairment
or severe disability

Newspaper for people with different types of
disability, carers and professionals, and anyone
interested in disability. News and comment on
anything of interest in the disability field: benefits,
services, equipment, jobs, politics, motoring,
holidays, sport, relationships, the arts. All regular
contributors have a disability (unless they are a
parent of someone with a disability). Preliminary
letter or email desirable. Founded 1984.

Diva

Millivres Prowler Ltd, Spectrum House,
32-34 Gordon House Road, London NW5 1LP
tel 020-7424 7400 *fax* 020-7424 7401
email edit@divamag.co.uk
website www.divamag.com
Editor Gillian Rodgerson
Monthly £2.25

Lesbian life and culture: articles, features, news,
short fiction. Length: 1000–2000 words (articles/
features); 300–500 words (news); 1000–2000 words
(short stories). Illustrations: colour and b&w.
Payment: £10 per 100 words; £30–£50 per photo;
£25–£80 per drawing. Founded 1994.

Diver

55 High Street, Teddington, Middlesex TW11 8HA
tel 020-8943 4288 *fax* 020-8943 4312
email enquiries@divermag.co.uk
website divernet@www.divernet.com
Editor Nigel Eaton
Monthly £3.20

Articles on sub aqua diving and related developments. Length: 1500–4000 words. Illustrations: line,
half-tone and colour. Payment: by arrangement.
Founded 1953.

Dogs Today

Pet Subjects Ltd, Town Mill, Bagshot Road,
Chobham, Surrey GU24 8BZ
tel (01276) 858880 *fax* (01276) 858860
email dogstoday@dial.pipex.com
Editor Beverley Cuddy
Monthly £2.95

Study of magazine essential before submitting ideas.
Interested in human interest dog stories, celebrity
interviews, holiday features and anything unusual –
all must be entertaining and informative and
accompanied by illustrations. Length: 800–1200
words. Illustrations: colour, preferably transparencies or digital, colour cartoons. Payment:
negotiable. Founded 1990.

Dorset Life – The Dorset Magazine

7 The Leanne, Sandford Lane, Wareham,
Dorset BH20 4DY
tel (01929) 551264 *fax* (01929) 552099
email office@dorsetlife.co.uk
Editor John Newth
Monthly £2

Articles (500–1200 words), photos (colour) and line
drawings with a specifically Dorset theme. Payment:
by arrangement. Founded 1967.

Drapers

EMAP Communications, Greater London House,
Hampstead Road, London NW1 7EJ
tel 020-7391 3300 *fax* 020-7391 3403
email drapers@emap.com
website www.drapersrecord.com
Editor-in-Chief Eric Musgrave
Weekly £2.75

Business editorial aimed at fashion retailers, large
and small. Payment: by negotiation. Illustrations:
colour and b&w photos. Founded 1887.

Early Music

Oxford University Press, 70 Baker Street,
London W1M 7DN
tel 020-7616 5902 *fax* 020-7616 5901
email jnl.early-music@oup.co.uk
website www.em.oupjournals.org
Editor Tess Knighton
Quarterly £10.50 (£46 p.a., institutions £92 p.a.)

Lively, informative and scholarly articles on aspects
of medieval, renaissance, baroque and classical
music. Payment: £20 per 1000 words. Illustrations:
line, half-tone, colour. Founded 1973.

East Lothian Life

1 Beveridge Row, Belhaven, Dunbar,
East Lothian EH42 1TP
tel/fax (01368) 863593
email info@east-lothian-life.co.uk
website www.east-lothian-life.co.uk
Editor Pauline Jaffray
Quarterly £2.50

Articles and features with an East Lothian slant.
Length: up to 1000 words. Illustrations: b&w
photos, line, cartoons. Payment: negotiable.
Founded 1989.

Eastern Art Report

Eastern Art Publishing Group, PO Box 13666,
27 Wallorton Gardens, London SW14 8WF

tel 020-8392 1122 *fax* 020-8392 1422
email ear@eapgroup.com
Managing Sajid Rizvi, *Send material to* Shirley Rizvi,
Executive Editor
Bi-monthly £6 (£30 p.a. individual, £60 p.a.
institutions)

Original, well-researched articles on all aspects of
the visual arts – Buddhist, Islamic, Judaic, Indian,
Chinese and Japanese; reviews. Length of articles:
min. 1500 words. Illustrations: colour transparencies,
b&w photos; no responsibility accepted for
unsolicited material. Payment: by arrangement.
Founded 1989.

Eastern Eye
Ethnic Media Group, Unit 2,
65 Whitechapel Road,
London E1 1DU
tel 020-7650 2000 *fax* 020-7650 2001
Editor Mujibul Islam
Weekly 70p

Articles, features and news of interest to British
Asians. Magazine covers music, fashion, film gossip.
Freelance material considered. Illustrations: colour.
Founded 1989.

The Ecologist
Unit 18, Chelsea Wharf, 15 Lots Road,
London SW10 0QJ
tel 020-7351 3578 *fax* 020-7351 3617
email sally@theecologist.org
Editors Zac Goldsmith
10 p.a. £3.50

Fully referenced articles on economic, social and
environmental affairs from an ecological
standpoint. Study magazine first for level and
approach. Length: 1000–5000 words. Illustrations:
line, half-tone. Payment: by arrangement.

Economica
STICERD, London School of Economics,
Houghton Street, London WC2A 2AE
tel 020-7955 7855 *fax* 020-7955 6951
Editors Prof F.A. Cowell, Prof Alan Manning,
Prof Tore Ellingsen
Quarterly £28 (apply for subscription rates)

Learned journal covering the fields of economics,
economic history and statistics. Payment: none.
Founded 1921; New Series 1934.

The Economist
25 St James's Street,
London SW1A 1HG
tel 020-7830 7000
website www.economist.com
Editor Bill Emmott
Weekly £2.90

Articles staff-written. Founded 1843.

The Edge
65 Guinness Buildings, London W6 8BD
tel 020-7460 9444
email davec@theedge.abelgratis.co.uk
website www.theedge.abelgratis.co.uk
Editor David Clark
Quarterly £4

Interviews, features, reviews: books, films, music,
modern popular culture; imaginative fiction –
science fiction, modern urban fiction, horror, etc.
Return postage essential. Payment: £30–£300
negotiable.

Edinburgh Review
22A Buccleugh Place, Edinburgh EH8 9LN
tel/fax 0131-651 1415
email Edinburgh.Review@ed.ac.uk
Editor Alex Thomson
Tri-annual £17 p.a. (individual)

Fiction, poetry, clearly written articles on Scottish
and international cultural and philosophical ideas.
Payment: by arrangement. Founded 1969.

Education Journal
17 Park Road, Hampton Hill, Middlesex TW12 1HE
tel/fax 020-8979 9473
Editor George Low
Monthly £38 p.a.

Features on policy, management and professional
development issues. Major documents and reports
gutted down to a brief digest; documents and
research listings. Research section combining original
reports and updates on research projects. Coverage of
parliamentary debates and answers to parliamentary
questions, giving statistical data by LEA. Reference
section that includes coverage of all circulars,
conference reports and opinion column. Length:
1000 words. Illustrations: photos, cartoons. Payment:
by arrangement. Founded 1903; relaunched 1996.

EE Times
CMP Europe Ltd, City Reach, 5 Greenwich View
Place, Millharbour, London E14 9NN
tel 020-7861 6417 *fax* 020-7861 6253
email cedwards@cmp-europe.com
Editor Chris Edwards
Weekly £3.25 (£85 p.a.)

News, reviews and features on the electronics
industry. Length: 2000 words (features), 200 words
(news). Illustrations: colour transparencies, colour
and b&w artwork and cartoons. Payment: variable.
Founded 1978.

Electrical Review
Cumulus Business Media, Anne Boleyn House,
9-13 Ewell Road, Cheam, Surrey SM3 8BZ
tel 020-8652 8736 *fax* 020-8652 8951
email b.evett@cumulusmedia.co.uk

Managing Editor Bill Evett
Fortnightly £3.50

Technical and business articles on electrical and control engineering; outside contributions considered. Electrical news welcomed. Illustrations: photos and drawings, cartoons. Payment: according to merit. Founded 1872.

Electrical Times

Cumulus Business Media,
Anne Boleyn House,
9-13 Ewell Road, Cheam,
Surrey SM3 8BZ
tel 020-8652 8736 *fax* 020-8652 8972
email b.evett@cumulusmedia.co.uk
Managing Editor Bill Evett
Monthly £3.50

Business and technical articles of interest to contractors and installers in the electrical industries and business services engineers, with illustrations as necessary. Length: 750–1000 words. Payment: negotiable. Illustrations: line, half-tone, colour, cartoons. Founded 1892.

Elle (UK)

Hachette Filipacchi UK, 16-18 Berners Street,
London W1T 3LN
tel 020-7150 7000 *fax* 020-7150 7670
Editor Sarah Bailey
Monthly £2.80

Commissioned material only. Payment: by arrangement. Illustrations: colour. Founded 1985.

Embroidery

The Embroiderers' Guild, PO Box 42B,
East Molesey, Surrey KT8 9BB
email pppinpod@aol.com
website www.embroderersguild.com/embroidery
6 p.a. £4.75 (£28.50 p.a.)

Illustrated features on contemporary textile art. Reports on internationally renowned makers. In-depth articles on ethnographic embroidery. Looks inside important collections, and at the history and social history of embroidery. Plus book and exhibition reviews, news and opportunities. Payment: by arrangement.

Empire

Endeavour House, 189 Shaftesbury Avenue,
London WC2H 8JG
tel 020-7439 9011 *fax* 020-7859 8613
website www.empireonline.com
Editor Colin Kennedy
Monthly £3

Guide to film and video: articles, features, news. Length: various. Illustrations: colour and b&w photos. Payment: approx. £300 per 1000 words; varies for illustrations. Founded 1989.

The Engineer

Centaur Communications Ltd, St Giles House,
50 Poland Street, London W1F 7AX
tel 020-7970 4106 *fax* 020-7970 4189
email george.coupe@centaur.co.uk
website www.e4engineering.com
Editor Sean Brierley
50 p.a. Controlled circulation (£118 p.a.)

Features and news on innovation and technology, including profiles, analysis. Length: news up to 800 words, features average 1000 words. Illustrations: colour transparencies or prints, artwork, line diagrams, graphs. Payment: by negotiation. Founded 1856.

Engineering

Gillard Welch Ltd, 355 Station Road, Dorridge,
Solihull B93 8EY
tel (01564) 771772 *fax* (01564) 774776
Editor Jonathan Ward
12 p.a. £8

'For innovators in technology, manufacturing and management': features and news. Contributions considered on all aspects of engineering. Illustrations: colour. Founded 1866.

The English Garden

Romsey Publishing Ltd, Jubilee House,
2 Jubilee Place, London SW3 3TQ
tel 020-7751 4800 *fax* 020-7751 4848
email theenglishgarden@romseypublishing.com
Editor Julia Watson
Monthly £3.20

Features and photography on English gardens, plant genera and garden design. Send written synopsis. Length: 1000 words. Illustrations: colour photos and artwork. Payment: variable. Founded 1997.

Envoi

44 Rudyard Road, Biddulph Moor, Stoke-on-Trent,
Staffs. ST8 7JN
tel (01782) 517892
Editor Roger Elkin
3 p.a. £15 p.a.

New poetry, including sequences, collaborative works and translations, reviews, articles on modern poets and poetic style; poetry competitions; adjudicator's reports. Sample copy: £3.00. Payment: one complimentary copy. Founded 1957.

The Erotic Review

4th Floor, Maddox House, 1 Maddox Street,
London W1S 2PZ
tel 020-7439 8999 *fax* 020-7437 3528
email info@theeroticreview.co.uk
website www.theeroticreview.co.uk
Editor Rowan Pelling, *Send material to* Susanna Forrest, Assistant Editor

Monthly £3.50

Up-market literary magazine for sensualists and libertines. Length: 1000 words (articles and features), 1000–2000 (short stories). Illustrations: colour and b&w prints, artwork and cartoons. Payment: £50–£75 (articles and features), £50–£75 (short stories); £50 (prints and artwork), £40 (cartoons). Founded 1997.

ES Magazine – see Evening Standard in Regional newspapers UK and Ireland, page 11

Esquire

National Magazine House, 72 Broadwick Street, London W1F 9EP
tel 020-7439 5000 *fax* 020-7439 5675
Editor Simon Tiffin
Monthly £3.40

Quality men's general interest magazine – articles, features. No unsolicited material or short stories. Length: various. Illustrations: colour and b&w photos, line. Payment: by arrangement. Founded 1991.

Essential Water Garden

Aceville Publications Ltd, 25 Phoenix Court, Hawkins Road, The Hythe, Colchester, Essex CO2 8JY
tel (01206) 505977 *fax* (01206) 505985
email demelzashea@genie.co.uk
Editor Demelza Shea
10 p.a. £2.80

Magazine for owners of all styles and sizes of water gardens, including fish-stocked pools. Practical projects and seasonal solutions. Illustrated step-by-step projects considered; also regular readers' garden feature. Illustrations: colour. Length: approx. 1000 words. Payment: by arrangement. Founded 1998.

Essentials

IPC Media, King's Reach Tower, Stamford Street, London SE1 9LS
tel 020-7261 6970
Editor Karen Livermore
Monthly £2.30

Features, plus fashion, health and beauty, cookery. Illustrations: colour. Payment: by negotiation. Founded 1988.

Essex Life & Countryside

Dugard House, Peartree Road, Stanway, Colchester CO3 5JX
tel (01206) 571348 *fax* (01206) 366982
Editor Carmen Konopka
Monthly £2.50

Features with Essex emphasis. Length: up to 1200

words. Illustrations: colour photos. Payment: negotiable. Founded 1952.

Essex Magazine and East Anglian Life

Acorn Magazines Ltd, The Old County School, Northgate Street, Bury St Edmunds, Suffolk IP33 1HP
tel (01284) 701190 *fax* (01284) 701680
Editor Pippa Bastin
Monthly £2.30

Magazine for residents of Essex and East Anglia covering history, people, places, environment, events, homes and gardens. Considers unsolicited material; no acknowledgement. Welcomes ideas for articles and features. Length: 1500 words features/ articles. Illustrations: colour. Payment: £100 per 1500-word feature/article; £50 for front cover image. Founded 1999.

European Chemical News

Reed Business Information, Quadrant House, The Quadrant, Sutton, Surrey SM2 5AS
tel 020-8652 8147 *fax* 020-8652 3375
email ecne@rbi.co.uk
Editor John Baker
Weekly £365 p.a. Europe (£410 p.a. overseas)

Articles and features concerning business, markets and investments in the chemical industry. Length: 1000–2000 words; news items up to 400 words. Payment: £150–£200 per 1000 words.

Eventing

IPC Media, Room 2005, King's Reach Tower, Stamford Street, London SE1 9LS
tel 020-7261 5388 *fax* 020-7261 5429
Editor Amanda Gee
Monthly £3.30

News, articles, features, event reports and opinion pieces – all with bias towards the sport of horse trials. Mostly commissioned, but all ideas welcome. Length: up to 1500 words. Illustrations: colour and b&w, mostly commissioned. Payment: by arrangement. Founded 1984.

Evergreen

PO Box 52, Cheltenham, Glos. GL50 1YQ
tel (01242) 537900 *fax* (01242) 537901
Editor Roy Faiers
Quarterly £3.50

Articles about Britain's famous people and infamous characters, its natural beauty, towns and villages, history, traditions, odd customs, legends, folklore, etc; regular articles on old films, songs, radio programmes and variety acts. Length 250–2000 words. Also 'meaningful rather than clever' poetry. Illustrations: colour transparencies. Payment: £15 per 1000 words, £4 poems. Founded 1985.

Everyday Practical Electronics

Wimborne Publishing Ltd, 408 Wimborne Road East, Ferndown, Dorset BH22 9ND
tel (01202) 873872 *fax* (01202) 874562
email editorial@epemag.wimborne.co.uk
website www.epemag.wimborne.co.uk
Editor Mike Kenward
Monthly £2.95

Constructional and theoretical articles aimed at the student and hobbyist. Length: 1000–5500 words. Payment: £55–£90 per 1000 words. Illustrations: line, half-tone. Founded 1971.

Executive PA

11 Southwark Street, London SE1 1RQ
tel 020-7089 5880 *fax* 020-7089 5855
email michael@executivepa.net
Editor Sara Evans
Quarterly Complimentary

Business to business for working senior secretaries. Length: 700–1400 words. Illustrations: colour. Payment: £140 per 1000 words. Founded 1991.

Executive Woman

Saleworld Ltd, 2 Chantry Place, Harrow, Middlesex HA3 6NY
tel 020-8420 1210 *fax* 020-8420 1691/3
email info@execwoman.com
website www.execwoman.com
Editor Angela Giveon
Bi-monthly £2.50

News and features with a holistic approach to the world of successful working women. Strong business features; articles on management, personnel, networking and mentoring. Length: 500–1000 words. Illustrations: colour and b&w. Payment: £150 per 1000 words; £50–£100. Founded 1987.

The Face

EMAP Élan Ltd, Exmouth House, Pine Street, London EC1R 0JL
tel 020-7689 9999 *fax* 020-7689 0300
Editor Neil Stevenson
Monthly £2.70

Articles on music, fashion, films, popular youth culture. Contributors must be familiar with the magazine, its audience and culture. Illustrations: half-tone, colour. Payment: £250 per 1000 words; illustrations approx. £150 per page. Founded 1980.

Family Law

21 St Thomas Street, Bristol BS1 6JS
tel 0117-923 0600 *fax* 0117-925 0486
email familylaw@jordanpublishing.co.uk
website www.familylaw.co.uk
Editors Elizabeth Walsh, Miles McColl
Monthly £150 p.a.

Articles dealing with all aspects of the law as it affects the family, written from a legal or socio-legal point of view. Length: from 1000 words. Payment: by arrangement. No illustrations. Founded 1971.

Family Tree Magazine

61 Great Whyte, Ramsey, Huntingdon, Cambs. PE26 1HJ
tel (01487) 814050
email lesboon@family-tree.co.uk
website www.family-tree.co.uk
Editorial Manager Sue Fearn
Monthly £2.50 (£27.50 p.a.)

Articles on any genealogically related topics. Payment: £40 per 1000 words. Founded 1984.

Farmers Weekly

Reed Business Information, Quadrant House, The Quadrant, Sutton, Surrey SM2 5AS
tel 020-8652 4911 *fax* 020-8652 4005
email farmers.weekly@rbi.co.uk
website www.fwi.co.uk
Editor Stephen Howe
Weekly £1.65

Articles on agriculture from freelance contributors will be accepted subject to negotiation. Founded 1934.

Fasttrack

1-3 Frederick's Place, London EC2R 8AB
tel 0161-817 3400 *fax* 0161-817 3401
email editor@fasttrack-digital.com
website www.goldensquare.com
Editor Marion Ainge
6 p.a. £15 p.a.

Upbeat magazine targeted mainly at female professional and executive personnel in the 20–40 age group. News and features – success stories, career changes, mentoring, current workplace issues, training opportunities, etc. Founded 1995.

FHM (For Him Magazine)

EMAP Élan Network, Mappin House, 4 Winsley Street, London W1W 8HF
tel 020-7436 1515 *fax* 020-7343 3000
email dan.elk@fhm.com
website www.fhm.com
Editor David Davies
Monthly £3.10

Features, fashion, grooming, travel (adventure) and men's interests. Length: 1200–2000 words. Illustrations: colour and b&w photos, line and colour artwork. Payment: by negotiation. Founded 1987.

The Field

IPC Media Ltd, King's Reach Tower, Stamford Street, London SE1 9LS
tel 020-7261 5198 *fax* 020-7261 5358

website www.thefield.co.uk
Monthly £3.20

Specific, topical and informed features on the British countryside and country pursuits, including natural history, field sports, gardening and rural conservation. Overseas subjects considered but opportunities for such articles are limited. No fiction or children's material. Articles, length 800–2000 words, by outside contributors considered; also topical 'shorts' of 200–300 words on all countryside matters. Illustrations: colour photos of a high standard. Payment: on merit. Founded 1853.

Film Review

Visual Imagination Ltd, 9 Blades Court, Deodar Road, London SW15 2NU
tel 020-8875 1520 *fax* 020-8875 1588
email filmreview@visimag.com
Editor Neil Corry
Monthly £3

Features and interviews on mainstream cinema; film and video reviews. No fiction. Length: 1000–3000 words (features), 350 words (reviews). Illustrations: colour and b&w. Payment: £80 per 1000 words; £20 for first image, £10 per additional image. Founded 1950.

Financial Adviser

FT Finance Ltd, Maple House, 149 Tottenham Court Road, London W1P 9LL
tel 020-7896 2525 *fax* 020-7896 2699/2588
Editor Hal Austin
Weekly (£90 p.a.) Free to financial intermediaries working in financial services

Topical personal finance news and features. Length: variable. Payment: by arrangement. Founded 1987.

Financial Mail on Sunday – see Mail on Sunday in National newspapers UK and Ireland, page 3

Fire

Queensway House, 2 Queensway, Redhill, Surrey RH1 1QS
tel (01737) 855431 *fax* (01737) 855418
Editor Andrew Lynch
Monthly £6.95 (£61 p.a.)

Articles on firefighting and fire prevention from acknowledged experts only. Length: 600 words. No unsolicited contributions. Illustrations: dramatic firefighting or fire brigade rescue colour photos. Also *Fire International*. Payment: by arrangement. Founded 1908.

Fishing News

Telephone House, 69-77 Paul Street, London EC2A 4LQ
tel 020-7017 4531 *fax* 020-7017 4536
email tim.oliver@informa.com

Editor Tim Oliver
Weekly £1.10

News and features on all aspects of the commercial fishing industry. Length: up to 1000 words (features), up to 500 words (news). Illustrations: colour and b&w photos. Payment: negotiable. Founded 1913

The Fix

(formerly Zene)
TTA Press, 5 Martins Lane, Witcham, Ely, Cambs. CB6 2LB
email ttapress@aol.com
website www.ttapress.com
Editor Andy Cox
Bi-monthly 15 p.a. (subscription only)

Reviews of short fiction, in-depth coverage of the world's magazines (both large and small) plus interviews, columns, news and views. Hundreds of markets for writers in every issue. Submissions welcome. Payment: negotiable. Founded 1995.

Flight International

Reed Business Information Ltd, Quadrant House, The Quadrant, Sutton, Surrey SM2 5AS
tel 020-8652 3842 *fax* 020-8652 3840
email flight.international@rbi.co.uk
website www.flightinternational.com
Editor Murdo Morrison
Weekly £2.40

Deals with all branches of aerospace: operational and technical articles, illustrated by photos, engineering cutaway drawings; also news, paragraphs, reports of lectures, etc. News press days: Thurs, Fri. Illustrations: tone, line, colour. Payment: by agreement. Founded 1909.

Flora International

The Fishing Lodge Studio, 77 Bulbridge Road, Wilton, Salisbury, Wilts. SP2 0LE
tel/fax (01722) 743207
email floramag@aol.com
Editor Maureen Foster
Bi-monthly £2.99

Magazine for flower arrangers and florists. Also features flower-related articles, flower arrangers' gardens and flower-related crafts. Will consider unsolicited material. Welcomes ideas for articles and features. Length: approx. 1000 words (articles/features). Illustrations: transparencies and colour prints, b&w cartoons. Payment: £50 (words), £15 illustrations. Founded 1974.

Fly-Fishing & Fly-Tying

Rolling River Publications, Aberfeldy Road, Kenmore, Perthshire PH15 2HF
tel/fax (01887) 830526
email MarkB.ffft@btinternet.com

website www.flyfishing-and-flytying.co.uk
Editor Mark Bowler
11 p.a. £2.60

Fly-fishing and fly-tying articles, fishery features, limited short stories, fishing travel. Length: 800–2000 words. Illustrations: colour photos. Payment: by arrangement. Founded 1990.

Focus
Origin Publishing, 14th Floor, Tower House, Fairfax Street, Bristol BS1 3BN
tel 0117-927 9009 *fax* 0117-934 9008
Editor Emma Bayley
Monthly £3.25

'The magazine of science and discovery.' Articles, features and news with a science-based or technical slant. All material is commissioned. Length: 1000–3000 words (features), 50–200 words (news). Illustrations: colour prints, transparencies and artwork. Payment: £150–£200 per 1000 words; £200 per full-page photo (negotiable). Founded 1992.

Folio
64-65 North Road, St Andrews, Bristol BS6 5AQ
tel 0117-942 8491 *fax* 0117-942 0369
email editor@venue.co.uk
website www.venue.co.uk
Editor Dave Higgitt
Monthly Free

Articles, features, interviews and news on people, places and events with a local connection (Bristol, Bath and Cheltenham area). No short stories or poems. Unsolicited material considered. Length: 600–2000 words (features), variable (news). Illustrations: colour and b&w. Payment: by negotiation. Founded 1994.

Football Picture Story Library
D.C. Thomson & Co. Ltd, Albert Square, Dundee DD1 9QJ
tel (01382) 223131 *fax* (01382) 322214
185 Fleet Street, London EC4A 2HS
tel 020-7400 1030 *fax* 020-7400 1089
2 p.m. 90p

Football stories for boys told in pictures.

For Women
Fantasy Publications, 4 Selsdon Way, London E14 9GL
tel 020-7308 5363
Fiction Editor Elizabeth Coldwell
6-weekly £3.50

Women's magazine with erotic emphasis. Features on sex and health; erotic fiction and photos. Erotic fiction welcomed on spec. Fiction guidelines on receipt of sae. Length: 2000–3000 words. Illustrations: colour and b&w photos. Payment: £150 per story. Founded 1992.

Fortean Times
Box 2409, London NW5 4NP
tel 020-7687 7002 *fax* 020-7687 7099
email david.sutton@ifgmags.com
website www.forteantimes.com/
Editors David Sutton
Monthly £3.20

Journal of strange phenomena, experiences, related subjects and philosophies. Articles, features, news, reviews. Length: 500–5000 words; longer by arrangement. Illustrations: colour photos, line and tone art, cartoons. Payment: by negotiation. Founded 1973.

Fortnight – An Independent Review of Politics and the Arts
11 University Road, Belfast BT7 1NA
tel 028-9023 2353/9032 4141 *fax* 028-9023 2650
email editor@fortnight.org
website www.fortnight.org
Editor Malachi O'Doherty
Monthly £2.20

Current affairs analysis, reportage, opinion pieces, cultural criticism, book reviews, poems. Illustrations: line, half-tone, cartoons. Payment: by arrangement. Founded 1970.

FourFourTwo
Haymarket Leisure Publications Ltd, 38-42 Hampton Road, Teddington TW11 0JE
tel 020-8267 5337 *fax* 020-8267 5019
Editor Mat Snow
Monthly £3.20

Football magazine with 'adult' approach: interviews, in-depth features, issues pieces, odd and witty material. Length: 2000–3000 (features), 100–500 words (news/latest score). Illustrations: colour transparencies and artwork, b&w prints. Payment: £200 per 1000 words. Founded 1994.

FRANCE Magazine
Community Media Ltd, Cumberland House, Oriel Road, Cheltenham, Glos. GL50 1BB
tel (01242) 216050 *fax* (01242) 216074
email editorial@francemag.com
website www.francemag.com
Editor Philip Faiers
Bi-monthly £3.99

Informed quality features and articles on the real France, ranging from cuisine to customs to architecture to exploring the hidden France. Length: 800–2000 words. Illustrations: colour transparencies (mounted and captioned). Payment: £100 per 1000 words; £50 per page/pro rata for illustrations. Founded 1989.

Freelance Market News
Sevendale House, 7 Dale Street, Manchester M1 1JB

tel 0161-228 2362 ext. 210 *fax* 0161-228 3533
email fmn@writersbureau.com
Editor Angela Cox
11 p.a.

Information on UK and overseas publications with editorial content, submission requirements and contact details. News of editorial requirements for writers. Features on the craft of writing, competitions, letters page. Founded 1968.

Freelance Photographer

(formerly Photon)
Icon Publications Ltd,
Maxwell Place, Maxwell Lane, Kelso,
Roxburghshire TD5 7BB
tel (01573) 226032 *fax* (01573) 226000
email david@maxwellplace.demon.co.uk
website www.freelancephotographer.co.uk/photon/
Editor David Kilpatrick
6 p.a. £2.95

Illustrated features on professional and craft photography. All material commissioned. Length: 750–2500 words. Illustrations: b&w and colour photos. Payment: £50–£300 per feature, including photos. Founded 1989.

The Friend

New Premier House, 150 Southampton Row,
London WC1B 5BQ
tel 020-7387 7549
email editorial@thefriend.org
website www.thefriend.org
Editor Harry Albright
Weekly £1.20

Material of interest to the Religious Society of Friends and like-minded people; political, social, economic or devotional, considered from outside contributors. Length: up to 1200 words. Illustrations: b&w or colour prints, b&w line drawings. Payment: not usually but will negotiate a small fee with professional writers. Founded 1843.

Fun Size Beano – see The Beano

Funsize Dandy – see The Dandy

The Furrow

St Patrick's College, Maynooth, Co. Kildare,
Republic of Ireland
tel (01) 7083741 *fax* (01) 7083908
email furrow.office@may.ie
website www.thefurrow.ie
Editor Rev. Ronan Drury
Monthly €2.16

Religious, pastoral, theological, social articles. Length: up to 3000 words. Payment: average €20 per page (450 words). Illustrations: line, half-tone. Founded 1950.

The Garden

4th Floor, Churchgate, New Road,
Peterborough PE1 1TT
tel (01733) 775775 *fax* (01733) 775819
email thegarden@rhs.org.uk
Editor Ian Hodgson
Monthly £3.75

Journal of The Royal Horticultural Society. Features of horticultural or botanical interest on a wide range of subjects. Commissioned material only. Length: 1200–2500 words. Illustrations: 35mm or medium format colour transparencies, occasional b&w prints, botanical line drawings; digital images are not accepted for features. Payment: varies. Founded 1866.

Garden Answers

EMAP Active Ltd, Bretton Court, Bretton,
Peterborough PE3 8DZ
tel (01733) 264666 *fax* (01733) 282695
Editor Nicola Dela-Croix
Monthly £2.70

Commissioned features and articles on all aspects of gardening. Study of magazine essential. Approach by letter with examples of published work. Length: 750 words. Illustrations: colour transparencies and artwork. Payment: by negotiation. Founded 1982.

Garden News

EMAP Active Ltd, Apex House, Oundle Road,
Peterborough PE2 9NP
tel (01733) 898100 *fax* (01733) 466857
email sarah.page@ecm.emap.com
Editor Sarah Page
Weekly £1

Up-to-date information on everything to do with plants, growing and gardening. Illustrations: line, colour, cartoons. Payment: by negotiation. Founded 1958.

Gay Times

Ground Floor, Worldwide House,
116-134 Bayham Street, London NW1 0BA
tel 020-7482 2576 *fax* 020-7284 0329
email edit@gaytimes.co.uk
Editor Vicky Powell
Monthly £2.95

Feature articles, full news and review coverage of all aspects of gay and lesbian life. Length: up to 2000 words. Illustrations: colour, line and half-tone, cartoons. Payment: by arrangement. Founded 1982.

Geographical Journal

Royal Geographical Society (with the Institute of British Geographers), Kensington Gore,
London SW7 2AR
tel 020-7591 3026 *fax* 020-7591 3001
email journals@rgs.org

Editor Prof A. Millinglon
4 p.a. £30 (post free), (£81 p.a.)

Papers on all aspects of geography and development of current interest and concern. Large reviews section. Illustrations: photos, maps, diagrams. Founded 1893.

Geographical Magazine

(under licence from the Royal Geographical Society)
Campion Interactive Publishing Ltd, Unit 11,
Pall Mall Deposit, 124-8 Barlby Road,
London W10 6BL
tel 020-8960 6400 *fax* 020-8960 6004
email magazine@geographical.co.uk
website www.geographical.co.uk
Deputy Editor Geordie Torr
Monthly £3.25

Covers travel, culture, wildlife, exploration, science and history. Illustrations: top quality transparencies, vintage material. Payment: by negotiation. Founded 1935.

Geological Magazine

Cambridge University Press, The Edinburgh Building, Shaftesbury Road, Cambridge CB2 2RU
tel (01223) 312393
Editors Prof I.N. McCave, Dr N.H. Woodcock,
Dr M.J. Bickle, Dr G.E. Budd
Bi-monthly (£253 p.a. institutions, £45 p.a. students, US$412 USA/Canada/Mexico)

Original articles on all earth science topics containing the results of independent research by experts. Also reviews and notices of current geological literature, correspondence on geological subjects – illustrated. Length: variable. Payment: none. Founded 1864.

Gibbons Stamp Monthly

Stanley Gibbons Ltd, 5 Parkside, Ringwood,
Hants BH24 3SH
tel (01425) 472363 *fax* (01425) 470247
email hjefferies@stanleygibbons.co.uk
Editor Hugh Jefferies
Monthly £2.40 (£28.80 p.a.)

Articles on philatelic topics. Contact the Editor first. Length: 500–2500 words. Payment: by arrangement, £35 or more per 1000 words. Illustrations: photos, line, stamps or covers.

Girl About Town Magazine

Independent Magazines, Independent House,
191 Marsh Wall, London E14 9RS
tel 020-7005 5000 *fax* 020-7005 5333
Editor-in-Chief Bill Williamson
Weekly Free

Articles of general interest to women. Length: about 1100–1500 words. Payment: negotiable. Founded 1972.

Girl Talk – see page 295

Glamour

The Condé Nast Publications Ltd,
6-8 Old Bond Street, London W15 4PH
tel 020-7499 9080 *fax* 020-7491 2551
email features@glamourmagazine.co.uk
website www.glamour.com
Editor Jo Elvin, *Features Editor* Miranda Levy
Monthly £1.90

Lifestyle magazine containing fashion, beauty, real life features and celebrity news aimed at women aged 18–34. Feature ideas welcome; approach with brief outline. Length: 500–800 words. Payment: by arrangement. Founded 2001.

Golf Monthly

IPC Magazines Ltd, King's Reach Tower,
Stamford Street, London SE1 9LS
tel 020-7261 7237 *fax* 020-7261 7240
email golfmonthly@ipcmedia.com
Editor Jane Carter
Monthly £3.25

Original articles on golf considered (not reports), golf clinics, handy hints. Illustrations: half-tone, colour, cartoons. Payment: by arrangement. Founded 1911.

Golf Weekly

EMAP Active Ltd, Bushfield House, Orton Centre, Peterborough PE2 5UW
tel (01733) 237111 *fax* (01733) 288025
email peter.masters@emap.com
Editor Peter Masters
Weekly £2.25

News, tournament reports and articles on golf of interest to golfers. Payment: 15p per word published. Illustrations: photos of golf news and new courses.

Golf World

EMAP Active Ltd, Bushfield House, Orton Centre, Peterborough PE2 5UW
tel (01733) 237111 *fax* (01733) 288025
Publishing Editor-in-Chief Dave Clarke
Monthly £3.30

Expert golf instructional articles, 500–3000 words; general interest articles, personality features 500–3000 words. No fiction. No unsolicited material. Payment: by negotiation. Illustrations: line, half-tone, colour, cartoons. Founded 1962.

Good Housekeeping

National Magazine House, 72 Broadwick Street,
London W1F 9EP
tel 020-7439 5000 *fax* 020-7439 5591
website www.natmags.co.uk
Editor-in-Chief Lindsay Nicholson

Monthly £2.80

Articles on topics of interest to intelligent women. No unsolicited features or stories accepted; approach by letter only. Homes, fashion, beauty and food covered by staff writers. Payment: magazine standards. Illustrations: commissioned. Founded 1922.

GQ

Condé Nast Publications, Vogue House, Hanover Square, London W1S 1JU
tel 020-7499 9080 *fax* 020-7495 1679
website www.gq/magazine.co.uk
Editor Dylan Jones
Monthly £3.10

Style, fashion and general interest magazine for men. Illustrations: b&w and colour photos, line drawings, cartoons. Payment: by arrangement. Founded 1988.

Granta

2-3 Hanover Yard, Noel Road, London N1 8BE
tel 020-7704 9776 *fax* 020-7704 0474
website www.granta.com
Editor Ian Jack
Quarterly £9.99 (£26.95 p.a.)

Original literary fiction, non-fiction and journalism. Study magazine before submitting work. No poems, essays or reviews. Length: determined by content. Illustrations: photos. Payment: by arrangement. Founded 1889; new series 1979.

Green Futures

Overseas House, 19-23 Ironmonger Row, London EC1V 3QN
email post@greenfutures.org.uk
website www.greenfutures.org.uk
Editor Martin Wright, *Send material to* Hannah Bullock, Editorial Assistant
Bi-monthly £22 p.a. individuals, £30 p.a. organisations, £38 p.a. businesses (subscription only)

Articles and features on environmental solutions and sustainable futures for people in government, business and higher education. Length: 800–1000 words. Payment: 'reasonable'. Specially commissions most material. Welcomes ideas for articles and features. Illustrations: high-res digital photos and transparencies. Founded 1996.

Greetings Today

(formerly Greetings Magazine)
Lema Publishing, Unit No. 1, Queen Mary's Avenue, Watford, Herts. WD18 7JR
tel (01923) 250909 *fax* (01923) 250995
Publisher-in-Chief Malcolm Naish, *Editor* Vicky Denton

Monthly £45 p.a. (other rates on application)

Articles, features and news related to the greetings card industry; includes Artists Directory for aspiring artists wishing to attract the eye of publishers. Mainly written in-house; some material taken from outside. Length: varies. Illustrations: line, colour and b&w photos. Payment: by arrangement. Founded 1999; first published 1972.

The Grocer

(incorporating CTN – Confectioner, Tobacconist, Newsagent)
William Reed Publishing Ltd, Broadfield Park, Crawley, West Sussex RH11 9RT
tel (01293) 613400 *fax* (01293) 610333
email grocer.editorial@william-reed.co.uk
website www.foodanddrink.co.uk
Editor Julian Hunt
Weekly £1.30

Trade journal: articles or news or illustrations of general interest to the grocery and provision trades. Payment: by arrangement. Founded 1861.

The Grower

Nexus Media Ltd, Nexus House, Azalea Drive, Swanley, Kent BR8 8HU
tel (01322) 660070 *fax* (01322) 616324
email editor.horticulture@nexusmedia.com
Editor Peter Rogers
Weekly £1.35

News and practical articles on commercial horticulture, covering all sectors including fruit, vegetable, salad crop and ornamentals. Founded 1923.

Guiding Magazine

17-19 Buckingham Palace Road, London SW1W 0PT
tel 020-7834 6242 *fax* 020-7828 8317
website www.girlguiding.org.uk
Editor Victoria Wheater
Monthly

Official magazine of Girlguiding UK. Articles of interest to women of all ages, with special emphasis on youth work and the Guide Movement. Articles on simple crafts, games and the outdoors especially welcome. Length: 300–400 words. Illustrations: line, half-tone, colour. Payment: £70 per 1000 words; £100 full colour spread.

H&E Naturist

New Freedom Publications Ltd, Burlington Court, Carlisle Street, Goole, East Yorkshire DN14 5EG
tel (01405) 769712 *fax* (01405) 763815
email newfreedom@btinternet.com
website www.healthandefficiency.co.uk
Editor Mark Nisbet
Monthly £3.25

Articles on naturist travel, clubs, beaches and naturist lifestyle experiences from the UK, Europe and the world. Length: 700–1500 words. Illustrations: line, colour transparencies and prints featuring naturists in natural settings; also cartoons, humorous fillers and features with naturist themes. Payment: by negotiation but guidelines for contributors and basic payment rates available on request.

Hairflair
Hairflair Magazines Ltd, Freebournes House, Freebournes Road, Witham, Essex CM8 3US
tel (01376) 534557 *fax* (01376) 534546
Editor Ruth Page
Bi-monthly £2.60

Hair, beauty, fashion – and related features – for the 16–35 age group. Preliminary letter essential. Length: 800–1000 words. Illustrations: colour and b&w photos. Payment: negotiable. Founded 1985.

Hampshire – The County Magazine
74 Bedford Place, Southampton SO15 2DF
tel 023-8022 3591/8033 3457
Monthly £2

Factual articles concerning all aspects of Hampshire, past and present. Length: 400–1000 words. Payment: by arrangement. Illustrations: mainly colour photos. Founded 1960.

Harpers & Queen
National Magazine House, 72 Broadwick Street, London W1F 9EP
tel 020-7439 5000 *fax* 020-7439 5506
Editor Lucy Yeomans
Monthly £3.30

Features, fashion, beauty, art, theatre, films, travel, interior decoration – all commissioned. Illustrations: line and wash, full colour and 2- and 3-colour, and photos. Founded 1929.

Health Club Management
Leisure Media Company Ltd, Portmill House, Portmill Lane, Hitchin, Herts. SG5 1DJ
tel (01462) 471920 *fax* (01462) 433909
email catherinelarner@leisuremedia.com
website www.leisuremedia.co.uk
Editor Catherine Larner
Monthly £48 p.a. with *Leisure Management* magazine

Official publication of the Fitness Industry Association. Articles on the operation of health clubs, day spas, fitness and sports centres. Items on consumer issues and lifestyle trends as they affect club management are welcomed. Length: up to 1500 words. Illustrations: colour and b&w photos. Payment: by arrangement. Founded 1995.

Health & Fitness
Highbury WViP, 53-79 Highgate Road, London NW5 1TW
tel 020-7331 1000 *fax* 020-7331 1108
email editorial@hfonline.co.uk
website www.hfonline.co.uk
Editor Mary Comber
Monthly £2.60

Articles on all aspects of health and fitness. Illustrations: line, half-tone, colour. Payment: by arrangement. Founded 1984.

Hello!
Wellington House, 69-71 Upper Ground, London SE1 9PQ
tel 020-7667 8700 *fax* 020-7667 8716
Editor Ronnie Whelan
Weekly £1.85

News-based features – showbusiness, celebrity, royalty; exclusive interviews. Payment: by arrangement. Illustrated. Founded 1988.

Here's Health
EMAP Esprit, Greater London House, Hampstead Road, London NW1 7EJ
tel 020-7347 1893 *fax* 020-7347 1897
Editor Sarah Wilson
Monthly £2.60

Articles on alternative medicine, complementary health, holistic living, environment, nutrition and natural treatment success stories. Preliminary letter and clippings essential. Length: 750–1800 words. Payment: on publication.

Hertfordshire Countryside
Beaumonde Publications Ltd, PO Box 5, Hitchin, Herts. SG5 1GJ
tel (01462) 431237 *fax* (01462) 422015
email info@hertscountryside.co.uk
Editor Sandra Small
Monthly £1.25

Articles of county interest. No poetry, puzzles or crosswords. Length: approx. 1000 words. Payment: £30 per 1000 words. Illustrations: line, half-tone. Founded 1946.

Hi-Fi News
IPC Country & Leisure Media Ltd, Focus House, Dingwall Avenue, Croydon CR9 2TA
tel 020-8774 0846 *fax* 020-8774 0940
email hi-finews@ipcmedia.com
Editor Steve Harris
Monthly £3.50

Articles on all aspects of high-quality sound recording and reproduction; also extensive record review section and supporting musical feature articles. Audio matter is essentially technical, but should be presented in a manner suitable for music lovers interested in the nature of sound. Length: 2000–3000 words. Illustrations: line, half-tone. Payment: by arrangement. Founded 1956.

History Today

20 Old Compton Street,
London W1D 4TW
tel 020-7534 8000
email admin@historytoday.com
website http://admin@historytoday.com
Editor Peter Furtado
Monthly £3.60

History in the widest sense – political, economic, social, biography, relating past to present; world history as well as British. Length: articles 3500 words; shorter news/views pieces 600–1200 words. Illustrations: from prints and original photos. Please do not send original material until publication is agreed. Accepts freelance contributions dealing with genuinely new historical and archaeological research. Payment: by arrangement. Founded 1951.

Home

SPL Publishing Ltd, Berwick House,
8-10 Knoll Rise, Orpington, Kent BR6 0PS
tel (01689) 887253 *fax* (01689) 896847
email jwooderson@splpublishing.co.uk
website www.splpublishing.co.uk
Editor Sarah Giles, *Send material to* Kate Sleeman, Features Editor
Monthly £3.20

Home interest magazine for women aged 25–55. Specially commissions most material. Welcomes ideas for articles and features. Founded 1995.

Home and Family

The Mothers' Union, Mary Sumner House,
24 Tufton Street, London SW1P 3RB
tel 020-7222 5533 *fax* 020-7222 1591
Editor Jill Worth
Quarterly £1.50

Short articles related to Christian family life. Payment: approx. £70 per 1000 words. Illustrations: colour photos. Founded 1954.

Home Words

G.J. Palmer & Sons Ltd, St Mary's Works,
St Mary's Plain, Norwich, Norfolk NR3 3BH
tel (01603) 612914 *fax* (01603) 624483
email admin@scm-canterburypress.co.uk
Publisher G.A. Knights, *Editor* Terence Handley MacMath, *Poetry Editor* D.H.W. Grubb
Monthly

Illustrated C of E magazine insert. Articles of popular Christian interest with an Anglican slant (450 words) with relevant photos or illustrations. Payment: by arrangement. Founded 1870.

Homes and Gardens

IPC Magazines Ltd, King's Reach Tower,
Stamford Street, London SE1 9LS
tel 020-7261 5000 *fax* 020-7261 6247
Editor Isobel McKenzie-Price
Monthly £2.90

Articles on home interest or design, particularly well-designed British interiors (snapshots should be submitted). Length: articles, 900–1000 words. Illustrations: all types. Payment: generous, but exceptional work required; varies. Founded 1919.

Homestyle

Essential Publishing, The Tower, Phoenix Square, Colchester, Essex CO4 9PE
tel (01206) 796911 *fax* (01206) 796922
website www.essentialhomes.com
Editor Sally Narraway
Monthly £1.90

Ideas and practical features on home and garden improvements. Merchandise reviews. Length: 2–6 page spreads. Illustrations: colour transparencies, digital images. Payment: by negotiation. Founded 1992.

Horse & Hound

IPC Media Ltd, King's Reach Tower,
Stamford Street, London SE1 9LS
tel 020-7261 6315 *fax* 020-7261 5429
email jenny_sims@ipcmedia.com
website www.horseandhound.co.uk
Editor Lucy Higginson
Weekly £1.85

Special articles, news items, photos, on all matters appertaining to equestrian sports. Payment: by negotiation.

Horse and Rider

Haslemere House, Lower Street, Haslemere, Surrey GU27 2PE
tel (01428) 651551 *fax* (01428) 653888
email djm@dj-murphy.demon.co.uk
website www.horseandridermagazine.co.uk
Editor Alison Bridge
Monthly £2.70

Sophisticated magazine covering all forms of equestrian activity at home and abroad. Good writing and technical accuracy essential. Length: 1500–2000 words. Illustrations: photos and drawings, the latter usually commissioned. Payment: by arrangement. Founded 1959.

Horticulture Week

Haymarket Magazines Ltd, 174 Hammersmith Road, London W6 7JP
tel 020-8267 4977
Editor Pete Weston
Weekly £1.75 (£75 p.a.)

News, technical and business journal for the nursery and garden centre trade, landscape industry and public parks and sports ground staff. Outside contributions considered. No fiction. Length: 500–1500 words. Illustrations: line, half-tone, colour. Payment: by arrangement.

Hortus

Bryan's Ground, Stapleton, Nr Presteigne, Herefordshire LD8 2LP
tel (01544) 260001 *fax* (01544) 260015
email all@hortus.co.uk
website www.hortus.co.uk
Editor David Wheeler
Quarterly £32 p.a. (UK)

Articles on decorative horticulture: plants, gardens, history, design, literature, people; book reviews. Length: 1500–5000 words, longer by arrangement. Illustrations: line, half-tone and wood-engravings. Payment: by arrangement. Founded 1987.

Hospital Doctor

Reed Healthcare Publishing, Quadrant House, The Quadrant, Sutton, Surrey SM2 5AS
tel 020-8652 8745 *fax* 020-8652 8701
email hospital.doctor@rbi.co.uk
Editor Mike Broad
Weekly Free to 40,000 doctors. (£89 p.a.)

Commissioned features of interest to all grades and specialities of hospital doctors; demand for news tip-offs. Length: features 800–1500 words. Illustrations: colour photos, transparencies, cartoons and commissioned artwork. Payment: £165 per 1000 words, £16 per 100 words (news). Founded c.1977.

Hot Press

13 Trinity Street, Dublin 2, Republic of Ireland
tel (01) 2411500 *fax* (01) 2411539
email info@hotpress.ie
website www.hotpress.com
Editor Niall Stokes
Fortnightly €3.17

High-quality, investigative stories, or punchily written offbeat pieces, of interest to 16–39 year-olds, including politics, music, sport, sex, religion – whatever's happening on the street. Length: varies. Illustrations: colour with some b&w. Payment: by negotiation. Founded 1977.

Hotdog

Paragon House, St Peter's Road, Bournemouth BH1 2JS
tel (01202) 299900 *fax* (01202) 299955
email andymc@paragon.co.uk
website www.hotdog-magazine.co.uk
Editor Andy McDermott
13 p.a. £3.99

In-depth news and features for film fanatics. Specially commissions most material but will consider unsolicited material. Welcomes ideas for articles and features. Length: 1500–3000 words (features), 200–1000 words (news). Payment: 20p per word. Founded 2000.

Hotel and Catering Review

Jemma Publications Ltd, Marino House, 52 Glasthule Road, Sandycove, Co. Dublin
tel (01) 2800000 *fax* (01) 2801818
email fcorr@homenet.ie
Editor Frank Corr
Monthly IR£22 p.a.

Short news and trade news pieces. Length: approx. 200 words. Features. Payment: £100 per 1000 words. Illustrations: half-tone, cartoons.

House & Garden

Vogue House, Hanover Square, London W1S 1JU
tel 020-7499 9080 *fax* 020-7629 2907
Editor Susan Crewe
Monthly £3

Articles (always commissioned), on subjects relating to domestic architecture, interior decorating, furnishing, gardening, household equipment, food and wine.

House Beautiful

National Magazine Co. Ltd, National Magazine House, 72 Broadwick Street, London W1F 9EP
tel 020-7439 5000 *fax* 020-7439 5595
Editor Sarah Whelan
Monthly £2.40

Specialist 'home' features for the homes of today. Preliminary study of magazine advisable. Payment: according to merit. Illustrated. Founded 1989.

Housebuilder

56-64 Leonard Street, London EC2A 4JX
tel 020-7608 5130
email ben.roskrow@house-builder.co.uk
website www.house-builder.co.uk
Editor Ben Roskrow, *Send material to* Allison Heller
11 p.a. £66 p.a.

Official Journal of the HouseBuilders Federation published in association with the National House-Building Council. Technical articles on design, construction and equipment of dwellings, estate planning and development, and technical aspects of house-building, aimed at those engaged in house and flat construction and the development of housing estates. Preliminary letter advisable. Length: articles from 500 words, preferably with illustrations. Payment: by arrangement. Illustrations: photos, plans, construction details, cartoons.

HQ Poetry Magazine
(The Haiku Quarterly)
39 Exmouth Street, Swindon SN1 3PU
tel (01793) 523927
Editor Kevin Bailey
3–4 p.a. £2.80 (4 issues £10 p.a. UK, £13 p.a. non-UK)
International in scope, publishes both experimental
and traditional work. About one third of the
content is devoted to haikuesque and imagistic
poetry. Plus review section and articles. Payment:
small. Founded 1990.

i-D Magazine
124 Tabernacle Street, London EC2A 4SA
tel 020-7490 9710 *fax* 020-7251 2225
email editor@i-Dmagazine.co.uk
Editor Avril Mair
Monthly £2.80
International fashion orientated magazine. Includes
music, art, design and film. Illustrations: colour and
b&w photos. Payment: £100 per 1000 words; photos
£50 per page. Founded 1980.

Ideal Home
IPC Media Ltd, King's Reach Tower,
Stamford Street, London SE1 9LS
tel 020-7261 5000 *fax* 020-7261 6697
Acting Editor Jane Parbury
Monthly £2.60
Lifestyle magazine, articles usually commissioned.
Contributors advised to study editorial content
before submitting material. Payment: according to
material. Illustrations: usually commissioned.
Founded 1920.

The Illustrated London News
20 Upper Ground, London SE1 9PF
tel 020-7805 5555 *fax* 020-7805 5911
Editor Alison Booth
2-3 p.a. £2.50
Two special issues published annually: Summer and
Christmas, plus occasional additional issues to tie in
with major events. Focuses on London and the UK:
culture, the arts, people, dining, fashion, entertainment. All material commissioned but ideas welcome.
Founded 1842.

In Balance Health & Lifestyle Magazine
Pintail Media Ltd, 50 Parkway, Welwyn Garden City,
Herts. AL8 6HH
tel (01707) 339007
email vrb@inbalancemagazine.com
website www.inbalancemagazine.com
Editor Val Reynolds Brown
Bi-monthly £1.50
Health and lifestyle magazine with therapy listings.
Features on alternative therapies and related
environmental issues. Founded 1990.

In Britain
Romsey Publishing Group, Jubilee House,
2 Jubilee Place, London SW3 3TQ
tel 020-7751 4800 *fax* 020-7751 4848
email inbritain@romseypublishing.com
website www.inbritain.co.uk
Editor Andrea Spain
Monthly £2.95 (£23.70 p.a. UK/Europe; $33 US)
Upmarket features magazine about places and
people in Britain. Very limited freelance material is
accepted. Illustrated. Payment: by arrangement.
Founded 1930.

In Dublin
6-7 Camden Place, Dublin 2, Republic of Ireland
tel (01) 4784322 *fax* (01) 4781055
Editor Tom Galvin
Fortnightly €2.48
Dublin-related news features, oddball items,
humour and interviews. Length: 500–1000 words.
Payment: €120 per 1000 words. Illustrated. Founded
1976.

In Style
Time Life International Inc., 5th Floor, Brettenham
House, Lancaster Place, London WC2E 7TL
tel 020-7322 1510 *fax* 020-7322 1511
Editor Dee Nolan, *Features & Fashion Features
Director* Vanessa Friedman
Monthly £2.70
Fashion, beauty and celebrity lifestyle magazine for
style-conscious women aged 25–44. Welcomes ideas
for articles and features. Payment: by arrangement.
Founded 2001.

The Independent Magazine – see The Independent in National newspapers UK and Ireland, page 3

Index on Censorship
Lancaster House, 33 Islington High Street,
London N1 9LH
tel 020-7278 2313 *fax* 020-7278 1878
email judith@indexoncensorship.org
website www.indexoncensorship.org
Editor-in-Chief Ursula Owen, *Send material to*
Natasha Schmidt, Editorial Co-ordinator
Quarterly £9.50 (£32 p.a.)
Articles up to 3000 words dealing with all aspects of
free speech and political censorship. Illustrations:
b&w, cartoons. Payment: £75 per 1000 words.
Founded 1972.

Infant Projects
Scholastic Ltd, Villiers House, Clarendon Avenue,
Leamington Spa, Warks. CV32 5PR
tel (01926) 887799 *fax* (01926) 337322

Editor Jeremy Sugden
Bi-monthly £3.15

Practical articles suggesting project activities for teachers of children aged 4–7; material mostly commissioned. Length: 500–1000 words. Illustrations: colour photos and line illustrations, colour posters. Payment: by arrangement. Founded 1978.

Inspirations For Your Home

SPL Publishing Ltd, Berwick House,
8-10 Knoll Rise, Orpington, Kent BR6 0PS
tel (01689) 837200
Editor Andrée Frieze
Monthly £2.90

Inspirational features on all aspects of home interest – home design, cookery, decorating, makeovers. Length: 800–1000 words. Payment: by arrangement. Founded 1993.

Insurance Age

Informa Group plc, Informa House,
30-32 Mortimer Street, London W1W 7RE
tel 020-7017 4129 *fax* 020-7436 8397
email jon.guy@informa.com
website www.insuranceage.com
Editor Jon Guy
Monthly £5

News and features on general insurance and the broker market, personal, commercial, health and Lloyd's of London. Illustrations: transparencies. Payment: by negotiation. Founded 1979.

Insurance Brokers' Monthly

7 Stourbridge Road, Lye, Stourbridge,
West Midlands DY9 7DG
tel (01384) 895228 *fax* (01384) 893666
email info@brokersmonthly.co.uk
website www.brokersmonthly.co.uk
Editor Brian Susman
Monthly £4

Articles of technical and non-technical interest to insurance brokers and others engaged in the insurance industry. Occasional articles of general interest to the City, on finance, etc. Length: 1000–1500 words. Payment: from £40 per 1000 words on last day of month following publication. Authoritative material written under true name and qualification receives highest payment. Illustrations: line and half-tone. Founded 1950.

InterMedia

International Institute of Communications,
35 Portland Place, London W1B 1AE
tel 020-7323 9622 *fax* 020-7323 9623
email martin@iicom.org
Editor Martin Sims
Bi-monthly £70 p.a. individuals, £150 p.a. library subscription

International journal concerned with policies, events, trends and research in the field of communications, broadcasting, telecommunications and associated issues, particularly cultural and social. Preliminary letter essential. Illustrations: b&w line. Payment: by arrangement. Founded 1970.

International Affairs

Royal Institute of International Affairs,
Chatham House, 10 St James's Square,
London SW1Y 4LE
tel 020-7957 5700 *fax* 020-7957 5710
email IA-CH@riia.org
website www.riia.org
Editor Caroline Soper
5 p.a. £16 (£50 p.a.individuals, £184 p.a. institutions)

Serious long-term articles on international affairs; approx. 100 books reviewed each quarter. Preliminary letter advisable. Article length: average 7000 words. Illustrations: none. Payment: by arrangement. Founded 1922.

Internet

EMAP Automotive Ltd, Priory Court,
30-32 Farringdon Lane, London EC1R 3AU
tel 020-7017 3691
website www.internet-magazine.com
Editor Dave Wilby
Monthly £3.75

Internet magazine for the serious home user market and professional small business sector. No unsolicited contributions. Payment: by arrangement. Founded 1994.

Internet Made Easy

Paragon Publishing, Paragon House, St Peters Road,
Bournemouth BH1 2JS
tel (01202) 299900 *fax* (01202) 299955
email dominicb@paragon.co.uk
website www.paragon.co.uk
Editor Dominic Brookman
Monthly £3.99

'The easiest guide to using the Net'. Includes practical tutorials on internet software; reviews of websites; net hardware and software; internet news and features. Send paragraph summaries for features to Editor in first instance. Payment: varies. Founded 1999.

Interzone

217 Preston Drove, Brighton, East Sussex BN1 6FL
tel (01273) 504710
website www.sfsite.com/interzone
Editor David Pringle
Monthly £3 (£34 p.a.)

Science fiction and fantasy short stories, articles, interviews and reviews. Read magazine before submitting. Length: 2000–6000 words. Illustrations: line, half-tone, colour. Payment: by arrangement. Founded 1982.

Investors Chronicle

Maple House, 149 Tottenham Court Road, London W1T 7LB
tel 020-7896 2525 *fax* 020-7896 2078
Editor Matthew Vincent
Weekly £3.25

Journal covering investment and personal finance. Occasional outside contributions for surveys are accepted. Payment: by negotiation.

Ireland of the Welcomes

Fáilte Ireland, Baggot Street Bridge, Dublin 2, Republic of Ireland
tel (01) 6024000 *fax* (01) 6024335
email iow@bordfailte.ie
website www.irelandofthewelcomes.com
Editor Letitia Pollard
Bi-monthly €3.17

Articles on cultural, sporting or topographical aspects of Ireland; designed to arouse interest in Irish holidays. Mostly commissioned – preliminary letter advised. No unsolicited MSS. Length: 1200–1800 words. Payment: by arrangement. Illustrations: scenic and topical transparencies, line drawings, some cartoons. Founded 1952.

Ireland's Own

Channing House, Upper Rowe Street, Wexford, Republic of Ireland
tel (053) 40140 *fax* (053) 340191
email irelands.own@peoplenews.ie
Editors Sean Nolan, Phil Murphy
Weekly €90 cents

Short stories: non-experimental, traditional with an Irish orientation (2000–2500 words); articles of interest to Irish readers at home and abroad (750–1000 words); general and literary articles (750–1000 words). Monthly special bumper editions, each devoted to a particular seasonal topic. Suggestions for new features considered. Payment: varies according to quality and length. Illustrations: photos, cartoons. Founded 1902.

Irish Farmers Journal

Irish Farm Centre, Bluebell, Dublin 12, Republic of Ireland
tel (01) 4199500 *fax* (01) 4520876
email editdept@ifj.ie
website www.farmersjournal.ie
Editor Matthew Dempsey
Weekly €1.90

Readable, technical articles on any aspect of farming. Length: 700–1000 words. Payment: £100–£150 per article. Illustrated. Founded 1948.

Irish Journal of Medical Science

Royal Academy of Medicine, 6 Kildare Street, Dublin 2, Republic of Ireland
tel (01) 6623706 *fax* (01) 6611684
email journal@rami.ie
website www.iformix.com
Send material to Mr Thomas N. Walsh
Quarterly €35 (€130 p.a. EU, €160 p.a. outside EU)

Official Organ of the Royal Academy of Medicine in Ireland. Original contributions in medicine, surgery, midwifery, public health, etc; reviews of professional books, reports of medical societies, etc. Illustrations: line, half-tone, colour.

Irish Medical Times

24-26 Upper Ormond Quay, Dublin 7, Republic of Ireland
tel (01) 8176300 *fax* (01) 8176345
email editor@imt.ie
website www.imt.ie
Editor Aindreas McEntee
Weekly €4.25 (€198 p.a.)

Medical articles, also humorous articles with medical slant. Length: 850–1000 words. Payment: £60 per 1000 words. Illustrations: line, half-tone, colour, cartoons.

Irish Printer

Jemma Publications Ltd, 52 Glasthule Road, Sandycove, Co. Dublin, Republic of Ireland
tel (01) 2800000 *fax* (01) 2801818
email n.tynan@jemma.ie
Editor Nigel Tynan
Monthly €60.95 p.a. (€76.18 UK/overseas)

Technical articles and news of interest to the printing industry. Length: 800–1000 words. Illustrations: colour and b&w photos. Payment: €140 per 1000 words; photos £30. Founded 1974.

Irish Tatler

Smurfit Publications Ltd, 2 Clanwilliam Court, Lower Mount Street, Dublin 2, Republic of Ireland
tel (01) 2405367 *fax* (01) 6619757
email feeback@ivenus.com
website www.ivenus.com
Editor Vanessa Harriss
Monthly €2

General interest women's magazine: beauty, interiors, fashion, cookery, current affairs, reportage and celebrity interviews. Length: 2000–4000 words. In association with ivenus.com. Payment: by arrangement.

J–17

EMAP Élan, Endeavour House, 189 Shaftesbury Avenue, London WC2H 8JG
tel 020-7208 3408 *fax* 020-7208 3590
Editor Anna-Louise Weatherby

Monthly £2

Articles of interest to girls aged 14–17: fashion, beauty, and various features; investigative pieces; quizzes; celebrities and advice. Payment: by arrangement. Illustrations: colour. Founded 1983.

Jack Magazine

IFG Publishing, 9 Dallington Street, London EC1V 0BQ
tel 020-7687 7000 *fax* 020-7687 7099
email jack@ifgmags.com
kimberly.taylorbennett@ifgmags.com
website www.jackmagazine.co.uk
Editor James Brown, *Send material to* Kimberly Taylor-Bennett, Editorial Assistant
Monthly £2.50

'Magazine for intelligent men.' Wide-ranging content, from humour to sport, from nature to war to conspiracy theories. Requirements vary. Will consider unsolicited material. Welcomes ideas for articles and features. Payment: varies. Founded 2002.

Jane's Defence Weekly

Sentinel House, 163 Brighton Road, Coulsdon, Surrey CR5 2YH
tel 020-8700 3700 *fax* 020-8763 1007
website http//jdw.janes.com
Editor Clifford Beal
Weekly £220 p.a. (5-year archive on CD-Rom)

International defence news; military equipment; budget analysis, industry, military technology, business, political, defence market intelligence. Payment: minimum £200 per 1000 words used. Illustrations: line, half-tone, colour. Founded 1984.

Jazz Journal International

Jazz Journal Ltd, 3 and 3A Forest Road, Loughton, Essex IG10 1DR
tel 020-8532 0456/0678 *fax* 020-8532 0440
Publisher/Editor-in-Chief Eddie Cook
Monthly £3.50

Articles on jazz, record reviews. Telephone or write before submitting material. Payment: by arrangement. Illustrations: photos. Founded 1948.

Jewish Chronicle

25 Furnival Street, London EC4A 1JT
tel 020-7415 1500
Editor Edward J. Temko
Weekly 60p

Authentic and exclusive news stories and articles of Jewish interest from 500–1500 words are considered. Includes a lively arts and leisure section and regular travel pages. Payment: by arrangement. Illustrations: of Jewish interest, either topical or feature. Founded 1841.

The Jewish Quarterly

PO Box 2078, London W1A 1JR
tel/fax 020-8830 5367 (editorial)
Editor Matthew Reisz
Quarterly £4.95 (£25 p.a., £35 p.a. Europe, £45 p.a. overseas)

Articles of Jewish interest, literature, history, music, politics, poetry, book reviews, fiction. Illustrations: half-tone. Founded 1953.

Jewish Telegraph

Telegraph House, 11 Park Hill, Bury Old Road, Prestwich, Manchester M25 0HH
tel 0161-740 9321 *fax* 0161-740 9325
email mail@jewishtelegraph.com
website www.jewishtelegraph.com
1 Shaftesbury Avenue, Leeds LS8 1DR
tel 0113-295 6000 *fax* 0113-295 6006
Harold House, Dunbabin Road, Liverpool L15 6XL
tel 0151-475 6666 *fax* 0151-475 2222
May Terrace, Giffnock, Glasgow G46 6LD
tel 0141-621 4422 *fax* 0141-621 4333
Editor Paul Harris
Weekly Man. 35p, Leeds 25p, Liverpool 25p, Glasgow 40p

Non-fiction articles of Jewish interest, especially humour. Exclusive Jewish news stories and pictures, international, national and local. Length: 1000–1500 words. Payment: by arrangement. Illustrations: line, half-tone, cartoons. Founded 1950.

Journal of Alternative and Complementary Medicine

9 Rickett Street, London SW6 1RU
tel 020-7385 0012 *fax* 020-7385 4566
Editor Graeme Miller
Monthly £2.95 (£33.50 p.a.)

Feature articles (up to 2000 words) and news stories (up to 250 words). Unsolicited material welcome but not eligible for payment unless commissioned. Illustrations: line, half-tone, colour. Payment: by negotiation. Founded 1983.

Junior Education

Scholastic Ltd, Villiers House, Clarendon Avenue, Leamington Spa, Warks. CV32 5PR
tel (01926) 887799 *fax* (01926) 883331
email juniored@scholastic.co.uk
Editor Tracy Lomas
Monthly £3.75

For teachers of 7–11 year-olds. Articles by specialists on practical teaching ideas, coverage of primary education news; posters; photocopiable material for the classroom. Length: 800–1000 words. Payment: by arrangement. Illustrated with photos and drawings; includes colour poster. Founded 1977.

Junior Focus

Scholastic Ltd, Villiers House, Clarendon Avenue, Leamington Spa, Warks. CV32 5PR
tel (01926) 887799 *fax* (01926) 883331
email jfocus@scholastic.co.uk
Editor Tracy Lomas
Monthly £3.75

Aimed at teachers of 7–11 year-olds, each issue is based on a theme, closely linked to the National Curriculum. Includes A1 and A3 full-colour posters, 12 pages of photocopiable material and 16 pages of articles. All material commissioned. Length: 800 words. Illustrations: photos and drawings. Payment: £100 per double-page spread; varies for illustrations. Founded 1982.

Junior Magazine

Beach Magazines & Publishing Ltd,
4 Cromwell Place, London SW7 2JE
tel 020-7761 8900 *fax* 020-7761 8901
email editorial@juniormagazine.co.uk
website www.juniormagazine.co.uk
Editor Catherine O'Dolan
Monthly £2.90

Glossy up-market parenting magazine aimed at mothers of children aged 0–8 and reflects the shift in today's society towards older mothers and fathers who have established their careers and homes. Intelligent and insightful features and the best in fashion. Specially commissions most material. Welcomes ideas for articles and features. Payment: £150 per 1000 words (articles/features/short fiction), £300 per feature (colour and b&w photos/artwork). Founded 1998.

Justice of the Peace

LexisNexis UK, 35 Chancery Lane,
London WC2A 1EL
tel 020-7400 2828 *fax* 020-7400 2805
email jpn@butterworths.com
Editor Adrian Turner, *Send material to* Diana Rose
Weekly £239 p.a.

Professional journal. Articles on magisterial and local government law and associated subjects including family law, criminology, medico-legal matters, penology, police, probation. Information on articles and contributions sent on request. Length: 3000 words. Payment: £200 per feature article or £20 per column (articles). Founded 1837.

Kent Life

25A Pudding Lane, Maidstone, Kent ME14 1PA
tel (01622) 762818 *fax* (01622) 663294
email ian.trevett@archant.co.uk
kate.cowling@kent-life.co.uk
website www.kent-life.co.uk
Editor Ian Trevett, *Assistant Editor* Kate Cowling
Monthly £2.25

Local lifestyle magazine 'celebrating the best of county life'. Features local people, social events and entertainment and promotes local towns and villages, walks and heritage. Will consider unsolicited material. Welcomes ideas for articles and features. Length: 1000 words (articles/features), 200 words (news), 500 words (short fiction). Illustrations: transparencies, colour and b&w prints, colour artwork. Payment: negotiable.

Kerrang!

EMAP Performance 2001, PO Box 2930,
London W1A 6DZ
tel 020-7436 1515 *fax* 020-7312 8910
Editor Ashley Bird
Weekly £1.70

News, reviews and interviews; music with attitude. All material commissioned. Illustrations: colour. Payment: by arrangement. Founded 1981.

Kids Alive! (The Young Soldier)

The Salvation Army, 101 Newington Causeway,
London SE1 6BN
tel 020-7367 4910 *fax* 020-7367 4710
email kidsalive@salvationarmy.org.uk
Editor Ken Nesbitt
Weekly 50p (£25 p.a. including free membership of the Kids Alive! Club)

Children's magazine: stories, pictures, cartoon strips, puzzles, etc; Christian-based with emphasis on education re addictive substances. Payment: by arrangement. Illustrations: half-tone, line and 4-colour line, cartoons. Founded 1881.

Kids Out

Time Out Guides Ltd, Universal House,
251 Tottenham Court Road, London W1T 7AB
tel 020-7813 6018 *fax* 020-7813 6153
email meldakin@timeout.com
Editor Melanie Dakin
Monthly £2.50

Contains a comprehensive calendar of events in London for families, plus travel, education and parenting articles of interest to parents of under 16 year-olds in the London area. Also restaurant, game, book, software, film, shops and product reviews. For picture requirements call Kerri Miles 020-7813 6089. Length: 200–8000 words. Payment: £100 per 1000 words. Founded 1995.

Kitchen Garden

12 Orchard Lane, Woodnewton,
Peterborough PE8 5EE
tel (01780) 470097 *fax* (01780) 470550
website www.kitchengarden.co.uk
Editor Andrew Blackford
Monthly £2.90

Magazine for people with a passion for growing

their own vegetables, fruit and herbs. Includes practical tips and inspirational ideas. Specially commissions most material. Welcomes ideas for articles and features. Length: 700–2000 (articles/features). Illustrations: colour transparencies, prints and artwork; all commissioned. Payment: varies. Founded 1997.

The Lady
39-40 Bedford Street, London WC2E 9ER
tel 020-7379 4717 *fax* 020-7836 4620
website www.lady.co.uk
Editor Arline Usden
Weekly 85p

British and foreign travel, countryside, human-interest, celebrity interviews, animals, cookery, art and antiques, historic-interest and commemorative articles (preliminary letter advisable for articles dealing with anniversaries). Send proposals for articles by post or fax; do not phone. Length: 900–1200 words; Viewpoint: 500 words. Annual Short Story Competition in October with prize of £1000 plus. Winning entries printed in magazine. Payment: by arrangement. Founded 1885.

Lancashire Magazine
33 Beverley Road, Driffield, Yorkshire YO25 6SD
tel/fax (01377) 253232
Editor Winston Halstead
Bi-monthly £1.60

Articles about people, life and character of all parts of Lancashire. Length: 1000 words. Payment: £35–£40 approx. per published page. Illustrations: line, half-tone, colour. Founded 1977.

Lancet
32 Jamestown Road, London NW1 7BY
tel 020-7424 4910 *fax* 020-7424 4911
website www.thelancet.com
Editor Dr Richard Horton
Weekly £5

Research papers, review articles, editorials, correspondence and commentaries on international medicine, medical research and policy. Consult the Editor before submitting material. Founded 1823.

Land & Liberty
Suite 427, The London Fruit Exchange, Brushfield Street, London E1 6EL
tel 020-7377 8885 *fax* 020-7377 8886
email editor@LandandLiberty.org.uk
website www.LandandLiberty.org.uk
Editor Peter Gibb
Quarterly £3.75 (£15 p.a.)

Explores how common wealth can be used sustainably as public revenue to enhance and balance relationships between the individual, the community and the environment. Articles on land

economics, land taxation, land prices, land speculation as they relate to housing, the economy, production, politics. Study of journal essential. Length: up to 3000 words. Payment: by arrangement. Illustrations: half-tone. Founded 1894.

The Lawyer
Centaur Communications Group, 50 Poland Street, London W1V 4AX
tel 020-7970 4614 *fax* 020-7970 4640
email lawyer.edit@chiron.co.uk
website www.thelawyer.com
Editor Catrin Griffiths
Weekly £1.75 (£60 p.a.)

News, articles, features and views relevant to the legal profession. Length: 600–900 words. Illustrations: as agreed. Payment: £125–£150 per 1000 words. Founded 1987.

Legal Week
Global Professional Media Ltd,
99 Charterhouse Street, London EC1M 6HR
tel 020-7566 5600 *fax* 020-7253 8505
email jmalpas@gpmuk.com
website www.legalweek.net
Editor John Malpas
Weekly £2.45

News and features aimed at business lawyers. Length: 750–1000 words (features), 300 words (news). Payment: £150 upwards (features), £75–£100 (news). Considers unsolicited material and welcomes ideas for articles and features. Founded 1999.

Legal Director
Monthly

News and features for in-house lawyers.

Legal IT
Monthly

News and features for IT decision-makers in the legal industry.

The Leisure Manager
The Institute of Leisure and Amenity Management, ILAM House, Lower Basildon, Reading, Berks. RG8 9NE
tel (01491) 874800 *fax* (01491) 874801
email leisuremanager@ilam.co.uk
website www.ilam.co.uk
Editor Jonathan Ives
Monthly £40 p.a. (£50 p.a. overseas)

Official Journal of The Institute of Leisure and Amenity Management. Articles on amenity, children's play, tourism, leisure, parks, entertainment, recreation and sports management, cultural services. Payment: by arrangement. Illustrations: line, half-tone. Founded 1985.

Leisure Painter

63-65 High Street, Tenterden, Kent TN30 6BD
tel (01580) 763315 *fax* (01580) 765411
Editor Jane Stroud
Monthly £2.60

Instructional articles on painting and fine art.
Payment: £75 per 1000 words. Illustrations: line,
half-tone, colour, original artwork. Founded 1967.

Leviathan Quarterly

Bears Hay Farm, Brookhay Lane, Fradley,
Lichfield WS13 8RG
tel (01543) 411161 *fax* (01543) 410679
email leviathanmh@hotmail.com
Editor Michael Hulse
Quarterly £5.95

Fiction, essays, poetry, criticism, interviews,
photographs, drawings and symposia aimed at
readers interested in literature and art. Considers
unsolicited material. Length: 500–8000 words.
Illustrations: b&w photos and artwork. Payment:
negotiable. Founded 2001.

Life & Work: Magazine of the Church of Scotland

121 George Street, Edinburgh EH2 4YN
tel 0131-225 5722 *fax* 0131-240 2207
email lifework@dial.pipex.com
Editor Lynne Robertson
Monthly £1.20

Articles not exceeding 1200 words and news;
occasional stories. Study the magazine and contact
the Editor first. Payment: up to £100 per 1000
words, or by arrangement. Illustrations: photos and
line drawings, colour illustrations, cartoons.

Lincolnshire Life

PO Box 81, Lincoln LN1 1HD
tel (01522) 527127 *fax* (01522) 560035
email editorial@lincolnshirelife.co.uk
website www.lincolnshirelife.co.uk
Editor Judy Theobald
Monthly £1.85

Articles and news of county interest. Approach in
writing. Length: up to 1600 words. Illustrations:
colour photos and line drawings. Payment: varies.
Founded 1961.

The Linguist

The Institute of Linguists, Saxon House,
48 Southwark Street, London SE1 1UN
tel 020-7226 2822
email linguist@patricia.treasure.co.uk
website www.linguistonline.co.uk
Editor Pat Treasure
Bi-monthly £6 (£30 p.a.)

Articles of interest to professional linguists in
translating, interpreting and teaching fields. Articles
usually contributed, but payment by arrangement.

All contributors have special knowledge of the
subjects with which they deal. Length: 1500–2000
words. Illustrations: line, half-tone.

The List

The List Ltd, 14 High Street,
Edinburgh EH1 1TE
tel 0131-558 1191 *fax* 0131-557 8500
email editor@list.co.uk
Editor Mark Fisher
Fortnightly £2.20

Events guide for Glasgow and Edinburgh covering
film, theatre, music, clubs, books, city life, art, and
TV and video. Considers unsolicited material and
welcomes ideas. Length: 200 words (articles), 800
words and above (features). Illustrations:
transparencies and colour prints. Payment: £20
(articles), from £60 (features); £25–£50. Founded
1985.

The Literary Review

44 Lexington Street, London W1F 0LW
tel 020-7437 9392 *fax* 020-7734 1844
Editor Nancy Sladek
Monthly £3 (£30 p.a.)

Reviews, articles of cultural interest, interviews,
profiles, monthly poetry competition. Material
mostly commissioned. Length: articles and reviews
800–1500 words. Illustrations: line and b&w photos.
Payment: £25 per article; none for illustrations.
Founded 1979.

Loaded

IPC Media Ltd, King's Reach Tower,
Stamford Street, London SE1 9LS
tel 020-7261 5000 *fax* 020-7261 5557
email tammy_butt@ipc.co.uk (features)
johnny-cigarettes@ipcmedia.com (handbook)
website www.uploaded.com
Editor Scott Manson
Monthly £2.90

Magazine for men aged 18–30. Music, sport, sex,
humour, travel, fashion, hard news and popular
culture. Address longer features (2000 words) to
Features Editor, and shorter items to Handbook
Editor. Payment: by arrangement. Founded 1994.

LOGOS

5 Beechwood Drive, Marlow,
Bucks. SL7 2DH
tel/fax (01628) 477577
email logos-marlow@dial.pipex.com
Editor Gordon Graham
Quarterly £45 p.a. (£108 p.a. institutions)

In-depth articles on publishing, librarianship and
bookselling with international or interdisciplinary
appeal. Length: 3500–7000 words. Payment: 25
offprints/copy of issue. Founded 1990.

The London Magazine: A Review of Literature and the Arts

32 Addison Grove, London W4 1ER
tel 020-8400 5882 *fax* 020-8994 1713
email editorial@londonmagazine.ukf.net
website www.londonmagazine.ukf.net
Publisher Christopher Arkell, *Editor* Sebastian Barker
Bi-monthly £6.95 (£32 p.a.)

Poems, stories (2000–5000 words), memoirs, critical articles, features on art, photography, theatre, music, architecture. Sae essential (3 IRCs from abroad). Submissions by email are not accepted except when agreed with the Editor. Payment: by arrangement. Founded 1732.

London Review of Books

28 Little Russell Street, London WC1A 2HN
tel 020-7209 1101 *fax* 020-7209 1102
email edit@lrb.co.uk
Editor Mary-Kay Wilmers
Fortnightly £2.95

Features, essays, poems. Payment: by arrangement. Founded 1979.

Lothian Life

Ballencrieff Cottage, Ballencrieff Toll, Bathgate, West Lothian EH48 4LD
tel (01506) 632728 *fax* (01506) 635444
email editor@lothianlife.co.uk
website www.lothianlife.co.uk
Editor Susan Coon
Quarterly £2

Articles, profiles etc with a Lothians angle. Length: 800–3000 words. Illustrations: colour and b&w photos, b&w artwork and cartoons. Payment: £20 per 1000 words. Founded 1995.

MacUser

Dennis Publishing Ltd, 30 Cleveland Street, London W1T 4JD
tel 020-7907 6000 *fax* 020-7907 6369
email edit@macuser.co.uk
website www.macuser.co.uk
Editor Ian Betteridge
Fortnightly £3.50

News, reviews, tutorials and features on Apple Macintosh computer products and topics of interest to their users. Commissioned reviews of products compatible with Mac computers required. Occasional requirement for features relating to Mac-based design and publishing and general computing and internet issues. Ideas welcome. Length: 2000–5000 words (features), approx. 500 words (news), 300–2500 words (reviews). Illustrations: commissioned from Mac-based designers. Payment: £190 per 1000 words; competitive (artwork). Founded 1985.

Macworld

IDG Communications, 99 Gray's Inn Road, London WC1X 8TY
tel 020-7831 9252
email editor@macworld.co.uk
website www.macworld.co.uk
Editor Simon Jary
Every 4 weeks £4.99

All aspects of Apple Macintosh computing, primarily for professional users: industry news, product testing, tips and how-to features. Specially commissions most material. Welcomes ideas for articles and features. Payment: £210 per 1000 words. Digital pictures only. Founded 1989.

Making Music

VViP Highgate Studios, 53–79 Highgate Road, London NW5 1TW
tel 020-7331 1170 *fax* 020-7331 1273
website www.makingmusic.co.uk
Editor Paul Fowler
Monthly £18 p.a.

Technical, musicianly and instrumental features on rock, pop, blues, dance, world, jazz, soul; little classical. Length: 500–2500 words. Payment: £95 per 1000 words. Illustrations: colour, including cartoons and photos. Founded 1986.

Management Today

174 Hammersmith Road, London W6 7JP
tel 020-8267 4610 *fax* 020-7267 4966
Editor Matthew Gwyther
Monthly £40 p.a.

Company profiles and analysis – columns from 1000 words, features up to 3000 words. Payment: £330 per 1000 words. Illustrations: colour transparencies, always commissioned. Founded 1966.

Marie Claire

European Magazines Ltd, 2 Hatfields, London SE1 9PG
tel 020-7261 5240 *fax* 020-7261 5277
email marieclaire@ipcmedia.com
Editor Marie O'Riordan
Monthly £2.60

Feature articles of interest to today's woman; plus fashion, beauty, health, food, drink and travel. Commissioned material only. Payment: by negotiation. Illustrated in colour. Founded 1988.

Market Newsletter

Bureau of Freelance Photographers, Focus House, 497 Green Lanes, London N13 4BP
tel 020-8882 3315/6 *fax* 020-8886 5174
email info@thebfp.com
website www.thebfp.com
Editor John Tracy

Monthly Private circulation
Current information on markets and editorial requirements of interest to writers and photographers. Founded 1965.

Marketing Week
St Giles House, 50 Poland Street, London W1F 7AX
tel 020-7970 4000 *fax* 020-7970 6721
website www.marketing-week.co.uk
Editor Stuart Smith
Weekly £2.30

Aimed at marketing management. Accepts occasional features and analysis. Length: 1000–2000 words. Payment: £200 per 1000 words. Founded 1978.

Maxim
Dennis Publishing Ltd, 30 Cleveland Street, London W1T 4JD
tel 020-7907 6410 *fax* 020-7907 6439
email editorial.maxim@dennis.co.uk
website www.maxim-magazine.co.uk
Editor Tom Loxley
Monthly £3.20

Glossy men's lifestyle magazine with news, features and articles. All material is commissioned. Length: 1500–2500 words (features), 150–500 words (news). Illustrations: transparencies. Payment: by negotiation. Founded 1995.

Medal News
Token Publishing Ltd, Orchard House, Duchy Road, Heathpark, Honiton, Devon EX14 1YD
tel (01404) 46972 *fax* (01404) 44788
email info@tokenpublishing.com
website www.tokenpublishing.com
Editor John Mussell
10 p.a. £2.95

Well-researched articles on military history with a bias towards medals. Length: up to 2000 words. Illustrations: b&w preferred. Payment: £25 per 1000 words; none for illustrations. Founded 1989.

Media Week
Quantum Business Media Ltd, Quantum House, 19 Scarbrook Road, Croydon CR9 1LX
tel 020-8565 4317 *fax* 020-8565 4394
email mweeked@mediaweek.co.uk
Editor Tim Burrowes
Weekly £1.85

News and analysis of UK advertising media industry. Illustrations: full colour and b&w. Founded 1985.

Men Only
2 Archer Street, London W1V 8JJ
tel 020-7292 8000 *fax* 020-7734 5030
Publisher Paul Raymond, *Editor* Nat Saunders
Monthly £2.60

High-quality glamour photography; explicit sex stories (no erotic fiction); male interest features – sport, humour, entertainment, hedonism! Proposals welcome. Payment: by arrangement. Founded 1971.

Men's Health
Rodale Press Ltd, 7-10 Chandos Street, London W1M 0AD
tel 020-7291 6000 *fax* 020-7291 6053
website www.menshealth.co.uk
Editor Simon Geller
10 p.a. £3.20

Active pursuits, grooming, fitness, fashion, sex, career and general men's interest issues. Length 1000–4000 words. Ideas on any subject welcome. No unsolicited MSS. Payment: by arrangement. Founded 1994.

Methodist Recorder
122 Golden Lane, London EC1Y 0TL
tel 020-7251 8414
email editorial@methodistrecorder.co.uk
website www.methodistrecorder.co.uk
Managing Editor Moira Sleight
Weekly 65p

Methodist newspaper; ecumenically involved. Limited opportunities for freelance contributors. Preliminary letter advised. Founded 1861.

Military Modelling
Nexus Special Interests Ltd, Nexus House, Azalea Drive, Swanley, Kent BR8 8HU
tel (01322) 660070 *fax* (01322) 667633
Editor Ken Jones
Monthly £2.75

Articles on military modelling. Length: up to 2000 words. Payment: by arrangement. Illustrations: line, half-tone, colour.

Minor Monthly
Poundbury Publishing Ltd, Peverill Avenue East, Poundbury, Dorchester, Dorset DT1 3WE
tel (01305) 756397 *fax* (01305) 756395
email brian@poundbury.co.uk
website www.minormonthly.com
Editor Brian J. Elliott
Monthly £2.40

Magazine for the Morris Minor owner and enthusiast: news, features, profiles and workshops. Specially commissions most material but will consider unsolicited material. Length: 1000 words (articles/features). Illustrations: colour prints. Payment: negotiable. Founded 1995.

Mixmag
EMAP plc, Mappin House, 4 Winsley Street, London W1N 8HF

tel 020-7436 1515 *fax* 020-7312 8977
email mixmag@emap.com
website www.mixmag.net
Editor Viv Crask
Monthly £3.85

Dance music and clubbing magazine. Considers unsolicited material. Length: 300–1000 words (articles), 2500–3000 (features). Payment: £200 per 1000 words. Illustrations: colour and b&w. Founded 1984.

Mizz

IPC Magazines Ltd, King's Reach Tower, Stamford Street, London SE1 9LS
tel 020-7261 6319 *fax* 020-7261 6032
email mizz@ipcmedia.com
website www.ipcmedia.com
Editor Sharon Christal
Fortnightly £1.50

Articles on any subject of interest to girls aged 10–14. Approach in writing. Payment: by arrangement. Illustrated. Founded 1985.

Model Boats

Nexus Special Interests Ltd, Nexus House, Azalea Drive, Swanley, Kent BR8 8HU
tel (01322) 660070 *fax* (01322) 667633
Editor John L. Cundell *tel* (01525) 382847
13 p.a. £2.70

Articles, drawings, plans, sketches of model boats. Payment: £25 per page; plans £100. Illustrations: line, half-tone. Founded 1964.

Model Engineer

Nexus Special Interests Ltd, Nexus House, Azalea Drive, Swanley, Kent BR8 8HU
tel (01322) 660070 *fax* (01322) 667633
Editor Mike Chrisp
Fortnightly £2.30

Detailed description of the construction of models, small workshop equipment, machine tools and small electrical and mechanical devices; articles on small power engineering, mechanics, electricity, workshop methods, clocks and experiments. Payment: up to £40 per page. Illustrations: line, half-tone, colour. Founded 1898.

Modern Language Review

Modern Humanities Research Association, c/o Maney Publishing, Hudson Road, Leeds LS9 7DL
Quarterly Price on application to money@money.co.uk

Articles and reviews of a scholarly or specialist character on English, Romance, Germanic and Slavonic languages and literatures. Payment: none, but offprints are given. Founded 1905.

Modern Painters

3rd Floor, 52 Bermondsey Street, London SE1 3UD
tel 020-7407 9246 *fax* 020-7407 9242
email info@modernpainters.co.uk
website www.modernpainters.co.uk
Editor Karen Wright
Quarterly £5.99

Journal of modern and contemporary fine arts and architecture – commissioned articles and features; also interviews. Length: 1000–2500 words. Payment: £100 per 1000 words. Illustrated. Founded 1986.

Modern Woman Nationwide

Meath Chronicle Ltd, Market Square, Navan, Co. Meath, Republic of Ireland
tel (046) 79600 *fax* (046) 23565
Editor Margot Davis
Monthly €63 cents

Articles and features on a wide range of subjects of interest to women over the age of 18 (e.g. politics, religion, health and sex). Length: 200–1000 words. Illustrations: colour and b&w photos, line drawings and cartoons. Payment: NUJ rates. Founded 1984.

Mojo

EMAP Metro, Mappin House, 4 Winsley Street, London W1W 8HF
tel 020-7436 1515 *fax* 020-7312 8296
email mojo@emap.com
website www.mojo4music.com
Editor Phil Alexander
Monthly £3.80

Serious rock music magazine: interviews, news and reviews of books, live shows and albums. Length: up to 10,000 words. Illustrations: colour and b&w photos, colour caricatures. Payment: £250 per 1000 words; £200–£400 illustrations. Founded 1993.

MoneyMarketing

Centaur Communications, St Giles House, 50 Poland Street, London W1T 3QN
tel 020-7970 4000 *fax* 020-7943 8097
Editor John Lappin
Weekly £1.75

News, features, surveys and viewpoints. Length: features from 900 words. Illustrations: b&w photos, colour and b&w line. Payment: by arrangement. Founded 1985.

Moneywise

RD Publications Ltd, 11 Westferry Circus, Canary Wharf, London E14 4HE
tel 020-7715 8465 *fax* 020-7715 8725
website www.moneywise.co.uk
Editor David Ellis, *Send material to* Dominic Hiatt, Features Editor
Monthly £3.50

Financial and consumer interest features, articles

and news stories. No unsolicited MSS. Length: 1500–2000 words. Illustrations: willing to see designers, illustrators and photographers for fresh new ideas. Payment: by arrangement. Founded 1990.

More!

EMAP Élan, Endeavour House,
189 Shaftesbury Avenue, London WC2H 8JG
tel 020-7208 3165 *fax* 020-7208 3595
Editor Alison Hall
Fortnightly £1.45

Celebrities, fun, gossip and sexy features, how-to articles aimed at young women, including 'Men Unzipped' section. Serialised erotic fiction. Study of magazine essential. Length: 900–1100 words. Payment: £150 per 1000 words. Founded 1988.

Mother & Baby

EMAP Esprit, Greater London House,
Hampstead Road, London NW1 7EJ
tel 020-7347 1869
website www.motherandbaby.co.uk
Editor Dani Zur
Monthly £1.99

Features and practical information including pregnancy and birth and babycare advice. Expert attribution plus real-life stories. Length: 1000–1500 words. Payment: by negotiation. Illustrated. Founded 1956.

Motor Boat and Yachting

IPC Media Ltd, King's Reach Tower,
Stamford Street, London SE1 9LS
tel 020-7261 5333 *fax* 020-7261 5419
email mby@ipcmedia.com
website www.mby.com
Editor Tom Isitt
Monthly £3.50

General interest as well as specialist motor boating material welcomed. Features up to 2000 words considered on all sea-going aspects. Payment: varies. Illustrations: photos (mostly colour and transparencies preferred). Founded 1904.

Motor Boats Monthly

IPC Magazines Ltd, King's Reach Tower,
Stamford Street, London SE1 9LS
tel 020-7261 7256 *fax* 020-7261 7900
email mbm@ipcmedia.com
website www.motorboatsmonthly.co.uk
Editor Jane Kavanagh
Monthly £3.25

News on motorboating in the UK and Europe, cruising features and anecdotal stories. Mostly commissioned – send synopsis to the Editor. Length: news up to 200 words, features up to 4000 words. Illustrations: colour transparencies. Payment: by arrangement. Founded 1987.

Motor Caravan Magazine

IPC Country & Leisure, Focus House,
Dingwall Avenue, Croydon CR9 2TA
tel 020-8774 0752 *fax* 020-8774 0939
email simon-collis@ipcmedia.com
Editor Simon Collis
Monthly £2.95

Practical features, touring features (home and abroad), motorhome tests. Length: up to 1500 words. Payment: £60 per page. Illustrations: line, half-tone, colour, cartoons. Founded 1985.

Motor Cycle News

EMAP Active Ltd, Media House,
Peterborough Business Park, Lynchwood,
Peterborough PE2 6EA
tel (01733) 468000 *fax* (01733) 468028
email mcn@emap.com
website www.motorcyclenews.com
Editor Adam Duckworth
Weekly £1.60

Features (up to 1000 words), photos and news stories of interest to motorcyclists. Founded 1955.

Motorcaravan Motorhome Monthly (MMM)

PO Box 88, Tiverton, Devon EX16 7ZN
email mmmeditor@warnersgroup.co.uk
website www.mmmonline.co.uk
Editor Mike Jago
Monthly £2.95

Articles including motorcaravan travel, owner reports and DIY. Length: up to 2500 words. Payment: by arrangement. Illustrations: line, half-tone, colour prints and transparencies. Founded 1966 as *Motor Caravan and Camping*.

Ms London

Independent Magazines, Independent House,
191 Marsh Wall, London E14 9RS
tel 020-7005 5000 *fax* 020-7005 5333
Editor-in-Chief Bill Williamson
Weekly Free

Features and lifestyle pieces of interest to young professional working women with a contemporary London bias. All material commissioned. Length: 800–1400 words. Illustrations: no unsolicited illustrations; enquire first. Payment: by negotiation. Founded 1968.

Mslexia

PO Box 656, Newcastle upon Tyne NE99 1PZ
tel 0191-261 6656 *fax* 0191-261 6636
email postbag@mslexia.demon.co.uk
website www.mslexia.co.uk
Editor Debbie Taylor, *Send material to* Melanie Ashby
4 p.a. £18.75 p.a.

Magazine for women writers which combines features and advice about writing, with new fiction and poetry by women. Considers unsolicited material. Length: up to 3000 words (short stories), articles/features by negotiation, up to 6 poems. Illustrations: mono art, photos, colour transparencies. Payment: by negotiation. Founded 1998.

Music Teacher

Rhinegold Publishing Ltd,
241 Shaftesbury Avenue,
London WC2H 8TF
tel 020-7333 1747 *fax* 020-7333 1769
email music.teacher@rhinegold.co.uk
Editor Lucien Jenkins
Monthly £3.75

Information and articles for both school and private music teachers, including reviews of books, music, CD-Roms, videos and other music–education resources. Articles and illustrations must both have a teacher, as well as a musical, interest. Length: articles 1000–2000 words. Payment: £120 per 1000 words. Founded 1908.

Music Week

United Business Media International,
7th Floor, Ludgate House, 245 Blackfriars Road,
London SE1 9UR
tel 020-7579 4143 *fax* 020-7579 4011
email mwnews@ubminternational.com
Editor Ajax Scott
Weekly £3.60 (£160 p.a.)

News and features on all aspects of producing, manufacturing, marketing and retailing music. Payment: by negotiation. Founded 1959.

Musical Opinion

2 Princes Road, St Leonards-on-Sea,
East Sussex TN37 6EL
tel (01424) 715167 *fax* (01424) 712214
email musicalopinion2@aol.com
Editor Denby Richards
Bi-monthly £5 (£28 p.a.)

Suggestions for contributions of musical interest, scholastic, educational, anniversaries and ethnic. Dance, video, CD, opera, festival, book, music reviews. All editorial matter must be commissioned. Payment: on publication. Illustrations: colour photos. Founded 1877.

Musical Times

22 Gibson Square, London N1 0RD
Editor Antony Bye
4 p.a. For subscription rates *tel* (01442) 879097

Musical articles, reviews, 500–6000 words. All material commissioned; no unsolicited material. Illustrations: music. Founded 1844.

My Weekly

D.C. Thomson & Co. Ltd, 80 Kingsway East,
Dundee DD4 8SL
tel (01382) 223131 *fax* (01382) 452491
email myweekly@dcthomson.co.uk
185 Fleet Street, London EC4A 2HS
tel 020-7400 1030 *fax* 020-7400 1089
Editor H.G. Watson
Weekly 60p

Serials, from 20,000–60,000 words, suitable for family reading. Short complete stories of 1000–3500 words with humorous, romantic or strong emotional themes. Articles on TV stars and on all subjects of women's interest. Contributions should appeal to women everywhere. Payment: on acceptance. Illustrations: colour and b&w. Founded 1910.

My Weekly Story Collection

D.C. Thomson & Co. Ltd, Albert Square,
Dundee DD1 9QJ
tel (01382) 223131 *fax* (01382) 322214
185 Fleet Street, London EC4A 2HS
tel 020-7400 1030 *fax* 020-7400 1089
Editor Dorothy Hunter
4 p.m. 90p

25,000–30,000-word romantic stories aimed at the adult market. Payment: by arrangement; competitive for the market. No illustrations.

The National Trust Magazine

The National Trust, 36 Queen Anne's Gate,
London SW1H 9AS
tel 020-7222 9251 *fax* 020-7222 5097
website www.nationaltrust.org.uk
Editor Gaynor Aaltonen
3 p.a. Free to members

News and features on the conservation of historic houses, coasts and countryside in the UK. No unsolicited articles. Length: 1000 words (features), 200 words (news). Illustrations: colour transparencies and artwork. Payment: by arrangement; picture library rates. Founded 1969.

Natural World

EMAP Active Ltd, Bushfield House, Orton Centre,
Peterborough PE2 5UW
tel (01733) 237111 *fax* (01733) 465658
Editor Trevor Lawson
3 p.a. Free to members

National magazine of the Wildlife Trusts. Short articles on the work of the UK's 47 wildlife trusts. Unsolicited MSS not accepted. Length: up to 1200 words. Payment: by arrangement. Illustrations: line, colour. Founded 1981.

Naturalist

The University, Bradford BD7 1DP
tel (01274) 234212 *fax* (01274) 234231

email m.r.d.seaward@bradford.ac.uk
Editor Prof M.R.D. Seaward MSc, PhD, DSc
Quarterly £20 p.a.

Original papers on all kinds of British natural history subjects, including various aspects of geology, archaeology and environmental science. Length: immaterial. Illustrations: photos and line drawings. Payment: none. Founded 1875.

Nature

Macmillan Magazines Ltd, The Macmillan Building, 4 Crinan Street, London N1 9XW
tel 020-7833 4000 *fax* 020-7843 4596
email nature@nature.com
website www.nature.com
Editor Philip Campbell
Weekly £5.45

Devoted to scientific matters and to their bearing upon public affairs. All contributors of articles have specialised knowledge of the subjects with which they deal. Illustrations: line, half-tone. Founded 1869.

Nautical Magazine

Brown, Son & Ferguson Ltd, 4-10 Darnley Street, Glasgow G41 2SD
tel 0141-429 1234 *fax* 0141-420 1694
email info@skipper.co.uk
website www.skipper.co.uk
Editor L. Ingram-Brown
Monthly £29.40 p.a. (£33 p.a. overseas)

Articles relating to nautical and shipping profession, from 1500–2000 words; also translations. Payment: by arrangement. No illustrations. Founded 1832.

Needlecraft

Future Publishing Ltd, 30 Monmouth Street, Bath BA1 2BW
tel (01225) 442244 *fax* (01225) 732398
email debora.bradley@futurenet.co.uk
Editor Debora Bradley
Monthly £3.20

Mainly project-based stitching designs with step-by-step instructions. Features with tight stitching focus (e.g. technique, personality). Length: 1000 words. Illustrated. Payment: £150–£200. Founded 1991.

.net The Internet Magazine

Future Publishing Ltd, Beaufort Court, 30 Monmouth Street, Bath BA1 2BW
tel (01225) 442244 *fax* (01225) 732291
email netmag@futurenet.co.uk
website www.netmag.co.uk
Editor Paul Douglas
Monthly CD edition £4.49

Articles, features and news on the internet. Length: 1000–3000 words. Payment: negotiable. Illustrations: colour. Founded 1994.

New Beacon

RNIB, 224 Great Portland Street, London W1N 6AA
tel 020-7388 1266
Editor Ann Lee
Monthly £2

Articles on all aspects of living with a visual impairment (blindness or partial sight). Published in clear print, braille, disk and tape editions. Length: from 500 words. Payment: by arrangement. Illustrations: half-tone. Founded 1930; as *Beacon* 1917.

New Humanist

1 Gower Street, London WC1E 6HD
tel 020-7436 1151
email frank.jordans@newhumanist.org.uk
website www.newhumanist.org.uk
Editor Frank Jordans
Bimonthly £2.50

Articles on current affairs, philosophy, science, literature and humanism. Length: 500–1500 words. Illustrations: b&w photos. Payment: nominal. Founded 1885.

New Impact

Anser House of Marlow, Courtyard Offices, 140 Oxford Road, Marlow, Bucks. SL7 2NT
tel (01628) 481581 *fax* (01628) 475570
Managing Editor Elaine Sihera
5 p.a. £48 p.a. business; £35 p.a. individual; £20 p.a. colleges, min. 2 subscriptions

'Promoting enterprise, training and diversity.' Articles, features and news on any aspect of training, business and women's issues to suit a multicultural audience; also profiles of personalities, short stories. Length: 900–1000 words. Illustrations: b&w photos if related to profiles. Payment: none. Founded 1993.

New Internationalist

55 Rectory Road, Oxford OX4 1BW
tel (01865) 728181 *fax* (01865) 793152
email ni@newint.org
website www.newint.org
Editors Vanessa Baird, Katharine Ainger, David Ransom
Monthly £2.95 (£28.85 p.a.)

World issues, ranging from food to feminism to peace – examines one subject each month. Length: up to 2000 words. Illustrations: line, half-tone, colour, cartoons. Payment: £80 per 1000 words. Founded 1973.

New Law Journal

LexisNexis Butterworths Tolley, Halsbury House, 35 Chancery Lane, London WC2A 1EL
tel 020-7400 2500 *fax* 020-7400 2583
email newlaw.journal@butterworths.com

Editor Jane Maynard, *Assistant Editor* Alex Godfree
48 p.a. £4.75

Articles and news on all aspects of the legal profession. Length: up to 2000 words. Payment: by arrangement.

New Musical Express

(incorporating Melody Maker)
IPC Magazines Ltd, 25th Floor,
King's Reach Tower, Stamford Street,
London SE1 9LS
tel 020-7261 5000 *fax* 020-7261 5185
Editor Conor McNicholas
Weekly £1.50

Authoritative articles and news stories on the world's rock and movie personalities. Length: by arrangement. Preliminary letter or phone call desirable. Payment: by arrangement. Illustrations: action photos with strong news angle of recording personalities, cartoons.

New Scientist

RBI Ltd, 151 Wardour Street,
London W1F 8WE
tel 020-8652 3500 *fax* 020-7331 2777
email enquiries@newscientist.com
website www.NewScientist.com
Editor Jeremy Webb
Weekly £2.20

Authoritative articles of topical importance on all aspects of science and technology. Intending contributors should study recent copies of the magazine and initially send only a 200-word synopsis of their idea. NB: Does not publish non-peer reviewed theories, poems or crosswords. Payment: varies but average £300 per 1000 words. Illustrations: all styles, cartoons; contact art deptartment.

New Statesman

(formerly New Statesman & Society)
Victoria Station House, 191 Victoria Street,
London SW1E 5NE
tel 020-7828 1232 *fax* 020-7828 1881
email info@newstatesman.co.uk
Editor Peter Wilby
Weekly £2.40

Interested in news, reportage and analysis of current political and social issues at home and overseas, plus book reviews, general articles and coverage of the arts, environment and science seen from the perspective of the British Left but written in a stylish, witty and unpredictable way. Length: strictly according to the value of the piece. Illustrations: commissioned for specific articles, though artists' samples considered for future reference; occasional cartoons. Payment: by agreement. Founded 1913.

New Theatre Quarterly

Oldstairs, Kingsdown, Deal,
Kent CT14 8ES
email simontrussler@lineone.net
Editors Clive Barker, Simon Trussler
Quarterly £19 (£32 p.a.)

Articles, interviews, documentation, reference material covering all aspects of live theatre. An informed, factual and serious approach essential. Preliminary discussion and synopsis desirable. Payment: by arrangement. Illustrations: line, half-tone. Founded 1985; as *Theatre Quarterly* 1971.

New Welsh Review

PO Box 170, Aberystwyth,
Ceredigion SJ23 1WZ
tel (01970) 626230
email nwr@welshnet.co.uk
Editor Francesca Rhydderch
Quarterly £5.40 (£20 p.a., £38 2 yrs)

Literary – critical articles, short stories, poems, book reviews, interviews and profiles. Especially, but not exclusively, concerned with Welsh writing in English. Theatre in Wales section. Length: up to 3000 words (articles). Illustrations: colour. Payment: £50 per 1000 words (articles); £25 per poem, £75 per short story, £40 per review, £60 per illustration. Founded 1988.

New Woman

EMAP Élan, Endeavour House,
189 Shaftesbury Avenue, London WC2H 8JG
tel 020-7437 9011 *fax* 020-7208 3585
email lizzi.hosking@hotmail.com
website www.newwoman.co.uk
Editor Sara Cremer
Monthly £2.60

Features up to 2000 words. Occasionally accepts unsolicited articles; enclose sae for return. No fiction. Payment: at or above NUJ rates. Illustrated. Founded 1988.

The New Writer

PO Box 60, Cranbrook, Kent TN17 2ZR
tel (01580) 212626 *fax* (01580) 212041
email editor@thenewwriter.com
website www.thenewwriter.com
Editor Suzanne Ruthven *Publisher* Merric Davidson
6 p.a. £3.95

Features, short stories from guest writers and from subscribers, poems, news and reviews. Seeks forward-looking articles on all aspects of the written word that demonstrate the writer's grasp of contemporary writing and current editorial/publishing policies. Length: approx. 1000 words (articles), longer pieces considered; 1000–2000 words (features). Payment: £20 per 1000 words (articles), £10 (stories), £3 (poems). Founded 1996.

The Newspaper

Young Media Ltd, PO Box 121, Tonbridge,
Kent TN12 5ZR
tel (01622) 871036 *fax* (01622) 871927
email simon@young-media.co.uk
website www.thenewspaper.org.uk
Editor Simon Hobbs
6 p.a. Free

Newspaper aimed at 8–14 year-old schoolchildren
for use as part of the National Curriculum.
Contains similar columns as in any national daily
newspaper. Length: 800–1000 words for features
and short stories (fiction). Payment: £250 per item.
Illustrations: colour. Founded 1999.

Night and Day – see Mail on Sunday in National
newspapers UK and Ireland, page 3

19

IPC Magazines Ltd, King's Reach Tower,
Stamford Street, London SE1 9LS
tel 020-7261 6410
Editor Helen Bazuaye
Monthly £2.40

Glossy fashion and general interest magazine for
young women aged 16–22, including beauty,
celebrities and social features of strong contemporary interest. All illustrations commissioned.
Payment: by arrangement. Founded 1968.

Now

IPC Media Ltd, King's Reach Tower,
Stamford Street, London SE1 9LS
tel 020-7261 7366 *fax* 020-7261 6789
Editor Jane Ennis
Weekly £1.10

Showbiz magazine of celebrity gossip, news,
fashion, health and cookery. Most articles are
commissioned or are written by in-house writers.
Founded 1996.

Nursery Education

Scholastic Ltd, Villiers House,
Clarendon Avenue, Leamington Spa,
Warks. CV32 5PR
tel (01926) 887799 *fax* (01926) 883331
email earlyyears@scholastic.co.uk
website www.scholastic.co.uk
Editor Susan Howard
Monthly £3.75

Practical theme-based activities for educators
working with 3–5 year-olds. All ideas based on the
Early Learning Goals. Material mostly commissioned. Length: 500–1000 words. Illustrations:
colour and b&w; colour posters. Payment: by
arrangement. Founded 1997.

Nursery World

Admiral House, 66-68 East Smithfield,
London E1W 1BX
tel 020-7782 3120
Editor Liz Roberts
Weekly £1.20

For all grades of primary school, nursery and child
care staff, nannies, foster parents and all concerned
with the care of expectant mothers, babies and
young children. Authoritative and informative
articles, 800 or 1600 words, and photos, on all
aspects of child welfare and early education, from
0–8 years, in the UK. Practical ideas and leisure
crafts. No short stories. Payment: by arrangement.
Illustrations: line, half-tone, colour.

Nursing Times

EMAP Healthcare, Greater London House,
Hampstead Road, London NW1 7EJ
tel 020-7874 0500 *fax* 020-7874 0505
Editor Rachel Downey
Weekly £1.10

Articles of clinical interest, nursing education and
nursing policy. Illustrated articles not longer than
2000 words. Contributions from other than health
professionals sometimes accepted. Press day:
Monday. Illustrations: photos, line, cartoons.
Payment: NUJ rates; by arrangement for illustrations. Founded 1905.

Observer Magazine – see The Observer in National
newspapers UK and Ireland, page 3

Office Secretary (OS Magazine)

Peebles Media Group, 1st Floor, 63 High Street,
Witney, Oxon OX28 6HS
tel (01993) 775545 *fax* (01993) 778884
email paul.ormond@peeblesmedia.com
website www.peeblesmedia.com
Editor Louise Hackett
Bi-monthly £20 p.a.

Serious features on anything of interest to senior
secretaries and executive PAs. No unsolicited MSS;
ideas only. Illustrations: colour transparencies and
prints. Payment: by negotiation. Founded 1986.

OK! Magazine

Northern & Shell plc, Ludgate House,
245 Blackfriars Road, London SE1 9UX
tel 020-7928 8000 *fax* 020-7579 4607
Editor Nic McCarthy
Weekly £1.85

Exclusive celebrity interviews and photographs.
Submit ideas in writing. Length: 1000 words.
Illustrations: colour. Payment: £150–£250,000 per
feature. Founded 1993.

The Oldie
65 Newman Street, London W1T 3EG
tel 020-7436 8801 *fax* 020-7436 8804
email theoldie@theoldie.co.uk
website www.theoldie.co.uk
Editor Richard Ingrams
Monthly £2.75

General interest magazine reflecting attitudes of older people but aimed at a wider audience. Welcomes features (800–2000 words) on all subjects. Enclose sae for reply/return of MSS. No poetry. Illustrations: welcomes b&w and colour cartoons. Payment: approx. £80–£100 per 1000 words; minimum £50 for cartoons. Founded 1992.

Opera
36 Black Lion Lane, London W6 9BE
tel 020-8563 8893 *fax* 020-8563 8635
email editor@operamag.clara.co.uk
website www.opera.co.uk
Editor John Allison
13 p.a. £3.70

Articles on general subjects appertaining to opera; reviews; criticisms. Length: up to 2000 words. Payment: by arrangement. Illustrations: photos.

Opera Now
241 Shaftesbury Avenue, London WC2H 8TF
tel 020-7333 1740 *fax* 020-7333 1769
email opera.now@rhinegold.co.uk
website www.rhinegold.co.uk
Editor Ashutosh Khandekar
Bi-monthly £4.95

Articles, news, reviews on opera. All material commissioned only. Length: 150–1500 words. Illustrations: colour and b&w photos, line, cartoons. Payment: £120 per 1000 words. Founded 1989.

Orbis
17 Greenhow Avenue, West Kirby,
Wirral CH48 5EL
tel 0151-625 1446
email carolebaldock@hotmail.com
Editor Carole Baldock
Quarterly £4, £15 p.a.; £5/€9/$9, €32/$32 overseas

Poetry, prose (1000 words), news, reviews, views, letters. Up to 4 poems by post; via email, overseas only, up to 2 in body (no attachments). Enclose sae/2 IRCs with all correspondence. Payment: £40, £30, £20 Editor's Choice; £50 Readers' Award. Founded 1968.

Organic Gardening
Sandvoe, North Roe, Shetland ZE2 9RY
tel (01806) 533319
email organic.gardening@virgin.net
Editor Gaby Bartai Bevan
Monthly £2.65

Articles on all aspects of gardening by experienced organic gardeners. Unsolicited material welcome. Length: 600–2000 words. Illustrations: digital images, transparencies, colour photos, line drawings, cartoons. Payment: by arrangement. Founded 1988.

Other Poetry
29 Western Hill, Durham DH1 4RL
tel 0191-386 4058
website www.otherpoetry.com
Editors Michael Standen (managing), Richard Kell, Peter Bennet, James Roderick Burns
3 p.a. £4.50 (£13/$30 p.a.)

Poetry. Submit up to 6 poems with sae. Payment: £5 per poem. Founded 1979.

Our Dogs
Oxford Road Station Approach,
Manchester M60 1SX
tel 0161-236 2660 *fax* 0161-236 5534/0892
Editor William Moores
Weekly £1.60

Articles and news on the breeding and showing of pedigree dogs. Illustrations: b&w photos. Payment: by negotiation; £10 per photo. Founded 1895.

Outposts Poetry Quarterly
22 Whitewell Road, Frome, Somerset BA11 4EL
tel/fax (01373) 466653
Editor Roland John *Founder* Howard Sergeant MBE,
Send material to M. Pargitter
Quarterly £4 (£14 p.a.)

Poems, essays and critical articles on poets and their work; poetry competitions. Payment: by arrangement. Founded 1943.

Oxford Poetry
Magdalen College, Oxford OX1 4AU
email editors@oxfordpoetry.co.uk
website www.oxfordpoetry.co.uk
Editors Kelly Grovier, Carmen Bogan, Sarah Hesketh (business & subscriptions)
3 p.a. £3 (£9 p.a.)

Previously unpublished poems and translations, both unsolicited and commissioned; interviews, articles and reviews. Payment: none. Founded 1910; refounded 1983.

Park Home & Holiday Caravan
(formerly Mobile & Holiday Homes)
Link House, Dingwall Avenue, Croydon CR9 2TA
tel 020-8774 0600 *fax* 020-8774 0939
email phhc@ipcmedia.com
Editor Anne Webb
Monthly £2.40

Informative articles on residential mobile homes (park homes) and holiday static caravans – personal experience articles, site features, news items. No

preliminary letter. Payment: by arrangement.
Illustrations: line, half-tone, colour transparencies,
cartoons. Founded 1960.

PC Advisor

IDG Communications Ltd, 5th Floor,
85 Tottenham Court Road, London W1T 4TQ
tel 020-7291 5920 *fax* 020-7580 1935
email pcadvisor_letters@idg.com
website www.pcadvisor.co.uk
Editor Andrew Charlesworth
Monthly CD edition £2.99, DVD edition £4.99

Aimed at PC-proficient individuals who are looking
for IT solutions that will enhance their productivity
at work and at home. Includes information on the
latest hardware and software and advice on how to
use PCs to maximum effect. Features are commissioned; unsolicited material may be considered.
Length: 1500–3000 words (features). Illustrations:
colour artwork. Payment: £200 per 1000 words;
artwork £200 (A5), £300 (A4). Founded 1995.

PC Answers

Future Publishing Ltd, 30 Monmouth Street,
Bath BA1 2BW
tel (01225) 442244 *fax* (01225) 732295
email pcanswers@futurenet.co.uk
website www.pcanswers.co.uk
Editor Nick Peers
13 p.a. £4.99

Reviews, news and practical/how-to features for
home PC users, excluding games. Length: 2500
words (features). Illustrations: colour. Payment: by
negotiation. Founded 1991.

PCS View

Public and Commercial Services Union,
160 Falcon Road, London SW11 2LN
tel 020-7924 2727 *fax* 020-7924 1847
email editor@pcs.org.uk
website www.pcs.org.uk
Editor Sharon Breen
10 p.a. Free to members

Well-written articles on civil service, trade union
and general subjects considered. Send ideas for
consideration before submitting full article. Length:
600 words. Also photos and humorous drawings of
interest to civil servants. Illustrations: line, half-
tone. Payment: NUJ rates.

Peace News

5 Caledonian Road, London N1 9DX
tel 020-7278 3344 *fax* 020-7278 0444
email editorial@peacenews.info
website www.peacenews.info
Submit material to The Editor
Quarterly £2.50

Political articles based on nonviolence in every

aspect of human life. Illustrations: line, half-tone.
No payment. Founded 1936.

Peninsular Magazine

Cherrybite Publications, Linden Cottage,
45 Burton Road, Little Neston,
Cheshire CH64 4AE
tel 0151-353 0967
email helicon@globalnet.co.uk
website www.cherrybite.co.uk
Editor Shelagh Nugent
Quarterly £3.50

Short story magazine: essential to read a current
issue before sending MSS. Regular competitions
with prizes. Length: up to 4000 words. Payment: £5
per 1000 words. Founded 1996.

Pensions World

LexisNexis UK, Tolley House, 2 Addiscombe Road,
Croydon CR9 5AF
tel 020-8686 9141 *fax* 020-8212 1970
email stephanie.hawthorne@lexisnexis.co.uk
website www.pensionsworld.co.uk
Editor Stephanie Hawthorne
Monthly £84 p.a.

Specialist articles on pensions, investment and law.
No unsolicited articles; all material is commissioned.
Length: 1500 words. Payment: by negotiation.
Founded 1972.

People Magazine – see The People in National newspapers UK and Ireland, page 3

People Management

Personnel Publications Ltd, 1 Benjamin Street,
London EC1M 5EA
tel 020-7296 4200 *fax* 020-7296 4215
email editorial@peoplemanagement.co.uk
website www.peoplemanagement.co.uk
Editor Steve Crabb
Fortnightly £5 (£88 p.a.)

Journal of the Chartered Institute of Personnel and
Development. News items and feature articles on
recruitment and selection, training and development; pay and performance management; industrial
psychology; employee relations; employment law;
working practices and new practical ideas in
personnel management in industry and commerce.
Length: up to 2500 words. Payment: by arrangement. Illustrations: contact art editor.

People's Friend

D.C. Thomson & Co. Ltd, 80 Kingsway East,
Dundee DD4 8SL
tel (01382) 223131 *fax* (01382) 452491
185 Fleet Street, London EC4A 2HS
tel 020-7400 1030 *fax* 020-7400 1089
Send material to The Editor

Weekly 60p

Fiction magazine for women of all ages. Includes personal and home interests, especially knitting and cookery. Serials (60,000–70,000 words) and complete stories (1500–3000 words) of strong romantic and emotional appeal. Considers stories for children. No preliminary letter required. Illustrations: colour and b&w. Payment: on acceptance. Founded 1869.

People's Friend Story Collection

D.C. Thomson & Co. Ltd, 2 Albert Square, Dundee DD1 9QJ
tel (01382) 223131 *fax* (01382) 322214
185 Fleet Street, London EC4A 2HS
tel 020-7400 1030 *fax* 020-7400 1089
Editor Shirley Blair
2 p.m. £1.20

50,000–55,000-word family and romantic stories aimed at 30+ age group. Payment: by arrangement. No illustrations.

Perfect Home

Fox Publishing Ltd, Lion House, Red Lion Street, Richmond, Surrey TW9 1RE
tel 020-8332 9090 *fax* 020-8332 9991
email zena.alli@fox-publishing.com
Editor Zena Alli
Monthly £2.80

Home-related features: readers' homes, makeovers, DIY, product testing/reviews, gardening. Length: 800–1000 words. Payment: by merit. Illustrated. Founded 1992.

Period Living & Traditional Homes

EMAP East, Mappin House, 4 Winsley Street, London W1W 8HF
tel 020-7343 8775 *fax* 020-7343 8710
Editor Sharon Parsons
Monthly £2.95

Articles and features on decoration, furnishings, renovation of period homes; gardens, crafts, decorating in a period style. Illustrated. Payment: varies, according to work required. Founded 1990.

Personal Computer World

VNU House, 32-34 Broadwick Street, London W1A 2HG
tel 020-7316 9000 *fax* 020-7316 9313
email dylan_armbrust@pcw.co.uk
website www.pcw.co.uk
Editor Dylan Armbrust
Monthly £3.25

Articles about computers, reviews, features and how-to advice. Length: 800–5000 words. Payment: from £150 per 1000 words. Illustrations: line, half-tone, colour. Founded 1978.

Personal Finance

Charterhouse Communications, Arnold House, 36-41 Holywell Lane, London EC2A 3SF
tel 020-7827 5454 *fax* 020-7827 0567
email martin.fagan@charterhouse-communications.co.uk
Editor Martin Fagan
Monthly £2.75

Articles and features on savings and investment, general family finance, of interest both to new investors and financially aware readers. All material commissioned: submit ideas in writing to the Editor in first instance. Illustrations: colour and b&w photos, colour line drawings. Payment: £200 per 1000 words; illustrations by negotiation. Founded 1994.

Picture Postcard Monthly

15 Debdale Lane, Keyworth, Nottingham NG12 5HT
tel 0115-937 4079 *fax* 0115-937 6197
email reflections@argonet.co.uk
website www.postcardcollecting.co.uk
Editor Brian Lund
Monthly £2.40 (£28 p.a.)

Articles, news and features for collectors of old or modern picture postcards. Length: 500–2000 words. Illustrations: colour and b&w. Payment: £27 per 1000 words; 50p per print. Founded 1978.

Pig Farming

United Business Media International, Sovereign House, Sovereign Way, Tonbridge, Kent TN9 1RW
tel 020-8309 7000 *fax* (01732) 377128
Editor Roger Abbott
Monthly £28 p.a.

Practical, well-illustrated articles on all aspects of pigmeat production required, particularly those dealing with new ideas in pig management, feeding, housing, health and hygiene, product innovation and marketing. Length: 800–1200 words. Payment: by arrangement. Illustrations: line, half-tone, colour.

Pilot

PO Box 313, Teddington, Middlesex TW11 9WD
tel 020-8977 6595 *fax* 020-8977 5881
email pilotmagazine@pilotweb.co.uk
website www.pilotweb.co.uk
Editor Philip Whiteman
Monthly £3.25

Feature articles on general aviation, private and business flying. Illustrations: line, half-tone, colour, cartoons. Payment: £125–£1000 per article on acceptance; £30 per photo. Founded 1968.

The Pink Paper

2nd Floor, Medius House, 63-69 New Oxford Street, London WC1A 1DN
tel 020-7845 4300
email editorial @pinkpaper.com

Editor Tris Reid-Smith
Weekly Free

National news magazine for lesbians and gay men. Features (500–1000 words) and news (100–500 words) plus lifestyle section (features 350–1000 words) on any gay-related subject. Illustrations: b&w photos and line plus colour 'scene' photos. Payment: £40–£90 for words; £30–£60 for illustrations. Founded 1987.

Planet

PO Box 44, Aberystwyth, Ceredigion SY23 3ZZ
tel (01970) 611255 *fax* (01970) 611197
email planet.enquiries@planetmagazine.org.uk
website www.planetmagazine.org.uk
Editor John Barnie
6 p.a. £3.25 (£15 p.a.)

Short stories, poems, topical articles on Welsh current affairs, politics, the environment and society. New literature in English. Length of articles: 1000–3500 words. Payment: £40 per 1000 words for prose; £25 minimum per poem. Illustrations: line, half-tone, cartoons. Founded 1970–9; relaunched 1985.

PN Review

(formerly Poetry Nation)
Carcanet Press Ltd, 4th Floor, Conavon Court, 12 Blackfriars Street, Manchester M3 5BQ
tel 0161-834 8730 *fax* 0161-832 0084
email pnr@carcanet.u-net.com
website www.carcanet.co.uk
Editor Michael Schmidt
6 p.a. £4.99 (£29.50 p.a.)

Poems, essays, reviews, translations. Submissions by post only. Payment: by arrangement. Founded 1973.

Poetry Ireland Review/Éigse Éireann

Bermingham Tower, Upper Yard, Dublin Castle, Dublin 2, Republic of Ireland
tel (01) 671 4632 *fax* (01) 671 4634
email poetry@iol.ie
Managing Editor Joseph Woods
Quarterly €7.99 (€30.50/$52 p.a.)

Poetry. Features and articles by arrangement. Payment: €32 per contribution or one year's subscription; €51 reviews. Founded 1981.

Poetry London

1A Jewel Road, London E17 4QU
tel/fax 020-8521 0776
email editors@poetrylondon.co.uk
website www.poetrylondon.co.uk
Editors Pascale Petit, Scott Verner, Martha Kapos, *Send material to* Andre Harris, Business Manager
3 p.a. £11 p.a.

Poems of the highest standard, articles/ reviews on any aspect of modern poetry. Comprehensive

listings of poetry events and resources. Contributors must be knowledgeable about contemporary poetry. Payment: £20 minimum. Founded 1988.

Poetry Nottingham International

PO Box 6740, Nottingham NG5 1QG
Editor Julie Lumsden
Quarterly £2.75 (£10 p.a. UK, 17 p.a. overseas)

Poems; letters; articles up to 500 words on current issues in the poetry world. Payment: one complimentary copy. Founded 1946.

Poetry Review

22 Betterton Street, London WC2H 9BX
tel 020-7420 9880 *fax* 020-7240 4818
email poetryreview@poetrysociety.org.uk
website www.poetrysociety.org.uk
Editors Robert Potts, David Herd
Quarterly £30 p.a. (£40 p.a. institutions, schools and libraries)

Poems, features and reviews; also cartoons. Send no more than 6 poems with sae. Preliminary study of magazine essential. Payment: £40 per poem.

Poetry Wales

38-40 Nolton Street, Bridgend CF31 3BN
tel (01656) 663018 *fax* (01656) 649226
email poetrywales@seren-books.com
websites www.seren-books.com
www.poetrywales.co.uk
Editor Robert Minhinnick, *Reviews Editor* Amy Wack
Quarterly £4 (£16 p.a.)

Poetry, criticism and commentary from Wales and around the world. Payment: by arrangement. Founded 1965.

Police Journal

Vathek Publishing, 5 Millennium Court, Derby Road, Douglas, Isle of Man IM2 3EW
tel (01624) 863256 *fax* (01624) 863254
email mlw@vathek.com
Publisher Mairwen Lloyd-Williams
Quarterly £76 p.a.

Articles of technical or professional interest to the Police Service throughout the world. Payment: none. Illustrations: line drawings. Founded 1928.

Police Review

Jane's Information Group, The Quadrangle, 1st Floor, 180 Wardour Street, London W1F 8FY
tel 020-7851 9701 *fax* 020-7287 4765
Editor Catriona Marchant
Weekly £1.75

News and features of interest to the police and legal professions. Length: 200–1500 words. Illustrations: colour photos, line, cartoons. Payment: NUJ rates. Founded 1893.

The Political Quarterly

Blackwell Publishers Ltd, 108 Cowley Road,
Oxford OX4 1JF
tel (01865) 791100
website www.blackwellpublishers.co.uk
Editors Tony Wright MP, Prof Andrew Gamble,
Literary Editor Prof Donald Sassoon
Assistant Editor Gillian Bromley, 3 Fernhill Close,
Kidlington, Oxford OX5 1BB
4 p.a. (£111 p.a. institutions, £21 p.a. individuals)

Topical aspects of national and international politics
and public administration; takes a progressive, but
not a party, point of view. Send articles to Assistant
Editor. Length: average 5000 words. Payment: about
£100 per article. Founded 1930.

Pony Magazine

Haslemere House, Lower Street, Haslemere,
Surrey GU27 2PE
tel (01428) 651551 *fax* (01428) 653888
Editor Janet Rising
Monthly £1.99

Lively articles and short stories with a horsy theme
aimed at readers aged 8–16 . Technical accuracy and
young, fresh writing essential. Length: up to 800
words. Payment: by arrangement. Illustrations:
drawings (commissioned), photos, cartoons.
Founded 1949.

Popular Crafts

Nexus Special Interests Ltd, Nexus House,
Azalea Drive, Swanley, Kent BR8 8HU
tel (01322) 660070 *fax* (01322) 616319
email debbie.moss@nexusmedia.com
website www.popularcrafts.com
Editor Debbie Moss
Monthly £2.95

Covers all kinds of crafts. Projects with full
instructions, profiles and successes of craftspeople,
news on craft group activities, readers' homes,
celebrity interviews, general craft-related articles.
Welcomes written outlines of ideas. Payment: by
arrangement. Illustrated.

Post Magazine & Insurance Week

Timothy Benn Publishing Ltd, 39 Earlham Street,
London WC2H 9LD
tel 020-7306 7000 *fax* 020-7306 7101
email postmag@benn.co.uk
website www.postmag.co.uk
www.insurancewindow.net
Editor Anthony Gould
Weekly £3 (£142 p.a.)

Commissioned specialist articles on topics of
interest to insurance professionals; news, especially
from overseas stringers. Illustrations: colour photos
and illustrations, colour and b&w cartoons and line
drawings. Payment: £200 per 1000 words; photos

£30–£120, cartoons/line by negotiation. Founded
1840.

Poultry World

Quadrant House, The Quadrant, Sutton,
Surrey SM2 5AS
tel 020-8652 4020 *fax* 020-8652 4042
email poultry.world@rbi.co.uk
Editor John Farrant
Monthly £2.40

Articles on poultry breeding, production, marketing
and packaging. News of international poultry
interest. Payment: by arrangement. Illustrations:
photos, line.

PR Week

Haymarket Marketing Publications,
174 Hammersmith Road, London W6 7JP
tel 020-8267 4520 *fax* 020-8267 4509
Editor Kate Nicholas
Weekly Controlled circulation; £1.85 (£72 p.a.)

News and features on public relations. Length:
approx. 800–3000 words. Payment: £185 per 1000
words. Illustrations: colour and b&w. Founded
1984.

Practical Boat Owner

Westover House, West Quay Road, Poole,
Dorset BH15 1JG
tel (01202) 440820
email pbo@ipcmedia.com
website www.pbo.co.uk
Editor Sarah Norbury
Monthly £3.20

Hints, tips and practical articles for cruising
skippers – power and sail. Send synopsis first.
Payment: by negotiation. Illustrations: photos or
drawings. Founded 1967.

Practical Caravan

Haymarket Magazines Ltd, 60 Waldegrave Road,
Teddington, Middlesex TW11 8LG
tel 020-8267 5629 *fax* 020-8267 5725
email practical.caravan@haynet.com
website www.practicalcaravan.com
Editor Carl Rodgerson
Monthly £3.15

Caravan-related travelogues, human interest
features, technical and DIY matters. Length:
1500–2500. Illustrations: colour. Payment: £120 per
1000 words; negotiable. Founded 1967.

Practical Fishkeeping

EMAP Active Ltd, Bretton Court, Bretton,
Peterborough PE3 8DZ
tel (01733) 264666
website www.practicalfishkeeping.co.uk
Editor Karen Youngs

Monthly £2.95

Practical fishkeeping in tropical and coldwater aquaria and ponds. Heavy emphasis on inspiration and involvement. Good colour photography always needed, and used. No verse or humour, no personal biographical accounts of fishkeeping unless practical. Payment: by worth. Founded 1966.

Practical Householder

WVIP, Highgate Studios, 53-79 Highgate Road, London NW5 1TW
tel 020-7331 1138 *fax* 020-7331 1269
Editor John McGowan
Monthly £2.15

Articles about 1500 words in length, about practical matters concerning home improvement. Payment: according to subject. Illustrations: line, half-tone. Founded 1955.

Practical Parenting

IPC Media Ltd, King's Reach Tower, Stamford Street, London SE1 9LS
tel 020-7261 5058 *fax* 020-7261 6542
Editor Sara Pates
Monthly £2.20

Articles on parenting, baby and childcare, health, psychology, education, children's activities, personal birth/parenting experiences. Send synopsis, with sae. Illustrations: commissioned only; colour: photos, line. Payment: by agreement. Founded 1987.

Practical Photography

EMAP Active Ltd, Bretton Court, Bretton, Peterborough PE3 8DZ
tel (01733) 264666 *fax* (01733) 465246
email practical.photography@emap.com
Editor Will Cheung, *Associate Editor* Andrew James
Monthly £3.10

Aimed at anyone who seeks to take excellent quality pictures. Excellent potential for freelance pictures: must be first rate – technically and pictorially – and have some relevance to photographic technique. Freelance ideas for words welcome (the more unusual ideas stand the greatest chance of success). Send synopsis of feature ideas in first instance. Payment: negotiable but typically £80 per page and £120 per 1000 words. Founded 1959.

Practical Wireless

PW Publishing Ltd, Arrowsmith Court, Station Approach, Broadstone, Dorset BH18 8PW
tel (01202) 659910 *fax* (01202) 659950
email rob@pwpublishing.ltd.uk
Editor Rob Mannion G3XFD
Monthly £2.85

Articles on the practical and theoretical aspects of amateur radio and communications. Constructional projects. Write or email for advice and author's guide. Illustrations: in b&w and colour; photos, line drawings and wash half-tone for offset litho. Payment: by arrangement. Founded 1932.

Practical Woodworking

Nexus Special Interests Ltd, Nexus House, Azalea Drive, Swanley, Kent BR8 8HU
tel (01322) 660070 *fax* (01322) 616319
email mark.chisholm@nexusmedia.com
Editor Mark Chisholm
Monthly £2.75

Articles of a practical nature covering any aspect of woodworking, including woodworking projects, tools, joints or timber technology. Payment: £75 per published page. Illustrated.

The Practising Midwife

(formerly Modern Midwife)
54 Siward Road, Bromley BR2 9JZ
tel 020-8466 1037
email prac.mid@ntlworld.com
Editor Jennifer Hall, *Managing Editor* Vivienne Riddoch
Monthly £35 p.a.

Disseminates research-based material to a wide professional audience. Research and review papers, viewpoints and news items pertaining to midwifery, maternity care, women's health and neonatal health with both a national and an international perspective. All articles submitted are anonymously reviewed by at least 2 external acknowledged experts. Length: 1000–2000 words (articles); 150–400 words (news); up to 1000 words (viewpoints). Illustrations: colour transparencies and artwork. Payment: by arrangement. Founded 1991.

The Practitioner

CMP Information Ltd, City Reach, 5 Greenwich View Place, Millharbour, London E14 9NN
tel 020-7861 6478 *fax* 020-7861 6544
email gmatkin@cmpinformation.com
Editor Gavin Atkin
Monthly £12.60 (£82.50 p.a. UK, $194.25 overseas)

Articles of interest to GPs and vocational registrars, and others in the medical profession. Payment: approx. £200 per 1500 words. Founded 1868.

Prediction

IPC Country & Leisure, Focus House, Dingwall Avenue, Croydon CR9 2TA
tel 020-8774 0600 *fax* 020-8774 0939
Editor Tania Ahsan
Monthly £2.80

Articles on astrology and all esoteric subjects. Length: up to 2000 words. Payment: by arrangement. Illustrations: large-format colour transparencies or photos. Founded 1936.

Press Gazette

Quantum Business Media Ltd,
Quantum House, 19 Scarbrook Road,
Croydon CR9 1LX
tel 020-8565 4200 *fax* 020-8565 4395
Editor Ian Reeves
Weekly £2.30

News and features of interest to journalists and
others working in the media. Length: 1200 words
(features), 300 words (news). Payment: approx.
£200 (features), news stories negotiable. Founded
1965.

Pride Magazine

Hamilton House, 55 Battersea Bridge Road,
London SW11 3AX
tel 020-7228 3110 *fax* 020-7228 3130
Managing Editor Delali Damanka
Monthly £2.80

Lifestyle magazine incorporating fashion and
beauty, travel, food and entertaining articles for the
young woman of colour. Length: 1000–3000 words.
Illustrations: colour photos and drawings. Payment:
£100 per 1000 words. Founded 1993; relaunched
1997, 1998.

Priests & People

Blackfriars, 64 St Giles, Oxford OX1 3LY
tel (01865) 514845
Editor Rev. D.C. Sanders OP
Monthly £2.50

Journal of pastoral theology especially for parish
ministers and for Christians of English-speaking
countries. Illustrations: occasional b&w photos.
Length and payment by arrangement.

Prima

National Magazine Company, 72 Broadwick Street,
London W1F 9EP
tel 020-7439 5000 *fax* 020-7312 4100
Editor Maire Fahey
Monthly £2

Articles on fashion, crafts, health and beauty,
cookery; features. Founded 1986.

Prima Baby

National Magazine Co Ltd, 72 Broadwick Street,
London W1F 9EP
tel 020-7312 3852 *fax* 020-7312 3744
email prima.baby@natmags.co.uk
Editor Julie Goodwin
Monthly £1.95

Magazine for women covering all aspects of
pregnancy and childbirth and life with children
aged up to 3 years; plus health, beauty, fashion.
Length: up to 1500 words. Illustrations: colour
transparencies. Payment: by arrangement. Founded
1994.

Printing World

CMP Information, Sovereign House, Sovereign Way,
Tonbridge, Kent TN9 1RW
tel (01732) 377329 *fax* (01732) 377552
Editor Gareth Ward
Weekly £2.75 (£94.50 p.a., overseas £142 p.a.)

Commercial, technical, financial and labour news
covering all aspects of the printing industry in the
UK and abroad. Outside contributions. Payment: by
arrangement. Illustrations: line, half-tone, colour,
cartoons. Founded 1878.

Private Eye

6 Carlisle Street, London W1V 5RG
tel 020-7437 4017 *fax* 020-7437 0705
email strobes@private-eye.co.uk
website www.private-eye.co.uk
Editor Ian Hislop
Fortnightly £1.20

Satire. Payment: by arrangement. Illustrations: b&w,
line, cartoons. Founded 1961.

Professional Nurse

EMAP Healthcare Ltd, Greater London House,
Hampstead Road, London NW1 7EJ
tel 020-7874 0384 *fax* 020-7874 0386
email pn@healthcare.emap.co.uk
Editor Carolyn Scott
Monthly £39 p.a.

Clinical articles of interest to the professional nurse.
Length: articles: 2000–3000 words; letters: 250–500
words. Payment: by arrangement. Illustrations:
commissioned. Founded 1985.

Professional Photographer

Archant Specialist Ltd, The Mill,
Bearwalden Business Park, Wendens Ambo,
Saffron Walden, Essex CB11 4GB
tel (01799) 544246 *fax* (01799) 544201
Editor Steve Hynes
Monthly £3.10

Articles on professional photography, including
technical articles, photographer profiles and
coverage of issues affecting the industry. Length:
1000–2000 words. Illustrations: colour and b&w
prints and transparencies, or digital files; diagrams
if appropriate. Payment: from £200. Founded 1961.

Prospect

Prospect Publishing Ltd, 2 Bloomsbury Place,
London WC1A 2QA
tel 020-7255 1281 *fax* 020-7255 1279
email editorial@prospect-magazine.co.uk
website www.prospect-magazine.co.uk
Editor David Goodhart
Monthly £3.99

Political and cultural monthly magazine. Essays,
features, special reports, reviews, short stories,

opinions/analysis. Length: 3000–6000 words (essays, special reports, short stories), 1000 words (opinions). Illustrations: colour and b&w. Payment: by negotiation. Founded 1995.

Publishing News

39 Store Street, London WC1E 7DS
tel 020-7692 2900
website www.publishingnews.co.uk
Editor Jane Ellis, *Managing Editor* Rodney Burbeck, *Associate Editor* Liz Thomson
Weekly £2

Articles and news items on the book publishing and bookselling industry. Payment: £120 per 1000 words. Founded 1979.

Pulse

CMP Information Ltd, City Reach,
5 Greenwich View Place, Millharbour,
London E14 9NN
tel 020-7861 6483 *fax* 020-7861 6257
email pulse@cmpinformation.com
Editor Howard Griffiths
Weekly £141.25 p.a.

Articles and photos of direct interest to GPs. Purely clinical material can only be accepted from medically qualified authors. Length: up to 750 words. Payment: £150 average. Illustrations: b&w and colour photos. Founded 1959.

Q Magazine

EMAP Performance, Mappin House,
4 Winsley Street, London W1W 8HF
tel 020-7436 1515 *fax* 020-7312 8247
email q@ecm.emap.com
website www.q4music.com
Editor Paul Rees
Monthly £3.40

Glossy modern guide to more than just rock music. All material commissioned. Length: 1200–2500 words. Illustrations: colour and b&w photos. Payment: £185 per 1000 words; illustrations by arrangement. Founded 1986.

QWF

PO Box 1768, Rugby CV21 4ZA
tel (01788) 334302
email jo@qwfmagazine.co.uk
website www.qwfmagazine.co.uk
Editor Jo Good, *Send material to* Sally Zigmond, Assistant Editor, 18 Warwick Crescent, Harrogate, North Yorkshire HG2 8JA
Bi-monthly £3.95 (£23 p.a.)

Thought-provoking short stories by female writers (no traditional romances, domestic crises or mainstream fiction) and articles of general interest. Study magazine first. Length: up to 4000 words. Payment: £5 (articles), £10 (short stories). Annual short story competition (up to 5000 words) in any style or genre, on any theme; first prize: £200. Founded 1994.

RA Magazine

Royal Academy of Arts, Burlington House,
Piccadilly, London W1J 0BD
tel 020-7300 5820 *fax* 020-7300 5881
email ramagazine@royalacademy.org.uk
website www.royalacademy.org.uk
Editor Sarah Greenberg
Quarterly £4.50

Visual arts and culture articles relating to the Royal Academy of Arts and the international arts scene. Length: 500–1800 words. Illustrations: consult the Editor. Payment: £200 per 1000 words; illustrations by negotiation. Founded 1983.

Racing Post

Trinity Mirror, Floor 23, One Canada Square,
Canary Wharf, London E14 5AP
tel 020-7293 3291 *fax* 020-7293 3758
email editor@racingpost.co.uk
website www.racingpost.co.uk
Editor Chris Smith
Mon–Fri €1.15, Sat €1.35

News on horseracing, greyhound racing and sports betting. Founded 1986.

Radio Control Models and Electronics

Nexus Special Interests Ltd, Nexus House,
Azalea Drive, Swanley, Kent BR8 8HU
tel (01322) 660070 *fax* (01322) 667633
Editor Graham Ashby
Monthly £2.85

Well-illustrated articles on topics related to radio control. Payment: £45 per published page. Illustrations: line, half-tone. Founded 1960.

Radio Times

BBC Worldwide Ltd, 80 Wood Lane,
London W12 0TT
tel 020-8433 3400 *fax* 020-8433 3160
email radio.times@bbc.co.uk
website www.radiotimes.com
Editor Gill Hudson
Weekly 88p

Articles that preview the week's programmes on British TV and radio. All articles are specially commissioned – ideas and synopses are welcomed but not unsolicited MSS. Length: 600–2500 words. Payment: by arrangement. Illustrations: mostly in colour; photos, graphic designs or drawings.
SmartTV
Editor Liz Vercoe
Termly
Children's version of *Radio Times*.

Rail

EMAP Active Publications, Bretton Court, Bretton, Peterborough PE3 8DZ
tel (01733) 264666 *fax* (01733) 282720
email rail@emap.com
Managing Editor Nigel Harris
Fortnightly £2.40

News and in-depth features on current UK railway operations. Length: 2000–3000 words (features), 250–400 words (news). Illustrations: colour and b&w photos and artwork. Payment: £75 per 1000 words; £20 per photo except cover (£70). Founded 1981.

Railway Gazette International

Reed Business Information, Quadrant House, The Quadrant, Sutton, Surrey SM2 5AS
tel 020-8652 8608 *fax* 020-8652 3738
website www.railwaygazette.com
Editor Murray Hughes
Monthly £70 p.a.

Deals with management, engineering, operation and finance of railways worldwide. Articles of practical interest on these subjects are considered and paid for if accepted. Illustrated articles, of 1000–3000 words, are preferred. A preliminary letter is required.

Railway Magazine

IPC Media Ltd, King's Reach Tower, Stamford Street, London SE1 9LS
tel 020-7261 5821 *fax* 020-7261 5269
Editor Nick Pigott
Monthly £3.05

Illustrated magazine dealing with all railway subjects; no fiction or verse. Articles from 1500–2000 words accompanied by photos. Preliminary letter desirable. Payment: by arrangement. Illustrations: colour transparencies, half-tone and line. Founded 1897.

The Rambler

The Ramblers' Association, 2nd Floor, Camelford House, 87-90 Albert Embankment, London SE1 7TW
tel 020-7339 8500 *fax* 020-7339 8501
email ramblers@london.ramblers.org.uk
website www.ramblers.org.uk
Editor Christopher Sparrow
Quarterly Free to members

Magazine of the Ramblers' Association. Articles on walking, access to countryside and related issues. Material mostly commissioned. Length: about 700 words. Illustrations: colour photos, cartoons. Payment: by agreement. Founded 1935.

Reader's Digest

The Reader's Digest Association Ltd, 11 Westferry Circus, Canary Wharf, London E14 4HE
tel 020-7715 8000
email excerpts@readersdigest.co.uk
website www.readersdigest.co.uk
Editor-in-Chief Katherine Walker
Monthly £2.95

Original anecdotes – £200 for up to 150 words – are required for humorous features. Booklet 'Writing for Reader's Digest' available £4.50 post free.

Real

H. Bauer Publishing, Academic House, 24-28 Oval Road, London NW1 7DT
tel 020-7241 8392 *fax* 020-7241 8090
email real.life@bauer.co.uk
Editor Sian Rees, *Commissioning Editor* Kate Thompson
Fortnightly £1

Fashion, beauty, health issues and lifestyle features for women aged 25–40 and real life celebrity profiles. Will consider unsolicited material. Approach Commissioning Editor with ideas and outlines. Payment: by arrangement. Founded 2001.

Reality

Redemptorist Publications, Orwell Road, Rathgar, Dublin 6, Republic of Ireland
tel (01) 4922488 *fax* (01) 4922654
email info@redemptoristpublications.com
website www.redemptoristpublications.com
Editor Rev. Gerry Moloney CSSR
Monthly €1.25

Illustrated magazine for Christian living. Illustrated articles on all aspects of modern life, including family, youth, religion, leisure. Length: 1000–1500 words. Payment: by arrangement; average £50 per 1000 words. Founded 1936.

Record Collector

45 St Mary's Road, London W5 5RQ
tel 020-8579 1082 *fax* 020-8566 2024
email andy.davis@dpgmags.co.uk
website www.recordcollectormag.com
Editor Andy Davis
Monthly £3.30

Covers all areas of music, with the focus on collectable releases and the reissues market. Specially commissions most material but will consider unsolicited material. Welcomes ideas for articles and features. Length: 2000 (articles/features), 200 (news). Illustrations: transparencies, colour and b&w prints, scans of rare records; all commissioned. Payment: negotiable. Founded 1980.

Red

Hachette Filipacchi UK Ltd, 16-18 Berners Street, London W1T 3LN
tel 020-7150 7000 *fax* 020-7150 7001
Editor Trish Halpin, *Send material to* Victoria

Harper, Features Editor
Monthly £2.90

High-quality articles on topics of interest to women aged 35–45: humour, memoirs, interviews and well-researched investigative features. Approach with ideas in writing in first instance. Length: 1500 words upwards. Illustrations: transparencies. Payment:NUJ rates. Founded 1998.

Red Pepper
Socialist Newspaper (Publications) Ltd,
1B Waterlow Road, London N19 5NJ
email redpepper@redpepper.org.uk
website www.redpepper.org.uk
Editor Hilary Wainwright, Send material to David Castle, Deputy Editor
Monthly £1.95

Independent radical magazine: news and features on politics, culture and everyday life of interest to the left and greens. Material mostly commissioned. Length: news/news features 200–800 words, other features 800–2000 words. Illustrations: b&w photos, cartoons, graphics. Payment: for investigations, otherwise only exceptionally. Founded 1994.

Reform
(published by United Reformed Church)
86 Tavistock Place, London WC1H 9RT
tel 020-7916 8630 fax 020-7916 2021 (fao 'Reform')
email reform@urc.org.uk
Editor David Lawrence
Monthly £1.30 (£11.50 p.a.)

Articles of religious or social comment. Length: 600–1000 words. Illustrations: line, half-tone, colour, cartoons. Payment: by arrangement. Founded 1972.

Report
ATL, 7 Northumberland Street,
London WC2N 5RD
tel 020-7782 1517 fax 020-7925 0529
email info@atl.org.uk
website www.askatl.org.uk
Editor Heather Pinnell
10 p.a. £2.50 (£15 p.a. UK; £27 p.a. overseas)

The magazine from the Association of Teachers and Lecturers (ATL). Features, articles, comment, news about nursery, primary, secondary and further education. Payment: minimum £120 per 1000 words.

Restaurant Magazine
3rd Floor, 9 Carnaby Street, London W1F 9PE
tel 020-7434 9190 fax 020-7434 4517
email editorial@restaurantmagazine.co.uk
Editor Chris Maillard
Bi-weekly £1.95

Articles, features and news on the restaurant trade. Specially commissions most material. Welcomes

ideas for articles and features. Illustrations: colour transparencies, prints and artwork. Payment: variable. Founded 2001.

Retail Week
EMAP Retail, 33-39 Bowling Green Lane,
London EC1R 0DA
tel 020-7520 1500 fax 020-7520 1752
Editor Neill Denny
Weekly Controlled circulation (£105 p.a.)

Features and news stories on all aspects of retail management. Length: up to 1000 words. Illustrations: colour photos. Payment: by arrangement. Founded 1988.

Review – see Mail on Sunday in National newspapers UK and Ireland, page 3

The Rialto
PO Box 309, Aylsham, Norwich NR11 6LN
website www.therialto.co.uk
Editor Michael Mackmin
3 p.a. £4.25 (£12 p.a., £9 p.a. low income)

Poetry and criticism. Sae essential. Payment: by arrangement. Founded 1984.

Right Start
McMillan-Scott plc, 10 Savoy Street,
London WC2E 7HR
tel 020-7878 2338 fax 020-7379 6261
Editor Lynette Lowthian
Bi-monthly £2.10

Features on all aspects of pre-school and infant education, child health and behaviour. No unsolicited MSS. Length: 800–1500 words. Illustrations: colour photos, line. Payment: varies. Founded 1989.

Royal National Institute of the Blind
PO Box 173, Peterborough, Cambs. PE2 6WS
tel (0845) 7023153 fax (01733) 371555
email cservices@rnib.org.uk
website www.rnib.org.uk/wesupply/magazine/welcome.htm
textphone (0845) 7585691

Published by the Royal National Institute of the Blind, the following titles are available via email, on floppy disk and in braille, unless otherwise stated. 3FM (email and braille), Absolutely Boys, Absolutely Girls, Access IT, After Hours (braille), Aphra, BBC On Air, Big Print newspaper (large print), Blast Off! (children's magazine; disk and braille), Braille at Bedtime (braille), Broadcast Times (email and disk), Broadcast Times Christmas Special (email and disk), Busy Solicitor's Digest (disk and braille), Channels of Blessing (disk and braille), Chess Magazine (braille), Christmas Cracker (disk and braille), Christmas Radio Guide (email and braille), Christmas Television

Guide (email and braille), *Compute IT, Contention, Conundrum* (disk and braille), *Cricket Fixtures, Daily Bread* (disk and braille), *E-Access Bulletin* (email only), *Eye Contact* (print, email, disk, cassette tape), *Football Fixtures, Good Vibrations, Money Matters, Music Magazine* (disk and braille), *New Beacon* (print, email, disk, cassette tape, braille), *New Literature on Sight Problems* (print, email, disk, cassette tape, braille), *Physiotherapy* (disk, cassette tape, braille), *Physiotherapy Frontline* (cassette tape), *Physiotherapists' Quarterly* (braille), *Piano Tuners' Quarterly* (large print, email, disk, cassette tape, braille), *Progress, Proms Guide, Radio Guide* (email and braille), *Ready, Steady, Read* (for new readers of braille), *Rhetoric, Scientific Enquiry* (disk and braille), *Shaping Up, Shop Window, Shop Window Christmas Guide, Short Stories, Slugs & Snails* (for teenage boys; disk and braille), *Soundings* (cassette tape), *SP, Sugar & Spice* (for teenage girls; disk and braille), *Tape Medical Bulletin* (cassette tape), *Television Guide* (email and braille), *Theological Times* (disk, cassette tape, braille), *Upbeat, You & Your Child, Visability* (print, email, disk, cassette tape), *Vision* (clear print, email, disk, cassette tape, braille), *Welcome to a world of...* (email, disk, www.rnib.org.uk, cassette tape, braille).

Rugby World

IPC Media Ltd, Kings Reach Tower, Stamford Street, London SE1 9LS
tel 020-7261 6830 *fax* 020-7261 5419
email Paul_Morgan@ipcmedia.com
Editor Paul Morgan
Monthly £3.10

Features and exclusive news stories on rugby. Length: approx. 1200 words. Illustrations: colour photos, cartoons. Payment: £120. Founded 1960.

Runner's World

Rodale Ltd, 7-10 Chandos Street, London W1M 0AD
tel 020-7291 6000 *fax* 020-7291 6080
email rwedit@rodale.co.uk
website www.runnersworld.co.uk
Editor Steven Seaton
Monthly £3

Articles on jogging, running, health and fitness. Payment: by arrangement. Illustrations: line, half-tone, colour. Founded 1979.

Running Fitness

Kelsey Publishing Ltd, Arcade Chambers, Westgate Arcade, Peterborough PE1 1PY
tel (01733) 347559 *fax* (01733) 352749
email paul.larkins@kelsey.co.uk
Editor Paul Larkins
Monthly £3

Practical articles on all aspects of running lifestyle,

especially road running training and events, and advice on health, fitness and injury. Illustrations: colour photos, cartoons. Payment: by negotiation. Founded 1985.

RUSI Journal

Whitehall, London SW1A 2ET
tel 020-7930 5854 *fax* 020-7321 0943
email journal@rusi.org
website www.rusi.org
Editor Dr Terence McNamee
Bi-monthly £7.50

Journal of the Royal United Services Institute for Defence Studies. Articles on international security, the military sciences, defence technology and procurement, and military history; also book reviews and correspondence. Length: 3000–3500 words. Illustrations: b&w photos, colour transparencies, maps and diagrams. Payment: £12.50 per printed page upon publication.

S:2 Magazine – see Sunday Express in National newspapers UK, page 3

Safety Education

Royal Society for the Prevention of Accidents, Edgbaston Park, 353 Bristol Road, Birmingham B5 7ST
tel 0121-248 2000 *fax* 0121-248 2001
website www.rospa.org.uk
Editor Janice Cave
3 p.a. £10.50 p.a. for members of Safety Education Department (£12.50 p.a. non-members)

Articles on every aspect of good practice in safety education including safety of teachers and pupils in school, and the teaching of road, home, water, leisure and personal safety by means of established subjects on the school curriculum. All ages. Founded as *Child Safety* 1937; became *Safety Training* 1940; 1966.

Saga Magazine

Saga Publishing Ltd, The Saga Building, Enbrook Park, Folkestone, Kent CT20 3SE
tel (01303) 771523 *fax* (01303) 776699
Editor Emma Soames
Monthly £16.95 p.a. Subscription only

General interest magazine aimed at the intelligent, literate 50+ reader. Wide range of articles from human interest, 'real life' stories, intriguing overseas interest (not travel), some natural history, celebrity interviews, photographic book extracts – all relevant to 50+ audience. Articles mostly commissioned or written in-house, but genuine exclusives welcome. Illustrations: colour, digital media; mainly commissioned but top-quality photo feature suggestions sometimes accepted. Payment: competitive rate, by negotiation. Founded 1984.

Sainsbury's Magazine

New Crane Publishing, 20 Upper Ground,
London SE1 9PD
tel 020-7633 0266 *fax* 020-7401 9423
Editor Sue Robinson
Monthly £1

Features: general, food and drink, health, beauty,
homes; all material commissioned. Length: from
1500 words. Illustrations: colour and b&w photos
and line illustrations. Payment: varies; £300 per full
page for illustrations. Founded 1993.

Satellite Times

Everpage Ltd, The Stables, West Hill Grange,
North Road, Horsforth, Leeds LS18 5HG
tel 0113-258 5008 *fax* 0113-258 9745
email info@satellitetimes.co.uk
Editor-in-Chief Juliet Cross
Monthly £2.30

TV and film personality articles and interviews,
sports articles, music, competitions. Payment: from
£120 per 1000 words. Founded 1988.

Saturday – see Daily Record in National newspapers UK and Ireland, page 3

Saturday – see Daily Express in National newspapers UK and Ireland, page 3

The School Librarian

The School Library Association, Unit 2,
Lotmead Business Village, Lotmead Farm,
Wanborough, Swindon SN4 0UY
tel (01793) 791787 *fax* (01793) 791786
email info@sla.org.uk
website www.sla.org.uk
Editor Ray Lonsdale, DILS, University of Wales,
Aberystwyth, Ceredigion SY23 3AS
Quarterly Free to members (£55 p.a.)

Official journal of the School Library Association.
Articles on school library management, use and
skills, and on authors and illustrators, literacy,
publishing. Reviews of books, CD-Roms, websites
and other library resources from preschool to adult.
Length: 1800–3000 words (articles). Payment: by
arrangement. Founded 1937.

Science Progress

Science Reviews, PO Box 314, St Albans,
Herts. AL1 4ZG
tel/fax (01727) 847323
email scilet@scilet.com
Editors Prof David Phillips, Prof Robin Rowbury
Quarterly £195 p.a. ($300 p.a. overseas)

Articles of 6000 words on new scientific
developments, written so as to be intelligible to
workers in other disciplines. Imperative to submit

synopsis before full-length article. Payment: by
arrangement. Illustrations: line, half-tone.

Scientific Computing World

Cambridge Publishers Ltd, 53-54 Sydney Street,
Cambridge CB2 3HX
tel (01223) 477411 *fax* (01223) 327356
website www.scientific-computing.com
Editor Dr Tom Wilkie
6 p.a. Free to qualifying subscribers

Features on hardware and software developments
for the scientific community, plus news articles and
reviews. Length: 800–2000 words. Illustrations:
colour transparencies, photos, electronic graphics.
Payment: by negotiation. Founded 1994.

The Scots Magazine

D.C. Thomson & Co. Ltd, 2 Albert Square,
Dundee DD1 9QJ
tel (01382) 223131 *fax* (01382) 322214
email mail@scotsmagazine.com
website www.scotsmagazine.com
Monthly £1.40

Articles on all subjects of Scottish interest. Short
stories, poetry, but must be Scottish. Illustrations:
colour and b&w photos. Payment: £22 per 1000
words; from £12–£40. Founded 1739.

Scottish Book Collector

8 Lauriston Street, Edinburgh EH3 9DJ
tel 0131-228 4837 *fax* 0131-228 3904
email jennie@scotbooksmag.demon.co.uk
website www.scotbooksmag.demon.co.uk
Editor Jennie Renton
Quarterly £3

Articles on book collecting; literary/bibliographical
articles, features on writers. Length: 1500–2500
words. Payment: £25 per article. Founded 1987.

The Scottish Farmer

SMG Magazines Ltd, 200 Renfield Street,
Glasgow G2 3PR
tel 0141-302 7700 *fax* 0141-302 7799
Editor Alasdair Fletcher
Weekly £1.50

Articles on agricultural subjects. Length: 1000–1500
words. Payment: £80 per 1000 words. Illustrations:
line, half-tone, colour. Founded 1893.

Scottish Field

Special Publications, Craigcrook Castle,
Craigcrook Road, Edinburgh EH4 3PE
tel 0131-312 4550 *fax* 0131-312 4551
email editor@scottishfield.co.uk
Editor Archie Mackenzie
Monthly £3

Will consider all material with a Scottish link and
good photos. Payment: by negotiation. Founded 1903.

Scottish Home and Country

42A Heriot Row, Edinburgh EH3 6ES
tel 0131-225 1724 *fax* 0131-225 8129
email magazine@swri.demon.co.uk
website www.swri.org.uk
Editor Liz Ferguson
Monthly 90p

Articles on crafts, cookery, travel, personal
experience, DIY; humorous rural stories; fashion,
health, books. Length: up to 1000 words, preferably
illustrated. Illustrations: colour prints/transparencies,
b&w, cartoons. Payment: by arrangement.
Founded 1924.

Scottish Memories

Lang Syne Publishers Ltd,
Strathclyde Business Centre,
120 Carstairs Street, Glasgow G40 4DJ
tel 0141-554 9944 *fax* 0141-554 9955
email scottish-memories@aol.com
website www.scottish-memories.co.uk
Editor George Forbes
Monthly £2.25

Features on any aspect of Scottish nostalgia or history,
from primeval times to the 1990s. Contact the
Editor with an outline in first instance. Length: 1000
words. Illustrations: colour and b&w. Payment: £70
per 1000 words; £20 per photo. Founded 1993.

Scouting Magazine

Gilwell House, Gilwell Park, London E4 7QW
tel 020-8433 7100 *fax* 020-8433 7103
Editor Anna Sorensen
Monthly £2.15

Magazine of the Scout Association. Ideas, news,
views, features and programme resources for
Leaders and Supporters. Training material, accounts
of Scouting events and articles of general interest
with Scouting connections. Illustrations: photos –
action shots preferred rather than static posed shots
for use with articles or as fillers or cover potential,
cartoons. Payment: on publication by arrangement.

Screen International

EMAP Business Publishing, 33-39 Bowling Green
Lane, London EC1R 0DA
tel 020-7505 8080 *fax* 020-7505 8117
email ScreenInternational@compuserve.com
website www.screendaily.com
Managing Editor Leo Barraclough
Weekly £2.50

International news and features on the international
film business. No unsolicited material. Length:
variable. Payment: by arrangement.

Scuba World

Freestyle Publications Ltd, Alexander House,
Ling Road, Tower Park, Poole, Dorset BH12 4NZ

tel (01202) 735090 *fax* (01202) 733969
email fraines@freepubs.co.uk
website www.freepubs.co.uk
Editor Frank Raines
Monthly £3

The official magazine of the Sub-Aqua Association.
Articles, features, news and short stories related to
diving. Unsolicited material welcome. Length:
1300–1400 words (articles/features); 200–300 words
(news); 800 words (short stories); 2000 words
(interviews). Payment: negotiable. Founded 1990.

Sea Angler

EMAP Active Ltd, Bushfield House, Orton Centre,
Peterborough PE2 5UW
tel (01733) 237111 *fax* (01733) 465658
Editor Mel Russ
Monthly £2.60

Topical articles on all aspects of sea-fishing around
the British Isles. Payment: by arrangement. Illustrations: colour. Founded 1973.

Sea Breezes

Media House, Tromode, Douglas,
Isle of Man IM4 4SB
tel (01624) 626018 *fax* (01624) 696573
Editor A.C. Douglas
Monthly £2.50

Factual articles on ships and the sea past and
present, preferably illustrated. Length: up to 4000
words. Illustrations: line, half-tone, colour.
Payment: by arrangement. Founded 1919.

Sewing World

Traplet Publications Ltd, Traplet House,
Severn Drive, Upton Upon Seven,
Worcs. WR8 0JL
tel (01684) 595300 *fax* (01684) 594586
email sw@traplet.co.uk
Editor Wendy Gardiner
Monthly £2.95

'Sewing magazine for sewing machine enthusiasts.'
Articles and step-by-step projects. Length:
1000–1500 words (articles). Illustrations: colour.
Payment: £100 per article including illustrations.
Founded 1995.

She

National Magazine House, 72 Broadwick Street,
London W1F 9EP
tel 020-7439 5000 *fax* 020-7312 3981
Editor Eve Cameron, *Send material to* Cayte
Williams, Features Editor
Monthly £2.70

No unsolicited MSS. Ideas with synopses welcome
on subjects ranging from health and relationships
to child care. Payment: NUJ freelance rates.
Illustrations: photos. Founded 1955.

SHERLOCK

(formerly Sherlock Holmes – The Detective
Magazine)
Overdale, 69 Greenhead Road,
Huddersfield HD1 4ER
tel/fax (01484) 426957
email overdale@btinternet.com
Editor David Stuart Davies
6 p.a. £3.95

Articles relating to Sherlock Holmes, crime fiction
and writers. Also short stories. Contact the Editor
with ideas/synopsis in the first instance. Length:
1800 words (articles), 6000–7000 words (short
stories). Payment: by negotiation. Founded 1991.

Ships Monthly

IPC Country & Leisure (Marine),
222 Branston Road, Burton-on-Trent,
Staffs. DE14 3BT
tel (01283) 542721 *fax* (01283) 546436
Editor Iain Wakefield
Monthly £2.60 plus 4 special issues @ £3.35

Illustrated articles of shipping interest – both
mercantile and naval, preferably of 20th and 21st
century ships. Well-researched, factual material only.
No short stories or poetry. 'Notes for Contributors'
available. Mainly commissioned material; preliminary letter essential, with sae. Payment: by arrangement. Illustrations: half-tone and line, colour
transparencies and prints. Founded 1966.

Shoot

IPC Magazines Ltd, King's Reach Tower,
Stamford Street, London SE1 9LS
tel 020-7261 6287 *fax* 020-7261 6019
Editor Colin Mitchell
Monthly £2.60

Football magazine. Features, profiles of big names
in football. Length: 500–2000 words (features).
Illustrations: colour transparencies. Payment:
negotiable. Founded 1969.

Shooting Times and Country Magazine

IPC Magazines Ltd, King's Reach Tower,
Stamford Street, London SE1 9LS
tel 020-7261 6180 *fax* 020-7261 7179
Editor Julian Murray-Evans
Weekly £1.70

Articles on fieldsports, especially shooting, and on
related natural history and countryside topics.
Unsolicited MSS not encouraged. Length: up to
2000 words. Payment: by arrangement. Illustrations:
photos, drawings, colour transparencies. Founded
1882.

The Shop: A Magazine of Poetry

Skeagh, Schull, Co. Cork, Republic of Ireland
email wakeman@iolfree.ie

Editors John and Hilary Wakeman
3 p.a. €19 p.a.

Poems on any subject in any form and occasional
essays on poetry, especially Irish poetry. No
submissions by email. No illustrations required.
Length: 2000–3000 words (essays); any (poems).
Payment: by arrangement. Founded 1999.

The Short Wave Magazine

Arrowsmith Court, Station Approach, Broadstone,
Dorset BH18 8PW
tel (01202) 659910 *fax* (01202) 659950
email kevin.nice@pwpublishing.ltd.uk
website www.pwpublishing.ltd.uk
Editor Kevin Nice
Monthly £3.25 (£36 p.a.)

Technical and semi-technical articles, 500–5000
words, on design, construction and operation of
radio receiving equipment. Radio-related photo
features welcome. Payment: £55 per page.
Illustrations: line, half-tone, colour. Founded 1937.

Shout

D.C. Thomson & Co. Ltd, Albert Square,
Dundee DD1 9QJ
tel (01382) 223131 *fax* (01382) 200880
email shout@dcthomson.co.uk
185 Fleet Street, London EC4A 2HS
tel 020-7400 1030 *fax* 020-7400 1089
Editor-in-Chief Jackie Brown
Fortnightly £1.60

Colour gravure magazine for 11–14 year-old girls.
Pop, film and 'soap' features and pin-ups; general
features of teen interest; emotional features, fashion
and beauty advice. Illustrations: colour transparencies. Payment: on acceptance. Founded 1993.

The Shropshire Magazine

77 Wyle Cop, Shrewsbury, Shropshire SY1 1UT
tel (01743) 361979 *fax* (01743) 362128
Editor Keith Parker
Monthly £1.50

Articles on topics related to Shropshire, including
countryside, history, characters, legends, education,
food; also home and garden features. Length: up to
1500 words. Illustrations: colour. Founded 1950.

Sight and Sound

British Film Institute, 21 Stephen Street,
London W1T 1LN
tel 020-7255 1444 *fax* 020-7436 2327
Editor Nick James
Monthly £3.25

Topical and critical articles on the cinema of any
country; reviews of every film theatrically released
in the UK; book reviews; reviews of every video
released; regular columns from around the world.
Length: 1000–5000 words. Payment: by

arrangement. Illustrations: relevant photos, cartoons. Founded 1932.

The Sign

G.J. Palmer & Sons Ltd, St Mary's Works, St Mary's Plain, Norwich, Norfolk NR3 3BH
tel (01603) 615995 *fax* (01603) 624483
email terencestalbans@aol.com
Publisher G.A. Knights, *Editor* Terence Handley MacMath, *Poetry Editor* D.H.W. Grubb
Monthly 5p

Leading national insert for C of E parish magazines. Articles of interest to parishes. Items should bear the author's name and address; return postage essential or send by email. Length: up to 450 words, accompanied by photos/illustrations. Payment: by arrangement. Founded 1905.

Ski and Board

The Ski Club of Great Britain, The White House, 57-63 Church Road, London SW19 5SB
tel (0845) 4580780 *fax* (0845) 4580781
email s&b@skiclub.co.uk
website www.skiclub.co.uk
Editor Arnie Wilson
Monthly (Oct-Jan) £2.95

Articles, features, news, true life stories, ski tips, equipment reviews, resort reports – all in connection with skiing and snowboarding. Welcomes ideas for articles and features. Length: 600–2000 words. Illustrations: colour transparencies, colour and b&w artwork and cartoons. Payment: £200 per 1000 words; £100–£200 per photo/illustration. Founded 1903.

The Skier and The Snowboarder Magazine

Mountain Marketing Ltd, PO Box 386, Sevenoaks, Kent TN13 1AQ
tel (0845) 3108303 *fax* (01732) 779266
email skierandsnowboarder@hotmail.com
Editor Frank Baldwin
5 p.a. (July-May) £2.95

Ski features, based around a good story. Length: 800–1000 words. Illustrations: colour action ski photos. Payment: by negotiation. Founded 1984.

Slimmer, Healthier, Fitter

Aceville Publications Ltd, Castle House, 97 High Street, Colchester CO1 1TH
tel (01206) 505972 *fax* (01206) 505935
email slimmer@aceville.com hmulley@aceville.co.uk
Editor Helen Mulley
10 p.a. £2.10

Features on health, nutrition, slimming. Personal weight loss stories. Sae essential. Length: 600 or 1200 words. Payment: by arrangement. Founded 1972.

Slimming Magazine

EMAP Esprit, Greater London House, Hampstead Road, London NW1 7EJ
tel 020-7347 1854 *fax* 020-7347 1863
Editor Rashmi Madan
11 p.a. £2.10

Articles on psychology, lifestyle and health related to diet and nutrition. Approach the Editor in writing with ideas. Length: 1000–1500 words. Payment: by negotiation. Founded 1969.

Smallholder

Hook House, Hook Road, Wimblington, March, Cambs. PE15 0QL
tel/fax (01354) 741182
email edit@smallholder.co.uk
website www.smallholder.co.uk
Editor Liz Wright
Monthly £2.60

Articles of relevance to small farmers about livestock and crops, organics, conservation, poultry, equipment. Items relating to the countryside considered. Send for copy. Payment: £30 per 1000 words or by arrangement. Illustrations: line, half-tone, cartoons. Founded 1985.

Smash Hits

EMAP Performance, Mappin House, 4 Winsley Street, London W1W 8HF
tel 020-7436 1515 *fax* 020-7636 5792
email smash-hits@emap.com
Editor Lisa Smosarski
Fortnightly £1.90

News interviews and posters of pop, TV and film stars. Illustrations: colour photos. Payment: varies.

Snooker Scene

Cavalier House, 202 Hagley Road, Edgbaston, Birmingham B16 9PQ
tel 0121-454 2931 *fax* 0121-452 1822
email editor@snookerscene.com
website www.snookerscene.com
Editor Clive Everton
Monthly £2.50 (£25 p.a.)

News and articles about the snooker and billiards scene for readers with more than a casual interest in the games. Payment: by arrangement. Illustrations: photos. Founded 1971.

Snoop

Snoop Publications Ltd, 5A High Street, Southall, Middlesex UB1 3HA
tel 020-8571 7700 *fax* 020-8571 6006
email editor@snooplife.com
website www.snooplife.com
Editor Raj Kaushal
Monthly £3

Entertainment and lifestyle magazine for second and

third generation UK Asians (16–35 year-olds): interviews, music, films, fashion, gossip and gigs. Features and articles by arrangement. Founded 1997.

Solicitors Journal

Wilmington Business Information Ltd, Paulton House, 8 Shepherdess Walk, London N1 7LB
tel 020-7490 0049 *fax* 020-7324 2366
email editorial@solicitorsjournal.co.uk
Weekly £189 for 48 issues

Articles, by practising lawyers or specialist journalists, on subjects of practical interest to solicitors. Articles on spec should be sent on disk or by email. Length: up to 1800 words. Payment: by negotiation. Founded 1856.

Somerset Magazine

Eastern Counties Newspapers, 23 Market Street, Crewkerne, Somerset TA18 7JU
tel (01460) 270011 *fax* (01460) 270022
Managing Publisher Jenny Nicholls
Monthly £2.25

Articles, features with particular reference to Somerset locations, facilities and other interests. Length: 1000–1500 words. Illustrations: half-tone, colour. Payment: by arrangement. Founded 1977 as *Somerset & West.*

The Songwriter

International Songwriters Association, PO Box 46, Limerick City, Republic of Ireland
tel (061) 228837
Editor James D. Liddane
Monthly

Articles on songwriting and interviews with music publishers and recording company executives. Length: 400–5000 words. Payment: by arrangement. Illustrations: photos. Founded 1967.

Songwriting and Composing

Sovereign House, 12 Trewartha Road, Praa Sands, Penzance, Cornwall TR20 9ST
tel (01736) 762826 *fax* (01736) 763328
email songmag@aol.com
website www.songwriters-guild.co.uk
General Secretary Carole Jones
Quarterly Free to members

Magazine of the Guild of International Songwriters and Composers. Short stories, articles, letters relating to songwriting, publishing, recording and the music industry. Payment: negotiable upon content £25–£60. Illustrations: line, half-tone. Founded 1986.

The Spark Magazine

Blue Sax Publishing Ltd, 86-88 Colston Street, Bristol BS1 5BB

tel 0117-914 3434 *fax* 0117-914 3444
email john@thespark.co.uk
website www.thespark.co.uk
Editor John Dawson
Quarterly Free

'A free... thinking magazine about positive change for the West Country.' Features on health, fitness, the environment, social and community issues. Welcomes ideas for features and articles. Send A4 envelope for writers' guidelines or see website. Length: varies. Illustrations: colour cover. Payment: £6.50 per 100 words. Founded 1993.

The Spectator

56 Doughty Street, London WC1N 2LL
tel 020-7405 1706 *fax* 020-7242-0603
Editor Boris Johnson, *Publisher* Kimberly Fortier
Weekly £2.40

Articles on current affairs, politics, the arts; book reviews. Illustrations: colour and b&w, cartoons. Payment: on merit. Founded 1828.

Spectrum Magazine – see Scotland on Sunday in National newspapers UK and Ireland, page 3

Sport First

20-26 Brunswick Place, London N1 6DZ
tel 020-7490 7575 *fax* 020-7490 7666
email editorial@sportfirst.com
website www.sportfirst.com
Editor James Eastham
Weekly 60p

Tabloid Sunday newspaper covering all sports. Length: 800 words (articles), 300–800 words (news). No unsolicited contributions. Payment: £150 per 1000 words. Founded 1998.

Springboard

8 Landrock Road, London N8 9HP
tel 020-8340 8356
email springboardmag@aol.com
Editor Fiona Mallin-Robinson
Quarterly £15 p.a.

Short fiction, poetry and articles on writing, competition news and markets. Aims to support and encourage writers. Competitions in every issue (free to subscribers) with winning stories, poems and articles receiving prize money and publication. Unsolicited material is accepted but writers should read at least one issue first. Founded 1990.

The Squash Player

460 Bath Road, Longford, Middlesex UB7 0EB
tel (01753) 775511 *fax* (01753) 775512
email editor@squashplayer.co.uk
Editor Ian McKenzie
10 p.a. £40 p.a.

Covers all aspects of playing squash. All features are commissioned – discuss ideas with the Editor. Length: 1000–1500 words. Illustrations: unusual photos (e.g. celebrities), cartoons. Payment: £75 per 1000 words; £25–£40 for illustrations. Founded 1971.

Staffordshire Life Magazine

Staffordshire Newsletter Ltd, The Publishing Centre, Derby Street, Stafford ST16 2DT
tel (01785) 257700 *fax* (01785) 253287
email editor@staffordshirelife.co.uk
Editor Philip Thurlow-Craig
11 p.a. £1.75

County magazine for Staffordshire. Historical articles; features on county personalities. No short stories. Contact the Editor in the first instance. Length: 500–800 words. Illustrations: colour transparencies and prints. Founded 1948; relaunched 1980.

The Stage

(incorporating Television Today)
Stage House, 47 Bermondsey Street,
London SE1 3XT
tel 020-7403 1818 *fax* 020-7357 9287
email editor@thestage.co.uk
website www.thestage.co.uk
Editor Brian Attwood
Weekly £1

Original and interesting articles on professional stage and broadcasting topics may be sent for the Editor's consideration. Length: 500–900 words. Payment: £100 per 1000 words. Founded 1880.

Stamp Lover

National Philatelic Society, British Philatelic Centre, 107 Charterhouse Street, London EC1M 6PT
tel 020-7336 0882
email nps@philately.org.uk
Editor Michael Furnell
6 p.a. £2

Original articles on stamps and postal history. Illustrations: line, half-tone. Payment: by arrangement. Founded 1908.

Stamp Magazine

IPC Media Ltd, Focus Network, 9 Dingwall Avenue, Croydon CR9 2TA
tel 020-8774 0772 *fax* 020-8774 0939
Editor Steve Fairclough
Monthly £2.40

Informative articles and exclusive news items on stamp collecting and postal history. No preliminary letter. Payment: by arrangement. Illustrations: line, half-tone, colour. Founded 1934.

Stand Magazine

School of English, University of Leeds,
Leeds LS2 9JT
tel 0113-233 4794 *fax* 0113-233 4791
email stand@leeds.ac.uk
website http://saturn.vcu.edu/~dlatane/stand.html
Managing Editor Jon Glover
Quarterly £6.50 plus p&p (£25 p.a.)

Poetry, short stories, translations, literary criticism. Send sae/IRCs for return. Payment: £50 per 1000 words (prose); £20 per poem. Founded 1952.

Staple

35 Carr Road, Walkley, Sheffield S6 2WY
Editors Elizabeth Barrett, Ann Atkinson
3 p.a. £10 p.a. (£15 p.a. overseas)

Poetry, short fiction, articles and reviews. Payment: £5 per poem, £10 fiction/articles. Founded 1982.

Starburst

Visual Imagination Ltd, 9 Blades Court, Deodar Road, London SW15 2NU
tel 020-8875 1520 *fax* 020-8875 1588
email starburst@vismag.com
website www.wisimag.com
Editor Andrew Cartmel
Monthly plus 4 specials p.a. £3.25

Features and interviews on all aspects of science fiction. Length: 2000 words. Illustrations: colour and b&w photos. Payment: £80 per 1000 words; £10–£20 per image. Founded 1977.

The Strad

Orpheus Publications, SMG, 3 Waterhouse Square, 138-142 Holborn, London EC1N 2NY
tel 020-7882 1040 *fax* 020-7882 1020
email thestrad@orpheuspublications.com
website www.thestrad.com
Editor Naomi Sadler
12 p.a. £3.75

Features, news and reviews for string instrument players, teachers, makers and enthusiasts – both professional and amateur. Specially commissions most material but will consider unsolicited material. Welcomes ideas for articles and features. Length: 1000–2000 (articles/features), 100–150 (news). Payment: £150–£300 (articles/features), varies for news. Illustrations: transparencies, colour and b&w prints and artwork, colour cartoons; all commissioned. Founded 1890.

Studies, An Irish quarterly review

35 Lower Leeson Street, Dublin 2,
Republic of Ireland
tel (01) 6766785 *fax* (01) 6762984
email studies@s-j.ie
website www.studiesirishreview.com
Editor Rev. Fergus O'Donoghue SJ
Quarterly €6.35

General review of social comment, literature, history, the arts. Articles written by specialists for the general reader. Critical book reviews. Preliminary letter. Length: 4000 words. Founded 1912.

Studio Sound

Miller Freeman Entertainment Ltd, 8 Montague Close, London SE1 9UR *tel* 020-7940 8500 *fax* 020-7407 7102 *Editor* Tim Goodyer Monthly £5

Articles on all aspects of professional sound recording. Technical and operational features on the functional aspects of sound recording, AV postproduction and broadcast; general features on studio affairs. Length: widely variable. Payment: by arrangement. Illustrations: line, half-tone, colour. Founded 1959.

Suffolk Norfolk Life

Today Magazines Ltd, The Publishing House, Station Road, Framlingham, Suffolk IP13 9EE *tel* (01728) 622030 *fax* (01728) 622031 *email* todaymagazines@btopenworld.com *website* www.today-magazines.com *Editor* William Locks Monthly £1.50

Articles relevant to Suffolk and Norfolk – current topics plus historical items, art, leisure, etc. Considers unsolicited material and welcomes ideas for articles and features. Length: 900–1000 words. Illustrations: transparencies, colour and b&w prints, b&w artwork and cartoons. Payment: £30–£50 per article. Founded 1989.

Sugar

Hachette Filipacchi, 64 North Row, London W1K 7LL *tel* 020-7150 7000 *fax* 020-7150 7001 *Editor* Claire Irvin Monthly £2.20

Magazine for young women aged 12–17. Fashion, beauty, entertainment, features. Send synopsis first. Will consider unsolicited material. Interested in real-life stories (1200 words), quizzes. Payment: negotiable. Founded 1994.

Sunday Express 'S' Magazine – see Sunday Express in National newspapers UK and Ireland, page 3

Sunday Magazine – see News of the World in National newspapers UK and Ireland, page 3

The Sunday Post Magazine – see Sunday Post in National newspapers UK and Ireland, page 3

The Sunday Review – see Independent on Sunday in National newspapers UK and Ireland, page 3

Sunday Telegraph Magazine – see Sunday Telegraph in National newspapers UK and Ireland, page 3

The Sunday Times Magazine – see The Sunday Times in National newspapers UK and Ireland, page 3

Swimming Magazine

(formerly Swimming Times) Swimming Times Ltd, Harold Fern House, Derby Square, Loughborough LE11 5AL *tel* (01509) 618766 *fax* (01509) 618768 *Editor* Peter Hassall Monthly £2 (£22 p.a.)

Official journal of the Amateur Swimming Association and the Institute of Swimming Teachers and Coaches. Reports of major events and championships; news and features on all aspects of swimming including synchronised swimming, diving and water polo, etc; accompanying photos where appropriate; short fiction with a swimming theme. Unsolicited material welcome. Length: 800–1500 words. Payment: by arrangement. Founded 1923.

The Tablet

1 King Street Cloisters, Clifton Walk, London W6 0QZ *tel* 020-8748 8484 *fax* 020-8748 1550 *email* thetablet@thetablet.co.uk *website* www.thetablet.co.uk/ *Editor* John Wilkins Weekly £1.55

The senior Catholic weekly. Religion, philosophy, politics, society, books and arts. International coverage. Freelance work welcomed. Length: 1500 words. Illustrations: cartoons. Payment: by arrangement. Founded 1840.

Take a Break

H. Bauer Publishing Ltd, Academic House, 24-28 Oval Road, London NW1 7DT *tel* 020-7241 8000 *fax* 020-7241 8052 *Editor* John Dale Weekly 68p

Lively, tabloid women's weekly. True life features, celebrities, health and beauty, family, travel; short stories (up to 1500 words); lots of puzzles. Payment: by arrangement. Illustrated. Founded 1990.

Take a Break's Take a Puzzle

H. Bauer Publishing, Academic House, 24-28 Oval Road, London NW1 7DT *tel* 020-7241 8229 *fax* 020-7241 8009 *email* take.puzzle@bauer.co.uk *Editor* Rachel Plumridge Monthly £1.55

Puzzles. Fresh ideas always welcome. Illustrations: colour transparencies and b&w prints and artwork. Work supplied on Mac-compatible disk preferred. Payment: from £25 per puzzle, £30–£90 for picture puzzles and for illustrations not an integral part of a puzzle. Founded 1991.

TATE

The Condé Nast Publications Ltd, Vogue House, Hanover Square, London W1S 1JU
tel 020-7499 9080 *fax* 020-7460 6406
email czamani@condenast.co.uk
Editor Robert Violette
Bi-monthly £4

Independent visual arts magazine: features, news, interviews, reviews, previews and opinion pieces. Length: up to 3000 words but always commissioned. Illustrations: colour and b&w photos. Payment: negotiable. Founded 1993; relaunched 2002.

Tatler

Vogue House, Hanover Square, London W1S 1JU
tel 020-7499 9080 *fax* 020-7409 0451
website www.tatler.co.uk
Editor Geordie Greig
Monthly £3.30

Smart society magazine favouring sharp articles, profiles, fashion and the arts. Illustrations: colour, b&w, but all commissioned. Founded 1709.

The Teacher

National Union of Teachers, Hamilton House, Mabledon Place, London WC1H 9BD
tel 020-7380 4708 *fax* 020-7383 7230
Editor Mitch Howard
8 p.a. Free to NUT members

Articles, features and news of interest to all those involved in the teaching profession. Length: 750 words. Payment: NUJ rates to NUJ members. Founded 1872.

Technology Ireland

Enterprise Ireland, Strand Road, Dublin 4, Republic of Ireland
tel (01) 206 6337 *fax* (01) 206 6342
email tecnology.ireland@enterprise-ireland.com
website www.technologyireland.ie
Editor Tom Kennedy, Mary Sweetman, Sean Dute
Monthly €48 p.a. (IR£38 p.a. overseas)

Articles, features, reviews, news on current business, innovation and technology. Length: 1500–2000 words. Illustrations: line, half-tone, colour. Payment: varies. Founded 1969.

Telegraph Magazine – see The Daily Telegraph in National newspapers UK and Ireland, page 3

Television

Reed Business Information Ltd, Quadrant House, The Quadrant, Sutton, Surrey SM2 5AS
tel 020-8652 8120 *fax* 020-8652 8956
Monthly £2.80

Articles on the technical aspects of domestic TV and video equipment, especially servicing, long-distance TV, constructional projects, satellite TV, video recording, teletext and viewdata, test equipment, monitors. Payment: by arrangement. Illustrations: photos and line drawings for litho. Founded 1950.

Tempo

Cambridge University Press, The Edinburgh Building, Shaftesbury Road, Cambridge CB2 2RU
Editorial address PO Box 171, Herne Bay, Kent CT6 6WD
email macval@compuserve.com
Editor Calum MacDonald
Quarterly £4.99 (£20 p.a.)

Authoritative articles on contemporary music. Length: 2000–4000 words. Payment: by arrangement. Illustrations: music type, occasional photographic or musical supplements.

Tennis World

Umbrella Media, 5 Blythe Mews, Olympia, London W14 0HW
tel 020-7605 0000 *fax* 020-7605 0020
email charlotte.james@umbrellamedia.com
Editor Charlotte James
Monthly £2.50

Tournament reports, topical features, personality profiles, instructional articles. Length: 600–1500 words. Payment: by arrangement. Illustrations: line, half-tone, colour.

TGO (The Great Outdoors) Magazine

SMG Magazines Ltd, 200 Renfield Street, Glasgow G2 3PR
tel 0141-302 7700 *fax* 0141-302 7799
email cameron.mcneish@smg.plc.uk
Editor Cameron McNeish
Monthly £2.95

Articles on walking or lightweight camping in specific areas, preferably illustrated. Length: 1200–1800 words. Payment: by arrangement. Illustrations: colour. Founded 1978.

that's life!

H. Bauer Publishing Ltd, Academic House, 24-28 Oval Road, London NW1 7DT
tel 020-7241 8000 *fax* 020-7241 8008
Editor Jo Checkley
Weekly 63p

Dramatic true life stories about women. Length: average 1000 words. Illustrations: colour photos and cartoons. Payment: £750. Founded 1995.

Therapy Weekly

EMAP Healthcare Ltd, Greater London House, Hampstead Road, London NW1 7EJ
tel 020-7874 0360 *fax* 020-7874 0368
Editor Steve Bagshaw
Weekly Free to NHS and local authority therapists (£47.50 p.a.)

Articles of interest to chartered physiotherapists, occupational therapists and speech and language therapists. Guidelines to contributors available. Send proposals only initially. Length: up to 1000 words. Illustrations: colour and b&w photos, line, cartoons. Payment: by arrangement. Founded 1974 as *Therapy*.

The Third Alternative

TTA Press, 5 Martins Lane, Witcham, Ely, Cambs. CB6 2LB
tel (01353) 777931
email ttapress@aol.com
website www.ttapress.com
Editor Andy Cox
Bi-monthly £3.95 (£21 for 6 issues)

Extraordinary new fiction: science fiction, fantasy, horror, slipstream. Also interviews with, and profiles of, authors and film-makers. Send sae with all submissions. Considers unsolicited material and welcomes ideas for articles and features. Length: 3000–4000 words (articles and features), short stories unrestricted. Illustrations: send samples and portfolios. Payment: £30 per 1000 words on acceptance. Founded 1994.

Third Way

St Peter's, Sumner Road, Harrow, Middlesex HA1 4BX
tel 020-8423 8494 *fax* 020-8423 5367
email editor@thirdway.org.uk
10 p.a. £2.90

Aims to present biblical perspectives on the political, social and cultural issues of the day. Payment: by arrangement on publication. Founded 1977.

This Caring Business

1 St Thomas' Road, Hastings, East Sussex TN34 3LG
tel (01424) 718406 *fax* (01424) 718460
email vivshep@aol.com
Editor Vivien Shepherd
Monthly £50 p.a.

Specialist contributions relating to the commercial aspects of nursing and residential care, including hospitals. Payment: £100 per 1000 words. Illustrations: line, half-tone. Founded 1985.

This England

PO Box 52, Cheltenham, Glos. GL50 1YQ
tel (01242) 537900
Editor Roy Faiers
Quarterly £4

Articles on towns, villages, traditions, customs, legends, crafts of England; stories of people. Length: 250–2000 words. Payment: £25 per page and pro rata. Illustrations: line, half-tone, colour. Founded 1968.

Time Out

Time Out Group Ltd, Universal House, 251 Tottenham Court Road, London W1T 7AB
tel 020-7813 3000 *fax* 020-7813 6001
website www.timeout.com
Editor Laura Lee Davies
Weekly £2.20

Listings magazine for London covering all areas of the arts, plus articles of consumer and news interest. Illustrations: colour and b&w. Payment by negotiation. Founded 1968.

The Times Educational Supplement

Admiral House, 66-68 East Smithfield, London E1W 1BX
tel 020-7782 3000 *fax* 020-7782 3202 (news), 020-7782 3919 (features)
email friday@tes.co.uk (feature outlines), teacher@tes.co.uk (curriculum-related outlines)
website www.tes.co.uk
Editor Bob Doe
Weekly £1.20

Articles on education written with special knowledge or experience; news items; books, arts and equipment reviews. Advisable to check with news or picture editor before submitting. Outlines of feature ideas should be faxed or emailed. Illustrations: suitable photos and drawings of educational interest, cartoons. Payment: standard rates, or by arrangement.

Times Educational Supplement Scotland

Scott House, 10 South St Andrew Street, Edinburgh EH2 2AZ
tel 0131-557 1133 *fax* 0131-558 1155
Editor Neil Munro
Weekly £1.20

Articles on education, preferably 800–1000 words, written with special knowledge or experience. News items about Scottish educational affairs. Illustrations: line, half-tone. Payment: by arrangement. Founded 1965.

Times Higher Education Supplement

Admiral House, 66-68 East Smithfield, London E1W 1BX
tel 020-7782 3000 *fax* 020-7782 3300

Editor John O'Leary
Weekly £1.20

Articles on higher education written with special knowledge or experience, or articles dealing with academic topics. Also news items. Illustrations: suitable photos and drawings of educational interest. Payment: by arrangement. Founded 1971.

The Times Literary Supplement

Admiral House, 66-68 East Smithfield,
London E1W 1BX
tel 020-7782 3000 *fax* 020-7782 3100
Editor Peter Stothard
Weekly £2.40

Will consider poems for publication, literary discoveries and articles, particularly of an opinionated kind, on literary and cultural affairs. Payment: by arrangement.

The Times Magazine – see The Times in National newspapers UK and Ireland, page 3

Today's Fishkeeper

(formerly Aquarist and Pondkeeper)
TRMG Ltd, 1 Forum Place, Winchester Court,
Hatfield, Herts. AL10 0RN
tel (01707) 273999 *fax* (01707) 276555
Editor Derek Lambert
Monthly £2.95

Magazine for both the advanced and novice fishkeeper. A team of experts provides selected items that cover the full spectrum of aquarium and pond life, including fish (tropical, cold water, marine, discus and koi), reptiles and amphibians, plants, products and services. Illustrations: colour photos and diagrams. Payment: phone (01858) 438817 for details. Founded 1924.

Today's Golfer

EMAP Active Ltd, Bushfield House, Orton Centre,
Peterborough PE2 5UW
tel (01733) 237111 *fax* (01733) 288014
Editor Paul Hamblin
Monthly £3.20

Specialist features and articles on golf instruction, equipment and courses. Founded 1988.

Today's Pilot

Key Publishing Ltd, PO Box 100, Stamford,
Lincs. PE9 1XQ
tel (01780) 755131 *fax* (01780) 757261
email dave.unwin@keypublishing.com
website www.todayspilot.co.uk
Editor Dave Unwin
Monthly £3.20

General aviation magazine providing information and inspiration for the recreational aviator.

Considers unsolicited material. Submit suggestions or an outline in the first instance. Length: 3000 words (articles/features), 1000 words (news). Illustrations: colour. Payment: negotiable (words); £20 per image. Founded 2000.

Top of the Pops – see page 295

Top Santé Health & Beauty

EMAP Elán, Endeavour House,
189 Shaftesbury Avenue, London WC2H 8JG
tel 020-7437 9011 *fax* 020-7208 3514
Editor Juliette Kellow
Monthly £2.10

Articles, features and news on all aspects of health and beauty. Ideas welcome. No unsolicited features. Illustrations: colour photos and drawings. Payment: £350 per 1300 words; illustrations by arrangement. Founded 1993.

Total DVD

Highbury WViP, Unit 601, Highgate Studios,
53-79 Highgate Road, London NW5 1TW
tel 020-7331 1000 *fax* 020-7331 1242
email chris.jenkins@wvip.co.uk
website www.totaldvd.net
Editor Chris Jenkins
Monthly £3.99

DVD reviews, home entertainment, equipment reviews, news and features. Length: 800–2500 words (articles/features), 100–500 words (news). Payment: £120 per 1000 words. Illustrations: transparencies or digital. Founded 1999.

Total Film

99 Baker Street, London W1U 6FP
tel 020-7317 2600 *fax* 020-7317 0275
email totalfilm@futurenet.co.uk
Editor Matt Mueller
Monthly £3

Movie magazine covering all aspects of film. Email ideas before submitting material. Not seeking interviews or reviews. Length: 400 words (news items); 1000 words (funny features). Payment: £150 per 1000 words; up to £1500 per picture. Founded 1996.

Trail

(formerly Trail Walker)
EMAP Active Ltd, Bretton Court, Bretton,
Peterborough PE3 8DZ
tel (01733) 264666 *fax* (01733) 282653
email trail@emap.com
Editor Guy Procter
Monthly £3.10

Outdoor activity magazine focusing mainly on high level walking with some scrambling, moutain biking and climbing. Very limited opportunities for freelances.

Traveller

Wexas Ltd, 45 Brompton Road, London SW3 1DE
tel 020-7589 0500 *fax* 020-7581 1357
email traveller@wexas.com
website www.traveller.org.uk
Editor Jonathan Lorie
Quarterly Free to Wexas members; back numbers £3
(£3.50 overseas), payable to Wexas

Adventurous and authentic travel writing. Narrative
features describe personal journeys to remarkable
places. Unsolicited material considered if prose and
pictures are excellent. See website for guidelines.
Length: 800 words. Illustrations: transparencies,
b&w prints. Payment: £150 per 1000 words; colour
£50 (£100 cover). Founded 1970.

Tribune

9 Arkwright Road, London NW3 6AN
tel 020-7433 6410
email george@tribpub.demon.co.uk
Editor Mark Seddon, *Reviews Editor* Caroline Rees
Weekly £1.25

Political, literary, with Socialist outlook. Informative
articles (about 900 words), news stories (250–300
words). No unsolicited reviews or fiction. Payment:
by arrangement. Illustrations: cartoons, photos.

Trout and Salmon

EMAP Active Ltd, Bushfield House, Orton Centre,
Peterborough PE2 5UW
tel (01733) 237111 *fax* (01733) 465820
email sandy.leventon@emap.com
Editor Sandy Leventon
Monthly £2.80

Articles of good quality with strong trout or salmon
angling interest. Length: 400–2000 words,
accompanied if possible by colour transparencies or
good quality colour prints. Payment: by arrangement. Illustrations: line, colour transparencies and
prints,cartoons. Founded 1955.

Truck & Driver

Reed Business Information, Quadrant House,
The Quadrant, Sutton, Surrey SM2 5AS
tel 020-7652 3682 *fax* 020-7652 8988
Editor Dave Young
Monthly £2.10

News, articles on trucks, personalities and features
of interest to truck drivers. Words (on disk or
electronically) and picture packages preferred.
Length: approx. 2000 words. Illustrations: colour
transparencies and artwork, cartoons. Payment:
negotiable. Founded 1984.

Trucking

A & S Publishing, Messenger House,
35 St Michael's Square, Gloucester GL1 1HX
tel (01452) 317750 *fax* (01452) 415817

Editor Richard Simpson
Monthly £2.20

For truck drivers, owner–drivers and operators:
news, articles, features and technical advice. Length:
750–2500 words. Illustrations: mostly 35mm colour
transparencies. Payment: by negotiation. Founded
1983.

TV Quick

H. Bauer Publishing Ltd, Academic House,
24-28 Oval Road, London NW1 7DT
tel 020-7241 8000 *fax* 020-7241 8066
website www.bauer.co.uk
Editor Lori Miles
Weekly 65p

TV listings magazine featuring TV-related material.
Payment: by arrangement. Founded 1991.

TVTimes Magazine

IPC Media Ltd, 10th Floor, King's Reach Tower,
Stamford Street, London SE1 9LS
tel 020-7261 7000 *fax* 020-7261 7777
Editor Mike Hollingsworth
Weekly 70p

Features with an affinity to ITV, BBC1, BBC2,
Channels 4 and 5, satellite and radio personalities
and TV generally. Length: by arrangement. Photographs: commissioned only. Payment: by arrangement.

U magazine

Smurfit Communications, 2 Clanwilliam Court,
Lower Mount Street, Dublin 2, Republic of Ireland
tel (01) 240 5300 *fax* (01) 661 9757
email letters@umagazine.ie
Editor Fionnuala McCarthy
Monthly €3.43

Fashion and beauty magazine for 18–25 year-old
Irish women, with celebrity interviews, talent
profiles, real-life stories, sex and relationship
features, plus regular pages on the club scene,
movies, music and film. Also travel, interiors,
health, food, horoscopes. Material mostly
commissioned. Payment: varies. Founded 1978.

Ulster Business

Greer Publications, 5B Edgewater Business Park,
Edgewater Road, Belfast Harbour Estate,
Belfast BT3 9JQ
tel 028-9078 3223 *fax* 028-9078 3210
email russellcampbell@greenpublications.com
website www.ulsterbusiness.com
Editor Russell Campbell
Monthly £2.30

Feature-based magazine with general business-
related editorial for management level and above.
Specially commissions most material but will
consider unsolicited material. Welcomes ideas for
articles and features. Length: 800 words (articles),

1500 words (features). Payment: £60–£80 (articles), £120 (features). No illustrations required. Founded 1987.

Ulster Grocer

Greer Publications, 5B Edgewater Business Park, Belfast Harbour Estate, Belfast BT3 9JQ
tel 028-9078 3200 *fax* 028-9078 3210
email kathyj@writenow.prestel.co.uk
Editor Kathy Jensen
Monthly Controlled circulation

Topical features (1000–1500 words) on food/grocery retailing and exhibitions; news (200 words) with a Northern Ireland basis. All features commissioned; no speculative articles accepted. Illustrations: colour photos. Payment: features £275, product news £160. Founded 1972.

Under Five Contact

Pre-school Learning Alliance, 69 Kings Cross Road, London WC1X 9LL
tel 020-7833 0991 *fax* 020-7837 4942
email editor.u5c@pre-school.org.uk
Contact The Editor
10 p.a. £30 p.a.

Articles on the role of adults – especially parents/preschool workers – in young children's learning and development, including children from all cultures and those with special needs. Length: 750 words. Payment: £60 per article. Founded 1962.

The Universe

1st Floor, St James's Buildings, Oxford Street, Manchester M1 6FP
tel 0161-236 8856 *fax* 0161-236 8530
Editor Joe Kelly
Weekly 70p

Catholic Sunday newspaper. News stories, features and photos on all aspects of Catholic life required; also cartoons. MSS should not be submitted without sae. Payment: by arrangement. Founded 1860.

Vanity Fair

The Condé Nast Publications Ltd, Vogue House, Hanover Square, London W1S 1JU
tel 020-7499 9080 *fax* 020-7493 1962
website www.vanityfair.co.uk
London Editor Henry Porter
tel 020-7221 6228 *fax* 020-7221 6269
Monthly £3

Media, glamour and politics for grown-up readers. No unsolicited material. Payment: by arrangement. Illustrated.

The Vegan

The Vegan Society, Donald Watson House, 7 Battle Road, St Leonards-on-Sea, East Sussex TN37 7AA
tel (01424) 427393 *fax* (01424) 717064
email editor@vegansociety.com
website www.vegansociety.com
Editor Rick Savage
Quarterly £2.50

Articles on health, nutrition, cookery, vegan lifestyle, land use, animal rights. Length: approx. 1000 words. Payment: by arrangement. Illustrations: photos, cartoons, line drawings – foods, animals, livestock systems, crops, people, events; colour for cover. Founded 1944.

Venue

Venue Publishing, 64-65 North Road, Bristol BS6 5AQ
tel 0117-942 8491 *fax* 0117-942 0369
email editor@venue.co.uk
website www.venue.co.uk
Editor Dave Higgitt
Weekly £1.20

Listings magazine for Bristol and Bath combining comprehensive entertainment information with local features, profiles and interviews. Length: by agreement. Illustrations: colour. Payment: £8.50 per 100 words. Founded 1982.

Veterinary Review

John C. Alborough Ltd, Lion Lane, Needham Market, Suffolk IP6 8NT
tel (01449) 723800 *fax* (01449) 723801
email enquiries@jca.uk.com
Editor David Watson
Monthly £60 p.a.

News, articles – both topical and general – and product listings for veterinarians. Payment: negotiable.

Animal Health News
Editor Rachael Porter
Bi-monthly £30 p.a.

News, articles and product listings for the agricultural supply trade.

Viz Comic

PO Box 1PT, Newcastle upon Tyne NE99 1PT
fax 0191-241 4244
email viz@viz.co.uk
website www.viz.co.uk
Contact Editorial Cabinet
10 p.a. £1.95

Cartoons, spoof tabloid articles, spoof advertisements. Illustrations: half-tone, line, cartoons. Payment: £300 per page (cartoons). Founded 1979.

Vogue

Vogue House, Hanover Square, London W1S 1JU
tel 020-7499 9080 *fax* 020-7408 0559
website www.vogue.co.uk

Editor Alexandra Shulman
Monthly £3.20

Fashion, beauty, health, decorating, art, theatre, films, literature, music, travel, food and wine. Length: articles from 1000 words. Illustrated.

The Voice

Blue Star House, 234-244 Stockwell Road, London SW9 9UG
tel 020-7737 7377 *fax* 020-7274 8994
email newsdesk@the-voice.co.uk
Group Editor Deidre Forbes
Weekly 75p

News, general and arts features of interest to black readers. Illustrations: colour and b&w photos. Founded 1982.

woman2woman
Last Mon of each month

Supplement addressing the needs and aspirations of young Black Britons with a focus on a female readership.

Wanderlust

PO Box 1832, Windsor SL4 1YT
tel (01753) 620426
website www.wanderlust.co.uk
Editor Lyn Hughes
Bi-monthly £3.50

Features on independent, adventure and special-interest travel. Send sae or visit website for 'Guidelines for contributors'. Length: up to 2500 words. Illustrations: high-quality colour slides (send stocklist first). Payment: by arrangement. Founded 1993.

The War Cry

The Salvation Army, 101 Newington Causeway, London SE1 6BN
tel 020-7367 4900 *fax* 020-7367 4710
email warcry@salvationarmy.org.uk
website www.salvationarmy.org/warcry
Editor Major Nigel Bovey
Weekly 20p (£26 p.a.)

Voluntary contributions: Christian comment on contemporary issues, human interest stories of personal Christian faith; puzzles. Illustrations: line and photos, cartoons. Founded 1879.

Water Gardener

TRMG, Winchester Court, 1 Forum Place, Hatfield, Herts. AL10 0RN
tel (01707) 273999 *fax* (01707) 276555
email christina@trmg.co.uk
Editor Christina Guthrie
Monthly £2.95

Magazine for water gardeners of all levels of expertise. Covers ponds and water features of all sizes; also fish and wildlife. Will consider unsolicited

material. Welcomes ideas for articles and features. Length: 1000 words (articles), 1500 words (features) 200 words (news). Illustrations: transparencies and colour prints. Payment: varies.

Waterways World

Waterways World Ltd, 151 Station Street, Burton-on-Trent, Staffs. DE14 1BG
tel (01283) 742952 *fax* (01283) 742957
email hugh.potter@wwonline.co.uk
Editor Hugh Potter
Monthly £2.75

Feature articles on all aspects of inland waterways in Britain and abroad, including historical material; factual and technical articles preferred. No short stories or poetry. Send sae for 'Notes for WW Contributors'. Payment: £42 per 1000 words. Illustrations: colour transparencies or prints, line. Founded 1972.

Wedding and Home

IPC Magazines Ltd, King's Reach Tower, Stamford Street, London SE1 9LS
tel 020-7261 7471 *fax* 020-7261 7459
email weddingandhome@ipcmedia.com
Editor Kate Barlow, *Deputy Editor* Helen Salmon
Bi-monthly £4.10

Ideas and inspiration for modern brides. Fashion and beauty, information for grooms, real life weddings, planning advice, gift list ideas and honeymoon features. Unsolicited features not accepted. Founded 1985.

Weekend – see The Guardian in National newspapers UK and Ireland, page 3

The Weekly News

D.C. Thomson & Co. Ltd, Albert Square, Dundee DD1 9QJ
tel (01382) 223131
137 Chapel Street, Manchester M3 6AA
tel 0161-834 5122
144 Port Dundas Road, Glasgow G4 0HZ
tel 0141-332 9933
185 Fleet Street, London EC4A 2HS
tel 020-7400 1030
Send material to Rod Cameron, Deputy Editor
Weekly 52p

Real-life dramas of around 1000 words told in the first person. Non-fiction series with lively themes or about interesting people. Keynote throughout is strong human interest. General interest fiction. Illustrations: cartoons. Payment: on acceptance.

Weight Watchers Magazine

Bloomsbury House Ltd, 1 Cecil Court, 49-55 London Road, Enfield, Middlesex EN2 6DN
tel 020-8342 2222 *fax* 020-8342 2223

Editor Pat Kane
8 p.a. £1.95

Features: health, beauty, news, astrology; food-orientated articles; success stories. All material commissioned. Length: ½–3 pages. Illustrations: colour photos and cartoons. Payment: by arrangement.

What Camcorder

(formerly Video Camera)
Highbury WViP, 53-79 Highgate Road,
London NW5 1TW
tel 020-7331 1000 *fax* 020-7331 1242
email jake.williams@wvip.co.uk
Editor Jake Williams
Monthly £3.25

Technique articles aimed at the beginner on how to use camcorders and equipment tests of camcorders and accessories. Material mostly commissioned. Length: 1000–1800 words. Illustrations: colour photos, diagrams. Payment: £95 per 1000 words; £70 per page for illustrations. Founded 2000.

What Car?

Haymarket Motoring Magazines Ltd,
60 Waldegrave Road, Teddington,
Middlesex TW11 8LG
tel 020-8267 5688 *fax* 020-8267 5750
Editor Rob Aherne
Monthly £3.60

Road tests, buying guide, consumer stories and used car features. No unsolicited material. Illustrations: colour and b&w photos, line drawings. Payment: by negotiation. Founded 1973.

What Laptop & Handheld PC

Crimson Publishing, 14 Northfields,
London SW18 1UU
tel 020-8875 5600 *fax* 020-8875 5601
email letters@whatlaptop.co.uk
website www.whatlaptop.co.uk
Editor Ian Delaney
Monthly £2.99

Non-technical news, reviews and help for anyone who wants to buy or has bought a portable computer. Discuss ideas for features with the Editor in the first instance; welcomes ideas for features. Length: up to 1600 words. Payment: by arrangement. Founded 1999.

What's on TV

IPC Media Ltd, 10th Floor, King's Reach Tower,
Stamford Street, London SE1 9LS
tel 020-7261 7769 *fax* 020-7261 7739
Editor Mike Hollingsworth
Weekly 45p

Features on TV programmes and personalities. All material commissioned. Length: up to 500 words.

Illustrations: colour and b&w photos, cartoons. Payment: by agreement. Founded 1991.

WI Home and Country

104 New King's Road, London SW6 4LY
tel 020-7731 5777 *fax* 020-7736 4061
Editor Susan Seager
Monthly £1.54

Journal of the National Federation of Women's Institutes for England and Wales. Publishes material related to the Federation's and members' activities; also considers articles of general interest to women, particularly country women, e.g. craft, environment, humour, health, rural life stories, of 800–1200 words. Illustrations: colour and b&w photos and drawings, cartoons. Payment: by arrangement. Founded 1919.

Wine

Quest Magazines Ltd, Wilmington Publishing,
6-8 Underwood Street, London N1 7JQ
tel 020-7549 2572 *fax* 020-7549 8622
email wine@wilmington.co.uk
Editor Catharine Lowe
12 p.a. £3.30

Articles, features and news on new developments in wine and spirits; travelogues, tastings and profiles. Illustrations: colour. Payment: £200 per 1000 words. Founded 1983.

The Wisden Cricketer

The New Boathouse, 136-142 Bramley Road,
London W10 6SR
tel 020-7565 3080 *fax* 020-7565 3090
Editor Emma John, Stephen Fay
Monthly £3.25

Cricket articles of exceptional interest (unsolicited pieces seldom used). Length: up to 3000 words. Payment: by arrangement. Illustrations: half-tone, colour.

Woman

IPC Media, King's Reach Tower, Stamford Street,
London SE1 9LS
tel 020-7261 5000 *fax* 020-7261 5997
Editor Carole Russell
Weekly 72p

Human interest stories and practical articles of varying length on all subjects of interest to women. Payment: by arrangement. Illustrations: colour transparencies and photos. Founded 1937.

Woman Alive

(formerly Christian Woman)
Christian Media Centre Ltd, Garcia Estate,
Canterbury Road, Worthing,
West Sussex BN13 1EH
tel (01903) 821082 *fax* (01903) 821081

email womanalive@christianmedia.org.uk
Editor Jackie Stead
Monthly £2

Aimed at women aged 25 upwards. Celebrity interviews, topical features, Christian issues, 'Day in the life of' profiles of women in interesting occupations, Christian testimonies, fashion, beauty, health, crafts. Unsolicited material should include colour slides or photos. Length: 'Day in the life of'/testimonies 750 words, interviews/features 1300 words. Payment: £72 per 1000 words published. Founded 1982.

Woman and Home
(incorporating Living)
IPC Magazines Ltd, King's Reach Tower, Stamford Street, London SE1 9LS
tel 020-7261 5000 *fax* 020-7261 7346
Acting Editor Sue James
Monthly £2.60

Centres on the personal and home interests of the lively minded mature, modern woman. Articles dealing with fashion, beauty, leisure pursuits, gardening, home style; features on topical issues, people and places. Fiction: complete stories from 3000–4500 words in length. Illustrations: commissioned colour photos and sketches. Please note: non-commissioned work is rarely accepted and regrettably cannot be returned. Founded 1926.

The Woman Writer
c/o Jenny Lisney, 4 Larch Way, Haywards Heath, West Sussex RH16 3TY
email swwriters@aol.com
website www.swwj.co.uk
Editor Jenny Lisney
6 p.a. Free to members

Periodical of the Society of Women Writers and Journalists. See under Societies section for further information. Founded 1894.

Woman's Own
IPC Connect Ltd, King's Reach Tower, Stamford Street, London SE1 9LS
tel 020-7261 5000
Editor Elsa McAlonan
Weekly 72p

Modern women's magazine aimed at the 20–35 age group. No unsolicited features or fiction. Illustrations: colour and b&w: interior decorating and furnishing, fashion. Address work to relevant department editor. Payment: by arrangement.

Woman's Way
Smurfit Communications, 2 Clanwilliam Court, Lower Mount Street, Dublin 2, Republic of Ireland
tel (01) 240 5300 *fax* (01) 662 2979
email ltaylor@smurfit-comms.ie

Editor Lucy Taylor
Weekly €1.30

Human interest, personality interviews, features on fashion, beauty, celebrities and investigations, short stories. Length: 1800 words. Payment: approx. €65–€130. Founded 1963.

Woman's Weekly
IPC Media Ltd, King's Reach Tower, Stamford Street, London SE1 9LS
tel (0870) 4445000 *fax* 020-7261 6322
Editor Gilly Sinclair
Weekly 68p

Lively, family-interest magazine. One serial, averaging 4000 words each instalment, of general emotional interest, and several short stories of 1000–2500 words of general emotional interest. Celebrity and strong human interest features; also inspirational and entertaining personal stories. Payment: by arrangement. Illustrations: full colour fiction illustrations, small sketches and photos. Founded 1911.

Woman's Weekly Fiction Special
IPC Media Ltd, King's Reach, Stamford Street, London SE1 9LS
tel (0870) 4445000 *fax* 020-7261 6322
Editor Olwen Rice
Bi-monthly £1.40

At least 25 stories each issue of 1000–10,000 words of varied emotional interest, including romance, humour and mystery. Payment: by arrangement. Illustrations: full colour. Founded 1998.

Women's Health
WVIP, 53-79 Highgate Road, London NW5 1TW
tel 020-7331 1000 *fax* 020-7331 1108
email tracey.smith@highburywv.com
Editor Tracey Smith
Monthly £2.60

Lifestyle magazine for women covering a wide range of issues from fashion and fitness to health and beauty, including alternative therapies and food. Length: 1200–1800 words. Payment: by negotiation. Founded 1998.

The Woodworker
Nexus Special Interests Ltd, Nexus House, Azalea Drive, Swanley, Kent BR8 8HU
tel (01322) 660070
Editor Mark Ramuz
Monthly £2.65

For the craft and professional woodworker. Practical illustrated articles on cabinet work, carpentry, wood polishing, wood turning, wood carving, rural crafts, craft history, antique and period furniture; also wooden toys and models, musical instruments; timber procurement, conditioning, seasoning; tool, machinery and equipment reviews. Payment: by arrangement. Illustrations: line drawings and photos.

The Word

Divine Word Missionaries, 3 Pembroke Road, Dublin 4, Republic of Ireland
tel/fax (01) 6606646
email editor@theword.ie
Editor Garry O'Sullivan
Monthly €1

General interest magazine with religious emphasis. Illustrated articles up to 2000 words and good picture features. Payment: by arrangement. Illustrations: photos and large colour transparencies. Founded 1936.

Workbox Magazine

Ebony Media Ltd, PO Box 25, Liskeard, Cornwall PL14 6XX
tel (01579) 340100 *fax* (01579) 340400
email workbox@ebony.co.uk
website www.ebony.co.uk/workbox
Editor Victor Briggs
Bi-monthly £2.25

Features, of any length, on all aspects of needlecrafts. No 'how-to' articles. Send sae with enquiries and submissions. Illustrations: good colour transparencies. Payment: by agreement. Founded 1984.

World Fishing

Nexus Media Ltd, Nexus House, Azalea Drive, Swanley, Kent BR8 8HU
tel (01322) 667633 *fax* (01322) 616324
Editor Mark Say
Monthly £49 p.a.

International journal of commercial fishing. Technical and management emphasis on catching, processing and marketing of fish and related products; fishery operations and vessels covered worldwide. Length: 500–1500 words. Payment: by arrangement. Illustrations: photos and diagrams for litho reproduction. Founded 1952.

The World of Interiors

The Condé Nast Publications Ltd, Vogue House, Hanover Square, London W1S 1JU
tel 020-7499 9080 *fax* 020-7493 4013
email interiors@condenast.co.uk
website www.worldofinteriors.co.uk
Editor Rupert Thomas
Monthly £3.60

All material commissioned: send synopsis/visual reference for article ideas. Length: 1000–1500 words. Illustrations: colour photos. Payment: £500 per 1000 words; photos £125 per page. Founded 1981.

World Soccer

IPC Media Ltd, King's Reach Tower, Stamford Street, London SE1 9LS
tel 020-7261 5737 *fax* 020-7261 7474
Editor Gavin Hamilton
Monthly £2.90

Articles, features, news concerning football, its personalities and worldwide development. Length: 600–2000 words. Payment: by arrangement. Founded 1960.

The World Today

The Royal Institute of International Affairs, Chatham House, 10 St James's Square, London SW1Y 4LE
tel 020-7957 5712 *fax* 020-7957 5710
email wt@riia.org
website www.theworldtoday.org
Editor Graham Walker, *Send material to* Michelle Mannion, Assistant Editor
Monthly £2.50

Analysis of international issues and current events by journalists, diplomats, politicians and academics. Length: 1400–2300 words. Payment: nominal. Founded 1945.

World's Children

Save the Children, 17 Grove Lane, London SE5 8RD
tel 020-7703 5400 *fax* 020-7708 2508
email publications@scfuk.org.uk
website www.savethechildren.org.uk
Contact Frances Ellery (Head of Publications)
Quarterly Sent free to regular donors

Magazine of Save the Children. Articles on child welfare and rights, related to Save the Children's work overseas and in the UK. No unsolicited features. Illustrations: colour and b&w photos. Founded 1920.

Writers' Forum

(incorporating World Wide Writers)
Writers' International Ltd, PO Box 3229, Bournemouth BH1 1ZS
website www.writers-forum.com
Publisher John Jenkins
10 p.a. £3 (£28 p.a., £40 Europe)

Welcomes articles on any aspect of the craft and business of writing. Length: 800–2000 words. Payment: by arrangement. Poetry and short story competitions in each issue. Founded 1993.

Writers' News

PO Box 168, Wellington Street, Leeds LS1 1RF
tel 0113-238 8333 *fax* 0113-238 8330
Editor Derek Hudson
Monthly £44.90 p.a. (£39.90 p.a. CC/DD)

News, competitions and articles on all aspects of

writing. Length: 400–1500 words. Illustrations: colour, line, half-tone. Payment: by arrangement. Founded 1989.

Writing Magazine

PO Box 168, Wellington Street, Leeds LS1 1RF
tel 0113-238 8333 *fax* 0113-238 8330
Editor Derek Hudson
Bi-monthly £3 (free to *Writers' News* subscribers)

Articles on all aspects of writing. Length: 400–1500 words. Illustrations: full colour, line, half-tone. Payment: by arrangement. Founded 1992.

Yachting Monthly

IPC Media Ltd, Room 2215, King's Reach Tower, Stamford Street, London SE1 9LS
tel 020-7261 6040 *fax* 020-7261 7555
Editor Paul Gelder
Monthly £3.30

Articles on all aspects of seamanship, navigation, the handling of sailing craft, and their design, construction and equipment. Well-written narrative accounts of cruises in yachts. Length: up to 2250 words (articles), up to 2500 words (narratives). Illustrations: colour transparencies and prints, cartoons. Payment: quoted on acceptance. Founded 1906.

Yachting World

IPC Media Ltd, King's Reach Tower, Stamford Street, London SE1 9LS
tel 020-7261 6800 *fax* 020-7261 6818
email yachting_world@ipc.media.com
website www.yachting-world.com
Editor Andrew Bray
Monthly £3.50

Practical articles of an original nature, dealing with sailing and boats. Length: 1500–2000 words. Payment: varies. Illustrations: colour transparencies, drawings, cartoons. Founded 1894.

Yachts and Yachting

196 Eastern Esplanade, Southend-on-Sea, Essex SS1 3AB
tel (01702) 582245 *fax* (01702) 588434
email editorial@yachtsandyachting.com
website www.yachtsandyachting.com
Editor Gael Pawson
Fortnightly £3.20

Short articles which should be technically correct. Payment: by arrangement. Illustrations: line, half-tone, colour. Founded 1947.

Yorkshire Ridings Magazine

33 Beverley Road, Driffield, Yorkshire YO25 6SD
tel/fax (01377) 253232
Editor Winston Halstead
Bi-monthly £1.40

Articles exclusively about people, life and character of the 3 Ridings of Yorkshire. Length: up to 1000 words. Payment: approx. £35–£40 per published page. Illustrations: colour, b&w photos; prints preferred. Founded 1964.

You – see Mail on Sunday in National newspapers UK and Ireland, page 3

You & Your Wedding

NatMag Specialist Media (AIM) Ltd, National Magazine House, 72 Broadwick Street, London W1F 9EP
tel 020-7439 5000 *fax* 020-7439 2985
website www.youandyourwedding.co.uk
Editor Carole Hamilton, *Send material to* Debbie Codd, Associate Editor
Bi-monthly £4.25

Articles, features and news covering all aspects of planning a wedding. Submit ideas in writing only. Illustrations: colour. Payment: £300 per 1000 words.

Young People Now

National Youth Agency, 17-23 Albion Street, Leicester LE1 6GD
tel 0116-285 3760 *fax* 0116-285 3775
email ypn@nya.org.uk
website www.nya.org.uk
Editor Tim Burke
Monthly £2 (£22.80 p.a.)

Informative articles, highlighting issues of concern to all those who work with young people, including youth workers, probation and social services, Connexions Service, teachers and volunteers. Guidelines for contributors available on request. Founded 1989.

Young Writer

Glebe House, Weobley, Herefordshire HR4 8SD
tel/fax (01544) 318901
email editor@youngwriter.org
website www.youngwriter.org
Editor Kate Jones
3 p.a. £2.75 (£7.50 for 3 issues)

Specialist magazine for young writers under 18 years: ideas for them and writing by them. Includes interviews by children with famous writers, fiction and non-fiction pieces, poetry; also explores words and grammar, issues related to writing (e.g. dyslexia), plus competitions with prizes. Length: 750 or 1500 words (features), up to 400 words (news), 750 words (short stories – unless specified otherwise in a competition), poetry of any length. Illustrations: colour – drawings by children, snapshots to accompany features. Payment: most children's material is published without payment; £25–£100 (features); £15 (cover cartoon). Founded 1995.

Your Cat Magazine

BPG (Stamford) Ltd, Roebuck House,
33 Broad Street, Stamford, Lincs. PE9 1RB
tel (01780) 766199 *fax* (01780) 766416
email suebpgroup@talk21.com
Editor Sue Parslow
Monthly £2.65

Practical advice on the care of cats and kittens,
general interest items and news on cats, and true life
tales and fiction. Length: 800–1500 words (articles),
200–300 (news), up to 1000 (short stories).
Illustrations: colour transparencies and prints.
Payment: £80 per 1000 words. Founded 1994.

Your Dog Magazine

BPG (Stamford) Ltd, Roebuck House,
 33 Broad Street, Stamford, Lincs. PE9 1RB
tel (01780) 766199 *fax* (01780) 766416
email sarahbpgroup@talk21.com
Editor Sarah Wright
Monthly £2.95

Articles and information of interest to dog lovers;
features on all aspects of pet dogs. Length: approx.
1500 words. Illustrations: colour transparencies,
prints and line drawings. Payment: £80 per 1000
words. Founded 1994.

Your Horse

Emap Active, Bretton Court, Bretton,
Peterborough PE3 8DZ
tel (01733) 264666 *fax* (01733) 465100
email amanda.stevenson@emap.com
Editor Amanda Stevenson
Every 4 weeks £2.75

Practical horse care and riding advice for the leisure
rider and horse owner. Send feature ideas with
examples of previous published writing. Specially
commissions most material. Welcomes ideas for
articles and features. Length: 1500 words. Payment:
£120per 1000 words.

Yours

EMAP Esprit Ltd, Bretton Court,
Peterborough PE3 8DZ
tel (01733) 264666 *fax* (01733) 465353
Editor Valery McConnell
Monthly £1.15

Features and news about and/or of interest to the
over-60s age group, including nostalgia and short
stories. Study of magazine essential; approach in
writing in first instance. Length: articles up to 1000
words, short stories up to 1800 words. Illustrations:
preferably colour transparencies/prints but will
consider good b&w prints/line drawings, cartoons.
Payment: at the Editor's discretion or by agreement.
Founded 1973.

Zest

National Magazine House, 72 Broadwick Street,
London W1F 9EP
tel 020-7439 5000 *fax* 020-7312 3750
email zest.mail@natmags.co.uk
Editor Alison Pylkkanen, *Send material to* Susie
Whalley, Feature Editor
Monthly £2.80

Health and beauty magazine. Commissioned
material only: health, fitness and beauty, features,
news and shorts. Length: 50–2000 words.
Illustrations: colour and b&w photos and line.
Payment: by arrangement. Founded 1994.

Newspapers and magazines overseas

Listings are given for newspapers and magazines in Australia (below), Canada (page 102), New Zealand (page 105) and South Africa (page 107). For information on submitting material to the USA, see page 109. Newspapers are listed under the towns in which they are published.

AUSTRALIA

(Adelaide) Advertiser
121 King William Street, Adelaide, SA 5000
tel (08) 8206 2000 *fax* (08) 8206 3669
London office PO Box 481, 1 Virginia Street, London E1 9BD
tel 020-7702 1355 *fax* 020-7702 1384
Editor Mel Mansell
Daily Mon–Fri 90c, Sat $1.30

Descriptive and news background material, 400–800 words, preferably with pictures; also cartoons. Founded 1858.

(Adelaide) Sunday Mail
121 King William Street, Adelaide, SA 5000
postal address GPO Box 339, Adelaide, SA 5001
tel (08) 8206 2000 *fax* (08) 8206 3646
website www.sundaymail.com.au
Editor Karen Porter
Sun $1.50

Founded 1912.

AQ – Journal of Contemporary Analysis
Australian Institute of Political Science,
PO Box 145, Balmain, NSW 2041
tel (02) 9810 5642 *fax* (02) 9810 2406
website www.aips.net.au
6 p.a. $60.50 p.a. individuals/schools, $104.50 p.a. organisations ($120 overseas)

Peer-reviewed articles for the informed non-specialist on politics, law, economics, social issues, etc. Length: 3500 words preferred. Payment: none. Founded 1929.

Art and Australia
Fine Art Publishing Pty Ltd, 42 Chandos Street, St Leonards, NSW 2065
tel (02) 9966 8400 *fax* (02) 9966 0355
email info@finearts.com.au
website www.artaustralia.com
Editor Laura Murray Cree
Quarterly $17.50, $108 p.a.

Articles with a contemporary perspective on Australia's traditional and current art, and on international art of Australian relevance, plus exhibition and book reviews. Length: 2000–3000 words (articles), 600–1200 words (reviews).

Payment: $250 per 1000 words. Colour transparencies. Founded 1916 as *Art in Australia*.

Art Monthly Australia
GPO Box 804, Canberra, ACT 2601
tel (02) 6125 3988 *fax* (02) 6125 9794
email art.monthly@anu.edu.au
website www.artmonthly.org.au
Editor Deborah Clark
10 p.a. March–Dec $6.00

Contemporary visual arts: reviews, commentary, news and book reviews. Specially commissions most material but will consider unsolicited material. Welcomes ideas for articles and features. Length: negotiable. Payment: $200 per 1000 words. Founded 1987.

Australian Bookseller & Publisher
Thorpe-Bowker, Building C3, 85 Turner Street, Port Melbourne, Victoria 3207
tel (03) 8645 0300 *fax* (03) 8645 0333
email bookseller.publisher@thorpe.com.au
website www.thorpe.com.au
Editor Joanne Shiells
Monthly $90 p.a. ($110 p.a. NZ/Asia; $150 p.a. USA/Canada; $140 p.a. UK/Europe)

Founded 1921.

Australian Camera
Horwitz Publications Pty Ltd, 55 Chandos Street, St Leonards, NSW 2065
tel (02) 9901 6100 *fax* (02) 9901 6198
email paulb@horwitz.com.au
Editor Paul Burrows
Monthly $5.95

Magazine for amateur photographers and digital imaging enthusiasts covering techniques, test reports, new products. Considers unsolicited material. Welcomes ideas for articles and features. Length: 750–1500 words (features/articles). Illustrations: colour prints and transparencies. Payment: $300–$500. Founded 1979.

The Australian Financial Review
GPO Box 506, Sydney, NSW 2001
tel (02) 9282 2512 *fax* (02) 9282 3137
Editor Glenn Burge
London office 1 Bath Street, London EC1V 9LB
tel 020-7688 2777 *fax* 020-7688 3499

New York office Suite 1720, 317 Madison Avenue,
New York, NY 10017
tel 212-398-9494
Daily Mon–Fri $2.20

Investment business and economic news and
reviews; government and politics, production,
banking, commercial, and Stock Exchange statistics;
company analysis. General features in Friday
Weekend Review supplement.

Australian Flying

Yaffa Publishing Group, 17-21 Bellevue Street,
Surry Hills, NSW 2010
tel (02) 9281 2333 *fax* (02) 9281 2750
email shelleyross@yaffa.com.au
Editor Shelley Ross
London office 2 Milford Road, London W13 9HZ
tel 020-8579 4836
Contact Robert Logan
6 p.a. $5.95

Covers the Australian aviation industry, from light
aircraft to airliners. Payment: by arrangement.

Australian Geographic

PO Box 321, Terrey Hills, NSW 2084
tel (02) 9473 6777 *fax* (02) 9473 6701
website www.australiangeographic.com.au
Managing Editor Terri Cowley
Quarterly $49.50 p.a.

Articles and features about Australia, particularly
life, technology and wildlife in remote parts of the
country. Material mostly commissioned. Length:
articles, 300–800 words, features, 2000–3000 words.
Illustrations: all commissioned. Payment: from $500
per 1000 words; illustrations by negotiation.
Founded 1986.

Australian Home Beautiful

Private Bag 9700, North Sydney, NSW 2059
tel (02) 9464 3218 *fax* (02) 9464 3263
email homebeaut@pacpubs.com.au
Editor Andrea Jones
Monthly $5.90

Interior decoration, furnishing, gardening, cookery,
etc. Unsolicited MSS not accepted. Founded 1925.

Australian House and Garden

54 Park Street, Sydney, NSW 1028
postal address GPO Box 4088, Sydney, NSW 1028
tel (02) 9282 8456 *fax* (02) 9267 4912
email h@ampcaacp.com.au
website www.acp.com.au
Editor Anny Friis
Monthly $5.95

Factual articles dealing with interior decorating,
home design, gardening, wine, food. Preliminary
letter essential. Payment: by arrangement. Illustrations: line, half-tone, colour. Founded 1948.

Australian Journal of International Affairs

Department of International Relations,
RSPAS, Australian National University,
Canberra, ACT 0200
tel (06) 249 2169 *fax* (06) 279 8010
Editor Dr Ramesh Thakur, Vice-Rector (Peace &
Governance), United Nations University,
53-70 Jingumae 5-chome, Shibuya-ku,
Tokyo 150-8925, Japan
3 p.a. Personal rate A$64 p.a., institutions A$132
p.a. (Australia); other rates on application

Scholarly articles on international affairs. Length:
3000–7000 words. Payment: none.

Australian Journal of Politics and History

School of Political Science and International Studies
and the Department of History, University of
Queensland, St Lucia, Queensland 4067
tel (07) 3365 3163 *fax* (07) 3365 1388
email i.ward@mailbox.uq.edu.au
Editor Ian Ward and Andrew Bonnell
4 p.a. $66/£38 p.a. individuals; $144/£110
institutions

Australian, European, Asian, Pacific and international articles. Special feature: regular surveys of
Australian Foreign Policy and State and Commonwealth politics. Length: 8000 words max. Illustrations: line, only when necessary. Payment: none.

Australian Photography

Yaffa Publishing Group, 17-21 Bellevue Street,
Surry Hills, NSW 2010
tel (02) 9281 2333 *fax* (02) 9281 2750
email robertkeeley@yaffa.com.au
Editor Robert Keeley
London office 2 Milford Road, London W13 9HZ
tel 020-8579 4836
Contact Robert Logan
Monthly $5.95

Illustrated articles: picture-taking techniques,
technical. Length: 1200–2500 words with colour
and/or b&w prints or slides. Payment: $80 per page.
Founded 1950.

Australian Powerboat

Yaffa Publishing Group, GPO Box 606, Sydney,
NSW 2001
tel (02) 9281 2333 *fax* (02) 9281 2750
Editor Graham Lloyd
London office 2 Milford Road, London W13 9HZ
tel 020-8579 4836
Contact Robert Logan
Bi-monthly $5.20

Articles and news on boats and boating, racing,
water skiing and products. Length: 1500 words
(articles), 200 words (news). Illustrations: colour
(transparencies preferred). Payment: $100 per 1000
words; from $30. Founded 1976.

The Australian Women's Weekly
Australian Consolidated Press Ltd, 54 Park Street,
Sydney, NSW 1028
postal address GPO Box 4178, Sydney, NSW 1028
tel (02) 9282 8000 *fax* (02) 9267 4459
email dthomas@acp.com.au
Editor Deborah Thomas
Monthly $5.20

Fiction and features. Length: fiction 1000–5000
words; features 1000–4000 words plus colour or
b&w photos. Payment: according to length and
merit. Fiction illustrations: sketches by own artists
and freelances.

The Big Issue Australia
GPO Box 4911VV, Melbourne, Victoria 3001
tel (03) 9663 4522 *fax* (03) 9663 4252
email editor@bigissue.org.au
Editor Rachel Antony
Fortnightly $3

Profiles and features of general interest and on
social issues, plus international and local news, arts
reviews. No fiction. Length: 1000–2500 words
(features), up to 900 words (news), 250 words
(reviews). Payment: 15c per word (features and
news), $30 (reviews). Colour and b&w cartoons
(approx. $100); photos $150–$200. Founded 1996.

(Brisbane) The Courier-Mail
Queensland Newspapers Pty Ltd, Campbell Street,
Bowen Hills, Brisbane, Queensland 4006
tel (07) 3666 8000 *fax* (07) 3666 6696
email cmletters@qnp.newsltd.com.au
website www.news.com.au
Editor-in-Chief C. Mitchell
Daily $1

(Brisbane) The Sunday Mail
Queensland Newspapers Pty Ltd, PO Box 130,
Campbell Street, Bowen Hills, Brisbane,
Queensland 4006
tel 300 304 020 *fax* (07) 3666 6787
email smletters@qnp.newsltd.com.au
Editor Michael Prain
Sun $1.60

Anything of general interest. Length: up to 1500
words. Illustrations: line, photos, b&w and colour,
cartoons. Rejected MSS returned if postage enclosed.

Dance Australia
Yaffa Publishing Group, Box 606, GPO Sydney,
NSW 2001
tel (02) 9281 2333 *fax* (02) 9281 2750
email dance@yaffa.com.au
Editor Karen van Ulzen
London office 2 Milford Road, London W13 9HZ
tel 020-8579 4836
Contact Robert Logan

Bi-monthly $5.50

Articles and features on all aspects of dance in
Australia. Material mostly commissioned, but will
consider unsolicited contributions. Illustrations:
b&w photos, line drawings, cartoons. Payment:
$200 per 1000 words; illustrations by negotiation.
Founded 1980.

Dolly
GPO Box 5201, Sydney, NSW 2001
tel (02) 9282 8437 *fax* (02) 9267 4911
website www.ninemsn.com.au/dolly
Editor Virginia Knight
Monthly $4.60

Features on teen fashion, health and beauty,
personalities, music, social issues and how to cope
with growing up, etc. Length: not less than 1000
words. Illustrations: colour, b&w, line, cartoons.
Payment: by arrangement. Founded 1970.

EA Today Magazine
PO Box 199, Alexandria, NSW 1435
tel (02) 9353 0620 *fax* (02) 9353 0613
email electaus@fpc.com.au
website www.electronicsaustralia.com.au
Editor Graham Cattley
Monthly $6.95

Articles on technical TV and radio, hi-fi, popular
electronics. Length: up to 2000 words. Payment: by
arrangement. Illustrations: line, half-tone, cartoons.

Geo Australasia
Hallmark Editions, PO Box 84, Hampton,
Victoria 3188
tel (03) 9555 7377 *fax* (03) 9555 7599
email hallmark@halledit.com.au
website www.geo.com.au
Editor Peter Stirling
Bi-monthly $7.95 ($55 p.a. surface mail, $85 p.a.
airmail)

Non-fiction articles on wildlife, adventure, culture
and lifestyles, natural history and the environment
in Australia, New Zealand, the Pacific and SE Asia.
Length: 1500–3000 words. Payment: $600–$1500 by
arrangement. Illustrations: photos, colour transparencies. Founded 1978.

Harper's Bazaar
ACP Publishing Pty Ltd, 54 Park Street, Sydney,
NSW 2000
tel (02) 9282 8703 *fax* (02) 9267 4456
email bazaar@acp.com.au
Editor Karin Upton Baker
10 p.a. $6.50

Fashion, health and beauty, celebrity news, plus
features. Length: 3000 words. Illustrations: colour
and b&w photos. Payment: $500 per 1000 words;
$150. Founded 1998.

HQ Magazine
35-51 Mitchell Street, McMahons Point, NSW 2060
tel (02) 9464 2604 *fax* (02) 9464 3504
email hq@pacpubs.com.au
Editor Ms Alex Craig
Bi-monthly $7.95

General interest features and profiles for a literate readership. Length: 1500–5000 words. Illustrations: colour and b&w photos. Payment: by negotiation. Founded 1989.

(Launceston) Examiner
Box 99, PO Launceston, Tasmania 7250
tel (03) 633 67111 *fax* (03) 633 47328
Editor Rod Scott
Daily $1

Accepts freelance material. Payment: by arrangement.

Meanjin
Meanjin Company Ltd, 131 Barry Street, Carlton, Victoria 3054
tel (03) 8344 6950 *fax* (03) 9347 2550
email meanjin@unimelb.edu.au
website www.meanjin.unimelb.edu.au
Editor Dr Ian Britain
Quarterly $19.95

Cultural commentary, fiction, poetry, essays and discussion of contemporary issues, e.g. biography, drugs, travel. See website for submission guidelines. Payment: $50 per poetry item, min. $100 prose. Founded 1941.

(Melbourne) Age
The Age Company Ltd, 250 Spencer Street, Melbourne, Victoria 3000
tel (03) 9600 4211 *fax* (03) 9601 2412
London office 1 Bath Street, London EC1V 9LB
tel 020-7688 2777 *fax* 020-7688 3499
Editor-in-Chief Michael Gawenda, *Deputy Editor* Simon Mann
Daily Mon–Fri $1.10, Sat $1.90, Sun $1.50

Independent liberal morning daily; room occasionally for outside matter. *Good Weekend* and *Sunday Life* (illustrated weekend magazines); *Insight*; *A2* (includes literary reviews). Accepts occasional freelance material.

(Melbourne) Herald Sun
HWT Tower, 40 City Road, Southbank, Victoria 3006
tel (03) 9292 1686 *fax* (03) 9292 2112
Editor Peter Blunden
Send material to Darrell Richardson, Syndications Manager
Daily Mon–Fri $1, Sat $1.20, Sun $1.50

Accepts freelance articles, preferably with illustrations. Length: up to 750 words. Illustrations: half-tone, line, cartoons. Payment: on merit.

(Melbourne) Sunday Herald Sun
HWT Tower, 40 City Road, Southbank, Victoria 3006
tel (03) 9292 2000 *fax* (03) 9292 2080
Editor Alan Howe
Weekly $1.50

Accepts freelance articles, preferably with illustrations. Length: up to 2000 words. Illustrations: colour. Payment: on merit.

New Woman
Level 6, 187 Thomas Street, Haymarket, NSW 2000
tel (02) 9581 9400 *fax* (02) 9211 9540
Editor Sue Wheeler
Monthly $5.95

Irreverent and humorous style of magazine for the single, professional woman aged 25–35. Includes celebrity gossip, fashion, beauty, sex and relationships, and entertainment reviews. Founded 1989.

NW Magazine
54 Park Street, Sydney, NSW 2000
tel (02) 9282 8285 *fax* (02) 9264 6005
Editor Louisa Hatfield
Weekly $3.50

News and features on celebrities, food, new products, fashion and astrology. Illustrated. Payment: by negotiation. Founded 1993.

Overland
PO Box 14146, Melbourne, Victoria 8001
tel (03) 9688 4163 *fax* (03) 9687 7614
email overland@vu.edu.au
Editors Nathan Hollier, Kath Wilson
Quarterly $42 p.a.

Literary and cultural. Australian material preferred. Payment: by arrangement. Illustrations: line, half-tone, cartoons.

People Magazine
GPO Box 2860, Sydney, NSW 2000
tel (02) 9288 9648 *fax* (02) 9283 6179
Editor Tom Foster
Weekly $3.30

National weekly news-pictorial. Mainly celebrity stories. Photos depicting exciting happenings, glamour, show business, unusual occupations, rites, customs. Payment: $300 per page, text and photos.

(Perth) The Sunday Times
34-40 Stirling Street, Perth, Western Australia 6000
tel (08) 9326 8476 *fax* (08) 9226 8316
Editor Brett McCarthy
Sun $1.30

Topical articles to 800 words. Payment: on acceptance. Founded 1897.

(Perth) The West Australian

50 Hasler Road, Osborne Park,
Western Australia 6017
tel (08) 9482 3111 *fax* (08) 9482 3452
website www.thewest.com.au
Editor Brian Rogers
Daily Mon–Fri 88c, Sat $1.60

Articles and sketches about people and events in
Australia and abroad. Length: 300–700 words.
Payment: Award rates or better. Illustrations: line,
half-tone. Founded 1833.

Quadrant

437 Darling Street, Balmain, NSW 2041
postal address PO Box 82, Balmain, NSW 2041
tel (02) 9818 1155 *fax* (02) 9818 1422
email quadrnt@ozemail.com.au
Editor P.P. McGuinness
Literary Editor Les Murray
Monthly $6.50

Articles, short stories, verse, etc. Prose length: 2000–
5000 words. Payment: min. $90 articles/stories, $60
reviews, $40 poems; illustrations by arrangement.

Reader's Digest (Australia)

PO Box 4353, Sydney, NSW 2001
tel (02) 9690 6111 *fax* (02) 9690 6211
Editor-in-Chief Thomas Moore
Monthly $5.79 (inc. GST)

Articles on Australian subjects by commission only.
No unsolicited MSS accepted. Length: 2500–5000
words. Payment: up to $6000 per article; brief filler
paragraphs, $50–$250. Illustrations: half-tone,
colour.

Rock

Wild Publications Pty Ltd, PO Box 415, Prahran,
Victoria 3181
tel (03) 9826 8482 *fax* (03) 9826 3787
email rock@wild.com.au
website www.rock.com.au
Editor Chris Baxter
Quarterly $8.99

Australian rockclimbing and mountaineering
articles, features and news. Length: 2000 words
(articles/features), 200 words (news). Illustrations:
colour transparencies. Payment: $85 per page
(words and pictures). Founded 1978.

Scuba Diver

Yaffa Publishing Group, 17-21 Bellevue Street,
Surry Hills, NSW 2010
tel (02) 9281 2333 *fax* (02) 9281 2750
email yaffa@flex.com.au
Editor Sue Crowe
London office 2 Milford Road, London W13 9HZ
tel 020-8579 4836
Contact Robert Logan

Bi-monthly $6.50

News, features, articles and short stories on scuba
diving. Length: 1500 words (articles/features),
300–800 words (news), 800–1000 words (short stories).
Illustrations: colour. Payment: $70 per page,
negotiable (words and pictures).

The Sun-Herald

GPO Box 506, Sydney, NSW 2001
tel (02) 9282 2822 *fax* (02) 9282 2151
London office John Fairfax (UK) Ltd, 1 Bath Street,
London EC1V 9LB
tel 020-7688 2777 *fax* 020-7688 3499
Editor Philip McLean
Weekly $1.50

Topical articles to 1000 words; news plus sections
on current affairs, entertainment, finance, sport and
travel. Payment: by arrangement.

(Sydney) The Daily Telegraph

News Ltd, 2 Holt Street, Surry Hills, NSW 2010
tel (02) 9288 3000 *fax* (02) 9288 3311
Editor-in-Chief Col Allan
Daily Mon–Fri 90c, Sat $1.20

Modern feature articles and series of Australian or
world interest. Length: 1000–2000 words. Payment:
according to merit/length.

The Sydney Morning Herald

PO Box 506, Sydney, NSW 2001
tel (02) 9282 2858
London office 1 Bath Street, London EC1V 9LB
tel 020-7688 2777 *fax* 020-7688 3499
Editor Phil Scott
Daily $1.10

Saturday edition has pages of literary criticism and
also magazine articles, plus glossy colour magazine.
Topical articles 600–4000 words. Payment: varies,
but minimum $100 per 1000 words. Illustrations:
all types. Founded 1831.

(Sydney) The Sunday Telegraph

News Ltd, 2 Holt Street, Surry Hills, Sydney,
NSW 2010
tel (02) 9288 3000 *fax* (02) 9288 3311
Editor Jeni Cooper
Daily $1.50

News and features. Illustrations: transparencies.
Payment: varies. Founded 1935.

Vive

125-127 Little Eveleigh Street, Redfern,
NSW 2016
tel (02) 9318 0500 *fax* (02) 9318 1140
email vive@pol.net.au
Editor Angie Buttrose
Bi-monthly $5.95

A business/lifestyle publication aimed at successful executive women. Content includes business profiles, career-related features, travel, food, beauty, working mothers. Specially commissions most material. Welcomes ideas for articles and features. Do not send unsolicited material. Length: 1500–2000 words (articles/features). Payment: 65c per word. Illustrations: transparencies, colour and b&w prints and artwork; all commissioned. Founded 1996.

Vogue Australia

170 Pacific Highway, Greenwich, NSW 2065
postal address Locked Bag 2550, Crows Nest, NSW 1585
tel (02) 9964 3817 *fax* (02) 9964 3763
Editor Kirstie Clements
Monthly $5.90

Articles and features on fashion, beauty, health, business, people and the arts of interest to the modern woman of style and high spending power. Ideas welcome. Length: from 1000 words. Illustrations: colour and b&w. Founded 1959.

Wild

Wild Publications Pty Ltd, PO Box 415, Prahran, Victoria 3181
tel (03) 9826 8482 *fax* (03) 9826 3787
email wild@wild.com.au
website www.wild.com.au
Editor Chris Baxter
4 p.a. $7.99

'Australia's wilderness adventure magazine.' Illustrated articles of first-hand experiences of the Australian wilderness, plus book and track reviews, product tests. See website for guidelines for contributors. Length: 2500 words (articles), 200 words (news). Colour transparencies. Payment: $125 per published page. Founded 1981.

Woman's Day

54-58 Park Street, Sydney, NSW 2000
tel (02) 9282 8000 *fax* (02) 9267 4360
Editor-in-Chief Philip Barker
Weekly $3.30

National women's magazine; news, show business, fiction, fashion, general articles, cookery, home economy.

CANADA

The Beaver: Canada's History Magazine

Canada's National History Society, Suite 478, 167 Lombard Avenue, Winnipeg, Manitoba R3B 0T6
tel 204-988-9300 *fax* 204-988-9309
website www.historysociety.ca
Editor Annalee Greenberg
Bi-monthly $29.95 p.a. ($37.95 USA, $44.95 p.a. elsewhere)

Articles, historical and modern, on Canadian history. Length: 1500–3000 words, with illustrations. Payment: on acceptance. Illustrations: b&w and colour archival photos or drawings. Founded 1920.

C international contemporary art

PO Box 5, Station B, Toronto, Ontario M5T 2T2
tel 416-539-9495 *fax* 416-539-9903
email general@cmagazine.com
Quarterly US$8.25

Arts and artists' projects, features, reviews. Accepts submissions. Length: features (varies), reviews (500 words). Illustrations: transparencies, photos. Payment: $250–$500 features, $100 reviews. Founded 1972.

Canadian Literature

University of British Columbia, Buchanan E158, 1866 Main Mall, Vancouver, BC V6T 1Z1
tel 604-882-2780 *fax* 604-822-5504
Editor E.M. Kröller
4 p.a. $45 p.a. individual; $60 p.a. institutions (outside Canada add $20 postage)

Articles on Canadian writers and writing in English and French. No fiction. Length: up to 5000 words. Payment: none. Founded 1959.

Canadian Theatre Review (CTR)

Drama Program, University of Guelph, Guelph, Ontario N1G 2W1
Contact Editorial Committee
Quarterly $10.50 ($35 p.a.)

Feature and review articles on Canadian theatre aimed at theatre professionals, academics and general audience; book and play reviews. Send MSS accompanied by PC compatible disk. Length: 2000–3000 words. Illustrations: b&w. Payment: $200–$275 (features/articles), $75 (book/play reviews). Founded 1974.

Canadian Writer's Journal

PO Box 5180, New Liskeard, Ontario P0J 1P0
tel 705-647-5424 *fax* 705-647-8366
email cwj@cwj.ca
website www.cwj.ca
Editor Deborah Ranchuk
Bi-monthly $35 p.a.

News on markets and articles on writers' aspirations for dedicated apprentice and professional Canadian writers. Considers unsolicited material. Founded 1984.

Chatelaine
1 Mount Pleasant Road, Toronto, Ontario M4Y 2Y5
tel 416-764-1888
Editor Rona Maynard
Monthly $2.99

Women's interest articles; Canadian angle preferred. Payment: on acceptance; from $1000.

The Dalhousie Review
Dalhousie University, Halifax, Nova Scotia B3H 3J5
tel 902-494-2541 *fax* 902-494-3561
email Dalhousie.Review@dal.ca
website www.dal.ca/~dalrev/
Associate Editors Ronald Huebert, Trevor Ross
3 p.a. ($32.10 p.a., $85.60 for 3 years; ($40/$100 outside Canada)

Articles on history, literature, political science, philosophy, sociology, popular culture, fine arts; short fiction; verse; book reviews. Usually not more than 3 stories and 10–12 poems in any one issue. Length: prose, up to 5000 words; verse, less than 40 words. Contributors receive 2 copies of issue and 10 offprints of their work.

Equinox
11450 Albert-Hudon Blvd, Montreal, Montreal, QC H1G 3J9
tel 514-327-4464 *fax* 514-327-0514
email eqxmag@globetrotter.net
Editor Martin Silverstone
Bi-monthly ($22.95 p.a. Canada; Can.$29 p.a. USA; Can.$35 elsewhere)

Magazine of discovery in science, human cultures, technology and geography. Accepts articles on hard science topics (length: 250–350 words); welcomes queries (2–3-page outline) for specific assignments. No phone queries please. Illustrations: colour transparencies. Payment: by arrangement. Founded 1982.

The Fiddlehead
Campus House, 11 Garland Court,
UNB PO Box 4400, Frederiction, NB E3B 5A3
tel 506-453-3501
email fid@nbnet.nb.ca
website www.lib.unb.ca/texts/fiddlehead
Editor Ross Leckie
Quarterly US$10 (US$25 p.a.)

Reviews, poetry, short stories. Payment: approx. $20 per printed page. Founded 1945.

(Hamilton) The Spectator
44 Frid Street, Hamilton, Ontario L8N 3G3
tel 905-526-3333
website www.hamiltonspectator.com
Publisher Ms Jagoda S. Pike

Daily Mon–Fri 75c Sat $1.75

Articles of general interest, political analysis and background; interviews, stories of Canadians abroad. Length: 800 words maximum. Payment: rate varies. Founded 1846.

Inuit Art Quarterly
2081 Merivale Road, Ottawa, Ontario K2G 1G9
tel 613-224-8189 *fax* 613-224-2907
email iaq@inuitart.org
website www.inuitart.org
Editor Marybelle Mitchell
Quarterly $6.25

Features, original research, artists' perspectives, news. Freelance contributors are expected to have a thorough knowledge of the arts. Length: varies. Illustrations: colour and b&w photos and line. Payment: by arrangement. Founded 1985.

Journal of Canadian Studies
Trent University, Peterborough, Ontario K9J 7B8
tel 705-748-1279 *fax* 705-748-1110
email jcs_rec@trentu.ca
Editors Stephen Bocking, Jill Smith
Quarterly US$50 p.a. (US$60 p.a. institutions)

Major academic review of Canadian studies. Articles of general as well as scholarly interest on history, politics, literature, society, arts. Length: 7000–10,000 words.

The Malahat Review
University of Victoria, PO Box 1700 STN CSC, Victoria, BC V8W 2Y2
tel 250-721-8524
email malahat@uvic.ca (queries only)
website www.malahatreview.com
Editor Marlene Cookshaw
Quarterly $30 p.a. ($40 p.a. overseas)

Short stories, poetry, short plays, reviews. Payment: $30 per magazine page. Illustrations: half-tone. Founded 1967.

Performing Arts & Entertainment in Canada (PA&E)
104 Glenrose Avenue, Toronto, Ontario M4T 1K8
tel 416-484-4534 *fax* 416-484-6214
Sarah Hood, *Send material to* George Hencz
Quarterly $8 p.a. ($14 p.a. elsewhere)

Feature articles on Canadian theatre, music, dance and film artists and organisations; technical articles on scenery, lighting, make-up, costumes, etc. Length: 600–1200 words. Payment: $150–$175, one month after publication. Illustrations: b&w photos, colour slides. Founded 1961.

Photo Life
1 Dundas Street West, Suite 2500, PO Box 84, Toronto, Ontario M5G 1Z3
tel 800-905-7468 *fax* 800-664-2739

email editor@photolife.com
website www.photolife.com
Editors Anita Dammer, Darwin Wiggett
6 p.a. $4.50 Can., US$3.95

Covers all aspects of photography of interest to amateur and professional photographers. Length: 800–1500 words. Illustrations: colour and b&w photos. Payment: by arrangement. Founded 1976.

Queen's Quarterly

Queen's University, Kingston, Ontario K7L 3N6
tel 613-533-2667 *fax* 613-533-6822
email qquarter@post.queensu.ca
website http://info.queensu.ca/quarterly
Editor Dr Boris Castel
Quarterly $6.50 ($20 p.a.; $40 p.a. institutions)

A multidisciplinary scholarly journal aimed at the general educated reader – articles, short stories and poems. Length: 2500–3500 words (articles), 2000 (stories). Payment: by negotiation. Founded 1893.

Quill & Quire

70 The Esplanade, Suite 210, Toronto, Ontario M5E 1R2
tel 416-360-0044 *fax* 416-955-0794
email info@quillandquire.com
Editor Scott Anderson
12 p.a. $59.95 p.a. (outside Canada $95p.a.)

Articles of interest about the Canadian book trade. Payment: from $100. Illustrations: line, half-tone. Subscription includes Canadian Publishers Directory (2 p.a.). Founded 1935.

Reader's Digest (Canada)

1100 René Levesque Blvd. W, Montreal, Quebec H3B 5H5
tel 514-940-0751
Editor Murray Lewis
Monthly $3.25

Original articles on all subjects of broad general appeal, thoroughly researched and professionally written. Outline or query only. Length: 3000 words approx. Payment: from $2700. Also previously published material. Illustrations: line, half-tone, colour.

(Toronto) The Globe and Mail

444 Front Street West, Toronto, Ontario M5V 2S9
Publisher Phillip Crawley, *Editor-in-Chief* Edward Greenspon
Daily 60c

Unsolicited material considered. Payment: by arrangement. Founded 1844.

Toronto Life

59 Front Street East, Toronto, Ontario M5E 1B3
tel 416-364-3333 *fax* 416-861-1169
website www.torontolife.com
Editor John Macfarlane

Monthly $3.95

Articles, profiles on Toronto and Torontonians. Illustrations: line, half-tone, colour. Founded 1966.

Toronto Star

One Yonge Street, Toronto, Ontario M5E 1E6
tel 416-367-2000
website www.thestar.com
London office Level 4A, PO Box 495, Virginia Street, London E1 9XY
tel 020-7833 0791
Daily Mon–Fri 30c, Sat $1, Sun 75c

Features, life, world/national politics. Payment: by arrangement. Founded 1892.

(Vancouver) Province

200 Granville Street, Suite 1, Vancouver, BC V6C 3N3
tel 604-605-2063 *fax* 604-606-2720
Editor-in-Chief Vivienne Sosnowski
Daily Mon–Fri 70c, Sun $1.40

Founded 1898.

Vancouver Sun

200 Granville Street, Vancouver, BC V6C 3N3
tel 604-605-2180 *fax* 604-605-2323
email nreynolds@png.canwest.com
website www.vancouversun.com
London office Canwest News, 8 Heath Mansions, Hampstead Grove, London NW3 6SL
tel 020-7435 5103
Editor-in-Chief Neil Reynolds
Daily Mon–Thu 75c; Fri, Sat $1.40

Mix arts magazine. Travel, Op-Ed pieces considered. Payment: by arrangement.

Wascana Review of Contemporary Poetry & Short Fiction

c/o English Department, University of Regina, Regina, Sask. S4S 0A2
tel 306-585-4302 *fax* 306-585-4827
website www.uregina.ca/wrhome.htm
Editor Michael Trussler
Bi-annual $10 p.a. ($12 p.a. outside Canada)

Criticism, short stories, poetry, reviews. MSS from freelance writers welcome. Length: prose, not more than 6000 words; verse, up to 100 lines. Payment: $3 per page for prose; $10 per printed page for verse; $3 per page for reviews. Contributors also receive 2 free copies and a year's subscription. Founded 1966.

Winnipeg Free Press

1355 Mountain Avenue, Winnipeg, MB R2X 3B6
tel 204-697-7000 *fax* 204-697-7412
website www.winnipegfreepress.com
Editor Nicholas Hirst
Daily Mon–Fri 25c, Sat $1.25, Sun 35c

Some freelance articles. Payment: $100. Founded 1872.

NEW ZEALAND

(Auckland) New Zealand Herald
PO Box 32, Auckland
tel (09) 379 5050 *fax* (09) 373 6421
email editor@herald.co.nz
website www.nzherald.co.nz
Editor Tim Murphy *Editor-in-Chief* Gavin Ellis
Daily Mon–Fri $1.20, Weekend $2.50

Topical and informative articles 800–1100 words.
Payment: minimum $150–$300. Illustrations:
colour negatives or prints. Founded 1863.

(Auckland) Sunday News
PO Box 1327, Auckland
tel (09) 302 1300 *fax* (09) 358 3003
email editor@sunday-news.co.nz
Editor Clive Nelson
Sun $1.10

News, sport and showbiz, especially with New
Zealand interest. Illustrations: colour and b&w
photos. Founded 1963.

(Auckland) Sunday Star-Times
News Media Auckland Ltd, PO Box 1327,
Auckland 1
tel (09) 302 1300 *fax* (09) 309 0258
email feedback@star-times.co.nz
Editor Suzanne Chetwin
Sun $1.50

(Christchurch) The Press
Private Bag 4722, Christchurch
tel (03) 379 0940 *fax* (03) 364 8238
email editorial@press.co.nz
Editor Paul Thompson
Daily Mon–Fri 90c, Sat $1.50

Articles of general interest not more than 800
words. Illustrations: photos and line drawings,
cartoons. Payment: by arrangement.

(Dunedin) Otago Daily Times
PO Box 181, Dunedin
tel (03) 477 4760 *fax* (03) 474 7422
email odt.editor@alliedpress.co.nz
website www.odt.co.nz
Editor R.L. Charteris
Daily 80c

Any articles of general interest up to 1000 words,
but preference is given to NZ writers. Topical
illustrations and personalities. Payment: current NZ
rates. Founded 1861.

Hawke's Bay Today
PO Box 180, Karamu Road North, Hastings
tel (06) 878 5155 *fax* (06) 876 0655
Editor L. Pierard
Daily 70c

Limited requirements. Payment: $50 upwards for
articles, $15 upwards for photos. Illustrations: web
offset.

(Invercargill) The Southland Times
PO Box 805, Invercargill
tel (03) 218 1909 *fax* (03) 214 9905
email editor@stl.co.nz
website www.press.co.nz
Editor F.L. Tulett
Daily Mon–Fri 70c, Sat 80c

Articles of up to 800 words on topics of Southland
interest. Payment: by arrangement. Illustrations:
line, half-tone, colour, cartoons. Founded 1862.

Management Magazine
Profile Publishing, PO Box 5544, Auckland
tel (09) 630 8940 *fax* (09) 630 1046
email sprofile@iconz.co.nz
Editor Sherrill Tapsell
Monthly $5.95

Articles on the practice of management skills and
techniques, individual and company profiles,
coverage of business trends and topics. A
NZ/Australian angle or application preferred.
Length: 2000 words. Payment: by arrangement;
minimum 23c per word. Illustrations: photos, line
drawings.

The Nelson Mail
PO Box 244, 15 Bridge Street, Nelson
tel (03) 548 7079 *fax* (03) 546 2802
email nml@nelsonmail.co.nz
Editor Bill Moore
Daily 70c

Features, articles on NZ subjects. Length: 500–1000
words. Payment: up to $100 per 1000 words.
Illustrations: half-tone, colour.

(New Plymouth) The Daily News
PO Box 444, Currie Street, New Plymouth
tel (06) 758 0559 *fax* (06) 758 6849
email editor@tnl.co.nz
Editor Lance G. Butcher
Daily 90c

Articles preferably with a Taranaki connection.
Payment: by negotiation. Illustrations: half-tone,
cartoons. Founded 1857.

New Zealand Woman's Day
Private Bag 92512, Auckland
tel (09) 308 2718 *fax* (09) 357 0978
Editor Louise Wright
Weekly $3.25

Celebrity interviews, exclusive news stories, short
stories, gossip. Length: 1000 words. Illustrations:
colour transparencies; payment according to use.
Payment: by arrangement. Founded 1989.

New Zealand Woman's Weekly

PO Box 90-119 AMC, Auckland 1
tel (09) 360 3820 *fax* (09) 360 3829
email editor@nzww.co.nz
Editor Rowan Dixon
Weekly $3.25

Articles and features of general interest to women aged 30+ and their families: celebrities, news, health, food, fashion, DIY and home improvement, short stories. Considers unsolicited material and welcomes ideas for features and articles. Length: 800–2000 words (features/articles), 500–1500 (fiction). Illustrations: colour. Payment: 20th of month or on publication. Founded 1932.

NZ House & Garden

PO Box 6341, Wellesley Street, Auckland
tel (09) 353 1010 *fax* (09) 353 1020
Editor Kate Coughlan
Monthly $8.95

Upmarket magazine that celebrates New Zealand's most interesting houses and beautiful gardens. Inspiration for food and entertaining, and a resource for decor. Considers unsolicited material. Welcomes ideas for articles and features. Length: 500–800 words. Payment: $400. Illustrations: colour transparencies. Founded 1994.

She

Private Bag 92512, Wellesley Street,
Auckland 1036
tel (09) 308 2735 *fax* (09) 302 0667
email she@acpnz.co.nz
Editor Leonie Dale
Monthly $6.20

Lifestyle magazine for women aged 25–40. Length: 1000–2000 words (features and profiles). Illustrations: colour. Payment: negotiable. Founded 1996.

Straight Furrow

Rural Press, PO Box 4233, Auckland
tel (09) 376 9786 *fax* (09) 376 9780
Editor Susan Topless

Fortnightly News and features of interest to the farming/rural sector with emphasis on agri-political issues. Length: 500 words news, 1000 words features. Illustrations: colour and b&w photos. Payment: 30c per published word; $15 per published photo. Founded 1933.

Takahe

Takahe Collective Trust, PO Box 13335,
Christchurch 8001
tel (03) 359 8133
3 p.a. $25 for 4 issues ($35 international)

Quality short fiction and poetry by both new and established writers. Payment: approx. $30 per issue. Founded 1989.

The Timaru Herald

PO Box 46, Bank Street, Timaru
tel (03) 684 4129 *fax* (03) 688 1042
email editor@timaruherald.co.nz
Editor D.H. Wood
Daily 65c

Topical articles. Payment: by arrangement. Illustrations: colour or b&w prints.

(Wellington) The Dominion Post

PO Box 3740, 40 Boulcott Street, Wellington
tel (04) 474 0000 *fax* (04) 474 0350,
(04) 474 0185 (editor)
email editor@dompost.co.nz
website www.stuff.co.nz
Editor Tim Pankhurst
Daily Mon–Fri $1, Sat $1.50

General topical articles, 600 words. Payment: NZ current rates or by arrangement. News illustrations, cartoons. Founded 2002 with the merger of *The Dominion* and *The Evening Post*.

Your Home and Garden

Australian Consolidated Press (New Zealand) Ltd,
Private Bag 92512, Wellesley Street, Auckland
tel (09) 308 2700 *fax* (09) 377 6725
Editor Claire McCall
Monthly $6.20

Advice, ideas and projects for homeowners – interiors and gardens. Length: 1000 words. Illustrations: good quality colour transparencies. Payment: 30c per word/ $75 per transparency. Founded 1991.

SOUTH AFRICA

Bona

Caxton Magazines, PO Box 32083, Mobeni 4060, KwaZulu-Natal
tel (031) 910-5745
Monthly R6.95

Articles on human drama, sport, music, medical, social and consumer issues of interest to black people. Length: up to 2000 words. Payment: by arrangement. Illustrations: colour prints, occasionally cartoons.

(Cape Town) Cape Times

Newspaper House, 5th Floor, 122 St George's Mall, Cape Town 8001
postal address PO Box 56, Cape Town 8000
tel (021) 488-4911 *fax* (021) 488 4744
website www.iol.co.za
Editor Chris Whitfield
London office Mediaforce Ltd, 1 Gunpowder Square, Fleet Street, London EC4A 3EP
tel 020-7583 2100 *fax* 020-7353 2111
Daily R3.10

Contributions must be suitable for a daily newspaper and must not exceed 800 words. Illustrations: photos of outstanding South African interest. Founded 1876.

Car

PO Box 180, Howard Place 7450
tel (021) 530-3153 *fax* (021) 532-2698
email car@rsp.co.za
website www.cartoday.com
Editor John Wright
Monthly R16.95

New car announcements with pictures and full colour features of motoring interest. Payment: by arrangement. Illustrations: colour, cartoons. Founded 1957.

Daily Dispatch

Dispatch Media (Pty) Ltd, 35 Caxton Street, East London 5201
postal address PO Box 131, East London 5200
tel (043) 702-2000 *fax* (043) 743 5155
email eledit@iafrica.com
website www.dispatch.co.za
Editor Gavin Stewart
Daily Mon–Sat R2

Newspaper for the Eastern Cape region. Features of general interest, especially successful development projects in developing countries. Contributions welcome. Illustrations: colour and b&w photographs, artwork, cartoons; provides research facility for a fee to authors and publications. Length: approx. 1000 words (features). Payment: R350; R100 photographs. Founded 1872.

(Durban) The Mercury

Independent Newspapers KwaZulu-Natal Ltd, PO Box 47549, Durban 4000
tel (031) 308-2258 *fax* (031) 308-2306
Editor D. Canning
Daily Mon–Fri R3.60

Serious background news and inside details of world events. Length: 700–900 words. Illustrations: photos of general interest. Founded 1852.

Farmer's Weekly

Caxton Magazines, PO Box 1797, Pinegowie, Johannesburg 2123
tel (011) 889-0836
email farmersweekly@caxton.co.za
Editor Chris Burgess
Weekly R7.95

Articles, generally illustrated, up to 1000 words, on all aspects of practical farming and research with particular reference to conditions in Southern Africa. Includes women's section which accepts suitable, illustrated articles. Illustrations: line, halftone, colour, cartoons. Payment: according to merit. Founded 1911.

Femina Magazine

Associated Magazines, Box 3647, Cape Town 8000
tel (021) 464-6200 *fax* (021) 461 4290
email femina@assocmags.co.za
Editor Clare O'Donoghue
Monthly R15.95

For busy young professionals, often with families. Humour, personalities, real-life drama, medical breakthroughs, popular science, news-breaking stories and human interest. Payment: by arrangement.

Garden and Home

Caxton Magazines, PO Box 32083, Mobeni 4060
tel (031) 910-5713
Editor Les Abercrombie
Monthly R17.95

Well-illustrated articles on gardening suitable for southern hemisphere. Articles for home section on furnishings, decor ideas, food. Payment: by arrangement. Illustrations: half-tone, colour, cartoons.

Independent Newspapers (South Africa) Ltd

PO Box 56, Cape Town 8000
tel (021) 488-4911 *fax* (021) 488-4762
website www.iol.co.za
Cape Town **Argus** Daily R2.70
Saturday Argus R5.60
Sunday Argus R5.60
Cape Times Daily R3.10

Accepts articles of general and South African interest; also cartoons. Payment: in accordance with an editor's assessment.

Independent Newspapers Gauteng

PO Box 1014, Johannesburg 2000
tel (011) 633-9111 *fax* (011) 836-8398
website www.iol.co.za
Johannesburg **The Star** Daily R2.40
Saturday Star R3.20
Sunday Independent R6
Pretoria **Pretoria News** Daily R2.50

Accepts articles of general and South African interest; also cartoons. Payment: in accordance with an editor's assessment.

Independent Newspapers Kwa-Zulu Natal Ltd

18 Osborne Street, Greyville, Durban 4023
tel (031) 308-2400 *fax* (031) 308-2427
website www.iol.co.za
Durban **Daily News** R2.40
Ilanga Bi-weekly R1.40
The Mercury Daily R3.20
The Post Bi-weekly R3.40
Independent on Saturday R3.20

Accepts articles of general and South African interest; also cartoons. Payment: in accordance with an editor's assessment.

(Johannesburg) Sunday Times

PO Box 1742, Saxonwold 2132
tel (011) 280-5102 *fax* (011) 280-5111
email suntimes@sundaytimes.co.za
Editor M.W. Robertson
Sun R6

Illustrated articles of political or human interest, from a South African angle if possible. Maximum 1000 words long and 2–3 photos. Shorter essays, stories and articles of a light nature from 500–750 words. Payment: average rate £100 a column. Illustrations: colour and b&w photos, line drawings.

Living and Loving

Caxton Magazines, PO Box 32083, Mobeni 4060, KwaZulu-Natal
tel (031) 910-5785/6
Editor Fiona Wayman
Monthly R11.95

Parenting magazine: from pregnancy to preschool. Articles about behaviour and development in the first 7 years of life. First-person parenting experiences – pregnancy and the growing child. Medical news/breakthroughs of interest to parents worldwide. Payment: by merit, on acceptance and publication. Founded 1970.

Natal Witness

Box 362, Pietermaritzburg, KwaZulu-Natal 3201
tel (033) 355-1111 *fax* (033) 355-1122
email features@witness.co.za
Editor J.H. Conyngham
Daily R2.80

Accepts topical articles. All material should be submitted direct to the Editor in Pietermaritzburg. Length: 500–1000 words. Payment: average of R400 per 1000 words. Founded 1846.

Southern Cross

PO Box 2372, Cape Town 8000
tel (021) 465-5007 *fax* (021) 465-3850
email scross@global.co.za
Editor Gunther Simmermacher
Weekly R3

National English-language Catholic weekly. Catholic news reports, world and South African. Length: 550-word articles. Illustrations: photos of Catholic interest from freelance contributors. Payment: 12c per word; illustrations R23.10.

Woman's Value

Media 24, PO Box 1802, Cape Town 8000
tel (021) 406-2205 *fax* (021) 406-2929
email tleroux@womansvalue.com
website www.womansvalue.com
Editor Terena le Roux
Monthly R13.95

Features on beauty, food, finance, knitting, needlecraft, crafts, home and garden, health and parenting; short stories. 600-word accounts of experiences published on the 'My own story' page. Length: up to 1400 words (features/stories). Payment: R1.30 per word. Colour transparencies. Founded 1980.

World Airnews

PO Box 35082, Northway, Durban 4065
tel (031) 564-1319 *fax* (031) 563-7115
Editor Tom Chalmers
Monthly £36 p.a.

Aviation news and features with an African angle. Payment: by negotiation.

Your Family

PO Box 473016, Parklands 2121, Gauteng
tel (011) 889-0749
Editor Patti Garlick
Monthly R10.95

Cookery, knitting, crochet and homecrafts. Family drama, happy ending. Payment: by arrangement. Illustrations: continuous tone, colour and line, cartoons.

USA

The *Yearbook* does not contain a detailed list of US magazines and journals. The Overseas volume of *Willings Press Guide* is the most useful general reference guide to US publications, available in most reference libraries. For readers with a particular interest in the US market, the publications listed here will be helpful (please make payments to the US in US funds).

When submitting material to US journals, include a covering letter, together with return postage in the form of International Reply Coupons (IRC). IRCs can be exchanged in any foreign country for stamps representing the minimum postage payable on a letter sent from one country to another. Make it clear what rights are being offered for sale as some editors like to purchase MSS outright, thus securing world copyright, i.e. the traditional British market as well as the US market. Send the MSS direct to the US office of the journal and not to any London office.

In many cases it is best to send a preliminary letter giving a rough outline of your article or story (enclose IRCs for a reply). Most magazines will send a leaflet giving guidance to authors.

American Markets Newsletter

175 Westland Drive,
Glasgow G14 9JQ
email sheila.oconnor@juno.com
Editor Sheila O'Connor
6 p.a. £34 p.a. (£63 for 2 years)

Editorial guidelines for US, Canadian and other overseas markets, plus information on press trips, non-fiction/fiction markets and writers' tips. Free syndication. Sample issue £5.95 (payable to S. O'Connor).

Willings Press Guide

Waymaker Ltd, Chess House, 34 Germain Street, Chesham, Bucks. HP5 1SJ
tel 0870-7360010 (UK), (1494) 797225 (int.)
fax 0870-7360011 (UK), (1494) 797224
email willings@waymaker.co.uk
website www.willingspress.com
£265 2-volume set; or £180 UK volume, £190 international volume

Two volumes contain details of over 50,000 newspapers, broadcasters, periodicals and special interest titles in the UK and internationally. Usually available at local reference libraries or direct from the publisher. Also available as an online product.

The Writer

Kalmbach Publishing Co., 21027 Crossroads Circle, PO Box 1612, Waukesha, WI 53187
tel 262-796-8776 *fax* 262-796-8468
website www.writermag.com
Monthly $29 p.a. ($39 p.a. Canada and foreign)

Contains articles of instruction on all writing fields, lists of markets for MSS and special features of interest to freelance writers everywhere. The Writer Books also publishes books on writing fiction, non-fiction, poetry, articles, plays, etc.

Writer's Digest

Writer's Digest Books, 1507 Dana Avenue, Hamilton, OH 45207-1005
tel 513-531-2690 *fax* 513-531-2902
email writersdigest@fwpubs.com
website www.writersdigest.com
($36 plus $10 surface post, $75 airmail)

Monthly magazine for writers who want to write better and sell more; aims to inform, instruct and inspire the freelance.

Writer's Digest Books

(address above)

Also publishes annually *Novel and Short Story Writer's Market, Children's Writer's and Illustrator's Market, Poet's Market, Photographer's Market, Artist's & Graphic Designer's Market, Guide to Literary Agents* and many other books on creating and selling writing and illustrations.

The Writer's Handbook

The Writer Books, Kalmbach Publishing Co., Dept W1966, 21027 Crossroads Circle, PO Box 986, Waukesha, WI 53187
tel 262-796-8776 *fax* 262-796-0126
website www.kalmbach.com
$29.95 plus $5.50 shipping & handling; $7.50 s&h plus 7% GST Canada; $10.50 s&h foreign

Contains more than 3000 quality magazine and book markets, and hundreds of additional literary resources, plus 60 articles with advice from America's most successful writers.

Writer's Market

Writer's Digest Books (address above)
website www.writersmarket.com
($27.99 plus $4 p&p)

An annual guidebook giving editorial requirements and other details of over 4000 US markets for freelance writing. Also available on website.

Writing for newspapers

Richard Keeble outlines the huge scope for freelance journalists writing for newspapers.

Every week more than 160 million newspapers are either sold or given away in Britain. The national mainstream press comprises 10 morning dailies and 10 Sundays. The broadsheets (*Daily Telegraph, Financial Times, Guardian, Independent, The Times*) sell around 2.82 million copies daily, the mid-market tabloids (*Daily Mail, Daily Express*) 3.35 million, and the red top tabloids (*Daily Star, Daily Mirror, Sun*) 6.22 million. On Sundays, the broadsheets (*Observer, Independent on Sunday, Sunday Telegraph and Sunday Times*) sell 2.88 million copies; the *Mail on Sunday* and *Sunday Express* 3.21 million; while the *News of the World, Sunday Mirror, Sunday People* and *Sunday Sport* sell 7.07 million. At the local level, 37.5 million regional dailies are sold or given away every week, while over six million local paid-for weeklies and 30 million free weeklies are distributed. In addition, there are a vast range of alternative peace-movement, ethnic-minority, religious and leftist newspapers.

Newspapers clearly offer writers an enormous range of opportunities. And freelancing has its definite attractions. As a freelance you can often work from home and so avoid the hassles of office politics and commuting. You can develop a specialist interest. You may have a particular knowledge of wines (built up through attending tasting classes, holidays and reading) and be familiar with some prominent names in the business. Writing reviews and features in this area for the few specialist newspaper sections could well prove financially (and personally) rewarding.

The freelance challenge

Yet launching into a freelance career is not easy. Many freelances are former full-time staffers who have developed a specialism, sent out linage (freelance copy paid by the line) to nationals and then, through either choice or redundancy, taken the plunge and gone solo or started a small agency. With newspapers increasingly laying off experienced full-time staffers, competition amongst freelances has intensified. And while freelances enjoy certain 'freedoms' not permitted to staff writers, they still cannot avoid the constraints and ethical dilemmas that all journalists face. For instance, you may be very critical of the political and ethical stances of the mainstream press. Thus you may decide to contribute (largely unpaid) to an ethnic-minority, left-wing, religious, peace-movement or environmental newspaper or news magazine and gain your money from other employment. One of the greatest journalists of the last century, George Orwell, committed himself to small-scale, left-wing, literary journals and largely ignored the seductive appeal of Fleet Street. It was his deliberate political choice. Or you may be happy to sell your copy to a Rupert Murdoch-owned newspaper (such as *The Times* or *Sunday Times*). But always be fully aware there are political and ethical implications behind your journalistic decisions.

Why contacts are crucial

Very few freelances are generalists. They instead develop a specialism (or a discreet range of linked specialisms) and become valuable to editors because of their specialist knowledge, experience and contacts. Thus your major task in launching into a freelance career is to build up a contacts book containing sources' phone numbers, addresses, fax and pager numbers, email and website details. You may have to go to meetings, conferences and press launches, and/or ring up spokespersons of political parties, companies and campaigning bodies. All this takes a lot of time. But from your sources will come ideas for stories, details of events to attend, quotes, and specialist (and hopefully exclusive) information. Many freelances place contact details on a computer database as a back-up while those investigating sensitive issues (such as national security, spying, the arms and drugs trade, share dealings) tend to keep details of important exclusive sources in their heads. Police have been known to raid the homes and computers of journalists involved in sensitive areas and thus every step has to be taken to preserve the anonymity of such contacts.

The skills of interviewing are crucial to all freelances. You normally have to prepare in advance of the meeting and be confident enough in the subject to maintain a flowing interview – while recording accurately at the same time. It's far from easy. You may be tempted to use a tape recorder. But what if it breaks down at the crucial moment? For all interviews you need to make a written note. You may not have the time to learn a shorthand technique such as Teeline (in which 100 words a minute is the industry standard) but you do need to develop your own reliable rapid writing technique.

Get to know the market for your specialist area of interest. Study the different writing styles, the lengths of the sentences and articles in the differing publications. Try to establish, by examining byline patterns, the amount of freelance work accepted and in which particular areas. Analyse the advertising in the publications to get a feel for the intended target readership. Read recent issues carefully to get an idea of the stories covered and, more importantly, not covered. See who are the prominent sources used in stories and those who have been missed or marginalised. Get used to creating files of cuttings. Well-maintained filing cabinets can be invaluable research tools. And when you read documents, journal articles and books, file the notes from these too. But don't become over-reliant on cuttings. Journalists often report inaccurately so checking is usually necessary. Significantly, in its March 1992 report, the Press Complaints Commission (the watchdog promoting an ethical Code of Practice for print journalists) commented: "Cuttings are an essential part of newspaper research but too many journalists now seem to act in the belief that to copy from 10 old stories is better than to write a new one with confirmation by proper fresh enquiry."

The need for imaginative flair

As a freelance you will have to develop a special journalistic imagination. Ideas will be your lifeblood. A new report highlights a national survey showing students are increasingly going without sleep and as a result their academic work and health are suffering. Do a local follow-up: go to the colleges and universities in your area and interview students, counsellors, lecturers, etc about the issues involved. Better still, take the opposite line and do a feature for the women's section of a Sunday newspaper highlighting career women who need only a few hours sleep a day – and yet still thrive. Or take a major international story such as the dispute between the two nuclear-armed neighbours India and Pakistan. Again think local. Many British cities have Indian and Pakistani communities but their views have been largely ignored. So why not interview people from these countries about the issues? Are they afraid? What do they see as the political factors behind the crisis and what are their solutions? Are there any human interest angles to help humanise the reports? In all these cases you have to move quickly while the issues are still newsworthy.

A lot of starting-up freelances imagine a life sitting at home bashing out on the computer words of wisdom on a range of topics to an admiring public. But it is rare for a freelance career to start in this way. Columnists tend to be experienced journalists, novelists, comedians or other media celebrities and their views are seen by editors to carry authority. As a result they can command substantial salaries. *The Times* columnist Matthew Parris was rumoured to have turned down £300,000 a year to work for the *Independent* while Suzanne Moore was reported to receive £140,000 a year for one column a week for the *Mail on Sunday*. But there are exceptions to this rule. A local newspaper may want to carry an opinionated column from a reader presenting a particular viewpoint – such as that of a youngster, a football fan or an asylum seeker. In this way the paper is striving to make its mark on the local community, with a column aimed at getting people talking – and possibly provoking letters (for or against).

The rewards of reviewing

Arts reviewing for local papers has its obvious attractions. Most journalists come from humanities backgrounds (resulting in the unfortunate marginalisation of science news in the press) and so there tends to be fierce competition for these posts. Most will be filled by staffers or experienced freelances. But if you have the necessary specialist knowledge, have built up contacts in the area and can write in a lively, original way, you may well find an opening. Reviews serve many functions. They provide basic information: for example, that a play has just opened and can be seen at the theatre indicated. For people who intend to see, read or hear a work (or in the case of broadcasting have already seen or heard it), the review gives an opinion carrying some authority to compare with their own. Yet usually the vast majority of readers will never experience directly the work under review. A concert may have been attended by no more than a hundred people. The review must then exist as a piece of writing in its own right. It must entice the reader through the colour and quality of its prose.

All newspapers have their own house style. This is outlined in a document called the stylebook (occasionally handbook or sheet), though it is increasingly carried onscreen and on the newspaper's website. For instance, you can check out the *Guardian's* stylebook on its website. Stylebooks tend to focus on such elements as spellings (gaol or jail?, Gaddafi or Khadaffi?), punctuation, abbreviations, the use of capitals, titles, Americanisms to avoid, the handling of quotations. Ethical issues, such as the handling of anonymous quotes or how to refer to people with disabilities, can also be covered. Take a close look at your target publications and study their styles. Freelances are not expected to present copy perfectly according to style: sub-editors are on hand to prepare copy for publication. But if your copy shows some awareness of the house style, then the editors will be impressed.

Some basic requirements

As a freelance you will need internet access on your computer. Most copy is now supplied via email and companies are increasingly supplying press releases through email. You will also need an accountant to advise on tax liabilities, and a pension plan. If you become particularly successful you will have to pay VAT. Most freelances keep in regular touch with their local tax inspector. Remember to log for tax purposes all relevant expenses, such as stationery, office equipment, book and travel expenses. Christopher Browne (in his book *The Journalist's Handbook*, A & C Black, 1999) suggests that beginning freelances should negotiate an overdraft facility of at least £3000 to £4000 with their bank manager after presenting them with a business plan drawn up by an accountant. Membership of the freelance branch of the National Union of Journalists (NUJ) is worth considering. The NUJ, along with local education centres, runs courses for starting-up freelances which can help develop skills and confidence.

Journalism remains a job carrying enormous personal rewards. It is difficult, challenging (politically, ethically, physically) and fun. It requires a formidable range of knowledge and skills. And journalists need to be curious, persistent, imaginative and daring. In the words of Nicholas Tomalin, the *Sunday Times* foreign correspondent killed on the Golan Hights in 1973, journalists should cultivate "rat-like cunning, a plausible manner and a little literary ability". There is a glamorous side to the job, which Hollywood has helped to promote. No wonder the queues for entering the industry are so long.

Richard Keeble is Professor of Journalism at Lincoln University. His publications include *The Newspapers Handbook* (Routledge, 3rd edn 2001) and *Ethics for Journalists* (Routledge, 2001).

Further reading

Randall, David, *The Universal Journalist*, Pluto, 2nd edn 2000

Hicks, Wynford, with Harriett Gilbert and Sally Adams, *Writing for Journalists*, Routledge, 1999

Adams, Sally, *Interviewing for Journalists*, Routledge, 2001

Hicks, Wynford, *English for Journalists*, Routledge, 2nd edn 1997

Pilger, John, *Hidden Agendas*, Vintage, 1998

Peak, Steve (ed), *Media Guide 2003*, Guardian Books in association with Atlantic Books, annually updated

Writing for magazines

Richard Keeble explains the different types of features that magazines run and offers advice to freelance writers on how to approach writing for magazines.

There are well over 9000 mainstream magazines published in Britain – and many hundreds of alternative publications. Research suggests that weekly consumer magazines are read by 39% of adults and monthlies by 48%. Yet while there appears to be an enormous variety of publications, the sector is dominated by just two companies: IPC and EMAP. IPC was sold by Reed Elsevier to Cinven, an investment company, in January 1998 for £860 million and then to AOL Time Warner for £1.3 billion in August 2001. Magazine publishing is clearly big business!

The differing genres

Freelancing for magazines will normally involve writing features. So it's important from the outset to have a clear idea about the different journalistic genres. Each will have its own writing style, research strategy, tone, and place in the publication. Here is a selection of the genres you might expect to find in a representative range of magazines.

Hard news

Hard news has the highest status in newspapers and tends to be on the front pages, while magazines may have an opening section carrying hard news. Hard news features usually open with the most striking details and the information given subsequently is generally of lesser importance. Some background details may be needed to make the news intelligible but description, analysis, comment and the subjective 'I' of the reporter are either excluded or included only briefly.

Soft news

Here the news element is strong and prominent at or near the opening but is treated in a lighter way. Largely based on factual information and quotations, the writing is nonetheless more colourful, with an emphasis on description and comment. The tone, established in the intro (opening) section, may be witty or ironic. The separation of hard and soft news emerged in the second half of the nineteenth century: the first, linked to notions of accuracy, objectivity, neutrality, was used for transmitting information; the second was more an entertainment genre. Magazine opening sections usually adopt this softer approach to news.

News features

A news feature is usually longer than a straight news story. The news angle is prominent, though not necessarily in the opening section, and quotes again are important. It can contain analysis, comment, descriptions, historical background detail, eye-witness reporting and deeper coverage of the issues and the range of sources.

Timeless features

These have no specific news angle; the special interest is provided by the subject or sources. For example, such a feature could explore young people's experiences of dealing with sexually transmitted diseases or coming out in terms of sexual orientation.

Backgrounder/preview/curtain-raiser features

Here the emphasis is not so much on reporting the news as on explaining it, or setting the scene for an event about to happen. For instance, if a major anti-globalisation demonstration is planned for mid-July, that month's magazine (produced well in advance) might carry a feature highlighting the historical background, the arguments of the protestors, the range of voices expected on the march, the hopes of the organisers and the predicted turn-out, and so on. A retrospective is a similar feature looking back on an event.

Colour features

These concentrate on descriptive, eye-witness reporting, quotations and the build-up of factual details. They need not have a strong news angle. You may visit Highgate cemetery and describe (for a travel or tourist magazine) your experience of walking through it and talking to people. What do they think of Karl Marx, who is buried there?

Eye-witness news features

These are based on your observations of a newsy event, incorporating such elements as description, conversations, interviews, analysis and comment. You may accompany a rock star for a week as they tour the country and describe the experience for a rock magazine.

Profiles (sometimes called interviews)

These are portraits in words, usually based on interviews with the subject and sometimes also with their friends, critics, relations, work colleagues.

Reviews

Reviews include descriptions and assessments of works of art, television programmes, exhibitions, books, theatre shows, CDs, rock gigs and so on.

Lifestyle features

Lifestyle features include advice columns (such as on health or education matters, gardening or computer problems).

Comment pieces

If you have an original voice, confidence in your personal writing style and a wide range of interests, then you might well aim to become a columnist. Editorials, on the other hand, reflect the institutional voice of the publication and are rarely written by freelances.

Getting ideas

You must be immersed in your specialist area, regularly reading and building up cuttings files from the relevant publications, websites, press releases, newsletters of pressure groups, etc. You will need to generate a network of contacts at public events, informal social gatherings, conferences, press launches. And ideas will emerge from conversations with friends and family. Remember your best resources are your own experiences. You have a teenage son who is showing no interest in politics; you could then plan a feature looking at the broader picture, talking to teachers, the youngsters themselves, other parents and political commentators. After 20 years in the same rat-race job you (your family, four dogs and three cats) are quitting to live simply in a remote cottage in Northumbria; so why not write about it?

Developing magazine feature ideas from news reports needs a special imaginative flair. A report from a university media monitoring unit criticises the increasing intrusiveness of the paparazzi photographers. A daily or weekly newspaper (working to relatively short deadlines) will follow up the report, interviewing editors and photographers and placing the current controversy in its historical context. A magazine writer, on the other hand, will have the luxury of a slightly longer deadline – and this throws up opportunities. You could spend a week on the back of a paparazzi's motorbike zooming about the streets of London and describe the experience, the feelings of the photographer and the people they shoot. The feature could involve eye-witness descriptions, dialogue, factual details: as you describe your movements around London so your copy is given extra movement and colour.

The ethical/political challenge
Always be aware of the ethical/political dilemmas stories can throw up. You are planning a vox pop (a collection of snappy quotes usually accompanied by photographs) about the work of paparazzi photographers: think about the range of people to be shown, in terms of race, gender, age and authority. If someone will speak to you only 'off the record' what do you do? How important is it for your feature to present a balancing range of views? One of your sources is an outspoken racist or sexist: how do you deal with their quotes? And so on.

The feature package
It's often best to think in terms of producing not just one single article (of say 2500 words) but a package of contrasting features. These will have different lengths and tones and will provide the sub-editor with material for a more interesting layout. Thus the paparazzi package might contain the main eye-witness, participatory feature (1200 words), a background piece outlining the history of the paparazzi and ending with their alleged role in the death of Princess Diana and the ensuing controversy (700 words) and a profile of a prominent photographer who argues strongly for (or against) legislation to restrain intrusive photographers (600 words).

The structure of the feature
The opening section
Most features do not start with the traditional five Ws (who, what, where, when, why) and the H (how) of the hard news opening section. The writing can be

more flexible – but there is still an urgency needed in the copy to attract the attention of the reader. One of the most popular devices for helping the reader understand a complex event or issue is to begin by focusing on the experience or views of an individual. You are writing a piece about poverty on a bleak housing estate in Manchester, so you focus on the plight of an elderly woman, shivering in her unheated semi and terrified of the yobs who have raided her home three times over the last year and thrown fireworks through her letterbox.

According to the convention in the UK, most news stories don't begin with direct quotations. But features – and in particular profiles – often do. Quotes are useful because they can be colourful, succinct, and convey a lot about the personality of the person quoted. Thus a feature about 'flexploitation' (as employers are increasingly using flexi-time working arrangements to extend their exploitation of white-collar staff) could begin: 'We all sit in rows now. You log in and log out – even for your 20-minute lunch break. It's more like clocking in at a factory.'

The 'I' of the reporter is only rarely prominent in news intros. But the tone of magazine features (and not just those by regular columnists) can be far more personal, idiosyncratic, even witty. A feature exploring an issue such as fox-hunting, or debt in the developing world, can open with your views; an intro section for a piece about hairdressing can focus on a recent bad experience; and so on. Similarly, while news reports hardly ever begin with a question, features often do. Thus a feature about the boom in ski-ing in the Alps in the New Year could start: 'Have you tried to secure your travel ticket for the Alps yet?'

The body of the text

While colour, description, opinion, analysis, narrative, quotes, dialogue and historical context may be important in features, they are all still built on the cement of factual or emotional accuracy and a clear sense of structure. Just as in news stories the most important information comes first, with the less important details thereafter, so the body of the feature text is usually intended to expand on an opening section. At the same time, the writing styles of magazine features can be far more colourful. Emotional tones (angry, witty, ironic, condemnatory, adulatory) can vary along with textual rhythms. Indeed, before launching into your writing, as well as planning the structure, it is crucial to identify the emotional core of the piece. Try always to be as authentic as possible (within the constraints of the editorial policy of your target publication).

The closing section

A hard news story carries information in the order of its news value. The last paragraph is the least important and can be cut without destroying the overall impact. Features can be different, with the final section carrying its own, crucial significance. One feature may explore a range of views or experiences and conclude by passing a comment on them; another may argue a case and come to a conclusion in the final section. The final paragraph may raise a pointed question, contain a striking direct quote, summarise an argument or look ahead to a possible future.

Pitching ideas

You can choose to write or phone in your idea to a commissioning editor. There is no hard rule here. But even after you have spoken to an editor, they may well want you to spell out the idea by fax, letter or email. Make sure the grammar, spelling, facts, and punctuation in your proposal (as in your copy) are spot on. And don't be tempted to spell out the idea at length. The essential idea should be summarised in one paragraph at most: 'With Martin Scorsese's *Gangs of New York* due to be released in two months, my 1200-word feature will look critically at the way in which Hollywood has represented street gangs in the past.' Don't be vague. Don't say: 'I propose a feature about prostitution in inner cities.' Rather: 'A report published this week has highlighted the rise of prostitution in inner cities. To what extend are students (both male and female) funding their studies through prostitution?'

Dangers

Publications may steal your ideas and give them to someone else to follow up. And the freelance has absolutely no protection in law against this kind of theft. While written work can be copyrighted, ideas can occur to two people at the same time. One solution is to provide only a bare minimum of background details before the idea is accepted. Personal contact with the commissioning editor also helps create mutual trust and confidence. The best solution is to prove your abilities to the publication with a series of stories, sent on spec or to commission, so they will be concerned not to lose your work to other competitors. Make sure you have a copy of all submitted work. If it is rejected you may want to rework it with some new angles/quotes for a different publication. And be persistent: remember that *Gone with the Wind* was rejected 25 times before it was published.

Payment

How much should you expect to be paid? Well, the National Union of Journalists draws up a regularly updated list of minimum freelance rates which will give you some idea of what to expect. And remember that if you are a self-employed freelance you own the copyright to your work. This does not mean refusing further use of the material: you can license it, giving permission for a specific use for an agreed fee. Whatever freelancing you end up doing, enjoy the ethical, political, writing challenges. It's not easy but the personal rewards can be substantial. Good luck!

Richard Keeble is Professor of Journalism at Lincoln University. He has feelanced for a range of publications including *Tribune*, *Press Gazette*, *Peace News*, the *Journalist* and MediaLens.org.

Further reading

McKay, Jenny, *The Magazines Handbook*, Routledge, 2000
Willings Press Guide, Media Information Ltd, annual
Hennessy, Brendan, *Writing Feature Articles*, Focal Press, 3rd edn 1997
Hicks, Wynford, with Harriett Gilbert and Sally Adams, *Writing for Journalists*, Routledge, 1999

ndicates human interest picture stories; topical
*v*ell-illustrated background articles and series;
*•*graphic features dealing with science, people,
nalities, glamour; genre pictures for
tising; condensations and serialisations of
*s*elling fiction and non-fiction; cartoons, comic
, film and TV rights, merchandising and
paper graphics online.

*C*anadian Press

*c*iated Press House, 12 Norwich Street,
on EC4A 1QE
*2*0-7353 6355 *fax* 020-7583 4238
Correspondent Helen Branswell

on Bureau of the national news agency of
da. Founded 1919.

*Ce*ritext

*b*oadway Studios, 28 Tooting High Street,
on SW17 0RG
x 020-8672 5100
info@celebritext.com
te www.celebritext.com
ct Lee Howard

*a*lises in music, film and TV celebrity
*v*iews. Commission: 50%. Founded 2000.

*ra*l Press Features

le Way, Bristol BS99 7HD
17-934 3600 *fax* 0117-934 3642
*mail@central-press.co.uk
te www.central-press.co.uk
r Dominic Moody

lies features, cartoons, crosswords, horoscopes
*g*raphics strips to newspapers, magazines and
publications (including internet sites) in 50
*t*ries. Included in over 100 daily and weekly
es are columns of international interest on
h and beauty, medicine, employment, sports,
e and home, motoring, computers, film and
*, children's features, gardening, celebrity
es, food and drink, finance and law. Also runs
*l*iamentary service as well as supplying
*c*ial material for advertising features.

dra S. Perera

ra, 437 Pethiyagoda, Kelaniya-11600,
nka
9-911885 *fax* 94-1-323910/674-737/674-738
*C*HANDRA PERERA
cinetraww@dialogsl.net comsvc01@slt.lk ATTN
*D*RA PERERA
ra Worldwide Createch (Pvt) Ltd,
*r*d floor, 10B YMBA Building, Fort,
*m*bo 1, Sri Lanka
1-323910

and TV news, news films on Sri Lanka and
*v*es, colour and b&w photo news and features,

photographic and film coverages, screenplays and
scripts for TV and films, press clippings.
Broadcasting, TV and newspapers; journalistic
features, news, broadcasting and TV interviews.

Children's Express UK

Exmouth House, 3-11 Pine Street,
London EC1R 0JH
tel 020-7833 2577 *fax* 020-7278 7722
email enquiries@childrensexpress.btinternet.com
website www.childrens-express.org
Chief Executive Christopher Wyld, *Chairman*
Stephanie Williams

Offers young people aged 8–18 the opportunity to
write on issues of importance to them, for
newspapers, radio and TV. It operates after school
and at weekends. Founded 1995.

Daily & Sunday Telegraph Syndication

The Telegraph Group Ltd, 1 Canada Square,
Canary Wharf, London E14 5DT
tel 020-7538 7505 *fax* 020-7538 7319
email syndicat@telegraph.co.uk
website http://syndication.telegraph.co.uk

News, features, photography; worldwide
distribution and representation.

Environmental & Occupational Health Research Foundation

Penrose House, Birtles Road, Whirley,
Cheshire SK10 3JQ
tel/fax (01625) 615323
email eorhfl@aol.com
Managing Editor Peggy Bentham

Undertakes individual commissions and syndicates
articles to diverse science and technology journals
and general consumer media. Peer reviewed and
accredited contributors from academia and
professional institutions.

Euro-Digest Features

34A Compton Avenue, Brighton BN1 3PS
tel (01273) 233615 *fax* (01273) 203622
Directors Edward Whitehead, Andrew C.F.
Whitehead, Kirsty Tranter

Represents European press. Human interest and
travel features. Occasional news items. Particularly
interested in material from Scotland, Northern
Ireland and Wales. Commission: by arrangement,
according to subject, etc.

Europa-Press

Sveavägen 47, 2nd Floor, Box 6410, S-113 82,
Stockholm
tel 8-34 94 35 *fax* 8-34 80 79
email tord@europapress.se
Managing Director Tord Steinsvik

Syndicates, news and press agen

Before submitting material, you are strongly advised to make preliminary enquirie: ascertain terms of work. Strictly speaking, syndication is the selling and resellin previously published work although some news and press agencies handle original

Academic File Information Services

Eastern Art Publishing Group,
PO Box 13666, 27 Wallorton Gardens,
London SW14 8WF
tel 020-8392 1122 *fax* 020-8392 1422
email afis@eapgroup.com
website www.eapgroup.com
Managing Editor Sajid Rizvi, *Executive Editor* Shirley Rizvi

Feature and photo syndication with special reference to the developing world and immigrant communities in the West. Founded 1985.

Advance Features

Stubbs Wood Cottage, Hammerwood,
East Grinstead, West Sussex RH19 3QE
tel/fax (01342) 850480
website www.advancefeatures.uk.com
Managing Editor Peter Norman

Crosswords: daily, weekly and theme; general puzzles. Daily and weekly cartoons for the regional, national and overseas press (not single cartoons).

Alpha incorporating London News Service

63 Gee Street, London EC1V 3RS
tel 020-7336 0632 *fax* 020-7253 8419
Managing Director Ray Blumire

Worldwide syndication of features and photos.

The Associated Press Ltd

(News Department), The Associated Press House,
12 Norwich Street, London EC4A 1BP
tel 020-7353 1515 *fax* 020-7353 8118

Atlantic Syndication

17-18 Haywards Place, London EC1R 0EQ
tel 020-7566 0360 *fax* 020-7566 0388
Contact Nick York

Worldwide syndication of newspaper features, photos, cartoons, strips and book serialisations. Agency represents the international syndication of Associated Newspapers (*Daily Mail, Mail on Sunday, Evening Standard*).

Australian Associated Press

12 Norwich Street, London EC4A 1QJ
tel 020-7353 0153 *fax* 020-7583 3563

News service to the Australian, New Zealand and Pacific Island press, radio and TV. Founded 1935.

Brainwarp

PO Box 51, Newton-le-Willows,
Merseyside WA3 3NZ
tel (01942) 271817
email trixie@brainwarp.com
website www.brainwarp.com
Partners Trixie Roberts, Tony Roberts

Supplies original crosswords, brainteaser searches, quizzes and word games to edit printed page. Commission: standard fees syndicated work; customised work nego Founded 1987.

Bulls Presstjänst AB

Tulegatan 39, Box 6519, S-11383 Stockh Sweden
tel (08) 55520600 *fax* (08) 55520665
email kontakt@bulls.se
website www.bulls.se
Bulls Pressedienst GmbH
Eysseneckstrasse 50, D-60322 Frankfur Germany
tel (069) 959 270 *fax* (069) 959 27111
email sales@bullspress.de
Bulls Pressetjeneste A/S
Ebbells Gate 3, N-0183 Oslo, Norway
tel 22 98 26 60 *fax* 22 20 49 78
email bullsosl@online.no
Bulls Pressetjeneste
Ostbanegade 9, 1th, DK-2100 Copen Denmark
tel 35 38 90 99 *fax* 35 38 25 16
email kjartan@bulls.dk
Oy Fennopress AB – a Bulls compar
Arabianranta 6, FIN-00560, Helsink
tel (09) 612 96 50 *fax* (09) 656 092
email ilkka@bullspress.fi
Bulls Press
ul. Chocimska 28, Pokoj 509, 00-79 Poland
tel (22) 845 90 10 *fax* (22) 845 90 1
email krzysztof@bulls.com.pl
Bulls Press
Narva MNT 7D, EE 10117 Tallin, I
tel (372) 66 96 737 *fax* (372) 66 01
email bulls@delfi.ee

Market newspapers, magazines, we advertising agencies in Sweden, D Finland, Iceland, Poland, The Balt Austria and German-speaking Sw

Market: newspapers, magazines, weeklies and websites in Sweden, Denmark, Norway, Finland, and the Baltic states. Syndicates high-quality features of international appeal such as topical articles, photofeatures – b&w and colour, women's features, short stories, serial novels, non-fiction stories and serials with strong human interest, crime articles, popular science, cartoons, comic strips.

Europress Features (UK)
18 St Chads Road, Didsbury,
Nr Manchester M20 9WH
tel 0161-445 2945
email freddy_12_gb@hotmail.com

Representation of newspapers and magazines in Europe, Australia, United States. Syndication of top-flight features with exclusive illustrations – human interest stories – showbusiness personalities. 30–35% commission on sales of material successfully accepted; 40% on exclusive illustrations.

Express Enterprises
(division of Express Newspapers plc)
Ludgate House, 245 Blackfriars Road,
London SE1 9UX
tel 020-7922 7903 *fax* 020-7922 7871

Text and pictures from all Express titles. Archive from 1900. Numerous strips and political cartoons. Material handled worldwide for freelance journalists.

Frontline Photo Press Agency
18 Wall Street, Norwood, South Australia 5067
postal address PO Box 162, Kent Town, SA 5071
tel (08) 8333 2691 *fax* (08) 8364 0604
email info@frontline.net.au
website www.frontline.net.au
Director Carlo Irlitti

Photographic press agency. Services provided: news, interviews, features, articles and photos for newspapers, magazines and other media. Digital photo wire services.

Syndicates sports, celebrity, travel, men's, women's, human and general interest features and articles with photos. Welcomes approaches from individuals and organisations abroad. Assignments undertaken. Rates negotiable. Founded 1988.

Gemini News Service
9 White Lion Street, London N1 9PD
tel 020-7278 1111 *fax* 020-7278 0345
email gemini@panoslondon.org.uk
website www.gemininewsservice.com
Editor Dipankar De Sarkar

Network of freelance contributors and specialist writers all over the world. Specialists in news-features of international, topical and development interest. Preferred length 800–1200 words.

Graphic Syndication
4 Reyntiens View, Odiham,
Hants RG29 1AF
tel (01256) 703004
email sensible@screaming.net
Manager M. Flanagan

Cartoon strips and single frames supplied to newspapers and magazines in Britain and overseas. Terms: 50%. Founded 1981.

Hayters Teamwork
Image House, Station Road,
London N17 9LR
tel 020-8808 3300 *fax* 020-8808 1122
email sport@haytersteamwork.com
website www.hayters.com
Managing Director Nick Callow, *Chief Executive* Gerry Cox

Sports news, features and data supplied to all branches of the media. Commission: negotiable according to merit. Founded 1955.

India-International News Service
Head office Jute House, 12 India Exchange Place,
Kolkata 700001, India
tel 22209563
Proprietor Eur Ing H. Kothari BSc, DWP(Lond), FIMechE, FIE, FVI, FInstD(Lond), FRAS, FRSA

'Calcutta Letters' and Air Mail news service from Calcutta. Specialists in industrial and technical news.

INS (International News Service) and Irish News Service
UK office 7 King's Avenue, Minnis Bay,
Birchington-on-Sea, East Kent CT7 9QL
tel (01843) 845022
Editor and Managing Director Barry J. Hardy PC,
Photo Editor Jan Vanek, *Secretary* K.T. Byrne

News, sport, book and magazine reviews (please forward copies), TV, radio, photographic department; also equipment for TV films, etc.

International Fashion Press Agency
Penrose House, Birtles Road, Whirley,
Cheshire SK10 3JQ
tel/fax (01625) 615323
email ifpressagy@aol.com
Directors P. Bentham (managing), P. Dyson,
S. Fagette, L.C. Mottershead, L.B. Fell, T.R. Fox

Monitors and photographs international fashion collections and developments in textile and fashion industry. Specialist writers on health, fitness, beauty and personalities. Undertakes individual commissioned features. Supplies syndicated columns/pages to press, radio and TV (NUJ staff writers and photographers).

International Press Agency (Pty) Ltd
Sunrise House, 56 Morningside, Ndabeni 7405,
South Africa
tel (021) 531 1926 *fax* (021) 531 8789
email inpra@iafrica.com
Manager Mrs T. Temple
UK office 12 Marion Court, 134-142 Tooting High
Street, London SW17 0RU
tel 020-8767 4828
Managing Editor Mrs U.A. Barnett PhD

South African agents for many leading British,
American and continental press firms for the
syndication of comic strips, cartoons, jokes, feature
articles, short stories, serials, press photos for the
South African market. Founded 1934.

J.W. Crabtree and Son
Cheapside Chambers, 43 Cheapside,
Bradford BD1 4HP
tel (01274) 732937 (office), (01535) 655288 (home)
fax (01274) 732937

News and sport. Founded 1919.

Joker Feature Service (JFS)
PO Box 253, 6040 AG, Roermond,
The Netherlands
tel (0475) 337338 *fax* (0475) 315663
email j.f.s@tip.nl
Managing Director Ruud Kerstens

Feature articles, serial rights, tests, cartoons, comic
strips and illustrations, puzzles. Handles TV
features, books, internet sites; also production for
merchandising.

Knight Features
20 Crescent Grove, London SW4 7AH
tel 020-7622 1467 *fax* 020-7622 1522
email peter@knightfeatures.co.uk
website www.knightfeatures.co.uk
Director Peter Knight, *Associates* Ann King-Hall,
Gaby Martin, Andrew Knight, Samantha Ferris

Worldwide selling of strip cartoons and major
features and serialisations. Exclusive agent in UK
and Republic of Ireland for United Feature
Syndicate and Newspaper Enterprise Association of
New York. Founded 1985.

London News Service – see Alpha incorporating London News Service

Maharaja Features Pvt. Ltd
5-226 Sion Road East,
Bombay 400022, India
tel 22-4097951 *fax* 22-4097801
email mahafeat@bom2.vsnl.net.in
website www.welcomeindia.com/maharaja
Editor Mrs R. Ravi, *Managing Editor* K.R.N. Swamy

Syndicates feature and pictorial material, of interest
to Asian readers, to newspapers and magazines in
India, UK and abroad. Specialists in well-researched
articles on India by eminent authorities for
publication in prestige journals throughout the
world. Also topical features 1000–1500 words.
Illustrations: b&w prints and colour transparencies.

Mirrorpix
22nd Floor, 1 Canada Square, Canary Wharf,
London E14 5AP
tel 020-7293 3700 *fax* 020-7293 2712
email desk@mirrorpix.com
website www.mirrorpix.com
Contact Sales desk

Images of the past 100 years by photographers of
the *Daily Mirror* and her sister titles which
document both the light and dark sides of British
life: people, places, events and movements.

National Association of Press Agencies (NAPA)
41 Lansdowne Crescent, Leamington Spa,
Warks. CV32 4PR
tel (01926) 424181 *fax* (01926) 424760
website www.napa.org.uk
Directors Denis Cassidy, Chris Johnson, Barrie
Tracey, John Quinn

NAPA is a network of independent, established and
experienced press agencies serving newspapers,
magazines, TV and radio networks. Founded 1983.

National Sports Reporting
10 Elmete Grange, Menston, Ilkley,
West Yorkshire LS29 6LA
tel (01943) 884228
email 100654.463@compuserve.com
Editor Christopher Harte, *Managers* Michael
Latham (Northern Region), David Fox (South West
Region), Diana Harding (South East Region), Dave
Hammond (Scotland)

News and reporting service for sporting events.
Research facilities for radio and TV, particularly
sports documentaries. Commission: NUJ rates.
Founded 1994.

Neil Bradley Puzzles
Linden House, 73 Upper Marehay, Ripley,
Derbyshire DE5 8JF
tel (01773) 741500 *fax* (01773) 741555
email bradcart@aol.com
Director Neil Bradley

Supplies visual puzzles to national and regional
press; emphasis placed on variety and topicality
with work based on current media listings. Work
supplied on disk or prints to Mac or PC. Daily
single frame and strip cartoons. Contact for free
booklet and disk demo. Founded 1981.

New Blitz Literary & TV Agency
Via di Panico 67, 00186 Rome, Italy
postal address CP 30047-00193, Rome 47, Italy
tel/fax (06) 686 4859
email blitzgacs@inwind.it
Manager Giovanni A.S. Congiu

Syndicates worldwide: cartoons, comic strips, humorous books with drawings, feature and pictorial material, topical, environment, travel. Average rates of commission 60/40%, monthly report of sales, payment 60 days after the date of monthly report.

Pixfeatures
5 Latimer Road, Barnet, Herts. EN5 5NU
tel 020-8449 9946 *fax* 020-8441 2725
Contact Peter Wickman
Spanish office tel 00349 6642 5312, *Contact* Roy Wickman

News agency and picture library. Specialises in selling Spanish pictures and features to British and European press.

The Press Association
292 Vauxhall Bridge Road, London SW1V 1AE
tel 020-7963 7000 *fax* 020-7963 7192
website www.pa.press.net
Chief Executive/Editor-in-Chief Paul Potts, *Managing Director* Steven Brown

PA News Fast and accurate news, photography and information to print, broadcast and electronic media in the UK and Ireland.

PA Sport In-depth coverage of national and regional sports, transmitting a huge range of stories, results, pictures and updates every day.

PA Listings Page- and screen-ready information from daily guides to 7-day supplements on sports results, TV and radio listings, arts and entertainment, financial and weather listings tailored to suit requirements.

PA Digital Top quality content including news and sport for a wide range of multimedia customers.

PA WeatherCentre Continuously updated information on present and future weather conditions; consultancy services for media and industry. Founded 1868.

Press Features Syndicate
9 Paradise Close, Eastbourne,
East Sussex BN20 8BT
tel (01323) 728760
Editor Harry Gresty

Specialises in photo-features, both b&w and colour. Seeks human interest, oddity, glamour, pin-ups, scientific, medical, etc material suitable for marketing through own branches in London,

San Francisco, Paris, Hamburg, Milan, Stockholm, Amsterdam (for Benelux), Helsinki.

Press Gang News
137 Endlesham Road, London SW12 8JN
tel 020-8673 4229 020-8673 7778 *fax* 020-8673 3205
email mail@pressgangnews.co.uk
website www.pressgangnews.co.uk
Partners Mark Christy, Sarah Christy

National news, features and photographic news agency. Seeks good journalists and photographers; considers material from freelance journalists. Keen to receive stories, press releases, etc from individual members of the public and from organisations, etc. Founded 1996.

Rann Communication
Level 1, 18-20 Grenfell Street, Adelaide, SA 5000, Australia
postal address GPO Box 958, Adelaide, SA 5000, Australia
tel (08) 8211 7771 *fax* (08) 8212 2272
email chrisrann@rann.com.au
Proprietor C.F. Rann

Full range of professional PR, press releases, special newsletters, commercial and political intelligence, media monitoring. Welcomes approaches from organisations requiring PR representation or press release distribution. Founded 1982.

Reuters Group plc
85 Fleet Street, London EC4P 4AJ
tel 020-7250 1122

Southern News Service
Exchange House, Hindhead,
Surrey GU26 6AA
tel (01428) 607330 *fax* (01428) 606351
email denis@cassidyandleigh.com
Partners Denis Cassidy and Donald Leigh

News stories, features and court coverage. Full picture service, digital and ISDN. Public relations words and pictures. Founded 1960.

UK Features
38 The Woodlands, Esher, Surrey KT10 8DB
tel 020-8398 5676 *fax* 020-8398 9051
email robincorry@ukfeatures.com
Proprietor Robin Corry

Human interest and general features. Payment: £150–£250 for an early tip-off. Founded 1979.

United Press UK Ltd
Prince Consort House, 27-29 Albert Embankment, London SE1 7TJ
tel 020-7820 4183 (editorial), 020-7820 4180 (admin) *fax* 020-7820 4190
email www.upi.com

Universal Pictorial Press & Agency

29-31 Saffron Hill, London EC1N 8SW
tel 020-7421 6000 *fax* 020-7421 6006
email charles.taylor@photoshot.com
Managing Director Charles Taylor

Photographic news agency and picture library: the UK's leading archive for British and international personalities from 1944 to present. Digital archive from 1994. Founded 1929.

Visual Humour

5 Greymouth Close, Stockton-on-Tees TS18 5LF
tel/fax (01642) 581847
email peterdodsworth@btclick.com
website enquiries@businesscartoons.co.uk
Contact Peter Dodsworth

Daily and weekly humorous cartoon strips; also single panel cartoon features (not gag cartoons) for possible syndication in the UK and abroad. Picture puzzles also considered. Submit photocopy samples only initially, with sae. Founded 1984.

Books

Submitting material

Each year, thousands of typescripts are submitted to publishers by hopeful authors but only a small proportion are accepted for publication. Some are needlessly rejected either because they were sent to an inappropriate publisher, or because the publisher's submission procedure was not followed. We give here some guidelines to consider before submitting material.

First, and most importantly, choose the right publisher. It is a waste of time and money to send the typescript (or manuscript, abbreviated to MS) of a novel to a publisher which publishes no fiction, or poetry to one who publishes no verse. By studying the entries in the *Yearbook*, examining publishers' lists of publications, or by looking for the names of suitable publishers in the relevant sections in libraries and bookshops, you will find the names of several publishers which might be interested in seeing your material.

Secondly, approach the publisher in the way they prefer. Many publishers will not accept unsolicited material – you must enquire first if they would be willing to read the whole work. A few publishers are prepared to speak on the telephone, allowing you to describe, briefly, the work on offer. Most prefer a preliminary letter; and many publishers, particularly of fiction, will only consider material submitted through a literary agent. It has to be said that some publishing houses, the larger ones in particular, may well employ all three methods!

Enclose a synopsis of the work, and two or three sample chapters, with your preliminary letter, plus return postage (or International Reply Coupons if you are writing from outside the country or if you are submitting material from the UK to the Republic of Ireland; for further information *tel* (08457) 223344). Writers have been known to send out such letters in duplicated form, an approach unlikely to stimulate a publisher's interest. Remember, also, that whilst every reasonable care will be taken of material in the publishers' possession, responsibility cannot be accepted if material is lost or damaged. Never send your only copy of the typescript. For more information, see *Dos and don'ts on approaching a publisher* on page 217. An alphabetical listing of publishers' names and addresses follows on page 127.

Fiction
See page 685 for a list of *Publishers of fiction*, by fiction genre. A full list of literary agents starts on page 348.

Children's books
The market for children's books is considered in *Writing and the children's book market* on page 226. The list of *Children's book publishers and packagers* on page 688 includes publishers of poetry for children and teenage fiction. A list of *Literary agents for children's books* is on page 692.

Poetry

Publishers which consider poetry for adults are listed on page 691. See also *Getting poetry published* on page 261 and *Poetry organisations* on page 267.

Small presses

It is beyond the scope of the *Yearbook* to list all the many smaller publishers which have either a limited output, or that specialise in poetry, avant-garde or other fringe publishing. However, some of the better-known small poetry houses are included.

Self-publishing

Authors are strongly advised not to pay for the publication of their work. A reputable firm of publishers will undertake publication at its own expense, except possibly for works of an academic nature. See *Doing it on your own* on page 234 for an introduction to self-publishing and *Vanity publishing* on page 247.

Publishers' contracts

Following a publishing company's firm interest in a MS, a publisher's contract is drawn up between the author and the publisher (see *Publishing agreements*, page 591). If the author is not entirely happy with the contract presented to them or wishes to take advice, he/she could ask their literary agent, the Society of Authors or the Writers' Guild of Great Britain to check the contract on their behalf – providing the author has an agent and/or is a member of those organisations. Otherwise, the author can either check it for himself (for guidance, see *An Author's Guide to Publishing* and *Understanding Publishers' Contracts*, both books by Michael Legat; see page 591), or seek advice from a solicitor. Before consulting a solicitor, make sure that they are familiar with publishing agreements and can give informed advice. Many local firms have little or no experience of such work and their opinion can often be of limited value and the cost may outweigh any possible gains. See *Editorial, literary and production services* for practitioners who undertake these legal services.

See also ...

- Book publishers in *Australia* (page 193); in *Canada* (page 196); in *New Zealand* (page 199); in *South Africa* (page 201); and in the *USA* (page 203)
- *Ghostwriting*, page 221
- *Who owns whom in publishing*, page 250
- *Top one hundred chart of 2002 paperback fastsellers*, page 252
- *Book packagers*, page 187
- *How to get an agent*, page 345
- *Literary agents*, page 348
- *E-publishing*, page 525
- *The writer's toolkit*, page 543

Book publishers UK and Ireland

*Member of the Publishers Association or Scottish Publishers Association
†Member of the Irish Book Publishers' Association

A & C Black Publishers Ltd*
37 Soho Square, London W1D 3QZ
tel 020-7758 0200 *fax* 020-7758 0222
email enquiries@acblack.com
website www.acblack.com
Chairman Nigel Newton, *Managing Director* Jill
Coleman, *Directors* Colin Adams, Jenny Aspinall,
Charles Black, Sarah Fecher (children's books),
Oscar Heini (production), Paul Langridge (rights),
Janet Murphy (Adlard Coles Nautical), Kathy
Rooney, Terry Rouelett (distribution), David
Wightman (sales), Jonathan Glasspool (reference)

Children's and educational books (including music)
for 3–15 years (preliminary enquiry appreciated –
fiction guidelines available on request); ceramics,
art and craft, drama, ornithology, reference (*Who's
Who*, *Whitaker's Almanack*), sport, theatre, travel,
books for writers. Subsidiary of Bloomsbury
Publishing plc. Founded 1807.

Adlard Coles Nautical (imprint)
Nautical.

Andrew Brodie (imprint)
Children's, educational.

Christopher Helm (imprint)
Ornithology.

The Herbert Press (imprint)
Visual arts.

Pica Press (imprint)
Ornithology.

T & AD Poyser (imprint)
Ornithology, natural history.

Thomas Reed (imprint)
Nautical.

AA Publishing
Automobile Association, Fanum House,
Basingstoke, Hants RG21 4EA
tel (0990) 448866 *fax* (01256) 322575
website www.theAA.com
Managing Director Stephen Mesquita, *Editorial
Director* Michael Buttler

Travel, atlases, maps, leisure interests, including
Essential Guides, Spiral Guides, City Packs and
Explorer Travel Guides. Founded 1979.

Abacus – see Time Warner Books UK

ABC-Clio Europe
(formerly Clio Press Ltd)
Old Clarendon Ironworks, 35A Great
Clarendon Street, Oxford OX2 6AT
tel (01865) 311350 *fax* (01865) 311358
email oxford@abc-clio.ltd.uk
website www.abc-clio.com
Senior Acquisitions Editor Dr Robert G. Neville

General and academic reference: encyclopedias in
history, mythology, literature, ethnic studies;
bibliography. Publishes *The Clio Montessori Series*,
and CD-Rom and web versions of abstracting
services in American studies and history. Branch of
ABC-CLIO Inc. Founded 1971.

Absolute Classics – see Oberon Books

Absolute Press
Scarborough House, 29 James Street West,
Bath BA1 2BT
tel (01225) 316013 *fax* (01225) 445836
email sales@absolutepress.co.uk
website www.absolutepress.co.uk
Publisher Jon Croft, *Directors* Amanda Bennett
(sales), Meg Avent (editorial)

General list: cookery, food-related topics, wine,
lifestyle, popular culture, travel, gay travel. No
fiction. *Outlines* series of monographs on gay and
lesbian artists. No unsolicited MSS. Founded 1979.

Academic Press – see Elsevier Ltd

Academy Editions – acquired by Wiley Europe Ltd

Access Press – see HarperCollins Publishers

Ace Books – see Age Concern Books

Acorn Editions – see James Clarke & Co. Ltd

Actinic Press – see Cressrelles Publishing Co. Ltd

Addison-Wesley – see Pearson Education

Adlard Coles Nautical – see A & C Black Publishers Ltd

Age Concern Books
(formerly Ace Books)
Age Concern England, 1268 London Road,
London SW16 4ER

tel 020-8765 7200 *fax* 020-8765 7211
email books@ace.org.uk
Publisher Richard Holloway

Health and care, advice, finance, gerontology. Founded 1973.

Aidan Ellis Publishing

Whinfield, Herbert Road, Salcombe,
Devon TQ8 8HN
tel (01548) 842755 *fax* (01548) 844356
email aidan@aepub.demon.co.uk
website www.aepub.co.uk
Publisher Aidan Ellis

Non-fiction: gardening, maritime, biography, general. Founded 1971.

Airlife Publishing – see The Crowood Press

Aladdin/Watts – see The Watts Publishing Group Ltd

Allen Lane – see Penguin Group (UK)

Allison & Busby Ltd

Suite 111, Bon Marché Centre,
241-251 Ferndale Road, London SW9 8BJ
tel 020-7738 7888 *fax* 020-7733 4244
email all@allisonbusby.co.uk
website www.allisonandbusby.ltd.uk
Publishing Director David Shelley, *Editor* Debbie Hatfield, *Press Officer* Fiona Hague

Literary fiction, crime fiction. Biography and history with a literary theme. Writers' Guides. New proposals accepted (send synopsis and sample pages initially) but sae essential.

The Alpha Press – see Sussex Academic Press

Amber Lane Press Ltd

Church Street, Charlbury,
Oxon OX7 3PR
tel/fax (01608) 810024
email info@amberlanepress.co.uk
Chairman Brian Clark, *Director/Managing Editor* Judith Scott

Plays, theatre, music. Founded 1978.

AN The Artists Information Company

1st Floor, 7-15 Pink Lane,
Newcastle upon Tyne NE1 5DW
tel 0191-241 8000 *fax* 0191-241 8001
email edit@anpubs.demon.co.uk
website www.anweb.co.uk
AN Editor Gillian Nicol

Provides information, advice and critical debate on contemporary visual arts practice through *AN magazine* (monthly), its website, and a programme of artists' training and professional development for Northern England. Founded 1980.

Andersen Press Ltd*

20 Vauxhall Bridge Road, London SW1V 2SA
tel 020-7840 8700 (editorial) *fax* 020-7233 6263
email andersenpress@randomhouse.co.uk
website www.andersenpress.co.uk
Managing Director/Publisher Klaus Flugge, *Directors* Philip Durrance, Joëlle Flugge (company secretary), Janice Thomson (editorial)

Children's books: picture books, novelties, junior and teenage fiction (send synopsis and first 3 chapters with sae); no short stories or poetry. International co-productions. Founded 1976.

André Deutsch – see Carlton Publishing Group

Andrew Brodie – see A & C Black Publishers Ltd

The Angels' Share – see Neil Wilson Publishing Ltd

Anness Publishing

88-89 Blackfriars Road, London SE1 8HA
tel 020-7401 2077 *fax* 020-7633 9499
Managing Director Paul Anness, *Publisher* Joanna Lorenz

Practical illustrated books on lifestyle, cookery, crafts, gardening, Mind, Body & Spirit, health and children's non-fiction. Founded 1989.

Aquamarine (hardback imprint)

Lifestyle, cookery, crafts and gardening.

Hermes House (imprint)

Illustrated promotional books on practical subjects.

Lorenz Books (hardback imprint)

Lifestyle, cookery, crafts, gardening, Mind, Body & Spirit, health and children's non-fiction.

Southwater (paperback imprint)

Lifestyle, cookery, crafts, gardening, Mind, Body & Spirit, health and children's non-fiction.

Antique Collectors' Club Ltd

Sandy Lane, Old Martlesham, Woodbridge,
Suffolk IP12 4SD
tel (01394) 389950 *fax* (01394) 389999
email sales@antique-acc.com
website www.antique-acc.com
Managing Director Diana Steel

Fine art, antiques, gardening and garden history, architecture. Founded 1966.

Anvil Books/The Children's Press†

45 Palmerston Road, Dublin 6,
Republic of Ireland
tel (01) 4973628 *fax* (01) 4968263
Directors Rena Dardis (managing), Margaret Dardis (editorial)

Anvil: Irish history and biography. Only considers MSS by Irish-based authors and of Irish interest.

Send synopsis with IRCs (no UK stamps); unsolicited MSS not returned. Children's Press: adventure, fiction, ages 9–14. Founded 1964.

Anvil Press Poetry
Neptune House, 70 Royal Hill, London SE10 8RF
tel 020-8469 3033 *fax* 020-8469 3363
email anvil@anvilpresspoetry.com
website www.anvilpresspoetry.com
Director Peter Jay
Poetry. Submissions only with sae. Founded 1968.

Apple Press – see Quarto Publishing plc in Book packagers, page 191

Appletree Press Ltd*†
14 Howard Street South, Belfast BT7 1AP
tel 028-9024 3074 *fax* 028-9024 6756
email reception@appletree.ie
website www.appletree.ie
Director John Murphy

Gift books, biography, cookery, guidebooks, history, Irish interest, literary criticism, music, photographic, social studies, sport, travel. Founded 1974.

Aquamarine – see Anness Publishing

Arc Publications
Nanholme Mill, Shaw Wood Road, Todmorden, Lancs. OL14 6DA
tel (01706) 812338 *fax* (01706) 818948
Partners Rosemary Jones, Tony Ward (general editor), Angela Jarman, *Associate Editors* John Kinsella (international), Jean Boase-Beier (translation), Jo Shapcott (UK)
Poetry. MSS with sae only. List is full for next 2 years.

Arcadia Books Ltd
15-16 Nassau Street, London W1W 7AB
tel/fax 020-7436 9898
email info@arcadiabooks.co.uk
website www.arcadiabooks.co.uk
Managing Director Gary Pulsifer, *Publishing Director* Daniela de Groote

Original paperback fiction, fiction in translation, autobiography, biography, travel, gender studies, gay books. Submissions via literary agents only. *Sunday Times* Small Publisher of the Year 2002/03. Founded 1996.

Architectural Press – see Elsevier Ltd

Arcturus – see W. Foulsham & Co. Ltd

Arkana – former imprint of Penguin Press

Arrow Books Ltd – see Random House Group Ltd

Arthur James Ltd – incorporated into John Hunt Publishing Ltd

Ashgate Publishing Ltd
Gower House, Croft Road, Aldershot, Hants GU11 3HR
tel (01252) 331551 *fax* (01252) 344405
email info@ashgatepub.co.uk
Editors Sarah Markham (social sciences), Katherine Hodkinson (social work and public service), John Hindley (aviation management), Thomas Gray (history), Pamela Edwardes (art history), Rachel Lynch (music and literary studies), Sarah Lloyd (philosophy and theology), Val Rose (regional science), Kirsten Howgate (politics and international relations), John Irwin (legal studies)

Publishes a wide range of academic research in the social sciences and humanities, professional practice publications in the management of business and public services, and illustrated books on art, architecture and design. Founded 1967.

Gower (imprint)
Editor Jonathan Norman
Business, management and training.

Lund Humphries (imprint)
Editor Lucy Myers
Art and design.

Variorum (imprint)
Editor John Smedley
History.

Ashmolean Museum Publications
Beaumont Street, Oxford OX1 2PH
tel (01865) 278010 *fax* (01865) 278018
website www.ashmol.ox.ac.uk
Contact Susan Moss

Fine and applied art of Europe and Asia, archaeology, history, numismatics. No unsolicited MSS. Photographic archive. Founded 1683.

Aslib (The Association for Information Management)
Temple Chambers, 3-7 Temple Avenue, London EC4Y 0HP
tel 020-7583 8900 *fax* 020-7583 8401
website www.aslib.com

For books contact Taylor & Francis 020-7842 2400; for journals contact Emerald (01206) 796351; for *Managing Information* magazine contact Graham Coult (editor) 020-7583 8900, www.managinginformation.com

Aspect Guides – see Bloomsbury Publishing Plc

Associated University Presses – see Golden Cockerel Press Ltd

Atlantic Books

Ormond House, 26-27 Boswell Street,
London WC1N 3JZ
tel 020-7269 1610 *fax* 020-7430 0916
email enquiries@groveatlantic.co.uk
Managing Director/Publisher Toby Mundy

Literary fiction, history, current affairs, biography, politics, reference, autobiography; *Guardian* and *Observer* books. No unsolicited submissions. Wholly owned subsidiary of **Grove/Atlantic Inc.**, New York. Founded 2000.

Atlantic Europe Publishing Co. Ltd

Greys Court Farm, Greys Court,
Henley-on-Thames, Oxon RG9 4PG
tel (01491) 628188 *fax* (01491) 628189
email info@atlanticeurope.com
website www.AtlanticEurope.com
Directors Dr B.J. Knapp, D.L.R. McCrae

Children's colour illustrated information books, co-editions and primary class books: science, geography, technology, mathematics, history. No MSS accepted by post. In the first instance email. Founded 1990.

Atom – see Time Warner Books UK

Attic Press – see Cork University Press

Aureus Publishing Ltd

Castle Court, Castle-upon-Alun,
Vale of Glamorgan CF32 0TN
tel/fax (01656) 880033
email info@aureus.co.uk
website www.aureus.co.uk
Director Meuryn Hughes

Rock and pop, autobiography, sport, aviation, religion; also music. Founded 1993.

Aurum Press Ltd

25 Bedford Avenue, London WC1B 3AT
tel 020-7637 3225 *fax* 020-7580 2469
email firstname.surname@aurumpress.co.uk
website www.aurumpress.co.uk
Directors Bill McCreadie (managing), Piers Burnett (editorial), Graham Eames (sales), Sheila Murphy (non-executive), Khalil Abu-Shawareb (non-executive)

General, illustrated and non-illustrated adult non-fiction: biography and memoirs, military, visual arts, film, sport, travel, fashion, home interest. Imprints: Argentum (photography), Jacqui Small (lifestyle). Founded 1977.

Award Publications Ltd

1st Floor, 27 Longford Street, London NW1 3DZ
tel 020-7388 7800 *fax* 020-7388 7887
Managing Director Ron Wilkinson

Children's books: full colour picture story books; early learning, information and activity books. No unsolicited material. Founded 1954.

Azure Books – see Society for Promoting Christian Knowledge

B.T. Batsford Ltd – see Chrysalis Books Group

Bailliere Tindall – see Elsevier Ltd

Bantam – see Transworld Publishers Ltd

Bantam Children's – see Random House Group Ltd

Bantam Press – see Transworld Publishers Ltd

Barefoot Books Ltd

124 Walcot Street, Bath BA1 5BG
tel (01225) 322400 *fax* (01225) 322499
email info@barefootbooks.co.uk
website www.barefootbooks.co.uk
Publisher Tessa Strickland

Children's picture books and audiobooks: myth, legend, fairytale. No unsolicited MSS. Founded 1993.

Barrie & Jenkins – former imprint of Random House Group Ltd

Barry Rose Law Publishers Ltd

Little London, Chichester, West Sussex PO19 1PG
tel (01243) 783637 *fax* (01243) 779278
email books@barry-rose-law.co.uk

Law, local government, police, legal history. Founded 1972.

Countrywise Press Ltd

Reprints in paperback of hardcover books from Barry Rose; some non-law titles.

Bartholomew – see HarperCollins Publishers

BBC Audiobooks Ltd*

St James House, The Square, Lower Bristol Road,
Bath BA2 3SB
tel (01225) 335336 *fax* (01225) 422585
website www.bbcaudiobooks.com
Directors Paul Dempsey (managing), Jan Paterson (publishing), Rachel Stammers (marketing)

Large print books and complete and unabridged audiobooks: general fiction, crime, romance, mystery/thrillers, westerns, non-fiction. Does not publish original books. Imprints: Chivers Large Print, Chivers Audio Books, Black Dagger Crime, Windsor Large Print, Galaxy Children's Large Print. Formed in 2002 from the amalgamation of Chivers Press, Cover To Cover and BBC Radio Collection.

BBC Radio Collection – see BBC Audiobooks Ltd

BBC Worldwide Ltd – see page 294

Belitha Press – see Chrysalis Children's Books

Bell & Hyman Ltd – acquired by HarperCollins Publishers

Berg Publishers
1st Floor, Angel Court, 81 St Clements Street, Oxford OX4 1AW
tel (01865) 245104 *fax* (01865) 791165
email enquiry@bergpublishers.com
Managing Director Kathryn Earle

Social anthropology, cultural studies, sport, dress and fashion studies, European studies, politics, history. Founded 1983.

Berkswell Publishing Co. Ltd
PO Box 420, Warminster, Wilts. BA12 9XB
tel (01985) 840189 *fax* (01985) 840243
email churchwardens@btinternet.com
Directors J.N.G. Stidolph, S.A. Abbott

Books of local interest, field sports. Ideas and MSS welcome.

Berlitz Publishing Co. Ltd – see Insight Guides/Berlitz Publishing

Bernard Babani (Publishing) Ltd
The Grampians, Shepherds Bush Road, London W6 7NF
tel 020-7603 2581/7296 *fax* 020-7603 8203
Directors S. Babani, M.H. Babani

Practical handbooks on radio, electronics and computing.

BFI Publishing
British Film Institute, 21 Stephen Street, London W1P 2LN
tel 020-7255 1444 *fax* 020-7636 2516
website www.bfi.org.uk
Head of Publishing Andrew Lockett

Film and media studies; general books on films and directors. Founded 1982.

Big Fish – see Chrysalis Children's Books

BIOS Scientific Publishers – see Taylor & Francis Group plc

Birlinn Ltd*
West Newington House, 10 Newington Road, Edinburgh EH9 1QS
tel 0131-668 4371 *fax* 0131-668 4466

email info@birlinn.co.uk
website www.birlinn.co.uk
Directors Hugh Andrew, Hubert Andrew, Neville Moir, Ronnie Shanks

Scottish history, local interest/history, Scottish humour, guides, military, adventure, history, archaeology, vernacular architecture, sport, general non-fiction. Founded 1992.
John Donald (imprint)
Polygon (imprint)

New international and Scottish fiction, poetry, short stories, popular Scottish and international general interest. No unsolicited poetry accepted.

Birnbaum – see HarperCollins Publishers

Black Ace Books
PO Box 6557, Forfar DD8 2YS
tel (01307) 465096 *fax* (01307) 465494
website www.blackacebooks.com
Publisher Hunter Steele, *Art, Publicity and Sales* Boo Wood

Fiction, Scottish and general; new editions of outstanding recent fiction. Some biography, history, psychology and philosophy. No submissions without first visiting website for latest list details and requirements. Imprints: Black Ace Books, Black Ace Paperbacks. Founded 1991.

Black Lace – see Virgin Books Ltd

Black Swan – see Transworld Publishers Ltd

BlackAmber Books Ltd
3 Queen Square, London WC1N 3AU
tel 020-7278 2488 *fax* 020-7278 8864
email info@blackamber.com
website www.blackamber.com
Publisher Rosemarie Hudson

Literary fiction and non-fiction and work in translation by British and European Black and Asian writers. For novel submissions send one-page synopsis together with first 3 chapters and sae; for non-fiction, send a detailed outline with some accompanying material plus a one-page CV and sae. Founded 1998.

Blackstaff Press Ltd
4c Heron Wharf, Sydenham Business Park, Belfast BT3 9LE
tel 028-9045 5006 *fax* 028-9046 6237
email info@blackstaffpress.com
website www.blackstaffpress.com
Managing Editor Patsy Horton

Fiction, poetry, biography, history, politics, natural history, humour, education. Founded 1971.

Blackstone Press Ltd – acquired by Oxford University Press

The Blackwater Press – see Folens Publishing Company

Blackwell Publishing Ltd*
9600 Garsington Road, Oxford OX4 2DQ
tel (01865) 776868 *fax* (01865) 714591
website www.blackwellpublishing.com
Also at 108 Cowley Road, Oxford OX4 1JF
tel (01865) 791100 *fax* (01865) 791347
Chairman Nigel Blackwell, *President* Robert Campbell, *Chief Executive* René Olivieri

Books and journals in medicine, veterinary medicine, dentistry, nursing and allied health, science (particularly biology, chemistry and geology), social sciences, business and humanities. Journals are delivered online through Blackwell Synergy. Formed by merging Blackwell Science (founded 1939) and Blackwell Publishers (founded 1922).

Blake Publishing
(incorporating Smith Gryphon Ltd)
3 Bramber Court, 2 Bramber Road,
London W14 9PB
tel 020-7381 0666 *fax* 020-7381 6868
email words@blake.co.uk

Popular non-fiction, including biographies and true crime. No unsolicited fiction. Founded 1991.

Bloodaxe Books Ltd
Highgreen, Tarset, Northumberland NE48 1RP
tel (01434) 240500 *fax* (01434) 240505
email editor@bloodaxebooks.demon.co.uk
Directors Neil Astley, Simon Thirsk

Poetry, literary criticism. No submissions from new authors this year. Founded 1978.

Bloomsbury Publishing Plc*
38 Soho Square, London W1D 3HB
tel 020-7494 2111 *fax* 020-7434 0151
website www.bloomsburymagazine.com
Chairman and Chief Executive Nigel Newton,
Directors Liz Calder (publishing), Alexandra Pringle (publishing), Kathleen Farrar (international), Karen Rinaldi (Bloomsbury USA), Kathy Rooney (reference), David Ward (sales), Minna Fry (marketing), Rosamund de la Hey (children's marketing), Katie Collins (publicity), Ruth Logan (rights), Penny Edwards (production), Arzu Tahsin (paperbacks), Sarah Odedina (children's), Colin Adams (finance), Will Webb (design), Jill Coleman

Fiction, biography, illustrated, reference, travel, children's, trade paperback and mass market paperback. Founded 1986.

Aspect Guides (imprint)
email info@aspectguides.com
website www.aspectguides.com
Travel guides including the *French Entrée* series, *Everybody's Guides, Access Guides, Before You Go.*

Peter Collin (imprint)
email info@petercollin.com
website www.petercollin.com
Specialised dictionaries covering many subjects – from business to computing, medicine to tourism, law to banking. Bilingual language dictionaries in various subjects and languages.

Boatswain Press Ltd – now Nautical Data Ltd

Bodley Head Children's Books – see Random House Group Ltd

Booth-Clibborn Editions
12 Percy Street, London W1T 1DW
tel 020-7637 4255 *fax* 020-7637 4251
email info@booth-clibborn.com
website www.booth-clibborn-editions.co.uk

Illustrated books on art, popular culture, graphic design, photography. Founded 1974.

Bounty – see Octopus Publishing Group

Bowker
Windsor Court, East Grinstead House,
East Grinstead, West Sussex RH19 1XA
tel (01342) 336149 *fax* (01342) 336192
email customer.services@bowker.co.uk
website www.bowker.co.uk
Managing Director Jacki Heppard

Print and electronic publishers of bibliographies and serials databases, trade and reference directories and library and information titles. Part of the Cambridge Information Group.

Boxtree – see Macmillan Publishers Ltd

Boydell & Brewer Ltd
PO Box 9, Woodbridge,
Suffolk IP12 3DF

Medieval studies, history, literature, archaeology, art history. No unsolicited MSS. Founded 1969.

Bradt Travel Guides Ltd
19 High Street, Chalfont St Peter, Bucks SL9 9QE
tel (01753) 893444 *fax* (01753) 892333
email info@bradt-travelguides.com
website www.bradt-travelguides.com
Managing Director Hilary Bradt

Guides for the adventurous traveller who seeks off-beat places and 'the dreamer who would like to travel there but never will'.

Brandon/Mount Eagle Publications
(incorporating Brandon Book Publishers Ltd, 1982)
Cooleen, Dingle, Co. Kerry,
Republic of Ireland
tel (353) 66 9151463 *fax* (353) 66 9151234
Publisher Steve MacDonogh

Fiction, biography and current affairs. No
unsolicited MSS.

Brassey's (UK) Ltd – see Chrysalis Books Group

Breedon Books Publishing Co. Ltd
Breedon House, 3 The Parker Centre,
Mansfield Road, Derby DE21 4SZ
tel (01332) 384235 *fax* (01332) 292755
email anton@breedonbooks.co.uk
Directors Anton Rippon (chairman and editorial),
Patricia Rippon, Graham Hales (production)

Heritage, local history, archive photography, local
guidebooks, sports history – especially soccer. No
fiction. Preliminary letter essential. Founded 1981.

Breese Books Ltd
10 Hanover Crescent,
Brighton BN2 9SB
tel (01273) 687555
email martin@sherlockholmes.co.uk
website www.sherlockholmes.co.uk
Publisher Martin Breese

Conjuring books, Sherlock Holmes pastiches and
Breese's Guide to Modern First Editions. All work is
commissioned and unsolicited submissions are not
required. Founded 1980.

Brilliant Publications*
1 Church View, Sparrow Hall Farm, Edlesborough,
Dunstable LU6 2ES
tel (01525) 229720 *fax* (01525) 229725
email editorial@brilliantpublications.co.uk
website www.brilliantpublications.co.uk
Managing Director Priscilla Hannaford

Resource books for teachers and others concerned
with the education of 0–13 year-olds. All areas of
the curriculum published. Study catalogue or visit
website before sending proposal. Founded 1993.

Britannica.co.uk.ltd – see Encyclopaedia Britannica (UK) Ltd

The British Library (Publications)*
Publishing Office, The British Library,
96 Euston Road, London NW1 2DB
tel 020-7412 7704 *fax* 020-7412 7768
email blpublications@bl.uk
website www.bl.uk
Managers David Way (publishing), Lara Speicher
(managing editor), Catherine Britton (sales and
marketing)

Book arts, bibliography, music, maps, oriental,
manuscript studies, history, literature, facsimiles,
audiovisual, and multimedia CD-Rom. Founded
1973.

British Museum Company Ltd*
46 Bloomsbury Street, London WC1B 3QQ
tel 020-7323 1234 *fax* 020-7436 7315
website www.britishmuseumcompany.co.uk
Managing Director Andrew Thatcher, *Director of
Publishing* Alasdair MacLeod

General and specialised adult and children's books
on art history, archaeology, numismatics, history,
oriental art and archaeology, horology, ethnography.
Division of The British Museum Company Ltd.
Founded 1973.

Brockhampton Press – see Caxton Publishing Group

Brown, Son & Ferguson, Ltd*
4-10 Darnley Street, Glasgow G41 2SD
tel 0141-429 1234 (24 hours) *fax* 0141-420 1694
email info@skipper.co.uk
website www.skipper.co.uk
Editorial Director L. Ingram-Brown

Nautical books; plays; Scout, Cub Scout, Brownie
Guide and Guide story books. Founded 1860.

Brunner-Routledge – see Psychology Press Ltd

Bryntirion Press
(formerly Evangelical Press of Wales)
Bryntirion, Bridgend CF31 4DX
tel (01656) 655886 *fax* (01656) 665919
email office@emw.org.uk
website www.emw.org.uk
Press Manager Huw Kinsey

Theology and religion (in English and Welsh).
Founded 1955.

Burns & Oates – see The Continuum International Publishing Group Ltd

Buster Books – see Michael O'Mara Books Ltd

Butterworth-Heinemann – see Elsevier Ltd

C. Hurst & Co. (Publishers) Ltd*
38 King Street, London WC2E 8JZ
tel 020-7240 2666, (night) 020-7624 8713
fax 020-7240 2667
email hurst@atlas.co.uk
website www.hurstpub.co.uk
Directors Christopher Hurst, Michael Dwyer

Scholarly 'area studies' covering contemporary
history, politics, sociology and religion of Europe,

former USSR, Middle East, Asia and Africa. Founded 1967.

C.J. Fallon†

Lucan Road, Palmerstown, Dublin 20, Republic of Ireland
tel (01) 6166400 *fax* (01) 6166499
email editorial@cjfallon.ie
Executive Directors H.J. McNicholas (managing), P. Tolan (financial), N. White (editorial)

Educational text books. Founded 1927.

The C.W. Daniel Company Ltd

1 Church Path, Saffron Walden, Essex CB10 1JP
tel (01799) 521909 *fax* (01799) 513462
email cwdaniel@dial.pipex.com
website www.cwdaniel.com
Directors Ian Miller, Jane Miller

Natural healing, Bach Flower Remedies, homoeopathy, aromatherapy, mysticism. Founded 1902.

Health Science Press (imprint)
Directors Ian Miller, Jane Miller

Homoeopathy.

L.N. Fowler & Co Ltd (imprint)
Directors Ian Miller, Jane Miller

Mysticism, astrology.

Neville Spearman Publishers (imprint)
Editorial Director Sebastian Hobnut

Mysticism, metaphysical.

Cadogan Guides

Highlands House, 165 The Broadway, London SW19 1NE
tel 020-8544 8051 *fax* 020-8544 8081
email info.cadogan@virgin.net
website www.cadoganguides.com
Managing Editor Christine Stroyan

Travel guides. Founded 1982.

Calder Publications Ltd

51 The Cut, London SE1 8LF
tel 020-7633 0599 *fax* 020-7928 5930
email info@calderpublications.com
website www.calderpublications.com
Directors John Calder, Toby Fenton

European, international and British fiction and plays, art, literary, music and social criticism, biography and autobiography, essays, humanities and social sciences, European classics. No unsolicited MSS. Inquiry letters must include an sae. Series include: *English National Opera Guides, Scottish Library, New Writing and Writers, Opera Library, Historical Perspectives, Thought Bites.*

Calmann & King Ltd – see Laurence King Publishing Ltd

Cambridge University Press*

The Edinburgh Building, Shaftesbury Road, Cambridge CB2 2RU
tel (01223) 312393 *fax* (01223) 315052
email information@cambridge.org
website www.cambridge.org
Chief Executive of the Press Stephen R.R. Bourne

Anthropology and archaeology, art and architecture, astronomy, biological sciences, classical studies, computer science, dictionaries, earth sciences, economics, educational (primary, secondary, tertiary), e-learning products, engineering, film, English language teaching, history, language and literature, law, mathematics, medical sciences, music, philosophy, physical sciences, politics, psychology, reference, technology, social sciences, theology, religion. Journals (humanities, social sciences, STM). The Bible and Prayer Book. Founded 1534.

Cameron & Hollis

PO Box 1, Moffat, Dumfriesshire DG10 9SU
tel (01683) 220808 *fax* (01683) 220012
email editorial@cameronbooks.co.uk
website www.cameronbooks.co.uk
Directors Ian A. Cameron, Jill Hollis

Modern art, decorative art, collecting and film (serious critical works only). Founded 1979.

Campbell Books – see Macmillan Publishers Ltd

Canongate Books Ltd*

14 High Street, Edinburgh EH1 1TE
tel 0131-557 5111 *fax* 0131-557 5211
email info@canongate.co.uk
website www.canongate.net
Publisher Jamie Byng, *Directors* David Graham (managing), Judy Moir (editorial), Caroline Graham (production)

Adult general non-fiction and fiction: literary fiction, translated fiction, music, travel, mountaineering, Scottish interest, philosophy, religion, history and biography. No unsolicited MSS. Founded 1973.

Canongate Classics (imprint)
Senior Editor Rory Watson

Reprint series of key works of Scottish literature ranging from fiction to poetry, to biography, philosophy and travel.

Canopus Publishing Ltd

27 Queen Square, Bristol BS1 4ND
tel 0117-922 6660
email robin@canopusbooks.com

website www.canopusbooks.com
Director Robin Rees
Popular science and astronomy. Founded 1999.

Canterbury Press Norwich*
St Mary's Works, St Mary's Plain, Norwich,
Norfolk NR3 3BH
tel (01603) 612914 *fax* (01603) 624483
email admin@scm-canterburypress.co.uk
website www.scm-canterburypress.co.uk
Publisher Christine Smith

Religious doctrine, theology, liturgy, general
interest, reference, diary, guide and resource,
histories and associated topics, hymn books.
Division of SCM–Canterbury Press Ltd, a
subsidiary of Hymns Ancient & Modern Ltd.

Carcanet Press Ltd
4th Floor, Alliance House, 28-34 Cross Street,
Manchester M2 7AQ
tel 0161-834 8730 *fax* 0161-832 0084
email pnr@carcanet.u-net.com
website www.carcanet.co.uk
Director Michael Schmidt

Poetry, *Fyfield* series, Oxford Poets, translations.
Founded 1969.

Carlton Publishing Group
20 Mortimer Street,
London W1T 3JW
tel 020-7612 0400 *fax* 020-7612 0401
email enquiries@carltonbooks.co.uk
website www.carlton.com
Managing Director Jonathan Goodman, *Editorial
Director* Piers Murray Hill

No unsolicited MSS; synopses and ideas welcome.
Imprints: Carlton Books, André Deutsch, Granada
Media, Manchester United Books, Prion Books.
Owned by Carlton Communications. Founded
1992.

André Deutsch (division)

Autobiography, biography, history, current affairs,
the arts.

Carlton Books (division)

Illustrated leisure and entertainment books aimed
at the mass market: TV tie-ins, lifestyle (fashion,
beauty, health and wellbeing), popular science,
design, history, music, sport, puzzles.

Granada Media (division)

Manchester United Books (division)

Cassell Illustrated – see Octopus Publishing Group

Cassell Military – see Weidenfeld & Nicolson

Cassell Reference – see Weidenfeld & Nicolson

Cat's Whiskers – see The Watts Publishing Group Ltd

Catholic Truth Society
40-46 Harleyford Road, London SE11 5AY
tel 020-7640 0042 *fax* 020-7640 0046
email editorial@cts-online.org.uk
website www.cts-online.org.uk
Chairman Most Rev. Peter Smith DCL, LLB,
General Secretary Fergal Martin LLB, LLM

General books of Roman Catholic and Christian
interest, bibles, prayer books, RE, and booklets of
doctrinal, historical, devotional or social interest.
MSS of 11,000–15,000 words with up to 6
illustrations considered for publication as
pamphlets. Founded 1868.

Cavendish Publishing Ltd*
The Glass House, Wharton Street,
London WC1X 9PX
tel 020-7278 8000 *fax* 020-7278 8080
email info@cavendishpublishing.com
website www.cavendishpublishing.com
Executive Chairman Sonny Leong, *Managing
Director* Jeremy Stein, *Marketing Director* Ruth
Phillips, *Managing Editor* Cara Annett

A wide range of legal and medico–legal books and
journals. Imprints: Birkbeck Law Press, Glass House
Press, UCL Press. Founded 1990.

Caxton Publishing Group
20 Bloomsbury Street,
London WC1B 3QA
tel 020-7636 7171 *fax* 020-7636 1922
Directors John Maxwell (managing), Jack Cooper
(deputy managing)

Reprints, promotional books, remainders. Imprints:
Caxton Editions, Brockhampton Press, Knight
Paperbacks.

CBD Research Ltd
15 Wickham Road, Beckenham,
Kent BR3 5JS
tel 020-8650 7745 *fax* 020-8650 0768
email cbd@cbdresearch.com
website www.cbdresearch.com
Directors G.P. Henderson, S.P.A. Henderson,
A.J.W. Henderson

Directories, reference books, bibliographies, guides
to business and statistical information. Founded
1961.

Chancery House Press (imprint)

Unusual non-fiction/reference works. Preliminary
letter and synopsis with return postage essential.

Centaur Press – acquired by Open Gate Press

Century – see Random House Group Ltd

Chambers Harrap Publishers Ltd

7 Hopetoun Crescent, Edinburgh EH7 4AY
tel 0131-556 5929 fax 0131-556 5313
email admin@chambersharrap.co.uk
Managing Director Maurice Shepherd, Publishing Manager Patrick White

English language and bilingual dictionaries, reference, word games. No unsolicited MSS. Write enclosing CV and synopsis.

Chancery House Press – see CBD Research Ltd

Chapman Publishing

4 Broughton Place, Edinburgh EH1 3RX
tel 0131-557 2207 fax 0131-556 9565
email chapman-pub@blueyonder.co.uk
website www.chapman-pub.co.uk
Editor Joy Hendry

Poetry and drama: Chapman New Writing Series. Founded 1970.

Charles Knight – see LexisNexis Butterworths Tolley

Chartered Institute of Personnel and Development

CIPD Publishing, CIPD House, Camp Road, London SW19 4UX
tel 020-8263 3382 fax 020-8263 3850
email publish@cipd.co.uk
website www.cipd.co.uk/publications
Publishing Manager Sarah Brown

Personnel management, training and development.

Chatto & Windus – see Random House Group Ltd

Cherrytree Books – see Zero to Ten Ltd

The Chicken House – see Egmont Books

Child's Play (International) Ltd

Ashworth Road, Bridgemead, Swindon, Wilts. SN5 7YD
tel (01793) 616286 fax (01793) 512795
email allday@childs-play.com
website www.childs-play.com
Chairman Adriana Twinn, Publisher Neil Burden

Children's educational books: board picture, activity and play books; fiction and non-fiction. Founded 1972.

Chivers Press – see BBC Audiobooks Ltd

Christian Education*

(incorporating RE Today and International Bible Reading Association)
1020 Bristol Road, Selly Oak, Birmingham B26 6LB
tel 0121-472 4242 fax 0121-472 7575
email enquiries@christianeducation.org.uk
website www.christianeducation.org.uk

Publications and services for teachers of RE including RE Today magazine, curriculum booklets and British Journal of Religious Education, training material for children and youth workers in the Church. Worship resources for use in primary schools. Christian drama and musicals, Activity Club material and Bible reading resources.

Christopher Davies Publishers Ltd

PO Box 403, Swansea SA1 4YF
tel/fax (01792) 648825
email editor@cdaviesbookswales.com
website www.cdaviesbookswales.com
Directors Christopher Talfan Davies (editorial), K.E.T. Colayera, D.M. Davies

History, leisure, sport and general books of Welsh interest, Triskele Books. Founded 1949.

Christopher Helm – see A & C Black Publishers Ltd

Chrysalis Books Group

The Chrysalis Building, Bramley Road, London W10 6SP
tel 020-7314 1400 fax 020-7221 6455

Part of Chrysalis Group plc.

B.T. Batsford (imprint)
email batsford@chrysalisbooks.co.uk
website www.batsford.com
Director Roger Huggins

Chess and bridge, art techniques, film, fashion and costume, practical craft, gardening, embroidery, lace, woodwork.

Brassey's (UK) Ltd (imprint)
website www.brasseys.com
Editorial John Lee

Military technology, military history and illustrated military reference works.

Collins & Brown (imprint)
Directors Will Steeds (publishing), Frank Chambers (international rights), Richard Samson (UK sales and marketing)

Lifestyle and interiors, gardening, photography, practical arts, health and beauty, hobbies and crafts, natural history, history, ancient civilisation and general interest.

Conway Maritime Press (imprint)
Editorial John Lee

Highly illustrated reference books on naval history and maritime culture, ship design and ship modelling.

Paper Tiger (imprint)
Contact Colin Ziegler

Science fiction and fantasy art.

Pavilion Books Ltd (imprint)
UK Sales and Marketing Director Richard Samson
Cookery, gardening, travel, humour, sport, photography, art.

Putnam Aeronautical Books (imprint)
Editorial John Lee
Highly illustrated reference books on specialist aviation histories and studies of aerospace manufacturers.

Robson Books (imprint)
Publisher Jeremy Robson
General non-fiction, biography, music, humour, sport. Unsolicited MSS discouraged; ideas with synopses welcome with sae.

Salamander (imprint)
Directors Jo Mesham (publishing)
Cookery, crafts, military, natural history, music, gardening, hobbies, transport, sports.

Vega (imprint)
Publisher Will Steeds
Mind, Body & Spirit.

Chrysalis Children's Books

The Chrysalis Building, Bramley Road, London W10 6SP
tel 020-7221 2213
email childrens@chrysalisbooks.co.uk
website www.chrysalisbooks.co.uk
Head of Children's Books Steve Evans, *Publisher* Chester Fisher

Belitha Press, Big Fish, David Bennett Books, Learning World, Pavilion Children's Books and Zig Zag are now known collectively as Chrysalis Children's Books. Titles range from illustrated educational books covering all areas of the curriculum to reference and information books for the home and school. Lively information and story books for the under 5 age group; lavishly illustrated, high-quality picture books for older children; educational guides for parents; interactive non-fiction and novelty books. Founded 2003.

Churchill Livingstone – see Elsevier Ltd

Cicerone Press

2 Police Square, Milnthorpe, Cumbria LA7 7PY
tel (01539) 562069 *fax* (01539) 563417
email info@cicerone.co.uk
website www.cicerone.co.uk
Managing Director Jonathan Williams

Guidebooks: walking, trekking, mountaineering, climbing, cycling, etc in Britain and worldwide.

Cico Books

32 Great Sutton Street, London EC1V 0NB
tel 020-7253 7960 *fax* 020-7253 7967

email mail@cicobooks.co.uk
Directors Mark Collins (managing), Lucinda Richards (publishing)
Lifestyle and interiors and Mind, Body & Spirit. Founded 1999.

Cima Books – now Cico Books

Clarendon Press – former imprint of Oxford University Press

Classic Publications – see Ian Allan Publishing Ltd

Clive Bingley Ltd – see Facet Publishing

Cló Iar-Chonnachta Teo.[†]

Indreabhán, Conamara, Co. Galway, Republic of Ireland
tel (091) 593307 *fax* (091) 593362
email cic@iol.ie
website www.cic.ie
Director Micheál Ó Conghaile, *General Manager* Deirdre O'Toole

Irish-language – novels, short stories, plays, poetry, songs, history; cassettes (writers reading from their works in Irish and English). Promotes the translation of contemporary Irish fiction and poetry into other languages. Founded 1985.

CMP Information Ltd

Riverbank House, Angel Lane, Tonbridge, Kent TN9 1SE
tel (01732) 377591 *fax* (01732) 368324

Directories for business and industry, including *Benn's Media* and *The Knowledge*, guides for the media and film and TV markets respectively. Subsidiary of United Business Media.

Co & Bear Productions*

565 Fulham Road, London SW6 1ES
tel 020-7385 0888 *fax* 020-7385 0101
email info@cobear.co.uk
Publisher Beatrice Vincenzini

High-quality illustrated books on lifestyle, photography, art. Imprints: Scriptum Editions, Cartago. Founded 1996.

Colin Smythe Ltd*

PO Box 6, Gerrards Cross, Bucks. SL9 8XA
tel (01753) 886000 *fax* (01753) 886469
website www.colinsmythe.co.uk
Directors Colin Smythe (managing and editorial), Peter Bander van Duren, A. Norman Jeffares, Ann Saddlemyer, Leslie Hayward

Biography, phaleristics, heraldry, Irish literature and literary criticism, folklore, crafts and history. Founded 1966.

Collins – see HarperCollins Publishers

Collins & Brown – see Chrysalis Books Group

Collins Crime – see HarperCollins Publishers

Collins Dictionaries/COBUILD – see HarperCollins Publishers

Collins Gem – see HarperCollins Publishers

Collins Jet – see HarperCollins Publishers

Collins New Naturalist Library – see HarperCollins Publishers

Collins Picture Books – see HarperCollins Publishers

Collins Teacher – see HarperCollins Publishers

Collins Willow – see HarperCollins Publishers

Collins/Times Maps and Atlases – see HarperCollins Publishers

Colourpoint Books*
Unit D5, Ards Business Centre, Jubilee Road, Newtownards, Co. Down BT23 4YH
tel (028) 9182 0505 *fax* (028) 9182 1900
email info@colourpoint.co.uk
website www.colourpoint.co.uk
Directors Sheila Johnston (commissioning editor), Norman Johnston (transport editor), Malcolm Johnston, Wesley Johnston, *Administrator* Michelle Chambers, *Sales Manager* Lawrence Greer

Educational textbooks; transport – shipping, aviation, buses, road and railways; religion; Irish and general interest. Initial approach in writing please, with full details of proposal and sample chapters. Include return postage. Founded 1993.

The Columba Press†
55A Spruce Avenue, Stillorgan Industrial Park, Blackrock, Co. Dublin, Republic of Ireland
tel (1) 2942556 *fax* (1) 2942564
email info@columba.ie
website www.columba.ie
Publisher and Managing Director Seán O'Boyle

Religion (Roman Catholic and Anglican) including pastoral handbooks, spirituality, theology, liturgy and prayer; counselling and self-help. Founded 1985.

Conran Octopus – see Octopus Publishing Group

Constable & Robinson Ltd*
3 The Lanchesters, 162 Fulham Palace Road, London W6 9ER

tel 020-8741 3663 *fax* 020-8748 7562
email enquiries@constablerobinson.com
website www.constablerobinson.com
Non-Executive Chairman Benjamin Glazebrook, *Managing Director* Nick Robinson, *Directors* Jan Chamier, Nova Jayne Heath, Adrian Andrews

Unsolicited sample chapters, synopses and ideas welcome with return postage. Do not send MSS; no email submissions. Founded 1890 (Constable); 1983 (Robinson).

Constable (imprint: hardbacks)
Editorial Director Carol O'Brien

Biography, fiction, general and military history, travel and endurance, climbing, landscape photography, psychology.

Robinson (imprint: paperbacks)
Crime fiction, *Daily Telegraph* health books, the Mammoth series, psychology, true crime, military history, *Smarties* children's books.

Constable Publishers – see Constable & Robinson Ltd

Consumers' Association – see Which? Ltd

The Continuum International Publishing Group Ltd
The Tower Building, 11 York Road, London SE1 7NX
tel 020-7922 0880 *fax* 020-7922 0881
email info@continuumbooks.com
website www.continuumbooks.com
Chairman & Ceo Philip J. Sturrock, *Directors* Robin Baird-Smith (publishing: religious and general), Philip Law (editorial: academic, religious, biblical studies and theology), Anthony Haynes (editorial: professional and philosophy), Janet Joyce (publishing: journals and humanities), Frank Roney (finance), Ed Suthon (sales and marketing), Benn Linfield (publishing services)

Serious non-fiction, academic and professional, including scholarly monographs and educational texts and reference works in history, politics and social thought; literature, criticism, performing arts; religion and spirituality; education, psychology, women's studies, business. Imprints: Continuum, Burns & Oates, T&T Clark, Handsel Press, Mowbray: Morehouse, Sheffield Academic Press.

Conway Maritime Press – see Chrysalis Books Group

Corgi – see Transworld Publishers Ltd

Corgi Children's Books – see Random House Group Ltd

Cork University Press[†]

Crawford Business Park, Crosses Green, Cork,
Republic of Ireland
tel (021) 4902980 *fax* (021) 4315329
email corkunip@ucc.ie
website www.corkuniversitypress.com
Publisher Sara Wilbourne

Irish literature, history, cultural studies, medieval
studies, English literature, musicology, poetry,
translations. Founded 1925.

Attic Press (imprint)
tel (021) 4321725
email S.Wilbourne@ucc.ie

Books by and about women in the areas of social
and political comment, women's studies, reference
guides and handbooks.

Coronet – see Hodder Headline Ltd

Council for British Archaeology

Bowes Morrell House, 111 Walmgate,
York YO1 9WA
tel (01904) 671417 *fax* (01904) 671384
email info@britarch.ac.uk
website www.britarch.ac.uk
Director George Lambrick, *Publications Officer* Jane
Thorniley-Walker

British archaeology – academic; practical
handbooks; general interest archaeology. Founded
1944.

Countryside Books

2 Highfield Avenue, Newbury, Berks. RG14 5DS
tel (01635) 43816 *fax* (01635) 551004
website www.countrysidebooks.co.uk
Partners Nicholas Battle, Suzanne Battle

Books of local or regional interest, usually on a
county basis: walking, outdoor activities, local
history; also genealogy, aviation. Founded 1976.

Countrywise Press Ltd – see Barry Rose Law Publishers Ltd

Cover to Cover – see BBC Audiobooks Ltd

CRC Press – see Taylor & Francis Group plc

Crescent Moon Publishing

PO Box 393, Maidstone, Kent ME14 5XU
tel (01622) 729593
email jrobinson@crescentmoon.org.uk
website www.crescentmoon.org.uk
Director Jeremy Robinson, *Editors* C. Hughes,
B.D. Barnacle

Literature, poetry, fine art, cultural studies, media,
cinema, feminism. Submit sample chapters or 6
poems plus sae, not complete MSS. Founded 1988.

Cressrelles Publishing Co. Ltd

10 Station Road Industrial Estate, Colwall, Malvern,
Herefordshire WR13 6RN
tel/fax (01684) 540154
email simonsmith@cressrelles4drama.fsbusiness.co.uk
Directors Leslie Smith, Simon Smith

General publishing. Founded 1973.

Actinic Press (imprint)
Chiropody.

J. Garnet Miller (imprint)
Plays and theatre textbooks.

Kenyon-Deane (imprint)
Plays and drama textbooks for amateur dramatic
societies. Plays for women.

Croner.CCH Group Ltd

145 London Road, Kingston-upon-Thames,
Surrey KT2 6SR
tel (0870) 2415719 *fax* 020-8247 1184
email info@.croner.cch.co.uk
website www.croner.cch.co.uk
Managing Director Hans Thijs

Law, taxation, finance, insurance, looseleaf and
online information services. Founded 1948.

Crown House Publishing Ltd*

Crown Buildings, Bancyfelin,
Carmarthen SA33 5ND
tel (01267) 211345 *fax* (01267) 211882
email books@crownhouse.co.uk
website www.crownhouse.co.uk
Directors Martin Roberts (chairman), Glenys
Roberts, David Bowman, Karen Bowman

Psychotherapy, life skills, business, education,
training, health. Founded 1998.

The Crowood Press

The Stable Block, Ramsbury, Marlborough,
Wilts. SN8 2HR
tel (01672) 520320 *fax* (01672) 520280
email enquiries@crowood.com
website www.crowood.com
Directors John Dennis (chairman), Ken Hathaway
(managing)

Sport, motoring, aviation, military, climbing,
walking, fishing, country sports, farming, natural
history, gardening, DIY, crafts, dogs, equestrian,
games. Founded 1982.

Airlife Publishing (imprint)
Aviation, technical and general, military, military
history.

Current Science Group

34-42 Cleveland Street, London W1T 4LB
tel 020-7323 0323 *fax* 020-7580 1938
email csg@cursci.co.uk

website www.current-science-group.com
Chairman Vitek Tracz

Biological sciences, medicine, pharmaceutical science, internet communities, electronic publishing.

Curzon Press Ltd – now RoutledgeCurzon – see Taylor & Francis Group plc

Cygnus Arts – see Golden Cockerel Press Ltd

D.C. Thomson & Co. Ltd – Publications
2 Albert Square, Dundee DD1 9QJ
London office 185 Fleet Street,
London EC4A 2HS

Publishers of newspapers and periodicals. Children's books (annuals), based on weekly magazine characters; fiction. For fiction guidelines, send a large sae to Central Fiction Dept.

Dalesman Publishing Co. Ltd
Stable Courtyard, Broughton Hall, Skipton,
North Yorkshire BD23 3AE
tel (01756) 701381 *fax* (01756) 701326
email editorial@dalesman.co.uk
Chairman T.J. Benn, *Chief Executive* C.G. Benn,
Managing Director R. Flanagan

Countryside books and magazines covering the North of England. Founded 1939.

Darton, Longman & Todd Ltd*
1 Spencer Court, 140-142 Wandsworth High Street,
London SW18 4JJ
tel 020-8875 0155 *fax* 020-8875 0133
email editorial@darton-longman-todd.co.uk
Editorial Director Brendan Walsh

Religious books and bibles, including the following themes: bible study, spirituality, prayer and meditation, anthologies, daily readings, healing, counselling and pastoral care, bereavement, personal growth, mission, political, environmental and social issues, biography/autobiography, theological and historical studies. Founded 1959.

Darwen Finlayson Ltd – see Phillimore & Co. Ltd

David & Charles Children's Books – see Gullane Children's Books

David & Charles Ltd
Brunel House, Newton Abbot, Devon TQ12 4PU
tel (01626) 323200 *fax* (01626) 323319
Acting Managing Director Budge Wallis, *Publishing Director* Sara Domville

High-quality illustrated non-fiction specialising in crafts, hobbies, art techniques, gardening, natural history, equestrian, DIY, photography. Founded 1960.

David Bennett Books – see Chrysalis Children's Books

David Fickling Books – see Random House Group Ltd

David Fulton Publishers Ltd*
Chiswick Centre, 414 Chiswick High Road,
London W4 5TF
tel 020-8996 3610 *fax* 020-8996 3622
email mail@fultonpublishers.co.uk
website www.fultonpublishers.co.uk
Chairman David Fulton, *Publishing Director* Christopher Glennie, *Marketing Director* Rachael Robertson

Initial and continuing teacher education (special needs, primary and secondary), educational management and psychology. Unsolicited MSS not returned. Part of Granada Learning Ltd. Founded 1987.

Dean – see Egmont Books

Dedalus Ltd
24 St Judith's Lane, Sawtry,
Cambs. PE28 5XE
tel/fax (01487) 832382
email DedalusLimited@compuserve.com
website www.dedalusbooks.com
Chairman Juri Gabriel, *Directors* Eric Lane (managing), Robert Irwin (editorial), Lindsay Thomas (marketing), Mike Mitchell (translations)

Original fiction in English and in translation; Dedalus European Classics, Dedalus concept books. Founded 1983.

diehard
91-93 Main Street, Callander FK17 8BQ
tel (01877) 339449
website www.poetryscotland.co.uk
Directors Ian William King (managing), Sally Evans King (marketing)

Scottish poetry. Founded 1993.

Digital Press – see Elsevier Ltd

Discovery Walking Guides Ltd
10 Tennyson Close, Dallington,
Northampton NN5 7HJ
tel/fax (01604) 752576
website www.walking.demon.co.uk/
Chairman Rosamund C. Brawn

'Warm island' walking guides and plant and flower guides to European holiday destinations; 'Tour & Trail' digital cartographic large-scale maps, 'Drive' touring maps, '34 Walks' guide books. Founded 1994.

Dorling Kindersley – see Penguin Group (UK)

Doubleday (UK) – see Transworld Publishers Ltd

Doubleday Children's Books – see Random House Group Ltd

Dref Wen
28 Church Road, Whitchurch,
Cardiff CF14 2EA
tel 029-2061 7860 *fax* 029-2061 0507
Directors Roger Boore, Anne Boore, Gwilym Boore,
Alun Boore

Original Welsh language novels for children and
adult learners. Original, adaptations and
translations of foreign and English language full-
colour picture story books for children. Educational
material for primary/secondary schoolchildren in
Wales and England. Founded 1970.

Dublar Scripts
204 Mercer Way, Romsey, Hants SO51 7QJ
tel (01794) 501377 *fax* (01794) 502538
email scripts@dublar.freeserve.co.uk
website www.dublar.co.uk
Managing Director Robert Heather

Pantomimes. Imprint: Sleepy Hollow Pantomimes.
Founded 1994.

Duncan Baird Publishers
6th Floor, Castle House, 75-76 Wells Street,
London W1T 3QH
tel 020-7323 2229 *fax* 020-7580 5692
Directors Duncan Baird (managing), Bob Saxton
(editorial), Roger Walton (art), Alex Mitchell
(international sales), Ryan Tring (financial)

Non-fiction, illustrated reference. Founded 1992.

Dunedin Academic Press*
Hudson House, 8 Albany Street,
Edinburgh EH1 3QB
tel 0131-473 2397 *fax* (01250) 870937
email mail@dunedinacademicpress.co.uk
website www.dunedinacademicpress.co.uk
Director Anthony Kinahan

All types of academic books and books of Scottish
interest. Founded 2000.

Dunitz – see Taylor & Francis Group plc

Earthlight – see Simon & Schuster

Earthscan Publications Ltd – see Kogan Page Ltd

East-West Publications (UK) Ltd
8 Caledonia Street, London N1 9DZ
tel 020-7837 5061 *fax* 020-7278 4429

Chairman L.W. Carp
General non-fiction, Eastern studies, sufism. No
unsolicited MSS; please write first. Founded 1977.

Ebury Press – see Random House Group Ltd

Eden – see Transworld Publishers Ltd

Edinburgh University Press*
22 George Square, Edinburgh EH8 9LF
tel 0131-650 4218 *fax* 0131-662 0053
Chairman Tim Rix, *Managing Director* Timothy
Wright, *Editorial Director* Ms Jackie Jones

Academic publishers of scholarly books and
journals: media and cultural studies, Islamic studies,
geography, history, linguistics, literary studies,
philosophy, politics, Scottish studies, American
studies, religious studies, classical and ancient
history. Trade: Scottish language, literature and
culture, Scottish history and politics.

Éditions Aubrey Walter
27 Old Gloucester Street, London WC1 3XX
email aubrey@gmppubs.co.uk
Publisher Aubrey Walter

Visual work by gay artists and photographers,
usually in the form of a monograph showcasing one
artist's work. Work may be submitted on disk,
email, transparency, photocopy or photograph.

The Educational Company of Ireland†
Ballymount Road, Walkinstown, Dublin 12,
Republic of Ireland
tel (01) 4500611 *fax* (01) 4500993
email info@edco.ie
website www.edco.ie
Executive Directors F.J. Maguire (chief executive),
R. McLoughlin, *Financial Controller* A. Harrold,
Sales and Marketing Manager M. Harford-Hughes,
Publisher F. Fahy

Trading unit of Smurfit Ireland Ltd. Educational
MSS on all subjects in English or Irish language.

Educational Explorers
PO Box 3391, Winnersh,
Wokingham RG41 5ZD
tel 0118-978 9680 *fax* 0118-978 2335
email explorers@cuisenaire.co.uk
website www.cuisenaire.co.uk
Directors M.J. Hollyfield, D.M. Gattegno

Educational, mathematics: *Numbers in colour with
Cuisenaire Rods*, languages: *The Silent Way*, literacy,
reading: *Words in Colour*; educational films. No
unsolicited material. Founded 1962.

Edward Arnold – now part of Hodder Arnold – see Hodder Headline Ltd

Edward Elgar Publishing Ltd

Glensanda House, Montpellier Parade, Cheltenham, Glos. GL50 1UA
tel (01242) 226934 *fax* (01242) 262111
email info@e-elgar.co.uk
website www.e-elgar.co.uk
Managing Director Edward Elgar

Economics and other social sciences. Founded 1986.

Egmont Books*

239 Kensington High Street, London W8 6SA
tel 020-7761 3500 *fax* 020-7761 3510
email firstname.surname@ecb.egmont.com
Chief Executive Julie Goldsmith, *Managing Director* Fiona Clarke

Children's books: picture books, fiction (ages 4–16), illustrated non-fiction, licensed character list. Publishes under Egmont and Dean.

The Chicken House

2 Palmer Street, Frome, Somerset BA11 1DS
tel (01373) 454488 *fax* (01373) 454499
email chickenhouse@doublecluck.com
Managing Director Barry Cunningham

Fiction and non-fiction for 7+, picture books. An Egmont joint venture company.

Element – see HarperCollins Publishers

11:9 – see Neil Wilson Publishing Ltd

Elliot Right Way Books

Kingswood Buildings, Brighton Road,
Lower Kingswood, Tadworth,
Surrey KT20 6TD
tel (01737) 832202 *fax* (01737) 830311
email info@right-way.co.uk
website www.right-way.co.uk
Managing Directors Clive Elliot, Malcolm Elliot

Independent publishers of practical non-fiction 'how to' paperbacks. The low-price *Right Way* and *Right Way Plus* series include games, pastimes, horses, pets, motoring, sport, health, business, public speaking and jokes, financial and legal, cookery and etiquette. Similar subjects are covered in the *Clarion* series of large-format paperbacks, sold in supermarkets and bargain bookshops. No freelance proofreaders or editors required. Founded 1946.

ELM Publications

Seaton House, Kings Ripton, Huntingdon,
Cambs. PE28 2NJ
tel (01487) 773238 *fax* (01487) 773359
email elm@elm-training.co.uk
website www.elm-training.co.uk
Managing Director Sheila Ritchie

Educational books and resources; books and training aids (tutor's packs and software) for business and management; software simulations; library and information studies. Actively seeking good, tested management skills training materials. Telephone in the first instance, rather than send MSS. Founded 1977.

Elm Tree Books – former imprint of Hamish Hamilton/Penguin

Elsevier Ltd*

(incorporating Pergamon Press and Harcourt Publishers International)
The Boulevard, Langford Lane, Kidlington,
Oxford OX5 1GB
tel (01865) 843000 *fax* (01865) 843010
website www.elsevier.com
Coo Gavin Howe, *Ceo Science & Technology (Books & Journals)* Arie Jongejan, *Ceo Health Sciences Division (Books & Journals)* Brian Nairn

Academic and professional reference books; scientific, technical and medical books, journals, CD-Roms and magazines. No unsolicited MSS, but synopses and project proposals welcome. Imprints: Academic Press, Architectural Press, Bailliere Tindall, Butterworth-Heinemann, Churchill Livingstone, Digital Press, Elsevier, Elsevier Advanced Technology, Focal Press, Gulf Professional Press, JAI, Made Simple Books, Morgan Kauffman, Mosby, Newnes, North-Holland, Pergamon, W.B. Saunders. Division of Reed Elsevier, Amsterdam.

Elsevier Ltd (Butterworth Heinemann)

Linacre House, Jordan Hill, Oxford OX2 8DP
tel (01865) 310366 *fax* (01865) 314541
website www.bh.com
Managing Director Philip Shaw

Books and electronic products across business, technical, medical fields for students and professionals.

Elsevier Ltd (Health Sciences)

32 Jamestown Road, London NW1 7BY
tel 020-7424 4200 *fax* 020-7483 2293
websites www.elsevier.com www.elsevierhealth.com
Managing Director, Health Sciences Dominic Vaughan

Scientific, technical and medical books and journals. No unsolicited MSS but synopses and project proposals welcome. Imprints: Bailliere Tindall, Churchill Livingstone, Elsevier, Mosby, Pergamon, W.B. Saunders.

Academic Press (division)
Managing Director Jan Velterop

Academic and reference.

Baillière Tindall Ltd (division)
Managing Director Andrew Stevenson

Medical, veterinary, nursing, pharmaceutical books and journals.

Churchill Livingstone (division)
Managing Director Andrew Stevenson

Medical, nursing, pharmaceutical books and journals.

Dryden Press (division)
Managing Director Peter H. Lengemann

Educational books (college, university), economics, business.

Holt Rinehart & Winston (division)
Managing Director Peter H. Lengemann

Educational books.

Mosby International (division)
6th Floor, Lynton House, 7-12 Tavistock Square, London WC1H 9LB
tel 020-7388 7676 *fax* 020-7391 6555
Managing Director Derrick Holman

W.B. Saunders Co. Ltd (division)
Managing Director Andrew Stevenson

Medical and scientific.

Encyclopaedia Britannica (UK) Ltd
2nd Floor, Unity Wharf, Mill Street, London SE1 2BH
tel 020-7500 7800 *fax* 020-7500 7878
email enquiries@britannica.co.uk
website www.britannica.co.uk
Managing Director Leah Mansoor, *Sales & Marketing Director* Jane Helps

Enitharmon Press
26B Caversham Road, London NW5 2DU
tel 020-7482 5967 *fax* 020-7284 1787
email books@enitharmon.co.uk
website www.enitharmon.co.uk
Director Stephen Stuart-Smith

Poetry, literary criticism, fiction, translations, artists' books. No unsolicited MSS. No freelance editors or proofreaders required. Founded 1967.

Epworth Press
c/o Methodist Publishing House,
4 John Wesley Road, Peterborough PE4 6ZP
tel (01733) 325002 *fax* (01733) 384180
Commissioning Editor Dr Natalie Watson

Religion, theology, church history, worship, Bible commentaries.

Estates – see HarperCollins Publishers

Euromonitor plc
60-61 Britton Street, London EC1M 5UX
tel 020-7251 8024 *fax* 020-7608 3149
email info@euromonitor.com
website www.euromonitor.com

Directors T.J. Fenwick (managing), R.N. Senior (chairman)

Business and commercial reference, marketing information, European and International Surveys, directories. Founded 1972.

Europa Publications Ltd
11 New Fetter Lane, London EC4P 4EE
tel 020-7583 9855 *fax* 020-7842 2249
email sales@europapublications.co.uk
Directors R. Horton (managing), P. Kelly (editorial), *General Manager* J.G. North

Directories, international relations, reference, yearbooks. A member of **Taylor & Francis Group plc**.

Evangelical Press of Wales – see Bryntirion Press

Evans Brothers Ltd*
2A Portman Mansions, Chiltern Street, London W1V 6NR
tel 020-7487 0920 *fax* 020-7487 0921
email sales@evansbooks.co.uk
website www.evansbooks.co.uk
Directors S.T. Pawley (managing), Brian D. Jones (international publishing), A.O. Ojora (Nigeria), *UK Publisher* Su Swallow

Educational books, particularly preschool, school library and teachers' books for the UK, including the Rainbows series of graded information books for 5–8 year-olds; primary and secondary for Africa, the Caribbean and Brazil. Part of the Evans Publishing Group. Founded 1908.

Everyman – see The Orion Publishing Group Ltd

Everyman's Library
Gloucester Mansions, 140A Shaftesbury Avenue, London WC2H 8HD
tel 020-7539 7600 *fax* 020-7379 4060
Publisher David Campbell

Everyman's Library (clothbound reprints of the classics); *Everyman's Library Children's Classics*; *Everyman's Library Pocket Poets*; *Everyman Guides*; *Everyman City Guides*; *Everyman City Map Guides*; *Everyman Chess*. No unsolicited submissions. An imprint of **Alfred A. Knopf**.

Exley Publications Ltd
16 Chalk Hill, Watford, Herts. WD19 4BG
tel (01923) 250505 *fax* (01923) 818733/249795
Directors Dalton Exley, Helen Exley (editorial), Lincoln Exley, Richard Exley

Popular colour giftbooks for an international market. No unsolicited MSS. Founded 1976.

Expert Books – see Transworld Publishers Ltd

Faber & Faber Ltd*

3 Queen Square, London WC1N 3AU
tel 020-7465 0045 fax 020-7465 0034
website www.faber.co.uk
Chief Executive Stephen Page, Directors John Bodley, Walter Donohue, Valerie Eliot, Laurence Longe, Julian Loose, Nigel Marsh, Jon Riley, David Tebbutt

High-quality general fiction and non-fiction; all forms of creative writing, including plays. Write to Sales Dept for current catalogues. Unsolicited submissions for the children's list not accepted. For information on submission procedure ring 020-7465 0189. For practical and security reasons submissions by fax or on disk cannot be accepted, except by special arrangement. Allow 6–8 weeks for a response. Freelance editors and proofreaders without in-house experience need not apply.

Fabian Society

11 Dartmouth Street, London SW1H 9BN
tel 020-7227 4900 fax 020-7976 7153
email info@fabian-society.org.uk
website www.fabian-society.org.uk
General Secretary Michael Jacobs

Current affairs, political thought, economics, education, environment, foreign affairs, social policy. Also controls NCLC Publishing Society Ltd. Founded 1884.

Facet Publishing*

7 Ridgmount Street, London WC1E 7AE
tel 020-7255 0590 fax 020-7255 0591
email info@facetpublishing.co.uk
website www.facetpublishing.co.uk
Managing Director Janet Liebster

Library and information science, information technology, reference works, directories, bibliographies.

Clive Bingley Ltd (imprint)

Library and information science, reference works.

Library Association Publishing (imprint)

Library and information science, information technology, reference works, directories, bibliographies.

Falmer Press – now RoutledgeFalmer, see Taylor & Francis Group plc

Fernhurst Books

Duke's Path, High Street, Arundel, West Sussex BN18 9AJ
tel (01903) 882277 fax (01903) 882715
email sales@fernhurstbooks.co.uk
website www.fernhurstbooks.co.uk
Publisher Tim Davison

Sailing, watersports. Founded 1979.

Financial Times Prentice Hall – see Pearson Education

First and Best in Education Ltd

(incorporating Hamilton House Publishing)
Earlstrees Court, Earlstrees Road, Corby, Northants. NN17 4HH
tel (01536) 399004 fax (01536) 399012
email info@firstandbest.co.uk
website www.firstandbest.co.uk
Contact Anne Cockburn (editor)

Education-related books (no fiction). Currently actively recruiting new writers for schools; ideas welcome. Sae must accompany submissions. Founded 1992.

Fitzroy-Dearborn – see Taylor & Francis Group plc

Five Star – see Serpent's Tail

Flambard Press

Stable Cottage, East Fourstones, Hexham, Northumberland NE47 5DX
tel (01434) 674360 fax (01434) 674178
Managing Editor Peter Lewis, Deputy Editor Margaret Lewis

Poetry and fiction (literary and crime). Only hard-copy submissions with sae considered. Preliminary letter required. Founded 1990.

Flame – see Hodder Headline Ltd

Flamingo – see HarperCollins Publishers

Flicks Books

29 Bradford Road, Trowbridge, Wilts. BA14 9AN
tel (01225) 767728
email flicks.books@dial.pipex.com
Partners Matthew Stevens (publisher), Aletta Stevens

Cinema, TV, related media. Founded 1986.

Floris Books*

15 Harrison Gardens, Edinburgh EH11 1SH
tel 0131-337 2372 fax 0131-347 9919
email floris@florisbooks.co.uk
Editors Christopher Moore, Gale Winskill

Religion, science, Celtic studies, craft; children's books: picture and board books, activity books. Founded 1978.

Flyways (imprint)

Children's fiction paperbacks for the more able reader.

Kelpies (imprint)

Children's fiction from Scotland.

Flyways – see Floris Books

Focal Press – see Elsevier Ltd

Fodor Guides – see Random House Group Ltd

Folens Ltd*
Apex Business Centre, Boscombe Road,
Dunstable LU5 4RL
tel (0870) 609 1237 *fax* (0870) 609 1236
email folens@folens.com
website www.folens.com
Managing Director Malcolm Watson

Primary and secondary educational books, learn at home books. Founded 1987.

Folens Publishing Company
Hibernian Industrial Estate,
Greenhills Road, Tallaght, Dublin 24,
Republic of Ireland
tel (01) 4137200 *fax* (01) 4137282
Chairman Dirk Folens, *Directors* John O'Connor (managing), Margaret Burns (secondary), Deirdre Whelan (primary)

Educational (primary, secondary, comprehensive, technical, in English and Irish).

The Blackwater Press† (imprint)

General non-fiction, Irish interest.

Fontana Press – former imprint of HarperCollins Publishers

Foulsham – see W. Foulsham & Co. Ltd

Foundery Press – see Methodist Publishing House

The Foundry*
Crabtree Hall, Crabtree Lane, London SW6 6TY
tel 020-7386 4700 *fax* 020-7386 4701
email info@foundry.co.uk
website www.foundry.co.uk
Managing Director Frances Bodiam,
Publisher/Creative Director Nick Wells

Reference, art, cookery, education. Founded 1992.

Four Courts Press†
7 Malpas Street, Dublin 8,
Republic of Ireland
tel (01) 4534668 *fax* (01) 4534672
email info@four-courts-press.ie
website www.four-courts-press.ie
Managing Director Michael Adams

Academic books in the humanities, especially history, Celtic and medieval studies, art, theology. Founded 1970.

Fourth Estate – see HarperCollins Publishers

Framework Press Educational Publishers Ltd*
Heinemann, Halley Court, Jordan Hill,
Oxford OX2 8EJ
tel (01865) 314194 *fax* (01865) 314116
email nigel.kelly@repp.co.uk
Publisher Nigel Kelly

School management, professional development, raising attainment, PSHE and Citizenship. Founded 1983.

Frances Lincoln Ltd
4 Torriano Mews, Torriano Avenue,
London NW5 2RZ
tel 020-7284 4009 *fax* 020-7485 0490
email reception@frances-lincoln.com
Directors John Nicoll (managing), Anne Fraser (editorial, adult books), Janetta Otter-Barry (editorial, children's books)

Illustrated, international co-editions: gardening, interiors, health, spirituality, art, gift, children's books. Founded 1977.

Frank Cass & Co. Ltd
Crown House, 47 Chase Side, Southgate,
London N14 5BP
tel 020-8920 2100 *fax* 020-8447 8548
email info@frankcass.com
website www.frankcass.com
Directors Frank Cass (chairman), Stewart Cass (managing), A.E. Cass, H.J. Osen, M.P. Zaidner, Hon. C. Callman

History, economic and social history, military and strategic studies, politics, international affairs, development studies, African studies, Middle East studies, sports studies, law, business management and academic journals in all of these fields.

Woburn Press (imprint)
Educational.

Franklin Watts – see The Watts Publishing Group Ltd

Free Association Books
57 Warren Street, London W1T 5NR
tel 020-7388 3182 *fax* 020-7388 3187
email fab@fa-b.com
website www.fa-b.com
Publisher and Managing Director T.E. Brown

Social sciences, psychoanalysis, psychotherapy, counselling, cultural studies, social welfare, addiction studies, child and adolescent studies. Also contemporary fiction, including works in translation. No poetry, science fiction or fantasy. Founded 1984.

Free Press – see Simon & Schuster

FT Law & Tax – incorporated into Sweet & Maxwell

Gaia Books Ltd
66 Charlotte Street,
London W1P 1LR
tel (01453) 752985 *fax* (01453) 752987
Managing Director Joss Pearson
Illustrated reference books on ecology, natural living, health, mind. Submissions (outline, author biography and sample chapter) with sae to managing director.

Gairm Publications
(incorporating Alex MacLaren & Sons)
29 Waterloo Street, Glasgow G2 6BZ
tel/fax 0141-221 1971
Editorial Director Derick Thomson
(Gaelic and Gaelic-related only) dictionaries, language books, novels, poetry, music, children's books, quarterly magazine, *Gairm*. Founded 1952.

The Gallery Press
Loughcrew, Oldcastle, Co. Meath,
Republic of Ireland
tel/fax (049) 8541779
email gallery@indigo.ie
Editor/Publisher Peter Fallon
Poetry, drama, occasionally fiction, by Irish authors only at this time. Founded 1970.

Garland Science – see Taylor & Francis Group plc

Garnet Publishing Ltd
8 Southern Court, South Street,
Reading RG1 4QS
tel (01189) 597847 *fax* (01189) 597356
email enquiries@garnet-ithaca.demon.co.uk
Editorial Manager Emma G. Hawker
Art, architecture, photography, fiction, religious studies, travel and general, mainly on Middle and Far East, and Islam. Founded 1991.

Ithaca Press (imprint)
Post-graduate academic works, especially on the Middle East.

South Street Press (imprint)
Non-fiction, including *Behind the Headlines* series.

Gateway Books – see Gill & Macmillan Ltd

The Gay Men's Press
(Millivres Prowler Ltd)
PO Box 3220, Brighton BN2 5AU
tel (01273) 672823 *fax* 01273) 672159
email peterburton@easicom.com
Commissioning Editor Peter Burton
Gay-related issues: primarily fiction from literary to popular; limited non-fiction.

Geddes & Grosset*
David Dale House,
New Lanark ML11 9DJ
tel (01555) 665000 *fax* (01555) 665694
email info@gandg.sol.co.uk
Publishers Ron Grosset, Mike Miller
Popular reference, children's non-fiction and activity books. Founded 1988.

Geographia – now Bartholomew – see HarperCollins Publishers

George Allen & Unwin Publishers – acquired by HarperCollins Publishers

George Ronald
46 High Street, Kidlington, Oxon OX5 2DN
tel/fax (01235) 529137
email sales@grpubl.demon.co.uk
website www.grbooks.com
Managers W. Momen, E. Leith
Religion, specialising in the Baha'i Faith. Founded 1939.

Gerald Duckworth & Co. Ltd
61 Frith Street, London W1D 3JL
tel 020-7434 4242 *fax* 020-7434 4420
email info@duckworth-publishers.co.uk
website www.ducknet.co.uk
Directors Peter Mayer (chairman), Gillian Hawkins (managing), Deborah Blake (editorial)
General trade publishers with a strong academic division (no fiction). Imprints: Bristol Classical Press and Chatham Publishing; naval and maritime history. Founded 1898.

Giles de la Mare Publishers Ltd
PO Box 25351, London NW5 1ZT
tel 020-7485 2533 *fax* 020-7485 2534
email gilesdelamare@dial.pipex.com
Chairman Giles de la Mare
Non-fiction: art, architecture, biography, history, music, travel. Telephone before submitting MSS. Founded 1995.

Gill & Macmillan Ltd[†]
Hume Avenue, Park West, Dublin 12,
Republic of Ireland
tel (01) 500 9500 *fax* (01) 500 9599
website www.gillmacmillan.ie
Biography or memoirs, educational (secondary, university), history, literature, cookery, current affairs, guidebooks, popular fiction. Founded 1968.

Gateway Books (imprint)
Spirituality, ecology, metaphysics and alternative science.

Newleaf (imprint)

Mind, Body & Spirit, popular psychology, self-help, health and healing, lifestyle.

Tivoli (imprint)

Popular fiction.

Ginn & Co. – see Harcourt Education Ltd

Godsfield Press Ltd

Laurel House, Station Approach, Alresford, Hants SO24 9JH
tel (01962) 736677 *fax* (01962) 738610
email enquiries@godsfieldpress.com
website www.godsfieldpress.com
Publisher Debbie Thorpe

Highly illustrated books for adults in the area of Mind, Body & Spirit with an emphasis on practical application and personal spiritual awareness. Founded 1994.

Golden Cockerel Press Ltd

Unit 304, 50 Westminster Bridge Road, London SE1 7QY
tel 020-7953 8770 *fax* 020-7953 8738
email aup.uk@btinternet.com
Contact Tamar Lindesay

Academic.

Associated University Presses (imprint)

Literary criticism, art, music, history, film, theology, philosophy, Jewish studies, politics, sociology.

Cygnus Arts (imprint)

The arts.

The Goldsmith Press

Newbridge, Co. Kildare, Republic of Ireland
tel (045) 433613 *fax* (045) 434648
email de@iol.ie
website www.irishpoems.com
Directors V. Abbott, D. Egan, *Secretary* B. Ennis

Literature, art, Irish interest, poetry. Unsolicited MSS not returned. Founded 1972.

Gollancz – see The Orion Publishing Group Ltd

Gomer Press

Llandysul, Ceredigion SA44 4QL
tel (01559) 362371 *fax* (01559) 363758
email gwasg@gomer.co.uk
website www.gomer.co.uk
Directors Jonathan Lewis, John H. Lewis, *Editors* Mairwen Prys Jones, Bethan Mair, Gordon Jones, Ceri Wyn Jones

Literature and non-fiction with a Welsh background or relevance: biography, history, aspects of Welsh culture, children's books. No unsolicited MSS; preliminary enquiry essential. Founded 1892.

Government Supplies Agency

Publications Division, Office of Public Works, 51 St Stephen's Green, Dublin 2, Republic of Ireland
tel (01) 6476000 *fax* (01) 6476843

Irish government publications.

Gower – see Ashgate Publishing Ltd

Grafton – now HarperCollins Paperbacks

Graham & Whiteside Ltd

High Holborn House, 50-51 Bedford Row, London WC1R 4LR
tel 020-7067 2500 *fax* 020-7067 2600
email sales@major-co-data.com
Directors A.M.W. Graham, R.M. Whiteside, P.L. Murphy

Directories for international business and professional markets. Founded 1995.

Granada Media – see Carlton Publishing Group

Granta Publications

2-3 Hanover Yard, Noel Road, London N1 8BE
tel 020-7704 9776 *fax* 020-7354 3469
website www.granta.com
Editorial Director George Miller, *Magazine Editor* Ian Jack

Literary fiction, memoir, political non-fiction, travel, history, etc. Founded 1982.

Green Books

Foxhole, Dartington, Totnes, Devon TQ9 6EB
tel (01803) 863260 *fax* (01803) 863843
email edit@greenbooks.co.uk
website www.greenbooks.co.uk
Publisher John Elford

Environment (practical and philosophical). No fiction or children's books. No MSS; submit synopsis with covering letter, preferably by email. Founded 1987.

Green Print – see Merlin Press Ltd

Greenhill Books/Lionel Leventhal Ltd

Park House, 1 Russell Gardens, London NW11 9NN
tel 020-8458 6314 *fax* 020-8905 5245
email info@greenhillbooks.com
website www.greenhillbooks.com
Managing Director Lionel Leventhal, *Deputy Managing Director* Mark Wray

Military history. Founded 1984.

Gresham Books Ltd

46 Victoria Road, Oxford OX2 7QD
tel (01865) 513582 *fax* (01865) 512718

email greshambks@btinternet.com
website www.gresham-books.co.uk
Chief Executive Paul Lewis

Hymn books, Prayer books, Service books, school histories.

Grub Street Publishing
The Basement, 10 Chivalry Road,
London SW11 1HT
tel 020-7924 3966/738 1008 *fax* 020-7738 1009
email post@grubstreet.co.uk
website www.grubstreet.co.uk
Principals John B. Davies, Anne Dolamore

Adult non-fiction: military, aviation history, cookery, wine. Founded 1992.

Guild of Master Craftsman Publications Ltd
166 High Street, Lewes, East Sussex BN7 1XU
tel (01273) 477374 *fax* (01273) 478606
Joint Managing Directors Jennifer Phillips, Jonathan Phillips

Practical, illustrated crafts, including photography, needlecrafts, dolls' houses, woodworking and other leisure and hobby subjects. Founded 1979.

Guinness World Records
338 Euston Road, London NW1 3BD
tel 020-7891 4567 *fax* 020-7891 4501

Guinness World Records, British Hit Singles, Guinness World Records Prime Time TV shows. A Hit Entertainment company. Founded 1954.

Gullane Children's Books
Winchester House, 259-269 Old Marylebone Road,
London NW1 5XJ
tel 020-7616 7200 *fax* 020-7616 7201
Directors Alison Ritchie (editorial), Paula Burgess (art)

Picture books, novelty books, board books, and giftsets for under-7 age group. A Gullane Entertainment company.

Gwasg Bryntirion Press – see Bryntirion Press

Gwasg y Dref Wen – see Dref Wen

Hachette Illustrated – see Octopus Publishing Group

Haldane Mason Ltd
PO Box 34196, London NW10 3YB
tel 020-8459 2131 *fax* 020-8728 1216
email info@haldane.mason.com
Directors Ron Samuel, Sydney Francis

Illustrated general non-fiction: children's, cookery, health, New Age, lifestyle, popular reference, sport. Opportunities for freelances. Founded 1992.

Hambledon and London
102 Gloucester Avenue, London NW1 8HX
tel 020-7586 0817 *fax* 020-7586 9970
email office@hambledon.co.uk
website www.hambledon.co.uk
Managing Director Martin Sheppard, *Commissioning Director* Tony Morris

History. *The Sunday Times* Small Publisher of the Year 2001–2. Founded in 1980 as Hambledon Press.

Hamilton House Publishing – see First and Best in Education Ltd

Hamish Hamilton – see Penguin Group (UK)

Hamlyn – see Octopus Publishing Group

Handsel Press – see The Continuum International Publishing Group Ltd

Harcourt Education Ltd*
Halley Court, Jordan Hill, Oxford OX2 8EJ
tel (01865) 310533 *fax* (01865) 314641
email uk.schools@harcourteducation.co.uk
website www.harcourteducation.co.uk
Chief Executive John Philbin

Division of Reed Elsevier (UK) Ltd.

Ginn & Co. (imprint)
fax (01865) 314189
Managing Director Paul Shuter

Textbook/other educational resources for primary schools.

Heinemann Educational (imprint)
Managing Director Bob Osborne

Textbooks, literature and other educational resources for all levels.

Rigby Heinemann (imprint)
fax (01865) 314189
Managing Director Paul Shuter

Textbook/other educational resources for primary schools.

Harcourt Publishers Ltd – see Elsevier Ltd (Health Sciences)

Harlequin Mills & Boon Ltd*
Eton House, 18-24 Paradise Road, Richmond,
Surrey TW9 1SR
tel 020-8288 2800 *fax* 020-8288 2899
Directors Andy Low (managing), Stuart Barber (financial), Angela Meredith (production), Alan Dawson (retail sales and marketing), Karin Stoecker (editorial), Liz Bulow (direct marketing), Mike Creffield (information technology), Jackie McGee (human resources)

Founded 1908.

Historical™ (imprint)
Senior Editor L. Fildew
Romance fiction.

Medical™ (imprint)
Senior Editor S. Hodgson
Romance fiction.

Mira Books® (imprint)
Senior Editor L. Fildew
Women's fiction.

Modern Romance (imprint)
Senior Editor Tessa Shapcott
Contemporary romance fiction in paperback and hardback.

Red Dress Ink™ (imprint)
Senior Editor Samantha Bell
Contemporary women's fiction with energy and attitude.

Silhouette® (imprint)
Editorial Manager L. Stonehouse
Popular romantic women's fiction.

Tender Romance (imprint)
Associate Senior Editor Bryoney Green
Contemporary romance fiction in paperback and hardback.

Harold Starke Publishers Ltd*
Pixey Green, Stadbroke, Eye, Suffolk IP21 5NG
tel (01379) 388334 *fax* (01379) 388335
email red@eclat.force9.co.uk
Directors Naomi Galinski (editorial)
Specialist, scientific, medical, reference.

HarperCollins Audio – see HarperCollins Publishers

HarperCollins Entertainment – see HarperCollins Publishers

HarperCollins Publishers*
77-85 Fulham Palace Road, London W6 8JB
tel 020-8741 7070 *fax* 020-8307 4440
website www.fireandwater.com
Ceo/Publisher Victoria Barnsley

All fiction and trade non-fiction must be submitted through an agent. Unsolicited submissions should be made in the form of a typewritten synopsis. Founded 1819.

HarperCollins General Books (division)
Managing Director Amanda Ridout

HarperFiction (division)
Publisher Lynne Drew

HarperCollins (imprint)
General trade fiction and women's fiction.

Collins Crime (imprint)
Publishing Director Julia Wisdom

Voyager (imprint)
Publishing Director Jane Johnson
Science fiction/fantasy.

HarperPress (division)
Managing Director/Publisher Caroline Michel, *Associate Publisher/Editor-in-Chief* Christopher Potter, *Associate Publishing Director* Nicky Eaton

Flamingo (imprint)
Publishing Director Philip Gwyn Jones
Original and engaging literary fiction and topical non-fiction.

Fourth Estate (imprint)
Publishing Director Nick Pearson
Current affairs, literature, popular culture, fiction, humour, politics, science, popular reference.

HarperCollins (imprint)
Publishing Director Michael Fishwick
General trade non-fiction.

HarperEntertainment (division)
Managing Director/Publisher Trevor Dolby

HarperCollins Entertainment (imprint)
Media-related books from film companions to autobiographies and TV tie-ins.

Collins Willow (imprint)
Publishing Director Michael Doggart
Sport.

HarperCollins Audio (imprint)
Publishing Director Rosalie George
Selection of fiction and non-fiction recordings of adult and children's titles by famous name readers.

Estates
Publishing Director David Brawn
Authors include Agatha Christie, J.R.R. Tolkien, C.S. Lewis. Imprint: Tolkien.

Thorsons/Element (division and imprint)
Managing Director Belinda Budge, *Publishing Director* Wanda Whiteley
Mind, Body & Spirit.

HarperCollins Children's (division)
Managing Director Sally Gritten, *Publishing Directors* Gillie Russell (fiction), Venetia Davie (properties), Sue Buswell (picture books)
Quality picture books and book and tape sets for under 7s; fiction for age 6 up to young adult. Imprints: Lions, Collins Picture Books, Collins Jet, Collins Teacher.

Collins (division)
Managing Director Thomas Webster, *Publishing Director, Collins Reference* Sarah Bailey
Reference, including encyclopedias, guides and handbooks, phrase books and manuals on popular reference, art instruction, illustrated, cookery and wine, crafts, DIY, gardening, military, natural

history, pet care, Scottish, pastimes. Imprints:
Collins, Collins Gem, Collins New Naturalist
Library, Jane's, Times Books.

Collins/Times Maps and Atlases (division and
imprint)
Publishing Directors Juliet Lawler (international
titles), Mike Cottingham (UK titles)

Maps, atlases, street plans and leisure guides.
Imprints: Access Press, Bartholomew, Birnbaum,
Nicholson.

Collins Dictionaries/COBUILD (division and
imprint)
Publishing Director Lorna Sinclair Knight

Bilingual and English dictionaries, English
dictionaries for foreign learners.

Collins Education (division)
Managing Director Jim Green

Books, CD-Roms and online material for UK
schools and colleges.

Letterland (imprint)

Home learning titles from preschool to further
education.

Harrap – see Chambers Harrap Publishers Ltd

Harvey Miller Publishers
Christchurch Lodge, Christchurch Passage,
London NW3 1JG
tel 020-7794 8947 *fax* 020-7794 9907
email johan.van.der.beke@brepols.com
website www.brepols.com
Publisher Johan Van der Beke

Art history. Imprint of Brepols Publishers.

The Harvill Press – see Random House Group Ltd

Haynes Publishing
Sparkford, Yeovil, Somerset BA22 7JJ
tel (01963) 440635 *fax* (01963) 440023
website www.haynes.co.uk
Directors J.H. Haynes (chairman), J. Haynes
(managing), D.J. Hermelin, M. Minter, M.J. Hughes,
G.R. Cook, J. Bunkham, M. Webb

Car and motorcycle service and repair manuals, car
handbooks/servicing guides; DIY books for the
home; car, motorcycle, motorsport and leisure
activities.

Haynes Motor Trade Division (imprint)
Editorial Director Matthew Minter

Car and motorcycle service and repair manuals and
technical data books.

Haynes Special Interest Publishing Division (imprint)
Editorial Director Mark Hughes

Cars, motorcycles, motorsport, related biographies,
practical maintenance and renovation.

Headland Publications
Editorial office Ty Coch, Galltegfa, Llanfwrog,
Ruthin, Denbighshire LL15 2AR
and 38 York Avenue, West Kirby,
Wirral CH48 3JF
Director and Editor Gladys Mary Coles

Poetry, anthologies of poetry and prose. No
unsolicited MSS. Founded 1970.

Headline – see Hodder Headline Ltd

Headline Book Publishing Ltd – see Hodder
Headline Ltd

Headway – see Hodder Headline Ltd

Health Science Press – see The C.W. Daniel
Company Ltd

Heinemann Educational – see Harcourt Education
Ltd

Heinemann English Language Teaching – now
Macmillan Heinemann English Language Teaching

Heinemann Young Books – former imprint of
Egmont Books

The Herbert Press – see A & C Black Publishers Ltd

Hermes House – see Anness Publishing

Highbury Nexus Special Interests Ltd
Nexus House, Azalea Drive, Swanley,
Kent BR8 8HU
tel (01322) 660070 *fax* (01322) 616319
Publisher Dawn Frosdick-Hopley

Modelling, model engineering, woodworking,
aviation, military, boats, crafts.

Hilmarton Manor Press
Calne, Wilts. SN11 8SB
tel (01249) 760208 *fax* (01249) 760379
email mailorder@hilmartonpress.co.uk
website www.hilmartonpress.co.uk
Editorial Director Charles Baile de Laperriere

Fine art, antiques, visual arts, wine, *Who's Who in
Art.* Founded 1964.

Hippo – see Scholastic Children's Books

Hippopotamus Press
22 Whitewell Road, Frome,
Somerset BA11 4EL
tel/fax (01373) 466653
Editors Roland John, Anna Martin

Poetry, essays, criticism. Publishes *Outposts Poetry Quarterly*. Poetry submissions from new writers welcome. Founded 1974.

Historical™ – see Harlequin Mills & Boon Ltd

Hobsons Publishing plc

Challenger House, 42 Adler Street,
London E1 1EE
tel 020-7958 5000 *fax* 020-7958 5001
website www.hobsons.com
Chairman Martin Morgan, *Directors* Chris Letcher (managing), Frances Halliwell, David Harrington, Tanja Kuveljic

Database publisher of educational and careers information under licence to CRAC (Careers Research and Advisory Centre). Founded 1974.

Hodder & Stoughton – see Hodder Headline Ltd

Hodder Children's Books – see Hodder Headline Ltd

Hodder Christian – see Hodder Headline Ltd

Hodder Gibson

2A Christie Street, Paisley PA1 1NB
tel 0141-848 1609 *fax* 0141-889 6315
email hoddergibson@hodder.co.uk
website www.hodderheadline.co.uk
www.madaboutbooks.com
Managing Director John Mitchell

Educational books specifically for Scotland. No unsolicited MSS. Formed by an amalgamation of Robert Gibson & Sons (Glasgow) and the Scottish branch of Hodder & Stoughton Educational. Part of the Hodder Headline Group.

Hodder Headline Ltd*

338 Euston Road, London NW1 3BH
tel 020-7873 6000 *fax* 020-7873 6024
Chairman Richard Handover, *Group Chief Executive* Tim Hely Hutchinson, *Directors* Martin Neild (managing, Headline), Jamie Hodder-Williams (managing, Hodder & Stoughton General), Charles Nettleton (managing, Hodder & Stoughton Religious), Malcolm Edwards (managing, Australia and New Zealand), Philip Walters (managing, Hodder Arnold), Colin Fairbain (finance), David Kewley (interim managing, Bookpoint), Mary Tapissier (group personnel/training/admin)
Founded 1986.

Headline Book Publishing Ltd (division)
Managing Director Martin Neild, *Publishing Directors* Jane Morpeth (fiction), Heather Holden-Brown (non-fiction)

Publishes under Headline and Review. Commercial and literary fiction (hardback and paperback), and popular non-fiction including autobiography, biography, food and wine, gardening, history, popular science, sport, TV tie-ins.

Hodder Children's Books (division)
Managing Director Charles Nettleton, *Publishing Director* Margaret Conroy, *Editorial Directors* Anne McNeil, Anne Clark

Publishes under Hodder Children's Books (picture books, fiction and non-fiction) and Hodder Wayland (illustrated non-fiction and reference).

Hodder Arnold (division)
Directors Philip Walters (managing), Elisabeth Tribe (schools publishing), Katie Roden (consumer education), Georgina Bentliff (health sciences), Mary Attree (journals and reference books), Alyssum Ross (production & design), Catherine Newman (sales & marketing)

Publishes under Hodder & Stoughton Educational, Teach Yourself, Headway. Textbooks for the primary, secondary, tertiary and further education sectors and for self-improvement. Academic and professional books and journals.

Hodder & Stoughton General (division)
Managing Director Jamie Hodder-Williams, *Publisher* Nick Sawyers, *Non-fiction* Rowena Webb, *Sceptre* Carole Welch, *Fiction* Carolyn Mays, *Audio* Rupert Lancaster

Publishes under Hodder & Stoughton, Coronet, Flame, New English Library, Sceptre, Lir, Mobius. Commercial and literary fiction; biography, autobiography, history, self-help, humour, Mind, Body & Spirit, travel and other general interest non-fiction; audio. All unsolicited MSS to the Submissions Editor, Betty Schwartz.

Hodder & Stoughton Religious (division)
Managing Director Charles Nettleton, *Publishing Director* Judith Longman

Publishes under New International Version of the Bible, Hodder Christian Books, Help Yourself, Bibles. Christian books, biography, self-help, gift, health.

Hodder Wayland – see Hodder Headline Ltd

Hogarth Press – former imprint of Random House Group Ltd

Hollis Publishing Ltd

Harlequin House, 7 High Street, Teddington,
Middlesex TW11 8EL
tel 020-8977 7711 *fax* 020-8977 1133
email gary@hollis-pr.co.uk
website www.hollis-pr.co.uk
Managing Director Gary Zabel

Publications include *Hollis Press & PR Annual*, *Hollis Sponsorship Yearbook*, *Advertisers Annual*, *Marketing Handbook*, Hollis Europe, *A.S.K. Hollis*

(Directory of Associations) and *SHOWCASE* (International Music Business Guide).

Honno Ltd (Welsh Women's Press)
Honno Editorial Office,
c/o Canolfan Merched y Wawr,
Vulcan Street, Aberystwyth,
Ceredigion SY23 1JB
tel/fax (01970) 623150
email post@honno.co.uk
website www.honno.co.uk
Editor Janet Thomas

Literature written by women in Wales or with a Welsh connection. All subjects considered – fiction, non-fiction, poetry, autobiographies. Honno is a community co-operative. Founded 1986.

Hopscotch Educational Publishing Ltd*
Unit 2, 56 Pickwick Road, Corsham,
Wilts. SN13 9BX
tel (01249) 701701 *fax* (01249) 701987
email sales@hopscotchbooks.com
website www.hopscotchbooks.com
Editorial Director Margot O'Keeffe, *Creative Director* Frances Mackay

National Curriculum subjects for primary teachers. Founded 1997.

House of Lochar
Isle of Colonsay, Argyll PA61 7YR
tel/fax (01951) 200232
email lochar@colonsay.org.uk
website www.houseoflochar.com
Managing Director Georgina Hobhouse, *Editorial Director* Kevin Byrne

Scottish history, transport, Scottish literature. Founded 1995.

How To Books Ltd
3 Newtec Place, Magdalen Road,
Oxford OX4 1RE
tel (01865) 793806 *fax* (01865) 248780
email info@howtobooks.co.uk
website www.howtobooks.co.uk
Publisher and Managing Director Giles Lewis,
Commissioning Editor Nikki Read

Reference. Practical books that inspire. Subjects covered include small business and self-employment, business and management, career development, living and working abroad, home and family reference, personal development, study skills and student guides, creative writing. Book proposals welcome. Founded 1991.

Hugo's Language Books – see Penguin Group (UK)

Hunt & Thorpe – now incorporated into John Hunt Publishing Ltd

Hutchinson – see Random House Group Ltd

Hutchinson Children's Books – see Random House Group Ltd

I.B.Tauris & Co. Ltd
6 Salem Road, London W2 4BU
tel 020-7243 1225 *fax* 020-7243 1226
email mail@ibtauris.com
website www.ibtauris.com
Chairman/Publisher Iradj Bagherzade, *Managing Director* Jonathan McDonnell

History, biography, politics, international relations, current affairs, Middle East, cultural and media studies, film, art, archaeology, travel guides. Founded 1983.

Tauris Academic Studies (imprint)

Academic monographs on history, political science and social sciences.

Tauris Parke Books (imprint)

Illustrated books on architecture, design, photography, cultural history and travel.

Tauris Parke Paperbacks (imprint)

Non-fiction trade paperbacks: biography, history, travel, cinema, art, cultural history.

Ian Allan Publishing Ltd
Riverdene Business Park, Molesey Road,
Hersham, Surrey KT12 4RG
tel (01932) 266600 *fax* (01932) 266601
email info@ianallanpub.co.uk
website www.ianallanpublishing.com
Publishing Manager Peter Waller

Transport: railways, aircraft, shipping, road; naval and military history; reference books and magazines; sport and cycling guides; no fiction.

Classic Publications (imprint)

Transport, aviation.

Midland Publishing (imprint)

Transport: railways, aviation; naval and military history.

Oxford Publishing Company (imprint)

Transport: railways, road.

ICSA Publishing Ltd*
16 Park Crescent, London W1B 1AH
tel 020-7612 7020 *fax* 020-7323 1132
email icsa.pub@icsa.co.uk
website www.icsapublishing.co.uk
Joint Managing Directors Clare Grist Taylor, Susan Richards

Publishing company of the Institute of Chartered Secretaries and Administrators. Professional business information for the corporate, public and not-for-profit sectors in a range of formats. Founded 1981.

In Pinn – see Neil Wilson Publishing Ltd

Insight Guides/Berlitz Publishing

58 Borough High Street, London SE1 1XF
tel 020-7403 0284 fax 020-7403 0290
website www.insightguides.com
Managing Director Jeremy Westwood

Travel, language and related multimedia. Founded 1970.

Institute of Physics Publishing

Dirac House, Temple Back, Bristol BS1 6BE
tel 0117-929 7481 fax 0117-930 1186
email john-navas@iop.org
website www.bookmarkphysics.iop.org
Editorial Manager John Navas

Monographs, graduate texts, conference proceedings and reference works in physics and physics-related science and technology; also popular science titles.

Institute of Public Administration†

Vergemount Hall, Clonskeagh, Dublin 6, Republic of Ireland
tel (01) 2403600 fax (01) 2698644
email jarmstrong@ipa.ie
website www.ipa.ie
Editor Jennifer Armstrong

Government, economics, politics, law, public management, social policy and administrative history. Founded 1957.

Inter-Varsity Press*

38 De Montfort Street, Leicester LE1 7GP
tel 0116-255 1754 fax 0116-254 2044
email ivp@uccf.org.uk
website www.ivpbooks.com
Managing Editor S. Carter

Theology and religion.

Irish Academic Press Ltd

44 Northumberland Road, Ballsbridge, Dublin 4, Republic of Ireland
tel (01) 6688244 fax (01) 6601610
email info@iap.ie
website www.iap.ie
Directors Stewart Cass, Frank Cass, Michael Philip Zaidner, Administrator Rachel Milotte

Publishes under the imprints Irish University Press and Irish Academic Press. Scholarly books especially in 19th and 20th century history, literature, heritage and culture. Founded 1974.

IRS/Eclipse – see LexisNexis Butterworths Tolley

The Islamic Foundation

Markfield Conference Centre, Ratby Lane, Markfield, Leics. LE67 9SY

tel (01530) 244944 fax (01530) 244946
Director General Dr Manazir Ahsan, Deputy Director Chowdhury Mueen-Uddin

Books on Islam for adults and children. Founded 1973.

Ithaca Press – see Garnet Publishing Ltd

J. Garnet Miller – see Cressrelles Publishing Co. Ltd

J. Whitaker & Sons Ltd – see VNU Entertainment Media UK Ltd

J.A. Allen

Clerkenwell House, 45-47 Clerkenwell Green, London EC1R 0HT
tel 020-7251 2661 fax 020-7490 4958
email allen@halebooks.com
Publisher Caroline Burt

Horse and equestrianism including bloodstock breeding, racing, polo, dressage, horse care, carriage driving, breeds, veterinary and farriery. Books usually commissioned but willing to consider any serious, specialist MSS on the horse and related subjects. Imprint of Robert Hale Ltd. Founded 1926.

J.M. Dent – now incorporated into Weidenfeld & Nicolson

JAI – see Elsevier Ltd

James Clarke & Co. Ltd*

PO Box 60, Cambridge CB1 2NT
tel (01223) 350865 fax (01223) 366951
email publishing@lutterworth.com
website www.lutterworth.com
Managing Director Adrian Brink

Theology, academic, reference books. Founded 1859.

Acorn Editions (imprint)
Sponsored books.

Lutterworth Press (subsidiary)
The arts, biography, children's books (fiction, non-fiction, picture, rewards), educational, environmental, general, history, leisure, philosophy, science, sociology, theology and religion.

Patrick Hardy Books (imprint)
Children's fiction.

James Currey Ltd

73 Botley Road, Oxford OX2 0BS
tel (01865) 244111 fax (01865) 246454
Directors James Currey, Prof Wendy James FBA, Dr Douglas H. Johnson, Keith Sambrook

Academic studies of Africa, Caribbean, Third World: history, anthropology, archaeology, economics, agriculture, politics, literary criticism, sociology. Founded 1985.

James Nisbet & Co. Ltd
Pirton Court, Hitchin, Herts. SG5 3QA
tel/fax (01462) 713444
Directors Miss E.M. Mackenzie-Wood,
Mrs A.A.C. Bierrum

Business management. Founded 1810.

Jane's – see HarperCollins Publishers

Jane's Information Group
163 Brighton Road, Coulsdon,
Surrey CR5 2YH
tel 020-8700 3700 *fax* 020-8763 1005
website www.janes.com
Managing Director Alfred Rolington

Professional publishers in hardcopy and electronic multimedia of military, aviation, naval, defence, non-fiction, reference, police, geo-political. Consumer books in association with **HarperCollins Publishers**.

Jarrold Publishing
(incorporating Pitkin and Unichrome brands)
Whitefriars, Norwich NR3 1TR
tel (01603) 763300 *fax* (01603) 662748
Directors Margot Russell-King (managing), Heather Hook (commercial – heritage & leisure), David Loombe (finance), Steve Plackett (production)

UK travel guidebooks, pictorial books and calendars. Unsolicited MSS, synopses and ideas welcome but approach in writing before submitting to Sarah Letts, Managing Editor. Division of Jarrold & Sons Ltd. Founded 1770.

Jessica Kingsley Publishers*
116 Pentonville Road, London N1 9JB
tel 020-7833 2307 *fax* 020-7837 2917
email post@jkp.com
website www.jkp.com
Directors Jessica Kingsley (managing), Amy Lankester-Owen (editorial), Barbara Martin (sales)

Psychology, psychotherapy, psychiatry, arts therapies, social work, special needs (especially autism and Asperger Syndrome), education, law. Founded 1987.

John Blake Publishing Ltd
(incorporating Metro Books)
3 Bramber Court, 2 Bramber Road,
London W14 9PB
tel 020-7381 0666 *fax* 020-7381 6868
email words@blake.co.uk

Popular non-fiction, including biographies, true crime, food and drink, health. No unsolicited fiction. Acquired Metro Publishing Ltd 2001.

John Donald – see Birlinn Ltd

John Hunt Publishing Ltd
(incorporating Hunt & Thorpe, Arthur James Ltd)
46A West Street, New Alresford,
Hants SO24 9AU
tel (01962) 736880 *fax* (01962) 736881
email john@johnhunt-publishing.com
Director John Hunt

Children's and adult religious, full colour books for the international market. MSS welcome; send sae. Founded 1989.

O-Books (imprint)
Global spirituality.

John Libbey & Co. Ltd
PO Box 276, Eastleigh SO50 5YS
tel (01342) 315440 *fax* (023) 8065 0259
email johnlibbey@aol.com
Director John Libbey

Film/cinema, animation. Founded 1979.

John Murray (Publishers) Ltd*
338 Euston Road, London NW1 3BH
tel 020-7873 6000
Managing Director Roland Philipps

General: biography and autobiography, letters and diaries, travel, exploration, general history, fiction. No unsolicited MSS. Founded 1768; acquired by **Hodder Headline Ltd** 2002.

Jonathan Cape – see Random House Group Ltd

Jonathan Cape Children's Books – see Random House Group Ltd

Jordan Publishing Ltd
21 St Thomas Street, Bristol BS1 6JS
tel 0117-923 0600 *fax* 0117-925 0486
website www.jordanpublishing.co.uk
Managing Director Richard Hudson

Law and business administration. Also specialist Family Law imprint (including the *Family Law Journal*). Books, looseleaf services, serials, CD-Roms and online.

Josef Weinberger Plays Ltd
12-14 Mortimer Street,
London W1T 3JJ
tel 020-7580 2827 *fax* 020-7436 9016
email general.info@jwmail.co.uk
website www.josef-weinberger.com

Stage plays only, in both acting and trade editions. Preliminary letter essential.

The Journeyman Press – see Pluto Press

Karnak House
300 Westbourne Park Road,
London W11 1EH
tel/fax 020-7243 3620
email karnakhouse@aol.com
website www.karnakhouse.co.uk
Directors Amon Saba Saakana (managing), Seheri
Sujai (art)

Specialists in African/Caribbean studies worldwide:
anthropology, education, Egyptology, fiction,
history, language, linguistics, literary criticism,
music, philosophy, prehistory. Founded 1979.

Kelpies – see Floris Books

The Kenilworth Press Ltd
Addington, Buckingham MK18 2JR
tel (0129 671) 5101 *fax* (0129 671) 5148
email mail@kenilworthpress.co.uk
website www.kenilworthpress.co.uk
Directors David Blunt, Deirdre Blunt

Equestrian, including official publications for the
British Horse Society. Founded 1989. Incorporates
Threshold Books; founded 1970.

Kenneth Mason Publications Ltd
The Book Barn, Westbourne,
Hants PO10 8RS
tel (01243) 377977 *fax* (01243) 379136
Directors Kenneth Mason (chairman), Piers Mason
(managing), Michael Mason, Anthea Mason

Nautical, slimming, health, fitness; technical
journals. Founded 1958.

Kenyon-Deane – see Cressrelles Publishing Co. Ltd

Kevin Mayhew Ltd
Buxhall, Suffolk IP14 3BW
tel (01449) 737978 *fax* (01449) 737834
email info@kevinmayhewltd.com
Directors Kevin Mayhew (chairman), Gordon Carter
(managing) Ray Gilbert (purchasing), Paul Smith
(sales)

Christianity: prayer and spirituality, pastoral care,
preaching, liturgy worship, children's, youth work,
drama, instant art. Music: hymns, organ and choral,
contemporary worship, piano and instrumental.
Contact Editorial Dept before sending MSS/synopses.
Founded 1976.

Kingfisher Publications plc
(formerly Larousse plc)
New Penderel House, 283-288 High Holborn,
London WC1V 7HZ
tel 020-7903 9999 *fax* 020-7242 4979
email sales@kingfisherpub.co.uk
Directors Géraud de Durand (finance), John Richards
(production)

Kingfisher (imprint)
Publishing Director, Non-fiction Gillian Denton,
Acting Publishing Director, Fiction Suzanne Carnell
Children's books. No unsolicited MSS or synopses
considered.

Kluwer Academic/Plenum Publishers*
241 Borough High Street,
London SE1 1GB
tel 020-7940 7490 *fax* 020-7940 7495
email mail@plenum.co.uk
website www.wkap.nl
Publishing Director Dr Ken Derham, *Senior
Publishing Editor* Joanna Lawrence

Postgraduate, professional scientific, technical and
medical, and reference books. Founded 1966.

Knight Paperbacks – see Caxton Publishing Group

Knockabout Comics
10 Acklam Road, London W10 5QZ
tel 020-8969 2945 *fax* 020-8968 7614
email knockcomic@aol.com
website www.knockabout.com
Editors Tony Bennett, Carol Bennett

Humorous and satirical graphic novels for an adult
readership. Founded 1975.

Kogan Page Ltd*
120 Pentonville Road,
London N1 9JN
tel 020-7278 0433 *fax* 020-7837 6348
website www.kogan.page.co.uk
website www.earthscan.co.uk *Managing Director*
Philip Kogan, *Directors* Pauline Goodwin
(editorial), Peter Chadwick (production and
editorial), Gordon Watts (financial), Philip Mudd
(editorial), Julie McNair (sales)

Education, training, educational and training
technology, journals, business and management,
human resource management, transport and
distribution, marketing, sales, advertising and PR,
finance and accounting, directories, small business,
careers and vocational, personal finance,
environment. Founded 1967.

Earthscan Publications Ltd (subsidiary)
website www.earthscan.com
Directors Philip Kogan, Jonathan Sinclair-Wilson
(editorial)

Third World and environmental issues: politics,
sociology, environment, economics, current events,
geography, health.

Kogan Page Science Ltd (subsidiary)
Directors Philip Kogan

Engineering science, physics, chemistry, structural
engineering, communication science, materials
science.

Penton Press (imprint)
Director Philip Kogan

Engineering science, materials science, surface technology, information systems and networks.

Kyle Cathie Ltd
122 Arlington Road, London NW1 7HP
tel 020-7692 7215 *fax* 020-7692 7260
email general.enquiries@kyle-cathie.com
website www.kylecathie.com
Publisher and Managing Director Kyle Cathie

Health, beauty, food and drink, gardening, reference, style, design, Mind, Body & Spirit. Founded 1990.

L.N. Fowler & Co. Ltd – see The C.W. Daniel Company Ltd

Ladybird – see Penguin Group (UK)

Laurence King Publishing Ltd*
(formerly Calmann & King Ltd)
71 Great Russell Street, London WC1B 3BP
tel 020-7430 8850 *fax* 020-7430 8880
email enquiries@laurenceking.co.uk
website www.laurenceking.co.uk
Directors Robin Hyman (chairman), Laurence King (managing), Lesley Ripley Greenfield (editorial: college and fine arts), Philip Cooper (editorial: architecture and design), Judith Rasmussen (production), John Stoddart (financial)

Illustrated books on art, architecture, design, graphic design, film and photography. Founded 1976.

Lawrence & Wishart Ltd
99A Wallis Road, London E9 5LN
tel 020-8533 2506 *fax* 020-8533 7369
email lw@l-w-bks.demon.co.uk
website www.l-w-bks.co.uk
Directors S. Davison (editorial), J. Rodrigues, B. Kirsch, M. Seaton, J. Rutherford, A. Greenaway, G. Andrews

Cultural studies, current affairs, history, socialism and Marxism, political philosophy, politics, popular culture.

Learning World – see Chrysalis Children's Books

Lennard Publishing
Windmill Cottage, Mackerye End, Harpenden, Herts. AL5 5DR
tel (01582) 715866
email stephenson@lennardqap.co.uk
Directors K.A.A. Stephenson, R.H. Stephenson

Sponsored books, special commissions. No unsolicited MSS. Division of Lennard Associates Ltd.

Letterland – see HarperCollins Publishers

Letts Educational*
Chiswick Centre, 414 Chiswick High Road, London W4 5TF
tel 020-8996 3333 *fax* 020-8742 8390
email mail@lettsed.co.uk
website www.lettsed.co.uk/
Directors Stephen Baker (managing), Wayne Davies (publishing), Andrew Thraves (publishing), Lee Warren (finance)

Accountancy and taxation; children's; computer science; economics; educational and textbooks; industry, business and management; mathematics and statistics; vocational training and careers; homework and revision books. Associate and subsidiary companies: Granada Learning, nferNelson, Black Cat, Granada Media, Semerc. Founded 1979.

Lewis Masonic
Riverdene Business Park, Molesey Road, Hersham, Surrey KT12 4RG
tel (01932) 266600 *fax* (01932) 266601

Masonic books; *Masonic Square Magazine*. Founded 1870.

LexisNexis Butterworths Tolley
Halsbury House, 35 Chancery Lane, London WC2A 1EL
tel 020-7400 2500 *fax* 020-7400 2842
email customer_services@butterworths.com
website www.kingfisherpub.com
Directors John Richards (managing), Anne Maire Ryan (editorial)

Division of Reed Elsevier (UK) Ltd. Founded 1974.

Butterworths (imprint)

Legal and tax and accountancy books, journals, looseleaf and electronic services.

Charles Knight (imprint)

Looseleaf legal works and periodicals on local government law, construction law and technical subjects.

IRS/Eclipse (imprint)

Company and employment law.

Tolley (imprint)

Law, taxation, accountancy, business.

Library Association Publishing – see Facet Publishing

Libris Ltd
26 Lady Margaret Road, London NW5 2XL
tel 020-7482 2390 *fax* 020-7485 2730
Directors Nicholas Jacobs, S.A. Kitzinger

Literature, literary biography, German studies, bilingual poetry. Founded 1986.

The Lilliput Press Ltd[†]
62-63 Sitric Road, Dublin 7, Republic of Ireland
tel (01) 6711647 *fax* (01) 6711233
email info@lilliputpress.ie
website www.lilliputpress.ie
Managing Director Antony T. Farrell

General and Irish literature: essays, biography/ autobiography, fiction, criticism; Irish history; philosophy; contemporary culture; nature and environment. Founded 1984.

Lion Publishing plc*
Mayfield House, 256 Banbury Road, Oxford OX2 7DH
tel (01865) 302750 *fax* (01865) 302757
email enquiries@lion-publishing.co.uk
website www.lion-publishing.co.uk
Directors Paul Clifford (managing & editorial), Denis Cole, Tony Wales, John O'Nions, Roy McCloughry

Reference, paperbacks, illustrated children's books, educational, gift books, religion and theology; all reflecting a Christian position. No adult fiction. Send preliminary letter before submitting MSS. Founded 1971.

Lions – see HarperCollins Publishers

Lir – see Hodder Headline Ltd

Little Tiger Press – see Magi Publications

Little, Brown and Company (UK) – see Time Warner Books UK

Liverpool University Press
4 Cambridge Street, Liverpool L69 7ZU
tel 0151-794 2233 *fax* 0151-794 2235
email robblo@liv.ac.uk
website www.liverpool-unipress.co.uk
Publisher Robin Bloxsidge

Academic and scholarly books in a range of disciplines. Special interests: art history, European and American literature, science fiction criticism, all fields of history, archaeology, sociology. New series established include *Liverpool Latin American Studies* and *Studies in Social and Political Thought*. Founded 1899.

Livewire – see The Women's Press

Logaston Press
Little Logaston, Logaston, Woonton, Almeley, Herefordshire HR3 6QH
tel (01544) 327344

email logastonp@aol.com
Proprietor Andy Johnson

History, social history, archaeology and guides to rural west Midlands and central and south Wales. Founded 1985.

Lonely Planet Publications
72-82 Rosebery Avenue,
London EC1R 4RW
tel 020-7841 9000 *fax* 020-7841 9001
email go@lonelyplanet.co.uk
website www.lonelyplanet.com/
Directors Tony Wheeler, Maureen Wheeler, *UK General Manager* John Sadler

Country and regional guidebooks, city guides, *Best Of* citybreak guides, city maps, phrasebooks, walking guides, diving and snorkelling guides, pictorial books, health guides, food guides, cycling guides, wildlife guides, first-time travel guides, classic overland routes, and travel photography. Also digital travel guides (*CitySync*), a commercial slide library (Lonely Planet Images) and a TV company. London office established 1991.

Longman – see Pearson Education

Lorenz Books – see Anness Publishing

Lund Humphries – see Ashgate Publishing Ltd

Lutterworth Press – see James Clarke & Co. Ltd

Macdonald Young Books – now Hodder Children's Books – see Hodder Headline Ltd

McGraw-Hill Education*
McGraw-Hill House, Shoppenhangers Road, Maidenhead, Berks. SL6 2QL
tel (01628) 502500 *fax* (01628) 770224
email (contact)@mcgraw-hill.com
website www.mcgraw-hill.co.uk
Directors Simon Allen (managing – EMEA), Alan Martin (operations), Rupert Mitchell (professional, Northern Europe), Murray St Leger (higher education sales & marketing, Northern Europe), Melissa Rosati (higher education, editorial)

Technical, scientific, professional reference.
Open University Press (imprint)
Social sciences.

Macmillan Children's Books Ltd – see Macmillan Publishers Ltd

Macmillan Education Ltd – see Macmillan Publishers Ltd

Macmillan Heinemann English Language Teaching – see Macmillan Publishers Ltd

Macmillan Publishers Ltd*

The Macmillan Building, 4 Crinan Street,
London N1 9XW
tel 020-7833 4000 *fax* 020-7843 4640
Chief Executive Richard Charkin, *Directors*
M. Barnard, C.J. Paterson, G.R.U. Todd, D. North,
Dr A. Thomas, D.J.G. Knight

Macmillan Children's Books Ltd (division)
20 New Wharf Road, London N1 9RR
tel 020-7014 6000 *fax* 020-7014 6001
Managing Director Kate Wilson, *Editorial Director
(Picture Books and Gift Books)* Suzanne Carnell,
Editorial Director (Campbell Books) Camilla Reid,
Publishing Director (Fiction, Non-Fiction and Poetry)
Sarah Davies, *Associate Publisher (Fiction)* Marion
Lloyd, *Associate Publisher (Picture Books and Gift
Books)* Alison Green

Publishes under Macmillan, **Pan**, Campbell Books,
Young Picador. Picture books, fiction, poetry, non-
fiction, early learning, pop-up, novelty, board
books. No unsolicited material.

Pan Macmillan (division)
20 New Wharf Road, London N1 9RR
tel 020-7014 6000 *fax* 020-7014 6001
Managing Director David North, *Editorial Directors*
Imogen Taylor (fiction), Peter Lavery (TOR (UK)
and thrillers), Georgina Morley (non-fiction),
Publishing Manager (Macmillan Audio) Alison
Muirden, *Publishing Director (Macmillan, Pan and
Picador)* Maria Rejt

Novels, crime, science fiction, fantasy and horror.
Autobiography, biography, business, gift books,
health and beauty, history, humour, natural history,
travel, philosophy, politics and world affairs,
psychology, theatre and film, gardening and
cookery, encyclopedias. Publishes under **Boxtree**,
Macmillan, **Pan**, **Picador**, **Sidgwick & Jackson**.
Founded 1843.

Boxtree (imprint)
fax 020-7881 8280
Publisher, Channel 4 Books Emma Marriott

TV and film tie-ins (adult and children's non-
fiction); illustrated and general non-fiction; mass
market paperbacks linked to TV, film, rock and
sporting events; humour.

Pan (imprint)
Publisher Peter Lavery

Fiction: novels, crime, science fiction, fantasy and
horror. Non-fiction: sports, theatre and film, travel,
gardening and cookery, encyclopedias, general.
Founded 1947.

Picador (imprint)
Publishing Director Andrew Kidd

Literary international fiction and non-fiction,
poetry. Founded 1972.

Sidgwick & Jackson (imprint)
Publisher Ingrid Connell

Military and war, music, pop and rock. MSS,
synopses and ideas welcome. Send to submissions
editor, with return postage. Founded 1908.

Macmillan Education Ltd (division)
Macmillan Oxford, Between Towns Road,
Oxford OX4 3PP
tel (01865) 405700 *fax* (01865) 405701
Chairman Christopher Paterson, *Managing Director*
Christopher Harrison, *Publishing Directors* Sue Bale,
Alison Hubert, *Finance Director* Paul Emmett,
Production Director John Peacock, *IT Director* Ian
Johnstone

English language teaching materials. School and
college textbooks and materials in all subjects for
international markets.

Macmillan Heinemann English Language Teaching
Macmillan Oxford, Between Towns Road,
Oxford OX4 3PP
tel (01865) 405700 *fax* (01865) 405701
Chairman Christopher Paterson, *Managing Director*
Christopher Harrison, *Director, ELT Publishing* Sue
Bale

English language teaching materials.

Palgrave Macmillan Ltd (division)
Managing Director Dominic Knight, *Publishing
Directors* Frances Arnold (College), Sam Burridge
(Scholarly and Reference), David Bull (Journals),
Sales and Marketing Directors Margaret Hewinson,
Garrett Kiely, *Operations Director* John Peacock,
Finance Director Richard Hartgill

Textbooks, monographs and journals in academic
and professional subjects.

Made Simple Books – see Elsevier Ltd

Magi Publications

1 The Coda Centre, 189 Munster Road,
London SW6 6AW
tel 020-7385 6333 *fax* 020-7385 7333
website www.littletigerpress.com
Publisher Monty Bhatia, *Editors* Ramona Reihill,
Jude Evans

Little Tiger Press (imprint)
email info@littletiger.co.uk

Quality children's picture books and novelty books.
New material will be considered from authors and
illustrators; see website for guidelines. Founded
1987.

Mainstream Publishing Co. (Edinburgh) Ltd*

7 Albany Street, Edinburgh EH1 3UG
tel 0131-557 2959 *fax* 0131-556 8720

email enquiries@mainstreampublishing.com
website www.mainstreampublishing.com
Directors Bill Campbell, Peter MacKenzie, Fiona
Brownlee (marketing), Sharon Atherton (publicity),
Ray Cowie (sales), Neil Graham (production), Ailsa
Bathgate (editorial)

Biography, autobiography, art, photography, sport,
health, guidebooks, humour, literature, current
affairs, history, politics. Founded 1978.

Mainstream Sport (imprint)

Sport.

Mammoth – former imprint of Egmont Books

Management Books 2000 Ltd
(incorporating Mercury Books)
Forge House, Limes Road, Kemble, Cirencester,
Glos. GL7 6AD
tel (01285) 771441 *fax* (01285) 771055
email M.B.2000@virgin.net
website www.mb2000.com
Directors N. Dale-Harris, R. Hartman, *Publisher*
James Alexander

Practical books for working managers and business
professionals: management, business and lifeskills,
and sponsored titles. Unsolicited MSS, synopses and
ideas for books welcome.

Manchester United Books – see Carlton Publishing Group

Manchester University Press*
Oxford Road, Manchester M13 9NR
tel 0161-275 2310 *fax* 0161-274 3346
email mup@man.ac.uk
website www.manchesteruniversitypress.co.uk
Chief Executive David Rodgers, *Head of Editorial*
Matthew Frost

Works of academic scholarship: literary criticism,
cultural studies, media studies, art history, design,
architecture, history, politics, economics, international law, modern language texts. Textbooks and
monographs. Founded 1904.

Mandrake of Oxford
PO Box 250, Oxford OX1 1AP
tel (01865) 243671 *fax* (01865) 432929
email mandrake@mandrake.uk.net
website www.mandrake.uk.net
Directors Mogg Morgan, Kym Morgan

Occult and bizarre. Founded 1986.

Manson Publishing Ltd*
73 Corringham Road, London NW11 7DL
tel 020-8905 5150 *fax* 020-8201 9233
email manson@man-pub.demon.co.uk
website www.manson-publishing.co.uk

Managing Director Michael Manson
Medical, scientific, veterinary. Founded 1992.

Mantra
5 Alexandra Grove, London N12 8NU
tel 020-8445 5123 *fax* 020-8446 7745
email sales@mantrapublishing.com
website www.mantralingua.com
Managing Director M. Chatterji

Children's multicultural picture books; multilingual
friezes/posters; dual language books/cassettes; South
Asian literature/teenage fiction; CD-Roms and
videos. Founded 1984.

Marino Books – see The Mercier Press

Marion Boyars Publishers Ltd
24 Lacy Road, London SW15 1NL
tel 020-8788 9522 *fax* 020-8789 8122
email marion.boyars@talk21.com
website www.marionboyars.co.uk
Directors Catheryn Kilgarriff, Ken Hollings
(editorial)

Literary fiction, film, memoirs, travel, cultural
studies, jazz, music. Will only consider fiction
submitted through an agent. Founded 1975.

Marshall Pickering – former imprint of HarperCollins Publishers

Martin Books – see Simon & Schuster

Mary Glasgow – former imprint of Nelson Thornes Ltd

Medical™ – see Harlequin Mills & Boon Ltd

Mentor Books†
43 Furze Road, Sandyford Industrial Estate,
Dublin 18, Republic of Ireland
tel (353) 1-2952112 *fax* (353) 1-2952114
email all@mentorbooks.ie
website www.mentorbooks.ie
Managing Director Daniel McCarthy, *Managing
Editor* Claire Haugh

General: fiction, non-fiction, children's, guidebooks,
biographies, history. Educational (secondary):
languages, history, geography, business, maths,
science. No unsolicited MSS. Founded 1979.

The Mercat Press*
10 Coates Crescent, Edinburgh EH3 7AL
tel 0131-225 5324 *fax* 0131-226 6632
email enquiries@mercatpress.com
Managing Editors Seán Costello, Tom Johnstone

Scottish books of general and academic interest. No
new poetry. Founded 1970.

The Mercier Press[†]
Douglas Village, Cork,
Republic of Ireland
tel (021) 4899858 *fax* (021) 4899887
email books@mercierpress.ie
website www.mercierpress.ie
Directors G. Eaton (chairman), J.F. Spillane
(managing), M.P. Feehan, J. O'Donoghue

Irish literature, folklore, history, politics, humour,
education, theology, law, current affairs, health,
mind and spirit, general non-fiction. Imprint:
Marino Books. Founded 1944.

Merehurst Ltd – see Murdoch Books UK Ltd

Merlin Press Ltd
PO Box 30705, London WC2E 8QD
tel 020-7836 3020 *fax* 020-7497 0309
email info@merlinpress.co.uk
website www.merlinpress.co.uk
Managing Director Anthony Zurbrugg

Radical history and social studies. Letters/synopses
only please.

Green Print (imprint)

Green politics and the environment.

Merlin Unwin Books
Palmers House, 7 Corve Street, Ludlow,
Shropshire SY8 1DB
tel (01584) 877456 *fax* (01584) 877457
email books@merlinunwin.co.uk
website www.countrybooksdirect.com
Proprietor Merlin Unwin

Fishing and country books. Founded 1990.

Merrell Publishers Ltd
42 Southwark Street, London SE1 1UN
tel 020-7403 2047 *fax* 020-7407 1333
email mail@merrellpublishers.com
website www.merrellpublishers.com
Publisher Hugh Merrell, *Editorial Director* Julian
Honer, *Sales & Marketing Director* Emilie Nangle

High-quality illustrated books on all aspects of
visual culture, including art, architecture,
photography and design.

Methodist Publishing House
4 John Wesley Road, Werrington,
Peterborough PE4 6ZP
tel (01733) 325002 *fax* (01733) 384180
email sales@mph.org.uk
Chief Executive Martin Stone

Hymn and service books, general religious titles,
church supplies. Founded 1773.

Foundery Press (imprint)

Ecumenical titles.

Methuen Academic – now incorporated into Routledge, see Taylor & Francis Group plc

Methuen Children's Books – former imprint of Egmont Books

Methuen Publishing Ltd
215 Vauxhall Bridge Road, London SW1V 1EJ
tel 020-7798 1600 *fax* 020-7828 2098
Managing Director Peter Tummons, *Publishing
Director* Max Eilenberg, *Sales Manager* Haydn Jones,
Publicity Manager Margot Weale

Literary fiction and non-fiction: biography,
autobiography, travel, history, sport, drama,
humour, film, performing arts, plays. No unsolicited
MSS.

Metro Publishing Ltd – see John Blake Publishing Ltd

Michael Joseph – see Penguin Group (UK)

Michael O'Mara Books Ltd
9 Lion Yard, Tremadoc Road,
London SW4 7NQ
tel 020-7720 8643 *fax* 020-7627 8953
website www.mombooks.com
Chairman Michael O'Mara, *Managing Director*
Lesley O'Mara

General non-fiction: biography, humour, history,
ancient history, anthologies and royal books.
Founded 1985.

Buster Books (imprint)

Young children's novelty books.

Michelin Travel Publications
Hannay House, 39 Clarendon Road, Watford,
Herts. WD17 1JA
tel (01923) 205240 *fax* (01923) 205241
website www.viamichelin.com
Head of Travel Publications J. Lewis

Tourist guides, maps and atlases, hotel and
restaurant guides.

Midland Publishing – see Ian Allan Publishing Ltd

Milestone Publications
62 Murray Road, Horndean,
Waterlooville PO8 9JL
tel (023) 9259 7440 *fax* (023) 9259 1975
email info@gosschinaclub.co.uk
website www.gosscrestedchina.co.uk
Managing Director Lynda J. Pine

Goss & Crested heraldic china, antique porcelain.
Publishing and bookselling division of Goss &
Crested China Club. Founded 1967.

Miller's – see Octopus Publishing Group

Miller Freeman Information Services – now CMP Information Ltd

Mills & Boon – see Harlequin Mills & Boon Ltd

Mira Books® – see Harlequin Mills & Boon Ltd

The MIT Press – see page 209

Mitchell Beazley – see Octopus Publishing Group

Mobius – see Hodder Headline Ltd

Modern Romance – see Harlequin Mills & Boon Ltd

Mojo Books – former imprint of Canongate Books Ltd

Monarch Books
Concorde House, Grenville Place,
London NW7 3SA
tel 020-8959 3668 *fax* 020-8959 3678
email tonyc@angushudson.com
website www.angushudson.com
Editorial Director Tony Collins

Christian books: issues of faith and society;
leadership, mission, evangelism. Submit synopsis/2
sample chapters only with return postage.

Morgan Kauffman – see Elsevier Ltd

Morrigan Book Company
Killala, Co. Mayo, Republic of Ireland
tel/fax (096) 32555
email morrigan@online.ie
Publisher Gerry Kennedy, *Administrator* Hilary
Kennedy, *Editor* Gillian Brennan

Non-fiction: general Irish interest, biography,
history, local history, folklore and mythology.
Founded 1979.

Mosby – see Elsevier Ltd

Mount Eagle Publications Ltd – see
Brandon/Mount Eagle Publications

Mowbray: Morehouse – see The Continuum International Publishing Group Ltd

MQ Publications Ltd
12 The Ivories, 6-8 Northampton Street,
London N1 2HY
tel 020-7359 2244 *fax* 020-7359 1616
email mail@mqpublications.com
website www.mqpublications.com
Ceo Zaro Weil

Lifestyle, Mind, Body & Spirit, inspirational,
photography, cookery, popular culture, biography,
gift books. Founded 1993.

Murdoch Books UK Ltd
Ferry House, 51-57 Lacy Road,
London SW15 1PR
tel 020-8355 1480 *fax* 020-8355 1499
Ceo Juliet Rogers, *Publisher* Kay Scarlett

Cookery, gardening, DIY, homes and interiors,
crafts and hobbies, cake decorating. Imprint:
Merehurst Ltd.

National Christian Education Council – see
Christian Education

The National Trust
36 Queen Anne's Gate, London SW1H 9AS
tel 020-7222 9251 *fax* 020-7447 6641
Publisher Margaret Willes

History, cookery, architecture, gardening,
guidebooks, children's non-fiction. No unsolicited
MSS. Founded 1895.

The Natural History Museum Publishing Division
Cromwell Road, London SW7 5BD
tel 020-7942 5336 *fax* 020-7942 5010
email publishing@nhm.ac.uk
website www.nhm.ac.uk/publishing

Natural sciences; entomology, botany, geology,
mineralogy, palaeontology, zoology, history of
natural history. Founded 1881.

Nautical Books – now Adlard Coles Nautical – see A
& C Black Publishers Ltd

Nautical Data Ltd
The Book Barn, Westbourne, Hants PO10 8RS
tel (01243) 377977 *fax* (01243) 379136
Directors Piers Mason, Michael Benson-Colpi

Yachting titles, nautical almanacs.

Naxos AudioBooks
18 High Street, Welwyn, Herts. AL6 9EQ
tel (01438) 717808 *fax* (01438) 717809
email naxos_audiobooks@compuserve.com
website www.naxosaudiobooks.com
Managing Director Nicolas Soames

Classic literature, modern fiction, non-fiction,
drama and poetry on CD and cassette. Also junior
classics and classical music. Founded 1994.

NCVO Publications
(incorporating Bedford Square Press)
Regent's Wharf, 8 All Saints Street,
London N1 9RL
tel 020-7713 6161 *fax* 020-7713 6300

email ncvo@ncvo-vol.org.uk
website www.ncvo-vol.org.uk
Head of Publications Maria Kane

Imprint of the National Council for Voluntary Organisations. Practical guides, reference books, directories and policy studies on voluntary sector concerns including management, employment, trustee development, legal and finance. No unsolicited MSS accepted.

Neate Publishing*
33 Downside Road, Winchester SO22 5LT
tel (01962) 841479 *fax* (01962) 841743
email bobbie@neatepublishing.co.uk
website www.neatepublishing.co.uk
Directors Bobbie Neate (managing), Ann Langran, Maggie Threadingham

Non-fiction books and posters for primary children. Founded 1999.

Neil Wilson Publishing Ltd*
303 The Pentagon Centre, 36 Washington Street, Glasgow G3 8AZ
tel 0141-221 1117 *fax* 0141-221 5363
email info@nwp.co.uk
website www.nwp.co.uk
Managing Director Neil Wilson

The Angels' Share (imprint)
website www.angelshare.co.uk

Whisky-related matters (leisure, reference, history, memoir); other food and drink categories.

11:9 (imprint)
tel 0141-204 1109
website www.11-9.co.uk

Scottish Arts Council/National Lottery-funded project to bring new Scottish fiction writing to the marketplace.

In Pinn (imprint)
website www.theinpinn.co.uk

The outdoors: travel, hillwalking, climbing.

NWP (imprint)

Scottish interest subjects including history, biography, culture and reference.

The Vital Spark (imprint)
website www.vitalspark.co.uk

Scottish humour.

Nelson Thornes Ltd*
Delta Place, 27 Bath Road, Cheltenham, Glos. GL53 7TH
tel (01242) 267100 *fax* (01242) 221914
email name@nelsonthornes.com
website www.nelsonthornes.com
Directors Oliver Gadsby, David Vincent, Adrian Ford

Print and electronic publishers for the educational market: primary, secondary, further education,

professional. Part of the Wolters Kluwer Group of Companies.

Neville Spearman Publishers – see The C.W. Daniel Company Ltd

New Beacon Books
76 Stroud Green Road, London N4 3EN
tel 020-7272 4889 *fax* 020-7281 4662
Directors John La Rose, Sarah White, Michael La Rose, Janice Durham

Small specialist publishers: general non-fiction, fiction, poetry, critical writings, concerning the Caribbean, Africa, African–America and Black Britain. No unsolicited MSS. Founded 1966.

New Cavendish Books
3 Denbigh Road, London W11 2SJ
tel 020-7229 6765 *fax* 020-7792 0027
email sales@cavbooks.co.uk
website www.newcavendishbooks.co.uk

Specialist books for the collector; art reference, Thai guidebooks. Founded 1973.

River Books (associate imprint)
The art and architecture of Southeast Asia.

New English Library – see Hodder Headline Ltd

New Holland Publishers (UK) Ltd*
Garfield House, 86 Edgware Road, London W2 2EA
tel 020-7724 7773 *fax* 020-7258 1293
email postmaster@nhpub.co.uk
website www.newhollandpublishers.com
Managing Director John Beaufoy

Illustrated non-fiction books on natural history, travel, cookery, needlecrafts and handicrafts, interior design, DIY, gardening, fishing, Mind, Body & Spirit, travel guides, sport, general books. New proposals accepted (send CV and synopsis and sample chapters in first instance; sae essential).

New Island Books
2 Brookside, Dundrum Road, Dundrum, Dublin 14, Republic of Ireland
tel (01) 2986867/2989937 *fax* (01) 2982783
email staff@newisland.ie
Directors Edwin Higel (managing), Fergal Stanley

Fiction, poetry, drama, humour, biography, current affairs. Founded 1992.

New Playwrights' Network
10 Station Road Industrial Estate, Colwall, Nr Malvern, Herefordshire WR13 6RN
tel/fax (01684) 540154
email simonsmith@cressrelles4drama.fsbusiness.co.uk
Publishing Director Leslie Smith

General plays for the amateur, one-act and full length.

New Theatre Publications/The Playwright Co-operative
13 Mossgrove Road, Timperley, Altringham, Cheshire WA15 6LF
tel (08700) 275297
email plays4theatre@btinternet.com
website www.plays4theatre.com
Directors Paul Beard, Ian Hornby

Plays for the professional and amateur stage. Submissions encouraged. Founded 1987.

Newleaf – see Gill & Macmillan Ltd

Newnes – see Elsevier Ltd

Nexus – see Virgin Books Ltd

nferNelson Publishing Co. Ltd*
The Chiswick Centre, 414 Chiswick High Road, London W4 5TF
tel (0845) 6021937 *fax* 020-8996 3660
email information@nfer-nelson.co.uk
website www.nfer-nelson.co.uk
General Manager Tim Cornford

Testing and assessment services for education and health care, including literacy, numeracy, thinking skills, ability, learning support and online testing. Founded 1981.

Nia – see the X Press

Nicholas Brealey Publishing
3-5 Spafield Street, London EC1R 4QB
tel 020-7239 0360 *fax* 020-7239 0370
email rights@nbrealey-books.com
website www.nbrealey-books.com
Managing Director Nicholas Brealey

Business, intelligent self-help, popular psychology, cross-cultural studies. Founded 1992.

Nicholson – see HarperCollins Publishers

Nick Hern Books Ltd
The Glasshouse, 49A Goldhawk Road, London W12 8QP
tel 020-8749 4953 *fax* 020-8735 0250
email info@nickhernbooks.demon.co.uk
website www.nickhernbooks.co.uk
Publisher Nick Hern

Theatre, professionally produced plays, screenplays. Initial letter required. Founded 1988.

NMSI
Science Museum, Exhibition Road, London SW7 2DD
tel 020-7942 4361 *fax* 020-7942 4362
email publicat@nmsi.ac.uk
website www.nmsi.ac.uk/publications
Publications Manager Ela Ginalska

History of science and technology, public understanding of science, history of photography, railway history, museum guides.

North-Holland – see Elsevier Ltd

Northcote House Publishers Ltd
Horndon House, Horndon, Tavistock, Devon PL19 9NQ
tel (01822) 810066 *fax* (01822) 810034
email northcote.house@virgin.net
website www.northcotehouse.com
Directors B.R.W. Hulme, A.V. Hulme (secretary)

Education and education management, educational dance and drama, literary criticism (*Writers and their Work*). Founded 1985.

NWP – see Neil Wilson Publishing Ltd

O-Books – see John Hunt Publishing Ltd

Oak Tree Press
19 Rutland Street, Cork, Republic of Ireland
tel (021) 431 3855 *fax* (021) 431 3496
email info@oaktreepress.com
website www.oaktreepress.com
Directors Brian O'Kane, Rita O'Kane, Ron Immink

Business management, enterprise, accountancy and finance, law. Founded 1991.

Oberon Books
(incorporating Absolute Classics)
521 Caledonian Road, London N7 9RH
tel 020-7607 3637 *fax* 020-7607 3629
email oberon.books@btinternet.com
website www.oberonbooks.com
Managing Director Charles Glanville, *Publisher* James Hogan, *Editor* Dan Steward

New and classic play texts, programme texts and general theatre and performing arts books. Founded 1986.

The O'Brien Press Ltd
20 Victoria Road, Rathgar, Dublin 6, Republic of Ireland
tel (01) 492 3333 *fax* (01) 492 2777
email books@obrien.ie
website www.obrien.ie
Directors Michael O'Brien, Ide ní Laoghaire, Ivan O'Brien

Adult: business, true crime, biography, music, travel, sport, Celtic subjects, food and drink, history, humour, politics, reference. Children's: fiction for every age from tiny tots to teenage; illustrated fiction series – *Pandas* (age 5+), *Flyers* (age 6+) and *Red Flag* (8+); substantial novels (10+) – contemporary, historical, fantasy. Some non-fiction, mainly historical and art and craft, resource books for teachers. No poetry, adult fiction or academic. Unsolicited MSS (sample chapters only), synopses and ideas for books welcome – submissions will not be returned. Founded 1974.

The Octagon Press Ltd
PO Box 227, London N6 4EW
tel 020-8348 9392 *fax* 020-8341 5971
email octagon@schredds.demon.co.uk
website www.octagonpress.com
Managing Director George R. Schrager

Psychology, philosophy, Eastern religion. Unsolicited MSS not accepted. Founded 1972.

Octopus Publishing Group
2-4 Heron Quays, London E14 4JP
tel 020-7531 8400 *fax* 020-7531 8650
email firstname.lastname@octopus-publishing.co.uk
website www.octopus-publishing.co.uk
Chief Executive Derek Freeman, *Executive Directors* Laura Bamford, Helen Barlow

Bounty (imprint)
tel 020-7531 8601 *fax* 020-7531 8607
email bountybooksinfo-bp@bountybooks.co.uk
Publisher/Managing Director Alison Goff

Promotional publishing, adult books.

Hachette Illustrated (imprint)
tel 020-7531 8602 *fax* 020-7531 8607
website www.hachette-illustrated.co.uk
Sales & Publishing Director Rebecca de Rafael

Illustrated reference.

Conran Octopus (imprint)
tel 020-7531 8628 *fax* 020-7531 8627
email info-co@conran-octopus.co.uk
website www.conran-octopus.co.uk
Publishing Director Lorraine Dickie

Quality illustrated books, particularly lifestyle, cookery, gardening.

Hamlyn (imprint)
tel 020-7531 8573 *fax* 020-7537 0514
email info-ho@hamlyn.co.uk
website www.hamlyn.co.uk
Publisher/Managing Director Alison Goff

Popular illustrated non-fiction, particularly cookery, health and parenting, home and garden, sport and reference.

Miller's (imprint)
The Cellars, High Street, Tenterden,
Kent TN30 6BN
tel (01580) 766411 *fax* (01580) 766100
email firstname.lastname@millers.uk.com
Publisher/Managing Director Jane Aspden

Quality illustrated books on antiques and collectables.

Mitchell Beazley (imprint)
tel 020-7531 8400 *fax* 020-7531 8650
email info-mb@mitchell-beazley.co.uk
Publisher/Managing Director Jane Aspden

Quality illustrated books, particularly antiques, gardening, craft and interiors, wine.

Philip's (imprint)
tel 020-7531 8459 *fax* 020-7531 8460
email george.philip@philips-maps.co.uk
website www.philips-maps.co.uk
Publisher/Managing Director John Gaisford

Atlases, maps, astronomy, encyclopedias, globes.

Cassell Illustrated (imprint)
tel 020-7531 8400 *fax* 020-7531 8650
email info-ci@cassell-illustrated.co.uk
website www.cassell-illustrated.co.uk
Publishing Director Polly Powell

Illustrated books for the international market specialising in gardening, history and heritage, health and humour.

Oldcastle Books Ltd
18 Coleswood Road, Harpenden, Herts AL5 1EP
tel/fax (01582) 761264
email ion@noexit.co.uk
website www.noexit.co.uk
www.pocketessentials.com www.highstakes.com
Director Ion Mills

Imprints: No Exit Press (crime fiction), High Stakes (gambling), Pocket Essentials (reference guides). Founded 1985.

The Oleander Press
16 Orchard Street, Cambridge CB1 1JT
tel (01223) 357768
website www.oleanderpress.com
Managing Director Dr Jeremy Toner

Travel, language, literature, Libya, Arabia and Middle East, Cambridgeshire, history, humour, reference. Preliminary letter required before submitting MSS; please send sae for reply. Founded 1960.

Omnibus Press/Music Sales Ltd
8-9 Frith Street, London W1D 3JB
tel 020-7434 0066 *fax* 020-7434 3310
email music@musicsales.co.uk
Chief Editor Chris Charlesworth

Rock music biographies, books about music. Founded 1976.

On Stream Publications Ltd
Currabaha, Cloghroe, Blarney, Co. Cork,
Republic of Ireland
tel/fax (353) 21-4385798

email info@onstream.ie
website www.onstream.ie
Owner Rosalind Crowley

Cookery, wine, travel, human interest non-fiction, local history, academic and practical books. Founded 1986.

Oneworld Publications
185 Banbury Road, Oxford OX2 7AR
tel (01865) 310597 *fax* (01865) 310598
email info@oneworld-publications.com
website www.oneworld-publications.com
Directors Juliet Mabey (publisher), Novin Doostdar (publisher), Helen Coward (managing)

Religion, world religions, inter-religious dialogue, Islamic studies, philosophy, history, psychology, self-help, popular science. Founded 1984.

Onlywomen Press Ltd
40 St Lawrence Terrace, London W10 5ST
tel 020-8354 0796 *fax* 020-8960 2817
email onlywomenpress@aol.com
Managing Director Lilian Mohin

Lesbian feminist: theory, fiction, poetry, crime fiction and cultural criticism. Founded 1974.

Open Books Publishing Ltd
Willow Cottage, Cudworth, Nr Ilminster, Somerset TA19 0PS
tel/fax (01460) 52565
email patrickta@aol.com
Directors P. Taylor (managing), C. Taylor

Gardening. Founded 1974.

Open Gate Press*
(incorporating Centaur Press, founded 1954)
51 Achilles Road, London NW6 1DZ
tel 020-7431 4391 *fax* 020-7431 5129
email books@opengatepress.co.uk
website www.opengatepress.co.uk
Directors Jeannie Cohen, Elisabeth Petersdorff, George Frankl, Sandra Lovell

Psychoanalysis, philosophy, social sciences, religion, animal welfare, the environment. Founded 1988.

Open University Press – see McGraw-Hill Education

Orbit – see Time Warner Books UK

Orchard Books – see The Watts Publishing Group Ltd

The Orion Publishing Group Ltd*
Orion House, 5 Upper St Martin's Lane, London WC2H 9EA
tel 020-7240 3444 *fax* 020-7379 6158
Directors Jean-Louis Lisimachio (chairman), Anthony Cheetham (chief executive), Peter Roche (managing)

No unsolicited MSS; approach in writing in first instance. Founded 1992.

Orion Paperbacks (division)
Managing Director Susan Lamb

Mass market fiction and non-fiction under **Everyman, Orion** and **Phoenix** imprints.

Orion Trade (division)
Directors Malcolm Edwards (managing), Jane Wood (publishing), Alan Samson

Hardcover fiction (popular fiction in all categories), non-fiction and audio.

Gollancz (imprint)
Contact Simon Spanton, Jo Fletcher

Science fiction and fantasy.

Orion Children's Books (division)
Publisher Fiona Kennedy

Children's fiction and non-fiction.

Osprey Publishing Ltd*
Elms Court, Chapel Way, Botley,
Oxford OX2 9LP
tel (01865) 727022 *fax* (01865) 727017/727019
email info@ospreypublishing.com
website www.ospreypublishing.com
Managing Director William Shepherd, *Finance Director* Sarah Lough, *Director, American Operations* Bill Corsa

Illustrated history, military history and military aviation from around the world. Founded 1969.

Oxford Publishing Company – see Ian Allan Publishing Ltd

Oxford University Press*
Great Clarendon Street,
Oxford OX2 6DP
tel (01865) 556767 *fax* (01865) 556646
email enquiry@oup.com
website www.oup.com
Chief Executive and Secretary to the Delegates Henry Reece, *Group Finance Director* Roger Boning, *Academic Division Managing Director* Ivon Asquith, *UK Educational Division Managing Director* Kate Harris, *ELT Division Managing Director* Peter Mothersole, *UK Personnel Director* John Williams

Anthropology, archaeology, architecture, art, belles-lettres, bibles, bibliography, children's books (fiction, non-fiction, picture), commerce, current affairs, dictionaries, drama, economics, educational (infants, primary, secondary, technical, university), English language teaching, electronic publishing, essays, foreign language learning, general history, hymn and service books, journals, law, maps and atlases, medical, music, oriental, philosophy, political economy, prayer books, reference, science, sociology, theology and religion; educational software; *Grove Dictionaries of Music & Art*. Trade paperbacks published under the imprint of Oxford Paperbacks. Founded 1478.

Paladin – now Flamingo – see HarperCollins Publishers

Palgrave Publishers Ltd – see Macmillan Publishers Ltd

Pan – see Macmillan Publishers Ltd

Pan Macmillan – see Macmillan Publishers Ltd

Pandora Press – see Rivers Oram Press

Paper Tiger – see Chrysalis Books Group

Parthenon Press – see Taylor & Francis Group plc

Paternoster
PO Box 300, Carlisle, Cumbria CA3 0QS
tel (01228) 512512 *fax* (01228) 593388
email info@paternoster-publishing.com
Publisher Mark Finnie

Biblical studies, Christian theology, ethics, history, mission. Imprints: Paternoster Press, Authentic Lifestyle, Partnership, Regnum, Rutherford House, Challenge, Paternoster Periodicals, SP Media.

Patrick Hardy Books – see James Clarke & Co. Ltd

Patrick Stephens Ltd – see Sutton Publishing Ltd

Paul Chapman Publishing Ltd
6 Bonhill Street, London EC2A 4PU
tel 020-7374 0645 *fax* 020-7374 8741
website www.paulchapmanpublishing.co.uk
Consultant P.R. Chapman, *Commissioning Editor* Marianne Lagrange

Education. Subsidiary of SAGE Publications Ltd.

Pavilion Books Ltd – see Chrysalis Books Group

Pavilion Children's Books – see Chrysalis Children's Books

Pavilion Publishing (Brighton) Ltd
The Ironworks, Cheapside,
Brighton BN1 4GD
tel (01273) 623222 *fax* (01273) 625526
email info@pavpub.com
website www.pavpub.com
Directors Chris Parker, Julie Gibson, Loretta Harrison

Health and social care training resources: learning disability, mental health, community care

management, older people, looked-after young people, community justice, drugs, supported housing. Founded 1987.

Payback Press – former imprint of Canongate Books Ltd

Pearson Education*
Edinburgh Gate, Harlow, Essex CM20 2JE
tel (01279) 623623 *fax* (01279) 431059
email firstname.lastname@pearsoned-ema.com
website www.pearsoned.com
President, Pearson Education Ltd Rod Bristow

Materials for school pupils, students and practitioners globally. Imprints include Longman, Financial Times Prentice Hall, Addison-Wesley, Prentice Hall.

Pelham Books – former imprint of Michael Joseph/Penguin

Pen & Sword Books Ltd
47 Church Street, Barnsley,
South Yorkshire S70 2AS
tel (01226) 734222 *fax* (01226) 734438
email charles@pen-and-sword.co.uk
website www.pen-and-sword.co.uk
Managing Director Charles Hewitt, *Publishing Manager* Henry Wilson, *Commissioning Editors* Peter Coles, Rupert Harding

Military history, aviation history, naval and maritime, general history, local history. Imprints: Leo Cooper, Pen & Sword Military Classics, Pen & Sword Aviation, Pen & Sword Naval & Maritime.

Wharncliffe* (imprint)
Local history.

Penguin Group (UK)*
80 Strand, London WC2R 0RL
tel 020-7010 3000 *fax* 020-7010 6060
website www.penguin.co.uk
Ceo Anthony Forbes Watson, *Managing Directors* Helen Fraser (Penguin), Andrew Welham (Dorling Kindersley)

Owned by Pearson plc.

Penguin General Books (division)
Managing Director Tom Weldon, *Publishing Directors* Tony Lacey (Penguin), Juliet Annan (Viking/Penguin), Simon Prosser (Hamish Hamilton/Penguin), Louise Moore (Michael Joseph/Penguin)

No unsolicited MSS or synopses.

Hamish Hamilton (imprint)
Fiction, belles-lettres, biography and memoirs, current affairs, history, literature, politics, travel. No unsolicited MSS or synopses.

Michael Joseph (imprint)

Biography and memoirs, current affairs, fiction, history, humour, travel, health, spirituality and relationships, sports, general leisure, illustrated books. No unsolicited MSS or synopses.

Penguin (imprint)

Adult paperback books – wide range of fiction, non-fiction, TV and film tie-ins. No unsolicited MSS or synopses.

Viking (imprint)

Fiction, general non-fiction; literature, biography, autobiography, current affairs, history, travel, popular culture, reference. No unsolicited MSS or synopses.

Penguin Press (division)

Managing Director Stefan McGrath, *Publishing Directors* Stuart Proffitt, Nigel Wilcockson, Simon Winder

Serious adult non-fiction, reference, specialist and classics. Imprint: Allen Lane. Series: Penguin Classics, Penguin Modern Classics. No unsolicited MSS or synopses.

Puffin (division)

Managing Director Francesca Dow, *Publishing Directors* Rebecca McNally (fiction), Mandy Suhr (picture books), Clare Hulton (non-fiction)

Children's paperback and hardback books: wide range of picture books, board books and novelties; fiction; non-fiction and popular culture. No unsolicited MSS or synopses.

Warne (division)

websites www.ladybird.co.uk www.funwithspot.com www.flowerfairies.com www.peterrabbit.com *Managing Director* Sally Floyer, *Publishing Directors* Stephanie Barton, Susan Winton

Specialises in preschool illustrated developmental books for 0–6, non-fiction 0–8; licensed brands; children's classic publishing and merchandising properties. No unsolicited MSS.

Dorling Kindersley (division)

Managing Director Andrew Welham, *Publisher* Christopher Davis, *Adult Publisher* John Roberts, *Children's Publisher* Miriam Farbry, *DK Designs* Sophie Mitchell

Illustrated non-fiction for adults and children: gardening, medical, travel, food and drink, Mind, Body & Spirit, history, reference, pregnancy and childcare, antiques, preschool, 5–8, 8+.

Hugo's Language Books (imprint)

Hugo's language books and courses.

Rough Guides (division)

website www.roughguides.com *Managing Director* Kevin Fitzgerald, *Publisher* Mark Ellingham, *Travel Publisher* Martin Dunford, *Reference Publisher* Jonathan Buckley

Travel and modern culture.

Penton Press – see Kogan Page Ltd

Pergamon – see Elsevier Ltd

Peter Collin – see Bloomsbury Publishing Plc

Peter Halban Publishers Ltd

22 Golden Square, London W1F 9JW
tel 020-7437 9300 *fax* 020-7437 9512
email books@halbanpublishers.com
website www.halbanpublishers.com
Directors Martine Halban, Peter Halban

General non-fiction; history and biography; Jewish subjects and Middle East. No unsolicited MSS considered; preliminary letter essential. Founded 1986.

Peter Owen Ltd

73 Kenway Road, London SW5 0RE
tel 020-7373 5628/370 6093 *fax* 020-7373 6760
email admin@peterowen.com
website www.peterowen.com
Directors Peter L. Owen (managing), Antonia Owen (editorial)

Art, belles lettres, biography, literary fiction, general non-fiction, sociology, theatre. No highly illustrated books. Do not send fiction without first speaking to the Editorial Dept unless it is by an established novelist. First novels rarely published.

Peterloo Poets

The Old Chapel, Sand Lane, Calstock, Cornwall PL18 9QX
tel (01822) 833473 *fax* (01822) 833989
email poets@peterloo.fsnet.co.uk
website www.peterloopoets.co.uk
Publishing Director Harry Chambers, *Trustees* Brian Perman, David Selzer, Rose Taw, *Honorary President* Charles Causley CBE

Poetry. Founded 1976.

Phaidon Press Ltd

Regent's Wharf, All Saints Street, London N1 9PA
tel 020-7843 1000 *fax* 020-7843 1010
Chairman/Publisher Richard Schlagman, *Managing Director* Andrew Price, *Deputy Publisher* Amanda Renshaw, *Directors* Frances Johnson, Nigel Watts-Morgan, James Booth-Clibborn, Karen Stein

Quality books on the visual arts, including fine art and art history, architecture, design, decorative arts, photography, music, fashion, film.

Philip Wilson Publishers Ltd

7 Deane House, 27 Greenwood Place, London NW5 1LB
tel 020-7284 3088 *fax* 020-7284 3099
email pwilson@philip-wilson.co.uk

website www.philip-wilson.co.uk
Chairman P. Wilson, *Director* S. Prohaska, *Managing Editor* C. Venables, *Production Manager* N. Turpin
Fine and applied art, collecting, museums. Founded 1975.

Philip's – see Octopus Publishing Group

Phillimore & Co. Ltd
(incorporating Darwen Finlayson Ltd)
Shopwyke Manor Barn, Chichester,
West Sussex PO20 2BG
tel (01243) 787636 *fax* (01243) 787639
email bookshop@phillimore.co.uk
website www.phillimore.co.uk
Directors Philip Harris JP (chairman), Noel Osborne MA, FSA (managing), Hilary Clifford Brown (marketing), Nicola Willmot (production)

Local and family history; architectural history, archaeology, genealogy and heraldry; also Darwen County History series and History from the Sources series. Founded 1897.

Phoenix – see The Orion Publishing Group Ltd

Piatkus Books
5 Windmill Street, London W1T 2JA
tel 020-7631 0710 *fax* 020-7436 7137
email info@piatkus.co.uk
website www.piatkus.co.uk
Managing Director Judy Piatkus, *Directors* Philip Cotterell (marketing), Gill Bailey (editorial)

Fiction, biography, history, sport, memoirs, self-help, health, Mind, Body & Spirit, business, careers, women's interest, how-to and practical, popular psychology, cookery, parenting and childcare, paranormal. Imprints: Piatkus, Portrait. Founded 1979.

Pica Press – see A & C Black Publishers Ltd

Picador – see Macmillan Publishers Ltd

Piccadilly Press
5 Castle Road, London NW1 8PR
tel 020-7267 4492 *fax* 020-7267 4493
email books@piccadillypress.co.uk
website www.piccadillypress.co.uk
Directors Brenda Gardner (publisher and managing), Philip Durrance (secretary)

Early picture books, parental advice trade paperbacks, trade paperback teenage non-fiction and humorous teenage fiction. Founded 1983.

Pimlico – see Random House Group Ltd

Pipers' Ash Ltd
Pipers' Ash, Church Road, Christian Malford,
Chippenham, Wilts. SN15 4BW

tel (01249) 720563 *fax* (0870) 0568916
email pipersash@supamasu.com
website www.supamasu.com
Editorial Director Alfred Tyson

Poetry, contemporary short stories, science fiction stories; short novels, biographies, plays, philosophy, translations, children's, general non-fiction. New authors with talent and potential encouraged. Founded 1976.

Pitkin Unichrome Ltd – see Jarrold Publishing

Pitman Publishing – now Financial Times Prentice Hall; see Pearson Education

The Playwrights Publishing Company
70 Nottingham Road, Burton Joyce, Notts. NG14 5AL
tel 0115-931 3356
email playwrightspublishingco@yahoo.co.uk
website www.geocities.com/playwrightspublishingco
Proprietor Liz Breeze, *Consultant* Tony Breeze

One-act and full-length drama: serious work and comedies, for mixed cast, all women or schools. Reading fee unless professionally produced; sae required. Founded 1990.

Plexus Publishing Ltd
55A Clapham Common Southside, London SW4 9BX
tel 020-7622 2440 *fax* 020-7622 2441
email plexus@plexusuk.demon.co.uk
website www.plexusbooks.com
Directors Terence Porter (managing), Sandra Wake (editorial)

Film, music, biography, popular culture, fashion. Imprint: Eel Pie. Founded 1973.

Pluto Press*
345 Archway Road, London N6 5AA
tel 020-8348 2724 *fax* 020-8348 9133
email pluto@plutobooks.com
website www.plutobooks.com
Directors Roger van Zwanenberg (managing), Anne Beech (editorial), *Head of Sales* Simon Liebesny, *Head of Marketing* Melanie Patrick

Sociology, economics, history, politics, cultural, international, women's studies, legal studies, Irish studies, Black studies, Third World and development, anthropology, media studies. Imprint: Journeyman Press. Founded 1968.

Pocket Books – see Simon & Schuster

Point – see Scholastic Children's Books

The Policy Press
University of Bristol, 4th Floor, Beacon House,
Queen's Road, Bristol BS8 1QU
tel 0117-331 4054 *fax* 0117-331 4093

email tpp-info@bristol.ac.uk
website www.policypress.org.uk
Publishing Director Alison Shaw, *Editorial and Production Manager* Dawn Louise Rushen, *Marketing and Sales Manager* Julia Mortimer

Social science publisher, specialising in social and public policy, social work and social welfare. Founded 1996.

Policy Studies Institute (PSI)
100 Park Village East, London NW1 3SR
tel 020-7468 0468 *fax* 020-7388 0914
email pubs@psi.org.uk

Economic, cultural, social and environmental policy, political institutions, social sciences.

Polity Press
65 Bridge Street, Cambridge CB2 1UR
tel (01223) 324315 *fax* (01223) 461385
website www.polity.co.uk
Directors Anthony Giddens, David Held, John Thompson

Social and political theory, politics, sociology, history, psychology, media and cultural studies, philosophy, literary theory, feminism, human geography, anthropology. Founded 1983.

Polygon – see Birlinn Ltd

Poolbeg Group Services Ltd
123 Grange Hill, Baldoyle, Dublin 13, Republic of Ireland
tel (01) 8321477 *fax* (01) 8321430
email poolbeg@poolbeg.com
Directors Kieran Devlin (managing), Philip MacDermott (chairman), Paula Campbell (publisher)

Commercial fiction, non-fiction, current affairs. Imprint: Poolbeg. Founded 1976.

Portland Press Ltd
59 Portland Place, London W1B 1QW
tel 020-7580 5530 *fax* 020-7323 1136
email editorial@portlandpress.com
website www.portlandpress.com
Directors Rhonda C. Oliver (managing), Chris J. Finch (finance), John Day (IT), Adam Marshall (marketing)

Biochemistry and molecular life science books for graduate, post-graduate and research students. Illustrated science books for children: Making Sense of Science series. Founded 1990.

Prentice Hall – see Pearson Education

Princeton University Press – Europe
3 Market Place, Woodstock, Oxon OX20 1SY
tel (01993) 814500 *fax* (01993) 814504

email admin@pupress.co.uk
website http://pup.princeton.edu
Publishing Director – Europe Richard Baggaley

Economics, finance and mathematics. Part of Princeton University Press, USA. European office founded 1999.

Prion Books – see Carlton Publishing Group

Profile Books Ltd
58A Hatton Garden, London EC1N 8LX
tel 020-7404 3001 *fax* 020-7404 3003
email info@profilebooks.co.uk
website www.profilebooks.co.uk
Publisher and Managing Director Andrew Franklin, *Editorial Director* Stephen Brough

General non-fiction: current affairs, politics, social sciences, history, psychology, business, management. Also publishes in association with the *Economist* and the *London Review of Books*. No unsolicited MSS; phone or send preliminary letter. Founded 1996.

Psychology Press Ltd
27 Church Road, Hove, East Sussex BN3 2FA
tel (01273) 207411 *fax* (01273) 205612
email info@psypress.co.uk
website www.psypress.co.uk

Psychology textbooks and monographs. A member of the **Taylor and Francis Group plc**.

Brunner-Routledge (imprint)

Clinical psychology and psychiatry.

Puffin – see Penguin Group (UK)

Pushkin Press*
123 Biddulph Mansions, Elgin Avenue, London W9 1HU
tel 020-7266 9136 *fax* 020-7266 2718
email petra@pushkinpress.com
Owner Melissa Ulfane

Continental European literature in translation. Founded 1997.

Putnam Aeronautical Books – see Chrysalis Books Group

Quadrille Publishing
5th Floor, Alhambra House, 27-31 Charing Cross Road, London WC2H 0LS
tel 020-7839 7117 *fax* 020-7839 7118
Directors Alison Cathie (managing), Jane O'Shea and Anne Furniss (editorial), Helen Lewis (art), David Kemp (commercial), Vincent Smith (production)

Illustrated non-fiction: cookery, craft, health and medical, gardening, interiors, magic. Founded 1994.

Quantum – see W. Foulsham & Co. Ltd

Quartet Books Ltd
27 Goodge Street, London W1T 2LD
tel 020-7636 3992 *fax* 020-7637 1866
email quartetbooks@easynet.co.uk
Chairman N.I. Attallah, *Managing Director* Jeremy
Beale, *Publishing Director* Stella Kane

General fiction and non-fiction, foreign literature in
translation, classical music, jazz, contemporary
music, biography. Member of the Namara Group.
Founded 1972.

Queen Anne Press
Windmill Cottage, Mackerye End, Harpenden,
Herts. AL5 5DR
tel (01582) 715866
email stephenson@lennardqap.co.uk
Directors K.A.A. Stephenson, R.H. Stephenson

Sporting yearbooks, sponsored titles and special
commissions. No unsolicited MSS. Division of
Lennard Associates Ltd.

Quiller Publishing Ltd
Wykey House, Wykey, Shrewsbury, Shrops. SY4 1JA
tel (01939) 261616 *fax* (01939) 261606
email info@quillerbooks.com
website www.swanhillbooks.com
Managing Director Andrew Johnston

Quiller Press (imprint)

Specialises in sponsored books and publications
sold through non-book trade channels as well as
bookshops: architecture, biography, business and
industry, collecting, cookery, DIY, gardening,
guidebooks, humour, reference, sports, travel, wines
and spirits.

Swan Hill Press (imprint)

Country and field sports activities, including
fishing, cookery, shooting, falconry, equestrian,
gundog training, natural history.

Radcliffe Medical Press Ltd
18 Marcham Road, Abingdon, Oxon OX14 1AA
tel (01235) 528820 *fax* (01235) 528830
email contact.us@radcliffemed.com
website www.radcliffe-oxford.com
Directors Andrew Bax (managing), Gill Nineham
(editorial), Margaret McKeown (financial), Gregory
Moxon (marketing)

Primary care, child health, palliative care, nursing,
pharmacy, dentistry, healthcare organisation and
management. Founded 1987.

Ragged Bears Publishing Ltd
Milborne Wick, Sherborne, Dorset DT9 4PW
tel (01963) 251600 *fax* (01963) 250889
email info@raggedbears.co.uk

website www.raggedbears.co.uk
Managing Director Henrietta Stickland, *Submissions
Editor* Barbara Lamb

Preschool and primary age picture and novelty
books. Takes very few unsolicited ideas as the list is
small. Send sae for return of MSS; do not send
original artwork. Imprints: Ragged Bears,
Spindlewood. Founded 1984.

Random House Audio Books – see Random House Group Ltd

Random House Business Books – see Random House Group Ltd

Random House Children's Books – see Random House Group Ltd

Random House Group Ltd*
20 Vauxhall Bridge Road, London SW1V 2SA
tel 020-7840 8400 *fax* 020-7233 8791
email randomhouse.co.uk
Chairman/Ceo Gail Rebuck, *Directors* Simon Master
(deputy chairman), Ian Hudson (managing), Larry
Finlay (managing, Transworld), Mark Gardiner
(finance), Brian Davies (managing director, overseas
operations), Alfred Willmann (group bibliographic),
Clare Harington (group communications)

Subsidiary of Bertelsmann AG.

Arrow Books Ltd (imprint)
tel 020-7840 8518 *fax* 020-7821 7387
Publishing Director Susan Sandon

Fiction, non-fiction, romance, humour, film tie-ins.

Bantam Children's (imprint)
Publisher Philippa Dickinson

Paperback young adult books and series.

Century (imprint)
tel 020-7840 8554 *fax* 020-7233 6127
Directors Richard Cable (managing), Mark Booth
(publishing), Kate Elton (publishing), Oliver
Johnson (editorial), Charlotte Bush (publicity)

Fiction, biography, autobiography, general non-
fiction.

Chatto & Windus (imprint)
tel 020-7840 8522 *fax* 020-7233 6123
Directors Alison Samuel (publishing), Penny Hoare,
Tasja Dorkofikis (publicity)

Art, belles-lettres, biography and memoirs, current
affairs, drama, essays, fiction, history, poetry,
politics, philosophy, translations, travel, hardbacks
and paperbacks. No unsolicited MSS.

Ebury Press (imprint of Ebury Division)
tel 020-7840 8400 *fax* 020-7840 8406
Directors Fiona MacIntyre (publisher), Jake
Lingwood (senior publishing)

General non-fiction, autobiography, popular history, sport, travel writing, popular science, humour, film and TV tie-ins, music, travel guides, reference, cookery, lifestyle, health and beauty.

Fodor Guides (imprint of **Ebury Press**)
Worldwide annual travel guides.

The Harvill Press (imprint)
Publisher Christopher MacLehose

English-language and world literature in translation (literary fiction, non-fiction and some narrative thrillers); monographs in the fields of ethnography, art, horticulture and natural history. Unsolicited MSS only accepted with sae. Founded 1946.

Hutchinson (imprint)
tel 020-7840 8564 *fax* 020-7233 6127
Directors Sue Freestone (publishing), Anthony Whittome, Paul Sidey (editorial), Sarah Whale (publicity)

Fiction and non-fiction: biography, memoirs, thrillers, crime, general history, politics, travel, adventure.

Jonathan Cape (imprint)
tel 020-7840 8576 *fax* 020-7233 6117
Directors Dan Franklin (managing), Robin Robertson, Rebecca Linsley (publicity)

Biography and memoirs, current affairs, drama, fiction, history, poetry, travel. Imprint: Yellow Jersey Press (sport).

Pimlico (imprint)
tel 020-7840 8630 *fax* 020-7233 6117
Publishing Director Will Sulkin

History, biography, literature.

Vintage (imprint)
tel 020-7840 8400
Publisher Rachel Cugnoni, *Associate Publishing Director* Will Sulkin

Quality fiction and non-fiction.

William Heinemann (imprint)
tel 020-7840 8400 *fax* 020-7233 6127
Directors Ravi Mirchandani, Andy McKillop (publishing), Cassie Chadderton (publicity)

Fiction and general non-fiction: crime, thrillers, women's fiction, literary fiction, translations, history, biography, science. No unsolicited MSS and synopses considered.

Random House Audio Books
tel 020-7840 8419 *fax* 020-7233 6127
Editor Georgia Marnham

Random House Business Books
tel 020-7840 8550 *fax* 020-7840 6127
Publishing Director Clare Smith

Business strategy and management, personal and career development, business narrative and general finance.

Rider (imprint of Ebury Division)
tel 020-7840 8400 *fax* 020-7840 8406
Publishing Director Fiona MacIntyre, *Publishing Director* Judith Kendra

Buddhism, spirituality and personal development, healing, travel, ancient wisdom, paranormal, divination.

Secker and Warburg (imprint)
tel 020-7840 8649 *fax* 020-7233 6117
Directors Geoff Mulligan (editorial), Tasja Dorkofikis (publicity)

Literary fiction, general non-fiction. No unsolicited MSS/synopses.

Vermilion (imprint of Ebury Division)
tel 020-7840 8400 *fax* 020-7840 8406
Directors Fiona MacIntyre (publisher), Amanda Hemmings (editorial)

Personal development, relationships, parenting, pregnancy and childcare, health, diet and fitness, sex, beauty.

Random House Children's Books (division)
61-63 Uxbridge Road, London W5 5SA
tel 020-8579 2652 *fax* 020-8579 5479
Managing Director Philippa Dickinson, *Publishing Director – Fiction* Annie Eaton, *Publishing Director – Picture Books* Caroline Roberts, *Publisher – Doubleday Picture Books* Penny Walker, *Senior Commissioning Editor – Fiction* Alex Antscherl, *Senior Commissioning Editor – Picture Books* Natascha Biebow, *Commissioning Editor – Jonathan Cape Picture Books* Helen Mackenzie-Smith, *Associate Publisher – Jonathan Cape Picture Books* Ian Craig, *Associate Publisher – Jonathan Cape Fiction* Delia Huddy, *Publisher – Jonathan Cape* Tom Maschler, *Publicity Director* Clare Hall-Craggs

Publishes picture books, fiction, poetry, non-fiction and audio cassettes under Bodley Head Children's Books, Corgi Children's Books, Doubleday Children's Books, Hutchinson Children's Books, Jonathan Cape Children's Books, Red Fox Children's Books, David Fickling Books.

David Fickling Books (imprint)
31 Beaumont Street, Oxford OX1 2NP
tel (01865) 339000 *fax* (01865) 339009
email dfickling@randomhouse.co.uk
Publisher David Fickling, *Editor* Bella Pearson

Quality children's fiction and picture books.

Transworld Publishers (division)
See page 180.

Ransom Publishing Ltd

Rose Cottage, Howe Hill, Watlington, Oxon OX49 5HB
tel (01491) 613711 *fax* (01491) 613733
email ransom@ransompublishing.co.uk
website www.ransom.co.uk

Directors Jenny Ertle (managing), Steve Rickard (creative)

Preschool and primary literacy including special needs. Range of multimedia from preschool to secondary for literacy, numeracy and science. Founded 1995.

The Reader's Digest Association Ltd*
11 Westferry Circus, Canary Wharf, London E14 4HE
tel 020-7715 8000 *fax* 020-7715 8600
Managing Director A.T. Lynam-Smith, *Editorial Directors* Katherine Walker (magazine), Cortina Butler (books)

Monthly magazine, condensed and series books; also DIY, computers, puzzles, gardening, medical, handicrafts, law, touring guides, encyclopedias, dictionaries, nature, folklore, atlases, cookery, music; videos.

Reaktion Books
77-79 Farringdon Road, London EC1M 3JU
tel 020-7404 9930 *fax* 020-7404 9931
email info@reaktionbooks.co.uk
website www.reaktionbooks.co.uk
Editorial Director Michael R. Leaman

Art history, design, architecture, history, cultural studies, film studies, Asian studies, travel writing, photography. Founded 1985.

Rebel Inc. – former imprint of Canongate Books Ltd

Red Dress Ink™ – see Harlequin Mills & Boon Ltd

Red Fox Children's Books – see Random House Group Ltd

Reed Books – now Octopus Publishing Group

Reed Business Information
Windsor Court, East Grinstead House, Wood Street, East Grinstead, West Sussex RH19 1XA
tel (01342) 326972 *fax* (01342) 335612
email information@reedinfo.co.uk
website www.reedbusiness.com
Managing Director John Minch

Directories and reference books covering professional and industrial sectors, including *Kompass*, *Kelly's*, *Dial* and *The Bankers' Almanac*. Part of Reed Elsevier plc. Founded 1983.

Reed Educational and Professional Publishing Ltd – see Harcourt Education Ltd

Religious and Moral Education Press
St Mary's Works, St Mary's Plain, Norwich, Norfolk NR3 3BH

tel (01603) 612914 *fax* (01603) 624483
email admin@scm-canterburypress.co.uk
website www.scm-canterburypress.co.uk
Publisher Mary Mears

Books for primary and secondary school pupils, college students, and teachers on religious, moral, personal and social education. Division of SCM–Canterbury Press Ltd, a subsidiary of Hymns Ancient & Modern Ltd.

Review – see Hodder Headline Ltd

Reynolds & Hearn Ltd
61A Priory Road, Kew, Richmond, Surrey TW9 3DH
tel 020-8940 5198 *fax* 020-8940 7679
email richardreynolds@btconnect.com
website www.rhbooks.com
Directors Richard Reynolds (managing), Marcus Hearn (editorial), David O'Leary, Geoffrey Wolfson

Film, TV, music, entertainment, media. Founded 1999.

Rider – see Random House Group Ltd

Rigby Heinemann – see Harcourt Education Ltd

Rivelin Grapheme Press
Merlin House, Church Street, Hungerford, Berks. RG17 0JG
tel (01488) 684645 *fax* (01488) 683018
Director Snowdon Barnett

Poetry. Send introductory letter enclosing one short poem. Founded 1984.

River Books – see New Cavendish Books

Rivers Oram Press
144 Hemingford Road, London N1 1DE
tel 020-7607 0823 *fax* 020-7609 2776
email ro@riversoram.demon.co.uk
Directors Elizabeth Rivers Fidlon (managing), Anthony Harris

Non-ficton: social and political science, current affairs, social history, gender studies, sexual politics, cultural studies and photography. Founded 1991.

Pandora Press (imprint)
Managing Editor Caroline Lazar

Feminist press publishing. General non-fiction: biography, arts, media, health, current affairs, reference and sexual politics.

Robert Gibson & Sons Glasgow Ltd – see Hodder Gibson

Robert Hale Ltd
Clerkenwell House, 45-47 Clerkenwell Green, London EC1R 0HT

tel 020-7251 2661 *fax* 020-7490 4958
email enquire@halebooks.com
website www.halebooks.com
Directors John Hale (managing and editorial),
Robert Kynaston (financial), Martin Kendall
(marketing)
Adult general non-fiction and fiction. Founded 1936.

Robinson – see Constable & Robinson Ltd

Robson Books – see Chrysalis Books Group

Rough Guides – see Penguin Group (UK)

Roundhouse Publishing Ltd
Millstone, Limers Lane, Northam,
North Devon EX39 2RG
tel (01237) 474474 *fax* (01237) 474774
email roundhouse.group@ukgateway.net
website www.roundhouse.net
Publisher Alan T. Goodworth

Film, cinema, and performing arts; reference books.
No unsolicited MSS. Founded 1991.

Route
School Lane, Glasshoughton, Castleford,
West Yorkshire WF10 4QH
tel (01977) 603028 *fax* (01977) 512819
email books@route-online.com
website www.route-online.com
www.openingline.co.uk www.artcircus.org.uk
Contact Ian Daley

Fiction imprint of Yorkshire Art Circus. Specialises
in contemporary fiction and has a commitment to
new writing. Looking for novels/novellas and
publishes an annual collection of short fiction
(check for current theme). Unsolicited MSS
discouraged; send for fact sheet or visit website for
submission guidelines. Also manages the writers
programme, The Opening Line. Route Events
facilitate the development of performance poetry.

Routledge – see Taylor & Francis Group plc

RoutledgeCurzon – see Taylor & Francis Group plc

RoutledgeFalmer – see Taylor & Francis Group plc

Royal National Institute of the Blind
PO Box 173, Peterborough,
Cambs. PE2 6WS
tel (0845) 7023153 *fax* (01733) 371555
email cservices@rnib.org.uk
website www.rnib.org.uk
textphone (0845) 7585691

Magazines, catalogues and books for blind and
partially sighted people, to support daily living,
leisure, learning and employment reading needs.

Produced in braille, audio, large/legible print, disk
and Moon. For complete list of magazines see
page 77. Founded 1868.

Ryland Peters & Small
Kirkman House, 12-14 Whitfield Street,
London W1T 2RP
tel 020-7436 9090 *fax* 020-7436 9790
email info@rps.co.uk
website www.rylandpeters.com
Directors David Peters (managing), Alison Starling
(publishing), Gabriella Le Grazie (art), Joanna
Everard (rights), Meryl Silbert (production)

High-quality illustrated books on food and drink,
lifestyle, interior design, Mind, Body & Spirit,
gardening. Founded 1995.

S.B. Publications
c/o 19 Grove Road, Seaford,
East Sussex BN25 1TP
tel (01323) 893498 *fax* (01323) 893860
email sales@sbpublications.swinternet.co.uk
website www.sbpublications.swinternet.co.uk
Proprietor Lindsay Woods

Local history, local themes (e.g. walking books,
guides), maritime history, transport, specific
themes. Founded 1987.

SAGE Publications Ltd*
6 Bonhill Street, London EC2A 4PU
tel 020-7374 0645 *fax* 020-7374 8741
email info@sagepub.co.uk
website www.sagepub.co.uk
Directors Stephen Barr (managing), Katharine
Jackson, Ian Eastment, Mike Birch, Ziyad Marar,
Richard Fidczuk, Michael Melody (USA), Sara
Miller McCune (USA), Paul R. Chapman

Social sciences, behavioural sciences, humanities,
STM, software. Founded 1971.

Saint Andrew Press*
121 George Street, Edinburgh EH2 4YN
tel 0131-240 2253 *fax* 0131-220 3113
email standrewpress@cofscotland.org.uk
website www.standrewpress.com
Head of Publishing Ann Crawford

Publishing house of the Church of Scotland:
publishes books that explore Christianity,
spirituality, faith and ethical and moral issues, as
well as more general works of fiction and non-
fiction; children's.

St Pauls
St Pauls Publishing, 187 Battersea Bridge Road,
London SW11 3AS
tel 020-7978 4300 *fax* 020-7978 4370
email editions@stpauls.org.uk
website www.stpauls.ie

Theology, ethics, spirituality, biography, education, general books of Roman Catholic and Christian interest. Founded 1948.

Salamander – see Chrysalis Books Group

Salariya Book Company Ltd

Book House, 25 Marlborough Place, Brighton BN1 1UB
tel (01273) 603306 fax (01273) 693857
email salariya@salariya.com
website www.salariya.com
Director David Salariya

Children's non-fiction. Imprint: Book House. Founded 1989.

Samuel French Ltd*

52 Fitzroy Street, London W1T 5JR
tel 020-7387 9373 fax 020-7387 2161
email theatre@samuelfrench-london.co.uk
website www.samuelfrench-london.co.uk
Directors Charles R. Van Nostrand (chairman, USA), Vivien Goodwin (managing), Amanda Smith, Paul Taylor, Consultant John Bedding

Publishers of plays and agents for the collection of royalties. Founded 1830.

Scala Publishers

Gloucester Mansions, 140A Shaftesbury Avenue, London WC2H 8HD
tel 020-7539 7600 fax 020-7836 5756
email info@scalapublishers.com
Chairman David Campbell, Directors Miranda Harrison (editorial), Henry Channon, Jan Baily, Antony White, Director of Museum Publications Jennifer Wright

Art, architecture, guides to museums and art galleries, antiques. Founded 1992.

Sceptre – see Hodder Headline Ltd

Schofield & Sims Ltd

Dogley Mill, Fenay Bridge, Huddersfield HD8 0NQ
tel (01484) 607080 fax (01484) 606815
email schofield_and_sims@compuserve.com
Managing Director J. Stephen Platts

Educational: nursery, infants, primary; posters. Founded 1901.

Scholastic Children's Books*

Commonwealth House, 1-19 New Oxford Street, London WC1A 1NU
tel 020-7421 9000 fax 020-7421 9001
email publicity@scholastic.co.uk
Publisher Richard Scrivener

Imprint of Scholastic Ltd.

Hippo (imprint)
Children's paperbacks – fiction and non-fiction. No unsolicited MSS.

Point (imprint)
Fiction for 12+.

Scholastic Press (imprint)
Literary fiction and picture books.

Scholastic Ltd*

Villiers House, Clarendon Avenue, Leamington Spa, Warks. CV32 5PR
tel (01926) 887799 fax (01926) 883331
website www.scholastic.co.uk
Directors Ian Ronald (managing), M.R. Robinson (USA), R.M. Spaulding (USA), D.J. Walsh (USA)

Children's Division
Publisher Richard Scrivener
See Scholastic Children's Books.

Direct Marketing
Managing Director, Book Fair Division & Book Club Division Miles Stevens-Hoare, Managing Director, Trade Sales and Marketing Gavin Lang
Children's book clubs and school book fairs.

Educational Division
Publishing Director Anne Peel
Publishers of books for teachers (Bright Ideas and other series), primary classroom resources and magazines for teachers (Child Education, Junior Education and others). Founded 1964.

Scholastic Press – see Scholastic Children's Books

Science Museum Publications – see NMSI

SCM Press*

9-17 St Albans Place, London N1 0NX
tel 020-7359 8033 fax 020-7359 0049
email admin@scm-canterburypress.co.uk
website www.scm-canterburypress.co.uk
Publishing Director Christine Smith

Theological books with special emphasis on text and reference books and contemporary theology for both students and clergy. Division of SCM-Canterbury Press Ltd. Founded 1929.

Scottish Children's Press

Unit 13D, Newbattle Abbey Business Annexe, Newbattle Road, Dalkeith EH22 3LJ
tel 0131-660 4757 fax 0131-660 6414
email info@scottishbooks.com
website www.scottishbooks.com
Directors Avril Gray, Brian Pugh

Scottish fiction, Scottish non-fiction and Scots language, children's writing. Unsolicited MSS not accepted; send letter, telephone or email before sending material.

SCP Publishers Ltd*

(trading as Scottish Cultural Press)
Unit 13D, Newbattle Abbey Business Annexe,
Newbattle Road, Dalkeith EH22 3LJ
tel 0131-660 6366 *fax* 0131-660 6414
email info@scottishbooks.com
website www.scottishbooks.com
Directors Brian Pugh, Avril Gray

Literature, poetry, history, archaeology, biography
and environmental history. Unsolicited MSS not
accepted; send letter, telephone or email before
sending material. Founded 1992.

Scribner – see Simon & Schuster

Scripture Union

207-209 Queensway, Bletchley, Milton Keynes,
Bucks. MK2 2EB
tel (01908) 856000 *fax* (01908) 856111
email postmaster@scriptureunion.org.uk

Christian books and Bible reading materials for
people of all ages; educational and worship
resources for churches; children's fiction and non-
fiction; adult non-fiction. Founded 1867.

Seafarer Books

102 Redwald Road, Rendlesham, Woodbridge,
Suffolk IP12 2TE
tel (01394) 420789
email info@seafarerbooks.com
website www.seafarerbooks.com
Commissioning Editor Patricia Eve

Books on traditional sailing, mainly narrative.

Search Press Ltd

Wellwood, North Farm Road, Tunbridge Wells,
Kent TN2 3DR
tel (01892) 510850 *fax* (01892) 515903
email searchpress@searchpress.com
Directors Martin de la Bédoyère (managing),
Rosalind Dace (editorial)

Arts, crafts, leisure, gardening. Founded 1970.

Secker and Warburg – see Random House Group Ltd

Seren

First Floor, 38-40 Nolton Street, Bridgend CF31 3BN
tel (01656) 663018 *fax* (01656) 649226
email seren@seren-books.com
Director Mick Felton

Poetry, fiction, drama, history, film, literary
criticism, biography, art – mostly with relevance to
Wales. Founded 1981.

Serpent's Tail

4 Blackstock Mews, London N4 2BT

tel 020-7354 1949 *fax* 020-7704 6467
email info@serpentstail.com
website www.serpentstail.com
Director Peter Ayrton

Fiction and non-fiction in paperback; literary and
non-mainstream work, and work in translation. No
unsolicited MSS. Imprint: Five Star. Founded 1986.

Seven Dials – see Weidenfeld & Nicolson

Severn House Publishers

9-15 High Street, Sutton, Surrey SM1 1DF
tel 020-8770 3930 *fax* 020-8770 3850
email editorial@severnhouse.com
website www.severnhouse.com
Chairman Edwin Buckhalter, *Publishing Director*
Amanda Stewart

Hardcover adult fiction for the library market:
romances, crime, thrillers, detective, adventure, war,
science fiction. No unsolicited MSS.

Sheffield Academic Press – see The Continuum International Publishing Group Ltd

Sheldon Press – see Society for Promoting Christian Knowledge

Sheldrake Press

188 Cavendish Road, London SW12 0DA
tel 020-8675 1767 *fax* 020-8675 7736
email mail@sheldrakepress.demon.co.uk
website www.sheldrakepress.demon.co.uk
Publisher J.S. Rigge

History, travel, architecture, cookery, music;
stationery. Founded 1979.

Shepheard-Walwyn (Publishers) Ltd

Suite 604, 50 Westminster Bridge Road,
London SE1 7QY
tel 020-7721 7666 *fax* 020-7721 7667
email books@shepheard-walwyn.co.uk
website www.shepheard-walwyn.co.uk
Directors A.R.A. Werner, M.M. Werner

History, biography, political economy, philosophy;
illustrated gift books; Scottish interest. Founded 1971.

Shire Publications Ltd

Cromwell House, Church Street,
Princes Risborough, Bucks. HP27 9AA
tel (01844) 344301 *fax* (01844) 347080
email shire@shirebooks.co.uk
website www.shirebooks.co.uk
Director J.W. Rotheroe

Discovering paperbacks, Shire Albums, Shire
Archaeology, Shire Natural History, Shire
Ethnography, Shire Egyptology, Shire Garden
History. Founded 1962.

Short Books Ltd
15 Highbury Terrace, London N5 1UP
tel 020-7226 1607 *fax* 020-7226 4169
email rebecca@sbco.demon.co.uk
website www.theshortbookco.com
Editorial Directors Rebecca Nicolson, Aurea
Carpenter

Short (mostly less than 40,000 words) books of
non-fiction bridging the gap between journalism
and publishing: history, biography, essays,
reportage. Founded 1999.

Sidgwick & Jackson – see Macmillan Publishers Ltd

Sigma Press
5 Alton Road, Wilmslow,
Cheshire SK9 5DY
tel/fax (01625) 531035
email info@sigmapress.co.uk
website www.sigmapress.co.uk
Partners Graham Beech, Diana Beech

Leisure: country walking, cycling, regional heritage,
sport, cookery, health, folklore; biographies.
Founded 1979.

Signet Books – former imprint of Michael Joseph/Penguin

Silhouette® – see Harlequin Mills & Boon Ltd

Simon & Schuster*
Africa House, 64-78 Kingsway,
London WC2B 6AH
tel 020-7316 1900 *fax* 020-7316 0331/2
website www.simonsays.co.uk
Directors Ian Chapman (managing), Suzanne
Baboneau (publishing), Caroline Proud (sales and
marketing), Diane Spivey (rights), Ingrid Selberg
(children's publishing)

Commercial and literary fiction; general and serious
non-fiction; children's. No unsolicited MSS.
Founded 1986.

Earthlight (imprint)

Science fiction and fantasy.

Free Press (imprint)

Serious adult non-fiction: history, biography,
current affairs, science.

Martin Books (imprint)

Mass market non-fiction.

Pocket Books (imprint)

Mass-market fiction and non-fiction paperbacks.

Scribner (imprint)

Literary fiction and non-fiction.

Simon & Schuster Audioworks

Fiction, non-fiction and business.

Simon & Schuster Children's Publishing
Fiction and non-fiction.

Skoob Russell Square
10 Brunswick Centre, off Bernard Street,
London WC1N 1AE
tel 020-7278 8760 *fax* 020-7278 3137
email books@skoob.com
website www.skoob.com
Editorial M. Lovell

Literary guides, cultural studies, oriental literature.
No unsolicited material. Founded 1979.

Smith Gryphon Ltd – see Blake Publishing

Society for Promoting Christian Knowledge*
Holy Trinity Church, Marylebone Road,
London NW1 4DU
tel 020-7643 0382 *fax* 020-7643 0391
email publishing@spck.org.uk
Director of Publishing Simon Kingston

Founded 1698.

Azure Books (imprint)
Editor Alison Barr

Biography and letters, personal growth and
relationships, history, humour, spirituality, travel.

Sheldon Press (imprint)
Editorial Director Joanna Moriarty

Popular medicine, health, self-help, psychology.

SPCK (imprint)
Editorial Director Joanna Moriarty

Theology and academic, liturgy, prayer, spirituality,
biblical studies, educational resources, mission,
gospel and culture.

Society of Genealogists Enterprises Ltd
14 Charterhouse Buildings, Goswell Road,
London EC1M 7BA
tel 020-7251 8799 *fax* 020-7250 1800
email sales@sog.org.uk
website www.sog.org.uk/
Chief Executive June Perrin

Local and family history books, fiche, disks, CDs,
software and magazines plus extensive library
facilities.

South Street Press – see Garnet Publishing Ltd

Southwater – see Anness Publishing

Souvenir Press Ltd
43 Great Russell Street,
London WC1B 3PD
tel 020-7580 9307/8
Managing Director Ernest Hecht

Archaeology, biography and memoirs, educational

(secondary, technical), general, humour, practical handbooks, psychiatry, psychology, sociology, sports, games and hobbies, travel, supernatural, parapsychology, illustrated books. No unsolicited fiction or children's books; initial enquiry by telephone essential.

SPCK – see Society for Promoting Christian Knowledge

Spellmount Ltd
The Old Rectory, Staplehurst,
Kent TN12 0AZ
tel (01580) 893730 *fax* (01580) 893731
email enquiries@spellmount.com
website www.spellmount.com
Proprietor Jamie A.G. Wilson

Ancients, 15th through to 20th century history/military history. Send sae with submissions please. Founded 1984.

Spindlewood – see Ragged Bears Publishing Ltd

Spon Press – see Taylor & Francis Group plc

Springer-Verlag London Ltd
Sweetapple House, Catteshall Road, Godalming,
Surrey GU7 3DJ
tel (01483) 418800 *fax* (01483) 415151
email postmaster@svl.co.uk
website www.springer.co.uk
Managing Director John Watson, *Executive Directors* D. Goetz, R. Gebauer

Medicine, computing, engineering, astronomy, mathematics. Founded 1972.

Stacey International
128 Kensington Church Street,
London W8 4BH
tel 020-7221 7166 *fax* 020-7792 9288
email enquiries@stacey-international.co.uk

Illustrated non-fiction, encyclopedic books on regions and countries, Islamic and Arab subjects, world affairs, children's books, art, travel, belles-lettres. Founded 1974.

Stainer & Bell Ltd
PO Box 110, Victoria House, 23 Gruneisen Road,
London N3 1DZ
tel 020-8343 3303 *fax* 020-843 3024
email post@stainer.co.uk
website www.stainer.co.uk
Directors Keith Wakefield (joint managing), Carol Wakefield (joint managing and secretary), Peter Braley, Antony Kearns, Andrew Pratt, Nicholas Williams

Books on music, religious communication. Founded 1907.

Stanley Gibbons Publications
Parkside, Christchurch Road, Ringwood,
Hants BH24 3SH
tel (01425) 472363 *fax* (01425) 470247
email sales@stangib.demon.co.uk
Chief Executive T. McQuillan

Philatelic handbooks, stamp catalogues and albums, *Gibbons Stamp Monthly*. Founded 1856.

Stanley Paul – former imprint of Random House Group Ltd

Stanley Thornes (Publishers) Ltd – see Nelson Thornes Ltd

Stationery Office (Ireland) – see Government Supplies Agency

Stenlake Publishing*
54-58 Mill Square, Catrine Ayrshire KA5 6RD
tel (01290) 552233 *fax* (01290) 551122
email sales@stenlake.co.uk
website www.stenlake.co.uk
Proprietor Richard Stenlake, *Editorial Director* Oliver van Helden

Local history, railways, transport, aviation, canals, mining. Founded 1997.

Stride Publications
11 Sylvan Road, Exeter, Devon EX4 6EW
email editor@stridebooks.co.uk
website www.stridebooks.co.uk
Managing Editor Rupert M. Loydell

Poetry, literary experimental novels and short fiction collections, contemporary music and visual arts, interviews. No submissions are currently being sought. Founded 1980.

Summersdale Publishers Ltd
46 West Street, Chichester, West Sussex PO19 1RP
tel (01243) 771107 *fax* (01243) 786300
email info@summersdale.com
liz@summersdale.com
website www.summersdale.com
Commissioning Editor Elizabeth Kershaw

Travel literature, martial arts, biography and history, humour and gift books. No poetry or children's literature. Founded 1990.

Sunflower Books
12 Kendrick Mews, London SW7 3HG
tel/fax 020-7589 1862
email mail@sunflowerbooks.co.uk
website www.sunflowerbooks.co.uk/
Directors P.A. Underwood (editorial),
J.G. Underwood, S.J. Seccombe

Travel guidebooks.

Sussex Academic Press
PO Box 2950, Brighton BN2 5SP
tel (01273) 699533 *fax* (01273) 621262
email edit@sussex-academic.co.uk
website www.sussex-academic.co.uk
Editorial Director Anthony Grahame

Theology and religion, British history and Middle East studies. Founded 1994.

The Alpha Press (imprint)
Religion, history, sport.

Sutton Publishing Ltd
Phoenix Mill, Thrupp, Stroud, Glos. GL5 2BU
tel (01453) 731114 *fax* (01453) 731117
email publishing@sutton-publishing.co.uk
website www.suttonpublishing.co.uk
Managing Director Jeremy Yates-Round, *Editorial* Jaqueline Mitchell (biography), Christopher Feeney (general history), Jonathan Alconer (military), Simon Fletcher (local history)

General academic and specialist publishers of high-quality illustrated books: history, military, biography, archaeology, heritage. Owned by Haynes Publishing. Founded 1978.

Patrick Stephens Ltd (imprint)

Aviation, maritime and military. New titles and new editions now published under Sutton imprint.

Swan Hill Press – see Quiller Publishing Ltd

Swedenborg Society
20-21 Bloomsbury Way, London WC1A 2TH
tel 020-7405 7986 *fax* 020-7831 5848
email swed.soc@netmatters.co.uk
website www.swedenborg.co.uk

The Writings of Swedenborg.

Sweet & Maxwell*
100 Avenue Road, London NW3 3PF
tel 020-7393 7000 *fax* 020-7393 7010
Directors Wendy Beecham (managing), Jim Glover, Aris Kassimatis, Hilary Lambert, Wendy Newman, Martin Redfern, Jackie Rhodes

Law. Part of Thomson Legal & Regulatory (Europe) Ltd. Founded 1799; incorporated 1889.

T & AD Poyser – see A & C Black Publishers Ltd

T&T Clark – see The Continuum International Publishing Group Ltd

Take That Ltd
PO Box 200, Harrogate, North Yorkshire HG1 2YR
tel (01423) 507545 *fax* (01423) 526035
email sales@takethat.co.uk
website www.takethat.co.uk
Managing Director Chris Brown

Internet/computing, business, finance, gambling. Send sae with synopsis/samples. Founded 1986.

Tamarind Ltd
PO Box 52, Northwood, Middlesex HA6 1UN
tel 020-8866 8808 *fax* 020-8866 5627
email info@tamarindbooks.co.uk
website www.tamarindbooks.co.uk
Managing Director Verna Wilkins

Multicultural children's picture books and posters. All books give a high positive profile to black children. Unsolicited material welcome with return postage. Founded 1987.

Tango Books – imprint of Sadie Fields Productions Ltd, see page 191

Tarquin Publications
Stradbroke, Diss, Norfolk IP21 5JP
tel (01379) 384218 *fax* (01379) 384289
email tarquin-books.demon.co.uk
website www.tarquin-books.demon.co.uk
Partners Gerald Jenkins, Margaret Jenkins

Mathematics and mathematical models; paper cutting, paper engineering and pop-up books for intelligent children. No unsolicited MSS; send suggestion or synopsis in first instance. Founded 1970.

Tate Publishing
The Lodge, Millbank, London SW1P 4RG
tel 020-7887 8869/70 *fax* 020-7887 8878
email tgpl@tate.org.uk
website www.tate.org.uk
Chief Executive Celia Clear, *Publishing Director* Roger Thorp, *Senior Manager* Brian McGahon, *Production Manager* Tim Holton, *Head of Licensing* Jo Matthews, *Head of Products* Rosey Blackmore

Publishers for Tate in London, Liverpool and St Ives. Exhibition catalogues, art books (contemporary, modern and from 1500 if British) and diaries, posters, etc. Also product development, picture library and licensing. Division of Tate Enterprises Ltd. Founded 1995.

Tauris Academic Studies – see I.B.Tauris & Co. Ltd

Tauris Parke Books and Paperbacks – see I.B.Tauris & Co. Ltd

Taylor & Francis Group plc*
11 New Fetter Lane, London EC4P 4EE
tel 020-7583 9855 *fax* 020-7842 2298
email info@tandf.co.uk
website www.tandf.co.uk
Chief Executive David J. Smith, *Managing Director, Taylor & Francis Books Ltd* Roger Horton

The company is making its books available through the Taylor & Francis Electronic Library imprint.

BIOS Scientific Publishers (imprint)

Bioscience textbooks.

CRC Press (imprint)

Engineering and science books.

Dunitz (imprint)

Medical books.

Europa Publications Ltd (imprint)

See page 143.

Fitzroy-Dearborn (imprint)

Reference and academic encyclopedias and handbooks.

Garland Science (imprint)

Science textbooks and scholarly works.

Parthenon Press (imprint)

Medical books.

Psychology Press Ltd

See page 169.

Routledge (imprint)
website www.routledge.com

Addiction, anthropology, archaeology, Asian studies, business, classical studies, counselling, criminology, development and environment, dictionaries, economics, education, geography, health, history, Japanese studies, library science, language, linguistics, literary criticism, media and culture, nursing, performance studies, philosophy, politics, psychiatry, psychology, reference, social administration, social studies/sociology, women's studies.

RoutlegeCurzon (imprint)

Academic/scholarly books in the social sciences, particularly Asian studies.

RoutledgeFalmer (imprint)

Education books.

Spon Press (imprint)

Architecture, civil engineering, construction, leisure and recreation management, sports science.

Taylor & Francis (imprint)

Educational (university), science: physics, mathematics, chemistry, electronics, natural history, pharmacology and drug metabolism, toxicology, technology, history of science, ergonomics, production engineering, remote sensing, geographic information systems.

Teach Yourself – see Hodder Headline Ltd

Telegraph Books
Telegraph Group Ltd, 1 Canada Square, Canary Wharf, London E14 5DT
tel 020-7538 6826 *fax* 020-7538 6064

Publisher Morven Knowles

Business, personal finance, crosswords, sport, travel and guides, cookery, health, general, gardening, history – usually by *Telegraph* journalists and contributors, and co-published with major publishing houses. Founded 1920.

The Templar Company plc – see Book packagers, page 192

Tempus Publishing Group Ltd
The Mill, Brimscombe Port, Stroud, Glos. GL5 2QG
tel (01453) 883300 *fax* (01453) 883233
Directors Richard Joseph (chief executive), Geoff Holmes (operations, USA), Chris McLaren (editorial sales & marketing), Paul Raffle (finance), Mike Walton (operations, Europe)

Local and national history throughout the British Isles; USA (Arcadia Publishing Inc.); modern; mediaeval; archaeology; sport; industrial and transport history. Founded 1993.

Tender Romance – see Harlequin Mills & Boon Ltd

Terence Dalton Ltd
Water Street, Lavenham, Sudbury, Suffolk CO10 9RN
tel (01787) 249289 *fax* (01787) 248267
Directors T.A.J. Dalton, E.H. Whitehair

Non-fiction.

Thames & Hudson Ltd*
181A High Holborn, London WC1V 7QX
tel 020-7845 5000 *fax* 020-7845 5050
email sales@thameshudson.co.uk
website www.thamesandhudson.com
Directors T. Neurath (managing), E. Bates, C. Kaine, C. Ferguson, J. Camplin, P. Hughes, S. Baron, B. Meek, P. Meades, J. Neurath, T. Evans, T. Naylor, N. Stangos, N. Palfreyman

Illustrated non-fiction for an international audience, especially art, architecture, graphic design, garden and landscape design, archaeology, cultural history, historical reference, fashion, photography, ethnic arts, mythology and religion.

Thames Publishing
c/o William Elkin Music Services, Station Road Industrial Estate, Salhouse, Norwich NR13 6NS
tel (01603) 721302 *fax* (01603) 721801
email sales@elkinmusic.co.uk
website www.elkinmusic.co.uk
Publishing Manager E.B. Bishop

Books about music (not pop), particularly British composers and musicians. Preliminary letter essential. Founded 1970.

Thomas Cook Publishing

PO Box 227, Units 19-21, The Thomas Cook
Business Park, Peterborough PE3 8XX
tel (01733) 416477 *fax* (01733) 416688
email publishing-sales@thomascook.com
website www.thomascookpublishing.com
Managing Director Donald Greig
Travel guides, rail maps and timetables. Founded
1875.

Thomas Nelson Ltd – see Nelson Thornes Ltd

Thomas Reed – see A & C Black Publishers Ltd

Thomson Round Hall

43 Fitzwilliam Place, Dublin 2,
Republic of Ireland
tel (01) 6625301 *fax* (01) 6625302
email info@roundhall.ie
Director and General Manager Elanor McGarry
Law. Part of Thomson Legal & Regulatory (Europe)
Ltd.

Thorsons/Element – see HarperCollins Publishers

Time Warner Books UK*

(formerly Little, Brown and Company (UK))
Brettenham House, Lancaster Place,
London WC2E 7EN
tel 020-7911 8000 *fax* 020-7911 8100
Chief Executive David Young, *Directors* Ursula
Mackenzie (publisher), Barbara Boote (editorial),
Richard Beswick (editorial), David Kent (sales),
Nigel Batt (financial), Terry Jackson (marketing),
Stephen Roberts (commercial)
Hardback and paperback fiction and general non-
fiction. No unsolicited MSS. Founded 1988.

Abacus (division)
Editorial Director Richard Beswick
Trade paperbacks.

Atom (division)
Editor Ben Sharpe
Young adult paperbacks.

Orbit (imprint)
Editorial Director Tim Holman
Science fiction and fantasy paperbacks.

Virago (division)
Publisher Lennie Goodings

Fiction, including Modern Classics Series,
biography, autobiography and general non-fiction
which highlight all aspects of women's lives.

Warner (division)
Editorial Directors Barbara Boote, Alan Samson,
Hilary Hale

Paperbacks: original fiction and non-fiction;
reprints.

X Libris (imprint)
Editor Sarah Shrubb
Erotic fiction for women.

Times Books – see HarperCollins Publishers

Titan Books

144 Southwark Street, London SE1 0UP
tel 020-7620 0200 *fax* 020-7620 0032
email readerfeedback@titanemail.com
Publisher and Managing Director Nick Landau,
Editorial Director Katy Wild

Graphic novels, including *Simpsons* and *Batman*,
featuring comic strip material; film and TV tie-ins
and cinema reference books, including *Star Wars*
and *Star Trek*. No fiction or children's proposals and
no unsolicited material without preliminary letter
please; send large sae for current author guidelines.
Division of Titan Publishing Group Ltd. Founded
1981.

Tivoli – see Gill & Macmillan Ltd

Tolkien – see HarperCollins Publishers

Tolley – see LexisNexis Butterworths Tolley

TownHouse, Dublin†

Trinity House, Charleston Road, Ranelagh,
Dublin 6, Republic of Ireland
tel (01) 4972399 *fax* (01) 4970927
email books@townhouse.ie
Directors Treasa Coady, Jim Coady

General illustrated non-fiction, popular and literary
fiction, art, archaeology and biography. Imprints:
TownHouse, Simon and Schuster/TownHouse,
Pocket/TownHouse, Scribner/TownHouse,
Earthlight/TownHouse. Founded 1981.

Transworld Publishers*

61-63 Uxbridge Road, London W5 5SA
tel 020-8579 2652 *fax* 020-8579 5479
email info@transworld-publishers.co.uk
website www.booksattransworld.co.uk
Managing Director Larry Finlay, *Publisher* Patrick
Janson-Smith, *Deputy Publisher* Bill Scott-Kerr,
Senior Publishing Director Francesca Liversidge

Division of **Random House Group Ltd**; subsidiary
of Bertelsmann AG. No unsolicited MSS accepted.

Bantam (imprint)
Senior Publishing Director Francesca Liversidge
Paperback general fiction and non-fiction, Mind,
Body & Spirit, self-help, travel.

Bantam Press (imprint)
Publishing Director Sally Gaminara
Fiction, general, cookery, business, crime, health
and diet, history, humour, military, music,

paranormal, self-help, science, travel and adventure, biography and autobiography.

Black Swan (imprint)
Deputy Publisher Bill Scott-Kerr

Paperback quality fiction.

Corgi (imprint)
Deputy Publisher Bill Scott-Kerr

Paperback general fiction and non-fiction.

Doubleday (UK) (imprint)
Publishing Director Marianne Velmans

Literary fiction and non-fiction.

Eden (imprint)
Managing Editor Katrina Whone

Environmental: the Eden Project.

Expert Books (imprint)
Co-ordinator Gareth Pottle

Gardening and DIY.

Treehouse Children's Books

2nd Floor Offices, Old Brewhouse,
Lower Charlton Trading Estate, Shepton Mallet,
Somerset BA4 5QE
tel (01749) 330529 *fax* (01749) 330544
email richard.powell4@virgin.net
Editorial Director Richard Powell

Preschool children's books and novelty books.
Imprint of Emma Treehouse Ltd. Founded 1989.

Trentham Books Ltd*

Westview House, 734 London Road, Oakhill,
Stoke-on-Trent, Staffs. ST4 5NP
tel (01782) 745567 *fax* (01782) 745553
email tb@trentham.books.co.uk
website www.trentham-books.co.uk
Editorial office 28 Hillside Gardens,
London N6 5ST
tel 020-8348 2174
Directors Dr Gillian Klein (editorial), Barbara
Wiggins (executive)

Education (including specialist fields – multi-ethnic
issues, equal opportunities, bullying, design and
technology, early years), social policy, sociology of
education, European education, women's studies.
Does not publish books for use by parents or
children, or fiction, biography, reminiscences and
poetry. Founded 1978.

Trotman & Company Ltd

2 The Green, Richmond,
Surrey TW9 1PL
tel 020-8486 1150 *fax* 020-8486 1161
website www.trotmanpublishing.co.uk
Managing Director Toby Trotman, *Editorial Director*
Mina Patria, *Commissioning Editor* Rachel Lockhart

Independent advice and guidance on careers and
higher education. Founded 1970.

TSO (The Stationery Office)*

Head office St Crispins, Duke Street,
Norwich NR3 1PD
tel (0870) 6005522 *fax* (0870) 6005533
website www.tso.co.uk
Chief Executive Ian Burns, *Coo* Fred Perkins,
Commercial Director Peter Miller, *Sales & Marketing
Director* J. Hook

Publishing and information management services:
business, current affairs, directories, general,
pharmaceutical, professional, reference, National
Curriculum, Learning to Drive.

Ulric Publishing

PO Box 55, Church Stretton, Shrops. SY6 6WR
tel (01694) 781354 *fax* (01694) 781372
email books@ulric-publishing.com
website www.ulric-publishing.com
Directors Ulric Woodhams, Elizabeth Follows

Military and political history – World War Two;
automobilia – classic cars; travel – unique
adventures. No unsolicited MSS. Founded 1992.

University of Exeter Press

Reed Hall, Streatham Drive, Exeter,
Devon EX4 4QR
tel (01392) 263066 *fax* (01392) 263064
email uep@exeter.ac.uk
website www.ex.ac.uk/uep/
Publisher Simon Baker

Academic and scholarly books on history, local
history (Exeter and the South West), archaeology,
classical studies, English literature, film history,
performance studies, medieval studies, linguistics,
modern languages, European studies, maritime
studies, mining history. Founded 1958.

University of Wales Press

10 Columbus Walk, Brigantine Place,
Cardiff CF10 4UP
tel 029-2049 6899 *fax* 029-2049 6108
email press@press.wales.ac.uk
website www.wales.ac.uk/press
Director Susan Jenkins

Academic and educational (Welsh and English).
Publishers of *Welsh History Review, Studia Celtica,
Llên Cymru, Efrydiau Athronyddol, Contemporary
Wales, Welsh Journal of Education, Journal of Celtic
Linguistics, ALT-J (Association for Learning
Technology Journal), Kantian Review.* Founded 1922.

Unwin Hyman Academic – incorporated into
Routledge; see Taylor & Francis Group plc

Unwin Hyman Ltd – acquired by HarperCollins
Publishers

Usborne Publishing*
Usborne House, 83-85 Saffron Hill,
London EC1N 8RT
tel 020-7430 2800 *fax* 020-7430 1562
email mail@usborne.co.uk
website www.usborne.com
Directors Peter Usborne, Jenny Tyler (editorial),
Robert Jones, Keith Ball, David Harte, Lorna Hunt

Children's books: reference, practical, computers,
craft, natural history, science, languages, history,
geography, preschool, fiction. Founded 1973.

V&A Publications
160 Brompton Road, London SW3 1HW
tel 020-7942 2966 *fax* 020-7942 2977
website www.vandashop.co.uk/books
Head of Publications Mary Butler

Popular and scholarly books on fine and decorative
arts, architecture, contemporary design, fashion and
photography. Founded 1980.

Vallentine Mitchell
Crown House, 47 Chase Side, London N14 5BP
tel 020-8920 2100 *fax* 020-8447 8548
email info@vmbooks.com
website www.vmbooks.com
Directors Frank Cass (chairman), Stewart Cass, A.E.
Cass, H.J. Osen, Hon. C.V. Callman, M.P. Zaidner

Jewish history, Jewish thought, Judaism, Holocaust
studies.

Variorum – see Ashgate Publishing Ltd

Vega – see Chrysalis Books Group

Veritas Publications†
Veritas House, 7-8 Lower Abbey Street, Dublin 1,
Republic of Ireland
tel (01) 8788177 *fax* (01) 8786507
email publications@veritas.ie
website www.veritas.ie

Liturgical and Church resources, religious school
books for primary and post-primary levels,
biographies, academic studies, and general books on
religious, moral and social issues.

Vermilion – see Random House Group Ltd

Verso Ltd
6 Meard Street, London W1F 0EG
tel 020-7437 3546 *fax* 020-7734 0059
email verso@verso.co.uk
Directors George Galfalvi (executive chairman),
Gavin Everall (sales and marketing), Robin
Blackburn, Tariq Ali, Perry Anderson

Politics, sociology, economics, history, philosophy,
cultural studies. Founded 1970.

Victor Gollancz Ltd – now incorporated into The Orion Publishing Group Ltd

Viking – see Penguin Group (UK)

Vintage – see Random House Group Ltd

Virago – see Time Warner Books UK

Virgin Books Ltd
Thames Wharf Studios, Rainville Road,
London W6 9HA
tel 020-7386 3300 *fax* 020-7386 3360
Directors K.T. Forster (managing), Sir Richard
Branson, *Management* Carolyn Thorne (editorial
director, illustrated), James Parker (rights), Jamie
Moore (marketing), Becke Parker (publicity), Ray
Mudie (sales)

Virgin (imprint)
Editorial Carolyn Thorne (general), Jonathan Taylor
(sport), Stuart Slater (music), Kirstie Addis
(general), Mark Wallace (general)

Popular culture: entertainment, showbiz, arts, film
and TV, music, humour, biography and autobiography, popular reference, true crime, sport, travel.

Black Lace (imprint)
Senior Editor Kerri Sharp

Erotic fiction by women for women.

Nexus (imprint)
Editor Paul Copperwaite

Erotic fiction.

Virtue Books Ltd
Edward House, Tenter Street,
Rotherham S60 1LB
tel (01709) 365005 *fax* (01709) 829982
email info@virtue.co.uk
website www.virtue.co.uk
Directors Peter E. Russum, Margaret H. Russum

Books for the professional chef: catering and drink.

The Vital Spark – see Neil Wilson Publishing Ltd

VNR – see Wiley Europe Ltd

VNU Entertainment Media UK Ltd*
Endeavour House, 189 Shaftesbury Avenue,
London WC2H 8TJ
tel 020-7420 6000 *fax* 020-7836 2909
Directors Jonathan Nowell, Howard Lander

Reference including *The Bookseller* (1858),
Whitaker's Books in Print (1874), and other book
trade directories.

Voyager – see HarperCollins Publishers

W. Foulsham & Co. Ltd
The Publishing House, Bennetts Close, Slough,
Berks. SL1 5AP
tel (01753) 526769 *fax* (01753) 535003
Managing Director B.A.R. Belasco, *Editorial Director*
W. Hobson

Life issues. General know-how, cookery, health and
alternative therapies, hobbies and games, gardening,
sport, travel guides, DIY, collectibles, popular new
age. Founded 1819.

Arcturus (imprint)
Military, art and drawing, popular psychology.

Foulsham (imprint)

Quantum (imprint)
Mind, Body & Spirit, popular philosophy and
practical psychology.

W.B. Saunders – see Elsevier Ltd

W.H. Allen – acquired by Virgin Books Ltd

W.H. Freeman
Palgrave Publishers Ltd, Houndmills, Basingstoke,
Hants RG21 6XS
tel (01256) 332807 *fax* (01256) 330688

Science, medicine, economics, psychology,
archaeology.

W.W. Norton & Company
Castle House, 75-76 Wells Street,
London W1T 3QT
tel 020-7323 1579 *fax* 020-7436 4553
Managing Director Alan Cameron

English and American literature, economics, music,
psychology, science. Founded 1980.

Walker Books Ltd*
87 Vauxhall Walk, London SE11 5HJ
tel 020-7793 0909 *fax* 020-7587 1123
email mail@walkerbooks.co.uk
website www.walkerbooks.co.uk
Directors David Heatherwick, David Lloyd, Karen
Lotz, Roger Alexander (non-executive), Michel
Blake, Sarah Foster, Harold G. Gould OBE (non-
executive), Mike McGrath, Henryk Wesolowski, Jane
Winterbotham, *Company Secretary* Richard
Wilkinson

Children's: picture books, non-fiction and novelty
titles; junior and teenage fiction. Founded 1979.

Wallflower Press
5 Pond Street, London NW3 2PN
tel 020-7431 6622 *fax* 020-7435 6522
email info@wallflowerpress.co.uk
website www.wallflowerpress.co.uk
Editorial Director Yoram Allon, *Technical Director*
Howard Seal

The moving image: cinema, TV, screen arts –
academic and popular. Founded 1999.

Warburg Institute
University of London, Woburn Square,
London WC1H 0AB
tel 020-7862 8949 *fax* 020-7862 8955
email warburg@sas.ac.uk
website www.sas.ac.uk/warburg/

Cultural and intellectual history, with special
reference to the history of the classical tradition.

Ward Lock – former imprint of Weidenfeld & Nicolson

Ward Lock Educational Co. Ltd
BIC Ling Kee House, 1 Christopher Road,
East Grinstead, West Sussex RH19 3BT
tel (01342) 318980 *fax* (01342) 410980
email wle@lingkee.com
website www.wardlockeducational.com
Directors Au Bak Ling (chairman, Hong Kong),
Au King Kwok (Hong Kong), Au Wai Kwok (Hong
Kong), Albert Kw Au (Hong Kong), *General
Manager* Penny Kitchenham

Primary and secondary pupil materials, Kent
Mathematics Project: KMP BASIC and KMP Main
series covering Reception to GCSE, Reading
Workshops, Take Part Series and Take Part Starters,
teachers' books, music books, Target Series for the
National Curriculum: Target Science and Target
Geography, religious education. Founded 1952.

Warne – see Penguin Group (UK)

Warner – see Time Warner Books UK

Warner/Chappell Plays Ltd – see Josef Weinberger Plays Ltd

The Watts Publishing Group Ltd*
96 Leonard Street, London EC2A 4XD
tel 020-7739 2929 *fax* 020-7739 2318
email gm@wattspub.co.uk
website www.wattspublishing.co.uk
Directors Marlene Johnson (managing), Philippa
Stewart (publishing, Franklin Watts), Clare
Somerville (sales), Elaine Ward (production), Zosia
Knopp (rights)

Cat's Whiskers (imprint)
Publishing Director Philippa Stewart
Children's picture books.

Franklin Watts (division)
Publishing Director Philippa Stewart
Children's illustrated non-fiction, reference,
education. Imprint: Aladdin/Watts.

Orchard Books (division)
Publishing Director Ann-Janine Murtaugh

Children's picture books, fiction, poetry, novelty books, board books.

Wayland – now Hodder Wayland – see Hodder Headline Ltd

Websters International Publishers Ltd

2nd Floor, Axe & Bottle Court,
70 Newcomen Street, London SE1 1YT
tel 020-7940 4700 *fax* 020-7940 4701
website www.websters.co.uk www.ozclarke.com
Chairman and Publisher Adrian Webster, *Managing Director* Jean-Luc Barbanneau, *Publishing Director* Susannah Webster

Wine, food, travel, health. Founded 1983.

Weidenfeld & Nicolson

Orion House, 5 Upper St Martin's Lane,
London WC2H 9EA
tel 020-7240 3444 *fax* 020-7379 6158
Publishing Director Richard Milner

Biography and autobiography, current affairs, history, travel, fiction, literary fiction. Part of the **Orion Publishing Group Ltd**.

Weidenfeld & Nicolson Illustrated
Editor-in-Chief Michael Dover

Quality illustrated non-fiction: gardening, cookery, wine, art and design, health and lifestyle, history, popular culture, archaeology, British heritage, literature, fashion, architecture, natural history, sport and adventure.

Cassell Military (imprint)
Publishing Director Ian Drury

Military history and militaria.

Cassell Reference (imprint)
Publishing Director Richard Milbank

Language and general interest reference. In association with Peter Crawley: *Master Bridge Series*.

Seven Dials (imprint)
Managing Editor Nic Cheetham

Quality illustrated paperbacks: food and drink, gardening, heritage, history, lifestyle, art.

Welsh Academic Press*

PO Box 733, Cardiff CF14 2YX
tel 029-2056 0343 *fax* 029-2056 1931
email post@welsh-academic-press.com
website www.welsh-academic-press.com
Managing Director Ashley Drake

History, politics, biography, Celtic studies. Founded 1994.

Wharncliffe – see Pen & Sword Books Ltd

Which? Ltd

2 Marylebone Road, London NW1 4DF
tel 020-7770 7000 *fax* 020-7770 7660
email books@which.net
Chief Executive Sheila McKechnie, *Head of Which? Books* Robert Gray

Part of Consumers' Association. Founded 1957.

Which? Books (imprint)

Travel, restaurant, hotel and wine guides, medicine, law and personal finance for the layman, gardening, careers, DIY – all branded *Which? Books*.

Whittet Books Ltd

Hill Farm, Stonham Road, Cotton, Stowmarket,
Suffolk IP14 4RQ
tel (01449) 781877 *fax* (01449) 781898
email annabel@whittet.dircon.co.uk
Directors Annabel Whittet, John Whittet

Natural history, countryside, poultry, livestock, pets, horses. Founded 1976.

Whurr Publishers Ltd*

19B Compton Terrace,
London N1 2UN
tel 020-7359 5979 *fax* 020-7226 5290
email info@whurr.co.uk
Director Anne Bassett

Disorders of human communication, medicine, psychology, psychiatry, psychotherapy, occupational therapy, physiotherapy, nursing, for professional markets only. Founded 1987.

Wiley Europe Ltd*

(incorporating Interscience Publishers)
The Atrium, Southern Gate, Chichester,
West Sussex PO19 8SQ
tel (01243) 779777 *fax* (01243) 775878
email europe@wiley.co.uk
website www.wileyeurope.com
Managing Director/Senior Vice President J.H. Jarvis, *Director, STM Publishing* M. Davis, *Senior Vice President, P&T Publishing* S. Smith

Physics, chemistry, mathematics, statistics, engineering, architecture, computer science, biology, medicine, earth science, psychology, business, economics, finance. Imprints: Betty Crocker, Bible, Capstone, CliffsNotes, Current Protocols, Ernst & Sohn, ExpressExec, For Dummies, Frommer's, Howell Book House, Interscience, Jossey–Bass, J.K. Lasser, Pfeiffer, Red Hat Press, Scripta Technica, The Unofficial Guide, Visual, Webster's New World, Wiley Academy, Wiley–Interscience, Wiley–Liss, ValuSource, WILEY–VCH, VNR.

William Heinemann – see Random House Group Ltd

William Reed Directories

Broadfield Park, Crawley,
West Sussex RH11 9RT
tel (01293) 610488 *fax* (01293) 610310
email directories@william-reed.co.uk
website www.william-reed.co.uk
Director Mark de Lange, *Editorial Manager* Sulann
Staniford, *Group Sales Manager* Simon Hughes

Publishers of leading business-to-business
directories and reports, including *The Grocer
Directory of Buyers and Retailers* and *The Grocer
Directory of Manufacturers and Suppliers.*

The Windrush Press

Windrush House, Adlestrop, Moreton-in-Marsh,
Glos. GL56 0YN
tel (01608) 658758 *fax* (01608) 659345
email victoriama.huxley@btinternet.com
website www.windrushpress.com
Managing Director Geoffrey Smith, *Publishing
Director* Victoria Huxley

History, biography, *The Traveller's History* series,
ancient mysteries. Publishes in association with the
Orion Group. Founded 1987.

Woburn Press – see Frank Cass & Co. Ltd

The Women's Press

Top Floor, 27 Goodge Street, London W1P 2LD
tel 020-7580 7806 *fax* 020-7637 1866
website www.the-womens-press.com
Managing Director Charlotte Gascoigne

Books by women in the areas of literary and crime
fiction, biography and autobiography, health,
culture, politics, handbooks, literary criticism,
psychology and self-help, the arts. Founded 1978.

Livewire (imprint)

Books for teenagers and young women.

Wooden Books

The Walkmill, Cascob, Presteigne,
Powys LD8 2NT
website www.woodenbooks.com
Directors John Martineau (managing), Anthony
Brandt (secretary), Michael Glickman (overseas)

Magic, mathematics, ancient sciences, esoteric.
Illustrators and cartoonists needed. Founded 1996.

Woodhead Publishing Ltd

Abington Hall, Abington, Cambridge CB1 6AH
tel (01223) 891358 *fax* (01223) 893694
email wp@woodhead-publishing.com
website www.woodhead-publishing.com
Managing Director Martin Woodhead

Engineering, materials, welding, textiles,
commodities, food science and technology,
environmental science. Founded 1989.

Wordsworth Editions Ltd

8B East Street, Ware, Herts. SG12 9HJ
tel (01920) 465167 *fax* (01920) 462267
email enquiries@wordsworth-editions.com
website www.wordsworth.editions.com
Directors Michael Trayler (managing), Helen Trayler
(operations), Dennis Hart (sales)

Reprints of classic books: literary, children's,
exploration, military; myth, legend and folklore;
poetry; reference. Founded 1987.

X Libris – see Time Warner Books UK

The X Press

PO Box 25694, London N17 6FP
tel 020-8801 2100 *fax* 020-8885 1322
email vibes@xpress.co.uk
Editorial Director Dotun Adebayo, *Marketing
Director* Steve Pope

Black interest popular novels, particularly reflecting
contemporary ethnic experiences. *Black Classics*
series: reprints of classic novels by black writers.
Founded 1992.

Nia (imprint)

Literary black fiction.

Y Lolfa Cyf.

Talybont, Ceredigion SY24 5AP
tel (01970) 832304 *fax* (01970) 832782
email ylolfa@ylolfa.com
website www.ylolfa.com
Director Garmon Gruffudd, *Editor* Lefi Gruffudd

Welsh-language popular fiction and non-fiction,
music, children's books; Welsh-language tutors;
Welsh politics in English and a range of Welsh-
interest books for the tourist market. Founded
1967.

Yale University Press London*

47 Bedford Square, London WC1B 3DP
tel 020-7079 4900 *fax* 020-7079 4901
email firstname.lastname@yaleup.co.uk
Managing Director John Nicoll

Art, architecture, history, economics, political
science, literary criticism, Asian and African studies,
religion, philosophy, psychology, history of science.
Founded 1961.

Yellow Jersey Press – see Random House Group Ltd

Young Picador – see Macmillan Publishers Ltd

Zed Books Ltd

7 Cynthia Street, London N1 9JF
tel 020-7837 4014 (general) *fax* 020-7833 3960
email zed@zedbooks.demon.co.uk
website www.zedbooks.demon.co.uk

Editors Robert Molteno, Barbara Clarke

Social sciences on international issues; women's studies, politics, development and environmental studies; area studies (Africa, Asia, Caribbean, Latin America, Middle East and the Pacific). Founded 1976.

Zero to Ten Ltd*

2A Portman Mansions, Chiltern Street, London W1U 6NR
tel 020-7487 0920 *fax* 020-7487 0921
email sales@evansbrothers.co.uk
Publishing Director Anna McQuinn

Non-fiction for children aged 0–10: board books, toddler books, first story books, etc. Part of the Evans Publishing Group. Founded 1997.

Cherrytree Books (imprint)
UK Publisher Su Swallow

Non-fiction children's books for schools and the trade.

See also...
- *Publishers of fiction,* page 685
- *Children's book publishers and packagers,* page 688
- *Audiobook publishers,* page 691
- *Publishers of plays,* page 691
- *Publishers of poetry,* page 691

Zig Zag – see Chrysalis Children's Books

Zoë Books Ltd

15 Worthy Lane, Winchester,
Hants SO23 7AB
tel (01962) 851318
email enquiries@zoebooks.co.uk
website www.zoebooks.co.uk
Directors I.Z. Dawson (managing publishing), C.W. Dawson, J.T. Dawson

Publishers of children's information books for the school and library markets in the UK; specialists in co-editions for world markets. No unsolicited MSS. No opportunities for freelances. Founded 1990.

Book packagers

Many modern illustrated books are created by book packagers, whose special skills are in the areas of book design and graphic content. In-house desk editors and art editors match up the expertise of specialist writers, artists and photographers who usually work on a freelance basis.

act-two ltd – now John Brown Junior

Aetos Ltd
69 Warminster Road, Bathampton,
Bath & NE Somerset BA2 6RU
tel (01225) 425745 *fax* (01225) 444966
email ron@aetos.co.uk
General Manager Athina Adams-Florou, *Publishing Manager* Ron Adams

Full packaging/production service, from original concept to delivery of film or finished copies. Specialises in illustrated educational and general interest books. Publishers' commissions undertaken. Opportunities for freelances.

Aladdin Books Ltd
28 Percy Street, London W1P 0LD
tel 020-7323 3319 *fax* 020-7323 4829
email aladdin@dircon.co.uk
Directors Charles Nicholas, Bibby Whittaker

Full design and book packaging facility specialising in children's non-fiction and reference. Founded 1980.

Albion Press Ltd
Spring Hill, Idbury, Oxon OX7 6RU
tel (01993) 831094 *fax* (01993) 831982
Directors Emma Bradford, Neil Philip

Quality integrated illustrated titles. Specialises in children's books. Supply finished books. Publishers' commissions undertaken. No unsolicited MSS. Founded 1984.

Alphabet & Image Ltd
Marston House, Marston Magna, Yeovil,
Somerset BA22 8DH
tel (01935) 851331 *fax* (01935) 851372
Directors Anthony Birks-Hay, Leslie Birks-Hay

Complete editorial, picture research, photographic, design and production service for illustrated books on ceramics, fine art, horticulture, architecture, history, etc. Imprint: Marston House. Founded 1972.

Amber Books Ltd
Bradley's Close, 74-77 White Lion Street,
London N1 9PF
tel 020-7520 7600 *fax* 020-7520 7606/7607
email enquiries@amberbooks.co.uk
website www.amberbooks.co.uk
Managing Director Stasz Gnych, *Deputy Managing Director* Sara Ballard, *Publishing Manager* Charles Catton, *Head of Production* Peter Thompson, *Design Manager* Mark Batley

Illustrated non-fiction. Subject areas include military, aviation, transport, crime, general reference and maritime. Opportunities for freelances. Imprints: Brown Books Ltd. Founded 1989.

Andromeda Oxford Ltd
11-13 The Vineyard, Abingdon, Oxon OX14 3PX
tel (01235) 550296 *fax* (01235) 550330
email mail@andromeda.co.uk
website www.andromeda.co.uk
Directors David Holyoak (managing), Graham Bateman (publishing), Clive Sparling (production), Simon Matthews (finance), Christopher Collier (sales), Linda Cole (creative)

Produces for the international market adult and junior reference books: history, natural history, geography, science, art; children's information and activity books. Founded 1986.

Angus Hudson Ltd
Concorde House, Grenville Place,
London NW7 3SA
tel 020-8959 3668 *fax* 020-8959 3678
email coed@angushudson.com
website www.angushudson.com
Directors Nicholas Jones (managing), Stephen Price (production), Rodney Shepherd (operations), Geoffrey Benge

Adult and children's Christian books including international co-editions. Publishing imprints: Candle Books, Monarch Books. Founded 1971.

BCS Publishing Ltd
2nd Floor, Temple Court, 109 Oxford Road,
Cowley, Oxford OX4 2ER
tel (01865) 770099 *fax* (01865) 770050
email bcs-publishing@dsl.pipex.com
Managing and Art Director Steve McCurdy

Specialises in the preparation of illustrated non-fiction; provides a full creative, design, editorial and production service. Opportunities for freelances. Commissioned work undertaken.

Bender Richardson White

PO Box 266, Uxbridge,
Middlesex UB9 5NX
tel (01895) 832444 fax (01895) 835213
email brw@brw.co.uk
Partners Lionel Bender, Kim Richardson, Ben White

Specialises in children's natural history, science and family information. Opportunities for freelances. Founded 1990.

BLA Publishing Ltd

BIC Ling Kee House, 1 Christopher Road,
East Grinstead, West Sussex RH19 3BT
tel (01342) 318980 fax (01342) 410980
Directors Au Bak Ling (chairman, Hong Kong), Albert Kw Au (Hong Kong)

High-quality illustrated reference books, particularly science dictionaries and encyclopedias, for the international market. Founded 1981.

The Book Guild Ltd

Temple House, 25 High Street, Lewes,
East Sussex BN7 2LU
tel (01273) 472534 fax (01273) 476472
email info@bookguild.co.uk
website www.bookguild.co.uk
Directors G.M. Nissen CBE (chairman), Carol Biss (managing), Anthony Nissen, Jane Nissen, David Ross, Paul White (financial), Janet Wrench (production)

Offers a range of publishing options: a comprehensive package for authors incorporating editorial, design, production, marketing, publicity and distribution; editorial and production only for authors requiring private editions; or a complete service for companies and organisations requiring books for internal or promotional purposes – from brief to finished book. Founded 1982.

Book Packaging and Marketing

1 Church Street, Bakesley, Towcester,
Northants. NN12 8RA
tel/fax (01327) 861300
Proprietor Martin F. Marix Evans

Illustrated general and informational non-fiction and reference for adults, especially military history, travel, countryside. Product development and project management; editorial and marketing consultancy. Very limited opportunities for freelances. Founded 1990.

Breslich & Foss Ltd

2A Union Court, 20-22 Union Road,
London SW4 6JP
tel 020-7819 3990 fax 020-7819 3998
Directors Paula G. Breslich, K.B. Dunning

Books produced from MS to bound copy stage from in-house ideas. Specialising in the arts, crafts,

gardening, health, gift and novelty, children's. Founded 1978.

Bridgewater Book Company

The Old Candlemakers, West Street, Lewes,
East Sussex BN7 2NZ
tel (01273) 403120 fax (01273) 487441
email (surname)@bridgewaterbooks.co.uk
website www.bridgewaterbooks.co.uk
Directors Terry Jeavons (managing), Peter Bridgewater, Jenny Manstead

Provides full editorial, design (and where required, production) service to publishing clients. Specialises in building entire lists of illustrated books in all subject areas; developing individual titles; designing jackets/covers; producing sales material; rebranding. Opportunities for freelances. Part of the Ivy Publishing Group.

Brown Packaging Books Ltd

Bradley's Close, 74-77 White Lion Street,
London N1 9PF
tel 020-7520 7600 fax 020-7520 7606/7607
email enquiries@amberbooks.co.uk
website www.amberbooks.co.uk
Managing Director Stasz Gnych, Deputy Managing Director Sara Ballard, Managing Editor Charles Catton, Head of Production Peter Thompson, Design Manager Mark Batley

Highly illustrated non-fiction. Subject areas include military, aviation, transport, crime, general reference and maritime. Opportunities for freelances. Imprint: Brown Books Ltd. Founded 1989.

The Brown Reference Group Plc

8 Chapel Place, Rivington Street,
London EC2A 3DQ
tel 020-7920 7500 fax 020-7920 7501
email info@brownreference.com
website www.brownreference.com
Managing Director Sharon Hutton

Book, partwork and continuity set packaging services for trade, promotional and international publishers. Opportunities for freelances. Founded 1989.

Brown Wells & Jacobs Ltd

Foresters Hall, 25-27 Westow Street,
London SE19 3RY
tel 020-8771 5115 fax 020-8771 9994
email graham@popking.demon.co.uk
website www.bwj.org
Director Graham Brown

Design, editorial, illustration and production of high-quality non-fiction illustrated children's books. Specialities include pop-ups and novelties. Opportunities for freelances. Founded 1979.

Cambridge Language Services Ltd

Greystones, Allendale, Northumberland NE47 9PX
tel/fax (01434) 683200
email paul@oakleaf.demon.co.uk
Managing Director Paul Procter

Suppliers to publishers, societies and other
organisations of customised database management
systems, with advanced retrieval mechanisms, and
electronic publishing systems for the preparation of
dictionaries, reference books, encyclopedias,
catalogues, journals, archives. PC (windows) based.
Founded 1982.

Cambridge Publishing Management Ltd

149B Histon Road, Cambridge CB4 3JD
tel (01223) 367288 *fax* (01223) 368237
email initial.surname@cambridgepm.co.uk
website www.cambridgepm.co.uk
Managing Director Jackie Dobbyne, *Publishing
Director* Julia Morris

Creative and highly skilled editorial and book
production company. Specialises in complete
project management of education, ELT, travel and
illustrated non-fiction titles, from MS to delivery of
film or final files on disks. Opportunities for
freelances. Founded 1999.

Cameron & Hollis

PO Box 1, Moffat, Dumfriesshire DG10 9SU
tel (01683) 220808 *fax* (01683) 220012
email editorial@cameronbooks.co.uk
website www.cameronbooks.co.uk
Directors Ian A. Cameron, Jill Hollis

Illustrated non-fiction: fine arts (including
environmental and land art), film, the decorative
arts, crafts, architecture, design, antiques, collecting,
natural history, environmental studies, social
history, food. Founded 1976.
Edition: Design, editing, typesetting, production
work from concept to finished book for galleries,
museums, institutions and other publishers.
Founded 1975.

Canopus Publishing Ltd

27 Queen Square, Bristol BS1 4ND
tel/fax 0117-922 6660
email robin@canopusbooks.com
website www.canopusbooks.com
Director Robin Rees

Highly illustrated popular science and astronomy
titles for international markets. Founded 1999.

Carroll & Brown Ltd

20 Lonsdale Road, London NW6 6RD
tel 020-7372 0900 *fax* 020-7372 0460
email mail@carrollandbrown.co.uk
Directors Amy Carroll (managing), Denise Brown
(creative)

Editorial and design through to final film and
printing of cookery, health, craft, Mind, Body &
Spirit, and lifestyle titles. Opportunities for
freelances. Founded 1989.

Cowley Robinson Ltd

8 Belmont, Bath BA1 5DZ
tel (01225) 339999 *fax* (01225) 339995
Directors Lee Robinson (chairman), Stewart Cowley
(publishing), Rob Kendrew (production)

Children's international co-editions. Novelty format
creation. Licence and character publishing
developments. Information and early learning.
Founded 1998.

Design Eye Ltd

4th Floor, The Fitzpatrick Building,
188-194 York Way, London N7 9QP
tel 020-7700 7654 *fax* 020-7700 3890
Managing Director Jeffrey Nobbs

Packager and publisher of interactive kit books for
adults and children: arts and crafts, science, history
and fiction. Opportunities for freelances. Member
of the Quarto Group. Founded 1988.

Diagram Visual Information Ltd

195 Kentish Town Road, London NW5 2JU
tel 020-7482 3633 *fax* 020-7482 4932
email diagramvis@aol.com
Director Bruce Robertson

Research, writing, design and illustration of
reference books, supplied as film or disk.
Opportunities for freelances. Founded 1967.

Eddison Sadd Editions Ltd

St Chad's House, 148 King's Cross Road,
London WC1X 9DH
tel 020-7837 1968 *fax* 020-7837 2025
email reception@eddisonsadd.co.uk
Directors Nick Eddison, Ian Jackson, David Owen,
Elaine Partington, Charles James, Susan Cole

Illustrated non-fiction books and kits for the
international co-edition market. Broad, popular list
with emphasis on Mind, Body & Spirit and
complementary health. Founded 1982.

First Rank Publishing

51 Cuckfield Road, Hurstpierpoint, Hassocks,
West Sussex BN6 9RR
tel (01273) 834680 *fax* (01273) 831629
email byronajacobs@aol.com
Proprietor Byron Jacobs

Packager and publisher of sports, games and leisure
books. No unsolicited MSS but ideas and synopses
welcome. Payment usually fees. Also provides
editorial, production and typesetting services.
Founded 1996.

Focus Publishing

11A St Botolph's Road, Sevenoaks, Kent TN13 3AJ
tel (01732) 742456 *fax* (01732) 743381
email focus-publishing@netway.co.uk
website www.focus-publishing.co.uk
Partners Guy Croton, Caroline Watson

Illustrated non-fiction: gardening, wine and food, sex
and health, sport, aviation, DIY and crafts, transport.
Opportunities for freelances. Founded 1997.

Graham-Cameron Publishing & Illustration

The Studio, 23 Holt Road, Sheringham,
Norfolk NR26 8NB
tel (01263) 821333 *fax* (01263) 821334
email forename@graham-cameron.com
and 59 Redvers Road, Brighton BN2 4BF
tel (01273) 385890
Directors Mike Graham-Cameron, Helen Graham-
Cameron, Duncan Graham-Cameron

Educational and children's books; information
publications; sponsored publications. Illustration
agency with 37 artists. Do not send unsolicited
MSS. Founded 1984.

Hardlines Ltd

Park Street, Charlbury, Oxon OX7 3PS
tel (01608) 811255 *fax* (01608) 811442
email info@hardlines.co.uk
website www.hardlines.co.uk
Managing Director R. Hickey, *Directors* P. Wilkinson,
G. Walker

Primary, secondary academic education (geography,
science, modern languages) and co-editions (travel
guides, gardening, cookery). Multimedia (CD-Rom
programming and animations). Opportunities for
freelances. Founded 1985.

Hart McLeod Ltd

14 Greenside, Waterbeach, Cambridge CB5 9HP
tel (01223) 861495 *fax* (01223) 862902
email inhouse@hartmcleod.co.uk
website www.hartmcleod.co.uk
Directors Graham Hart, Chris McLeod

Primarily educational and general non-fiction with
particular experience of revision books, school texts,
ELT. Opportunities for freelances. Founded 1985.

The Ivy Press Ltd

The Old Candlemakers, West Street, Lewes,
East Sussex BN7 2NZ
tel (01273) 487440 *fax* (01273) 487441
email surname@ivypress.co.uk
Directors Peter Bridgewater, Jenny Manstead, Terry
Jeavons, Sophie Collins

Packagers of illustrated trade books on art, lifestyle,
popular culture, design, health and Mind, Body &
Spirit. Opportunities for authors and freelances.
Founded 1995.

John Brown Junior

The New Boathouse, 136-142 Bramley Road,
London W10 6SR
tel 020-7565 3000 *fax* 020-7565 3060
website www.jbcp.co.uk
Directors Dean Fitzpatrick (managing), Andrew
Jarvis, Paul Colbert, Jeremy Leslie

Creative development and packaging of children's
products including books, magazines, partworks,
CD-Roms and websites.

Lennard Books

Windmill Cottage, Mackerye End, Harpenden,
Herts. AL5 5DR
tel (01582) 715866
email stephenson@lennardqap.co.uk
Directors K.A.A. Stephenson, R.H. Stephenson

Commissioned projects only. Division of Lennard
Associates Ltd.

Lexus Ltd

60 Brook Street, Glasgow G40 2AB
tel 0141-556 0440 *fax* 0141-556 2202
email peterterrell@ukonline.co.uk
Director P.M. Terrell

Reference book publishing (especially bilingual
dictionaries) as contractor, packager, consultant;
translation. Founded 1980.

Lionheart Books – now incorporated into Bender Richardson White

Market House Books Ltd

2 Market House, Market Square, Aylesbury,
Bucks. HP20 1TN
tel (01296) 484911 *fax* (01296) 437073
email books@mhbref.com
website www.mhbref.com
Directors Dr Alan Isaacs, Dr John Daintith,
P.C. Sapsed

Compilation of dictionaries, encyclopedias, and
reference books. Founded 1970.

Marshall Cavendish Partworks Ltd

119 Wardour Street, London W1F 0UW
tel 020-7734 6710 *fax* 020-7734 6221
website www.marshallcavendish.co.uk
Group Editor Rebecca Fry

Cookery, crafts, gardening, do-it-yourself, history,
children's interests, general illustrated non-fiction.
Founded 1969.

Marshall Editions Ltd

The Old Brewery, 6 Blundell Street, London N7 9BH
tel 020-7700 6700 *fax* 020-7700 4191
email info@marshalleditions.com

Highly illustrated non-fiction for adults and

children, including history, health, gardening, home design, pets, natural history, popular science.

Mathew Price Ltd
The Old Glove Factory, Bristol Road, Sherborne, Dorset DT9 4HP
tel (01935) 816010 *fax* (01935) 816310
email mathewp@mathewprice.com
Chairman Mathew Price

Illustrated fiction and non-fiction children's books for all ages for the international market. Specialist in flap, pop-up, paper-engineered titles. Founded 1983.

Monkey Puzzle Media Ltd
Gissing's Farm, Fressingfield, Eye, Suffolk IP21 5SH
tel (01379) 588044 *fax* (01379) 588055
email rgc@ndirect.co.uk
Director Roger Goddard-Coote

High-quality illustrated children's and adult non-fiction for trade, institutional and mass markets worldwide. Publishers' commissions undertaken.

Orpheus Books Ltd
2 Church Green, Witney, Oxon OX28 4AW
tel (01993) 774949 *fax* (01993) 700330
email info@orpheusbooks.com
website www.orpheusbooks.com
Executive Director Nicholas Harris (editorial, design and marketing)

Children's illustrated non-fiction/reference. Opportunities for freelance artists. Founded 1992.

Pinwheel Ltd
Station House, 8-13 Swiss Terrace,
London NW6 4RR
tel 020-7586 5100 *fax* 020-7483 1999
email angela.brooksbank@pinwheel.co.uk
shaheen.bilgrami@pinwheel.co.uk
website www.pinwheel.co.uk
Art Director Angela Brooksbank, *Commissioning Editor* Shaheen Bilgrami

Novelty books for children under 5. Opportunities for freelances. Founded 1995.

Playne Books Ltd
Chapel House, Trefin, Haverfordwest,
Pembrokeshire SA62 5AU
tel (01348) 837073 *fax* (01348) 837063
email playne.books@virgin.net
Design and Production David Playne, *Editor* Gill Davies

Specialises in highly illustrated adult non-fiction and books for very young children. All stages of production undertaken from initial concept (editorial, design and manufacture) to delivery of completed books. Include sae for return of work. Founded 1987.

The Puzzle House
Ivy Cottage, Battlesea Green, Stradbroke,
Suffolk IP21 5NE
tel/fax (01379) 384656
email puzzlehouse@btinternet.com
website www.thepuzzlehouse.co.uk
Partners Roy Preston and Sue Preston

Specialist editorial service creating crossword, quiz and puzzle books for children and adults. Founded 1988.

Quarto Children's Books Ltd
3rd Floor, The Fitzpatrick Building,
188-194 York Way, London N7 9QP
tel 020-7607 3322 *fax* 020-7700 2951
Editorial Director Beck Ward, *Managing Director* Jeffrey Nobbs

Highly illustrated children's non-fiction.
Apple Press (imprint)
Leisure, domestic and craft pursuits; cookery, gardening, sport, transport, children's.

Quarto Publishing plc/Quintet Publishing Ltd
The Old Brewery, 6 Blundell Street, London N7 9BH
tel 020-7700 6700 *fax* 020-7700 4191
Publisher (Quarto) Piers Spence, *Publisher (Quintet)* Oliver Salzmann, *Directors* L.F. Orbach, R.J. Morley, M.J. Mousley

International co-editions. Founded 1976/1984.

Roger Coote Publishing
Gissing's Farm, Fressingfield, Eye, Suffolk IP21 5SH
tel (01379) 588044 *fax* (01379) 588055
email rgc@ndirect.co.uk
Director Roger Goddard-Coote

High-quality illustrated children's non-fiction titles for trade, institutional and international markets. Commissions undertaken. Freelance opportunities for editors and designers. Founded 1989.

Sadie Fields Productions Ltd
3D West Point, 36-37 Warple Way, London W3 0RG
tel 020-8996 9970 *fax* 020-8996 9977
email sales@tangobooks.co.uk
Directors Sheri Safran, David Fielder

Creates and produces international co-editions of books, plus pop-up, touch-and-feel, and other novelty books for children. Imprint: Tango Books. Founded 1983.

Savitri Books Ltd
25 Lisle Lane, Ely, Cambridgeshire CB7 4AS
tel/fax (01353) 654327
email munni@savitribooks.demon.co.uk
Director Mrinalini S. Srivastava

Packaging, publishing, design, production. Founded 1983.

Studio Cactus Ltd

13 Southgate Street, Winchester, Hants SO23 9DZ
tel (01962) 878600 *fax* (01962) 850209
email mail@studiocactus.co.uk
website www.studiocactus.co.uk
Editorial Director Damien Moore, *Art Director*
Amanda Lunn

High-quality illustrated non-fiction books for the
international market. Undertakes book
packaging/production service, from initial concept
to delivery of final electronic files. Opportunities for
freelances. Founded 1998.

Tangerine Designs Ltd

2 High Street, Freshford, Bath BA2 7WE
tel (01225) 722382 *fax* (01225) 722856
email tangerinedesigns@aol.com
website www.tangerinedesigns.co.uk
Managing Director Christine Swift

Packagers and co-edition publishers of children's
novelty books including licensed titles. Innovative
new concepts sought. Foreign rights and co-edition
agent to publishers. Freelance enquiries invited (in
writing only). Founded 2000.

The Templar Company plc

Pippbrook Mill, London Road, Dorking,
Surrey RH4 1JE
tel (01306) 876361 *fax* (01306) 889097
email info@templar.co.uk
website www.templarco.co.uk
Directors Amanda Wood, Ruth Huddleston, Elaine
Hunt

Children's gift, novelty, picture and illustrated
information books; most titles aimed at
international co-edition market. Established links
with major co-publishers in USA, Australia and
throughout Europe. Imprints: Templar Publishing,
Amazing Baby.

Toucan Books Ltd

3rd Floor, 89 Charterhouse Street,
London EC1M 6HR
tel 020-7250 3388 *fax* 020-7250 3123
Directors Robert Sackville West, Ellen Dupont,
Adam Nicolson, Jane MacAndrew

International co-editions; editorial, design and
production services. Founded 1985.

Treehouse Children's Books

2nd Floor Offices, Old Brewhouse,
Lower Charlton Trading Estate, Shepton Mallet,
Somerset BA4 5QE
tel (01749) 330529 *fax* (01749) 330544
Directors Richard Powell (editorial), Dawn Powell,
Deborah Bailey, David Bailey (sales)

Packager and co-edition publisher of novelty
preschool children's books. Opportunities for
freelance artists. Imprint of Emma Treehouse Ltd.
Founded 1989.

Tucker Slingsby Ltd

Roebuck House, 288 Upper Richmond Road West,
London SW14 7JG
tel 020-8876 6310 *fax* 020-8876 4104
email firstname@tuckerslingsby.co.uk
Directors Janet Slingsby, Del Tucker

Packager specialising in highly illustrated books and
magazines. Creation, editorial and design to disk,
film or finished copy of children's books, magazines
and general interest adult titles. Commissioned
work undertaken. Opportunities for freelances and
picture book artists. Founded 1993.

Ventura Publishing Ltd

80 Strand, London WC2R 0RL
tel 020-7010 3000 *fax* 020-7010 6707
email funwithspot@penguin.co.uk
website www.funwithspot.com
Managing Director Sally Floyer

Specialises in production of the *Spot* books by
Eric Hill.

Wordwright Books

8 St Johns Road, Saxmundham,
Suffolk IP17 1BE
tel (01728) 604204 *fax* (01728) 604029
email wordwright@clara.co.uk
Director Charles Perkins

Full packaging/production service – from concept
to delivery of film or finished copies. Produces
illustrated non-fiction. Also assesses and prepares
MSS for the US market. Publishes a small general
fiction list. Founded 1987.

Working Partners Ltd

1 Albion Place, London W6 0QT
tel 020-8748 7477 *fax* 020-8748 7450
email enquiries@workingpartnersltd.co.uk
website www.workingpartnersltd.co.uk
Chairman Ben Baglio, *Managing Director* Chris
Snowdon, *Creative Director* Rod Ritchie, *Editorial
Director* Deborah Smith

Children's and young adult fiction – series, trilogies,
single titles. Founded 1995.

Book publishers overseas

Listings are given for book publishers in Australia (below), Canada (page 196), New Zealand (page 199), South Africa (page 201) and the USA (page 203).

AUSTRALIA

Member of the Australian Publishers Association

Access Press

54 Railway Parade, Bassendean, Western Australia 6054
postal address PO Box 446, Bassendean, Western Australia 6054
tel (08) 9379 3188 *fax* (08) 9379 3199
Managing Editor Helen Weller

Australiana, poetry, children's, history, general. Commissioned works and privately financed books published and distributed. Founded 1974.

Allen & Unwin Pty Ltd*

83 Alexander Street, Crows Nest, NSW 2065
postal address PO Box 8500, St Leonards, NSW 1590
tel (02) 8425 0100 *fax* (02) 9906 2218
email info@allenandunwin.com
website www.allenandunwin.com

General trade, including fiction and children's books, academic, especially social science and history.

The Australian Council for Educational Research Ltd*

19 Prospect Hill Road, Private Bag 55, Camberwell, Victoria 3124
tel (03) 9277 5555 *fax* (03) 9277 5500
email info@acer.edu.au
website www.acerpress.com.au

Range of books and kits: for teachers, trainee teachers, parents, psychologists, counsellors, students of education, researchers.

Blackwell Publishing Asia Pty Ltd

550 Swanston Street, Carlton South, Victoria 3053
tel (03) 9347 0300 *fax* (03) 9347 5001
email info@blackwellpublishing.com
website www.blackwellpublishingasia.com
Group President Mark Robertson

Medical, healthcare, life, earth sciences, professional.

Cambridge University Press Australian Branch*

477 Williamstown Road, Port Melbourne, Victoria 3207
tel (03) 8671 1411 *fax* (03) 9676 9955

email info@cambridge.edu.au
website www.cambridge.edu.au
Director Sandra McComb

Academic, educational, reference, English as a second language.

Dominie Pty Ltd

Drama Department, 8 Cross Street, Brookvale, NSW 2100
tel (02) 9905 0201 *fax* (02) 9905 5209
email dominie@dominie.com.au
website www.dominie.com.au

Australian representatives of publishers of plays and agents for the collection of royalties for Samuel French Ltd, incorporating Hanbury Plays and Samuel French Inc., The Society of Authors, Bakers Plays of Boston, Nick Hern Books, Pioneer Drama and Dramatic Publishing.

Harcourt Australia Pty Ltd*

30-52 Smidmore Street, Marrickville, NSW 2204
tel (02) 9517 8999 *fax* (02) 9550 6007
Managing Director Fergus Hall

Novels, children's, academic, medical and scientific books. Imprints: Harcourt Brace; Holt, Rinehart and Winston; W.B. Saunders/Balliere Tindall; Saunders College; The Psychological Corporation; Academic Press, Churchill Livingstone; Morgan Kaufmann; Industrial Press; Technomic Publishing, Mosby. Established 1972.

Harcourt Education Australia*

22 Salmon Street, Port Melbourne, Victoria 3207
tel (03) 9245 7111 *fax* (03) 9245 7333
Managing Director David O'Brien

Curriculum-based textbooks and classroom resources for the states of Australia and across all syllabus areas from kindergarten to Year 12. Imprints: Rigby, Heinemann, CIS, Barrie Publishing, Heinemann Library. Division of Reed Elsevier Australia. Founded 1982.

HarperCollins Publishers (Australia) Pty Limited Group*

25-31 Ryde Road, Pymble, NSW 2073
postal address PO Box 321, Pymble, NSW 2073
tel (02) 9952 5000 *fax* (02) 9952 5555
Managing Director Brian Murray

Literary fiction and non-fiction, popular fiction,

reference, biography, autobiography, current affairs, sport, lifestyle, health/self-help, humour, true crime, travel, Australiana, history, business, gift/stationery, religion.

Hill of Content Publishing Co. Pty Ltd – see Michelle Anderson Publishing Pty Ltd

Hodder Headline Australia Pty Ltd*

Level 22, 201 Kent Street, Sydney, NSW 2000
tel (02) 8248 0800 *fax* (02) 2848 0810
email auspub@hha.com.au
website www.hha.com.au
Directors Malcolm Edwards (managing), Lisa Highton, Mary Drum, David Cocking

General, children's. No unsolicited MSS.

John Wiley & Sons Australia Ltd*

33 Park Road, Milton, Queensland 4064
tel (07) 3859 9755 *fax* (07) 3859 9715
email brisbane@johnwiley.com.au
website www.johnwiley.com.au
Managing Director P. Donoughue

Educational, technical, atlases, professional, reference, trade. Imprints: John Wiley & Sons, Jacaranda Press. Founded 1954.

Kangaroo Press – see Simon & Schuster (Australia) Pty Ltd

Lawbook Co.

PO Box 3502, Rozelle, NSW 2039
tel (02) 8587 7000 *fax* (02) 8587 7100
email service@thomson.com.au
website www.lawbookco.com.au

Law.

LexisNexis Butterworths Australia*

Tower 2, 475-495 Victoria Avenue, Chatswood, NSW 2067
postal address Level 9, Locked Bag 2222, Chatswood Delivery Centre, Chatswood, NSW 2067
tel (02) 9422 2222 *fax* (02) 9422 2444
website www.butterworths.com.au
Managing Director Murray Hamilton, *Editorial/ Deputy Managing Director* J. Broadfoot

Legal, tax and commercial. Division of Reed International Books Australia Pty Ltd.

Lonely Planet Publications*

Corner Maribyrnong and Parker Streets, Footscray 3011, Victoria
tel (03) 8379 8000 *fax* (03) 8379 8079
email talk2us@lonelyplanet.com.au
website www.lonelyplanet.com

Travel guidebooks, phrasebooks, travel literature, pictorial books, city maps; diving and snorkelling, walking, health, restaurant, pre-departure guide-books, world food, condensed pocket guides. Offices in London, Paris and Oakland, USA. Founded 1973.

Lothian Books*

132 Albert Road, South Melbourne, Victoria 3205
tel 613-9694-4900 *fax* 613-9645-0705
email books@lothian.com.au
website www.lothian.com.au
Chairman/Managing Director P. Lothian, *Director* B. Hilliard

Juveniles, health, gardening, reference, Australian history, business, sport, biography, New Age, humour, Buddhism.

Macmillan Education Australia Pty Ltd*

Melbourne office Locked Bag 1, Prahran, Victoria 3181
tel (03) 9825 1025 *fax* (03) 9825 1010
email mea@macmillan.com.au
Sydney office Level 2, St Martin's Tower, 31 Market Street, Sydney, NSW 2000
tel (02) 9285 9200 *fax* (02) 9285 9290
email measyd@macmillan.com.au
Directors Richard Charkin (chief executive – UK), Ross Gibb (executive chairman), Shane Armstrong (managing), Peter Huntley (sales), Sandra Iversen (primary publishing), Rex Parry (secondary publishing), George Smith (production), *Company Secretary/Financial Controller* Terry White

Educational books.

Melbourne University Publishing

268 Drummond Street, Carlton, Victoria 3053
postal address PO Box 1167, Carlton South, Victoria 3053
tel (03) 9342 0300 *fax* (03) 9342 0399
email mup-info@unimelb.edu.au
website www.mup.com.au
Ceo/Publisher Louise Adler

Academic, scholastic and cultural; educational textbooks and books of reference. Imprint: Miegunyah Press. Founded 1922.

Michelle Anderson Publishing Pty Ltd*

PO Box 6032, Chapel Street North, South Yarra 3141
tel (03) 9826 9028 *fax* (03) 9826 8552
email mapubl@bigpond.net.au
website www.michelleandersonpublishing.com
Directors M. Slamen, Michelle Anderson

General health and mind/body, children's. Licensed imprint of Hill of Content.

Mimosa Publications Pty Ltd – see Weldon Russell Pty Ltd

Pan Macmillan Australia Pty Ltd*

Level 18, 31 Market Street, Sydney, NSW 2000
tel (02) 9285 9100 *fax* (02) 9285 9190
email pansyd@macmillan.com.au
website www.macmillan.com.au
Directors Ross Gibb (chairman), James Fraser
(publishing), Roxarne Burns (publishing), Siv Toigo
(finance), Peter Phillips (sales), Jeannine Fowler
(publicity and marketing)

Commercial and literary fiction; children's fiction,
non-fiction and character products; non-fiction;
sport.

Penguin Books Australia Ltd*

250 Camberwell Road, Camberwell,
Victoria 3124
postal address PO Box 701, Hawthorn,
Victoria 3122
tel (03) 9811 2400 *fax* (03) 9811 2620
Ceo P.J. Field, *Publishing Director* R.P. Sessions

Fiction, general non-fiction, current affairs,
sociology, economics, environmental, travel guides,
anthropology, politics, children's, health, cookery,
gardening, pictorial and general books relating to
Australia. Imprints: Penguin Books, Viking.
Founded 1946.

Random House Australia Pty Ltd*

20 Alfred Street, Milsons Point,
NSW 2061
tel (02) 9954 9966 *fax* (02) 9954 4562
email random@randomhouse.com.au
website www.randomhouse.com.au
Managing Director Margaret Seale, *Coo* Andrew
Davis, *Head of Publishing, Random House* Jane
Palfreyman, *Head of Publishing, Bantam Doubleday*
Fiona Henderson, *Children's Commissioning Editor*
Eva Mills, *Illustrated Publisher* Steve Barnett, *Sales &
Marketing Director* Carol Davidson, *Commercial
Manager* Daren Chan, *Rights Manager* Nerrilee Weir

General fiction and non-fiction; children's,
illustrated. MSS submissions – for Random House
and Transworld Publishing, unsolicited non-fiction
accepted, unbound in hard copy addressed to
Submissions Editor. Fiction submissions are only
accepted from previously published authors, or
authors represented by an agent or accompanied by
a report from an accredited assessment service.
Imprints: Arrow, Avon, Ballantine, Bantam, Black
Swan, Broadway, Century, Chatto & Windus, Corgi,
Crown, Dell, Doubleday, Ebury, Fodor, Heinemann,
Hutchinson, Jonathan Cape, Knopf, Mammoth UK,
Minerva, Pantheon, Pavilion, Pimlico, Random
House, Red Fox, Rider, Vermillion, Vintage, Virgin.
Agencies: BBC Worldwide. Subsidiary of
Bertelsmann AG.

Samuel French Ltd – see Dominie Pty Ltd

Scholastic Australia Pty Ltd*

PO Box 579, Gosford, NSW 2250
tel (02) 4328 3555 *fax* (02) 4323 3827
website www.scholastic.com.au
Managing Director Ken Jolly

Children's fiction/non-fiction; educational materials
for elementary schools, teacher reference. Founded
1968.

Simon & Schuster (Australia) Pty Ltd*

20 Barcoo Street, East Roseville,
NSW 2069
postal address PO Box 507, East Roseville,
NSW 2069
tel (02) 9415 9900 *fax* (02) 9417 4292
Managing Director/Publisher Jon Attenborough

General non-fiction including anthropology, child
care, hobbies, house and home, how-to, craft,
biography, motivation, management, outdoor
recreation, sport, travel. Imprints: Simon & Schuster
Australia, Kangaroo Press.

Thomson Learning Australia*

102 Dodds Street, Southbank,
Victoria 3006
tel (03) 9685 4111 *fax* (03) 9685 4199
email customerservice@thomsonlearning.com.au
website www.thomsonlearning.com.au

Educational books.

Transworld Publishers (Aust) Pty Ltd – merged with Random House Australia Pty Ltd

University of Queensland Press

PO Box 6042, St Lucia,
Queensland 4067
tel (07) 3365 2127 *fax* (07) 3365 7579
email uqp@uqp.uq.edu.au
website www.uqp.uq.edu.au
General Manager L.C. Muller

Scholarly works, tertiary texts, indigenous
Australian writing, Australian fiction, young adult
fiction, poetry, history, general interest. Founded
1948.

University of Western Australia Press*

UWA, 35 Stirling Hwy, Crawley 6009,
Western Australia
tel (08) 9380 3670 *fax* (08) 9380 1027
email uwap@cyllene.uwa.edu.au
website www.uwapress.uwa.edu.au

Natural history, history, maritime history, critical
studies, women's studies, general non-fiction,
contemporary issues, children's picture books,
young fiction. Imprints: Cygnet Books, Staples,
Tuart House, UWA Press. Founded 1954.

UNSW Press*

University of New South Wales,
UNSW Sydney NSW 2052
tel (02) 9664 0900 *fax* (02) 9664 5420
email info.press@unsw.edu.au
website www.unswpress.com.au
Managing Director Dr Robin Derricourt, *Publishing Manager* John Elliot

Science, ecology, natural history, botany and horticulture; cultural studies, politics, history; general reference; tertiary textbooks. Founded 1962.

Viking – see Penguin Books Australia Ltd

Wild & Woolley Pty Ltd*

PO Box 41, Glebe, NSW 2037
tel (02) 9692 0166 *fax* (02) 9552 4320
website www.fastbooks.com.au
Director Pat Woolley

Offers short-run paperback printing, promotion, marketing and distribution for self-publishing writers. Founded 1974.

Wrightbooks Pty Ltd – acquired by John Wiley & Sons Australia Ltd*

CANADA

*Member of the Canadian Publishers' Council
†Member of the Association of Canadian Publishers

Addison-Wesley Canada – merged with Prentice Hall Canada to form Pearson Education Canada

Annick Press Ltd†

15 Patricia Avenue, Toronto, Ontario M2M 1H9
tel 416-221-4802 *fax* 416-221-8400
email annick@annickpress.com
website www.annickpress.com
Co-editors Rick Wilks, Colleen MacMillan

Preschool to juvenile fiction and non-fiction. Founded 1975.

Butterworths Canada Ltd – see Lexis Nexis Canada Inc.

CDG Books Canada Inc.

99 Yorkville Avenue, Suite 400, Toronto, Ontario M5R 3K5
tel 416-963-8830 *fax* 416-923-4821

Trade book publishers. Founded 1905.

The Charlton Press

PO Box 820, Station Willowdale B, North York, Ontario M2K 2R1
tel 416-488-1418 *fax* 416-488-4656
email chpress@charltonpress.com
website www.charltonpress.com
President W.K. Cross

Collectibles, Numismatics, Sportscard price catalogues. Founded 1952.

Doubleday Canada*

1 Toronto Street, Suite 300, Toronto, Ontario M5C 2V6
tel 416-364-4449 *fax* 416-957-1587
website www.randomhouse.ca
Chairman John Neale, *Publisher* Maya Mavjee

General trade non-fiction: current affairs, politics; fiction; children's illustrated. Division of **Random House of Canada Ltd.** Founded 1942.

Douglas & McIntyre Ltd†

2323 Quebec Street, Suite 201, Vancouver, BC V5T 4S7
tel 604-254-7191 *fax* 604-254-9099
email dm@douglas-mcintyre.com

General list, including Greystone Books imprint: Canadian biography, art and architecture, natural history, history, native studies, Canadian fiction. Children's division (Groundwood Books) specialises in fiction and illustrated flats. No unsolicited MSS. Founded 1964.

ECW Press Ltd†

2120 Queen Street E, Suite 200, Toronto,
Ontario M4E 1E2
tel 416-694-3348 *fax* 416-698-9906
email info@ecwpress.com
website www.ecwpress.com
President Jack David, *Secretary-Treasurer* Robert Lecker

Popular culture, sports, humour, general trade books, biographies, guidebooks. Founded 1979.

Fitzhenry & Whiteside Ltd

195 Allstate Parkway, Markham,
Ontario L3R 4T8
tel 905-477-9700 *fax* 905-477-9179
email godwit@fitzhenry.ca
tel 1-800-387-9776 (toll free)
fax 1-800-260-9777 (toll free)
Director Sharon Fitzhenry

Trade, educational, children's books. Founded 1966.

Gage Learning Corporation†

164 Commander Boulevard, Toronto,
Ontario M1S 3C7
tel 416-293-8141 *fax* 416-293-9009

Publishers of elementary and secondary school textbooks; professional and reference materials. Founded 1844.

Gold Eagle Books – see Harlequin Enterprises Ltd

Harcourt Canada Ltd*

55 Horner Avenue, Toronto,
Ontario M8Z 4X6
tel 416-255-4491 *fax* 416-255-4046
email firstname_lastname@harcourt.com
website www.harcourtcanada.com
President Wendy Cochran

Educational materials from K–Grade 12, testing and assessment. Imprints: Harcourt Religion (formerly Brown-ROA), Harcourt Brace & Company, Holt, Rinehart and Winston, MeadowBrook Press, The Psychological Corporation, Therapy Skill Builders/Communications Skill Builders. Founded 1922.

Harlequin Enterprises Ltd*

225 Duncan Mill Road, Don Mills,
Ontario M3B 3K9
tel 416-445-5860 *fax* 416-445-8655
website www.eharlequin.com
President & Publisher Donna Hayes, *Vice President, Editorial* Isabel Swift

Women's fiction, romance, action adventure, mystery. Founded 1949.

Gold Eagle Books (imprint)
Editorial Director Randall Toye

Series action adventure fiction.

Harlequin Books (imprint)
Editorial Director Tara Gavin

Contemporary and historical romance fiction in series.

Mira Books (imprint)
Editorial Director Dianne Moggy

Women's fiction: contemporary and historical dramas, family sagas, romantic suspense and relationship novels.

Red Dress Ink (imprint)
Editorial Director Tara Gavin

Women's fiction for the 20-somethings.

Silhouette Books (imprint)
Editorial Director Tara Gavin

Contemporary romance fiction in series.

Steeple Hill (imprint)
Editorial Director Tara Gavin

Contemporary inspirational romantic fiction in series.

Worldwide Mystery (imprint)
Editorial Director Randall Toye

Contemporary mystery fiction. Reprints only.

HarperCollins Publishers Ltd*

Suite 2900, Hazelton Lanes,
55 Avenue Road, Toronto,
Ontario M5R 3L2
tel 416-975-9334 *fax* 416-975-9884
website www.harpercanada.com
President David Kent

Publishers of literary fiction and non-fiction, business books, history, politics, biography, spiritual and children's books. Founded 1989.

Irwin Publishing Ltd

325 Humber College Blvd, Toronto,
Ontario M9W 7C3
tel 416-798-0424 *fax* 416-798-1384
email irwin@irwin-pub.com
President Brian O'Donnell, *Chairman* Jack Stoddart

Educational books at the elementary, high school and college levels.

Key Porter Books Ltd†

70 The Esplanade, 3rd Floor, Toronto,
Ontario M5E 1R2
tel 416-862-7777 *fax* 416-862-2304
email aporter@keyporter.com
website www.keyporter.com
Publisher/Ceo Anna Porter, *President* Diane Davy, *Editor-in-Chief* Clare McKeon

Fiction, nature, history, Canadian politics, conservation, humour, biography, autobiography, health, children's books. Founded 1981.

Kids Can Press Ltd†
29 Birch Avenue, Toronto, Ontario M4V 1E2
tel 416-925-5437 *fax* 416-960-5437
email info@kidscan.com
Publisher Valerie Hussey
Juvenile/young adult books.

Knopf Canada – see Random House of Canada Ltd*

Lexis Nexis Canada Inc.
75 Clegg Road, Markham, Ontario L6G 1A1
tel 905-479-2665 *fax* 905-479-2826
email info@lexisnexis.ca

Law and accountancy. Division of Reed Elsevier plc.

Lone Pine Publishing
10145-81 Avenue, Edmonton, Alberta T6E 1W9
tel 780-433-9333 *fax* 780-433-9646
website www.lonepinepublishing.com
Chairman Grant Kennedy, *President* Shane Kennedy

Natural history, recreation and wildlife guidebooks, gardening, popular history. Founded 1980.

McClelland & Stewart Ltd†
481 University Avenue, Suite 900, Toronto,
Ontario M5G 2E9
tel 416-598-1114 *fax* 416-598-7764
website www.mcclelland.com
Chairman Avie Bennett, *President/Publisher* Douglas M. Gibson

General. Founded 1906.

McGill-Queen's University Press†
3430 McTavish Street, Montreal, Quebec H3A 1X9
tel 514-398-3750 *fax* 514-398-4333
email mqup@post.queensu.ca
website www.mqup.ca
Queen's University, Kingston, Ontario K7L 3N6
tel 613-533-2155 *fax* 613-533-6822
email mqup@qucdn.queensu.ca

Academic, non-fiction, poetry. Founded 1969.

McGraw-Hill Ryerson Ltd*
300 Water Street, Whitby, Ontario L1N 9B6
tel 905-430-5000 *fax* 905-430-5020
website www.mcgrawhill.ca

Educational and trade books.

Mira Books – see Harlequin Enterprises Ltd

Nelson*
(formerly Nelson Thomson Learning)
1120 Birchmount Road, Toronto, Ontario M1K 5G4
tel 416-752-9100 *fax* 416-752-9646
President/Ceo George W. Bergquist, *Senior Vice President, Finance/Cfo* Lesley Gouldie, *Senior Vice President, School* Greg Pilon, *Vice President, Higher*

Education Ron Kelly, *Vice President, Media Services* Susan Cline, *Vice President, Operations* Ed Berman, *Vice President, Human Resources* Marlene Nyilassy, *Editorial Director, Higher Education* Evelyn Veitch, *Director of Publishing, School* David Steele, *Director of Marketing, Higher Education* James Rozsa, *Director of Sales, School* James Reeve, *Director of Information Systems & Technology* Bruce Sharron

Educational publishing: school (K–12), college and university, career education, measurement and guidance, professional and reference, ESL titles. Founded 1914.

Oberon Press
400-350 Sparks Street, Suite 400, Ottawa,
Ontario K1R 7S8
tel/fax 613-238-3275
website www3.sympatico.ca.oberon

General.

Oxford University Press, Canada*
70 Wynford Drive, Don Mills, Ontario M3C 1J9
tel 416-441-2941 *fax* 416-444-0427
website www.oup.com/ca
President Joanna Gertler

General, educational and academic.

Pearson Education Canada*
(formerly Prentice Hall Canada and Addison-Wesley Canada)
26 Prince Andrew Place, Toronto,
Ontario M3C 2T8
tel 416-447-5101 *fax* 416-443-0948
website www.pearsoned.ca
President Tony Vander Woude

Academic, technical, educational, children's and adult, trade.

Penguin Books Canada Ltd*
10 Alcorn Avenue, Suite 300, Toronto,
Ontario M4V 3B2
tel 416-925-2249 *fax* 416-925-0068
website www.penguin.ca
President Ed Carson

Literary fiction, memoir, non-fiction (history, business, current events). Founded 1974.

Pippin Publishing Corporation
Suite 232, 85 Ellesmere Road, Toronto,
Ontario M1R 4B9
tel 416-510-2918 *fax* 416-510-3359
email jld@pippinpub.com
website www.pippinpub.com
President/Editorial Director Jonathan Lovat Dickson

ESL/EFL, teacher reference, adult basic education, school texts (all subjects), general trade (non-fiction).

Random House of Canada Ltd*
One Toronto Street, Suite 300, Toronto,
Ontario M5C 2V6
tel 416-364 4449 *fax* 416-364-6863
website www.randomhouse.com
Chairman John Neale
Imprints: Ballantine Canada, Doubleday Canada,
Knopf Canada, Random House Canada, Seal Books,
Vintage Canada. Subsidiary of Bertelsmann AG.
Founded 1944.

Knopf Canada (imprint/division)
Literary fiction and non-fiction.

Red Dress Ink – see Harlequin Enterprises Ltd

Silhouette Books – see Harlequin Enterprises Ltd

Steeple Hill – see Harlequin Enterprises Ltd

Stoddart Publishing Co. Ltd
895 Don Mills Road, 400-2 Park Centre, Toronto,
Ontario M3C 1W3
tel 416-445-3333 *fax* 416-445-5967
email cservice@genpub.com
website www.stoddartpub.com
Chairman Jack E. Stoddart
Fiction and non-fiction. Founded 1984.

Tundra Books Inc.†
481 University Avenue, Suite 900, Toronto,
Ontario M5G 2E9
tel 416-598-4786 *fax* 416-598-0247
High quality children's picture books.

University of Toronto Press Inc.†
10 St Mary Street, Suite 700, Toronto,
Ontario M4Y 2W8
tel 416-978-2239 *fax* 416-978-4738
email publishing@utpress.utoronto.ca
website www.utpress.utoronto.ca
President/Publisher George L. Meadows

Worldwide Mystery – see Harlequin Enterprises Ltd

NEW ZEALAND
**Member of the New Zealand Book
Publishers' Association*

Auckland University Press*
University of Auckland, Private Bag 92019, Auckland
tel (09) 373-7528 *fax* (09) 373-7465
email aup@auckland.ac.nz
website www.auckland.ac.nz/aup
Director Elizabeth Caffin

NZ history, NZ poetry, Maori and Pacific studies,
politics, sociology, literary criticism, art history,
biography, media studies, women's studies. Founded
1966.

Bush Press Communications Ltd
4 Bayview Road, Hauraki Corner, Takapuna
postal address PO Box 33-029, Takapuna,
Auckland 1309
tel/fax (09) 486-2667
email bush.press@clear.net.nz
Governing Director/Publisher Gordon Ell ONZM

NZ non-fiction, particularly outdoor, nature, travel,
architecture, crafts, Maori, popular history;
children's non-fiction. Founded 1979.

The Caxton Press
113 Victoria Street, Christchurch
postal address PO Box 25-088, Christchurch
tel (03) 366-8516 *fax* (03) 365-7840
Director E.B. Bascand
Biography, history, natural history, travel,
gardening. Founded 1935.

David Bateman Ltd*
30 Tarndale Grove, Bush Road, Albany, Auckland
postal address PO Box 100242, North Shore Mail
Centre, Auckland 1330
tel (09) 415-7664 *fax* (09) 415-8892
email bateman@bateman.co.nz
website www.bateman.co.nz
Chairman/Publisher David L. Bateman, *Directors*
Janet Bateman, Paul Bateman (joint managing),
Paul Parkinson (joint managing)

Natural history, gardening, encyclopedias, sport, art,
cookery, historical, juvenile, travel, motoring,
maritime history, business, art, lifestyle. Founded
1979.

Dunmore Press Ltd*
PO Box 5115, Palmerston North
tel (06) 358-7169 *fax* (06) 357-9242
email dunmore@xtra.co.nz
website www.dunmore.co.nz
Directors Murray Gatenby, Sharmian Firth

Education, history, sociology, business studies,
general non-fiction. Founded 1970.

Godwit Publishing Ltd – acquired by Random House New Zealand Ltd

HarperCollins Publishers (New Zealand) Ltd
PO Box 1, Auckland
tel (09) 443-9400 *fax* (09) 443-9403
website www.harpercollins.co.nz
Publishers of general literature, non-fiction, reference, children's.

Hodder Moa Beckett Publishers Ltd
PO Box 100-749, North Shore Mail Centre, Auckland 1330
tel (09) 478-1000 *fax* (09) 478-1010
email admin@hoddermoa.co.nz
Managing Director Kevin Chapman, *Executive Editor* Warren Adler
Sport, gardening, cooking, travel, atlases, general.

LexisNexis NZ Ltd*
205-207 Victoria Street, Wellington 1
postal address PO Box 472, Wellington 1
tel (04) 385-1479 *fax* (04) 385-1598
email Russell.Gray@lexisnexis.co.nz
website www.lexisnexis.co.nz
Managing Director Russell Gray
Law, business, academic.

Mallinson Rendel Publishers Ltd
Level 5, 15 Courteny Place, PO Box 9409, Wellington
tel (04) 802-5012 *fax* (04) 802-5013
email publisher@mallinsonrendel.co.nz
Director Ann Mallinson
Children's books. Founded 1980.

Nelson Price Milburn Ltd
1 Te Puni Street, Petone
postal addres PO Box 38-945, Wellington Mail Centre, Wellington
tel (04) 568-7179 *fax* (04) 568-2115
email npm@xtra.co.nz
Children's fiction, primary school texts, especially school readers and maths, secondary educational.

New Zealand Council for Educational Research*
Box 3237, Education House,
178-182 Willis Street,
Wellington 1
tel (04) 384-7939 *fax* (04) 384-7933
email info@nzcer.org.nz
website www.nzcer.org.nz
Director Robyn Baker, *Publisher* Bev Webber
Education, including educational policy and institutions, early childhood education, educational achievement tests, Maori education, curriculum and assessment, etc. Founded 1934.

Pearson Education New Zealand Ltd*
Private Bag 102908, North Shore Mail Centre, Glenfield, Auckland 10
tel (09) 444-4968 *fax* (09) 444-4957
email rosemary.stagg@pearsoned.co.nz
NZ educational books.

Random House New Zealand Ltd
Private Bag 102950, North Shore Mail Centre, Auckland 10
tel (09) 444-7197 *fax* (09) 444-7524
Managing Director M. Moynahan
Fiction, general non-fiction, gardening, cooking, art, business, health. Subsidiary of Bertelsmann AG. Founded 1977.

Reed Publishing (New Zealand) Ltd*
(incorporating Reed Consumer Books and Heinemann Education)
39 Rawene Road, Private Bag 34901, Birkenhead, Auckland 10
tel (09) 441 2960 *fax* (09) 480-4999
Chairman John Philbin, *Managing Director* Alan Smith
NZ literature, specialist and general titles, primary, secondary and tertiary textbooks. Imprints: BBC, Egmont, Brimax, Butterworth-Heinemann, CIS Heinemann, Conran, Philip's, Ginn UK, Heinemann Australia, Heinemann NZ, Heinemann UK, Heinemann USA, Huia Jasons, Kyle Cathie, Longacre, Mammoth, Mitchell Beazley, Quadrille, Reed NZ, Rigby Australia, Rigby USA, Virgin Publishing.

Scholastic New Zealand Ltd
21 Lady Ruby Drive, East Tamaki, Auckland
postal address Private Bag 94407, Greenmount, Auckland
tel (09) 274-8112 *fax* (09) 274-8114
General Manager David Peagram, *Publishing Manager* Christine Dale
Children's books. Founded 1962.

Shortland Publications
10 Cawley Street, Ellerslie, Auckland 5
tel (09) 526-6200 *fax* (09) 526-4448
Submissions Louise Williams, Shortland Publications, Private Bag 11904, Ellerslie, Auckland 5
email Louise_Williams@mcgraw-hill.com
International primary reading market: potential authors should familiarise themselves with Shortland products. Currently seeking submissions for: *Emergent/early and fluency reading material* – 8–24pp, stories need to be simple and to feature supports for the child learning to read, e.g. repetition of vocabulary and sentence structure.
Short fiction (ages 9–12) – MSS up to 1500 words

long. Looking for fresh ideas. *Cocky Circle* – 24pp read-to books for 2–6 year-olds. Stories must lend themselves to a different illustration on each page. Fantasy and humour are always good sellers. All submissions should cater for an international market; include sae. Founded 1984.

University of Otago Press
University of Otago, PO Box 56, Dunedin
tel/fax (03) 479-8807 (03) 479-8385
email university.press@otago.ac.nz
Managing Editor Wendy Harrex
Student texts and scholarly works in many disciplines and general books, including Maori and women's studies, natural history and environmental studies, health and fiction. Also publishes journals including *Landfall* and the *Women's Studies Journal*. Founded 1958.

Victoria University Press*
Victoria University of Wellington, PO Box 600, Wellington
tel (04) 463-6580 *fax* (04) 463-6581
email victoria-press@vuw.ac.nz
website www.vuw.ac.nz/vup
Publisher Fergus Barrowman
Academic, scholarly books on NZ history, sociology, law; Maori language; fiction, plays, poetry. Founded 1974.

Viking Sevenseas Ltd
201A Rosetta Road, Raumati
tel/fax (04) 902-8240
email vikings@paradise.net.nz
Managing Director M.B. Riley
Natural history books on New Zealand only.

SOUTH AFRICA
*Member of the Publishers' Association of South Africa

Ad Donker (Pty) Ltd – see Jonathan Ball Publishers (Pty) Ltd

Cambridge University Press*
Dock House, Portswood Ridge, Victoria & Alfred Waterfront, Cape Town 8001
tel (021) 419-8414
email information@cup.co.za
website www.cambridge.org
Director Hanri Pieterse
African Branch of CUP, responsible for sub-Saharan Africa and English-speaking Caribbean. Publishes distance learning material and textbooks for various African countries, as well as primary reading materials in 28 local African languages.

David Philip Publishers (Pty) Ltd*
PO Box 23408, Claremont 7735, Western Cape
tel (21) 6744-136 *fax* (21) 6743-358
email information@dpp.co.za
website www.dpp.co.za
Managing & Marketing Director Bridget Impey,
Publishing Director Russell Martin, *Non-executive Directors* David Philip, Marie Philip, Wilmot James, G.J. Gerwel, Njabulo Ndebele, Steve Kromberg, Alec Davis, Mike Tissong, Mike Siluma, Zwelakhe Sisulu
Academic, history, social sciences, politics, biography, belles-lettres, reference books, fiction, cartoons, educationa. Founded 1971.

Delta Books – see Jonathan Ball Publishers (Pty) Ltd

Jacklin Enterprises (Pty) Ltd
PO Box 521, Parklands 2121
tel (011) 265-4200 *fax* (011) 314-2984
email mjacklin@jacklin.co.za
Managing Director M.A.C. Jacklin
Children's fiction and non-fiction; Afrikaans large print books. Subjects include aviation, natural history, romance, general science, technology and transportation. Imprints: Mike Jacklin, Kennis Onbeperk, Daan Retief.

Jonathan Ball Publishers (Pty) Ltd
10-14 Watkins Street, Denver Ext. 4, Johannesburg
postal address Box 33977, Jeppestown 2043
tel (011) 622-2900 *fax* (011) 622-3553
Ad Donker (imprint)
Africana, literature, history, academic.
Jonathan Ball (imprint)
General publications, reference books, South African business, history, politics.

Delta Books (imprint)
General South African trade non-fiction.

Juta & Company Ltd*
PO Box 14373, Kenwyn 7790, Cape Town
tel (021) 797-5101 *fax* (021) 762-0248
email books@juta.co.za
website www.juta.co.za
Ceo Rory Wilson

School, academic, professional, law and electronic.
Founded 1853.

Maskew Miller Longman (Pty) Ltd*
c/o Forest Drive & Logan Way, Pinelands 7405,
Cape Town
postal address PO Box 396, Cape Town 8000
tel (021) 531-7750 *fax* (021) 531-4877
email administrator@mml.co.za
website www.mml.co.za
Educational and general publishers.

Oxford University Press Southern Africa*
Vasco Boulevard, N1 City, Cape Town 7460
postal address PO Box 12119, N1 City,
Cape Town 7463
tel (021) 595-4400 *fax* (021) 595-4430
email oxford.za@oup.com
Managing Director Kate McCallum

Ravan Press
c/o Macmillan SA, Old Trafford 4,
Isle of Houghton, Houghton 2198
postal address PO Box 32484,
Braamfontein 2017
tel (011) 484-0916 *fax* (011) 484-3129

South African studies: history, politics, social
studies; fiction, literature, biography. Founded 1972.

Shuter and Shooter Publishers (Pty) Ltd*
230 Church Street, Pietermaritzburg 3201,
KwaZulu-Natal
postal address PO Box 109, Pietermaritzburg 3200,
KwaZulu-Natal
tel (033) 3946-830/3948-881 *fax* (033) 3427-419
email dryder@shuter.co.za
website www.shuter.co.za
Publishing Director D.F. Ryder

Primary and secondary educational, science,
biology, history, maths, geography, English,
Afrikaans, biblical studies, music, teacher training,
agriculture, accounting, early childhood,
dictionaries, African languages. Founded 1925.

Struik Publishers (Pty) Ltd
Cornelius Struik House, 80 McKenzie Street,
Cape Town 8001
tel (021) 462-4360 *fax* (021) 462-4379
Managing Director Steve Connolly

General illustrated non-fiction. Division of New
Holland Publishing (Pty) Ltd.

Unisa Press*
PO Box 392, Pretoria 0003
tel (012) 429-3051 *fax* (012) 429-3221
email unisa-press@unisa.ac.za
website www.unisa.ac.za/dept/press/ index.html
Head Phoebe Van Der Walt

Theology and all academic disciplines. Publishers of
University of South Africa. Imprint: UNISA.
Founded 1957.

University of Natal Press*
Private Bag X01, Scottsville,
3209 KwaZulu-Natal
tel (033) 260 5226 *fax* (33) 260 5801
email books@nu.ac.za
website www.unpress.co.za
Publisher Glenn Cowley

Southern African social, political, economic and
military history, gender, natural sciences, African
poetry and literature, genealogy, education,
biography. Founded 1948.

Van Schaik Publishers*
PO Box 12681, Hatfield, Pretoria 0028
tel (012) 342-2765 *fax* (012) 430-3563
email vanschaik@vanschaiknet.com
website www.vanschaiknet.com

Publishers of school books in English, Afrikaans
and African languages. Specialists in textbooks and
books for the corporate market. Founded 1914.

Witwatersrand University Press*
PO Wits, Johannesburg 2050
tel (011) 484-5910 *fax* (011) 484-5971
email klippv@wup.wits.ac.za
website http://witspress.wits.ac.za

Zebra Press
80 McKenzie Street Gardens, Cape Town 8001
postal address PO Box 1144, Cape Town 8000
tel (021) 462-4360 *fax* (021) 462-4379
email moniquev@zebrapress.co.za
website www.zebrapress.co.za

Business, contemporary, humour. Imprint of Struik
Publishers. Division of New Holland Publishing
(South Africa) (Pty) Ltd, a member of Johnnic
Publishing Ltd.

USA

Member of the Association of American Publishers Inc.

Abbeville Press

116 West 23rd Street, Suite 500, New York, NY 10011
tel 646-375-2039 *fax* 646-375-2040
website www.abbeville.com
Publisher/President Robert Abrams

Art and illustrated books. Founded 1977.

Abingdon Press

PO Box 801, Nashville, TN 37202-0801
tel 615-749-6404 *fax* 615-749-6512
website www.abingdon.org
Senior Vice President, Publishing Harriett Jane Olson

General interest, professional, academic and reference – primarily directed to the religious market.

Applause Theatre and Cinema Book Publishers

151 West 46th Street, 8th Floor, New York, NY 10036
tel 212-575-9265 *fax* 646-562-5852
website www.applausebooks.com
Ceo John Cerullo

Performing arts. Founded 1980.

Arcade Publishing

141 Fifth Avenue, New York, NY 10010
tel 212-475-2633 *fax* 212-353-8148
email arcadeinfo@arcadepub.com
website www.arcadepub.com
President/Editor-in-Chief Richard Seaver,
Publisher/Marketing Director Jeannette Seaver,
General Manager/Executive Editor Cal Barksdale,
Editors Greg Comer, Darcy Falkenhagen, *Publicity* Casey Ebro

General trade, including adult hard cover and paperbacks. No unsolicited MSS.

Atlantic Monthly Press – see Grove/Atlantic Inc.

Avery – see The Putnam Publishing Group

Avon Books – see HarperCollins Publishers

The Ballantine Publishing Group*

1540 Broadway, New York, NY 10036
tel 212-782-9000 *fax* 212-302-7985
website www.randomhouse.com
President/Publisher Gina Centrello

Trade and mass-market general fiction, science fiction and non-fiction. Imprints: Ballantine Books, Ballantine Wellspring, Del Rey, Fawcett, Ivy, Library of Contemporary Thought, One World. Division of **Random House Inc.**

Bantam Dell Publishing Group*

1540 Broadway, New York, NY 10036
tel 212-782-9000 *fax* 212-302-7985
website www.randomhouse.com
President/Publisher Irwyn Applebaum

General fiction and non-fiction. Imprints: Bantam Hardcover, Bantam Mass Market, Bantam Trade Paperback, Crimeline, Delacorte Press, Dell, Delta, Dial Press, Domain, DTP, Fanfare, Island, Spectra. Division of **Random House Inc.**

Barron's Educational Series Inc.

250 Wireless Boulevard, Hauppage, NY 11788
tel 516-434-3311 *fax* 516-434-3723
website www.barronseduc.com
Chairman/Ceo Manuel H. Barron,
President/Publisher Ellen Sibley

Test preparation, juvenile, cookbooks, Mind, Body & Spirit, crafts, business, pets, gardening, family and health, art, study guides, school guides. Founded 1941.

Beacon Press

25 Beacon Street, Boston, MA 02108
tel 617-742-2110 *fax* 617-723-3097
website www.beacon.org
Director Helene Atwan

General non-fiction in fields of religion, ethics, philosophy, current affairs, gender studies, environmental concerns, African–American studies, anthropology and women's studies, nature.

Berkley Publishing Group

375 Hudson Street, New York, NY 10014
tel 212-366-2000 *fax* 212-366-2666
email online@penguinputnam.com
website www.penguinputnam.com
President, Mass Market Paperbacks Leslie Gelbman

Fiction and general non-fiction. Imprints: Ace Books, Berkley Books, Boulevard, Diamond Books, HP Books, Jam, Jove, Perigee, Prime Crime, Riverhead Books (trade paperback). Division of **Penguin Putnam Inc.** Founded 1954.

Berkley Books (imprint)
President and Publisher Leslie Gelbman

Fiction and general non-fiction for adults. Imprints: Ace Books, Berkley Books, Boulevard Books, Diamond Books, Jam, Jove, Prime Crime. Founded 1954.

HP Books (imprint)
Editorial Director, Automotive Michael Lutfy

Non-fiction trade paperbacks. Founded 1964.

Perigee Books (imprint)
Vice President/Publisher John Duff

Non-fiction paperbacks: psychology, spirituality, reference, etc. Founded 1980.

Riverhead Books (Trade Paperback)
Editor Christopher Knutsen

Fiction and general non-fiction for adults. Founded 1995.

Betterway Books – see Writer's Digest Books

Bloomsbury USA

Suite 300, 175 Fifth Avenue, New York, NY 10010
tel 212-674-5151 *fax* 212-780-0115
Publisher and Editorial Director, Adult Books Karen Rinaldi, *Deputy Editorial Director, Adult Books* Colin Dickerman, *Editorial Director, Children's Books* Victoria Arms, *Director of Marketing and Publicity (Children's)* Kate Kubert

Literary fiction, general non-fiction, children's books. Branch of **Bloomsbury UK**. Founded 1998.

BlueHen – see The Putnam Publishing Group

Boyds Mills Press

815 Church Street, Honesdale, PA 18431
tel 570-253-1164 *fax* 570-253-0179
website www.boydsmillpress.com
Publisher Kent Brown Jr, *President* Clay Winters, *Editorial Director* Larry Rosler, *Art Director* Tim Gillner

Fiction, non-fiction, and poetry trade books for children. Founded 1990.

Burford Books

PO Box 388, Short Hills, NJ 07078
tel 973-258-0960 *fax* 973-258-0113
email info@burfordbooks.com
website www.burfordbooks.com
President Peter Burford

Outdoor activities: golf, sports, fitness, nature, travel. Founded 1997.

Cambridge University Press*

(North American Branch)
40 West 20th Street, New York, NY 10011
tel 212-924-3900 *fax* 212-691-3239
website www.cambridge.org
Director Richard L. Ziemacki

Candlewick Press

2067 Massachusetts Avenue, Cambridge, MA 02140
tel 617-661-3330 *fax* 617-661-0565
website www.candlewick.com
Editorial Director/Associate Publisher Liz Bicknell, *Executive Editor* Mary Lee Donovan, *Editorial Director (novelty)* Joan Powers, *Editor-at-Large* Amy Ehrlich

Children's books 6 months–14 years: board books, picture books, novels, non-fiction, novelty books. Submit material through a literary agent. Subsidiary of **Walker Books Ltd**, UK. Founded 1991.

Carroll & Graf Publishers Inc.

161 William Street, 16th Floor, New York, NY 10038
tel 646-375-2570 *fax* 646-375-2571
website www.carrollandgraf.com
President/Publisher Herman Graf, *Subrights* Martine Ballen, *Foreign Rights* Lena Dixon

Mystery and crime, popular fiction, history, biography, literature, literary fiction. Founded 1983.

Chronicle Books

85 Second Street, 6th Floor, San Francisco, CA 94105
tel 415-537-4200 *fax* 415-537-4460
website www.chroniclebooks.com
Chairman and Ceo Nion McEvoy, *Publisher* Jack Jensen, *Associate Publishers* Christine Carswell, Debra Laude, Victoria Rock

Cooking, art, fiction, general, children's, gift, new media, gardening, regional, nature. Founded 1967.

Coffee House Press

27 N 4th Street, Suite 400, Minneapolis, MN 55401
tel 612-338-0125 *fax* 612-338-4004
UK Representation Nancy Green Madia
tel 212-864-0425 *fax* 212-316-2121

Literary fiction and poetry; collectors' editions. Founded 1984.

Columbia University Press*

61 West 62nd Street, New York, NY 10023
tel 212-459-0600 *fax* 212-459-3677
website www.columbia.edu/cu/cup
UK Office 1 Oldlands Way, Bognor Regis, West Sussex PO22 9SA
tel (0243) 842165 *fax* (0243) 842167
Editorial Director Jennifer Crewe

General reference works in print and electronic formats, translations and serious non-fiction of more general interest.

Concordia Publishing House

3558 S Jefferson Avenue, St Louis, MO 63118
tel 314-268-1000 *fax* 314-268-1329

Religious books, Lutheran perspective. Few freelance MSS accepted; query first. Founded 1869.

Contemporary Books

130 East Randolph Street, Suite 900, Chicago, IL 60601
tel 312-233-6520 *fax* 312-233-7570
Vice President Philip Ruppel

Non-fiction. Imprints: Contemporary Books, Lowell House, Passport Books, VGM Career Books. Division of the McGraw-Hill Companies.

The Continuum International Publishing Group Inc.
370 Lexington Avenue, New York, NY 10017-6503
tel 212-953-5858 *fax* 212-953-5944
email contin@tiac.net
website www.continuum-books.com
Chairman/Publisher Philip Sturrock
General non-fiction, education, literature, psychology, politics, sociology, literary criticism, religious studies. Founded 1999.

Cornell University Press*
(including ILR Press and Comstock Publishing Associates)
Sage House, 512 East State Street, Ithaca, NY 14850
tel 607-277-2338 *fax* 607-277-2374
email cupressinfo@cornell.edu
website www.cornellpress.cornell.edu
Director John G. Ackerman
Scholarly books. Founded 1869.

Council Oak Books
1615 S. Baltimore Avenue, Suite 3, Tulsa, OK 74119
tel 918-587-6454 *fax* 918-583-4995
email jclark@counciloakbooks.com
website www.counciloakbooks.com
Publishing Director Melissa Lilly, *Editor-in-Chief* Paulette Millichap
Non-fiction: native American, multicultural, life skills, life accounts, Earth awareness, meditation. Founded 1984.

The Countryman Press
PO Box 748, Rte 12N, Mount Tom Building, Woodstock, VT 05091
tel 802-457-4826 *fax* 802-457-1678
email countrymanpress@wwnorton.com
website www.countrymanpress.com
Editorial Director Kermit Hummel
Outdoor recreation guides for anglers, hikers, cyclists, canoeists and kayakers, US travel guides, New England non-fiction, how-to books, country living books, books on nature and the environment, classic reprints and general non-fiction. No unsolicited MSS. Division of **W.W. Norton & Co. Inc.** Founded 1973.

Crown Publishing Group*
299 Park Avenue, New York, NY 10170
tel 212-572-2408 *fax* 212-940-7408
President/Publisher Jenny Frost
General fiction, non-fiction, illustrated books. Imprints: Bell Tower, Clarkson Potter, Crown Publishers Inc., Harmony Books, Three Rivers Press. Division of **Random House Inc.**

D.C. Heath and Co. – acquired by Houghton Mifflin Company

David R. Godine, Publisher Inc.
9 Hamilton Place, Boston, MA 02108
tel 617-451-9600 *fax* 617-350-0250
email info@godine.com
website www.godine.com
President David R. Godine
Fiction, photography, poetry, art, biography, children's, essays, history, typography, architecture, nature and gardening, music, cooking, words and writing, and mysteries. No unsolicited MSS. Founded 1970.

DAW Books Inc.
375 Hudson Street, 3rd Floor, New York, NY 10014
tel 212-366-2096 *fax* 212-366-2090
email daw@penguinputnam.com
website www.dawbooks.com
Publishers Elizabeth R. Wollheim, Sheila E. Gilbert
Science fiction, fantasy, horror, mainstream thrillers: originals and reprints. Imprints: DAW/Fantasy, DAW/Fiction, DAW/Science Fiction. Affiliate of **Penguin Putnam Inc.** Founded 1971.

Dial Books for Young Readers – see Penguin Putnam Books for Young Readers

Doubleday Broadway Publishing Group*
1540 Broadway, New York, NY 10036
tel 212-782-9000 *fax* 212-302-7985
website www.randomhouse.com
President/Publisher Stephen Rubin
General fiction and non-fiction. Imprints: Anchor Bible Dictionary, Anchor Bible Reference Library, Currency, Doubleday, Doubleday Bible Commentary, Doubleday/Galilee, Doubleday/Image, Nan A. Talese, The New Jerusalem Bible. Division of **Random House Inc.**

Dover Publications Inc.
31 E 2nd Street, Mineola, NY 11501
tel 516-294-7000 *fax* 516-742-5049
Vice-President, Editorial Paul Negri
Art, architecture, antiques, crafts, juvenile, food, history, folklore, literary classics, mystery, language, music, math and science, nature, design and ready-to-use art. Founded 1941.

Dutton
(formerly Dutton/Signet)
375 Hudson Street, New York, NY 10014
tel 212-366-2000 *fax* 212-366-2666
email online@penguinputnam.com
website www.penguinputnam.com
Vice President/Editor-in-Chief Brian Tart

Fiction and general non-fiction for adults. Imprint: Dutton. Division of **Penguin Putman Inc.**

Dutton Children's Books – see Penguin Putnam Books for Young Readers

Facts On File Inc.
132 West 31st Street, 17th Floor, New York, NY 10001-2006
tel 212-967 8800 *fax* 212-967 9196
President Mark McDonnell, *Editorial Director* Laurie E. Likoff

General reference books and services for colleges, libraries, schools and general public. Founded 1940.

Farrar, Straus and Giroux
19 Union Square West, New York, NY 10003
tel 212-741-6900 *fax* 212-633-9385
website www.fsgbooks.com
President/Publisher Jonathan Galassi, *Editor-in-Chief* John Glusman

General publishers.

Fodor's Travel Publications Inc. – see Random House Inc.

Four Walls Eight Windows*
39 West 14th Street, Room 503, New York, NY 10011
tel 212-206-8965 *fax* 212-206-8799
email edit@4w8w.com
website www.4w8w.com
Publisher John Oakes

Fiction, history, current affairs, biography, environment, health. No unsolicited submissions accepted. Founded 1987.

Franklin Watts
90 Sherman Turnpike, Danbury, CT 06816
tel 203-797-3500 *fax* 203-797-6986

School and library books for grades K–12.

Frederick Warne – see Penguin Putnam Books for Young Readers

G.P. Putnam's Sons (adult) – see The Putnam Publishing Group

G.P. Putnam's Sons (children's) – see Penguin Putnam Books for Young Readers

Getty Publications*
1200 Getty Center Drive, Suite 500, Los Angeles, CA 90049-1682
tel 310-440-7365 *fax* 310-440-7758
email pubsinfo@getty.edu

website www.getty.edu/bookstore
Publisher Christopher Hudson, *General Manager* Kara Kirk, *Editor-in-Chief* Mark Greenberg

Art, art history, architecture, classical art and archaeology, conservation. Founded 1958.

Golden Books Family Entertainment
888 Seventh Avenue, New York, NY 10106
tel 212-547-6700 *fax* 212-547-6788
website www.goldenbooks.com
Chairman/Ceo Richard E. Snyder, *Coo* Richard Collins, *President* Steve Weitzer

Children's books, educational workbooks and products, electronic books and software, children's videos. Founded 1907.

Greenwillow Books – see HarperCollins Publishers

Grosset & Dunlap – see Penguin Putnam Books for Young Readers

Grove/Atlantic Inc.*
841 Broadway, New York, NY 10003-4793
tel 212-614-7850 *fax* 212-614-7886
Publisher Morgan Entrekin

MSS of permanent interest, fiction, biography, autobiography, history, current affairs, social science, belles-lettres, natural history. Imprints: Atlantic Monthly Press, Grove Press.

Harcourt Trade Division*
525 B Street, Suite 1900, San Diego, CA 92101
tel 619-231-6616 *fax* 619-699-6320
website www.harcourtbrace.com
President/Publisher, Adult Books Dan Farley, *Vice President/Publisher, Children's Books* Louise Pelan

General publishers. Fiction, history, biography, etc. Division of Harcourt Inc.

HarperCollins Publishers*
10 East 53rd Street, New York, NY 10022
tel 212-207-7000 *fax* 212-207-7145
website www.harpercollins.com
HarperCollins SanFrancisco 1160 Battery Street, San Francisco, CA 94111
tel 415-477-4400 *fax* 415-477-4444
President/Ceo Jane Friedman

Fiction, history, biography, poetry, science, travel, cookbooks, juvenile, educational, business, technical and religious. No unsolicited material; all submissions must come through a literary agent. Founded 1817.

HarperCollins General Books Group (division)
President/Publisher Cathy Hemming

HarperInformation (division)

Imprints: HarperBusiness, HarperResource, Access, William Morrow Cookbooks.

HarperSanFrancisco (division)
Imprint: HarperSanFrancisco.

HarperTrade (division)
Imprints: HarperCollins, Perennial, Cliff Street Books, Ecco, Quill, Amistad, HarperAudio, Large Print Editions, Rayo, Fourth Estate, ReganBooks and PerfectBound (e-books).

Morrow/Avon (division)
Imprints: William Morrow, Avon, HarperTorch, Eos, HarperEntertainment.

HarperCollins Children's Books Group
1350 6th Avenue, New York, NY 10019
tel 212-261-6500
President/Publisher Susan Katz

Imprints: Greenwillow Books, Joanna Cotler Books, Laura Geringer Books, HarperCollins Children's Books, HarperFestival, HarperTrophy, Avon, HarperTempest.

Harry N. Abrams Inc.*
100 Fifth Avenue, New York, NY 10011
tel 212-206-7715 *fax* 212-645-8437
website www.abramsbooks.com
Ceo/President Steve Parr

Art and architecture, photography, natural sciences, performing arts, children's books. No fiction. Founded 1949.

Harvard University Press*
79 Garden Street, Cambridge, MA 02138-1499
tel 617-495 2600 *fax* 617-495-5898
website www.hup.harvard.edu
Director William P. Sisler, *Editor-in-Chief/ Assistant Director* Aida D. Donald

History, philosophy, literary criticism, politics, economics, sociology, music, science, classics, social sciences, behavioural sciences, law.

Hastings House/Daytrips Publishers
2601 Wells Avenue, Suite 161, Fern Park, FL 32730
tel 407-339-3600 *fax* 407-339-5900
email hastings_daytrips@earthlink.net
website www.HastingsHouseBooks.com
Publisher Peter Leers

Travel.

Henry Holt and Company LLC*
115 West 18th Street, New York, NY 10011
tel 212-886-9200 *fax* 212-633-0748
website www.henryholt.com
President/Publisher John Sterling

History, biography, nature, science, self-help, novels, mysteries; books for young readers; trade paperback line, computer books. Founded 1866.

Hill and Wang
19 Union Square West, New York, NY 10003
tel 212-741-6900 *fax* 212-633-9385
website www.fsgbooks.com
Publisher Elisabeth Sifton, *Editor* Thomas LeBien

General non-fiction, history, public affairs. Division of **Farrar, Straus and Giroux**. Founded 1956.

Hippocrene Books Inc.
171 Madison Avenue, New York, NY 10016
tel 212-685-4371 *fax* 212-779-9338
email orders@hippocrenebooks.com
website www.hippocrenebooks.com
President/Editorial Director George Blagowidow

Foreign language books, international cookbooks, foreign language dictionaries, love poetry, travel, military history, Polonia, general trade. Founded 1971.

Holiday House
425 Madison Avenue, New York, NY 10017
tel 212-688-0085
President John Briggs, *Vice-President/Editor-in-Chief* Regina Griffin

General children's books. Send query letter before submitting MSS. Always include sae. No multiple submissions. Founded 1935.

Houghton Mifflin Company*
222 Berkeley Street, Boston, MA 02116
tel 617-351-5000

Fiction and non-fiction – cookbooks, history, political science, biography, nature (Peterson Guides), and gardening guides; reference, both adult and juvenile. No unsolicited MSS. Imprints: Mariner (original and reprint paperbacks); Houghton Mifflin Children's Books; Clarion (juvenile); American Heritage® Dictionaries. Founded 1832.

HP Books – see Berkley Publishing Group

Hyperion*
77 West 66 Street, New York, NY 10023-6298
tel 212-456-0110 *fax* 212-456-0157
website www.hyperionbooks.com
President Robert Miller, *Vice-President/Publisher* Ellen Archer, *Vice-President/Publisher (Hyperion Books for Children)* Lisa Holton

General fiction and non-fiction, children's books. Division of Buena Vista Publishing, formerly Disney Book Publishing Inc. Founded 1990.

Indiana University Press
601 North Morton Street, Bloomington, IN 47404-3797
tel 812-855-8817 *fax* 812-855-8507
email iupress@indiana.edu

website www.indiana.edu/~iupress
Director Peter-John Leone

African studies, Russian and East European studies, music, history, women's studies, Jewish studies, African–American studies, film, folklore, philosophy, medical ethics, archaeology, anthropology, paleontology. Reference and high level trade books. Founded 1950.

International Marine Publishing
PO Box 220, Camden, Maine 04843
tel 207-236-4837 *fax* 207-236-6314
email nancy_dowling@mcgraw-hill.com
website www.internationalmarine.com
www.raggedmountainpress.com
Editorial Director Jonathan F. Eaton

Imprints: International Marine (boats, boating and sailing); Ragged Mountain Press (sport, adventure/ travel, natural history). Division of the McGraw-Hill Companies. Founded 1992.

Jeremy P. Tarcher – see The Putnam Publishing Group

John Wiley & Sons Inc.*
111 River Street, Hoboken, NJ 07030-5773
tel 201-748-6000 *fax* 201-748-6088
email info@wiley.com
website www.wiley.com
President/Ceo William J. Pesce

Specialises in scientific and technical books and journals, textbooks and educational materials for colleges and universities, as well as professional and consumer books and subscription services. Subjects include business, computer science, electronics, engineering, environmental studies, reference books, science, social sciences, multimedia, and trade paperbacks. Founded 1807.

The Johns Hopkins University Press*
2715 North Charles Street, Baltimore, MD 21218-4319
tel 410-516-6971 *fax* 410-516-6968
Director James D. Jordan

History, literary criticism, classics, politics, environmental studies, biology, medical genetics, consumer health, religion, physics, astronomy, mathematics, education. Founded 1878.

Knopf Publishing Group*
299 Park Avenue, New York, NY 10170
tel 212-572-2600 *fax* 212-572-8700
website www.randomhouse.com
President Sonny Mehta

General literature, fiction, belles-lettres, sociology, politics, history, nature, science, etc. Imprints: Alfred A. Knopf Inc., Anchor, Everyman's Library,

Pantheon Books, Schocken Books, Vintage Books. Division of **Random House Inc.**

Krause Publications
700 East State Street, Iola, WI 54990-0001
tel 715-445-2214 *fax* 715-445-4087
email info@Krause.com
website www.Krause.com
Acquisitions Editors Julie Stephani (sewing/crafts), Donald Gulbrandsen (transportation/firearms/ outdoors), Paul Kennedy (antiques/collectibles)

Antiques and collectibles: coins, stamps, automobiles, toys, trains, firearms, comics, records; sewing and crafts, ceramics, outdoors, hunting.

Little, Brown & Company*
1271 Avenue of the Americas, New York, NY 10020
tel 212-522-8700
Chief Executive Larry Kirshbaum

General literature, fiction, non-fiction, biography, history, trade paperbacks, books for boys and girls. Art and photography books under the Bulfinch Press imprint. Imprint of AOL Time Warner Book Group.

Llewellyn Publications
PO Box 64383, St Paul, MN 55164-0383
email info@llewellyn.com
website www.llewellyn.com
President Carl Llewellyn Weschcke, *Vice President* Gabriel Weschcke

New Age, occult, astrology, magic. Founded 1901.

The Lyons Press
246 Goose Lane, Guilford, CT 06437
tel 203-458-4500
President/Publisher Tony Lyons

Outdoor sport, natural history, sports, art, general fiction and non-fiction. Founded 1978.

McGraw-Hill*
1221 Avenue of Americas, New York, NY 10020
tel 212-512-2000
website www.mcgraw-hill.com
Group Vice-President Theodore Nardin

Professional and reference: engineering, scientific, business, architecture, encyclopedias; college textbooks; high school and vocational textbooks: business, secretarial, career; trade books; training materials for industry. Division of The McGraw-Hill Companies.

McPherson & Company
PO Box 1126, Kingston, NY 12402
tel/fax 845-331-5807
email bmcpher@ulster.net
website www.mcphersonco.com

Publisher Bruce R. McPherson

Literary fiction; non-fiction: art criticism, writings by artists, film-making, etc; occasional general titles (e.g. anthropology). No poetry. No unsolicited MSS; query first. Founded 1974.

Merrell Publishers Ltd
49 West 24th Street, 8th Floor, New York, NY 10010
tel 212-929-8344 *fax* 212-929-8346
email jb@merrellpublishersusa.com
website www.merrellpublishers.com
US Director Joan Brookbank

High-quality illustrated books on all aspects of visual culture, including art, architecture, photography and design.

Microsoft Press*
One Microsoft Way, Redmond, WA 98052-6399
tel 425-882-8080 *fax* 425-936-7329
website www.microsoft.com
Publisher James Brown, *Editorial Director* Kim Fields

Computer books. Division of Microsoft Corp. Founded 1983.

Milkweed Editions
1011 Washington Avenue South, Suite 300, Minneapolis, MN 55415
tel 612-332-3192 *fax* 612-215-2550
websites www.milkweed.org www.worldashome.org
Editor H. Emerson Blake

Fiction, poetry, essays, the natural world, children's novels (ages 8–14). Founded 1979.

The MIT Press*
5 Cambridge Center, Cambridge, MA 02142-1493
tel 617-253-5646 *fax* 617-258-6779
website mitpress.mit.edu
Director Frank Urbanowski, *Editor-in-Chief* Laurence Cohen

Architecture, art and design, cognitive sciences, neuroscience, linguistics, computer science and artificial intelligence, economics and finance, philosophy, environment and ecology, natural history. Founded 1961.

Morehouse Publishing Co.
PO Box 1321, Harrisburg, PA 17105
tel 717-541-8130 *fax* 717-541-8128
email kquigley@morehousegroup.com
website www.morehousegroup.com
President Kenneth Quigley, *Publisher* Debra Farrington

Religious books, spirituality, children's.

The Naiad Press Inc.
PO Box 10543, Tallahassee, FL 32302
tel 850-539-5965 *fax* 850-539-9731
website www.naiadpress.com
Ceo Barbara Grier

Lesbian fiction; non-fiction: bibliographies, biographies, essays. Founded 1973.

NAL
375 Hudson Street, New York, NY 10014
tel 212-366-2000 *fax* 212-366-2666
email online@penguinputnam.com
website www.penguinputnam.com
President, Mass Market Paperbacks Leslie Gelbman, *Vice President/Publisher* Kara Welch

Fiction and general non-fiction. Imprints: Mentor, Meridian, New American Library, Onyx, Roc, Signet, Signet Classics, Topaz. Division of **Penguin Putnam Inc.** Founded 1948

North Light Books – see Writer's Digest Books

Orchard Books
555 Broadway, New York, NY 10012
tel 212-343-6782 *fax* 212-343-4890
website www.scholastic.com
Editorial Director Ken Geist

Books for children and young adults; picture books, fiction. Imprint of **Scholastic Inc.** Founded 1987.

Ottenheimer Publishers Inc.
5 Park Center Court, Suite 300, Onwings Mill, MD 21117
tel 410-902-9100 *fax* 410-902-7210
Directors Allan T. Hirsh, Jr, Allan T. Hirsh, III

Juvenile and adult non-fiction, reference. Founded 1890.

The Overlook Press*
141 Wooster Street, New York, New York 10012
tel 212-673-2210 *fax* 212-673-2296
website www.overlookpress.com
President and Publisher Peter Mayer, *Publishing Director* Tracy Carns

Non-fiction, fiction, children's books.

Oxford University Press Inc.*
198 Madison Avenue, New York, NY 10016
tel 212-726-6000 *fax* 212-726-6455
website www.oup-usa.org

Scholarly, professional, reference, bibles, college textbooks, religion, medical, music.

Pantheon Books – imprint of Knopf Publishing Group

Paragon House Publishers
2285 University Avenue West, Suite 200, St Paul, MN 55114
tel 651-644-3087 *fax* 651-644-0997
email rby@paragonhouse.com
website www.paragonhouse.com

Executive Director Gordon L. Anderson

Textbooks in philosophy and religion; general non-fiction. Member of the **Continuum International Publishing Group Inc.**

Peachtree Publishers Ltd

1700 Chattahoochee Avenue, Atlanta,
GA 30318-2112
tel 404-876-8761 *fax* 404-875-2578
email hello@peachtree-online.com
website www.peachtree-online.com
President and Publisher Margaret Quinlin, *Editorial Director* Kathy Landwehr

Children's picture books, novels and non-fiction books. Adult non-fiction subjects include self-help, parenting, education, health, regional guides. No adult fiction. For children's books, send complete MS; for all others, send query letter with 3 sample chapters and table of contents to Helen Harriss with sase for response and/or return of material. Founded 1977.

Pelican Publishing Company*

PO Box 3110, Gretna, LA 70054
tel 504-368-1175 *fax* 504-368-1195
email editorial@pelicanpub.com
website www.pelicanpub.com www.epelican.com
Publisher/President Milburn Calhoun

Art and architecture, cookbooks, travel, history, business, children's. Founded 1926.

Penguin AudioBooks – see Viking Penguin

Penguin Books – see Viking Penguin

Penguin Putnam Books for Young Readers*

345 Hudson Street, New York, NY 10014
tel 212-366-2000 *fax* 212-366-2666
email online@penguinputnam.com
website www.penguinputnam.com
President Douglas Whiteman

Children's: picture books, board and novelty books, young adult novels, mass merchandise products. Imprints: Dial Books for Young Readers, Dutton Children's Books, Dutton Interactive, Phyllis Fogelman Books, Grosset & Dunlap, PaperStar, Philomel, Planet Dexter, Platt & Munk, Playskool, Price Stern Sloan, PSS, Puffin Books, G.P. Putnam's Sons, Viking Children's Books, Frederick Warne. Division of **Penguin Putnam Inc.** Founded 1997.

Dial Books for Young Readers (imprint)
fax 212-414-3394
President/Publisher Nancy Paulsen, *Editorial Director* Laura Hornik, *Vice President/Publisher, Phyllis Fogelman Books* Phyllis Fogelman

Children's fiction and non-fiction, picture books, board books, interactive books, novels.

Dutton Children's Books (imprint)
President/Publisher Stephanie Lurie, *Editorial Director, Dutton Children's Trade* Donna Brooks

Picture books, young adult novels, non-fiction photographic books. Founded 1852.

Grosset & Dunlap (imprint)
President/Publisher, Grosset & Dunlap Debra Dorfman

Children's: picture books, activity books, fiction and non-fiction. Imprints: Grosset & Dunlap, Platt & Munk, Somerville House USA, Planet Dexter. Founded 1898.

Price Stern Sloan (imprint)
Vice President/Publisher Jon Anderson

Children's books: novelty/lift-flaps, activity books, middle-grade fiction, middle-grade and YA non-fiction, cutting-edge graphic readers, picture books, books plus. Imprints: Crazy Games, Doodle Art, Planet Dexter, Serendipity, Troubador Press, Wee Sing. Founded 1963.

Puffin Books (imprint)
President/Publisher Tracy Tang, *Associate Publisher/Managing Editor* Gerard Mancini

Children's paperbacks. Founded 1935.

G.P. Putnam's Sons (imprint)
President/Publisher Nancy Paulsen

Children's hardcover and paperback books. Imprints: G.P. Putnam's Sons, Philomel Books, PaperStar. Founded 1838.

Viking Children's Books (imprint)
President Regina Hayes

Fiction, non-fiction, picture books. Founded 1925.

Frederick Warne (imprint)

Original publisher of Beatrix Potter's *Tales of Peter Rabbit*. Founded 1865.

Penguin Putnam Inc.*

(formerly Penguin USA and Putnam Berkley)
375 Hudson Street, New York,
NY10014
tel 212-366-2000 *fax* 212-366-2666
email online@penguinputnam.com
website www.penguinputnam.com
President, The Penguin Group David Wan, *President* Susan Pearson Kennedy, *Ceo* David Shanks

Publisher of consumer books in both hardcover and paperback for adults and children; also produces maps, calendars, audiobooks and mass merchandise products. Adult imprints: Ace, Ace/Putnam, Allen Lane The Penguin Press, Avery, Berkley Books, BlueHen, Boulevard, DAW, Dutton, Grosset/Putnam, HP Books, Jove, Mentor, Meridian, Onyx, Penguin, Penguin Classics, Penguin Compass, Perigee, Plume, Prime Crime, Price Stern Sloan Inc., Putnam, G.P. Putnam's Sons, Riverhead Books, Roc, Signet, Signet

Classics, Jeremy P. Tarcher, Topaz, Viking, Viking Compass, Viking Studio, Marian Wood Books. Children's imprints: Dial Books for Young Readers, Dutton Children's Books, Grosset & Dunlap, PaperStar, Philomel Books, Planet Dexter, Price Stern Sloan Inc., Puffin, G.P. Putnam's Sons, Viking Children's Books, Wee Sing, Frederick Warne. Divisions: Berkley Publishing Group, Dutton, Plume, NAL, Penguin Putnam Books for Young Readers, The Putnam Publishing Group, Viking Penguin.

Penn State University Press*

820 North University Drive, USB1, Suite C, University Park, PA 16802
tel 814-865-1327 *fax* 814-863-1408
website www.psupress.org
Editor-in-Chief Peter Potter

Art history, literary criticism, religious studies, philosophy, political science, sociology, history, Russian and East European studies, Latin American studies and medieval studies. Founded 1956.

Perigee Books – see Berkley Publishing Group

The Permanent Press and Second Chance Press

4170 Noyac Road, Sag Harbor, NY 11963
tel 631-725-1101 *fax* 631-725-8215
website www.thepermanentpress.com
Directors Martin Shepard, Judith Shepard
Quality fiction. Founded 1978.

Plume

375 Hudson Street, New York, NY 10014
tel 212-366-2000 *fax* 212-366-2666
email online@penguinputnam.com
website www.penguinputnam.com
Publisher Kathryn Court, *President* Clare Ferraro, *Editor-in-Chief* Trena Keating

Fiction and general non-fiction for adults. Division of Penguin Putnam Inc.

Pocket Books*

1230 Avenue of the Americas, New York, NY 10020
tel 212-698-7000 *fax* 212-698-7007
website www.SimonSays.com
President/Publisher Judith M. Curr, *Vice President/Editorial Director* Emily Bestler

General fiction and non-fiction, trade hardcovers and paperbacks, mass market paperbacks. Imprints: Archway Paperbacks, Minstrel Books. Division of Simon & Schuster Adult Publishing Group. Founded 1939.

Price Stern Sloan – see Penguin Putnam Books for Young Readers

Princeton University Press*

Princeton, NJ 08540
postal address 41 William Street, Princeton, NJ 08540
tel 609-258-4900 *fax* 609-258-6305
website www.pup.princeton.edu
Director Walter Lippincott, *Editors-in-Chief* Terry Vaughn (humanities/social sciences), Sam Elworthy (Science Group)

Scholarly and scientific books on all subjects. Founded 1905.

Puffin Books – see Penguin Putnam Books for Young Readers

The Putnam Publishing Group

375 Hudson Street, New York, NY 10014
tel 212-366-2000 *fax* 212-366-2666
email online@penguinputnam.com
website www.penguinputnam.com

General trade books for adults; books on cassette. Imprints: Avery, BlueHen, G.P. Putnam's Sons, Riverhead Books, Jeremy P. Tarcher, Tarcher/Penguin, Putnam Berkley Audio, Marian Wood Books. Division of Penguin Putnam Inc.

R.R. Bowker*

630 Central Avenue, New Providence, NJ 07974
tel 908-286-1090 *fax* 908-219-0098
website www.bowker.com
President Michael Cairns

Bibliographies and reference tools for the book trade and literary and library worlds, available in hardcopy, on microfiche, online and CD-Rom. Reference books for music, art, business, computer industry, cable industry and information industry. Division of Cambridge Information Group.

Rand McNally

PO Box 7600, Chicago, IL 60680
tel 847-329-2178
Chairman John Macomber, *President/Ceo* Norman E. Wells, Jr

Maps, guides, atlases, educational publications, globes and children's geographical titles and atlases in print and electronic formats.

Random House Inc.*

1540 Broadway, New York, NY 10036
tel 212-782-9000 *fax* 212-302-7985
299 Park Avenue, New York, NY 10170, *and* 280 Park Avenue, New York, NY 10017
tel 212-572-2600 *fax* 212-572-8700
website www.randomhouse.com
Chairman/Ceo Peter Olson, *President/Coo* Erik Engstrom

General fiction and non-fiction, children's books. Subsidiary of Bertelsmann AG.

Random House Audio Publishing Group (division)
President Jenny Frost

BDD Audio Publishing, Random House Audio Publishing.

Random House Children's Media Group (division)
President Kristina Peterson

Imprints: Children's Publishing (Crown Books for Young Readers, CTW Publishing, Delacorte Press, Disney Books, Doubleday Books for Young Readers, Dragonfly Books, First Choice Chapter Books, Knopf Books for Young Readers, Knopf Paperbacks, Laurel-Leaf, Picture Yearling, Random House Children's Publishing, Skylark, Starfire, Yearling Books); Children's Media.

Random House Diversified Publishing Group (division)
President Jenny Frost

Random House Large Print Publishing; Random House Value Publishing (Children's Classics, Crescent Books, Derrydale, Gramercy Books, Testament Books, Wings Books).

The Random House Information Group (division)
President Bonnie Ammer

Imprints: Fodor's Travel Publications, Living Language, Princeton Review, Random House Reference, Random House Puzzles and Games.

Random House Trade Publishing Group (division)
President/Editor-in-Chief Ann Godoff

Imprints: Random House Adult Trade Books, The Modern Library, Villard Books.

Riverhead Books (Hardcover) – see The Putnam Publishing Group

Riverhead Books (Trade Paperback) – see Berkley Publishing Group

Rizzoli International Publications Inc.
300 Park Avenue South, New York, NY 10010
tel 212-387-3400 *fax* 212-387-3535
Publisher Marta Hallett

Art, architecture, photography, fashion, gardening, design, gift books, cookbooks. Founded 1976.

Rodale Book Group
400 South 10th Street, Emmaus, PA 18098
tel 610-967-5171 *fax* 610-967-8961
Executive Editor, Rodale General Books Stephanie Tade, *Editor-in-Chief, Women's Health Books* Tami Booth, *Executive Editor, Home Arts Books* Ellen Phillips, *Executive Editor, Lifestyle Books* Margot Schupf, *Executive Editor, Men's Health/Sports & Fitness Books* Jeremy Katz, *Senior Editor, Parenting Books* Lou Cinquino

General health, women's health, men's health, senior health, alternative health, fitness, healthy cooking, gardening, pets, spirituality/inspiration, trade health, biography, memoir, current affairs, science, parenting, organics, lifestyle, self-help, how-to, home arts. Founded 1932.

Rough Guides – see Viking Penguin

Routledge
29 West 35th Street, New York, NY 10001
tel 212-216-7800 *fax* 212-563-2269
Vice President and Publisher Linda Hollick, *Vice President and Publishing Director, Humanities* William P. Germano, *Publishing Director, Social Sciences* Karen Wolny, *Publishing Director, Reference* Sylvia K. Miller

Music, history, psychology and psychiatry, politics, women's studies, education, sociology, urban studies, religion, lesbian and gay studies, film, media, literary and cultural studies, reference. Subsidiary of Taylor & Francis Books Inc.

Running Press Book Publishers
125 S 22 St, Philadelphia, PA 19103-4399
tel 215-567-5080 *fax* 215-568 2919
President Stuart Teacher, *Publisher* Carlo DeVito, *Design Director* Bill Jones, *Production Director* Peter Horodowich, *Editorial Director* Jennifer Worick

Art, craft/how-to, general non-fiction, children's books. Imprints: Courage Books, Running Press Miniature Editions. Founded 1972.

Rutgers University Press*
100 Joyce Kilmer Avenue, Piscataway, NJ 08854-8099
tel 732-445-7762 *fax* 732-445-7039
website http://rutgerspress.rutgers.edu
Directors Marlie Wasserman, *Editor-in-Chief* Leslie Mitchner

Women's studies, anthropology, film and media studies, sociology, public health, popular science, cultural studies, literature, religion, history of medicine, Asian–American studies, African–American studies, American history, American studies, art history, regional titles. Founded 1936.

St Martin's Press Inc.*
175 Fifth Avenue, New York, NY 10010
tel 212-674-5151 *fax* 212-420-9314
website www.stmartins.com
President John Sargent

Trade, reference, college.

Samuel French Inc.
45 West 25th Street, New York, NY 10010
tel 212-206-8990 *fax* 212-206-1429

Play publishers and authors' representatives (dramatic).

Schocken Books – imprint of Knopf Publishing Group

Scholastic Inc.*

555 Broadway, New York, NY 10012
tel 212-343-6100 *fax* 212-343-6930
website www.scholastic.com
Chairman/President/Ceo Richard Robinson,
Executive Vice President, Book Group Barbara
Marcus, *Executive Vice President, Scholastic
Entertainment* Deborah Forte, *Executive Vice
President, Educational Publishing* Julie McGee

Innovative textbooks, magazines, technology and
teacher materials for use in both school and the
home. Founded 1920.

Scribner – imprint of Simon & Schuster Adult Publishing Group

Sheridan House Inc.*

145 Palisade Street, Dobbs Ferry, NY 10522
tel 914-693-2410 *fax* 914-693-0776
email sheribks@aol.com
website www.sheridanhouse.com
President Lothar Simon

Sailing, nautical, travel. Founded 1940.

Simon & Schuster Adult Publishing Group*

1230 Avenue of the Americas, New York, NY 10020
tel 212-698-7000 *fax* 212-698-7007
President/Publisher Carolyn K. Reidy

General fiction and non-fiction. Imprints: Fireside,
The Free Press, Kaplan, MTV®, PB Press, Pocket
Books, Scribner, Scribner Paperback Fiction, S&S
Libros en Espanol, Simon & Schuster, S&S Source,
Sonnet, Star Trek®, Touchstone, Wall Street Journal
Books, Washington Square Press VHI®. Division of
Simon & Schuster. Founded 1924.

Simon & Schuster Children's Publishing Division*

1230 Avenue of the Americas, New York, NY 10020
tel 212-698-2112 *fax* 212-698-2793
President Kristina Peterson

Preschool to young adult, fiction and non-fiction,
trade, library and mass market. Imprints: Aladdin
Paperbacks, Atheneum Books for Young Readers,
Little Simon, Margaret K. McElderry Books, Simon
& Schuster Books for Young Readers, Simon
Spotlight. Division of Simon & Schuster. Founded
1924.

Soho Press Inc.

853 Broadway, New York, NY 10003
tel 212-260-1900 *fax* 212-260-1902
email soho@sohopress.com
website www.sohopress.com
Publisher Juris Jurjevics, *Associate Publisher* Laura
Hruska

Literary fiction, commercial fiction, mystery,
thrillers, travel, memoir, general non-fiction.
Founded 1986.

Stackpole Books

5067 Ritter Road, Mechanicsburg, PA 17055-6921
tel 717-796-0411 *fax* 717-796-0412
email sales@stackpolebooks.com
website www.stackpolebooks.com
Directors David Detweiler (chairman), David Ritter
(president), Judith Schnell (editorial)

Nature, outdoor sports, Pennsylvania, crafts and
hobbies, history, military history. Founded 1930.

Stanford University Press*

Palo Alto, CA 94304-1124
tel 650-723-9434 *fax* 650-725-3457
website www.sup.org
Director Geoffrey Burn

Scholarly non-fiction, college text, professional.

Strawberry Hill Press

21 Isis Street, Apt 102, San Francisco,
CA 94103-4365
President Jean-Louis Brindamour PhD, *Executive
Vice-President/Art Director* Ku Fu-Sheng, *Treasurer*
Edward E. Serres

Health, self-help, cookbooks, philosophy, religion,
history, drama, science and technology, biography,
mystery, Third World. No unsolicited MSS;
preliminary letter and return postage essential.
Founded 1973.

Ten Speed Press

PO Box 7123, Berkeley, CA 94707
tel 510-559-1600 *fax* 510-524-1052
email order@tenspeed.com
website www.tenspeed.com
President Philip Wood, *Publisher and Vice President*
Kirsty Melville

Career/business, cooking, general non-fiction,
health, women's interest, self-help, practical guides,
children's. Founded 1971.

Theatre Arts Books

29 West 35th Street, New York, NY 10001
tel 212-216-7877
Publishing Director William Germano

Theatre, performance, dance and allied books –
acting techniques, voice, movement, costume, etc;
a few plays. Imprint of **Routledge**.

Thomas Nelson Publisher

501 Nelson Place, Nashville, TN 37214-1000
tel 615-889-9000 *fax* 615-391-5225
*Executive Vice President, Thomas Nelson Publishing
Group* Lee Gessner

Bibles, religious, non-fiction and fiction general trade books. Founded 1798.

Tor Books
175 Fifth Avenue, 14th Floor, New York, NY 10010
tel 212-388-0100 *fax* 212-388-0191

Fiction: general, historical, western, suspense, mystery, horror, science fiction, fantasy, humour, juvenile, classics (English language); non-fiction: adult and juvenile. Affiliate of St Martin's Press Inc. Founded 1980.

Tuttle Publishing/Periplus Editions
153 Milk Street, Boston, MA 02109
tel 617-951-4080 *fax* 617-951-4045
website www.tuttlepublishing.com
Periplus Editions, 5 Little Road 08-01, Singapore 536983
tel 65-280-3320 *fax* 65-280-6290
Ceo Eric Oey, *Editorial Director* Ed Walters

Asian art, culture, cooking, gardening, Eastern philosophy, martial arts, health. Founded 1948.

United Publishers Group – see Hastings House Book Publishers

The University of Alabama Press
Box 870380, Tuscaloosa, AL 35487
tel 205-348-5180 *fax* 205-348-9201
Director Daniel J.J. Ross, *Managing Editor* Kristin Harpster Lawrence

American and Southern history, African–American studies, religion, rhetoric and communication, Judaic studies, literary criticism, anthropology and archaeology. Founded 1945.

The University of Arkansas Press
The University of Arkansas, 201 Ozark Avenue, Fayetteville, AR 72701
tel 479-575-3246 *fax* 479-575-6044
email uaprinfo@cavern.uark.edu
Director Lawrence J. Malley

History, humanities, literary criticism, Middle East studies, African–American studies, poetry. Founded 1980.

University of Chicago Press*
1427 East 60th Street, Chicago, IL 60637
tel 773-702-7700 *fax* 773-702-2705
Director Paula Barker Duffy

Scholarly books and monographs, religious and scientific books, general trade books, and 44 scholarly journals.

University of Illinois Press*
1325 South Oak Street, Champaign, IL 61820
tel 217-333-0950 *fax* 217-244-8082

Director Willis G. Regier

American studies (history, music, literature, religion), working-class and ethnic studies, communications, regional studies, architecture, philosophy and women's studies. Founded 1918.

The University of Massachusetts Press
PO Box 429, Amherst, MA 01004-0429
tel 413-545-2217 *fax* 413-545-1226
website www.umass.edu/umpress
Director Bruce G. Wilcox

Scholarly books and works of general interest: American studies and history, black and ethnic studies, women's studies, cultural criticism, architecture and environmental design, literary criticism, poetry, fiction, philosophy, political science, sociology, books of regional interest. Founded 1964.

The University of Michigan Press
839 Greene Street, PO Box 1104, Ann Arbor, MI 48106-1104
tel 734-764-4388 *fax* 734-615-1540
email um.press@umich.edu
website www.press.umich.edu/
Director Philip Pochoda, *Assistant Director* Mary Erwin, *Executive Editor* LeAnn Fields, *Managing Editor* Christina Milton

Scholarly and general interest works in literary and cultural theory, classics, history, theatre, women's studies, political science, law, American history, American studies, anthropology, economics, jazz; textbooks in English as a second language; regional trade titles. Founded 1930.

University of Missouri Press
2910 LeMone Boulevard, Columbia, MO 65201
tel 573-882-7641 *fax* 573-884-4498
website www.system.missouri.edu/upress
Director/Editor-in-Chief Beverly Jarrett, *Acquisitions Editor* Clair Willcox

American and European history, African American studies, American, British and Latin American literary criticism, journalism, political philosophy, art history, regional studies; short fiction. Founded 1958.

University of New Mexico Press
1720 Lomas Boulevard NE, Albuquerque, NM 87131-1591
tel 505-277-2346 *fax* 505-277-9270
email unmpress@unm.edu
website www.unmpress.com
Director Luther Wilson

Western history, anthropology and archaeology, Latin American studies, photography, multicultural literature, poetry. Founded 1929.

The University of North Carolina Press*
PO Box 2288, 116 South Boundary Street,
Chapel Hill, NC 27514
tel 919-966-3561 *fax* 919-966-3829
Director Kate Douglas Torrey

American history, American studies, Southern
studies, European history, women's studies, Latin
American studies, political science, anthropology
and folklore, classics, regional trade. Founded 1922.

University of Oklahoma Press
1005 Asp Avenue, Norman, OK 73019-6051
tel 405-325-2000 *fax* 405-325-4000
Director John N. Drayton

History of American West, American Indian studies,
Mesoamerican studies, classical studies, women's
studies, natural history, political science. Founded
1928.

University of Pennsylvania Press
4200 Pine Street, Philadelphia, PA 19104-4011
tel 215-898-6261 *fax* 215-898-0404
website www.upenn.edu/pennpress
Director Eric Halpern

American and European history, anthropology, art,
architecture, business, cultural studies, ancient
studies, human rights, literature, health,
Pennsylvania regional studies. Founded 1890.

University of Tennessee Press*
110 Conference Center Building, Knoxville,
TN 37996-4108
tel 865-974-3321 *fax* 865-974-3724
email harris@utk.edu
website www.utpress.org
Director Jennifer Siler

American studies: African–American studies,
Appalachian studies, history, religion, literature,
historical archaeology, folklore, vernacular
architecture, material culture. Founded 1940.

University of Texas Press*
PO Box 7819, Austin, TX 78713-7819
tel 512-471-7233 *fax* 512-232-7178
email utpress@uts.cc.utexas.edu
website www.utexas.edu/utpress/
Director Joanna Hitchcock, *Assistant Director and
Editor-in-Chief* Theresa May, *Assistant Director and
Financial Officer* Joyce Lewandowski, *Assistant
Director and Design/Production Manager* David
Cavazos

Scholarly non-fiction: anthropology, classics and the
Ancient World, conservation and the environment,
film and media studies, geography, Latin American
and Latino studies, Middle Eastern studies, natural
history, ornithology, Texas and Western studies.
Founded 1950.

University of Washington Press
PO Box 50096, Seattle, WA 98145-5096
tel 206-543-4050 *fax* 206-543-3932
Director Patrick Soden

Anthropology, Asian–American studies, Asian
studies, art and art history, aviation history,
environmental studies, forest history, Jewish studies,
literary criticism, marine sciences, Middle East
studies, music, regional studies, including history
and culture of the Pacific Northwest and Alaska,
Native American studies, resource management and
public policy, Russian and East European studies,
Scandinavian studies. Founded 1909.

University Press of Kansas
2501 West 15th Street, Lawrence, KS 66049-3905
tel 785-864-4154 *fax* 785-864-4586
email upress@ku.edu
website www.kansaspress.ku.edu
Director Fred Woodward, *Editor-in-Chief* Michael
Briggs, *Senior Production Editor* Melinda Wirkus,
Assistant Director/Marketing Manager Susan K.
Schott

American history (political, social, cultural,
environmental), military history, American political
thought, American presidency studies, law and
constitutional history, political science. Founded
1946.

Van Nostrand Reinhold – acquired by John Wiley & Sons

Viking – see Viking Penguin

Viking Children's Books – see Penguin Putnam Books for Young Readers

Viking Penguin
375 Hudson Street, New York, NY 10014
tel 212-366-2000 *fax* 212-366-2666
email online@penguinputnam.com
website www.penguinputnam.com
Chairman Susan Petersen Kennedy, *President* Clare
Ferraro

Fiction and general non-fiction for adults. Imprints:
Stephen Greene Press, Pelham, Penguin Books,
Penguin Classics, Penguin Compass, Rough Guides,
Viking, Viking Compass, Penguin AudioBooks,
Allen Lane The Penguin Press. Division of **Penguin
Putnam Inc.** Founded 1975.

Penguin AudioBooks (imprint)
Senior Editor David Highfill

Imprints: Penguin AudioBooks, Penguin
HighBridge Audio. Founded 1990.

Penguin Books (imprint)
President/Publisher Kathryn Court

Fiction and general non-fiction for adults. Imprints: Penguin, Penguin Classics, Penguin Compass, Penguin 20th Century Classics. Founded 1935.

Rough Guides (imprint)
345 Hudson Street, New York, NY 10014
tel 212-414-3635 *fax* 212-414-3352
email rough@panix.com
website www.roughguides.com
Publisher Martin Dunford

Trade paperbacks, travel guides, phrasebooks, music reference, music CDs and internet reference. Founded 1982.

Viking (imprint)
Associate Publisher Paul Slovak

Fiction and general non-fiction for adults. Founded 1925.

W.W. Norton & Company Inc.

500 Fifth Avenue, New York, NY 10110
tel 212-354-5500 *fax* 212-869-0856
website www.wwnorton.com

General fiction and non-fiction, music, boating, psychiatry, economics, family therapy, social work, reprints, college texts, science.

Walker & Co.

435 Hudson Street, New York, NY 10014
tel 212-727-8300 *fax* 212-727-0984
website www.walkerbooks.com
Publisher George Gibson, *Mystery* Michael Seidman, *Juvenile* Emily Easton

General publishers, biography, popular science, health, business, mystery, history, juveniles. Founded 1960.

Walter H. Baker Company

PO Box 699222, Quincy, MA 02269
tel 617-745-0805 *fax* 617-745-9891
website www.bakersplays.com
President Charles Van Nostrand, *General Manager* Kurt Gombar, *UK Agent* Samuel French Ltd

Plays and books on the theatre. Also agents for plays. Founded 1845.

Warner Books Inc.*

1271 Avenue of the Americas, New York, NY 10020
tel 212-522-7200 *fax* 212-522-7991
website www.twbookmark.com
Ceo Laurence K. Kirshbaum,
President/Coo/Publisher Maureen Mahon Egen

Paperback originals and reprints, fiction and non-fiction, trade paperbacks and hardcover books, audio books, gift books. Subsidiary of AOL Time Warner Book Group. Founded 1961.

WaterBrook Press*

2375 Telstar Drive, Suite 160, Colorado Springs, CO 80920
tel 719-590-4999 *fax* 719-590-8977
website www.waterbrookpress.com
President Stephen Cobb

Broad range of Christian fiction and non-fiction. Imprint: Shaw Books. Division of **Random House Inc.**

Watson-Guptill Publications

770 Broadway, New York, NY 10003
tel 646-654-5000 *fax* 646-654-5487
email info@watsonguptill.com
website www.watsonguptill.com
Director of Sales & Marketing Charles Whang, *Senior Acquisitions Editors* Candy Raney, Bob Nirkind, Victoria Craven, Joy Aquilino

Art, crafts, how-to, comic/cartooning, photography, performing arts, architecture and interior design, graphic design, music, entertainment, writing, reference, children's. Imprints: Amphoto Books, Back Stage Books, Billboard Books, Watson-Guptill, Whitney Library of Design. Founded 1937.

Westminster John Knox Press

100 Witherspoon Street, Louisville, KY 40202-1396
tel 502-569-5052 *fax* 502-569-5113
email wjk@presbypub.com
website www.wjkbooks.com
Director Jack Keller

Religious, academic, reference, general.

William Morrow – see HarperCollins Publishers

Writer's Digest Books

4700 E. Galbraith Road, Cincinnati, OH 45236
tel 513-531-2690 *fax* 513-891-7185

Market Directories, books for writers, photographers and songwriters.

Betterway Books (imprint)

How-to in home building, remodelling, woodworking, home organisation, theatre, genealogy.

North Light Books (imprint)

Fine art, decorative art, crafts, graphic arts instruction books.

Yale University Press*

302 Temple Street, New Haven, CT 06511
postal address PO Box 209040, New Haven, CT 06520
tel 203-432-0960 *fax* 203-432-0948/2394
email firstname.lastname@yale.edu
website www.yale.edu/yup/
Director John G. Ryden

Scholarly books and art books.

Dos and don'ts on approaching a publisher

You want the book you've written to be published. So how do you set about it? Where will you send the typescript? Probably to a publisher, but to which one? Michael Legat offers guidelines on how to proceed.

Finding a publisher

Do your market research in public libraries and bookshops, and especially in *Writers' and Artists' Yearbook*, to find out which publishers bring out the kind of book you have written. While looking at the *Yearbook* entries, note which publishers are willing to consider books submitted to them directly, rather than through an agent, and which require a letter of enquiry first. Incidentally, if you are hoping to interest an agent, they almost all want an enquiry letter first.

```
                    10 Any Street, Any Town,
                                   Any County

Messrs Dickens and Thackray,
83 Demy Street,
London WC45 9BM              12th March

Dear Sirs,

May I please send for your consider-
ation the novel I have written.

Yours sincerely,


L. Hopeful
```

This letter is far too brief. It gives no information about the kind of novel the author wishes to submit, nor of its length, it doesn't include a sae, and it doesn't even reveal the writer's sex. And since the writer doesn't use a question mark and has misspelt 'Thackeray', it's a good bet that the book will need meticulous and time-consuming copy-editing.

Enquiry letters

An enquiry letter should be business-like. Don't grovel ('it would be an honour to be published by so distinguished a firm'), don't make jokes ('my Mum says it's smashing, but maybe you'll think she's prejudiced'), don't be aggressive ('I have chosen you to publish my book, kindly send me your terms by return'). It is a good idea to write to whichever editor in the publishing house is responsible for books of the kind you have written (a phone call will provide this information – but take care to get the right title and spelling of the editor's name). Enclose a stamped addressed envelope. Look at the examples of the two poor enquiry letters followed by a good one on page 219.

You may have noticed that none of the letters refers to sending a disk or email. Such submissions may well become standard in a few years' time, but that stage has not yet been reached. However, once a book has been accepted, the publisher will certainly want a copy of the book on disk if it is available.

Presentation

Assuming that a publishing firm agrees to look at your book, the editor will expect to see a well-presented typescript (sometimes called a manuscript, abbreviated to MS). Here are some dos and don'ts about its appearance.

Use a typewriter or a word processor, or get a secretarial service to translate your handwriting on to a disk. Don't expect a publisher to read a handwritten script,

```
                    12 Any Street, Any Town,
                                   Any County

Messrs Dickens and Thackeray,
83 Demy Street,
London WC45 9BM              14th March

Dear Sirs,

May I please send you the novel I
have written, which I want to get
published? It's called Wendy Chiltern.
That's the name of the heroine. I am
a 76-year-old grandmother, but all my
friends say that I am very young for
my age and I can certainly claim to
be 'with it'. I belong to the
Townswomen's Guild, and I do a lot of
work at the local Church, and I play
Bridge regularly, so you can tell my
mind's still as sharp as ever.

I have been writing ever since I was
a little girl, without trying to get
anything published, but my friends
have persuaded me to try my luck with
this book. One of them said it was
better than anything by Jackie Collins.
Any publisher would jump at it, she
said. They are all so enthusiastic,
that I just had to 'have a go'…

The book is 57 pages long. It is
properly typed, and all the spelling
mistakes have been corrected. I
should tell you that I am aware that
the novel has some faults. It is just
a little slow to get started, but
once you're into it I am sure you
won't be able to put it down.

If your reply is favourable, I shall
bring the typescript to your office
and perhaps you could spare me a few
minutes to talk about it.

Yours sincerely,


Louise Hopeless (Mrs)
```

This letter is far too long, and includes masses of irrelevant information about the author. The fact that the lady's friends said they liked the book is no recommendation – what else are they going to say to their friend? And no editor is going to be tempted by a slow beginning, however honest it may be for the author to point it out. The book is almost certainly typed in single spacing with minuscule margins, and even so will be a long way short of book-length. And publishers do not spend time interviewing would-be authors – the lady should leave the typescript at reception, and let it speak for itself.

even if you have a fine Italian hand.

Choose a good quality white A4 paper (preferably not continuous listing paper, or if you must use it, at least separate the pages and remove the perforated edges). Whatever paper you use don't type on both sides, and don't use single spacing (which publishers abhor, and usually refuse to read) – one side of the paper only and double spacing is the rule. And do leave a good margin, at least 3 cm, all around the text, using the same margins throughout, so as to have the same number of lines on each page (except at the beginning and end of chapters). Double spacing and good margins allow space for your last-minute corrections to the typescript, for any copy-editor's amendments, and for instructions to the printer. And, not least in importance, a typescript in that style is much easier to read.

Always begin chapters on a new page. Justify on the left hand side only. Don't use blank lines between paragraphs (in the style of most typed letters nowadays), but indent the first line of each paragraph a few spaces. Blank lines should be used only to indicate a change of subject, or time, or scene, or viewpoint.

Be consistent in your choice of variant spellings, capitalisation, use of subheadings, etc. Make up your mind whether you are going to use -ise or -ize suffixes, for example, and whether, if 'village hall' appears in your text, you will type 'village hall' or Village Hall'.

For plays, use capitals for character names and underline stage directions or print them in italics. Use single spacing for dialogue, but leave a blank line between one character's speech and that of the next character to speak.

Poetry should be typed in exactly the way that the poem would appear in a printed version, using single or double spacing and various indentations as the poet wishes.

Organising the pages

Number the pages (or 'folios', as publishers like to call them) straight through from beginning to end. Don't start each chapter at folio 1. If you need to include an extra folio after, say, folio 27, call it folio 27a and write at the foot of folio 27: 'Folio 27a follows'. Then write at the foot of 27a: 'Folio 28 follows'. Obviously, if you want to insert more than one page, you would use '27a', '27b', '27c', and so on. Some writers like to use part of the book's title as well as the folio number: 'Harry 27', for example, but this is not essential.

Create a title page for the book, showing the title and your name or pseudonym. Add your name and address in the bottom right hand corner, and also type it on the last folio of the typescript, in case the first folio becomes detached. You can also add a word count, if you wish (if using the word-counting facility on your word processor, round the figure up or down to the nearest thousand or five thousand). If you want to include a list of your previously published books, a dedication, a quotation, a list of contents or of illustrations, an assertion of your moral rights, or any similar material, use a separate page for each item. Leave these pages unnumbered or use small roman figures – i, ii, iii, etc – so that the first folio to have an Arabic number will be the first page of your text.

When fastening the typescript together, don't use pins (which scratch),

```
                        14 Any Street, Any Town,
                                       Any County

Ms Ann Clarke,
Messrs Dickens and Thackeray,
83 Demy Street,
London WC45 9BM              16th March

Dear Ms Clarke,

May I please send you my novel, My
Son, my Son, for your kind
consideration? It is approximately
87,000 words in length and is a
contemporary story, telling of the
devastating effect on the marriage of
the central characters when their 17-
year-old son announces that he is
gay. It is aimed at the same market
as that of Joanna Trollope, although
my characters might be described as a
little further down the class scale.

I have written a number of articles
which have been published not only in
my local newspaper, but in a couple of
cases in 'The Lady', and once in 'The
Observer'. This is my first work of
fiction, but I have two other novels
with similar backgrounds in mind.

I enclose a sae and look forward to
hearing from you. Perhaps you will
let me know whether you would prefer
to see a synopsis and specimen
chapters, or the entire book.

Yours sincerely,

Lucilla Possible
```

A good enquiry letter. The writer has (we can presume) found out to whom to address the letter, and how the lady spells her name. The letter is brief, but gives a clear picture of what the novel is about, and suggests its possible market, telling the publisher all that is necessary at this stage. It makes the two points that the writer has had some success with her work (do always include such details, provided that they are for professional publications), and that she intends to write other books. It also asks about the possibility of sending a synopsis and specimen chapters rather than the complete book, and that is in fact the way in which most publishers nowadays like to see new material (especially for non-fiction books, but also for novels). Of course, no enquiry letter, however satisfactory, can guarantee a favourable response, but at least with this one no editorial hackles should rise.

paperclips (which pick up other papers from a busy editor's desk), or staples (which make it difficult to read). Don't ever fasten the pages together in one solid lump, and it's best to avoid ring binders too. Don't use plastic folders – they are slippery and can very easily cascade off a pile on the editor's desk (which won't please the editor). Almost all publishers prefer to handle each folio separately, so put the typescript into a wallet-type folder, or more than one if necessary. Put the title of the book and your name and address on the outside of the folder.

If illustrations form a large part of your book and you expect to provide them yourself they should be included with the typescript, and equally a selection should accompany a synopsis and specimen chapters. Send copies rather than originals. If your book is for children don't complete all the illustrations until the publisher has decided on the size of the book and the number of illustrations. If you have a friend who wants to supply illustrations for your book, do make sure that they will be up to publishing standard before you accept the offer. You may put off a children's publisher by suggesting an illustrator – they like to choose.

Waiting for a decision

Many publishers take what seems to be an unconscionable time to give a verdict on typescripts submitted to them. However, a decision whether or not to publish may not be easy, and several readings and consultations with other departments in the publishing house often have to take place before the editor can be sure of the answer. If you have heard nothing after two months, send a polite letter of enquiry; if you get no response, ask for your typescript back, and try another publisher.

Don't expect to be given reasons for rejection. Publishers do not have time to spend on books and authors which they are not going to publish. However, if the rejection letter contains any compliments on your work, you can take them at face value – publishers tend not to encourage authors unless they mean it.

Copyright material

Copyright exists as soon as you (or anyone else) records anything original to you on paper or film or disk. If you want to quote or otherwise use any material which is someone else's copyright, even if it is a short extract, you will have to get permission to do so, and possibly pay a fee. This applies not only to the text of a book, but also to letters and photographs, the copyright of which belongs to the letter-writer and photographer respectively. You must always give full acknowledgement to the source of the material. Use copyright material without such clearance and acknowledgement, and you are guilty of plagiarism – and another name for plagiarism is stealing. There are some circumstances in which you may use small amounts of text under a rule called 'Fair Dealing'. If your book has been accepted for publication, the publisher will be able to give you advice on the matter. (See also articles on copyright starting on page 603.)

Proofs

When your book is accepted by a publisher you may be asked to do further work on it, and a copy-editor will probably check the typescript line by line and word by word. As the author you should see the final copy before it goes to the printer, and this is almost your last chance to make any changes, whether they are simply the correction of literals or are more extensive than that.

At a later stage you will be sent proofs from the printer, which you will have to read with great care. Any errors which the printer has made are corrected without charge, but if you alter anything else, the publisher will have to pay for the changes and will be entitled to pass on to you any costs which exceed 10–15% of the cost of composition (i.e. the setting of the book in type). That sounds as though it gives you a lot of leeway, but alterations at proof stage are hugely expensive, so avoid them if you possibly can.

Michael Legat became a full-time writer after a long and successful publishing career. He is the author of a number of highly regarded books on publishing and writing.

See also...
- *Submitting material,* page 125
- *Writing and the children's book market,* page 226
- *How to get an agent,* page 345
- *Copyright questions,* page 603
- *UK copyright law,* page 606

Ghostwriting

It is possible for an unknown writer to make a living as a full-time ghostwriter. Andrew Crofts shares some of his secrets on how to do it.

Why do it?
The greatest problem facing any professional writer is finding a steady supply of ideas and subjects so dazzlingly certain to appeal to the book-buying public that publishers are eager to buy. Not only are saleable ideas in short supply, it also takes an inordinate amount of time to research a new subject deeply enough to be able to sell it successfully. You might spend months researching a subject from a number of different sources and still be unable to find a buyer.

One answer is to collaborate with other people who lack writing skills and experience but have good stories to tell, either as fiction or non-fiction, or possess all the necessary information to create a book.

These people can be found in a number of places. They might be celebrities, who would impress publishers because of their notoriety, or ordinary people who have undergone extraordinary experiences. Alternatively, they might be experts in subjects that the public want to know more about.

It's much easier for publishers to market books by celebrities or established experts than those by unknown writers. Apart from a handful of literary stars, few people buy books because of the authors' names, and the media have a limited amount of space in which to write about them. But if you write the autobiography of a soap star, controversial politician or sporting hero, the resulting book will be widely written and talked about in the media. While the author is spending several weeks being whistled around all day from breakfast television to late night television, the ghost can stay comfortably at home and get on with their next project.

The speed with which you can gather the information for a ghosted book means that you can produce far more publishable material in the course of a year than if you were researching each book in order to write them under your own name. Publishers are also willing to pay higher advances because they can see how they will market the book once it is written. Ghosting makes it quite possible for an unknown writer to make a good full-time living as an author. It also provides you with broad writing experience and helps you to build contacts in the publishing industry to whom you can then sell other projects of your own.

Of all the advantages that ghosting offers, however, the greatest must be the opportunities that ghosts get to meet people of interest. It's a licence to ask the sort of impertinent questions that you truly want to know the answers to, and to be allowed inside some of the most extraordinary stories.

Ghosting a book for someone is like being paid to be educated by the best teachers in the world. Imagine, for instance, being asked to ghost *The Origin of the Species* for Darwin, or *The Decline and Fall of the Roman Empire* for Gibbon; being paid to learn everything that is in their heads and then turning their thoughts, words and notes into book form. Could there be a better form of education?

How to start

The first step could be to approach people you would like to ghost for and offer your services. That might mean your favourite celebrities, who you could write to care of their agents or television companies. It might be people you have read about in the press and who you think have stories that could be developed into books. It's usually possible to find some way of getting a letter or email to them.

A more practical first step, however, might be to approach people who you come across in everyday life and who have an expertise that you think would be popular with a wider audience. If you've been on a course, for instance, find out if the trainer has thought of turning their message into book form. Would a garage mechanic who's good at explaining why your car isn't working be able to supply the material for a book on car maintenance? What about your doctor doing a book on healthcare for a specialist sector of the market? The options are endless.

Anyone who has access to a captive marketplace, like training companies or public speakers, has a ready-made market for books. There are companies who might want to produce books by their chief executives for distribution to employees as well as to the outside world and public relations departments who would relish the idea of getting their clients' messages to wider audiences.

If you're already a writer in another field, approach your existing contacts. A show business journalist, for instance, has access to actors and singers. A sports writer can approach sportspeople they've interviewed in the past. People will nearly always prefer to work with a ghost they already know and trust and feel they have a rapport with, than with a stranger.

At the same time as approaching potential authors, you should also be letting the publishing world know that you're available to work as a ghost. Write to the literary agents and publishers listed in this *Yearbook* to let them know what your experience is and how they can contact you. They will often have clients who they know are not capable of doing their own writing.

How to sell projects

It's unusual for any publisher to buy a book idea without seeing a synopsis and some sample material. Once you're experienced you will sometimes be able to charge for writing synopses, but at the beginning it's probably wise to offer to do it for free in order to get projects off the ground.

A synopsis must be a hard-selling document that gives the publisher all the reasons why they should commission the book. It might be worth preparing a one- or two-page version first in order to catch their attention and then a longer document (between 5000 and 10,000 words usually suffices) in order to get the message across. It must give the publishers confidence that the book will be written to a high standard and delivered on time. It must be something that their sales teams can immediately see how to sell. Give a brief biography of the author and demonstrate how promotable they will be.

Involve a literary agent, firstly because most publishers don't like dealing directly with authors and secondly because the agent can handle all the money side of the relationship, removing potential conflicts between the author and ghost.

Whenever possible, have one good agent representing both parties in the arrangement. The agent's prime interest will then be in getting the book well published, not in encouraging the ghost and the author to fight one another for larger shares of the resulting royalties. The agent can also act as a conciliatory go-between should the relationship between author and ghost break down.

Who pays the ghost?

How the ghost gets paid will depend largely on how speculative the project is and on the wishes of the author. It might be that the author is sufficiently confident of the book's success to suggest paying the ghost a fee. How much that fee will be depends on what the author can afford, what they are willing to pay and what the ghost is willing to do the job for. In other words, it's open for negotiation.

If the project already has a publisher and there is no speculative work involved, then it may be that the publisher will suggest a fee. Then there will be little or no room for negotiation. Any writer starting out should accept any book that is offered, even if the money is low, simply in order to build up a track record.

Where there is no publisher involved at the outset, and the author has no money, then suggest splitting all the proceeds 50/50, which includes advances, royalties and foreign rights sales, serialisation fees and payments for film and television rights.

If the author is a celebrity and it's obvious the book will make a large amount of money the ghost might have to accept a lower percentage, or a percentage that will become lower once he or she has received a pre-agreed amount; e.g. the proceeds might be split 50/50 until the ghost has received £50,000, at which stage his or her share might then drop to 40%, and might then drop again at £100,000.

It would be unwise to write an entire book unless some money has been forthcoming, either from a publisher or from the author, but there are cases where even this risk is worth taking. With fiction it is nearly always necessary to write the whole book before any publisher will make an offer, making it a highly risky business. Go into it with your eyes open, knowing that it is closer to buying a lottery ticket than earning a living.

What skills does a ghost need?

Ghosts must suppress their own egos completely when working on an autobiography – a good discipline for any writer. You're fulfilling a similar function to a barrister in court, using your skills to plead the case of your client. Authors need ghosts who will not challenge them, but will simply listen to what they have to say and understand why they did what they did. If the ghost wishes to be critical of the subject then they must step back and create an objective biography, not an autobiography.

It is essential for the ghost to make the subject feel completely comfortable in his or her company. If they think the ghost is going to criticise them, judge them or argue with them they will not relax, open up or talk honestly. It's not the ghost's job to try to make them change their opinions about anything or anyone, but rather to encourage them to tell their story in the most interesting and coherent way possible. The ghost must be able to coax them off their hobbyhorses and persuade them to answer all the questions that the eventual readers are likely to ask. The author must not sound bitter. Part of the ghost's job is to ensure that the author remains attractive and interesting to the reader.

Once the voice is on tape the ghost then has to create what amounts to an 80,000-word monologue, just as a playwright might do, staying completely in the author's character at all times, using the sort of vocabulary the author would use and expressing the same views, ideas and prejudices.

It's important that a ghost is interested in the subject; otherwise the project will become unbearable. Imagine spending that much time talking to someone who bores you, and then having to go away and write it out all over again.

A ghost must also be able to see the structure of a book from early on in the process. He or she then needs to be able to guide the subject into providing the right material, keeping them on track and clearing up any inconsistencies in the telling of the tale.

The ghosting process

Sometimes the author has already produced some written material that can provide the bulk of the background. More often the ghost will have a clean slate to work from.

How many hours of taping will be required depends on how succinct the author can be persuaded to be and how quickly the ghost can master the subject. I find that 10–20 hours of useful taping is generally enough to produce a strong first draft. For autobiographies it's important to get them to tell you the story chronologically, so that you know what they have and have not experienced at each stage of the tale. The sequence can always be changed for dramatic effect once the actual writing commences.

It is usually preferable to interview them on their own home ground, where they will be at their most relaxed and least guarded. You will also get a better idea of what their lives are like.

The first draft should be shown to no one until the author has okayed it. They have final veto on what should and shouldn't be in the final draft. Only if they're confident that they have the final say will they be completely open and honest with you. The ghost can advise and warn, but the author has the last word. (Once given the power to make changes they nearly always decide they can't actually think of a better way of putting things and leave the manuscript virtually untouched). If there is arguing to be done, let it be done by the agent and the publisher.

A ghost must expect no glory. Enjoy the experience of the researching and the writing and of being paid to do pleasant work. Sometimes your name will get mentioned on the cover of a book and sometimes it will appear only on the flyleaf. Sometimes you will get a mention in the acknowledgements and sometimes you will not appear at all. You may get billed as 'co-author', but it is more likely to say 'By Big Shot with Joe Bloggs' or 'as told to Joe Bloggs'. It's always useful to have your name there but it can never be allowed to become a problem if it disappears.

Why publishers use ghosts

Publishers like to use ghostwriters because they know they will be able to rely on them as professionals. They want to know that the book will arrive on time in a publishable form, conforming as nearly as possible to the synopsis or the brief.

Frequently the authors of the books are busy people and hard to get hold of. Sometimes they are temperamental. The publishers consequently rely on the ghosts to act as go-betweens and to make the process of publication as smooth as possible.

The ghost is also the subject's best friend in the publishing business. During the long months when the agent is trying to sell the project and the phone doesn't ring, he or she will assure them that this is perfectly normal and doesn't mean they will never find a publisher. When the publisher wants to change the title or favours a cover in the subject's least favourite colour, the ghost will again have to be there to assure them that it will all be okay on the night. Then, when the book comes out and the subject can't find it on the front table in any of their local book shops, the ghost will have to explain the economics of the business to them and try to dissuade them from ringing the publisher and ranting and raving.

Ghosting is an endlessly varied, interesting and rewarding job – relish every opportunity you are given to practice it.

Andrew Crofts was described in the *Independent* as 'the king of modern ghosts'. He has published over 40 ghosted books and has even written a novel, *Maisie's Amazing Maids* (Stratus Books 2001) with a ghostwriter as the central character. He is also the author of *The Freelance Writer's Handbook – How to make money and enjoy life* (Piatkus 2002).

Writing and the children's book market

Over 10,000 new children's titles are published in the UK every year. Chris Kloet suggests how a potential author can best ensure that their work is published.

Children's book publishing can be difficult for the first-time writer to break into. It is a diverse, overcrowded market, with many thousands of titles currently in print, available both in the UK and from elsewhere via the internet. Children's publishers tend to fill their lists with commissioned books by writers they publish regularly, so they may lack space or be reluctant to take a risk with an untried author. This is a selective, highly competitive, market-led business. Since every new book is expected to meet its projected sales target, your writing must demonstrate solid sales potential, as well as strength and originality, if it is to stand a chance of being published.

Is your work right for today's market? Literary tastes and fashions change. Publishers cater to children whose reading is now almost certainly different from that of your own childhood. In the present electronic media-driven age, few want cosy tales about fairies and bunnies, jolly talking cars or magic teapots. Nor anything remotely imitative. Editors choose original, lively material – something witty, innovative and pacey. They look for polished writing with a fresh, contemporary voice that speaks directly and engages today's critical, media-savvy young readers, who are often easily bored.

Develop a sense of the market so that you can judge the potential for your work. Read widely and critically across the children's book spectrum for an overview, especially noting recent titles. Visit dedicated children's books websites, such as Achuka. As you read, pay attention to the different categories, series, genres and publishers' imprints. This will help you to pinpoint likely publishers. Before submitting your typescript, ensure that your targeted publisher currently publishes in your particular form or genre. Request catalogues from their marketing department; check out their website. Consult the publisher's entry under *Book publishers UK and Ireland* (see page 127). Many publishing houses now stipulate 'No unsolicited MSS or synopses'. Don't spend your time and postage sending work to them; choose instead a publisher who accepts unsolicited work.

You might consider approaching a literary agent who knows market trends, publishers' lists and the faces behind them. Most editors regard agents as filters and may prefer submissions from them, knowing that a preliminary critical eye has been cast over them.

Picture books

Books for babies and toddlers are often board books and novelties. Unless you are also a professional illustrator (see *Illustrating for children's books*, page 230) they present few opportunities for a writer. Picture books are aimed at children aged between two and five or six, and are usually 32 pages long, giving 12–14 double-page spreads, and illustrated in colour.

Although a story written for this format should be simple, it must be structured, with a compelling beginning, middle and end. The theme should interest and be appropriate for the age and experience of its audience. As the text is likely to be reread, it should possess a satisfying rhythm (but beware of rhymes). Ideally, it should be fewer than 1000 words (and could be much shorter), must offer scope for illustration and, finally, it needs strong international appeal. Reproducing full-colour artwork is costly and the originating publisher must be confident of achieving co-productions with publishers overseas, to keep unit costs down. It has to be said: it is a tough field.

Submit a picture book text typed either on single-sided A4 sheets, showing page breaks, or as a series of numbered pages, each with its own text. Do not go into details about illustrations, but simply note anything that is not obvious from the text that needs to be included in the pictures.

Younger fiction

This area of publishing presents opportunities for the new writer. It covers stories written for the post-picture book stage, when children are reading their first whole novels. Texts vary in length and complexity, depending on the age and fluency of the reader, but tend to be between 1000 and 6000 words long.

Publishers bring out titles under the umbrella of various series, each targeted at a particular level of reading experience and competency. Categories are: beginning or first readers, developing or newly confident, confident, and fluent readers. Note that these are not the same as reading schemes published for the schools market and do not require such a restricted vocabulary. Stories for the bottom end of the age range are usually short, straight-through narratives illustrated throughout in colour, whereas those for older children are broken down into chapters and may be illustrated in black and white. The table on page 228 lists publishers' requirements for some currently published series. Check that your material is correct in terms of length and interest level when approaching a publisher with a submission for a series.

Genre fiction

Another area in children's publishing is that of genre fiction. Usually published in paperback series, titles are sometimes the work of a single author, but might also be novels from several authors writing in a similar vein. Some fiction aimed at teenagers is published in genre series although it is much less popular than in recent years.

General fiction

Many novels for children aged 9–12 are published, not in series, but as 'standalone' titles, each judged on its own merits. The scope for different types of stories is wide – adventure stories, fantasies, historical novels, science fiction, ghost and horror stories, humour, and stories of everyday life. Generally, their length is 20,000– 40,000 words. This is a rough guide and is by no means fixed. For example, J.K. Rowling's phenomenally successful *Harry Potter* novels weigh in at between 300–750 closely printed pages, and publishers now seem more

Publisher	Series name	Length	Age group	Comments
Andersen Press	Tigers	3000–5000 words 64 pages	6–9	B&w illustrations throughout
A & C Black	Black Cats	12,000–14,000 words 96 pages	10–12	Short novels; b&w illustrations
	Chameleons	1200 words 48 pages	5–7	Colour illustrations throughout
Bloomsbury	Young Fiction	2500 words 64 pages	5–7	B&w illustrations throughout
	Middle Fiction	6000 words 64 pages	7–9	B&w illustrations throughout
Collins Children's Books	Roaring Good Reads	2000–8000 words	7–9	B&w illustrations throughout
	Collins Voyager	20,000 words+	9–14	Fantasy
	Collins Flamingo	30,000–60,000 words	13–16	Contemporary fiction
Egmont Books	Blue Bananas	1000 words 48 pages	5+	Colour illustrations
	Red Bananas	2000 words 48 pages	6+	Colour illustrations
	Yellow Bananas	3000 words 48 pages	7+	Colour illustrations
	Go Bananas	1000–3000 words 48 pages	5–7	Curriculum-based strand
Franklin Watts	Leapfrog	180 words 32 pages	4–6	Colour illustrations throughout
	Hopscotch	350–400 words 32 pages	5–7	Colour illustrations throughout
Hodder Children's Books	Bite	35,000+ words	12+	Contemporary fiction
	Silver	35,000+ words	10+	Fantasy and science fiction
	Signature	35,000+ words	11+	Literary fiction
Kingfisher	I Am Reading	1200 words 48 pages	5–7	Colour illustrations throughout
Orchard Books	Crunchies	1000–1500 words	5–7	B&w line illustrations
	Colour Crunchies	1000–1500 words	5–7	Colour illustrations
	Super Crunchies	5000 words	7–9	B&w line illustrations
	Orchard Storybooks	7000–15,000	8–11	B&w line illustrations
	Red Apples	20,000–25,000 words	9–11	
	Black Apples	30,000–40,000 words	12+	
Penguin Group	Colour Young Puffin	1000–2500 words 32–64 pages	5–8	Colour illustrations
	Young Puffin	8000–10,000 words 96–128 pages	7–9	B&w line illustrations
Scholastic Children's Books	Young Hippo	3500–10,000 words 64–96 pages	6–9	B&w illustrations throughout
	Hippo	15,000–25,000 words	8–12	
	Point	30,000 words	12+	
Walker Books	Sprinters	2000 words	6–8	B&w illustrations throughout
	Junior fiction	15,000–25,000 words	8–12	
	Teenage fiction	25,000–40,000 words	12+	

willing to publish longer texts, particularly fantasies, which are often published as hefty trilogies.

Perhaps more than in other areas of juvenile fiction, the individual editor's tastes will play a significant part in the publishing decision, i.e they want authors' work which *they* like. They, and their sales and marketing departments, also need to feel confident of a new writer's ability to go on to write further books for their lists – nobody is keen to invest in an author who is just a one-book wonder.

When submitting your work it is probably best to send the entire typescript (see *Dos and don'ts on approaching a publisher*, page 217). Although some people advise sending in a synopsis with the first three chapters, a prospective publisher will need to see whether you can sustain a reader's interest to the end of the book.

Teenage fiction

As noted earlier, some of the published output for teenaged readers is published in series. Increasingly, publishers are targeting this area of the market with edgy, hard-hitting novels about contemporary teenagers, which they publish as standalone titles. There is also a current vogue for 'young adult' novels that have a crossover appeal to an adult readership. This is particularly true of certain types of historical fiction by writers such as Jamila Gavin, Adele Geras and Kevin Crossley-Holland, and of several fantasy writers. For example, Philip Pullman's *The Amber Spyglass* was the first children's book to be the overall winner of the Whitbread Book of the Year award.

Non-fiction

The last few years have seen fundamental and striking changes in the type of information books published for the young. Hitherto the province, by and large, of specialist publishers catering for the educational market, the field has now broadened to encompass an astonishing range of presentations and formats which are attractive to the young reader. Although the illustrated text book approach still has its place in schools, increasingly, children are wooed into learning about many topics via entertaining and accessible paperback series such as the *Horrible Histories* published by Scholastic, and a host of similar series from other publishers. In writing for this market, it goes without saying that you must research your subject thoroughly and be able to put it across clearly, with an engaging style. Familiarise yourself with the relevant parts of the National Curriculum. Check out the various series and ask the publishers for any guidelines. You will be well advised to check that there is a market for your book before you actually write it, as researching a subject can be both time consuming and costly. Submit a proposal to your targeted publisher, outlining the subject matter and the level of treatment, and your ideas about the audience for your book.

Chris Kloet worked as Children's Publisher (1984–97) at Victor Gollancz Ltd, and is now Editor-at-Large at Walker Books. She has written and reviewed children's books and has lectured widely on the subject.

Illustrating for children's books

The world of children's publishing is big business. The huge range of books published each year all carry artwork – lots of it. Maggie Mundy offers guidance for people who are at the start of their career in illustrating for children's books.

The portfolio

Your portfolio should reflect the best of you and your work, and should speak for itself. Keep its content simple – if too many styles are included, for instance, your work will not leave a lasting impression.

Include some artwork other than those carried out for college projects, e.g. an illustration from a timeless classic to show your abilities, and something modern which reflects your own taste and the area in which you wish to work.

If your strength is for black and white illustration, include pieces with and without tone and with or without a wash. Some publishers want line and tone and some want only line. As cross hatching and stippling can add a lot of extra time to an illustration deadline, it might be advisable to leave out these samples. If you can, include a selection of humour as it can be used effectively in educational books and elsewhere. It is best not to sign and date your work: some artworks can stand the test of time and still look good after a year or two, but if it looks dated … so is the illustrator!

An A3 portfolio is probably the ideal size. Place your best piece of artwork on the opening page and your next best piece on the last page. See *Freelancing for beginners* on page 381 for further information on portfolio presentation.

Looking at the market

Start by looking thoroughly at what is being published today for children. Take your studies to branches of big retail chains, some independent bookshops, as well as your local library (a helpful librarian should be able to tell you which are the most borrowed books). Absorb the picture books, explore the novelty books, look at the variety of colour covers, and note the range of black line illustrations inside books for children and teenagers. Make a list of the publishers you think may be able to use your particular style.

By making these investigations you will gain an insight into not only the current trends and styles but also the much favoured, oft-published classic children's literature. Most importantly, it will help you identify your market.

In books for a young age range every picture must tell the story – some books have no text and the illustrations say it all. Artwork should be uncluttered, shapes clear, and colour bright. If this does not appeal to you, go up a year or two and note the extra details that are added to the artwork (which still tells the story). Children now need to see more than just clear shapes: they need extra details added to the scene – e.g. a quirky spider hanging around, or a mouse under the bed.

Children are your most critical audience: never think that you can get away with 'any old thing'. Indeed, at the Bologna Book Fair it is a panel of children which judges what they consider to be the best picture book.

Current trends
Innovative publishers are always on the lookout for something new in illustration styles: something completely different from the tried and tested. More and more they are turning to European and overseas illustrators, often sourced from the Bologna Book Fair exhibitions and illustrators catalogue.

Always strive to improve on your work. Don't be afraid to try out something different and to work it up into acceptable examples. Above all, don't get left behind.

Making approaches for work

With your portfolio arranged and your target audience in mind, compile a list of publishing houses, packagers and magazines which you think may be suitable for your work.

An agent should know exactly where to place your work, and this may be the easier option (see below). However, you may wish to market yourself by making and going to appointments until you crack your first job.

Alternatively, you could make up a simple broadsheet comprising a black and white and two or three colour illustrations, together with your contact details, and have it colour photocopied or printed. Another inexpensive option is to have your own CDs made up and to send them instead. Send a copy to either the Art Director, the Creative Director or the Senior Commissioning Editor (for picture books) of each potential client on your list. Try to find out the name of the person you would like to see your work. Wait at least a week and then follow up your mailing with a phone call to ask if someone would like to see your portfolio.

Also consider investing in your own website which you can easily update yourself (see *Setting up a website*, page 530).

Know your capabilities

Know your strengths, but be even more aware of your weaknesses. You will gain far more respect if you admit to not being able to draw something particularly well than by going ahead and producing an embarrassing piece of artwork and having it rejected. You will be remembered for your professional honesty and that client may well try to give you a job where you can use your expertise.

Publishers need to know that you can turn out imaginative, creative artwork while closely following a text or brief, and be able to meet their deadline. It may take an illustrator three weeks to prepare roughs for 32 pages, three weeks to finish the artwork, plus a week to make any corrections. In addition, time has to be allowed for the roughs to be returned. On this basis, how many books can an illustrator realistically take on? Scheduling is of paramount importance (see below).

You will need to become familiar with 'publishing speak' – terms such as gutters, full bleed, holding line, overlays, vignettes, tps, etc. If you don't know the meaning of a term, ask – after all, if you have only recently left college you will not be expected to know all the jargon.

In the course of your work you will have to deal with such issues as contracts, copyright, royalties, public lending rights, rejection fees, etc. The Association of Illustrators, which exists to give help to illustrators in all areas, is well worth joining.

Organising your workload

When you have reached the stage when you have jobs coming through on a fairly regular basis, organise a comprehensive schedule for yourself so you do not overburden yourself with work. Include on it when roughs have to be submitted, how much work you can fit in while waiting for their approval, the deadline for the artwork, and so on. A wall chart can be helpful for this but another system may work better for you. It is totally unacceptable to deliver artwork late. If you think that you might run over time with your work, let your client know in advance as it may be possible to reach a new agreement for delivery.

Payment

There are two ways in which an illustrator may be paid for a commission for a book: a flat fee on receipt and acceptance of the artwork, or by an advance against a royalty of future sales. The advance offered could be less than a flat fee but it may result in higher earnings overall. If the book sells well, the illustrator will receive royalty payments twice a year for as long the book is in print.

You need to know from the outset how you are going to be paid. If it is by a flat fee, you may be given an artwork order with a number to be quoted when you invoice. Always read through orders to make sure you understand the terms and conditions. If you haven't been paid within 30 days, send a statement to remind the client, or make a quick phone call to ask when you can expect to receive payment.

With a royalty offer, a contract will be drawn up and this must be checked carefully. One of the clauses will state the breakdown of how and when you will be paid.

Once you have illustrated your first book you should register with the Public Lending Right Office (see page 602) so that you can receive a yearly payment on all UK library borrowings. You will need to cooperate with the author regarding percentages before submitting your own form. The PLR office will give you a reference number, and you then submit details to them of each book you illustrate. It mounts up and is a nice little earner!

Agents

The role of the agent is to represent the illustrator to the best of their ability and to the illustrator's best advantage. A good agent knows the marketplace and will promote illustrators' work where it will count. An agent may ask you to do one or two sample pieces to strengthen your portfolio, giving them a better chance of securing work for you.

Generally speaking, agents will look after you, your work schedules, payments, contracts, royalties, copyright issues, and try to ensure you have a regular flow of work which you not only enjoy but will stretch your talents to taking on bigger and better jobs. Without exposing your weaknesses, check that you have adequate time in which to do a job and that you are paid a fair rate for the work.

Some illustrators manage well without an agent, and having one is not necessarily a pathway to fame and fortune. Choose carefully: you need to both like and trust the agent and vice versa.

Agents' charges range from 25% to 30%. Find out from the outset how much a prospective agent will charge.

Finally

Do not be downhearted if progress is at first slow. Everyone starts by serving an apprenticeship, and it is a great opportunity to learn, absorb and soak up as much of the business as possible. Ask questions, get all the advice you can, and use what you learn to improve your craft and thereby your chances of landing a job. Publishers are always on the lookout for fresh talent and new ideas, and one day your talent will be the one they want.

Maggie Mundy has been representing illustrators for children's books since 1983. Her agency represents 25 European and British illustrators for children's books.

See also...

Doing it on your own

Reasons for self-publishing are varied. Many highly respected comtemporary and past authors have published their own works. Peter Finch introduces the concept and outlines the implications of such an undertaking.

Why bother?

You've tried all the usual channels and been turned down; your work is uncommercial, specialised, technical, out of fashion; you are concerned with art while everyone else is obsessed with cash; you need a book out quickly; you want to take up small publishing as a hobby; you've heard that publishers make a lot of money out of their authors and you'd like a slice – all reason enough. But be sure you understand what you are doing before you begin.

But isn't this cheating? It can't be real publishing – where is the critical judgement? Publishing is a respectable activity carried out by firms of specialists. Writers of any ability never get involved.

But they do. Start self-publishing and you'll be in good historical company: Horace Walpole, Balzac, Walt Whitman, Virginia Woolf, Gertrude Stein, John Galsworthy, Rudyard Kipling, Beatrix Potter, Lord Byron, Thomas Paine, Mark Twain, Upton Sinclair, W.H. Davies, Zane Grey, Ezra Pound, D.H. Lawrence, William Carlos Williams, Alexander Pope, Robbie Burns, James Joyce, Anaïs Nin and Lawrence Stern. All these at some time in their careers dabbled in doing it themselves. William Blake did nothing else. He even made his own ink, handprinted his pages and got Mrs Blake to sew on the covers.

But today it's different?

Not necessarily. This is not vanity publishing we're talking about although if all you want to do is produce a pamphlet of poems to give away to friends then self-publishing will be the cheapest way. Doing it yourself today can be a valid form of business enterprise. Being twice shortlisted for major literary prizes sharpened Timothy Mo's acumen. Turning his back on mass-market paperbacks, he published *Brownout on Breadfruit Boulevard* on his own. Billy Hopkin's Headline bestseller of Lancashire life, *High Hopes*, began as a self-published title. Susan Hill self-produced her short stories, *Listening to the Orchestra*, and as an example to us all Jill Paton Walsh's self-published *Knowledge of Angels* was shortlisted for the Booker Prize.

Can anyone do it?

Certainly. If you are a writer then a fair number of the required qualities will already be in hand. The more able and practical you are then the cheaper the process will be. The utterly inept will need to pay others to help them, but it will still be self-publishing in the end.

Where do I start?

With research. Read up on the subject. Make sure you know what the parts of a book are. Terms like *verso*, *recto*, font, typeface and point size all have to lose their mystery. You will not need to become an expert but you will need a certain familiarity. Don't rush. Learn.

What about ISBN numbers?
International Standard Book Numbers – a standard bibliographic code, individual to each book published, are used by booksellers and librarians alike. They are issued by the Standard Book Numbering Agency at a cost of £60 plus VAT for ten. Self-publishers may balk at this apparently inordinate expense but the ISBN is the device used by the trade to track titles and if you are serious about your book should be regarded as essential. The Agency issues a free information pack; see *FAQs about ISBNs* on page 596.

Next?
Put your book together – be it the typed pages of your novel, your selected poems or your story of how it was sailing round the world – and see how large a volume it will make. If you have no real idea of what your book should look like, go to your local bookshop and hunt out a few contemporary examples of volumes produced in a style you would like to emulate. Take your typescript and your examples round to a number of local printers and ask for a quote.

How much?
It depends. How long is a piece of string? Unit cost is important: the larger the number of copies you have printed the less each will cost. Print too many and the total bill will be enormous. Printing has gone through a revolution in recent years. The arrival of POD (Printing on Demand) and other digital technologies have reduced costs and, for the first time, made short runs economic. But books are still not cheap.

Can I make it cost less?
Yes. Do some of the work yourself. If you want to publish poems and you are prepared to use a text set by a word processor, you will make a considerable saving. Many word processing programs have publishing facilities which will enhance the look of your text. Could you accept home production, run the pages off on an office photocopier, then staple the sheets? Editions made this way can be very presentable.

For longer texts keyed in on a word processor, savings can be made by supplying the work as a digital file directly to a printer. They can import your text into their program without the need for any rekeying. But be prepared to shop around.

Home binding, if your abilities lie in that direction, can save a fair bit. What it all comes down to is the standard of production you want and indeed at whom your book is aimed. Books for the commercial marketplace need to look like their fellows; specialist publications can afford to be more eccentric.

Who decides how it looks?
You do. No one should ever ask a printer simply to produce a book. You should plan the design of your publication with as much care as you would a house extension. Spend as much time and money as you can on the cover. It is the part of the book your buyer will see first. If you're stuck, employ a book designer.

How many copies should I produce?

Poetry books sell about 300 copies, new novels sometimes manage 1000, literary paperbacks 10,000, mass-market blockbusters over a million. But that is generally where there is a sales team and whole distribution organisation behind the book. Do not, on the one hand, end up with a prohibitively high unit cost by ordering too few copies. One hundred of anything is usually a waste of time. On the other hand can you really sell 3000? Will shops buy in dozens? They will probably only want twos and threes. Take care. Research your market first.

How do I sell it?

With all your might. This is perhaps the hardest part of publishing. It is certainly as time consuming as both the writing of the work and the printing of it put together. To succeed here you need a certain flair and you should definitely not be of a retiring nature. If you intend selling through the trade (and even if you don't you are bound to come into contact with bookshop orders at some stage), your costing must be correct and worked out in advance. Shops will want at least 35% (with national chains asking for even more) of the selling price as discount. You'll need about the same again to cover your distribution, promotion and other overheads, leaving the final third to cover production costs and any profit you may wish to make. Multiply your unit production cost by at least four. Commerical publishers often multiply by as much as nine.

Do not expect the trade to pay your carriage costs. Your terms should be 35% post free on everything bar single copy orders. Penalise these by reducing your discount to 25%. Some shops will suggest that you sell copies to them on sale or return. This means that they only pay you for what they sell and then only after they've sold it. This is a common practice with certain categories of publications and often the only way to get independent books into certain shops; but from the self-publisher's point of view it should be avoided if at all possible. Cash in hand is best but expect to have your invoices paid by cheque at a later date. Buy a duplicate pad in order to keep track of what's going on. Phone the shops you have decided should take your book or turn up in person and ask to see the buyer. Letters and sample copies sent by post will get ignored. Get a freelance distributor to handle all of this for you if you can. But expect to be

Low print run printers

Start by asking a few local printers for quotes. It is also worth trying:

Able Publishing
13 Station Road, Knebworth, Herts SG3 6AP
tel (01438) 814316 *fax* (01438) 815232
email fp@ablepublishing.co.uk
website www.ablepublishing.co.uk

Biddles Ltd – Short Run Printing
Woodbridge Park Estate, Woodbridge Road,
Guildford, Surrey GU1 1DA
tel (01483) 502224/(01553) 769072
fax (01483) 576150
email shortrun@biddles.co.uk
website www.biddles.co.uk

The Better Book Company
Warblington Lodge, The Gardens, Warblington,
Havant, Hants PO9 2XH
tel 023-9248 1160 *fax* 023-9249 2819
email editors@better-book.co.uk

Antony Rowe Ltd
Bumper's Farm, Chippenham, Wilts. SN14 6LH
tel (01249) 659705 *fax* (01249) 445535
email sales@antonyrowe.co.uk
website www.antonyrowe.co.uk

disappointed. Independent book representatives willing to take on a one-off title are as rare as hen's teeth. If you can contract one they will want another 12% or so commission on top of the shops' discount – but expect to have to go it alone.

What about promotion?
A vital aspect often overlooked by beginners. Send out as many review copies as you can, all accompanied by slips quoting selling price and name and address of the publisher. Never admit to being that person yourself. Invent a name: it will give your operation a professional feel. Ring up newspapers and local radio stations ostensibly to check that your copy has arrived but really to see if they are prepared to give your book space. Buying advertising space rarely pays for itself but good local promotion with 100% effort will generate dividends.

What about depositing copies at the British Library?
Under the Copyright Acts the British Library, the Bodleian Library, Oxford, the University Library, Cambridge, the National Library of Scotland, the Library of Trinity College Dublin and the National Library of Wales are all entitled to a free copy of your book which must be sent to them within one month of publication. One copy should go direct to the Legal Deposit Office at the British Library, Boston Spa, Wetherby, West Yorkshire LS23 7BY. The other libraries use an agent, Carryl M. Allardice, Agent for the Copyright Libraries, 100 Euston Street, London NW1 2HQ. Contact her directly to find out how many copies she requires.

What if I can't manage all this myself?
You can employ others to do it for you. If you are a novelist and you opt for a package covering everything, it could set you back more than £10,000. A number of publishers and associations advertise such services in writers' journals and in the Sunday classifieds. 'Authors. Publish with us.' is a typical ploy. They will do a competent job for you, certainly, but you will still end up having to do the bulk of the selling yourself. It is a costly route, fraught with difficulty. Do the job on your own if you possibly can.

And what if it goes wrong?
Put all the unsolds under the bed or give them away. It has happened to lots of us. Even the big companies who are experienced at these things have their regular flops. It was an adventure and you did get your book published. On the other hand you may be so successful that you'll be at the London Book Fair selling the film rights and wondering if you've reprinted enough.

Can the internet help?
The web has yet to take the place of traditional print. However, a good number of authors are setting up their own home pages. From these they advertise themselves and their works, and offer downloadable samples and, in some cases, their complete books. No one has yet made a fortune here and the number of 'hits' some sites claim to get are questionable. Nonetheless, this method of self-promotion comes highly recommended. Self-publishers, if they are not already familiar with the internet, should get on board now. *The Internet: A Writer's Guide* (see further reading) is a good place to start; see also *Setting up a website* on page 530.

Currently, the internet is thick with operators offering to promote or publish work electronically. These range from companies which post sample chapters and then charge readers a fee for the complete work to professional e-book developers who offer books fully formatted for use on hand-held PDAs (Personal Digital Assistants) and other devices (see *E-publishing*, page 525). The jury is still out on where this flux of technological change is going, but if you'd like to test the waters, visit Jane Dorner's site at www.internetwriter.co.uk or romance writer Mary Wolf's list of e-publishers at http://my. coredcs.com/~mermaid/epub.html.

Peter Finch runs Academi, the Welsh National Literature Promotion Agency and Society of Writers. He is a poet, former bookseller and small publisher and author of the *How to Publish Yourself*. His website contains further advice for self-publishers (www.peterfinch.co.uk).

Further reading

Baverstock, Alison, *Marketing Your Book: An Author's Guide*, A & C Black, 2001

Coleman, Vernon, *How to Publish Your Own Book*, Blue Books, 1999

Dawes, John (ed.), *The Best of Write to Publish!*, John Dawes Publications, 2002

Domanski, Peter and Irvine, Philip, *A Practical Guide to Publishing Books Using Your PC*, Domanski-Irvine Books, 1997

Dorner, Jane, *The Internet: A Writer's Guide*, A & C Black, 2nd edn, 2001

Finch, Peter, *How to Publish Yourself*, Allison & Busby, 4th edn, 2000

Ross, Tom and Marilyn, *The Complete Guide to Self-Publishing*, Writer's Digest Books, 4th edn, 2002

Spicer, Robert, *Publishing a Book*, How To Books, 3rd edn, 1998, o.p.

Woll, Thomas, *Publishing for Profit*, Kogan Page, 2000

Helping to market your book

Authors can enhance their publisher's efforts to sell their book and in this article
Alison Baverstock offers guidance on how they can help. The information is also
relevant to self publishers.

Having a book accepted for publication is immensely satisfying – all the more so
if in the process you have amassed a thick pile of rejection letters spanning
several years. At this stage, some authors decide that, having committed
themselves to work with a professional publishing house, this is the end of their
involvement in the process. They will move on thankfully to the writing of their
next book.

Once you have delivered your manuscript, and it has been accepted for
publication, a publisher should handle all aspects of your book's subsequent
development, from copy-editing and production to promotion and distribution.
But there is a sound pragmatism in remaining vigilant. When it comes to the
marketing of your book, there is a huge amount that you can do to help it sell.

The challenging marketplace

Each year in Britain alone, over 100,000 books get published or come out in new
editions. All compete for the attention of the same review editors, the same stock
buyers in bookshops, and the largely static number of regular book-buying
members of the general public. It follows that anything an author can do to help
'position' the book, to make it sound different, or just more interesting than
those it competes with, will be a huge advantage.

The marketing of books is not usually an area of high spending and there are
many reasons why. Books are cheap (a novel costs about the same as a cinema
ticket, and much less than a round of drinks), the publishers' profit margins are
low, booksellers claim a percentage of the purchase price as discount (35–50%),
and books sell in relatively small quantities (a mass market novel selling 15,000
copies may be considered a 'bestseller' – compare that with the sales figures for
CDs or computer games). Your publisher will probably try to make maximum
use of (free) publicity to stimulate demand using low-cost marketing
techniques. They are far more likely to arrange for the insertion of a simple
leaflet as a loose insert in a relevant publication, or organise a specific mailing to
members of a relevant society, than book television or billboard advertising.
Your assistance in helping them reach the market could be most important.

Examine your resources

Think in detail about what resources you have at your disposal that would help
make your book sell, and tell your publisher. Most houses send out an Authors'
Publicity Form about six months before publication, asking you for details of
your book and how you feel it can best be marketed. Whilst the house will
probably not be able to fulfil all your ambitions (mass market advertising is not
possible for every book), they will be particularly interested in your contacts. For

example, were you at school with the person who is now a features writer on *The Times*? Even if you have not spoken since, they may still remember your name. Do your children attend the same school as a contact on your local paper? Do you belong to a society or professional organisation that produces a newsletter for members, organises a conference or regular dining club? All these communication channels provide opportunities for publishers to send information on your book to potential purchasers.

Even greater things may be achieved if you set up the arrangements yourself. Can you arrange for an editorial mention of your book in a society journal (which will carry more weight than an advertisement) or organise for your publisher to take advertising space at a reduced rate? Remember that the less it costs your publishing house to reach each potential customer, the more of the market they will be able to cover out of their planned budgetary spend.

Offer a peg to your publisher

In trying to stimulate demand for a book, publishers try to achieve publicity (or coverage in the media) at the time of publication. The most usual way of getting this is for the in-house publicist to write a press release about you and your book and send this out to journalists in the hope that they will be interested enough to write about you, or even better decide to interview you.

Your publishing house will need 'pegs' on which to hang stories about you and your book, and it is helpful if you volunteer these rather than waiting to be asked. So, think back over your career and life in general. What is interesting about you? Are there any stories that arise out of the research for the book; incidents that give a flavour of the book and you as a writer?

Try to look at your life as others might see it; events or capabilities you take for granted might greatly interest other people. For example, novelist Catherine Jones is married to a former soldier, and has moved house 15 times in 20 years. In that time she has produced three children and has had appointments with over 40 different classroom teachers. She speaks about her life in a very matter of fact way, but when she wrote her first novel, *Army Wives* (Piatkus), the media were quite fascinated by a world they clearly knew nothing about. They found military jargon particularly compelling, and this proved a wonderful (and headline-producing) peg on which to promote her book.

Make yourself available

For a mass market title, any publicity that can be achieved will need to be orchestrated at the time of publication. By this time the publisher will hopefully have persuaded booksellers to take stock and the books will be in the shops. If the publicity is successful, but peaks before the books are available to buy, you have entirely missed the boat. If there is no publicity on publication, and no consequent demand, the bookseller has the right to return the books to the publisher and receive a credit note. And in these circumstances it will be *extremely* difficult to persuade them to restock the title having been let down once.

Timing is therefore absolutely crucial, so make yourself available at the time of publication (this is not the time to take your well-earned break). Remember too that, unless you are a very big star, each different newspaper or programme approached will consider its own requirements exclusively, and will not be interested in your own personal scheduling. Not all journalists work every day, and even if they do they like to decide on their own priorities. If you ask for an interview to be rescheduled, it may be dropped completely.

Don't assume that only coverage in the national media is worth having and turn your nose up at local radio and newspapers; they can reach a very wide audience and be particularly effective in prompting sales. You may be able to extend the amount of time and space you get by suggesting a competition or reader/listener offer. Local journalists usually have a much friendlier approach than those who work on the nationals, so if you are a novice to the publicity process this can be a much easier start, and an opportunity to build your confidence.

Contributing text for marketing

At several stages in the production process your publisher may request your input. You may be asked to provide text for the book jacket or for an author profile, to check information that will be included in the publisher's annual catalogue, or to provide biographical information for their website.

Think in detail about the words you have been asked for, who will read them and in what circumstances, and then craft what you write accordingly. For example, the text on a fiction book jacket (or 'blurb') should not retell the story or give away the plot; rather it should send signals that convey atmosphere, whet the appetite of the reader and show what kind of book they can expect. The potential customer is likely to be reading the blurb in a hurry, perhaps whilst standing in a bookshop being jostled by other shoppers, so it is best to keep it brief.

A non-fiction blurb should establish what the book will do for the reader and what your qualifications are for writing it. Again, keep the details short. The key factor is relevance – what have you done, and what are you qualified to do, that is relevant to the publication in hand?

For both categories of book a third party recommendation will help enormously as this provides objective proof of what a book is like and how useful it is. When books have come out as hardbacks, then extracts from the review coverage can be used on the paperback edition. For previously unpublished authors, a relevant quotation is very helpful instead. Do you know anyone established in the appropriate field who could provide an endorsement for what you have written? Can you contact them and ask them to help? The endorsement does not have to be from someone famous, just someone relevant. For example, a children's book endorsed as a gripping read by a 10-year-old child, or an educational text endorsed by a student who had just passed her exams could both be effective.

You may be asked to check your details in a publisher's catalogue. Bear in mind that your entry will sit alongside everything else they publish, so it must be factual and clear.

If you are asked to write website copy, be sure to look at the relevant site before you draft something. Think about the context in which your material will be seen and read (by whom, how often and for how long) and use this information as the basis for writing.

Marketing after publication

Although most of the effort in marketing your book will inevitably occur at the time of publication (because next month's schedule will bring forward further titles that need the marketing department's attention), there is a great deal of opportunity to carry on selling your book afterwards.

So, if you are asked to speak at a conference or run a training course, ask if your book can be included in the package available to delegates, either as part of the overall price or at a reduced rate. Ask the publishing house for simple flyers (leaflets) on your book which you can hand out on suitable occasions. Then ask the organisers to put a copy inside the delegate pack, on every seat, or in a pile at the back of the hall (or preferably all three!).

Give your publishing house the details of speaking engagements or conferences at which they could usefully mount a display of all their titles (your own included). Even though they published your book, you cannot reasonably expect them to be specialists in every specific field you know intimately, so give them *all* the details they need. For a conference this would include the full title (not just the initials you refer to it by), the organiser's address and contact numbers (not the chairperson's address to which you should send associated papers), the precise dates and times, and any associated deadlines (e.g. stand bookings placed before a certain date may be cheaper). Finally, try to plan ahead rather than passing on key details at the last minute (this is one of publishers' most common complaints about authors!).

When authors get together they will moan about their publishers. But if that energy is channelled into helping promote the books, everyone benefits!

After 10 years in publishing **Alison Baverstock** set up her own marketing consultancy, specialising in running campaigns for the book trade and training publishers to market more effectively. She is a well-established speaker on the book business and has written widely on how to market books. Her most recent title is *Marketing Your Book: An Author's Guide* (A & C Black 2001). She may be contacted at baverstockjam@cwcom.net

Book distribution

Despite the large number of bookshops in the UK, a published book is not guaranteed a place in one of them. Mike Petty charts the journey a book may take from publisher to bookshop and offers reasons why so many books don't reach the high street.

"Why aren't my books in the shops?" The *cri de coeur* is a familiar one (not just from authors, I might add – their editors are prone to similar gripes). There has been an explosion in bookshop numbers in the last decade or so: as of December 2002 there were 93 Ottakar's branches as opposed to nine in 1992, 61 Borders/Books Etc as against 10 Books Etc, and 204 Waterstone's branches as against 178 Waterstone's/Dillon's. Over the same period WHSmith began to take their claim to be Britain's largest booksellers reasonably seriously. I doubt, however, whether the majority of writers would feel that their lot has improved accordingly; there is no particular evidence that the number of book buyers has risen, and spending on books as a percentage of household expenditure fell between 1985 and 1998.

The mechanics of book distribution are, in outline, simple enough. Anywhere between six and three months before publication all books are subscribed either by sales management or reps to customers, whether individual shops, the head office teams of the chains, or wholesalers. ('Customers' in publisher-speak are people who sell books, not people who buy them from bookshops.) The salespeople will have been primed by their editorial and marketing colleagues as to the qualities and saleability (in theory) of each title, and will be wielding at the very least a jacket and an information sheet bearing the salient details. The customer, if sufficiently impressed by the presentation and the author's sales history, if any, will order a quantity ranging from one to many thousands, plus associated paraphernalia such as dumpbins, posters, etc and these will be delivered in time for publication.

(A publication date, by the way, has very little significance these days, except of course for the author, especially if there is a party or a dinner in the offing. Otherwise it is largely a matter of administrative convenience for publishers and booksellers since, unless specifically asked not to for some reason to do with newsworthiness, bookshops will place stock on sale as soon as they receive it. Books hanging around in stockrooms do not earn money.)

Distribution centres

A modern book distribution centre is a vast, echoing place, its offices full of the clatter of computer operators, its warehouse area crammed with racks carrying pallets of books stacked up to a hundred feet high, while the air is filled with the sound of forklift trucks and transistor radios. Littlehampton Book Services (LBS), a typical large distribution centre, handles Canongate, Serpent's Tail, Aurum, Watts, Kyle Cathie and Atlantic among others, as well as owners Orion, whose imprints include Weidenfeld and Nicolson, Gollancz and several paperback lists.

The figures are astounding. According to Bridget Radnedge, Publishing Services Director at LBS, the warehouse contains about 25,000 different titles at any one time (out of a database of around 150,000 titles), which translates to somewhere between 25 and 28 million books. Seven to eight thousand separate orders are received per week and are turned round in an average of 3–4 days. In 2002, 34.8 million books were despatched, an average of 650,000 a week. 'Goods In' sees anything up to 400 pallets a day (including 3.6 million returns in 2002), delivered by 20 or so trucks. LBS operates 24 hours a day, though the small hours are reserved for housekeeping chores such as replenishing the forward picking racks, where new and fast-moving titles are stored for easy despatch. These figures will be duplicated at the other half a dozen or so vast distribution centres round the country – and LBS are currently operating at 85% of capacity.

But the mechanics of book distribution do not always work as smoothly as they should. In spite of the best efforts of publishers, warehouses, transport firms, wholesalers and booksellers, the process is best thought of as an obstacle race. The winners will appear in the shops in decent quantities – and, in an ideal world reappear there – while the losers will fall at one of quite a few hurdles along the way.

Small- and medium-size publishers, unable to afford the serious expense of their own warehouses, sign up with one or other of the big boys. In its three warehouses The Book Service (TBS, formerly known as Tiptree Book Services) handles all the Random House and Transworld imprints and dozens of others besides, including Time Warner, Mainstream, Virgin, Lonely Planet, Piatkus, Taschen and the AA. A recent recruit is Faber & Faber, who until recently had their own warehouse. If these larger businesses get into trouble, the knock-on effects for their clients can be serious. The changeover to a new computer system is a frequent and apparently inevitable cause for complaint, as is a tendency to overstretch resources in the pursuit of margin. LBS celebrated winning the British Book Award for Distributor of the Year back in January 1998 by expanding their client list. By Christmas of that year their systems were seriously overloaded, they were operating from four sites, and there was talk of books left out in the rain because there was no space under cover. The year ended in a welter of recriminations and threatened lawsuits. Martin Evans, an experienced logistics troubleshooter, was brought in to sort things out, which he did most effectively. But the after-effects, in the shape of compensation claims, lingered for Orion and their French owners Hachette for some time.

Centralised ordering and promotions

The increasing centralisation of ordering is another obstacle. In rare cases as much as 90% of a book's UK subscription can go to perhaps a dozen key accounts, leaving the balance to be fought over by the on-the-road sales force which traditionally has been the main means of communication with individual bookshops. While in most cases the percentage will be lower than this, there is no doubt that in recent years – and in particular since the collapse of the Net Book Agreement – the balance has shifted significantly towards centralised buying. By 'key accounts' is meant wholesalers (the biggest are THE, Gardners and Bertrams); specialised wholesalers such as Thomas Cork and Aspen who supply supermarkets, motorways and airports; WHSmith; supermarkets who are not otherwise supplied; and – increasingly – the online booksellers. Many of these, such as Blackwell's, Foyles and WHSmith, have their terrestrial counterparts, while others, most notably Amazon, do not. Between centralisation of ordering on the one hand, and increased penetration of the independents by wholesalers on the other, the future for reps is not rosy.

Chains such as Waterstone's are also centralising promotions, leading to the homogenisation of high street bookselling. The range of stock that used to be one of the glories of Waterstone's in particular has inevitably suffered. Promotions such as '3 for 2' or BOGOF (Buy One Get One Free), which are such a common feature in all the chains, arguably get more copies of fewer titles into the hands of more people, but at some cost, one suspects, to the publishers' margins and the authors' royalty accounts. Supermarkets take the process a stage further; if you are one of the few (largely high-profile) authors stocked by the likes of Tesco and Asda you can take pleasure in the expansion – at least in theory – of your readership, but you are entitled to ask whether even your publisher is making any money, let alone you yourself.

Publishers

Of course not all the obstacles to literary success lie along the supply chain; some can be laid at the door of the publishers themselves. It is self-evident that booksellers will be disinclined to give a book much shelf space if they feel that the publishers aren't putting any promotion behind it. The higher the advance, the more will be spent on promotion, and the more customers – retailers, wholesalers, library suppliers, etc – will be disposed to give that book adequate display.

Decisions are taken as a book makes its stately way through the publication process – at acquisition meetings, marketing meetings, sales meetings – which can affect its ultimate profile in the marketplace. The author can achieve sudden fame – or notoriety – in another field, for instance, or someone powerful and influential will read a proof and pronounce favourably on it. This sort of thing can provide a boost to the morale of the people whose job it is to sell and market books, and this 'buzz' is passed on to the customers and ultimately to the public. As an editor I would often reflect ruefully on the fact that my enthusiastic advocacy in-house seemed to carry less weight than three lines in the *Bookseller* from paperback pundit Sarah Broadhurst, happy though I was to find her agreeing with me.

On the other hand, it can happen that, for no reason that anybody can put their finger on, a book seems to wither on the vine in the months between acquisition and publication. (Failure to come up with a jacket that anybody likes can be a reason.) "Surely we didn't really think we were going to sell that many," someone will say, the print run will be cut (to the accompaniment of outraged bleats from its editor), and the book's chances of making any kind of showing in the marketplace cut accordingly.

And, of course, there are returns, which like the poor are always with us. As the old joke has it: publishers don't sell books, they merely lend them to booksellers. One of the insoluble paradoxes that afflict the book trade is that if a publisher *does* put some energy into selling a book into the trade, an avalanche of returns can be its only reward. "The fact has always remained that an unsaleable book is an unsaleable book no matter how it is dressed up; and it is better not to have it in the supply chain at all, getting in the way of books that do have a market," said Peter Kilborn of Book Industry Communication, an organisation set up by the Publishers Association, Booksellers Association and Library Association (now called CILIP, the Chartered Institute of Library and Information Professionals) and the British Library, and charged *inter alia* with finding a solution to the returns problem. Kilborn's rather Darwinian view is not the whole truth, of course – an unsaleable book is not necessarily a bad book, as any author will tell you. In fact you could make a case for saying that if a book is good enough it will sooner or later be remaindered. But until the problem is solved, a decent showing in a bookshop is only a temporary phenomenon; if the books do not sell quickly enough they will be on their way back to the warehouse in months if not weeks.

Too many books?

So what can the poor author do? While it is certainly the responsibility of publishers to make sure that their products are to be found in bookshops (and far too many books are not so much published as simply made available should anybody happen to want them), it has at least become more possible for authors to make a difference. Online booksellers, while no more immune to cock-ups than their terrestrial counterparts, have made a huge difference to the sheer *availability* of books; the access they offer to writers and their public is absolutely unprecedented. The fact that selling books has been in the forefront of the internet revolution suggests that there is a close correlation between internet users and bookbuyers, and they are out there to be blandished and cajoled. Any author who has a website should make a point of linking to Amazon, or one of the other online booksellers, at the very least. The upcoming print-on-demand revolution means (in theory, at least) that no book need ever go out of print.

"Why isn't my book in the shops?" Everybody seems to agree that too many books are published, though nobody seems disposed to do anything about it, least of all publishers and writers. (Writers may not be incurable optimists, but publishers are.) If your book isn't in the shops, it may simply be that either you or your publisher has failed to differentiate it sufficiently from all the other books in its field, whatever it might be. The odds are not, sadly, on your side. Then again, it's a book trade fact of life that everybody complains; authors complain about publishers and agents, booksellers complain about publishers, publishers complain about absolutely everybody. Yet year after year new discoveries are made, reputations are made, even fortunes are made occasionally. Nothing seems to put writers off writing, including, I trust, the foregoing!

Mike Petty was formerly Editorial Director at Picador, Chatto & Windus, Abacus, Bloomsbury and Victor Gollancz. He now runs the publication programme for the Eden Project. An earlier version of this article appeared in *The Author*, the magazine of the Society of Authors.

Vanity publishing

Mainstream publishers invest their own money in the entire publishing process. In contrast, vanity publishers require an up-front payment. Johnathon Clifford highlights the perils of vanity publishing.

My research into vanity publishing began in 1990 when a 12-year old girl wrote to me in my position as founder and Senior Trustee of the National Poetry Foundation, saying she had found a publisher willing to publish her poetry. I telephoned the 'publisher' under the guise of an aspiring author, and this call was all it took for them to agree to publish my poetry. Their offer was 100 copies of a 38-page book for a fee of £1900, with no need for them to see my poetry first.

Definition of vanity publishing

"Vanity publishing, also self-styled (often inaccurately) as 'subsidy', 'joint-venture', 'shared-responsibility' or even 'self' publishing, is a service whereby authors are charged to have their work published. Vanity publishers generally offer to publish a book for a specific fee, or offer to include short stories, poems or other literary or artistic material in an anthology, which the authors are then invited to buy."

– Advertising Standards Authority definition of vanity publishing, 1997

Since then, I have written *Vanity Press & The Proper Poetry Publishers*, a book based on my extensive feedback from vanity companies, assisted the Advertising Standards Authority and collaborated in the making of television and radio programmes. In 1999, I was invited to the House of Lords to talk about the problem of vanity publishing and the need for a change in the law to stop 'rogue traders' in the publishing world. Despite receiving letters of support from 58 MPs, a change to the existing law has yet to be implemented. As a consequence, I set up an 'awareness campaign' consisting of a website and a free advice pack in an effort to protect aspiring authors. The pack, apart from highlighting the business practices of vanity publishers, gives advice on finding a mainstream publisher, internet publishing, the market for short stories and self-publishing. To date, I have sent copies to almost 14,000 individual authors worldwide.

The perils of vanity publishing

'Vanity publisher' is a phrase I coined in the early 1960s when two American companies were advertising widely in the British press offering to publish poems for £9 and £12 per poem, respectively. Since then the term has also come to mean 'any company that charges a client to publish a book'.

Mainstream publishers invest in the promotion of a book and make their profit from the sale of copies of the book. Vanity publishers, on the other hand, make money from up-front charges. One of the main drawbacks of being published by a vanity publisher is its lack of credibility within the industry. The majority of booksellers and library suppliers are loath to handle vanity books and few reviewers are willing to consider a book published in this way. The Business Unit Director of one of the UK's biggest booksellers wrote: "We do not buy from vanity publishers except in exceptional circumstances. Their books are, with one or two exceptions, badly produced, over-priced, have poor, uncompetitive jackets and usually have no marketing support."

I have amassed an extensive collection of documentation from authors who have approached some of the 60-plus vanity publishers operating in the UK. It consists of vanity publishers' initial promotional letters, subsequent written promises, the contracts and letters of complaint from the author, and the vanity publishers' response to those complaints. In recent years, court judgements have found that some vanity publishers are guilty of 'gross misrepresentation of the services they offer' and, as a result, some have been successfully sued and some forced into 'voluntary' liquidation – often only to swiftly reappear under different names.

How vanity publishers operate

Mainstream publishers never advertise for authors and almost never charge a client, whether known or unknown. Vanity publishers place advertisements wherever they possibly can inviting authors to submit manuscripts. Almost without exception, when authors submit work the vanity publisher will reply that they would like to publish the book but that, as an unknown, the author will have to pay towards the cost. Vanity publishers may tell the author they are very selective in the authors they accept and praise the work, but this is false flattery. I have not been able to find one person during the last 12 years, anywhere in the world, who has been turned down by a vanity publisher – however poorly written their book is. The vanity publisher may state that this is the way many famous authors in the past set out. This is untrue: not one of the quoted 'famous authors' started their writing career by paying a vanity publisher. The BBC programme *Southern Eye* reported that many authors had been sent exactly the same 'glowing report', whatever the subject or quality of their book.

Vanity publishers have charged aspiring authors anything from £1800 up to (in one recorded instance) £20,000 for publishing their book. Many authors have borrowed thousands of pounds on the strength of promised 'returning royalties', as authors are often led to believe that the vanity publisher's marketing department will sell their book for them and that they will recoup their outlay via this service. In December 1997, *Private Eye* ran an article about three authors, one of whom had paid £2400 and the other two £1800 each to a vanity publisher, on the basis that their books would command a 'high level of royalties'. These royalties amounted to £16.35, £21.28 and £47.30 respectively. When the authors complained they each received a threatening letter from the vanity publisher's solicitor. The same company's business practices was a topic featured on the BBC programme *Watchdog* in November 2002.

Some vanity publishers are now asking their clients to pay a 'subvention'. The standard dictionary definition of the word subvention is 'a grant, aid or subsidy paid by a government to an educational institution', so the term is meaningless when used in the context of vanity publishing. The bottom line, however the request for payment is worded, is that the author will bear the full cost of publishing the book. Not a share of, or a subsidy towards, but all the costs and a profit margin on top.

Few vanity publishers quote for a fixed number of copies, leaving the author with little idea what they have paid for. Vanity publishers may simply keep manuscripts 'on file' and only print-on-demand, making it difficult to deliver copies quickly enough to the outlets who *do* order them. There are also companies who propose that once book sales have reached a certain 'target' figure, the client's outlay will be refunded. The number of copies required to be sold is always well in excess of a realistic target.

Some companies claim that part of the service they offer is to send copies of your book to Whitakers, the Copyright Receipt Office and the British Library. In fact, this is a legal requirement for all UK publishers. Other companies claim a 'special' relationship which enables them to supply information on your book to particular outlets on the internet. But Amazon.co.uk, the biggest internet bookseller, does not support this and writes: "Books are listed on Amazon.co.uk's website in a number of ways – we take feeds from BookData and Whitakers (who automatically update these details on our website) as well as from several wholesalers".

Authors choosing to vanity publish should be aware that as soon as their last instalment has been paid, the vanity publisher has made maximum profit and does not need to sell a single copy of the author's book.

Self-publishing

Another way for an author to see their book in print is to self-publish. For self-publishing an author independently funds publication, employing professionals to undertake elements of the process which they cannot do. Most authors are unable to design text pages or covers themselves and will need experts to print the book and (if required) market and promote it. Self-publishing is particularly suited to authors wanting only a few copies.

Since self-publishing has become more widespread, some vanity publishers have misleadingly passed themselves off as self-publishers. However, there is little any vanity publisher can do that the author cannot do better. True self-publishing gives the author much greater control over the production and dissemination of the book. If authors choose to self-publish they should view the whole process, not as money invested to make a return, but as money spent on a pleasurable hobby which will hopefully have been an enjoyable experience.

Finally...

Aspiring authors should be careful not to be taken in by the promises of some vanity publishers which have so often proved false. The legal phrase 'Caveat Emptor' (Buyer Beware) here becomes 'Caveat Scriptor' – 'Author Beware!'

Johnathon Clifford may be contacted on *tel* (01329) 822218 or at johnathonclifford@vanitypublishing.info

Who owns whom in publishing

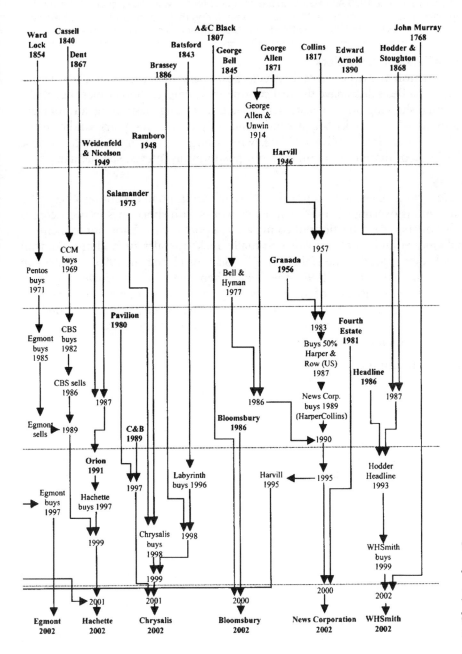

© Christopher Gasson

Top one hundred chart of 2002 paperback fastsellers

Every year since 1979 Alex Hamilton has compiled for the *Guardian* a chart of the 100 topselling paperbacks published for the first time during that year by British publishers. For readers new to it he describes its terms of reference, and sets the context.

Bestsellers and fastsellers

A distinction must be made between 'bestsellers' and the term used here – 'fastsellers'. Bestsellers have the real commercial pedigree. Sometimes they make a strong showing in the fastseller lane, but among bestselling authors are hundreds whose books began slowly and only over many years vindicate the faith of the original publisher. D.H. Lawrence and George Orwell are two whose sales in their lifetimes were modest, but posthumous interest spectacular.

Poetry

While serious poets never repeat Lord Byron's triumph in becoming a bestseller and 'famous overnight', and the only two works with short lines in two decades of fastsellers were collections of comic verse, a poet such as Eliot, not to mention Shakespeare and Chaucer, will eventually rack up sales in millions. And an outside event, such as the Nobel Prize for Seamus Heaney in 1995, produces an immediate harvest. In 1998, the year when the Oxford University Press announced the closure of its poetry section to save money, the late Poet Laureate, Ted Hughes, with the last book of his life, *Birthday Letters*, headed the hardcover selling lists with 145,000 copies, and won every award for which the book could qualify.

Fiction and non-fiction

The staple of publishing has long been Bibles, classic authors, cookbooks, dictionaries and other reference books. Although fiction dominates counter sales and library borrowings, the top individual titles for the 20th century, with figures over 20 million copies, include most of these categories. For example, the *Guinness Book of Records*, over many editions, passed 85 million copies. However, gross figures of 50 to 300 million copies are claimed for worldwide hardcover, paperback and translation editions of prolific authors such as Agatha Christie, Alistair MacLean, Mickey Spillane, Stephen King and Catherine Cookson. In all her long writing life Cookson was never off the lists, and her running Transworld sale when she died in 1998 was 53.5 million, with seven unpublished titles to come. The last is included in this year's list.

The fastseller list on pages 254–7 is limited to paperbacks that appeared for the first time in 2002 from British publishers. These are defined in the trade as 'frontlist', and those that remain in print become 'backlist'. It is tempting to enter backlist titles revived as screen tie-ins (e.g. Keneally's *Schindler's Ark* and Harris's *Silence of the Lambs* that both tripled their sales, to 800,000 and 1,580,000 respectively), but except when the figure is very large, I exclude them. In 2002 the publishers of *Lord of the Rings* made a gigantic harvest of 12 million copies of Tolkien titles.

Looking at the figures

From 1979 until the 1990s recession there were always between 102 and 125 titles that passed the 100,000 mark, conveniently round for those who make comparisons, but the figure is rising: this year there were 163. The expansion results partly from widespread competitive discounting by chain booksellers, supermarket interest, and the focus of many high street bookshops. Ubiquitous 'top 10' charts reinforce the successes (of the frontlist, that is; the backlist tends to suffer).

A distortion for titles published at the end of the year looks likely, but actually it rarely makes much difference. Electronic stock control enables booksellers to match ordering to demand. The significant sale of new paperbacks, particularly by established authors, takes place within a few weeks of their appearance, although a few do enter the magic circle of bestsellers: *Captain Corelli's Mandolin* by Louis de Bernières has gone on to sell 2 million copies after achieving only 60,000 in its first year.

The authors

Over 20 years, the lists indicate conservative attitudes among buyers. Fewer than 10% of authors generally come from outside the Anglo-American axis (though it divides this year 53–34). Few appear in the top 25 who have not appeared somewhere on the list in previous years. (2001 provided three exceptions; this year there is only one, Pamela Stephenson's biography of her husband Billy Connolly.) Once established on it, authors have only to turn in a regular supply of similar works to stay there. However, like typecast actors, they may find too late that they are captives of the market. One author trapped in his own formula was thriller writer Peter Cheyney, who gave his publisher a book unlike his others and was told to bury it, lest it confuse his loyal following.

Leading figures of the 1980s were Wilbur Smith (more than 25 novels past the million, 30 million sales), Stephen King (25 million), Dick Francis (19 million), Barbara Taylor Bradford, Len Deighton, Catherine Cookson, Jeffrey Archer, Danielle Steel and Victoria Holt. To these (minus Holt, who died) the 1990s added regular front-runners in John Grisham and Maeve Binchy, with Patricia Cornwell and Jilly Cooper as top 10 reliables. J.K. Rowling is the outstanding newcomer of this decade, but Ian Rankin and possibly Ian McEwan have also fixed themselves in top positions. Cookson, King and Steel are the only three in every list since 1979. Such authors' names are like a brand. While only seven of 2000 titles were volumes of short stories, two had sales over 750,000, because they were by Frederick Forsyth and Jeffrey Archer, and two reached 500,000 (Archer and Rosamund Pilcher).

More than half the buyers of books have always been women but for most of the 1980s hardly more than a quarter of the authors were. In the 1990s their presence gradually increased, and in 2000 they at last achieved parity, to reach 53% in 2001 – only to fall back the next year, mysteriously, to 41%.

No	Title	Genre	Author	Imprint
1	A Painted House	Novel	John Grisham (US)	Arrow
2	Billy	Biog.	Pamela Stephenson (Aus.)	HarperCollins
3	Atonement	Novel	Ian McEwan (Br.)	Vintage
4	How To Be Good	Novel	Nick Hornby (Br.)	Penguin
5	Warlock	Adventure	Wilbur Smith (SA)	Pan
6	Five Quarters of the Orange	Novel	Joanne Harris (Br.)	Black Swan
7	Resurrection Men	Crime	Ian Rankin (Br.)	Orion
8	One for My Baby	Novel	Tony Parsons (Br.)	HarperCollins
9	A Man Named Dave	Autobiog.	Dave Pelzer (US)	Orion
10	Dead Famous	Novel	Ben Elton (Br.)	Black Swan
11	Dreamcatcher	Chiller	Stephen King (US)	NEL
12	Violets Are Blue	Thriller	James Patterson (US)	Headline
13	1st to Die	Thriller	James Patterson (US)	Headline
14	Detox for Life	Health	Carol Vorderman (Br.)	Virgin
15	On Green Dolphin Street	Novel	Sebastian Faulks (Br.)	Vintage
16	Something Dangerous	Saga	Penny Vincenzi (Br.)	Orion
17	Faceless	Novel	Martina Cole (Br.)	Headline
18	The Woman Who Left	Saga	Josephine Cox (Br.)	Headline
19	Black House	Horror	S. King & P. Straub (US)	HarperCollins
20	The Kiss	Novel	Danielle Steel (US)	Corgi
21	Acid Row	Crime	Minette Walters (Br.)	Pan
22	Lone Eagle	Novel	Danielle Steel (US)	Corgi
23	Isle of Dogs	Crime	Patricia Cornwell (US)	Time Warner
24	Thief of Time	Fantasy	Terry Pratchett (Br.)	Corgi
25	Death in Holy Orders	Crime	P.D. James (Br.)	Penguin
26	City of Bones	Thriller	Michael Connelly (US)	Orion
27	Fatal Voyage	Crime	Kathy Reichs (US)	Arrow
28	Leap of Faith	Novel	Danielle Steel (US)	Corgi
29	Tell No One	Thriller	Harlan Coben (US)	Orion
30	The Silent Lady	Saga	Catherine Cookson (Br.)	Corgi
31	Adam and Eve and Pinch Me	Crime	Ruth Rendell (Br.)	Arrow
32	Fame Fatale	'Chicklit'	Wendy Holden (Br.)	Headline
33	Father Unknown	Saga	Lesley Pearse (Br.)	Penguin
34	The Last Time They Met	Novel	Anita Shreve (US)	Abacus
35	The Smoke Jumper	Novel	Nicholas Evans (Br.)	Corgi
36	Jinnie	Saga	Josephine Cox (Br.)	Headline
37	The Sigma Protocol	Thriller	Robert Ludlum (US)	Orion
38	Stupid White Men	Polemic	Michael Moore (US)	Penguin
39	Amazing Maurice & his Rodents	Juvenile	Terry Pratchett (Br.)	Corgi
40	Shopaholic Ties the Knot	Novel	Sophie Kinsella (Br.)	Black Swan
41	Frank Skinner	Autobiog.	Frank Skinner (Br.)	Arrow
42	Babyville	Mum lit	Jane Green (Br.)	Penguin
43	The Veteran	Thriller	Frederick Forsyth (Br.)	Corgi
44	Once	Thriller	James Herbert (Br.)	Pan
45	Blood Hunt	Thriller	Ian Rankin (Br.)	Orion
46	Under the Duvet	Autobiog.	Marian Keyes (Ire.)	Penguin
47	Maura's Game	Novel	Martina Cole (Br.)	Headline
48	The Road to Nab End	Autobiog.	William Woodruff (US)	Abacus
49	Artemis Fowl	Juvenile	Eoin Colfer (Ire.)	Puffin
50	Traitor to Memory	Crime	Elizabeth George (US)	NEL

RRP	Month	Home	Export	Total	Gross	No
£6.99	Jan	591,304	302,391	893,695	£6,246,928	1
£6.99	July	794,849	25,208	820,057	£5,732,198	2
£7.99	May	615,247	163,403	778,650	£6,221,414	3
£6.99	Apr	604,322	167,461	771,783	£5,394,763	4
£6.99	May	330,466	284,756	615,222	£4,300,402	5
£6.99	Jan	450,307	119,156	569,463	£3,980,546	6
£6.99	Oct	384,379	178,545	562,924	£3,934,839	7
£6.99	May	518,652	32,058	550,710	£3,849,463	8
£6.99	Apr	432,111	105,808	537,919	£3,760,054	9
£6.99	July	466,901	59,414	526,315	£3,678,942	10
£6.99	June	382,706	99,117	481,823	£3,367,943	11
£6.99	July	405,468	75,634	481,102	£3,362,903	12
£6.99	Apr	369,564	87,135	456,699	£3,192,326	13
£10.99	Jan	287,800	112,000	399,800	£4,393,802	14
£6.99	May	360,865	38,626	399,491	£2,792,442	15
£6.99	May	236,842	156,700	393,542	£2,750,859	16
£6.99	May	316,781	59,338	376,119	£2,629,072	17
£5.99	Feb	339,370	32,481	371,851	£2,227,387	18
£6.99	Sept	294,238	77,117	371,355	£2,595,771	19
£6.99	Nov	301,046	65,523	366,569	£2,562,317	20
£6.99	Aug	236,828	128,869	365,697	£2,556,222	21
£6.99	Feb	289,177	76,052	365,229	£2,552,951	22
£6.99	June	255,578	102,408	357,986	£2,502,322	23
£6.99	May	263,641	92,640	356,281	£2,490,404	24
£6.99	Sept	243,658	107,388	351,046	£2,453,812	25
£6.99	Nov	240,305	109,127	349,432	£2,442,530	26
£6.99	Apr	254,683	82,408	337,091	£2,356,266	27
£5.99	Aug	281,889	53,759	335,648	£2,010,532	28
£5.99	Jan	277,426	55,965	333,391	£1,997,012	29
£5.99	Apr	229,081	88,605	317,686	£1,902,939	30
£6.99	June	260,416	55,576	315,992	£2,208,784	31
£5.99	June	289,860	21,285	311,145	£1,863,759	32
£6.99	Feb	283,638	26,789	310,427	£2,169,885	33
£6.99	Jan	244,812	65,065	309,877	£2,166,040	34
£6.99	June	230,531	77,040	307,571	£2,149,921	35
£6.99	Oct	290,254	16,363	306,617	£2,143,253	36
£6.99	Aug	170,613	131,799	302,412	£2,113,860	37
£7.99	Oct	278,262	18,936	297,198	£2,374,612	38
£5.99	Nov	255,172	38,157	293,329	£1,757,041	39
£6.99	July	271,721	21,496	293,217	£2,049,587	40
£6.99	May	284,574	1,928	286,502	£2,002,649	41
£6.99	May	242,007	42,499	284,506	£1,988,697	42
£6.99	Sept	188,054	93,265	281,319	£1,966,420	43
£6.99	May	263,934	17,280	281,214	£1,965,686	44
£5.99	Jan	218,023	59,280	277,303	£1,661,045	45
£6.99	July	193,390	83,603	276,993	£1,936,181	46
£10.99	Oct	242,436	22,424	264,860	£2,910,811	47
£6.99	Jan	252,273	2,123	254,396	£1,778,228	48
£4.99	Mar	198,079	55,299	253,378	£1,264,356	49
£6.99	July	167,210	85,505	252,715	£1,766,478	50

No	Title	Genre	Author	Imprint
51	Last Light	Thriller	Andy McNab (Br.)	Corgi
52	What She Wants	Novel	Cathy Kelly (Ire.)	HarperCollins
53	Jackdaws	Thriller	Ken Follett (Br.)	Pan
54	Triumph of Katy Byrne	Novel	Barbara Taylor Bradford (Br.)	HarperCollins
55	Sea Glass	Novel	Anita Shreve (US)	Abacus
56	The Nanny Diaries	Novel	McLaughlin & Kraus (US)	Penguin
57	Valhalla Rising	Thriller	Clive Cussler (US)	Penguin
58	Pursuit of Happiness	Novel	Douglas Kennedy (US)	Arrow
59	The Watchman	Thriller	Chris Ryan (Br.)	Arrow
60	Rebecca's Tale	Novel	Sally Beauman (Br.)	Time Warner
61	Learning to Fly	Autobiog.	Victoria Beckham (Br.)	Penguin
62	True History of the Kelly Gang	Novel	Peter Carey (Aus.)	Faber
63	Red Room	Crime	Nicci French (Br.)	Penguin
64	The Blue Nowhere	Thriller	Jeffery Deaver (US)	Coronet
65	The Corrections	Novel	Jonathan Franzen (US)	Fourth Estate
66	Midnight Runner	Thriller	Jack Higgins (Br.)	HarperCollins
67	Precious Time	Romance	Erica James (Br.)	Orion
68	The Other Boleyn Girl	Hist. novel	Philippa Gregory (Br.)	HarperCollins
69	Flesh and Blood	Thriller	Jonathan Kellerman (US)	Headline
70	Sharpe's Prey	Hist. novel	Bernard Cornwell (Br.)	HarperCollins
71	Robbie Williams: Somebody ...	Autobiog.	Robbie Williams (Br.)	Ebury
72	Staying at Daisy's	'Chicklit'	Jill Mansell (Br.)	Headline
73	The House on Lonely Street	Saga	Lyn Andrews (Br.)	Headline
74	The Chestnut Tree	Novel	Charlotte Bingham (Br.)	Bantam
75	Back When We Were Grownups	Novel	Anne Tyler (US)	Vintage
76	The Killing Kind	Thriller	John Connolly (Ire.)	Coronet
77	Hollywood Wives: New Generation	Novel	Jackie Collins (Br.)	Pocket
78	The Fourth Hand	Novel	John Irving (US)	Black Swan
79	A Parrot in the Pepper Tree	Travel	Chris Stewart (Br.)	Sort of...
80	Love and Promise	Saga	Lyn Andrews (Br.)	Headline
81	Fast Food Nation	Polemic	Eric Schlosser (US)	Penguin
82	Portrait in Sepia	Novel	Isabel Allende (Chile)	Flamingo
83	Dinner for Two	'Ladlit'	Mike Gayle (UK)	Flame
84	Gallows Thief	Hist. novel	Bernard Cornwell (Br.)	HarperCollins
85	Francesca's Party	Novel	Patricia Scanlan (Ire.)	Bantam
86	Falling Angels	Hist. novel	Tracy Chevalier (US)	HarperCollins
87	Just Between Us	Novel	Cathy Kelly (Ire.)	HarperCollins
88	One Door Away from Heaven	Thriller	Dean Koontz (US)	Headline
89	Give Me Ten Seconds	Autobiog.	John Sergeant (Br.)	Pan
90	Big Night Out	Anthology	Jessica Adams et al (Br.)	HarperCollins
91	The Forgotten	Thriller	Faye Kellerman (US)	Headline
92	George Best: Blessed	Autobiog.	George Best (Ire.)	Ebury
93	Porno	Novel	Irvine Welsh (Br.)	Cape
94	The Potter's House	Novel	Rosie Thomas (Br.)	Arrow
95	Help Yourself	Autobiog.	Dave Peltzer (US)	HarperCollins
96	Last Man Standing	Thriller	David Baldacci (US)	Pocket
97	Protect and Defend	Novel	Richard North Patterson (US)	Arrow
98	The Map that Changed the World	Biog.	Simon Winchester (Br.)	Penguin
99	Keys of Hell	Thriller	Jack Higgins (Br.)	HarperCollins
100	The Boy Next Door	Novel	E. Lloyd & J. Rees (Br.)	Arrow

RRP	Month	Home	Export	Total	Gross	No
£6.99	Oct	207,935	43,336	251,271	£1,756,384	**51**
£6.99	Apr	170,643	78,782	249,425	£1,743,481	**52**
£6.99	Sept	148,952	99,822	248,774	£1,738,930	**53**
£6.99	Feb	144,832	99,445	244,277	£1,707,496	**54**
£6.99	Nov	187,908	55,009	242,917	£1,697,990	**55**
£6.99	Mar	148,003	94,791	242,794	£1,697,130	**56**
£6.99	Aug	167,035	75,114	242,149	£1,692,622	**57**
£6.99	Sept	202,539	39,252	241,791	£1,690,119	**58**
£6.99	June	201,224	39,884	241,108	£1,685,345	**59**
£6.99	May	216,528	23,915	240,443	£1,680,697	**60**
£6.99	July	224,850	13,953	238,803	£1,669,233	**61**
£7.99	Jan	169,762	63,462	233,224	£1,863,460	**62**
£6.99	Feb	149,311	78,587	227,898	£1,593,007	**63**
£6.99	May	160,903	60,200	221,103	£1,545,510	**64**
£7.99	Sept	190,578	28,867	219,445	£1,753,366	**65**
£5.99	Oct	179,312	36,826	216,138	£1,294,667	**66**
£5.99	June	165,529	48,393	213,922	£1,281,393	**67**
£6.99	Oct	183,086	29,587	212,673	£1,486,584	**68**
£6.99	Sept	165,453	44,915	210,368	£1,470,472	**69**
£6.99	June	170,195	39,470	209,665	£1,465,558	**70**
£7.99	Oct	196,922	12,567	209,489	£1,673,817	**71**
£5.99	Aug	191,888	17,590	209,478	£1,254,773	**72**
£5.99	Feb	204,465	4,141	208,606	£1,249,550	**73**
£5.99	Aug	174,261	33,832	208,093	£1,246,477	**74**
£6.99	July	176,326	31,139	207,465	£1,450,180	**75**
£6.99	Jan	162,475	43,877	206,352	£1,442,400	**76**
£6.99	May	158,439	47,076	205,515	£1,436,550	**77**
£6.99	June	124,009	78,115	202,124	£1,412,847	**78**
£6.99	May	185,672	12,746	198,418	£1,386,942	**79**
£5.99	Sept	196,928	1,202	198,130	£1,186,799	**80**
£7.99	Apr	159,738	31,740	191,478	£1,529,909	**81**
£6.99	July	166,177	25,168	191,345	£1,337,502	**82**
£6.99	Aug	167,290	23,590	190,880	£1,334,251	**83**
£5.99	Aug	153,092	33,613	186,705	£1,118,363	**84**
£5.99	May	172,700	12,924	185,624	£1,111,888	**85**
£6.99	June	157,769	26,845	184,614	£1,290,452	**86**
£10.99	Oct	146,339	38,221	184,560	£2,028,314	**87**
£6.99	Aug	133,397	49,882	183,279	£1,281,120	**88**
£7.99	Aug	180,140	1,256	181,396	£1,449,354	**89**
£6.99	July	145,884	34,893	180,777	£1,263,631	**90**
£5.99	Feb	136,953	42,348	179,301	£1,074,013	**91**
£7.99	Aug	175,213	3,521	178,734	£1,428,085	**92**
£10.00	Aug	138,115	39,692	177,807	£1,778,070	**93**
£6.99	Mar	160,085	17,176	177,261	£1,239,054	**94**
£6.99	Mar	157,271	16,058	173,329	£1,211,570	**95**
£6.99	June	88,989	82,610	171,599	£1,199,477	**96**
£6.99	Feb	123,851	45,679	169,530	£1,185,015	**97**
£7.99	July	105,050	62,828	167,878	£1,341,345	**98**
£5.99	Mar	93,428	74,370	167,798	£1,005,110	**99**
£6.99	Feb	145,166	20,892	166,058	£1,160,745	**100**

Genres

More than 80 of the top 100 paperback fastsellers are always fiction. Regular elements of the non-fiction remainder have dealt in diets, horoscopes, jokes, showbiz lives and, latterly, history. Cookery books, being basically tools in daily use, are essentially hardcover bestsellers (with more than 6 million in three years for Jamie Oliver's cookbooks). Of fiction, genres fill most slots, particularly thrillers (30 this year), crime, horror, family sagas and a mixed bag of romances. The 'chicklit' fashion for humorous accounts of young women's urban experience, sharing flats, holding a job, finding a man, is evolving into 'mumlit' – and in due course perhaps 'nanlit'. The chicklit pioneer, *Bridget Jones's Diary*, has now passed 3.5 million.

Though there is a lesser vogue for 'ladlit', there is no longer an obvious category of the 'men's fiction', once supplied by authors such as Mickey Spillane and Harold Robbins (world sales reached 130 million in his 1970s heyday). Currently the heroics of SAS men, typified by Andy McNab, are the substitute. In the 1970s and early 1980s, with authors such as Russell Braddon and Sven Hassel, hot war outsold sex. But the balloon of the cold war spy story, inflated by Ian Fleming and crewed by Len Deighton, John le Carré, *et al*, fell with the Berlin Wall. Much depends on the policies of the White House and the Kremlin, and the aftermath of recent terrorist action. An interesting development is the arrival of polemics on global issues, typified here by the books of Michael Moore and Eric Schlosser.

Science fantasy does better than experimental science fiction. Westerns never figured, despite the fame of Zane Grey, Louis L'Amour and J.T. Edson. Contrary to widespread opinion, erotica have never made publishers an opulent living. Imprints dedicated to soft porn must be content with sales of around 25,000, and their living is made more precarious by material on the internet. Comic books, on the edge of being non-books, and collections of cartoonists of genius, appear *passim*, and quickly fade. Travellers' tales had no significant presence until the American Bill Bryson's flattering farewell journey around Britain sold more copies in one year (1996) than any other travelogue had in 20. But newcomer Pete McCarthy has the best mileage since, followed by Chris Stewart, with the distinction of an imprint specially created for his books.

Heavyweight to juvenile

Literary authors such as Ian McEwan, John Irving and Jonathan Franzen were never common on the list. However, in recent years the Booker Prize has brought winners in (witness Peter Carey, and Arundati Roy in 1998, the highest to date). When it works, this award seems to establish books rather than authors, and not all winners reappear. Still, the potential of non-category fiction is evinced by Humberto Eco's *The Name of the Rose*, Tom Wolfe's *The Bonfire of the Vanities*, Salman Rushdie's *Midnight's Children*, and Zadie Smith's first novel *White Teeth*, all with well over half a million copies.

The phenomenon at the century's end was a series by J.K. Rowling about a schoolboy wizard called Harry Potter. With four of seven Potter titles published, they sell 50,000 copies a week in Britain. (The fifth book was published in June 2003 and is reputed to have sold 1.6 million copies on the first day.) Together with Philip Pullman's award-winning trilogy *His Dark Materials*, they have boosted the status of children's book publishing and the total claimed for 40 countries is 80 million. Rowling quickly became as popular with children as the late Roald Dahl and Terry Pratchett, who is equally at home on the wilder shores of technology, and whose 45 titles with Transworld sell 1,850,000 copies a year. Mention must also be made of American horror writer R.L.Stine, claiming worldwide sales of 220 million for 60 children's books.

The year 2002

The new element for the trade in recent years has been freedom from retail price maintenance and widespread discounting on top hardcover titles. For a few, surprisingly high figures are reported. (Thus, Harris's grotesque thriller *Hannibal* sold 800,000 copies, and Sir Alex Ferguson's *Managing My Life* 600,000). The topselling hardcovers of 2002 were mainly celebrity memoirs of, for example, the Irish footballer Roy Keane (542,193 copies), and the Formula One commentator Murray Walker with *Unless I'm Very Much Mistaken* (468,234 copies). Paperbacks are less affected, but perhaps 20% should be deducted from the aggregate money gross shown. The most common price point has stayed on £6.99, though few customers will have paid full price.

In a market with a surplus of books, the fastsellers' performance seems still the most stable element. The total number of units, 30,247,358, is remarkably similar to the 2000 figures, but nearly 3 million down on 2001, which included a Potter surge. (The first 25 titles account for 12.5 million books and £89.5 million). Export sank a further two percentage points from its record low of 22% last year. Ostensibly, the total gross is £213,097,699, but my guess is that between £25 million and £30 million were given away in discounts on these 100 titles alone. All in the name of market share.

Alex Hamilton is a journalist and award-winning travel writer, and the author of several novels and volumes of short stories.

Book clubs

Artists' Choice

Artists' Choice Ltd, PO Box 3, Huntingdon,
Cambs. PE28 0QX
tel (01832) 710201 *fax* (01832) 710488
websites www.artists-choice.co.uk
www.acaward.com

Quarterly.

Baker Books

Manfield Park, Cranleigh, Surrey GU6 8NU
tel (01483) 267888 *fax* (01483) 267409
email bakerbooks@dial.pipex.com
website www.bakerbooks.co.uk

School book clubs for children aged 3–13. Operates
in the UK and reaches English medium schools
overseas.

BCA

Greater London House, Hampstead Road,
London NW1 7TZ
tel 020-7760 6500 *fax* 020-7760 6901
websites www.bol.com www.booksdirect.co.uk

Ancient & Medieval History Book Club, Arts Guild,
Book Club of Ireland, Books for Children,
Computer Book Club, English Book Club, Escape
(The Fiction Club), Fantasy & SF Book Club, The
History Guild, Home Software World, Just Good
Books, Mango, Military and Aviation Book Society,
Mind Body & Spirit, The Mystery & Thriller Club,
QPD (Quality Paperbacks Direct), The Railway
Book Club, The Softback Preview, Taste (A Fresh
Approach to Food), World Books.

Cygnus Book Club

PO Box 15, Llandeilo,
Carmarthenshire SA19 6YX
tel (01550) 777977/777701 *fax* (01550) 777569
email enquiries@cygnus-books.co.uk
website www.cygnus-books.co.uk

Includes psychology and self-help, diet, health and
exercise, world religions, new economics and
education, green issues, mythology, spirituality.
Monthly.

The Folio Society

44 Eagle Street, London WC1R 4FS
tel 020-7400 4222 *fax* 020-7400 4242
website www.foliosoc.co.uk

Fine editions of classic literature.

Letterbox Library

71-73 Allen Road, London N16 8RY
tel 020-7503 4801 *fax* 020-7503 4800
email info@letterboxlibrary.com
website www.letterboxlibrary.com

Multicultural and non-sexist children's books.

The Poetry Book Society

Book House, 45 East Hill, London SW18 2QZ
tel 020-8870 8403 *fax* 020-8870 0865
email info@poetrybooks.co.uk
website www.poetrybooks.co.uk

Quarterly. See pages 267.

Readers' Union Ltd

Brunel House, Ford Close, Newton Abbot,
Devon TQ12 4PU
tel (01626) 323200 *fax* (01626) 323318

Includes Country Sports Book Society, The Craft
Club, Craftsman Book Society, Equestrian Book
Society, Gardeners Book Society, Needlecrafts with
Cross Stitch Book Society, Photographic Book
Society.

The Red House Book Club

Windrush Park, Witney, Oxon OX29 0XD
tel (01993) 893456 *fax* (01993) 893424
website www.redhouse.co.uk

Mail order book supplier specialising in children's
and parenting books. Also available online.

Writers' Bookshelf

PO Box 168, Wellington Street, Leeds LS1 1RF
tel 0113-238 8333 *fax* 0113-238 8330
email janet.davison@writersnews.co.uk

Books for writers.

Poetry

Getting poetry published

Michael Schmidt examines the challenges for poets who wish to see their work published.

Start with this axiom: you have not come here to make money.

I write as a publisher who has spent over 30 years not making money out of poetry, and as a quondam poet whose rewards were never material, either. Money may be a consequence, but only in a few cases, usually obtained in the form of grants and bursaries, when a career is well beyond the point at which an article such as this is of interest.

In the old days, right up through the 1950s, there was a popular tradition of verse writing: people kept commonplace books for friends to write lines in when visiting. Or folk composed ballads, Christmas poems, dialect eclogues, limericks. Verse was part of social engagement. It took itself seriously in formal terms but made no pretence of being 'art'. There was a level of competence in making conventional verses, sometimes beyond English, in Latin or Greek, and most people could tell a good piece of verse from a bad one. Jane Austen's family was given to playful versing. In second-hand bookshops you find tomes with verse inscriptions. Like weekend painters, verse writers expressed themselves clearly and skilfully, bringing direct, strictly occasional pleasure to another person or a group. The ambition to Get Published At All Costs had not set in. Now it has; it has been endemic for three decades. The social space for verse has almost vanished, and with it the popular versifying skills. Such a loss has consequences. Dr Johnson in *The Life of Savage* reflects that 'negligence and irregularity, long continued, will make knowledge useless, wit ridiculous, and genius contemptible'. The creative writing culture of reception nowadays seems to be defined less as readership or audience, more as 'market'. Is this change regrettable? Yes. Has it brought any benefits? To the art of poetry, to poetry readership, very few.

Even today, weekend painters know their work will never hang in the Tate; amateur musicians (singers, instrumentalists, composers) content themselves with making music as an end in itself. But the occasional versifier is a dying breed, like the red squirrel, replaced by the interloping grey who, a year into writing, submits work to a dozen editors at once, declaring it to be original, relevant, topical. In the twinkling of an eye these strident creatures absorb, without troubling to learn names, the art of Chaucer, Spenser, Milton, Cowper, Dickinson, Walcott, Rich. Their opinion of modern poetry is low. But then they do not base their opinion on a very large sample. They will have heard of the market leaders and remember some of the poetry read at school.

As an editor at a small publishing house I receive over 2000 full manuscripts a year (and many more submissions for *PN Review*). Telephone calls, letters and emails ask what kind of poetry we publish, whether we publish poetry at all, or how much it will cost to have poems printed. Few poets submitting are aware of the editorial contents of a poetry publisher's list, despite websites and other resources offering this information. Many have read, perhaps in this volume, which publishers have a poetry list and try, without doing a smidgen of research. Without reading. Few seem aware of how large a shoal of wannabe poets surrounds the little flotilla of publishers, editors and other validators. Poetry becomes a means to an end, not an end in itself: to be a poet, go for prizes, give readings and all the peripheral rewards which in the end poison and parch the individual spring, assuming it has more than illusory water in it.

Publishing in book form

An article of this kind usually proffers advice: how to present a manuscript, how to address an editor, what to expect from a contract, etc. I'd rather try to give writers who believe they have a body of publishable work a realistic sense of the chance of publication, and a realistic preparation for its aftermath, assuming the first goal is achieved. Better to counsel realism than foster illusion.

First, the chances of book publication. More than 1000 new books of verse are published each year, but few are marketed or sold and fewer still reviewed. A list like the one I edit, with 40 poetry titles a year, accommodates at most two or three first collections. Other substantial poetry publishers go for a year or five without adding new names to their lists. Few first collections sell over 1000 copies. Indeed, some may sell fewer than 300. The book trade has become resistant to all but the market leaders in poetry; few independent presses get their poets even into some of the leading chains.

The ecology of poetry publishing, as distinct from that of standard trade publishing, is based more and more narrowly on events. A poet can publish his or her own work, paying a printer to do the job and selling at readings. But then, who is going to invite a self-published poet to read? A poet can go to one of the vanity presses and pay a more substantial sum for the promise of exposure. Again, such publication capitalises on illusion and, as the title proclaims, vanity (see *Vanity publishing*, page 247).

There *are* new opportunities which can be valuable. Any poet is free to post work on the web, in both text and voice form, inviting response. It's quite cheap to do so and response is almost immediate. There are electronic magazines as well. In a sense, the withering away of the poetry book trade is a harbinger of the wider impact of the web. Unfortunately, the web is not discriminating and it is hard to know how a critical take on work self-published on the web will develop. At every stage, it seems to me, poets are tempted to succumb, in their eagerness for publication, to acts of desperation. Publish and be damned! Luck would be a fine thing. There is not even a sufficient audience to damn new work on the web. The question must be, how to publish and be sufficiently visible to *be* damned, or welcomed, as the case may be. But we are getting ahead of ourselves: the first question must be the quality of the work and the motive of the writer.

Before looking for a publisher, writers of verse (as of anything else) should interrogate themselves. *Why* do I want to be published in book form? Is it mere whim or is my work genuinely original? The only way you can answer these questions is by wide reading, not only of contemporaries but also of poets from the past. To be able to judge your art, you must understand it, as you would any other. What makes my work original? In a few instances subject matter in itself can be sufficiently interesting to justify a book, but this is rare: it has more to do with the accidents of birth and upbringing than with any choices a poet might make. Originality is expressed in diction, prosody and form. It need not be dazzling. Edward Thomas recognised Robert Frost's originality, reviewing *North of Boston* in 1914: 'This is one of the most revolutionary books of modern times, but one of the quietest and least aggressive. It speaks, and it is poetry.'

A poet who sets out to get published without understanding in depth the art practised, and the nature of the work intended for publication, is on a hiding to very little. Chances are that such a poet will make decisions that ensure the poetry remains unread.

Ask, before you solicit editorial judgment, to whom your poetry is likely to appeal: To friends and family? The local community (is it in dialect, locally relevant in some way)? To a religious group? Is your work sufficiently distinctive to appeal beyond those groups from which your identity is derived?

Seeking critical appraisal

If a spouse, relation, teacher or friend, commends your verse, it will be gratifying, but how informed are they, and is their response to you as writer or to the writing? Is it courtesy or real validation? Kind Sir John Betjeman used to write a note to anyone who sent him poems saying 'you show potential' or 'talent'. Thousands of poets thus commended would take his endorsement and include it for the next 20 years with each magazine and volume submission. The commendation of a kind writer is, alas, not worth the paper it is written on. If an established writer believes in your work, he or she will make it a mission to send your work to an editor.

It is important to get a critical purchase on your work, not to overestimate it. Some poets accept that their level is, say, among small magazines; they are content to exist there in a community of similarly committed writers. They do not try for the 'better magazines', knowing they haven't a chance of getting in. They may blame those magazines as elitist and cliquish and no doubt some of them are, but elites and cliques that are permeable to quality. Finding one's level is an early stage in establishing peace of mind: always to aim too high and so to invite rebuff finally undermines self-respect.

Never ask an editor for comments and criticisms unless you are willing to take them. I am often been asked for 'a serious appraisal'. When work seems genuinely interesting I offer detailed advice, and often receive back angry letters or defences of work I have risked commenting upon. A poem works or fails to work; no amount of arguifying can convert an experienced reader. I may come to understand more clearly what the intention of a poem *was*, and therefore better to understand how far short it has fallen.

Magazines, the internet and broadcasting

Most editors advise new writers to seek publication in magazines first. This is mixed advice. It assumes the poet writes 'filler' poems, the fast food that can be served up in a weekly journal. If you are published in magazines the editor does not respect, it may diminish his or her respect for your work. It is crucial, especially if you are not prolific, to try for publication in places where (a) the work will be widely read and (b) publication will increase your visibility. The *Times Literary Supplement* and *London Review of Books* have a curious and unpredictable taste; several specialised journals are worth trying, *Poetry Review, London Magazine, Stand, Poetry London, The North* and *PN Review* among them. It is crucial to subscribe to journals you find congenial, read them regularly and get a sense of the wider world of contemporary publication. Among foreign magazines worth close attention are *Parnassus, Raritan* and *Salt*.

Publication in web magazines can be satisfying; it can also be dangerous for your copyright (the work slips out of your control), and few editors of my acquaintance credit the web as a place to look for poems. Remember that a poem first published on the web is unlikely to be published in a reputable magazine.

Broadcasting is as unpredictable a medium of dissemination as the web. There are slots for various kinds of poetry on radio: dramatic, lyric, etc. Look at the broadcasting schedules, familiarise yourself with the poetry programmes and producers, locally and nationally. On many networks a broadcast poem is heard by quite a large, if not a discriminating or informed, audience. Editors have been known to track down poems heard in broadcast, especially in the poet's own voice if that poet is a good performer.

The importance of market research

Where should you do your market research for a book publisher? In your personal library of modern poetry books (you ought to have one, with books by favourite authors from a variety of imprints). Most publishers have editorial priorities which are more or less coherent, expressed in anthologies or in the general choice offered. The chief imprints are Faber, Picador, Penguin, Cape and Chatto among larger players, and Arc, Anvil, Bloodaxe, Carcanet, Enitharmon and Seren among the independents. Many other valuable outlets exist. The Poetry Book Society makes a convenient selection and has useful catalogues, but trusting a book club's choices is no safer for the poetry than for the fiction lover. Always read *beyond*.

Poetry magazines

The North
The Poetry Business, The Studio, Byram Arcade, Westgate, Huddersfield HD1 1ND

Parnassus Literary Magazine
Taylor University, English Dept., 236 West Reade Avenue, Upland, IN 46989-1001, USA
tel 765-998-5141 *fax* 765-998-4930

Raritan Literary Magazine
Rutgers – The State University of New Jersey, 31 Mine Street, New Brunswick, NJ 08903, USA
tel 732-932-7887 *fax* 732-932-7855

Salt Literary Magazine
PO Box 202, Applecross, Western Australia 6153
email jvk20@hermes.cam.ac.uk
Editor John Kinsella
Details for the other magazines mentioned in the article may be found in either *Magazines UK and Ireland* starting on page 21 or *Poetry organisations*, which follows this article.

In approaching journal editors or publishers it is important to indicate that you know who they are, and why you have chosen them over others. A brief letter is sufficient. If you practise multiple submissions, warn the editors to whom you write. Some editors follow a geological time-scale in replying. If you have not had a reply in six weeks, feel free to send your work elsewhere, but should the first editor accept it in the end, you must immediately withdraw it from other editors.

Success is slow: a hundred rejections may precede an acceptance. Or acceptance may never quite come. If it doesn't, how do you deal with failure? Many wannabe poets who cannot get visibly published develop a strategy of blame. It is not, they insist, the quality of the work that deprives them of readership, it is the cabals that control the avenues of transmission. Jonathan Swift knew this:

If on Parnassus' top you sit,
You rarely bite, are always bit:
Each poet of inferior size
On you shall rail and criticise ...

Other poets study 'the market' and try to follow the latest fashion. Runt-Raines, runt-Muldoons and Motions, have given way to runt-Duffys and Armitages. Aping success can seem to work: in my late 'teens, when the *New Statesman* had rejected me several times, I wrote a poem in what I took to be the style of Ted Walker, a poet popular with the magazine's poetry editor. Sure enough, my verse was accepted. I had the same experience with *Poetry Now* on radio. The editor loved what he called 'the macabre' and I delivered precisely that. Such poems, cynically composed, had a short half-life. Imitation is part of any serious apprenticeship, but publishing unacknowledged imitations, especially if they are written not to develop skills but to achieve publication, is a form of failure.

Dealing with success

Assuming the Muses of publication smile, how do you deal with success? Success can be failure postponed. A book is edited, designed, published, and then falls into a black hole of neglect. A book is published and receives negative reviews. A book is published, receives good reviews, but fails to sell. A book is published, receives good reviews, sells, but the next book does less well and there is a future of diminishing returns. The judge at the pearly gates will declare, 'It is the sort of verse which was modern in its time'.

Real success is rare and has little to do with the strategies outlined here. No poet living in the UK at this time makes a living solely from writing poems. Most write and teach, or write and perform, or have a day job, or write in other genres (novels, radio and television plays, journalism) as well as poetry. Assuming the poetry is good and/or well received, there will be invitations to perform. Fees vary from about £100 to £1000, depending on the occasion and the venue. A poet who is a good performer will read once or twice a week for a period of time and sell more books than a poet who cannot perform convincingly, even if the latter's poems are better. Indeed some apparently substantial reputations are based on performance skills rather than on the quality of the poetry.

Real success is judged less by the marketplace, more by a culture of reception which gradually grows alert to new work and explores it. It may be, if the work you are writing is original and challenging, that you will have to develop your own means of transmission on paper (a magazine, a pamphlet or book publishing house) or on the web. As long as the vehicles you create exist to serve not only your own work, but poetry more widely, whether the writing of fellow radicals or neglected texts from the past that helped shape your perspectives and formal approaches. The creation of such vehicles means that you retain control of production and dissemination; eventually the endeavour, particular and general, is acknowledged, the work read. You are in dialogue with readers.

The endorsement of an Establishment consisting of the larger publishers, specialist lists, journals and the academy, is not a guarantee of quality. What is a guarantee is a readership which will go out of its way to get hold of your work – a poem in a magazine, a pamphlet, an e-poem, a book – and will invest time and creative energy in reading you and taking bearings from what you propose.

It would be churlish of me not to mention that many poets spend their time and resources on entering competitions, and competitions are a way (the three or four major ones) of making yourself briefly visible. A competition-winning poem is not 'news that stays news', as Pound said poetry ought to be, but mere news. Mere news with money attached: not to be sneezed at. There is also the matter of fees and advances. For a 24-line poem published in a journal, payment will vary from £30 to £500, depending on the outlet. The advance for a book of poems, especially a first collection, will vary from £300 to £3000, with the occasional mad exception.

In negotiating a publishing contract, it is worth remembering that the greatest value your poems will have in the long term for you, as for your publisher, is unlikely to be the book sales. What will matter in the end, assuming your work becomes established, is the subsidiary rights: anthology, quotation, broadcasting, electronic, translation. Several poetic estates live handsomely on subsidiary rights income. For three decades I have been publishing William Carlos Williams' poetry.

So much depends
upon

a red wheel
barrow...

Eight simple lines have earned Williams' estate, and his publisher, between £27 and £35 per week over that period.

Michael Schmidt is editor of *PN Review* and director of Carcanet Press.

Poetry organisations

Poetry is one of the easiest writing art forms to begin with, though the hardest to excel at or earn any money from. Many organisations offer advice, information and resources to writers and readers at all levels, and as many as possible are included here. Jules Mann, Director of the Poetry Society, lists below the organisations which can help poets take their poetry further.

Where to get involved

The Poetry Society
22 Betterton Street, London WC2H 9BX
tel 020-7420 9880 *fax* 020-7240 4818
email info@poetrysociety.org.uk
website www.poetrysociety.org.uk

The Poetry Society was set up to help poetry and poets thrive in Britain and is a registered charity funded by the Arts Council England. The Society offers advice and information to all, with a more comprehensive level of information available to members. Membership is open to anyone interested in poetry and includes 4 issues each of the magazine *Poetry Review* and the newsletter *Poetry News*.

The Society also publishes education resources (see later); promotes National Poetry Day; runs a critical service called Poetry Prescription (£50 for 100 lines – 20% discount to members); provides an education advisory and training service, school membership, youth membership and a thriving website. A range of events and readings take place at the Poetry Café and the Poetry Studio at the Society's headquarters in Covent Garden.

Competitions run by the Society include the National Poetry Competition, the largest open poetry competition in Britain each year with a first prize of £5000, the biannual Corneliu M. Popescu Prize for European Poetry Translation and the Foyle Young Poets of the Year Award. Membership: £35 full, £25 concessions. Founded 1909.

Poetry Ireland
Upper Yard, Dublin Castle, Dublin 1,
Republic of Ireland
tel (01) 671 4632
email poetry@iol.ie
website www.poetryireland.ie

Poetry Ireland is the national poetry organisation for Ireland. It is grant-aided by both the Northern and Southern Arts Councils of Ireland and is a resource centre with the Austin Clarke Library of over 10,000 titles. It publishes the quarterly magazine *Poetry Ireland Review* and the bi-monthly newsletter *Poetry Ireland News*. Poetry Ireland organises readings in Dublin and nationally, and runs a Writers-in-Schools Scheme.

The Poetry Book Society
Book House, 45 East Hill, London SW18 2QZ
tel 020-8870 8403 *fax* 020-8870 0865
email info@poetrybooks.co.uk
website www.poetrybooks.co.uk
Chair Maura Dooley, *Director* Chris Holyfield

This unique book club for readers of poetry was founded in 1953 by T.S. Eliot, and is funded by the Arts Council England. Every quarter, selectors choose one outstanding publication (the PBS Choice), and recommend 4 other titles. Members can receive some or all of these books free and are also offered substantial discounts on other poetry books. The Poetry Book Society also administers the T.S. Eliot Prize (see page 514), produces the quarterly membership magazine, the *Bulletin*, and has an education service providing teaching materials for primary and secondary schools. Write for details.

The British Haiku Society
Lenacre Ford, Woolhope, Hereford HR1 4RF
Secretary David Walker
tel (01432) 860328
email davidawalker@btinternet.com
website www.britishhaikusociety.org

The Society runs 'The Hackett' annual haiku competition; organises tutorials, workshops and critical comment; and provides information to promote the appreciation of haiku, senryu, tanka and renga. It publishes the journal *Blithe Spirit* (4 p.a.), a newsletter for its members called the *Brief* (4 p.a.), as well as books and the *Haiku Kit* – a teachers' guide for schools suitable for all age groups. Write for membership details. Founded 1990.

Survivors Poetry
Diorama Arts Centre, 34 Osnaburgh Street,
London NW1 3ND
tel 020-7916 5317 *fax* 020-7916 0830
email survivor@survivorspoetry.org.uk

Survivors Poetry provides poetry workshops, performances, readings, publishing, networking and training for survivors of mental distress in London and the UK. Survivors Poetry is funded by the Arts Council England and was founded in 1991 by

4 poets who have had first-hand experience of the mental health system. It works in partnership with local and national arts, mental health, community, statutory and disability organisations. Its outreach project has established a network of 30 writers' groups in the UK.

Where to get information

Your local library should have information about the local poetry scene. Many libraries are actively involved in promoting poetry as well as having modern poetry available for loan. Local librarians promote writing activities with, for example, projects like Poetry on Loan and Poetry Places information points in West Midlands Libraries.

The Poetry Library

Level 5, Royal Festival Hall, London SE1 8XX
tel 020-7921 0943/0664 *fax* 020-7921 0939
email poetrylibrary@rfh.org.uk
website www.poetrylibrary.org.uk

The principal roles of the Poetry Library are to collect and preserve all poetry published in the UK since about 1912 and to act as a public lending library. The Library also keeps a wide range of international poetry. It has 2 copies of each title available and a collection of about 40,000 titles in English and English translation. The Library also provides an education service (see page 270).

Founded in 1953 by the Arts Council, the Library runs an active information service, which includes a unique noticeboard for lost quotations, and tracing authors and publishers from extracts of poems. Current awareness lists are available for magazines, publishers, competitions, bookshops, groups and workshops, evening classes and festivals on receipt of a large sae. The Library also stocks a full range of British poetry magazines as well as a selection from abroad. When visiting the Library, look out for the Voice Box, a performance space for literature; a programme is available from 020-7921 0906. Open 11am–8pm Tuesday to Sunday. Membership: free with proof of identity and current address.

The Northern Poetry Library

County Library, The Willows, Morpeth, Northumberland NE61 1TA
tel (01670) 534514 (poetry enquiries)
tel (01670) 534524 (poetry dept)

The Northern Poetry Library has over 14,000 titles and magazines covering poetry published since 1945. For information about epic through to classic poetry, a full text database is available of all poetry from 600–1900. A postal lending service is available to members, who pay for return postage. Membership is free to anyone living in the areas of Tyne and Wear, Durham, Northumberland, Cumbria and Cleveland. Founded 1968.

The Scottish Poetry Library

5 Crichton's Close, Canongate, Edinburgh EH8 8DT
tel 0131-557 2876 *fax* 0131-557 8393
email inquiries@spl.org.uk
website www.spl.org.uk

The Scottish Poetry Library is run along similar lines to the Poetry Library in London. It specialises in 20th century poetry written in Scotland, in Scots, Gaelic and English. It also collects some pre-20th-century poetry and contemporary poetry from all over the world. Information and advice is given, and visits by individuals, groups and schools are welcome. Borrowing is free of charge and there is a membership scheme (£20 p.a.), which includes use of the members' reading room and a regular newsletter. It has branches in libraries and arts centres throughout Scotland and also runs a library touring service. Readings and exhibitions are regularly organised, particularly during the Edinburgh Festival. Founded 1984.

Poeziecentrum

Hoornstraat 11, B-9000 Ghent, Belgium
tel 0032 9 225 2225 *fax* 0032 9 225 9054

Poeziecentrum (poetry centre) offers general information about translated and non-translated poetry. It has a library of 20,000 titles (including English, Scottish, American, Canadian and South African poetry), 600 magazines and 5000 archives including press cuttings, periodicals and biographical information. It also promotes the study of poetry (particularly in schools), offers advice on writing, publishing and competitions, and publishes many collections, including its own magazine *Poezierant* (bi-monthly). Founded 1980.

Arts Council England

website www.artscouncil.org.uk
Arts Council England has 9 regional offices and local literature officers can provide information on local poetry groups, workshops and societies (see page 444). Some give grant aid to local publishers and magazines and help fund festivals, literature projects and readings, and some run critical services.

The internet

You can get many links with good internet poetry magazines through the following:

The Poetry Kit

website www.poetrykit.org

The Poetry Society of America

website www.poetrysociety.org

Where to get poetry books

See the Poetry Book Society on page 267. The Poetry Library provides a list of bookshops which stock poetry. For second-hand mail order poetry books try:

Peter Riley

27 Sturton Street, Cambridge CB1 2QG
tel (01223) 576422
email priley@dircon.co.uk

The Poetry Bookshop

The Ice House, Brook Street,
Hay-on-Wye HR3 5BQ
tel (01497) 821812

Where to celebrate poetry

Festival information should be available from Arts Council England offices (see page 444). See also *Literature festivals* on page 518.

The British Council

Information Officer, Literature Dept,
The British Council, 11 Portland Place,
London W1N 4EJ
tel 020-7930 8466 *fax* 020-7389 3199
website www.britishcouncil.org/arts/literature

Send a large sae or visit the website for a list of forthcoming festivals.

Where to perform

In London, Express Excess and Vice Verso are 2 of the liveliest venues and they regularly feature the best performers, while Poetry Unplugged at the Poetry Café is famous for its weekly open mike nights (Tuesdays 7.30pm). Other performance venues listed below have readings. For up-to-date information, read *Time Out* and *What's On in London*).

Apples and Snakes Performance Poetry

Battersea Arts Centre, Lavender Hill, London SW11
tel 020-7223 2223

Coffee House Poetry

Troubadour Coffee House, 265 Old Brompton Road, London SW5
tel 020-7370 1434

Express Excess

The Enterprise, 2 Haverstock Hill, London NW3
tel 020-7485 2659

Poetry Café

22 Betterton Street, London WC2
tel 020-7420 9888

Vice Verso

Bread and Roses, 68 Clapham Manor Street,
London SW4
tel 020-8341 6085

Voice Box

Level 5, Royal Festival Hall, London SE1
tel 020-7960 4242

For venues outside London, check local listings, and ask at libraries and Arts Council England offices (see page 444).

Competitions

There are now hundreds of competitions to enter and as the prizes increase, the highest being £5000 (first prize in the National Poetry Competition and the Arvon Foundation International Poetry Competition), so does the prestige associated with winning such competitions.

To decide which competitions are worth entering, make sure you know who the judges are and think twice before paying large sums for an anthology of 'winning' poems which will only be read by entrants wanting to see their own work in print. The Poetry Library publishes a list of competitions each month (available free on receipt of a large sae). See also *Getting poetry published* on page 261 and *Prizes and awards* on page 493.

Literary prizes are given annually to published poets and as such are non-competitive. An A–Z guide to literary prizes can be found on the Booktrust website (www.booktrust.org.uk).

Where to write poetry

The Arvon Foundation

The Arvon Foundation at Lumb Bank
Hebden Bridge, West Yorkshire HX7 6DF
tel (01422) 843714 *fax* (01422) 843714
website www.arvonfoundation.org
The Arvon Foundation at Totleigh Barton
Sheepwash, Beaworthy, Devon EX21 5NS
tel (01409) 231338 fax (01409) 231144
The Arvon Foundation at Moniack Mhor
Teavarren, Kiltarlity, Beauly,
Inverness-shire IV4 7HT
tel (01463) 741675 *fax* (01463) 741733

The Arvon Foundation's 3 centres run 5-day residential courses throughout the year to anyone over the age of 16, providing the opportunity to live and work with professional writers. Writing genres explored include poetry, narrative, drama, writing for children, song writing and the performing arts. Bursaries are available to those receiving benefits. Founded in 1968.

The Poetry School

1a Jewel Road, London E17 4QU
tel/fax 020-8223 0401 *tel* 020-8985 0090
email poetryschl@aol.com

Using London venues, the Poetry School offers a core programme of tuition in reading and writing poetry. It provides a forum to share experience, develop skills and extend appreciation of both traditional and innovative aspects of poetry.

The Poet's House/Teach na hÉigse

Clonbarra, Falcarragh, County Donegal, Republic of Ireland
tel 00 353 74 65470 *fax* 00 353 74 65471
email phouse@iol.ie

The Poet's House runs 3 10-day poetry courses in July and August. An MA degree in creative writing is validated by Lancaster University, and the Irish Language Faculty includes Cathal O'Searcaigh. The poetry faculty comprises 30 writers, including Paul Durcan and John Montagu.

Ty Newydd

Taliesin Trust, Ty Newydd, Llanystumdwy, Criccieth, Gwynedd LL52 0LW
tel (01766) 522811 *fax* (01766) 523095
email tynewydd@dial.pipex.com

Ty Newydd runs week-long writing courses encompassing a wide variety of genres, including poetry, and caters for all levels, from beginners to published poets. All the courses are tutored by published writers. Writing retreats are also available.

Write Away

East Midlands Arts, Mountfields House, Epinal Way, Loughborough, Leics. LE11 0QE
tel (01509) 218292 *fax* (01509) 262214
website www.arts.org.uk
Contact Lisa Pacynko

A varied programme of residential writing courses. Details on application.

Groups on the internet

It is worth searching for discussion groups and chat rooms on the internet. There are plenty of them; John Kinsella's is highly recommended, which is junk mail-resistant and highly informative:

John Kinsella's

email poetryetc@jiscmail.ac.uk

The Poetry Kit

website www.poetrykit.org/wkshops2.htm

Local groups

Local groups vary enormously so it is worth shopping around to find one that suits your poetry. Up-to-date information can be obtained from Art Council England regional offfices (see page 444).

The Poetry Library publishes a list of groups for the Greater London area which will be sent out on receipt of a large sae.

Help for young poets and teachers

The Poetry Library

Children's Section, Royal Festival Hall, London SE1 8XX
tel 020-7921 0664
website www.poetrylibrary.org.uk

For young poets, the Poetry Library has about 4000 books incorporating the SIGNAL Collection of Children's Poetry. It also has a multimedia children's section, from which cassettes and videos are available to engage children's interest in poetry.

The Poetry Library has an education service for teachers and writing groups. Its information file covers all aspects of poetry in education. There is a separate collection of books and materials for teachers and poets who work with children in schools, and teachers may join a special membership scheme to borrow books for the classroom.

National Association of Writers in Education (NAWE)

PO Box 1, Sheriff Hutton, York YO60 7YU
tel/fax (01653) 618429
email paul@nawe.co.uk
website www.nawe.co.uk

NAWE is a national organisation, which aims to widen the scope of writing in education, and coordinate activities between writers, teachers and funding bodies. It publishes the magazine *Writing in Education* and is author of a writers' database which can identify writers who fit the given criteria (e.g. speaks several languages, works well with special needs, etc) for schools, colleges and the community. Publishes *Reading the Applause: Reflections on Performance Poetry by Various Artists*. Write for membership details.

Poetry Society Education

The Poetry Society, 22 Betterton Street, London WC2H 9BX
tel 020-7420 9894 *fax* 020-7240 4818
email education@poetrysociety.org.uk
website www.poetrysociety.org.uk

For over 30 years the Poetry Society has been introducing poets into classrooms, providing teachers' resources and producing colourful, accessible publications for pupils. A publication celebrating National Poetry Day is sent free to schools, giving an insight into the best of contemporary poetry.

Schools membership (£50 secondary, £30 primary) offers publications, training opportunities for teachers and poets, a free subscription to *Poems on the Underground* and a consultancy service giving advice on working with poets in the classroom. *Poetryclass*, an INSET training project funded by the DfES, employs poets to train teachers at primary and secondary level. People aged 11–18 can join the Society and receive poetry books and posters, quarterly copies of *Poetry News*, and a Young Writer's Pack giving advice on developing writing skills.

Poetry Society publications for schools include *The Poetry Book for Primary Schools* and *Jumpstart Poetry in the Secondary School*, a young poets pack and posters for school Key Stage 1 to GCSE requirements. A full catalogue of poetry resources, details of youth membership, the Foyle Young Poets of the Year Award, school membership and education residencies are available from the Education Department.

Young poetry competitions

Children's competitions are included in the competition list provided by the Poetry Library (free on receipt of a large sae).

Foyle Young Poets of the Year Award

The Poetry Society, 22 Betterton Street, London WC2H 9BX
tel 020-7420 9894 *fax* 020-7240 4818
email education@poetrysociety.org.uk
website www.poetrysociety.org.uk
Free entry for 11–18 year-olds with unique prizes.

Further reading

Baldwin, Michael, *The Way to Write Poetry*, Hamish Hamilton, 1982, o.p.

Chisholm, Alison, *The Craft of Writing Poetry*, Allison & Busby, 1997, repr. 2001

Chisholm, Alison, *A Practical Poetry Course*, Allison & Busby, 1997

Corti, Doris, *Writing Poetry*, Writers News Library of Writing/Thomas & Lochar, 1994

Fairfax, John, and John Moat, *The Way to Write*, Elm Tree Books, 2nd edn revised, 1998

Finch, Peter, *How to Publish Your Poetry*, Allison & Busby, 2nd edn, 1998

Forbes, Peter, *Scanning the Century*, Penguin Books, 2000

Hamilton, Ian, *The Oxford Companion to Twentieth Century Poetry in English*, OUP, 1996

Hyland, Paul, *Getting into Poetry*, Bloodaxe, 2nd edn, 1997

Livingstone, Dinah, *Poetry Handbook for Readers and Writers*, Macmillan, 1992

O'Brien, Sean, *The Firebox*, Picador, 1998

Reading the Applause: Reflections on Performance Poetry by Various Artists, NAWE, 1999

Riggs, Thomas (ed.), *Contemporary Poets*, St James Press, 7th edn, 2000

Roberts, Philip Davies, *How Poetry Works*, Penguin Books, 2nd edn, 2000

Sansom, Peter, *Writing Poems*, Bloodaxe, 1994, reprinted 1997

Sweeney Matthew, and John Williams, *Teach Yourself Writing Poetry*, Hodder and Stoughton, 1997 (new edn due Dec 2003)

Whitworth, John, *Writing Poetry*, A & C Black, 2001

USA

Breen, Nancy, *Poet's Market*, Writer's Digest Books, USA, 2004 (due Aug 2003)

Fulton, Len, *Directory of Poetry Publishers*, Dustbooks, USA, 19th edn, 2003–4

Fulton, Len, *The International Directory of Little Magazines and Small Presses*, Dustbooks, USA, 39th edn, 2003–4

Preminger, Alex, *New Princeton Encyclopedia of Poetry and Poetics*, Princeton University Press, 3rd edn, 1993

See also...

● *Publishers of poetry*, page 691

Television, film and radio

Adaptations from books

Although every writer wants to create their own work and find their own voice, adaptation is a good way both to generate income and to learn about how to write for other formats. It can also be a chance for a writer to raise their profile, with a successful adaptation sometimes leading to an original commission. Kate Sinclair explains.

Although every writer wants to create their own work and find their own voice, adaptation is a good way both to generate income and to learn about the disciplines of different media: how to write for other formats.

Writers may be approached to adapt their own work from one medium to another during their career. For example, John Mortimer originally wrote *A Voyage Round My Father* for the radio and later adapted it for stage, film and finally, for television. There are also opportunities for both writers and directors to adapt someone else's work from one performance medium to another or from a novel to any of the above.

Every year classic novels are made into adaptations for all media. These may be for the theatre, such as Helen Edmundson's version of *War and Peace* (Shared Experience/RNT), or for radio such as *Rob Roy* (the Classic Serial, Radio 4). Television carries dramatisations like *The Forsyte Saga* (ITV) or *Daniel Deronda* (BBC), and film features screenplays such as Terence Davies' version of Edith Wharton's *The House of Mirth*. Although these are usually costly to produce, involving large casts and – particularly in the visual media – the considerable expense of recreating the period in which they were written, they command loyal audiences and seem to be in steady demand. These classic projects also generate significant income both from DVD/video sales and from sales to overseas companies and networks. Some adapters are as well known as writers who concentrate on their own work. For example, Andrew Davis has become almost a household name for his television dramatisations of *Pride and Prejudice*, *The Way of the World* and, most recently, *Dr Zhivago*.

Producers in radio, television and film are also in regular contact with publishers and literary agents to keep abreast of contemporary novels which may work well in another format. I currently work as the Book Scout for Channel 4 to find books, both fiction and non-fiction, which may become television dramas or feature films. The BBC employs a Books Executive to identify suitable material for their Serials and Film Departments. Both radio producers and film companies are also sent potential books by the publicity departments of publishing houses. Writers may also make direct approaches to producers and commissioners with material that they feel they can successfully transcribe for that particular medium.

There is clearly, then, a market for adaptations of all types, with the added stimulus to the adapter of exploring technically how another writer writes – their use of language, the way they structure a narrative, their characterisation. There is the opportunity to learn from the skill and subtlety of great writers and there is the challenge of finding ways to transport a story from one form to another, with all the creative possibilities that this presents.

What to adapt, and why?

Just because a narrative works in one format doesn't guarantee that it will in another. Form and story are often inextricably bound together. Something works as a radio play precisely because it appeals to a listening audience and is able to exploit the possibilities of sound. A novel may have a reflective subject, or concentrate on a character's inner thoughts, and not on external action. While this may be fine for reading quietly alone, it could leave a theatre, television or film audience bored and longing for something to happen.

There are some stories, however, which seem to work in almost any media and which have almost become universal (though different treatments bring out diverse aspects of the original). For example, Henry James's *The Turn of the Screw* was written as a novella. It subsequently became a much-performed opera, with a libretto by Myfanwy Piper and music by Benjamin Britten; an acclaimed film, re-titled *The Innocents* with the screenplay by John Mortimer; and a recent television adaptation for ITV by Nick Dear. What makes a narrative like this transmute so successfully?

At the most simplistic level it must be dramatic. Radio, television and film, like the theatre, need drama to hold their audiences. Aristotle's premise that 'all drama is action', and should have protagonists whom we identify with, antagonists who oppose them, and the reversals, climaxes and resolutions which typify a dramatic structure. This is not necessarily the case for a novel; it is easy to be seduced by a tale that has personal resonance or beautiful language and forget the basic template which has, after all, worked for thousands of years. Reminding yourself of this when considering the suitability of any material for adaptation could spare you a rejection or a great deal of later reworking.

Knowing the media

The other important consideration is a detailed knowledge of the final medium. The adapter needs to understand why that particular story is specifically suited to it and ideally have experience of writing for that form, as well as an awareness of the current market for the project. It is vital to know precisely what is currently being produced and by whom. Staff and policies change very quickly, so the more up-to-date your research is, the better your chance of creating a successful adaptation and being able to get it accepted.

If you are adapting for the theatre, how often do you go and when was the last time you saw a production that wasn't originally written for the stage? As well as observing how successful it was, both artistically and in box office terms, would you know whether that company or theatre regularly programmes adaptations, and if so, what sort? Do they, like Shared Experience, have a reputation primarily for classics, or do they, like the Loft at the Royal National Theatre, or The Royal

Exchange, Manchester, produce versions of contemporary novels? Are you sufficiently aware of the tastes of the current artistic director and the identity of the theatre to know whether to send your project to the Royal Shakespeare Company, the West Yorkshire Playhouse or Southwark Playhouse? This is not necessarily just a question of scale or level, but more a reflection of contemporary trends and the specific policy of each of these institutions. Whilst the overall remit of a theatre or company may remain the same – if they are funded to produce only new plays, it is unlikely that this will alter – individual personnel and fashions will change regularly and it is important to keep in touch.

Television and radio

The same holds true for all the other media and, if anything, is even more important in radio and television. All of the broadcast media are now subject to the rigorous demands of ratings, which in turn make for extremely precise scheduling. Programmes have strong identities, and conversations with producers and commissioners will inevitably involve a discussion of which slot a project is suited to and what has recently been shown or broadcast. Up-to-the-minute knowledge of the work being produced by a company or broadcaster is therefore essential.

For example, BBC Radio 3's *Wire* is specifically for new work by contemporary writers and therefore isn't suitable for a classic adaptation of a novel. Radio 4 produces the Classic Serial on Sunday afternoons and *Women's Hour* has a regular serialisation slot that can be contemporary or classic and is often an adapted novel. Biographies or autobiographies are also frequently abridged and read on Radio 4 at 9.45am on weekdays. For a detailed knowledge of this output there can be no substitute for studying the *Radio Times*, seeing what is programmed, and listening to what gets produced in which slots. Being able to envisage the eventual destination for a chosen adaptation helps you to choose the right project and place it successfully.

In television this process of research is more complex. As well as strong competition between the BBC and the larger independent broadcasters (ITV, Channel 4, Carlton, Granada, etc) to secure an audience, there is also considerable rivalry between the hundreds of independent production companies to receive commissions. The ratings war means that scheduling is paramount and big dramatic adaptations are often programmed at exactly the same time on BBC 2 and ITV. Familiarity with the output of each channel is crucial when suggesting projects for adaptation, either to a commissioner or a production company. Again, watching dramatisations and noting what format they are in, who is producing them, and when they are being broadcast, is all part of the job.

As a general rule it is helpful to know that both adaptations and writing commissioned directly for television, tend to be divided into several basic categories (not including soaps). Single dramas are usually high profile, broadcast at peak times and are about two hours long. Series consist of a number of weekly parts shown over several weeks (3, 4, 6, 8 and 10 are all common), each part lasting anywhere between 30 and 60 minutes; there has also recently been a trend for fewer 90-minute-long episodes. Finally there are two-part dramas or event pieces which take place on consecutive nights with each part between one and two hours long. The percentage of adaptations will generally be lower than newly commissioned drama, although this is entirely dependent upon the type of slot and the broadcaster. For example, the BBC has approximately double the budget per hour for drama that Channel 4 has, and produces many more dramatisations of classic novels. Likewise, ITV has currently been producing regular serialisations of classics and single adaptations in association with HSBC. Channel 4, when it commissions adaptations, tends to focus on cutting-edge contemporary novels, such as *White Teeth* by Zadie Smith, adapted by Simon Burke. And there are of course always exceptions to all these trends, which is why it is necessary to be an aware and regular viewer.

If you want to adapt for film, the nature of what will work and when, seems to be more open-ended, though it is of course important to go regularly to the cinema and know what has been produced recently. This may be to do with the nature of distribution – the fact that most films are on in a number of cinemas for several weeks – and the time it takes to make a film – often years between the initial idea and eventual screening. However, you still need to keep up-to-date with who is producing what and when. This will enable you both to latch on to the coat tails of a fashion, and to avoid doing a lot of unnecessary work on an adaptation that someone else is in the middle of filming.

The rights

Once you have selected your material and medium, it is vital to establish who has the rights to the original and whether these are available for negotiation. Sometimes this involves a bit of detective work. If the writer is dead, it is necessary to find out whether there is an estate and if the work is still subject to copyright.

Copyright law is extremely complex. In the UK it has altered from 50 to 70 years, so some texts that were out of copyright have gone back in again (for further information see *UK copyright law*, page 606). This varies, however, around the world so it is essential therefore that you seek expert advice concerning the current rules of copyright for any potential project, depending on the country of origin.

It is usually possible to begin the search for the copyright holder and source of rights from the imprint page of the novel, play, film script, etc. If this information is not given, try the publisher, the Society of Authors or the Writers' Guild.

In the case of a living writer, you will need to establish who their literary agent is – if they have one – and contact them to see if adaptation is possible and how much it will cost. The scale of costs will depend upon the medium. Rights for a stage adaptation are often separate from film or television options. If a book or play has already been optioned, this means that it is probably not available for a period of at least 12–18 months. Should the purchaser of the option choose not to renew, or fail to produce the adaptation within the required timescale, rights may become available again. Many agreements include an extension clause for a further fixed time period, however, and this is particularly common in film as the end-product is rarely produced within 18 months.

Large film companies, particularly in Hollywood, will often buy the rights to a book or script outright, sometimes for a substantial sum. The proposed version may never get made but legally the original will not be available for adaptation by anyone else. If the writer or material is famous enough, or if they have a good agent, a time limit will be part of the original agreement. Complete buy-outs are less common in the UK.

The cost of acquiring rights varies significantly with the scale of the project, the profile of the writer and the intended medium. Usually an initial payment will be needed to secure the rights for a fixed period, followed by the same amount again, should an extension be necessary. In addition, there is nearly always some form of royalty for the original writer or estate in the form of a percentage of the overall profits of the final production, film, or broadcast. This will normally have a 'bottom ceiling' – a minimum amount or reserve – which must be paid whether or not the final work is financially successful. With television, film or radio, there may be a further payment for repeats and in the theatre the rate may well alter if the production transfers. Sometimes, with a low-budget production such as a fringe show or short film, a writer or estate will waive any initial rights fee and only expect a royalty.

Legalities aside, time spent forming a relationship with the writer of the original, or whoever manages their estate, has other another much more important function, a creative one, that of getting closer to the source material.

How to adapt

I don't believe it is possible to lay down a set of rules for adapting, any more than one could invent a meaningful template for creative writing. The only observation I can offer, therefore, is personal and a reflection of my own taste.

When I recommend or commission an adaptation, either to direct in the theatre, or for television and film, my first requirement is that something in the original story has hooked me and I want to see the original given another life and another audience. I have to be able to imagine that it has the potential to work dramatically in a different format and can often already see or hear fragments of it.

At this stage I ask myself a lot of questions about the material. Why should it be done in another medium? How is it possible to achieve this particular part of the narrative, this character, this tone, this sequence of action, in a way that is different but still truthful, a sort of creative equivalent, like a metaphor. For me, it is all about thinking laterally and being enthused about the new possibilities another form will generate from the original, or vice versa.

This process generally leads me back to the source, be it book, film or play, in order to dig over everything about it and its writer. As well as looking at other adaptations to see what parts of the original have been enhanced or cut, I like to meet and talk to the writer. If they are no longer alive I try to find out about them from books and/or people who knew them. I want to know what interested them; what were they thinking when they were writing; even what they looked at every day. If possible, I like to go and visit the places they have written about or the place in which they wrote. This process of total immersion helps me to get under the skin of the original.

While this is entirely personal, it raises an interesting question which I believe any adapter needs to answer for themselves. How closely do you wish to replicate the original material and how much do you intend to depart from it? Choosing not to stick closely to the source may be the most creative decision you make but you must understand why you are doing it and what the effect will be. After all, two different trains of thought, styles and imaginations need to be fused together for this transformation to be complete and it is important that the balance between them works. I once spoke to a writer who was commissioned to adapt a well-known myth for Hollywood.

Successful collaborations

Here is an entirely subjective list of my personal favourites among recent successful collaborations, by way of example.

Film
Trainspotting (Irvine Welsh, screenplay John Hodges)
Persuasion (Jane Austen, screenplay Nick Dear)

Television
The Way of the World (Anthony Trollope, adaptation Andrew Davies)
The Forsyte Saga (John Galsworthy, adaptation Stephen Mallatratt)
Brideshead Revisited (Evelyn Waugh, adaptation John Mortimer)
The Buddha of Suburbia (Hanif Kureshi, adaptation Roger Michell and Hanif Kureshi)
Longitude (Dava Sobel, adaptation Charles Sturridge)

Theatre
The Mill on the Floss (George Eliot, adaptation Helen Edmundson)
Nana (Emile Zola, adaptation Pam Gems)
The Magic Toyshop (Angela Carter, adaptation Bryony Lavery)

Radio
The Old Curiosity Shop (Charles Dickens, adaptation Mike Walker)

Several drafts later, when he had been asked to alter all the key elements of the story to the point where it was unrecognisable, he decided to quit. It was the right decision and the film was a flop.

While respect for the writer and the source material is fundamental, there are of course lots of examples where enormous lateral and creative changes have been made to make a story work to optimum effect in its new medium. What matters ultimately is the integrity of the final product. At its best, it is like a marriage of two minds, celebrating the talents of both writer and adapter in an equally creative partnership.

Kate Sinclair is the Book Scout for Channel 4. She has also worked as a director in theatre and radio.

Writing for television

Writing for television can be an extremely rewarding career. Anji Loman Field says anyone with the right aptitude and attitude can succeed, and here she gives sound advice for the potential screenwriter.

The markets

There are various openings for new writers in television, but apart from competitions and special projects these are hardly ever advertised. The BBC's latest information on opportunities for new writers can be found at www.bbc.co.uk/writersroom. The openings fall into four categories:

Single drama

There are fewer slots nowadays for the single play – a 30- or even 60-minute one-off drama is highly unlikely to find a market. Occasionally broadcasters will gather single 90-minute plays together under a collective banner (e.g. Screens One and Two; Love Bites; Obsession) but it's best to think of individual projects as either standalone 90-minute television films, two-parters or even four-parters. It's always worth asking television companies for their guidelines on single drama and film. Channel 4 is currently commissioning 30-minute dramas from new writers via its Independent Film & Video department.

Series and serials

Although it has been known for a new writer to sell an original series or serial, it is a relatively rare occurrence. Writers with a track record of writing for existing strands are far more likely to be taken seriously. Long-running soaps like *EastEnders*, *Emmerdale* and *Family Affairs* are often in the market for new writers, but check first. If the door is open, a good 'calling card script' is usually the way in. Submit an original piece of work in a similar genre that is at least an hour long and shows your ability to create believable characters, write sparkling dialogue and tell a compelling story. You may be invited to try out for one of these long-running shows.

Dramatisations/adaptations

A new writer is extremely unlikely to be commissioned to adapt or dramatise someone else's work for television. However, if there's something you really want to adapt and you can afford to take out an 'option' on the rights (or already own them, if it is your own novel or play) then write the script on spec. If you have a good script and can show that you own the rights, you could succeed.

Situation comedy

This is the one area where production companies and broadcasters are desperate for new talent, and there are often competitions open to new writers. If you are a good comedy writer and market your work well, you will undoubtedly succeed (see 'Writing situation comedy' below).

Aptitude and attitude

The first prerequisite in writing for television is that you enjoy the medium, and actually watch the kinds of shows that you would be interested in writing for. A cynical approach will always show through. And before sitting down to write that first television script, arm yourself with the appropriate skills by examining the medium as a whole.

● **Tape the kind of show you'd like to write for and analyse it.** How many scenes are there? What length are they? How much of the story happens 'off camera'? Knowing the answers to these questions will help you to understand the grammar of screen, and enable you to write a more professional script.

● **Study the structure of story telling.** There are plenty of books on the subject, and although it is never a good idea to follow structural paradigms to the letter, absorb as much information as possible so that the essential 'rules' on character, motivation and plot filter through into your writing.

● **Read scripts.** Some are published in book form, but a huge variety of scripts are also available from specialist book shops such as Offstage (*tel* 020-7485 4996), the Screenwriter's Store (*tel* 020-8469 2244) and the internet.

● **If you want to write sitcom, see as many live recordings of shows as possible.** This enables you to understand the techniques involved in television production, and particularly the physical constraints imposed by the studio. Free tickets for sitcom recordings are always available – phone the broadcasters for information.

● **Be realistic.** Don't make your first project too ambitious in terms of screen time, locations or special effects. If you can 'contain the action' and make your first script affordable to shoot, it is far more likely to be taken seriously.

Learning the craft

Even the most successful and experienced screenwriters say they never stop learning. Some have been lucky enough to learn the skill of writing for the screen in a subliminal way. For example, Lynda La Plante (*Prime Suspect*) was an actress with plenty of opportunity for studying scripts and production techniques before she turned her hand to writing; John Sullivan (*Only Fools and Horses*) worked in the props department at the BBC on countless sitcoms, and used to take the scripts home to study. But there are other ways to learn. Script workshops are particularly useful.

There are many courses and workshops available. These range from small self-help groups, where writers give each other feedback on their work, to full- and part-time Screenwriting MA courses at universities (e.g. in London, Sheffield, Leicester, Bournemouth, Manchester and Leeds). Evening classes are springing up in local colleges, and there are even script workshops on the internet. Workshops can help in the following ways:

● **Discipline.** The hardest thing most writers ever have to do is sit down and face that blank screen or page. Joining a script workshop – where you *have* to deliver an outline or a treatment, or the next 20 pages of your script by a certain date – provides the push that so many writers need.

● **Feedback.** Reading and giving feedback on other people's work helps you to focus on getting your own script right. It is also good to get used to the idea of showing your own work to others and getting their feedback. Television writing is generally a collaborative process and writers need to be pleasant to work with, and receptive to ideas. Knowing when to argue a point and when to concede are crucial skills which can be developed in good writing workshops.

● **Rewriting.** Learn to Love the Rewrite. It is such a major achievement to get to the end of a first draft that it is all too easy to rush to the post box and send it off to several production companies at once. *Four Weddings and a Funeral,* a Channel 4-funded project, went through 17 rewrites before finally reaching the screen. So before you post your masterpiece:

● Leave it to 'settle' for a few days and do something completely different – allow your head to clear completely. Then re-read the script from beginning to end – from as objective a viewpoint as possible – and make necessary changes.

● Get feedback so that you're sure your script is ready to send. Be warned: knowing how to read and analyse a script properly is a particular skill. Unless they are equipped in this area, *never* ask your friends or relations to read your script. Their comments could either lull you into a false sense of security or destroy your confidence for ever. Feedback from other writers in your workshop group is best. There are some organisations (including the Screenwriters' Workshop) which offer a professional script feedback service for a moderate fee.

Writing situation comedy

Situation comedy writing is the most lucrative area of television, and deservedly so. Have you ever tried making an audience laugh several times a minute for 25 minutes for at least six weeks running, and maybe (in the case of *Last of the Summer Wine*) for 20 long years?

Despite its name, sitcom is less about situation and much more about character. It is better to start with funny and engaging characters in mind and then (if it isn't part and parcel of the character) find the perfect situation in which to place them than it is to begin with the premise 'nobody's ever set a sitcom in a nuclear power station before'. It is not the setting that makes the audience laugh, it is the characters.

A good exercise in seeing if you can write funny material is to write an episode of an existing sitcom. If *Fawlty Towers* is your all-time favourite, study a few episodes and then try your own. It will never get made, but you'll learn a lot in the process – and sample scripts like this are often useful as calling card scripts. Some of the broadcast companies issue guidelines on writing situation comedy. Phone the comedy departments at the BBC, LWT and Carlton for information, and for Channel 4's excellent 'beginners' guide to sitcom writing' pack contact Broadcasting Support Services (*tel* 0161-277 7000).

Competitions

Broadcasters occasionally run writing competitions or 'new writing initiatives'. Check their websites – and general screenwriters' websites – for up-to-date information. Also, watch out for annual awards run by organisations such as PAWS (People's Awareness of Science, *tel* 020-8214 1543), the BBC Talent (www.bbc.co.uk/talent), and the Orange Prize for Screenwriting (www.orangeprize.com *tel* (07970) 111999). Details can be found in the trade press and via relevant websites and screenwriting organisations. See also *Prizes and awards* section on page 493.

Breaking in

Do you need an agent?

Many new writers are keen to get an agent before they attempt to sell anything, but this can be an arduous process and there are few agents prepared to take on a completely untried writer.

The best way to get an agent is to first get an offer of a deal on a project. Most *bona fide* production companies and broadcasters will happily recommend a selection of agents to writers they want to do business with. If you can phone an agent and say 'so-and-so wants to option/ commission my project and has recommended you as an agent' s/he is far more likely to be interested. And at that point you can pick and choose the agent who is right for you, rather than going with the first one to say "yes".

Selling yourself

Once you are sure you have a good script, where do you send it? If you've done your homework, you will already know which channel is the most likely to be interested. But sometimes it is better to send to an independent production company rather than directly to a broadcaster, so do a bit more research. Check out the companies that are making the kind of show you've written and approach them first.

A preliminary letter or phone call can save you time and money because some smaller companies simply don't have the resources to read unsolicited material. If you feel that a certain production company is absolutely right for your project, write a letter giving a brief synopsis of the project and asking if they will read the script. If they agree, your script will join the 'solicited' pile. And if it fits the bill,

Useful information

Euroscript
Suffolk House, 1-8 Whitfield Place,
London W1T 5JU
tel/fax 020-7387 5880
email info@euroscript.co.uk
website www.euroscript.co.uk
A script development organisation aiming to place great screenplays at the heart of the industry. Originally funded by the European Union's Media II programme, the service is now worldwide. Professional development support is provided for screenwriters, producers and production companies through consultancy, Film Story Competition (deadlines: 30 April and 31 October each year) and international workshops.

London Film & Video Development Agency
114 Whitfield Street, London W1T 5EF
tel 020-7383 7755 *fax* 020-7383 7745
(incorporating the London Production Fund
tel 020-7383 7766)
email lfvda@lfvda.demon.co.uk
website www.lfvda.demon.co.uk
Offers grants that enable writers, producers and directors to make their projects. Consult website or send sae for further information.

National Association of Television Program Executives (NATPE)
452 Oakleigh Road North, London N20 0RZ
tel 020-8361 3793 *fax* 020-8368 3824
website www.natpe.org
Contact Pam Smithard
Non-profit TV programming and content association dedicated to the continued growth and success of the global TV marketplace. Year-round activities include the annual conference and exhibition, which reaches tens of thousands of key decisionmakers in virtually every sector of the TV industry.

Useful information (cont.)

PACT (Producers Alliance for Cinema and Television)
45 Mortimer Street, London W1W 8HJ
tel 020-7331 6000 *fax* 020-7331 6700
email enquiries@pact.co.uk
website www.pact.co.uk
Serves the feature film and independent TV production sector. The *PACT Directory* lists contacts in all areas (£30 to non-members). (See also page 470.)

Arts Council England regional offices
Many regional offices offer grants that enable writers, producers and directors to make their projects (see page 444).

The Screenwriters' Workshop
(formerly London Screenwriters' Workshop)
Suffolk House, 1-8 Whitfield Place, London W1T 5JU
tel/fax 020-7387 5511
email screenoffice@tiscali.co.uk
website www.lsw.org.uk
Runs regular courses, workshops and events; publishes a quarterly newsletter. Educational charity. (See also page 477.)

The Spotlight
7 Leicester Place, London WC2H 7RJ
tel 020-7437 7631 *fax* 020-7437 7631
email info@splotlightcd.com
website www.splotlightcd.com
Publishes a book called *Contacts*, which contains useful information and contact addresses.

The Writers' Guild of Great Britain
15 Britannia Street, London WC1X 9JN
tel 020-7833 0777 *fax* 020-7833 4777
email admin@writersguild.org.uk
website www.writersguild.org.uk
Trade union-affiliated organisation for professional writers. Negotiates rates for TV drama with the BBC and the ITV Network Centre. (See also page 490.)

they may even pick it up and develop it. But don't expect overnight results. It can sometimes take many months before scripts are even read by small and/or busy companies.

Sending your script directly to a broadcaster can lead to a commission, but unless you target a particular producer whose work you admire you will probably have less control over who you work with.

Being 'discovered'
If you can get your work 'rehearse-read' by actors in front of an audience it will help your writing, and may even lead to discovery. Many script readings are attended by development executives from television and production companies and there are many stories of individuals being picked up from such projects. TAPS (Television Arts Performance Showcase) (*tel* 01932 592151), Player–Playwrights (*tel* 020-8883 0371) and the Screenwriters' Workshop, all organise rehearsed readings.

Development hell
This is the place between finding someone who wants to produce your script and waiting for the 'suits' at the television companies to give the final go-ahead for the project. In the meantime you will have been paid, perhaps just an option fee, or maybe a commission fee for a script or two.

Either way, *never put all your eggs in one development basket*. Aim eventually to have several projects bubbling under for every one that comes to the boil.

A realistic optimism is required for this game. Don't believe anything wonderful will happen until you actually have that signed contract in front of you. In the meantime keep writing, keep marketing and, if you possibly can, keep making contacts in the industry. If you're good at schmoozing, go to as many industry events as possible and make new contacts. If you can send a script to a producer with a covering letter saying 'I heard your talk the other day ...' you will immediately arouse interest.

Coping with rejection

The standard rejection letter is the worst part of this business. When it is accompanied by your returned script – looking decidedly un-read – it is very easy to become disillusioned. The trick is this: change your mental attitude to the point where if you don't receive at least one rejection letter in the post every day, you feel rejected! So long as you are absolutely sure that your work is good, keep sending it out. Sooner or later you'll get a nicer, more personalised rejection letter, and then eventually perhaps even a cup of tea with the producer ...

Selling ideas

Completely new writers do occasionally sell ideas but are much more likely to sell the idea alone, i.e. the 'format rights', and will probably end up not writing the script. If you have a great calling card script or two, or have had a few episodes of something produced, your ideas will be taken much more seriously. At this stage you might well sell a project on the basis of a short outline or synopsis, and be paid to write the script(s).

All scripts must be typed and properly formatted if they are to be taken seriously. If you dread the practical aspects of getting your script onto the page it might be worth investing in a screenwriting software program for your computer. They take the pain out of screenwriting by auto-formatting and numbering the pages and scenes, thus enabling you to move scenes around and restructure your script with ease. Such facilities allow writers to concentrate wholly on the creative process and can therefore be quite liberating, even for those who type well. Contact the Screenwriters' Store for details and advice.

Summary

Writing for television is not generally something that can be taken up as a hobby. It may look easy but huge amounts of work and commitment are required in order to succeed. If that doesn't put you off, and it is what you really want to do, then go for it. And good luck!

Anji **Loman Field** worked as a television producer for several years before turning to writing. She has since written drama, comedy drama and animation for film, television and radio, and has taught writing at the Screenwriters' Workshop, the Royal College of Art and the London Institute.

Further reading

Friedmann, Julian, *How to Make Money Scriptwriting*, Intellect Books, 2000
Kelsey, Gerald, *Writing for Television*, A & C Black, 3rd edn, 1999
Seger, Linda, *Making a Good Script Great*, Samuel French Inc. (pbk), 1994
Vogler, Christopher, *The Writer's Journey*, Pan, 2nd revised edn, (pbk), 1999
Wolfe, Ronald, *Writing Comedy*, Robert Hale, 2003

Writing drama for radio

Writing drama for radio allows a freedom which none of the other performing arts can give. Lee Hall guides the radio drama writer to submit a script which will be both well received and merit production.

With upwards of 300 hours of radio drama commissioned each year, radio is an insatiable medium and, therefore, one which is constantly seeking new blood. It is no surprise to find that many of our most eminent dramatists, such as Pinter and Stoppard, did important radio work early in their careers.

Although the centrality of radio has been eclipsed somewhat by television and fringe theatre, it continues to launch new writers, and its products often find popular recognition in other media (for example, the film version of Anthony Mingella's *Truly Madly Deeply*). Because radio is often cited as the discoverer and springboard of so many talents, this should not obscure the fact that many writers make a living primarily out of their radio writing and the work itself is massively popular, with plays regularly getting audiences of over 500,000 people.

For the dramatist, the medium offers a variety of work which is difficult to find anywhere else: serials, dramatisations, new commissions of various lengths (from a couple of minutes to several hours), musicals, soap operas, adaptations of the classics, as well as a real enthusiasm to examine new forms.

Because it is no more expensive to be in the Hindu Kush than to be in a laundrette in Deptford, the scope of the world is only limited by the imagination of the writer. However, though radio drama in the 'Fifties and 'Sixties was an important conduit for absurdism, there is a perceived notion that radio drama on the BBC is domestic, Home Counties and endlessly trotting out psychological trauma in a rather naturalistic fashion. This is not a fair assessment of the true range of work presented. The BBC itself is anxious to challenge this idea and as the face of broadcasting changes, there is a conscious move to attract new audiences with new kinds of work.

Get to know the form

Listen to as many plays as possible, read plays that are in print, and try to analyse what works, what doesn't and why. This may seem obvious, but it is easy to fall back on your preconceived notions of what radio plays are. The more you hear other people's successes and failures, the more tools you will have to discriminate when it comes to your own work.

Plays on radio tend to fit into specific time slots: 30, 60, 75, 90 minutes, and each slot will have a different feel – an afternoon play will be targeted at a different audience from one at 10.30pm.

A radio play will be chosen on artistic grounds but nevertheless a writer should be familiar with the market. This should not be seen as an invitation merely to copy forms or to try to make your play 'fit', but an opportunity to gain some sense of what the producers are dealing with. Producers are looking for new and fresh voices, ones which are unique, open new areas or challenge certain preconceptions. This is not to suggest you should be wilfully idiosyncratic but to be aware that it is the individuality of your 'voice' that people will notice.

Write what you feel strongly about, in the way that most attracts you. It should be bold, personal, entertaining, challenging and stimulating. Radio has the scope to explore drama that wouldn't get produced in theatres or on television, so treat it as the most radical forum for new writing. How many times have you listened to the radio with the sense that you've heard it all before? Never feel limited by what exists but be aware how your voice can enrich the possibilities of the future.

Who to approach
Opportunities for writing for radio in the UK are dominated by the BBC. Whilst there are increasing opportunities with independent stations, BBC Radio Drama overwhelms the field. Its output is huge. The variety of the work – from soaps to the classics – makes it the true national repertory for drama in its broadest sense. However, the BBC is increasingly commissioning productions from independent producers, so you can:
● send your unsolicited script to the BBC 'writersroom' (formerly the New Writing Initiative; see page 293) where it will be assessed by a reader. If they find it of interest they will put you in contact with a suitable producer.
● approach a producer directly. This may be a producer at the BBC or at an independent company (see page 324). Both will give a personal response based on their own taste, rather than an institutional one.

Producers have a broad role: they find new writers, develop projects, edit the script, cast the actors, record and edit the play, and even write up the blurb for the *Radio Times*. Because of this intense involvement, the producer needs to have a strong personal interest in the writer or writing when they take on a project.

The system of commissioning programmes at the BBC is such that staff producers or independent production companies offer projects to commissioning editors to decide upon. Thus, a writer must be linked to a producer in the first instance to either get their play produced or get a commission for a new piece of work. Therefore, going direct to a producer can be a convenient short cut, but it requires more preparation.

Approaching a producer
Discovering and developing the work of new writers is only a small part of a producer's responsibilities, so be selective. Do your homework – there is little point in sending your sci-fi series to a producer who exclusively produces one-off period comedies.

To help decide which producer will be the most receptive to your work, become familiar with the work of each producer you are intersted in and the type of writers they work with. Use the *Radio Times* to help with your research and listen to as many of their plays as possible. It is well worth the effort in order to be sure to send your play to the right person. If you can quote the reasons why you've chosen them in particular, it can only help to get a congenial reception. It will also give you confidence in their response, as the comments – good or bad – will be from someone you respect.

Submitting your work

Don't stuff your manuscript into an envelope as soon as you've written 'The End'. You owe it to yourself to get the script into the best possible state before anyone sees it. First impressions matter and time spent refining will pay dividends in attracting attention.

Ask a person you trust to give you some feedback. Try to edit the work yourself, cutting things that don't work and spending time revising and reinventing anything which you think could be better. Make sure that what you send is the best you can possibly do.

Producers have mountains of scripts to read. The more bulky your tome the less enthusiastically it will be received. (It's better to send a sparkling 10-page sample than your whole 300-page masterpiece.) Try to make the first scene excellent. The more you can surprise, engage or delight in the first few pages, the more chance the rest will be carefully read. The adage that a reader can tell whether a play is any good after the first three pages might be wholly inaccurate but it reflects a cynicism versed by the practice of script reading. The reader will probably approach your script with the expectation that it is unsuitable, and part of getting noticed is jolting them out of their complacency.

Have your script presentably typed. Make sure your letter of introduction is well informed and shows that you haven't just picked a name at random. Do not send it to more than one producer at a time, as this is considered bad etiquette. And don't expect an instantaneous response – it may take a couple of months before you receive a reply. Don't be afraid of calling up if they keep you waiting for an unreasonable length of time, but don't badger people as this will inevitably be counterproductive.

Finally

Don't be discouraged by rejection and *don't* assume that because one person has rejected your script that it is no good. It is all a question of taste. Use the criticism positively to help your work, not as a personal attack.

Lee Hall has written several plays for BBC Radio, including the award-winning *Spoonface Steinberg*, which he has since adapted for TV and theatre. His translations of theatre plays include Brecht's *Mr Puntilla and His Man Matti* and *Mother Courage*, and Goldoni's *The Servant with Two Masters*. His play *Cooking with Elvis* was nominated for an Olivier Award for Best New Comedy, and his screenplay for *Billy Elliot* was Oscar nominated.

Digital broadcasting

Digital broadcasting is expanding rapidly. David Teather introduces this new media and looks at the implications for writers.

Digital broadcasting offers choice from hundreds of channels and the chance to offer interactive services to viewers. As many as 10 digital services are able to occupy the frequency previously occupied by one analogue service. Picture quality is far sharper using digital transmission.

Interactive services are so far only being used for e-commerce – for instance, Sky's television shopping and banking service Open. But a number of broadcasters are beginning to explore different ways of using the services for entertainment. In its coverage of Wimbledon, for instance, the BBC used the Sky Digital service to allow viewers to choose which court they wanted to watch. Ultimately, viewers will be able to link straight from a programme to associated websites, merchandising or online discussion points covering issues raised in a show. Digital transmission costs are also much lower which makes it more commercially viable for niche channels to exist.

The story so far

The first company to launch digital services was Sky which now has 7 million digital subscribers. Its customer numbers for pay-TV stations had plateaued, but are now rising again as a result of digital broadcasting.

Of the cable companies, Telewest began its digital services at the end of 1999 and NTL (which now owns Cable & Wireless) started in mid 2000. The plug was pulled on ITV Digital, a joint venture between Carlton Communications and Granada which enabled digital services to be sent via traditional roof-top aerials, in April 2002. It has been replaced by Freeview, a joint venture between the BBC, BSkyB and Crown Castle, which offers around 30 channels. The service is free as the name suggests and is being received by around 1.3 million homes. Former ITV Digital subscribers can receive it through their existing set top boxes, while new viewers simply need to buy a box or own a digital television set.

The uptake of digital services was given a huge boost when the fierce competition for subscribers led Sky to scrap the £200 charge for the set-top boxes needed to unscramble the digital signal.

The government is aiming to switch off analogue and would like to do so before 2010. By that time, digital set-top boxes should have been replaced by television sets able to receive digital signals – but sales so far have been slow. The switch-off date for analogue is highly political because it will cause an inevitable outcry when old sets become useless.

Free-to-air channels

There are a number of free-to-air channels. The BBC has controversially set up a number of new channels: BBC3, aimed at the youth market; BBC4, an arts-based channel; and BBC News 24 which – as the name suggests – screens news

24 hours a day. Rival companies such as Sky have argued that the licence fee should not be used to prop up stations like News 24 in a commercial marketplace. During the day, BBC3 and BBC4 run two children's channels, Cbeebies, for a preschool audience and CBBC for older children. The BBC has committed around £300 million to digital services: BBC3 has the biggest budget of £53 million, BBC4 has a budget of £32 million and the

The technical explanation

The BBC offers this definition:"Digital Broadcasting is transmission by converting sound and picture into binary digits – a series of ones and noughts. Digital signals are more robust than analogue signals and can occupy parts of the spectrum unavail-able to analogue. A process of compression also allows many digital services within the space taken by one analogue service."

children's channels have a combined budget of £20 million. UK History, a documentary-based channel is also available on Freeview. Each of the channels is a mixture of repeats from other mainstream channels and new commissions.

ITV Network's ITV2 also shows catch-up episodes of programmes like *Coronation Street*, as well trumpeting a large number of US imports. All of the existing five free-to-air channels are also available in digital format. Other channels on Freeview include Sky News, QVC and Full On Entertainment.

Video-on-demand

The next step in the digital revolution is video-on-demand. A number of companies are offering services, including the cable companies and Kingston Communications, which runs a joint venture over telephone wires with BSkyB in Hull. Users are able to download films or television programmes at will, and fast forward, pause and rewind them. Programme-makers like the BBC have already sold packages to some of the video-on-demand firms and writers need to consider the implications for the potential sell-on of copyright.

Video-on-demand could become widespread with the advent of a technology called ADSL (Asymmetrical Digital Subscriber Line), which upgrades existing copper telephone wires for high bandwidth use such as pay-TV without the need to dig up roads. ADSL is becoming more widely available on BT's networks. A ban on broadcasting being carried over BT's lines has now been lifted but costs are still prohibitively high.

Digital technology in the next few years will enable video-quality film to be sent over mobile phone networks. The mobile phone industry has the networks in place and is beginning to sell the necessary handsets after many delays.

New channels, new opportunities?

The explosion of new channels may suggest that there will be an equally huge demand for new writing talent to help fill the extra airtime. Through a joint venture with Flextech Television, the BBC has six pay-TV channels, including UK Gold, UK Play and UK Drama. The evidence so far, however, is that money is being spent largely on three things: sports rights, movies and US imports. Most original programming on pay-TV channels is very low budget and is far more likely to be a cookery or pop music show than original drama.

Unfortunately, rather than playing to their own strengths, the BBC and ITV appear to be drawn into competing with the entertainment channels at their level. "Once upon a time the BBC set the standards of quality and everyone else had to try and compete," says one writer. "That doesn't happen any more. Now the BBC competes with the others for crap."

The level of competition among broadcasters now also means that where original drama is being commissioned it is often low budget. In fact, many writers believe that in the short term digital technology has not opened opportunities at all and see the future as pretty bleak. Management gurus, though, maintain that 'content is king' and that those broadcasters who triumph will be the ones who produce the most compelling programming.

Copyrights

The Writers' Guild notes a recent case where a writer saw a 30-year-old show he had penned being repeated again and again on a pay-TV channel and demanded to know why he wasn't being paid. It turned out that he had signed his rights away in 1972.

If the explosion of channels made possible by digital technology isn't leading to a wave of new commissioning then writers could at least hope for healthier repeat fees. The culture of broadcasters forcing writers to sign away their rights for a lump sum so that they can show a programme whenever they like is becoming increasingly prevalent. The usual royalty is 5.6% of the sale price, which gives the owner the right to show the programme a set number of times over a given period.

Broadcasters blame the need to sell to the US market programmes which are unencumbered by copyright issues. When selling work, writers should remember how many more times, potentially, a programme will appear on air because of the growth in distribution platforms, and therefore at least try to protect their rights. The rapid changes in technology has also led writers' unions to recommend that contracts over the shortest space of time possible are agreed.

Original programming

There are at last some encouraging signs, however, led by Channel 4 and followed by Sky. Channel 4 has long supported new writing talent through its backing of British film and has found its own pay-TV distribution outlet with FilmFour.

Sky One has a total budget of around £90 million but its efforts in original programming have met with mixed results – probably the most successful has been the football drama *Dream Team*. However, Sky's original programming has largely been forced upon it as the cost of acquiring top US content has soared due to increased competition – the reason why it lost the rights to show *Friends* and *ER*, two of Sky One's biggest ratings pullers, to Channel 4. Channel 4 is commissioning original programming for its digital entertainment channel, E4.

Sky attempted to launch its own film business, Sky Pictures, but abandoned the project after its first few films met with tepid reviews and box office sales. NTL, Britain's largest cable company, has dipped its toe into original programming but like its rival, Telewest, is in a precarious financial position and more in cost-cutting than commissioning mode.

Digital radio

The attributes of digital radio are similar to those of television. It was supposed to be the next revolution, but it has yet to catch on. The growth of stations is still in its infancy. In London, for instance, there will be three so-called 'multiplexes' of eight stations awarded to various consortia of existing radio groups. Interactive services will be on offer with the most obvious for radio including up-to-date traffic or weather reports displayed on a digital monitor on request. Digital radio could also lead to music or programming on demand similar to that of digital television programming.

A number of stations are now being broadcast in both digital and analogue as well as a growing number in digital alone. The BBC has launched five new radio stations, including one devoted to the spoken word, BBC7. So far, though, the industry has been held back by the prohibitive cost of hardware – the radios currently cost around £300.

David Teather is at the *Guardian*.

BBC network television and radio

For more information visit the BBC website: www.bbc.co.uk

The new structure

Major restructuring, introduced by BBC Director-General Greg Dyke on 3 April 2000, resulted in the creation of four programming divisions:
- Drama, Entertainment and Children;
- Factual and Learning;
- Sport; and
- News.

BBC Broadcast and BBC Production have been abolished. In the areas of sport, children's and education, commissioning and programme-making are now integrated. A New Media division is now developing the BBC's interactive television online activities.

Television genre commissioners in drama, entertainment and features now work with the television channel controllers to strengthen the BBC's output in these areas.

The disbanding of the Independent Commissioning Group has not diminished the value the BBC now places on the contribution of independents. However, in future they will take the same commissioning routes as in-house producers.

The restructuring also gives output guarantees for in-house departments, including Nations and English Regions, and longer term commissions to enable better planning and a greater focus on creativity.

website www.bbc.co.uk
Director of New Media & Technology Ashley Highfield
Director, Television Jana Bennett
Director, Sport Peter Salmon
Controller, BBC 1 Lorraine Heggessy
Controller, BBC 2 Jane Root
Controller, BBC Choice Stuart Murphy
Controller, BBC4 Roly Keating
Controller, Children's (CBBC) Dorothy Prior
Director, Radio Jenny Abramsky
Controller, Radio 1 Andy Parfitt
Controller, Radio 2 Jim Moir
Controller, Radio 3 Roger Wright
Controller, Radio 4 Helen Boaden
Controller, Radio 5 Live Bob Shennan

Drama, Entertainment and Children

Director Alan Yentob

Drama

BBC Television Centre, Centre House,
Wood Lane, London W12 7SB
tel 020-8743 8000

Drama Development in the North

BBC New Broadcasting House, Oxford Road,
Manchester M60 1SJ
tel 0161-200 2020

BBC Broadcasting Centre
Pebble Mill Road, Birmingham B5 7QQ
tel 0121-432 8888

Drama has departments in London, Birmingham and Manchester and produces a broad range of plays, serials, series and readings for TV, film, BBC Radio 3, BBC Radio 4 and BBC World Service.

The Manchester team also operates radio drama workshops, primarily for writers in the North of England. For further information contact Drama Development in the North.

The Birmingham radio team reads the unsolicited scripts of writers in the Midlands, East Anglia and South West but does not have a formal new writing department.

Controller, Continuing Drama Series Mal Young
Head of Films and Single Drama David Thompson
Head of Drama Serials Laura Mackie
Head of Development Television Series Serena Cullen
Head of Development Television Serials Sarah Brown
Controller, Drama Commissioning Jane Tranter
Head of Independents Drama Gareth Neame
Controller, Innovation and Factual Drama Susan Spindler
Senior Executive Producer, Drama Serials Hilary Salmon
Head of Development Films Tracey Scoffield
Head of Casting, Drama Series Jane Deitch
Head of Radio Drama and New Services tbc
Executive Producer Radio Drama and Editor, The Archers, Birmingham Vanessa Whitburn
Executive Producer Radio Drama, Manchester Sue Roberts
Head of Drama, BBC World Service Gordon House

Entertainment

BBC Television Centre, Wood Lane,
London W12 7RJ
tel 020-8743 8000
website www.bbc.co.uk/entertainment
Controller, Entertainment Commissioning Jane Lush
Editor, Radio Entertainment John Pidgeon
Head of Comedy Sophie Clark-Jervoise
Head of Comedy Entertainment Jon Plowman
Editor, Comedy Development Micheal Jacob
Editor, Comedy Allen Keaton
Head of Music Entertainment Trevor Dann

Children's

BBC Television Centre, Wood Lane,
London W12 7RJ
tel 020-8743 8000

There are opportunities for new writers in this
highly competitive area. Unsolicited material is read
by the department, preferably in the form of
synopses of ideas. The preferred genres are
contemporary comedy and drama.

Controller, Children's Programmes Dorothy Prior
Head of Drama Elaine Sperber
Head of Entertainment Anne Gildost
Development Executive Amanda Gabbites

BBC writersroom

3rd Floor, 1 Mortimer Street, London W1T 3JA
tel 020-7765 0756
website www.bbc.co.uk/writersroom

Unsolicited scripts for TV drama and narrative
comedy, films, single plays and radio drama and
comedy are co-ordinated by BBC writersroom
(formerly the New Writing Initiative). The
department produces *Writers' Guidelines*, a detailed
information pack which includes advice on how to
write radio and TV scripts, current trends, available
markets, contacts, free audience opportunities and
further reading (available by sending an A4 first
class sae to the address above). Since competition is
fierce, writers are strongly advised to read the
guidelines before submitting scripts one at a time.
All writers submitting scripts are considered for the
initiative's highly targeted writing schemes and
workshops. The website offers further advice,
interviews, and free downloadable scripts and
formatting templates.

New Writing Co-ordinator Jessica Dromgoole

Factual and Learning

Director John Willis

General Factual

BBC Television Centre, Wood Lane,
London W12 7RJ
tel 020-8743 8000

Controller, Commissioning Nicola Moody
Controller, General Factual Anne Morrison
Head of Production, General Factual Steve Wallis
Managing Editor, General Factual Donna Taberer

Entertainment and Features, Manchester

BBC New Broadcasting House, PO Box 27,
Oxford Road, Manchester M60 1SJ
tel 0161-200 2020

A network TV department responsible for a wide
range of factual, entertainment and music
programming. The department is also committed to
spotting new comedy talent in the North West.

Managing Editor Helen Bullash
Editor, Entertainment Phil Parsons
Executive Producers (entertainment and comedy)
   Caroline Roberts, Robin Ashbrook

General Factual, Bristol

BBC Broadcasting House, Whiteladies Road,
Bristol BS8 2LR
tel 0117-9732211

Produces a range of factual leisure, documentary
and animation programmes for radio and TV along
with supporting websites.

Head of Programmes, General Factual, Bristol Mark
   Hill
Creative Director Andy Batten-Foster
Joint Editors, Radio Fiona Couper, Elizabeth Burke
Executive Producer, Animation Helen Nabarro
Managing Editor Kalpna Woolf

Network Production, Birmingham

BBC Birmingham, The Mailbox, Royal Mail Street,
Birmingham B1 1XL
tel 0121-432 8888

A vast range of radio and TV programming which
encompasses Asian, consumer affairs, leisure,
lifestyle, motoring, music and rural affairs.

Head of Programmes (General Factual) Tessa Finch
Managing Editor (Factual and Learning) Jane Booth
Editor, Factual Radio and Countryfile Andrew
   Thorman
Editor, Radio Drama and The Archers Vanessa
   Whitburn
Editor, Specialist Programmes, Radio 2 Dave Barber

Specialist Factual

BBC White City, 201 Wood Lane,
London W12 7TS
tel 020-8752 5252

Controller Keith Scholey
Commissioner Emma Swain
Head of Production Kelvin Jones
Managing Editor Clare Brigstocke

Natural History Unit

BBC Broadcasting House, Whiteladies Road,
Bristol BS8 2LR
tel 0117-9732211

Makes specialist programmes with established
experts.

Head of Natural History Unit Neil Nightingale
Head of Development Alistair Fothergill
Commercial Director Ailish Heneberry
Editor Radio Julian Hector

Religion and Ethics

BBC New Broadcasting House, PO Box 27,
Oxford Road, Manchester M60 1SJ
tel 0161-200 2020

Produces a wide range of religious, moral and
ethical programmes for radio and TV which, while
recognising Christianity as the UK's dominant faith,
explores a wide range of faiths and issues.
Head of Religion and Ethics Alan Bookbinder

News

BBC Television Centre, Wood Lane,
London W12 7RJ
tel 020-8743 8000

BBC News is the biggest news organisation in the
world with over 2000 journalists, 50 bureaux
worldwide and 13 networks and services across TV,
radio and new media.
Director, News Richard Sambrook
Assistant Director and Head of Political Programmes
Mark Damazer
Head of Current Affairs Peter Horrocks
Head of Radio News Steve Mitchell
Head of New Media Richard Deverell
Head of TV News Roger Mosey
Head of Newsgathering Adrian Van Klaveren
Executive Editor Radio Daily Current Affairs Anne
Koch
Managing News Editor, News 24 Peter Knowles

Sport

BBC Television Centre, Wood Lane,
London W12 7RJ
tel 020-8743 8000

Multimedia coverage of a wide range of sports in
the UK and worldwide.
Director, Sport Peter Salmon
Director of Sports Rights and Finance Dominic Coles
Head of Programmes and Planning Pat Younge
Head of Football and Boxing Niall Sloane
Head of Radio Gordon Turnbull
Head of Major Events Dave Gordon
Head of General Sport Barbara Slater
Head of Sports News, Development and Interactive
Andrew Thompson

World Service

Bush House, PO Box 76, Strand, London WC2B 4PH
tel 020-7557 2941 *fax* 020-7557 1912
email worldservice.press@bbc.co.uk
website www.bbc.co.uk/worldservice

BBC World Service provides radio services in
English and 42 other languages, via short wave and
in an increasing number of cities around the world,
on MW and FM. The English service is also
available 24 hours a day in real audio on the
internet. Classic contemporary drama, novels, short
stories, soap operas and poetry are all a feature of

its English service, plus a wide range of arts,
documentaries, education, features, music, religious
affairs, science, sports and youth programmes. In
addition, BBC World Service provides on-the-spot
coverage of world news, giving a global perspective
of international events.
Director, BBC World Service Mark Byford
*Director, English Network and News and Programme
Commissioning* Phil Harding

Worldwide

BBC Woodlands, 80 Wood Lane, London W12 0TT
tel 020-8433 2000 *fax* 020-8749 0538
website www.bbcworldwide.com

BBC Worldwide Ltd is the commercial arm of the
BBC. It makes money from broadcast-related
businesses and returns cash to the BBC to invest in
new programming. Publishing forms a significant
part of its activities.
Chief Executive Rupert Gavin
Managing Director, UK Regions and Deputy CE
Peter Teague

Audio tapes and CDs

BBC Audiobooks, St James House, The Square,
Lower Bristol Road, Bath BA2 3SB
email radio.collection@bbc.co.uk

Around 130 audio tapes and CDs of BBC radio and
TV programmes are released every year, mainly
comedy, readings and dramatised serials. Over 800
titles are on CD and tape. Pitch ideas to:
Publishing Director Jan Paterson

Books

Ideas for books that would extend audience
enjoyment of a BBC radio or TV programme
should be pitched, according to subject matter, via a
short synopsis to:
Commissioning Editor, Factual Sally Potter
Commissioning Editor, Factual/Drama Emma
Shackleton
Commissioning Editors, Lifestyle Vivien Bowler,
Nicky Copeland
Commissioning Editor, Sport and Entertainment
Benn Dunn

Magazines

Freelance contributions are regularly used by BBC
Worldwide magazines, but the use of unsolicited
material is rare as the editorial links closely to BBC
programme content. Ideas for articles that clearly fit
the remit of a magazine should be pitched via a
short written summary to the Editor.
Eve Jane Bruton
Gardens Illustrated Clare Foster
Radio Times Gill Hudson
BBC Good Food Orlando Murrin
BBC Gardeners' World Adam Pasco

BBC Good Homes Julie Savill
BBC History Magazine Greg Neale
BBC Homes & Antiques Mary Carroll
BBC Top Gear Magazine Michael Harvey
BBC Music Magazine Helen Wallace
BBC Wildlife Magazine Rosamund Kidman Cox
(BBC Bristol address)

All ideas for BBC children's and teen magazines
(*Top of the Pops, It's Hot, Girl Talk, popgirl, BBC
Learning is Fun, Noddy, BBC Toybox, Teletubbies,
Bob the Builder* and *Tweenies*) should be sent to the
magazine concerned.

Nations and Regions
BBC Broadcasting House, Portland Place,
London W1A 1AA
tel 020-7580 4468

BBC Nations and Regions is responsible for around
80% of all the BBC's domestic output – about 7000
hours of TV and over 250,000 of radio. BBC
Northern Ireland, BBC Scotland and BBC Wales
produce a growing number of programmes for the
BBC's TV and radio networks, as well as providing
comprehensive services for viewers and listeners in
their own nations. The BBC's English Regions are
responsible for 11 TV regional news and current
affairs services across England; for 40 BBC local
radio stations and 40 local 'Where I Live' websites
with their emphasis on news and information for
their local communities.
Director, Nations and Regions Pat Loughrey

BBC Northern Ireland
BBC Broadcasting House, Ormeau Avenue,
Belfast BT2 8HQ
tel 028-9033 8000
website www.bbc.co.uk/ni

BBC Northern Ireland produces a broad spectrum of
radio and TV programmes, both for the BBC's
networks and for its home audience. Output includes
news and current affairs, documentaries, education,
entertainment, sport, music, Irish language and
religious programmes. It also has a thriving drama
department which reads unsolicited scripts across all
genre, i.e. single, serials, series, feature films and the
short film scheme *Northern Lights*, which is aimed at
new talent from within Northern Ireland.

In addition to making network radio programmes,
broadcasting on BBC Radio 1, 2, 3, 4, and 5 Live
and BBC World Service, BBC Northern Ireland also
makes programmes for its local radio listeners.
Controller, BBC Northern Ireland Anna Carragher
Head of Broadcasting Tim Cooke
Head of News and Current Affairs Andrew Colman
Head of Factual and Learning Bruce Batten
Entertainment and Events Mike Edgar
Head of Drama Robert Cooper
Editor, Radio Foyle Ana Leddy

Head of Marketing and Development Peter Johnston
Head of Resources Stephen Beckett

BBC Radio Ulster
BBC Broadcasting House, Ormeau Avenue,
Belfast BT2 8HQ
tel 028-9033 8000

BBC Radio Foyle
8 Northland Road, Londonderry BT48 7JO
tel 028-7126 2244

BBC Scotland
BBC Broadcasting House, Queen Margaret Drive,
Glasgow G12 8DG
tel 0141-339 8844
website www.bbc.co.uk/scotland

BBC Scotland is the BBC's most varied production
centre outside London, providing BBC TV and radio
networks and BBC World Service with pivotal
drama, comedy, entertainment, children's, leisure,
documentaries, religion, education, arts, music,
special events news, current affairs and political
coverage. Internet development is also a key element
of production activity. Its drama department, along
with Scottish Screen, is responsible for the highly
successful initiative, *Tartan Shorts*, which promotes
film-making in the nation and provides a platform
for emerging Scottish creative talent, including
actors, writers, directors and producers.

In addition to making network output, more
than 850 hours of TV programming per year is
transmitted on BBC1 Scotland and BBC2 Scotland,
including the Scottish soap *River City*, broadcast
twice weekly on BBC1 Scotland. BBC Radio
Scotland is the country's only national radio station,
and is on air 18 hours a day, 7 days a week. Local
programmes are also broadcast on Radio Scotland's
FM frequency in the Northern Isles, and there are
daily local bulletins for listeners in the Highlands,
Grampian, Borders, and the southwest. BBC Radio
Nan Gaidheal provides a Gaelic service on a
separate FM frequency for around 40 hours a week.
Controller, BBC Scotland John McCormick
Head of Programmes Ken MacQuarrie
Head of Network Programmes Colin Cameron
Head of News and Current Affairs Blair Jenkins
Head of Drama Barbara McKissack

BBC Radio Scotland
BBC Broadcasting House, Queen Margaret Drive,
Glasgow G12 8DG
tel 0141-338 8844

BBC Radio Nan Gaidheal
Rosebank, Church Street, Stornoway,
Isle of Lewis PA87 2LS
tel (0851) 705000

BBC Wales

BBC Broadcasting House, Llandaff, Cardiff CF5 2YQ
tel 029-2032 2000
website www.bbc.co.uk/wales

BBC Wales provides a wide range of services in Welsh and in English, on radio, TV and online. This includes more than 20 hours a week of programmes on BBC1 Wales and BBC2 Wales including the new BBC Wales digital services. Regular output includes the flagship news programme *Wales Today*, the current affairs strand *Week In Week Out*, and the rugby magazine *Scrum V*. A further 10 hours are shown on the Welsh-language channel S4C including the news programme *Newyddion*, the nightly drama serial *Pobol y Cwm* plus a range of programmes for schools. Its 2 radio stations, BBC Radio Wales, broadcasting in English, and BBC Radio Cymru, broadcasting in Welsh, each provide 20 hours a day of news, entertainment, music and sports output. Political coverage on all services has expanded as a result of the creation of the National Assembly for Wales. BBC Wales also makes popular drama, documentaries, education and music programmes for audiences throughout the UK, including the biennial *Cardiff Singer of the World* competition, accompanied by the BBC National Orchestra of Wales.

Controller, BBC Wales Menna Richards
Head of Programmes (English) Clare Hudson
Head of Programmes (Welsh) Keith Jones
Head of Marketing and Communications Huw Roberts
Head of News and Current Affairs Mark O'Callaghan
Editor, Radio Wales Julie Barton
Editor, Radio Cymru Aled Glynne Davis
Head of Drama Matthew Robinson
Head of Sport Nigel Walker
Head of Factual Adrian Davis
Head of Arts Paul Islwyn Thomas
Head of Music David Jackson
Music Director, BBC National Orchestra of Wales David Murray

BBC Radio Cymru (Welsh language)

BBC Broadcasting House, Llandaff, Cardiff CF5 2YQ
tel 029-2032 2000

BBC Radio Wales (English language)

BBC Broadcasting House, Llandaff, Cardiff CF5 2YQ
tel 029-2032 2000

BBC regional television and local radio

The BBC's English Regions are responsible for 11 TV regional news and current affairs services across England, and for 40 BBC local radio stations with their emphasis on news and information for their local communities.

BBC English regions (TV and radio)

BBC Birmingham, The Mailbox, Royal Mail Street, Birmingham B1 1XL
tel 0121-432 8888
Controller, English Regions Andy Griffee
Head of Programming Craig Henderson
Head of New Services Julie Allen

BBC East

St Catherine's Close, All Saints Green, Norwich NR1 3ND
tel (01603) 619331
Head of Regional and Local Programmes David Holdsworth

BBC Radio Cambridgeshire

PO Box 96, Hills Road, Cambridge CB2 1LD
tel (01223) 259696
email cambs@bbc.co.uk

BBC Essex

198 New London Road, Chelmsford CM2 9AB
tel (01245) 616000
email essex@bbc.co.uk

BBC Radio Norfolk

The Forum, Millennium Place, Norwich NR2 1TF
tel (01603) 617411
email norfolk@bbc.co.uk

BBC Radio Northampton

Broadcasting House, Abington Street, Northampton NN1 2BE
tel (01604) 239100
email northampton@bbc.co.uk

BBC Radio Suffolk

Broadcasting House, St Matthew's Street, Ipswich IP1 3EP
tel (01473) 250000
email suffolk@bbc.co.uk

BBC Three Counties Radio

PO Box 3CR, Luton, Beds. LU1 5XL
tel (01582) 637400
email 3cr@bbc.co.uk

BBC East Midlands

London Road, Nottingham NG2 4UU
tel 0115-955 0500
Head of Regional and Local Programmes Alison Ford

BBC Radio Derby

PO Box 269, Derby DE1 3HL
tel (01332) 361111
email radio.derby@bbc.co.uk

BBC Radio Leicester

Epic House, Charles Street, Leicester LE1 3SH
tel 0116-251 6688
email radioleicester@bbc.co.uk

BBC Radio Lincolnshire

Radio Buildings, PO Box 219, Newport, Lincoln LN1 3XY
tel (01522) 511411
email radio.lincolnshire@bbc.co.uk

BBC Radio Nottingham

London Road, Nottingham NG2 4UU
tel 0115-955 0500
email radio.nottingham@bbc.co.uk

BBC South East

The Great Hall, Mount Pleasant Road, Tunbridge Wells, Kent TN1 1QQ
tel (01892) 675550
Head of Regional and Local Programmes Laura Ellis

BBC London 94.9 FM

35c Marylebone High Street, London W1A 4LG
tel 020-7224 2424
email yourlondon@bbc.co.uk

BBC Radio Kent

The Great Hall, Mount Pleasant Road, Tunbridge Wells, Kent TN1 1QQ
tel (01892) 675550
email radio.kent@bbc.co.uk

BBC South East London

35c Marylebone High Street, London W1A 4LG
tel 020-7224 2424
email yourlondon@bbc.co.uk

BBC Southern Counties Radio
Broadcasting Centre, Guildford GU2 5AP
tel (01483) 306306
email southern.counties.radio@bbc.co.uk

BBC North
Broadcasting Centre, Woodhouse Lane,
Leeds LS2 9PX
tel 0113-244 1188
Head of Regional and Local Programmes Colin Philpott

BBC Radio Humberside
9 Chapel Street, Hull HU1 3NU
tel (01482) 323232
email radio.humberside@bbc.co.uk

BBC Radio Leeds
Broadcasting Centre, Woodhouse Lane,
Leeds LS2 9PN
tel 0113-244 2131
email radio.leeds@bbc.co.uk

BBC Radio Sheffield
54 Shoreham Street, Sheffield S1 4RS
tel 0114-273 1171
email radio.sheffield@bbc.co.uk

BBC North Yorkshire – Radio York
20 Bootham Row, York YO3 7BR
tel (01904) 641351
email radio.york@bbc.co.uk

BBC North East and Cumbria
Broadcasting Centre, Barrack Road,
Newcastle upon Tyne NE99 2NE
tel 0191-232 1313
Head of Regional and Local Programmes Olwyn
Hocking

BBC Radio Cleveland
PO Box 95FM, Newport Road,
Middlesbrough TS1 5DG
tel (01642) 225211
email radio.cleveland@bbc.co.uk

BBC Radio Cumbria
Annetwell Street, Carlisle CA3 8BB
tel (01228) 592444
email radio.cumbria@bbc.co.uk

BBC Radio Newcastle
Broadcasting Centre, Barrack Road,
Newcastle upon Tyne NE99 1RN
tel 0191-232 4141
email radio.newcastle@bbc.co.uk

BBC North West
New Broadcasting House, Oxford Road,
Manchester M60 1SJ
tel 0161-200 2020
Head of Regional and Local Programmes Martin
Brooks

BBC GMR
PO Box 951, Oxford Road,
Manchester M60 1SD
tel 0161-200 2000
email gmr@bbc.co.uk

BBC Radio Lancashire
26 Darwen Street, Blackburn, Lancs. BB2 EA
tel (01254) 262411
email radio.lancashire@bbc.co.uk

BBC Radio Merseyside
55 Paradise Street, Liverpool L1 3BP
tel 0151-708 5500
email radio.merseyside@bbc.co.uk

BBC South
Broadcasting House, Havelock Road,
Southampton SO14 7PW
tel 023-80226201
Head of Regional and Local Programmes Eve Turner

BBC Radio Berkshire
PO Box 1044, Reading, Berks. RG4 8FH
tel 0118-946 4200
email radio.berkshire@bbc.co.uk

BBC Radio Oxford
PO Box 95.2, Oxford OX2 7YL
tel (08459) 311444
email radio.oxford@bbc.co.uk

BBC Radio Solent
Broadcasting House, Havelock Road,
Southampton SO14 7PW
tel 023-8063 1311
email radio.solent@bbc.co.uk

BBC South West
Broadcasting House, Seymour Road,
Mannamead, Plymouth PL3 5BD
tel (01752) 229201
Head of Regional and Local Programmes Leo Devine

BBC Radio Cornwall
Phoenix Wharf, Truro, Cornwall TR1 1UA
tel (01872) 275421
email radio.cornwall@bbc.co.uk

BBC Radio Devon
PO Box 1034, Plymouth PL3 5BD
tel (01752) 260323
PO Box 1034, Exeter EX4 4DB
tel (01392) 215651
email radio.devon@bbc.co.uk

BBC Radio Guernsey
Bulwer Avenue, St Sampsons, Guernsey GY2 4LA
tel (01481) 728977
email radio.guernsey@bbc.co.uk

BBC Radio Jersey
18 Parade Road, St Helier, Jersey JE2 3PL
tel (01534) 870000
email radio.jersey@bbc.co.uk

BBC West
Broadcasting House, Whiteladies Road,
Bristol BS8 2LR
tel 0117-973 2211
Head of Regional and Local Programmes Andrew
  Wilson

BBC Radio Bristol
PO Box 194, Bristol BS99 7QT
tel 0117-974 1111
email radio.bristol@bbc.co.uk

BBC Radio Gloucestershire
London Road, Gloucester GL1 1SW
tel (01452) 308585
email radio.gloucestershire@bbc.co.uk

BBC Radio Somerset Sound
(part of Radio Bristol)
14-15 Paul Street, Taunton, Somerset TA1 3PF
(01823) 252437
email somerset@bbc.co.uk

BBC Wiltshire and BBC Radio Swindon
PO Box 1234, Swindon SN1 3RW
tel (01793) 513626
email wiltshire.sound@bbc.co.uk

BBC West Midlands
Pebble Mill Road, Birmingham B5 7QQ
tel 0121-432 8888
Head of Regional and Local Programmes Roy Roberts

BBC Radio Coventry WM (Coventry)
Holt Court, 1 Greyfriars Road, Coventry CV1 2WR
tel (02476) 860086
email coventry@bbc.co.uk warwickshire@bbc.co.uk

BBC Hereford & Worcester
Hylton Road, Worcester WR2 5WW
tel (01905) 748485
email bbchw@bbc.co.uk

BBC Radio Shropshire
2-4 Boscobel Drive, Shrewsbury SY1 3TT
tel (01743) 248484
email radio.shropshire@bbc.co.uk

BBC Radio Stoke
Cheapside, Hanley, Stoke on Trent ST1 1JJ
tel (01782) 208080
email radio.stoke@bbc.co.uk

BBC Radio WM (Birmingham)
The Mailbox, Royal Mail Street,
Birmingham B1 1XL
tel 0121-432 8484
email radio.wm@bbc.co.uk

BBC broadcasting rights and terms

Contributors are advised to check latest details of fees with the BBC.

Rights and terms – television

Specially written material

Fees for submitted material are paid on acceptance. For commissioned material, half the fee is paid on commissioning and half on acceptance as being suitable for television. All fees are subject to negotiation above the minima.

In November 2002 a new TV script agreement was introduced. It replaced the old BBC/Guild script agreement for dramatic scripts of 15 minutes and over. The terms were agreed with the PMA and the Writers' Guild. The most significant changes are:

● On First Day of Principal Photography an advance payment of either 15% or 115% of script fee will be made against:

(a) repeats/commercial exploitation: 100% of script fee plus/or

(b) 5-year licence of Public Service use (excluding BBC1 and BBC2): 15%

(a) only applies to scripts commissioned for BBC1 or BBC2 (but excludes long-running series; (b) applies to BBC1 and BBC2 commissions and also scripts for BBC3 and BBC4 and long-running series on BBC1 and BBC2. Rates for BBC4 may be up to 50% less than those quoted below for specially written material.

● Rates for one performance of a 60-minute original television play are a minimum of £6800 for a play written by a beginner and a 'going rate' of £8500 for an established writer, or *pro rata* for shorter or longer timings.

● Fees for a 50-minute episode in a series during the same period are a minimum of £5120 for a beginner and a 'going rate' of £6400 for an established writer.

● Fees for a 50-minute dramatisation are a minimum of £3680 for a beginner and a 'going rate' of £4600 for an established writer.

● Fees for a 50-minute adaptation of an existing stage play or other dramatic work are a minimum of £2240 for a beginner and a 'going rate' of £2800 for an established writer.

Specially written light entertainment sketch material

● The rates for sketch material range from £40 per minute for beginners with a 'going rate' of £70 for established writers.

● The fee for a quickie or news item is half the amount of the writer's per minute rate.

● Fees for submitted material are payable on acceptance and for commissioned material half on signature and half on acceptance.

Published material

● Prose works: £20.64 per minute.
● Poems: £23.97 per half minute.

Stage plays and source material for television
- Fees for stage plays and source novels are negotiable.

Rights and terms – radio
Specially written material
Fees are assessed on the basis of the type of material, its length, the author's status and experience in writing for radio. Fees for submitted material are paid on acceptance. For commissioned material, half the fee is paid on commissioning and half on acceptance as being suitable for broadcasting.
- Rates for specially written radio dramas in English (other than educational programmes) are £46.42 a minute for beginners and a 'going rate' of £70.66 a minute for established writers. This rate covers two broadcasts.

Specially written short stories
- Fees range from £143 for 15 minutes.

Published material
Domestic radio
- Dramatic works: £14.02 per minute.
- Prose works: £14.02 per minute.
- Prose works required for dramatisation: £10.93 per minute.
- Poems: £14.02 per half minute.

World Service Radio (English)
- Dramatic works: £7.02 per minute for broadcasts within a seven-day period.
- Prose works: £7.02 per minute for broadcasts within a seven-day period.
- Prose works required for dramatisation: £5.47 per minute for broadcasts within a seven-day period.
- Poems: £7.02 per half minute for broadcasts within a seven-day period.
- Foreign Language Services are approximately one-fifth of the rate for English Language Services.

Television and radio
Repeats in BBC programmes
- Further proportionate fees are payable for repeats.

Use abroad of recordings of BBC programmes
If the BBC sends abroad recordings of its programmes for use by overseas broadcasting organisations on their own networks or stations, further payments accrue to the author, usually in the form of additional percentages of the basic fee paid for the initial performance or a royalty based on the percentage of the distributors' receipts. This can apply to both sound and television programmes.

Value Added Tax
There is a self-billing system for VAT which covers radio, World Service and television for programmes made in London.

Talks for television

Contributors to talks will be offered the standard television talks contract which provides the BBC certain rights to broadcast the material in a complete, abridged and/or translated manner, and which provides for the payment of further fees for additional usage of the material whether by television, domestic radio or external broadcasting. The contract also covers the assignment of material and limited publication rights. Alternatively, a contract taking in all standard rights may be negotiated. Fees are arranged by the contract authorities in London and the Regions.

Talks for radio

Contributors to talks for domestic radio and World Service broadcasting may be offered either:
- the standard talks contract which takes rights and provides for residual payments, as does the television standard contract; or
- an STC (Short Talks Contract) which takes all rights except print publication rights where the airtime of the contribution does not exceed five minutes and which has set fees or disturbance money payable; or
- an NFC (No Fee Contract) where no payment is made which provides an acknowledgement that a contribution may be used by the BBC.

Independent national television

BSkyB
Grant Way, Isleworth, Middlesex TW7 5QD
tel 020-7705 3000 *fax* 020-7705 3030/3113
website www.sky.com

Channel 5 Broadcasting Ltd
22 Long Acre, London WC2E 9LY
tel 020-7550 5555 *fax* 020-7550 5554
website www.channel5.co.uk

The fifth and last national 'free-to-air' terrestrial 24-hour TV channel. Commissions a wide range of programmes to suit all tastes.

Channel 4 Television Corporation
124 Horseferry Road, London SW1P 2TX
tel 020-7396 4444 *fax* 020-7306 8347
website www.channel4.com

Commissions and purchases programmes (it does not make them) for broadcast during the whole week throughout the UK (except Wales). Also broadcasts subscription film channel FilmFour and digital entertainment channel E4.

GMTV
London Television Centre, Upper Ground, London SE1 9TT
tel 020-7827 7000 *fax* 020-7827 7001
website www.gm.tv.

GMTV1 is ITV's national breakfast TV service, 6.00–9.25am, 7 days a week. GMTV2 is GMTV's cable and digital channel shown on ITV2 daily 6.00–9.25am.

Independent Television Commission (ITC)
33 Foley Street, London W1W 7TL
tel 020-7255 3000 *fax* 020-7306 7800
email publicaffairs@itc.org.uk
website www.itc.co.uk

Licenses and regulates all commercially funded TV services in the UK, including cable and satellite services as well as terrestrial services.

ITN
200 Gray's Inn Road, London WC1X 8XZ
tel 020-7833 3000
website www.itn.co.uk

Provides the national news programmes for ITV, Channel 4 and Channel 5.

ITV Network Ltd
200 Gray's Inn Road, London WC1X 8HF
tel 020-7843 8000 *fax* 020-7843 8158
website www.itv.co.uk

NTL
NTL House, Bartley Wood Business Park, Bartley Way, Hook, Hants RG27 9UP
tel (01256) 752000 *fax* (01256) 752100
website www.ntl.co.uk

S4C
Parc Ty Glas, Llanishen, Cardiff CF14 5DU
tel 029-20747444 *fax* 029-20754444
email s4c@s4c.co.uk
website www.s4c.co.uk

The Welsh Fourth Channel. S4C's analogue service broadcasts 32 hours per week in Welsh: 22 hours are commissioned from independent producers and 10 hours are produced by the BBC. Most of Channel 4's output is rescheduled to complete this service. S4C's digital service broadcasts 12 hours per day in Welsh.

Teletext Ltd
Building 10, Chiswick Park, 566 Chiswick High Road, London W4 5TS
tel (0870) 731 3000 *fax* (0870) 731 3001
email editor@teletext.co.uk
website www.teletext.co.uk

Independent regional television

It is advisable to check before submitting any ideas/material – in all cases, scripts are preferred to synopses. Programmes should be planned with natural breaks for the insertion of advertisements. These companies also provide some programmes for Channel 4.

Anglia Television Ltd

Anglia House, Norwich NR1 3JG
tel (01603) 615151 *fax* (01603) 631032
email angliatv@angliatv.com
website www.angliatv.com

Provides programmes for the East of England, daytime discussion programmes, documentaries and factual programmes for UK and international broadcasters.

Border Television Ltd

The Television Centre, Carlisle CA1 3NT
tel (01228) 25101
website www.border-tv.com

Provides programmes for, Cumbria, the Borders and the Isle of Man, during the whole week. Ideas for programmes, but not drama programmes, are considered from outside sources. Suggestions should be sent to Neil Robinson, Controller of Programmes.

Carlton Broadcasting

101 St Martin's Lane, London WC2N 4AZ
tel 020-7240 4000 *fax* 020-7240 4171

Provides ITV programmes for London and the South East from Monday to Friday.

Carlton Broadcasting, Central Region

Gas Street, Birmingham B1 2JT
tel 0121-643 9898 *fax* 0121-643 4897
website www.carlton.com
Carlton Studios, Lenton Lane,
Nottingham NG7 2NA
tel 0115-986 3322 *fax* 0115-964 5552
Unit 9, Windrush Court, Abingdon Business Park,
Abingdon, Oxon OX1 1SA
tel (01235) 554123 *fax* (01235) 524024

Provides ITV programmes for the East, West and South Midlands 7 days a week.

Carlton Broadcasting, West Country Region

Langage Science Park, Plymouth PL7 5BQ
tel (01752) 333333 *fax* (01752) 333444
email info@westcountry.co.uk

ITV franchise holder that provides programmes for South West England throughout the week. In-house production mainly news, regional current affairs and topical features; other regional features commissioned from independent producers.

Channel Television

The Television Centre, St Helier, Jersey JE1 3ZD
tel (01534) 816816 *fax* (01534) 816817
Television House, St Sampson's, Guernsey GY2 4LA
tel (01481) 241888 *fax* (01481) 241889
email broadcast@channeltv.co.uk
website www.channeltv.co.uk

Channel Television, the smallest ITV broadcaster, produces 5.5 hours of local programmes each week relating to Channel Islands news, events and current affairs.

Grampian Television plc

Craigshaw Business Park, West Tullos,
Aberdeen AB12 3QH
tel (01224) 848848 *fax* (01224) 848800
email gtv@grampiantv.co.uk
Harbour Chambers, Dock Street, Dundee DD1 3HW
tel (01382) 591000 *fax* (01382) 591010
23-25 Huntly Street, Inverness IV3 5PR
tel (01463) 242624

Provides programmes for North Scotland during the whole week.

Granada Television Ltd

Granada Television Centre, Manchester M60 9EA
tel 0161-832 7211 and
Upper Ground, London SE1 9LT
tel 020-7620 1620

The ITV franchise holder for the North West of England. Produces programmes across a broad range for both its region and the ITV Network. Writers are advised to make their approach through agents who would have some knowledge of Granada's current requirements.

HTV Ltd

HTV Wales, The Television Centre,
Culverhouse Cross, Cardiff CF5 6XJ
tel 029-2059 0590 and
email public.relations@htv-wales.co.uk
website www.htvwales.com
HTV West, The Television Centre, Bristol BS4 3HG
tel 01179-722 722
email presspr@htv-west.co.uk
website www.htvwest.com

Provides programmes for Wales and West of England during the whole week. Produces programmes for home and international sales.

LWT

The London Television Centre, London SE1 9LT
tel 020-7620 1620
website www.granadamedia.com

Broadcasts to Greater London and much of the
Home Counties area from Friday 5.15pm to
Monday 6.00am (excluding 6.00–9.25am on
Sat/Sun).

Meridian Broadcasting

Television Centre, Southampton, Hants SO14 0PZ
tel 023-8022 2555 *fax* 023-8033 5050
website www.meridiantv.com

The ITV franchise holder for the South and South
East. Broadcasts local news to 3 separate sub-
regions, provides a wide range of quality award-
winning regional programmes, and makes a
significant contribution to the ITV networks and
other channels.

SMG TV Productions

200 Renfield Street, Glasgow G2 3PR
tel 0141-300 3000 *fax* 0141-300 3580
website www.smg.plc.uk

Wholly owned subsidiary of SMG plc, making
drama and other programmes for the ITV network.
SMG TV Productions also includes Ginger
Television.
• Material (STV): ideas and formats for long-form
series with or without a Scottish flavour. Approach
Controller of Drama, Eric Coulter.

• Material (Ginger): produces compelling
programmes for groups of all ages. Programming
includes *TFI Friday* and *The Priory*. Contact:
Elizabeth Partuka.

Tyne Tees Television Ltd

The Television Centre, City Road,
Newcastle upon Tyne NE1 2AL
tel 0191-261 0181 *fax* 0191-261 2302
email tyne.tees@granadamedia.com

Serving the North of England 7 days a week,
24 hours a day.

UTV

Ormeau Road, Belfast, Northern Ireland BT7 1EB
tel 028-9032 8122 *fax* 028-9024 6695
email info@u.tv
website www.u.tv

Provides programmes for Northern Ireland.

Yorkshire Television Ltd

The Television Centre, Leeds LS3 1JS
tel 0113-243 8283 *fax* 0113-244 5107

Yorkshire Television is a Network Company which
produces many programmes for the ITV Network
and the Yorkshire area 7 days a week. Material
preferred submitted through agents. Wholly owned
subsidiary of Granada plc.

Television and film producers

Jean McConnell advises on submitting a screenplay for consideration.

The recommended approach for placing material is through a recognised literary agent (see page 692). Most film companies have a story department to which material can be sent for consideration by its editors. If you choose to submit material direct, first check with the company to make sure it is worth your while.

Many of the feature films these days are based on already best-selling books. However, there are some companies, particularly those with a television outlet, which will sometimes accept unsolicited material if it seems to be exceptionally original.

When a writer submits material direct to a company, some of the larger ones – usually those based in the United States – may request that a Release Form be signed before they are prepared to read it. This document is ostensibly designed to absolve the company from any charge of plagiarism if they should be working on a similar idea; and also to limit their liability in the event of any legal action. Writers must make up their own minds whether they wish to sign this but, in principle, it is not recommended.

It should be noted that there are a number of independent companies making films specifically for television presentation. These are included in the list below of companies currently in active production.

Jean McConnell is a founder member of the Writers' Guild of Great Britain. She has written screenplays, radio and stage plays, and books. She is a member of the Crime Writers' Association and the Society of Women Writers and Journalists.

Aardman Animations
Gas Ferry Road, Bristol BS1 6UN
tel 0117-984 8485 *fax* 0117-984 8486
website www.aardman.com
Head of Script Development Mike Cooper, *Development Executive (Shorts & Series)* Helen Brunsdon

Specialists in model animation. No unsolicited treatments. Founded 1972.

Absolutely Productions
Craven House 226, 121 Kingsway, London WC2B 6PA
tel 020-7930 3113 *fax* 020-7930 4114
email info@absolutely-uk.com
website www.absolutely-uk.com
Contact Miles Bullough

Drama and comedy screenplays for cinema and TV, and TV entertainment programmes. Unsolicited scripts are not accepted. Founded 1989.

British Lion
Pinewood Studios, Iver, Bucks. SL0 0NH
tel (01753) 651700 *fax* (01753) 656844
website www.britishlionfilms.com
Contact Peter Snell

Screenplays and treatments for cinema. No unsolicited material. Founded 1927.

Brook Lapping Productions Ltd
6 Anglers Lane, London NW5 3DG
tel 020-7428 3100 *fax* 020-7284 0626
website www.brooklapping.com
Directors Anne Lapping, Brian Lapping, Norma Percy, Alex Connock, Sam Cash

TV documentaries and current affairs.

Carlton Television Productions
35-38 Portman Square, London W1H 0NU
tel 020-7486 6688 *fax* 020-7486 1132
Director of Programmes Steve Hewlett

Comprises Carlton Television Productions, Planet 24 and Action Time and makes programmes for all UK major broadcasters (ITV, BBC, Channel 4, Channel 5 and Sky) and regional programmes for Carlton Central, Carlton London and Carlton Westcountry. Carlton Television Productions' Drama department encourages the submission of scripts and outlines from professional writers through an agent.

Catalyst Film and Television International Ltd
Brook Green Studios, 186 Shepherds Bush Road,
London W6 7NL
tel 020-7603 7030 *fax* 020-7603 9519
Contact Head of Drama Development

Screenplays/novels for adaptation for film and TV.
Will only consider material submitted through an
agent or publisher. Founded 1991.

Celador Productions Ltd
39 Long Acre, London WC2E 9LG
tel 020-7240 8101 *fax* 020-7845 9541

Unsolicited scripts are not accepted.

Chatsworth Television Ltd
97-99 Dean Street, London W1D 3TE
tel 020-7734 4302 *fax* 020-7437 3301
email television@chatsworth-tv.co.uk
website www.chatsworth-tv.co.uk
Managing Director Malcolm Heyworth

Entertainment, factual and drama. Sister companies
in TV distribution and licensing. Founded 1980.

Children's Film and Television Foundation Ltd
Elstree Film and Television Studios,
Borehamwood, Herts. WD6 1JG
tel 020-8953 0844 *fax* 020-8207 0860
email annahome@cftf.onyxnet.co.uk

Involved in the development and co-production of
films for children and the family, both for the
theatric market and for TV.

Collingwood O'Hare Entertainment and Convergence Productions
10-14 Crown Street, London W3 8SB
tel 020-8993 3666 *fax* 020-8993 9595
email info@crownstreet.co.uk
Contact Helen Stroud, Head of Development

Animation series for children (COE), documentary
series, and drama films and series (Convergence).
Limited development capacity – generates own
ideas/projects. Prefers material to be submitted
through an agent. Founded 1988.

Company Pictures
Suffolk House, 1-8 Whitfield Place, London W1T 5JU
tel 020-7380 3900 *fax* 020-7380 1166
email enquiries@companypictures.co.uk
Contact George Faber, Charles Pattinson, Max
Massenbach

Screenplays for TV drama and feature films. All
material should be submitted through an agent.
Founded 1997.

Cosgrove Hall Films Ltd
8 Albany Road, Chorlton-Cum-Hardy,
Manchester M21 0AW

tel 0161-882 2500 *fax* 0161-882 2555
email animation@chf.co.uk
Contact Nicola Davies, Assistant Script Editor

Screenplays for cinema and TV for animation
(drawn, model or CGI) or a 'live action'/animation
mix. Series material especially welcome, preschool
to adult. Founded 1976.

Ecosse Films Ltd
Brigade House, 8 Parsons Green,
London SW6 4TN
tel 020-7371 0290 *fax* 020-7736 3436
website www.ecossefilms.com

High-quality films and dramas for cinema and TV.
Material is considered only if it is submitted
through an agent. Founded 1988.

Endemol
Shepherd's Building Central, Charecrost Way,
London W14 0EE
tel (0870) 333 1700 *fax* (0870) 333 1800

Entertainment, documentary, drama, children's arts,
news, current affairs, religion.

Fairwater Films Ltd
68 Vista Rise, Llandaff, Cardiff CF5 2SD
tel/fax 029-2057 8488
email tbarnes@netcomuk.co.uk
Managing Director Tony Barnes

Animation for cinema and TV; live action
entertainment. All material should be submitted
through an agent. Founded 1982.

Feelgood Fiction Ltd
49 Goldhawk Road, London W12 8QP
tel 020-8746 2535 *fax* 020-8740 6177
email feelgood@feelgoodfiction.co.uk
Managing Director Philip Clarke, *Drama Producer*
Laurence Bowen

Film and TV drama.

The First Film Company Ltd
38 Great Windmill Street, London W1D 7LU
tel 020-7439 1640 *fax* 020-7437 2062
Producers Roger Randall-Cutler, Robert Cheek

Screenplays for cinema. All material should be
submitted through an agent. Founded 1984.

Focus Films Ltd
The Rotunda Studios,
rear of 116-118 Finchley Road,
London NW3 5HT
tel 020-7435 9004 *fax* 020-7431 3562
email focus@pupix.demon.co.uk
Contact Lucinda Van Rie

Screenplays for cinema. Will only consider material
submitted through an agent. Founded 1982.

Front Page Films
507 Riverbank House, 1 Putney Bridge Approach,
London SW6 3JD
Contact Script Editor
Screenplays for cinema. Founded 1985.

Gaia Communictions
Sanctuary House, 35 Harding Avenue, Eastbourne,
East Sussex BN22 8PL
tel (01323) 727183 *fax* (01323) 734809
email production@gaiacommunications.co.uk
website www.gaiacommunications.co.uk
Directors Robert Armstrong, Loni von Grüner
Specialises in Southeast regional documentary
programmes, particularly historical and tourist.
Founded 1987.

Greenwich Village Productions
14 Greenwich Church Street, London SE10 9BJ
tel 020-8853 5100 *fax* 020-8293 3001
email info@greenwichvillage.tv
website www.greenwichvillage.tv
Creative Director John Taylor
Drama, short films, arts documentaries and
features. Unsolicited scripts only via agents.

Hartswood Films
Twickenham Studios, The Barons, St Margaret's,
Twickenham, Middlesex TW1 2AW
tel 020-8607 8736 *fax* 020-8607 8744
Producers Beryl Vertue, Sue Vertue, Elaine Cameron
Screenplays for cinema and TV; comedy and drama.
No unsolicited material. Founded 1981.

Hat Trick Productions Ltd
10 Livonia Street, London W1F 8AF
tel 020-7434 2451 *fax* 020-7287 9791
website www.hattrick.com
Contact Denise O'Donoghue
Situation and drama comedy series and light
entertainment shows. Founded 1986.

Ignition Films Ltd
1 Wickham Court, Bristol BS16 1DQ
tel 0117-958 3087 *fax* 0117-965 7674
email ignition@blueyonder.co.uk
website www.ignition.pwp.blueyonder.co.uk
Contact Alison Sterling
Screenplays for cinema and TV. Material only
accepted through agents. Founded 1999.

Illuminations
19-20 Rheidol Mews, Rheidol Terrace,
London N1 8NU
tel 020-7288 8400 *fax* 020-7359 1151
email linda@illumin.co.uk
website www.illumin.co.uk
Contact Linda Zuck

Cultural documentaries, arts and entertainment for
broadcast TV. Founded 1982.

The Jim Henson Company
30 Oval Road, London NW1 7DE
tel 020-7428 4000 *fax* 020-7428 4001
website www.henson.com
President, Jim Henson Television Europe Angus
Fletcher, *Director of Development, Jim Henson
Television* Sophie Finston, *International
Development Co-ordinator* Clare Lewis
Screenplays for cinema and TV; fantasy, family and
children's programmes – usually involving puppetry
or animatronics. All material should be submitted
through an agent. Founded 1979.

Little Bird Company Ltd
9 Grafton Mews, London W1P 5LG
tel 020-7380 3980 *fax* 020-7380 3981
email firstname@littlebird.co.uk
Contact N. Mirza
Screenplays for cinema and TV. No unsolicited
material. Founded 1982.

Little Dancer Ltd
Avonway, 3 Naseby Road, London SE19 3JJ
tel 020-8653 9343
email Littdan99@cs.com
Producer Robert Smith
Screenplays for cinema and TV; drama. Founded 1992.

LWT and United Productions
London TV Centre, Upper Ground, London SE1 9LT
tel 020-7620 1620
Controller of Drama Michele Buck
Producers of TV and film. Founded 1996.

Malone Gill Productions Ltd
27 Campden Hill Road, London W8 7DX
tel 020-7937 0557 *fax* 020-7376 1727
email malonegill@aol.com
Contact Georgina Denison
TV programmes. Founded 1978.

Mark Forstater Productions Ltd
27 Lonsdale Road, London NW6 6RA
tel 020-7624 1123 *fax* 020-7624 1124
Contact Rosie Homan
Film and TV production. No unsolicited scripts.

Maya Vision International Ltd
43 New Oxford Street, London WC1A 1BH
tel 020-7836 1113 *fax* 020-7836 5169
email info@mayavisionint.com
website www.mayavisionint.com
Producer/Director Rebecca Dobbs
Features, TV dramas and documentaries. No
unsolicited scripts. Founded 1982/3.

Mike Hopwood Productions Ltd

Winton House, Stoke Road, Stoke-on-Trent ST4 2RW
tel (01782) 848800 *fax* (01782) 749447
Contact Development Executive

Screenplays for cinema; drama and factual TV programmes. No unsolicited material. Founded 1991.

Monogram Productions Ltd

45-49 Mortimer Street, London W1W 8HX
tel 020-7470 0035
Managing Director Eileen Quinn

Screenplays for cinema and TV; drama series and serials only. All material should be submitted through an agent. Founded 1997; merged with Scottish Independent Wark Clements 2001.

MW Entertainments

48 Dean Street, London W1D 5BF
tel 020-7734 7707 *fax* 020-7734 7727
email mw@michaelwhite.co.uk

Screenplays for cinema. Treatments and synopses only. Founded 1963.

Noel Gay Television

Shepperton Studios, Studios Road, Shepperton, Middlesex TW17 0QD
tel (01932) 592569 *fax* (01932) 592172
Contact Lesley McKirdy

Treatments for TV; entertainment, comedy and drama. Founded 1987.

Pearson

1 Stephen Street, London W1F 1PJ
tel 020-7691 6000 *fax* 020-7691 6100

Light entertainment, drama and children's TV programmes.

Penumbra Productions Ltd

80 Brondesbury Road, London NW6 6RX
tel 020-7328 4550 *fax* 020-7328 3844
email nazpenumbra@aol.com
Contact H.O. Nazareth

Contemporary social-issue drama and docs for feature films and TV; non-broadcast videos to commissions. Send synopsis only, not scripts, preferably by email. Founded 1981.

Picture Palace Films Ltd

13 Egbert Street, London NW1 8LJ
tel 020-7586 8763 *fax* 020-7586 9048
email info@picturepalace.com
website www.picturepalace.com
Contact Malcolm Craddock

Screenplays for cinema and TV; low budget films; TV drama series. Material only considered if submitted through an agent. Founded 1971.

Planet 24 Productions Ltd

35-38 Portman Square, London W1H 0NU
tel 020-7486 6268 *fax* 020-7612 0679
website www.planet24.com
Managing Director Ed Forsdick

Light entertainment, factual entertainment, music, features and computer animation. Wholly owned subsidiary of Carlton Communications Plc.

Portobello Pictures Ltd

PO Box 31579, London W11 3YA
tel 020-7379 5566 *fax* 020-7379 5599
Contact Eric Abraham

Screenplays for cinema. Founded 1987.

Praxis Films Ltd

PO Box 290, Market Rasen, Lincs. LN3 6BB
tel/fax (01472) 399976
email info@praxisfilms.com
website www.praxisfilms.com
Contact Lori Wheeler, Head of Development

Documentaries, news, current affairs, all factual genres for TV. No drama/movies. Proposals via website preferred. Founded 1985.

RDF Television

The Gloucester Building, Kensington Village, Avonmore Road, London W14 8RF
tel 020-7013 4000 *fax* 020-7013 4001

Light entertainment, documentary, drama, arts, news, current affairs, religion.

September Films Ltd

Glen House, 22 Glenthorne Road, London W6 0NG
tel 020-8563 9393 *fax* 020-8741 7214
email september@septemberfilms.com
website www.septemberfilms.com
Head of Production Elaine Day, *Head of Drama and Film Development* Nadine Mellor

Factual entertainment and documentary specialists expanding into TV drama and film. Founded 1993.

SH Production

Green Dene Cottage, Honeysuckle Bottom, East Horsley, Surrey KT24 5TD
tel/fax (01483) 281792
Contact Robert Symes

Broadcast and non-broadcast commercial material, English and German voiceovers for films, video production. Founded 1988.

Specific Films

25 Rathbone Street, London W1T 1NQ
tel 020-7580 7476 *fax* 020-7494 2676
email info@specificfilms.com
Contact Michael Hamlyn

Feature-length films.

Spice Factory UK Ltd
81 The Promenade, Peacehaven,
East Sussex BN10 8LS
tel (01273) 585275 *fax* (01273) 585304
email script@spicefactory.co.uk
Contact Lucy Shuttleworth, Head of Development

Feature film production company. No unsolicited submissions. Founded 1995.

Talisman Films Ltd
5 Addison Place, London W11 4RJ
tel 020-7603 7474 *fax* 020-7602 7422
email email@talismanfilms.com
Contact Richard Jackson

Screenplays for cinema and TV. Material only considered if submitted through an agent. Single page treatments accepted. Founded 1991.

TalkBack Productions
20-21 Newman Street, London W1T 1PG
tel 020-7861 8000 *fax* 020-7861 8001

TV situation comedies and comedy dramas, features, straight drama. Send unsolicited material to PA to Managing Director; material through an agent to Peter Fincham. Founded 1981.

Tiger Aspect Productions
Drama and *Tiger Aspect Pictures* 5 Soho Square, London W1V 5DE
tel 020-7434 0672 *fax* 020-7544 1665
Comedy 7 Soho Street, London W1D 3DQ
tel 020-7434 0700 *fax* 020-7434 1798
email general@tigeraspect.co.uk
website www.tigeraspect.co.uk

TV drama, comedy and sitcoms. All material should be submitted through an agent. Founded 1993.

Twentieth Century Fox Productions Ltd
Twentieth Century House, 31-32 Soho Square, London W1D 3AP
tel 020-7437 7766 *fax* 020-7434 2170

Will not consider unsolicited material.

Twenty Twenty Television
20 Kentish Town Road, London NW1 9NX
tel 020-7284 2020 *fax* 020-7284 1810
email mail@twentytwenty.tv
Executive Producer Claudia Milne

Current affairs, documentaries, science and educational programmes, drama. Founded 1982.

Twofour Productions Ltd
Quay West Studios, Old Newnham,
Plymouth PL7 5BH
tel (01752) 333900 *fax* (01752) 344224
email enq@twofour.co.uk
website www.twofour.co.uk
Contact Melanie Leach, Development Dept

Factual, factual entertainment, leisure and lifestyle, and children's TV programmes. Founded 1987.

The Walt Disney Company Ltd
3 Queen Caroline Street, London W6 9PE
tel 020-8222 1000 *fax* 020-8222 2795

Screenplays not accepted by London office. Must be submitted by an agent to The Walt Disney Studios in Burbank, California.

Warner Bros. Productions Ltd
Warner House, 98 Theobald's Road,
London WC1X 8WB
tel 020-7984 5000

Screenplays for cinema. Will only consider material submitted through an agent.

Warner Sisters Film & TV Ltd
The Cottage, Pall Mall Deposit, 124 Barlby Road, London W10 6BL
tel 020-8960 3550 *fax* 020-8960 3880

Screenplays for cinema and TV; TV programmes. All material should be submitted through an agent. Founded 1984.

Working Title Films
Films 76 Oxford Street, London W1D 1BS
tel 020-7307 3000 *fax* 020-7307 3003
website www.workingtitlefilms.com
Chairmen Tim Bevan and Eric Fellner,
Head of Development Debra Hayward (films)
TV 77 Shaftesbury Avenue, London W1V 8HQ
tel 020-7494 4001 *fax* 020-7255 8600
Head of Television Simon Wright
WT2 76 Oxford Street, London W1D 1BS
Head of Development Natascha Wharton

Screenplays for films; TV drama and comedy; low budget films (WT2).

World Productions Ltd
Eagle House, 50 Marshall Street,
London W1F 9BQ
tel 020-7734 3536 *fax* 020-7758 7000
email firstname@world-productions.com
website www.world-productions.com
Contact Office Manager

Screenplays for TV; TV drama series and serials; feature films.

Zenith Entertainment Ltd
43-45 Dorset Street, London W1U 7NA
tel 020-7224 2440 *fax* 020-7224 3194
email general@zenith-entertainment.co.uk

Screenplays for cinema; TV drama. No unsolicited scripts.

Independent national radio

Atlantic 252
1 Stephen Street, London W1T 1AT
tel 020-7691 5252 *fax* 020-7691 5232
email programming@atlantic252.com
website www.atlantic252.com

Broadcast from Southern Ireland but with two-thirds of its audience in the UK. Founded 1989.

Commercial Radio Companies Association (CRCA)
77 Shaftesbury Avenue, London W1D 5DU
tel 020-7306 2603 *fax* 020-7470 0062
email info@crca.co.uk
website www.crca.co.uk

The trade body for UK commercial radio representing commercial radio to Government, the Radio Authority (see below), copyright societies and other organisations concerned with radio. It is a source of advice to members and acts as a clearing house for radio information. CRCA runs the Radio Advertising Clearance Centre. It jointly owns Radio Joint Audience Research Ltd (RAJAR) with the BBC and JICRIT Ltd (an electronic means of buying, selling and accounting for radio advertisements) with the IPA. CRCA is a founder member of the Association of European Radios (AER), which lobbies European institutions on behalf of commercial radio.

Classic FM
7 Swallow Place, London W1B 2AG
tel 020-7343 9000 *fax* 020-7344 2700
email enquiries@classicfm.co.uk
website www.classicfm.com

Classical music, national and international news.

Digital One Ltd
7 Swallow Place, London W1R 7AA
tel 020-7518 2620 *fax* 020-7518 2605
email info@digitalone.co.uk
website www.ukdigitalradio.com

Commercial digital radio multiplex operator. Founded 1999.

IRN (Independent Radio News)
6th Floor, 200 Gray's Inn Road, London WC1X 8XZ
tel 020-7430 4090 *fax* 020-7430 4092
email news@irn.co.uk
website www.irn.co.uk

National news provider to all UK commercial radio stations, including live news bulletins, sport and financial news, and coverage of the House of Commons.

Oneword
Landseer House, 19 Charing Cross Road, London WC2H 0ES
tel 020-7976 3030 *fax* 020-7930 9460
email info@oneword.co.uk
website www.oneword.co.uk
Programme Manager Christina Captieux

The first commercial national radio station to be exclusively dedicated to the transmission of books, plays, comedy and discussion. Broadcasts 7 days a week on Sky (channel 877), Freeview (channel 85), NTL (channel 893), DAB digital radio and streams live on the internet. Founded 2000.

The Radio Authority
Holbrook House, 14 Great Queen Street, London WC2B 5DG
tel 020-7430 2724 *fax* 020-7405 7062
email info@radioauthority.org.uk
website www.radioauthority.org.uk

Licenses and regulates independent radio. Plans frequencies, awards licences, regulates programming and advertising, and plays an active role in the discussion and formulation of policies which affect the Independent Radio industry and its listeners.

From December 2003 Ofcom (the Office of Communications) will be the new regulator responsible for broadcasting, telecommunications and spectrum in the UK. The Communications Bill, which is likely to become an Act in the summer of 2003, will transfer the functions of the 5 existing regulatory bodies currently responsible for these sectors – the Radio Authority, the Independent Television Commission, the Broadcasting Standards Commission, the Office of Telecommunications (Oftel), the Radiocommunications Agency – to Ofcom. See page 587.

TalkSPORT
18 Hatfields, London SE1 8DJ
tel 020-7959 7800 *fax* 020-7959 7874
website www.talksport.net

Sports commentary, comments and coverage.

Virgin 1215
1 Golden Square, London W1F 9DJ
tel 020-7434 1215 *fax* 020-7434 1197
email reception@virginradio.co.uk
website www.virginradio.co.uk

Rock and contemporary music.

Independent local radio

Refer to the Office of Communications for more details.

*Stations offering some/occasional opportunities for creative input from local writers. Check with the station before submitting material.

ENGLAND

Alton/Haslemere
Delta FM 102 *and* 97.1, Prospect Place, Mill Lane, Alton GU34 2SY
tel (01420) 544444 *fax* (01420) 544044
email studio@deltaradio.co.uk
website www.deltaradio.co.uk

Aylesbury
Mix 96, Friars Square Studios, 11 Bourbon Street, Aylesbury, Bucks. HP20 2PZ
tel (01296) 399396 *fax* (01296) 398988
email mix@mix96.co.uk
website www.mix96.co.uk

Barnstaple
Lantern FM, Unit 2B, Lauder Lane, Barnstaple, Devon EX31 3TA
tel (01271) 340340 *fax* (01271) 340345
email lanternfm@musicradio.com

Basingstoke
107.6 Kestrel FM, 2nd Floor, Paddington House, The Walks Shopping Centre, Basingstoke RG21 7LJ
tel (01256) 694000 *fax* (01256) 694111
website www.kestrelfm.com

Bassetlaw
Trax 107.9 FM, PO Box 444, Worksop, Notts. S80 1GP
tel (01909) 500611 *fax* (01909) 500445
website www.trax.fm.co.uk

Bath
Bath FM, Station House, Ashley Avenue, Lower Weston, Bath BA1 3DS
tel (01225) 471571 *fax* (01225) 471681
website www.bath.fm

Bedford
96.9 Chiltern FM, 55 Goldington Road, Bedford MK40 3LT
tel (01234) 272400 *fax* (01234) 325137

Birmingham
96.4 FM BRMB *and* Capital Gold (1152 AM), 9 Brindleyplace, 4 Oozells Square, Birmingham B1 2DJ
tel 0121-245 5000 *fax* 0121-245 5245
email info@brmb.co.uk
website www.brmb.co.uk

Birmingham
Galaxy 102.2, 1 The Square, 111 Broad Street, Birmingham B15 1AS
tel 0121-695 0000 *fax* 0121-695 0055
email firstname.surname@galaxy1022.co.uk
website www.galaxy1022.co.uk

Birmingham
Radio XL 1296 AM, KMS House, Bradford Street, Birmingham B12 0JD
tel 0121-753 5353 *fax* 0121-753 3111
email arun@radioxl.net

Blackpool
Radio Wave 96.5, 965 Mowbray Drive, Blackpool, Lancs. FY3 7JR
tel (01253) 304965 *fax* (01253) 301965
email sales@thewavefm.co.uk
website www.thewavefm.co.uk

Bolton & Bury
Tower FM, The Mill, Brownlow Way, Bolton BL1 2RA
tel (01204) 387000 *fax* (01204) 534065
website www.towerfm.co.uk

Bournemouth
2CR FM *and* Classic Gold 828, 5 Southcote Road, Bournemouth BH1 3LR
tel (01202) 259259 *fax* (01202) 255244
email sales@musicradio.co.uk
website www.koko.com

Bradford
Sunrise FM, Sunrise House, 30 Chapel Street, Little Germany, Bradford BD1 5DN
tel (01274) 735043 *fax* (01274) 728534
website www.sunriseradio.fm

Bradford, Huddersfield & Halifax
Classic Gold 1278/1530 AM *and* The Pulse, Pennine House, Forster Square, Bradford BD1 5NE
tel (01274) 203040 *fax* (01274) 203130
email general@pulse.co.uk
website www.pulse.co.uk

Bridgwater
BCR FM, Royal Clarence House, York Building,
High Street, Bridgwater, Somerset TA6 4WE
tel (01278) 727701 *fax* (01278) 727705
email studio@bcrfm.co.uk
website www.bcrfm.co.uk

Bridlington
Yorkshire Coast Radio – Bridlington, PO Box 1024,
Harbour Road, Bridlington, East Yorkshire YO15 2YR
tel (01262) 404400 *fax* (01262) 404404
website www.yorkshirecoastradio.com

Brighton*
Juice 107, PO Box 107, Brighton BN1 1QG
tel (01273) 386107 *fax* (01273) 273107
website www.nonstopjuice.com

Brighton/Eastbourne & Hastings
Capital Gold (1323 and 945) *and* Southern FM,
Radio House, PO Box 2000, Brighton BN41 2SS
tel (01273) 430111 *fax* (01273) 430098
website www.capitalgolddigital.com

Bristol
Star 107.3, Bristol Evening Post Building,
Temple Way, Bristol BS99 7HD
tel 0117-910 6600 *fax* 0117-925 0941
website www.star1073.co.uk

Bristol & Bath
Classic Gold 1260 AM *and* GWR FM, PO Box 2000,
Swindon SN4 7EX
tel (01793) 842600 *fax* (01793) 842602
email reception@classicgold.musicradio.com
website www.classicgolddigital.co.uk www.koko.com

Burgess Hill & Haywards Heath
Bright 106.4, The Market Place Shopping Centre,
Burgess Hill, West Sussex RH15 9NP
tel (01444) 248127 *fax* (01444) 248553
website www.bright1064.com

Burnley
2BR, Imex, Lomeshaye Business Village, Netson,
Lancs BB9 7DR
tel (01282) 690000 *fax* (01282) 69001
website www.2br.co.uk

Cambridge
Star 107.9, Radio House, Sturton Street,
Cambridge CB1 2QF
tel (01223) 722300 *fax* (01223) 577686
email firstname.surname@star1079.co.uk
website www.star1079.co.uk

Cambridge & Newmarket
Q103 FM, Enterprise House, The Vision Park,
Chivers Way, Histon, Cambridge CB4 9WW

tel (01223) 235255 *fax* (01223) 235161
email reception@q103.musicradio.com

Canterbury
106 CTFM Radio, 16 Lower Bridge Street,
Canterbury, Kent CT1 2HQ
tel (01227) 789106 *fax* (01227) 785106
email e-mail@ctfm.co.uk
website www.ctfm.co.uk

Carlisle
CFM, PO Box 964, Carlisle CA1 3NG
tel (01228) 818964 *fax* (01228) 819444
email news@cfmradio.com
website www.cfmradio.com

Chelmsford
Dream 107.7 FM, 6th Floor, Cater House,
High Street, Chelmsford, Essex CM1 1AL
tel (01245) 259400 *fax* (01245) 259558
email reception@dream107.com
website www.dream107.com

Cheltenham
Star 107.5 FM, Cheltenham Film Studios, 1st Floor,
West Suite, Arle Court, Matherley Lane,
Cheltenham, Glos. GL51 6PN
tel (01242) 699555 *fax* (01242) 699666
website www.star1075.co.uk

Chester
Chester FM, The Racecourse, Chester CH1 2LY
tel (01244) 394218 *fax* (01244) 394214
website www.chester-fm.com

Chester
Dee 106.3 Ltd, 2 Chantry Court, Chester CH1 4QN
tel (01244) 391000 *fax* (01244) 391010
website www.dee1063.com

Chesterfield & North Derbyshire
Peak 107 FM, Radio House, Foxwood Road,
Chesterfield S41 9RF
tel (01246) 269107 (01246) 269933
email info@peak107.com
website www.peak107.com

Chichester, Bognor Regis & Littlehampton
Spirit FM 96.6 *and* 102.3, Dukes Court,
Bognor Road, Chichester, West Sussex PO19 8FX
tel (01243) 773600 *fax* (01243) 786464
email info@spiritfm.net
website www.spiritfm.net

Colchester
SGR Colchester, Abbeygate Two, 9 Whitewell Road,
Colchester CO2 7DE
tel (01206) 575859 *fax* (01206) 561199

Cornwall, Plymouth & West Devon
Pirate FM102·2/8, Carn Brea Studios, Wilson Way,
Redruth, Cornwall TR15 3XX
tel (01209) 314400 *fax* (01209) 314345
email enquiries@piratefm102.co.uk
website www.piratefm.co.uk

Coventry
Classic Gold 1359 *and* Mercia FM, Hertford Place,
Coventry CV1 3TT
tel (01203) 868200 *fax* (01203) 868202
website www.classicgolddigital.com

Coventry
Kix 96, Watch Close, Spon Street,
Coventry CV1 3LN
tel 024-7652 5656 *fax* 024-7655 1744
email kix962@aol.com
website www.kix.fm

Darlington
Alpha 103.2, Radio House, 11 Woodland Road,
Darlington, Co. Durham DL3 7BJ
tel (01325) 255552 *fax* (01325) 255551
email admin@alpharadio.demon.co.uk
website www.alpha1032.net

Derby
Ram FM, 35-36 Irongate, Derby DE1 3GA
tel (01332) 851100 *fax* (01332) 851199

Doncaster
Trax FM, PO Box 444, Doncaster DN4 5GW
tel (01302) 341166 *fax* (01302) 326104
website www.traxfm.co.uk

Dover & Folkestone
Neptune Radio, PO Box 1068, Dover CT16 1GB
tel (01304) 202505 *fax* (01304) 212717
website www.neptuneradio.co.uk

East of England
Vibe FM, Reflection House, The Anderson Centre,
Olding Road, Bury St Edmunds IP33 3TA
tel (01284) 718800 *fax* (01284) 718839
email general@vibefm.co.uk
website www.vibefm.co.uk

East Lancashire
Asian Sound Radio, Globe House, Southall Street,
Manchester M3 1LG
tel 0161-288 1000 *fax* 0161-288 9000
website www.asiansoundradio.co.uk

East Midlands
106 Century FM, City Link, Nottingham NG2 4NG
tel 0115-910 6100 *fax* 0115-910 6107
email info106@centuryfm.com
website www.centuryfm.com

Eastbourne*
107.5 Sovereign Radio, 14 St Mary's Walk,
Hailsham, East Sussex BN27 1AF
tel (01323) 442700 *fax* (01323) 442866
email info@1075sovereignradio.co.uk
website www.1075sovereignradio.co.uk

Exeter & Torbay
Classic Gold Digital 666/954 *and* Gemini FM,
Hawthorn House, Exeter Business Park,
Exeter EX1 3QS
tel (01392) 444444 *fax* (01392) 354202
email colin.slade@musicradio.com
website www.classicgolddigital.com

Fenland*
Star 107.1 *and* 107.5, 5 Church Mews, Wisbech,
Cambs. PE13 1HL
tel (01945) 464465 *fax* (01945) 464464
email mail@star1071.co.uk
website www.star1071.co.uk

Gloucestershire
Severn Sound *and* Classic Gold 774, Bridge Studios,
Eastgate Centre, Gloucester GL1 1SS
tel (01452) 313200 *fax* (01452) 313213
email reception@severnsound-musicradio.com
website www.classicgolddigital.com

Great Yarmouth & Lowestoft
The Beach, PO Box 103.4, Lowestoft NR32 2TL
tel (0845) 3451035 *fax* (0845) 3451036
website www.thebeach.co.uk

Greater London
Heart 106·2, The Chrysalis Building, Bramley Road,
London W10 6SP
tel 020-7468 1062 *fax* 020-7470 1065
website www.heart1062.co.uk

Greater London
Jazz FM 102.2, 26-27 Castlereagh Street,
London W1H 5DL
tel 020-7706 4100 *fax* 020-7723 9742
email info@jazzfm.com
website www.jazzfm.com

Greater London
Kiss 100 FM *and* Magic 105.4 FM, Mappin House,
4 Winsley Street, London W1W 8HF
Magic tel 020-7955 1054 *fax* 020-7975 8165
Kiss tel 020-7975 8100 *fax* 020-7975 8150
website www.kiss100.com

Greater London
LBC 1152 AM *and* ITN News Direct 97·3 FM,
200 Gray's Inn Road, London WC1X 8XZ
tel 020-7973 1152 *fax* 020-7312 8503
website www.lbc.co.uk www.newsdirect.com

Greater London
Millennium 106.8 FM, 2-6 Basildon Road,
Abbey Wood, London SE2 0EW
tel 020-8311 3112 *fax* 020-8312 1930
website www.millennium1068.com

Greater London
95.8 Capital FM *and* Capital Gold (1548),
30 Leicester Square, London WC2H 7LA
tel 020-7766 6000 *fax* 020-7766 6100
website www.capitalfm.com

Greater London
963/972 Liberty Radio, Liberty House, The Grove,
London E15 1EL
tel 020-8221 4040 *fax* 020-8221 4044
website www.libertyradio.co.uk

Greater London*
Premier Christian Radio, 22 Chapter Street,
London SW1P 4NP
tel 020-7316 1300 *fax* 020-7233 6706
email premier@premier.org.uk
website www.premier.org.uk

Greater London
Ritz 1035 AM, 33-35 Wembley Hill Road,
Wembley, Middlesex HA9 8RT
tel 020-8733 1300 *fax* 020-8733 1393
website www.ritz1035.com

Greater London
Spectrum Radio, 4 Ingate Place, London SW8 3NS
tel 020-7627 4433 *fax* 020-7627 3409
email name@spectrumradio.net
website www.spectrumradio.net

Greater London
Sunrise Radio, Sunrise House, Merrick Road,
Southall, Middlesex UB2 4AU
tel 020-8574 6666 *fax* 020-8813 9800
website www.sunriseradio.com

Greater London
Virgin 105.8, 1 Golden Square, London W1F 9DJ
tel 020-7434 1215 *fax* 020-7434 1197
email reception@virginradio.co.uk
website www.virginradio.co.uk

Greater London
Xfm, 30 Leicester Square, London WC2H 7LA
tel 020-7766 6600 *fax* 020-7766 6601
website www.xfm.co.uk

Greater Manchester, Merseyside & South & Central Lancashire
Galaxy 102, 5th Floor, The Triangle, Hanging Ditch,
Manchester M4 3TR

tel 0161-279 0300 *fax* 0161-279 0301
website www.galaxy102.co.uk

Grimsby, Cleethorpes, Immingham
Compass FM, 26A Wellengate, Grimsby DN32 0RA
tel (01472) 346666 *fax* (01472) 508811
email enquiries@compassfm.co.uk
website www.compassfm.co.uk

Guernsey
Island FM, 12 Westerbrook, St Sampson,
Guernsey GY2 4QQ, Channel Islands
tel (01481) 242000 *fax* (01481) 249676
email firstname@islandfm.guernsey.net
website www.islandfm.guernsey.net

Guildford
County Sound Radio 1566 AM *and* 96.4 The Eagle,
Dolphin House, North Street, Guildford GU1 4AA
tel (01483) 300964 *fax* (01483) 531612
email onair@countrysound.co.uk

Harlow
Mercury FM, Latton Bush Centre, Southern Way,
Harlow, Essex CM18 7BU
tel (01279) 432415 *fax* (01279) 445289
email studios@ten17.co.uk

Harrogate
97.2 Stray FM, The Hamlet, Hornbeam Park Avenue,
Harrogate HG2 8RE
tel (01423) 522972 *fax* (01423) 522922
website www.strayfm.com

Hastings
107.8 Arrow FM, Priory Meadow Centre, Hastings,
East Sussex TN34 1PJ
tel (01424) 461177 *fax* (01424) 422662
email info@arrowfm.co.uk
website www.arrowfm.co.uk

Havering
Soul City 107.5 FM, Lambourne House,
7 Western Road, Romford, Essex RM1 3LD
tel (0870) 6071075 *fax* (0870) 2403286
website www.soulcity.com

Hereford & Worcester
Classic Gold 954/1530, PO Box 262,
Worcester WR6 5ZE
tel (01905) 740600 *fax* (01905) 740608
and 18 Broad Street, Hereford HR4 9AP
tel (01432) 360246 *fax* (01432) 360247
website www.themagicam.com

Hereford, Worcester & Kidderminster
Wyvern FM, 5 Barbourne Terrace, Worcester WR1 3JZ
tel (01905) 612212 *fax* (01905) 746637
website www.koko.com

Hertford, Ware, Hatfield, Welwyn Garden City & Stevenage

Hertbeat fm, The Pump House, Knebworth Park, Herts SG3 6HQ
tel (01438) 810900 *fax* (01438) 815100
email info@hertbeat.com
website www.hertbeat.com

High Wycombe

Swan FM, PO Box 1170, High Wycombe HP13 6YT
tel (01494) 446611 *fax* (01494) 445400
website www.swanfm.co.uk

Hinckley, Nuneaton & surrounding area

Fosseway Radio, PO Box 107, Hinckley, Leics. LE10 1WR
tel (01455) 614151 *fax* (01455) 616888
email enquiries@fossewayradio.co.uk
website www.fossewayradio.co.uk

Huddersfield

Home 107.9, The Old Stableblock, Lockwood Park, Huddersfield HD1 3UR
tel (01484) 321107 *fax* (01484) 311107
email info@home1079.com
website www.home1079.com

Humberside

Magic 1161 AM *and* 96.9 Viking FM, The Boathouse, Commercial Road, Hull HU1 2SG
tel (01482) 325141 *fax* (01482) 593067
website www.magic1161.co.uk www.vikingfm.co.uk

Ipswich & Bury St Edmunds

SGR-FM *and* Classic Gold Amber (Suffolk), Alpha Business Park, 6-12 White House Road, Ipswich IP1 5LT
tel (01473) 461000 *fax* (01473) 741200
website www.koko.com

Isle of Man*

Manx Radio, PO Box 1368, Broadcasting House, Douglas, Isle of Man IM99 1SW
tel (01624) 682600 *fax* (01624) 682604
email postbox@manxradio.com
website www.manxradio.com www.radiott.com

Isle of Wight

Isle of Wight Radio, Dodnor Park, Newport PO30 5XE
tel (01983) 822557 *fax* (01983) 822109
email admin@iwradio.co.uk
website www.iwradio.co.uk

Jersey

Channel 103 FM, 6 Tunnell Street, St Helier, Jersey JE2 4LU, Channel Islands
tel (01534) 888103 *fax* (01534) 887799
email chan103@itl.net
website www.channel103.com

Kendal & Windermere

Lakeland Radio, Lakeland Food Park, Plum Garths, Crook Road, Kendal LA8 8QJ
tel (01539) 737380 *fax* (01539) 737390
website www.lakelandradio.co.uk

Kent

Capital Gold (1242 and 603) *and* Invicta FM, Radio House, John Wilson Business Park, Whitstable, Kent CT5 3QX
tel (01227) 772004 *fax* (01227) 771558
email info@invictaradio.co.uk
website www.capitalgold.com

Kettering, Corby, Wellingborough*

Connect FM, Unit 1, PO Box 1074, Centre 2000, Kettering, Northants. NN16 8PU
tel (01536) 412413 *fax* (01536) 517390
email info@connectfm.co.uk
website www.connectfm.co.uk

Kings Lynn

KL.FM 96·7, 18 Blackfriars Street, Kings Lynn, Norfolk PE30 1NN
tel (01553) 772777 *fax* (01553) 766453
email klfmradio.co.uk
website www.klfm967.co.uk

Kingston upon Thames

107.8 FM Thames, Brentham House, 45c High Street, Hampton Wick, Kingston upon Thames KT1 4DG
tel 020-8288 1300 *fax* 020-8288 1312
email info@thamesradio.com
website www.thamesradio.com

Knowsley*

KCR 106.7 FM, The Studios, Cables Retail Park, Prescot, Knowsley L34 5SW
tel 0151-290 1501 *fax* 0151-290 1505
website www.ker.fm

Leeds

96.3 Aire FM *and* Magic 828, 51 Burley Road, Leeds LS3 1LR
tel 0113-283 5500 *fax* 0113-283 5501
website www.airefm.com

Leicester

Leicester Sound, Granville House, Granville Road, Leicester LE1 7RW
tel 0116-256 1300 *fax* 0116-256 1303
email leicesterfm@musicradio.com

Leicester

Sabras, Radio House, 63 Melton Road, Leicester LE4 6PN
tel 0116-261 0666 *fax* 0116-266 7776
website www.sabrasradio.com

Lincolnshire & Newark*
Lincs FM, Witham Park, Waterside South,
Lincoln LN5 7JN
tel (01522) 549900 *fax* (01522) 549911
email enquiries@lincsfm.co.uk
website www.lincsfm.co.uk

Liverpool
Juice 107.6, 27 Fleet Street, Liverpool L1 4AR
tel 0151-707 3107 *fax* 0151-707 3109
email mail@juiceliverpool.com
website www.juice.fm

Liverpool
Radio City 96·7 *and* Magic 1548, St Johns Beacon,
1 Houghton Street, Liverpool L1 1RL
tel 0151-472 6800 *fax* 0151-472 6821
website www.radiocity.co.uk

London (Lewisham)
Fusion 107.3, Astra House, Arklow Road,
London SE14 6EB
tel 020-8691 9202 *fax* 020-8691 9193
website www.fusion1073.com

London (North & South)
Choice FM, 291-299 Borough High Street,
London SE1 1JG
tel 020-7378 3969 (South London), 020-8348 1033
(North London) *fax* 020-7378 3911 (South
London), 020-7378 3911 (North London)
email info@choicefm.net
website www.choicefm.net

London (North)
London Greek Radio, Florentia Village, Vale Road,
London N4 1TD
tel 020-8800 8001 *fax* 020-8800 8005
email sales@lgr.co.uk
website www.lgr.co.uk

London (North)
London Turkish Radio, 185ʙ High Road,
London N22 6BA
tel 020-8881 0606/2020 *fax* 020-8881 5151
email info@londonturkishradio.com
website www.londonturkishradio.com

Loughborough, Charnwood and North West Leicestershire
107 Oak FM, 7 Waldron Court, Prince William Road,
Loughborough LE11 5GD
tel (01509) 211711 *fax* (01509) 246107
website www.oak.fm

Ludlow
Sunshine 855, Unit 11, Burway Trading Estate,
Ludlow, Shropshire SY8 1EN
tel (01584) 873795 *fax* (01584) 875900

email sunshine855@ukonline.co.uk
website www.sunshine855.com

Luton
97.6 Chiltern FM *and* Classic Gold 792/828
(Bedford & Luton), Chiltern Road, Dunstable,
Beds. LU6 1HQ
tel (01582) 676200 *fax* (01582) 676201
website www.koko.com www.classicgolddigital.com

Macclesfield
Silk FM, Radio House, Bridge Street, Macclesfield,
Cheshire SK11 6DJ
tel (01625) 268000 *fax* (01625) 269010
email mail@silkfm.com
website www.silkfm.com

Manchester
Capital Gold 1458 AM, Laser House, Waterfront
Quay, Salford Quays, Manchester M5 2XN
tel 0161-400 0105 *fax* 0161-400 1105
website www.capitalgolddigital.com

Manchester
Key 103 *and* Magic 1152, Castle Quay, Castlefield,
Manchester M5 4PR
tel 0161-288 5000 *fax* 0161-288 5001
website www.key.com

Mansfield & Ashfield
Mansfield 103.2 FM, The Media Suite,
Brunts Business Centre, Samuel Brunts Way,
Mansfield, Notts. NG18 2AH
tel (01623) 646666 *fax* (01623) 660606
email info@mansfield103.co.uk

Medway towns
Mercury 107.9 FM, Berkeley House, 186 High Street,
Rochester ME1 1EY
tel (01634) 841111 *fax* (01634) 841122
website www.koko.com

Milton Keynes
FM 103 Horizon, Broadcast Centre, Vincent Avenue,
Crownhill Industry, Milton Keynes MK8 0AB
tel (01908) 269111 *fax* (01908) 564063
email fm103horizon@musicradio
website www.koko.com

Morecambe Bay
The Bay 96.9 FM, PO Box 969, St George's Quay,
Lancaster LA1 3LD
tel (01524) 848747 *fax* (01524) 848787
website www.thebay.fm

Newbury*
Kick FM, The Studios, 42 Bone Lane, Newbury,
Berks. RG14 5SD
tel (01635) 841600 *fax* (01635) 841010

email mail@kickfm.com
website www.kickfm.com

North East England

Century Radio, Century House, PO Box 100,
Gateshead NE8 2YX
tel 0191-477 6666 *fax* 0191-477 5660
website www.centuryfm.co.uk

North East England

Galaxy 105-106, Kingfisher Way,
Silverlink Business Park,
Tyne & Wear NE28 9NX
tel 0191-206 8000 *fax* 0191-206 8080
email mail@galaxy1056.co.uk
website www.galaxy1056.co.uk

North West England

105.4 Century FM, Laser House, Waterfront Quay,
Salford Quays, Manchester M5 2XW
tel 0161-400 0105 *fax* 0161-400 1105
email info1054@centuryfm.co.uk
website www.centuryfm.co.uk

North West England

Jazz FM 100.4, 8 Exchange Quay, Manchester M5 3EJ
tel 0161-877 1004 *fax* 0161-877 1005
email jazzinfo@jazzfm.com
website www.jazzfm.com

Northampton

Northants 96 *and* Classic Gold 1557,
19-21 St Edmunds Road, Northampton NN1 5DY
tel (01604) 795600 *fax* (01604) 795601
email reception@northants96.musicradio.com
website www.koko.com www.classicgolddigital.com

Norwich

Broadland 102·4 FM *and* Classic Gold Amber,
St George's Plain, 47-49 Colegate, Norwich NR3 1DB
tel (01603) 630621 *fax* (01603) 671175
website www.koko.com

Nottingham & Derby

96 Trent FM *and* Classic Gold Gem,
29-31 Castle Gate, Nottingham NG1 7AP
tel 0115-952 7000 *fax* 0115-912 9302
email firstname.surname@musicradio.com
website www.koko.com

Oldham

96.2 The Revolution, PO Box 962, Oldham OL1 3JF
tel 0161-621 6500 *fax* 0161-621 6521
website www.revolutiononhire.co.uk

Oxford

Fusion 107.9, Suite 41, Westgate Centre,
Oxford OX1 1PD
tel (01865) 724442 *fax* (01865) 726161

email mail@oxygen.demon.co.uk
website www.fashion1079.com

Oxford & Banbury

FOX FM, Brush House, Pony Road, Oxford OX4 2XR
tel (01865) 871000 *fax* (01865) 871036
email fox@foxfm.co.uk
website www.foxfm.co.uk

Peterborough

Classic Gold 1332 AM *and* 102·7 Hereward FM,
PO Box 225, Queensgate Centre,
Peterborough PE1 1XJ
tel (01733) 460460 *fax* (01733) 281445
website www.classicgolddigital.com

Peterborough

Lite FM, 2nd Floor, 5 Church Street,
Peterborough PE1 1XB
tel (01733) 898106 *fax* (01733) 898107
website www.litefm.co.uk

Plymouth

Classic Gold 1152 *and* 97FM Plymouth Sound,
Earl's Acre, Plymouth PL3 4HX
tel (01752) 275600 *fax* (01752) 275605
website www.classicgolddigital.com

Poole, Bournemouth & surrounding area*

Fire 107.6 FM, Quadrant Studios,
Old Christchurch Road, Bournemouth BH1 2AD
tel (01202) 318100 *fax* (01202) 318110
website www.fire1076.com

Portsmouth, Havant, Gosport & Fareham*

107.4 The Quay, PO Box 1074, Portsmouth PO2 8YG
tel (02392) 364141 *fax* (02392) 364151
website www.quayradio.com

Preston & Blackpool

Magic 999 *and* Rock FM, PO Box 999/PO Box 974,
Preston, Lancs. PR1 1XR
tel (01772) 556301 *fax* (01772) 201917
website www.rockfm.co.uk

Reading, Basingstoke & Andover

2-TEN FM *and* Classic Gold 1431/1485,
PO Box 2020, Reading RG31 7FG
tel 0118-945 4400 *fax* 0118-928 8513
email mail2tenfm@musicradio.com
website www.classicgolddigital.com

Reigate & Crawley

102.7 Mercury FM *and* Classic Gold 1521,
The Stanley Centre, Kelvin Way, Crawley,
West Sussex RH10 9SE
tel (01293) 519161 *fax* (01293) 560927
website www.koko.com

Rugby
107.1 Rugby FM, Suites 4-6, Dunsmore Business
Centre, Spring Street, Rugby CV21 3HH
tel (01788) 541100 *fax* (01788) 541070
website www.rugbyfm.co.uk

Rutland*
Rutland Radio, 40 Melton Road, Oakham,
Rutland LE15 6AY
tel (01572) 757868 *fax* (01572) 757744
email enquiries@rutlandradio.co.uk
website www.rutlandradio.co.uk

Salisbury
Spire FM, City Hall Studios, Malthouse Lane,
Salisbury, Wilts. SP2 7QQ
tel (01722) 416644 *fax* (01722) 416688
email admin@spirefm.co.uk
website www.spirefm.co.uk

Scarborough
Yorkshire Coast Radio, PO Box 962, Scarborough,
North Yorkshire YO12 5YX
tel (01723) 500962 *fax* (01723) 501050
email info@yorkshirecoastradio.com
website www.yorkshirecoastradio.com

Severn Estuary
Vibe 101, 1 Passage Street, Bristol BS2 0JF
tel 0117-901 0101 *fax* 0117-984 3204
website www.vibe101.co.uk

Shaftesbury
97.4 Vale FM, Longmead, Shaftesbury SP7 8QQ
tel (01747) 855711 *fax* (01747) 855722
website www.valefm.co.uk

Slough, Windsor & Maidenhead
Star 106·6, The Observatory Shopping Centre,
Slough, Berks. SL1 1LH
tel (01753) 551066 *fax* (01753) 512277
email onair@1066starfm.co.uk
website www.starfm.co.uk

Solent area
Wave 105.2 FM, 5 Manor Court, Barnes Wallis Road,
Segensworth East, Fareham PO15 5TH
tel (01489) 481057 *fax* (01489) 481100
website www.wave105.com

South & West Yorkshire
Real Radio, Sterling Court, Capitol Park,
Leeds WF3 1EL *tel* 0113-238 1114 *fax* 0113-238 1911
website www.realradiofm.com

South Hampshire
Capital Gold (1170/1557), Ocean FM *and* Power FM,
Radio House, Whittle Avenue, Segensworth West,
Fareham PO15 5SH

tel (01489) 589911 *fax* (01489) 589453
websites www.capitalgolddigital.com oceanfm.com

South Yorkshire
Hallam FM *and* Magic AM, Radio House,
900 Herries Road, Sheffield, S6 1RH
tel 0114-209 1000 *fax* 0114-285 3159
email programmes@hallamfm.co.uk
website www.clickhallam.com

Southampton
SouthCity FM, City Studios, Marsh Lane,
Southampton SO14 3ST
tel 023-8022 0020 *fax* 023-8022 0060
email info@southcityfm.co.uk
website www.southcityfm.co.uk

South-East Staffordshire
Centre FM, 5-6 Aldergate, Tamworth, Staffs B79 7DJ
tel (01827) 318000 *fax* (01827) 318002
website www.centre.fm

Southend & Chelmsford
Classic Gold Breeze *and* Essex FM, Radio House,
Clifftown Road, Southend-on-Sea, Essex SS1 1SX
tel (01702) 333711 *fax* (01702) 345224
website www.classicgolddigital.com

Southern Gloucestershire
Star 107 FM, Brunel Mall, London Road, Stroud,
Glos. GL5 2BP
tel (01453) 767369 *fax* (01453) 757107
email admin@star107.co.uk
website www.star107.co.uk

Southport
107.9 Dune FM, The Power Station, Victoria Way,
Southport PR8 1RR
tel (01704) 502500 *fax* (01704) 502540
email info@dunefm.co.uk
website www.dunefm.co.uk

Stockport
Imagine FM, Regent House, Heaton Lane,
Stockport SK4 1BX
tel 0161-609 1400 *fax* 0161-609 1401
email recipient@imaginefm.net

Stoke-on-Trent
Signal One *and* Signal 2, Stoke Road,
Stoke-on-Trent ST4 2SR
tel (01782) 441300 *fax* (01782) 441301
email initialsurname@signalradio.com
website www.signal1.co.uk

Stratford upon Avon*
FM 102 – The Bear, The Guard House Studios,
Banbury Road, Stratford upon Avon CV37 7HX
tel (01789) 262636 *fax* (01789) 263102

email info@thebear.co.uk
website www.thebear.co.uk

Sunderland*
Sun FM, PO Box 1034, Sunderland SR5 2YL
tel 0191-548 1034 *fax* 0191-548 7171
email progs@sun-fm.com
website www.sun-fm.com

Swindon
Classic Gold 936/1161, Lime Kiln Lane, Lime Kiln,
Wootton Bassett, Swindon SN4 7EX
tel 0117-984 3200 *fax* 0117-984 3202
email reception@classicgold.musicradio.com
website www.classicgolddigital.com

Swindon & West Wiltshire
GWR FM 97.2, PO Box 2000, Swindon SN4 7EX
tel (01793) 842600 *fax* (01793) 842602
website www.koko.com

Teesside
TFM *and* Magic 1170, Radio House, Yale Crescent,
Thornaby, Stockton-on-Tees TS17 6AA
tel (01642) 888222 *fax* (01642) 868288

Telford*
Telford FM, PO Box 1074, Telford TF3 3WG
tel (01952) 280011 *fax* (01952) 280010
website www.telfordfm.co.uk

Tendring*
Dream 100 FM, Northgate House, St Peters Street,
Colchester CO1 1HT
tel (01206) 764466 *fax* (01206) 715102
email info@dream100.com
website www.dream100.com

Thanet
TLR, Imperial House, 2-14 High Street, Margate,
Kent CT9 1DH
tel (01843) 220222 *fax* (01843) 299666
email reception@tlr.fm.co.uk
website www.tlr.fm.co.uk

Tunbridge Wells & Sevenoaks
KM–FM, 1 East Street, Tonbridge, Kent TN9 1AR
tel (01732) 369200 *fax* (01732) 369201
website www.koko.com

Tyne & Wear
Magic 1152 *and* Metro FM, Longrigg, Swalwell,
Newcastle upon Tyne NE99 1BB
tel 0191-420 0971 *fax* 0191-488 9222
website www.metroradio.com

Wakefield
Ridings FM, PO Box 333, Monckton Road,
Wakefield WF2 7YQ

tel (01924) 367177 *fax* (01924) 367133
email enquiries@ridingsfm.co.uk

Warminster
107.5 3TR FM, Riverside Studios, Boreham Hill,
Bistopstrow, Warminster BA12 9HQ
tel (01985) 211111 *fax* (01985) 211110
website www.3trfm.com

Warrington, Widnes & Runcorn
107.2 Wire FM, Warrington Business Park,
Long Lane, Warrington WA2 8TX
tel (01925) 445545 *fax* (01925) 657705
email info@wirefm.com
website www.wirefm.com

Watford & South Herts.
Watford's Mercury 96.6, Unit 5, The Metro Centre,
Dwight Road, Watford WD18 9UP
tel (01923) 205470 *fax* (01923) 205471
email firstname.surname@creation.com
website www.koko.com

West Cumbria
CFM, PO Box 964, Carlisle CA1 3NG
tel (01228) 818964 *fax* (01228) 819444
email reception@cfmradio.com
website www.cfmradio.com

West Midlands
100·7 Heart FM, 1 The Square, 111 Broad Street,
Birmingham B15 1AS
tel 0121-695 0000 *fax* 0121-696 1007
email heartfm@heartfm.co.uk
website www.heartfm.co.uk

West Midlands*
Saga 105.7 FM, 3rd Floor, Crown House, Beaufort
Court, 123 Hagley Road, Birmingham B16 8LD
tel 0121-452 1057 *fax* 0121-452 3222
website www.saga1057fm.co.uk

West Somerset
Quay West Radio, Harbour Studios, The Esplanade,
Watchet, Somerset TA23 0AJ
tel (01984) 634900 *fax* (01984) 634811
email studio@quaywestradio.com

Weston-Super-Mare
Star 107.7 FM, 11 Beaconsfield Road,
Weston-Super-Mare BS23 1YE
tel (01934) 624455 *fax* (01934) 629922
website www.star1077.co.uk

Weymouth & Dorchester
Wessex FM, Radio House, Trinity Street, Dorchester,
Dorset DT1 1DJ
tel (01305) 250333 *fax* (01305) 250052
website www.wessexfm.co.uk

Wigan & St Helens

102.4 Wish FM, Orrell Lodge, Orrell Road,
Wigan WN5 8HJ
tel (01942) 761024 *fax* (01942) 777694
email studio@wish_fm.com

Winchester*

Win FM, PO Box 1072, The Brooks,
Winchester SO23 8FT
tel (01962) 841071 *fax* (01962) 841079
website www.winfm.co.uk

Wirral

Wirral's Buzz 97.1, Media House, Claughton Road,
Birkenhead CH41 6EY
tel 0151-650 1700 *fax* 0151-647 5427
website www.thebuzz971.co.uk

Wolverhampton

107.7 The Wolf, 10th Floor, Mander House,
Wolverhampton WV1 3NE
tel (01902) 571070 *fax* (01902) 571079
email studio@thewolf.co.uk
website www.thewolf.co.uk

Wolverhampton, Shrewsbury & Telford

Beacon Radio FM *and* Classic Gold WABC,
267 Tettenhall Road, Wolverhampton WV6 0DE
tel (01902) 461300 *fax* (01902) 461299
website www.classicgolddigital.com

Yeovil & Taunton

Orchard FM, Haygrove House,
Taunton TA3 7BT
tel (01823) 338448 *fax* (01823) 368318
website www.koko.com

York

Minster FM, PO Box 123, Dunnington,
York YO19 5ZX
tel (01904) 488888 *fax* (01904) 481088
email general@minsterfm.co.uk
website www.minsterfm.co.uk

Yorkshire

Galaxy 105, Josephs Well, Hanover Walk,
off Park Lane, Leeds LS3 1AB
tel 0113-213 0105 *fax* 0113-213 1055
email mail@galaxy105.co.uk
website www.galaxy105.co.uk

Yorkshire Dales & East Lancs.

Fresh Radio Ltd, Firth Street,
Skipton BD23 2PT
tel (01756) 799991 *fax* (01756) 799771
PO Box 1413, Richmond DL10 4WY
tel (01748) 821134 *fax* (01748) 821144
email info@freshradio.co.uk
website www.freshradio.co.uk

NORTHERN IRELAND

Belfast

Citybeat 96.7, 46 Stranmillis Embankment,
Belfast BT9 5FN
tel 028-9020 5967 *fax* 028-9020 0023
website www.citybeat.co.uk

Coleraine*

Q97.2 Causeway Coast Radio, 24 Cloyfin Road,
Coleraine BT52 2NU
tel 028-703 59100 *fax* 028-703 26666
website www.q972.fm

Londonderry

Q102·9 FM, The Riverview Suite, 87 Rossdowney
Road, Waterside, Londonderry BT47 5SU
tel 028-7134 4449 *fax* 028-7131 1177
website www.q102.fm

Mid Ulster

Mid FM, 15 Drumanee Road, Bellaghy,
Co. Londonderry BT45 8LE
tel 028-9020 5967
email midfm@hotmail.com

Northern Ireland

Cool FM, PO Box 974, Belfast BT1 1RT
tel (01247) 817181 *fax* (01247) 814974
email music@coolfm.co.uk
website www.coolfm.co.uk

Northern Ireland

Downtown Radio, Newtownards,
Co. Down BT23 4ES
tel 028-9181 5555 *fax* 028-9181 8913
email programmes@downtown.co.uk
website www.downtown.co.uk

Omagh & Enniskillen

Q101.2 FM Radio West, 42A Market Street, Omagh,
Co. Tyrone BT78 1EH
tel 028-8224 5777
1 Belmore Mews, Enniskillen,
Co. Permangh BT74 6AA
tel 028-6632 0676 *fax* 028-6632 0777
Head Office The Riverview Suite,
87 Rossdowney Road, Waterside,
Londonderry BT47 5SU

SCOTLAND

Aberdeen

Northsound One *and* Northsound Two,
45 Kings Gate, Aberdeen AB15 4EL
tel (01224) 337000 *fax* (01224) 400003
email northsound@srh.co.uk
website www.northsound.co.uk

Arbroath/Carnoustie
RNA FM, Radio North Angus, Arbroath Infirmary,
Rosemount Road, Arbroath, Angus DD11 2AT
tel (01241) 879660 *fax* (01241) 439664
website www.radionorthangus.co.uk

Ayr
West FM *and* West Sound AM, Radio House,
54A Holmston Road, Ayr KA7 3BE
tel (01292) 283662 *fax* (01292) 283665
websites www.westonline.com
www west-sound.co.uk

The Borders
Radio Borders, Tweedside Park,
Galashiels TD1 3TD
tel (01896) 759444 *fax* (01896) 759494
website www.radioborders.com

Central Scotland
Beat 106 Ltd, The Four Winds Pavilion,
Pacific Quay, Glasgow G51 1EB
tel 0141-566 6106 *fax* 0141-566 6110
email info@beat106.com
website www.beat106.com

Central Scotland*
Real Radio, PO Box 101, Parkway Court,
Glasgow Business Park, Glasgow G69 6GA
tel 0141-781 1011 *fax* 0141-781 1112
email firstname.surname@realradiofm.com
website www.realradio.com

Dumbarton
Castle Rock FM 103, Pioneer Park Studios, Unit 3,
80 Castlegreen Street, Dumbarton G82 1JB
tel (01389) 734422 *fax* (01389) 734380
email info@castlerockfm.com
website www.castlerockfm.com

Dumfries & Galloway
South West Sound, Unit 40, The Loreburne Centre,
High Street, Dumfries DG1 2BD
tel (01387) 250999 *fax* (01387) 265629
website www.westsound.co.uk

Dundee*
Wave 102 FM, 8 South Tay Street,
Dundee DD1 1PA
tel (01382) 901000 *fax* (01382) 900999
email studio@wave102.co.uk
website www.wave102.co.uk

Dundee/Perth*
Tay AM* *and* Tay FM, 6 North Isla Street,
Dundee DD3 7JQ
tel (01382) 200800 *fax* (01382) 423252
email tayam@radiotay.co.uk
website www.radiotay.co.uk

Edinburgh
Forthone *and* Forth 2, Forth House, Forth Street,
Edinburgh EH1 3LE
tel 0131-556 9255 *fax* 0131-558 3277
email info@forthone.com info@forth2.com
website www.forthone.com www.forth2.com

Fife
Kingdom FM, Haig House, Haig Business Park,
Balgonie Road, Markinch, Fife KY7 6AQ
tel (01592) 753753 *fax* (01592) 612022
email kingdomfm@aol.com
website www.kingdomfm.co.uk

Fort William & Parts of Lochaber
Nevis Radio, Ben Nevis Estate, Fort William PH33 6PR
tel (01397) 700007 *fax* (01397) 701007
email studio@nevisradio.co.uk
website www.nevisradio.co.uk

Glasgow
Clyde 1 *and* Clyde 2, Clydebank Business Park,
Clydebank, Glasgow G81 2RX
tel 0141-565 2200 *fax* 0141-565 2265
website www.clyde1.com www.clyde2.com

Inverness
Moray Firth Radio (MFR), PO Box 271,
Scorguie Place, Inverness IV3 8UJ
tel (01463) 224433 *fax* (01463) 243224
website www.mfr.co.uk

Inverurie
NECR, Town House, Kintore, Inverurie AB51 0UX
tel (01467) 632909 *fax* (01467) 632969
email necrradio102.ifmsales@supanet.com

Kintyre, Islay & Jura
Argyll FM, 27-29 Longrow, Campbelltown,
Argyll PA28 6ER
tel (01586) 551800 *fax* (01586) 551888
email argyllfm1065@aol.com

Lanarkshire
Clan FM, Radio House, Rowantree Avenue,
Newhouse Industrial Estate, Newhouse,
Lanarkshire ML1 5RX
tel (01698) 733107 *fax* (01698) 733318
website www.clanfm.com

Oban*
Oban FM, 132 George Street, Oban, Argyll PA34 5NT
tel (01631) 570057 *fax* (01631) 570530
email us@oban-fm.freeserve.co.uk

Paisley
96.3 QFM, 65 Sussex Street, Kinning Park,
Glasgow G41 1DX
tel 0141-429 9430 *fax* 0141-429 9431

Peterhead
Waves Radio Peterhead, Unit 2, Blackhouse
Industrial Estate, Peterhead AB42 1BW
tel (01779) 491012 *fax* (01779) 490802
email waves@radiophd.freeserve.co.uk
website www.wavesfm.com

Pitlochry & Aberfeldy*
Heartland FM, Atholl Curling Rink, Lower Oakfield,
Pitlochry, Perthshire PH16 5HQ
tel (01796) 474040 *fax* (01796) 474007
website www.heartlandfm.co.uk

Shetland
SIBC, Market Street, Lerwick, Shetland ZE1 0JN
tel (01595) 695299 *fax* (01595) 695696
email info@sibc.co.uk
website www.sibc.co.uk

Stirling & Falkirk
Central FM, 201 High Street, Falkirk FK1 1DU
tel (01324) 611164 *fax* (01324) 611168
website www.centralfm.co.uk

Ullapool*
Lochbroom FM, Mill Street, Ullapool,
Ross-shire IV26 2UN
tel (01854) 613131 *fax* (01854) 613132
email radio@lochbroomfm.co.uk
website www.lochbroomfm.co.uk

Western Isles
Isles FM, PO Box 333, Stornoway,
Isle of Lewis HS1 2PU
tel (01851) 703333 *fax* (01851) 703322
email studio@isles.fm
website www.isles.fm

WALES

Bridgend
Bridge 106.3 FM, Cumbria House, Wyndham Street,
Bridgend CF31 1EY
tel (01656) 647777 *fax* (01656) 673611
website www.bridge.fm

Caernarfon
Champion 103 FM, Llys y Dderwen, Parc Menai,
Bangor, Gwynedd LL57 4BN
tel (01248) 671888 *fax* (01248) 671971
email sarah.smithard@musicradio.com

Cardiff & Newport
Red Dragon FM *and* Capital Gold AM,
Atlantic Wharf, Cardiff CF10 4DJ
tel 029-2066 2066 *fax* 029-2066 2060
website www.reddragonfm.co.uk
www.capitalgolddigital.com

Ceredigion*
Radio Ceredigion, Yr Hen Ysgol Gymraeg, Ffordd
Alexandra, Aberystwyth, Ceredigion SY23 1LF
tel (01970) 627999 *fax* (01970) 627206
email news@ceredigionradio.co.uk

Heads of South Wales Valleys
Valleys Radio, Festival Park, Victoria,
Ebbw Vale NP23 8XW
tel (01495) 301116 *fax* (01495) 300710
email admin@valleysradio.co.uk
website www.valleysradio.co.uk

Montgomeryshire
Radio Maldwyn, The Studios, The Park, Newtown,
Powys SY16 2NZ
tel (01686) 623555 *fax* (01686) 623666
email radio.maldwyn@ukonline.co.uk
website www.magic756.net

North Wales Coast
Coast FM, Media House, Conway Road,
Colwyn Bay LL28 5AB
tel (01492) 534555 *fax* (01492) 535248

Pembrokeshire
Radio Pembrokeshire, 14 Old School, Narberth,
Pembrokeshire SA67 7DU
tel/fax (01834) 869292
email enquiries@radiopembrokeshire.com
website www.radiopembrokeshire.com

South Wales Region
Real Radio, PO Box 6105, Ty-Nant Court,
Cardiff CF15 8YF
tel 029-2031 5100 *fax* 029-2031 5150
website www.realradio.com

Swansea
Swansea Sound, PO Box 1170, Victoria Road,
Gowerton, Swansea SA4 3AB
tel (01792) 511170 *fax* (01792) 511171
email info@swanseasound.co.uk
website www.swanseasound.co.uk

Swansea
The Wave 96·4 FM, PO Box 964, Victoria Road,
Gowerton, Swansea SA4 3AB
tel (01792) 511964 *fax* (01792) 511965
email info@thewave.co.uk
website www.thewave.co.uk

Wrexham & Chester
MFM 103.4 *and* Classic Gold Marcher 1260,
The Studios, Mold Road, Gwersyllt,
Wrexham LL11 4AF
tel (01978) 752202 *fax* (01978) 722209
website www.classicgolddigital.com
www.mfradio.co.uk

Independent radio producers

Many writers approach independent production companies direct and, increasingly, BBC Radio is commissioning independent producers to make programmes.

Cork Campus Radio

Level 3, Áras na Mac Léinn, University College Cork, Cork City, Republic of Ireland
tel (021) 4902170 *fax* (021) 4903108
email radio@ucc.ie
Contact Sinéad O'Donnell, Station Manager

Actively produces dramatic works by new writers; stories of 1800-2000 words from the annual Fallen Leaves Short Story Competition; and the weekly *On the Road* documentary series. Oxygen 2001 SMEDIA Award winner – best student radio station. Founded 1995.

Fast Forward Productions

22 Fleshmarket Close, Edinburgh EH1 1DY
tel 0131-220 0200 *fax* 0131-220 2297
Producer Adrian Quine

Aviation. Founded 1994.

Festival Productions Ltd

11 Old Steine, Brighton BN1 1EJ
tel (01273) 669595 *fax* (01273) 669596
email post@festivalradio.com
website www.festivalradio.com
Managing Director Steve Stark

Plays, docs, features and programmes. Founded 1989.

The Fiction Factory

14 Greenwich Church Street, London SE10 9BJ
tel 020-8853 5100 *fax* 020-8293 3001
email radio@fictionfactory.co.uk
website www.fictionfactory.co.uk
Creative Director John Taylor

Plays, dramatisations, readings, documentaries and features mainly for BBC network radio and the World Service. Original radio drama scripts considered if targeted at existing BBC slots. Script reading fee except for submissions from established writers – some student exemptions. No charge for considering programme ideas and outlines. Founded 1993.

Heavy Entertainment Ltd

Canalot Studios, 222 Kensal Road, London W10 5BN
tel 020-8960 9001/2 *fax* 020-8960 9003
Company Directors David Roper, Davy Nougarède

Audiobooks, radio documentaries and commercials. Showreels and promotional audio and video. Two studios available for hire. Founded 1992.

Mediatracks

93 Columbia Way, Blackburn, Lancs. BB2 7EA
tel (01254) 691197 *fax* (01254) 723505
email info@mediatracks.co.uk
Contact Steve Johnson

Music and general interest docs for BBC local radio network. Founded 1987.

Mike Hopwood Productions Ltd

Winton House, Stoke Road, Stoke-on-Trent ST4 2RW
tel (01782) 848800 *fax* (01782) 749447
Editor Mike Hopwood

Plays, docs, comedy, soaps, light entertainment. No unsolicited material. Founded 1991.

Penumbra Productions Ltd

80 Brondesbury Road, London NW6 6RX
tel 020-7328 4550 *fax* 020-7328 3844
email nazpenumbra@aol.com
Contact H.O. Nazareth

Drama and documentaries for Radio 3 only. Send synopses by email. Founded 1981.

Quantum Radio Productions Ltd

22 Fleshmarket Close, Edinburgh EH1 1DY
tel 0131-220 0200 *fax* 0131-220 2297
email quine@quantumradio.demon.co.uk
Producer Adrian Quine

Sponsored syndicated radio programmes.

SH Radio

Green Dene Cottage, Honeysuckle Bottom, East Horsley, Surrey KT24 5TD
tel (01483) 283223 *fax* (01483) 281792
Contact Robert Symes

Broadcast and non-broadcast commercial material (English and German). Founded 1988.

Smooth Operations

PO Box 286, Cambridge CB1 7XW
tel (01223) 244544 *fax* (01223) 244384
email nick@smoothoperations.com
Contact Nick Barraclough
6 Millgate, Delph, Oldham OL3 5JG
tel (01457) 873752 *fax* (01457) 878500
email john@smoothoperations.com
website www.smoothoperations.com
Contact John Leonard

Music-based docs and series and online content provision for BBC radio. Founded 1992.

Testbed Productions
5th Floor, 14-16 Great Portland Street, London W1N 5AB
tel 020-7436 0555 *fax* 020-7436 2800
Directors Viv Black, Nick Baker

Docs and other programmes; ideas for interviews, feature series, magazine, plays and panel/quiz games. Founded 1992.

Whistledown Productions Ltd
PO Box 36633, London SE1 4NQ
tel 020-7922 1120 *fax* 020-7261 0939
Contact David Prest, Managing Director

Social, historical and popular culture documentaries as well as authored narratives, biographical features and magazine programmes for BBC network radio. Also syndicated tapes and other work for commercial companies. Founded 1998.

Television and radio overseas

Opportunities are outlined here for submitting material to television and radio companies in Australia, Canada, Republic of Ireland, New Zealand and South Africa.

AUSTRALIA

Australian Broadcasting Corporation (ABC)
Box 9994, Sydney, NSW 2001
tel 612-9333-1500 *fax* 612-9333-5305
email comments@your.abc.net.au
website www.abc.net.au
Manager for Europe Australian Broadcasting Corporation, 54 Portland Place, London W1N 4DY

Provides TV, radio and online programmes in a national broadcasting service; and operates Radio Australia internationally.

ABC TV restricts its production resources to work closely related to the Australian environment. ABC radio also looks principally to Australian writers for the basis of its drama output. However, ABC radio is interested in reading or auditioning new creative material of a high quality from overseas sources and this may be submitted in script or taped form. No journalistic material is required. Talks on international affairs are commissioned.

Commercial Radio Australia Ltd
Level 5, 88 Foveaux Street, Surry Hills, NSW 2010
tel (02) 9281 6577 *fax* (02) 9281 6599
email mail@commercialradio.com.au
website www.commercialradio.com.au
Ceo Joan Warner

Industry body for commercial radio stations within Australia. See website.

Federation of Australian Commercial Television Stations (FACTS)
44 Avenue Road, Mosman, NSW 2088
tel (02) 9960 2622 *fax* (02) 9969 3520
Ceo Julie Flynn

Represents all 48 commercial TV stations.

CANADA

Canadian Broadcasting Corporation
250 Lanark Avenue, PO Box 3220, Stn. 'C', Ottawa, Ontario K1Y 1E4
tel 613-724-1200
email commho@ottawa.cbc.ca
website www.cbc.radio-canada.ca

CTV Inc.
9 Channel Nine Court, Scarborough, Ontario M1S 4B5
tel 416-332-5000 *fax* 416-332-6314

IRELAND

Broadcasting Commission of Ireland
(formerly IRTC)
2-5 Warrington Place, Dublin 2, Republic of Ireland
tel (01) 676 0966 *fax* (01) 676 0948
email info@bci.ie
website www.bci.ie

Under the Irish Broadcasting Act 2001, the name and role of the Independent Radio & Television Commission (IRTC) was changed to the Broadcasting Commission of Ireland. Consequentially, it now has a much expanded remit. In addition to its functions contained in the Radio & Television Act 1988, its new functions include the licensing of new TV services on terrestrial, cable, MMDS and satellite platforms, as well as the development of codes of programming and advertising standards for TV and radio services.

To date, its activities have included the establishment of:
• an independent TV programme service (TV3);
• a national radio service (100-102 Today FM);

- 23 local commercial radio services;
- 2 special interest radio services;
- 14 community/community of interest radio services;
- 7 hospital/institutional radio services;
- approximately 20 short-term special event licences per annum.

It is envisaged that further licences will be granted for both commercial and non-commercial radio stations.

Radio Telefís Éireann (RTÉ)

Donnybrook, Dublin 4, Republic of Ireland
tel (01) 208 3111 *fax* (01) 208 3080
email press@rte.ie
website www.rte.ie

The Irish national broadcasting service operating radio and TV.

Television Ongoing production of an urban drama serial. Currently of interest: drama series for mainstream audiences, serials (preferably contemporary) and situation comedies (preferably set in Ireland or of strong Irish interest), with preferred length of commercial half hour or one hour. Proposals for serials and series suitable for a young adult Network 2 audience, either cutting edge or humorous, which could exploit a low-cost DV production model are of particular interest. Full scripts will not be considered – treatments and series/serial outlines only, except in cases where projects are already part funded. Before submitting material to the Drama or Entertainment departments, authors are advised to write to the department in question to establish initial interest, timing of commissioning rounds, etc.

Radio Ongoing production of hour-long dramas each week. Occasional full 2-hour productions and seasons of drama. Short stories (length 13–14 minutes) in Irish or English suitable for broadcasting; plays (running 28 or 58 minutes) are welcome. Guidelines on writing for radio drama are available from the RTÉ Radio Drama Department, Radio Centre, Donnybrook, Dublin 4.

NEW ZEALAND

The Radio Network of New Zealand Ltd

Private Bag 92198, Auckland
tel (09) 373-0000 *fax* (09) 367-4650
Ceo John McElhinney

A radio company controlling a NZ-wide group of commercial radio stations in metropolitan and provincial markets. The station brand groups are

Newstalk ZB, Classic Hits, ZM, Easy Listening i, Hauraki, Radio Sports Network, and Community.

Television New Zealand Ltd

PO Box 3819, Auckland
tel (09) 916-7000 *fax* (09) 379-4907
website www.tvnz.co.nz
Chairman Ross Armstrong, *Ceo* Ian Fraser

A Crown-owned company, TVNZ is charged with operating a commercially successful TV business, acting with social responsibility in the provision of quality services. Of particular importance is the provision of TV programmes which reflect and foster New Zealand's identity and culture, and which are in the overall national interest. TVNZ broadcasts on 2 nationwide channels with a web presence via the organisation's internet portal, nzoom.com

Local and international activities include programme production, outside broadcasting services (through subsidiary company Moving Pictures), multimedia development, merchandising, Teletext, signal distribution and programming supply and transmission consultancy services in Australia, South-East Asia and the Pacific.

SOUTH AFRICA

South African Broadcasting Corporation (SABC)

Private Bag X1, Auckland Park 2006
tel (011) 714-9111 *fax* (011) 714-3106
website www.sabc.co.za

Television Operates 6 TV services (4 free-to-air and 2 pay-TV). Three of the free-to-air channels, SABC1, SABC2 and SABC3, accept scripts in English for drama and comedy, either for one-off programmes or series.

Radio Operates 19 internal radio networks and one external radio service. The service which makes the greatest use of written material in English is SAFM.

Drama One-hour plays of all kinds welcomed. Half-hour plays are occasionally broadcast.

Short stories Short stories of all kinds (1500–1800 words) are welcomed.

Children's programmes Short stories, plays and serials (maximum 15 minutes) may be submitted.

Talks Most are locally commissioned, but outstanding material of particular interest may be submitted (3–10 minutes).

Theatre

Writing for the theatre

Writing for the theatre is a competitive market but thoroughly researching this market will improve the chances of your work being accepted. Christopher William Hill offers guidance.

If anybody ever attempts to convince you that writing for the theatre is a soft career option, ignore them and walk away. It is a competitive market and it would be wrong to suggest otherwise. There are many more playwrights than producing theatres. Although the odds are stacked against you, it is still sometimes possible to scrape a living as a playwright. Of course, there are a number of ways in which you can improve the chances of your work being accepted.

Research your market
It is important to try to understand why a theatre company may produce one play and reject another (due to size of theatre, casting limitations, preferences of the artistic management, etc). Go to the theatre as regularly as possible and read as many plays, contemporary and classic, as you can. In addition, theatre reviews in national and regional newspapers can be extremely useful. *Theatre Record* (fortnightly; *tel* 020-8737 8489, *email* editor@theatrerecord.demon.co.uk *website* www.theatrerecord.com, *Editor and Publisher* Ian Herbert) provides comprehensive press cuttings for West End and regional plays. *The Stage* (weekly), gives informed background to current and forthcoming theatre productions.

The Royal National Theatre and the Theatre Museum in Covent Garden both hold video-taped recordings of many recent London theatre productions. It is only possible to view these recording on site (subject to appointment) but, again, it is a helpful way of expanding your knowledge of contemporary British theatre.

On a more practical level, many theatres offer writing classes. This is an important way of making contact with a theatre and fellow dramatists. Contrary to popular myth, most writers benefit from time away from their draughty garrets.

A number of 'self-help' books on play writing are available, offering advice on every aspect of writing for the theatre. Each author will have a different approach to his or her work, and it is worth spending time finding a book which is suitable for you. As well as providing practical tips on constructing a script, many books also offer reassurance that all the emotions experienced by a playwright (elation, writer's block, despair, etc) are shared by even the most experienced dramatists.

Constructing your script
When writing your play it is worth bearing in mind a number of practical considerations. First and foremost, write the play that you want to write and trust in your own view of the world. Be wary of trying to surf dramatic trends. If you are conscious of a trend developing you have almost certainly missed it.

Be conscious of the cost of mounting a production. It usually follows that the more characters you write into a play, the more actors you need to play them. A script requiring more than six actors may seem prohibitive to a theatre company. From time to time writers will submit plays with casts of 18 plus, and whilst an extremely well-established writer may (occasionally, but rarely) get away with this, an unknown playwright stands little or no chance of having his or her script accepted. Character doubling (with actors playing multiple roles) can be a pragmatic way of negotiating the casting hurdle. This is often a matter for discussion between writer, director and producer, prior to production.

Beware the famous theatrical adage 'you got to have a gimmick'. Never let anybody convince you that innovation is a bad thing but try not to innovate just for the sake of it. The best way to get noticed is by writing a good play. Be careful of using cynical marketing ploys in order to sell your work. Plays with a strong regional voice are eagerly received by many theatre companies, but do not attempt to 'regionalise' a play that you have already written in order to pitch it at a specific theatre.

It is easy to forget that the primary objective in the theatre is to entertain. Try to grab the audience's attention as quickly as possible. Many scripts suffer from elaborate 'set-up' before the drama of the play can actually begin. A laborious introduction to character and situation is a guaranteed way of losing your audience (metaphorically and physically).

No matter how tightly plotted a play is, it will always be undermined by poor dialogue. Strangely, many writers are apt to forget that dialogue is written to be spoken. It is often useful to read your work aloud, especially if you are new to play writing. If a line is difficult to read, re-write it. Try not to produce 'interchangeable' dialogue. Each character should have their own distinctive voice, tone, rhythm and thought processes (spoken and unspoken). Check back through the play. How easy is it to distinguish between characters?

Do not overload the script with stage directions. Detailed notes about set design and lighting requirements will often be ignored. Ultimately, it is the job of the director to realise your work on stage and, whilst your input will undoubtedly be canvassed, it is not your responsibility to produce the play. It is the director's job to direct and the designer's job to design. Similarly, actors object to detailed notes in the script, indicating how their lines should be delivered.

Reviewing your work

Resist the temptation to start editing your play the moment you have finished writing. Apart from missing glaring errors in the script, you can easily lose sight of the essential qualities of the play, and edit simply for the sake of editing. Allow it to sit for a few weeks before doing anything more. It is very easy to find yourself swept along on a tide of euphoria as you finish writing, but this can be delusional.

Viewing your own work with a truly objective eye is always difficult, but it is an ability that can be cultivated with time. It may be easier to accept constructive criticism from someone whose opinion you value, before entrusting your script to the tender mercies of a theatre's literary department. Make any alterations to your script that you consider appropriate. There will rarely be an opportunity to re-submit a rejected script.

Approaching theatre companies

Once you are satisfied that your script is ready to send out, stop and take stock. Remember, it is not necessary to have an agent in order to send your work to a theatre. Although an agent's relationship with a director or literary manager may result in a faster response to a script, lack of representation should not count against you. Theatre companies are always on the lookout for new talent. However, it is important to bear in mind that a number of opinions about your work will have been formed before the script is even opened.

Many of the initial obstacles you need to overcome are not related to the script itself. Even envelopes and cover letters present problems for the unwary. Never forget that literary managers are sensitive creatures. A script addressed 'dear sir or madam' is an indication that the play is being sent out as a circular, with no specific focus. A bit of research helps avoid this embarrassment. Do not email your script unless a theatre expressly requests that you do this. Even in this technological age, it is still preferable to send a script by post.

Avoid unnecessary script embellishments. A simple cover letter, brief outline of previous work and a clean (white) A4 play text is all that is expected. Fancy binding, photographs, CDs, projected set designs, casting suggestions, etc, will have a strangely dispiriting effect on the script reader. Allow the play to speak for itself. It should go without saying (but unfortunately does not) that all text must be printed in black ink. The use of multi-coloured inks to distinguish between characters will undoubtedly show you up as a novice. Colour blind literary managers will be disinclined to sympathise with you.

You do not need to invest in costly script-formatting software as there is no professionally approved standard for the layout of play texts. A number of software programmes offer script templates; these are also downloadable from the internet. A cursory glance through a handful of contemporary play scripts will reveal the myriad of different page layouts employed by playwrights and publishers. Find the layout that is right for you. Allow wide margins, with space at the head and foot of each page. Secure the script in such a way that pages can be turned easily and make sure that each page is numbered.

Waiting for a response

Once your script has been delivered into the hands of a theatre company, do be prepared to wait. Many theatres will write to acknowledge receipt of the script. Some theatres will also give an indication of how long it will take them to offer a response. If you have heard nothing after six months it might be worth dropping the theatre a line (if only to retrieve your script), but do take into account the sheer volume of scripts they receive.

When the theatre company finally responds, you are unlikely to be offered in-depth analysis of your work, unless they show an interest in producing the play.

Again, this is due to the vast quantity of unsolicited material they receive. In certain cases, brief comments may be offered. Companies which focus exclusively on new writing may provide more detailed script reports.

Some theatres offer a script-reading service, providing a comprehensive response to the play for a small fee. This can be one of the most effective ways of gaining objective professional advice about your work. Although charging for this feedback may seem mercenary, it is important to remember that script readers are paid very little for their services. Many readers have considerable knowledge of the theatre and their advice can be invaluable to a new writer.

Even if a script is unsuitable, an artistic director or literary manager may still want to meet with the writer. Although this will not necessarily lead to future production, it is an indication that they see you as a writer of promise. This is a good opportunity to forge a relationship with a theatre, and may result in a speedier response to any work you submit in the future. Unless the theatre requests a re-write, a play that is re-written as a result of feedback from the literary department will almost certainly be returned unread.

There is nothing more depressing than the thud of returned play scripts dropping through the letterbox. Choosing a play for production is a subjective process, reflecting the tastes of the literary department and the predilections of the theatre company. Even good plays are rejected. Try not to be disheartened by your first rejection letter. Chances are you will have to endure many more.

Although your play may have been read more than once and discussed at a readers panel meeting, the literary manager's decision is final. There are stories (sadly not apocryphal) of playwrights attempting to employ strong-arm tactics in order to gain production of their work. This is a risky gambit. There is a subtle distinction between single-minded dedication to your work and psychosis. Be careful not to cross this line. Allow a day of mourning for your rejected script, then move on.

In production

On the other hand, what if a theatre is interested in producing your play? Do not feel pressured into making an immediate decision. It is easy, especially if you have never had your work produced, to succumb to flattery. Bide your time. It is worth considering that many theatres enjoy the kudos of premiering new work, but once your play has had its first production (unless it is a runaway success) other theatres may be reluctant to produce it.

If a theatre expresses an interest in commissioning you or optioning an existing play (offering a fixed term within which to produce your play), it is advisable to seek the professional advice of an agent. However, this can take time, so do not lose heart if an agent is not immediately forthcoming. Most theatres will offer an agreed standard contract, which provides a degree of security for the writer and the theatre. If in doubt, consider taking independent legal advice or contact the Writers' Guild.

Do not despair if you are rejected by an agent. Many agencies are simply too busy with existing clients to take on new writers. An agent may enjoy your work but not feel enthusiastic enough to represent you. It is a question of personal taste. Persevere until you find an agent who is as enthusiastic about your work as you are.

Once a theatre has optioned your work, things can move quickly. Even the largest of theatre companies may discover holes in their programming which need to be filled. Conversely, you may have to wait a considerable period of time before your work can be staged. Either way, in principle you should have the right to agree on a director and designer for your play. In practice this may never happen. Many theatres rely on staff directors, or a pool of tried and tested practitioners. Financial considerations can also be restrictive.

The relationship between the writer and director is, of course, vital to the success of a production. Try not to be precious about your work. Be as objective as possible. Cuts or re-writes will often be suggested, before or during the rehearsal process. This is not an attempt to undermine the writer, but an opportunity to consolidate the script. Of course, if you have any reservations about a script alteration, talk to the director or literary manager about it. Changes to the script cannot be made without your express approval, but do not pull rank just for the sake of it.

Insist on access to the publicity material a theatre produces for your play. It is a contractual obligation and the theatre should honour this. In many cases the marketing department will approach you for blurb (for flyers and press releases). This is the first contact most audience members will have with your play, and you will want to make sure that your work is accurately represented.

Again, if you are unhappy about any aspect of the production, speak to the director. Most problems can be easily rectified if nipped in the bud.

Selling your script

Although you would be hard pressed to find a playwright who took up the profession for financial gain, money is still a consideration. In the case of a non-commissioned play, the majority of the fee will be paid on signature of the contract, with a final sum payable on acceptance of the play. This gives the producing theatre the opportunity to request any revisions to the script before agreeing to production. A proportion of the fee will be a non-returnable advance against royalties. In most cases the royalty will be 8% of the net box office receipts.

If a theatre commissions a play from scratch, the fee should be paid in the following way: roughly half of the total fee on signature of the contract; a further quarter of the fee on completion of the first draft; the final quarter on acceptance of the script for production. Again, a proportion of the fee will be a non-returnable advance against royalties. As with a non-commissioned play, the royalty will normally be 8% of net box office receipts.

It is this final sum of the commission fee which is the most difficult to predict. When is a play ready for production? How long is a piece of string? You may well find that you spend anywhere between six and 18 months, even longer, restructuring your play so that it is suitable for production. Only in exceptional cases will the first draft of a script be accepted. Some theatres may never produce the resulting play, although the 'policy' of over-commissioning is perhaps not such a prevalent evil as writers are often led to believe. Of greater concern is the tendency to option a play, then leave the playwright waiting indefinitely for the work to be produced.

A commission does not guarantee production. Once a script has been rejected, all rights revert to the writer, who will then be entitled to offer the script to another company.

Financially, it is important to pace yourself. The commission fee may have to last you a considerable period of time. Tempting though it may be, resist the urge to cash your first cheque and embark on a shopping spree.

Many established writers choose not to write to commission, preferring instead to write a play as and when the muse takes them. For a young or relatively inexperienced writer this may not be the most practical way of keeping body and soul together.

Playing the field

Even if you have managed to secure the services of an agent, this is no guarantee of work. It is in a playwright's best interests to actively seek employment.

Nowadays, it would be extremely unusual for a writer's first play to be offered a West End run. A play which proves itself in the regions may be offered a transfer, but this would be the exception, not the rule. However, there are a number of fringe venues in London that may provide an opportunity to see your work staged. This will not necessarily result in overnight success, but it can often bring your work to the attention of reviewers and other theatre companies.

There is also a vibrant theatrical community at work outside London. Regional theatres are keen to foster links with local writers, and this can be a very good way of establishing yourself as a playwright. Many subsidised touring companies may also consider commissioning work, although this will usually be tailored to specific considerations, such as the number of performers in the company, suitability for touring, etc.

Although persistence will not always be rewarded, it is certainly an approach worth trying. If all else fails, turn impresario and produce your own work. Many playwrights have established themselves in this way, forming their own companies and producing plays on the fringe circuit. Without a production a play is little more than a blueprint.

Christopher William Hill is a recent recipient of an Arts Council Theatre Writing Bursary and has been writer-in-residence at Plymouth Theatre Royal (Pearson Playwrights' Scheme Bursary). He has worked as a degree lecturer, reader and script editor. His stage plays include *Multiplex*, *Lam*, *Song of the Western Men* and *Blood Red, Saffron Yellow*.

Theatre producers

This list is divided into London theatres (below), provincial theatres (page 336) and touring companies (page 341). See also *Writing for the theatre* on page 327 and *Literary agents for television, film, radio and theatre* on page 692.

There are various types of theatre companies and it is helpful to know what they include. Metropolitan new writing theatre companies are largely London-based theatres which specialise in new writing (Hampstead Theatre, Royal Court, Bush Theatre, Soho Theatre, etc). Regional repertory theatre companies are theatres based in towns and cities across the country which may do new plays as part of their repertoire. Commercial producing managements are unsubsidised profit-making theatre producers who may occasionally be interested in new plays to take on tour or to present in the West End. Small and/or middle-scale touring companies are companies (mostly touring) which may exist to explore or promote specific themes or are geared towards specific kinds of audiences.

Individuals also have a role. Independent theatre practitioners include, for example, actors who may be looking for interesting plays in which to appear. Independent theatre producers include, for example, young directors or producers who are looking for plays to produce at the onset of their career. There are also drama schools and amateur dramatics companies.

LONDON

Bill Kenwright Ltd
BKL House, 106 Harrow Road, London W2 1RR
tel 020-7446 6200 *fax* 020-7446 6222
email info@kenwright.com
Managing Director Bill Kenwright, *Deputy Managing Director* Simon Meadon

Commercial producing management presenting revivals and new works for the West End and for touring theatres.

Bush Theatre
Shepherd's Bush Green, London W12 8QD
tel 020-7602 3703 *fax* 020-7602 7614
email info@bushtheatre.co.uk
website www.bushtheatre.co.uk
Literary Manager Nicola Wilson

Welcomes unsolicited full-length stage scripts (plus one small and one large sae). Commissions writers, including those at an early stage in their career. Produces 9 premieres a year.

Finborough Theatre
118 Finborough Road, London SW10 9ED
tel 020-7244 7439 *fax* 020-7835 1853
email admin@finboroughtheatre.co.uk
website www.finboroughtheatre.co.uk
Artistic Director Neil McPherson

A new writing venue. Also presents revivals of neglected 20th century plays, music theatre and recently has staged UK premieres of foreign work, particularly from Ireland, the USA and Canada. The theatre building has been recently refurbished. The theatre is also available for hire and the fee is sometimes negotiable to encourage interesting work. Unsolicited scripts can no longer be accepted. Founded 1980.

Hampstead Theatre
Eton Avenue, London NW3 3EU
tel 020-7449 4200 *fax* 020-7449 4201
website www.hampsteadtheatre.com
Contact Jeanie O'Hare, Literary Manager

The newly opened theatre has been designed with writers in mind. It allows for bold and flexible staging within an intimate auditorium. The artistic policy is the production of the best British and international new plays. All plays are read and discussed, with feedback given to all writers with potential. It usually takes 2–3 months to respond. Include postage with submissions. No plays accepted by email. For futher details see website.

King's Head Theatre
115 Upper Street, London N1 1QN
tel 020-7226 8561 *fax* 020-7226 8507
website www.kingsheadtheatre.org
Contact Dan Crawford, Artistic Director

Off-West End theatre producing revivals and new works. No unsolicited submissions.

Lyric Hammersmith
King Street, London W6 0QL
tel (08700) 500511 *fax* 020-8741 5965
email enquiries@lyric.co.uk
website www.lyric.co.uk
Directors Simon Mellor, Neil Bartlett

A producing theatre as well as a receiving venue for work by new writers, translators, performers and composers. Unsolicited scripts for in-house productions not accepted.

Man in the Moon Theatre
392 King's Road, London SW3 5UZ
tel 020-7351 5701 *fax* 020-7351 1873
Programming Director Nick Elsen

65-seat theatre. Part of each season is reserved for new writing which links with the season theme. Phone theatre for details. Plays scheduled in seasons of 3–4 months for in-house productions.

Michael Codron Plays Ltd
Aldwych Theatre Offices, Aldwych,
London WC2B 4DF
tel 020-7240 8291 *fax* 020-7240 8467

Michael White
48 Dean Street, London W1D 5BF
tel 020-7734 7707 *fax* 020-7734 7727

Moral Support
Studio 2, Greville House, 35 Greville Street,
London EC1N 8TB
tel (07958) 418515
website www.moralsupportonline.org
Contact Zoe Klinger

The company brings together writers, musicians and other freelance practitioners to create new work with the emphasis on producing new writing and performance styles, to be performed in a variety of locations. Its performance technique has been described as 'an utterly original theatrical language'. Available for commissions of new plays, performance and dance. Established 1997.

The Old Red Lion Theatre
418 St John Street, London EC1V 4NJ
tel/fax 020-7833 3053
Artistic Director Melanie Tait

Interested in contemporary pieces, especially from unproduced writers. No funding: incoming

production company pays to rent the theatre. Sae essential with enquiries. Founded 1977.

Orange Tree Theatre
1 Clarence Street, Richmond, Surrey TW9 2SA
tel 020-8940 0141 *fax* 020-8332 0369
email admin@orange-tree.demon.co.uk
website www.orangetreetheatre.co.uk

Producing venue. The theatre does not currently have a literary manager and no longer has a studio theatre. New works presented generally come from agents or through writers' groups.

Polka Theatre for Children
240 The Broadway, London SW19 1SB
tel 020-8545 8320 *fax* 020-8545 8365
email info@polkatheatre.com
website www.polkatheatre.com
Artistic Director Annie Wood, *Director of New Writing* Richard Shannon

Exclusively for children, the Main Theatre seats 300 and The Adventure Theatre seats 80. Programmed for 18 months to 2 years in advance. Theatre of new writing, with targeted commissions; contact Director of New Writing. Founded 1967.

The Questors Theatre
Mattock Lane, London W5 5BQ
tel 020-8567 0011 *fax* 020-8567 8736
email nw@questors.org.uk
website www.questors.org.uk
Theatre Manager Paul Maurel, *Contact for new work* Evan Rule

Largest community theatre in Europe producing around 20 shows a year, specialising in modern and classical world drama. No unsolicited scripts.

Really Useful Theatres
Manor House, 21 Soho Square, London W1D 3QP
tel 020-7494 5200 *fax* 020-7434 1217
email info@rutheatres.com
website www.rutheatres.com
Production Director Nica Burns

Owns 13 West End theatres: Adelphi, Apollo, Cambridge, Duchess, Garrick, Gielgud, Her Majesty's, London Palladium, Lyric Shaftesbury Avenue, New London, Palace, Queens and Theatre Royal Drury Lane. Now commissions new plays from both established writers and new talent. Founded 1978.

Robert Fox Ltd
6 Beauchamp Place, London SW3 1NG
tel 020-7584 6855 *fax* 020-7225 1638
email rf@robertfoxltd.com

Independent theatre and film production company. Stages productions mainly in the West End and on Broadway. Welcomes scripts from new writers. Founded 1980.

Royal Court Theatre

(English Stage Company Ltd)
Sloane Square, London SW1W 8AS
tel 020-7565 5050 *fax* 020-7565 5002
Literary Manager Graham Whybrow

New plays.

Royal National Theatre

South Bank, London SE1 9PX
tel 020-7452 3323 *fax* 020-7452 3350
Literary Manager Jack Bradley

Limited opportunity for the production of
unsolicited material, but submissions welcome.
No synopses or treatments. Send to Literary
Manager, together with an sae with return postage
for the script.

Royal Shakespeare Company

1 Earlham Street, London WC2H 9LL
tel 020-7845 0515 *fax* 020-7845 0505
Artistic Director Michael Boyd, *Dramaturg* Paul
Sirett

The RSC is a classical theatre company based in
Stratford-upon-Avon. It has recently transformed
itself to create the opportunity for different
ensemble companies to work on distinct projects
that will open both in Stratford and at various
venues in London. The Company also has an
annual residency in Newcastle and tours both
nationally and internationally.

As well as Shakespeare, English classics and
foreign classics in translation, ambitious new plays
counterpoint the RSC's repertory, especially those
which celebrate language. The Dramaturgy
Department is proactive rather than reactive, and
seeks out the plays and playwrights it wishes to
commission. It will read translations of classic
foreign works submitted, or of contemporary works
where theoriginal writer and/or translator is known.
It is unable to read unsolicited works from less
established writers, and can only return scripts if an
sae is enclosed with the submission.

Soho Theatre and Writers' Centre

21 Dean Street, London W1D 3NE
tel 020-7287 5060 *fax* 020-7287 5061
email writers@sohotheatre.com
website www.sohotheatre.com
Artistic Director Abigail Morris

Always on the look out for new plays and
playwrights and welcome unsolicited scripts. These
are read by a professional panel who write a
detailed critical report. Also offer various levels of
workshop facilities, including rehearsed reading and
platform performances, for promising playwrights,
and in-depth script development with the Artistic
Director and Literary Manager. See also the Verity
Bargate Award on page 515.

Tabard Theatre

2 Bath Road, London W4 1LW
tel 020-8995 6035 *fax* 020-8994 5985

The theatre will be under new management from
August 2003.

TEG Productions

11-15 Betterton Street, London WC2H 9BP
tel 020-7379 1066 *fax* 020-7836 9454
email teg@plays.demon.co.uk
Contact Jeremy Meadow

Produces 2–4 new plays with commercial potential
and revivals per year, all with 'star' casting.
Welcomes scripts from new writers. Founded 1997.

Theatre of Comedy Company

Shaftesbury Theatre, 210 Shaftesbury Avenue,
London WC2H 8DP
tel 020-7379 3345 *fax* 020-7836 8181
Contact Keith Murray

Commercial producing management creating a
broad range of plays. Welcomes new scripts from
writers. Founded 1983.

Theatre Royal, Stratford East

Gerry Raffles Square, London E15 1BN
tel 020-8534 7374 *fax* 020-8534 8381
website www.stratfordeast.com
Artistic Director Philip Hedley, *Deputy Director*
Mr Kerry Michael

Middle-scale producing theatre. Specialises in new
writing: currently developing contemporary British
musicals. Welcomes new plays that are unproduced,
full in length, and which relate to its diverse
multicultural, Black and Asian audience.

The Tricycle Theatre Company

Tricycle Theatre, 269 Kilburn High Road,
London NW6 7JR
tel 020-7372 6611 *fax* 020-7328 0795
Contact Nicolas Kent

Metropolitan new writing theatre company with
particular focus on Black and Irish writing. Script-
reading service but fee charged for unsolicited
scripts.

Triumph Proscenium Productions Ltd

Suite 4, Waldorf Chambers, 11 Aldwych,
London WC2B 4DA
tel 020-7343 8800 *fax* 020-7343 8801
email dcwtpp@aol.com

Unicorn Theatre for Children

Admin offices St Mark's Studios,
Chillingworth Road, London N7 8QJ
tel 020-7700 0702 *fax* 020-7700 3870
email admin@unicorntheatre.com
website www.unicorntheatre.com

Administrative Director Christopher Moxon, *Artistic Director* Tony Graham, *Associate Director* Emily Gray, *Literary Manager* Carl Miller, *Associate Artist (Literary)* Charles Way

Six productions a year for children aged 4–12 and their families – new writing and adaptations.

Warehouse Theatre

Dingwall Road, Croydon CR0 2NF
tel 020-8681 1257 *fax* 020-8688 6699
email info@warehousetheatre.co.uk
website www.warehousetheatre.co.uk
Artistic Director Ted Craig

South London's premier new writing theatre. Seats 100. Produces 3–5 in-house plays a year and co-produces with companies which share the commitment to new work. It continues to build upon a tradition of discovering and nurturing new writers: activities include a monthly writers' workshop and the annual International Playwriting Festival (see page 521). Unsolicited scripts are welcome but it is more advisable to submit plays via the Festival. Also hosts youth theatre workshop, Saturday morning children's theatre and community outreach programme.

Young Vic Theatre Company

66 The Cut, London SE1 8LZ
tel 020-7922 8400 *fax* 020-7922 8401
email info@youngvic.org
website www.youngvic.org
General Manager Mark Feakins

Metropolitan producing theatre producing classic plays. Founded 1969.

PROVINCIAL

Abbey Theatre

26 Lower Abbey Street, Dublin 1,
Republic of Ireland
tel (01) 8872200 *fax* (01) 8729177
Artistic Director Ben Barnes, *Managing Director* Brian Jackson

Mainly produces plays written by Irish authors or on Irish subjects. Foreign classics are however regularly produced.

Actual Theatre

25 Hamilton Drive, Glasgow G12 8DN
tel/fax 0141-339 0654
Artistic Director Susan C. Triesman

Produces 'difficult and taboo subjects' as well as experimental theatre. Welcomes scripts from new writers. Founded 1980.

The Belgrade Theatre

Belgrade Square, Coventry CV1 1GS
tel 024-7625 6431 *fax* 024-7655 0680
email admin@belgrade.co.uk
website www.belgrade.co.uk
Contact Denise Atcheson

Produces new plays developed in conjunction with Theatre Absolute, through the Writing House.

Birmingham Repertory Theatre Ltd

Broad Street, Birmingham B1 2EP
tel 0121-245 2000 *fax* 0121-245 2100
email info@birmingham-rep.co.uk
website www.birmingham-rep.co.uk
Artistic Director Jonathon Church, *Executive Director* Stuart Rogers, *Associate Director (Literary)* Ben Payne

Aims to provide a platform for the best work from new writers from both within and beyond the West Midlands region. The development, commissioning and production of new writing takes place across the full range of the theatre's programme including: the Main House (capacity 830); the Door (capacity 190 max.), a space dedicated to new work; and its annual Community tours. Unsolicited submissions are welcome principally from the point of view of beginning a relationship with a writer. Priority in such development work is given to writers from the region.

The Bootleg Theatre Company

23 Burgess Green, Bishopdown, Salisbury, Wilts. SP1 3EL
tel (01722) 421476
email colin@bootlegtheatrecompany.fsnet.co.uk
Contact Colin Burden

Metropolitan new writing theatre company and independent theatre practitioner. Stages

2 productions per year. Welcomes scripts from new writers. Founded 1985.

Bristol Old Vic

Theatre Royal, King Street, Bristol BS1 4ED
tel 0117-949 3993 *fax* 0117-949 3996
website www.bristol-old-vic.co.uk
Associate Director Gareth Machin, *Executive Director* Sarah Smith

Programme includes class plays in the Theatre Royal (650 seats) and new writing in the New Vic Studio (150 seats). Plays must have enough popular appeal to attract an audience of significant size. Will read and report on unsolicited scripts for a fee of £25 per script.

Also seeks emerging talent to the Basement, a profit share venue (50 seats) committed to producing one-act plays by unproven writers. Will read plays free of charge but no report can be provided. New Vic Studio often receives productions of new plays from visiting companies.

The Byre Theatre of St Andrews

Abbey Street, St Andrews KY16 9LA
tel (01334) 476288 *fax* (01334) 475370
email enquiries@byretheatre.com
website www.byretheatre.com
Artistic Director Ken Alexander

Offers an exciting year-round programme of contemporary and classic drama, dance, concerts, opera, comedy and innovative education and community events. Operates a blend of in-house and touring productions. Maintains a policy of producing new and established work. Education programme caters for all ages with Youth workshops and Haydays (for 50+). Offers support for new writing through the Byre Writers, a well-established and successful playwrights group.

Chester Gateway Theatre Trust Ltd

Hamilton Place, Chester CH1 2BH
tel (01244) 318603 *fax* (01244) 317277
website www.gateway-theatre.org
Chief Executive Jasmine Hendry

Mid-scale theatre with 2 in-house productions per year. Also presents a diverse programme of theatre, dance, comedy and music. Education and access department undertakes schools drama tours and writers' workshops.

Chichester Festival Theatre Ltd

Chichester Festival Theatre, Oaklands Park, Chichester, West Sussex PO19 4AP
tel (01243) 784437 *fax* (01243) 787288
email admin@cft.org.uk
website www.cft.org.uk
Artistic Directors Martin Dungas, Ruth MacKenzie, Steven Pimlott

Festival Season March–Oct in Festival and Minerva Theatres together with a year-round education programme.

Clwyd Theatr Cymru

Mold, Flintshire CH7 1YA
tel (01352) 756331 *fax* (01352) 701558
email drama@celtic.co.uk
wjames@clwyd-theatr-cymru.co.uk
website www.clwyd-theatr-cymru.co.uk
Director Terry Hands, *Literary Manager* William James

Produces a season of plays each year performed by a core ensemble, along with tours throughout Wales (in English and Welsh). Plays are a mix of classics, revivals, contemporary drama and new writing. Considers plays by Welsh writers or with Welsh themes.

Colchester Mercury Theatre Ltd

Balkerne Gate, Colchester, Essex CO1 1PT
tel (01206) 577006 *fax* (01206) 769607
email mercury.theatre@virgin.net
Contact (Playwrights' Group) Adrian Stokes

Regional repertory theatre presenting works to a wide audience. Produces some new work, mainly commissioned. Runs local Playwrights' Group for adults with a serious commitment to writing plays.

The Coliseum Theatre

Fairbottom Street, Oldham OL1 3SW
tel 0161-624 1731 *fax* 0161-624 5318
Chief Executive Kevin Shaw

Interested in new work, particularly plays set in the North. Contact by letter with scenario initially.

Contact Theatre Company

Oxford Road, Manchester M15 6JA
tel 0161-274 3434 *fax* 0161-274 0640
Artistic Director John E. McGrath

Interested in working with and for young people aged 13–30. Send sae for writers' guidelines.

Derby Playhouse Ltd

Theatre Walk, Eagle Centre, Derby DE1 2NF
tel (01332) 363271 *fax* (01332) 547200
email admin@derbyplayhouse.co.uk
website www.derbyplayhouse.co.uk
Chief Executive Karen Hebden, *Creative Producer* Stephen Edwards

Regional repertory company. Unsolicited scripts: send a letter with synopsis, a resumé of your writing experience and any 10 pages of your script. A review of this material will determine whether a complete copy of the script is required.

Druid Theatre Company

Druid Theatre, Chapel Lane, Galway,
Republic of Ireland
tel (091) 568617/568660 *fax* (091) 563109
email info@druidtheatre.com
Artistic Director Garry Hynes, *Managing Director*
Fergal McGrath

Producing company presenting a wide range of
national and international plays. Emphasis on new
Irish writing.

The Dukes

Moor Lane, Lancaster LA1 1QE
tel (01524) 598505 *fax* (01524) 598519
Artistic Director Ian Hastings

Dundee Repertory Theatre

Tay Square, Dundee DD1 1PB
tel (01382) 227684
website www.dundeereptheatre.co.uk
Artistic Director Hamish Glen

Regional repertory theatre company. Concentrates
resources on commissions for contemporary
Scottish writers.

Everyman Theatre

Regent Street, Cheltenham, Glos. GL50 1HQ
tel (01242) 512515 *fax* (01242) 224305
email admin@everymantheatre.org.uk
website www.everymantheatre.org.uk
Chief Executive Philip Bernays, *Artistic Director* Sue
Colverd

Regional presenting and producing theatre
promoting a wide range of plays. Small-scale
experimental, youth and educational work
encouraged in The Other Space studio theatre.
Contact the Artistic Director before submitting
material.

Everyman and Playhouse Theatres

Liverpool and Merseyside Theatres Trust Ltd,
13 Hope Street, Liverpool L1 9BH
tel 0151-708 0338 *fax* 0151-709 0398
email info@everymanplayhouse.com
website www.everymanplayhouse.com
Executive Director Jo Beddoe, *General Manager* Tim
Brunsden

Produces and presents theatre.

Focus Theatre Company (Scotland)

c/o The Ramshorn Theatre, 98 Ingram Street,
Glasgow G1 1ES
tel 0141-552 3489 *fax* 0141-553 2036
email ramshorn.theatre@strath.ac.uk
Artistic Director Susan C. Triesman

Produces women's plays and feminist work. Also
holds workshops. Welcomes scripts from new
writers. Founded 1982.

Grand Theatre

Singleton Street, Swansea SA1 3QJ
tel (01792) 475242 *fax* (01792) 475379
email gary.iles@swansea.gov.uk
website www.swanseagrand.co.uk
General Manager Gary Iles

Regional receiving theatre.

Harrogate Theatre

Oxford Street, Harrogate,
North Yorkshire HG1 1QF
tel (01423) 502710 *fax* (01423) 563205
website www.harrogatetheatre.com
Associate Director Steve Ansell

Regional repertory theatre and touring company
producing both classic and contemporary plays.
Scripts welcome from writers within the Yorkshire
region; 10-page excerpts from writers outside the
Yorkshire region.

Haymarket Theatre Company

The Haymarket Theatre, Wote Street, Basingstoke,
Hants RG21 7NW
tel (01256) 323073 *fax* (01256) 357130
email info@haymarket.org.uk
website www.haymarket.org.uk

Produces up to 8 main house shows a year plus a
full and integrated education programme.
Interested in co-producing and up to 4 visiting
shows. Introducing a 3-year ensemble acting
company-in-residence from Aug 2003.

Leicester Haymarket Theatre

Belgrave Gate, Leicester LE1 3YQ
tel 0116-253 0021 *fax* 0116-251 3310
email enquiry@leicesterhaymarkettheatre.org
website www.leicesterhaymarkettheatre.org

Regional producing theatre company.

Library Theatre Company

St Peter's Square, Manchester M2 5PD
tel 0161-234 1913 *fax* 0161-228 6481
Contact Artistic Director

Contemporary drama, classics, plays for children.
Aims to produce drama which illuminates the
contemporary world; scripts from new writers
considered.

Live Theatre

27 Broad Chare, Quayside,
Newcastle upon Tyne NE1 3DF
tel 0191-232 1232
email info@live.org.uk
website www.live.org.uk
Enquiries Wendy Barnfather, *Script Submissions*
Jeremy Herrin

New writing theatre company and venue. Stages 3–4

productions per year of new writing, comedy, musical–comedy, etc.

LLt
Unity Theatre, 1 Hope Place, Liverpool L1 9BG
tel 0151-709 4332 *fax* 0151-709 7182
email lltpro@dircon.co.uk
Contact Paul Goetzee

New writing development company. Productions and showcases when funding permits. Promising scripts developed to production standard, and links created with other new writing theatres and organisations. Send sae for return of script. Founded 1983.

The New Theatre Co
The New Theatre, Temple Bar, 43 East Essex Street, Dublin 2, Republic of Ireland
tel (1) 6703361 *fax* (1) 6711943
email info@thenewtheatre.com
website www.thenewtheatre.com
Joint Artistic Directors Anthony Fox, Ronian Wilmot

Innovative theatre producing plays by classic as well as Irish writers whose work deals with issues pertaining to contemporary Irish society. Welcomes scripts from new writers. Founded 1997.

New Vic Theatre
Etruria Road, Newcastle under Lyme ST5 0JG
tel (01782) 717954 *fax* (01782) 712885
email admin@newvictheatre.org.uk
Artistic Director Gwenda Hughes, *General Manager* Nick Jones

Europe's first purpose built theatre-in-the-round, presenting classics, music theatre, contemporary plays, new plays.

The New Wolsey Theatre
Civic Drive, Ipswich, Suffolk IP1 2AS
tel (01473) 295911 *fax* (01473) 295910
Chief Executive Sarah Holmes, *Artistic Director* Peter Rowe, *Artistic Associate, Community & Education* Mary Swan

Mixed economy theatre. New writing and co-productions always condsidered.

Northcott Theatre
Stocker Road, Exeter, Devon EX4 4QB
tel (01392) 223999
Artistic Director Ben Crocker

Regional producing theatre company.

Northern Stage (Theatrical Productions) Ltd
Newcastle Playhouse, Barras Bridge, Newcastle upon Tyne NE1 1RH
tel 0191-232 3366 *fax* 0191-261 8093
email info@northernstage.com
website www.northernstage.com

Artistic Director Alan Lyddiard
Major company producing and presenting international work.

Nottingham Playhouse
Nottingham Theatre Trust Ltd, Wellington Circus, Nottingham NG1 5AF
tel 0115-947 4361 *fax* 0115-947 5759
website www.nottinghamplayhouse.co.uk/playhouse
Chief Executive Stephanie Sirr, *Artistic Director* Giles Croft

Works closely with communities of Nottingham and Nottinghamshire. Takes 6 months to read unsolicited MSS.

Nuffield Theatre
University Road, Southampton SO17 1TR
tel 023-8031 5500 *fax* 023-8031 5511
Script Executive tba

Repertory theatre producing straight plays and musicals, and some small-scale fringe work. Interested in new plays.

Octagon Theatre
Howell Croft South, Bolton BL1 1SB
tel (01204) 529407 *fax* (01204) 556502
Executive Director John Blackmore, *Operations Manager* Lesley Etherington, *Artistic Director* Mark Babych, *Associate/Activ8 Director* Sue Reddish

Fully flexible professional theatre. Year round programme of own productions and visiting companies.

The Palace Theatre Watford Ltd
Clarendon Road, Watford, Herts. WD17 1JZ
tel (01923) 235455 *fax* (01923) 819664
Contact Lawrence Till, Artistic Director

Regional repertory theatre. Produces 8 plays each year, both classic and contemporary drama. Welcomes synopses of new plays before submitting scripts.

Peacock Theatre
The Abbey Theatre, 26 Lower Abbey Street, Dublin 1, Republic of Ireland
tel (01) 8872200 *fax* (01) 8729177
Artistic Director Ben Barnes, *Managing Director* Brian Jackson, *Peacock Theatre Director* Ali Curran

Experimental theatre associated with the Abbey Theatre; mostly new writing.

Perth Theatre Ltd
185 High Street, Perth PH1 5UW
tel (01738) 472700 *fax* (01738) 624576
email theatre@perth.org.uk
website www.perth.org.uk/perth/theatre.htm
General Manager Paul Hackett

Combination of 3- and 4-weekly repertoire of plays and musicals, incoming tours, one-night variety events and studio productions.

Plymouth Theatre Royal

Theatre Royal, Royal Parade, Plymouth PL1 2TR
tel (01752) 230340 fax (01752) 225892
Chief Executive Adrian Vinken, Artistic Director Simon Stokes

Stages small, middle and large-scale drama and music theatre. Commissions and produces new plays. Unsolicited scripts with sae are read and responded to. Send one script at a time by post only; no email submissions.

Queen's Theatre, Hornchurch

(Havering Theatre Trust Ltd)
Billet Lane, Hornchurch, Essex RM11 1QT
tel (01708) 456118 fax (01708) 452348
email info@queens-theatre.co.uk
website www.queens-theatre.co.uk
Artistic Director Bob Carlton

500-seat producing theatre serving outer East London with permanent company of actors/musicians presenting 8 mainhouse and 2 TIE productions each year. Treatments welcome; unsolicited scripts may be returned unread. Queen's Theatre Writer's Group showcases new work Sept–March; contact Education & Outreach Manager for details.

The Ramshorn Theatre/Strathclyde Theatre Group

98 Ingram Street, Glasgow G1 1ES
tel 0141-552 3489 fax 0141-553 2036
email ramshorn.theatre@strath.ac.uk
Contact Susan C. Triesman (Director of Drama, University of Strathclyde)

Develops new writing (including experimental) through Ramshorn New Playwrights Initiative. Founded 1992.

Royal Exchange Theatre Company Ltd

St Ann's Square, Manchester M2 7DH
tel 0161-833 9333 fax 0161-832 0881
website www.royalexchange.co.uk
Executive Director Patricia Weller

Varied programme of major classics, new plays, musicals, contemporary British and European drama; also explores the creative work of diverse cultures.

Royal Lyceum Theatre Company

Royal Lyceum Theatre, Grindlay Street, Edinburgh EH3 9AX
tel 0131-248 4848 fax 0131-228 3955
email royallyceumtheatre@cableinet.co.uk
website www.lyceum.org.uk

Artistic Director Mark Thomson

Edinburgh's busiest repertory company, producing an all-year-round programme of classic, contemporary and new drama. Interested in work of Scottish writers.

Salisbury Playhouse

Malthouse Lane, Salisbury, Wilts. SP2 7RA
tel (01722) 320117 fax (01722) 421991
email info@salisburyplayhouse.com
Artistic Director Joanna Read

Regional repertory theatre producing a broad programme of classical and modern plays and new writing.

Scarborough Theatre Trust Ltd

Stephen Joseph Theatre, Westborough, Scarborough, North Yorkshire YO11 1JW
tel (01723) 370540 fax (01723) 360506
email enquiries@sjt.uk.com
website www.sjt.uk.com
Literary Manager Laura Harvey

Regional repertory theatre company which produces about 10 plays a year, many of which are premieres. The theatre has an excellent reputation for comedy. Plays should have a strong narrative and a desire to entertain, though nothing too lightweight will be considered. Enclose a sae with all submissions.

Sheffield Theatres

(Crucible, Crucible Studio & Lyceum)
55 Norfolk Street, Sheffield S1 1DA
tel 0114-249 5999 fax 0114-249 6003
Chief Executive Grahame Morris

Large-scale producing house with distinctive thrust stage; smallish studio; Victorian proscenium arch theatre used mainly for touring productions.

Sherman Theatre

Senghennydd Road, Cardiff CF24 4YE
tel 029-2064 6901 fax 029-2064 6902
General Manager Margaret Jones

Plays mainly for 15–25 age range, plus under 7's Christmas show. Founded 1974.

Show of Strength Theatre Company Ltd

74 Chessel Street, Bedminster, Bristol BS3 3DN
tel 0117-902 0235
Artistic Director Sheila Hannon

Small-scale company committed to producing new and unperformed work. Theatre season: Sept–Dec. Send sae for return of MSS. Founded 1986.

Theatre Royal

Windsor, Berks. SL4 1PS
tel (01753) 863444 fax (01753) 831673

Executive Producer Bill Kenwright, *Executive Director* Mark Piper

Regional producing theatre presenting a wide range of productions from classics to new plays.

Traverse Theatre
10 Cambridge Street, Edinburgh EH1 2ED
tel 0131-228 3223 *fax* 0131-229 8443
email roxana@traverse.co.uk hannah@traverse.co.uk
katherine@traverse.co.uk neil@traverse.co.uk
website www.traverse.co.uk
Literary Director Roxana Silbert, *Literary Development Officer* Hannah Rye, *International Literary Associate* Katherine Mendelsohn, *Literary Assistant* Neil Coull

Scotland's new writing theatre with a special interest in Scottish writers and writers based in Scotland. Will read unsolicited scripts but an sae must be included for return of script.

The West Yorkshire Playhouse
Playhouse Square, Quarry Hill, Leeds LS2 7UP
tel 0113-213 7800 *fax* 0113-213 7250
email mail@wyp.org.uk
Artistic Director Ian Brown, *Literary Manager* Alex Chisholm

Twin auditoria complex; community theatre. Has a policy of encouraging new writing from Yorkshire and Humberside region. Send script with an sae for its return to the Literary Manager.

York Citizens' Theatre Trust Ltd
Theatre Royal, St Leonard's Place, York YO1 7HD
tel (01904) 658162 *fax* (01904) 611534
Chief Executive Ludo Keston, *Artistic Director* Damian Cruden

Repertory productions, tours.

Yvonne Arnaud Theatre Management Ltd
Millbrook, Guildford, Surrey GU1 3UX
tel (01483) 440077 *fax* (01483) 564071
email yat@yvonne-arnaud.co.uk
website www.yvonne-arnaud.co.uk
Contact James Barber

Producing theatre which also receives productions.

TOURING COMPANIES

Actors Touring Company
Alford House, Aveline Street, London SE11 5DQ
tel 020-7735 8311 *fax* 020-7735 1031
email atc@atc-online.com
website www.atc-online.com
Executive Producer Emma Dunton

Small to medium-scale company producing innovative contemporary work for young audiences.

Compass Theatre Company
Carver Street Institute, 24 Rockingham Lane, Sheffield S1 4FW
tel 0114-275 5328 *fax* 0114-278 6931
email info@compasstheatrecompany.com
website www.compasstheatrecompany.com
Artistic Director Neil Sissons, *General Manager* Craig Dronfield

Touring classical theatre nationwide. Does not produce new plays.

Eastern Angles
Sir John Mills Theatre, Gatacre Road, Ipswich IP1 2LQ
tel (01473) 218202 *fax* (01473) 384999
email admin@easternangles.co.uk
website www.easternangles.co.uk
Contact Jill Streatfeild

Touring company producing new work with a regional theme. Stages 3 productions per year. Welcomes scripts from new writers. Founded 1982.

Graeae Theatre Company
Interchange Studios, Hampstead Town Hall Centre, 213 Haverstock Hill, London NW3 4QP
tel 020-7681 4755 *minicom* 020-7681 4757
fax 020-7681 4756
email info@graeae.org
website www.graeae.org
Executive Producer Roger Nelson, *Artistic Director* Jenny Sealey, *Administrator* Annette Cumper

Small-scale company. Welcomes scripts from disabled writers. Founded 1980.

The Hiss & Boo Company Ltd
1 Nyes Hill, Wineham Lane, Bolney, West Sussex RH17 5SD
tel (01444) 881707 *fax* (01444) 882057
email ian@hissboo.co.uk

Not much scope for new plays, but will consider comedy thrillers/chillers and plays/musicals for children. No unsolicited scripts – telephone first. Plays/synopses will be returned only if accompanied by an sae.

Hull Truck Theatre Co. Ltd
Hull Truck Theatre, Spring Street, Hull HU2 8RW
tel (01482) 224800 *fax* (01482) 581182

email admin@hulltruck.co.uk
website www.hulltruck.co.uk
Executive Director Joanne Gower, *Artistic Director* John Godber, *Associate Director* Gareth Tudor Price

World-renowned small-cast touring company presenting popular and accessible theatre. Produces some new work, mainly commissioned. Also presents the world premieres of the plays of John Godber, the company's Artistic Director.

The London Bubble
(Bubble Theatre Company)
3-5 Elephant Lane, London SE16 4JD
tel 020-7237 4434 *fax* 020-7231 2366
email admin@londonbubble.org.uk
website www.londonbubble.org.uk

M6 Theatre Company
Hamer C.P. School, Albert Royds Street, Rochdale, Lancs. OL16 2SU
tel (01706) 355898 *fax* (01706) 711700
email info@m6theatre.co.uk
Contact Jane Milne

Theatre-in-education company providing high quality theatre for children, young people and community audiences.

New Perspectives Theatre Company
The Old Library, Leeming Street, Mansfield, Notts. NG18 1NG
tel (01623) 635225 *fax* (01623) 635240
email info@newperspectives.co.uk
website www.newperspectives.co.uk
General Manager Cathy Leigh, *Theatre Writing Director* Esther Richardson

Has a policy of employing writers for new work. Also a founding partner of the Theatre Writing Partnership, with the Nottingham Playhouse, Leicester Haymarket Theatre, Northampton Theatre Trust and Derby Playhouse – developing new writing across the East Midlands.

New Victoria Theatre
The Peacocks, Woking, Surrey GU21 1GQ
tel (01483) 747422 *fax* (01483) 740477
Contact Michael Lynas *tel* (01908) 547599

Large-scale touring house. Interested to co-produce or produce.

NITRO
(formerly Black Theatre Co-operative Ltd)
6 Brewery Road, London N7 9NH
tel 020-7609 1331 *fax* 020-7609 1221
email info@nitro.co.uk
website www.nitro.co.uk
Artistic Director Felix Cross, *General Manager* Philip Bray

Commissions and produces new and innovative

musical theatre writing by black writers, that expresses the contemporary aspirations, cultures and issues that concern black people.

NTC Touring Theatre Company
(formerly Northumberland Theatre Company)
The Playhouse, Bondgate Without, Alnwick, Northumberland NE66 1PQ
tel (01665) 602586 *fax* (01665) 605837
email admin@ntc-touringtheatre.co.uk
website www.ntc-touringtheatre.co.uk
Artistic Director Gillian Hambleton

Performs a wide cross-section of work: new plays, extant scripts, classic and modern. Particularly interested in non-naturalism, physical theatre and plays with direct relevance to rural audiences.

Out of Joint
7 Thane Works, Thane Villas, London N7 7PH
tel 020-7609 0207 *fax* 020-7609 0203
email ojo@outofjoint.co.uk
website www.outofjoint.co.uk
Contact Max Stafford-Clark

Touring company producing new plays and some revivals. Welcomes scripts from writers. Founded 1993.

Oxford Stage Company
12 Mercer Street, London WC2H 9QD
tel 020-7438 9940 *fax* 020-7438 9941
email info@oxfordstage.co.uk
website www.oxfordstage.co.uk
Contact Development Producer

A middle-scale touring company presenting 3–4 productions per year: revivals of established masterpieces, modern classics, and new work.

Paines Plough
4th Floor, 43 Aldwych, London WC2B 4DN
tel 020-7240 4533 *fax* 020-7240 4534
email office@painesplough.com
website www.painesplough.com
Artistic Director Vicky Featherstone, *Associate Director* John Tiffany, *Literary Associate* Lucy Morrison

Tours new plays by British writers nationwide. The company believes that the playwright's voice should be at the centre of contemporary theatre and works with new and experienced writers. A programme of workshops and readings develops new work. Provides support for commissioned writers to push themselves, with the aim to produce the most ambitious and challenging of new theatre writing. Considers all unsolicited scripts from UK writers – send sae for return of script.

Proteus Theatre Company
Queen Mary's College, Cliddesden Road, Basingstoke, Hants RG21 3HF

tel (01256) 354541 *fax* (01256) 356186
email info@proteustheatre.com
website www.proteustheatre.com
Artistic Director Mark Helyar, *Associate Director*
Deborah Wilding, *General Manager* Julie Bladon

Small-scale touring company particularly
committed to new writing and new work, education
and community collaborations. Produces 3 touring
shows per year plus several community projects.
Founded 1979.

Quicksilver National Touring Theatre
4 Enfield Road, London N1 5AZ
tel 020-7241 2942 *fax* 020-7254 3119
email talktous@quicksilvertheatre.org
website www.quicksilvertheatre.org
Joint Artistic Director/Ceo Guy Holland, *Joint Artistic
Director* Carey English

A professional touring theatre company which
brings live theatre to theatres and schools all over
the country. Delivers good stories, original music,
kaleidoscopic design and poignant, often
humorous, new writing to entertain and make
children and adults think. Two to three new plays a
year for 3–5 year-olds, 7–11 year-olds and 6+ years
and families. Founded 1977.

Red Ladder Theatre Company
3 St Peters Buildings, York Street, Leeds LS9 8AU
tel 0113-245 5311 *fax* 0113-245 5351
email wendy@redladder.co.uk
website www.redladder.co.uk
Artistic Director Wendy Harris

Theatre performances for young people (14–25) in
youth clubs and small-scale theatre venues.
Commissions at least 2 new plays each year. Runs
the Asian Theatre School, an annual theatre training
programme for young Asians in Yorkshire.

Red Shift Theatre Company
TRG2 Trowbray House, 108 Weston Street,
London SE1 3QB
tel 020-7378 9787 *fax* 020-7378 9789
email mail@redshifttheatreco.co.uk
website www.redshifttheatreco.co.uk
Artistic Director Jonathan Holloway

Productions include adaptations, classics, new plays.
No commissions planned before 2004.

7:84 Theatre Company (Scotland)
333 Woodlands Road, Glasgow G3 6NG
tel 0141-334 6686 *fax* 0141-334 3369
email admin@784theatre.com
website www.784theatre.com

Presents 2–3 productions per year of political new
writing and relevant classical texts. Welcomes scripts
from new writers. Founded 1973.

Shared Experience Theatre
The Soho Laundry, 9 Dufour's Place,
London W1F 7SJ
tel 020-7434 9248 *fax* 020-7287 8763
email admin@setheatre.co.uk
website www.setheatre.co.uk
Joint Artistic Directors Nancy Meckler, Polly Teale

Middle-scale touring company presenting
2 productions per year: innovative adaptations or
translations of classic texts, and some new writing.
Tours nationally and internationally. Founded 1975.

Snap People's Theatre Trust
29 Raynham Road, Bishop's Stortford,
Herts. CM23 5PE
tel (01279) 461607 *fax* (01279) 506694
email info@snaptheatre.co.uk
Contact A. Graham

Produces theatre for young adults, children and
families. Emphasis on new writing. Welcomes
scripts from new writers. Founded 1979.

Solent Peoples Theatre (SPT)
135 St Mary Street, Southampton SO14 1NX
tel 023-8063 4381 *fax* 023-8063 5717
email solent@solentpeoples.demon.co.uk
General Manager Susan Carpenter

SPT has developed its artistic programme through
participatory projects, to incorporate a multimedia,
cross art form approach to theatre that will offer
richer opportunities and experience to both
community and company. Works with diverse
groups/individuals for whom an integrated
approach to the creation/presentation of new work
in performance makes that work more exciting,
relevant and accessible.

The Sphinx Theatre Co. Ltd
25 Short Street, London SE1 8LJ
tel 020-7401 9993/4 *fax* 020-7401 9995
Artistic Director Sue Parrish

Women writers only.

The Steam Industry
c/o Finborough Theatre, 118 Finborough Road,
London SW10 9ED
tel 020-7244 7439 *fax* 020-7835 1853
email steamindustry@finboroughtheatre.freeserve.co.uk
website www.steamindustry.co.uk
Artistic Director Phil Willmott

Produces new writing, radical adaptations of classic
texts and musicals. Unsolicited scripts are no longer
welcome. Founded 1994.

Talawa Theatre Company
3rd Floor, 23-25 Great Sutton Street,
London EC1V 0DN
tel 020-7251 6644 *fax* 020-7251 5969

email hq@talawa.com
Artistic Director Paulette Randall

Scripts from new writers considered. Particularly interested in scripts from black writers and plays portraying a black experience.

Theatre Absolute

57-61 Corporation Street, Coventry CV1 1GQ
tel (02476) 257380 *fax* (02476) 550680
email info@theatreabsolute.co.uk
website www.theatreabsolute.co.uk
Contact Julia Negus

Independent theatre producer of contemporary plays. Stages one premiere and tour over 2-year period. Founded 1992.

Theatre Centre

Units 7 & 8, Toynbee Workshops,
3 Gunthorpe Street, London E1 7RQ
tel 020-7377 0379 *fax* 020-7377 1376
email admin@theatre-centre.co.uk
website www.theatre-centre.co.uk
General Manager Jackie Alexis

New writing company producing and touring nationally and internationally. Professional theatre for young people – schools, arts centres, venues.

Theatre Workshop

34 Hamilton Place, Edinburgh EH3 5AX
tel 0131-225 7942 *fax* 0131-220 0112
Contact Robert Rae

Cutting edge, professional, inclusive theatre company. Plays include new writing/community/children's/disabled. Scripts from new writers considered.

Tiebreak Theatre Company

Heartsease High School, Marryat Road,
Norwich NR7 9DF
tel (01603) 435 209 *fax* (01603) 435 184
email info@tiebreak-theatre.com
website www.tiebreak-theatre.com
Contact Nicola Khandpur, General Manager

Presents 3 productions per year of children's and young people's theatre for schools and national venues. Founded 1981.

Literary agents

How to get an agent

New writers and illustrators wishing to have their work published frequently ask whether it is worth their while finding an agent. Philippa Milnes-Smith demystifies the role of the literary agent.

This article is for all those who are prepared to dedicate themselves to the pursuit of publication. If you are currently experiencing just a vague interest in being a writer or illustrator, stop reading now. You are unlikely to survive the rigorous commercial assessment to which your work will be subjected. If you are a children's writer or illustrator do not think that the process will be any easier. It's just as tough, if not tougher.

So, what is a literary agent and why would I want one?
You will probably already have noticed that contacts for many publishers are provided in the *Writers' & Artists' Yearbook*. This means that there is nothing to prevent you from pursuing publishers directly yourself. Indeed, if you can answer a confident 'yes' to all the questions below, and have the time and resources to devote to this objective, you probably don't need an agent:
1. Do you have a thorough understanding of the publishing market and its dynamics?
2. Do you know who are the best publishers for your book and why? Can you evaluate the pros and cons of each?
3. Are you financially numerate and confident of being able to negotiate the best commercial deal available in current market conditions?
4. Are you confident of being able to understand fully and negotiate a publishing or other media contract?
5. Do you enjoy the process of selling yourself and your work?
6. Do you want to spend your creative time on these activities?
An agent's job is to deal with all of the above on your behalf. A good agent will do all of these well.

So, is that is all an agent does?
Agents aren't all the same. Some will provide more editorial and creative support; some will help on longer term career planning; some will be subject specialists; some will involve themselves more on marketing and promotion. Such extras may well be taken into consideration in the commission rates charged.

I have decided I definitely do want an agent. Where do I begin?
When I left publishing and talked generally to the authors and illustrators I knew, a number of them said it was now more difficult to find an agent than a

publisher. Why is this? The answer is a commercial one. An agent will only take someone on if they can see how and why they are going to make money for the client and themselves. To survive, an agent needs to make commission and to do this they need projects they can sell. An agent also knows that if he/she does not sell a client's work, the relationship isn't going to last long.

So the agent just thinks about money?

Well, some agents may just think about money. And it might be all you care about. But good agents do also care about the quality of work and the clients they represent. They are professional people who commit themselves to doing the best job they can. They also know that good personal relationships count – and that they help everyone enjoy business more. This means that, if and when you get as far as talking to a prospective agent, you should ask yourself the questions: 'Do I have a good rapport with this person? Do I think we will get along? Do I understand and trust what they are saying?' Follow your instinct – more often than not it will be right.

So how do I convince an agent that I'm worth taking on?

Start with the basics. Make your approach professional. Make sure you only approach an appropriate agent who deals with the category of book you are writing/ illustrating. Phone to check to whom you should send your work and whether there are any particular ways your submission should be made (if it's not clear from the listings in this *Yearbook*). Only submit neat, typed work on single-sided A4 paper. Send a short covering letter with your manuscript explaining what it is, why you wrote it, what the intended audience is and providing any other *relevant* context. Always say if and why you are uniquely placed and qualified to write a particular book. Provide your professional credentials, if any. If you are writing an autobiography, justify why it is of public interest and why your experiences set you apart. Also, provide a CV (again, neat, typed, relevant) and a stamped addressed envelope for the return of your manuscript. Think of the whole thing in the same way as you would a job application, for which you would expect to prepare thoroughly in advance. You might only get one go at making your big sales pitch to an agent. Don't mess it up by being anything less than thorough.

And if I get to meet an agent?

Treat it like a job interview (although hopefully it will be more relaxed than this). Be prepared to talk about your work and yourself. An agent knows that a prepossessing personality in an author is a great asset for a publisher in terms of publicity and marketing – they will be looking to see how good your interpersonal skills are.

And if an agent turns my work down? Should I ask them to look again? People say you should not accept rejection.

No means no. Don't pester. It won't make an agent change his/her mind. Instead, move on to the next agency – the agent there might feel more positive. The agents who reject you may be wrong. But the loss is theirs.

Even if an agent turns my work down, isn't it worth asking for help with my creative direction?
No. Agents will often provide editorial advice for clients but will not do so for non-clients. Submissions are usually sorted into two piles of 'yes, worth seeing more' and 'rejections'. There is not another pile of 'promising writer but requires further tutoring'. Creative courses and writers' and artists' groups are better options to pursue for teaching and advice (see *Websites for writers*, page 536, *Creative writing courses*, page 551 and *Editorial, literary and production services*, page 553). It is, however, important to practise and develop your creative skills. You wouldn't expect to be able to play football without working at your ball skills or practise as a lawyer without studying to acquire the relevant knowledge. If you are looking to get your work published, you are going to have to compete with professional writers and artists – and those who have spent years working at their craft.

If I haven't put you off yet, it just remains for me to say good luck – and don't forget to buy plenty of stamps, envelopes and A4 paper.

Philippa Milnes-Smith is a literary agent and children's specialist at the agency LAW (Lucas Alexander Whitley). She was previously Managing Director of Puffin Books.

See also...

Literary agents UK and Ireland

*Full member of the Association of Authors' Agents

A & B Personal Management Ltd
Paurelle House, 91 Regent Street,
London W1B 4EL
tel 020-7734 6047/8 *fax* 020-7734 6318
Directors R.W. Ellis, R. Ellis

Full-length MSS. Scripts for TV, theatre, cinema;
also novels, fiction and non-fiction (home 12.5%,
overseas 15%), performance rights (12.5%). No
unsolicited material: write first before submitting
synopsis. No reading fee for synopsis, plays or
screenplays, but fee charged for full-length MSS.
Return postage required. Founded 1982.

A.M. Heath & Co. Ltd*
79 St Martin's Lane, London WC2N 4RE
tel 020-7836 4271 *fax* 020-7497 2561
Directors William Hamilton, Sara Fisher, Sarah
Molloy, Victoria Hobbs

Full-length MSS. Literary and commercial fiction
and non-fiction, children's (home 10–15%, USA
20%, translation 20%), performance rights (15%).
No science fiction, screenplays, poetry or short
stories except for established clients. No reading fee.
Agents in USA and all European countries and
Japan.

  Clients include Joan Aiken, Bella Bathurst, Anita
Brookner, Helen Cresswell, Patricia Duncker, Geoff
Dyer, Katie Fforde, Graham Hancock, Tobias Hill,
Hilary Mantel, Tim Pears, Ricardo Pinto, Susan
Price, Adam Thorpe, Barbara Trapido. Founded
1919.

A.P. Watt Ltd*
20 John Street, London WC1N 2DR
tel 020-7405 6774 *fax* 020-7831 2154 (books)
020-7430 1952 (drama)
email apw@apwatt.co.uk
website www.apwatt.co.uk
Directors Caradoc King, Linda Shaughnessy, Derek
Johns, Georgia Garrett, Nick Harris, Natasha
Fairweather, Jo Frank (Associate)

Full-length MSS; dramatic works for all media
(home 10%, USA and foreign 20% including
commission to foreign agent). No poetry. No
reading fee. No unsolicited MSS. Founded 1875.

Abbey Agency (Literary Services)
83 High Street, Graveley,
Cambridgeshire PE19 6PL
tel (01480) 839150
email admin@abbeyagency.co.uk
Proprietor Faith Dakin

General fiction and non-fiction. Full-length MSS
(home 10%, overseas 12.5%). Aims to encourage
new writers. Send preliminary letter with sae.
Reading fee charged for unpublished authors.

  Authors include Faustin Charles, Jeffrey Clark-
Meads, Kevin Dakin, Cyril Dowling, Cy Flood,
Derek M. Fox, Kathleen Sheehan-O'Connor.
Founded 1999; new management 2002.

Abner Stein*
10 Roland Gardens, London SW7 3PH
tel 020-7373 0456 *fax* 020-7370 6316
Contacts Abner Stein, Arabella Stein

Full-length and short MSS (home 10%, overseas
20%). No reading fee, but no unsolicited MSS;
preliminary letter and return postage required.

The Agency (London) Ltd*
24 Pottery Lane, London W11 4LZ
tel 020-7727 1346 *fax* 020-7727 9037
email info@theagency.co.uk
Executives Stephen Durbridge, Leah Schmidt,
Sebastian Born, Julia Kreitman, Bethan Evans,
Hilary Delamere (children's books), Katie Haines,
Ligeia Marsh

Represents writers for theatre, film, TV, radio and
children's book writers and illustrators. Also film
and TV rights in novels and non-fiction. Adult
novels represented only for existing clients.
Commission: 10% unless sub-agents employed
overseas; works in conjunction with agents in USA
and overseas. Strictly no unsolicited material. No
reading fee. Founded 1995.

Alan Brodie Representation Ltd
(incorporating Michael Imison Playwrights)
211 Piccadilly, London W1J 9HF
tel 020-7917 2871 *fax* 020-7917 2872
email info@alanbrodie.com
website www.alanbrodie.com
Directors Alan Brodie, Sarah McNair, Alison Lee

Specialises in stage plays, radio, TV, film (home
10%, overseas 15%); no prose fiction or general
MSS. Represented in all major countries. No
unsolicited scripts; recommendation from known
professional required.

Alexandra Nye, Writers & Agents
Craigower, 6 Kinnoull Avenue, Dunblane,
Perthshire FK15 9JB
tel (01786) 825114
Director Alexandra Nye

Literary fiction, Scottish history, biographies; no poetry or plays (home 10%, overseas 20%, translation 15%). Preliminary letter with synopsis preferred; sae essential for return. Reading fee for supply of detailed report on MSS. Founded 1991.

Andrew Lownie Literary Agency*

17 Sutherland Street, London SW1V 4JU
tel 020-7828 1274 *fax* 020-7828 7608
email lownie@globalnet.co.uk
website www.andrewlownie.co.uk
Director Andrew Lownie

Full-length MSS. Biography, history, reference, current affairs, and packaging journalists and celebrities for the book market (worldwide 15%). No reading fee; will suggest a revision.

Authors include Theo Aronson, Juliet Barker, the Joyce Cary Estate, Tom Devine, Peter Evans, David Fisher, Jonathan Fryer, Laurence Gardner, Timothy Good, Lawrence James, Robert Jobson, Leo McKinstry, Julian Maclaren-Ross Estate, Norma Major, Sir John Mills, Tom Pocock, Nick Pope, Martin Pugh, John Rae, Richard Rudgley, Desmond Seward, David Stafford, Andrew Wheatcroft, Alan Whicker; *The Oxford Classical Dictionary, The Cambridge Guide to Literature in English.* Founded 1988.

Andrew Mann Ltd*

(in association with Jane Conway-Gordon)
1 Old Compton Street, London W1D 5JA
tel 020-7734 4751 *fax* 020-7287 9264
Contacts Anne Dewe, Tina Betts, Sacha Elliot

Full-length MSS. Scripts for TV, cinema, radio and theatre (home 15%, USA and Europe 20%). Associated with agents worldwide. No reading fee, but no unsolicited MSS without preliminary enquiry and sae. Founded 1974.

Andrew Nurnberg Associates Ltd*

Clerkenwell House, 45-47 Clerkenwell Green, London EC1R 0HT
tel 020-7417 8800 *fax* 020-7417 8812
email all@nurnberg.co.uk

Specialises in the sale of translation rights of English and American authors into European languages. No reading fee.

Annette Green Authors' Agency

1 East Cliff Road, Tunbridge Wells, Kent TN4 9AD
tel (01892) 514275 *fax* (01892) 518124
email annettekgreen@aol.com
Partners Annette Green, David Smith

Full-length MSS (home 15%, overseas 20%). Literary and general fiction and non-fiction, popular culture, history, science, teenage fiction. No dramatic scripts, poetry, children's, SF or fantasy.

No reading fee. Preliminary letter, synopsis, sample chapter and sae essential.

Authors include Andrew Baker, Nick Barlay, Julia Bell, Bill Broady, Meg Cabot, Emma Gold, Justin Hill, Max Kinnings, Maria McCann, Adam MacQueen, Ian Marchant, Prof Charles Pasternak, Peter Shapiro, Owen Sheers, Rev. Victor Stock, Elizabeth Woodcraft. Founded 1998.

Anthony Sheil

29 Fernshaw Road, London SW10 0TG
tel 020-7351 7561 *fax* 020-7376 3594
email reception@gillonaitken.co.uk
Proprietor Anthony Sheil

Quality fiction and non-fiction (home 10%, overseas 20%). No reading fee. Works in conjunction with **Gillon Aitken Associates Ltd**.

Authors include Caroline Alexander, John Banville, Josephine Cox, John Fowles, John Keegan, Robert Wilson.

Antony Harwood Ltd

405 Riverbank House, 1 Putney Bridge Approach, London SW6 3JD
tel 020-7384 9209 *fax* 020-7384 9206
email mail@antonyharwood.com
Contacts Antony Harwood, James Macdonald Lockhart

General and genre fiction; general non-fiction (home 10%, overseas 20%). Will suggest revision. No reading fee.

Authors include Ethan Coen, Louise Doughty, Robert Edric, Peter F. Hamilton, Alan Hollinghurst, A.L. Kennedy, Douglas Kennedy, Chris Manby, George Monbiot, Tim Parks. Founded 2000.

Anubis Literary Agency

6 Birdhaven Close, Lighthorne Heath, Warks. CV35 0BE
tel/fax (01926) 642588
Contacts Steve Calcutt, Maggie Heavey

Genre fiction: crime, thrillers, horror, science fiction, fantasy (home 15%, USA/translation 20%). No other material considered. Send 50pp, a one-page synopsis and sae (essential). No reading fee. No telephone calls. Works with the **Marsh Agency Ltd** on translation rights.

Clients include Lesley Asquith, Georgie Hale, Anthea Ingham, Tim Lebbon, Adam Roberts, Steve Savile, Brett A. Savory, Zoe Sharp. Founded 1994.

Associated Publicity Holdings Ltd

7 Kensington Church Court, London W8 4SP
tel 020-7937 5277 *fax* 020-7937 2833
email Jonathan.Harris@aph-agent.demon.co.uk
Managing Director Jonathan G. Harris

Full-length MSS. Fiction and non-fiction, particularly sport, history, archaeology, biographies, thrillers and crime novels (home 15%, overseas 20%), performance, film and TV rights (15%). Send outline, 2 sample chapters and sae. Works with foreign agencies. No reading fee. Founded 1987.

Author Literary Agents

53 Talbot Road, London N6 4QX
tel 020-8341 0442 *mobile* (07989) 318245
email agile@authors.co.uk
Contact John Havergal

'Top-seller writing for page or screen' (writing: UK 15%, overseas/translations 25%; digital and other non-writing media: publishing 25%, advertising 33.3% – all rates plus VAT). Send half–one-page outline and just first chapter/scene/section. Sae essential for reply. No reading fee. Founded 1997.

Barbara Levy Literary Agency*

64 Greenhill, Hampstead High Street,
London NW3 5TZ
tel 020-7435 9046 *fax* 020-7431 2063
Director Barbara Levy, *Associate* John Selby (solicitor)

Full-length MSS. Fiction and general non-fiction (home 10%, overseas by arrangement). Film and TV rights for existing clients only. No reading fee, but preliminary letter with synopsis and sae essential. Translation rights handled by the **Marsh Agency Ltd**; works in conjunction with US agents. Founded 1986.

Blake Friedmann Literary, TV & Film Agency Ltd*

122 Arlington Road, London NW1 7HP
tel 020-7284 0408 *fax* 020-7284 0442
email firstname@blakefriedmann.co.uk
Directors Carole Blake, Julian Friedmann, Barbara Jones, Conrad Williams, Isobel Dixon

Full-length MSS. Fiction: thrillers, women's novels and literary fiction; non-fiction: investigative books, biography, travel; no poetry or plays (home 15%, overseas 20%). Specialises in film and TV rights; place journalism and short stories for existing clients only. Represented worldwide in 26 markets. Preliminary letter, synopsis and first 2 chapters preferred. No reading fee.

Authors include Gilbert Adair, Jane Asher, Edward Carey, Elizabeth Chadwick, Victoria Clayton, Barbara Erskine, Ann Granger, Maeve Haran, Ken Hom, Glenn Meade, Lawrence Norfolk, Gregory Norminton, Joseph O'Connor, Sheila O'Flanagan, Sian Rees, Michael Ridpath, Tim Sebastian, Julian Stockwin. Founded 1977.

Blanche Marvin

21A St John's Wood High Street,
London NW8 7NG
tel/fax 020-7722 2313

Full-length MSS (15%), performance rights. No reading fee but return postage essential.

Authors include Christopher Bond.

The Book Bureau Literary Agency

7 Duncairn Avenue, Bray, Co. Wicklow,
Republic of Ireland
tel (01) 276 4996 *fax* (01) 276 4834
email thebookbureau@oceanfree.net
Managing Director Geraldine Nichol

Full-length MSS (home 10%, USA 15%, translation 20%). Fiction preferred – thrillers, Irish novels, literary fiction, women's novels and general commercial. No horror, science fiction, children's or poetry. Strong editorial support. No reading fee. Preliminary letter, synopsis and 3 sample chapters. Return postage essential. Works with agents overseas.

BookBlast Ltd

PO Box 20184, London W10 5AU
tel 020-8968 3089 *fax* 020-8932 4087
Director G. de Chamberet

Full-length MSS (home 12%, overseas 20%), TV and radio (15%), film (20%). Fiction and non-fiction. No scripts, horror, crime, science fiction, fantasy, poetry, health, cookery, gardening, short stories, academic articles or children's books. Radio, TV and film rights sold mainly in works by existing clients. No unsolicited material; no submissions on disk, by fax or by email. Preliminary letter, synopsis, 3 sample chapters and biographical information. Return postage essential. No reading fee. Taking on very few new clients. Founded 1997.

Brie Burkeman*

14 Neville Court, Abbey Road, London NW8 9DD
tel (0709) 223 9113 *fax* (0709) 223 9111
email brie.burkeman@mail.com
Proprietor Brie Burkeman

Commercial and literary full-length fiction and non-fiction and film/TV/theatre scripts (home 15%, overseas 20%). No academic text, poetry, short stories, musicals or short films. No reading fee but return postage essential. Unsolicited email attachments will be deleted without opening. Also independent film and TV consultant to literary agents. Founded 2000.

Campbell Thomson & McLaughlin Ltd*

1 King's Mews, London WC1N 2JA
tel 020-7242 0958 *fax* 020-7242 2408
Directors John McLaughlin, Charlotte Bruton

Full-length book MSS (home 10%, overseas up to 20% including commission to foreign agent). No poetry, plays or TV/film scripts, short stories or children's books. Preliminary letter with sae essential. No unsolicited synopses or MSS. No reading fee. USA agents represented: Raines & Raines, the Fox Chase Agency, Inc. Representatives in most European countries.

Capel & Land Ltd*
29 Wardour Street, London W1D 6PS
tel 020-7734 2414 *fax* 020-7734 8101
email georgina@capelland.co.uk
Agents Georgina Capel (literary), Robert Caskie (film), Anita Land (TV)
Literary and commercial fiction, history, biography; film and TV (home/overseas 15%). No reading fee; will suggest revision.

Clients include Julie Burchill, Andrew Greig, Eamonn Holmes, Jean Marsh, Rt Hon. Dr Mo Mowlam, Cristina Odone, Jeremy Paxman, Henry Porter, Andrew Roberts, Simon Sebag Montefiore, Louis Theroux, Lucy Wadham. Founded 1999.

Caroline Davidson Literary Agency
5 Queen Anne's Gardens, London W4 1TU
tel 020-8995 5768 *fax* 020-8994 2770
Handles novels and non-fiction of high quality, including reference works (12.5%). Send preliminary letter with CV and detailed, well thought-out book proposal/synopsis and/or first 50pp of novel. Large sae with return postage essential. No reading fee. Quick response.

Authors include Susan Aldridge, Nigel Barlow, Anna Beer, Stuart Clark, Naomi Craft, Andrew Dalby, Emma Donoghue, Cindy Engel, Chris Greenhalgh, Paul Hillyard, Tom Jaine, Huon Mallalieu, Linda Somntag. Founded 1988.

Caroline Sheldon Literary Agency*
London office 71 Hillgate Place, London W8 7SS
tel 020-7727 9102
mailing address for MSS Thorley Manor Farm, Thorley, Yarmouth, Isle of Wight PO41 0SJ
tel (01983) 760205
Proprietor Caroline Sheldon
Full-length MSS. General fiction, women's fiction, and children's books (home 10%, overseas 20%). No reading fee. Synopsis and first 3 chapters with large sae in case of return required initially. Founded 1985.

Casarotto Ramsay & Associates Ltd
(formerly Margaret Ramsay Ltd and Casarotto Company Ltd)
National House, 60-66 Wardour Street, London W1V 4ND
tel 020-7287 4450 *fax* 020-7287 9128
email agents@casarotto.uk.com
Directors Jenne Casarotto, Giorgio Casarotto, Tom Erhardt, Tracey Hyde, Sara Pritchard, Mel Kenyon, Charlotte Kelly, Jodi Shields
MSS – theatre, films, TV, sound broadcasting only

(10%). Works in conjunction with agents in USA and other foreign countries. Preliminary letter essential. No reading fee.

Authors include Paul Abbott, Alan Ayckbourn, J.G. Ballard, Peter Barnes, Edward Bond, Caryl Churchill, Pam Gems, Christopher Hampton, David Hare, Nick Hornby, Amy Jenkins, Neil Jordan, Frank McGuiness, Phyllis Nagy, Mark Ravenhill, Willy Russell, Martin Sherman, Shawn Slovo, Fay Weldon, Timberlake Wertenbaker, David Wood. Founded 1989.

Cat Ledger Literary Agency*
20-21 Newman Street, London W1T 1PG
tel 020-7861 8226 *fax* 020-7861 8001
General non-fiction and fiction but no short stories, film/TV scripts, poetry or plays (home 10%, overseas 20%). No reading fee but preliminary letter, synopsis and sae essential. Represented in all foreign countries.

Celia Catchpole
56 Gilpin Avenue, London SW14 8QY
tel 020-8255 7200 *fax* 020-8288 0653
Specialises as agent for children's writers and illustrators (home 10% writers, 15% illustrators; overseas 20%). No unsolicited MSS. Founded 1996.

Chapman & Vincent*
The Mount, Sun Hill, Royston, Herts. SG8 9AT
tel (01763) 245005 *fax* (01763) 243033
email info@chapmanvincent.co.uk
Directors Jennifer Chapman, Gilly Vincent
Original non-fiction and (occasionally) quality fiction (home 15%; overseas 20%). No children's, genre fiction or poetry. No reading fee. Clients come mainly from personal recommendation. No phone calls; submissions by post only. Send synopsis and 2 sample chapters with sae.

Authors include George Carter, Leslie Geddes-Brown, Sara George, Rowley Leigh, John Miller, Dorit Peleg. Founded 1995.

Christine Green Authors' Agent*
6 Whitehorse Mews, Westminster Bridge Road, London SE1 7QD
tel 020-7401 8844 *fax* 020-7401 8860
website www.christinegreen.co.uk
Fiction and general non-fiction. Full-length MSS (home 10%, overseas 20%). Works in conjunction with agencies in Europe and Scandinavia. No reading fee, but preliminary letter and return postage essential. Founded 1984.

The Christopher Little Literary Agency*
10 Eel Brook Studios, 125 Moore Park Road, London SW6 4PS
tel 020-7736 4455 *fax* 020-7736 4490

email christopher@christopherlittle.net
christianname@christopherlittle.net
Contacts Christopher Little, Kellee Nunley, Emma
Schlesinger

Commercial and literary full-length fiction and
non-fiction (home 15%; USA, Canada, translation,
audio, motion picture 20%). No poetry, plays,
science fiction, fantasy, textbooks, illustrated
children's or short stories. Film scripts for
established clients only. No reading fee. No
unsolicited submissions. Founded 1979.

Christy & Moore Ltd – see Sheil Land Associates Ltd

Conville & Walsh Ltd*
118-120 Wardour Street, London W1V 3LA
tel 020-7287 3030 *fax* 020-7287 4545
email firstname@convilleandwalsh.com
Directors Clare Conville, Patrick Walsh (book
rights), Sam North (film/TV), Peter Tallack
(popular science)

Literary and commercial fiction plus serious and
narrative non-fiction. Particularly interested in first
novelists plus scientists, historians and journalists.
No reading fee.

Clients include Marina Benjamin, John
Burningham, Kate Cann, Helen Castor, Tom Conran,
Michael Cordy, Mike Dash, Prof John Emsley, Steve
Erikson, Katy Gardner, Christopher Hart, Dermot
Healy, James Holland, Tom Holland, Sebastian
Horsley, David Huggins, Guy Kennaway, Manjit
Kumar, P.J. Lynch, Hector Macdonald, Mark Mason,
Prof Arthur Miller, Harland Miller, Joshua Mowll,
Jacqui Murhall, Ruth Padel, D.B.C. Pierre, Rebbecca
Ray, Patrick Redmond, Candace Robb, Mark
Sanderson, Saira Shah, Tahir Shah, Nicky Singer,
Simon Singh, Doran Swade, Dr Richard Wiseman,
Adam Wishart, Isabel Wolff, and the Estate of
Francis Bacon. Founded 2000.

Coombs Moylett Literary Agency
3 Askew Road, London W12 9AA
tel 020-8740 0454 *fax* 020-8354 3065
Proprietor Lisa Moylett

Specialises in crime, thrillers, contemporary
women's fiction and literary fiction (home 10%;
overseas 15%). Send first 3 chapters and synopsis.
Will help with revision as appropriate. Return
postage essential.

Curtis Brown Group Ltd*
Haymarket House, 28-29 Haymarket,
London SW1Y 4SP
tel 020-7396 6600 *fax* 020-7396 0110
email cb@curtisbrown.co.uk
Chairman Paul Scherer, *Group Managing Director*
Jonathan Lloyd, *Financial Director* Mark
Collingbourne, *Australia: Managing Director* Fiona

Inglis, *Books London* Jonathan Lloyd, Anna Davis,
Jonny Geller, Hannah Griffiths, Ali Gunn, Camilla
Hornby, Anthea Morton-Saner, Peter Robinson,
Vivienne Schuster, Janice Swanson
Books Edinburgh 37 Queensferry Street,
Edinburgh EH2 4QS
tel 0131-225 1286/1288 *fax* 0131-225 1290
email cb@curtisbrown.co.uk
Contacts Giles Gordon, *Foreign Rights* Diana
Mackay, Carol Jackson, Kate Cooper,
Film/TV/Theatre Nick Marston (Managing Director,
Media Division), Ben Hall, Jo Phillips, *Presenters*
Sue Freathy, Julian Beynon

Agents for the negotiation in all markets of novels,
general non-fiction, children's books (home 10%,
overseas 20%) and associated rights (including
multimedia), as well as film, theatre, TV and radio
scripts. Outline for non-fiction and short synopsis
for fiction with 2–3 sample chapters and
autobiographical note. No reading fee. Return
postage essential. Also represents directors,
designers and presenters. Return postage essential.
Founded 1899.

Darley Anderson Literary, TV and Film Agency*
Estelle House, 11 Eustace Road,
London SW6 1JB
tel 020-7385 6653 *fax* 020-7386 5571
email darley.anderson@virgin.net
website www.darleyanderson.com
Contacts Darley Anderson, Lucie Whitehouse
(foreign rights), Elizabeth Wright (love stories and
'tear jerkers'/women's fiction), Carrie Neilson
(TV/film, children's books), Julia Churchill (non-
fiction), Rosi Bridge (finance)

Commercial fiction and non-fiction; children's
fiction; selected scripts for film and TV (home 15%,
USA/translation 20%, film/TV/radio 20%). No
poetry or academic books.

Special interests (fiction): all types of thrillers,
crime/mystery and young male fiction. All types of
American and Irish novels. All types of women's
fiction. Sagas, chick-lit; contemporary and literary.
Also comic fiction.

Special interests (non-fiction): celebrity
autobiographies, biographies, sports books, 'true-
life' women in jeopardy, revelatory history and
science, popular psychology, self improvement, diet,
beauty, health, fashion, animals, humour/cartoon,
cookery, gardening, inspirational, religious.

Send preliminary letter, synopsis and first
3 chapters. Return postage/sae essential for reply.
Disk and emailed submissions cannot be
considered. Overseas associates: APA Talent &
Literary Agency (LA/Hollywood), Liza Dawson
Literary Agency (New York) and 21 leading foreign
agents worldwide.

Clients include Liz Allen, Richard Asplin, Anne Baker, Catherine Barry, Paul Carson, Caroline Carver, Lee Child, Kira Cochrane, Martina Cole, John Connolly, Margaret Dickinson, Rose Doyle, Joan Jonker, Astrid Longhurst, Rani Manicka, Carole Matthews, Lesley Pearse, Lynda Page, Allan Pease, Adrian Plass, Carmen Reid, Mary Ryan, Rebecca Shaw, Peter Sheridan, Kwong Kuen Shan, Linda Taylor, Elizabeth Waite.

David Bolt Associates

12 Heath Drive, Send, Surrey GU23 7EP
tel/fax (01483) 721118

Specialises in biography, fiction, theology. Full-length MSS (home 10%, overseas 19%; all other rights including film, video and TV 10%). No unsolicited short stories or play scripts. Will sometimes suggest revision. Works in association with overseas agencies worldwide. Preliminary letter essential. Reading fee terms on application.

Authors include Chinua Achebe, David Bret, John Cannon, Keith Cory-Jones, Nicci Mackay, Joseph Rhymer, Colin Wilson.

David Godwin Associates – see DGA

David Grossman Literary Agency Ltd

118B Holland Park Avenue, London W11 4UA
tel 020-7221 2770 *fax* 020-7221 1445

Full-length MSS (home 10–15%, overseas 20% including foreign agent's commission), performance rights (15%). Works in conjunction with agents in New York, Los Angeles, Europe, Japan. No reading fee, but preliminary letter required. Founded 1976.

David Higham Associates Ltd*

(incorporating Murray Pollinger)
5-8 Lower John Street, Golden Square, London W1F 9HA
tel 020-7434 5900 *fax* 020-7437 1072
email dha@davidhigham.co.uk
website www.davidhigham.co.uk
Managing Director Anthony Goff, *Books* Veronique Baxter, Anthony Goff, Bruce Hunter, Jacqueline Korn, Caroline Walsh, *Foreign Rights* Ania Corless, *Film/TV/Theatre* Gemma Hirst, Nicky Lund, Georgina Ruffhead

Agents for the negotiation of all rights in fiction, general non-fiction, children's fiction and picture books, plays, film and TV scripts (home 15%, USA/translation 20%). Represented in all foreign markets. Preliminary letter and return postage essential. No reading fee. Founded 1935.

David O'Leary Literary Agency

10 Lansdowne Court, Lansdowne Rise, London W11 2NR
tel 020-7229 1623 *fax* 020-7727 9624

email d.o'leary@virgin.net

Popular and literary fiction and non-fiction. Special interests: Ireland, history, science (home 10%, overseas 20%, performance rights 15%). Will suggest revision; no reading fee. Write or call before submitting MSS; please enclose sae.

Authors include Alexander Cordell, David Crackanthorpe, Jim Lusby, Derek Malcolm, Ken Russell. Founded 1988.

Deborah Owen Ltd*

78 Narrow Street, Limehouse, London E14 8BP
tel 020-7987 5119/5441 *fax* 020-7538 4004
Contact Deborah Owen

Small agency specialising in representing authors direct around the world. International fiction and non-fiction – books which can be translated into a number of languages (home 10%, USA/translation 15%). No new authors.

Clients include Penelope Farmer, Amos Oz, Delia Smith. Founded 1971.

DGA

55 Monmouth Street, London WC2H 9DG
tel 020-7240 9992 *fax* 020-7395 6110
email assistant@davidgodwinassociates.co.uk
website www.davidgodwinassociates.co.uk
Directors David Godwin, Heather Godwin

Literary fiction and general non-fiction (home 10%, overseas 20%). No reading fee; send sae for return of MSS. Founded 1995.

Dinah Wiener Ltd*

12 Cornwall Grove, London W4 2LB
tel 020-8994 6011 *fax* 020-8994 6044

Full-length MSS only, fiction and general non-fiction (home 15%, overseas 20%), film and TV in association (15%). No plays, scripts, poetry, short stories or children's books. No reading fee, but preliminary letter and return postage essential.

Don Baker Associates

25 Eley Drive, Rottingdean, East Sussex BN2 7FH
tel/fax (01273) 386842
Directors Donald Baker, Katy Quayle

Full-length MSS. Fiction, film, TV and theatre scripts (home 12.5%, overseas 15%). Reading fee. Send sae. No unsolicited MSS. Founded 1996.

Dorian Literary Agency (DLA)*

Upper Thornehill, 27 Church Road, St Marychurch, Torquay, Devon TQ1 4QY
tel/fax (01803) 312095
Proprietor Dorothy Lumley

General fiction, and specialising in popular fiction: women's fiction from romance, historicals to contemporary; crime from historical to noir and thrillers; science fiction, fantasy (but cautious about humorous/soft fantasy, i.e. unicorns), dark fantasy and horror. Adult and young adult for over 10 years old. No poetry or drama (home 10–12.5%, USA 15%, translation 20%). No reading fee. Contact initially by post with 1–3 chapters and brief outline plus return postage/sae. No telephone calls, faxes or emails. Represents Fedogan & Bremer Publishers (USA) for UK/translation and Ethan Ellenberg Literary Agency (USA).

Authors include Gillian Bradshaw, Brian Lumley, Amy Myers, Stephen Jones, Rosemary Rowe. Founded 1986.

Duncan McAra

28 Beresford Gardens, Edinburgh EH5 3ES
tel/fax 0131-552 1558
email duncanmcara@hotmail.com

Literary fiction; non-fiction: art, architecture, archaeology, biography, military, Scottish, travel (home 10%, overseas 20%). Preliminary letter with sae essential. No reading fee. Founded 1988.

Ed Victor Ltd*

6 Bayley Street, Bedford Square, London WC1B 3HE
tel 020-7304 4100 *fax* 020-7304 4111
Executive Chairman Ed Victor, *Joint Managing Directors* Sophie Hicks, Margaret Phillips, *Directors* Carol Ryan, Graham C. Greene CBE, Leon Morgan, Hitesh Shah, *Editorial Director* Philippa Harrison

Fiction, non-fiction and children's books (home 15%, USA 15%, children's 10%, translation 20%). No short stories, poetry or film/TV scripts or plays. No reading fee. No unsolicited MSS. No response to submissions by email. Represented in all foreign markets.

Authors include Eoin Colfer, Sir Ranulph Fiennes, Frederick Forsyth, A.A. Gill, Josephine Hart, Jack Higgins, Erica Jong, Nigella Lawson, Kathy Lette, Allan Mallinson, Nigel Nicolson, Anne Robinson, and the Estates of Douglas Adams, Raymond Chandler, Dame Iris Murdoch, Sir Stephen Spender, Irving Wallace. Founded 1976.

Eddison Pearson Ltd

West Hill House, 6 Swains Lane, London N6 6QU
tel 020-7700 7763 *fax* 020-7700 7866
email enquiries@eddisonpearson.com
Contact Clare Pearson

Children's books and scripts, literary fiction and non-fiction, poetry (home 10%, overseas 15%). No unsolicited MSS. Enquire by letter enclosing brief writing sample and sae. Email enquiries welcome but no email submissions please. No reading fee. May suggest revision where appropriate.

Authors include Valerie Bloom, Michael Catchpool, Sue Heap, Sally Lloyd Jones, Robert Muchamore, Mary Murphy, Ruth Symes.

Edwards Fuglewicz*

49 Great Ormond Street, London WC1N 3HZ
tel 020-7405 6725 *fax* 020-7405 6726
Partners Ros Edwards and Helenka Fuglewicz

Literary and commercial fiction (but no children's fiction, science fiction, horror or fantasy); non-fiction: biography, history, popular culture (home 15%, USA/translation 20%). No unsolicited MSS or email submissions. No reading fee. Founded 1996.

Elisabeth Wilson

24 Thornhill Square, London N1 1BQ
fax 020-7609 6045

Rights agent and consultant; illustrated books, non-fiction (no children's). No reading fee. Founded 1979.

Elizabeth Puttick Literary Agency*

46 Brookfield Mansions, Highgate West Hill, London N6 6AT
tel 020-8340 6383 *fax* 020-8340 6384
email agency@puttick.com
website www.puttick.com
Director Elizabeth Puttick

Full-length MSS (home 15%, overseas 20%). General non-fiction with special interest in self-help, Mind, Body & Spirit, health, childcare, cookery, business, science, biography, history, current affairs, women's issues, illustrated books, TV and film tie-ins. No poetry, drama, children's books. No reading fee. Send preliminary letter with synopsis; return postage essential.

Authors include William Bloom, Robin Bloor, Ann-Marie Gallagher, Emma Restall Orr, Eddie and Debbie Shapiro. Founded 1995.

Elizabeth Roy Literary Agency

White Cottage, Greatford, Nr Stamford, Lincs. PE9 4PR
tel/fax (01778) 560672

Children's fiction and non-fiction – writers and illustrators (home 10–15%, overseas 20%). Preliminary letter, synopsis and sample chapters essential with names of publishers and agents previously contacted. Return postage essential. No reading fee. Founded 1990.

Elspeth Cochrane Personal Management

South Bank Commercial Centre, 140 Battersea Park Road, London SW11 4NB
tel 020-7622 0314 *fax* 020-7622 5815
email info@ecpma.com
Contact Elspeth Cochrane

Send synopsis with covering letter and sae in first instance (home and overseas 12.5%), performance rights (12.5%). No reading fee.

Authors include Nick Hennegan, Royce Ryton, Robert Tanitch. Founded 1960.

Eric Glass Ltd

25 Ladbroke Crescent, London W11 1PS
tel 020-7229 9500 *fax* 020-7229 6220
Director Janet Glass

Full-length MSS only; also theatre, films, TV, and sound broadcasting. No unsolicited MSS. Founded 1932.

Eunice McMullen Children's Literary Agent Ltd

Low Ibbotsholme Cottage, Off Bridge Lane,
Troutbeck Bridge, Windermere,
Cumbria LA23 1HU
tel (01539) 448551 *fax* (01539) 442289
email eunicemcmullen@totalise.co.uk
Director Eunice McMullen

All types of children's books, particularly picture books (home 10%, overseas 15%). No unsolicited scripts. Telephone enquiries only.

Authors include Wayne Anderson, Reg Cartwright, Sam Childs, Ross Collins, Jason Cockcroft, Charles Fuge, Maggie Kneen, David Melling, Sue Porter, Angela McAllister, Susan Winter, David Wood. Founded 1992.

Faith Evans Associates*

27 Park Avenue North, London N8 7RU
tel 020-8340 9920 *fax* 020-8340 9410

Small agency (home 15%, overseas 20%). New clients by personal recommendation only. Co-agents in most countries. No phone calls, scripts or unsolicited MSS.

Authors include Melissa Benn, Shyam Bhatia, Madeleine Bourdouxhe, Eleanor Bron, Carolyn Cassady, Caroline Conran, Helen Falconer, Alicia Foster, Midge Gillies, Ed Glinert, Cate Haste, Jim Kelly, Helena Kennedy, Seumas Milne, Tom Paulin, Sheila Rowbotham, Lorna Sage, Rebecca Stott, Hwee Hwee Tan, Harriet Walter, Elizabeth Wilson, Francesca Weisman. Founded 1987.

Felicity Bryan*

2A North Parade, Banbury Road, Oxford OX2 6LX
tel (01865) 513816 *fax* (01865) 310055

Fiction and general non-fiction (home 10%, overseas 20%). Translation rights handled by Andrew Nurnberg Associates; works in conjunction with US agents. No unsolicited submissions.

Felix De Wolfe

Garden Offices, 51 Maida Vale, London W9 1SD
tel 020-7289 5770 *fax* 020-7289 5731

Theatre, films, TV, sound broadcasting, fiction (home 10–15%, overseas 20%). No reading fee. Works in conjunction with many foreign agencies.

Film Rights Ltd

Mezzanine, Quadrant House, 80-82 Regent Street, London W1B 5AU

tel 020-7734 9911 *fax* 020-7734 0044
email information@filmrights.ltd.uk
website www.filmrights.ltd.uk
Directors Brendan Davis, Joan Potts

Theatre, films, TV and sound broadcasting (home 10%, overseas 15%). No reading fee. Represented in USA and abroad. Founded 1932.

Fox & Howard Literary Agency

4 Bramerton Street, London SW3 5JX
tel/fax 020-7352 8691
Partners Chelsey Fox, Charlotte Howard

General non-fiction: biography, history and popular culture, reference, business, Mind, Body & Spirit, health (home 15%, overseas 20%). No reading fee, but preliminary letter and synopsis with sae essential. Founded 1992.

Frances Kelly Agency*

111 Clifton Road, Kingston-upon-Thames, Surrey KT2 6PL
tel 020-8549 7830 *fax* 020-8547 0051

Full-length MSS. Non-fiction: general and academic, reference and professional books, all subjects (home 10%, overseas 20%), TV, radio (10%). No reading fee, but no unsolicited MSS; preliminary letter with synopsis, CV and return postage essential. Founded 1978.

Fraser & Dunlop Ltd, Fraser & Dunlop Scripts Ltd

– see PFD

French's

78 Loudoun Road, London NW8 0NA
tel 020-7483 4269 *fax* 020-7722 0754
Directors John French, Mark Taylor

All MSS; specialises in novels and screenplays (home/overseas 10%); theatre, films, TV, radio (10%). Reading service available, details on application. Sae must be enclosed with all MSS.

Futerman, Rose & Associates*

Heston Court Business Park, 19 Camp Road, London SW19 4UW
tel 020-8947 0188 *fax* 020-8605 2162
email guy@futermanrose.co.uk
website www.futermanrose.co.uk
Contact Guy Rose

Scripts for film and TV; commercial fiction and non-fiction with film potential, biography, show business, teenage fiction (15–20%). No unsolicited MSS. Send preliminary letter with a brief résumé, detailed synopsis and sae. Overseas associates.

Clients include Frank Dickens, Iain Duncan Smith, Royston Ellis, Charles Fourie, Russell Warren Howe, Sue Lenier, John McVicar, Angela Meredith, Valerie Grosvenor Myer, Michael O'Reilly, Paul

Rattigan, Yvonne Ridley, Frederick E. Smith, Gordon Thomas, Michael Walker, Mark White, Simon Woodham. Founded 1984.

Gillon Aitken Associates Ltd*

29 Fernshaw Road, London SW10 0TG
tel 020-7351 7561 *fax* 020-7376 3594
email reception@gillonaitken.co.uk
Contacts Gillon Aitken, Clare Alexander, Lesley Shaw (film/TV)

Fiction and non-fiction (home 10%, USA 20%, translation 20%, film/TV 10%). No plays, scripts or children's fiction unless by existing clients. Send preliminary letter with half-page synopsis and first 30pp of sample material and adequate return postage, in the first instance. No reading fee. Associated agents: Anthony Sheil, Mary Pachnos.

Clients include Caroline Alexander, John Banville, Pat Barker, Nicholas Blincoe, Gordon Burn, John Cornwell, Josephine Cox, Sarah Dunant, Susan Elderkin, Sebastian Faulks, Helen Fielding, John Fowles, Germaine Greer, Mark Haddon, Susan Howatch, LizJensen, John Keegan, Pete McCarthy, V.S. Naipaul, Jonathan Raban, Piers Paul Read, Michèle Roberts, Nicholas Shakespeare, Gillian Slovo, Matt Thorne, Colin Thubron, Salley Vickers, A.N. Wilson, Robert Wilson. Founded 1977.

Greene & Heaton Ltd*

37 Goldhawk Road, London W12 8QQ
tel 020-8749 0315 *fax* 020-8749 0318
email submissions@greeneheaton.co.uk
childrenssubmissions@greeneheaton.co.uk
Contacts Carol Heaton, Judith Murray, Antony Topping, Linda Davis (children's)

All types of fiction and non-fiction (home 10–15%, USA/translation 20%). No original scripts for theatre, film or TV. Send no more than a brief covering letter, synopsis and 3 chapters. No reply to unsolicited submissions without sae and/or return postage. Overseas associates worldwide.

Clients include Mark Barrowcliffe, Bill Bryson, Jan Dalley, Marcus du Sautoy, Hugh Fearnley-Whittingstall, Colin Forbes, Michael Frayn, P.D. James, Mary Morrissy, William Shawcross, Sarah Waters. Founded 1962.

Gregory & Company Authors' Agents*

3 Barb Mews, London W6 7PA
tel 020-7610 4676 *fax* 020-7610 4686
email info@gregoryandcompany.co.uk
website www.gregoryandcompany.co.uk
Contacts Jane Gregory, *Editorial* Broo Doherty, *Rights* Claire Morris

Fiction and general non-fiction (home 15%, USA/translation/radio/film/TV 20%). Special interests (fiction): literary, commercial, crime, suspense and thrillers. Particularly interested in

books which will also sell to publishers abroad. No original plays, film or TV scripts (only published books are sold to film and TV), science fiction, fantasy, poetry, academic or children's books. No reading fee. Editorial advice given to own authors. No unsolicited MSS: send preliminary letter with CV, synopsis, first 3 chapters and future writing plans plus return postage. Short submissions (3pp) by fax or email. Represented throughout Europe, Asia and USA. Founded 1987.

IMG Literary UK

The Pier House, Strand on the Green, London W4 3NN
tel 020-8233 5000 *fax* 020-8233 5001
Chairman Mark H. McCormack, *Agents* Sarah Wooldridge (London), Mark Reiter and Lisa Queen (New York), Fumiko Matsuki (Japan)

Celebrity books, sports-related books, commercial fiction, non-fiction and how-to business books (home 15%, USA 20%, elsewhere 25%). No theatre, children's, academic or poetry. No reading fee.

Intercontinental Literary Agency*

33 Bedford Street, London WC2E 9ED
tel 020-7379 6611 *fax* 020-7379 6790
email ila@ila-agency.co.uk
Contacts Nicki Kennedy, Sam Edenborough, Mary Esdaile

Represents translation rights for PFD, London, Harold Matson Company Inc., New York, the Turnbull Agency (John Irving) Inc., and Lucas Alexander Whitley Ltd. Founded 1965.

International Literary Representation & Management LLC

186 Bickenhall Mansions, Bickenhall Street, London W1U 6BX
tel 020-7224 1748 *fax* 020-7224 1802
email info@yesitive.com
website www.yesitive.com
Vice President for Europe Peter Cox

European office of US agency. Represents authors with major international potential. Commission by agreement. Only considers submissions if guidelines found on website have been followed. No unsolicited MSS. No radio or theatre scripts. No reading fee.

Clients include Martin Bell OBE, Brian Clegg, Brian Cruver, Caris Davis, Senator Orrin Hatch, Barbara Jacobs, Michael J. Nelson, Michelle Paver, Saxon Roach, David Soul. Founded 1993.

International Scripts

1A Kidbrooke Park Road, London SE3 0LR
tel 020-8319 8666 *fax* 020-8319 0801
Directors H.P. Tanner, J. Lawson

Specialises in full-length contemporary and women's fiction, biographies, business and general non-fiction (home 15%, overseas 20%), performance rights (15–20%); no poetry or short stories. Works with overseas agents. Preliminary letter and sae required. An editorial contribution plus return postage may be requested for reading MSS.

Authors include Jane Adams, Zita Adamson, Ashleigh Bingham, Simon Clark, Cory Daniells, Paul Devereux, Dr James Fleming, James Gibbins, Ed Gorman, Peter Haining, Julie Harris, Robert A. Heinlein, Anna Jacobs, Anne Jones, Richard Laymon, Nick Oldham, Christine Poulson, Mary Ryan, John and Anne Spencer, Janet Woods. Founded 1979.

J.M. Thurley Management
Archery House, 33 Archery Square, Walmer, Deal, Kent CT14 7JA
tel (01304) 371421 *fax* (01304) 371416
email JMThurley@aol.com
Contact Jon Thurley

Specialises in commercial and literary full-length fiction and commercial work for film and TV. No plays, poetry, short stories, articles or fantasy. No reading fee but preliminary letter and sae essential. Editorial/creative advice provided to clients (home 15%, overseas 20%). Links with leading US and European agents. Founded 1976.

Jacintha Alexander Associates – see LAW Ltd
(Lucas Alexander Whitley)

Jane Conway-Gordon*
(in association with Andrew Mann Ltd)
1 Old Compton Street, London W1D 5JA
tel 020-7494 0148 *fax* 020-7287 9264

Full length MSS, performance rights (home 15%, overseas 20%). Represented in all foreign countries. No reading fee but preliminary letter and return postage essential. Founded 1982.

Jane Judd Literary Agency*
18 Belitha Villas, London N1 1PD
tel 020-7607 0273 *fax* 020-7607 0623

General non-fiction and fiction (home 10%, overseas 20%). Special interests: women's fiction, crime, thrillers, narrative non-fiction. No short stories, film/TV scripts, poetry or plays. No reading fee, but preliminary letter with synopsis, first chapter and sae essential. Works with agents in USA and most foreign countries. Founded 1986.

Jane Turnbull*
13 Wendell Road, London W12 9RS
tel 020-8743 9580 *fax* 020-8749 6079

Fiction and non-fiction (home 10%, USA/translation 20%), performance rights (15%). No science fiction, romantic fiction, children's or

short stories. Works in conjunction with **Gillon Aitken Associates Ltd** for sale of translation rights. No reading fee. Preliminary letter and sae essential; no unsolicited MSS. Founded 1986.

Janet Fillingham Associates
52 Lowther Road, London SW13 9NU
tel 020-8748 5594 *fax* 020-8748 7374
email janet@jfillassoc.co.uk
Director Janet Fillingham

Film and TV only (home 10%, overseas 15–20%). Strictly no unsolicited MSS; professional recommendation required. Founded 1992.

Janklow & Nesbit (UK) Ltd
29 Adam & Eve Mews, London W8 6UG
tel 020-7376 2733 *fax* 020-7376 2915
email queries@janklow.co.uk
Agents Tif Loehnis, Claire Paterson

Commercial and literary fiction and non-fiction. No unsolicited MSS. Send informative covering letter and return postage with full outline (non-fiction), synopsis and 3 sample chapters (fiction). US and foreign rights handled by **Janklow & Nesbit Associates** in New York.

Jeffrey Simmons
15 Penn House, Lisson Green Estate, London NW8 8FX
tel 020-7224 8917 *fax* 020-7224 8918

Specialises in fiction (no science fiction, horror or fantasy), biography, autobiography, show business, personality books, law, crime, politics, world affairs. Full-length MSS (home from 10%, overseas from 15%). Will suggest revision. No reading fee, but preliminary letter essential.

Jennifer Luithlen Agency
88 Holmfield Road, Leicester LE2 1SB
tel 0116-273 8863 *fax* 0116-273 5697
Agents Jennifer Luithlen, Penny Luithlen

Not looking for new clients. Children's books; adult fiction: crime, historical, saga (home 10%, overseas 20%), performance rights (15%). Founded 1986.

Jill Foster Ltd
9 Barb Mews, Brook Green, London W6 7PA
tel 020-7602 1263 *fax* 020-7602 9336

Theatre, films, TV and sound broadcasting (12.5%). Particularly interested in film and TV comedy and drama. No novels or short stories. No reading fee. Preliminary letter essential. No submissions by email. Do not send material in the first instance. Founded 1978.

JMLA
The Basement, 94 Goldhurst Terrace, London NW6 3HS

tel 020-7372 8422 *fax* 020-7372 8423
Managing Director Judy Martin

Fiction, non-fiction, biography and popular culture (home 15%, overseas 20%). No plays, poetry, cookery, gardening or children's stories. Translation rights handled by the **Marsh Agency Ltd**. No reading fee, but sae required for all unsolicited MSS, together with details of publishing history. Founded 1990.

John Farquharson Ltd – see Curtis Brown Group Ltd

John Johnson (Authors' Agent)*
Clerkenwell House, 45-47 Clerkenwell Green, London EC1R 0HT
tel 020-7251 0125 *fax* 020-7251 2172
email johnjohnson@btinternet.com
Contacts Andrew Hewson

Full-length MSS (home 10%, USA 15–20%, translation 20%). General fiction and non-fiction. No science fiction, technical or academic material. Scripts from existing clients only. No unsolicited MSS; send preliminary letter and sae. No reading fee. Division of Johnson & Alcock Ltd. Founded 1956.

John Pawsey
60 High Street, Tarring, Worthing, West Sussex BN14 7NR
tel/fax (01903) 205167

General non-fiction, particularly biography, popular culture and sport; crime, thriller, suspense and genuinely original fiction only (home 10–15%, overseas 19–25%). No science fiction, fantasy, horror, poetry, short stories, journalism, children's or original film and stage scripts. Preliminary letter and return postage with all correspondence essential. Works in association with agencies in the USA, Europe and the Far East. Will suggest revision if MS sufficiently promising. No reading fee.

Authors include Jonathan Agnew, Jennie Bond, William Fotheringham, John Hale, Patricia Hall, Elwyn Hartley Edwards, Dr David Lewis. Founded 1981.

Jonathan Clowes Ltd*
10 Iron Bridge House, Bridge Approach, London NW1 8BD
tel 020-7722 7674 *fax* 020-7722 7677
Directors Jonathan Clowes, Ann Evans, Lisa Whadcock

Literary and commercial fiction and non-fiction, film, TV, theatre and radio (home 15%, overseas 20%). No reading fee. No unsolicited MSS. Works in association with agents overseas. Founded 1960.

Clients include Sir Kingsley Amis Estate, Dr David Bellamy, Bill Dare, Len Deighton, David Harsent, Elizabeth Jane Howard, Damian Lanigan, David Lawrence, Doris Lessing, David Nobbs, Gillian White.

Jonathan Williams Literary Agency
Rosney Mews, Upper Glenageary Road, Glenageary, Co. Dublin, Republic of Ireland
tel/fax (01) 2803482
Director Jonathan Williams

General fiction and non-fiction, preferably by Irish authors (home 10%). Will suggest revision; no reading fee unless a very fast decision is required. Return postage appreciated (no British stamps – please use IRCs). Sub-agents in Germany and Italy. Founded 1981.

Josef Weinberger Plays Ltd
(formerly Warner/Chappell Plays Ltd)
12-14 Mortimer Street, London W1T 3JJ
tel 020-7580 2827 *fax* 020-7436 9616

Specialises in stage plays. Works in conjunction with overseas agents. No unsolicited MSS; preliminary letter essential. Founded 1938.

Judith Chilcote Agency*
8 Wentworth Mansions, Keats Grove, London NW3 2RL
tel 020-7794 3717
email judybks@aol.com
Director Judith Chilcote

Commercial fiction, non-fiction – sports, self-help and health, cookery, autobiography and biography, current affairs, TV tie-ins (home 15%, overseas 20–25%). No short stories, science fiction, children's, poetry. Works in conjunction with overseas agents and New York affiliate. No reading fee but preliminary letter with 3 chapters only, CV and sae essential. Founded 1990.

Judith Murdoch Literary Agency*
19 Chalcot Square, London NW1 8YA
tel 020-7722 4197

Full-length fiction only (home 15%, overseas 20%). No thrillers, science fiction/fantasy, poetry, short stories or children's. Approach by letter, *not* telephone, sending the first 2 chapters and synopsis. Return postage/sae essential. Editorial advice given; no reading fee. Translation rights handled by the **Marsh Agency Ltd**. Founded 1993.

Judy Daish Associates Ltd
2 St Charles Place, London W10 6EG
tel 020-8964 8811 *fax* 020-8964 8966
Agents Judy Daish, Sara Stroud, Tracey Elliston

Theatre, film, TV, radio (rates by negotiation). No unsolicited MSS. No reading fee. Founded 1978.

Jüri Gabriel
35 Camberwell Grove, London SE5 8JA
tel/fax 020-7703 6186

Quality fiction and non-fiction (i.e. anything that shows wit and intelligence); radio, TV and film, but mainly selling these rights in existing works by existing clients. Full-length MSS (home 10%, overseas 20%), performance rights (10%); will suggest revision where appropriate. No short stories, articles, verse or books for children. No reading fee; return postage essential. Jüri Gabriel is the chairman of Dedalus (publishers).

Authors include Diana Constance, Miriam Dunne, Pat Gray, Robert Irwin, John Lucas, 'David Madsen', Richard Mankiewicz, David Miller, Andy Oaks, John Outram, Stefan Szymanski, Dr Terence White, Dr Robert Youngson.

Juvenilia

Avington, Winchester, Hants SO21 1DB
tel/fax (01962) 779656
email juvenilia@clara.co.uk
Contact Rosemary Bromley

Full-length MSS for the children's market, fiction and non-fiction (home 10%, overseas from 15%), illustration (10%), performance rights (10%). Short stories only if specifically for picture books, radio or TV. No unsolicited MSS; preliminary letter with sae and full details essential. Postage for acknowledge-ment and return of material imperative. No fax, telephone or email enquiries. Founded 1973.

Laura Morris Literary Agency

21 Highshore Road, London SE15 5AA
tel 020-7732 0153 *fax* 020-7732 9022
email laura.morris@ukgateway.net
Director Laura Morris

Literary fiction, film studies, biography, media, cookery, culture/art, humour (home 10%, overseas 20%). No unsolicitied MSS.

Authors include Peter Cowie, Laurence Marks and Maurice Gran, David Thomson, Brian Turner, Janni Visman. Founded 1998.

Laurence Fitch Ltd

(incorporating The London Play Company 1922)
Mezzanine, Quadrant House, 80-82 Regent Street, London W1B 5AU
tel 020-7734 9911 *fax* 020-7437 0561
email information@laurencefitch.com
website www.laurencefitch.com
Directors F.H.L. Fitch, Joan Potts, Brendan Davis

Theatre, films, TV and sound broadcasting (home 10%, overseas 15%). Also works with several agencies in USA and in Europe.

Authors include Carlo Ardito, John Chapman, Peter Coke; Ray Cooney, John Graham, Dawn Lowe-Watson, Glyn Robbins, Edward Taylor, and the Estate of the late Dodie Smith.

Lavinia Trevor*

The Glasshouse, 49A Goldhawk Road, London W12 8QP

tel 020-8749 8481 *fax* 020-8749 7377

Fiction and non-fiction, including popular science, for the general reader. No children's books or science fiction. No reading fee. Brief autobio-graphical letter and approx. first 50pp required plus sae. Founded 1993.

LAW Ltd (Lucas Alexander Whitley)*

(incorporating Jacintha Alexander Associates)
14 Vernon Street, London W14 0RJ
tel 020-7471 7900 *fax* 020-7471 7910
email firstname@lawagency.co.uk
Contacts Mark Lucas, Julian Alexander, Araminta Whitley, Philippa Milnes-Smith, Celia Hayley, Lucinda Cook, Peta Nightingale, Alice Saunders, Helen Mulligan

Full-length adult and children's commercial and literary fiction and non-fiction (home 15%, USA and translation 20%). No poetry, plays, textbooks, or fantasy. Film and TV scripts handled for established clients only. Unsolicited MSS considered; send brief covering letter, short synopsis and 2 sample chapters. Sae essential. No submissions by email. No reading fee. Overseas associates. Founded 1996.

LBLA (Lorella Belli Literary Agency)

54 Hartford House, 35 Tavistock Crescent, London W11 1AY
tel 020-7727 8547 *fax* (0870) 7874194
email info@lorellabelliagency.com
website www.lorellabelliagency.com
Proprietor Lorella Belli

Fiction and general non-fiction (home 15%, overseas 20%, dramatic 20%). Particularly interested in first-time writers, journalists, international and multicultural writing and books on Italy. No children's, science fiction, fantasy, academic, poetry, original scripts. No reading fee. May suggest revision. Works with overseas and dramatic associates.

Authors include Sean Bidder, Scott Capurro, Sean Coughlan, Dario Fo, Emily Griffin, Nisha Minhas, Rupert Steiner, Marcello Vannucci, Diana Winston. Founded 2002.

Limelight Management*

33 Newman Street, London W1T 1PY
tel 020-7637 2529 *fax* 020-7637 2538
email limelight.management@virgin.net
website www.limelightmanagement.com
Directors Fiona Lindsay, Linda Shanks

Full-length and short MSS. Food, wine, health, crafts, gardening, interior design (home 15%, overseas 20%), TV and radio rights (10-20%); will suggest revision where appropriate. No reading fee. Founded 1991.

The Lisa Richards Agency

46 Upper Baggot Street, Dublin 4,
Republic of Ireland
tel (01) 660 3534 *fax* (01) 660 3545
email fogrady@eircom.net
Contact Faith O'Grady

Fiction, non-fiction, children's (home 10%, UK
15%, overseas 20%). Translation rights handled by
the **Marsh Agency Ltd**. No reading fee.

Authors include June Considine, Tara Heavey,
Colm Keena, Martin Malone, Pauline McLynn,
Sarah O'Brien, David O'Doherty, Damien Owens,
Homan Potterton, Kevin Rafter, Annie Sparrow.
Founded 1998.

London Independent Books

26 Chalcot Crescent, London NW1 8YD
tel 020-7706 0486 *fax* 020-7724 3122
Proprietor Carolyn Whitaker

Specialises in commercial, fantasy and teenage
fiction, show business, travel. Full-length MSS
(home 15%, overseas 20%), films, TV and sound
broadcasting (15%). Will suggest revision of
promising MSS. No reading fee.

Authors include Eric Braun, Keith Gray, Tim
Mackintosh-Smith, Glenn Mitchell, Connie Monk,
Richard Morgan, Kevin Rushby, Emma Sinclair,
Chris Wooding. Founded 1971.

Louise Greenberg Books Ltd*

The End House, Church Crescent, London N3 1BG
tel 020-8349 1179 *fax* 020-8343 4559
email louisegreenberg@msn.com

Full-length MSS (home10%, overseas 20–25%).
Literary fiction and non-fiction. No reading fee.
Return postage and sae essential. No telephone
enquiries. Founded 1997.

Lucas Alexander Whitley – see LAW Ltd (Lucas Alexander Whitley)

Lutyens & Rubinstein*

231 Westbourne Park Road, London W11 1EB
tel 020-7792 4855 *fax* 020-7792 4833
Directors Sarah Lutyens, Felicity Rubinstein
Submissions Susannah Godman

Fiction and non-fiction, commercial and literary
(home 15%, overseas 20%). Send outline/2 sample
chapters and sae. No reading fee. Founded 1993.

Maggie Noach Literary Agency*

22 Dorville Crescent, London W6 0HJ
tel 020-8748 2926 *fax* 020-8748 8057
email m-noach@dircon.co.uk

Very few new clients taken on as it is considered
vital to give individual attention to each author's
work. High-quality full-length fiction; general non-

fiction (especially biography, travel, history);
children's books (text only) for reading age 8
upwards. Material submitted on an exclusive basis
preferred (home 15%, USA/translation generally
20%). No short stories, poetry, plays, screenplays,
cookery, gardening, Mind, Body & Spirit,
scientific/academic/specialist non-fiction or any
illustrated books. Send a brief description of the
book plus 2–3 sample chapters. Return postage
essential. Email attachments will not be opened and
faxed submissions will not be considered. No
reading fee. Founded 1982.

Maggie Pearlstine Associates Ltd*

31 Ashley Gardens, Ambrosden Avenue,
London SW1P 1QE
tel 020-7828 4212 *fax* 020-7834 5546
email post@pearlstine.co.uk

General non-fiction and fiction. Special interests:
history, current affairs, biography, health (home
10–12.5%; overseas, journalism and media 20%).
Translation rights handled by **Gillon Aitken
Associates Ltd**. No children's, poetry, horror, science
fiction, short stories or scripts. Seldom takes on new
authors. Prospective clients should write an
explanatory letter and enclose a sae and the first
chapter only. No submissions accepted by fax, email
or from abroad. No reading fee.

Authors include Debbie Beckerman, John Biffen,
Matthew Baylis, Kate Bingham, Menzies Campbell,
Robin Cook, Frank Dobson, Kim Fletcher, Roy
Hattersley, Rachel Holmes, Charles Kennedy, Mark
Leonard, Claire Macdonald, Eleanor Mills, Dr Raj
Persaud, Prof Lesley Regan, Hugo Rifkind, Winifred
Robinson, Jackie Rowley, Henrietta Spencer-
Churchill, Prof Alan Stewart, Prof Robert Winston.
Founded 1989.

Manuscript ReSearch

PO Box 33, Bicester, Oxon OX6 7PP
tel (01869) 323447 *fax* (01869) 324096
Proprietor T.G. Jenkins

Now concentrating on film/TV and radio scripts.
No reading fee, but sae for script return essential.
Founded 1988.

Margaret Hanbury*

27 Walcot Square, London SE11 4UB
tel 020-7735 7680 *fax* 020-7793 0316
email maggie@mhanbury.demon.co.uk

Personally run agency specialising in quality fiction
and non-fiction (home 15%, overseas 20%). No
unsolicited approaches this year.

Authors include George Alagiah, J.G. Ballard,
Simon Callow, Judith Lennox. Founded 1983.

Margaret Ramsay Ltd – now Casarotto Ramsay & Associates Ltd

Marjacq Scripts
34 Devonshire Place, London W1G 6JW
tel 020-7935 9499 *fax* 020-7935 9115
email enquiries@marjacq.com
website www.marjacq.com
Contact Asya Khan

Full-length MSS (home10%, overseas 20%). Crime, thrillers, science fiction, women's commercial fiction. No reading fee. Will suggest revision.

Authors include Benita Brown, Richard Craze, James Follett, Ros Jay, Jeannie Johnson, Elizabeth Lord, Michael Taylor, R.D. Wingfield. Founded 1974.

Mark Paterson & Associates – see Paterson Marsh Ltd

The Marsh Agency Ltd*
11-12 Dover Street, London W1S 4LJ
tel 020-7399 2800 *fax* 020-7399 2801
email enquiries@marsh-agency.co.uk
website www.marsh-agency.co.uk
Director Paul Marsh

Specialises in selling international rights in English and foreign language writing. Represents UK, USA and Canadian agencies and publishers, and some individual authors. Also UK rights for general fiction and non-fiction. No TV, film, radio, theatre, poetry or children's. Unsolicited submissions (outline and sample chapters) accepted by email. No reading fee. See also **Paterson Marsh Ltd**. Founded 1994.

Martinez Literary Agency
60 Oakwood Avenue,
London N14 6QL
tel 020-8886 5829
Contacts Françoise Budd, Mary Martinez

Fiction, children's books, arts and crafts, interior design, alternative health and complementary medicine, cookery, autobiographies, popular music, sport and memorabilia (home 15%; USA, overseas and translation 20%; performance rights 20%). No reading fee. Not accepting any new writers. Founded 1988.

Mary Clemmey Literary Agency*
6 Dunollie Road, London NW5 2XP
tel 020-7267 1290 *fax* 020-7482 7360

High-quality fiction and non-fiction with an international market (home 10%, overseas 20%), performance rights (15%). No children's books, science fiction or fantasy. TV, film, radio and theatre scripts from existing clients only. Works in conjunction with US agent. No reading fee. No unsolicited MSS. Approach by letter (including sae). Founded 1992.

MBA Literary Agents Ltd*
62 Grafton Way, London W1T 5DW
tel 020-7387 2076 *fax* 020-7387 2042
email firstname@mbalit.co.uk
Contacts Diana Tyler, John Richard Parker, Meg Davis, Laura Longrigg

Handles fiction and non-fiction, and TV, film, radio and theatre scripts (home 15%, overseas 20%; theatre, TV, radio 10%; films 10–20%). No unsolicited material. Works in conjunction with agents in most countries. UK representative for **Writers House LLC**, the Donald Maass Agency and the **Jabberwocky Literary Agency**.

Clients include Campbell Armstrong, A.L. Barker, *The Chap Magazine*, Estate of Harry Bowling, Jeffrey Caine, Glenn Chandler, Andrew Cowan, Patricia Finney, Maggie Furey, Sue Gee, Joanna Hines, the Estate of B.S. Johnson, Anne McCaffrey, Paul Magrs, Susan Oudot, Sir Roger Penrose, Anne Perry, Gervase Phinn, Iain Sinclair, Steve Strange, Mark Wallington, Douglas Watkinson, Paul Wilson, Valerie Windsor. Founded 1971.

Merric Davidson Literary Agency
12 Priors Heath, Goudhurst, Kent TN17 2RE
tel/fax (01580) 212041
email md@mdla.co.uk
Contacts Merric Davidson, Wendy Suffield

Specialising in contemporary adult fiction (home 10%, overseas 20%). No unsolicited MSS. Preliminary letter with synopsis, author information and sae. No initial reading fee, may suggest revision, subsequent editorial advice by arrangement.

Authors include Alys Clare, Francesca Clementis, Murray Davies, Harold Elletson, Alison Habens, Frankie Park, Mark Pepper, Simon Scarrow. Founded 1990.

Mic Cheetham Literary Agency
11-12 Dover Street, London W1S 4LJ
tel 020-7495 2002 *fax* 020-7495 5777
website www.miccheetham.com
Director Mic Cheetham, *Contact* Simon Kavanagh

General and literary fiction, science fiction, some non-fiction (home/overseas 10–20%); film, TV and radio rights (10–20%); will suggest revision. Works with the **Marsh Agency Ltd** for foreign rights. No unsolicited MSS. No reading fee. Founded 1994.

Michael Alcock Management*
Clerkenwell House, 45-47 Clerkenwell Green,
London EC1R 0HT
tel 020-7837 8137 *fax* 020-7837 8787
email alcockmgt@aol.com
Agents Michael Alcock, Anna Power

Fiction and non-fiction (home 15%, overseas 20%,

performance rights 15%). General non-fiction, mainly biography, history, current affairs, health and lifestyle; literary and commercial fiction. No reading fee. Send letter, CV including previous writing and media experience, and synopsis and first 3 chapters with sae. Overseas associates: **Andrew Nurnberg Associates**. Division of Johnson & Alcock Ltd.

Authors include Tamsin Blanchard, Barbara Currie, Tom Dixon, Yehudi Gordon, Mark Griffiths, Joanna Hall, Lisa Hilton, Lynne Robinson, Barnaby Rogerson, Barry Turner, Lowri Turner. Founded 1997.

Micheline Steinberg Associates
4th floor, 104 Great Portland Street, London W1W 6PE
tel 020-7631 1310 *fax* 020-7631 1146
email info@steinplays.com

Full-length MSS – theatre, films, TV, radio (home 10%, overseas 15%). Dramatic Associate for **Pollinger Ltd**; works in conjunction with agents in USA and other countries. No reading fee, but preliminary letter essential and return postage with MSS. Founded 1987.

Michelle Kass Associates*
36-38 Glasshouse Street, London W1B 5DL
tel 020-7439 1624 *fax* 020-7734 3394
Proprietor Michelle Kass

Full-length MSS. Literary fiction and drama scripts for film (home 10%, overseas 15–20%). Will suggest revision where appropriate. Works with agents overseas. No reading fee. Absolutely no unsolicited MSS without a preliminary phone call. Founded 1991.

Murray Pollinger – see David Higham Associates Ltd

New Authors Showcase
(Barrie James Literary Agency)
Rivendell, Kingsgate Close, Torquay, Devon TQ2 8QA
tel (01803) 326617
email mail@newauthors.org.uk
website www.newauthors.org.uk
Contact Barrie James

Internet site for new writers and poets to display their work to publishers. No reading fee but a small charge is made for display on the internet. No unsolicited MSS. First contact: send sae or email. Founded 1997.

Paterson Marsh Ltd*
(merged with the Marsh Agency Ltd 2001)
11-12 Dover Street, London W15 4LJ
tel 020-7399 2800 *fax* 020-7399 2801
email paterson@patersonmarsh.co.uk

website www.patersonmarsh.co.uk
Contacts Mark Paterson, Stephanie Ebdon

Book-length MSS; general but with special experience in psychoanalysis, psychotherapy, history and education (20% worldwide including sub-agents' commission). No fiction, articles or short stories except for existing clients. Preliminary letter with synopsis, sample material and return postage essential.

Authors include Sigmund Freud, Anna Freud, Hugh Brogan, Donald Winnicott, Peter Moss, Sir Arthur Evans, Dorothy Richardson, Hugh Schonfield, Georg Groddeck, Patrick Casement, John Seely. Founded 1955.

Peter Knight Agency
20 Crescent Grove, London SW4 7AH
tel 020-7622 1467 *fax* 020-7622 1522
email peter@knightfeatures.co.uk
website www.knightfeatures.co.uk
Director Peter Knight, *Associates* Ann King-Hall, Gaby Martin, Andrew Knight, Samantha Ferris

Motor sports, cartoon books, business, history and factual, biographical and autobiographical material. No poetry, science fiction or cookery. Overseas associates: United Media (USA), Auspac Media (Australia), Puzzle Company. No unsolicited MSS. Send letter accompanied by CV and sae with synopsis of proposed work.

Clients include Ralph Barker, Frank Dickens, John Dodd, Gray Jolliffe, Angus McGill, Chris Maslanka, Barbara Minto, Lisa Wild. Founded 1985.

The Peters Fraser and Dunlop Group Ltd – see PFD

PFD*
(incorporating A.D. Peters & Co. Ltd, Fraser & Dunlop Scripts Ltd, Fraser & Dunlop Ltd, June Hall Literary Agency Ltd, Watergate Film Services Ltd)
Drury House, 34-43 Russell Street, London WC2B 5HA
tel 020-7344 1000 *fax* 020-7836 9539
email postmaster@pfd.co.uk
website www.pfd.co.uk
Joint Chairmen Anthony Jones and Tim Corrie, *Managing Director* Anthony Baring, *Books* Caroline Dawnay, Michael Sissons, Pat Kavanagh, Charles Walker, Rosemary Canter, Rosemary Scoular, Robert Kirby, Simon Trewin, James Gill, *Serial* Pat Kavanagh, Carol Macarthur, *Film/TV* Tim Corrie, Anthony Jones, Norman North, Charles Walker, St John Donald, Natasha Galloway, Louisa Thompson, Jago Irwin, Lynda Mamy, *Actors* Maureen Vincent, Dallas Smith, Lindy King, Ruth Cooper, Ruth Young, Lucy Brazier, Kathryn Fleming, Duncan Hayes, *Theatre* Kenneth Ewing, St John Donald, Nicki Stoddart, Rosie Cobbe, *Children's* Rosemary Canter, *New Media* Rosemary Scoular,

Translation Rights Intercontinental Literary Agency, *US Illustrators' Representation* Harriet Kasak

Handles the full range of books including fiction, children's and non-fiction as well as scripts for film, theatre, radio and TV, actors and multimedia projects (home 10%; USA and translation 20%). Has 75 years of international experience in all media. Send a full outline for non-fiction and short synopsis for fiction with 2–3 sample chapters and autobiographical note. Screenplays/TV scripts should be addressed to the 'Film & Script Dept'. The Children's Dept accepts unsolicited written material in the form of a covering letter, brief plot summary and one paragraph only of text; submissions from illustrators are also welcome. Material submitted on an exclusive basis preferred; in any event it should be disclosed if material is being submitted to other agencies or publishers. Return postage essential. No reading fee. No guaranteed response to submissions by email.

Pollinger Ltd*

(formerly Laurence Pollinger Ltd, successor of Pearn, Pollinger and Higham)
9 Staple Inn, Holborn,
London WC1V 7QH
tel 020-7404 0342 *fax* 020-7242 5737
email info@pollingerltd.com
website www.pollingerltd.com
Chairman Paul Woolf, *Managing Director* Lesley Pollinger, *Rights Manager* Katy Loffman, *Children's List* Linda Jennings, *Consultant* Gerald Pollinger

All types of general trade adult and children's fiction and non-fiction; illustrators/photographers (home 15%, translation 20%). Unsolicited material considered only if preceded by letter or email. No reading fee. Overseas, media and theatrical associates.

Clients include Roy Apps, Derry Brabbs, Dougie Brimson, Michael Coleman, Michael Cox, Teresa Driscoll, Catherine Fisher, Philip Gross, Gene Kemp, Gary Latham, Alan McDonald, Gary Paulsen, Nicolas Rhea, Sue Welford; also the Estates of H.E. Bates, Louis Bromfield, Erskine Caldwell, Vera Chapman, D.H. Lawrence, John Masters, Alan Moorehead, W. Heath Robinson, William Saroyan, Clifford D. Simak and other notables. Founded 2002.

PVA Management Ltd

Hallow Park, Worcester WR2 6PG
tel (01905) 640663 *fax* (01905) 641842
email pva@pva.co.uk
Managing Director Paul Vaughan

Full-length MSS. Non-fiction only (home 15%, overseas 20%, performance rights 15%). Please send synopsis and sample chapters together with return postage.

Richard Hatton Ltd

29 Roehampton Gate,
London SW15 5JR
tel 020-8876 6699 *fax* 020-8876 8278
Director Richard Hatton

Stage plays; TV, cinema and radio scripts only. Preliminary letter with outline and sae only. Apply for reading fee rate. No unsolicited MSS. Founded 1954.

Richard Scott Simon Ltd – see Sheil Land Associates Ltd

Robert Dudley Agency

8 Abbotstone Road, London SW15 1QR
tel 020-8788 0938 *fax* 020-8780 3586
email rdudley@btinternet.com
Proprietor Robert Dudley

Specialises in history, biography, sport, humour, health, management, politics, IT and personal development (home 10%, overseas 15%; film/TV/radio 15%, 20%). No reading fee. Will suggest revision.

Authors include Steve Biko, Simon Caulrim, Clive Couldwell, Eva Kolinsky, David Osler, Tim Phillips, Sol Shulman. Founded 2000.

Robert Smith Literary Agency Ltd*

12 Bridge Wharf, 156 Caledonian Road,
London N1 9UU
tel 020-7278 2444 *fax* 020-7833 5680
email robertsmith.literaryagency@virgin.net
Directors Robert Smith, Anne Smith

Non-fiction: autobiography and biography, health and nutrition, cookery, lifestyle, popular culture, music, TV and film tie-ins, true crime, investigative journalism, illustrated books (home 15%, overseas 20%). No unsolicited MSS. No reading fee. Will suggest revision.

Authors include Carol Clerk, Stewart Evans, Neil and Christine Hamilton, James Haspiel, Chris Hutchins, Roberta Kray, Norman Parker, Mike Reid, Prof William Rubinstein, Keith Skinner, Douglas Thompson. Founded 1997.

Robin Wade Literary Agency

1 Cormorant Lodge, Thomas More Street,
London E1W 1AU
tel 020-7488 4171 *fax* 020-7488 4172
email rw@rwla.com
website www.rwla.com
Director Robin Wade, *Associate* Jo Kitching

General fiction and non-fiction, but no poetry, plays or short stories (home 10%, overseas 20%). Send descriptive preliminary email. No reading fee. Founded 2001.

Rochelle Stevens & Co.

2 Terretts Place, Upper Street,
London N1 1QZ
tel 020-7359 3900 *fax* 020-7354 5729
email info@rochellestevens.com
Proprietor Rochelle Stevens, *Associates* Frances
Arnold, Lucy Fawcett

Drama scripts for film, TV, theatre and radio (home
10%, overseas 15%). Preliminary letter, CV and sae
essential. No reading fee. Founded 1984.

The Rod Hall Agency Ltd

3 Charlotte Mews, London W1T 4DZ
tel 020-7637 0706 *fax* 020-7637 0807
email office@rodhallagency.com
website www.rodhallagency.com
Directors Rod Hall, Clare Barker, Charlotte Mann

Specialises in writers for stage, screen and radio but
also deals in TV and film rights in novels and non-
fiction (home 10%, overseas 15%). No reading fee.

Clients include Simon Beaufoy, Jeremy Brock,
Dario Fo, Susan Hill, Arthur Hopcraft, Liz
Lochhead, Martin McDonagh, Andrea Newman,
Simon Nye. Founded 1997.

Rogers, Coleridge & White Ltd*

20 Powis Mews, London W11 1JN
tel 020-7221 3717 *fax* 020-7229 9084
Directors Deborah Rogers, Gill Coleridge, Patricia
White (USA), David Miller, Laurence Laluyaux,
Consultant Ann Warnford-Davis, *USA Associate*
International Creative Management, Inc.

Full-length book MSS, including children's books
(home 10%, USA 15%, translation 20%). No
unsolicited MSS, and no submissions by fax or
email. Founded 1967.

Rosemary Bromley Literary Agency

Avington, Winchester, Hants SO21 1DB
tel/fax (01962) 779656
email rosemarybromley.juvenilia@clara.co.uk

Specialises in biography, travel, leisure, cookery,
health (home 10%, overseas from 15%). No poetry.
No unsolicited MSS. Send full details of work on
offer with return postage. No fax, telephone or
email enquiries. For children's books see **Juvenilia**.

Rosemary Sandberg Ltd

6 Bayley Street, London WC1B 3HB
tel 020-7304 4110 *fax* 020-7304 4109
Directors Rosemary Sandberg, Ed Victor

Children's – writers and illustrators, general fiction
and non-fiction. Absolutely no unsolicited MSS:
client list is full. Founded 1991.

Rosica Colin Ltd

1 Clareville Grove Mews, London SW7 5AH
tel 020-7370 1080 *fax* 020-7244 6441

Directors Sylvie Marston, Joanna Marston

All full-length MSS (excluding science fiction and
poetry); also theatre, film and sound broadcasting
(home 10%, overseas 10–20%). No reading fee, but
may take 3–4 months to consider full MSS. Send
synopsis only in first instance, with letter outlining
writing credits and whether MS has been previously
submitted, plus return postage.

Authors include Richard Aldington, Simone de
Beauvoir (in UK), Samuel Beckett (publication
rights), Steven Berkoff, Alan Brownjohn, Sandy
Brownjohn, Donald Campbell, Nick Dear, Neil
Donnelly, J.T. Edson, Bernard Farrell, Rainer Werner
Fassbinder (in UK), Jean Genet, Mary Halpin, Franz
Xaver Kroetz, Don McCamphill, Heiner Müller (in
UK), Graham Reid, Botho Strauss (in UK), Anthony
Vivis, Wim Wenders (in UK). Founded 1949.

Rupert Crew Ltd*

1A King's Mews, London WC1N 2JA
tel 020-7242 8586 *fax* 020-7831 7914
email rupertcrew@compuserve.com
Directors Doreen Montgomery, Caroline
Montgomery

International representation, handling volume and
subsidiary rights in fiction and non-fiction
properties (home 15%, elsewhere 20%); no plays,
poetry, journalism or short stories. No reading fee,
but preliminary letter and return postage essential.
Also acts independently as publishers' consultants.
Founded 1927 by F. Rupert Crew.

Saddler Literary Agency

9 Curzon Road, London W5 1NE
tel 020-8998 4868 *fax* 020-8998 8851
Proprietor John Saddler

Quality fiction and non-fiction (home 10%,
overseas 20%). No science fiction or fantasy. No
reading fee. Founded 2001.

Sarah Manson Literary Agent

6 Totnes Walk, London N2 0AD
tel 020-8883 3050
email smliteraryagent@aol.com
Proprietor Sarah Manson

Fiction for children and young adults (home 10%,
overseas 20%). Send brief email enquiry or
preliminary letter with sae. Founded 2002.

The Sayle Literary Agency

Bickerton House, 25-27 Bickerton Road,
London N19 5JT
tel 020-7263 8681 *fax* 020-7561 0529
Proprietor Rachel Calder

Fiction: general and crime. Non-fiction: current
affairs, social issues, travel, biographies, history
(home 15%, USA/translation 20%). No plays,
poetry, textbooks, children's, technical, legal or

medical books. No unsolicited MSS. No reading fee but preliminary letter and return postage essential. Overseas associates: Dunow & Carlson Agency, Darhansoff, Verrill and Feldman, Anne Edelstein Literary Agency, USA. Translation rights handled by the **Marsh Agency Ltd**. Film and TV rights handled by **Sayle Screen Ltd**.

Sayle Screen Ltd

11 Jubilee Place, London SW3 3TD
tel 020-7823 3883 *fax* 020-7823 3363
email info@saylescreen.com
website www.saylescreen.com
Agents Jane Villiers, Matthew Bates, Toby Moorcroft, Cathy Kehoe

Specialises in scripts for film, TV, theatre and radio (home 10%, overseas 15–20%). Works in conjunction with agents in New York and Los Angeles. No reading fee but preliminary letter and return postage essential. Represents film and TV rights in fiction and non-fiction for the **Sayle Literary Agency** and **BlackAmber** Books.

The Sharland Organisation Ltd

The Manor House, Manor Street, Raunds, Northants. NN9 6JW
tel (01933) 626600 *fax* (01933) 624860
email tsoshar@aol.com
Directors Mike Sharland, Alice Sharland

Specialises in film, TV, stage and radio rights throughout the world (home 15%, overseas 20%); also negotiates multimedia, interactive TV deals, speaking engagements and computer game contracts. Preliminary letter and return postage is essential. No reading fee. Works in conjunction with overseas agents. Founded 1988.

Sheil Land Associates Ltd*

(incorporating Richard Scott Simon Ltd 1971 and Christy & Moore Ltd 1912)
43 Doughty Street, London WC1N 2LH
tel 020-7405 9351 *fax* 020-7831 2127
email info@sheilland.co.uk
Agents UK and US Sonia Land, Luigi Bonomi, Vivien Green, Amanda Preston, *Film/theatre/TV* John Rush, Roland Baggott, *Foreign* Amelia Cummins, Vanessa Forbes

Full-length general, commercial, quality and literary fiction and non-fiction, including: social politics, history, military history, gardening, thrillers, crime, romance, drama, biography, travel, cookery, humour, UK and foreign estates (home 15%, USA/translation 20%). Also theatre, film, radio and TV scripts. Welcomes approaches from new clients either to start or to develop their careers. Preliminary letter with sae essential. No reading fee. Overseas associates: Georges Borchardt, Inc. (Richard Scott Simon). UK representatives for

Farrar, Straus & Giroux, Inc. US film and TV representation: CAA, APA and others.

Clients include Peter Ackroyd, Seve Ballesteros, Vincet Bhatia, Henry Blofeld, Melvyn Bragg, Stephanie Calman, Steven Carroll, Gennaro Contaldo, Catherine Cookson Estate, Anna del Conte, Elizabeth Corley, Seamus Deane, Charlie Dimmock, Alan Drury, Erik Durschmied, Alan Garner, Robert Green, Bonnie Greer, Susan Hill, Richard Holmes, HRH The Prince of Wales, John Humphrys, Mark Irving, Simon Kernick, James Long, Richard Mabey, Colin McDowell, Richard Madeley and Judy Finnigan, Patrick O'Brian Estate, Esther Rantzen, Pam Rhodes, Jean Rhys Estate, Steve Rider, Martin Riley, Colin Schindler, Tom Sharpe, Alan Sillitoe, Martin Stephen, Brian Sykes, Jeffrey Tayler, Rachel de Thame, Alan Titchmarsh, Rose Tremain, Phil Vickery, Tommy Walsh, John Wilsher, Paul Wilson, Chris Woodhead. Founded 1962.

Sheila Ableman Literary Agency

122 Arlington Road, London NW1 7HP
tel/fax 020-7485 3409
email sheila@ableman.freeserve.co.uk
Contact Sheila Ableman

Non-fiction including history, science, biography, autobiography (home 15%, USA/translation 20%). Specialises in TV tie-ins and ghost writing. Does not poetry, children's, cookery, gardening or sport. Unsolicited MSS welcome. Approach in writing with publishing history, CV, synopsis, 3 chapters and sae for return. No reading fee. Founded 2000.

Shelley Power Literary Agency Ltd*

13 rue du Pre Saint Gervais, 75019 Paris, France
tel 42 38 36 49 *fax* 40 40 70 08
email shelley.power@wanadoo.fr

General fiction and non-fiction. Full-length MSS (home 10%, USA and translation 19%). No children's books, poetry or plays. Works in conjunction with agents abroad. No reading fee, but preliminary letter with return postage as from UK or France essential. No submissions by email. Also based in the UK. Founded 1976.

Shirley Stewart Literary Agency

3rd Floor, 21 Denmark Street,
London WC2H 8NA
tel 020-7836 4440 *fax* 020-7836 3482
Director Shirley Stewart

Specialises in literary fiction and general non-fiction (home 10–15%, overseas 20%). No poetry, plays, film scripts, science fiction, fantasy or children's books. No reading fee. Send preliminary letter, synopsis and first 3 chapters plus return postage. Founded 1993.

Sinclair-Stevenson

3 South Terrace, London SW7 2TB
tel/fax 020-7581 2550
Directors Christopher Sinclair-Stevenson, Deborah Sinclair-Stevenson

Full-length MSS (home 10%, USA/translation 20%). General – no children's books. No reading fee; will suggest a revision. Founded 1995.

The Susie Adams Rights Agency

8 Sullivan Road, London SE11 4UH
tel 020-7582 6765 *fax* 020-7582 7279
email SusieARA@aol.com
Agent Susie Adams

Subsidiary rights agent on behalf of packagers and publishers: foreign language and co-editions worldwide, UK serial, book club, merchandise and other sub rights. No authors. Founded 1998.

The Susijn Agency

3rd Floor, 64 Great Titchfield Street, London W1W 7QH
tel 020-7580 6341 *fax* 020-7580 8626
email info@thesusijnagency.com
website www.thesusijnagency.com
Director Laura Susijn

Specialises in world rights in English and non-English language literature: literary fiction and general non-fiction (home 15%, overseas 20%, theatre/film/TV/ radio 15%). Send synopsis and 2 sample chapters. No reading fee.

Authors include Peter Ackroyd, Uzma Aslam Khan, Gilad Atemon, Robin Baker, Robert Craig, Radhika Jha, Anita Nair, Joydeep Roy-Bhattacharya, Karl Shaw, Paul Sussman, Alex Wheatle, Adam Zameenzad. Founded 1998.

Talent Media Group t/a ICM

Oxford House, 76 Oxford Street, London W1D 1BS
tel 020-7636 6565 *fax* 020-7323 0101
email writers@icmlondon.co.uk
Directors Duncan Heath, Susan Rodgers, Lyndsey Posner, Sally Long-Innes, Paul Lyon-Maris, *Literary Agents* Susan Rodgers, Jessica Sykes, Catherine King, Greg Hunt, Hugo Young, Michael McCoy, Duncan Heath, Paul Lyon-Maris

Specialises in scripts for film, theatre, TV, radio (home 10%, overseas 10%).

Tanja Howarth Literary Agency*

19 New Row, London WC2N 4LA
tel 020-7240 5553 *fax* 020-7379 0969
email tanja.howarth@virgin.net

Full-length MSS. General fiction and non-fiction, thrillers, contemporary and historical novels (home 15%, USA/translation 20%). No unsolicited MSS, and no submissions by fax or email. No reading fee. Specialists in handling German translation rights.

Represented in the USA by various agents. Founded 1970.

Tassy Barham Associates

23 Elgin Crescent, London W11 2JD
tel/fax 020-7229 8667
email t@ssybarham.freeserve.co.uk
Proprietor Tassy Barham

Specialises in representing British and American authors, agents and publishers in Brazil. Founded 1999.

The Tennyson Agency

10 Cleveland Avenue, London SW20 9EW
tel/fax 020-8543 5939
email agency@tenagy.co.uk
website www.tenagy.co.uk
Theatre, TV & Film Scripts Christopher Oxford, *Arts/Humanities* Adam Sheldon

Scripts and related material for theatre, film and TV, and selected fiction (home 15%, overseas 20%). No reading fee.

Clients include Vivienne Allen, Iain Grant, Julian Howell, Philip Hurd-Wood, Joanna Leigh, John Ryan, Walter Saunders, Diana Ward. Founded 2002.

Teresa Chris Literary Agency

43 Musard Road, London W6 8NR
tel 020-7386 0633
Director Teresa Chris

All fiction, especially crime, women's commercial, general and literary fiction; all non-fiction, especially biography, history, health, cooking, arts and crafts. No science fiction, horror, fantasy, short stories, poetry, academic books (home 10%, USA 15%, rest 20%). Own US office: Thompson & Chris Literary Agency. No reading fee. No unsolicited MSS. Send introductory letter describing work, first 3 chapters and sae. Founded 1988.

Toby Eady Associates Ltd

3rd Floor, 9 Orme Court, London W2 4RL
tel 020-7792 0092 *fax* 020-7792 0879
email toby@tobyeady.demon.co.uk
jessica@tobyeady.demon.co.uk
website www.tobyeadyassociates.co.uk
Contacts Toby Eady, Jessica Woollard

Fiction and non-fiction (home 15%, overseas 20%). Special interests: China, Middle East, Africa, India. No film/TV scripts or poetry. Approach by personal recommendation. Overseas associates for La Nouvelle Agence (France), Mohrbrooks (Germany), Jan Michael (Holland), The Buckman Agency (Italy, Spain, Portugal and Scandinavia), Joanne Wang (China).

Clients include Nada Awar Jarrar, Julia Blackburn, Mark Burnell, John Carey, Robert Carter, Bernard Cornwell, Jung Chang, Rana

Dasgupta, Fadia Faqir, Kuki Gallmann, Xiaolu Guo, Liu Hong, Wei Hui, Ma Jian, Julia Lovell, Robert Macfarlane, Francesca Marciano, Kanan Makiya, Linda Polman, Fiammetta Rocco, Deborah Scroggins, Rachel Seiffert, Ann Wroe, Xinran Xue. Founded 1968.

Uli Rushby-Smith Literary Agency

72 Plimsoll Road, London N4 2EE
tel/fax 020-7354 2718
Director Uli Rushby-Smith

Fiction and non-fiction, literary and commercial (home 15%, USA/foreign 20%). No poetry, plays or film scripts. Send outline, sample chapters (no disks) and return postage. No reading fee. UK representatives of **Curtis Brown Ltd**, New York (children's books) and Penguin Canada, Penguin South Africa, Columbia University Press (USA), Alice Toledo Agency (Netherlands). Founded 1993.

United Authors Ltd

11-15 Betterton Street, London WC2H 9BP
tel 020-7470 8886 *fax* 020-7470 8887
email utdauthors@clara.net

Fiction, non-fiction, children's, biography, travel. Full-length MSS (home 10%, overseas 15%), short MSS (12%/20%), film and radio (15%/20%), TV (15%/15%). Will suggest revision.

Authors include Charlotte Bingham, Terence Brady, Sydney Gilliatt, Peter Willet, and the Estate of John Bingham. Founded 1998.

Valerie Hoskins Associates

20 Charlotte Street, London W1T 2NA
tel 020-7637 4490 *fax* 020-7637 4493
email vha@vhassociates.co.uk
Proprietor Valerie Hoskins, *Agent* Rebecca Watson

Film, TV and radio; specialises in animation (home 12.5%, overseas max. 20%). No unsolicited MSS; preliminary letter essential. No reading fee, but sae essential. Works in conjunction with US agents.

Vanessa Holt Ltd*

59 Crescent Road, Leigh-on-Sea, Essex SS9 2PF
tel (01702) 473787 *fax* (01702) 471890
email vanessa@holtlimited.freeserve.co.uk

General adult fiction and non-fiction (home 15%, overseas 20%, TV/film/radio 15%). Works in conjunction with foreign agencies in all markets. No reading fee. No unsolicited MSS; send query letter first with sae. No overseas submissions. Founded 1989.

Watson, Little Ltd*

Capo Di Monte, Windmill Hill, London NW3 6RJ
tel 020-7431 0770 *fax* 020-7431 7225
email enquiries@watsonlittle.com
Directors Sheila Watson, Amanda Little, Sugra Zaman

Adult and children's fiction and non-fiction (home 15%, translation 19%, film/video/TV 10%). Fiction: commercial women's, crime and literary. Non-fiction special interests: history, science, popular psychology, self-help, business and general leisure books. No short stories, TV/play/film scripts or poetry. Not interested in purely academic writers. Send informative preliminary letter and synopsis with return postage. No unsolicited MSS. No reading fee. Works in conjunction with worldwide agents. Film and TV associates: the **Sharland Organisation Ltd** and Hurley Lowe Management.

WCA Licensing

3 Calais Street, London SE5 9LP
tel 020-7564 5898 *fax* 020-7564 3501
email ecollins@wca.co.uk
Partners Elaine Collins, Arabella Woods

Specialises in non-fiction: cookery, lifestyle, gardening, etc, TV tie-ins (home 15%, overseas 20%). No reading fee; will suggest a revision. Founded 1993.

William Morris Agency (UK) Ltd*

52-53 Poland Street, London W1F 7LX
tel 020-7534 6800 *fax* 020-7534 6900
website www.wma.com
Managing Director Stephanie Cabot

Worldwide theatrical and literary agency with offices in New York, Beverly Hills and Nashville, and associates in Sydney. Handles film and TV scripts, TV formats; fiction and general non-fiction (film/TV 10%, UK books 15%, USA books and translation 20%). No unsolicited material; MSS only when preceded by letter. No reading fee. London office founded 1965.

The Wylie Agency (UK) Ltd

17 Bedford Square, London WC1B 3JA
tel 020-7908 5900 *fax* 020-7908 5901
President Andrew Wylie

Literary fiction and non-fiction (home 10%, overseas 20%, USA 15%). No unsolicited MSS; send preliminary letter with 2 sample chapters and sae in first instance. Founded 1996.

Literary agents overseas

Before submitting material, writers are advised to send a preliminary letter with an sae or IRC (International Reply Coupon) and to ascertain terms. Listings for overseas literary agents other than in the USA start on page 376.

*Member of the Association of Authors' Representatives

USA

American Play Company Inc.
19 West 44th Street, Suite 1204, New York, NY 10036
tel 212-921-0545 *fax* 212-869-4032
President Sheldon Abend

AMG/Renaissance – see The Firm

The Angela Rinaldi Literary Agency*
PO Box 7877, Beverly Hill, CA 90212-7877
tel 310-842-7665 *fax* 310-877-3143
email amr@rinalditeray.com
President Angela Rinaldi

Mainstream and literary adult fiction; non-fiction (home 15%, overseas 20%). No reading fee. Founded 1994.

Anita D. McClellan Associates*
50 Stearns Street, Cambridge, MA 02138
tel 617-576-6950
Director Anita D. McClellan

General fiction and non-fiction. Full-length MSS (home 15%, overseas 20%). Will suggest revision for agency clients. No unsolicited MSS. Send preliminary letter and sase bearing US postage or IRC.

Ann Elmo Agency Inc.*
60 East 42nd Street, New York, NY 10165
tel 212-661-2880 *fax* 212-661-2883
Director Lettie Lee

Full-length fiction and non-fiction MSS (home 15%, overseas 20%), theatre (15%). Works with foreign agencies. No reading fee. Send query letter only with sase or IRC.

Austin Wahl Agency Inc.
1820 North 76th Court, Elmwood Park, IL 60707-3631
tel 708-456-2301 *fax* 708-456-2031
President Thomas Wahl

Full-length and short MSS (home 15%, overseas 20%), theatre, films, TV (10%). No reading fee; professional writers only. Founded 1935.

The Axelrod Agency*
49 Main Street, PO Box 357, Chatham, NY 12037
tel 518-392-2100 *fax* 518-392-2944
President Steven Axelrod

Full-length MSS. Fiction and non-fiction, software (home 15%, overseas 20%), film and TV rights (15%); will suggest revision where appropriate. Works with overseas agents. No reading fee. Founded 1983.

The Balkin Agency Inc.*
PO Box 222, Amherst, MA 01004
tel 413-548-9835 *fax* 413-548-9836
email balkin@crocker.com
Director Richard Balkin, *European and British Representative* Chandler Crawford Agency USA

Full-length MSS – adult non-fiction only (home 15%, overseas 20%). Query first. May suggest revision. No reading fee.

Barbara S. Kouts, Literary Agent*
PO Box 560, Bellport, NY 11713
tel 631-286-1278 *fax* 631-286-1538

Full-length MSS. Fiction and non-fiction, children's and adult (home 15%, overseas 20%); will suggest revision. Works with overseas agents. No reading fee. Send query letter first. Founded 1980.

Berman, Boals & Flynn Inc.*
208 West 30th Street, Suite 401, New York, NY 10001
tel 212-868-1068 *fax* 212-868-1052
Agents Judy Boals, Jim Flynn

Dramatic writing only (and only by recommendation).

Brandt & Hochman Literary Agents Inc.*
1501 Broadway, New York, NY 10036
tel 212-840-5760
British Representative A.M. Heath & Co. Ltd

Full-length and short MSS (home 15%, overseas 20%), performance rights (15%). No reading fee.

Carlisle & Company*
24 East 64 Street, New York, NY 10021
tel 212-813-1881 *fax* 212-813-9567

website www.carlisleco.com
Directors Michael V. Carlisle, Emma Parry, Christy D. Fletcher

Narrative non-fiction, science, history, biography, literary fiction (home 15%, overseas 20%). Founded 1998.

Carol Mann Agency*

55 Fifth Avenue, New York, NY 10003
tel 212-206-5635 *fax* 212-675-4809
Associates Carol Mann, James Fitzgerald, Kim Goldstein, Leyhla Ahuile

Psychology, popular history, biography, pop culture, general non-fiction; fiction (home 15%, overseas 20%). Works in conjunction with foreign agents. No reading fee. Founded 1977.

Curtis Brown Ltd*

10 Astor Place, New York, NY 10003
tel 212-473-5400
Ceo Timothy Knowlton, *Contact* Query Department
Branch office 1750 Montgomery Street, San Francisco, CA 94111
tel 415-954-8566
President Peter Ginsberg

Fiction and non-fiction, juvenile, film and TV rights. No unsolicited MSS; query first with sase. No reading fee; no handling fees.

Don Congdon Associates Inc.*

156 Fifth Avenue, Suite 625, New York, NY 10010
tel 212-645-1229 *fax* 212-727-2688
email dca@doncongdon.com
Agents Don Congdon, Michael Congdon, Susan Ramer, Cristina Concepcion

Full-length and short MSS. General fiction and non-fiction (home 15%, overseas 19%), performance rights (15%); will sometimes suggest revision. Works with co-agents overseas. No reading fee but no unsolicited MSS – query first with return postage or sase for reply. Does not accept phone calls from querying authors. Founded 1983.

Donadio & Ashworth Inc.*

121 West 27th Street, Suite 704, New York, NY 10001
tel 212-691-8077 *fax* 212-633-2837
Owner Candida Donadio, *Associates* Edward Hibbert, Neil Olson, Peter Steinberg, Ira Silverberg

Literary fiction and non-fiction.

Dunham Literary*

156 Fifth Avenue, Suite 625, New York, NY 10010-7002
website www.dunhamlit.com

Literary fiction and non-fiction, alternative spirituality, children's books (home 15%, overseas 20%). No reading fee. Founded 2000.

Dystel & Goderich Literary Management*

One Union Square West, New York, NY 10003
tel 212-627-9100 *fax* 212-627-9313
website www.dystel.com
Contacts Jane D. Dystel, Miriam Goderich, Stacey Glick, Michael Bourret, Jim McCarthy, Jessica Papin

Full-length and short MSS (home 15%, overseas 19%, film, TV and radio 15%). General fiction and non-fiction: literary and commercial fiction; narrative non-fiction; self-help; cookbooks; parenting; children's books; science fiction/fantasy. No reading fee. Founded 1991.

Ellen Levine Literary Agency Inc. – see Trident Media Group

The Evan Marshall Agency*

Six Tristam Place, Pine Brook, NJ 07058-9445
tel 973-882-1122 *fax* 973-882-3099
email evanmarshall@thenovelist.com
website www.thenovelist.com
President Evan Marshall

General fiction (home 15%, overseas 20%). Works in conjunction with overseas agents. Will suggest revision; no reading fee. Founded 1987.

Fifi Oscard Agency Inc.

110 W 40th Street, New York, NY 10018
tel 212-764-1100 *fax* 212-840-5019
email fifioscard@aol.com
Agents Fifi Oscard, Peter Sawyer, Carolyn French, Carmen La Via, Kevin McShane

Full-length MSS (home 15%, overseas 20%), theatrical performance rights (10%). Will suggest revision. Works in conjunction with many foreign agencies. No reading fee, but no unsolicited submissions.

The Firm

(formerly AMG/Renaissance)
9465 Wilshire Boulevard, Beverly Hills, CA 90212
tel 310-860-8000 *fax* 310-860-8132
Contacts Alan Nevins, Irv Schwartz, Michael Prevett

Full-length MSS. Fiction and non-fiction, plays (home 15%, overseas 20%), film and TV rights (home 10%, overseas 20%), performance rights. No unsolicited MSS; query first, submit outline. No reading fee. Founded 1934.

ForthWrite Literary Agency & Speaker's Bureau

23852 W. Pacific Coast Hwy, Suite 701, Malibu, CA 90265
tel 310-456-5698 *fax* 310-456-6589
email agent@kellermedia.com
website www.kellermedia.com
Owner Wendy Keller

Only non-fiction: business, self-help popular psychology, how-to. Subjects include: animals, art, horticulture/ gardening, archaeology, European history (especially English), biography, health (especially homeopathy and alternative medicines), parenting, coffee table (illustrated) books, crafts (bobbin lace, handicrafts, etc), nature, psychology. Send IRC with query. Response in 8 weeks. Founded 1988.

The Fox Chase Agency Inc.
Walnut Hill Plaza, Suite 140, 150 South Warner Road, King of Prussia, PA 19406
tel 610-341-9840 *fax* 610-341-9842

Frances Collin Literary Agent*
PO Box 33, Wayne, PA 19087-0033
tel 610-254-0555

Full-length MSS (specialisations of interest to UK writers: mysteries, women's fiction, history, biography, science fiction, fantasy) (home 15%, overseas 20%), performance rights (20%). No screenplays. No reading fee. No unsolicited MSS please. Letter queries must include sufficient IRCs. Works in conjunction with agents worldwide. Founded 1948; successor to Marie Rodell-Frances Collin Literary Agency.

Frederick Hill Bonnie Nadell Inc.
1842 Union Street, San Francisco, CA 94123
tel 415-921-2910 *fax* 415-921-2802
Branch office 505 North Robertson Blvd, Los Angeles, CA 90048
tel 310-860-9605 *fax* 310-860-9672

Full-length fiction and non-fiction (home 15%, overseas 20%). Send query letter initially. Works in conjunction with agents in Scandinavia, France, Germany, Holland, Japan, Spain. No reading fee. Founded 1979.

Gelfman Schneider Literary Agents Inc.*
250 West 57th Street, Suite 2515, New York, NY 10107
tel 212-245-1993 *fax* 212-245-8678
President Jane Gelfman, *Vice President* Deborah Schneider

Full-length and short MSS (home 15%, overseas 20%). Will suggest revision. No queries by fax. Works in conjunction with **Curtis Brown Group Ltd**, London.

Gelfman Schneider Literary Agents Inc.*
250 West 57th Street, Suite 2515, New York, NY 10107
tel 212-245-1993 *fax* 212-245-8678
Directors Jane Gelfman, Deborah Schneider

General adult fiction and non-fiction (home 15%, overseas 20%). Works in conjunction with **Curtis**

Brown, London. Will suggest revision. No reading fee but please send sase for return of material.

Georges Borchardt Inc.*
136 East 57th Street, New York, NY 10022
tel 212-753-5785 *fax* 212-838-6518
Directors Georges Borchardt, Anne Borchardt

Full-length and short MSS (home/British/ performance 15%, translations 20%). Agents in most foreign countries. No unsolicited MSS. No reading fee. Founded 1967.

Gerard McCauley Agency Inc.*
PO Box 844, Katonah, NY 10536
tel 914-232-5700

Specialises in history, biography, public affairs for the general reader.

Goodman Associates, Literary Agents*
500 West End Avenue, New York, NY 10024
tel 212-873-4806
Partners Arnold P. Goodman, Elise Simon Goodman

Adult book length fiction and non-fiction (home 15%, overseas 20%). No reading fee. Founded 1976.

Harold Matson Company Inc.*
276 Fifth Avenue, New York, NY 10001
tel 212-679-4490 *fax* 212-545-1224

Full-length MSS (home 15%, UK 19%, translation 19%). No unsolicited MSS. No reading fee. Founded 1937.

Harold Ober Associates Inc.*
425 Madison Avenue, New York, NY 10017
tel 212-759-8600 *fax* 212-759-9428
Directors Phyllis Westberg, Emma Sweeney, Knox Burger, Alex Smithline, Pamela Malpas

Full-length MSS (home 15%, British 20%, overseas 20%), performance rights (15%). Will suggest revision. No reading fee. Founded 1929.

The Helen Brann Agency Inc.*
94 Curtis Road, Bridgewater, CT 06752
tel 860-354-9580 *fax* 860-355-2572

Helen Merrill Ltd
295 Lafayette Street, Suite 915, New York, NY 10012
No unsolicited MSS. No books. No phone calls or faxes.

Helen Rees Literary Agency
123 N. Washington Street, Boston, MA 02114
tel 617-723 5232 *fax* 617-723 5211
email reesliterary@aol.com
Contact Joan Mazmanian, *Associates* Barbara Rifkind, Ann Collette

Business books, self-help, biography, autobiography, political, literary fiction (home 15%). Works with foreign agent. No reading fee. Submit query letter with sase. Founded 1982.

IMG Literary – see Mark Reiter IMG Literary

International Creative Management Inc.*
40 West 57th Street, New York, NY 10019
tel 212-556-5600 *fax* 212-556-5665
London office 4-6 Soho Square, London W1D 3PZ
tel 020-7432 0800 *fax* 020-7432 0808
No unsolicited MSS; send query letter.

James Peter Associates Inc.
PO Box 670, Tenafly, NJ 07670
tel 201-568-0760 *fax* 201-568-2959
email bertholtje@compuserve.com
Contacts Bert Holtje, Gene Brissie

Non-fiction, especially history, politics, popular culture, health, psychology, reference, biography (home 15%, overseas 20%). Foreign rights handled by: Bobbe Siegel, 41 West 83rd Street, New York, NY 10024. Will suggest revision. No reading fee. Founded 1971.

Janklow & Nesbit Associates
445 Park Avenue, New York, NY 10022
tel 212-421-1700 *fax* 212-980-3671, 212-355 1403
email postmaster@janklow.com
Partners Morton L. Janklow, Lynn Nesbit, *Senior Vice President* Anne Sibbald
Agents Tina Bennett, Amy Howell, Luke Janklow, Richard Morris, Eric Simonoff, *Foreign rights* Cullen Stanley, Dorothy Vincent, Cecile Barendsma, Kate Schafer

Commercial and literary fiction and non-fiction. No unsolicited MSS. Works in conjunction with Janklow & Nesbit (UK) Ltd. Founded 1989.

Jay Garon-Brooke Associates Inc. – see Pinder, Lane & Garon-Brooke Associates Ltd

JCA Literary Agency Inc.*
27 West 20th Street, Suite 1103, New York, NY 10011
tel 212-807-0888
Contacts Jeff Gerecke, Tony Outhwaite, Peter Steinberg

Adult fiction and non-fiction. No unsolicited MSS; query first.

Jean V. Naggar Literary Agency*
216 East 75th Street, Suite 1E, New York, NY 10021
tel 212-794-1082
President Jean V. Naggar, *Agents* Alice Tasman, Anne Engel, Jennifer Weltz (rights)

Mainstream commercial and literary fiction (no formula fiction); non-fiction: psychology, science, biography (home 15%, overseas 20%), performance rights (15%). Works in conjunction with foreign agents. No reading fee. Founded 1978.

Jeanne Fredericks Literary Agency Inc.*
221 Benedict Hill Road, New Canaan, CT 06840
tel/fax 203-972-3011
email jfredrks@optonline.net

Quality non-fiction, especially health, science, women's issues, gardening, antiques and decorative arts, biography, cookbooks, popular reference, business, natural history (home 15%, overseas 20%). No reading fee. Query first, enclosing sase. Member of Authors Guild. Founded 1997.

The Jeff Herman Agency LLC
PO Box 1522, Stockbldige, MA 01262
tel 413-298-0077 *fax* 413-298-8188
email jeff@jeffherman.com
website www.jeffherman.com

Business, reference, popular psychology, computers, health, spirituality, general non-fiction (home/overseas 15%); will suggest revision where appropriate. Works with overseas agents. No reading fee. Founded 1986.

Joan Daves Agency
21 West 26th Street, New York, NY 10010
tel 212-685-2663 *fax* 212-685-1781
Director Jennifer Lyons, *Assistant* Katie La Storia

Sample chapter or detailed outline of non-fiction projects (home 15%, overseas 20%, film 15%). No reading fee. Subsidiary of **Writers House LLC.** Founded in 1952 by Joan Daves.

John Hawkins & Associates Inc.*
(formerly Paul R. Reynolds Inc.)
71 West 23rd Street, Suite 1600, New York, NY 10010
tel 212-807-7040 *fax* 212-807-9555
website www.jhaliterary.com
President John Hawkins, *Vice-President* William Reiss, *Foreign Rights* Moses Cardona, *Permissions* Matthew Miele, *Other Agents* Warren Frazier, Anne Hawkins

Fiction, non-fiction, juvenile. No reading fee. Founded 1893.

The Joy Harris Literary Agency Inc.*
156 Fifth Avenue, Suite 617, New York, NY 10010-7002
tel 212-924-6269 *fax* 212-924-6609
email gen.office@jhlitagent.com
President Joy Harris

The Lazear Agency Inc./Talkback
800 Washington Avenue North, Suite 660,
Minneapolis, MN 55401
tel 612-332-8640 *fax* 612-332-4648
Contacts Jonathon Lazear, Wendy Lazear, Christi
Cardenas, Julie Mayo

Fiction: full-length MSS; non-fiction: proposals.
Adult fiction and non-fiction; film and TV rights;
foreign language rights; audio, video and electronic
rights (home 15%, overseas 20%). No reading fee.
No unsolicited MSS; 2–3 page query first with sase
for response. No faxed queries.

Talkback: A Speaker's Bureau: book packaging
and select entertainment management. Founded
1984.

Lescher & Lescher Ltd*
47 East 19th Street, New York, NY 10003
tel 212-529-1790 *fax* 212-529-2716
Directors Robert Lescher, Susan Lescher

Full-length and short MSS (home 15%, overseas
25%). No unsolicited MSS; query first with sase. No
reading fee. Founded 1966.

McIntosh & Otis Inc.*
353 Lexington Avenue, New York,
NY 10016
tel 212-687-7400 *fax* 212-687-6894
Adult Eugene H. Winick, Samuel L. Pinkus,
Elizabeth Winick, *Juvenile* Christina Biamonte,
Tracey Adams, *Film and TV* Evva Joan Pryor

Adult and juvenile literary fiction and non-fiction,
film and TV rights. No unsolicited MSS; query first
with outline, sample chapters and sase. No reading
fee. Founded 1928.

Margret McBride Literary Agency*
7744 Fay Avenue, Suite 201, La Jolla,
CA 92037
tel 858-454-1550 *fax* 858-454-2156
President Margret McBride

Business, mainstream fiction and non-fiction
(home 15%, overseas 25%). No poetry or children's
books. No reading fee. Submit query letter with sase
to Margret McBride. Founded 1981.

Maria Carvainis Agency Inc.*
1350 Avenue of the Americas, Suite 2905,
New York, NY 10019
tel 212-245-6365 *fax* 212-245-7196
President Maria Carvainis, *Executive Vice President*
Frances Kuffel

Adult fiction and non-fiction (home 15%, overseas
20%). Fiction: all categories except science fiction
and fantasy, especially literary and mainstream;
mystery, thrillers and suspense; historical, Regency,
contemporary women's, young adult. Non-fiction:
politics and film history, biography and memoir,

medicine and women's issues; business, finance,
psychology, popular science. Works in conjunction
with foreign, TV and movie agents. No reading fee.
Query first; no unsolicited MSS. No queries by fax
or email.

Mark Reiter IMG Literary
825 Seventh Avenue, 9th Floor, New York,
NY 10019
tel 212-489-5400 *fax* 212-246 1118

Fiction (no science fiction) and non-fiction. Send
query letter with sase.

The Marton Agency Inc.*
1 Union Square, Suite 612, New York,
NY 10003-3303
tel 212-255-1908 *fax* 212-691-9061
email info@martonagency.com
Owner Tonda Marton

Stage plays only.

Mary Yost Associates Inc.
59 East 54th Street, Suite 72, New York,
NY 10022
tel 212-980-4988

Full-length and short MSS (home and overseas
10%). Works with individual agents in all foreign
countries. Will suggest revision. No reading fee.
Founded 1958.

Mildred Marmur Associates Ltd*
2005 Palmer Avenue, PMB 127, Larchmont,
NY 10538-2469
tel 914-834-1170 *fax* 914-834-2840
email marmur@westnet.com,
lebowitz@westnet.com
President Mildred Marmur, *Associate* Jane Lebowitz

Serious non-fiction. Full-length and short MSS
(home licences 15%, overseas licences 20%,
performance rights 15%). Works with co-agents in
all major countries. No reading fee. Queries must
include sase or IRCs. Founded 1987.

Multimedia Product Development Inc.*
410 South Michigan Avenue, Suite 724,
Chicago, IL 60605
tel 312-922-3063 *fax* 312-922-1905
Contacts Jane Jordan Browne, Danielle Egan-Miller

General fiction and non-fiction (home 15%,
overseas 20%, performance rights 15%). Works in
conjunction with foreign agents. Will suggest
revision; no reading fee. Founded 1971.

New England Publishing Associates Inc.*
PO Box 5, Chester, CT 06412
tel 860-345-READ *fax* 860-345-3660
email nepa@nepa.com
website www.nepa.com

Contacts Elizabeth Frost-Knappman, Edward W. Knappman, Ron Formica, Kris Schiavi, Vicki Harlow

Serious non-fiction for the adult market (home 15%, overseas varies), performance rights (varies). Works in conjunction with foreign publishers. No reading fee; will suggest revision – if undertaken. Representatives: Scott Ferris (London); **Michael Meller Literary Agency** (Germany); A. Mediation Littéraire (France); **ACER Agencia Literaría** (Spain); **Andrew Nurnberg Associates** (Hungary). Dramatic rights: Joel Gotler.

Peter Elek Associates/The Content Company, Inc.
5111 JFK Boulevard East, West New York, NJ 07093
tel 201-558-0323 *fax* 201-558-0307
email info@theliteraryagency.com
website www.theliteraryagency.com
Directors Peter Elek, Helene W. Elek *Submissions* Lauren Mactas

Full-length fiction/non-fiction. Illustrated adult non-fiction: style, culture, popular history, popular science, current affairs; juvenile picture books (home 15%, overseas 20%), performance rights (20%); will sometimes suggest revision. Works with overseas agents. No reading fee. Experienced in licensing for multimedia, online and off-line. Founded 1979.

Philip G. Spitzer Literary Agency*
50 Talmage Farm Lane, East Hampton, NY 11937
tel 631-329-3650 *fax* 631-329-3651

General fiction and non-fiction; specialises in mystery/suspense, sports, politics, biography, social issues.

The Pimlico Agency Inc.
Box 20447, Cherokee Station, New York, NY 10021
tel 212-628-9729 *fax* 212-535-7861
Contacts Christopher Shepard, Catherine Brooks, *Directors* Kay McCauley, Kirby McCauley

Adult non-fiction and fiction. No unsolicited MSS.

Pinder, Lane & Garon-Brooke Associates Ltd
159 West 53rd Street, Suite 14, New York, NY 10019
tel 212-489-0880 *fax* 212-586-9346
London Representative Abner Stein

Specialises in fiction and non-fiction: biographies and lifestyle. Writer must be referred by an editor or a client. Will not read unsolicited MSS.

PMA Literary and Film Management Inc.
Old Chelsea Station, PO Box 1817, New York, NY 10011
tel 212-929-1222 *fax* 212-206-0238

email pmalitfilm@aol.com
website www.pmalitfilm.com
President Peter Miller, *Development Associate* Scott Hoffman

Full-length MSS. Specialises in commercial fiction (especially thrillers), true crime, non-fiction (all types), and all books with global publishing and film/TV potential (home 15%, overseas 25%), films, TV (10–20%). Works in conjunction with agents worldwide. Preliminary enquiry with career goals, synopsis and resumé essential. Founded 1976.

Ralph M. Vicinanza Ltd*
303 West 18th Street, New York, NY 10011
tel 212-924-7090
Contacts Ralph Vicinanza, Christopher Lotts, Christopher Schelling

Fiction: literary, women's, 'multicultural', popular (especially science fiction, fantasy, thrillers), children's. Non-fiction: history, business, science, biography, popular culture. Foreign rights specialists. New clients by professional recommendation only. No unsolicited MSS.

Rhoda Weyr Agency – see Dunham Literary

Richard Curtis Associates Inc.
171 East 74th Street, Floor 2, New York, NY 10021
tel 212-772-7363 *fax* 212-772-7393
website http://curtisagency.com
President Richard Curtis

All types of commercial non-fiction (home 15%, overseas 25%, film/TV 15%). Will suggest revision. No reading fee. Send sase with all queries. Foreign rights handled by Baror International. Founded 1970.

Robert A. Freedman Dramatic Agency Inc.*
(formerly Harold Freedman Brandt & Brandt Dramatic Dept. Inc.)
1501 Broadway, Suite 2310, New York, NY 10036
tel 212-840-5760

Plays, motion picture and TV scripts. Send letter of enquiry first, with sase. No reading fee.

Rosenstone/Wender*
38 East 29th Street, 10th Floor, New York, NY 10016
tel 212-725-9445 *fax* 212-725-9447
Contacts Phyllis Wender, Susan Perlman Cohen, Sonia Pabley

Fiction, non-fiction, film and TV rights. No unsolicited MSS; query first. No reading fee.

Roslyn Targ Literary Agency Inc.*
105 West 13th Street, New York, NY 10011
tel 212-206-9390 *fax* 212-989-6233
email roslyntarg@aol.com

Fiction and non-fiction: query with outline, publication history and CV. Fiction: query with synopsis or outline, and CV and publication history. All submissions require sase. No phone queries. Affiliates in most foreign countries. No reading fee.

Russell & Volkening Inc.*
50 West 29th Street, Suite 7E, New York, NY 10001
tel 212-684-6050 *fax* 212-889-3026
Contact Timothy Seldes

General fiction and non-fiction, film and TV rights. No screenplays. No unsolicited MSS; query first with letter and sase. No reading fee.

Samuel French Inc.*
45 West 25th Street, New York, NY 10010
tel 212-206-8990 *fax* 212-206-1429
President Charles R. Van Nostrand

Play publishers; authors' representatives. No reading fee.

Sandra Dijkstra Literary Agency*
PMB 515, 1155 Camino Del Mar, Del Mar, CA 92104-2605
tel 858-755-3115 *fax* 858-792-2822
President Sandra Dijkstra

Fiction and non-fiction: narrative, history, business, psychology, science, memoir/biography, contemporary, women's, suspense; selected children's projects (home 15%, overseas 20%). Works in conjunction with foreign and film agents. All submissions must include synopsis and sase (or IRC). No reading fee. Founded 1981.

Sandra Watt and Associates
8033 Sunset Boulevard, Suite 4053, Hollywood, CA 90046
tel 213-653-2339
Owner Sandra Watt

Lead women's fiction, suspense, mysteries, New Age, cyber-punk; psychological self-help, gardening, single-volume reference works; screenplays (home 15%, overseas 25%), films (10%). Works in conjunction with foreign agents. Will suggest revision; no reading fee; $100 marketing fee for unpublished authors. Founded 1978.

Sanford J. Greenburger Associates Inc.*
55 Fifth Avenue, New York, NY 10003
tel 212-206-5600 *fax* 212-463-8718
website www.greenburger.com
Contacts Heide Lange, Faith Hamlin, Theresa Park, Elyse Cheney, Daniel Mandel, PeterMcGuigan

Fiction and non-fiction, film and TV rights. No unsolicited MSS; query first. No reading fee.

Sarah Jane Freyman Literary Agency
(formerly Stepping Stone Literary Agency)
59 West 71st Street, Suite 9B, New York, NY 10023
tel 212-362-9277 *fax* 212-501-8240
email sjfs@aol.com
President Sarah Jane Freymann

Book-length fiction and general non-fiction. Special interest in serious non-fiction, mainstream commercial fiction, contemporary women's fiction, Latino-American, Asian-American, African American fiction and non-fiction. Non-fiction: women's issues, biography, health/fitness, psychology, self-help, spiritual, natural science, cookbooks, pop culture. Works in conjunction with **Abner Stein** in London. No reading fee. Founded 1974.

Scott Meredith Literary Agency LP
1675 Broadway, New York, NY 10019
tel 212-698-0785 *fax* 212-977-5997
website www.writingtosell.com
President Arthur Klebanoff, *Vice-President* Lisa J. Edwards, *Director, Subsidiary Rights* Barry N. Malzberg

Full-length and short MSS. General fiction and non-fiction. Single fee charged for readings, criticism and assistance in revision. Founded 1946.

The Shukat Company Ltd*
340 West 55th Street, Suite 1A, New York, NY 10019
tel 212-582-7614 *fax* 212-315-3752
email staff@shukat.com
President Scott Shukat, *Contacts* Maribel Rivas, Lysna Scriven-Marzani

Theatre, films, TV, radio (15%). No reading fee. No unsolicited material accepted.

The Spieler Agency
154 West 57th Street, Room 135, New York, NY 10019
tel 212-757-4439 *fax* 212-333-2019
email spieleragency@spieleragency.com
Directors F. Joseph Spieler, Lisa M. Ross, John F. Thornton, Deirdre Mullane

Full- and short-length MSS. History, politics, ecology, business, consumer reference, some fiction (home 15%, overseas 20%). No reading fee. Query first with sample and sase. Founded 1982.

Sterling Lord Literistic Inc.
65 Bleecker Street, New York, NY 10012
tel 212-780-6050 *fax* 212-780-6095
Directors Peter Matson, Sterling Lord, Philippa Brophy

Full-length and short MSS (home 15%, overseas 20%), performance rights (15%). Will suggest revision. No reading fee.

Susan Schulman Literary & Dramatic Agents Inc.*
454 West 44th Street, New York, NY 10036
tel 212-713-1633 *fax* 212-581-8830
email schulman@aol.com
2 Bryan Plaza, Washington Depot, CT 06794

Agents for negotiation in all markets (with co-agents) of fiction, general non-fiction, children's books, academic and professional works, and associated subsidiary rights including plays and film (home 15%, UK 7.5%, overseas 20%). No reading fee. Return postage required.

Trident Media Group*
41 Madison Avenue, New York, NY 10010
tel 212-899-0620
website www.tridentmediagroup.com
Executive Vice President Ellen Levine

Full-length MSS: biography, contemporary affairs, women's issues, history, science, literary and commercial fiction (home 15%, overseas 20%); in conjunction with co-agents, theatre, films, TV (15%). Will suggest revision. Works in conjunction with agents in Europe, Japan, Israel, Brazil, Argentina, Australia, Far East. No reading fee; preliminary letter and sase and US postage essential.

Virginia Barber Literary Agency Inc., The Writers Shop – see William Morris Agency Inc.

Wallace Literary Agency Inc.
177 East 70th Street, New York, NY 10021
tel 212-570-9090 *fax* 212-772-8979
Director Lois Wallace

No cookery, humour, how-to; film, TV, theatre for agency clients. Will suggest revision. No unsolicited MSS; no faxed queries. Will only answer queries with return postage. Founded 1988.

Watkins/Loomis Agency Inc.
133 East 35th Street, New York, NY 10016
tel 212-532-0080 *fax* 212-889-0506
President Gloria Loomis, *Contact* Katherine Fausset

Fiction and non-fiction. No unsolicited MSS; query first with sase. No reading fee. Representatives: **Abner Stein** (UK), the **Marsh Agency Ltd** (foreign).

Wecksler-Incomco
170 West End Avenue, New York, NY 10023
tel 212-787-2239 *fax* 212-496-7035
email jacinny@aol.com
President Sally Wecksler, *Associate* Joann Amparan-Close

Illustrated books, non-fiction, business books, some literary fiction, children's books (home 15%, overseas 20%); will suggest revision where appropriate. No reading fee. No submissions by fax or email: only hard copy will be read. Founded 1971.

William Morris Agency Inc.*
(incorporating the Writers Shop, formerly Virginia Barber Literary Agency)
1325 Avenue of the Americas, New York, NY 10019
tel 212-586-5100
Executive VP Owen Laster, *Senior VPs* Jennifer Rudolph Walsh, Suzanne Gluck, Virginia Barber, Joni Evans, Mel Berger, *Agents* Manie Barron, Jay Mandel, Tracy Fisher, *Foreign Rights Director* Tracy Fisher, *Foreign Rights Coordinator* Shana Kelly, *First Serial and Audio Manager* Karen Gerwin

General fiction and non-fiction (home 15%, overseas 20%, performance rights 15%). Will suggest revision. No reading fee.

Writers House LLC*
21 West 26th Street, New York, NY 10010
tel 212-685-2400 *fax* 212-685-1781
President Albert Zuckerman, *Executive Vice-President* Amy Berkower

Fiction and non-fiction, including all rights; film and TV rights. No screenplays or software. Write a one-page letter in first instance, saying what's wonderful about your book, what it is about and why you are the best person to write it. No reading fee. Founded 1974.

The Writers Shop – see William Morris Agency Inc.

The Wylie Agency Inc.
250 West 57th Street, New York, NY 10107
tel 212-246-0069 *fax* 212-586-8953
email mail@wylieagency.com
Directors Andrew Wylie (president), Sarah Chalfant

Literary fiction/non-fiction. No unsolicited MSS accepted. London office: the **Wylie Agency UK Ltd.**

Overseas literary agents – other

Most of the agents listed here work in association with an agent in London. Before submitting a typescript, writers are advised to send a preliminary letter and to ascertain terms.

ARGENTINA

International Editors Co.

Avenida Cabildo 1156, 1426 Buenos Aires
tel 54-11-4788-2992 *fax* 54-11-4786-0888

The Nancy H. Smith Literary Agency

(formerly The Lawrence Smith Agency)
Ayacucho 1867, 2B, Buenos Aires 1112
tel/fax (54 11) 4804 5508
email meg@interlink.com.ar
Contact Margaret Murray
London office 30 Acton Lane, London W4 5ED
tel 020-8995 4769 *fax* 020-8747 4012
email distobart@aol.com
Contact Diana Stobart

No reading fee. Founded 1938.

AUSTRALIA

Curtis Brown (Australia) Pty Ltd

PO Box 19, Paddington, Sydney, NSW 2021
tel (02) 9331 5301/9361 6161 *fax* (02) 9360 3935
email info@curtisbrown.com.au

No reading fee.

BRAZIL

Agência Literária Balcells Mello e Souza Riff/BMSR

Rua Visconde de Pirajá, 414 sl 1108 Ipanema, 22410-002 Rio de Janeiro, RJ
tel (55-21) 2287-6299 *fax* (55-21) 2267-6393
email lucia@bmsr.com.br
website www.bmsr.com.br
Contacts Lucia de Mello e Souza Riff

No reading fee.

Karin Schindler and Suely Pedro dos Santos Rights Representatives

Caixa Postal 19051, 04505-970 São Paulo, SP
tel 55-11-5041-9177 *fax* 55-11-5041-9077
email kschind@terr.com.br
suelypedrosantos@uol.com.br

CANADA

Acacia House Publishing Services Ltd

51 Acacia Road, Toronto, Ontario M4S 2K6
tel/fax 416-484-8356
email fhanna.acacia@rogers.com
Managing Director Mrs Frances A. Hanna, *Vice President* Bill Hanna

Literary fiction/non-fiction, quality commercial fiction, most non-fiction, except business books (15% English worldwide, 25% translation, performance 20%). No science fiction, horror or occult. Works with overseas agents. Query first with sample of 50pp max. Include return postage. No reading fee. Founded 1985.

Anne McDermid & Associates

92 Willcocks Street, Toronto, Ontario M5S 1C8
tel 416-324 8845 *fax* 416-324 8870
email anne@mcdermidagency.com
website www.mcdermidagency.com
Director Anne McDermid

Literary fiction and non-fiction, and quality commercial fiction; no children's literature (home 15%, US 15%, overseas 20%). No reading fee. Founded 1996.

Authors' Marketing Services Ltd

PO Box 84668, 2336 Bloor Street West, Toronto M65 4Z7
tel 416-763 8797 *fax* 416-763-1504
email authorslhoffman@cs.com
Director Larry Hoffman

Adult fiction, biography and autobiography (home 15%, overseas 20%). Reading fee charged for unpublished writers; will suggest a revision. Founded 1978.

EASTERN EUROPE

Andrew Nurnberg Associates Prague, s.r.o

Seifertova 81, 130 00 Prague 3, Czech Republic
tel (420) 2 22 78 20 41 *fax* (420) 2 22 78 23 08
email nurnprg@mbox.vol.cz
Contacts Petra Tobisková, Lucie Strakova

Aura-Pont, Theatrical and Literary Agency Ltd

Radlická 99, Prague 5, Czech Republic
tel/fax (420) 2 51 55 02 07
email aura-pont@aura-pont.cz
website www.aura-pont.cz
Director Zuzana Jezková

Handles authors' rights in books, theatre, film, TV, radio, software – both Czech and foreign (home 10%, overseas 15%). Founded 1990.

International Creative Management Inc.
Krátkého 1, 190 03 Prague 9, Czech Republic
tel (420) 2 83 89 15 87 *fax* (420) 2 83 89 35 99
email info@dilia.cz
website www.dilia.cz
Theatrical and literary agency.

Lex Copyright
Szemere utca 21, 1054 Budapest, Hungary
tel (36) 1 332 9340 *fax* (36) 1 331 6181
email lexcopy.bp@mail.datanet.hu
Director Dr Gyorgy Tibor Szanto

Specialises in representing American and British authors in Hungary. Founded 1991.

Lita
Mozartova 9, CS-81530, Bratislava, Slovakia
tel (421) 7 313623 *fax* (421) 7 580 2246

Slovak Literary Agency.

Prava I Prevodi Literary Agency Permissions & Rights Ltd
Koste Jovanovica 18, 11000 Belgrade, Yugoslavia
tel (381) 11 460 290 *fax* (381) 11 472 146
email ana@pip.co.yu office@pip.co.yu
Director Jovan Milenkovic, *Foreign Rights* Ana Milenkovic

Specialises in representing American and British authors in former Eastern Europe (15 languages). Founded 1983.

FRANCE

Agence Hoffman
77 Boulevard Saint-Michel, 75005 Paris
tel (1) 43 26 56 94 *fax* (1) 43 26 34 07
email hoffman@starnet.fr

Agence Michelle Lapautre
6 rue Jean Carriès, 75007 Paris
tel (1) 47 34 82 41 *fax* (1) 47 34 00 90
email lapautre@club-internet.fr

Bureau Littéraire International
1 rue Alfred Laurant, F-92100 Boulogne Billancourt
tel (1) 46 05 39 11
Contact Geneviéve Ulmann

La Nouvelle Agence
7 rue Corneille, 75006 Paris
tel (1) 43 25 85 60 *fax* (1) 43 25 47 98
email lnaparis@aol.com
Contact Mary Kling

GERMANY (see also SWITZERLAND)

Agence Hoffman
Bechsteinstrasse 2, 80804 Munich
tel 089-308 48 07 *fax* 089-308 21 08

Michael Meller Literary Agency
Sandstrasse 33, 80335 Munich
tel (089) 366371 *fax* (089) 366372
email info@melleragency.com
website www.melleragency.com

Full-length MSS. Fiction and non-fiction, screenplays for films and TV (home 15%, overseas 20%). Own US office. No reading fee. Founded 1988.

Thomas Schlück GmbH
Literary Agency, Hinter der Worth 12, Garbsen 30827
tel 05131-497560 *fax* 05131-497589
email mail@schlueckagent.com
website www.schlueckagent.com

No reading fee.

INDIA

Ajanta Books International
1 U.B. Jawahar Nagar, Bungalow Road, Delhi 110007
tel 7415016, 3926182 *fax* 91-11-7415016
email ajantabi@ndf.vsnl.net.in ajantabi@id.cth.net
Proprietor S. Balwant

Full-length MSS in social sciences and humanities (commission varies according to market – Indian books in Indian and foreign languages, foreign books into Indian languages). Will suggest revision; charges made if agency undertakes revision; reading fee. Founded 1975.

ISRAEL

I. Pikarski Ltd Literary Agency
200 Hayarkon Street, PO Box 4006, Tel Aviv 61040
tel 03-5270159/5231880 *fax* 03-5270160
email gabpikar@inter.net.il
Director Ilana Pikarski

General trade publishing and merchandising rights. Founded 1977.

ITALY

Agenzia Letteraria Internazionale SRL
Via Valpetrosa 1, 20123 Milano
tel (02) 865445, 861572 fax (02) 876222
email alidmb@tin.it

Eulama SRL
Via Guido de Ruggiero 28, 00142 Rome
tel (06) 540 73 09 fax (06) 540 87 72
email eulamaatiscalinet.it
Directors Harald Kahnemann, Karin von Prellwitz,
Norbert von Prellwitz, Pina Ocello von Prellwitz

International licensing agency representing
publishing houses, agents and authors of adult and
children's books worldwide. General and literary
fiction, non-fiction, academic works in humanities.
Promoting Italian, German and Spanish language
authors and publishers worldwide. Reading fee.
Founded 1962.

Grandi & Associati SRL
Via Caradosso 12, 20123 Milan
tel (02) 469 55 41/481 89 62 fax (02) 481 95108
email agenzia@grandieassociati.it
website www.grandieassociati.it
Directors Laura Grandi, Stefano Tettamanti

Provides publicity and foreign rights consultation
for publishers and authors as well as sub-agent
services; will suggest revision where appropriate.
Reading fee. Founded 1988.

ILA – International Literary Agency – USA
I-18010 Terzorio-IM
tel (018) 448 4048 fax (018) 448 7292
email libriggbooks@libero.it

Publishers' and authors' agent, interested only in
series of best-selling and mass market books by
proven, published authors with a track record. Also
interested in published books on antiques and
collectibles. No reading fee. Founded 1969.

New Blitz Literary & TV Agency
Via di Panico 67, 00186 Rome
postal address CP 30047-00193, Rome 47
tel/fax (06) 686 4859
email blitzgacs@inwind.it
Literary Department Giovanni A.S. Congiu

No reading fee.

JAPAN

The English Agency (Japan) Ltd
Sakuragi Building 4F, 6-7-3 Minami Aoyama,
Minato-ku, Tokyo 107-0062
tel 03-3406 5385 fax 03-3406 5387
Managing Director Hamish Macaskill

Handles work by English-language writers living in
Japan; arranges Japanese translations for
internationally established publishers, agents and
authors; arranges Japanese contracts for Japanese
versions of all media. Standard commission: 10%.
Own representatives in New York and London. No
reading fee. Founded 1979.

Orion Literary Agency
1-7-12-4F Kanda-Jimbocho, Chiyoda-ku,
Tokyo 101
tel 03-3295-1405 fax 03-3295-4366

NETHERLANDS

Auteursbureau Greta Baars-Jelgersma
Villa Beau Rivage, Maasstaete 40, 6585 CB,
Mook (L)
tel (024) 6963336 fax (024) 6963293

Literature; illustrated co-productions, including
children's, art, handicraft, hobby and nature
(home/overseas 20%). Works with overseas agents.
Occasionally charges a reading fee. Founded 1951.

Internationaal Literatuur Bureau B.V.
Postbus 10014, 1201 DA, Hilversum
tel (035) 621 35 00 fax (035) 621 57 71
email mkohn@planet.nl
website www.ilb.nu
Contacts Menno Kohn, Linda Kohn, Brigitte van der
Klaauw

NEW ZEALAND

Glenys Bean Writer's Agent
PO Box 60509, Titirangi, Auckland
tel (09) 812 8486 fax (09) 812 8188
email g.bean@clear.net.nz

Adult and children's fiction, educational, non-
fiction, film, TV, radio (10–20%). Send preliminary
letter, synopsis and sae. No reading fee. Represented
by Sanford Greenburger Associates Ltd (USA).
Translation/foreign rights: the Marsh Agency Ltd.
Founded 1989.

Richards Literary Agency
11 Channel View Road, Campbells Bay, Auckland 11
postal address PO Box 31-240, Milford, Auckland 9
tel/fax (09) 479-5681

email rla.richards@clear.net.nz
Partners Ray Richards, Nicky Richards Wallace

Full-length MSS, fiction, non-fiction, adult, juvenile, educational, academic books; films, TV, radio (home 10%, overseas 10–20%). Preliminary letter, synopsis with sae required. No reading fee. Co-agents in London and New York. Founded 1977.

PORTUGAL

Ilidio da Fonseca Matos
Avenida Gomes Pereira, 105-3°-B, 1500-326 Lisbon
tel (21) 716 2988 *fax* (21) 715 4445
email ilidio.matos@oninet.pt

No reading fee.

RUSSIA

Prava I Perevody
(Permissions and Rights Ltd, Moscow)
Bolshaya Bronnaya Street 6A, Moscow 103670
tel 095) 203 5280 *fax* (095) 203 0229
email prava@aha.ru
Director Konstantin Palchikov

Specialises in representing US and British authors in Russia, Latvia, Lithuania, Estonia and Ukraine. Founded 1993.

SCANDINAVIA

Bookman Literary Agency
Bastager 3, DK-2950 Vedbaek, Denmark
tel (45) 45 89 25 20 *fax* (45) 45 89 25 01
email ihl@bookman.dk

Handles rights in Denmark, Sweden, Norway, Finland and Iceland for foreign authors.

Gösta Dahl & Son, AB
Aladdinsvägan 14, S-167 61 Bromma, Sweden
tel 08 25 62 35 *fax* 08 25 11 18

Lennart Sane Agency AB
Holländareplan 9, S-374 34 Karlshamm, Sweden
tel 0454 123 56 *fax* 0454 149 20
Directors Lennart Sane, Elisabeth Sane, Ulf Töregård
Fiction, non-fiction, children's books. Founded 1969.

Leonhardt & Høier Literary Agency aps
Studiestraede 35, DK-1455 Copenhagen K, Denmark
tel 33 13 25 23 *fax* 33 13 49 92
email anneli@leonhardt-hoier.dk

No reading fee.

Sane Töregård Agency AB
Holländareplan 9, S-374 34 Karlshamn, Sweden
tel (46) 454 12356 *fax* (46) 454 14920
email ulf.toregard@sanetoregard.se
Directors Lennart Sane, Ulf Töregård

Represents authors, agents and publishers in Scandinavia and Holland for rights in fiction, non-fiction and children's books. Founded 1995.

SOUTH AFRICA

Frances Bond Literary Services
32B Stanley Teale Road, Westville North 3630, KwaZulu-Natal
postal address PO Box 223, Westville 3630
tel (031) 2624532 *fax* (031) 2622620
email fbond@mweb.co.za
Managing Editor Frances Bond, *Chief Editor* Eileen Molver

Full length MSS. Fiction and non-fiction; juvenile and children's literature. Consultancy service on contracts and copyright. Preliminary phone call or letter and sase required. Reading fee terms on application. Founded 1985.

Sandton Literary Agency
PO Box 785799, Sandton 2146
tel (011) 4428624
Directors J. Victoria Canning, M. Sutherland

Full-length MSS and screenplays; lecture agents. Professional editing. Reading fee for unpublished or self-published writers. Write enclosing sae or phone first. Works in conjunction with Renaissance-Swan Film Agency Inc., Los Angeles, USA. Founded 1982.

SPAIN

ACER Literary Agency
Amor de Dios 1, 28014 Madrid
tel 1-369-2061 *fax* 1-369-2052
Directors Elizabeth Atkins, Laure Merle d'Aubigné
Represents UK, US, French and German publishers for Spanish and Portuguese translation rights; represents Spanish- and Portuguese-language authors (home/overseas 10%). Will suggest revision where appropriate; £20 reading fee. Founded 1959.

Agencia Literaria Carmen Balcells S.A.
Diagonal 580, 08021 Barcelona
tel 93-200-89-33 *fax* 93-200-70-41
email ag-balcells@ag-balcells.com
Contact Gloria Gutiérrez

International Editors Co., S.A.
Rambla Catalunya 63, 3°-1a, 08007 Barcelona
tel 93-215-88-12 *fax* 93-487-35-83
email ieco@es.inter.net

Julio F. Yañez
Agencia Literaria S.L., Via Augusta 139, 6°-2a,
08021 Barcelona
tel 93-200-71-07, 93-200-54-43 *fax* 93-209-48-65
email yanezag@retemazil.es

Lennart Sane Agency AB
Paseo de Mejico 65, Las Cumbres-Elviria,
E-29600 Marbella (Malaga)
tel 95-283-41-80 *fax* 95-283-31-96
email lennart.sane@telia.com
Fiction, non-fiction, children's books, film and TV
scripts. Founded 1965.

Mercedes Casanovas Literary Agency
Iradier 24, 08017 Barcelona
tel 93-212-47-91 *fax* 93-417-90-37
Literature, non-fiction, children's books (home
10%, overseas 20%). Works with overseas agents.
No reading fee. Founded 1980.

RDC Agencia Literaria SL
C. Fernando VI, No 13-15, Madrid 28004
tel 91-308-55-85 *fax* 91-308-56-00
Director Raquel de la Concha
Representing foreign fiction, non-fiction, children's
books and Spanish authors. No reading fee.

SWITZERLAND

Liepman AG
Maienburgweg 23, CH-8044 Zürich
tel (01) 261 76 60 *fax* (01) 261 01 24
Contacts Eva Koralnik, Ruth Weibel
Represents authors, agents and publishers from all
over the world for German translation rights, and
selected international authors for world rights. No
reading fee.

Mohrbooks AG, Literary Agency
Klosbachstrasse 110, CH-8032 Zürich
tel (01) 244 8626 *fax* (01) 244 8627
email info@mohrbooks.com
website www.mohrbooks.com
Contacts Sabine Ibach, Sebastian Ritscher
No reading fee.

Niedieck Linder AG
Zollikerstrasse 87, Postbox, CH-8034 Zürich
tel (01) 381 65 92 *fax* (01) 381 65 13
website www.nlagency.ch
Represents German-language authors and Italian-
language authors on the German market as well as
major literary estates on a worldwide basis. No
reading fee.

Paul & Peter Fritz AG Literary Agency
Jupiterstrasse 1, CH-8032 Zürich
postal address Postfach 1773, CH-8032 Zürich
tel (01) 388 41 40 *fax* (01) 388 41 30
email info@fritzagency.com
Represents authors, agents and publishers in
German-language areas. No reading fee.

Art and illustration

Freelancing for beginners

Fig Taylor describes the opportunities open to freelance illustrators and discusses types of fee and how to negotiate one to your best advantage.

Full-time posts for illustrators are extremely rare. Because commissioners' needs tend to change on a regular basis, most artists have little choice but to freelance – offering their skills to a variety of clients in order to make a living.

Illustration is highly competitive and a professional attitude towards targeting, presenting, promoting and delivering your work will be vital to your success. Likewise, a realistic understanding of how the industry works and of your place within it will be key. Without adequate research into your chosen field(s) of interest, you may find yourself approaching inappropriate clients – a frustrating and disheartening experience for both parties and a waste of your time and money.

Who commissions illustration?

Magazines and newspapers

Whatever your illustrative ambitions, you are most likely to receive your first commissions from editorial clients. The comparatively modest fees involved allow art editors the freedom to take risks, so many are keen to commission newcomers. Briefs are generally fairly loose though deadlines can be short, particularly where daily and weekly publications are concerned. However, fast turnover also ensures a swift appearance in print, thus reassuring clients in other, more lucrative, spheres of your professional status. Given then that it is possible to use magazines as a springboard, it is essential to research them thoroughly when seeking to identify your own individual market. Collectively, editorial clients accommodate an infinite variety of illustrative styles and techniques. Don't limit your horizons by approaching only the most obvious titles and/or those you would read yourself. Consider also trade and professional journals, free publications and those available on subscription from membership organisations or charities. Seeking out as many potential clients as possible will benefit you in the long term.

Book publishing

With the exception of non-fiction, where the emphasis is on decorative, specialist and technical illustration, most publishers are predominantly interested in full-colour figurative work for use on covers. Strong, representational work, showing the figure in a narrative context, is invaluable to commissioners of mass market paperback fiction, especially historical romance, science fiction and fantasy – while the recent fashion illustration renaissance has strongly influenced the packaging of contemporary women's fiction. A broader range of styles can be accommodated by those smaller publishers and imprints specialising in literary, upmarket fiction. On the whole, publishing deadlines are civilised and mass market covers particularly well paid.

Children's publishers use a wide variety of styles, covering the gamut from baby books, activity and early learning, through to full-colour picture books, covers for young adults and black and white line illustrations for the 8–11 year-old age group. Author/illustrators are particularly welcomed by picture book publishers – though, whatever your style, you must be able to develop believable characters and sustain them throughout a narrative. See *Illustrating for children's books* on page 230.

Greeting cards

Many illustrators are interested in providing designs for cards and giftwrap. For specific information on the gift industry which, unlike the areas covered here, works on a speculative basis, see *Winning the greeting card game* on page 393.

Useful addresses

Archant Specialist
The Mill, Bearwalden Business Park, Wendens Ambo, Saffron Walden, Essex CB11 4GB
tel (01799) 544200
email editorial.graphicsintl@virgin.net
Publishes *Graphics International*.

Association of Illustrators
81 Leonard Street, London EC2A 4QS
tel 020-7613 4328 *fax* 020-7613 4417
email info@a-o-illustrators.demon.co.uk
website www.theaoi.com
Publishes *Survive – the Illustrators Guide to a Professional Career* and *Rights – the Illustrators Guide to Professional Practice and Images*. See also page 447.

Boomerang Media Ltd
PO Box 141, Aldershot, Hants GU12 4XX
tel (01252) 368368

BRAD Group
33-39 Bowling Green Lane, London EC1R 0DA
tel 020-7505 8000
website www.brad.co.uk
Publishes *ALF* (Account List File).

Centaur Communications
49-50 Poland Street, London W1V 4AX
tel 020-7439 4222
email patrick.burgoyne@centaur.co.uk
website www.creativereview.co.uk
www.design-week.co.uk
Publishes *Design Week* and *Creative Review*.

Design companies

Both designers and their clients (who are largely uncreative and will, ultimately, be footing the bill) will be impressed and reassured by relevant, published work so wait until you're in print before approaching them. Although fees are significantly higher than those in editorial and publishing, this third-party involvement generally results in a more restrictive brief. Deadlines may vary and styles favoured range from conceptual through to realistic, decorative, humorous and technical – with those involved in multimedia and web design favouring illustrators with animation skills.

Magazines such as *Design Week*, *Creative Review* (published by Centaur Communications) and *Graphics International* (published by Archant) will keep you abreast of developments in the design world and help you identify clients' individual areas of expertise. Meanwhile, *The Creative Handbook* (published by Reed Business Information and also available online), carries many listings. Individual contact names are also available at a price from database specialists

File FX, who can provide creative suppliers with up-to-date information on commissioning clients in all spheres.

Advertising agencies

As with design, you should ideally be in print before seeking advertising commissions. Fees can be high, deadlines short and clients extremely demanding. A wide range of styles are used and commissions might be incorporated into direct mail or press advertising, hoardings and poster sites or animated for television. Fees will vary, depending on whether a campaign is local or national.

Most agencies employ an art buyer to look at portfolios. A good one will know what each creative team is currently working on and may refer you to specific art directors. Agency listings and client details may be found in *ALF* (Account List File, published by the BRAD Group), while *Creative Review* and the weekly *Campaign* (published by Haymarket Business Publications) carry agency news.

Portfolio presentation

In general, UK commissioners prefer to see someone with a strong, consistent, recognisable style rather than an unfocused jack-of-all trades type. Thus, when assembling your professional portfolio, try to exclude samples which are, in your own eyes, weak, irrelevant, uncharacteristic or simply unenjoyable to do and focus on your strengths instead. Should you be one of those rare, multi-talented individuals who find it hard to limit themselves stylistically, try splitting conflicting work into separate portfolios geared towards different kinds of clients.

A lack of formal training need not be a handicap providing your portfolio accurately reflects the needs of the clients you target. Some illustrators find it useful to assemble 'mock-ups' using existing magazine layouts. By responding to the copy and replacing original images with your own illustrations, it is easier to see how your work will look in context. Eventually, as you become established you'll be able to augment these with published pieces.

Ideally, your folder should be of the zip-up, ring-bound variety and never exceed A2 in size as clients usually have little desk space. Complexity of style and diversity of subject matter will dictate how many samples to include but all should be neatly mounted on lightweight paper or card and placed inside protective plastic sleeves. High-quality photographs and laser copies are acceptable to clients but tacky out-of-focus snapshots are not. Also avoid including multiple sketchbooks and life drawings, which are anathema to clients. It will be taken for granted that you know how to draw from observation.

Interviews and beyond

Making appointments can be hard work but clients take a dim view of spontaneous visits from passing illustrators. Having established the contact name (either from a written source or by asking the company directly), clients are still best approached by letter or telephone call. Many publishing houses are happy to see freelances, though portfolio 'drop-offs' are also quite common. Some clients will automatically take photocopies of your work for reference. However, it's advisable to have some kind of promotional material to leave behind such as a CD, postcard or advertising tearsheet. Always ask an enthusiastic client if they know of others who might be interested in your work. Personal recommendation almost always guarantees an interview.

Cleanliness, punctuality and enthusiasm are more important to clients than how you dress – as is a professional attitude to taking and fulfilling a brief. A thorough understanding of each commission is paramount from the outset. You will need to know your client's requirements regarding roughs; format, size and flexibility of artwork; preferred medium; and whether the artwork is needed in colour or black and white. You will also need to know when the deadline is. Never, under any circumstances agree to undertake a commission unless you are certain you can deliver on time and always work within your limitations. Talent is nothing without reliability.

Self-promotion

There are many ways an illustrator can ensure their work stays uppermost in the industry's consciousness, some more expensive than others. Images can be emailed, put onto CD or posted on a website. Advertising in prestigious hardback annuals such as Elfande's *Contact Illustrators* and the Association of Illustrators' *Images* – which are distributed free to commissioners – can be effective but doesn't come cheap and, in the case of *Images*, only those professionally selected are permitted to buy pages for their winning entries. A more affordable – albeit one-off – alternative for newcomers is Elfande's softback springboard, *New Talent*, which also benefits from free distribution.

As commissioners increasingly turn to the internet for inspiration, websites are becoming a viable and affordable method of self-promotion (see *Setting up a website*, page 530). Advertisers in *Contact Illustrators* automatically qualify for a web portfolio of 12 images with links back to individual websites. This option is also open to *New Talent* advertisers at a discounted rate. Currently, it is also possible for illustrators to promote their work on the *Contact* website without appearing in either of the Elfande annuals. The Association of Illustrators (AOI) website features an archive of work from recent editions of *Images*. Both members and non-members can pay to appear in a similarly categorised Image File or the site's Directory, providing links and contact details.

Free publicity can be had courtesy of Boomerang Media Ltd, who will print appropriate images to go in postcard advertising racks. Distribution includes cafés, bars, cinemas, health clubs, universities and schools.

Be organised

Once you are up and running, it is imperative to keep organised records of all your commissions. Contracts can be verbal as well as written, though details – both financial and otherwise – should always be confirmed in writing and duplicated for your files. Likewise, keep corresponding client faxes, letters and order forms. AOI publications *Survive – the Illustrator's Guide to a Professional Career* and *Rights – the Illustrator's Guide to Professional Practice* offer a wealth of practical, legal and ethical information. Subjects covered include contracts, fee negotiation, agents, licences, royalties and copyright issues.

Money matters

The type of client, the purpose for which you are being commissioned and the usage of your work can all affect the fee you can expect to receive, as can your own professional attitude. Given that it is *extremely* inadvisable to undertake a commission without first agreeing on a fee, you will have to learn to be upfront about funds.

Licence *v.* copyright

Put simply, according to current EU legislation, copyright is the right to reproduce a piece of work anywhere, *ad infinitum*, for any purpose, for a period ending 70 years after the death of the person who created it. This makes it an extremely valuable commodity.

By law, copyright automatically belongs to you, the creator of your artwork, unless you agree to sell it to another party. In most cases, clients have no need to purchase it, and the recommended alternative is for you to grant them a licence instead, governing the precise usage of the artwork. This is far cheaper from the client's perspective and, should they subsequently decide to use your work for some purpose other than those outlined in your initial agreement, will benefit you too as a separate fee will have to be negotiated. It's also worth noting that even if you were ill-advised enough to sell the copyright, the artwork would still belong to you unless you had also agreed to sell that.

Rejection and cancellation fees

Most commissioners will not expect you to work for nothing unless you are involved in a speculative pitch, in which case it will be up to you to weigh up the pros and cons of your possible involvement. Assuming you have given a job your best shot – i.e. carried out the client's instructions to the letter – it's customary to receive a rejection fee even if the client doesn't care for the outcome: 25% is customary at developmental/rough stage and 50% at finished artwork stage. (Clear this with the client before you start, as there are exceptions to the rule.) Cancellation fees are paid when a job is terminated through no fault of the artist or, on occasion, even the client. Customary rates in this instance are 25% before rough stage, 33% on delivery of roughs and 100% on delivery of artwork.

Fixed *v.* negotiable fees

Editorial and publishing fees are almost always fixed with little, if any, room for haggling and are generally considerably lower than advertising and design fees, which tend to be negotiable. A national full-colour 48-sheet poster advertising Marks & Spencer is likely to pay more than a local black and white press ad plugging a poodle parlour. If, having paid your editorial dues, you find yourself hankering after commissions from the big boys, fee negotiation – confusing and complicated as it can sometimes be – will become a fact of life. However you choose to go about the business of cutting a deal, it will help if you disabuse yourself of the notion that the client is doing you a whopping favour by considering you for the job. Believe it or not, the client *needs* your skills to bring his/her ideas to life. In short, you are worth the money and the client knows it.

Pricing a commission

Before you can quote on a job, you'll need to know exactly what it entails. For what purpose is the work to be used? Will it be used several times and/or for more than one purpose? Will its use be local or national? For how long is the client intending to use it? Who is the client and how soon do they want the work? Are you up against anyone else (who could possibly undercut you)?

Next, ask the client what the budget is. Believe it or not there's a fair chance they might tell you. Whether they are forthcoming or not, don't feel you have to pluck a figure out of thin air or agree to their offer immediately. Play for time. Tell them you need to review your current workload and that you'll get back to them within a brief, specified period of time. If nothing else, haggling over the phone is less daunting than doing it face to face. If you've had no comparable commissions to date and are an AOI member, check out the going rate by calling them for pricing advice. Failing that, try speaking to a friendly client or a fellow illustrator who's worked on similar jobs.

When you begin negotiating, have in mind a bottom-line price you're prepared to do the job for and always ask for slightly more than your ideal fee as the client will invariably try to beat you down. You may find it useful to break down your asking price in order to explain exactly what it is the client is paying for. How you do this is up to you. Some people find it helpful to work out a daily rate incorporating overheads such as rent, heating, materials, travel and telephone charges, while others prefer to negotiate on a flat fee basis. There are also illustrators who charge extra for something needed yesterday, time spent researching, model hire if applicable and so on. It pays to be flexible, so if your initial quote exceeds the client's budget and you really want the job, tell them you are open to negotiation. If, on the other hand, the job looks suspiciously thankless, stick to your guns. If the client agrees to your exorbitant demands, the job might start to look more appetising.

Getting paid

Once you've traded terms and conditions, done the job and invoiced the client, you'll then have the unenviable task of getting your hands on your fee. It is customary to send your invoice to the accounts department stating payment within 30 days. It is also customary for them to ignore this entreaty, regardless of the wolf at your door, and pay you when it suits them. Magazines pay promptly, usually within 4–6 weeks; everyone else takes 60–90 days – no matter what.

Be methodical when chasing up your invoice. Send out a statement the moment your 30 days has elapsed and call the accounts department as soon as you like. Take names, note dates and the gist of their feeble excuses. ("It's in the post", "He's in a meeting", "He's on holiday and forgot to sign the cheque before he went"), and keep on chasing. Don't worry about your incessant nagging scuppering your plans of further commissions as these decisions are solely down to the art department, and they think you're a gem. Should payment still not be forthcoming three months down the line, it might be advisable to ask your commissioner to follow things up on your behalf. Chances are they'll be horrified you haven't been paid yet and things will be speedily resolved. In the meantime, you'll have had a good deal of practice talking money, which can only make things easier next time around.

And finally…

Basic book-keeping – making a simple, legible record of all your financial transactions, both incoming and outgoing – will be crucial to your sanity once the tax inspector starts to loom. It will also make your accountant's job easier, thereby saving you money. If your annual turnover is less than £15,000, it is unnecessary to provide the Inland Revenue with detailed accounts of your earnings. Information regarding your turnover, allowable expenses and net profit may simply be entered on your tax return. Although an accountant is not necessary to this process, many find it advantageous to employ one. The tax system is complicated and dealing with the Inland Revenue can be stressful, intimidating and time consuming. Accountants offer invaluable advice on tax allowances, National Insurance and tax assessments, as well as dealing expertly with the Inland Revenue on your behalf – thereby enabling you to attend to the business of illustrating. See *Income tax* on page 647, *Social security contributions* on page 660 and *Social security benefits* on page 669.

Fig Taylor initially began her career as an illustrators' agent in 1983. For 18 years she has been the resident 'portfolio surgeon' at the Association of Illustrators and also operates as a private consultant to non-AOI member artists. In addition, she lectures extensively in Business Awareness to BA and HND illustration students throughout the UK.

Art agents and commercial art studios

Before submitting work, artists are advised to make preliminary enquiries and to ascertain terms of work. Commission varies but averages 25–30%. The Association of Illustrators (see page 447) provides a valuable service for illustrators, agents and clients.

*Member of the Society of Artists Agents
†Member of the Association of Illustrators

Advocate†
Advocate Gallery, 372 Old York Road,
London SW18 1SP
tel (07000) 238622 *fax* 020-8874 7661
email mail@advocate-art.com
website www.advocate-art.com
Director Edward Burns

Represents 110 artists with 6 agents. Recently launched *Devil's Advocate*, representing alternative illustrators. Supplies work to book publishers, design and advertising agencies, greeting card and fine art publishers, ceramic manufacturers and potteries, and supplies editorial illustrations. Also has an original art gallery, a stock library and licensing agency for its art character 'Newton's Law'. Founded as a co-operative in 1996.

Allied Artists
New Richmond Gallery, 63 Sheen Road,
Richmond upon Thames TW9 1YJ
tel 020-8334 1010 *fax* 020-8334 9900
email info@alliedartists.ltd.uk
mary@umbrellapublishing.ca
website www.alliedartists.ltd.uk
www.umbrellapublishing.ca
Contacts Gary Mills, Mary Burtenshaw

Represents over 40 artists specialising in highly finished realistic figure illustrations, stylised juvenile illustrations for children's books, and cartoons for magazines, books, plates, prints, cards and advertising. Extensive library of stock illustrations.

Arena*†
Quantum Artists Ltd, 108 Leonard Street,
London EC2A 4RH
tel 020-7613 4040 *fax* 020-7613 1441
email info@arenaworks.com
website www.arenaworks.com
Contact Tamlyn Francis

Represents 35 artists working mostly for book covers, children's books and design groups. Average commission 30%. Founded 1970.

The Art Market*†
51 Oxford Drive, London SE1 2FB
tel 020-7407 8111 *fax* 020-7407 8222
email info@artmarketillustration.com

website www.artmarketillustration.com
Director Philip Reed

Represents 20 artists creating illustrations for publishing, design and advertising. Founded 1989.

The Artworks*
70 Rosaline Road, London SW6 7QT
tel 020-7610 1801 *fax* 020-7610 1811
email info@theartworksinc.com
website www.theartworksinc.com
Directors Allan Manham, Kit Taylor

Represents 30 artists. Undertakes artwork for illustrated gift books and children's books. Commission: 20%. Founded 1982.

Associated Freelance Artists Ltd
124 Elm Park Mansions, Park Walk,
London SW10 0AR
tel 020-7352 6890 *fax* 020-7352 8125
email pekes.afa@virgin.net
Directors Eva Morris, Doug FitzMaurice

Freelance illustrators mainly in children's educational fields, and some greeting cards.

Barry Everitt Associates
tel (01284) 828685
Contact Barry M. Everitt

Design and art resource specialising in licensing reproduction rights for greetings cards, fine art prints, calendars, giftware, etc. Always pleased to see the work of new and established artists and illustrators. Colour copies or photographs required initially with sae for return or reply, but telephone first for details.

Beehive Illustration†
42A Cricklade Street, Cirencester,
Glos. GL7 1JH
tel (01285) 885149 *fax* (01285) 641291
email info@beehiveillustration.co.uk
website www.beehiveillustration.co.uk
Owners Paul Beebee, Karen Beebee

Represents 40 artists specialising in education and general children's publishing illustration. Commission: 25%. Founded 1990.

Central Illustration Agency*[†]
36 Wellington Street, London WC2E 7BD
tel 020-7240 8925/836 1106 *fax* 020-7836 1177
email c.illustration.a@dial.pipex.com
website www.centralillustration.com
Director Brian Grimwood, Louisa St Pierre

Illustrations for design, publishing, animation and advertising. Commission: 30%. Founded 1983.

David Lewis Illustration Agency
Worlds End Studios, 134 Lots Road,
London SW10 0RJ
tel 020-7435 7762, *mobile* (07931) 824674
fax 020-7435 1945
email davidlewis34@hotmail.com
website www.davidlewisillustration.com
Director David Lewis, *Associate Director* Robin
Broadway

Considers all types of illustration for a variety of applications but mostly suitable for book and magazine publishers, design groups, recording companies and corporate institutions. Also offers a comprehensive selection of images suitable for subsidiary rights purposes. Send return postage with samples. Commission: 30%. Founded 1974.

Début Art[†]
30 Tottenham Street, London W1T 4RJ
tel 020-7636 1064 *fax* 020-7580 7017
email debutart@coningsbygallery.demon.co.uk
website www.debutart.com
Directors Andrew Coningsby, Luke Wilson,
Benjamin Cox

Represents 60 artists working in mixed media, digital, photographic 3D and 2D collage and montage. Commission: 25%. Founded 1985.

Folio Illustrators' & Designers' Agents*[†]
10 Gate Street, Lincoln's Inn Fields,
London WC2A 3HP
tel 020-7242 9562 *fax* 020-7242 1816
email all@folioart.co.uk
website www.folioart.co.uk

All areas of illustration. Send sae with samples. Founded 1976.

Frances McKay Illustration
14A Ravensdon Street, London SE11 4AR
tel 020-7820 6203 *fax* 020-7735 3303
email frances@francesmckay.com
website www.francesmckay.com
Proprietor Frances McKay

Represents 17+ artists for illustration mainly for children's books, magazines and products, greetings cards and stationery. Submit colour copies of recent work or email low-res scans; sae essential for return of all unsolicited samples. Commission: 25%–35%. Founded 1999.

Graham-Cameron Illustration[†]
The Studio, 23 Holt Road, Sheringham,
Norfolk NR26 8NB
tel (01263) 821333 *fax* (01263) 821334
and Duncan Graham-Cameron, Graham-Cameron
Illustration, 59 Redvers Road, Brighton BN2 4BF
tel (01273) 385890
email duncan@graham-cameron-illustration.com
Partners Mike Graham-Cameron, Helen
Graham-Cameron, Duncan Graham-Cameron

Represents 37 artists. Undertakes all forms of illustration for publishing and communications. Specialist in educational, information and children's books. Send sae with samples. Founded 1988.

The Guild of Aviation Artists
Trenchard House, 85 Farnborough Road,
Farnborough, Hants. GU14 6TF
tel (01252) 513123
email admin@gava.org.uk
website www.gava.org.uk
President Michael Turner PGAVA, *Secretary* Sue
Gardner

Professional body of 350 artists specialising in aviation art in all mediums. The Guild sells, commissions and exhibits members' work. Commission: 25%. Founded 1971.

Ian Fleming Associates*
64 Charlotte Street, London W1T 4QD
tel 020-7323 2030 *fax* 020-7323 3326
email fleming1@btclick.com
website www.ianflemingart.com
Directors Jon Rogers, Cariona Wydmanski

Represents 20 artists who work across the board – advertising, design and publishing. Commission: 33%. Founded 1971.

Illustration Ltd*[†]
2 Brooks Court, Cringle Street, London SW8 5BX
tel 020-7720 5202 *fax* 020-7720 5920
email team@illustrationweb.com
website www.illustrationweb.com
Contact Harry Lyon-Smith, Marie-Claire Carver,
Vanessa Dell

Illustrations and animation for international advertisers, designers, publishers and editorial clients. Commission: 33.3% or 25%.

Image by Design
34 Crescent Road, Luton, Beds. LU2 0AG
tel (01582) 890340 *fax* (01582) 896516
email enquiries@imagebydesign-licensing.co.uk
website www.imagebydesign-licensing.co.uk
Contact Lucy Brenham, Graham Dollman

Quality artwork for all products including prints, greeting cards, stationery, ceramics, etc. Commission: negotiable. Founded 1987.

The Inkshed*†
98 Columbia Road, London E2 7QB
tel 020-7613 2323 *fax* 020-7613 2726
email makecontact@inkshed.co.uk
website www.inkshed.co.uk
Partners Tim Woolgar, Jacqueline Hollister,
Contact Melanie Grimshaw, Abby Glassfield (agents)

Represents 30 artists who work across the board –
advertising, design, publishing, editorial.
Commission: 25%. Founded 1985.

John Hodgson Agency
38 Westminster Palace Gardens, Artillery Row,
London SW1P 1RR
tel 020-7580 3773 *fax* 020-7222 4468

Publishing (children's picture books) and
advertising. Send sae with samples. Commission:
25%. Founded 1965.

John Martin & Artists†
12 Haven Court, Hatfield Peverel, Chelmsford,
Essex CM3 2SD
tel (01245) 380337 *fax* (01245) 382055
email bernardjma@aol.com
website www.jm-a.co.uk
Contact Bernard Bowen-Davies

Represents 25 illustrators, mainly producing
artwork for children's fiction/ non-fiction and
educational books. Include return postage with
submissions. Founded 1956.

JWL
Parlington Hall, Aberford, West Yorkshire LS25 3EG
tel 0113-281 3913 *fax* 0113-281 3911
email info@jwl.uk.com
Managing Director Janet Woodward, *Manager*
Pamela Dash

International art licensing agency. Licensing
concepts, artwork and children's TV projects for
merchandise. Properties include *Rambling Ted*,
Kit 'n' Kin. Freelance contributions welcome but
ideas must be well developed. Samples with sae.

Kathy Jakeman Illustration†
Richmond Business Centre, 23-24 George Street,
Richmond, Surrey TW9 1HY
tel 020-8973 2000 *fax* (07071) 225 115
email kathy@kji.co.uk
website www.kji.co.uk

Illustration for publishing – especially children's;
also design, editorial and advertising. Do not send
samples by email. Commission: 25%.

Libba Jones Associates
Hopton Manor, Hopton, Nr Wirksworth,
Derbyshire DE4 4DF
tel (01629) 540353 *fax* (01629) 540577
email ljassociates@easynet.co.uk

website www.libbajonesassociates.com
Contacts Libba Jones, Ieuan Jones

High-quality artwork and design for china,
greetings cards and giftwrap, jigsaw puzzles,
calendars, prints, posters, stationery, book
illustration, fabric design. Submission of samples
required for consideration. Founded 1983.

Linda Rogers Associates†
PO Box 330, 163 Half Moon Lane, London SE24 9WB
tel 020-7501 9106 *fax* 020-7501 9175
email lr@lindarogers.net
website www.lindarogers.net
Partners Linda Rogers, Peter Sims, Jess Sims

Represents 65 illustrators and author/ illustrators in
all fields of illustration. Specialises in children's
books, educational, information books; adult leisure
books and magazines. Reply only with sae. Artwork
samples only viewed via post, *not* by email.
Commission: 25%. Founded 1973.

Maggie Mundy Illustrators' Agency
14 Ravenscourt Park Mansions, Dalling Road,
London W6 0HG
tel 020-8748 2029 *fax* 020-8748 0353
email maggiemundy@compuserve.com

Represents 20 artists in varying styles of illustration
for children's books. The Agency's books are closed.

Meiklejohn Illustration*†
5 Risborough Street, London SE1 0HF
tel 020-7593 0500 *fax* 020-7593 0501
email mjn@mjgrafix.demon.co.uk
website www.theartbook.com
www.meiklejohn.co.uk
Contacts Paul Meiklejohn, Malcolm Sanders

All types of illustration.

Michael Woodward Fine Art
Parlington Hall, Aberford, West Yorkshire LS25 3EG
tel 0113-281 3913 *fax* 0113-281 3911
email art@mwc.com
website www.woodward-fineart.co.uk
Managing Director Michael Woodward

Artist management company representing: Anthony
Christian, Terry Durham, Jude Roberts, David
Greenwood. Own publishing division. Artists
should send transparencies or laser copies of work
with biography, plus sae. Division of MWC Group.
Founded 1996.

N.E. Middleton
Richmond Business Centre, 23-24 George Street,
Richmond, Surrey TW9 1HY
tel 020-8973 2000 *fax* (07071) 225 115

Designs for greetings cards, stationery, prints,
calendars and china.

NB Illustration[†]
40 Bowling Green Lane, London EC1R 0NE
tel 020-7278 9131 *fax* 020-7278 9121
email info@nbillustration.co.uk
website www.nbillustration.co.uk
Directors Joe Najman, Charlotte Berens, Paul Najman

Represents 20+ artists and will consider all material for the commercial illustration market. Sae essential. Commission: 30%. Founded 2000.

The Organisation[†]
The Basement, 69 Caledonian Road, London N1 9BT
tel 020-7833 8268 *fax* 020-7833 8269
email organise@easynet.co.uk
website www.organisart.co.uk
Contact Lorraine Owen

Various styles of illustration supplied for book work in adult, children's and educational markets. Also for print, advertising, packaging and editorial. Average commission: 30%. Sae essential for unsolicited samples. Founded 1986.

Oxford Designers & Illustrators
Aristotle Lane, Oxford OX2 6TR
tel (01865) 512331 *fax* (01865) 512408
email richard@odi-illustration.co.uk
website www.o-d-i.com

Studio of 25 full-time illustrators working for publishers, business and industry. All types of artwork including science, technical, airbrush, graphic, medical, biological, botanical, natural history, figure, cartoon, maps, diagrams, and charts. Artwork supplied as PDF files or on a CD, Zip optical disk or ISDN, Mac or PC, with both b&w and colour proofs. Not an agency. Founded 1968.

Pennant Inc.[*†]
16 Littleton Street, London SW18 3SY
tel 020-8947 4002 *fax* 020-8946 7667
email matt@pennantinc.co.uk
website www.pennantinc.co.uk
Director Matthew Doyle

Illustrations for publishing, design and advertising. Samples must be accompanied by an sae. Commission: 30%. Founded 1992.

Pink Barge
13 Wyndham Place, London W1H 2PY
tel 020-7486 1053 *fax* 020-7262 1130
Director Maggee Barge

Represents 20 artists working in advertising, publishing and corporate art. Commission: 25%. Founded 1982.

Sarah Brown Agency
10 The Avenue, London W13 8PH
tel 020-8998 0390 *fax* 020-8843 1175
email sbagency@gxn.co.uk

website www.sbagency.com
Contact Brian Fennelly

Illustrations for publishing and advertising. Sae essential for unsolicited material. Commission: 25% UK, 33.3% USA. Founded 1977.

SGA Illustration Agency[†]
(formerly Simon Girling & Associates)
18 High Street, Hadleigh, Suffolk IP7 5AP
tel (01473) 824083 *fax* (01473) 827846
email info@sgadesignart.com
website www.sgadesignart.com

Represents over 50 illustrators. Mainly working within publishing (early learning through to teenage). Also manages projects from conception to final film. See website for portfolio of illustration samples. Commission: 30%. Founded 1985.

Specs Art[†]
93 London Road, Cheltenham, Glos. GL52 6HL
tel (01242) 515951 *fax* (01242) 518862
email roland@specsart.com
website www.specsart.com
Partners Roland Berry and Stephanie Prosser

High-quality illustration and animation work for advertisers, publishers and all other forms of visual communication. Specialises in licensed character illustration.

Temple Rogers Artists' Agency
120 Crofton Road, Orpington, Kent BR6 8HZ
tel (01689) 826249 *fax* (01689) 896312
Contact Patrick Kelleher

Illustrations for children's educational books and magazine illustrations. Commission: by arrangement.

Thorogood Illustration Ltd[†]
5 Dryden Street, London WC2E 9NW
tel 020-8859 7507, 020-8488 3195 *fax* 020-8333 7677
email draw@thorogood.net
website www.thorogood.net
Directors Doreen Thorogood, Stephen Thorogood

Represents 30 artists for advertising, design, publishing and animation work. Send return postage with samples. Commission: 30%. Founded 1977.

TWO:Design London Ltd
Studio 20, The Arches, Hartland Road, London NW1 8HR
tel 020-7267 1118 *fax* 020-7482 0221
email studio@twodesign.net
website www.twodesign.net
Directors Graham N. Peake, David M. Coventon

Studio providing comprehensive services: design, photography, image creation and manipulation, typesetting, artworking, marketing, point-of-sale material, etc. Specialists in general books, magazines and periodicals. Founded 1997.

Ulric Design

PO Box 55, Church Stretton, Shropshire SY6 6WR
tel (01694) 781354 *fax* (01694) 781372
Directors Ulric Woodhams, Elizabeth Follows

Studio offering high-quality bespoke graphics, corporate ID and illustration. Not an agency for artists.

Vicki Thomas Associates

195 Tollgate Road, London E6 5JY
tel 020-7511 5767 *fax* 020-7473 5177
email vickithomasassociates@yahoo.co.uk
website www.vickithomasassociates.com
Consultant Vicki Thomas

Considers the work of illustrators and designers working in greetings and gift industries, and promotes such work to gift, toy, publishing and related industries. Written application and b&w photocopies required. Commission: 30%. Founded 1985.

Wildlife Art Ltd†

The Lodge, Cargate Lane, Saxlingham Thorpe, Norwich NR15 1TU
tel (01508) 471500 *fax* (01508) 470391
email info@wildlife-art.co.uk

Illustrations of all things natural, including gardening and food. Clients range from children's/adults' books to design and advertising agencies. Sae must be included with work submitted for consideration. Commission: 30%. Founded 1992.

Winning the greeting card game

The UK population spends £1.2 billion a year on greeting cards yet finding a route into this fiercely competitive industry is not always easy. Jacqueline Brown steers artists through the greeting card maze. fee and how to negotiate one to your best advantage.

The UK greeting card industry leads the world on two counts – design and innovation and per capita send. On average people in the UK send 50 cards a year, 85% of which are bought by women.

But just how do you, as an artist, go about satisfying this voracious appetite of the card-sending public? There are two main options: either to become a greeting card publisher yourself or to supply existing greeting card publishers with your artwork and be paid a fee for doing so.

The idea of setting up your own greeting card publishing company may sound exciting, but this decision should not be taken lightly. Going down this route will involve taking on all the set up and running costs of a publishing company as well as the production, selling and administrative responsibilities. This often leaves little time for you to do what you do best – creating the artwork.

There are estimated to be around 800 greeting card publishers in the UK, ranging in size from one-person operations to multinational corporations, roughly 200 of which are regarded as 'serious' publishers (see page 397). Not all of them accept freelance artwork, but a great many do. Remember, whatever the size of the company, all publishers rely on good designs.

Finding the right publishers

While some publishers concentrate on producing a certain type of greeting card (e.g. humorous, fine art or juvenile), the majority publish a variety of greeting card ranges. Unfortunately, this makes it more difficult for you as an artist to target the most appropriate potential publishers for your work. There are various ways in which you can research the market, quickly improve your publisher knowledge and, therefore, reduce the amount of wasted correspondence:

● **Go shopping.** Browse the displays in card shops, newsagents and other high street shops, department stores and gift shops. This will not only give you an insight into what is already available but also which publishers

Some greeting card language

Own brand/bespoke publishers. These design specific to a retailer's needs.

Spring Seasons. The industry term to describe greeting cards for Valentine's Day, Mother's Day, Easter and Father's Day. Publishers generally launch these ranges all together in June/July.

Greeting card types. Traditional; cute or whimsical; contemporary/quirky art; juvenile; handmade or hand-finished; fine art; photographic, humorous.

Finishes and treatments. Artists will not be expected to know the production techniques and finishes, but a working knowledge is often an advantage. Some of the most commonly used finishes and treatments include: embossing (raised portion of a design), die-cutting (where the card is cut into a shape or includes an aperture), foiling (metallic film) and flitter (a glitter-like substance).

Further information

The Greeting Card Association

United House, North Road, London N7 9DP
tel 020-7619 0396
email gca@max-publishing.co.uk
website www.greetingcardassociation.org.uk
The UK trade association for greeting card
publishers. Its website contains leaflets on freelance
designing and writing for greeting cards complete
with lists of publishers which accept freelance work.

Trade fairs

Spring & Autumn Fairs Birmingham, NEC

Contact TPS *tel* 020-8277 5830
Takes place 1–5 Feb 2004, 5–8 Sept 2004

Top Drawer, Earls Court

Contact Clarion Events *tel* 020-7370 8374
Takes place 18–20 Jan 2004, May 2004, Sept 2004

Home and Gift, Harrogate

Contact Clarion Events *tel* 020-7370 8374
Takes place July 2004

Trade magazines

Greetings Today

(formerly Greetings Magazine)
Lema Publishing, Unit No. 1, Queen Mary's Avenue,
Watford, Herts. WD18 7JR
tel (01923) 250909 *fax* (01923) 250995
Publisher-in-Chief Malcolm Naish, *Editor* Vicky
Denton
Monthly £45 p.a. (other rates on application)
Articles, features and news related to the greetings
card industry. Includes Artists Directory for aspiring
artists wishing to attract the eye of publishers. Runs
seminars for small publishers and artists.

Progressive Greetings Worldwide

Max Publishing, United House, North Road,
London N7 9DP
tel 020-7700 6740 *fax* 020-7607 6411
12 p.a. (£40 p.a.)
The official magazine of the Greeting Card
Association. Provides an insight into the industry,
including an up-to-date list of publishers, a new
product section and a free showcase for artists and
illustrators. Special supplements include *Focus on Art
Cards, Focus on Humorous Cards, Focus on Words &
Sentiments, Focus on Kids* and *Focus on Giftwrap*.

Hosts The Henries, the greeting card industry
awards. The September edition includes details of
the finalists in the different categories and the
November issue features the winners.

may be interested in your work. Most
publishers include their contact details
on the backs of the cards.

● **Trade fairs.** There are a number of
trade exhibitions held during the year
at which publishers exhibit their
greeting card ranges to retailers and
overseas distributors. By visiting these
exhibitions, you will gain a broad
overview of the design trends in the
industry, as well as the current ranges
of individual publishers. Some publishers are willing to meet artists and
look through their portfolios on the
stand but others are not. If you believe
your work could be relevant for them,
ask for a contact name and follow it up
afterwards. Have a supply of business
cards handy, perhaps illustrated with
some of your work, to leave with
publishers.

Types of publishers

There are two broad categories of
publisher – wholesale and direct-to-
retail – each employing a different
method of distribution to reach the
retailer.

Wholesale publishers distribute their
products to the retailer via greeting
card wholesalers or cash-and-carry
outlets. They work on volume sales and
have a rapid turnover of designs, many
being used with a variety of different
captions. For example, the same floral
design may be used for cards for
mothers, grandmothers, aunts and
sisters. It is therefore usual for the artist
to leave a blank space on the design to
accommodate the caption. Until
recently, wholesale publishers were
generally only interested in traditional,
cute and juvenile designs, but they now
publish across the board, including
contemporary and humorous ranges.

Direct-to-retail (DTR) publishers supply retailers via sales agents or reps. Most greeting cards sold through specialist card shops and gift shops are supplied by DTR publishers, which range from multi-national corporations down to small, trendy niche publishing companies. These publishers market series of ranges based on distinctive design themes or characters. Categories of DTR cards include contemporary art/fun, fine art, humour, children's, photographic, traditional and handmade.

Approaching a publisher

Unfortunately, there is no standard way of approaching and submitting work to a card publisher. The first step is to establish that the publisher you wish to approach accepts work from freelance artists; then find out their requirements for submission and to whom it should be addressed.

It is always better to send several examples of your work to show the breadth of your artistic skills. Some publishers prefer to see finished designs while others are happy with well-presented sketches. Never send originals: instead send photocopies, laser copies or photographs, and include at least one design in colour. Never be tempted to sell similar designs to two publishers – a bad reputation will follow you around.

Some publishers will be looking to purchase individual designs for specific sending occasions while others will be more intent on looking for designs which could be developed to make up a range. Bear in mind that publishers work a long way in advance, e.g. Christmas ranges are launched to the retailers in January. Development of a range may take up to six months prior to launching.

Also remember that cards in retail outlets are rarely displayed in their entirety. Therefore, when designing a card make sure that some of the 'action' appears in the top half.

When interest is shown

Some publishers respond to submissions from artists immediately while others prefer to deal with them on a monthly basis. A publisher's response may be in the form of a request for more submissions of a specific design style or of a specific character. This speculative development work is usually carried out free of charge. Always meet your deadline (news travels fast in the industry).

A publisher interested in buying your artwork will probably then issue you with a contract. This may cover aspects such as the terms of payment; rights of usage of the design (e.g. is it just for greeting cards or will it include giftwrap and/or stationery?); territory of usage (most publishers want worldwide rights); and ownership of copyright or license period.

There is no set industry standard rate of pay for greeting card artists. Publishers pay artists either on a per design or per range basis in one of the following ways:

- **Flat fee.** A one-off payment is made to the artist for ownership of a design for an unlimited period. The industry standard is around £200–£250 for a single design, and payment on a sliding scale for more than one design.
- **Licensing fee.** The publisher is granted the right to use a piece of artwork for

a specified number of years, after which the full rights revert to the artist. Payment to the artist is approximately £150 upwards per design.

● **Licensing fee** plus royalty. As above plus a royalty payment on each card sold. Artists would generally receive a minimum of £100 for the licensing fee plus 3% of the trade price of each card sold.

● **Advance royalty deal.** A goodwill advance on royalties is paid to the artist. In the case of a range, the artist would receive a goodwill advance of say £500–£1000 plus 5% additional royalty payment once the threshold is reached.

● **Royalty only.** The artist receives regular royalty payments, generally paid quarterly, based on the number of cards sold. Artists should expect a sales report and royalty statement.

The fees stated above should only be regarded as a rough guideline. Fees and advances are generally paid on completion of artwork. Publishers which have worldwide rights pay royalties for sales overseas to artists, although these will be on a pro rata basis to the export trade price.

Jacqueline Brown is editor of *Progressive Greetings Worldwide* and general secretary of the Greeting Card Association.

Card and stationery publishers which accept illustrations and verses

Before submitting work, artists are advised to write giving details of the work they have to offer, and asking for requirements.

*Member of the Greeting Card Association

Andrew Brownsword Collection – see Hallmark Cards Plc

Card Connection Ltd*
Park House, South Street, Farnham, Surrey GU9 7QQ
tel (01252) 892300 *fax* (01252) 892363
email ho@card-connection.co.uk
website www.card-connection.co.uk
Managing Director Adrian Atkinson, *Senior Product and Marketing Manager* Alison Mahoney

Everyday and seasonal designs. Styles include cute, fun, traditional, floral, contemporary, graphic, art, photography. Submit colour copies. Humour designs and jokes. Sentiment verse. Founded 1992.

Carlton Cards Ltd*
Mill Street East, Dewsbury,
West Yorkshire WF12 9AW
tel (01924) 465200
website www.carltoncards.co.uk
Marketing Director Keith Auty, *Creative Director* Linda Marshall

All types of artwork, any size; submit as colour roughs, colour copies or transparencies. Especially interested in humorous artwork and ideas.

Caspari Ltd*
9 Shire Hill, Saffron Walden, Essex CB11 3AP
tel (01799) 513010 *fax* (01799) 513101
Managing Director Keith Entwisle

Traditional fine art/classic images; 5 x 4in transparencies. No verses. Founded 1990.

Charity Christmas Card Council*
221 St John Street, London EC1V 4LY
tel 020-7702 5090 *fax* 020-7702 5092
email karnthorsson@charitycards.org
website www.charitycards.org

Traditional and contemporary Christmas cards for the corporate market. Submit artwork on CD-Rom or 5 x 4in transparencies. No verses. Charitable not-for-profit organisation. Founded 1966.

The Classic Card Company Ltd – see Hallmark Cards Plc

Colour House Graphics*
58 Matilda Street, London N1 1BG
tel 020-7700 7780 *fax* 020-7700 7727
email colourhousegraphics@hotmail.com
website www.colourhousegraphics.com
Partners John Ellner and Margaret Ellner

Contemporary styles of painting of subjects relating to people's everyday lives. Particularly interested in sophisticated, loose, graphic styles. No verses. Founded 1990.

Felix Rosenstiel's Widow & Son Ltd
Fine Art Publishers, 33-35 Markham Street,
London SW3 3NR
tel 020-7352 3551 *fax* 020-7351 5300
email sales@felixr.com
website www.felixr.com

Invites offers of original oil paintings and strong watercolours of a professional standard for reproduction as picture prints for the picture framing trade. Any type of subject considered; send photographs of work.

Gallery Five Ltd*
121 King Street, London W6 9JG
tel 020-8741 8394 *fax* 020-8741 4444

Send samples of work FAO 'Gallery Five Art Studio'. Colour photocopies, Mac-formatted zip/CD acceptable, plus sae. Founded 1961.

Gemma International Ltd*
Linmar House, 6 East Portway, Andover,
Hants. SP10 3LU
tel (01264) 388400 *fax* (01264) 366243
website www.gemma-international.co.uk
Directors L. Rudd-Clarke, M. Rudd-Clarke, A. Parkin, T. Rudd-Clarke, W. O'Loughlin, R. Howard, K. Bishop

Cute, contemporary, leading-edge designs for children, teens and young adults, and mainstream adult humour. Considers humorous verses. Founded 1984.

Gibson Greetings International Ltd
Gibson House, Hortonwood 30, Telford,
Shropshire TF1 7YF

tel (01952) 608333 *fax* (01952) 605259
email jan_taylor@gibson-greetings.co.uk
Product Director Jan Taylor

All everyday and seasonal illustrations: cute, humorous, juvenile, traditional and contemporary designs, as well as surface pattern. Greeting card traditional and humorous verse. Founded 1991.

The Gordon Fraser Gallery – see Hallmark Cards Plc

Graphic Humour Ltd

4 Britannia House, Point Pleasant, Wallsend, Tyne & Wear NE28 6HA
tel 0191-295 4200 *fax* 0191-295 3916
email enquiries@graphic-humour.demon.co.uk
website www.graphic-humour.demon.co.uk

Risqué and everyday artwork ideas for greetings cards; short, humorous copy. Founded 1984.

Greetings Cards By Noel Tatt Ltd

t/a Noel Tatt Group, Appledown House, Barton Business Park, Appledown Way, New Dover Road, Canterbury, Kent CT1 3TE
tel (01227) 811600 *fax* (01227) 811601
email mail@noeltatt.co.uk
Directors Jarle Tatt, Diane Tatt, Richard Parsons, Ian Hylands

Greetings cards, giftwrap. Founded 1988.

Hallmark Cards Plc*

Hallmark House, Bingley Road, West Yorkshire BD9 8SD
email 1willi2@hallmark-uk.com
website www.hallmark.com
Submissions Mr Richmond Denton (illustrations), Paul Treacy (words)

Illustrations: all subjects considered. Submit colour copies and/or transparencies but not original artwork. Ensure that all work is named and include an sae. Words: verses, captions, jokes, etc considered.

Hanson White – UKG Speciality Products

9th Floor, Wettern House, 56 Dingwall Road, Croydon, Surrey CR0 0XH
tel 020-8260 1200 *fax* 020-8260 1213
email hannah.turpin@ukgsp.co.uk
david.blake@ukgsp.co.uk
Artwork Submissions Editor Hannah Turpin,
Copy Submissions Editor Hannah Turpin (everyday), David Blake (seasonal)

Humorous artwork and cartoons for greeting cards, including Christmas, Valentine's Day, Mother's Day and Father's Day. Humorous copy lines, punchline jokes, poems and rhymes; guidelines available. Founded 1958.

Jarrold Publishing

Whitefriars, Norwich NR3 1TR
tel (01603) 763300 *fax* (01603) 662748
email publishing@jarrold.com
website www.jarrold-publishing.co.uk
Managing Director Margot Russell-King

Decorative colour artwork – floral, kitchen, animals. Humour. Calendars only; no cards. Send sae with all submissions to Rose Joy. Founded 1770.

Jodds*

PO Box 353, Bicester, Oxon OX27 0GS
tel (01869) 278550 *fax* (01869) 278551
email design@joddscards.com
website www.joddscards.com
Partners M. Payne and J.S. Payne

Contemporary art style greetings cards; must give out a warm feel. Submit colour photocopies with sae. No verses. Founded 1988.

Leeds Postcards

4 Granby Road, Leeds LS6 3AS
email xtine@leedspostcards.com
website www.leedspostcards.com
Contact Christine Hankinson

Publisher and distributor of radical postcards for the wall and post.

Ling Design Ltd*

The Old Brewery, Newtown, Bradford on Avon, Wilts. BA15 1NF
tel (01225) 863991 *fax* (01225) 863992
email info@lingdesign.co.uk
website www.lingdesign.co.uk
Creative Director Kirsten Boyd

Artwork for greetings cards and giftwrap.

Medici*

Grafton House, Hyde Estate Road, London NW9 6JZ
tel 020-8205 2500 *fax* 020-8205 2552
email sales@medici.co.uk
website www.medici.co.uk
Contact The Art Department

Requirements: full colour or black and white paintings/sketches/etchings/designs suitable for reproduction as greeting cards. Send preliminary letter with brief details of work and colour copies only.

The Monster Factory*

Unit 207, Welsbach House, 3-9 Broomhill Road, London SW18 4JQ
tel 020-8875 9988 *fax* 020-8870 4488
email info@themonsterfactory.com
website www.themonsterfactory.com
Directors Martin Grix, Kate Eagar

Publishers of innovative stationery with a funky, design-led feel. Specialises in handmade ranges, unusual printing techniques and quirky illustration. Will consider original new concepts and fresh artwork styles with bags of character and humour. Do not send original artwork. No verses. Founded 2000.

Nigel Quiney Publications Ltd*
Cloudesley House, Shire Hill, Saffron Walden, Essex CB11 3FB
tel (01799) 520200 *fax* (01799) 520100
website www.nigelquiney.com
Contact Ms J. Arkinstall, Product & Marketing Director

Everyday and seasonal greetings cards and giftwrap including fine art, photographic, humour, fun art, contemporary and cute. Submit colour copies, photographs or transparencies: no original artwork.

The Paper House Group plc*
Waterwells Drive, Gloucester, Glos. GL2 4PH
tel (01452) 888999 *fax* (01452) 888912
email chris.hobbs@paperhouse.co.uk
website www.paperhouse.co.uk
Product Director Chris Wilcox

Publishers of greeting cards specialising in cartoon humour illustration, contemporary art styles and traditional verse design in special occasions and family birthday.

Paper Studios
4 Britannia House, Point Pleasant, Wallsend, Tyne and Wear NE28 6HA
tel 0191-295 4200 *fax* 0191-295 3916
email paperstudios@graphic-humour.demon.co.uk

Traditional, floral and cute designs for greetings cards for all occasions – artwork and 35mm transparencies. Verses considered. Founded 1999.

Paperlink Ltd*
356 Kennington Road, London SE11 4LD
tel 020-7582 8244 *fax* 020-7587 5212
email info@paperlinkcards.com
website www.paperlinkcards.com
Directors Louise Tighe, Jo Townsend, Tim Porte, Tim Purcell

Publishers of ranges of humorous and contemporary art greetings cards. Produce products under licence for charities. Founded 1986.

Pepperpot
Royston Road, Duxford, Cambridge CB2 4QY
tel (01223) 836825 *fax* (01223) 833321
Publishing Controller Linda Worsfold

Gift stationery, photo albums, gift cards. Colour illustrations; cute/traditional/floral. Submit original

artwork or 5 x 4in transparencies. No verses. Division of Copywrite Designs Ltd.

Pineapple Park Ltd*
58 Wilbury Way, Hitchin, Herts. SG4 0TP
tel (01462) 442021 *fax* (01462) 440418
email info@pineapplepark.co.uk
website www.pineapplepark.co.uk
Directors Peter M. Cockerline, Sarah M. Parker

Illustrations and photographs for publication as greetings cards. Contemporary, cute, humour: submit artwork or laser copies with sae. Photographic florals always needed. Humour copy/jokes accepted without artwork. Also concepts for ranges. Founded 1993.

Powell Publishing*
57 Coombe Valley Road, Dover, Kent CT17 0EX
tel (01304) 213999 *fax* (01304) 240151
email admin@powellprint.co.uk
website www.charitychristmascards.co.uk
Directors B.W. Powell (chairman), T.J. Paulett (managing)

Greetings card publishers. Interested in Christmas designs for the charity card market. Division of Powell Print Ltd.

Rainbow Cards Ltd*
Kingswood Business Park, Holyhead Road, Albrighton, Wolverhampton, West Midlands WV7 3AU
tel (01902) 376000 *fax* (01902) 376001
email sales@rainbowcards.co.uk
website www.rainbowcards.co.uk

Artwork for humorous and traditional greetings cards. Founded 1976.

Really Good*
Osney Mead, Oxford OX2 0ES
tel (01865) 246888 *fax* (01865) 246999
website www.reallygood.co.uk
Director David Hicks

Always looking for fun and funny artwork in a quirky or modern way to publish on cards, stationery or gifts. Send samples on paper rather than on disk, etc. Allow plenty of time for review. Founded 1987.

Royle Publications Ltd – see The Paper House Group plc

Santoro Graphics Ltd
Rotunda Point, 11 Hartfield Crescent, London SW19 3RL
tel 020-8781 1100 *fax* 020-8781 1101
email enquiries@santorographics.com
Directors Lucio Santoro, Meera Santoro (art)

Publishers of innovative and award-winning designs for greetings cards, giftwrap and gift stationery. Bold contemporary images with an international appeal. Subjects covered: quirky and humorous, whimsical, 'Fifties, 'Seventies, futuristic! Styles include traditional to stylised. Submit samples as colour photocopies, transparencies or on CD. Founded 1985.

Second Nature Ltd*
10 Malton Road, London W10 5UP
tel 020-8960 0212 *fax* 020-8960 8700
email rods@secondnature.co.uk
website www.secondnature.co.uk
Publishing Director Rod Schragger

Contemporary artwork for greetings cards and handmade cards; jokes for humorous range; short modern sentiment; verses. Founded 1981.

Solomon & Whitehead Ltd
Lynn Lane, Shenstone, Staffs. WS14 0DX
tel (01543) 480696 *fax* (01543) 481619
email sales@fineartgroup.co.uk

Fine art prints, limited editions and originals, framed and unframed.

Soul*
Osney Mead, Oxford OX2 0ES
tel (01865) 434444 *fax* (01865) 454444
website www.souluk.com
Director David Hicks

Publishers of contemporary, fine and quirky art. Allow plenty of time for review. Do not send originals. Sister company of Really Good.

Trumpet Limón
Osney Mead, Oxford OX2 0ES
tel (01865) 240140 *fax* (01865) 454444

Publishers of limited edition prints. Allow plenty of time for review. Do not send originals.

Valentines – see Hallmark Cards Plc

W.N. Sharpe Ltd – see Hallmark Cards Plc

Webb Ivory (Burton) Ltd
Queen Street, Burton-on-Trent, Staffs. DE14 3LP
tel (01283) 566311
email enquiries@webb-ivory.co.uk

High-quality Christmas cards and paper products.

Wishing Well Studios Ltd*
Kellet Close, Martland Park, Wigan,
Lancs. WN5 0LP
tel (01942) 218888 *fax* (01942) 218899
email info@wishingwell.co.uk
website www.wishingwell.co.uk
Directors David Evans, Brian Phillips

Traditional, cute, contemporary and humorous images. Send samples, colour photocopies or mock-ups, *not* originals. Considers verses and jokes.

Picture research

The freelance photographer

Becoming a successful freelance photographer is as much about marketing as photographic talent. Bruce Coleman and Ian Thraves discuss possibilities for the freelance photographer.

Having an outstanding portfolio is one thing, but to receive regular commissions takes a good business head and sound market knowledge. Although working as a professional photographer can be tough, it is undoubtedly one of the most interesting and rewarding ways of earning a living.

Entering professional photography

A good starting point is to embark on one of the many college courses available, which range from GCSE to degree level, and higher. These form a good foundation, though most teach only the technical aspects of photography and very few cover the basics of running a business. But a good college course will provide students with the opportunity to become familiar with photographic equipment and develop skills without the restrictions and pressures found in the workplace.

In certain fields, such as commercial photography, it is possible to learn the trade as an assistant to an established photographer. A photographer's assistant will undertake many varied tasks, including preparing camera equipment and lighting, building sets, obtaining props and organising locations, as well as general mundane chores. It usually takes only a year or two for an assistant to become a fully competent photographer, having during that time learnt many technical aspects of a particular field of photography and the fundamentals of running a successful business. There is, however, the danger of a long-standing assistant becoming a clone of the photographer worked for, and it is for this reason that some assistants prefer to gain experience with other photographers rather than working for just one for a long period of time. The Association of Photographers can help place an assistant.

However, in other fields of photography, such as photojournalism or wildlife photography, an assistant is not generally required, and photographers in these fields have to learn for themselves as they work.

Identifying your market

From the outset, identify which markets are most suitable for the kind of subjects you photograph. Study each market carefully and only offer images which suit the client's requirements.

Usually photographers who specialise in a particular field do better than those who generalise. By concentrating on one or two subject areas they become expert at what they do. Those who make a name for themselves are invariably specialists, and it is far easier for the images of, for example, an exceptional fashion photographer or an award-winning wildlife photographer to be remembered than the work of someone who covers a broad range of subjects.

In addition, photographers who produce work with individual style (e.g. by experimenting with camera angles or manipulating images to create unusual effects) are far more likely to make an impact. Alternative images which attract attention and can help sell a product are always sought after. This is especially true of advertising photography, but applies also to other markets such as book and magazine publishers, who are always seeking eye-catching images to use on front covers.

Promoting yourself

Effective self-promotion tells the market who you are and what service you offer. A first step should be to create an outstanding portfolio of images, tailored to appeal to the targeted market. Photographers targeting a few different markets should create an individual portfolio for each rather than presenting a single general one, including only a few relevant images. A portfolio containing between 10 and 20 images is enough for a potential client to judge a photographer's abilities.

Images should be presented in a format which the client is used to handling. Transparencies (perhaps duplicated to a larger size for easier viewing and general impact) are usually suitable for the editorial markets, but often more general companies prefer to view high-quality prints. Images can also be presented on CD-Rom and, unlike a traditional portfolio, can be left with potential clients to keep and refer to. Any published material (often referred to as 'tearsheets') should also be added to a portfolio. Tearsheets are often presented mounted and laminated in plastic.

Business cards and letterheads should be designed to reflect style and professionalism. Consider using a good graphic designer to design a logo for use on cards, letterheads and any other promotional literature. Many photographers produce postcard-size business cards and include an image as well as their name and logo.

Other than word of mouth, advertising is probably the best way of

Professional organisations

The Association of Photographers
Co-Secretary Gwen Thomas,
81 Leonard Street, London EC2A 4QS
tel 020-7739 6669 *fax* 020-7739 8707
email general@aophoto.co.uk
website www.the-aop.org
See page 447.

British Institute of Professional Photography
Fox Talbot House, Amwell End, Ware,
Herts. SG12 9HN
tel (01920) 464011
email bippware@aol.com
website www.bipp.com
See page 452.

Master Photographers Association
Jubilee House, 1 Chancery Lane, Darlington,
Co. Durham DL1 5QP
tel (01325) 356555 *fax* (01325) 357813
email info@mpauk.com
website www.mpauk.com
See page 467.

The Royal Photographic Society
The Octagon, Milsom Street, Bath BA1 1DN
tel (01225) 462841 *fax* (01225) 448688
email rps@rps.org
website www.rps.org
See page 475.

BAPLA (British Association of Picture Libraries and Agencies)
See page 448.

making your services known to potential clients. For a local market, a business directory such as *Yellow Pages* is a good start. Specialist directories in which photographers can advertise include *The Creative Handbook* and *Contact Photographers* (see page 404).

Cold calling by telephone is probably the most cost-effective and productive way of making contacts, and these should be followed up by an appointment for a personal visit (if possible) in order to show a portfolio of images. This helps to ensure you will not be forgotten.

Many photographers now use the internet as a medium to promote themselves. A cleverly designed website is a stylish and cost-effective way to expose a photographer's portfolio to a global market, as well as being a convenient way for a potential client to view a photographer's work. A personal website address can be added to business stationery and to other forms of advertising together with the usual address and telephone number information.

Creating a website is usually much cheaper than advertising using conventional published print media. However, its design should be carefully composed and is probably best left to a professional website designer (see *Setting up a website*, page 530). Although many images and details about your business can be placed on a website, one limiting factor is the time it can take to download the images due to the size of the files. Unless this is a relatively quick process the viewer may lose patience and cancel access to the site.

A well-organised exhibition of images is a very effective way of bringing your work to the attention of current and potential new clients. Throw a preview party with refreshments for friends, colleagues and specially invited guests from the industry. A show which is well reviewed by critics who write for newspapers and magazines can generate additional interest. Many photographic organisations have regular exhibitions. An excellent example is the Photographers Gallery in London, where work selected by the gallery board is exhibited free.

As a photographer's career develops, the budget for self-promotion should increase. Many established photographers will go as far as producing full-colour mailers, posters, and even calendars, which all contain examples of their work.

Digital photography

Digital photography and image-enhancement and manipulation using computer technology are now widely used in the photographic industry. Since the cost of digital cameras and other hardware can be considerably cheaper than using large quantities of film, many photographers are now using this technology.

There are various levels of quality produced by digital cameras and photographers should consider the requirements of their market prior to investing in expensive hardware which is prone to rapid change and improvement. At the cheaper level (£2000–£5000) the 35mm style digital cameras manufactured by companies such as Nikon and Canon can produce outstanding quality images suitable for many end uses. Cameras like these are now used predominantly for press and PR work, where maximum quality is not paramount and speed and convenience are the priority.

At a higher level, many commercial studio photographers have invested in a 'digital capture back', which is a high-quality chip which can be adapted to fit many of the conventional studio cameras. This system is far more expensive, but is capable of producing file sizes which closely compare in quality to a high-resolution scan from large format film. Thus the images are suitable for any end use, such as top-quality advertisements. Photographers thinking of supplying stock libraries with digital images should realise that it is this kind of quality which is normally required, as stock libraries are looking to supply a diverse range of markets, including advertising.

Image-enhancement and manipulation using a computer program such as Adobe Photoshop provides photographers with an on-screen darkroom where the possibilities for creating imaginative images are endless. As well as being useful for retouching purposes and creating photo compositions, it provides the photographer with an opportunity to create more unusual images. It is therefore especially useful for targeting the advertising market, where fantasy images are more important than reality.

Useful information

Bureau of Freelance Photographers

Focus House, 497 Green Lanes, London N13 4BP
tel 020-8882 3315 *fax* 020-8886 5174
website www.thebfp.com
Chief Executive John Tracy

Helps the freelance photographer by providing information on markets and a free advisory service. Publishes *Market Newsletter* (monthly). Membership: £45 p.a.

Directories

Reed Business Information

Windsor Court, East Grinstead House, Wood Street, East Grinstead, West Sussex RH19 1XA
tel (01342) 332034 *fax* (01342) 332037
Publishes *The Creative Handbook*.

Elfande Ltd

Surrey House, 31 Church Street, Leatherhead, Surrey KT22 8EF
tel (01372) 220300 *fax* (01372) 220340
email mail@contact-uk.com
website www.contact-uk.com
Publishes *Contact Photographers*.

Using a stock library

As well as undertaking commissions, photographers have the option of selling their images through a photographic stock library or agency. There are many stock libraries in the UK, some specialising in specific subject areas, such as wildlife photography, and others covering general subjects (see *Picture agencies and libraries*, page 407).

Stock libraries are fiercely competitive, all fighting for a share of the market, and it is therefore best to aim to place images with an established name, although competition amongst photographers will be strong. Each stock library has different specific requirements and established markets, so contact them first before making a submission. Some libraries will ask to see a few hundred images from a photographer in order to judge for consistency of quality and saleability. Stock libraries selling images through catalogues or over the internet will often consider an initial submission of just a few images, knowing that it is possible to accumulate significant fees from a small number of outstanding individual images marketed this way.

Images placed with a library remain the property of the photographer and libraries do not normally sell images outright to clients, but lease them for a specific use for a fee, from which commission is deducted. This means that a single image can accumulate many sales over a period of time. The commission rate is usually about 50% of every sale generated by the library. This may sound high, but it should be borne in mind that the library takes on all overheads, marketing costs and other responsibilities involved in the smooth running of a business, allowing the photographer the freedom to spend more time taking pictures.

Photographers should realise, however, that stock photography is a long-term investment and it can take some time for sales to build up to a significant income. Clearly, photographers who supply the right images for the market, and are prolific, are those who do well, and there are a good number of photographers who make their entire living as full-time stock photographers, never having to undertake commissioned work.

Royalty-free CD companies
Many stock libraries are now marketing royalty-free images on CD-Rom. These companies usually obtain images by purchasing them from photographers for a flat fee. Once a CD has been purchased by a client (usually at very low cost) they, in effect, own the images on the CD and are therefore able to reproduce them as many times as they wish, paying no further fees. Some royalty-free companies, however, do pay to photographers royalties related to CD sales in addition to a flat fee for the images. A typical CD may contain one hundred high-resolution reproduction-quality images in a variety of subject areas, including most specialist subjects.

Although photographers may be tempted to sell images to these companies in order to gain an instant fee, they should be aware that placing images with a traditional stock library can be far more fruitful financially in the long term, since a good image can accumulate very high fees over a period of time and go on selling for many years to come. Furthermore, the photographer always retains the rights to his or her own images.

Running your own library
Photographers choosing to market their own images or start up their own library have the advantage of retaining a full fee for every picture sale they make. But it is unlikely that an individual photographer could ever match the rates of an established library, or make the same volume of sales per image. However, the internet has opened a new marketing avenue for photographers, who now have the opportunity to sell their images worldwide. Previously, only an established stock library would have been able to do this. Before embarking on establishing a home library, photographers should be aware that the business of marketing images is essentially a desk job which involves a considerable amount of paperwork and time, which could be spent taking pictures.

When setting up a picture library, your first consideration should be whether to build up a library of your own images, or to take on other contributing photographers. Many photographers running their own libraries submit additional images to bigger libraries to increase the odds of making a good income. Often, a photographer's personal library is made up of work rejected by the larger libraries, which are usually only interested in images that will regularly sell and generate a high turnover. However, occasional sales can generate a significant amount of income for the individual. Furthermore, a photographer with a library of specialised subjects stands a good chance of gaining recognition with niche markets, which can be very lucrative if the competition for those particular subjects is low.

If you take on contributing photographers, the responsibility for another's work becomes yours, so it is important to draw up a contract with terms of business for both your contributing photographers and your clients. Loss or damage of images is the most important consideration when sending pictures to clients (most libraries will charge clients a fee of £400–£600 per image for loss or damage of originals). It is often worth checking that a company wishing to receive transparencies does have adequate insurance to cover these fees, which can amount to a considerable figure if a large quantity of images is lost or damaged. On no account should images be sent to companies which refuse to take responsibility for loss or damage, nor to private individuals, unless they are working on a freelance basis for an established company. It should also be clearly stated in your terms that all pictures in the client's possession become the client's responsibility until they are returned and inspected for damage by the library. Many libraries are now taking a safer approach to distributing images by scanning them first and then supplying them as digital files either on CD or direct to clients, usually via ISDN lines. In addition to being a much cheaper way of distributing images, the problem of loss or damage or original material is also eliminated.

Reproduction fees should also be established on a strict basis, bearing in mind that you owe it to your contributing photographers to command fees which are as high as possible when selling the rights to their images. It is also essential that you control how pictures will be used and the amount of exposure they will receive. The fees should be established according to the type of client using the image and how the image itself will be reproduced. Important factors to consider are where the image will appear, to what size it will be reproduced, the size of the print run, and the territorial rights required by the client. Many libraries also apply holding fees in cases where clients hold on to pictures for periods of time longer than a month.

Bruce Coleman is Chairman of Bruce Coleman The Natural World and past President of the British Association of Picture Libraries. Ian Thraves is a freelance photographer and former picture editor at Bruce Coleman The Natural World (www.thravesphoto.co.uk).

Picture agencies and libraries

As well as supplying images to picture editors, picture researchers and others who use pictures, picture agencies and libraries provide a service to the freelance photographer as one way of selling their work. Most of the agencies and libraries listed in this section take work from other photographers. To find which ones cover specific subjects see page 694.

*Member of the British Association of Picture Libraries and Agencies (BAPLA)

If you want to introduce your work to a library or agency, send samples on CDs or disks, or send tearsheets, duplicates or colour photocopies. Find out if they accept images via email or ISDN. Your work runs the risk of getting lost or damaged whilst in transit so never send unsolicited original material. To find out if agencies operate with analogue or digital files, or both, and which subject areas agencies and libraries cover, see the image/contact database of reputable and accredited libraries and agencies listed at the BAPLA (British Association of Picture Libraries and Agencies) website (www.bapla.org). BAPLA (see page 448) also supports the writer or freelance photographer through its free online job vacancy service – see the website for details.

See also ...
- *Card and stationery publishers which accept photographs*, page 437
- *Syndicates, news and press agencies*, page 119
- *The freelance photographer*, page 401
- *The picture research revolution*, page 439
- *National newspapers UK and Ireland*, page 3

A-Z Botanical Collection Ltd
192 Goswell Road, London EC1V 7DT
tel 020-7253 0991 *fax* 020-7253 0992
email azbotanical@yahoo.com
website www.idspicturedesk.com
Library Manager Anna Gibson

Colour transparencies of plant life worldwide, including named gardens, habitats, gardening, still life, romantic seasonal shots, fungi, pests and diseases, etc (6 x 6cm, 35mm, 5 x 4in).

A.A. & A. Ancient Art & Architecture Collection*
Suite 1, 1st Floor, 410-420 Rayners Lane, Pinner, Middlesex HA5 5DY
tel 020-8429 3131 *fax* 020-8429 4646
email library@aaacollection.co.uk
website www.aaacollection.com

Specialises in the history of civilisations of the Middle East, Mediterranean countries, Europe, Asia, Americas, from ancient times to recent past, their arts, architecture, beliefs and peoples.

Abode Interiors Picture Library*
Albion Court, 1 Pierce Street, Macclesfield, Cheshire SK11 6ER

tel (01625) 500070 *fax* (01625) 500910
email abodepix@appleonline.net
website www.abodepix.co.uk
Contact Judi Goodwin

Colour photo library specialising in English and Scottish house interiors of all styles, types and periods. High-quality material only; terms by agreement. Phone before sending material. Founded 1993.

Academic File News Photos
Eastern Art Publishing Group,
PO Box 13666, 27 Wallorton Gardens,
London SW14 8WF
tel 020-8392 1122 *fax* 020-8392 1422
email afis@eapgroup.com
website www.eapgroup.com
Director Sajid Rizvi

Daily news coverage in UK and general library of arts, cultures, people and places, with special reference to the Middle East, North Africa and Asia. New photographers welcomed to cover UK and abroad. Sample pictures accepted over email. Founded 1985.

Ace Stock Ltd*

Satellite House, 2 Salisbury Road,
London SW19 4EZ
tel 020-8944 9944 *fax* 020-8944 9940
email info@acestock.com
website www.acestock.com

General library: people, industry, business, travel,
commerce, skies, sport, music and natural history.
Worldwide syndication. Sae for enquiries. Very
selective editing policy. Terms: 50%.
Founded 1980.

Action Plus*

54-58 Tanner Street, London SE1 3PH
tel 020-7403 1558 *fax* 020-7403 1526
email info@actionplus.co.uk
website www.actionplus.co.uk

Specialist sports and action picture library.
Comprehensive collection of creative images,
including all aspects of 130 professional and
amateur sports worldwide. Covers all age groups, all
ethnic groups and all levels of ability. 35mm colour
stock and online digital archive. Terms: 50%.
Founded 1986.

Aerofilms*

Aerofilms Ltd, Gate Studios, Station Road,
Borehamwood, Herts. WD6 1EJ
tel 020-8207 0666 *fax* 020-8207 5433
email library@aerofilms.com

Comprehensive library – over 2.5 million photos
going back to 1919 – of vertical and oblique aerial
photographs of UK; large areas with complete
cover. Founded 1919.

Air Photo Supply

42 Sunningvale Avenue, Biggin Hill,
Kent TN16 3BX
tel (01959) 574872
email norman.rivett@virgin.net

Aircraft and associated subjects, Southeast England,
colour and monochrome. No other photographers'
material required. Founded 1963.

AKG London*

(The Arts and History Picture Library)
5 Melbray Mews, 158 Hurlingham Road,
London SW6 3NS
tel 020-7610 6103 *fax* 020-7610 6125
email enquiries@akg-london.co.uk
website www.akg-london.co.uk

Principal subjects covered: art, archaeology and
history. Exclusive UK and US representative for the
Archiv für Kunst und Geschichte (AKG) with full
access to the 10 million images held by AKG Berlin.
Also exclusively represents the Erich Lessing Culture
and Fine Art Archives in the UK. Founded 1994.

Dr Alan Beaumont

52 Squires Walk, Lowestoft, Suffolk NR32 4LA
tel (01502) 560126
email embeaumont@supernet.com

Worldwide collection of monochrome prints and
colour transparencies (35mm and 6 x 7cm) of
natural history, countryside, windmills and aircraft.
Brochure and subject lists available. No other
photographers required.

The Allan Wright Photo Library

The Stables, Parton, Castle Douglas,
Kirkcudbrightshire DG7 3NB
tel (016444) 470260 *fax* (016444) 470202
email allan@lyricalscotland.com
website www.lyricalscotland.com

Source of 'Lyrical Scotland' range of images
featuring all of Scotland. Founded 1986.

Allied Artists

5 Fauconberg Road, London W4 3JZ
tel 020-8995 5500 *fax* 020-8995 8844
email info@alliedartists.ltd.uk
website www.alliedartists.ltd.uk
Contacts Gary Mills, Mary Burtenshaw

Agency for illustrators specialising in a wide range
of styles for magazines, books, children's books and
advertising. Large colour library. Founded 1983.

Allsport UK – incorporated into Getty Images

American History Picture Library

3 Barton Buildings, Bath BA1 2JR
tel (01225) 334213 *fax* (01225) 480554

Photographs, engravings, colour transparencies
covering the exploration and social, political and
military history of North America from 15th to
20th century: conquistadors, civil war, railroads, the
Great Depression, advertisements, Prohibition and
gangsters, moon landings and space.

AMIS

(Atlas Mountains Information Services)
26 Kirkcaldy Road, Burntisland, Fife KY3 9HQ
tel (01592) 873546
Proprietor Hamish Brown MBE, FRSGS

Picture library on Moroccan sites, topography,
mountains, travel. Illustration service. Commissions
undertaken. No pictures purchased.

Ancient Egypt Picture Library*

6 Branden Drive, Knutsford, Cheshire WA16 8EJ
tel/fax (01565) 633106
email BobEgyptPL@aol.com

Images of Egypt, including most of the ancient sites
and views of modern Egypt. All photographs (over
30,000 colour transparencies) taken by an

Egyptologist, who can also provide full historical/archaeological information. Founded 1996.

Andalucía Slide Library

Apto 499, Estepona, Málaga 29680, Spain
tel (34) 952-793647 *fax* (34) 952-880138
email info@andaluciaslidelibrary.com
website www.andaluciaslidelibrary.com
Contact Michelle Chaplow

Colour transparencies (35mm and medium format) covering all aspects of Andalucía and Spain, principally its geography and culture. Also images of Portugal, Madeira, Malta. Commissions undertaken. Founded 1991.

Andes Press Agency*

26 Padbury Court, London E2 7EH
tel 020-7613 5417 *fax* 020-7739 3159
email apa@andespressagency.com
Director Carlos Reyes

Social, political and economic aspects of Latin America, Africa, Asia, Middle East, Europe and Britain; specialises in Latin America and contemporary world religions. Founded 1983.

Andrew N. Gagg's Photo Flora*

Town House Two, Fordbank Court, Henwick Road, Worcester WR2 5PF
tel (01905) 748515
email a.n.gagg@ntlworld.com
website http://homepage.ntlworld.com/a.n.gagg/photo/photoflora.html
Contact Andrew N. Gagg

Comprehensive collection of British and European wild plants. Travel: Egypt, India, Tibet, China, Nepal, Thailand, Mexico, Vietnam and Cambodia. Founded 1982.

Angela Hampton – Family Life Picture Library

Holly Tree House, The Street,
Walberton, Arundel,
West Sussex BN18 0PH
tel (01243) 555952 *mobile* (07880) 550653 *fax* (01243) 555952
Proprietor Angela Hampton

Contemporary lifestyle images including pregnancy, childbirth, babies and children, parenting, behaviour, education, medical, holidays, pets, families, couples, teenagers, women's health, men's health, retirement. Also domestic and farm animals. Around 100,000 colour transparencies. Founded 1991.

Animal Photography*

4 Marylebone Mews, New Cavendish Street, London W1G 8PY
tel 020-7935 0503 *fax* 020-7487 3038
email thompson@animal-photography.co.uk
website www.animal-photography.co.uk

Horses, dogs, cats, small pets, East Africa, Galapagos. Other photographers' work not represented. Founded 1955.

Ann and Bury Peerless*

22 King's Avenue, Minnis Bay, Birchington-on-Sea, Kent CT7 9QL
tel (01843) 841428 *fax* (01843) 848321

Art, craft (including textiles), archaeology, architecture, dance, iconography, miniature paintings, manuscripts, museum artefacts, social, cultural, agricultural, industrial, historical, political, educational, geographical subjects and travel in India,Pakistan, Bangladesh, Afghanistan, Burma, Cambodia, China, Egypt, Hong Kong, Indonesia (Borobudur, Java), Iran, Israel, Kenya, Libya, Malta, Malaysia, Morocco, Nepal, Russia (Moscow, St Petersburg, Samarkand and Bukhara, Uzbekistan), Sri Lanka, Spain, Sudan, Taiwan, Thailand, Tunisia, Uganda, Vietnam, Zambia and Zimbabwe. Specialist material on historical and world religions: Hinduism, Buddhism, Jainism, Judaism, Christianity, Confucianism, Islam, Sikhism, Taoism, Zoroastrianism (Parsees of India).

Ann Ronan Picture Library

Old Church Studios, Clifton, Deddington, Banbury, Oxon OX15 0PE
tel (01869) 338883 *fax* (01869) 338887

Woodcuts, engravings, etc social and political history plus history of science and technology, including military and space, literature and music.

The Anthony Blake Photo Library*

20 Blades Court, Deodar Road, London SW15 2NU
tel 020-8877 1123 *fax* 020-8877 9787
email info@abpl.co.uk
website www.abpl.co.uk

Food and wine images from around the world, including raw ingredients, finished dishes, shops, restaurants, markets, agriculture and viticulture. Commissions undertaken. Contributors welcome. Brochure available.

Aquarius Library*

PO Box 5, Hastings, East Sussex TN34 1HR
tel (01424) 721196 *fax* (01424) 717704
email aquarius.lib@clara.net
website www.aquariuscollection.com
Contact David Corkill

Showbusiness specialist library with over one million colour and b&w images: film stills, classic portraiture, candids, archive material to present. New material added every week. Downloadable website of TV & film stills. Division of SPM London Ltd.

Arcaid Architectural Photography and Picture Library*
Parc House, 25-37 Cowleaze Road,
Kingston upon Thames, Surrey KT2 6DZ
tel 020-8546 4352 fax 020-8541 5230
email arcaid@arcaid.co.uk
website www.arcaid.co.uk www.alamy.com/arcaid
'The built environment' – international collection:
architecture, interior design, lifestyle interiors,
gardens, travel, museums, historic and
contemporary. Terms: 50%.

Archivio Veneziano – see Venice Picture Library

Arctic Camera
66 Ashburnham Grove, London SE10 8UJ
tel/fax 020-8692 7651
email Derek.Fordham@btinternet.com
Contact Derek Fordham
Colour transparencies of all aspects of Arctic life
and environment. Founded 1978.

Ardea Wildlife & Pets*
35 Brodrick Road, London SW17 7DX
tel 020-8672 2067 fax 020-8672 8787
email ardea@ardea.co.uk
website www.ardea.co.uk
Contact Sophie Napier
Specialist worldwide natural history photographic
library of animals, birds, plants, fish, insects,
reptiles, worldwide scenics and domestic pets.

The Associated Press Ltd*
News Photo Department, The Associated Press
House, 12 Norwich Street, London EC4A 1BP
tel 020-7427 4260/4266, 020-7427 4263 (library
manager) fax 020-7427 4269
email london_photolibrary@ap.org
website www.apwideworld.com
News, features, sports, 20th century history,
personalities.

Australia Pictures
28 Sheen Common Drive, Richmond,
London TW10 5BN
tel/fax 020-7602 1989
Contact John Miles
Comprehensive library covering Australia,
Aboriginals and their art, indigenous peoples,
underwater, Tibet, Peru, Bolivia, Iran, Irian Jaya,
Pakistan, Yemen. Founded 1988.

Aviation Picture Library (Austin J. Brown)*
116 The Avenue, St Stephen's, London W13 8 JX
tel 020-8566 7712 cellphone (07860) 670073
fax 020-8566 7714
email avpix@aol.com
website www.aviationpictures.com

Worldwide aviation photographic library,
including dynamic views of aircraft. Aerial and
travel library including Europe, Caribbean, USA,
and East and West Africa. Material taken since 1960.
Specialising in air-to-air and air-to-ground
commissions. Chief photographers for Flyer
magazine. Founded 1970.

B. & B. Photographs
Prospect House, Clifford Chambers,
Stratford upon Avon, Warks. CV37 8HX
tel (01789) 298106 fax (01789) 292450
email BandBPhotographs@btinternet.com
35mm/medium format colour library of
horticulture (especially pests and diseases) and
geography (worldwide), natural history and
biological education. Other photographers' work
not represented. Founded 1974.

B.M. Totterdell Photography*
Constable Cottage, Burlings Lane, Knockholt,
Kent TN14 7PE
tel/fax (01959) 532001
email btrial@btinternet.com
Specialist volleyball library, covering all aspects of
the sport. Founded 1989.

Bandphoto Agency
(division of UPPA)
29-31 Saffron Hill, London EC1N 8SW
tel 020-7421 6000 fax 020-7421 6006
website www.uppa.co.uk
International news and feature picture service for
British and overseas publishers.

Barnaby's Picture Library – see Mary Evans Picture Library

Barnardo's Photographic Archive
Tanners Lane, Barkingside, Ilford, Essex IG6 1QG
tel 020-8550 8822 fax 020-8550 0429
Extensive collection of b&w and colour images
dating from 1874 to the present day covering social
history with the emphasis on children and child care.
Also 300 films dating from 1905. Founded 1874.

Barry Davies
Dyffryn, Bolahaul Road, Cwmffrwd, Carmarthen,
Carmarthenshire SA31 2LW
tel/fax (01267) 233625
Natural history, landscape, Egypt, children, outdoor
activities and general subjects. Formats 35mm,
6 x 6cm, 6 x 7cm, 6 x 17cm, 5 x 4in. Other
photographers' work not accepted. Founded 1983.

BBC Natural History Unit Picture Library – see Nature Picture Library

Bee Photographs – see Heritage & Natural History Photography

Bill Meadows Picture Library
11 Begonia Close, St Peters, Worcester WR5 3LZ
tel/fax (01905) 350801
Proprietor Bill Meadows

Aspects of Great Britain: general scenic including towns and villages; buildings and monuments; agricultural, industrial and building sites; urban scenes and services; misuse of the environment, vandalism, etc; recreational, 'people at play'; natural history subjects. 20,000 b&w photographs and 50,000 (6 x 6cm and 35mm) colour transparencies. Founded 1968.

The Billie Love Historical Collection
Reflections, 3 Winton Street, Ryde,
Isle of Wight PO33 2BX
tel (01983) 812572 *fax* (01983) 616515
Proprietor Billie Love

Photos (late 19th century–1930s), engravings, coloured lithographs, covering subjects from earliest times, people, places and events up to the Second World War; also more recent material. Founded 1969.

Bird Images
28 Carousel Walk, Sherburn in Elmet,
North Yorkshire LS25 6LP
tel/fax (01977) 684666
Principal P. Doherty

Specialist in the birds of Britain and Europe, including video footage from Europe and North America. Expert captioning service available. Founded 1989.

Bodleian Library*
Oxford OX1 3BG
Published slides and filmstrips
tel (01865) 277214/277152
fax (01865) 277187
email slidesales@bodley.ox.ac.uk
websites www.bodley.ox.ac.uk/dept/scwmss/wmss/
medieval/browse.htm
www.bodley.ox.ac.uk/dept/scwmss/wmss/medieval/
slides/cumulative.htm
www.bodley.ox.ac.uk/dept/scwmss/wmss/Orderfor
ms2002-UK-EU.pdf
www.bodley.ox.ac.uk/dept/scwmss/wmss/Orderfor
ms2002-World.pdf
Imaging Service
tel (01865) 277215/277061
fax (01865) 287127
email repro@bodley.ox.ac.uk
website www.bodley.ox.ac.uk/dept/imaging

Published slides and manuscripts: Library of 32,000 35mm colour transparencies in slides or filmstrips for immediate sale (not hire). There is an iconographical index to the images, which are mostly from medieval manuscripts.

Imaging Service: Large format transparencies more suitable for reproduction are available to order, as are copies, photographs and microfilm of any other items from the Bodleian's vast collections.

BookArt & Architecture Picture Library
1 Woodcock Lodge, Epping Green,
Hertford SG13 8ND
tel (01707) 875253 *fax* (01707) 875286
email sharpd@globalnet.co.uk

Modern and historic buildings, landscapes, works of named architects in Great Britain, Europe, Scandinavia, North America, India, Southeast Asia, Japan, North and East Africa; modern sculpture. Listed under style, place and personality. Founded 1991.

Boxing Picture Library
3 Barton Buildings, Bath BA1 2JR
tel (01225) 334213 *fax* (01225) 480554

Prints, engravings and photos of famous boxers, boxing personalities and famous fights from 18th century to recent years.

Brian and Sal Shuel – see Collections

Brian Gadsby Picture Library
17 route des Pyrénées, 65700 Labatut-Riviere,
Hautes Pyrénées, France
tel (33) 5 62 96 38 44
email GadsbyJB@aol.com

Colour transparencies (6 x 4.5cm, 35mm) and b&w prints. Wide range of subjects but emphasis on travel and the environment: UK, Europe (particularly France), Ecuador and Galapagos Islands, Patagonia, Sri Lanka. Natural history: mainly birds and plant life (wild and garden). Large wildfowl file. No other photographers' material required.

The Bridgeman Art Library*
17-19 Garway Road, London W2 4PH
tel 020-7727 4065 *fax* 020-7792 8509
email london@bridgeman.co.uk
website www.bridgeman.co.uk

Source of fine art images for publication. Acts as an agent for thousands of museums, galleries and private collections throughout the world. Every subject, era and style represented from cave paintings to pop art and beyond, including many historical events and personalities. Also offers research service and acts as copyright agent to a growing number of artists. Website catalogue and online ordering available. Founded 1972.

Britain on View*

Image Resource Centre, Thames Tower,
Black's Road, London W6 9EL
tel 020-8563 3120 *fax* 020-8563 3130
email pmortlock@bta.org.uk
website www.britainonview.com
Contact Paul Mortlock

Photo library of the British Tourist Authority.
British culture, society, events, landscapes, towns
and villages, tourist attractions.

British Library Picture Library*

96 Euston Road, London NW1 2DB
tel 020-7412 7614 *fax* 020-7412 7771
email picturelibrary@bl.uk
website www.bl.uk/imagesonline

Illustrative and historical material from
manuscripts, printed books, oriental and Indian
items, maps, music and philately. Fully searchable
website. Founded 1996.

Bruce Coleman Inc.

117 East 24th Street, New York,
NY 10010-2919, USA
tel 212-979-6252 *fax* 212-979-5468
email norman@bciusa.com
website www.bciusa.com
President Norman Owen Tomalin

Specialises in the natural world and travel destinations around it. All subjects required. Traditional
colour transparencies and digital stock media.

Bruce Coleman The Natural World

16 Chiltern Business Village, Arundel Road,
Uxbridge UB8 2SN
tel (01895) 467990 *fax* (01895) 467955
email library@brucecoleman.co.uk
website www.brucecoleman.co.uk

Creative images of nature, animals, landscapes,
space and wildlife. Catalogues available.

Bryan and Cherry Alexander Photography*

Higher Cottage, Manston, Sturminster Newton,
Dorset DT10 1EZ
tel (01258) 473006 *fax* (01258) 473333
email alexander@arcticphoto.co.uk
website www.arcticphoto.co.uk

Polar regions with emphasis on indigenous peoples
of the North. Landscape and wildlife: Alaska to
Siberia and Antarctica. Founded 1973.

C.M. Dixon*

The Orchard, Marley Lane, Kingston, Canterbury,
Kent CT4 6JH
tel (01227) 830075 *fax* (01227) 831135

Europe, Iceland, Jordan, Sri Lanka, Tunisia, Turkey,
former USSR. Main subjects include agriculture,
ancient art, archaeology, architecture, clouds,
geography, geology, history, horses, industry,
meteorology, mosaics, mountains, mythology,
occupations, people.

Camera Press Ltd*

21 Queen Elizabeth Street, London SE1 2PD
tel 020-7378 1300 *fax* 020-7278 5126

B&w prints and colour transparencies including
up-to-date coverage of British royalty, portraits of
world statesmen, politicians, entertainers, reportage,
humour, nature, pop, features. Terms: 50%.
Founded 1947.

CartoonStock*

Studio X, 25 Horsell Road, London N5 1XL
tel 020-7700 7080 *fax* 020-7700 7090
email admin@cartoonstock.com
website www.cartoonstock.com
Director Joel Mishon

Library of tens of thousands of cartoons and comic
illustration. B&w and colour cartoons by over 200
cartoonists whose work appears in national and
overseas newspapers and magazines and other
publications. Full database may be searched online.
Founded 1998.

Cephas Picture Library*

Hurst House, 157 Walton Road, East Molesey,
Surrey KT8 0DX
tel 020-8979 8647 or 07000 CEPHAS
fax 020-8224 8095
email mickrock@cephas.co.uk
website www.cephas.co.uk

Comprehensive library of food and drink photos:
wine and vineyards, spirits, beer and cider, food and
drink worldwide. Free catalogue available; specialist
knowledge.

Chandra S. Perera Cinetra

437 Pethiyagoda, Kelaniya-11600, Sri Lanka
tel (94) 1-911885 *fax* (94) 1-323910, 674737, 674738
email cinetraww@dialogsl.net comsvc01@slt.lk
Cinetra Worldwide Createch (Pvt) Ltd
126/3rd Floor, 10B, YMBA Building, Fort,
Colombo 1, Sri Lanka
tel/fax (94) 1-323910
Managing Director Chandra S. Perera

B&w and colour library including news, wildlife,
religious, social, political, sports, adventure,
environmental, forestry, nature and tourism.
Photographic and journalistic features on any
subject. Founded 1958.

Charles Tait Photo Library

Kelton, St Ola, Orkney KW15 1TR
tel (01856) 873738 *fax* (01856) 875313
email charles.tait@zetnet.co.uk

website www.charles-tait.co.uk

Colour photo library specialising in the Scottish islands, especially Orkney, Shetland, the Western Isles (including outliers) and Caithness. Archaeology, landscapes, seascapes, wildlife, crafts, industries, events, transport, and sites of interest. Also mainland Scotland and Hadrian's Wall, plus France, Venice, Alaska, and New England. Over 100,000 images in formats ranging from 35mm to 5 x 4in, including 70mm panoramic and 6 megapixel digital. Images available to browse online; high-res scans on CD and by email. Publisher of postcards, calendars, guidebooks. Founded 1978.

Chris Bonington Picture Library*

Badger Hill, Hesket Newmarket, Wigton, Cumbria CA7 8LA
tel (016974) 78286 *fax* (016974) 78238
email frances@bonington.com
website www.bonington.com
Manager Frances Daltrey

Mountains and mountaineering, climbers and climbing in Tibet, Nepal and the Himalayas. Includes the Peter Boardman and Joe Tasker collections. Founded 1988.

Chris Mattison

138 Dalewood Road, Sheffield S8 0EF
tel/fax 0114-236 4433
email chris.mattison@btinternet.com
website www.chris.mattison.btinternet.co.uk

Colour library specialising in reptiles and amphibians; other natural history subjects; habitats and landscapes in Africa, Southeast Asia, South America, USA, Mexico, Mediterranean. Captions or detailed copy supplied if required. No other photographers' material required.

Christine Foord

155B City Way, Rochester,
Kent ME1 2BE
tel/fax (01634) 847348

Colour picture library of over 1000 species of wild flowers. Also British insects, garden flowers, pests and diseases, lichen, mosses and cacti.

Christine Osborne Pictures – see World Religions Photo Library

Christopher Ware Photography

65 Trinity Street, Barry,
South Glamorgan CF62 7EX
tel (01446) 732816
Proprietor Christopher Ware

Colour and b&w photos of industry and transport of the southeast Wales area; also civil and military aircraft. Commissions undertaken. Founded 1970.

Chrysalis Images

64 Brewery Road, London N7 9NT
tel 020-7697 3000 *fax* 020-7697 3001
email tforshaw@chrysalisbooks.co.uk
Picture Manager Terry Forshaw

General collection including cookery, crafts, history, military, natural history, space, transport and travel. Founded 1996.

COI Photo Library – see Stockwave

Colin Garratt – see Railways – Milepost 92½

Colin Varndell Natural History Photography

The Happy Return, Whitecross, Netherbury, Bridport, Dorset DT6 5NH
tel (01308) 488341
email colin_varndell@hotmail.com
Proprietor Colin Varndell

UK wildlife and landscape with particular emphasis on birds, mammals, butterflies, wild flowers and habitats. 110,000 colour transparencies. Founded 1980.

Collections*

13 Woodberry Crescent, London N10 1PJ
tel 020-8883 0083 *fax* 020-8883 9215

The British Isles only: places, people, buildings, industry, leisure; specialist collections on customs, castles, bridges, London, plus an extensive collection on Ireland. Founded 1990.

Colorific/Getty Images News Services – incorporated into Getty Images

Corbis*

111 Salusbury Road, London NW6 6RG
tel 020-7644 7400 *fax* 020-7644 7401
email info@corbis.com
website www.corbis.com

Over 2.1 million images available online from a total of 65 million. The images are from professional photographers, museums, cultural institutions and public and private collections worldwide including the Bettmann Archive, Ansel Adams, Lynn Goldsmith, the Turnley Collection and Hulton Deutsch. Covers a wide range of subjects including celebrities and news. Founded 1989.

Country Collections Photolibrary

Unit 9, Ditton Priors Trading Estate, Bridgnorth, Shrops. WV16 6SS
tel (01746) 712533 *fax* (01746) 861330
Contact Robert Foster

Specialises in Celtic culture from stone circles to the present day. Also sundials and an expanding collection of rivers and streamside vegetation. Colour transparencies. Founded 1985.

Crafts Council Photostore®*

44A Pentonville Road, London N1 9BY
tel 020-7806 2503 *fax* 020-7833 4479
email photostore@craftscouncil.org.uk
website www.craftscouncil.org.uk/photostore

Comprehensive source of visual material for
contemporary British crafts. Spanning the last 30
years, subject areas cover: jewellery, ceramics,
furniture, glass, woodwork, paperwork,
bookbinding, domestic objects, decorative forms,
lettering, textiles, fashion accessories, basketry,
musical instruments and public art. Images can be
accessed through Photostore, the Craft Council's
interactive database, open during working hours
(no appointment necessary) and through regional
terminals. Founded 1973.

Das Photo

Chalet le Pin, Domaine de Bellevue 181,
6940 Septon, Belgium
tel/fax (32) 86-322426
Old School House, Llanfilo, Brecon,
Powys LD3 0RH
email dasphotogb@aol.com

Arab countries, Americas, Europe, Caribbean,
Southeast Asia, Amazon, world festivals,
archaeology, people, biblical, education, schools,
modern languages. Founded 1975.

Dave Lewis Nostalgia Collection

20 The Avenue, Starbeck, Harrogate,
North Yorkshire HG1 4QD
tel/fax (01423) 888642
email lewisattic@btinternet.com
website www.harrogate.com/davel

A collection of advertising, packaging, points of sale
and magazine reference from 1800–1970s. Founded
1995.

David Broadbent/Peak District Pictures

12 Thomas Street, Glossop, Derbyshire SK13 8QN
tel/fax (01457) 862997
email info@davidbroadbent.com
website www.davidbroadbent.com

The Peak District fully covered, landscape, natural
history, birds a speciality. Commissions undertaken.
New material welcome. Terms: 50%. Founded 1989.
David Broadbent/Birds
Highly stylised and pictorial library of British birds,
bird reserves and important wildlife landscapes.

David Hosking FRPS

Pages Green House, Wetheringsett, Stowmarket,
Suffolk IP14 5QA
tel (01728) 861113 *fax* (01728) 860222
email pictures@flpa-images.co.uk
website www.flpa-images.co.uk

Natural history subjects, especially birds covering

whole world. Also Dr D.P. Wilson's unique marine
photo collection.

David Williams Picture Library*

50 Burlington Avenue, Glasgow G12 0LH
tel 0141-339 7823 *fax* 0141-337 3031

Specialises in travel photography; wide coverage of
Scotland, Iceland and Spain. Also other European
countries and Western USA and Canada. Subjects
include: cities, towns, villages, 'tourist haunts',
buildings, landscapes and natural features; geology
and physical geography of Scotland and Iceland.
Commissions undertaken. Catalogue available.
Founded 1989.

Dawn Runnals Photographic Library

5 St Marys Terrace, Kenwyn Road, Truro,
Cornwall TR1 3SW
tel (01872) 279353

General library: land and seascapes, flora and fauna,
sport, animals, people, buildings, boats, harbours,
miscellaneous section; details of other subjects on
application. Other photographers' work not
accepted. Sae appreciated with enquiries. Founded
1985.

Dee Conway Ballet & Dance Picture Library

110 Sussex Way, London N7 6RR
tel 020-7272 7845 *fax* 020-7272 7966
email library@ddance.co.uk
website www.ddance.co.uk
Proprietor Dee Conway

Classical ballet, modern dance, flamenco, tango,
rock, jive, mime; dance from India, Africa, Russia,
China, Japan, Thailand; informal class pictures of
dance, music and drama. Colour and b&w images.
Founded 1995.

Dennis Davis Photography

9 Great Burrow Rise, Northam, Bideford,
Devon EX39 1TB
tel (01237) 475165

Gardens, wild and garden flowers, domestic
livestock including rare breeds and poultry,
agricultural landscapes, architecture – interiors and
exteriors, landscape, coastal, rural life. Commissions
welcomed. No other photographers required.
Founded 1984.

Douglas Dickins Photo Library

2 Wessex Gardens, London NW11 9RT
tel 020-8455 6221

Worldwide collection of colour transparencies
(mostly 6 x 6cm, some 35mm) and b&w prints
(10 x 8in originals), specialising in Asia, particularly
India and Indonesia; also USA, Canada, France,
Austria and Switzerland, Japan, China, Burma.
Founded 1946.

Earth Images Picture Library
Manor Cottages, Burnett, Keynsham,
Bristol BS31 2TF
tel/fax 0117-986 1144
Director Richard Arthur

Earth from Space (satellite remote sensing); earth science and art-in-science imagery – from cosmic to sub-atomic. Founded 1989.

Ecoscene*
The Oasts, Headley Lane, Passfield, Liphook,
Hants GU30 7RX
tel (01428) 751056 *fax* (01428) 751057
email sally@ecoscene.com
website www.ecoscene.com
Contact Sally Morgan

Specialists in environment and wildlife. Subjects include agriculture, conservation, energy, industry, pollution, habitats and habitat loss, sustainability, wildlife; worldwide coverage. Terms: 55% to photographer. Founded 1987.

Edinburgh Photographic Library*
Mercat International, 14 Garscube Terrace,
Edinburgh EH12 6BQ
tel 0131-337 7615 *fax* 0131-337 0303
email epl@mercat.co.uk
website www.mercat.co.uk
Proprietor James Young

15,000 colour transparency images of Scotland – castles, scenic, mountains, festivals, pipe bands. Founded 1986.

Education Photos*
April Cottage, Warners Lane, Albury Heath,
Guildford, Surrey GU5 9DE
tel/fax (01483) 203846
email johnwalmsley@educationphotos.co.uk
website www.educationphotos.co.uk
Proprietor John Walmsley

Digital photos of education, careers, portraits of ordinary people. Commissions undertaken. Founded 1987.

Elizabeth Linley Collection
The Elizabeth Linley Studio, 29 Dewlands,
Godstone, Surrey RH9 8BS
tel (01883) 742702, 742451
Contact Audrey I.B. Thomas

Prints, b&w photos and colour transparencies of 18th- and 19th-century artists, portraits, illustrations, theatre, society events, architecture.

English Heritage Photo Library*
23 Savile Row, London W1S 2ET
tel 020-7973 3338/3339 *fax* 020-7973 3027

Wide range of high-quality colour transparencies, ranging from ancient monuments to artefacts, legendary castles to stone circles, elegant interiors to industrial architecture and post-war listed buildings.

Environmental Investigation Agency*
62-63 Upper Street, London N1 0NY
tel 020-7354 7960 *fax* 020-7354 7961
email communications@eia-international.org
website www.eia-international.org
Communications Manager Mary Rice

Specialists in still and moving images of environmental crime, including the illegal trade in endangered species, ozone-depleting substances and illegal logging; also animals in their natural environment. Founded 1984.

Eric Whitehead Photography – see Snookerimages

Exile Images
1 Mill Row, West Hill Road, Brighton BN1 3SU
tel (01273) 208741 *fax* (01273) 382782
email pics@exileimages.co.uk
website www.exileimages.co.uk
Contact Howard Davies

Colour and b&w photos documenting refugees, asylum seekers, displaced peoples and conflicts worldwide. Also documentary photos of rural and urban lives in developing countries. Photos from 1988. CD-Rom available through website. 4000 images available from fully searchable website. Founded 2000.

Eyeline Photography
259 London Road, Cheltenham, Glos. GL52 6YG
tel (01242) 513567
email colin.jarman@btinternet.com

Sailing. Founded 1979.

FAMOUS Pictures & Features Agency*
13 Harwood Road, London SW6 4QP
tel 020-7731 9333 *fax* 020-7731 9330
email info@famous.uk.com
website www.famous.uk.com

Colour pictures and features library covering music, film and TV personalities. Terms: 50%. Founded 1990.

Feature-Pix Colour Library – see World Pictures

Financial Times Pictures
Number One, Southwark Bridge, London SE1 9HL
tel 020-7873 3671 *fax* 020-7873 4606
email photosynd@ft.com

Colour and b&w library serving the *Financial Times*. Specialises in world business, industry and commerce; world politicians and statespeople; cities and countries; plus many other subjects. Also

FT maps and graphics. All material available in colour and b&w, print and electronic formats. Library updated daily.

Fine Art Photographic Library*

Rawlings House, 2A Milner Street, London SW3 2PU
tel 020-7589 3127 *fax* 020-7584 1944
email info@fineartphotolibrary.com

Holds over 25,000 transparencies of paintings by British and European artists, from Old Masters to contemporary. Free brochure. CD-Rom available. Founded 1980.

FirePix International*

68 Arkles Lane, Anfield, Liverpool L4 2SP
tel/fax 0151-260 0111
email info@firepix.com
website www.firepix.com
Contact Tony Myers ARPS, GIFireE

Holds 23,000 images of fire and firefighters at work in the UK, USA, Japan and China. Established by photographer Tony Myers after 28 years in service with the British Fire Service. Many images are stored digitally; CD-Rom available. Founded 1995.

Fogden Wildlife Photographs*

Flat 1, 78 High Street, Perth PH1 5TH
tel/fax (01738) 580811
email susan.fogden@virgin.net
website www.fogdenphotos.com
Library Manager Susan Fogden

Wide coverage of natural history, including camouflage, warning coloration, mimicry, breeding strategies, feeding, animal/plant relationships, environmental studies, especially in rainforests and deserts. Founded 1980.

Forest Life Picture Library*

Forestry Commission, 231 Corstorphine Road, Edinburgh EH12 7AT
Picture Researcher Neill Campbell
tel 0131-314 6411
email neill.campbell@forestry.gsi.gov.uk
Business Manager Douglas Green
tel 0131-314 6200 *fax* 0131-314 6285
email douglas.green@forestry.gsi.gov.uk

Tree species, forest and woodland views and management, landscapes, wildlife, flora and fauna, conservation, sport and leisure. Founded 1983.

Format Photographers – see Panos Pictures and Photofusion*

Fortean Picture Library*

Henblas, Mwrog Street, Ruthin LL15 1LG
tel (01824) 707278 *fax* (01824) 705324
email janet.bord@forteanpix.demon.co.uk
website www.forteanpix.demon.co.uk

Colour and b&w pictures covering strange phenomena: UFOs, Loch Ness Monster, ghosts, Bigfoot, witchcraft, etc; also antiquities (especially in Britain – prehistoric and Roman sites, castles, churches).

Fotoccompli – The Picture Library

35 Birch Croft Road, Sutton Coldfield B75 6BP
tel 0121-378 1064 *fax* 0121-240 8950
email djgriffiths@lineone.net
website www.fotoccompli.com

Comprehensive library, ranging from abstracts to zoology, with added specialism of the building and construction industries. Terms: 50%. Minimum retention period: 3 years. Founded 1989.

Fotomas Index*

12 Pickhurst Rise, West Wickham, Kent BR4 0AL
tel 020-8776 2772 *fax* 020-8776 2236

Specialises in supplying pre-20th century (mostly pre-Victorian) illustrative material to publishing and academic worlds, and for TV and advertising. Complete production back-up for interior décor, exhibitions and locations.

Fotosports International

The Barn, Swanbourne, Bucks. MK17 0SL
tel (01296) 720773 *fax* (01296) 728181
email info@fotosports.com
website www.fotosports.com
Contact Roger Parker, Partner

250,000 b&w photos and 250,000 colour transparencies of sports: soccer (domestic, foreign, World Cup 1970s to present), tennis majors, Formula One motor racing, American football (inc. Superbowl) 1985–95; some golf, rugby, cricket. Founded 1968.

Frank Lane Picture Agency Ltd

Pages Green House, Wetheringsett, Stowmarket, Suffolk IP14 5QA
tel (01728) 860789 *fax* (01728) 860222
email pictures@flpa-images.co.uk
website www.flpa-images.co.uk

Natural history, ecology, environment, farming, geography, trees and weather.

Freelance Focus

39 Scotts Garth Close, Tickton, Beverley, East Yorkshire HU17 9RQ
tel/fax (01964) 501729
Contact Gary Hicks

UK/international network of photographers. Stock pictures covering most subjects, worldwide, at competitive rates. Assignments undertaken for all types of clients. Founded 1988.

Frontline Photo Press Agency

18 Wall Street, Norwood, SA 5067, Australia

postal address PO Box 162, Kent Town, SA 5071, Australia
tel (08) 8333 2691 *fax* (08) 8364 0604
email info@frontline.net.au
website www.frontline.net.au
Photo Editor Carlo Irlitti

Stock photo agency, picture library and photographic press agency with 400,000 images. Covers sport, people, personalities, travel, scenics, environmental, agricultural, industrial, natural history, concepts, science, medicine, social documentary and press images. Seeking worldwide stock contributors. Assignments undertaken. Prefers high-res image files on CD-Rom. Write, fax or email for submission guidelines, photo requirements and other details. Terms: 60% to photographer (stock); assignment rates negotiable. Founded 1988.

Galaxy Picture Library*
34 Fennels Way, Flackwell Heath, High Wycombe, Bucks. HP10 9BY
tel (01628) 521338 *fax* (01628) 520132
email robin@galaxypix.com
website www.galaxypix.com
Contact Robin Scagell

Astronomy: specialities include the night sky, amateur astronomy, astronomers and observatories. Founded 1992.

Garden Matters Photographic Library*
Marlham, Henley's Down, Battle, East Sussex TN33 9BN
tel (01424) 830566 *fax* (01424) 830224
email gardens@gmpix.com
website www.gmpix.com
Contact Dr John Feltwell

Plants 10,000 Over 10,000 scientifically named species and cultivars of garden flowers, wild plants, trees (over 1000 species), grasses, crops, herbs, spices, houseplants, carnivorous plants, climbers (especially Clematis), roses, geraniums and pelargoniums, and pests.

General gardening How-to, gardening techniques, garden design and embellishments, cottage gardens, USA designer-gardens, 200 garden portfolios from 16 states in the USA, 100 portfolios from 12 European countries. Several photographers now represented. Founded 1993.

Garden World Images*
(incorporating The Harry Smith Collection)
Grange Studio, Woodham Road, Battlesbridge, Wickford, Essex SS11 7QU
tel (01245) 325725 *fax* (01245) 429198
email info@gardenworldimages.com
website www.gardenworldimages.com
Partners Françoise Davis and Lisa Smith

All aspects of horticulture, including large and small gardens, specialist sections on all subjects including trees, fruit, vegetables, herbs, cacti, orchids, grasses, cultivated and wild flowers from all over the world, pests and diseases, action shots. Founded 1951.

Genesis Space Photo Library
Greenbanks, Robins Hill, Raleigh, Bideford, Devon EX39 3PA
tel (01237) 471960 *fax* (01237) 472060
email tim@spaceport.co.uk
website www.spaceport. co.uk
Contact Tim Furniss

Specialises in rockets, spacecraft, spacemen, Earth, Moon, planets, stars, galaxies, the Universe. Founded 1990.

Geo Aerial Photography*
4 Christian Fields, London SW16 3JZ
tel/fax 020-8764 6292, 0115-981 9418
email geo-aerial@geo-group.co.uk
website www.geo-group.co.uk
Director J.F.J. Douglas

Air-to-air and air-to-ground colour library: natural and cultural/man-made landscapes and individual features. Subjects from UK, Scandinavia, Middle East, Asia and Africa. Commissions undertaken. Terms: 50%. Founded 1992.

George A. Dey
Drumcairn, Aberdeen Road, Laurencekirk, Kincardineshire AB30 1AJ
tel (01561 37) 8845

Scottish Highland landscapes, Highland Games, forestry, seabirds, castles of Northeast Scotland, gardens, spring, autumn, winter scenes, veteran cars, North Holland, New Zealand (North Island). Mostly 35mm, some 6 x 6cm. Founded 1986.

GeoScience Features*
(incorporates K.S.F. and RIDA photolibraries)
6 Orchard Drive, Wye, Kent TN25 5AU
tel/fax (01233) 812707
email gsf@geoscience.demon.co.uk
website www.geoscience.demon.co.uk
Director Dr Basil Booth

Colour library (35mm to 5 x 4in). Animals, biology, birds, botany, chemistry, earth science, ecology, environment, geology, geography, habitats, landscapes, macro/micro, peoples, plants, travel, sky, weather, wildlife and zoology; Americas, Africa, Australasia, Europe, India, Southeast Asia. Over a third of a million colour images available as film or high-res digital images. CD-Rom available.

Geoslides*
4 Christian Fields, London SW16 3JZ
tel/fax 020-8764 6292 or 0115-981 9418
email geoslides@geo-group.co.uk

website www.geo-group.co.uk
Library Director John Douglas

Broadly based and substantial collections from Africa, Asia, Antarctic, Arctic and sub-Arctic areas, Australia (Blackwood Collection). Worldwide commissions undertaken. Terms: 50% on UK sales. Founded 1968.

Getty Images*

101 Bayham Street, London NW1 0AG
tel 0800-376 7977 *fax* 020-7544 3334
email sales@gettyimages.co.uk
website www.gettyimages.co.uk

Leading imagery company, creating and providing the largest collection of still and moving images to communication professionals – from sports and news photography to archival and contemporary. Collections include: Stone, Taxi, the Image Bank, Photodisc, Hulton Archive, Getty Images News & Sport, Digital Vision, National Geographic, FoodPix, Bridgeman Art Library. See website.

Gordon Wright Scottish Photo Library

25 Mayfield Road, Edinburgh EH9 2NQ
tel 0131-667 1300 *fax* 0131-667 1459
email info@scottish-books-photos.co.uk
website www.scottish-books-photos.co.uk
Managing Director Gordon Wright

Specialist library illustrating Scotland: cities, towns and villages; landscapes and landmarks including the Orkney Islands; Scottish nationalism, personalities and writers. 56,000 b&w photos and 11,000 colour transparencies. Founded 1960.

Greg Evans International Photo Library

ICS House, 32 Crossways, Silwood Road, Sunninghill, Ascot, Berks. SL5 0PL
tel 020-7636 8238 *fax* 020-7637 1439
email greg@gregevans.net
website www.gregevans.net

Comprehensive, general colour library with over 300,000 transparencies. Subjects include: abstract, aircraft, arts, animals, beaches, business, children, computers, couples, families, food/restaurant, women, industry, skies, sports (action and leisure), UK scenics, worldwide travel. Visitors welcome; combined commissions undertaken; no search fee. Photographers' submissions welcome. Searchable website. Free brochure/CD-Rom. Founded 1979.

Hamish Brown, Scottish Photographic

26 Kirkcaldy Road, Burntisland, Fife KY3 9HQ
tel (01592) 873546

Picture library on Scottish sites, topography, mountains, travel. Book illustrations. Commissions undertaken. No pictures purchased.

Harper Horticultural Slide Library

219 Robanna Drive, Seaford, VA 23696, USA
tel 757-898-6453 *fax* 757-890-9378
email pamharper@mindspring.com

160,000 35mm slides of plants, gardens and native habitats.

Heather Angel/Natural Visions*

Highways, 6 Vicarage Hill, Farnham, Surrey GU9 8HJ
tel (01252) 716700 *fax* (01252) 727464
email hangel@naturalvisions.co.uk
website www.naturalvisions.co.uk

Colour transparencies (35mm and 2¼in square) with worldwide coverage of natural history and biological subjects including animals, plants, natural habitats (deserts, polar regions, rainforests, wetlands, etc), landscapes, gardens, close-ups and underwater images; also man's impact on the environment – pollution, acid rain, urban wildlife, etc. Large China file including pandas in all seasons. Extensive water file (liquid, solid and vapour). Website holds over 12,000 images. Pictures cannot be supplied *gratis* for personal use.

Heritage & Natural History Photography

37 Plainwood Close, Summersdale, Chichester, West Sussex PO19 4YB
tel/fax (01243) 533822
Contact Dr John B. Free

Archaeology, history, agriculture: Arabia, China, India, Iran, Ireland, Japan, Kenya, Mediterranean countries, Mexico, Nepal, North America, Oman, Russia, Thailand, UK. Bees and bee keeping, insects and small invertebrates, tropical crops and flowers.

Holt Studios*

The Courtyard, 24 High Street, Hungerford, Berks. RG17 0NF
tel (01488) 683523 *fax* (01488) 683511
email library@holt-studios.co.uk
website www.holt-studios.co.uk

110,000 pictures on worldwide agriculture, horticulture, crops and associated pests (and their predators), diseases and deficiencies, farming people and practices, livestock, machinery, landscapes, diverse environments, natural flora and fauna. Extensive gardens and garden plants collection. Founded 1981.

Horizon International

Horizon International Images Ltd, Horizon House, Route de Picaterre, Alderney, Guernsey GY9 3UP
tel (01481) 822587 *fax* (01481) 823880
email mail@hrzn.com
website www.hrzn.com

Specialist stock library. Images include leisure and lifestyle, business and industry, science and medicine, environment and nature, world travel. Founded 1978.

Hortipix/PSP Image Library
49 Palmerston Avenue, Goring by Sea,
West Sussex BN12 4RN
tel (01903) 503147
email enquiries@peterstiles.com
websites www.peterstiles.com www.hortipix.co.uk

Stock image library specialising in pictures of plants, flowers, watergardening and most horticultural/gardening subjects. Also pictorial views of the Channel Islands and UK, tropical marine aquarium fish and invertebrates. Illustrated garden articles and commissioned horticultural photography.

Houses & Interiors Photographic Features Agency
192 Goswell Road, London EC1V 7DT
tel 020-7253 0991 *fax* 020-7253 0992
Contact Anna Gibson

Stylish house interiors and exteriors, people in their homes and gardens, home dossiers, renovations, architectural details, interior design, gardens and houseplants. Also step-by-step photographic sequences of DIY subjects, fresh and dried flower arrangements and gardening techniques. Food. Colour only. Commissions undertaken. Terms: 50%, negotiable. Founded 1985.

Hulton Archive – see Getty Images

Huntley Film Archive*
191 Wardour Street, London W1F 82E
tel 020-7287 8000 *fax* 020-7287 80001
email films@huntleyarchives.com
website www.huntleyarchives.com
Archivist Amanda Huntley

Documentary and cinema stills and movies. Founded 1984.

Hutchison Picture Library*
118B Holland Park Avenue, London W11 4UA
tel 020-7229 2743 *fax* 020-7792 0259
email library@hutchisonpic.demon.co.uk
website www.hutchisonpictures.co.uk

General colour library; worldwide subjects: agriculture, the environment, festivals, human relationships, industry, landscape, peoples, religion, towns, travel. Founded 1976.

The Illustrated London News Picture Library*
20 Upper Ground, London SE1 9PF
tel 020-7805 5585 *fax* 020-7805 5905
email iln.pictures@ilng.co.uk
website www.ilng.co.uk

Engravings, photos, illustrations in b&w and colour from 1842 to present day, especially 19th and 20th century social history, wars, portraits, royalty.

Collection includes the Seaco Picture Library of transport and travel images.

The Image Bank – see Getty Images

Image Diggers
618B Finchley Road, London NW11 7RR
tel/fax 020-8455 4564
email ziph@macunlimited.net
website http://imagediggers.netfirms.com
Contact Neil Hornick

Stills archive covering performing arts, popular culture, human interest, natural history, architecture, nautical, children and people, strange phenomena, etc. Also audio and video for research purposes, books, and ephemera including magazines, comic books, sheet music, postcards. Founded 1980.

Imagefinder Pte Ltd
228A South Bridge Road, Singapore 058777
tel (65) 324 3747 *fax* (65) 324 3748
email imagef@mbox4.singnet.com.sg
Director Rashidah Hamid

General photo library with strong focus on Asian-related material. Founded 1998.

Images of Africa Photobank*
11 The Windings, Lichfield, Staffs. WS13 7EX
tel (01543) 262898 *fax* (01543) 417154
email info@imagesofafrica.co.uk
website www.imagesofafrica.co.uk
Library Manager Jacquie Shipton, *Proprietor* David Keith Jones FRPS

135,000 images covering 19 African countries: Botswana, Chad, Egypt, Ethiopia, Kenya, Lesotho, Madagascar, Malawi, Morocco, Namibia, Rwanda, South Africa, Swaziland, Tanzania, Uganda, Zaire, Zambia, Zanzibar and Zimbabwe. Specialities: wildlife, people, landscapes, tourism, hotels and lodges, National Parks and Reserves. Terms: 50%. Founded 1983.

ImageState Pictor Ltd*
Ramillies House, 1-2 Ramillies Street,
London W1F 7LN
tel 020-7734 7344 *fax* 020-7434 0673
website www.imagestate.co.uk
Office Manager Julie Chamberlain

Contemporary rights-protected and royalty-free images, footage and music. Subjects include people, business, UK and world travel, industry and sport. Founded 1983.

Imperial War Museum*
Photograph Archive, Austral Street,
London SE11 4SL
tel 020-7416 5333/8 *fax* 020-7416 5355

email photos@iwm.org.uk
website www.iwm.org.uk
www.iwmcollections.org.uk

National archive of over 6 million photos, dealing with conflict in the 20th century involving the armed forces of Britain and the Commonwealth countries. Open by appointment Mon–Fri. Prints made to order. Founded 1917.

International Press Agency (Pty) Ltd

Sunrise House, 56 Morningside, Ndabeni 7405, South Africa
tel (021) 531 1926 *fax* (021) 531 8789
email inpra@iafrica.com

Press photos for South African market. Founded 1934.

The Irish Image Collection*

The Riggins, Dunshaughlin, Co Meath, Republic of Ireland
tel/fax (01) 8256623
email info@theirishimagecollection.ie
website www.theirishimagecollection.ie

Covers all 32 countries in Ireland and features diverse subjects: agriculture, pubs, sport, gardens, megalithic archaeology, tradition, many aspects of Irish life, etc. Fully searchable website.

Isle of Wight Pictures

60 York Street, Cowes, Isle of Wight PO31 7BS
tel (01983) 290366 *mobile* (07768) 877914
fax (01983) 290366
email patrick@patrickeden.co.uk
website www.patrickeden.co.uk
Proprietor Patrick Eden

Covers all aspects of the Isle of Wight, including landscape, aerial, industry, agriculture, tourism, Cowes Week, nautical aspects. Over 5000 pictures; any picture not on file can be shot to order. All images available as originals or in digital formats. Founded 1985.

Rev. J. Catling Allen

7 St Barnabas, The Beauchamp Community, Newland, Malvern WR13 5AX
tel (01684) 899390

Library of colour transparencies (35mm) and b&w photos of Bible Lands, including archaeological sites and the religions of Christianity, Islam and Judaism. Medieval abbeys and priories, cathedrals and churches in Britain. Also historic, rural and scenic Britain. (Not an agent or buyer.)

J.S. Library International

101A Brondesbury Park, London NW2 5JL
tel 020-8451 2668 *fax* 020-8459 0223/8517
email js@online24.co.uk

The J.S. Royal collection, Art collection, Hollywood

collection, Celebrity service, particularly authors. Travel, fauna and flora and general pictures. New photographers and material required. Assignments worldwide undertaken. Founded 1979.

James Davis Travel Photography

65 Brighton Road, Shoreham, West Sussex BN43 6RE
tel (01273) 452252 *fax* (01273) 440116
email library@eyeubiquitous.com
website www.eyeubiquitous.com
Proprietor Paul Seheult

Stock transparency library specialising in worldwide travel photos.

Japan Archive

9 Victoria Drive, Horsforth, Leeds LS18 4PN
tel 0113-258 3244 *fax* 0113-216 3441
email stephen.turnbull@virgin.net
website www.stephenturnbull.com
Contact S.R. Turnbull

Japan: modern, daily life, architecture, religion, history, personalities, gardens, natural world; European castles. Founded 1993.

Jason Hawkes Library*

Unit 68, 124-128 Barlby Road, London W10 6BL
tel 020-8960 7525 *fax* 020-8960 7253
email library@jasonhawkes.com
website www.jasonhawkes.com
Library Manager Chris Lacey

Aerial photography of London and Britain; also Europe, USA and Australia. Online searchable database of over 8000 images. Founded 1998.

Jazz Index

26 Fosse Way, London W13 0BZ
tel 020-8998 1232 *fax* 020-8998 2880
email christianhim@jazzindex.co.uk
website www. jazzindex.co.uk

Specialist photo library of jazz, blues and contemporary music. Comprehensive selection of archives material, atmospheric images of performers, portraits, smoky clubs, audiences, instruments. Terms: 50%. Founded 1979.

Joefilmbase.com

1 Town Mead Business Centre, William Morris Way, London SW6 2SZ
tel/fax 020-7751 0007
email joefilmbase@btconnect.com
website www.joefilmbase.com

General library: fashion, catwalk, people, business, ideas, art photos, business, traders, travel, dance, concerts, cars, boats, lifestyle, nature, worldwide. Transparencies only: 35mm, 6 x 7cm, etc. Founded 1991.

John Birdsall Social Issues Photo Library*
75 Raleigh Street, Nottingham NG7 4DL
tel 0115-978 2645 *fax* 0115-978 5546
email photos@johnbirdsall.co.uk
website www.johnbirdsall.co.uk
Contact Anna Grapes

Contemporary social documentary library covering children, youth, old age, health, families, disability, education, housing, work; also Nottingham and surrounding area; Spain, Cuba, India – commissions and stock pictures. Online catalogue searchable in both English and German. Founded 1980.

John Frost Newspapers
22B Rosemary Avenue, Enfield, Middlesex EN2 0SS
tel 020-8366 1392/0946 *fax* 020-8366 1379
email andrew@johnfrostnewspapers.com
website www.johnfrostnewspapers.co.uk

Headline stories from 80,000 British and overseas newspapers and 100,000 press cuttings reporting events since 1850.

John Glover Photography
The Oast Houses, Headley Lane, Passfield,
Hants GU30 7RX
tel (01428) 751925 *mobile* (07973) 307078
fax (01428) 751191
email john@glovphot.demon.co.uk
website www.glovphot.demon.co.uk

Gardens and gardening, from overall views of gardens to plant portraits with Latin names; UK landscapes including ancient sites, Stonehenge, etc. Founded 1979.

John Massey Stewart Picture Library
20 Hillway, London N6 6QA
tel 020-8341 3544 *fax* 020-8341 5292
email jms@gn.apc.org

Large collection Russia/USSR, including topography, people, culture, Siberia, plus Russian and Soviet history, 3000 pre-revolutionary PCs, etc. Also Britain, Europe (including Bulgaria, Poland, Slovenia and Turkey), Alaska, USA, Israel, Sinai desert, etc; and classical composers (portraits, houses, graves, monuments, etc).

John Vickers Theatre Collection
27 Shorrolds Road, London SW6 7TR
tel 020-7385 5774

Archives of British theatre and portraits of actors, writers and musicians by John Vickers from 1938–74.

Just Europe
50 Basingfield Road, Thames Ditton,
Surrey KT7 0PD
tel/fax 020-8398 2468
email justeurope@altavista.com

Specialises in Europe – major cities, towns, people and customs. Assignments undertaken; background information available; advice/research service. Founded 1989.

Katz Pictures Ltd*
109 Clifton Street, London EC2A 4LD
tel 020-7749 6000 *fax* 020-7749 6001
email info@katzpictures.com
website www.katzpictures.com

Images of people and world events from 1900s to contemporary.

Kilmartin House Trust
Kilmartin House, Kilmartin, Argyll PA31 8RQ
tel (01546) 510278 *fax* (01546) 510330
email museum@kilmartin.org
website www.kilmartin.org
Contact D.J. Adams McGilp

Ancient monuments, archaeological sites; artefacts and excavations. Aerial photographs of Mid Argyll. Colour prints and transparencies. Publishers of historical/archaeological works, including fiction. Founded 1994.

Lakeland Life Picture Library
Langsett, Lyndene Drive, Grange-over-Sands,
Cumbria LA11 6QP
tel (015395) 33565 (answerphone)
email davidwjones@ktdinternet.com
website www.lakelandlifepicturelibrary.co.uk

English Lake District: industries, crafts, sports, shows, customs, architecture, people. Also provides colour and b&w, illustrated articles. Not an agency. Catalogue available. Founded 1979.

Lebrecht Music Collection*
58B Carlton Hill, London NW8 0ES
tel 020-7625 5341 and 020-7372 8233
fax 020-7625 5341
email pictures@lebrecht.co.uk
website www.lebrecht.co.uk
Director Elbie Lebrecht

Colour and b&w images of music from antiquity to the 21st century: composers, musicians, opera singers, musical scores, concert halls and opera houses, instruments, world music, rock, pop, jazz, cinema. Founded 1992.

Lesley and Roy Adkins Picture Library
Ten Acre Wood, Heath Cross, Whitestone,
Exeter EX4 2HW
tel (01392) 811357 *fax* (01392) 811435
email mail@adkinsarchaeology.com
website www.adkinsarchaeology.com

Colour library covering archaeology, ancient history, history and heritage; prehistoric, Roman, Greek, Egyptian and medieval sites and monuments; landscape, countryside, architecture, towns, villages and religious monuments. Founded 1989.

Link Picture Library*
33 Greyhound Road, London W6 8NH
tel 020-7381 2261/2433 *fax* 020-7385 6244
email lib@linkpics.demon.co.uk
website www.linkpicturelibrary.com
Proprietor Orde Eliason

Specialist archives on Central and Southern Africa, India, China, Southeast Asia and Israel. Commissions accepted. Terms: 50%. Founded 1982.

London Metropolitan Archives
(formerly Greater London Record Office)
40 Northampton Road, London EC1R 0HB
tel 020-7332 3820 *minicom* 020-7278 8703
fax 020-7833 9136
email ask.lma@corpoflondon.gov.uk
website www.cityoflondon.gov.uk/lma

Largest local authority record office in the UK, with 32 miles of archives. Nearly 900 years of London history is contained in the records of London government, businesses, charities, hospitals, churches, etc. Collections include books, documents, photographs, maps and drawings. 100,000-volume reference library specialising in London history.

Lonely Planet Images*
website www.lonelyplanetimages.com
Australasia 90 Maribyrnong Street, Footscray, Victoria 3011
tel (03) 8379 8181 *fax* (03) 8379 8182
email lpi@lonelyplanet.com.au
Contact Ellen Burrows
Americas Lonely Planet Images, 150 Linden Street, Oakland, California 94607
tel 510-893-8555 *fax* 800-275-8555
email lpi@lonelyplanet.com
Contact Jain Lemos
Europe 72-82 Rosebery Avenue, London EC1R 4RW
tel 020-7841 9000 *fax* 020-7841 9001
email lpi@lonelyplanet.co.uk
Contact Miranda Duffy

Online collection of travel-related images. Searchable website.

Ludvigsen Library
Scoles Gate, Hawkedon, Suffolk IP29 4AU
tel/fax (01284) 789246
email karlcars@btinternet.com
Photographic resources Karl Ludvigsen

Specialist automotive and motor racing photo library. Includes much rare and unpublished material from John Dugdale, Edward Eves, Max le Grand, Peter Keen, Karl Ludvigsen, Rodolfo

Mailander, Ove Nielsen, Stanley Rosenthall and others. Founded 1984.

The MacQuitty International Collection*
7 Elm Lodge, River Gardens, Stevenage Road, London SW6 6NZ
tel/fax 020-7385 5606
email miranda.macquitty@btinternet.com

300,000 photos covering aspects of life in 70 countries: archaeology, art, buildings, flora and fauna, gardens, museums, people and occupations, scenery, religions, methods of transport, surgery, acupuncture, funeral customs, fishing, farming, dancing, music, crafts, sports, weddings, carnivals, food, drink, jewellery and oriental subjects. Period: 1920 to present day.

Mander & Mitchenson Theatre Collection*
Jerwood Library of the Performing Arts, King Charles Building, Old Royal Naval College, London SE10 9JF
tel 020-8305 4426 *fax* 020-8305 3993
email rmangan@tcm.ac.uk

Prints, drawings, photos, programmes, etc, theatre, opera, ballet, music hall, and other allied subjects including composers, playwrights, etc. All periods.

Marine Wildlife Photo Agency
Vine Villa, Mount Road, Llanfairfechan, North Wales LL33 0DW
tel/fax (01248) 681361
email info@marinewildlife.co.uk
website www.marinewildlife.co.uk
Proprietor Paul Kay

35mm and medium format images of UK and Irish (temperate) marine life and associated subjects (coastal services, environmental issues, etc). Subjects range from straight animal/plant portraits through to abstracts; also underwater scenic photos. Founded 1992.

Mark Gerson Photography
3 Regal Lane, Regents Park Road, London NW1 7TH
tel 020-7286 5894 *fax* 020-7267 9246
email mark.gerson@virgin.net

Portrait photographs of personalities, mainly literary, in colour and b&w from 1950 to the present. No other photographers' material required.

Martin and Dorothy Grace
40 Clipstone Avenue, Mapperley, Nottingham NG3 5JZ
tel 0115-920 8248 *fax* 0115-962 6802
email graces@lineone.net

General British natural history, specialising in native trees, shrubs, flowers, ferns, habitats and ecology. Founded 1984.

Mary Evans Picture Library*

59 Tranquil Vale, London SE3 0BS
tel 020-8318 0034 *fax* 020-8852 7211
email pictures@mepl.co.uk
website www.mepl.co.uk

Millions of historical illustrations documenting social, political, cultural, technical, geographical and biographical themes from ancient times to the 1970s. Photographs, original prints, and ephemera backed by a large international book and magazine collection. Special collections include the Sigmund Freud Collection, the Women's Library, the Meledin Collection (20th-century Russian history) and individual photographers active from the 1930s to the 1970s. Recent acquisitions include the Weimar Archive and Barnaby's Picture Library, which incorporates the Mustograph Agency. Colour brochure available. Compilers of the *Picture Researcher's Handbook*, published every 3 years by Pira International (www.piranet.com).

Medimage

32 Brooklyn Road, Coventry CV1 4JT
tel/fax (01203) 668562
email chambersking@ntlworld.com
Contact Anthony King

Specialist library of medium format transparencies of subjects in Mediterranean countries and the Czech Republic: agriculture, architecture, crafts, festivals, flora, industry, landscapes, markets, portraits, recreation, seascapes, sport and transport. Commissions undertaken. Other photographers' work not accepted. Founded 1992.

Merseyside Photo Library*

Suite 6, Egerton House, Tower Road, Birkenhead, Wirral CH41 1FN
tel 0151-650 6975 *fax* 0151-650 6976
email ron@merseywide.demon.co.uk
website www.merseysidephotolibrary.com
Operated by Ron Jones Associates

Library specialising in images of Liverpool and Merseyside but includes other destinations. Founded 1989.

Michael Cole Camerawork*

The Coach House, 27 The Avenue, Beckenham, Kent BR3 2DP
tel/fax 020-8658 6120
email mikecole@dircon.co.uk
website www.tennisphotos.com

Probably the largest and most comprehensive tennis library in the world comprising over half a million colour and b&w images. Includes over 50 years of the Wimbledon Championships. Founded 1945.

Michael Leach

Brookside, Kinnerley, Oswestry SY10 8DB
tel (01691) 682639 *fax* (01691) 682003
email mike.leach@lineone.net
website www.michael-leach.co.uk

General worldwide wildlife and natural history subjects, with particular emphasis on mammals (especially great apes) and urban wildlife. Comprehensive collection of owls from all over the world. No other photographers required.

Mick Sharp Photography

Eithinog, Waun, Penisarwaun, Caernarfon, Gwynedd LL55 3PW
tel/fax (01286) 872425
email mick.jean@virgin.net

Archaeology, ancient monuments, buildings, churches, countryside, environment, history, landscape, past cultures and topography. Emphasis on British Isles, but material also from other countries. Access to other specialist collections on related subjects. B&w prints from 5 x 4in negatives, and 35mm and 6 x 4.5cm colour transparencies. Founded 1981.

Microscopix

Middle Travelly, Beguildy, Nr Knighton, Powys LD7 1UW
tel (01547) 510242 *fax* (01547) 510317
email semages@microscopix.co.uk
website www.microscopix.co.uk

Scientific photo library specialising in scanning electron micrographs and photomicrographs for technical and aesthetic purposes. Commissioned work, both biological and non-biological, undertaken offering a wide variety of applicable microscopical techniques. Founded 1986.

Military History Picture Library

3 Barton Buildings, Bath BA1 2JR
tel (01225) 334213 *fax* (01225) 480554

Prints, engravings, photos, colour transparencies covering all aspects of warfare and uniforms from ancient times to the present.

Mirrorpix*

One Canada Square, Canary Wharf, London E14 5AP
tel 020-7293 3700 *fax* 020-7293 2712
email desk@mirrorpix.com
website www.mirrorpix.com
Contact Sales desk

Images of the past 100 years by photographers of the *Daily Mirror* and her sister titles which document both the light and dark sides of British life: people, places, events and movements.

Monitor Picture Library*

Monitor Press Features Ltd, The Forge, Roydon, Harlow, Essex CM19 5HH
tel (01279) 792700 *fax* (01279) 792600

email sales@monitorpicturelibrary.com
website www.monitorpicturelibrary.com
Contact Eleanore White, Stewart White

UK and international personalities 1850–1994. B&w and colour.

Motorcycles Unlimited
48 Lemsford Road, St Albans, Herts. AL1 3PR
tel (01727) 869001 *fax* (01727) 869014
email rolandbrown@motobike.demon.co.uk
Owner Roland Brown

Motorbikes of all kinds, from latest roadsters to classics, racers to tourers. Detailed information available on all machines pictured. Founded 1993.

Motoring Picture Library*
National Motor Museum, Beaulieu, Hants SO42 7ZN
tel (01590) 614656 *fax* (01590) 612655
email motoring.pictures@beaulieu.co.uk
website www.alamy.com/mpl
www.heritage-images.com

All aspects of motoring, cars, commercial vehicles, motor cycles, personalities, etc. Illustrations of period scenes and motor sport. Also large library of 5 x 4in and smaller colour transparencies of veteran, vintage and modern cars, commercial vehicles and motorcycles. Over 800,000 images in total.

Mountain Dynamics
Heathcourt, Morven Way, Monaltrie,
Ballater AB35 5SF
tel (013397) 55081 *fax* (013397) 55526
email gpa@globalnet.co.uk
Proprietor Graham P. Adams

Scottish and European mountains – from ground to summits – in panoramic (6 x 17cm), 5 x 4in and medium format. Commissions undertaken. Terms: 50%. Founded 1990.

Mountain Visions and Faces
25 The Mallards, Langstone, Havant,
Hants PO9 1SS
tel 023-9247 8441
email mtvisions@hotmail.com
website www.mountainvisions.co.uk
Contact Graham Elson, Roslyn Elson

Colour transparencies of mountaineering, skiing, and tourism in Europe, Africa, Himalayas, Arctic, Far East, South America and Australia. Does not act as agent for other photographers. Founded 1984.

Murray Wren Picture Library
3 Hallgate, London SE3 9SG
tel 020-8852 7556
email murraywren@aol.com

Outdoor nudes; nudist holiday resorts and activities in Europe and elsewhere; historic and erotic art of the nude through the ages. No new photographers required.

Museum of London*
London Wall, London EC2Y 5HN
tel 020-7814 5605 *fax* 020-7600 1058
email lpringle@museumoflondon.org.uk
website www.museumoflondon.org.uk
Picture Library Manager Lucy Pringle
London history.

The Mustograph Agency – see Mary Evans Picture Library

The National Archives Image Library*
The National Archives, Ruskin Avenue, Kew,
Surrey TW9 4DU
tel 020-8392 5225 *fax* 020-8392 5266
email image-library@nationalarchives.gov.uk
website www.nationalarchives.gov.uk/imagelibrary

Unique collection of millions of historical documents on a wide range of formats from 1086 to 1960s. Special collections include: Victorian and Edwardian advertisements and photographs, Second World War propaganda, military history, maps, decorative and technical designs and medieval illuminations. Founded 1995.

National Galleries of Scotland Picture Library*
The Dean Gallery, 73 Belford Road,
Edinburgh EH4 3DS
tel 0131-624 6258 *fax* 0131-623 7135
email picture.library@nationalgalleries.org
website www.nationalgalleries.org
Photographic & Licensing Manager Deborah Hunter

Fine art from Renaissance to present day. Specialist subjects include landscape, still life, portraits, genre, animals and costume.

National Maritime Museum Picture Library*
National Maritime Museum, Greenwich,
London SE10 9NF
email picturelibrary@nmm.ac.uk
website www.nmm.ac.uk
Contact David Taylor *tel* 020-8312 6631, Lucy Waitt *tel* 020-8312 6704

Maritime, transport, time and space and historic photographs.

National Museums & Galleries of Northern Ireland, Ulster Folk & Transport Museum
153 Bangor Road, Cultra, Holywood,
Co. Down BT18 0EU, Northern Ireland
tel 028-9042 8428 *fax* 028-9042 8728
email t.kenneth.anderson@talk21.com
Head of Dept of Photography T.K. Anderson

Photographs from 1850s to the present day, including the work of W.A. Green, Rose Shaw and

R.J. Welsh while he was under contract to Harland and Wolff Ltd. Subjects include Belfast shipbuilding (80,000 photographs, including 70 original negatives of the *Titanic*), road and rail transport, folk life, agriculture and the linen industry. B&w and colour (35mm, medium and large format). Founded 1962.

National Portrait Gallery Picture Library*
St Martin's Place, London WC2H 0HE
tel 020-7312 2474 *fax* 020-7312 2464
email picturelibrary@npg.org.uk
website www.npg.org.uk
Contact Tom Morgan

Portraits of the makers of British history, medieval to the present. The most comprehensive collection in the world: paintings, drawings, sculptures, engravings and photographs. Images supplied with definitive captions and rights clearance.

Natural History Photographic Agency – see NHPA Ltd

Natural Image
24 Newborough Road, Wimborne,
Dorset BH21 1RD
tel (01202) 849142 *fax* (01202) 848419
email bob.gibbons@which.net
Contact Dr Bob Gibbons

Colour library covering natural history, habitats, countryside and gardening (UK and worldwide); special emphasis on conservation. Commissions undertaken. Terms: 50%. Founded 1982.

The Nature and Landscape File
24 Southleigh Crescent, Leeds LS11 5TW
tel 0113-2715535 *mobile* (07866) 057823
website www.photosource.co.uk/photosource/
Nature&Landscape.htm
Proprietor Dr Mark Lucock

Natural history subjects and landscapes from around the world, especially the UK, southern Europe, North America. Specialises in photomacrographic images. 30,000 large- and small-format colour transparencies. Founded 1997.

Nature Picture Library*
(formerly BBC Natural History Unit Picture Library)
BBC Broadcasting House, Whiteladies Road,
Bristol BS8 2LR
tel 0117-9746720 *fax* 0117-9238166
email info@naturepl.com
website www.naturepl.com

Photographs illustrating all aspects of nature: mammals, birds, insects, reptiles, marine life, plants, landscapes, indigenous peoples, environmental issues and wildlife filming.

The Neil Williams Classical Collection
22 Avon, Hockley, Tamworth, Staffs. B77 5QA
tel/fax (01827) 286086
email neil@classicalcollection.co.uk
Proprietor Neil Williams PGC(Mus), BA Hons, DipMus

Specialises in classical music ephemera, including portraits of composers, musicians, conductors, opera singers, ballet stars, impresarios, and music-related literary figures. Old and sometimes rare photographs, postcards, antique prints, cigarette cards, stamps, concert programmes, Victorian newspapers, etc. Also modern photographs of composer references such as museums, statues, memorials, etc.

Other subjects: music in art, musical instruments, manuscripts, concert halls, opera houses and other music venues. Founded 1996.

New Blitz Literary & TV Agency
Via di Panico 67, 00186 Rome, Italy
postal address CP 30047-00193, Rome 47, Italy
tel/fax (06) 686 4859
email blitzgacs@inwind.it
Contact Giovanni A.S. Congiu

News and general library.

NHPA Ltd*
(Natural History Photographic Agency)
57 High Street, Ardingly,
West Sussex RH17 6TB
tel (01444) 892514 *fax* (01444) 892168
email nhpa@nhpa.co.uk
website www.nhpa.co.uk

Specialises in high-quality images covering all aspects of the natural world. Represents over 120 leading wildlife and environmental photographers with more than 200,000 pictures on file. Comprehensive coverage of British, European and worldwide nature and wildlife. Includes not only mainstream natural history subjects but rare and exotic species and conservation and environmental images, plus pets, agriculture, plants and marine life. Website holds over 15,000 hi-res images, available for download. *A–Z of Nature* catalogue and brochure available.

Northern Picture Library – see Stockwave

Operation Raleigh – see Raleigh International Picture Library

OSF Ltd, Photo Library*
(incorporating the Survival Anglia Photo Library)
Lower Road, Long Hanborough,
Oxon OX8 8LL
tel (01993) 881881 *fax* (01993) 882808
email enquiries@osf.uk.com
website www.osf.uk.com

Specialises in all aspects of the natural world, worldwide. Includes wildlife, underwater, science, landscapes, seascapes, plants, gardens, seasons, environment, country life, natural habitats, weather, space, adventure sports, domestic animals and pets. Film footage also available: natural world, wildlife, global locations, medical, science, time-lapse and special effects.

PA Photos*
292 Vauxhall Bridge Road,
London SW1V 1AE
tel 020-7963 7032/34/35 *fax* 020-7963 7066
email paphotos.research@pa.press.net
website www.paphotos.com

Over 6 million photos dating from the turn of the 20th century, covering news, sport, royalty and showbiz. Library updated daily. Searches undertaken, or customers are welcome to visit.

PAL (Performing Arts Library)
1st Floor, Production House, 25 Hackney Road,
London E2 7NX
tel 020-7749 4850 *fax* 020-7749 4858
email admin@peformingartslibrary.com
website www.performingartslibrary.com

Continually updated specialist image collection covering classical music, opera, theatre, musicals, instruments, festivals, venues, circus, ballet and contemporary dance. Almost one million images from late 19th century onwards.

Panos Pictures*
Studio 3B, 38 Southwark Street,
London SE1 1UN
tel 020-7234 0010 *fax* 020-7357 0094
email pics@panos.co.uk
website www.panos.co.uk

Third World and Eastern European documentary photos focusing on social, political and economic issues with a special emphasis on environment and development. Files on agriculture, conflict, education, energy, environment, family life, festivals, food, health, industry, landscape, people, politics, pollution, refugees, religions, rural life, transport, urban life, water, weather. Terms: 50%. Founded 1986.

Papilio Natural History & Travel Library
The Oasts, Headley Lane, Liphook,
Hants GU30 7RX
tel (01428) 751056 *fax* (01428) 751057
email library@papiliophotos.com
website www.papiliophotos.com
Contacts Vicki Coombs (library), Robert Pickett

Worldwide coverage of natural history and travel; commissions undertaken. More than 100,000 images held. Colour catalogue available. Founded 1988.

Pat Hodgson Library & Picture Research Agency
Jasmine Cottage, Spring Grove Road,
Richmond, Surrey TW10 6EH
tel/fax 020-8940 5986
email pat.hodgpix@virgin.net

Small collection of b&w historical engravings, book illustrations, ephemera, etc; some colour and modern photos. Subjects include history, Victoriana, ancient civilisations, occult, travel. Text written and research undertaken on any subject.

Peter Cumberlidge Photo Library
Sunways, Slapton, Kingsbridge, Devon TQ7 2PR
tel (01548) 580461 *fax* (01548) 580588
email info@petercumberlidge.co.uk
Contact Jane Cumberlidge

Nautical, travel and coastal colour transparencies 35mm and 6 x 6cm. Specialities: boats, harbours, marinas, inland waterways. Travel and holiday subjects in Northern Europe, the Mediterranean, and New England, USA. No other photographers' material required. Founded 1982.

Peter Dazeley*
The Studios, 5 Heathmans Road, London SW6 4TJ
tel 020-7736 3171 *fax* 020-7371 8876
email dazeleyp@aol.com

Extensive golf library dating from 1970. Colour and b&w coverage of major tournaments, with over 250,000 images of players, courses worldwide, action shots, portraits, trophies, including miscellaneous images: clubs, balls and teaching shots.

Peter Newark Picture Library
3 Barton Buildings, Bath BA1 2JR
tel (01225) 334213 *fax* (01225) 480554

One million pictures: engravings, prints, paintings and photographs on all aspects of world history from ancient times to the present.

Peter Sanders Photography Ltd*
24 Meades Lane, Chesham,
Bucks. HP5 1ND
tel (01494) 773674, 771372 *fax* (01494) 773674
email photos@petersanders.com
website www.petersanders.com

Specialises in the world of Islam, its cultures, lifestyles, architecture, landscapes, festivals and industry. Countries covered include: China, Egypt, India, Iran, Kenya, Kosovo, Kuwait, Mali, Mauritania, Morocco, Saudi Arabia, Spain, Sudan, Turkey, Turkmenistan, USA and Europe. Also other religions. Founded 1987.

Photo Link
126 Quarry Lane, Northfield, Birmingham B31 2QD
tel 0121-475 8712 *fax* 0121-604 0480
email vines@aviationphotolink.co.uk

website www.aviationphotolink.co.uk
Contact Mike Vines

Colour and b&w aviation library, covering subjects from 1909 to the present day. Specialises in air-to-air photography. Assignments undertaken. Over 10,000 aviation images from around the world are added every year. Can also research, advise and write aviation stories and press releases. Founded 1990.

Photo Resources
The Orchard, Marley Lane, Kingston, Canterbury, Kent CT4 6JH
tel (01227) 830075 *fax* (01227) 831135

Ancient civilisations, art, archaeology, world religions, myth, and museum objects covering the period from 30,000 BC to AD 1900. European birds, butterflies, trees.

Photofusion*
17A Electric Lane, London SW9 8LA
tel 020-7733 3500 *fax* 020-7738 5509
email library@photofusion.org
website www.photofusion.org

Covers all aspects of UK contemporary life with an emphasis on social and environment issues. Catalogue available. Photographers available for commission.

The Photolibrary Wales*
2 Bro-nant, Church Road, Pentyrch, Cardiff CF15 9QG
tel 029-2089 0311 *fax* 029-2089 2650
email info@photolibrarywales.com
website www.photolibrarywales.com
Director Steve Benbow

Comprehensive collection of contemporary images of Wales. Subjects include landscape, lifestyle, current affairs, sport, industry, people. Over 100 photographers represented. Digital files and transmission available. Colour transparencies and b&w prints. Commission: 50%. Founded 1998.

Photolibrary.com*
(formerly the Photographers' Library)
81A Endell Street, London WC2H 9AJ
tel 020-7836 5591 *fax* 020-7379 4650
website www.photolibrary.com

Requires digital material on all subjects. Submit via website.

Pictor International Ltd – see ImageState
Pictor Ltd

The Picture Company
100 Pondcroft Road, Knebworth, Herts. SG3 6DE
tel (01438) 814418 *mobile* (07850) 971491

fax (01438) 814418
email chrisbonass@hotmail.co.uk
website www.flightonfilm.co.uk
Contact Chris Bonass

Colour transparencies (2¼ x 2¼in and 35mm) of people and places worldwide. Taken by award-winning film and TV cameraman and largely unseen and unpublished. Also aviation pictures old and new, including air-to-air photography and a unique archive on 16mm film and broadcast videotape. Used by BBC, C4, etc. Assignments undertaken. Founded 1993.

Picture Research Service
Rich Research, One Bradby, 77 Carlton Hill, London NW8 9XE
tel/fax 020-7624 7755
Contact Diane Rich

Visuals found for all sectors of the media and publishing. Artwork and photography commissioned. Rights and permissions negotiated.

Picturepoint Ltd – see Topham Picturepoint

Picturesmiths Ltd*
Manor Farm Cottage, Main Road, Curbridge, Witney, Oxon OX29 7NT
tel (01993) 771907 *fax* (01993) 706383
email roger@picturesmiths.co.uk
website www.picturesmiths.co.uk
Managing Director Roger M. Smith

Plant photography, from portraits, close-ups and macrophotography to plant associations, colour themes and garden scenes. Colour transparencies. Founded 1997.

Pixfeatures
5 Latimer Road, Barnet, Herts. EN5 5NU
tel 020-8449 9946 *fax* 020-8441 2725
Contact Peter Wickman

Historical pictures and features covering big news events, royalty, showbiz. Travel (all countries). National newspapers' extensive collection of people in the news to 1970. *Stern* magazine features (before 1985). Documentary and historical photos. Special collections: Dukes of Windsor and Kent, Kennedys, Beatles, Keeler/Levy, trainrobbers, Second World War/Nazis. Terms: 50%.

Popperfoto (Paul Popper Ltd)*
The Old Mill, Overstone Farm, Overstone, Northampton NN6 0AB
tel (01604) 670670 *fax* (01604) 670635
email popperfoto@msn.com
website www.popperfoto.com
www.thegalleryatpopperfoto.com

Over 14 million images, covering 150 years of photographic history. Unrivalled archival material, world-famous sports library and extensive stock photography. Credit line includes Reuters, Bob Thomas Sports Photography, UPI, AFP and EPA, Acme, INP, Planet, Paul Popper, Exclusive News Agency, Victory Archive, Odhams Periodicals Library, *Illustrated*, Harris Picture Agency, and H.G. Ponting which holds the Scott 1910–12 Antarctic expedition material.

Colour from 1940, b&w from 1870 to present. Major subjects covered worldwide include: events, personalities, wars, royalty, sport, politics, transport, crime, history and social conditions. Popperfoto policy is to make material available, same day, to clients throughout the world. Mac-desk accessible. Researchers welcome by appointment. Free catalogue available.

POPPERFOTO Online includes half a million photos with delivery of full resolution images. *The Gallery at POPPERFOTO* features limited edition, hand-printed fine art photographs which can also be ordered online.

Premaphotos Wildlife

Amberstone, 1 Kirland Road, Bodmin, Cornwall PL30 5JQ
tel (01208) 78258 *fax* (01208) 72302
email pics@premaphotos.co.uk
website www.premaphotos.co.uk
Contact Dr Rod Preston-Mafham

Library of 35mm transparencies; wide range of natural history subjects from around the world, including camouflage, mimicry, warning coloration, parental care, courtship, mating, flowers, fruits, fungi, habitats (particularly rainforests and deserts), and many more. Specialists in invertebrate behaviour and cacti. Captions and copy can be provided. Founded 1978.

Press Association Photos – see PA Photos

Press Features Syndicate

9 Paradise Close, Eastbourne, East Sussex BN20 8BT
tel (01323) 728760

For full details see page 123.

Public Record Office Image Library – see The National Archives Image Library

Punch Cartoon Library & Archive*

87-135 Brompton Road, London SW1X 7XL
tel 020-7225 6710/6793 *fax* 020-7225 6712
email punch.library@harrods.com

Comprehensive collection of cartoons and illustrations, indexed under subject categories: humour, historical events, politics, fashion, sport, personalities, etc.

Railways – Milepost 92½*

Milepost 92½, Newton Harcourt, Leics. LE8 9FH
tel 0116-259 2068 *fax* 0116-259 3001
email contacts@milepost92-half.co.uk
website www.milepost92-half.co.uk

Comprehensive library representing all aspects of modern railway operations and scenic pictures from the UK and abroad. Includes Colin Garratt's collection of world steam trains as well as archive b&w photos. Welcomes contributing photographers and also archives, and markets picture collections on behalf of individuals. Founded 1969.

Raleigh International Picture Library

Raleigh House, 27 Parson's Green Lane, London SW6 4HZ
tel 020-7371 8585
email press@raleigh.org.uk
website www.raleighinternational.org
Contact Kate Davies

Stock colour images from around the world, especially remote landscapes, people and flora/fauna. Updated from expeditions 11 times a year. Open to researchers by appointment only, Mon–Fri, 9.30am–4.00pm.

Redferns Music Picture Library*

7 Bramley Road, London W10 6SZ
tel 020-7792 9914 *fax* 020-7792 0921
email info@redferns.com
website www.musicpictures.com
Contact Dede Millar

All styles of music, from 18th century classical composers to current Top 10, plus instruments, crowds, festivals and atmospherics. Brochure available. Pictures can be researched and sent digitally through website.

Retna Pictures Ltd*

West Complex, Pinewood Studios, Pinewood Road, Iver Heath, Bucks. SL0 0NH
tel (01753) 785450 *fax* (01753) 785451
email ukinfo@retna.com
website www.retna.com

Two libraries: celebrity (early and contemporary music, films and personalities) and lifestyle (people, family life, work, leisure and food). Founded 1984.

Retrograph Nostalgia Archive

Number 10, Hanover Crescent, Brighton BN2 9SB
tel/fax (01273) 687554
email retropix1@aol.com
website www.retrograph.com

Worldwide advertising, packaging, posters, postcards, decorative and fine art illustrations from 1880–1970. Special collections include Victoriana illustrations and scraps (1860–1901), fashion and beauty (1880–1975), RetroTravel Archive: travel and tourism, RetroGourmet Archive: food and drink (1890–1950). Research service and Image Consultancy services; RetroMontages: Victoriana montage design service. Free colour leaflets. Founded 1984.

Rex Features Ltd*
18 Vine Hill, London EC1R 5DZ
tel 020-7278 7294 *fax* 020-7837 4812
email rex@rexfeatures.com
websites www.rexfeatures.com www.timepix.com
Editorial Director Mike Selby, *Library Sales Manager* Glen Marks

International news and features photo agency and picture library serving more than 30 countries, and representing hundreds of photographers. Covers celebrity, news, human interest, pop and showbiz, etc. UK representative of TimePix, the picture archive of Time Inc. which includes the Mansell Collection, the British archive of historical images. Founded 1953.

Richard Welsby Photography
1 Breadalbane Terrace, Edinburgh EH11 2BW
tel/fax 0131-337 9975
email richard.welsby@orkney.com
website www.richardwelsby.com
Contact Richard Welsby

Specialist library of the Orkney Islands: business and industry, scenics, geology, archaeology and historic; wide coverage of flowers, plants and other natural history subjects; aerials. Founded 1984.

Ritmeyer Archaeological Design
114 Turners Avenue, Hawthorndene, Adelaide, SA 5051, Australia
tel (08) 8278 6865
email ritmeyer@adam.com.au
website www.templemountonline.com
Contact Leen and Kathleen Ritmeyer

Colour transparencies of the archaeology of the Holy Land with the emphasis on Jerusalem and the Temple Mount. Architectural reconstruction drawings of ancient sites, such as temples, synagogues, mosques and churches. Special collection of scenes of Jewish temple ritual illustrated on to-scale model of the first century temple in Jerusalem. Drawing commissions undertaken. Founded 1983.

Robert Harding Picture Library*
58-59 Great Marlborough Street, London W1F 7JY
tel 020-7478 4000 *fax* 020-7631 1070
email info@robertharding.com
website www.robertharding.com

Picture library with extensive range of subjects, including rights protected and royalty free, in particular travel, lifestyle, business and industry,

botany, science and medical. Full e-commerce website with over 120,000 searchable images. Free catalogue.

Roundhouse Ornithology Collection
Mathry Hill House, Mathry, Pembrokeshire SA62 5HB
tel/fax (01348) 837008
email John@stewartsmith.fsnet.co.uk
Contact John Stewart-Smith

Colour library specialising in birds of UK, Europe, Middle East (especially), North Africa, Far East and South America. Founded 1991.

Roy J. Westlake ARPS
West Country Photo Library, 31 Redwood Drive, Plympton, Plymouth PL7 2FS
tel/fax (01752) 336444

Specialises in all aspects of Devon, Cornwall, Dorset, Somerset and Wiltshire. Medium format transparencies of landscapes, seascapes, architecture, etc. Other photographers' work not required. Founded 1960.

Royal Collection*
Photographic Services, Windsor Castle, Windsor, Berks. SL4 1NJ
tel (01753) 868286 *fax* (01753) 620046
email photoservices@royalcollection.org.uk
website www.royal.gov.uk
Head of Photographic Services Miss Shruti Patel

Works of art comprising 10,000 pictures, enamels and miniatures, 20,000 drawings, 10,000 watercolours, 500,000 prints and thousands of pieces of furniture, sculpture, glass, porcelain, arms and armour, textiles and jewellery. Available for hire are a wide range of colour transparencies of items in the collection, including works by Van Dyck, Rembrandt, Holbein and Leonardo da Vinci, as well as b&w prints, for purchase. Orders, which should be as specific as possible, must be received in writing and are always treated as urgent.

Royal Geographical Society Picture Library*
1 Kensington Gore, London SW7 2AR
tel 020-7591 3060 *fax* 020-7591 3061
email pictures@rgs.org
website www.rgs.org/picturelibrary
Contact Picture Library Manager

Worldwide coverage of geography, travel, exploration, expeditions and cultural environment from 1870s to the present. Founded 1830.

The Royal Photographic Society
The Octagon, Milsom Street, Bath BA1 1DN
tel (01225) 462841 *fax* (01225) 469880
email sam@collection.rps.org
Contact Sam Johnson

History of photography from 1827 to the present day. Founded 1853.

The Royal Society for Asian Affairs
2 Belgrave Square, London SW1X 8PJ
tel 020-7235 5122 *fax* 020-7259 6771
email info@rsaa.org.uk
website www.rsaa.org.uk
Library of 19th and 20th century books on Asia, mainly central Asia and archive of original 19th and 20th century b&w photos, glass slides, etc of Asia. Publishes *Asian Affairs* (3 p.a.).

Royal Society of Chemistry Library and Information Centre*
Burlington House, Piccadilly, London W1J 0BA
tel 020-7440 3373 *fax* 020-7287 9798
email library@rsc.org
website www.rsc.org
Covers all aspects of chemistry information. Images collection dating from 1538 includes prints and photographs of famous chemists, *Vanity Fair* cartoons, scenes, lantern slides of similar subjects and colour photomicrographs of crystal structures. Founded 1841.

Royalpics – see Stockwave

RSPCA Photolibrary*
RSPCA Trading Ltd, Wilberforce Way, Southwater, Horsham, West Sussex RH13 9RS
tel 0870-754 0150 *fax* 0870-753 0048
email pictures@rspcaphotolibrary.com
website www.rspcaphotolibrary.com
Manager Andrew Forsyth
A comprehensive collection of natural history pictures representing the work of over 400 photographers, including the Wild Images collection. Its files include wild, domestic and farm animals, birds, marine life, veterinary work, animal welfare and environmental issues and a record of the work of the RSPCA. Founded 1993.

Russia and Eastern Images*
Sonning, Cheapside Lane, Denham, Uxbridge, Middlesex UB9 5AE
tel (01895) 833508 *fax* (01895) 831957
email easteuropix@btinternet.com
website www.easteuropix.com
Library Manager Mark Wadlow
Architecture, cities, landscapes, people and travel images covering Russia and the former Soviet Union. Excellent background knowledge available and Russian language spoken. Founded 1988.

S & G Press Agency Ltd
63 Gee Street, London EC1V 3RS
tel 020-7336 0632 *fax* 020-7253 8419

Press photos and vast photo library. Send photos, but negatives preferred.

S. & O. Mathews
Solent Cottage, High Street, Yarmouth, Isle of Wight PO41 0PN
tel (01983) 761983 *fax* (01983) 761982
email oliver@mathews-photography.com
website www.mathews-photography.com
Gardens, plants and landscapes.

Salamander Picture Library – see Chrysalis Images

Sarah Boait Photography and Picture Library
tel/fax (01409) 281354
email sarahboait@compuserve.com
website www.sarahboait.co.uk
Covers the British Isles, especially the West Country and locations from legend and folklore; also world travel, world religions. No contributors' work accepted.

Science Photo Library*
327-9 Harrow Road, London W9 3RB
tel 020-7432 1100 *fax* 020-7286 8668
email info@sciencephoto.com
website www.sciencephoto.com
Subjects include the human body, health and medicine, research, genetics, technology and industry, space exploration and astronomy, earth science, satellite imagery, environment, nature and wildlife and the history of science. Over 100,000 images available online. Founded 1979.

Science & Society Picture Library*
Science Museum, Exhibition Road, London SW7 2DD
tel 020-7942 4400 *fax* 020-7942 4401
email piclib@nmsi.ac.uk
website www.nmsi.ac.uk/piclib/
Subjects include: science and technology, medicine, industry, transport, social documentary and the media. Extensive collection; images drawn from the Science Museum in London, the National Railway Museum in York and the National Museum of Photography, Film and Television in Bradford. Free brochure available. Founded 1993.

Scope Features
26 St Cross Street, London EC1N 8UH
tel 020-7405 2997 *fax* 020-7831 4549
email images@scopefeatues.com
website www.scopefeatues.com
Colour images of personalities, particularly TV personalities. Scope Beauty: colour situations/beauty pictures.

Scotland in Focus Picture Library

Unit 5, Langlee Centre,
Marigold Drive, Galashiels,
Selkirkshire TD1 2LP
tel (01896) 755124 *fax* (01896) 752370
email library@scotfocus.sol.co.uk
website www.scotfocus.com

Specialist library offering thousands of stock images to illustrate every aspect of Scottish life and work.
Scottish Wildlife Library
Environmental and natural history. All Scottish material required on 35mm and upwards, medium format preferred. Photographers must enclose return postage. Terms: 50%. Founded 1988.

SCR Photo Library

Society for Co-operation in Russian and Soviet Studies, 320 Brixton Road, London SW9 6AB
tel 020-7274 2282 *fax* 020-7274 3230
email ruslibrary@scrss.org.uk
website www.scrss.org.uk

Russian and Soviet life and history. Comprehensive coverage of cultural subjects: art, theatre, folk art, costume, music; agriculture and industry, architecture, armed forces, education, history, places, politics, science, sport. Also material on contemporary life in Russia, the CIS and the Baltic states; posters and theatre props, artistic reference, advice. Research by appointment only. Founded 1924.

Seaco Picture Library – see The Illustrated London News Picture Library*

Sealand Aerial Photography Ltd*

Unit 2, Breadbares Barns, Clay Lane, Chichester, West Sussex PO18 8DJ
tel (01243) 576688 *fax* (01243) 575528
email info@sealandaerial.co.uk
website www.sealandaerial.co.uk

Aerial photo coverage of any subject that can be photographed from the air in the UK. Most stock on 2¼in format colour negative/transparency. Subjects constantly updated from new flying. Founded 1976.

Shout Picture Library

Mordene House, Merritts Hill, Illogan, Redruth, Cornwall TR16 4DF
tel (01209) 210525
email john@shoutpictures.com
website www.shoutpictures.com
Contact John Callan

Specialises in the emergency services: fire, police and ambulance. Also hospital, medical and trauma, education. Contact Library for password to the secure website. Commissions accepted. Founded 1994.

Simon Warner

Whitestone Farm, Stanbury, Keighley, West Yorkshire BD22 0JW
tel/fax (01535) 644644
email photos@simonwarner.co.uk
website www.simonwarner.co.uk

Landscape photographer with own stock pictures of northern England, North Wales and Northwest Scotland.

Sites, Sights and Cities

1 Manchester Court, Moreton-in-Marsh, Glos. GL56 0BY
tel/fax (01608) 652829
email paul.dev@tesco.net
Director Paul Devereux

Ancient monuments, mainly in Britain, Egypt, Greece and USA; city features in UK, Europe and USA; general nature shots. Founded 1990.

Skishoot – Offshoot*

Hall Place, Upper Woodcott, Whitchurch, Hants RG28 7PY
tel (01635) 255527 *fax* (01635) 255528
email skishootsnow@aol.com
website www.skishoot.co.uk
Librarians Jo Crossley, Kate Parker

Library specialising in all aspects of skiing and snowboarding. Also France, all year round. Assignments undertaken. Terms: 50%. Founded 1986.

Skyscan Photolibrary*

Oak House, Toddington, Cheltenham, Glos. GL54 5BY
tel (01242) 621357 *fax* (01242) 621343
email info@skyscan.co.uk
website www.skyscan.co.uk

Specialist aerial photolibrary now covering air-to-ground, aviation and aerial sports. Contributing photographers work from planes, helicopters, masts, balloons, gliders and other aerial platforms. Images can be placed in-house on an agency basis or retained by the photographer and requested for use on a brokerage basis; both terms: 50%. Founded 1984.

Snookerimages (Eric Whitehead Photography)

Postal Buildings, Ash Street, Bowness on Windermere, Cumbria LA23 3EB
tel (015394) 48894 *mobile* (07768) 808249
fax (015394) 48294
email eric@snookerimages.co.uk
website www.snookerimages.co.uk
Contact Eric Whitehead

Specialist picture library covering the sport of snooker. Over 20,000 images of all the professional players dating from 1984 to the present day: players away from the table in locations throughout the world as well as action images.

Society for Anglo-Chinese Understanding

Sally & Richard Greenhill Photo Library,
357 Liverpool Road, London N1 1NL
tel 020-7607 8549 *fax* 020-7607 7151
email sr.greenhill@virgin.net

Colour and b&w prints of China, late 1960s–1989.
Founded 1965.

Society for Co-operation in Russian and Soviet Studies – see SCR Photo Library

Sotheby's Picture Library*

34-35 New Bond Street, London W1A 2AA
tel 020-7293 5383 *fax* 020-7293 5062
email piclib.london@sothebys.com
Contact Sue Daly, Researcher

Art and antiques; Cecil Beaton archive of
photographs. Founded 1993.

Spectrum Colour Library

41-42 Berners Street, London W1T 3NB
tel 020-7637 1587 *fax* 020-7637 3681
website www.spectrumcolourlibrary.com

Extensive general library of high-quality
transparencies, for worldwide marketing, including
electronically. Photographer's information pack
available. Purchases photos and collections of
photos.

Sporting Pictures (UK) Ltd*

7A Lambs Conduit Passage,
London WC1R 4RG
tel 020-7405 4500 *fax* 020-7831 7991
email photos@sportingpictures.com
website www.sportingpictures.com
Director Crispin J. Thruston, *Contact* Sue Evans

Specialises in sports, sporting events, sportspersons,
amateur sport.

Steffi Schubert, Wildlife Conservation Collection Photographic Library

Bramble Cottage, Foxhill, St Cross,
South Elmham, Harleston,
Norfolk IP20 0NX
tel/fax (01986) 782279

All aspects of British wildlife and fauna. Founded
1990.

Stephen Benson Slide Bureau

45 Sugden Road, London SW11 5EB
tel 020-7223 8635
email info@avintageoccasion.com

World: agriculture, archaeology, architecture,
commerce, everyday life, culture, environment,
geography, science, tourism. Speciality: South
America, the Caribbean, Australasia, Nepal, Turkey,
Israel and Egypt. Assignments undertaken.

The Still Moving Picture Company*

8 Saxe Coburg Place, Edinburgh EH3 5BR
tel 0131-332 1123 *fax* 0131-332 9123
email info@stillmovingpictures.com
websites www.stillmovingpictures.com
www.stilldigital.co.uk

Over 150,000 pictures of Scotland and all things
Scottish; sport (Allsport agent for Scotland). Online
service via 'stilldigital' website. Founded 1991.

STILL PICTURES The Whole Earth Photo Library*

199 Shooters Hill Road, London SE3 8UL
tel 020-8858 8307 *fax* 020-8858 2049
email info@stillpictures.com
website www.stillpictures.com
Proprietor Mark Edwards

Specialises in people and the environment; the
Third World; nature; wildlife and habitats. Includes
industry, agriculture, indigenous peoples and
cultures, nature and endangered species. Terms:
50%. Founded 1970.

Stockwave

Headquarters Aylesbury office
tel (01296) 747878 *fax* (01296) 748648
email enquiries@stockwave.com
website www.stockwave.com www.royalpics.com

Collections encompassing Britain, Europe and the
world. British events (including social calendar),
social/political news, government, politicians,
industrial, tourism, science and technology, defence,
lifestyle, Royal family, film and stage personalities.
John Blake Picture Library
General topography of England, Europe and the
rest of the world. Landscapes, architecture,
churches, gardens, countryside, towns and villages.
Horse trials covered including Badminton and
Gatcombe Park.
COI Photo Library
Includes many important and previously unseen
images of Britain's government, political events,
interior views of the Houses of Parliament and 10
Downing Street, etc, British Royal archives, Festival
of Britain, industrial and manufacturing archives,
agriculture, education, defence.
Northern Picture Library
Northern England scenery; cities of Northern
England and Scotland; architecture and industrial
scenes of Northern England past and present.
Royalpics
Dedicated site for Royal pictures from Stockwave,
COI Archives and other major photo libraries.

Sue Cunningham Photographic*

56 Chatham Road, Kingston-upon-Thames,
Surrey KT1 3AA
tel 020-8541 3024 *fax* 020-8541 5388
email pictures@scphotographic.com

website www.scphotographic.com
International coverage on many subjects: Latin
America, Africa and Eastern Europe. Also Western
Europe, London (including aerial).

Survival Anglia Photo Library – see OSF Ltd, Photo Library

Sutcliffe Gallery
1 Flowergate, Whitby, North Yorkshire YO21 3BA
tel (01947) 602239 *fax* (01947) 820287
email photographs@sutcliffe-gallery.fsnet.co.uk
website www.sutcliffe-gallery.co.uk
Collection of 19th century photography, all by Frank
M. Sutcliffe Hon FRPS (1853–1941), especially
inshore fishing boats and fishing community; also
farming interests. Period covered 1872–1910.

Sylvia Cordaiy Photo Library*
45 Rotherstone, Devizes, Wilts. SN10 2DD
tel (01380) 728327 *fax* (01380) 728328
email info@sylvia-cordaiy.com
website www.sylvia-cordaiy.com
Worldwide travel and architecture, global
environmental topics, wildlife and domestic
animals, veterinary, comprehensive UK files, Paul
Kaye b&w archive. Terms: 50%. Founded 1990.

Sylvia Pitcher Photo Library
75 Bristol Road, London E7 8HG
tel/fax 020-8552 8308
email SPphotolibrary@aol.com
Musicians: blues, jazz, old-time country and
bluegrass, cajun and zydeco, soul and gospel, pop
(1960s and 1970s), plus related ephemera. Views
and details of the USA: countryside, 'small-town
America', shacks, railroads, rural Americana.
Archival: early 20th century – mainly cottonfields,
riverboats and various cities in the USA.
1960s–1970s: girls (both white and black) and
couples. Founded 1968.

Syndication International – see Mirrorpix

The Tank Museum Archive & Reference Library
The Tank Museum, Bovington, Dorset BH20 6JG
tel (01929) 462398 *fax* (01929) 462410
email librarian@tankmuseum.co.uk
website www.tankmuseum.co.uk
International collection, from 1900 to present, of
armoured fighting vehicles and military transport,
including tanks, armoured cars, personnel carriers,
cars, lorries and tractors, First and Second World
War Royal Armoured Corps War Diaries and
associated documents.

Telegraph Colour Library – incorporated into Getty Images

Theatre Museum
National Museum of the Performing Arts,
1E Tavistock Street, London WC2E 7PA
tel 020-7943 4700 *fax* 020-7943 4777
website http://theatremuseum.org
In addition to extensive public displays on live
entertainment and education programme, the
Museum has an unrivalled collection of
programmes, playbills, prints, photos, videos, texts
and press cuttings relating to performers and
productions from the 17th century onwards.
Available by appointment (book 3 weeks in
advance), free of charge through the Study Room.
Open Wed–Fri 10.30am–4.30pm. Reprographic
services available.

Thomas Cook Archives
19-21 Coningsby Road, Peterborough PE3 8SB
tel (01733) 402025 *fax* (01733) 402026
email paul.smith@thomascook.com
Company Archivist Paul Smith
History of travel and tourism in the late 19th and
early 20th centuries: posters, photos, brochure
covers (1851–1960). Founded 1999.

Tibet Pictures*
28 Sheen Common Drive, Richmond,
Surrey TW10 5BN
tel/fax 020-7602 1989
Contact Jonathan Miller
Specialises in the people, architecture, history,
religion and politics of Tibet. Also Yemen. Colour
and b&w. Founded 1992.

Tim Graham Picture Library
31 Ferncroft Avenue, London NW3 7PG
tel 020-7435 7693 *fax* 020-7431 4312
email mail@timgraham.co.uk
Royal Family in this country and on tours;
background pictures on royal homes, staff, hobbies,
sports, cars, etc; English and foreign country scenes;
international Heads of State, VIPs and celebrities.
Founded 1978.

Tim Woodcock
59 Stoodham, South Petherton,
Somerset TA13 5AS
tel (01460) 242788
email tim@timwoodcock.co.uk
website www.timwoodcock.co.uk
British and Eire landscape, seascape, architecture
and heritage; children, parenthood, adults and
education; gardens and containers; mountain
biking. Location commissions undertaken. Terms:
50%. Founded 1983.

Tony Stone Images – see Getty Images

Topham Picturepoint*

PO Box 33, Edenbridge, Kent TN8 5PB
tel (01732) 863939 *fax* (01732) 860215
email admin@topfoto.co.uk
website www.topfoto.co.uk

Eight million contemporary and historical images.
Delivery online if requested. New photographers –
sample submission of 50 transparencies; 5-year
contract, 50% commission.

Transworld/Scope – see Scope Features

Travel Ink Photo & Feature Library*

The Old Coach House, 14 High Street,
Goring-on-Thames, Nr Reading,
Berks. RG8 9AR
tel (01491) 873011 *fax* (01491) 875558
email info@travel-ink.co.uk
website www.travel-ink.co.uk

Travel, tourism and lifestyles covering around 150
countries – including the UK. Specialist sections
include Hong Kong (including construction of the
Tsing Ma Bridge), North Wales and Greece.
Founded 1988.

Travel Photo International

9 Halsall Green, Wirral CH63 9NA
tel/fax 0151-334 2300

Touristic interest including scenery, towns,
monuments, historic buildings, archaeological sites,
local people. Specialises in travel brochures and
books. Terms: 50%.

TRH Pictures

Bradley's Close, 74-77 White Lion Street,
London N1 9PF
tel 020-7520 7647 *fax* 020-7520 7606
email trh@trhpictures.co.uk
website www.trhpictures.co.uk
Director Ted Nevill

Specialises in colour transparencies and b&w
photos of the history of civil and military aviation,
modern warfare from the American Civil War,
transport on land and sea, and the exploration of
space. Commission: 50%. Founded 1983.

Tropix Photo Library*

156 Meols Parade, Meols, Wirral CH47 6AN
tel/fax 0151-632 1698
email tropixphoto@talk21.com
website www.tropix.co.uk

All aspects of tropics, sub-tropics and non-tropical
developing countries. Plus MerseySlides: photos of
Liverpool. Positive, progressive and model-released
images. Preliminary enquiry in writing essential,
preferably by email. Visit website for full submission
guidelines. No unsolicited material. Terms: 50%.
Founded 1982.

True North Picture Source

26 New Road, Hebden Bridge,
West Yorkshire HX7 8EF
tel (01422) 845532
email john@trunorth.demon.co.uk
Proprietor John Morrison

The life and landscape of the North of England. No
other photographers' work required. 30,000
transparencies (35mm and medium format).
Commissions undertaken. Founded 1992.

Ulster Folk & Transport Museum – see National Museums & Galleries of Northern Ireland, Ulster Folk & Transport Museum

Universal Pictorial Press & Agency (UPPA)

29-31 Saffron Hill, London EC1N 8SW
tel 020-7421 6000 *fax* 020-7421 6006
email charles.taylor@photoshot.com
website www.uppa.co.uk

Photo library containing notable Royal, political,
company, academic, legal, diplomatic, church,
military, pop, arts, entertainment and sports
personalities and well-known views and buildings.
Commercial, industrial, corporate and public
relations photo assignments undertaken. Founded
1929.

V&A Images*

Victoria & Albert Museum, Cromwell Road,
London SW7 2RL
tel 020-7942 2483/6/9 *fax* 020-7942 2482
email vanda.images@vam.ac.uk
website www.vandaimages.com

A vast collection of photographs from the world's
largest museum of decorative and applied arts,
reflecting culture and lifestyle spanning over 1000
years of history to the present time. Digital delivery
or large format transparencies of contemporary and
historical textiles, costumes and fashions, ceramics,
furniture, metalwork, glass, sculpture, toys and
games, design and photographs from around the
world. Unique photos include 1960s fashion by
John French, Harry Hammond's behind-the-scenes
pop idols, Houston Rogers' theatrical world of the
1930s–70s, images of royalty by Lafayette, and
images by Cecil Beaton and 19th century pioneer
photographers. Images from the inexhaustible
shelves of the National Art Library and Library of
Art & Design, and from the Theatre Museum and
Museum of Childhood are readily available.

Venice Picture Library*

(formerly Archivio Veneziano)
c/o The Bridgeman Art Library,
17-19 Garway Road, London W2 4PH
tel 020-7727 4065 *fax* 020-7792 8509
email london@bridgeman.co.uk

website www.bridgeman.co.uk
Contact Jenny Page

Specialises in Venice, covering most aspects of the city, islands and lagoon, especially architecture and the environment. Founded 1990.

Vidocq Photo Library
162 Burwell Meadow, Witney, Oxon OX28 5JJ
tel/fax (01993) 778518
email vidocq@which.net
website www.vidocq/languages.co.uk

Specialist in photographs for language and educational text books. Detailed coverage of France. Assignments undertaken. Founded 1983.

Visions in Golf
Noblethorpe Hall, Silkstone, Barnsley,
South Yorkshire S75 4NG
tel (01226) 791001 *fax* (0870) 831 1941
email mark@visionsingolf.freeserve.co.uk
Proprietor Mark Newcombe

Every aspect of worldwide golf, including an archive dating back to the late 19th century and world-famous golf courses. Over 250,000 colour transparencies and 5000 b&w images. Commission: 50%. Founded 1984.

Waterways Photo Library*
39 Manor Court Road, London W7 3EJ
tel 020-8840 1659 *fax* 020-8567 0605
email watphot39@aol.com
website www.waterwaysphotolibrary.com
Contact Derek Pratt

British inland waterways; canals, rivers; bridges, aqueducts, locks and all waterside architectural features; watersports; waterway holidays, boats, fishing; town and countryside scenes. No other photographers' work required. Founded 1976.

The Weimar Archive – see Mary Evans Picture Library

Welfare History Picture Library
Heatherbank Museum of Social Work, Caledonian University, Cowcaddens Road, Glasgow G4 0BA
tel 0141-331 8637 *fax* 0141-331 3005
email a.ramage@gcal.ac.uk
website www.lib.gcal.ac.uk/heatherbank/

Social history and social work, especially child welfare, poorhouses, prisons, hospitals, slum clearance, women's movement, social reformers and their work. Catalogue on request and on website. Founded 1975.

Wellcome Photo Library*
210 Euston Road, London NW1 2BE
fax 020-7611 8348 fax 020-7611 8577
email photolib@wellcome.ac.uk

website http://medphoto.wellcome.ac.uk
Library Manager Catherine Draycott

Leading source of images on the history of medicine, modern biomedical science and clinical medicine.

Werner Forman Archive*
36 Camden Square, London NW1 9XA
tel 020-7267 1034 *fax* 020-7267 6026
email wfa@btinternet.com
website www.werner-forman-archive.com

Art, architecture, archaeology, history and peoples of ancient, oriental and primitive cultures. Founded 1975.

Westcountry Pictures
10 Headon Gardens, Countess Wear, Exeter,
Devon EX2 6LE
tel (01392) 426640 *fax* (01392) 209080
email peter@cooperphotography.co.uk
website www.westcountrypictures.co.uk
Contact Peter Cooper

All aspects of Devon and Cornwall – culture, places, industry and leisure. Founded 1989.

Western Americana Picture Library
3 Barton Buildings, Bath BA1 2JR
tel (01225) 334213 *fax* (01225) 480554

Prints, engravings, photos and colour transparencies on the American West, cowboys, gunfighters, Indians, including pictures by Frederic Remington and Charles Russell, etc.

Wilderness Photographic Library*
Mill Barn, Broad Raine, Sedbergh,
Cumbria LA10 5ED
tel (015396) 20196 *fax* (015396) 21293
email wildernessphoto@bt.internet.com
Director John Noble FRGS

Specialist library in mountain and wilderness regions, especially polar. Associated aspects of people, places, natural history, geographical features, exploration and mountaineering, adventure sports, travel.

Wildlife Matters Photographic Library
Marlham, Henley's Down, Battle,
East Sussex TN33 9BN
tel (01424) 830566 *fax* (01424) 830224
email gardens@gmpix.com
website www.gmpix.com
Contact Dr John Feltwell

Ecology, conservation and environment; habitats and pollution; agriculture and horticulture; general natural history, entomology; Mediterranean wildlife; rainforests (Amazon, Central America, Costa Rica and Indonesia); aerial pics of countryside UK, Europe, USA. Founded 1980.

Windrush Photos*
99 Noah's Ark, Kemsing, Sevenoaks, Kent TN15 6PD
tel (01732) 763486 *fax* (01732) 763285
email dt@windrushphotos.demon.co.uk
Owner David Tipling

Worldwide wildlife and landscapes; birds a
speciality. Captioning and text services;
ornithological consultancy. Photographic and
features commissions undertaken. Terms: 50%.
Founded 1991.

Woodmansterne Publications Ltd*
1 The Boulevard, Blackmoor Lane, Watford,
Herts. WD18 8UW
tel (01923) 200600 *fax* (01923) 200601
email johanna@woodmansterne.co.uk

Britain, Europe, Holy Land; architecture, cathedral
and stately home interiors; general art subjects;
museum collections; volcanoes, transport, Space;
opera and ballet; major state occasions; British
heritage, contemporary artists.

World Pictures*
(formerly Feature-Pix Colour Library)
25 Gosfield Street, London W1W 6HQ
tel 020-7437 2121/436 0440 *fax* 020-7439 1307
email worldpictures@btinternet.com
website www.worldpictures.co.uk
Directors David Brenes, Carlo Irek

Over 600,000 medium and large format colour
transparencies aimed at travel and travel-related
markets. Extensive coverage of cities, countries and
specific resort areas, together with material of an
emotive nature, i.e. children, couples and families
on holiday, all types of winter and summer sporting
activities, motoring abroad, etc. Terms: 50%; major
contributing photographers 60%.

World Religions Photo Library*
53A Crimsworth Road, London SW8 4RJ
Tel/fax 020-7720 6951
email copix@clara.co.uk co@worldreligions.co.uk
website www.worldreligions.co.uk
www.middleeastpictures.com

Specialist stock on religions from more than 50
countries: major faiths, places of worship, rites of
passage, shrines, pilgrimage, sacred foods, culture
and ecclesiastical buildings – temples, churches,
mosques, etc. Also stocks the developing world:
Middle East/Arab States, North Africa, Central

Asian Republics, South Asia and Indian Ocean,
Southeast Asia, Pacific/Australia. Major files on
travel, crafts, agriculture, food, people. Member of
the British Guild of Travel Writers. Specialises in
illustrated editorial features. Welcomes submissions
from photographers covering any of these subjects.
The library is managed by Christine Osborne
Pictures (also proprietor of Middle East Pictures).

Yemen Pictures
Flat 2, Auriol Mansions, Edith Road,
London W14 0ST
tel/fax 020-7602 1989
Contact John Miles

Specialist colour library of Yemen, covering all
aspects of culture, people, architecture, dance, qat
and music. Also Africa, Australia, Middle East and
Asia. Founded 1995.

York Archaeological Trust Picture Library
Cromwell House, 13 Ogleforth,
York YO1 7FG
tel (01904) 663000 *fax* (01904) 663024
email ckyriacou@yorkarchaeology.co.uk
website www.yorkarchaeology.co.uk
Picture Librarian C. Kyriacou

York archaeology covering Romans, Dark Ages,
Vikings and Middle Ages; traditional crafts; scenes
of York and Yorkshire. Founded 1987.

Yorkshire Now!
4 Keelham Place, Denholme, Bradford,
West Yorks. BD13 4HL
tel/fax (01274) 831652
email rose@xelex.freeserve.co.uk
Proprietors Melvyn Strelitze, Rose White

B&w and colour images and videos of towns, cities,
industries, etc in Yorkshire. Commissions
undertaken. Founded 1998.

Zoological Society of London*
Regent's Park, London NW1 4RY
tel 020-7449 6293 *fax* 020-7586 5743
email library@zsl.org
website www.zsl.org
Librarian Ann Sylph

Archive collection of photographs, paintings and
prints, from the 16th century onwards, covering
almost all vertebrate animals, many now extinct or
rare, plus invertebrates. Founded 1826.

Card and stationery publishers which accept photographs

Before submitting work, photographers are advised to ascertain requirements, including terms and conditions. Only top quality material should be submitted; inferior work is never accepted. Postage for return of material should be enclosed.

*Member of the Greeting Card Association

Britannia Products Ltd
Dawson Lane, Dudley Hill, Bradford,
West Yorkshire BD4 6HW
tel (01274) 784200 *fax* (01274) 651218
Managing Director Steve McNally
Designs and manufactures greetings cards, giftwrap and calendars. Submit transparencies (5 x 4in). Brands: Fine Art Graphics, Paws for Thought, The Comedy Club, Just Kiddin', Academy, Mother Earth, Animates, Fleurs, Truffles. Division of Hallmark Cards (Holdings) Ltd. Founded 1980.

Card Connection Ltd*
Park House, South Street, Farnham, Surrey GU9 7QQ
tel (01252) 892300 *fax* (01252) 892363
email ho@cardconnection.co.uk
website www.card-connection.co.uk
Managing Director Adrian Atkinson, *Senior Product and Marketing Manager* Alison Mahoney
Cute, humour, traditional, floral, contemporary, photography. Submit colour copies or 5 x 4in transparencies of originals. Humour and sentimental verse. Founded 1992.

Caspari Ltd*
9 Shire Hill, Saffron Walden, Essex CB11 3AP
tel (01799) 513010 *fax* (01799) 513101
Managing Director Keith Entwisle
Traditional fine art/classic images; 5 x 4in transparencies. No verses. Founded 1990.

Chapter and Verse (International) Ltd
Granta House, 96 High Street, Linton,
Cambs. CB1 6JT
tel (01223) 891951 *fax* (01223) 894137
email sales@chapter-and-verse.sagehost.co.uk
Buildings, animals, flowers, scenic, or domestic subjects in series, suitable for greetings cards and postcards. All sizes of transparency. No verses. Founded 1981.

Hallmark Cards Plc*
Hallmark House, Bingley Road,
West Yorkshire BD9 8SD

email 1willi2@hallmark-uk.com
Submissions Mr Richmond Denton
All subjects suitable for greetings cards considered.

J. Salmon Ltd
100 London Road, Sevenoaks, Kent TN13 1BB
tel (01732) 452381 *fax* (01732) 450951
Picture postcards, calendars and local view booklets.

Nigel Quiney Publications Ltd
Cloudesley House, Shire Hill, Saffron Walden,
Essex CB11 3FB
tel (01799) 520200 *fax* (01799) 520100
website www.nigelquiney.com
Contact Ms J. Arkinstall, Product & Marketing Director
Everyday and seasonal greetings cards and giftwrap including fine art, photographic, humour, fun art, contemporary and cute. Submit colour copies, photographs or transparencies: no original artwork.

Pineapple Park
58 Wilbury Way, Hitchin,
Herts. SG4 0TP
tel (01462) 442021 *fax* (01462) 440418
email info@pineapplepark.co.uk
website www.pineapplepark.co.uk
Directors Peter M. Cockerline, Sarah H. Parker
Illustrations and photographs for publication as greetings cards. Contemporary, cute, humour: submit artwork or laser copies with sae. Photographic florals always needed. Humour copy/jokes accepted without artwork. Also concepts for ranges. Founded 1993.

Santoro Graphics Ltd
Rotunda Point, 11 Hartfield Crescent,
London SW19 3RL
tel 020-8781 110 *fax* 020-8781 1101
email enquiries@santorographics.com
website www.santorographics.com
Directors L. Santoro, M. Santoro
Publishers of innovative and award-winning designs

for greetings cards, giftwrap and gift stationery. Bold contemporary images with an international appeal. Subjects covered: b&w, colour floral, quirky and humorous, whimsical, 'Fifties, 'Seventies, futuristic! All formats accepted in both b&w and colour; transparencies ideally 5 x 4in but will accept 35mm. Founded 1985.

Scandecor Ltd

3 The Ermine Centre, Hurricane Close, Huntingdon, Cambs. PE29 6WY
tel (01480) 456395 *fax* (01480) 456269
email mail@scandecor-ltd.co.uk
Managing Director Derek Shirley

Transparencies all sizes. Founded 1967.

The picture research revolution

Julian Jackson describes how picture researchers have had to change the way they work since entering the 'digital age'.

Picture researchers find the images you see in books, magazines, on television shows and videos, and now on CD-Roms and the internet. For many years picture research was a relatively static profession. The procedures for contacting picture suppliers didn't change very much. The researcher would phone or fax a supplier with a request then a package of transparencies or prints would arrive in the post. Since entering the 'digital age' this has changed dramatically. Now picture researchers need to learn new skills in addition to the old ones. They need considerable internet search competencies. They also need enough technological knowledge to check that digital files are of sufficient quality for their use, which may be for a much wider variety of media. In an era of rapid technological change they need to keep an eye out for developments such as new file formats or software.

Courses and training

London School of Publishing
David Game House, 69 Notting Hill Gate, London W11 3JS
tel 020-7221 3399 fax 020-7243 1730
email lsp@easynet.co.uk
website www.publishing-school.co.uk
A 10-week evening course suitable for anyone wanting to pursue a career in picture research.

The Publishing Training Centre at Book House
45 East Hill, London SW18 2QZ
tel 020-8874 2718 fax 020-8870 8985
email publishing.training@bookhouse.co.uk
website www.train4publishing.co.uk
One-day picture research course suitable for those already working in publishing, aimed at those who already have some picture research experience. Also offers Picture Research by Distance Learning, a comprehensive course for home study.

Traditional picture research

There are two sorts of researchers: freelances, and salaried staff, sometimes called 'in-house' researchers. The way they both approach a job is the same. Generally most picture research assignments follow this pattern:
1. Briefing and creation of picture list.
2. The picture researcher contacts picture libraries, press agencies, photographers, museums, galleries or other picture sources, by phone, fax, email or personal visit.
3. Photography is commissioned, if appropriate.
4. Pictures arrive and are 'booked in'.
5. A preliminary selection is made, usually by the picture researcher, designer and editor working in concert.
6. Rejected pictures are returned to the library.
7. A final selection is made.
8. The picture researcher negotiates the fees, creates a list of contributors to be credited, and checks the proofs.
9. The picture researcher returns all the remaining unused pictures, and those used when they return from the printers or other production organisations.
10. The picture researcher keeps records and sends complementary copies or

'tearsheets' (the page that the supplier's picture was used on) to the various suppliers of the pictures.

This is a broad view of how all picture research assignments work, whether for traditional media such as books, or new media like CD-Roms. In some cases there might already be a fee structure in place so the researcher does not have to do fee negotiation.

Skills required

Picture researchers need to be organised, diligent, capable of leaps of the imagination when necessary ("I bet there's a museum devoted to shopping bags somewhere!"), and above all *diplomatic*. They need the ability to wheedle images out of sometimes unresponsive people: professional image libraries pride themselves on swift, efficient service, but picture researchers have to deal with museum staff, private collectors, individual photographers, PR people, and the odd complete nutter who just happens to own the rights to *the picture you must have*. Of all the skills necessary, this is the most vital.

A good picture researcher also needs diligence and good organisation. Diligence means keeping tabs on the pictures so they do not get lost. Though theoretically this isn't difficult, with large amounts of material and perhaps over-eager designers who take pictures from the files without telling you, transparencies do get lost. It isn't even necessary to lose the transparency: taking one out of its mount to scan, then losing the mount is often enough to mean hours of searching through delivery notes in order to track down which library it came from.

Though this is not often evident to outsiders, pictures are *valuable*. If a photographer has trekked to the Grand Canyon at dawn, and you lose the original, that picture is gone forever. A £400 replacement fee is not really too much in that particular case but some loss fees are much higher. While the occasional picture may go astray, the more a picture researcher keeps control over the situation, the fewer catastrophes will happen. For example, only give the designers selected images and keep the 'rejects', and note which images they have retained.

If you are a freelance and working from home there could be significant costs if you lose some pictures, so you need to take a careful look at your house contents insurance to see if that eventuality is covered. Once you deliver material to the client, then their insurance should cover it, but this is a point to note.

Useful directories

Picture Researcher's Handbook
by Hilary and Mary Evans, 7th edn, Pira

No picture researcher should be without this invaluable and comprehensive source of picture libraries worldwide. The book clearly lists where picture libraries are, the subjects they cover and addresses, websites, email addresses, telephone and fax numbers.

BAPLA Directory
BAPLA, 18 Vine Hill, London EC1R 5DZ
tel 020-7713 1780 *fax* 020-7713 1211

Lists all the current members of the British Association of Picture Libraries and Agencies (BAPLA).

Picture Research in a Digital Age
by Julian Jackson
website www.julianjackson.co.uk/pic_res_dig.htm

This e-book covers digital photography, scanning, searching the internet, and many other important topics to enable researchers to get the best out of the digital age. It is available online, and can be downloaded immediately.

Useful organisations

The Association of Photographers
See page 447.

BAPLA (British Association of Picture Libraries and Agencies)
See page 448.

DACS (The Design and Artists Copyright Society)
See page 623.

The Picture Research Association
See page 471.

The digital wave

Digitisation of files and the advent of the internet in general has caused a revolution in picture research. Agonised waits for a package of transparencies to arrive from Inner Mongolia are a thing of the past; now pictures can be sent by ISDN in seconds. Commissioning a photographer is streamlined when you can look at his or her portfolio online. Email is particularly convenient for dealing with suppliers in different time zones.

Like the famous 'butterfly' chaos theory, digitisation has caused a tornado which is roaring through the industry. Deadlines are shorter, leaving less time for considered decisions. Unlike transparencies, digital files can be unusable for a variety of invisible factors: for example, bad scanning, wrong resolution, corruption. These problems usually become evident at the last possible moment. Old-style picture researchers would have rejected a bad transparency or print at an early stage so these problems would have been avoided.

In recent years, picture researchers have had to learn powerful computer search skills and develop understandings of many technological concepts. For some this has been a difficult process that has lessened the enjoyment of the job. Unfortunately, one of the spin-offs from digitisation has been that employers may mistakenly believe that a researcher can do his or her job from behind a computer. However, it is estimated that only 3–5% of the pictures of major collections are currently digitised. The personal visit to a source to find images, and forge a relationship with the people there – often experts in their subject – is still an essential part of the job.

Old style *v.* digital

There are advantages and disadvantages to both ways of working. Most picture researchers will continue to handle prints and transparencies in the conventional manner alongside downloading, modifying, and transmitting digital files from their computer.

● One distinct advantage of digital files is that they can be instantly downloaded from the web or sent via ISDN, ADSL or other means.

● Working with digital files means that there are no time-consuming and tedious returns to do.

● Analogue media – prints, negatives and transparencies – can be immediately assessed for quality. To assess the quality of a digital file, further investigation is required.

● Intricate keywording systems often fail to find pictures which the library holds. Phoning the library's experienced staff may well be a better use of your time than spending hours wrestling with an online search system.

- Sometimes it is hard to keep track of digital files on a computer system, especially if the file name is just a number, as opposed to a descriptive name, such as 'Picture of Paris.jpg'.
- Negotiating fees remains the same. It is what the picture is *used* for, not whether it is analogue or digital, that is the main criterion.

Picture research now

Picture research has changed. Old-style methods of receiving transparencies in the post and viewing them on a lightbox are still valid, but the speed and convenience of digital files means that online picture research is becoming more and more of a necessity for researchers. Modern researchers need high levels of computer search skills to enable them to find the pictures they want, whether it's by searching the web generally, or accessing the online search systems of picture libraries.

Julian Jackson is a writer, internet expert and consultant to the UK picture research industry. He has close links with many companies and organisations within the photographic industry. His website is www.julianjackson.co.uk

Societies, prizes and festivals

Societies, associations and clubs

The societies, associations and clubs listed here will be of interest to both writers and artists. They include appreciation societies devoted to specific authors, professional bodies and national institutions. Some also offer prizes and awards (see page 493).

Academi (Welsh Academy)

Main Office 3rd Floor, Mount Stuart House, Mount Stuart Square, Cardiff CF10 5FQ
tel 029-2047 2266 *fax* 029-2049 2930
email post@academi.org
website www.academi.org
North West Wales Office Ty Newydd, Llanystumdwy, Criccieth, Gwynedd LL52 0LW
tel (01766) 522817 *fax* (01766) 523095
email academi.gog@dial.pipex.com
South West Wales Office Dylan Thomas Centre, Somerset Place, Swansea SA1 1RR
tel (01792) 463980 *fax* (01792) 463993
email academi.dylan.thomas@business.ntl.com
Chief Executive Peter Finch
Membership Associate: £15 p.a. (waged), £7.50 (unwaged)

Academi is the trading name of Yr Academi Gymreig, the Welsh National Literature Promotion Agency and Society of Writers. With funds mostly provided from public sources, it has been constitutionally independent since 1978. It runs courses, competitions (including the Cardiff International Poetry Competition), conferences, tours by authors, festivals and represents the interests of Welsh writers and Welsh writing both inside Wales and beyond. Its publications include *Taliesin* (3 p.a.), a literary journal in the Welsh language; *A470* (bi-monthly), a literature information magazine; *The Oxford Companion to the Literature of Wales*, *The Welsh Academy English–Welsh Dictionary*, and a variety of translated works.

In 1998 Academi took on a much enlarged role when it won the Arts Council of Wales's franchise to administer a range of schemes including Writers on Tour, Writers Residencies and Writing Squads for young people. It promotes an annual literary festival and runs a dedicated programme of literary activity. In addition, the Academi is in receipt of a lottery grant to publish the first *Encyclopaedia of Wales*. From 2003 Academi is also responsible for a range of services to writers in Wales including bursaries, critical advice, mentoring and the annual Book of the Year Award. Founded 1959.

Academic Writers Group – see The Society of Authors, page 487

Alliance of Literary Societies

Secretary Rosemary Culley, 22 Belmont Grove, Havant, Hants PO9 3PU
tel 023-9247 5855 *fax* (0870) 056 0330
email rosemary@sndc.demon.co.uk
website www.sndc.demon.co.uk
Open Book, Greta, Sandford Avenue, Church Stretton, Shropshire SY6 7AB
tel (01694) 722821
Editor Thelma Thompson
Membership Scale of charges depending on the size of the society

Membership comprises 100+ affiliated literary societies. Aims to act as a valuable liaison body between member societies as a means of sharing knowledge, skills and expertise, and may also act as a pressure group when necessary. The Alliance can assist in the preservation of buildings, places and objects having literary associations. Produces 2 newsletters a year, plus a literary magazine *Open Book* and a handbook.

American Society of Composers, Authors and Publishers

One Lincoln Plaza, New York, NY 10023, USA
tel 212-621-6000 *fax* 212-874 8480
President and Chairman Marilyn Bergman

American Society of Indexers (ASI)

10200 West 44th Avenue, Suite 304, Wheat Ridge, CO 80033, USA
tel 303-463-2887 *fax* 303-422-8894
email info@asindexing.org
website www.asindexing.org

Aims to increase awareness of the value of high-quality indexes and indexing; offer members access to educational resources that enable them to strengthen their indexing performance; keep members up to date on indexing technology; defend and safeguard the professional interests of indexers.

Angela Thirkell Society
Chairman Mrs I.J. Cox, 32 Murvagh Close,
Cheltenham, Glos. GL53 7QY
tel (01242) 251604
email penny.aldred@tesco.net
website www.angelathirkell.org/atuk.htm
Secretary Mrs P. Aldred, 54 Belmont Park,
London SE13 5BN
tel 020-8244 9339
Membership £7 p.a.; £10 from 2004

Aims 'to honour the memory of Angela Thirkell
(1890–1960) as a writer, and to make her works
available to new generations'. Publishes an *Annual
Journal*, and encourages Thirkell studies. Founded
1980.

The Arnold Bennett Society
Secretary Jean Potter, 106 Scotia Road, Burslem,
Stoke-on-Trent ST6 4ET
tel (01782) 816311
Membership £7 p.a. individuals, £9 p.a. family (plus
£2 if living outside EC)

Aims to promote the study and appreciation of the
life, works and times not only of Arnold Bennett
(1867–1931) himself, but also of other provincial
writers with particular relationship to North
Staffordshire.

The Arthur Conan Doyle Society
Organisers Christopher and Barbara Roden,
PO Box 1360, Ashcroft, B.C., Canada V0K 1A0
tel 250-453-2045 *fax* 250-453-2075
email ashtree@ash-tree.bc.ca
website www.ash-tree.bc.ca/acdsocy.html
Membership £16 p.a. (airmail extra)

Promotes the study of the life and works of Sir
Arthur Conan Doyle. Publishes *ACD* journal
(bi-annual) and occasional reprints of Conan Doyle
material. Occasional conventions. Founded 1989.

Artists Association of Ireland
43 Temple Bar, Dublin 2, Republic of Ireland
tel (01) 8740529 *fax* (01) 6771585
email info@artistsireland.com
website www.artistsireland.com
Contact Administrator
Membership £45 p.a.

Information and advice resource for professional
visual artists in Ireland. Publishes *Art Bulletin*
(6 p.a.), available on subscription. Founded 1981.

Arts Club
40 Dover Street, London W1S 4NP
tel 020-7499 8581 *fax* 020-7409 0913
website www.theartsclub.co.uk
Club Secretary Peter Kerrlish

For all those connected with or interested in the
arts, literature and science. Founded 1863.

Arts Council England
14 Great Peter Street, London SW1P 3NQ
tel (0845) 300 6200 *textphone* 020-7973 6564
fax 020-7973 6590
email enquiries@artscouncil.org.uk
website www.artscouncil.org.uk

Arts Council England is the national development
agency for the arts in England, distributing public
money from Government and the National Lottery.
The Council believes in the transforming power of
the arts – power to change the lives of people
throughout the country. Its ambition is to place the
arts at the heart of national life, reflecting the
country's rich and diverse cultural identity. The
Council wants people throughout England to
experience arts activities of the highest quality. It
believes that access to the arts goes hand-in-hand
with excellence.

Grants for the Arts, the new funding programme,
is available to individuals, organisations and
national touring companies.

Arts Council England has 9 regional offices
throughout England that distribute funding and
promote the arts within their region.

East
Eden House, 48-49 Bateman Street,
Cambridge CB2 1LR
tel (01223) 454400 *fax* (0870) 242 1271
email east@artscouncil.org.uk
textphone (01223) 306893

East Midlands
St Nicholas Court, 25-27 Castle Gate,
Nottingham NG1 7AR
tel 0115-989 7520 *fax* 0115-950 2467
email eastmidlands@artscouncil.org.uk

London
2 Pear Tree Court, London EC1R 0DS
tel 020-7608 6100 *fax* 020-7608 4100
email london@artscouncil.org.uk
textphone 020-7608 4101

North East
Central Square, Forth Street,
Newcastle upon Tyne NE1 3PJ
tel 0191-255 8500 *fax* 0191-230 1020
email northeast@artscouncil.org.uk
textphone 0191-255 8500

North West
Manchester House, 22 Bridge Street,
Manchester M3 3AB
tel 0161-834 6644 *fax* 0161-834 6969
email northwest@artscouncil.org.uk
textphone 0161-834 9131

South East
Sovereign House, Church Street, Brighton BN1 1RA
tel (01273) 763000 *fax* (0870) 2421257
email southeast@artscouncil.org.uk
textphone (01273) 710659

South West
Bradninch Place, Gandy Street, Exeter EX4 3LS
tel (01392) 218188 *fax* (01392) 229229
email southwest@artscouncil.org.uk
textphone (01392) 433503

West Midlands
82 Granville Street, Birmingham B1 2LH
tel 0121-631 3121 *fax* 0121-643 7239
email westmidlands@artscouncil.org.uk
textphone 0121-643 2815

Yorkshire
21 Bond Street, Dewsbury,
West Yorkshire WF13 1AX
tel (01924) 455555 *fax* (01924) 466522
email yorkshire@artscouncil.org.uk
textphone (01924) 438585

The Arts Council/An Chomhairle Ealaíon
Literature Officer, 70 Merrion Square, Dublin 2,
Republic of Ireland
tel (01) 6180200 *fax* (01) 6761302
website www.artscouncil.ie
Literature Officer Sinéad MacAodha, *Visual Arts
Officer* Oliver Dowling

The national development agency for the arts in
Ireland. Founded 1951.

Arts Council of Northern Ireland
MacNeice House, 77 Malone Road,
Belfast BT9 6AQ
tel 028-9038 5200 *fax* 028-90661715
website www.artscouncil-ni.org
Chief Executive Roisín McDonough, *Literature
Officer* Robbie Meredith, *Visual Arts Officer* Iain
Davidson

Promotes and encourages the arts throughout
Northern Ireland. Artists in drama, dance, music
and jazz, literature, the visual arts, traditional arts
and community arts, can apply for support for
specific schemes and projects. The value of the
grant will be set according to the aims of the
application. Applicants must have contributed
regularly to the artistic activities of the community,
with residency of at least one year in Northern
Ireland.

The Arts Council of Wales
9 Museum Place, Cardiff CF10 3NX
tel 029-2037 6500 *minicom* 029-2039 0027
fax 029-2022 1447
email info@artswales.org.uk
website www.artswales.org.uk
Chairman Sybil Crouch, *Chief Executive* Peter
Tyndall, *Deputy Chief Executive* Frances Medley,
Senior Officer: Dance Siri Wigdel, *Senior
Development Officer for Visual Arts* Emma Geliot,
Senior Development Officer for Crafts Nathalie Camus

National organisation with specific responsibility

for the funding and development of the arts in
Wales. ACW receives funding from the National
Assembly for Wales and also distributes the
National Lottery funds in Wales to the arts. From
these resources, ACW makes grants to support arts
activity and facilities. Some of the funds are
allocated in the form of annual revenue grants to
full-time arts organisations; also operates schemes
which provide financial and other forms of support
for individual activities or projects. Undertakes this
work in both the English and Welsh languages.

North Wales Regional Office
36 Princes Drive, Colwyn Bay LL29 8LA
minicom (01492) 532288
tel (01492) 533440 *fax* (01492) 533677

Mid and West Wales Regional Office
6 Gardd Llydaw, Jackson Lane,
Carmarthen SA31 1QD
minicom (01267) 223469
tel (01267) 234248 *fax* (01267) 233084

Aslib (The Association for Information Management)
Staple Hall, Stone House Court,
London EC3A 7PB
tel 020-7903 0000 *fax* 020-7903 0011
email aslib@aslib.com
website www.aslib.com
Ceo Roger Bowes

Actively promotes best practice in the management
of information resources. It represents its members
and lobbies on all aspects of the management of
and legislation concerning information at local,
national and international levels. Aslib provides
consultancy and information services, professional
development training, conferences, specialist
recruitment, internet products, and publishes
primary and secondary journals, conference
proceedings, directories and monographs.
Founded 1924.

Association for Scottish Literary Studies (ASLS)
c/o Dept of Scottish History, 9 University Gardens,
University of Glasgow G12 8QH
tel 0141-330 5309
email office@asls.org.uk
website www.asls.org.uk
Hon. President Alan MacGillivray, *Hon. Secretary*
Jim Alison, *Publishing Manager* Duncan Jones
Membership £34 p.a. individuals, £10 UK students,
£63 corporate

Promotes the study, teaching and writing of Scottish
literature and furthers the study of the languages of
Scotland. Publishes annually an edited text of
Scottish literature, an anthology of new Scottish
writing, a series of academic journals and a
Newsletter (2 p.a.). Also publishes *Scotnotes* –
comprehensive study guides to major Scottish

writers – literary texts and commentary cassettes designed to assist the classroom teacher, and a series of occasional papers. Organises 3 conferences a year. Founded 1970.

Association of American Correspondents in London (AACL)

Secretary Elizabeth Lea, c/o Time Magazine, Brettenham House, Lancaster Place, London WC2E 7TL
tel 020-7322 1084 *fax* 020-7322 1230

Association of American Publishers Inc.

71 Fifth Avenue, New York, NY 10003, USA
tel 212-255-0200 *fax* 212-255-7007
website www.publishers.org
President and Ceo Patricia S. Schroeder
Founded 1970.

Association of Art Historians (AAH)

70 Cowcross Street, London EC1M 6EJ
tel 020-7490 3211 *fax* 020-7490 3277
email admin@aah.org.uk
website www.aah.org.uk
Administrator Claire Davies
Membership Various options for personal membership; corporate membership available

Formed to promote the study of art history and ensure wider public recognition of the field. Publishes *Art History* journal, *The Art Book* magazine, *Bulletin* newsletter. Annual conference and book fair in March/April. Founded 1974.

Association of Assistant Librarians – see Career Development Group

The Association of Authors' Agents

2nd Floor, Drury House, 34-43 Russell Street, London WC2B 5HA
tel 020-7344 1000 *fax* 020-7836 9541
email aaa@pfd.co.uk
website www.agentsassoc.co.uk
President Derek Johns, *Vice President* Sara Fisher, *Treasurer* Paul Marsh, *Secretary* Simon Trewin

Maintains a code of professional practice to which all members commit themselves; holds regular meetings to discuss matters of common professional interest; provides a vehicle for representing the view of authors' agents in discussion of matters of common interest with other professional bodies. Founded 1974.

Association of Authors' Representatives Inc.

PO Box 237201, Ansonia Station, New York, NY 10023, USA
tel 212-252-3695
website www.aar-online.org
Founded 1991.

Association of British Science Writers

c/o British Association for the Advancement of Science, 23 Savile Row, London W1X 2NB
tel 020-7439 1205 *fax* 020-7973 3051
email absw@absw.org.uk
website www.absw.org.uk
Chairman Pallab Ghosh, *Administrator* Barbara Drillsma

Association of science writers, editors, and radio, film and TV producers concerned with the presentation and communication of science, technology and medicine. Aims to improve the standard of science writing and to assist its members in their work.

Association of Canadian Publishers

161 Eglinton Avenue East, Suite 702, Toronto, Ontario M4P 1J5, Canada
tel 416-487-6116 *fax* 416-487-8815
email info@canbook.org
website www.publishers.ca
Executive Director John P. Pelletier

Founded 1976; formerly Independent Publishers Association, 1971.

Association of Christian Writers

Administrator Mrs J.L. Kyriacou, All Saints Vicarage, 43 All Saints Close, Edmonton, London N9 9AT
tel 020-8884 4348
email admin@christianwriters.org.uk
Membership £20 p.a. (£17 DD)

Aims to see the quality of writing in every area of the media, either overtly Christian or shaped by a Christian perspective, reaching the widest range of people across the UK and beyond. To inspire and equip people to use their talents and skills with integrity to devise, write and market excellent material which comes from a Christian world view. Founded 1971.

Association of Freelance Editors, Proofreaders and Indexers

Contact Priscilla O'Connor, 3 The Lawn, Oldtown Mill, Celbridge, Co. Kildare, Republic of Ireland
tel (01) 6012850
email priscillaoconnor@eircom.net
website www.publishingireland.com

Provides information to publishers on freelances through a list of members and their qualifications. Also protects the interests of freelances, and provides social contact for isolated workers.

Association of Freelance Journalists

President Martin Scholes, 2 Glen Cottages, Brick Hill Lane, Beverley Glen, Ketley, Telford, Shrops. TF2 6SB
email afj@yahoo.com
website http://afj.home-page.org

Membership £30 p.a.

Aims to foster the interests of freelance journalists and news photographers, especially those on a low income, including those working as stringers, local correspondents, writers for specialist fields, etc. Founded 1996.

The Association of Illustrators

81 Leonard Street, London EC2A 4QS
tel 020-7613 4328 *fax* 020-7613 4417
website www.theaoi.com
Contact Membership Secretary

Exists to support illustrators, promote illustration and encourage professional standards in the industry. Publishes bi-monthly magazine; presents an annual programme of events; annual competition, exhibition and tour of Images – the Best of British Illustration (call for entries late spring). Founded 1973.

The Association of Learned and Professional Society Publishers

Secretary-General Sally Morris, South House, The Street, Clapham, Worthing, West Sussex BN13 3UU
tel (01903) 871 686 *fax* (01903) 871457
email sec-gen@alpsp.org
website www.alpsp.org
Membership Open to not-for-profit publishers and allied organisations

Represents not-for-profit publishers of scholarly and professional information. Founded 1972.

The Association of Photographers (AOP)

Co-Secretary Gwen Thomas, 81 Leonard Street, London EC2A 4QS
tel 020-7739 6669 *fax* 020-7739 8707
email general@aophoto.co.uk
website www.the-aop.org
Membership £250 p.a.

Exists to protect and promote the interests of fashion advertising and editorial photographers. Founded 1968.

Australia Council

PO Box 788, Strawberry Hills, NSW 2012, Australia
located at 372 Elizabeth Street, Surry Hills, NSW 2010, Australia
tel (02) 9215 9000 *fax* (02) 9215 9111
email mail@ozco.gov.au
website www.ozco.gov.au
Chairperson David Gonski

Provides a broad range of support for the arts in Australia, embracing music, theatre, literature, visual arts, crafts, Aboriginal arts, community and new media arts. It has 8 major Boards: Literature, Visual Arts/Craft, Music, Theatre, Dance, New Media, Community Cultural Development, Major

Performing Arts, as well as the Aboriginal and Torres Strait Islander Arts Board.

The Literature Board's chief objective is to support the writing of all forms of creative literature – novels, short stories, poetry, plays and literary non-fiction. It also assists with the publication of literary magazines, has a book publishing subsidies programme, and initiates and supports projects of many kinds designed to promote Australian literature both within Australia and abroad.

Australian Copyright Council

PO Box 1986, Strawberry Hills, NSW 2012, Australia
tel (02) 9318 1788 *fax* (02) 9698 3536
email info@copyright.org.au
website www.copyright.org.au

An independent non-profit organisation which aims to assist creators and other copyright owners to exercise their rights effectively; raise awareness in the community generally about the importance of copyright; research and identify areas of copyright law which are inadequate or unfair; seek changes to law and practice to enhance the effectiveness and fairness of copyright; foster cooperation amongst bodies representing creators and owners of copyright.

The Council comprises 23 organisations or associations of owners and creators of copyright material, including the Australian Society of Authors, the Australian Writers Guild and the Australian Book Publishers Association. Founded 1968.

Australian Library and Information Association

PO Box E441, Kingston, ACT 2604, Australia
tel (02) 6215 8222 *fax* (02) 6282 2249
email enquiry@alia.org.au
website www.alia.org.au
Executive Director Jennefer Nicholson

Aims to promote and improve the services of libraries and other information agencies; to improve the standard of library and information personnel and foster their professional interests; to represent the interests of members to governments, other organisations and the community; and to encourage people to contribute to the improvement of library and information services by supporting the association.

Australian Publishers Association (APA)

60/89 Jones Street, Ultimo, NSW 2007, Australia
tel (02) 9281 9788 *fax* (02) 9281 1073
email apa@publishers.asn.au
website www.publishers.asn.au
Chief Executive Susan Bridge

The Australian Society of Authors

PO Box 1566, Strawberry Hills NSW 2012, Australia
located at 98 Pitt Street, Redfern NSW 2016
tel (02) 9318 0877 *fax* (02) 9318 0530
email asa@asauthors.org
website www.asauthors.org
Executive Director José Borghino

Authors' Club (at The Arts Club)

40 Dover Street, London W1S 4NP
tel 020-7499 8581 *fax* 020-7409 0913
Secretary Ann de La Grange
Membership Apply to Secretary

Founded by Sir Walter Besant, the Authors' Club welcomes as members writers, publishers, critics, journalists, academics and anyone involved with literature. Administers the Authors' Club Best First Novel Award and the Sir Banister Fletcher Award. Founded 1891.

Authors' Licensing and Collecting Society – see page 620

AXIS

Visual Arts Information Service, Leeds Metropolitan University, 8 Queen Square, Leeds LS2 8AJ
tel (0870) 443 0701 *fax* (0870) 443 0703
AXIS Information Service (0870) 443 0702
email axis@lmu.ac.uk
website www.axisartists.org

Provides information on contemporary artists and makers living/working in Britain to national and international clients. The AXIS database features 16,000+ images by over 4000 artists (professionals and recent graduates). The database can be accessed on CD-Rom, online and on the AXIS Information Service line. Printouts of artist CVs, artwork images, and contact details are available to potential buyers, commissioners, exhibitors and collaborators. AXIS receives funding from the Arts Councils of England, Scotland and Wales. Founded 1991.

BAFTA (British Academy of Film and Television Arts)

195 Piccadilly, London W1J 9LN
tel 020-7734 0022 *fax* 020-7437 0473
email deborahb@bafta.org
website www.bafta.org
Chief Executive Amanda Berry
Membership £195 p.a., £98 (under age 30), £98 overseas, £88 country

The pre-eminent organisation in the UK for film, TV and interactive entertainment, recognising and promoting the achievement and endeavour of industry practitioners. BAFTA Awards are awarded annually by members to their peers in recognition of their skills and expertise. The Academy's premises provide club facilities with a 200-seat cinema and 40-seat preview theatre. Provides a full and varied programme of industry-related events, masterclasses, seminars and panel discussions, which are open to both members and non-members. Founded 1947.

BANA (Bath Area Network for Artists)

c/o 16A Broad Street, Bath BA1 5LJ
email enquiries@bana-arts.co.uk
website www.bana-arts.co.uk
Membership £10 p.a.

An artist-led organisation which encourages and promotes the arts in the Bath and North East Somerset area. Members include painters, printmakers, mixed media artists, photographers, illustrators, sculptors, glass artists, papermakers, ceramicists, digital artists, video artists, film-makers, performance artists and textile artists. Membership fee includes registration on database, newsletter, artist café, page on website and more. Founded 1999.

BAPLA (British Association of Picture Libraries and Agencies)

18 Vine Hill, London EC1R 5DZ
tel 020-7713 1780 *fax* 020-7713 1211
email enquiries@bapla.org.uk
website www.bapla.org
Chief Executive Linda Royles

Offers comprehensive information about finding, buying and selling pictures. Founded 1975.

The Beatrix Potter Society

9 Broadfields, Harpenden, Herts. AL5 2HJ
tel (01582) 769755
email beatrixpottersociety@tiscali.co.uk
website www.beatrixpottersociety.org.uk
Chairman Judy Taylor
Membership £15 p.a. UK, £20 overseas

Promotes the study and appreciation of the life and works of Beatrix Potter as author, artist, diarist, farmer and conservationist. Founded 1980.

The Beckford Society

Secretary Sidney Blackmore, 15 Healey Street, London NW1 8SR
tel 020-7267 7750 *fax* (01985) 213239
email sidney.blackmore@btinternet.com
Membership £10 p.a. minimum

Aims to promote an interest in the life and works of William Beckford of Fonthill (1760–1844) and his circle. Encourages Beckford studies and scholarship through exhibitions, lectures and publications, including *The Beckford Journal* (annual) and occasional newsletters. Founded 1995.

Bibliographical Society

c/o Institute of English Studies, Room 304, Senate House, Malet Street, London WC1E 7HU

tel 020-7389 2150
email secretary@bibsoc.org.uk
President M.M. Foot, *Hon. Secretary* D. Pearson
Acquisition and dissemination of information upon
subjects connected with historical bibliography.
Founded 1892.

The Blackpool Art Society

The Studio, Wilkinson Avenue, Blackpool FY3 9HB
President Marian Dodds
Hon. Secretary Wendy Slattery, 33 Leighton Avenue,
Fleetwood, Lancs FY7 8BP
tel (01253) 773769
Autumn exhibition (members' work only). Studio
meetings, practicals, lectures, etc, out-of-door
sketching, workshops. Founded 1884.

Book Publishers Association of New Zealand Inc.

PO Box 36477, Northcote, Auckland 1309,
New Zealand
tel (09) 480-2711 *fax* (09) 480-1130
email bpanz@copyright.co.nz
website www.bpanz.org.nz
President Kevin Chapman

Books Across the Sea

The English-Speaking Union of the Commonwealth,
Dartmouth House, 37 Charles Street,
London W1J 5ED
tel 020-7529 1550 *fax* 020-7495 6108
email esu@esu.org
website www.esu.org
The English Speaking Union of the United States,
144 East 39th Street, New York, NY 10016, USA
tel 212-818-1200 *fax* 212-867-4177
email info@english-speakingunion.org
World voluntary organisation devoted to the
promotion of international understanding and
friendship. Exchanges books with its corresponding
BAS Committees in New York, Russia and Australia.
The books are selected to reflect the life and culture
of each country and the best of its recent publishing
and writing. New selections are announced by the
bulletin, *The Ambassador Booklist.*

The Booksellers Association of the United Kingdom & Ireland Ltd

272 Vauxhall Bridge Road, London SW1V 1BA
tel 020-7802 0802 *fax* 020-7802 0803
email mail@booksellers.org.uk
Chief Executive T.E. Godfray
Founded 1895.

Booktrust

(formerly the National Book League, founded 1925)
Book House, 45 East Hill, London SW18 2QZ
tel 020-8516 2977 *fax* 020-8516 2998
email info@booktrust.org.uk

websites www.booktrust.org.uk
www.booktrusted.com
Chairman Trevor Glover, *Executive Director* Chris
Meade
Membership Booktrusted subscription: £25 p.a.
Booktrust is an independent charity bringing books
and people together. It exists to open up the world
of books and reading to people of all ages and
cultures. Its services and activities include the Book
Information Service, a unique specialist
information service for all queries on books and
reading (business callers are charged at £1.50 per
minute on 0906-516 1193, weekdays 10am–1pm).
Booktrust administers a number of literary prizes,
including the Orange, Booker, Commonwealth and
Nestlé Prizes and runs a series of reader
development projects.

The Children's Literature Team at Booktrust
offers advice and information on all aspects of
children's reading and books. The 'booktrusted'
website is dedicated to children's books and
resources for professionals working with young
readers, including annotated book lists, information
about organisations concerned with children's
books, publishers, children's book news and much
more. Booktrust also produces a range of
publications and resource materials for National
Children's Book Week. Subscribers receive 4 issues
of *Children's Books News* and a copy of *100 Best
Books 2002.* Booktrust also coordinates the national
Bookstart (books for babies) programme which
gives free advice and books to parents/carers
attending their baby's health checks.

The Bram Stoker Society

Regent House, Trinity College, Dublin 2,
Republic of Ireland
fax (01) 6719003 FAO David Lass
email dlass@tcd.ie
website www.vampyreempire.com
http://benecke.com/stoker.html
Treasurer Albert Power, 43 Castle Court,
Killiney Hill Road, Killiney, Co. Dublin,
Republic of Ireland
Hon. Secretary David Lass
Membership £10 p.a. UK, €10 EU, $20 USA/rest of
the world
Aims to promote the study and appreciation of
Bram Stoker's (1847–1912) works and his influence
in the areas of cinema, theatre and music, as well as
his importance in the Gothic horror genre.
Publishes an annual journal and an occasional
newsletter. Holds regular meetings with the
Society's affiliated body, the Bram Stoker Club, in
Trinity College, Dublin; and promotes an annual
summer school in Clontarf, Dublin, held on a
weekend in July. Founded 1980.

British Academy

10 Carlton House Terrace, London SW1Y 5AH
tel 020-7969 5200 *fax* 020-7969 5300
email secretary@britac.ac.uk
website www.britac.ac.uk
President Viscount Runciman, *Humanities Vice-President* The Revd Prof John Morrill, *Social Sciences Vice-President* Prof H.G. Genn, *Treasurer* Prof R.J.P. Kain, *Foreign Secretary* Prof C.N.J. Mann, *Publications Secretary* Dr D.J. McKitterick, *Research Secretary* Prof R.J. Bennett, *Secretary* P.W.H. Brown CBE

The national Academy for the humanities and social sciences: an independent and self-governing fellowship of scholars, elected for distinction and achievement in one or more branches of the academic disciplines that make up the humanities and social sciences. Its primary purpose is to promote research and scholarship in those areas: through research grants and other awards, the sponsorship of a number of research projects and of research institutes overseas; the award of prizes and medals; and the publication both of sponsored lectures and seminar papers and of fundamental texts and research aids prepared under the direction of Academy committees. It also acts as a forum for the discussion of issues of interest and concern to scholars in the humanities and the social sciences, and it provides advice to the Government and other public bodies. Founded 1901.

British Academy of Composers and Songwriters

British Music House, 25-27 Berners Street, London W1T 3LR
tel 020-7636 2929 *fax* 020-7636 2212
email info@britishacademy.com
website www.britishacademy.com
Contact Fergal Kilroy, Head of Membership

The Academy represents the interests of composers and songwriters across all genres, providing advice on professional and artistic matters. It administers a number of major awards and events, including the prestigious Ivor Novello Awards.

British American Arts Association (BAAA) – see Centre for Creative Communities

The British Association of Communicators in Business

Suite A, 1st floor, The Auriga Building, Davy Avenue, Knowl Hill, Milton Keynes MK5 8HG
tel (0870) 1217606 *fax* (0870) 1217601
email enquiries@cib.uk.com
website www.cib.uk.com

Aims to be the market leader for those involved in corporate media management and practice by providing professional, authoritative, dynamic, supportive and innovative services. Founded 1949.

British Association of Journalists

General Secretary Steve Turner, 88 Fleet Street, London EC4Y 1PJ
tel 020-7353 3003 *fax* 020-7353 2310
Membership £17.50 per month national newspaper staff, national broadcasting staff and national news agency staff; £10 p.m. other seniors including magazine journalists, PRs, freelances; £7.50 p.m. under age 24

Aims to protect and promote the industrial and professional interests of journalists. Founded 1992.

British Association of Picture Libraries and Agencies – see BAPLA

British Centre for Literary Translation

University of East Anglia, Norwich NR4 7TJ
tel (01603) 592785 *fax* (01603) 592737
email bclt@uea.ac.uk
website www.literarytranslation.com
Co-ordinator Catherine Fuller

Aims to promote literary translation and the status of the literary translator by working in the UK and overseas with translator associations and centres, cultural policymakers, teachers and researchers of literary translation, Arts Council England, publishers and the media, libraries and schools. Runs a translator-in-residence programme for translators to spend one calendar month in Norwich. Publishes new books in German, *Rearranging the World*, and the journal *In Other Words*. Founded 1989.

The British Copyright Council

Copyright House, 29-33 Berners Street, London W1T 3AB
tel (01986) 788 122 *fax* (01986) 788 847
email copyright@bcc2.demon.co.uk
Vice-Presidents Geoffrey Adams, Maureen Duffy, *Chairman* Prof Gerald Dworkin, *Vice Chairmen* Gwen Thomas, David Lester, Kate Pool, *Secretary* Janet Ibbotson, *Treasurer* Hugh Jones

Aims to defend and foster the true principles of creators' copyright and their acceptance throughout the world, to bring together bodies representing all who are interested in the protection of such copyright, and to keep watch on any legal or other changes which may require an amendment of the law.

The British Council

10 Spring Gardens, London SW1A 2BN
tel 020-7930 8466 *fax* 020-7839 6347
website www.britishcouncil.org
Chair Baroness Helena Kennedy QC, *Director-General* David Green, *Director Literature* Margaret Meyer, *Director Arts* Sue Harrison

The British Council connects people worldwide with learning opportunities and creative ideas from the UK, and builds lasting relationships between the UK and other countries. It works in 109 countries, where it has over 180 libraries and information centres, each catering to the needs of the local community with print and electronic resources. In 2002–03, 250,000 library members borrowed 6.5 million books and videos. British Council libraries not only provide information and materials to users, but also promote the latest UK publications.

Working in close collaboration with book trade associations, British Council offices organise book and electronic publishing exhibitions ranging from small, specialist displays to participation in major international book fairs. Other projects include Global Publishing Information, a collection of online publishing market reports on international markets compiled in collaboration with the Publishers Association. It also provides various resources on its website for those interested in finding out more about UK publishing.

Details of the British Council's many publications are available online (www.britishcouncil.org/publications/index.htm). The British Council is the agent for the Department for International Development (DFID) for book aid projects in developing countries, and is an authority on teaching English as a second or foreign language. It also gives advice and information on curriculum, methodology, materials and testing.

The British Council promotes British literature overseas through writers' tours, academic visits, seminars and exhibitions. It publishes *New Writing*, an annual anthology of unpublished short stories, poems, extracts from works in progress and essays; and a series of literary bibliographies, including *Eyes Wide Open: New Fiction from the UK 1999–2001, Hunting Down the Universe: A Bibliography of Popular Science and Literature,* and *Teaching Management Principles Using Literature.* Through its Literature Department, the British Council provides an overview of UK literature and a range of online resources on its literature website, www.britishcouncil.org/arts/literature. This includes a literary portal (http://literature.britishcouncil.org), directories of postgraduate and short courses in literature and creative writing, a directory of literary conferences, information about UK and Commonwealth authors (www.contemporarywriters.com and www.literarytranslation.com), including translation workshops. A worldwide online book club and reading group for adults, teenagers and children (www.encompassculture.com) was launched in May 2003, and also www.youngtranslators.com for young European translators. During 2003–04, creative writing projects that will result in e-books are being developed overseas.

The Visual Arts Department, part of the British Council's Arts Group, develops and enlarges overseas knowledge and appreciation of British achievement in the fields of painting, sculpture, printmaking, design, photography, the crafts and architecture, working closely with the British Council's overseas offices and with professional colleagues in the UK and abroad.

Further information about the work of the British Council is available from Press and Public Relations at the above address, or from British Council offices overseas.

The British Fantasy Society

201 Reddish Road, South Reddish,
Stockport SK5 7HR
tel 0161-476 5368 (after 6pm)
email faliol@yahoo.com
website www.britishfantasy.org.uk
President Ramsey Campbell, *Secretary* Robert Parkinson
Membership £25 p.a.

For devotees of fantasy, horror and related fields, in literature, art and the cinema. Publications include *British Fantasy Newsletter* (quarterly) featuring news and reviews and several annual booklets, including: *Dark Horizons; Masters of Fantasy* on individual authors. There is a small-press library and an annual convention and fantasy awards sponsored by the Society. Founded 1971.

British Film Institute (BFI)

21 Stephen Street, London W1T 1LN
tel 020-7255 1444 *24-hour*
BFI Events Line 0870-240 4050 *fax* 020-7436 0439
website www.bfi.org.uk
Chair Anthony Minghella CBE, *Acting Director* Adrian Wootton

The BFI offers opportunities for people to experience, learn and discover more about the world of film and moving image culture. It incorporates the BFI National Library, the magazine *Sight and Sound* (monthly), the BFI National Film Theatre, the annual London Film Festival, and the BFI London IMAX, and provides advice and support for regional cinemas and film festivals across the UK. The BFI also undertakes the preservation of, and promotes access to, films, TV programmes, computer games, museum collections, stills, posters and designs, and other special collections. Founded 1933.

British Guild of Beer Writers

Secretary Barry Bremner
tel (01462) 685844 *fax* (01462) 685783
email beer@bremner.tv
website www.beerguild.co.uk
Membership £40 p.a

Aims to improve standards in beer writing and at the same time extend public knowledge of beers and brewing. The Gold and Silver Tankard Awards are given annually to writers and broadcasters judged to have made the most valuable contribution to this end. Publishes a directory of members with details of their publications and their particular areas of interest, which is circulated to the media. Founded 1988.

The British Guild of Travel Writers

Hon. Secretary Melissa Shales, 178 Battersea Park Road, London SW11 4ND
tel 020-7720 9009
email bgtw@garlandintl.co.uk
website www.bgtw.org

Arranges meetings, discussions and visits for its 220 members (who are all professional travel journalists) to promote and encourage the public's interest in travel. Publishes a monthly newsletter (for members only), website and annual *Yearbook,* which contain details of members and lists travel industry PRs and contacts. Annual awards for journalism (members only) and the travel trade.

The British Haiku Society

Secretary David Walker, Lenacre Ford, Woolhope, Hereford HR1 4RF
tel (01432) 860328
email davidwalker@btinternet.com
website www.britishhaikusociety.org
Membership £25 p.a. UK, £28 Europe, £32 rest of world, £20 concession/unwaged

Aims to pioneer the appreciation and writing of haiku, senryu, renku and tanka in the UK and the rest of Europe, and to establish links with haiku societies throughout the world. Publishes the journal *Blithe Spirit,* and a newsletter, *The Brief,* and holds national events. Administers the biennial Sasakawa Prize (worth £2500), James W. Hackett International Award and the Nobuyuki Yuasa International English Haibun Contest. Founded 1990.

British Institute of Professional Photography

Fox Talbot House, Amwell End, Ware, Herts. SG12 9HN
tel (01920) 464011
email bippware@aol.com
website www.bipp.com

Exists to represent all who practise photography as a profession in any field; to improve the quality of photography; establish recognised examination qualifications and a high standard of conduct; to safeguard the interests of the public and the profession. Admission can be obtained either via examinations, or by submission of work and other information to the appropriate examining board. Fellows, Associates and Licentiates are entitled to the designation Incorporated Photographer or Incorporated Photographic Technician. Organises numerous meetings and conferences in various parts of the country throughout the year; publishes *The Photographer* journal (10 p.a.), and an annual Register of Members and *Guide to Buyers of Photography,* plus various pamphlets and leaflets on professional photography. Founded 1901; incorporated 1921.

British Interactive Media Association (BIMA)

Briarlea House, Southend Road, Billericay, Essex CM11 2PR
tel (01277) 658107 *fax* (0870) 0517842
email info@bima.co.uk
website www.bima.co.uk
Office Administrator Janice Cable
Membership Open to any organisation or individual with an interest in multimedia.
£650 p.a. commercial, £300 institutional, £160 individual plus VAT

Established to promote a wider understanding of the benefits of interactive multimedia to industry, government and education and to provide a regular forum for the exchange of views amongst members. Publishes regular newsletters. Founded 1984.

The British Science Fiction Association Ltd

Membership Secretary Estelle Roberts, 97 Sharp Street, Newland Avenue, Hull HU5 2AE
email bsfa@enterprise.net
President Arthur C. Clarke

For authors, publishers, booksellers and readers of science fiction, fantasy and allied genres. Publishes *Matrix,* an informal magazine of news and information; *Focus,* an amateur writers' magazine; *Vector,* a critical magazine and the Orbiter Service, a network of postal writers workshops. Trophies are awarded annually to the winner in each category of the BSFA Awards: best UK-published novel, best UK short story, best UK artwork and best UK non-fiction/anthology. Founded 1958.

British Society of Comedy Writers

President Kenneth Rock, 61 Parry Road, Ashmore Park, Wolverhampton, West Midlands WV11 2PS
tel/fax (01902) 722729
email info@bscw.co.uk
website www.bscw.co.uk
Membership £75 p.a. full, £40 p.a. subscriber

Aims to bring together writers and industry representatives in order to develop new projects and ideas. Holds an annual international comedy conference, networking days and workshops to train new writers to professional standards. A script reading service is available. Founded 1999.

British Society of Miniaturists
Director Margaret Simpson, Briargate,
2 The Brambles, Ilkley, West Yorkshire LS29 9DH
Membership By selection
'The world's oldest miniature society.' Holds 2 open
exhibitions a year. Founded 1895.

British Society of Painters in Oils, Pastels and Acrylics
Briargate, 2 The Brambles, Ilkley,
West Yorkshire LS29 9DH
Director Margaret Simpson
Membership By selection

Promotes interest and encourages high quality in
the work of painters in these media. Holds 2 open
exhibitions a year. Founded 1988.

British Watercolour Society
Director Margaret Simpson, Briargate,
2 The Brambles, Ilkley, West Yorkshire LS29 9DH
tel (01943) 609075

Promotes the best in traditional watercolour
painting. Holds 2 open exhibitions a year. Founded
1830.

Broadcasting Entertainment Cinematograph and Theatre Union (BECTU), Writers Section
373-377 Clapham Road, London SW9 9BT
tel 020-7346 0900 *fax* 020-7346 0901
email info@bectu.org.uk
website www.bectu.org.uk
General Secretary R. Bolton

Aims to defend the interests of writers in film, TV
and radio. By virtue of its industrial strength, the
Union is able to help its writer members to secure
favourable terms and conditions. In cases of
disputes with employers, the Union can intervene in
order to ensure an equitable settlement. Its
production agreement with PACT lays down
minimum terms for writers working in the
documentary area. Founded 1991.

Broadcasting Group – see the Society of Authors, page 487

The Brontë Society
Membership Secretary The Brontë Parsonage Museum,
Haworth, Keighley, West Yorkshire BD22 8DR
tel (01535) 642323 *fax* (01535) 647131
email bronte@bronte.prestel.co.uk
website www.bronte.org.uk

Acquisition, preservation, promotion of the
memoirs and literary remains of the Brontë family;
exhibitions of MSS and other subjects. Publishes
Brontë Studies (3 p.a.) and *The Brontë Gazette*
(bi-annual). Its Museum is open throughout
the year.

The Browning Society
Contact Dr Berry Chevasco, 52 Esmond Road,
Bedford Park, London W4 1JQ
tel 020-8995 4900
website www.browningsociety.org
Membership £15 p.a.

Aims to widen the appreciation and understanding
of the lives and poetry of Robert Browning and
Elizabeth Barrett Browning, and other Victorian
writers and poets. Founded 1881; refounded 1969.

Bureau of Freelance Photographers
Focus House, 497 Green Lanes, London N13 4BP
tel 020-8882 3315 *fax* 020-8886 5174
website www.thebfp.com
Chief Executive John Tracy
Membership £45 p.a. UK; £60 p.a. overseas

Exists to help the freelance photographer by
providing information on markets, and free
advisory service. Publishes *Market Newsletter*
(monthly). Founded 1965.

Byron Society (International)
Byron House, 6 Gertrude Street, London SW10 0JN
tel 020-7352 5112 *fax* 020-7352 1226
Hon. Director Mrs Elma Dangerfield CBE
Membership £20 p.a.

Aims to promote research into the life and works of
Lord Byron by seminars, discussions, lectures and
readings. Publishes *The Byron Journal* (annual,
£5.50 plus postage). Founded 1971.

Canadian Authors Association
PO Box 419, Campbellford, Ontario K0L 1L0,
Canada
tel 705-653-0323, 866-216-6222 (toll free)
fax 705-653-0593
email canauth@redden.on.ca
website www.CanAuthors.org/national.html
President Ishbel Moore, *Administrator* Alec
McEachern

Canadian Magazine Publishers Association
130 Spadina Avenue, Suite 202, Toronto,
Ontario M5V 2L4, Canada
tel 416-504-0274 *fax* 416-504-0437
email cmpainfo@cmpa.ca
website www.cmpa.ca www.magomania.com
President Mark Jamison

Founded 1973.

Canadian Publishers' Council
250 Merton Street, Suite 203, Toronto,
Ontario M4S 1B1, Canada
tel 416-322-7011 *fax* 416-322-6999
email pubadmin@pubcouncil.ca
website www.pubcouncil.ca
Executive Director Jacqueline Hushion

Career Development Group

(formerly Association of Assistant Librarians)
c/o CILIP, 7 Ridgmount Street, London WC1E 7AE
President Tracy Long, *Hon. Secretary* Joanna
Ball BA, MA, ALA

Publishes bibliographical aids, the journal *Impact*,
works on librarianship; and runs educational
courses. Founded 1895.

Careers Writers' Association

Membership Secretary Anne Goodman,
16 Caewal Road, Llandaff, Cardiff CF5 2BT
tel 029-2056 3444 *fax* 029-2065 8190
email anne.goodman5@ntlworld.com
website www.careerswriters.co.uk
Membership £20 p.a.

Society for established writers on the inter-related
topics of education, training and careers. Holds
occasional meetings on subjects of interest to
members, and circulates details of members to
information providers. Founded 1979.

Cartoonists Club of Great Britain

Secretary Richard Tomes, 29 Ulverley Crescent,
Olton, Solihull, West Midlands B92 8BJ
tel 0121-706 7652
email r.tomes@virgin.net
website www.ccgb.org.uk
Membership Fee on joining: full, provisional, or
associate £50; thereafter £35 p.a.

Aims to encourage social contact between members
and endeavours to promote the professional
standing and prestige of cartoonists.

Centerprise Literature Development Project

Centerprise Trust, 136-138 Kingsland High Street,
London E8 2NS
tel 020-7249 6572 *fax* 020-7923 1951
email sharoncenterlit@care4free.net
eva.centerlit@care4free.net
Contact Eva, Sharon

An advice and resource centre for writers of fiction
and poetry, servicing Central, East and North
London. Runs courses and workshops in creative
writing, organises poetry and book readings,
discussions and debates on literary and relevant
issues, writers' surgeries, and telephone information
on resources for writers in London. Publishes
Calabash newsletter for Writers of Black and Asian
origin. Funded by London Arts. See also page 551.
Founded 1995.

Centre for Creative Communities (CCC)

118 Commercial Street, London E1 6NF
tel 020-7247 5385 *fax* 020-7247 5256
email info@creativecommunities.org.uk
website www.creativecommunities.org.uk
Director Jennifer Williams

A non-profit-making organisation working in the
field of arts, education and community
development. Conducts research, organises
conferences, produces a quarterly newsletter and is
part of an international network of arts and
education organisations. Maintains a specialised
arts, education and community development
library. CCC is not a grant-giving organisation.

Charles Williams Society

Secretary Richard Sturch, 35 Broomfield,
Stacey Bushes, Milton Keynes MK12 6HA

To promote interest in the life and work of Charles
Walter Stansby Williams (1886–1945) and to make
his writings more easily available. Founded 1975.

The Chartered Institute of Journalists

General Secretary Christopher Underwood FCIJ, FRSA,
2 Dock Offices, Surrey Quays Road,
London SE16 2XU
tel 020-7252 1187 *fax* 020-7232 2302
email memberservices@ioj.co.uk
Membership £190 p.a. maximum, £95 trainees,
£130 affiliate

The senior organisation of the profession, the
Chartered Institute maintains an employment
register and has accumulated funds for the
assistance of members. A Freelance Division links
editors and publishers with freelances and a
Directory is published of freelance writers, with
their specialisations. There are special sections for
broadcasters, motoring correspondents, public
relations practitioners and overseas members.
Occasional contributors to the media may qualify
for election as Affiliates. Founded 1884;
incorporated by Royal Charter in 1890.

The Chartered Society of Designers

5 Bermondsey Street, London SE1 3UW
tel 020-7357 8088 *fax* 020-7407 9878
email csd@csd.org.uk
website www.designweb.co.uk/csd
Director Brian Lymbery

Works to promote and regulate standards of
competence, professional conduct and integrity,
including representation on government and official
bodies, design education and awards. The services
to members include general information,
publications, guidance on copyright and other
professional issues, access to professional indemnity
insurance, as well as the membership magazine *csd*.
Activities in the regions are included in an extensive
annual programme of events and training courses.

The Chesterton Society

Hon. Secretary Robert Hughes KHS,
11 Lawrence Leys, Bloxham, Nr Banbury,
Oxon OX15 4NU

tel (01295) 720869 *mobile* (07789) 752098
Membership £12.50 p.a.

Aims to promote interest in the life and work of G.K. Chesterton and those associated with him or influenced by his writings. Two lectures a year. Publishes the *Chesterton Quarterly Review* (4 p.a.). Founded 1974.

Children's Book Circle

c/o Rachel Wade, Hodder Children's Books, 338 Euston Road, London NW1 3BH
tel 020-7873 6000 *fax* 020-7873 6477
email rachel.wade@hodder.co.uk
Membership Secretary Nicola Wilkinson, Egmont Children's Books, 239 Kensington High Street, London W8 6SA
tel 020-7761 3500 *fax* 020-7761 3510
email nicola.wilkinson@ecb.egmont.com
Membership £15 p.a. if working inside M25; £12 outside

Provides a discussion forum for anybody involved with children's books. Monthly meetings are addressed by a panel of invited speakers and topics focus on current and controversial issues. Holds the annual Patrick Hardy lecture and administers the Eleanor Farjeon Award. Founded 1962.

Children's Books History Society

Secretary Mrs Pat Garrett, 25 Field Way, Hoddesdon, Herts. EN11 0QN
tel/fax (01992) 464885
email cbhs@abcgarrett.demon.co.uk
Membership £10 p.a.; apply for overseas rates

Aims 'to promote an appreciation of children's books, and to study their history, bibliography and literary content'. Holds approx. 6 meetings and produces 3 substantial *Newsletters* and an occasional paper per year. The Harvey Darton Award is given biennially for a book that extends knowledge of British children's literature of the past. Founded 1969.

Children's Writers and Illustrators Group – see the Society of Authors, page 487

CILIP (Chartered Institute of Library and Information Professionals)

7 Ridgmount Street, London WC1E 7AE
tel 020-7255 0500 *textphone* 020-7255 0505
fax 020-7255 0501
email info@cilip.org.uk
website www.cilip.org.uk
Chief Executive Bob McKee PhD, FRSA, MCLIP
Membership Varies according to income

CILIP was formed on 1 April 2002 following the unification of the Institution of Information Scientists and the Library Association. It is the leading membership body for library and information professionals, with around 23,000 members in the UK and overseas. Its monthly magazine *Update* is distributed free to members. The IIS was originally founded in 1958 and the LA in 1877.

Circle of Wine Writers

Secretary Andrea Warren, 166 Meadvale Road, London W5 1LS
tel 020-8930 0181 *fax* (01494) 670200
email administrator@winewriters.org
website www.winewriters.org
Membership By election, £35 p.a.

An association for those engaged in communicating about wines and spirits. Produces *Circle Update* newsletter (5 p.a.), organises tasting sessions as well as a programme of meetings and talks. Founded 1960.

Classical Association

Administrator Clare Roberts, Senate House, Malet Street, London WC1E 7HU
tel 020-7862 8706 *fax* 020-7862 8729
email croberts@sas.ac.uk
website www.sas.ac.uk/icls/classass

Exists to promote and sustain interest in classical studies, to maintain their rightful position in universities and schools, and to give scholars and teachers opportunities for meeting and discussing their problems.

Clé: The Irish Book Publishers' Association

43-44 Temple Bar, Dublin 2, Republic of Ireland
tel (01) 6707 393 *fax* (01) 6707 642
email info@publishingireland.com
website www.publishingireland.com
President Fergal Tobin, *Executive Director* Orla Martin

Comedy Writers Association UK (CWAUK)

Membership Secretary Mary Gamon, 12 Erskine Road, Colwyn Bay, Conwy, North Wales LL29 8EV
email info@cwauk.co.uk
website www.cwauk.co.uk
Membership £36 p.a. + one-off £5 registration fee.
Open to everyone interested in comedy writing

The largest group of independent comedy writers in the UK with contacts around the world. Holds one-day seminars with invited industry speakers. Provides advice on writing and career development, and monthly newsletter and monthly market information. Founded 1981.

Comhairle nan Leabhraichean/The Gaelic Books Council

22 Mansfield Street, Glasgow G11 5QP
tel 0141-337 6211 *fax* 0141-353 0515
email fios@gaelicbooks.net

website www.gaelicbooks.net
Chair Prof Donald E. Meek

Stimulates Scottish Gaelic publishing by awarding publication grants for new books, commissioning authors and providing editorial services and general assistance to writers and readers. Has its own bookshop of all Gaelic and Gaelic-related books in print and runs a book club; catalogue available. Founded 1968.

Comics Creators Guild

(formerly Society for Strip Illustration)
Postal address only 22 St James' Mansions, West End Lane, London NW6 2AA
website www.comicscreators.org.uk

Open to all those concerned with, or interested in, professional comics creation. Holds monthly meetings and publishes a newsletter (monthly), a Directory of Members' Work, Submission Guidelines for the major comics publishers, sample scripts for artists, a 'Guide to Contracts' and 'Getting Started in Comics', a beginners' guide to working in the industry, and *Comics Forum* (quarterly), a magazine of art and criticism.

Commonwealth Secretariat – see page 582

Copyright Clearance Center Inc.

222 Rosewood Drive, Danvers, MA 01923, USA
tel 978-750-8400 *fax* 978-750-4470
website www.copyright.com

Copyright Council of New Zealand Inc.

PO Box 36477, Northcote, Auckland 1309, New Zealand
tel (09) 480-2711 *fax* (09) 480-1130
Chairman Terence O'Neill-Joyce, *Secretary* Kathy Sheat

The Copyright Licensing Agency Ltd – see page 618

Crime Writers' Association

email secretary@thecwa.co.uk
website www.thecwa.co.uk
Membership Associate membership open to publishers, journalists, booksellers specialising in crime literature

For professional writers of crime novels, short stories, plays for stage, TV and radio, or of other serious works on crime. Publishes *Red Herrings* (monthly), available to members only. Founded 1953.

The Critics' Circle

Contact Catherine Cooper, Administrator, c/o 69 Marylebone Lane, London W1U 2PH
tel 020-7224 1410 (office hours)

President Charles Osborne, *Hon. General Secretary* Charles Hedges
Membership By invitation of the Council

Aims to promote the art of criticism, to uphold its integrity in practice, to foster and safeguard the professional interests of its members, to provide opportunities for social intercourse among them, and to support the advancement of the arts. Such invitations are issued only to persons engaged professionally, regularly and substantially in the writing or broadcasting of criticism of drama, music, films, dance and the visual arts. Founded 1913.

Cyngor Llyfrau Cymru – see Welsh Books Council

The D.H. Lawrence Society

Secretary Ron Faulks, 24 Briarwood Avenue, Nottingham NG3 6JQ
tel 0115-950 3008
Membership £11 p.a. UK, £13 Europe, £16 rest of world (under review)

Aims to bring together people interested in D.H. Lawrence (1885–1930), to encourage study of his work, and to provide information and guides for people visiting Eastwood. Founded 1974.

Deaf Broadcasting Council

70 Blacketts Wood Drive, Chorleywood, Rickmansworth, Herts. WD3 5QQ
tel (01923) 284538 (text phone only)
email rmyers@waitrose.com
website www.deafbroadcastingcouncil.org.uk
Policy & Liaison Ruth Myers

The Design and Artists Copyright Society Ltd – see page 623

Dickens Fellowship

The Dickens House, 48 Doughty Street, London WC1N 2LX
tel 020-7405 2127 *fax* 020-7831 5175
Joint Hon. Secretaries Dr Tony Williams, Thelma Grove
Membership On application

Based in house occupied by Dickens 1837–9; publishes *The Dickensian* (3 p.a.). Founded 1902.

Directory & Database Publishers Association

Secretary Rosemary Pettit, PO Box 23034, London W6 0RJ
tel 020-8846 9707
Membership £120–£1200 p.a.

Maintains a code of professional practice; aims to raise the standard and professional status of UK directory and database publishing and to protect (and promote) the legal, statutory and common interests of directory publishers; provides for the exchange of technical, commercial and management information between members. Founded 1970.

The Dorothy L. Sayers Society

Chairman Christopher J. Dean, Rose Cottage, Malthouse Lane, Hurstpierpoint, West Sussex BN6 9JY
tel (01273) 833444 *fax* (01273) 835988
website www.sayers.org.uk/
Secretaries Lenelle Davis, Jasmine Simeone
Membership £14 p.a. UK, £16.50 Europe, $28 USA

Aims to promote and encourage the study of the works of Dorothy L. Sayers; to collect archive materials and reminiscences about her and make them available to students and biographers; to hold an annual conference and other meetings; to publish proceedings, pamphlets and a bi-monthly bulletin. Founded 1976.

Dylan Thomas Society of Great Britain

5 Church Park, Mumbles, Swansea SA3 4DE
tel (01792) 520080
Chair Mrs E. Jenkins
Membership £5 p.a. single, £8 p.a. double

Aims to promote an interest in the works of Dylan Thomas (1914–53) and other Anglo–Welsh writers. Founded 1977.

The E.F. Benson Society

The Old Coach House, High Street, Rye, East Sussex TN31 7JF
tel (01797) 223114
Secretary Allan Downend
Membership £7.50 p.a. single, £8.50 2 people at same address, £12.50 overseas

Aims to promote interest in the author E.F. Benson and the Benson family. Arranges annual literary evening, annual outing to Rye (July) and other places of Benson interest, talks on the Bensons and exhibitions. Archive includes the Austin Seckersen Collection, transcriptions of the Benson diaries and letters. Publishes postcards, anthologies of Benson's works, a Benson biography and an annual journal, *The Dodo*. Also sells out-of-print Bensons to members. Founded 1984.

E.F. Benson: The Tilling Society

5 Friars Bank, Guestling, Hastings, East Sussex TN35 4EJ
fax (01424) 813237
Secretaries Cynthia and Tony Reavell
Membership £8 p.a., £10 overseas; full starters membership (inc. amalgamations of all back newsletters) £34, overseas £38

Aims to bring together enthusiasts, wherever they may live, for E.F. Benson and his Mapp & Lucia novels. Annual gathering in Rye. Publishes 2 journal-length newsletters a year. Founded 1982.

Early English Text Society

Christ Church, Oxford OX1 1DP
website www.eets.org.uk
Hon. Director Prof John Burrow *Executive Secretary* R.F.S. Hamer
Membership £15 p.a.

To bring unprinted early English literature within the reach of students in sound texts. Founded 1864.

The Eckhart Society

Summa, 22 Tippings Lane, Woodley, Reading, Berks. RG5 4RX
tel 0118-9690118
email ashleyyoung@aysumma.demon.co.uk
website www.eckhartsociety.org
Secretary Ashley Young
Membership £16 p.a.; £9 OAPs/students

Aims to promote the understanding and appreciation of Eckhart's writings and their importance for Christian thought and practice; to facilitate scholarly research into Eckhart's life and works; and to promote the study of Eckhart's teaching as a contribution to inter-religious dialogue. Founded 1987.

Edinburgh Bibliographical Society

c/o National Library of Scotland, George IV Bridge, Edinburgh EH1 1EW
tel 0131-226-4531
Secretary Dr W. McDougall, *Treasurer* P. Freshwater
Membership £10 p.a., £15 institutions; £5 full-time students

Encourages bibliographical activity through organising talks for members, particularly on bibliographical topics relating to Scotland, and visits to libraries. Also publishes *Transactions* (generally every 3 years, free to members) and other occasional publications. Founded 1890.

The Edith Nesbit Society

21 Churchfields, West Malling, Kent ME19 6RJ
email mmccarthy30@hotmail.com
website www.imagix.dial.pipex.com
Membership £6 p.a.; £12 organisations/overseas

Aims to promote an interest in the life and works of Edith Nesbit (1858–1924) by means of talks, a regular newsletter and and other publications, and visits to relevant places. Founded 1996.

Educational Writers Group – see the Society of Authors, page 487

The Edward Thomas Fellowship

1 Carfax, Undercliff Drive, St Lawrence, Isle of Wight PO38 1XG
tel (01983) 853366
Hon. Secretary Colin G. Thornton
Membership £7 p.a.

Aims to perpetuate the memory of Edward Thomas, poet and writer, foster an interest in his life and work, to assist in the preservation of places associated with him and to arrange events which extend fellowship amongst his admirers. Founded 1980.

English Association

University of Leicester, University Road, Leicester LE1 7RH
tel 0116-252 3982 *fax* 0116-252 2301
email engassoc@le.ac.uk
website www.le.ac.uk/engassoc/
Chair Elaine Treharne, *Chief Executive* Helen Lucas

Aims to further knowledge, understanding and enjoyment of English literature and the English language, by working towards a fuller recognition of English as an essential element in education and in the community at large; by encouraging the study of English literature and language by means of conferences, lectures and publications; and by fostering the discussion of methods of teaching English of all kinds.

English Speaking Board (International) Ltd

26A Princes Street, Southport PR8 1EQ
tel (01704) 501730 *fax* (01704) 539637
email admin@esbuk.org
website www.esbuk.org
President Christabel Burniston MBE, *Chairman* Prof Andrew Trott
Membership £25 p.a. individuals, £50 corporate

Aims to foster all activities concerned with oral communication. Offers assessment qualifications in practical speaking and listening skills for candidates at all levels in schools, vocational and business contexts; also for those with learning difficulties and those for whom English is an acquired language. Also provides training courses in teaching and delivery of oral communication. Offers membership to all those concerned with the development and expression of the English language. Members receive *Speaking English* (2 p.a.); articles are invited on any special aspect of spoken English.

The English-Speaking Union

Dartmouth House, 37 Charles Street, London W1J 5ED
tel 020-7529 1550 *fax* 020-7495 6108
email esu@esu.org
website www.esu.org
Director-General Mrs Valerie Mitchell OBE
Membership Various categories

Aims to promote international understanding and human achievement through the widening use of the English language throughout the world. The ESU is an educational charity which sponsors scholarships and exchanges, educational programmes promoting the effective use of English,

and a wide range of international and cultural events. Members contribute to its work across the world. Administers the Marsh Biography Award. See also Books Across the Sea. Founded 1918.

European Broadcasting Union

PO Box 45, Ancienne Route 17A, CH-1218 Grand Saconnex (Geneva), Switzerland
tel (22) 7172111 *fax* (22) 7174000
email ebu@ebu.ch
website www.ebu.ch
Secretary-General Mr Jean Stock

The largest professional association of national broadcasters. Working on behalf of its members in the European area, the EBU negotiates broadcasting rights for major sports events; operates the Eurovision and Euroradio networks; organises programme exchanges; stimulates and coordinates co-productions; and provides a full range of other operational, commercial, technical, legal and strategic services. Founded 1950.

Fabian Society

11 Dartmouth Street, London SW1H 9BN
tel 020-7227 4900 *fax* 020-7976 7153
email info@fabian-society.org.uk
website www.fabian-society.org.uk
General Secretary Michael Jacobs

Current affairs, political thought, economics, education, environment, foreign affairs, social policy. Also controls NCLC Publishing Society Ltd. Founded 1884.

Federation Against Copyright Theft Ltd (FACT)

7 Victory Business Centre, Worton Road, Isleworth, Middlesex TW7 6DB
tel 020-8568 6646 *fax* 020-8560 6364
email investigator@fact-uk.org.uk
Contact David Lowe, Director General

Aims to protect the interests of its members and others against infringement in the UK of copyright in cinematograph films, TV programmes and all forms of audiovisual recording. Founded 1982.

The Copyright Hotline offers advice and information to anyone who wants to use film, music or software copyrights. It is part of a collective initiative by FACT, Federation Against Software Theft (FAST), Music Publishers Association (MPA), Mechanical Copyright Protection Society (MCPS), Performing Right Society (PRS) and British Music Rights (BMR).

Federation of British Artists

17 Carlton House Terrace, London SW1Y 5BD
tel 020-7930 6844 *fax* 020-7839 7830
email info@mallgalleries.com
website www.mallgalleries.org.uk

Administers 9 major National Art Societies at the Mall Galleries, The Mall, London SW1.

Federation of European Publishers

204 avenue de Tervuren, 1150 Brussels, Belgium
tel (2) 770 11 10 *fax* (2) 771 20 71
email malemann@fep-fee.be
website www.fep-fee.be
President Anton C. Hilscher, *Director* Mechthild von Alemann

Represents the interests of European publishers on EU affairs; informs members on the development of EU policies which could affect the publishing industry. Founded 1967.

The Federation of Indian Publishers

18/1-C Institutional Area, Aruna Asaf Ali Marg (near JNU), New Delhi 110067, India
tel 26852263, 26964847 *fax* 26864054
email fipl@satyam.net.in

Federation of Spanish Publishers' Association

(Federación de Gremios de Editores de España)
Cea Bermúdez, 44-2° Dcha. 28003 Madrid, Spain
tel (91) 534 51 95 *fax* (91) 535 26 25
email fgee@fge.es
website www.federacioneditores.org
President Yoldi L'Ibeda, *Director* Antonio Avila

The Federation of Worker Writers and Community Publishers

Burslem School of Art, Queen Street, Stoke-on-Tent ST6 3EJ
tel/fax (01782) 822327
email thefwwcp@tiscali.co.uk
website www.thefwwcp.org.uk
Membership £40 p.a. funded groups; £20 unfunded

A network of writers groups and community publishers which promotes working-class writing and publishing. Founded 1976.

Financial Journalists' Group

Secretary, c/o Association of British Insurers, 51 Gresham Street, London EC2V 7HQ
tel 020-7216 7410
Chairman Chris Wheal
Membership No fee

Aims to give journalists working in the area of, or with an interest in, finance and financial services, a forum to learn more about some of the issues involved, and meet colleagues with similar interests. Founded 1997.

The Fine Art Trade Guild

16-18 Empress Place, London SW6 1TT
tel 020-7381 6616 *fax* 020-7381 2596
email information@fineart.co.uk
website www.fineart.co.uk

Managing Director Rosie Sumner

Promotes the sale of fine art prints and picture framing in the UK and overseas markets; establishes and raises standards amongst members and communicates these to the buying public. The Guild publishes *The Directory* and *Art Business Today*, the trade's longest established magazine, and various specialist books. Founded 1910.

First Film Foundation

Director Jonathan Rawlinson, 9 Bourlet Close, London W1W 7BP
tel 020-7580 2111 *fax* 020-7580 2116
email info@firstfilm.demon.co.uk
website www.firstfilm.co.uk

A charity that exists to help new British writers, producers and directors make their first feature film. Provides a range of unique educational and promotional programmes that give film-makers the contacts, knowledge and experience they need to achieve this goal. Founded 1987.

FOCAL International Ltd (Federation of Commercial AudioVisual Libraries International Ltd)

Pentax House, South Hill Avenue, South Harrow, Middlesex HA2 0DU
tel 020-8423 5853 *fax* 020-8933 4826
email info@focalint.org
website www.focalint.org
Commerical Manager Anne Johnson, *General Manager* Julie Lewis

Founded 1985.

The Folklore Society

The Warburg Institute, Woburn Square, London WC1E 0AB
tel 020-7862 8564
email folklore.society@talk21.com
website www.folklore-society.com
Hon. Secretary Dr Juliette Wood

Collection, recording and study of folklore. Founded 1878.

Foreign Press Association in London

Registered Office 11 Carlton House Terrace, London SW1Y 5AJ
tel 020-7930 0445 *fax* 020-7925 0469
email secretariat@foreign-press.org.uk
website www.foreign-press.org.uk
President Philippe Le Corre, *General Manager* Bob Jenner
Membership Entrance fee: £155; £145 p.a. Full membership open to overseas professional journalists residing in the UK; Associate membership available for British press and freelance journalists

Aims to promote the professional interests of its members. Founded 1888.

Francis Brett Young Society

Secretary Mrs J. Hadley, 92 Gower Road, Halesowen, West Midlands B62 9BT
tel 0121-422 8969
website www.fbysociety.co.uk
Membership £7 p.a., £70 p.a. life

Aims to provide opportunities for members to meet, correspond, and to share the enjoyment of the author's works. Publishes a journal (2 p.a). Founded 1979.

Free Painters & Sculptors

Registered office 14 John Street, London WC1N 2EB
Hon. Secretary Owen Legg, 152 Hadlow Road, Tonbridge, Kent TN9 1PB
Membership Secretary Joan Jago, 606 Nelson House, Dolphin Square, London SW1V 3NZ

Promotes group shows 4 times a year in prestigious galleries in London. Sponsors all that is exciting in contemporary art.

French Publishers' Association

(Syndicat National de l'Edition)
115 Blvd St Germain, 75006 Paris, France
tel (1) 44 41 40 50 *fax* (1) 44 41 40 77
website www.sne.fr

The Gaelic Books Council – see Comhairle nan Leabhraichean

Garden Writers Guild

Administrator Angela Clarke, c/o Institute of Horticulture, 14-15 Belgrave Square, London SW1X 8PS
tel/fax 020-7245 6943
email gwg@horticulture.org.uk
website www.gardenwriters.co.uk
Membership £40 p.a.

Aims to raise the standards of gardening communicators. Administers annual awards to encourage excellence in garden writing, trade and consumer press journalism, TV and radio broadcasting, as well as garden photography. Founded 1991.

The Gaskell Society

Far Yew Tree House, Over Tabley, Knutsford, Cheshire WA16 0HN
tel (01565) 634668
email JoanLeach@aol.com
website www.gaskellsociety.users.btopenworld.com
Hon. Secretary Mrs Joan Leach
Membership £12 p.a., £16 corporate and overseas

Promotes and encourages the study and appreciation of the work and life of Elizabeth Cleghorn Gaskell. Holds regular meetings in Knutsford, London, Manchester and Bath, visits and residential conferences; produces an annual Journal and bi-annual Newsletters. Founded 1985.

Gay Authors Workshop

Kathryn Byrd, BM Box 5700,
London WC1N 3XX
Membership £7 p.a., £3 unwaged

Exists to encourage writers who are lesbian, gay or bisexual. Quarterly newsletter. Founded 1978.

The George Borrow Society

Hon. Secretary Ms K.J. Cann, 21 Mulberry Close, Cambridge CB4 2AS
website www.clough5.fsnet.co.uk/gb.html
Membership £12.50 p.a.

Promotes knowledge of the life and works of George Borrow (1803–81), traveller and author. Publishes *Bulletin* (bi-annual). Founded 1991.

The George Eliot Fellowship

Secretary Mrs K.M. Adams, 71 Stepping Stones Road, Coventry CV5 8JT
tel 024-7659 2231
President Jonathan G. Ouvry
Membership £10 p.a.

Promotes an interest in the life and work of George Eliot (1819–80) and helps to extend her influence; arranges meetings; produces an annual journal, a quarterly newsletter and other publications. Awards the annual George Eliot Fellowship Prize (£250) for an essay on Eliot's life or work, which must be previously unpublished and not exceed 2500 words. Founded 1930.

German Publishers' and Booksellers' Association

(Börsenverein des Deutschen Buchhandels e.V.)
Postfach 100442, 60004 Frankfurt am Main, Germany
tel (069) 13060 *fax* (069) 1306201
email info@boev.de
website www.boersenverein.de
General Manager Dr Harald Heker

The Ghost Story Society

PO Box 1360, Ashcroft, British Columbia V0K 1A0, Canada
tel 250-453-2045 *fax* 250-453-2075
email ashtree@ash-tree.bc.ca
website www.ash-tree.bc.ca/GSS.html
Secretary Barbara Roden
Membership £20/US$30/Can.$36

Provides enthusiasts of the classic ghost story with a forum to discuss and appreciate the genre. Publishes *All Hallows* (3 p.a.) journal which contains news, articles, reviews and approx. 60pp of new fiction. Founded 1989.

Graham Greene Birthplace Trust

Secretary Ken Sherwood, Rhenigidale,
Ivy House Lane, Berkhamsted, Herts. HP4 2PP
tel (01442) 865158
email secretary@grahamgreenebt.org
website www.grahamgreenebt.org
Membership £7.50 p.a., £18 3 years

Exists to study the works of Graham Greene
(1904–91). The Trust promotes the Annual Graham
Greene Festival and Graham Greene trails. It
publishes a quarterly newsletter, occasional papers,
videos and CDs, and maintains a small archive. It
administers the Graham Greene Memorial Awards.
Special events and exhibitions are being planned to
celebrate the centenary of Greene's birth on
2 October 2004. Founded 1997.

Graphical, Paper & Media Union

Keys House, 63-67 Bromham Road,
Bedford MK40 2AG
tel (01234) 351521 *fax* (01234) 270580
email general@gpmu.org.uk
website www.gpmu.org.uk
General Secretary Tony Dubbins

The Greeting Card Association

United House, North Road, London N7 9DP
tel 020-7619 0396
website www.greetingcardassociation.org.uk
Administrator Sharon Little

See website for information on freelance designing
and writing for greeting cards. Official magazine:
Progressive Greetings Worldwide (12 p.a.). See page
394.

Guernsey Arts Council

La Fontaine, Courtil de la Fontaine, Kings Road,
St Peter Port, Guernsey GY1 1QB, CI
email tdguernsey@cwgsy.net eales@guernsey.net
Chairman Mrs Terry Domrille, *Secretary* Elizabeth
Eales *tel* (01481) 263189

Guild of Agricultural Journalists

Hon. General Secretary Don Gomery, Charmwood,
47 Court Meadow, East Sussex TN6 3LQ
tel (01892) 853187 *fax* (01892) 853551
email don.gomery@farmline.com
website www.gaj.org.uk
President Tony Pexton, *Chairman* Jonathan Page

Established to promote a high standard among
journalists who specialise in agricultural matters
and to assist them to increase their sources of
information and technical knowledge.

The Guild of Aviation Artists

(incorporating the Society of Aviation Artists)
Trenchard House, 85 Farnborough Road,
Farnborough, Hants. GU14 6TF

tel (01252) 513123 *fax* (01252) 510505
email admin@gava.org.uk
website www.gava.org.uk
President Michael Turner PGAvA,
Secretary/Administrator Susan Gardner
Membership £60 p.a. Full Members (by invitation),
£45 Associates, £25 Friends

Formed to promote aviation art through the
organisation of exhibitions and meetings. Holds
annual open exhibition in July in London; £1000
prize for 'Aviation Painting of the Year'. Quarterly
members' newsletter. Founded 1971.

Guild of Food Writers

Administrator Christina Thomas, 48 Crabtree Lane,
London SW6 6LW
tel 020-7610 1180 *fax* 020-7610 0299
email gfw@gfw.co.uk
website www.gfw.co.uk
Membership £70 p.a.

Aims to bring together professional food writers
including journalists, broadcasters and authors, to
print and issue an annual list of members, to extend
the range of members' knowledge and experience
by arranging discussions, tastings and visits, and to
encourage the development of new writers by every
means including competitions and awards. There
are 7 awards in 2004 and entry is not restricted to
members of the Guild. Founded 1984.

Guild of Health Writers

Administrator Jatinder Dua, 1 Broadmead Close,
Hampton, Middlesex TW12 3RT
tel/fax 020-8941 2977
email admin@healthwriters.com
website www.healthwriters.com
Membership £40 plus VAT p.a.

Brings together professional journalists dedicated to
providing accurate, broad-based information about
health and related subjects to the public. Publishes a
directory of members. Founded 1995.

The Guild of International Songwriters & Composers

Sovereign House, 12 Trewartha Road, Praa Sands,
Penzance, Cornwall TR20 9ST
tel (01736) 762826 *fax* (01736) 763328
email songmag@aol.com
website www.songwriters-guild.co.uk
Secretary Carole Ann Jones
Membership £42 p.a. UK, £50 EU/overseas

Gives advice to members on contractual and
copyright matters; assists with protection of
members rights; assists with analysis of members'
works; international collaboration register free to
members; outlines requirements to record
companies, publishers, artists. Publishes *Songwriting
& Composing* (quarterly).

The Guild of Motoring Artists

Administrator David Purvis, 71 Brook Court,
Watling Street, Radlett, Herts. WD7 7JA
tel (01923) 853803
email sharon@scott-fairweather.freeserve.co.uk
website www.newspress.co.uk/guild
Membership £27.50 p.a., £22.50 Associate, £18 Friend

To promote, publicise and develop motoring fine
art; to build a recognised group of artists interested
in motoring art, holding events and exchanging
ideas and support; to hold motoring art exhibitions.

The Guild of Motoring Writers

Contact General Secretary, 30 The Cravens,
Smallfield, Surrey RH6 9QS
tel (01342) 843294 *fax* (01342) 844093

Aims to raise the standard of motoring journalism.
For writers, broadcasters, photographers on matters
of motoring, but who are not connected with the
motor industry.

Guild of Railway Artists

Chief Executive Officer F.P. Hodges HON. GRA,
45 Dickins Road, Warwick CV34 5NS
tel (01926) 499246
email frank.hodges@tinyworld.co.uk
website www.railart.co.uk

Aims to forge a link between artists depicting
railway subjects and to give members a corporate
identity; also stages railway art exhibitions and
members' meetings. Founded 1979.

The H.G. Wells Society

Hon. General Secretary J.R. Hammond,
49 Beckingthorpe Drive, Bottesford,
Nottingham NG13 0DN
website http://hgwellsusa.50megs.com
Membership £16 p.a., £20 corporate

Promotes an active interest in and an appreciation
of the life, work and thought of H.G. Wells.
Publishes *The Wellsian* (annual) and *The Newsletter*
(bi-annual). Founded 1960.

Hakluyt Society

c/o The Map Library, The British Library,
96 Euston Road, London NW1 2DB
tel (01428) 641850 *fax* (01428) 641933
email office@hakluyt.com
website www.hakluyt.com
President Prof R.C. Bridges, *Hon. Secretary & Series
Editor* Prof W.F. Ryan

Publication of original narratives of voyages, travels,
naval expeditions, and other geographical records.
Founded 1846.

Harleian Society

College of Arms, Queen Victoria Street,
London EC4V 4BT

tel 020-7236 7728 *fax* 020-7248 6448
Chairman J. Brooke-Little CVO, MA, FSA,
Hon. Secretary T.H.S. Duke, Chester Herald of Arms

Instituted for transcribing, printing and publishing
the heraldic visitations of Counties, Parish Registers
and any manuscripts relating to genealogy, family
history and heraldry. Founded 1869.

The Henry Williamson Society

General Secretary Sue Cumming,
7 Monmouth Road, Dorchester, Dorset DT1 2DE
tel (01305) 264092
email zseagull@aol.com
website www.henrywilliamson.org
Membership Secretary Margaret Murphy,
16 Doran Drive, Redhill, Surrey RH1 6AX
tel (01737) 763228
email mm@misterman.freeserve.co.uk
Chairman Margaret White
Membership £12 p.a.

Aims to encourage a wider readership and greater
understanding of the literary heritage left by Henry
Williamson. Two meetings annually; also weekend
activities. Publishes an annual journal. Founded
1980.

Hesketh Hubbard Art Society

17 Carlton House Terrace, London SW1Y 5BD
tel 020-7930 6844 *fax* 020-7839 7830
website www.mallgalleries.org.uk
President Simon Whittle

Weekly life drawing classes open to all.

The Hilliard Society of Miniaturists

The Executive Officer Pauline Warner, Priory Lodge,
7 Priory Road, Wells, Somerset BA5 1SR
tel/fax (01749) 674472
website www.art-in-miniature.org
President Heather O. Catchpole RMS, pHSF, MASSA, MASF
Membership from £25 p.a.

Founded to increase knowledge and promote the
art of miniature painting. Annual Exhibition held in
June at Wells; seminars; Young People's Awards
(11–19 years); Newsletter. Member of the World
Federation of Miniaturists. Founded 1982.

Historical Novel Society

Secretary Richard Lee, Marine Cottage, The Strand,
Starcross, Devon EX6 8NY
tel (01626) 891962
email histnovel@aol.com
website www.historicalnovelsociety.com
Membership £18 p.a.

Promotes the historical novel via short story
competitions, conferences, a society magazine
Solander (2 p.a.) and reviews (*Historical Novels
Review*, quarterly). Membership is open to all and
includes eminent novelists. Founded 1997.

Hopkins Society

Secretary Oughtrington Rectory, Lymm,
Cheshire WA13 9JB
website www.hopkinsoc.freeserve.co.uk
Membership £7 p.a., £10 outside Europe

Aims to promote and celebrate the work of the poet
Gerard Manley Hopkins, to inform members about
the latest publications about Hopkins and to
support educational projects concerning his work.
Annual lecture held in North Wales in the spring;
publishes a newsletter (2 p.a.) Founded 1990.

Horror Writers Association (HWA)

PO Box 50577, Palo Alto, CA 94303, USA
email hwa@horror.org
website www.horror.org
UK Jo Fletcher, 24 Pearl Road,
London E17 4QZ
Membership $65 p.a. North America,
$75/£48 elsewhere

A worldwide organisation of writers and publishing
professionals dedicated to promoting the interests
of writers of horror and dark fantasy. There are 3
levels of membership: for new writers, established
writers and non-writing horror professionals.
Founded 1987.

Housman Society

80 New Road, Bromsgrove, Worcs. B60 2LA
tel (01527) 874136
email info@housman-society.co.uk
website www.housman-society.co.uk/
Chairman Jim Page
Membership £10 p.a.

Aims to foster interest in and promote knowledge
of A.E. Housman and his family. Sponsors a lecture
at the Guardian Hay Festival. Founded 1973.

Incorporated Society of Musicians

10 Stratford Place, London W1C 1AA
tel 020-7629 4413 *fax* 020-7408 1538
email membership@ism.org
website www.ism.org
President Prof John Morehen, *Chief Executive*
Neil Hoyle
Membership £108 p.a.

Professional body for musicians. Aims to promote
the art of music; protect the interests and raise the
standards of the musical profession; provide
services, support and advice for its members.
Publishes *Music Journal* (12 p.a.), a yearbook and
3 Registers of Specialists annually.

Independent Publishers Guild

PO Box 93, Royston, Herts. SG8 5GH
tel (01763) 247014 *fax* (01763) 246293
Membership £85 plus VAT p.a. Open to new and
established publishers and book packagers; supplier

membership is available to specialists in fields allied
to publishing (but not printers and binders)

Provides an information and contact network for
independent publishers. The IPG also voices the
concerns of member companies with the book
trade. Founded 1962.

Institute of Designers in Ireland

8 Merrion Square, Dublin 2, Republic of Ireland
tel (01) 7167885 *fax* (01) 7168736
Membership €171 p.a. full, €57 associate

Irish design profession's representative body,
covering every field of design. Details available
from the Honorary Secretary. Founded 1972.

Institute of Linguists

Saxon House, 48 Southwark Street,
London SE1 1UN
tel 020-7940 3100 *fax* 020-7940 3101
email info@iol.org.uk
website www.iol.org.uk

Professional association for translators, interpreters
and language tutors with 'Find-a-Linguist' website
service. International language examinations run by
its Educational Trust. One subsidiary NRPSI Ltd
manages the National Register of Public Service
Interpreters. Another, Language Services Ltd, offers
customised assessments and services.

The Institute of Translation & Interpreting (ITI)

Contact The Secretary, Fortina House,
South Fifth Street, Milton Keynes MK9 2EU
tel (01908) 325250 *fax* (01908) 325259
email info@iti.org.uk
website www.iti.org.uk

A professional association of translators and
interpreters which aims to promote the highest
standards in translating and interpreting. It has a
strong corporate membership and runs professional
development courses and conferences, sometimes in
conjunction with its language, regional and subject
networks. Membership is open to those with a
genuine and proven involvement in translation and
interpreting of all kinds, but particularly technical
and commercial translation. As a full and active
member of the International Federation of
Translators, it maintains good contacts with
translators and interpreters worldwide. ITI's
directory of members (online) and its bi-monthly
bulletin are available from the Secretariat.

The International Guild of Artists

Briargate, 2 The Brambles, Ilkley,
West Yorkshire LS29 9DH
Director Leslie Simpson FRSA

Organises 4 seasonal exhibitions per year for
3 national societies: Society of Miniaturists, British
Society of Painters in Oils, Pastels & Acrylics and

British Watercolour Society. Promotes these 3 societies in countries outside the British Isles.

International Publishers Association

3 avenue de Miremont, CH-1206 Geneva, Switzerland
tel (022) 346-30-18 *fax* (022) 347-57-17
President Pere Vicens, *Secretary-General* Mr Benoît Müller

Founded 1896.

International Society of Typographic Designers

Hon. Secretary Helen Cornish, Chapelfield Cottage, Randwick, Stroud, Glos. GL6 6HS
tel (01453) 759311 *fax* (01453) 767466
email helen.randwick@virgin.net
Chair Freda Sack FISTD

Advises and acts on matters of professional and educational practice, provides a better understanding of the typographic craft and the rapidly changing technology in the graphic industries by lectures, discussions and through the journal *Typographic*. Students of typography and graphic design are encouraged to gain membership of the Society by entering the annual student assessment project. Founded 1928.

International Theatre Exchange

c/o Drama Association of Wales, The Old Library, Singleton Road, Splott, Cardiff CF24 2ET
tel 029-2045 2200 *fax* 029-2045 2277
email aled.daw@virgin.net
website www.aitaiata.org
Secretariat Aled Rhys-Jones

Aims to encourage, foster and promote exchanges of theatre; student, educational, adult, theatre activities at international level. To organise international seminars, workshops, courses and conferences, and to collect and collate information of all types for national and international dissemination.

International Visual Communication Association (IVCA)

19 Pepper Street, Glengall Bridge, London E14 9RP
tel 020-7512 0571 *fax* 020-7512 0591
email info@ivca.org
website www.ivca.org
Membership Secretary Nick Gardiner
Membership From £175 p.a.

For those who use or supply visual communication. Aims to promote the industry and provide a collective voice; provides a range of services, publications and events to help existing and potential users to make the most of what video, film, multimedia and live events can offer their business. Founded 1987.

The Irish Book Publishers' Association – see Clé

The Irish Copyright Licensing Agency

19 Parnell Square, Dublin 1, Republic of Ireland
tel (01) 8729202 *fax* (01) 8722035
email icla@esatlink.com
Executive Director Samantha Holman

Licences schools and other users of copyright material to photocopy extracts of such material, and distributes the monies collected to the authors and publishers whose works have been copied. Founded 1992.

Irish Playwrights and Screenwriters Guild

(formerly the Society of Irish Playwrights)
Irish Writers' Centre, 19 Parnell Square, Dublin 1, Republic of Ireland
tel (01) 8721302 *fax* (01) 8726282
email moffatts@intigo.ie
Secretary Sean Moffatt

Represents writers' interests in theatre, radio and screenwriting. Founded 1969.

Irish Translators' Association

Irish Writers' Centre, 19 Parnell Square, Dublin 1, Republic of Ireland
tel (01) 8721302 *fax* (01) 8726282
email translation@eircom.net
website http://translatorsassociation.ie
Hon. Secretary Miriam Lee
Membership €30 p.a. ordinary, €15 student, €80 corporate

Promotes translation in Ireland, the translation of Irish authors abroad and the practical training of translators, and promotes the interests of translators. Catalogues the works of translators in areas of Irish interest; secures the awarding of prizes and bursaries for translators; and maintains a detailed register of translators. Founded 1986.

Irish Writers' Union/Comhar na Scríbhneoirí

Irish Writers' Centre, 19 Parnell Square, Dublin 1, Republic of Ireland
tel (01) 8721302 *fax* (01) 8726282
email info@writerscentre.ie
website www.ireland.writers.com
Chairman Conor Kostick, *Secretary* Anthony P. Quinn

The Union aims to advance the cause of writing as a profession, to achieve better remuneration and more favourable conditions for writers and to provide a means for the expression of the collective opinion of writers on matters affecting their profession. Founded 1986.

The J.B. Priestley Society

Secretary Rod Slater, 54 Framingham Road, Sale, Greater Manchester M33 3RJ
tel 0161-962 1477 (evening) *fax* 0161-905 3103
email priestleysociety@slatersweb.demon.co.uk
Membership £10 p.a. single, £15 family, £5 concessions

Aims to widen the knowledge, understanding and appreciation of the published works of J.B. Priestley (1894–1984) and to promote the study of his life and career. Holds lectures and discussions and shows films. Publishes a newsletter and journal. Organises walks to areas with Priestley connections, Annual Priestley Night and other social events. Founded 1997.

The James Hilton Society

Hon. Secretary Dr J.R. Hammond,
49 Beckingthorpe Drive, Bottesford,
Nottingham NG13 0DN
website www.jameshiltonsociety.co.uk
Membership £10 p.a. (£7 concessions)

Aims to promote interest in the life and work of novelist and scriptwriter James Hilton (1900–54). Publishes quarterly newsletter and organises conferences. Founded 2000.

The Jane Austen Society

Secretary Maggie Lane, 1 Brookleaze, Sea Mills,
Bristol BS9 2ET
email mlane@bgs.bristol.sch.uk
website www.janeaustensociety.org.uk
Membership £15 p.a. UK, £250 life; £18 overseas,
£300 life

Aims to promote interest in, and enjoyment of, Jane Austen's novels and letters. Regular publications, meetings and conferences. Twelve branches in UK. Founded 1940.

The John Buchan Society

Membership Secretary Russell Paterson,
Limpsfield, 16 Ranfurly Road, Bridge of Weir,
Renfrewshire PA11 3EL
tel (01505) 613116
Membership £10 p.a. full/overseas; other rates on application

Promotes a wider understanding and appreciation of the life and works of John Buchan. Encourages publication of a complete annotated edition of Buchan's works, and supports the John Buchan Centre and Museum at Broughton, Borders. Holds regular meetings and social gatherings; produces a Newsletter and a Journal. Founded 1979.

The John Clare Society

Hon. Secretary 9 The Chase, Ely,
Cambs. CB6 3DR
tel (01353) 668438
email moyse.helpston@talk21.com
website http://vzone.virgin.net/linda.curry/
jclaresociety
Membership £10 p.a. UK individual; other rates on application

Promotes a wider appreciation of the life and works of the poet John Clare. Founded 1981.

The John Masefield Society

Chairman Peter J.R. Carter, The Frith, Ledbury,
Herefordshire HR8 1LW
tel (01531) 633800 *fax* (01531) 631647
email petercarter@btinternet.com
website http://my.genie.co.uk/masefield
Membership £5 p.a., £10 overseas, £8 family/
institutions

Aims to stimulate interest in, and public awareness and enjoyment of, the life and works of the poet John Masefield. Holds an annual lecture and other, less formal, readings and gatherings; publishes an annual journal and frequent newsletters. Founded 1992.

The John Polidori Literary Society

Contact The Secretary, PO Box 6078,
Nottingham NG16 4HX
Founder/President Franklin Charles Bishop
Membership By invitation only

Promotes and encourages the appreciation of the life and works of Anglo-Italian John William Polidori MD (1795–1821) – novelist, poet, tragedian, philosopher, diarist, essayist, reviewer, traveller and one of the youngest ever students to obtain a medical degree at the age of 19. He introduced into English literature the icon of the vampire portrayed as an aristocratic, handsome seducer both cynical and amoral with his seminal work *The Vampyre – A Tale* (1819). The Society has a programme of republishing Polidori's literary works, including a recently found cache of previously unknown letters. The Society houses a collection of rare letters and memorabilia connected with Polidori. International membership. Founded 1990.

The Johnson Society

Johnson Birthplace Museum, Breadmarket Street,
Lichfield, Staffs. WS13 6LG
tel (01543) 264972
email honlitsec@lichfieldrambler.co.uk
website www.lichfieldrambler.co.uk
Hon. General Secretary Norma Hooper,
Hon. Literary Secretary John Dudley

Aims to encourage the study of the life and works of Dr Samuel Johnson; to preserve the memorials, associations, books, manuscripts and letters of Dr Johnson and his contemporaries; to work with the local council in the preservation of his birthplace.

Johnson Society of London

Secretary Mrs Zandra O'Donnell MA,
255 Baring Road, London SE12 0BQ
tel 020-8851 0173
President The Viscountess Eccles

Aims to study the life and works of Dr Johnson, and to perpetuate his memory in the city of his adoption. Founded 1928.

The Joseph Conrad Society (UK)

The Conradian, Dr Allan Simmons,
Dept of English, St Mary's College, Twickenham,
Middlesex TW1 4SX
Chairman Keith Carabine, *President* Philip Conrad,
Secretary Hugh Epstein, *Editor* Allan Simmons

Maintains close and friendly links with the Conrad
family. Activities include an annual international
conference; publication of *The Conradian* and a
series of pamphlets; and maintenance of a study
centre at the Polish Cultural Centre, 238-246 King
Street, London W6 0RF. Administers the Juliet
McLauchlan Prize: £100 annual award for the
winner of an essay competition. Founded 1973.

Keats-Shelley Memorial Association

Hon. Secretary David Leigh-Hunt, 1 Satchwell Walk,
Leamington Spa, Warks. CV32 4QE
tel (01926) 427400 *fax* (01926) 335133
Chairman Hon. Mrs H. Cullen
Membership £10 p.a. minimum

Owns and supports house in Rome where John
Keats died as a museum open to the public, and
celebrates the poets Keats, Shelley and Leigh Hunt.
Occasional meetings; poetry competitions; annual
Review, 2 literary awards, and progress reports.
Founded 1903.

Kent and Sussex Poetry Society

Contact John Arnold, 39 Rockington Way,
Crowborough, East Sussex TN6 2NJ
tel (01892) 662781
Secretary Joyce Mandel Walter
email joyce345@yahoo.co.uk
President Laurence Lerner, *Chairman* Clive Eastwood
Membership £10 p.a. full, £5 country members/
concessions

Based in Tunbridge Wells, the society was formed
to create a greater interest in poetry. Well-known
poets address the Society, a Folio of members' work
is produced and a full programme of recitals,
discussions, competitions and readings is provided.
See page 505 for details of Open Poetry
Competition. Founded 1946.

The Kipling Society

Hon. Secretary Jane Keskar, 6 Clifton Road,
London W9 1SS
tel 020-7286 0194
email jane@keskar.fsworld.co.uk
website www.kipling.org.uk
Membership Details on application

Aims to honour and extend the influence of
Rudyard Kipling (1865–1936), to assist in the study
of his writings, to hold discussion meetings, to
publish a quarterly journal, and to maintain a
Kipling Library in London and a Kipling Room in
The Grange, Rottingdean, near Brighton.

The Lancashire Authors' Association

General Secretary Eric Holt, 5 Quakerfields,
Westhoughton, Bolton BL5 2BJ
tel (01942) 791390
Membership £10 p.a.

'For writers and lovers of Lancashire literature and
history.' Publishes *The Record* (quarterly). Founded
1909.

League of Canadian Poets

54 Wolseley Street, 3rd Floor, Toronto,
Ontario M5T 1A5, Canada
tel 416-504-1657 *fax* 416-504 0096
email league@poets.ca
website www.poets.ca
Executive Director Edita Page

Aims to promote the interests of poets and to
advance Canadian poetry in Canada and abroad.
Administers 3 annual awards; operates the 'Poetry
Spoken Here' webstore; runs National Poetry
Month; publishes a newsletter and *Poetry Markets
for Canadians, Who's Who in The League of
Canadian Poets, Poets in the Classroom* (teaching
guide). Promotes and sells members' poetry books.
Founded 1966.

The Lewis Carroll Society

Secretary Alan White, 69 Cromwell Road, Hertford,
Herts. SG13 7DP
email alanwhite@tesco.net
website http://lewiscarrollsociety.org.uk
Membership £13 p.a. UK, £15 Europe,
£17 elsewhere; special rates for institutions

Aims to promote interest in the life and works of
Lewis Carroll (Revd Charles Lutwidge Dodgson)
and to encourage research. Activities include regular
meetings, exhibitions, and a publishing programme
that includes the first annotated, unexpurgated
edition of his diaries in 9 volumes, the Society's
journal *The Carrollian* (2 p.a.), a newsletter,
Bandersnatch (quarterly) and the *Lewis Carroll
Review* (occasional). Founded 1969.

Lewis Carroll Society (Daresbury)

Secretary Kenn Oultram, Clatterwick House,
Little Leigh, Northwich, Cheshire CW8 4RJ
tel (01606) 891303 (office), 781731 (evening)
Membership £5 p.a.

Aims to encourage an interest in the life and works
of Lewis Carroll, author of *Alice's Adventures.*
Meetings take place at Carroll's birth village
(Daresbury, Cheshire). Elects an annual 'Alice', who
is available for public engagements. Founded 1970.

Little Theatre Guild of Great Britain

Public Relations Officer Michael Shipley,
121 Darwen Road, Bromley Cross, Bolton BL7 9BG
tel (01204) 304103

Aims to promote closer cooperation amongst the little theatres constituting its membership; to act as coordinating and representative body on behalf of the little theatres; to maintain and advance the highest standards in the art of theatre; and to assist in encouraging the establishment of other little theatres. Yearbook available to non-members (£5).

The Malcolm Saville Society
Membership Secretary Richard Griffiths, 78A Windmill Road, Mortimer, Berks. RG7 3RL
email mystery@witchend.com
website www.witchend.com
Membership £7.50 p.a. UK and EU, £12 outside EU

Aims to remember and promote interest in the work of Malcolm Saville (1901–82), children's author. Regular social activities, book search, library, contact directory and magazine (3 p.a.). Founded 1994.

The Marlowe Society
Newsletter Editor & Webmaster Roger Hards, Venusmead, 36 Venus Street, Congnesbury, Bristol BS49 5EZ
tel (01934) 834780
email rogerhards@venusmead.go-plus.net
Membership £12 p.a., £7 concessions, £15/$26 overseas

Aims to extend appreciation and widen recognition of Christopher Marlowe (1564–93) as the foremost poet and dramatist preceding Shakespeare, whose development he influenced. Holds meetings and cultural visits, and issues a bi-annual magazine. Founded 1955.

Mary Webb Society
Secretary Sue Higginbotham, 8 The Knowe, Willaston, Neston, Cheshire CH64 1TA
tel 0151-327 5843
email suehigginbotham@yahoo.co.uk
website www.marywebb.2ya.com

For devotees of the literature and works of Mary Webb and of the beautiful Shropshire countryside of her novels. Publishes a bi-annual journal, organises summer schools and other events in various locations related to Webb's life and works. Archives, lectures; tours arranged for individuals and groups. Founded 1972.

Master Photographers Association
Jubilee House, 1 Chancery Lane, Darlington, Co. Durham DL1 5QP
tel (01325) 356555 *fax* (01325) 357813
email info@mpauk.com
website www.mpa@mpauk.com
Membership £110 p.a.

Exists to promote and protect professional photographers. Members qualify for awards of Licentiate, Associate and Fellowship.

Mechanical-Copyright Protection Society Ltd (MCPS)
Copyright House, 29-33 Berners Street, London W1T 3AB
tel 020-7580 5544, 020-8769 4400
fax 020-7306 4455 020-8769 8792
website www.mcps.co.uk
Chief Executive John Hutchinson

The Media Society
Secretary Peter Dannheisser, 56 Roseneath Road, London SW11 6AQ
tel/fax 020-7223 5631
Membership £35 p.a.

Exists to promote and encourage collective and independent research into the standards, performance, organisation and economics of the media and hold regular discussions, debates, etc on subjects of topical or special interest and concern to print and broadcast journalists and others working in or with the media. Founded 1973.

Mediawatch-UK
(formerly National Viewers' and Listeners' Association)
Director John C. Beyer, 3 Willow House, Kennington Road, Ashford, Kent TN24 0NR
tel (01233) 633936 *fax* (01233) 633836
email info@mediawatchuk.org
website www.mediawatchuk.org
Chairman John Milton Whatmore
Membership £10 p.a.

Aims to encourage viewers and listeners to react effectively to programme content; to initiate and stimulate public discussion and parliamentary debate concerning the effects of broadcasting, and other mass media, on the individual, the family and society; to secure – then uphold – effective legislation to control obscenity and pornography in the media. Founded 1965.

Medical Journalists Association
Hon. Secretary Sue Lowell, 101 Cambridge Gardens, London W10 6JE
tel 020-8968 1614 *fax* 020-8968 7910
email sue4382@aol.com
Chairman John Illman
Membership £30 p.a.

Aims to improve the quality and practice of health and medical journalism. Administers major awards for health and medical journalism and broadcasting. Publishes The *MJA Directory* and *MJA News* newsletter. Founded 1966.

Medical Writers Group – see the Society of Authors, page 487

The Mervyn Peake Society

Treasurer Frank Surry, 2 Mount Park Road, London W5 2RP
Hon. President Sebastian Peake, *Chairman* Brian Sibley
Membership £12 p.a. UK and Europe, £5 students, £16 all other countries

Devoted to recording the life and works of Mervyn Peake; publishes a journal and newsletter. Founded 1975.

Music Publishers Association Ltd

3rd Floor, Strandgate, 18-20 York Buildings, London WC2N 6JU
tel 020-7839 7779 *fax* 020-7839 7776
email info@mpaonline.org.uk
Chief Executive Sarah Faulder
Membership Details on request

Trade organisation representing over 200 UK music publisher members: promotes and safeguards its members' interests in copyright, trade and related matters. Sub-committees and groups deal with particular interests. Founded 1881.

National Acrylic Painters' Association (NAPA)

134 Rake Lane, Wallasey, Wirral, Merseyside CH45 1JW
tel/fax 0151-639 2980
Membership The Executive Council, c/o Alan Edwards, 6 Berwyn Boulevard, Bebington, Wirral CH63 5LR
tel 0151-645 8433
email alan.edwards420@ntlworld.com
websites www.art-arena.com/napa
www.napa-inter.org
www.watercolor-online.com/napa
www.napa-usa.org
President Alwyn Crawshaw, *Director/Founder* Kenneth J. Hodgson

Promotes interest in, and encourages excellence and innovation in, the work of painters in acrylic. Holds an annual exhibition and regional shows: awards are made. Worldwide membership. Publishes a newsletter known as the *International NAPA Newspages*. Founded 1985; American Division established 1995.

National Association of Press Agencies

The Administrator,
41 Lansdowne Crescent, Leamington Spa, Warks. CV32 4PR
tel (01926) 424181 *fax* (01926) 424760
website www.napa.co.uk
Membership £250 p.a.

Trade association representing the interests of the leading national news and photographic agencies. Founded 1983.

National Association of Writers' Groups

Headquarters The Arts Centre, Biddick Lane, Washington, Tyne and Wear NE38 2AB
Secretary Diane Wilson, 40 Burstall Hill, Bridlington, East Yorkshire YO16 7GA
tel/fax (01262) 609228
email nawg@tesco.net
website www.nawg.co.uk
Membership £20 p.a. plus £5 registration per group; £10 Associate individuals

Aims 'to advance the education of the general public throughout the UK, including the Channel Islands, by promoting the study and art of writing in all its aspects.' Publishes *Link* bi-monthly magazine. Annual Festival of Writing held in Durham 5–7 Sept 2003. Annual Creative Writing Competition. Founded 1995.

National Campaign for the Arts (NCA)

Pegasus House, 37-43 Sackville Street, London W1S 3EH
tel 020-7333 0375 *fax* 020-7333 0660
Director Victoria Todd, *Deputy Director* Anna Leatherdale
Membership £50 p.a., £25 unwaged; special rates for organisations

Independent advocacy and lobbying organisation that exists to promote the interests of the arts world in all its diversity. It is funded through membership subscriptions to ensure its independence. Founded 1985.

National Council for the Training of Journalists (NCTJ)

Latton Bush Centre, Southern Way, Harlow, Essex CM18 7BL
tel (01279) 430009 *fax* (01279) 438008
email info@nctj.com
website www.nctj.com

A registered charity which aims to advance the education and training of trainee journalists, including press photographers. Full-time courses run at 28 colleges/universities in the UK. Distance learning courses also available in newspaper and magazine journalism and sub-editing. Founded 1952.

National Literacy Trust

Swire House, 59 Buckingham Gate, London SW1E 6AJ
tel 020-7828 2435 *fax* 020-7931 9986
email contact@literacytrust.org.uk
websites www.literacytrust.org.uk www.rif.org.uk
www.readon.org.uk
Director Neil McClelland, *PA* Jacky Taylor

A registered charity that aims to make an independent, strategic contribution to the creation of a society in which all can enjoy the appropriate skills, confidence and pleasures of literacy to support their educational, economic, social and cultural goals. Maintains an extensive website with literacy issues, research news and a database detailing literacy practice nationwide; promotes and facilitates literacy partnerships; organises an annual conference, courses and training events; publishes quarterly magazine *Literacy Today* (£18 p.a.). Organised and implemented the National Year of Reading 1998–9 and is coordinating the National Reading Campaign. Runs Reading is Fundamental, UK which provides books free to children. Founded 1993.

National Society for Education in Art and Design

The Gatehouse, Corsham Court, Corsham, Wilts. SN13 0BZ
tel (01249) 714825 *fax* (01249) 716138
website www.nsead.org
General Secretary Dr John Steers NDD, ATC, AE, PhD

The leading national authority concerned with art, craft and design across all phases of education in the UK. Offers the benefits of membership of a professional association, a learned society and a trade union. Has representatives on National and Regional Committees concerned with Art and Design Education. Publishes *Journal of Art and Design Education* (3 p.a.; Blackwells). Founded 1888.

National Society of Painters, Sculptors and Printmakers

Hon. Secretary Gwen Spencer, 122 Copse Hill, London SW20 0NL
tel 020-8946 7878
website www.nationalsociety.co.uk

An annual exhibition at the Westminster Galleries (21–26 October 2003). Not an open exhibition but artists are welcome to apply for membership. Newsletter (2 p.a.) for members. Founded 1930.

National Union of Journalists

Head Office Headland House, 308-312 Gray's Inn Road, London WC1X 8DP
tel 020-7278 7916 *fax* 020-7837 8143
email acorn.house@nuj.org.uk

Trade union for working journalists with 28,000 members and 147 branches throughout the UK and the Republic of Ireland, and in Paris, Brussels, Geneva and the Netherlands. It covers the newspaper press, news agencies and broadcasting, the major part of periodical and book publishing, and a number of public relations departments and consultancies, information services and Prestel-Viewdata services. Administers disputes, unemployment, benevolent and provident benefits. Official publications: *The Journalist* (bi-monthly),

Freelance Directory, Freelance Fees Guide and policy pamphlets.

National Viewers' and Listeners' Association – see Mediawatch-UK

NCTJ – see National Council for the Training of Journalists

New English Art Club

17 Carlton House Terrace, London SW1Y 5BD
tel 020-7930 6844 *fax* 020-7839 7830
website www.mallgalleries.org.uk
President Ken Howard RA

For all those interested in the art of painting, and the promotion of fine arts. Open Annual Exhibition at the Mall Galleries, The Mall, London SW1, open to all working in painting, drawing, pastels and prints.

New Playwrights Trust – see Writernet

New Science Fiction Alliance (NSFA)

Chris Reed, BBR, PO Box 625, Sheffield S1 3GY
website www.bbr-online.com/catalogue
Publicity Officer Chris Reed

The NSFA is committed to supporting the work of new writers and artists by promoting independent and small press publications worldwide. It was founded by a group of independent publishers to give writers the opportunity to explore the small press and find the right market for their material. It offers a mail order service for magazines. Founded 1989.

New Writing North

7-8 Trinity Chare, Quayside, Newcastle upon Tyne NE1 3DF
tel 0191-232 9991 *fax* 0191-230 1883
email mail@newwritingnorth.com
website www.newwritingnorth.com
Director Claire Malcolm, *Administrator* Silvana Michelini

The literature development agency for the North East. Offers advice and support to writers of poetry, prose and plays. See website. Founded 1996.

New Zealand Writers Guild

PO Box 47886, Ponsonby, Auckland, New Zealand
tel (09) 360-1408 *fax* (09) 360-1409
email info@nzwritersguild.org.nz
website www.nzwritersguild.org.nz
Membership NZ$150-$400 full, $99 associate

Aims to represent the interests of New Zealand writers (TV, film, radio and theatre); to establish and improve minimum conditions of work and rates of compensation for writers; to provide professional services for members. Founded 1975.

Newspaper Press Fund
Dickens House, 35 Wathen Road, Dorking, Surrey RH4 1JY
tel (01306) 887511 *fax* (01306) 888212
website www.foundation.reuters.com/npf
Secretary David Ilott

For the relief of hardship amongst journalists, their widows and dependants. Financial assistance and retirement housing are provided.

The Newspaper Publishers Association Ltd
34 Southwark Bridge Road, London SE1 9EU
tel 020-7207 2200 *fax* 020-7928 2067

Newspaper Society
Bloomsbury House, 74-77 Great Russell Street, London WC1B 3DA
tel 020-7636 7014 *fax* 020-7631 5119
AdDoc DX35701 Bloomsbury
email ns@newspapersoc.org.uk
website www.newspapersoc.org.uk
Director David Newell

The Oscar Wilde Society
100 Peacock Street, Gravesend, Kent DA12 1EQ
tel (01474) 535 978
email vanessa@salome.co.uk
Secretary Vanessa Harris

Aims to promote knowledge, appreciation and study of the life, personality and works of the writer and wit Oscar Wilde (1854–1900). Activities include meetings, lectures, readings and exhibitions, and visits to associated locations. Members receive a journal, *The Wildean* (2 p.a.), and a newsletter, *Intentions* (6 p.a.). Founded 1990.

Outdoor Writers' Guild
Secretary Terry Marsh, PO Box 520, Bamber Bridge, Preston, Lancs. PR5 8LF
tel/fax (01772) 696732
email info@owg.org.uk
website www.owg.org.uk
Membership £60 p.a.

Aims to promote and maintain a high professional standard among writers, illustrators and photographers who specialise in outdoor activities; represents members' interests to representative bodies in the outdoor leisure industry; circulates members with news of media opportunities; provides a forum for members to meet colleagues and others in the outdoor leisure industry. Presents annual literary and photographic awards. Founded 1980.

The P.G. Wodehouse Society (UK)
Details Tony Ring, 34 Longfield, Great Missenden, Bucks. HP16 0EG
tel (01494) 864848 *fax* (01494) 863048
email tring@sauce34.freeserve.co.uk
website www.eclipse.co.uk/wodehouse
Membership £15 p.a.

Aims to promote enjoyment of P.G. Wodehouse (1881–1975). Publishes *Wooster Sauce* (quarterly) and *By The Way* papers (3 p.a.) which cover diverse subjects of Wodehousean interest. Holds events, entertainments and meetings throughout Britain. Founded 1997.

PACT (Producers Alliance for Cinema and Television)
45 Mortimer Street, London W1W 8HJ
tel 020-7331 6000 *fax* 020-7331 6700
email enquiries@pact.co.uk
website www.pact.co.uk
Chief Executive John McVay, *Information Manager* David Alan Mills
Pact Scotland
249 West George Street, Glasgow G2 4QE
tel 0141-222 4880 *fax* 0141-222 4881
email margaret@pact.co.uk
Head of Nations & Regions Margaret Scott

The main trade association for feature film and independent TV production companies. Represents the interests of over 1000 production companies throughout the UK: promotes and protects the commercial interests of its members; lobbies government and regulators on their behalf; negotiates terms of trade with broadcasters; provides a range of membership services including advice on business affairs, industrial relations and legal advice; operates a copyright registration service for members' proposals and treatments for films and TV programmes. Its representative office in Glasgow serves the interests of its regional members.

The Pastel Society
17 Carlton House Terrace, London SW1Y 5BD
tel 020-7930 6844 *fax* 020-7839 7830
website www.mallgalleries.org.uk
President Moira Huntly

Pastel and drawings in pencil or chalk. Annual Exhibition open to all artists working in dry media held at the Mall Galleries, London. Members elected from approved candidates' list. Founded 1899.

PEN, International
International Secretary Terry Carlbom, 9-10 Charterhouse Buildings, Goswell Road, London EC1M 7AT
tel 020-7253 4308 *fax* 020-7253 5711
email intpen@dircon.co.uk
website www.internatpen.org

International President Homero Aridjis
Membership Apply to Centres

A world association of writers. PEN was founded in 1921 by C.A. Dawson Scott under the presidency of John Galsworthy, to promote friendship and understanding between writers and to defend freedom of expression within and between all nations.

The initials PEN stand for Poets, Playwrights, Editors, Essayists, Novelists – but membership is open to all writers of standing (including translators), whether men or women, without distinction of creed or race, who subscribe to these fundamental principles. PEN takes no part in state or party politics. The International PEN Writers in Prison Committee works on behalf of writers imprisoned for exercising their right to freedom of expression, a right implicit in the PEN Charter to which all members subscribe. The International PEN Translations and Linguistic Rights Committee strives to promote the translations of works by writers in the lesser-known languages and to defend those languages. The Writers for Peace Committee exists to find ways in which writers can work for peaceful co-existence in the world. The Women Writers' Committee works to promote women's writing and publishing in developing countries. The Writers in Exile Network helps exiled writers. International Congresses are held most years. The 69th Congress will be held in Mexico City.

Membership of any one Centre implies membership of all Centres; at present 132 autonomous Centres exist throughout the world.

Associate membership is available for writers not yet eligible for full membership and for persons connected with literature. The English Centre has a programme of literary lectures, discussion, dinners and parties. A yearly Writers' Day is open to the public as are some literary lectures.

English PEN Centre
President Victoria Glendinning
Administrative Director Susanna Nicklin, Lancaster House, 33 Islington High Street, London N1 9LH
tel 020-7713 0023 *fax* 020-7713 0005
email enquiries@englishpen.org.uk
website www.pen.org.uk

Scottish PEN Centre
President Simon Berry, Greenleaf Editorial, 126 West Princess Street, Glasgow G84 9DB
tel/fax 0141-564 1958
email info@scottishpen.org
website www.scottishpen.org

Irish PEN Centre
President Brian Friel
Secretary Arthur Flynn, 26 Rosslyn, Killarney Road, Bray, Co. Wicklow, Republic of Ireland
tel (353) 1 282 8053

Performing Right Society Ltd (PRS)
Copyright House, 29-33 Berners Street, London W1T 3AB
tel 020-7580 5544 *fax* 020-7306 4455
website www.prs.co.uk
Chief Executive John Hutchinson

Periodical Publishers Association
Queens House, 28 Kingsway, London WC2B 6JR
tel 020-7404 4166 *fax* 020-7404 4167
email info1@ppa.co.uk
website www.ppa.co.uk
Chief Executive Ian Locks

The Personal Managers' Association Ltd
Liaison Secretary Angela Adler, 1 Summer Road, East Molesey, Surrey KT8 9LX
tel/fax 020-8398 9796
email aadler@thepma.com
Association of theatrical agents in the theatre, film and entertainment world generally.

The Picture Research Association
2 Culver Drive, Oxted, Surrey RH8 9HP
tel (01883) 730123 *fax* (01883) 730144
email pra@lippmann.co.uk
website www.picture-research.org.uk
Chair Charlotte Lippmann

Professional organisation of picture researchers and picture editors. Its aims are:
• to promote the recognition of picture research, management, editing, picture buying and supplying as a profession requiring particular skills and knowledge;
• to bring together all those involved in the picture profession and provide a forum for information exchange and interaction;
• to encourage publishers, TV and video production organisations, internet companies, and any other users of images to use the PRA freelance register and engage a member of PRA to obtain them, thus ensuring that professional standards are maintained;
• to advise those specifically wishing to embark on a profession in the research and supply of pictures for all types of visual media information, providing guidelines and standards in so doing.

Pier Playwrights
PO Box 141, Brighton, East Sussex BN2 1LZ
tel (01273) 625132
email admin@pierplaywrights.co.uk
website www.pierplaywrights.co.uk
Administrator Chris Taylor
Membership £15 p.a.

Aims to support and encourage writers and their writing for performance in all its forms. Activities include a script-reading service (members only), workshops from visiting professionals, and a monthly newsletter. Pier Playwrights is a registered charity supported by South East Arts and is open to all dramatic writers in South and South East England. Founded 1990.

Player-Playwrights

Secretary Peter Thompson, 9 Hillfield Park, London N10 3QT
tel 020-8883 0371
email p-p@dial.pipex.com
Membership £10 in first year and £6 thereafter (plus £1.50 per attendance)

Meets on Monday evenings upstairs at the Horse and Groom, 128 Great Portland Street, London W1. The society reads, performs and discusses plays and scripts submitted by members, with a view to assisting the writers in improving and marketing their work. Newcomers and new acting members are always welcome. Founded 1948.

Poetry Book Society

Book House, 45 East Hill, London SW18 2QZ
tel 020-8870 8403 *fax* 020-8870 0865
email info@poetrybooks.co.uk
website www.poetrybooks.co.uk
Chair Maura Dooley, *Director* Chris Holyfield

Foremost in getting books of new poetry to readers through quarterly selections, special offers, and 300-strong backlist which it sells at favourable rates to members. Website features over 1000 post-1950s poetry books for sale. Publishes *Bulletin* (quarterly) and runs the annual T.S. Eliot Prize for the best collection of new poetry. Operates as a charitable Book Club with annual membership (£10, £32, £125) open to all. Education resources for secondary schools and Children's Poetry Bookshelf for primary schools and libraries.

The Poetry Society

22 Betterton Street, London WC2H 9BX
tel 020-7420 9880 *fax* 020-7240 4818
email info@poetrysociety.org.uk
website www.poetrysociety.org.uk
Subscriptions Subscriptions and Membership Dept, Freepost 5410, London WC2H 9BR
tel 020-7420 9881 *fax* 020-7240 4818
Chair Richard Price, *Director* Jules Mann
Membership Open to all; national membership

Aims to help poets and poetry thrive in Britain today. Publishes *Poetry Review* (quarterly) and *Poetry News* (quarterly), has an information and imagination service, runs promotions and educational projects, helps to coordinate National Poetry Day and the annual National Poetry Competition (see page 508). Provides a unique critical service, Poetry Prescription, where poetry of up to 100 lines is appraised by a chosen poet. Runs

the Poetry Café at its premises in Covent Garden, which is also a venue for regular and one-off events, and is also available for hire for small readings and seminars (contact Jess York, *tel* 020-7420 9887). Founded 1909.

The Powys Society

Hon. Secretary Chris Gostick, Old School House, George Green Road, George Green, Wexham, Bucks. SL3 6BJ
tel (01753) 578632
email gostick@altavista.net
website www.powys-society.telinco.co.uk

Aims to promote the greater public recognition and enjoyment of the writings, thought and contribution to the arts of the Powys family, particularly John Cowper (1872–1963), Theodore (1875–1953) and Llewelyn (1884–1939) Powys, and the many other family members and their close friends. Publishes an annual scholarly journal (*The Powys Journal*) and 3 newsletters per year, and holds an annual weekend conference in August, as well as other activities. Founded 1967.

The Press Complaints Commission

Director Guy Black, 1 Salisbury Square, London EC4Y 8JB
tel 020-7353 1248 *Helpline tel* 020-7353 3732
fax 020-7353 8355
email pcc@pcc.org.uk
website www.pcc.org.uk
Acting Chairman Prof Robert Pinker

Independent body founded to oversee self-regulation of the Press. Deals with complaints by the public about the contents and conduct of British newspapers and magazines and advises editors on journalistic ethics. Complaints must be about the failure of newspapers or magazines to follow the letter or spirit of a Code of Practice, drafted by newspaper and magazine editors, adopted by the industry and supervised by the Commission. Founded 1991.

Printmakers Council

Clerkenwell Workshops, 31 Clerkenwell Close, London EC1R 0AT
tel/fax 020-7250 1927
President Stanley Jones, *Chair* Sheila Sloss
Membership £55 p.a., £27.50 students

Artist-led group which aims to promote the use of both traditional and innovative printmaking techniques by:
• holding exhibitions of prints;
• providing information on prints and printmaking to both its membership and the public;
• encouraging cooperation and exchanges between members, other associations and interested individuals. Founded 1965.

Private Libraries Association

Ravelston, South View Road, Pinner,
Middlesex HA5 3YD
website www.the-old-school.demon.co.uk/pla.htm
President Colin Franklin, *Hon. Editors* David
Chambers, Paul W. Nash, *Hon. Secretary* James
Brown
Membership £25 p.a.

International society of book collectors and private
libraries. Publications include *The Private Library*
(quarterly), annual *Private Press Books*, and other
books on book collecting. Founded 1956.

The Publishers Association

29B Montague Street, London WC1B 5BH
tel 020-7691 9191 *fax* 020-7691 9199
email mail@publishers.org.uk
website www.publishers.org.uk
Chief Executive Ronnie Williams OBE, *Director of
International and Trade Divisions (BDCI)* Ian Taylor,
*Director of Educational, Academic and Professional
Publishing* Graham Taylor
Founded 1896.

Publishers' Association of South Africa (PASA)

PO Box 22640, Fish Hoek 7974, South Africa
tel (021) 782-7677 *fax* (021) 782-7679
email pasa@publishsa.co.za
website www.publishsa.co.za/

Publishers Licensing Society Ltd (PLS)

37-41 Gower Street, London WC1E 6HH
tel 020-7299 7730 *fax* 020-7299 7780
email pls@pls.org.uk
website www.pls.org.uk
Chairman Robert Kiernan, *Chief Executive* Jens
Bammel

PLS has mandates from over 1600 publishers. These
non-exclusive licences allow PLS to include those
publishers' works as part of the repertoire offered to
licensees by CLA. The licences permit photocopying
and some digitisation of parts of copyright works.
The money collected from these licences is shared
between publishers and authors and PLS has
responsibility for distributing the publishers' share
to the mandating companies. PLS represents the
interests of a wide range of publishers from the
multinationals to the single-title publisher. Founded
1981.

Publishers Publicity Circle

Secretary/Treasurer Heather White,
65 Airedale Avenue, London W4 2NN
tel 020-8994 1881
email ppc-@lineone.net
website www.publisherspublicitycircle.co.uk

Enables all book publicists to meet and share
information regularly. Monthly meetings provide

a forum for press journalists, TV and radio
researchers and producers to meet publicists
collectively. Awards are presented for the best PR
campaigns. Monthly newsletter includes
recruitment advertising. Founded 1955.

The Radclyffe International Philosophical Association

BM-RIPhA, Old Gloucester Street,
London WC1N 3XX
email riphassoc@aol.com
President William Mann FRIPhA, *Secretary General*
John Khasseyan FRIPhA
Membership £30 p.a. (Fellows, Members and
Associates)

Aims to dignify those achievements which might
otherwise escape formal recognition; to promote
the interests and talent of its members; to
encourage their good fellowship; and to form a
medium for the exchange of ideas between
members. Published authors and artists usually
enter at Fellowship level. Founded 1955.

The Radio Academy

5 Market Place, London W1W 8AE
email info@radioacademy.org
website www.radioacademy.org
Director John Bradford

The professional association for those engaged in
the UK radio industry with over 2000 individual
members and 30 corporate patrons. Organises
conferences, seminars, debates, the annual UK
Radio Festival and social events for members in all
regions of theUK; publishes *Off Air* (quarterly)
newsletter and an annual *Yearbook*. Provides
administrative support for the Student Radio
Association and the Radio Studies Network and
organises a series of regional training events for
those interested in getting into radio.

Randolph Caldecott Society

Secretary Kenn Oultram, Clatterwick House,
Little Leigh, Northwich, Cheshire CW8 4RJ
tel (01606) 891303 (office), 781731 (evening)
Membership £7-£10 p.a.

Aims to encourage an interest in the life and works
of Randolph Caldecott, the Victorian artist,
illustrator and sculptor. Meetings held in Chester
and London. Liaises with the American Caldecott
Society. Founded 1983.

Regional Arts Offices – see Arts Council England

The Richard Jefferies Society

Hon. Secretary Phyllis Treitel, Eidsvoll,
Bedwells Heath, Boars Hill, Oxford OX1 5JE
tel (01865) 735678
Membership £7 p.a. Worldwide membership

Promotes interest in the life, works and associations of the naturalist and novelist, Richard Jefferies; helps to preserve buildings and memorials, and cooperates in the development of a Museum in his birthplace. Arranges regular meetings in Swindon, and occasionally elsewhere; organises outings and displays; publishes a Journal and a Newsletter in the spring and an Annual Report in September. Founded 1950.

Ridley Art Society
50 Crowborough Road, London SW17 9QQ
tel 020-8682 1212
email info@ridleyart.com
President Ken Howard RA, *Chairman* dickon

Represents a wide variety of attitudes towards the making of art. In recent years has sought to encourage younger artists. At least one central London Members' exhibition a year. Founded 1889.

The Robert Louis Stevenson Club
Secretary Margaret Bean, 37 Lauder Road, Edinburgh EH9 1UE
tel 0131-667 6256 *fax* 0131-662 0353
email MBeanConferences@aol.com
Membership £15 p.a., £100 10 years, £180 life

Aims to foster interest in Robert Louis Stevenson's life (1850–94) and works through various events and its newsletter. Founded 1920.

The Romantic Novelists' Association
Chairman Anthea Kenyon, 36 Eastgate, Hallaton, Market Harborough, Leics. LE16 8UB
tel/fax 020-7736 4968
website www.rna-uk.org
Hon. Secretary Mary de Laszlo, 57 Coniger Road, London SW6 3TB

Aims to raise the prestige of Romantic Authorship. Open to romantic and historical novelists. See also page 510.

Royal Academy of Arts
Piccadilly, London W1J 0BD
tel 020-7300 8000 *fax* 020-7300 8001
website www.royalacademy.org.uk
President Prof Phillip King, *Keeper* Brendan Neiland RA

Academicians (RA) are elected from the most distinguished artists in the UK. Holds major loan exhibitions throughout the year including the Annual Summer Exhibition (June–Aug). Also runs art schools for 60 postgraduate students in painting and sculpture.

Royal Birmingham Society of Artists
4 Brook Street, St Paul's, Birmingham B3 1SA
tel 0121-236 4353 *fax* 0121-236 4555
Membership Friends £20 p.a.

The Society has 2 floors of exhibition space and a craft gallery in the city centre. Members (RBSA) and Associates (ARBSA) are elected annually. Holds 4 Open Exhibitions: 3 all-media exhibitions (Spring, Summer and Winter) – send sae for schedules, available 6 weeks prior to Exhibition. A further Open £1000 First Prize Exhibition is held (June/July) for works in any media. Other substantial money prizes can be won with no preference given to Members and Associates. Also a varying programme of exhibitions throughout the year, including the Autumn Exhibition, open to Members and Associates, and 2 Friends Exhibitions (Feb and Aug). Friends of the RBSA are entitled to attend various functions and to submit work for the Annual Exhibitions.

Royal Institute of Oil Painters
17 Carlton House Terrace, London SW1Y 5BD
tel 020-7930 6844 *fax* 020-7839 7830
website www.mallgalleries.org.uk
President Olwen Tarrant

Promotes and encourages the art of painting in oils. Open Annual Exhibition at the Mall Galleries, The Mall, London SW1.

Royal Institute of Painters in Water Colours
17 Carlton House Terrace, London SW1Y 5BD
tel 020-7930 6844 *fax* 020-7839 7830
website www.mallgalleries.org.uk
President Ronald Maddox Hon. RWS
Membership Elected from approved candidates' list

Promotes the appreciation of watercolour painting in its traditional and contemporary forms, primarily by means of an annual exhibition at the Mall Galleries, The Mall, London SW1 of members' and non-members' work and also by members' exhibitions at selected venues in Britain and abroad. Founded 1831.

The Royal Literary Fund
3 Johnson's Court, off Fleet Street, London EC4A 3EA
tel 020-7353 7150 *fax* 020-7353 1350
email egunnrlf@globalnet.co.uk
website www.rlf.org.uk
President His Honour Sir Stephen Tumim, *General Secretary* Eileen Gunn

Founded in 1790, the Fund is the oldest charity serving literature, set up to help writers and their families who face hardship. It does not offer grants to writers who can earn their living in other ways, nor does it provide financial support for writing projects. But it sustains authors who have for one reason or another fallen on hard times – illness, family misfortune, or sheer loss of writing form. Applicants must have published work of approved literary merit, which may include important contributions to periodicals. The literary claim of every new applicant must be accepted by the General Committee before the question of need can be considered.

The Royal Musical Association
Secretary Dr Jeffrey Dean, 4 Chandos Road, Chorlton-cum-Hardy, Manchester M21 0ST
tel 0161-861 7542 *fax* 0161-861 7543
email jeffrey.dean@stingrayoffice.com
website www.rma.ac.uk

The Royal Photographic Society
The Octagon, Milsom Street, Bath BA1 1DN
tel (01225) 462841 *fax* (01225) 448688
email rps@rps.org
website www.rps.org
Open membership organisation which promotes the art and science of photography and electronic imagery. Publishes *The RPS Journal* (monthly) and *Imaging Science Journal* (quarterly). Founded 1853.

Royal Scottish Academy
The Mound, Edinburgh EH2 2YT
tel 0131-558 7097 *fax* 0131-557 6417
email info@royalscottishacademy.org
President Ian McKenzie Smith OBE, PRSA, *Secretary* Bill Scott RSA, *Treasurer* Isi Metzstein OBE, RSA

Academicians (RSA) and Associates (ARSA) and non-members may exhibit in the Annual Exhibition of Painting, Sculpture and Architecture, held approximately mid April–July; Festival Exhibition Aug–Oct. Royal Scottish Academy Student Exhibition held in March and the Salvesen Scholarship Exhibition in Nov–Dec. Founded 1826.

The Royal Society
6-9 Carlton House Terrace, London SW1Y 5AG
tel 020-7451 2500 *fax* 020-7930 2170
email press@royalsoc.ac.uk
website www.royalsoc.ac.uk
President Lord May of Oxford OM, AC, Kt, PRS, *Treasurer* Prof David Wallace CBE, FRS, *Biological Secretary* Prof P.P.G. Bateson FRS, *Physical Secretary* Prof John Enderby CBE, FRS, *Foreign Secretary* Prof Dame Julia Higgins DBE, FRS, FREng, *Executive Secretary* Mr S. Cox CVO

The Royal Society for Asian Affairs
2 Belgrave Square, London SW1X 8PJ
tel 020-7235 5122 *fax* 020-7259 6771
email info@rsaa.org.uk
website www.rsaa.org.uk
President The Lord Denman CBE, MC TD, *Chairman of Council* Sir Donald Hawley KCMG, MBE, *Secretary* David Easton MA, FRSA, FRGS
Membership £55 p.a. London, £45 more than 60 miles from London and overseas, £10 up to age 25

For the study of all Asia past and present; fortnightly lectures, etc; library. Publishes *Asian Affairs* (3 p.a.), free to members. Founded 1901.

Royal Society for the encouragement of Arts, Manufactures and Commerce (RSA)
8 John Adam Street, London WC2N 6EZ
tel 020-7930 5115 *fax* 020-7839 5805
email journal@rsa.org.uk
website www.rsa.org.uk
Chairman of Council Dr Neil Cross, *Director* Penny Egan, *Commercial Director* Chris Bond, *Programme Director* Dr Geoffrey Botting, *Communication Director* Paul Crake, *Director of Finance* Bernard Kelly, *Editor, RSA Journal* Morice Mendoza, *Press Officer* Barbara Ormston

With over 20,000 Fellows, the RSA sustains a forum for people from all walks of life to come together to address issues, shape new ideas and stimulate action. It works through projects, award schemes and its lecture programme, the proceedings of which are recorded in *RSA Journal*. Founded 1754.

Royal Society of British Artists
17 Carlton House Terrace, London SW1Y 5BD
tel 020-7930 6844 *fax* 020-7839 7830
website www.mallgalleries.org.uk
President Cav. Romeo di Girolamo, *Keeper* Alfred Daniels

Incorporated by Royal Charter for the purpose of encouraging the study and practice of the arts of painting, sculpture and architectural designs. Annual Open Exhibition at the Mall Galleries, The Mall, London SW1, open to artists working in any 2- or 3-dimensional medium.

Royal Society of Literature
Somerset House, Strand, London WC2R 1LA
tel 020-7845 4676 *fax* 020-7845 4679
email info@rslit.org
Chairman of Council Ronald Harwood CBE, FRSL, *Secretary* Maggie Fergusson
Membership £30 p.a.

For the promotion of literature and encouragement of writers by way of lectures, discussions, readings, and by publications. Administers the Royal Society of Literature Award under the W.H. Heinemann Bequest, the V.S. Pritchett Memorial Prize and the Winifred Holtby Memorial Prize. Founded 1820.

Royal Society of Marine Artists
17 Carlton House Terrace, London SW1Y 5BD
tel 020-7930 6844 *fax* 020-7839 7830
website www.mallgalleries.org.uk
President Bert Wright

Aims to promote and encourage marine painting. Open Annual Exhibition at the Mall Galleries, The Mall, London SW1 for any artists whose main interest is the sea, or tidal waters, or some object essentially connected therewith.

The Royal Society of Miniature Painters, Sculptors and Gravers

Executive Secretary Mrs Pam Henderson,
1 Knapp Cottages, Wyke, Gillingham,
Dorset SP8 4NQ
tel (01747) 825718; 020-7222 2723 (during exhibitions)
email hendersons@dial.pipex.com
website www.royal-miniature-society.org.uk
President Suzanne Lucas FLS, PRMS, FPSBA, *Treasurer* Alastair MacDonald, *Hon. Secretary* Barbara Penketh Simpson
Membership By selection and standard of work over a period of years (ARMS associate, RMS full member)

Annual Open Exhibition in November at the Westminster Gallery in London. Hand in Sept/Oct; schedules available in July (send sae). Applications and enquiries to the Executive Secretary. Founded 1895.

Royal Society of Painter-Printmakers

Bankside Gallery, 48 Hopton Street,
London SE1 9JH
tel 020-7928 7521
email info@banksidegallery.com
website www.banksidegallery.com
President Anita Kline PRE
Membership Open to British and overseas artists. An election of Associates is held annually; for particulars apply to the Secretary. Friends of the RSPP open to all those interested in artists' original printmaking.

The Society organises workshops and lectures on original printmaking; holds one members' exhibition per year. Founded 1880.

Royal Society of Portrait Painters

17 Carlton House Terrace, London SW1Y 5BD
tel 020-7930 6844 *fax* 020-7839 7830
President Andrew Festing

Annual Exhibition at the Mall Galleries, The Mall, London SW1, of members' work and that of selected non-members. Three high-profile artists' awards are made: the Ondaatje Prize for Portraiture (£10,000), the Carroll Foundation Young Portrait Painters Award (£3000), and the Prince of Wales Award for Portrait Drawing (£2000). Also commissions consultancy service. Founded 1891.

Royal Television Society

Holborn Hall, 100 Gray's Inn Road,
London WC1X 8AL
tel 020-7430 1000 *fax* 020-7430 0924
email membership@rts.org.uk
website www.rts.org.uk

Chief Executive Simon Albury, *Membership Services Manager* Deborah Halls
Membership £70 p.a.

The Society is a unique, central, independent forum to debate the art, science and politics of TV. Holds awards, conferences, dinners, lectures and workshops. Founded 1927.

Royal Watercolour Society

Bankside Gallery, 48 Hopton Street,
London SE1 9JH
tel 020-7928 7521
email info@banksidegallery.com
website www.banksidegallery.com
President Trevor Frankland, PRWS, RE
Membership Open to British and overseas artists. Election of Associates held annually; write to the Secretary for particulars. Friends of the RWS open to all those interested in watercolour painting

Arranges lectures on watercolour painting; organises residential/non-residential courses; holds open exhibition in summer. Exhibitions: spring and autumn. Founded 1804.

Royal West of England Academy

Queens Road, Clifton, Bristol BS8 1PX
tel 0117-973 5129 *fax* 0117-923 7874
website www.rwa.org.uk
President Derek Balmer

An art Academy/gallery whose objectives are to advance the education of the public in the fine arts and in particular to promote the appreciation and practice of the fine arts and to encourage and develop talent in the fine arts. Founded 1844.

The Ruskin Society

Hon. Secretary Dr C.J. Gamble, 49 Hallam Street,
London W1W 6JP
Membership £10 p.a.

Aims to encourage a wider understanding of John Ruskin (1819–1900) and his contemporaries. Organises lectures and events which seek to explain to the public the nature of Ruskin's theories and to place these in a modern context. Affiliated to the Ruskin Foundation. Founded 1997.

The Ruskin Society of London

Membership Secretary Mrs A. Hardy,
351 Woodstock Road, Oxford OX2 7NX
tel (01865) 310987/515962 *fax* (01865) 240448
Chairman and General Secretary Miss O.E. Forbes-Madden
Membership £10 p.a.

Promotes literary and biographical interest in John Ruskin and his contemporaries. Publishes an annual *Ruskin Gazette,* free to members. Members are also affiliated to other literary societies. Founded 1985.

SAA (Society for All Artists)

PO Box 50, Newark, Notts. NG23 5GY
tel (01949) 844050 *fax* (01949) 844051
email inspiration@saa.co.uk
website www.saa.co.uk
Membership £22.50–£42 p.a. including paintings
exhibition insurance and third party public liability,
£27.50 overseas

Aims to 'inform, encourage and inspire all who
want to paint', from complete beginners to
professionals; to promote friendship and
companionship amongst fellow artists. Holds
meetings and events locally and nationally,
organises painting holidays, workshops, local and
international exhibitions and competitions,
publishes newsletter *Paint* (quarterly) and *SAA
Home Shopping* catalogue. Founded 1992.

Scattered Authors Society

Secretary Anne Cassidy, 150 Wanstead Lane, Ilford,
Essex IG1 3SG
email anne.cassidy@cwcom.net

Aims to provide a forum for informal discussion,
contact and support for professional writers in
children's fiction. Founded 1998.

Scottish Arts Club

24 Rutland Square, Edinburgh EH1 2BW
tel 0131-229 8157 *fax* 0131-229 8887
email info@scottishartsclub.co.uk
website www.scottishartsclub.co.uk
Hon. Secretary Mhairi Kerr
tel 0131-229 8157
Membership £330 p.a. full; reductions available

Art, literature, music.

Scottish Arts Council

12 Manor Place, Edinburgh EH3 7DD
tel 0131-226 6051
Chairman James Boyle, *Director* Graham Berry,
Head of Literature Gavin Wallace, *Head of Visual
Arts* Amanda Catto

Principal channel for government funding of the
arts in Scotland, the Scottish Arts Council is funded
by the Scottish Executive. It aims to develop and
improve the knowledge, understanding and practice
of the arts, and to increase their accessibility
throughout Scotland. It offers about 1300 grants a
year to artists and arts organisations concerned with
the visual arts, drama, dance and mime, literature,
music, festivals, and traditional, ethnic and
community arts. It is also the distributor of
National Lottery funds to the arts in Scotland.

Scottish Book Trust (SBT)

Sandeman House, 55 High Street,
Edinburgh EH1 1SR
tel 0131-229 3663 *fax* 0131-228 4293

email info@scottishbooktrust.com
website www.scottishbooktrust.com

With a particular responsibility towards Scottish
writing, SBT exists to promote literature and
reading, and aims to reach (and create) a wider
reading public than has existed before. It also
organises exhibitions, readings and storytellings,
administers the Writers in Scotland scheme, operates
an extensive children's reference library available to
everyone and provides a book information service.
SBT has a range of publications and advises other
relevant art organisations. Founded 1960.

Scottish Daily Newspaper Society

48 Palmerston Place, Edinburgh EH12 5DE
tel 0131-220 4353 *fax* 0131-220 4344
email info@sdns.org.uk
Director J.B. Raeburn FCIS

Scottish Newspaper Publishers Association

48 Palmerston Place, Edinburgh EH12 5DE
tel 0131-220 4353 *fax* 0131-220 4344
email info@snpa.org.uk
website www.snpa.org.uk
Director J.B. Raeburn FCIS

Scottish Publishers Association

Scottish Book Centre, 137 Dundee Street,
Edinburgh EH11 1BG
tel 0131-228 6866 *fax* 0131-228 3220
email enquiries@scottishbooks.org
website www.scottishbooks.org
Director Lorraine Fannin, *Administrator* Carol
Lothian, *Member Services Manager* Liz Small,
Project Administrator Caroline Taylor
Founded 1973.

Scottish Screen

2nd Floor, 249 West George Street,
Glasgow G2 4QE
tel 0141-302 1700 *fax* 0141-302 1711
email info@scottishscreen.com
website www.scottishscreen.com
Information Manager Isabella Edgar

Develops, encourages and promotes every aspect of
film, TV and new media in Scotland through script
and company development, short film production,
distribution of National Lottery film production
finance, training, education, exhibition funding,
Film Commission Locations support and the
Scottish Screen Archive.

Screenwriters' Workshop

(formerly London Screenwriters' Workshop)
Suffolk House, 1-8 Whitfield Place,
London W1T 5JU
tel 020-7387 5511
email screenoffice@tisali.co.uk

website www.lsw.org.uk
Contact The Secretary
Membership £40 p.a.

Forum for contact, information and tuition, the SW helps new and established writers work successfully in the film and TV industry, and organises a continuous programme of activities, events, courses and seminars, all of which are reduced to members and open to non-members at reasonable rates. The SW is the largest screenwriting group in Europe and supports Euroscript, a Media II-funded organisation developing scripts for film and TV throughout the EU. Founded 1983.

SCRIBO

Contact K. & P. Sylvester, Flat 1, 31 Hamilton Road, Bournemouth BH1 4EQ
Membership Joining fee: £5 (send sae); no annual subscription

A postal forum for novelists (published and unpublished), SCRIBO aims to give friendly, informed encouragement and help, to discuss all matters of interest to novelists and to offer criticism via MSS folios: crime/thrillers, fantasy/SF, mainstream, aga-saga/popular women's fiction, plus literary folios. Founded 1971.

'Sean Dorman' Manuscript Society

Cherry Trees, Crosemere Road, Cockshutt, Ellesmere, Shropshire SY12 0JP
tel (01939) 270293
Director Mary Driver

Provides mutual help among writers and aspiring writers in the UK. By means of circulating MSS parcels, members receive constructive criticism of their own work and read and comment on the work of others. Each 'Circulator' has up to 9 participants and members' contributions may be in any medium: short stories, chapters of a novel, poetry, magazine articles, etc. Send sae for full details and application form. Founded 1957.

The Shaw Society

Secretary Barbara Smoker, 51 Farmfield Road, Downham, Bromley, Kent BR1 4NF
tel 020-8697 3619
email anthnyellis@aol.com
Membership £15/$30 p.a.

Improvement and diffusion of knowledge of the life and works of Bernard Shaw and his circle. Meetings in London; annual festival at Ayot St Lawrence in July. Publishes *The Shavian*.

The Sheila Kaye-Smith Society

Secretary Grace Chatfield, 5 Leeds Close, Ore Village, Hastings, East Sussex TN35 5BX
tel (01424) 437413 *fax* (01424) 883268
Membership £6 p.a. single, £9 joint

Aims to stimulate and widen interest in the work of the Sussex writer and novelist, Sheila Kaye-Smith (1887–1956). Produces *The Gleam* (annual) and occasional papers, and organises talks. Founded 1987.

The Sherlock Holmes Society of London

General enquiries Heather Owen, 64 Graham Road, London SW19 3SS
tel/fax 020-8540 7657
email heatherowen@tiscali.co.uk
website www.sherlock-holmes.org.uk
Membership R.J. Ellis, 13 Crofton Avenue, Orpington, Kent BR6 8DU
tel/fax (01689) 811314
email shsl221b@aol.com
President A.D. Howlett MA, LLB, *Chairman* Peter L. Horrocks MA
Membership £14 p.a. UK/Europe, £18 Far East, US$30.50 USA

Aims to bring together those who have a common interest as readers and students of the literature of Sherlock Holmes, and to encourage the pursuit of knowledge of the public and private lives of Sherlock Holmes and Dr Watson. Membership includes *The Sherlock Holmes Journal* (2 p.a.). Founded 1951.

Society for Editors and Proofreaders (SfEP)

(formerly Society of Freelance Editors and Proofreaders)
Office Riverbank House, 1 Putney Bridge Approach, London SW6 3JD
tel 020-7736 3278
email admin@sfep.org.uk
website www.sfep.org.uk

Works to promote high editorial standards and achieve recognition of its members' professional status, through local and national meetings, an annual conference, an email discussion group, a regular newsletter and a programme of reasonably priced workshops/training sessions. These sessions help newcomers to acquire basic skills, enable experienced editors to update their skills or broaden their competence, and also cover aspects of professional practice or business for the self-employed. An annual Directory of members' services is available. The Society supports moves towards recognised standards of training and accreditation for editors and proofreaders and has developed its own Accreditation in Proofreading qualification. It has close links with the Publishing Training Centre and the Society of Indexers, is represented on the BSI Technical Committee dealing with copy preparation and proof correction (BS 5261), and works to foster good relations with all relevant bodies and organisations in the UK and worldwide. Founded 1988.

Society for Strip Illustration – now Comics Creators Guild

The Society for Theatre Research

c/o The Theatre Museum, 1E Tavistock Street, London WC2E 7PR
email e.cottis@btinternet.com
website www.str.org.uk
Hon. Secretaries Eileen Cottis and Frances Dann

Publishes annual volumes and journal (3 p.a.), *Theatre Notebook*, holds lectures and makes annual research grants (current total sum approx. £4000). Starting in 1998, the Society's 50th anniversary, it awards an annual prize of £400 for the best book published in English on the historical or current practice of the British theatre.

Society of Artists Agents

44 Brookbank Avenue, London W7 3DW
tel/fax 020-8575 6572
email careyb@thesaa.com
website www.thesaa.com
Contact Carey Bennett

Formed to promote professionalism in the illustration industry and to forge closer links between clients and artists through an agreed set of guidelines. The Society believes in an ethical approach through proper terms and conditions, thereby protecting the interests of the artists and clients. Founded 1992.

The Society of Authors – see page 487

The Society of Botanical Artists

Executive Secretary Mrs Pam Henderson, 1 Knapp Cottages, Wyke, Gillingham, Dorset SP8 4NQ
tel (01747) 825718, 020-7222 2723 (during exhibitions)
email pam@soc-botanical-artists.org
website www.soc-botanical-artists.org
Founder President Suzanne Lucas FLS, PRMS, FPSBA,
Executive Vice President Margaret Stevens
Membership Through selection. £100 p.a.; £20 lay members

Aims to encourage the art of botanical painting. Annual Open Exhibition held after Easter at the Westminster Gallery, Central Hall Westminster, Storey's Gate, London SW1H 9NH; hand in Feb/March. Information and entrance forms available from the Executive Secretary from January, on receipt of sae. Founded 1985.

Society of Children's Book Writers and Illustrators (SCBWI)

Flat 3, 124 Norwood Road, London SE24 9AY
tel 020-8671 7539
email scbwi_bi@hotmail.com
website www.wordpool.co.uk/scbwi

Regional Adviser Natascha Biebow
Membership £44 p.a. plus a one-off fee of £7

An international network for the exchange of knowledge between professional writers, illustrators, editors, publishers, agents, librarians, educators, booksellers and others involved with literature for young people. Sponsors 2 annual conferences on writing and illustrating books and multimedia – in New York (February) and Los Angeles (summer) – as well as dozens of regional conferences and events throughout the world. Publishes a bi-monthly newsletter, *The Bulletin*, and information publications, and awards grants for works in progress. The SCBWI also presents the annual Golden Kite Award for the best fiction and non-fiction books, open both to published and unpublished writers and illustrators.

The SCBWI British Isles region meets quarterly for a speaker or workshop event. Also sponsors local critique groups and publishes *Words and Pictures* quarterly newsletter, which includes up-to-date events and marketing information and articles on the craft of children's writing and illustrating in the British Isles. The yearly Writer's Day and Illustrator's Day includes workshops and the opportunity to meet publishing professionals. Founded 1971.

The Society of Civil and Public Service Writers

Secretary Mrs J.M. Lewis, 17 The Green, Corby Glen, Grantham, Lincs. NG33 4NP
email joan@hykin.fsnet.co.uk
Membership £15 p.a.; Poetry Workshop add £3

Welcomes serving and retired members of the Civil Service, Armed Forces, Post Office and BT, the nursing profession, and other public servants. Members can be aspiring or published writers. Holds annual competitions for short stories, articles and poetry, plus occasional for longer works. Offers postal folios for short stories and articles; holds an AGM and occasional meetings; publishes *The Civil Service Author* (quarterly) magazine. Send sae for details. Founded 1935.

Society of Editors

Director Bob Satchwell, University Centre, Granta Place, Mill Lane, Cambridge CB2 1RU
tel (01223) 304080 *fax* (01223) 304090
email info@societyofeditors.org
website www.societyofeditors.org
Membership £230 p.a.

Formed from the merger of the Guild of Editors and the Association of British Editors, the Society has more than 450 members in national, regional and local newspapers, magazines, broadcasting, new media, journalism education and media law, campaigning for media freedom. Publishes *Briefing* (monthly). Founded 1999.

Society of Graphic Fine Art

18 Stiby Road, Yeovil, Somerset BA21 3EF
President David Brooke
Membership By election

A fine art society. Holds an annual open exhibition of work of high quality with an emphasis on good drawing, whether by pen, pencil (with our without wash), watercolour, pastel or any of the forms of printmaking. Founded 1919.

Society of Heraldic Arts

46 Reigate Road, Reigate,
Surrey RH2 0QN
tel (01737) 242945
website www.heraldic-arts.com
Secretary John Ferguson ARCA, SHA, DFACH, FRSA, FHS
Membership £12 p.a. associate, £17 craft

Aims to serve the interests of heraldic artists, craftsmen, designers and writers, to provide a 'shop window' for their work, to obtain commissions on their behalf and to act as a forum for the exchange of information and ideas. Also offers an information service to the public. Candidates for admission as craft members should be artists or craftsmen whose work comprises a substantial element of heraldry and is of a sufficiently high standard to satisfy the requirements of the Society's advisory council. Founded 1987.

Society of Indexers – see page 567

The Society of Limners

Founder/President Elizabeth Davys Wood MBE,
2 Glentrammon Close, Green Street Green,
Orpington, Kent BR6 6DL
tel (01689) 851158
email dionevenables@clara.net
Membership £30 p.a., £15 Friends (open to non-exhibitors); £45, £20 overseas

Aims to promote an interest in miniature painting (in any medium), calligraphy and heraldry and encourage their development to a high standard. New members are elected after the submission of 4 works of acceptable standard and guidelines are provided fornew artists. Members receive up to 4 newsletters a year and 2 annual exhibitions are arranged. Founded 1986.

The Society of Medical Writers

Chairman Dr David Brooks, The Barn,
Tonacliffe Road, Whitworth,
Lancs. OL12 8SJ
Secretary Mr Wilfred Hopkins, 633 Liverpool Road,
Southport PR8 3NG

Aims to recruit members from all branches of the medical profession, together with all professions allied to medicine, to foster interest in literature and in writing – not solely about medicine but also about art, history, music, theatre, etc. Members are encouraged to write fiction, poetry, plays, book reviews, etc. Publishes *The Writer* (2 p.a.); register of members and their writing interests published electronically each year. Holds an annual conference in which various aspects of literature and writing are explored in a relaxed and informal atmosphere. Founded 2001 as successor to the General Practitioner Writers Association.

Society of Scribes and Illuminators (SSI)

Hon. Secretary 6 Queen Square,
London WC1N 3AT
email scribe@calligraphyonline.org
website www.calligraphyonline.org
Membership £27 Lay members; £22 Friends

Aims to advance the crafts of writing and illumination. Holds regular exhibitions, provides opportunities for discussion, demonstration and sharing of research. Founded 1921.

The Society of Sussex Authors

Secretary Michael Legat, Bookends,
Lewes Road, Horsted Keynes,
Haywards Heath,
West Sussex RH17 7DP
tel/fax (01825) 790755
email michael@bookends.claranet.com
Membership £10 p.a. Open to writers living in Sussex who have had at least one book commercially published or who have worked extensively in journalism, radio, TV or the theatre

Aims to encourage social contact between members, and to promote interest in literature and authors. Founded 1969.

Society of Wildlife Artists

17 Carlton House Terrace,
London SW1Y 5BD
tel 020-7930 6844 *fax* 020-7839 7830
website www.mallgalleries.org.uk
President Bruce Pearson

Aims to promote and encourage the art of wildlife painting and sculpture. Open Annual Exhibition at the Mall Galleries, The Mall, London SW1, for any artist whose work depicts wildlife subjects (botanical and domestic animals are not admissable).

The Society of Women Artists

Executive Secretary 1 Knapp Cottages,
Wyke, Gillingham, Dorset SP8 4NQ
tel (01747) 825718 *fax* (01747) 826835
email hendersons@dial.pipex.com
website www.society-women-artists.org.uk
President Elizabeth Meek RMS, HS, FRSA
Membership Election by invitation, based on work submitted to the exhibition

Founded in 1855 when women were not considered as serious contributors to art and could not compete for professional honours, the Society continues to promote art by women. Receiving day end January for annual open exhibition held just before Easter at Westminster Gallery, Central Hall Westminster, Storey's Gate, London SW1H 9NH.

Society of Women Writers and Journalists

Secretary Zoe King, Calvers Farm, Thelveton, Diss, Norfolk IP21 4NG
tel (01379) 740550
email zoe@zoeking.com
Membership £35 p.a. town, £30 country, £25 overseas

For women writers: lectures, monthly workshops/ speakers; members' postal critique service. Publishes *The Woman Writer* (6 p.a.). Founded 1894.

Society of Young Publishers

Contact The Secretary, c/o The Bookseller, Endeavour House, 189 Shaftesbury Avenue, London WC2H 8TJ
email thesyp@thesyp.org.uk
website www.thesyp.org.uk
Membership Open to anyone employed in publishing or hoping to be soon; Associate membership available to those over the age of 35

Organises monthly speaker meetings at which senior figures talk on topics of key importance to the industry today, and social and other events. Runs a job database which matches candidates with potential employers. Meetings are held in Central London, usually on the last Wednesday of the month at 6.30pm. Also a branch in Oxford. Founded 1949.

South African Writers' Circle

Secretary Ann Carter, PO Box 115, Hillcrest 3650, South Africa
tel (031) 7655706
email brianduc@mweb.co.za
website www.sawc.sos.co.za
Membership R90 p.a. local, R100 overseas

Aims to help and encourage all writers, new and experienced, in the art of writing. Publishes a monthly *Newsletter*, and runs competitions with prizes for the winners. Founded 1960.

South & Mid Wales Association of Writers (SAMWAW)

Secretary Julian Rosser,
c/o IMC Consulting Group,
Denham House, Lambourne Crescent,
Cardiff CF14 5ZW
tel 029-2076 1170 *fax* 029-2076 1304
email info@imcconsultinggroup.co.uk
Membership £10 p.a. single, £15 joint

Aims to encourage the art of writing in all its forms, for both beginners and established writers. Offers a range of courses (see page 552). Publishes a newsletter and runs competitions, including the Mathew Prichard Award for Short Story Writing (see page 507). Founded 1965.

Southwest Scriptwriters

Secretary John Colborn *tel* 0117-909 5522
email southwest_scriptwriters@hotmail.com
website www.southwest-scriptwriters.co.uk
Membership £5 p.a.

Workshops members' drama scripts for stage, screen, radio and TV with the aim of improving their chances of professional production, meeting at the Bristol Old Vic. Also hosts regular talks by professional dramatists. Presents short annual seasons of script-in-hand performances of members' work at a major Bristol venue. Bi-monthly newsletter. Founded 1994.

Spoken Word Publishing Association (SWPA)

Administrator Zoe Howes,
Macmillan Audio Books, 20 New Wharf Road, London N1 9RR
tel 020-7014 6041
website www.swpa.co.uk
Membership £50–£600 p.a. plus VAT

The UK trade association for the spoken word industry, SWPA brings together all those involved – publishers, performers, producers, distributors, retailers, manufacturers. It aims to increase the profile of the spoken word in the media, the retail trade and among the general public, and to provide a forum for discussion. Founded 1994.

Sports Writers' Association of Great Britain (SWA)

Secretary Trevor Bond,
244 Perry Street, Billericay,
Essex CM12 0QP
tel (01277) 651708 *fax* (01277) 622890
email trevjanbondl@aol.com
website www.sportswriters.org.uk
Membership £23.50 p.a., £11.75 regional

Represents sports journalists across the country and is Britain's voice in international sporting affairs. Offers advice to members covering major events, acts as a consultant to organisers of major sporting events on media requirements. Member of the BOA Press Advisory Committee. Founded 1948.

Sussex Playwrights' Club

Hon. Secretary, 2 Brunswick Mews, Hove, East Sussex BN3 1HD
website www.newventure.org.uk

See 'features' page on website.

Swedish Publishers' Association
(Svenska Förläggareföreningen)
Drottninggaten 97, 2 tr.,
113 60 Stockholm, Sweden
tel 08-736 19 40 *fax* 08-736 19 44
email svf@forlagskansli.se
website www.forlagskansli.se
Director Kristina Ahlinder
Founded 1843.

The T.E. Lawrence Society
PO Box 728, Oxford OX2 6YP
website www.telsociety.org
Membership £18 p.a., £23 overseas
Promotes the memory of T.E. Lawrence and
furthers knowledge by research into his life;
publishes *Journal* (bi-annual) and *Newsletter*
(quarterly). Founded 1985.

The Tennyson Society
Hon. Secretary Kathleen Jefferson,
Brayford House, Lucy Tower Street,
Lincoln LN1 1XN
tel (01522) 552851 *fax* (01522) 552858
email linnet@lincolnshire.gov.uk
website www.tennysonsociety.org.uk
Membership £8 p.a., £10 family, £15 institutions
Promotes the study and understanding of the life
and work of the poet Alfred, Lord Tennyson and
supports the Tennyson Research Centre in Lincoln;
holds lectures, visits and seminars; publishes the
Tennyson Research Bulletin (annual), Monographs
and Occasional Papers; tapes/recordings available.
Founded 1960.

Theatre Writers' Union – incorporated into the Writers' Guild of Great Britain, page 490

The Thomas Hardy Society
PO Box 1438, Dorchester, Dorset DT1 1YH
tel/fax (01305) 251501
email info@hardysociety.org
website www.hardysociety.org
Membership £18 p.a., £22.50 overseas
Publishes *The Thomas Hardy Journal* (3 p.a.).
Biennial conference in Dorchester, 2004. Founded
1967.

Thomas Lovell Beddoes Society
11 Laund Nook, Belper,
Derbyshire DE56 1GY
tel (01773) 828066
email john@beddoes.demon.co.uk
website www.nortexinfo.net/mcdaniel/ tlb.htm
Aims to promote an interest in the life and works of
Thomas Lovell Beddoes (1803–49). The Society
promotes and undertakes Beddoes studies, and

disseminates and publishes useful research.
Founded 1994.

The Tolkien Society
Secretary Sally Kennett, 210 Prestbury Road,
Cheltenham, Glos. GL52 3ER
website www.tolkiensociety.org
Membership Secretary Trevor Reynolds,
65 Wentworth Crescent, Ash Vale,
Surrey GU12 5LF
email trevor@caerlas.demon.co.uk

The Translators Association
84 Drayton Gardens, London SW10 9SB
tel 020-7373 6642
email info@societyofauthors.org
website www.societyofauthors.org
Membership £75 p.a. (£70 DD), including
membership of the Society of Authors
Specialist unit within the membership of the
Society of Authors (see page 487), exclusively
concerned with the interests and special problems
of translators into English whose work is published
or performed commercially in Great Britain and
English-speaking countries overseas. Members are
entitled to general and legal advice on all questions
connected with their work, including remuneration
and contractual arrangements with publishers,
editors, broadcasting organisations. Publishes a
Quick Guide to literary translation (£2 to non-
members). Administers a range of translation
prizes. Founded 1958.

The Trollope Society
9A North Street, London SW4 0HN
tel 020-7720 6789 *fax* 020-978 1815
email trolsoc@barset.fsnet.co.uk
Chairman John Letts, *Secretary* Phyllis Eden
Membership £24 p.a., £240 life
Has produced the first ever complete edition of the
novels of Anthony Trollope (48 vols now available).
New 3-year extension will make this into the
'Complete Works' (60 vols by 2004). Founded 1987.

The Turner Society
BCM Box Turner, London WC1N 3XX
Chairman Eric Shanes
Membership £15 p.a.
Aims to foster a wider appreciation of all facets of
Turner's work; to encourage exhibitions of his
paintings, drawings and engravings. Publishes
Turner Society News (3 p.a.). Founded 1975.

United Society for Christian Literature
Albany House, 67 Sydenham Road, Guildford,
Surrey GU1 3RY
tel (01483) 888580 *fax* (01483) 888581
email headoffice@feedtheminds.org

website www.feedtheminds.org
Chairman John Clark

Exists to aid Christian literature principally in the world's poorest countries. Founded 1799.

Vampire Research Society

International Secretary Dennis Crawford,
3-22 Northwood Hall, Hornsey Lane,
London N6 5PH
email vampireresearchsociety@gothicpress.
freeserve.co.uk
Membership By invitation

The Society's sole purpose is to study and investigate vampirological phenomena, and publishes its research findings in books and academic reports. Holds the largest archive of vampire-related material in the world, to which membership allows access. Publishes a newsletter. Not affiliated to any other vampire interest group and remains aloof from the wider subculture. Founded 1970.

Ver Poets

Organiser/Editor May Badman, Haycroft,
61-63 Chiswell Green Lane, St Albans,
Herts. AL2 3AL
tel (01727) 867005 ·
email may.badman@virgin.net
Membership £12.50 p.a. UK, £15/$30 overseas

Encourages the writing and study of poetry as a part of our culture. Help and advice, assessment and comment on work are available on request. Holds meetings (fortnightly) in St Albans; organises workshops and competitions for members, and produces anthologies of members' work. The annual Open Competition (October) is also open to non-members. Founded 1966.

Virginia Woolf Society of Great Britain

Details Stuart N. Clarke, Fairhaven, Charnleys Lane,
Banks, Southport PR9 8HJ
tel/fax (01903) 764655
email snclarke@talk21.com
website http://orlando.jp.org/vwsgb/
Membership £12 p.a., £15 overseas

Acts as a forum for British admirers of Virginia Woolf (1882–1941) to meet, correspond and share their enjoyment of her work. Publishes the *Virginia Woolf Bulletin*. Founded 1998.

Visiting Arts

Bloomsbury House, 74-77 Great Russell Street,
London WC1B 3DA
tel 020-7291 1600 *fax* 020-7291 1616
email information@visitingarts.org.uk
website www.visitingarts.org.uk
Director Terry Sandell OBE

Works to ensure high-quality contemporary arts are brought into the UK from countries across the world and to extend the dialogue between UK artists and their overseas counterparts. Visiting Arts works with UK promoters, curators, managers, etc to develop the presentation of work from overseas in the UK. The projects it funds cover a large range of countries of origin, art forms, and venue sizes and locations, as Visiting Arts aims to place its resources strategically to ensure a higher profile to foreign arts and to extend the opportunities for audiences across the UK.

Activities include providing advice, information, training, consultancy, publications, special projects and project development, and covers the performing arts, visual, applied and media arts, crafts, design, literature, film, architecture and some museum activity.

Visiting Arts is an independent educational charity funded by the British Council, the Foreign and Commonwealth Office, the 4 national Arts Councils of England, Scotland, Wales and Northern Ireland and the Department for Culture, Media and Sport. Founded 1977.

Voice of the Listener & Viewer Ltd (VLV)

101 King's Drive, Gravesend,
Kent DA12 5BQ
tel (01474) 352835
Chairman Jocelyn Hay, *Administrative Secretary* Linda Forbes

Independent association representing the citizen and consumer interest in broadcasting and the interests of listeners and viewers on all broadcasting issues at UK and European level. Concerned to maintain the principle of public service plus independence, quality and diversity in British broadcasting. Has some 2000 individual members, nearly 30 charities as corporate members and more than 50 colleges in academic membership. Holds frequent public conferences all over UK. Maintains a panel of speakers. Holds the archives of the former Broadcasting Research Unit (1980–90), British Action for Children's Television (BACTV) 1988–94, as well as its own archive. Publishes a quarterly newsletter and briefings on broadcasting developments. Founded 1983.

The Walmsley Society

Secretary Fred Lane, April Cottage,
1 Brand Road, Hampden Park, Eastbourne,
East Sussex BN22 9PX
Membership Secretary Mrs Elizabeth Buckley,
21 The Crescent, Hipperholm, Halifax,
West Yorkshire HX3 8NQ

Aims to promote and encourage an appreciation of the literary and artistic heritage left to us by Leo and J. Ulric Walmsley. Founded 1985.

Welsh Academy – see Academi

Welsh Books Council/Cyngor Llyfrau Cymru
Castell Brychan, Aberystwyth,
Ceredigion SY23 2JB
tel (01970) 624151 *fax* (01970) 625385
email castellbrychan@cllc.org.uk
websites www.cllc.org.uk www.gwales.com
Director Gwerfyl Pierce Jones

Exists to promote Welsh-language and English-language books of Welsh interest. Editorial, design, marketing, distribution and children's books promotion services provided for publishers. Founded 1961

The West Country Writers' Association
Secretary Judy Joss, High Wotton, Wotton Lane, Lympstone, Exmouth, Devon EX8 5AY
tel (01395) 222749
email judy@josser.freeserve.co.uk
website www.westcountrywriters.co.uk
President Christopher Fry FRSL DLitt, *Chair* Dr David Keep
Membership Open to published authors, £10 p.a.

Aims to foster love of literature in the West Country and to give authors an opportunity of meeting to exchange news and views. Holds Annual Weekend Congress and Regional Meetings. Newsletter (2 p.a.).

Wilfred Owen Association
17 Belmont, Shrewsbury SY1 1TE
website www.1914-18.co.uk/owen
Membership £6 p.a. (£10 overseas), £15 groups/institutions, £4 concessions

Aims to commemorate the life and work of Wilfred Owen, and to encourage and enhance appreciation of his work through visits, public events, a newsletter and journal. Founded 1989.

The Wilkie Collins Society
Membership Secretary Paul Lewis, 4 Ernest Gardens, London W4 3QU
email paul@paullewis.co.uk
website www.wilkiecollins.org
Chairman Andrew Gasson
Membership £10 p.a. EU, £18 international

Aims to promote interest in the life and works of Wilkie Collins. Publishes a newsletter, an occasional scholarly journal and reprints of Collins's lesser known works. Founded 1981.

The William Cobbett Society
Chairman Molly Townsend, 10 Grenehurst Way, Petersfield, Hants GU31 4AZ
tel (01730) 262060
Membership £8 p.a.

Aims to make the life and work of William Cobbett better known. Founded 1976.

William Morris Society
Kelmscott House, 26 Upper Mall, London W6 9TA
tel 020-8741 3735 *fax* 020-8748 5207
email william.morris@care4free.net
website www.morrissociety.org
Secretary Peter Faulkner

Aims to spread knowledge of the life, work and ideas of William Morris; publishes *Newsletter* (quarterly) and *Journal* (2 p.a.). Library and collections open to the public Thurs and Sat, 2–5pm. Founded 1955.

Women in Publishing (WiP)
c/o 3 Gordon Road, London W5 2AD
email info@wipub.org.uk
website www.wipub.org.uk
Membership £25 p.a.

Promotes the status of women within publishing; encourages networking and mutual support among women; provides a forum for the discussion of ideas, trends and subjects to women in the trade; offers advice on publishing careers; supports and publicises women's achievements and successes. Each year WiP presents 2 awards: the Pandora Award is given in recognition of significant personal contributions to women in publishing, and the New Venture Award is presented to a recent venture which reflects the interests and concerns of women or minority groups in the 21st century. Founded 1979.

Women Writers Network
Membership Secretary Cathy Smith, 23 Prospect Road, London NW2 2JU
tel 020-7794 5861
Membership £45 p.a.; meetings only: £5 at door

London-based network serving both salaried and independent women writers from all disciplines, and providing a forum for the exchange of information, support and networking opportunities. Holds monthly meetings, workshops and publishes a newsletter and members' online Directory. Send sae for information. Founded 1985.

Worshipful Company of Stationers and Newspaper Makers
Stationers' Hall, London EC4M 7DD
tel 020-7248 2934 *fax* 020-7489 1975
Master C. Jonathan P. Straker, *Clerk* Brig. Denzil Sharp AFC

One of the Livery Companies of the City of London. Connected with the printing, publishing, bookselling, newspaper and allied trades. Founded 1557.

Writernet
(formerly New Playwrights Trust)
Cabin V, Clarendon Buildings, 25 Horsell Road, London N5 1XL

tel 020-7609 7474 *fax* 020-7609 7557
email writernet@btinternet.com
website www.writernet.org.uk
Executive Director Jonathan Meth
Membership Rates on application

Works with all new writing in all performance contexts. Provides writers for all forms of live and recorded performance – working at any stage of their career – with a range of services which enable them to pursue their careers better. Aims to network writers into and through the industry, principally by providing information, advice, guidance and career development training to meet the requirements of writers and producers alike. Also provides a wide range of producers who employ writers with the opportunity to make more informed choices to meet their needs. Writernet is an innovative interface between the writer and producer. Founded 1985.

The Writers Advice Centre for Children's Books
The Courtyard Studio, 43A Lesbourne Road, Reigate, Surrey RH2 7JS
tel (01737) 242999
email WritersAdvice@aol.com
Director Cherith Baldry

Editorial and marketing advice to children's writers. Founded 1994.

Writers' Circles Handbook
Contact Jill Dick, Oldacre, Horderns Park Road, Chapel-en-le-Frith, High Peak SK23 9SY
tel (01298) 812305
email oldacre@bt.internet.com
website www.btinternet.com/~oldacre

Handbook for writers' circles with information, articles, and a comprehensive list of all known circles and groups meeting in the UK. Some overseas entries too. Regular free updates available after initial purchase. Cost: £5 post free.

Writers Guild of America, East Inc. (WGAE)
Executive Director Mona Mangan, 555 West 57 Street, Suite 1230, New York, NY 10019, USA
tel 212-767-7800
Membership 1.5% of covered earnings

Represents writers in screen and TV for collective bargaining. It provides member services including pension and health, as well as educational and professional activities. Founded 1954.

Writers Guild of America, West Inc. (WGA)
Executive Director John McLean, 7000 West 3rd Street, Los Angeles, CA 90048, USA
tel 323-951-4000 *fax* 323-782-4800
website www.wga.org

Membership $2500 initiation, $25 quarterly, 1.5% of income annually

Union representing and servicing 9000 writers in film, broadcast, cable and multimedia industries for purposes of collective bargaining, contract administration and other services, and functions to protect and advance the economic, professional and creative interests of writers. Monthly publication, *Written By*, available by subscription. Founded 1933.

Writers Guild of Canada
123 Edward Street, Suite 1225, Toronto, Ontario M5G 1E2, Canada
tel 416-979-7907 *toll free* 1-800-567-9974
fax 416-979-9273
email info@wgc.ca
website www.wgc.ca
Executive Director Maureen Parker
Membership $150 p.a. plus 2% of fees earned in the Guild's jurisdiction

Represents over 1700 professional writers of film, TV, animation, radio, documentary and multimedia. Negotiates and administers collective agreements with independent producers as well as the CBC, TVO and NFB. The Guild also publishes *Canadian Screenwriter* magazine.

The Writers' Guild of Great Britain – see page 490

Writers in Oxford
Membership Secretary Rob Walters, 18 Paradise Square, Oxford OX1 1TW
tel (01865) 208930
email rob@satin.co.uk
Membership £20 p.a.

Exists to promote valuable discussion and social meetings among all kinds of published writers in and around Oxfordshire. Activities include: topical lunches and dinners, where subjects important to the writer are discussed; showcase evenings; parties. Publishes a regular newsletter, *The Oxford Writer*. Founded 1992.

The Writers' Union of Canada
40 Wellington Street East, 3rd Floor, Toronto, Ontario M5E 1C7, Canada
tel 416-703-8982 *fax* 416-504-7656
email info@writersunion.ca
website www.writersunion.ca

Yachting Journalists' Association
Secretary Barry Pickthall, Booker's Yard, The Street, Walberton, Arundel, West Sussex BN18 0PF
tel (01243) 555561 *fax* (01243) 555562
email ppl@mistral.co.uk
Membership £40 p.a.

Aims to further the interests of yachting, sail and power, and yachting journalism. Members vote annually for the Yachtsman of the Year, headline title of the British Nautical Awards, and the Young Sailor of the Year Award. Founded 1969.

The Yorkshire Dialect Society

Hon. Secretary Michael Park, 51 Stepney Avenue, Scarborough YO12 5BW
Membership £10 p.a.

Aims to encourage interest in: dialect speech, the writing of dialect verse, prose and drama; the publication and circulation of dialect literature; the study of the origins and the history of dialect and kindred subjects. Organises meetings; publishes *Transactions* (annual) and *The Summer Bulletin* free to members; list of other publications on request. Founded 1897.

The Society of Authors

The Society of Authors is an independent trade union, representing writers' interests in all aspects of the writing profession, particularly publishing, but also broadcasting, television and films, theatre and translation.

Founded over 100 years ago, the Society now has more than 7000 members. It has a professional staff, responsible to a Management Committee of 12 authors, and a Council (an advisory body meeting twice a year) consisting of 60 eminent writers. There are specialist groups within the Society to serve particular needs: the Academic Writers Group, the Broadcasting Group, the Children's Writers and Illustrators Group, the Educational Writers Group, the Medical Writers Group and the Translators Association (see page 482). There are also groups representing Scotland and the North of England.

"It does no harm to repeat, as often as you can, 'Without me the literary industry would not exist: the publishers, the agents, the sub-agents, the accountants, the libel lawyers, the departments of literature, the professors, the theses, the books of criticism, the reviewers, the book pages – all this vast and proliferating edifice is because of this small, patronised, put-down and underpaid person.'"
– *Doris Lessing*

What the Society does for members

Through its permanent staff (including a solicitor), the Society is able to give its members a comprehensive personal and professional service covering the business aspects of authorship, including:

- providing information about agents, publishers, and others concerned with the book trade, journalism, broadcasting and the performing arts;
- advising on negotiations, including the individual vetting of contracts, clause by clause, and assessing their terms both financial and otherwise;
- helping with members' queries, major or minor, over any aspect of the business of writing;
- taking up complaints on behalf of members on any issue concerned with the business of authorship;
- pursuing legal actions for breach of contract, copyright infringement, and the non-payment of royalties and fees, when the risk and cost preclude individual action by a member and issues of general concern to the profession are at stake;
- holding conferences, seminars, meetings and social occasions;
- producing a comprehensive range of publications, free of charge to members, including the Society's quarterly journal, *The Author*. *Quick Guides* cover many aspects of the profession such as: copyright, publishing contracts, libel, income tax, VAT, authors' agents, permissions, indexing, and the protection of titles. The Society also publishes occasional papers on subjects such as film agreements, packaged books, revised editions, multimedia, and vanity publishing.

Further membership benefits
Members have access to:
- the Retirement Benefit Scheme;
- a group Medical Insurance Scheme with BUPA;
- the Pension Fund (which offers discretionary pensions to a number of members);
- the Contingency Fund (which provides financial relief for authors or their dependents in sudden financial difficulties);
- free membership of the Authors' Licensing and Collecting Society (ALCS);
- books at special rates;
- membership of the Royal Over-Seas League at a discount.

The Society frequently secures improved conditions and better returns for members. It is common for members to report that, through the help and facilities offered, they have saved more, and sometimes substantially more, than their annual subscriptions (which are an allowable expense against income tax).

What the Society does for authors

The Society lobbies Members of Parliament, Ministers and Government Departments on all issues of concern to writers. Recent issues have included the operation and funding of Public Lending Right, the threat of VAT on books, copyright legislation and European Community initiatives. Concessions have also been obtained under various Finance Acts.

The Society litigates in matters of importance to authors. For example, the Society backed Andrew Boyle when he won his appeal against the Inland Revenue's attempt to tax the Whitbread Award.

The Society campaigns for better terms for writers. With the Writers' Guild, it has negotiated 'minimum terms agreements' with many leading publishers. The translators' section of the Society has also drawn up a minimum terms agreement for translators which has been adopted by Faber & Faber, and has been used on an individual basis by a number of other publishers.

The Society is recognised by the BBC for the purpose of negotiating rates for writers' contributions to radio drama, as well as for the

Membership

The Society of Authors

84 Drayton Gardens, London SW10 9SB
tel 020-7373 6642
email info@societyofauthors.org
website www.societyofauthors.org
General Secretary Mark Le Fanu

Membership at the discretion of the Committee of Management is open to authors who have had a full-length work published, broadcast or performed commercially in the UK. It is also open to authors who have had a full-length work accepted for publication, but not yet published; and those authors who have had occasional items broadcast or performed, or translations, articles, illustrations or short stories published. The owner or administrator of a deceased author's copyrights can become a member on behalf of the author's estate.

The annual subscription (which is tax deductible under Schedule D) is £80 (£75 by direct debit after the first year). There is a special rate for partners living at the same address. Authors under 35, who are not yet earning a significant income from their writing, may apply for membership at a lower subscription of £56. Authors over 65 may apply to pay at the reduced rate after their first year of membership.

Contact the Society for a membership booklet and copy of *The Author*.

broadcasting of published material. It was instrumental in setting up the ALCS (see page 620), which collects and distributes fees from reprography and other methods whereby copyright material is exploited without direct payment to the originators.

The Society keeps in close touch with the Arts Councils, the Association of Authors' Agents, the British Council, the Institute of Translation and Interpreting, the Department for Culture, Media and Sport, the National Union of Journalists, the Publishers Association and the Writers' Guild of Great Britain.

The Society is a member of the European Writers Congress, the British Copyright Council and the National Book Committee.

Awards

The Society of Authors administers:

● Travelling Scholarships which give honorary awards;

● four prizes for novels: the Betty Trask Awards, the Encore Award, the McKitterick Prize and the Sagittarius Prize;

● two prizes for a full-length published work: the Somerset Maugham Awards and the *Sunday Times* Young Writer of the Year Award;

● two poetry awards: the Eric Gregory Awards and the Cholmondeley Awards;

● the Tom-Gallon Award for short story writers;

● the Authors' Foundation and Kathleen Blundell Trust, which give grants to published authors working on their next book;

● the Richard Imison Award for a writer new to radio drama;

● awards for translations from French, German, Italian, Dutch, Portuguese, Spanish, Swedish and Japanese into English;

● the Francis Head Bequest for assisting authors who, through physical mishap, are temporarily unable to maintain themselves or their families.

The Writers' Guild of Great Britain

The Writers' Guild of Great Britain is the writers' trade union and is affiliated to the TUC.

The Writers' Guild of Great Britain is the writers' trade union, affiliated to the TUC, and represents writers' interests in film, television, radio, theatre and publishing. Formed in 1959 as the Screenwriters' Guild, the union gradually extended into all areas of freelance writing activity and copyright protection. In 1974, when book authors and stage dramatists became eligible for membership, substantial numbers joined. In June 1997 the Theatre Writers' Union membership unified with that of the Writers' Guild to create a larger, more powerful writers' union.

Apart from necessary dealings with Government and policies on legislative matters affecting writers, the Guild is, by constitution, non-political, has no involvement with any political party, and members pay no political levy.

The Guild employs a permanent secretary and staff and is administered by an Executive Council of 26 members. It has a national and regional/branch structure with committees representing Scotland, Wales, London and the South East, the North West, the North East, the Midlands and the South West of England. The Guild comprises practising professional writers in all media, united in common concern for one another and regulating the conditions under which they work.

The Writers' Guild and agreements

The Guild's basic function is to negotiate minimum terms in those areas in which its members work. Those agreements form the basis of the individual contracts signed by members. Further details are given below. The Guild also gives individual advice to its members on contracts and other matters which the writer encounters in his or her professional life.

Television

In 2002 the Guild concluded negotiations with the BBC for a new Television Script Commissioning Agreement. The new term came into effect on 1 November 2002. A new agreement for television production was also agreed with PACT (Producers Alliance of Cinema and Television) which came into effect on 1 February 2003.

The Guild has national agreements with the BBC, the ITV companies, PACT and TAC (representing Welsh language television producers). These agreements regulate minimum fees and going rates, copyright licence, credit terms and conditions for television plays, series and serials, dramatisations and adaptations. One of the Guild's most important achievements has been the establishment of pension rights for members. The BBC pays an additional 8% of the going rate on the understanding that the Guild member pays 5% of his or her fee. ITV companies now pay an additional 8% and the writer 5%.

The advent of digital and cable television channels and the creation of the BBC's commercial arm has seen the Guild in constant negotiation. The Guild now has agreements for all of the BBC's digital channels and for its joint venture channels.

In 1997, the Guild negotiated substantial revised terms and conditions for writers who are commissioned by the ITV companies. The new agreement includes a provision for the non-arms length sale of material to digital and cable channels, thus ensuring that writers receive market prices for the use of their material on these new channels.

Film

On 11 March 1985, an important agreement was signed with the two producer organisations: the British Film and Television Producers' Association and the Independent Programme Producers Association (now known as PACT). Since then there has been an industrial agreement which covers both independent television productions and independent film productions. Pension fund contributions have been negotiated for Guild members in the same way as for the BBC and ITV. The Agreement was renegotiated in February 1992 and negotiations on an updated agreement are in progress.

Radio

The Guild has a standard agreement for Radio Drama with the BBC, establishing a fee structure which is annually reviewed. The current agreement includes a Code of Practice which is important for establishing good working conditions for the writer working for the BBC. In December 1985 the BBC agreed to extend the pension scheme already established for television writers to include radio writers. In 1994 a comprehensive revision of the Agreement was undertaken. The Guild negotiated special agreements for the new daily serial on Radio 4, the new World Service soap West Way, the BBC Radio Wales soap Station Road, and for the online streaming of BBC Radio services.

Books

The Guild fought long, hard and successfully for the loans-based Public Lending Right to reimburse authors for books lent in libraries. This is now law and the Guild is constantly in touch with the Registrar of the scheme, which is administered from offices in Stockton-on-Tees. Together with the Society of Authors, the Guild has drawn up a draft Minimum Terms Book Agreement which has been widely circulated amongst publishers. A new model contract is in preparation.

Theatre

In 1979 the Guild, together with the Theatre Writers' Union, negotiated the first ever industrial agreement for theatre writers. The Theatres National Committee Agreement covers the Royal Shakespeare Company, the National Theatre Company and the English Stage Company.

In June 1986, a new agreement was signed with the Theatrical Management Association, which covers some 95 provincial theatres. In 1993, this agreement was comprehensively revised and included a provision for a year-on-year increase in fees in line with the Retail Price Index.

After many years of negotiation, an agreement was concluded in 1991 between the Guild and the Independent Theatre Council, which represents some 200 of the smaller and fringe theatres as well as educational, touring companies.

Other activities

The Guild is in constant touch with Government and national institutions wherever and whenever the interests of writers are in question or are being discussed. It holds cross-party Parliamentary lobbies with Equity and the Musicians Union to ensure that the various art forms they represent are properly cared for.

Working with the Federation of Entertainment Unions, the Guild makes its views known to Government bodies on a broader basis. It keeps in touch with the Arts Councils of Great Britain, the Independent Television Commission and other national bodies, and has close working relationships with Equity and the Musicians' Union.

Internationally, the Guild plays a leading role in the International Affiliation of Writers' Guilds, which includes the American Guilds East and West, the Canadian Guilds (French and English), and the Australian and New Zealand Guilds. When it is possible to make common cause, the Guilds act accordingly. The Guild takes a leading role in the European Writers' Congress, which is becoming increasingly important and successful. The Guild is becoming more involved with matters at European level where the harmonisation of copyright law and the regulation of a converged audiovisual/telecommunications are of immediate interest.

Membership

The Writers' Guild of Great Britain
(incorporating the Theatre Writers' Union)
15 Britannia Street, London WC1X 9JN
tel 020-7833 0777 *fax* 020-7833 4777
email admin@writersguild.org.uk
website www.writersguild.org.uk
General Secretary Bernie Corbett

Membership of the Guild is open to all persons entitled to claim a single piece of written work of any length for which payment has been received under written contract in terms not less favourable than those existing in current minimum terms agreements negotiated by the Guild. Candidate membership (£75) is open to all those who are taking their first steps into writing but who have not yet received a contract. The minimum subscription is currently £125 plus 1% of that part of an author's income earned from professional writing sources in the previous calendar year with a cap of £1250. All Full members are automatically members of the Authors Licensing and Collecting Society (ALCS). The Guild is a corporate member of the ALCS and maintains its links through representation on its board.

Members receive the *Writers' Bulletin*, which carries articles, letters and reports written by members. Other benefits include free entry to the British Library reading rooms, and reduced entry to the National Film Theatre.

Membership activities

The Guild in its day-to-day work takes up problems on behalf of individual members, gives advice on contracts, and helps with any problems which affect the lives of its members as professional writers. It now has a legal hotline so that members can quickly and easily seek legal advice. Regular Craft Meetings are held by all the Guild's specialist committees. This gives Guild members the opportunity of meeting those who control, work within, or affect the sphere of writing within which they work.

In conclusion

The writer is an isolated individual in a world in which individual voices are not always heard. The Guild brings together those writers in order to make common cause in respect of the many vitally important matters which are susceptible to influence only from the position of the collective strength which the Guild enjoys.

Prizes and awards

This list provides details of many British prizes, competitions and awards for writers and artists, including grants, bursaries and fellowships, as well as details of major international prizes. See page 700 for a quick reference to its contents.

ABSW/Glaxo Science Writers Awards
Details Barbara Drillsma,
Association of British Science Writers,
23 Savile Row, London W1X 2NB
tel 020-7439 1205 *fax* 020-7973 3051

Awards are given to the writers who, in the opinion of the judges, have done most to enhance the quality of science journalism. Entries will be accepted from specialist writers, newspaper reporters and freelances. There are 7 categories, each worth £2500. Organised in conjunction in the Association of British Science Writers. Closing date: 31 January. Founded 1966.

Alastair Salvesen Art Scholarship
Admin Secretary, The Royal Scottish Academy,
The Mound, Edinburgh EH2 2EL
tel 0131-558 7097 *fax* 0131-557 6417

The Scholarship consists of 2 parts:
• A 3–6 months travel scholarship of up to £10,000 depending on the plan submitted; and
• An exhibition in Nov/Dec organised by the Royal Scottish Academy.

Applicants must be painters aged 25–35 who have been trained at one of the 4 Scottish colleges of art; are currently living and working in Scotland; have worked for a minimum of 3 years outside a college or student environment; and have during 2003 had work accepted for an exhibition in the Annual Exhibition organised by certain Scottish

Further information

In the UK, details of awards for novels, short stories and works of non-fiction, as they are offered, will be found in such journals as *The Author*.

Booktrust
Book House, 45 East Hill,
London SW18 2QZ
tel 020-8516 2977 *fax* 020-8516 2998
email info@booktrust.org.uk
website www.booktrust.org.uk
The website has full details of literary prizes, awards and grants to writers.

institutes or, in a recognised gallery, have held a one-artist exhibition or participated in a group exhibition. Application forms available in December. Founded 1989.

The Alexander Prize
Literary Director, Royal Historical Society,
University College London, Gower Street,
London WC1E 6BT
tel 020-7387 7532 *fax* 020-7387 7532
email royalhistsoc@ucl.ac.uk
website www.rhs.ac.uk
An annual award of £250 or a silver medal for a paper based on original historical research. Candidates must either be under the age of 35 or be registered for a higher degree now or within the last 3 years. Closing date: 1 November each year.

Alfred Bradley Bursary Award
Details BBC Radio Drama Department,
BBC North, New Broadcasting House,
Oxford Road, Manchester M60 1SJ
tel 0161-244 4255
This biennial bursary of £6000 (over 2 years, plus a full commission for a radio play) is awarded to a writer resident in the North of England who has had a small amount of work published or produced. The scheme also allows for a group of finalists to receive small bursaries and develop ideas for radio drama commissions. Next closing date: November 2004. Founded 1992.

The Alfred Fagon Award
Details Roland Rees, Chair, 16 King's Grove,
London SE15 2NB
tel 020-7732 5608
email roland.rees@ukgateway.net
Submissions The Alfred Fagon Award,
The Royal Court Theatre, Sloane Square,
London SW1W 8AS
An annual award of £3500 for the best new play (which need not have been produced) for the theatre in English. TV and radio plays and film scripts will not be considered. Writers from the Caribbean or with Caribbean antecedents are eligible. Applicants should submit 2 copies of their play plus sae for return of their script and a CV which includes details of the writer's Caribbean connection. Closing date: end August. Founded 1997.

The André Simon Memorial Fund Book Awards

Details Tessa Hayward, 5 Sion Hill Place,
Bath BA1 5SJ
tel (01225) 336305 *fax* (01225) 421862
email tessa@tantraweb.co.uk

Two awards (£2000 each) are given annually, one
each for the best new book on food and on drink,
plus one Special Commendation of £1000 in either
category. Closing date: November each year.
Founded 1978.

Arthur C. Clarke Award

Details Paul Kincaid, 60 Bournemouth Road,
Folkestone, Kent CT19 5AZ
email arthurcclarkeaward@yahoo.co.uk
website www.clarkeaward.com

An annual award of £2003 plus engraved bookend
is given for the best science fiction novel with first
UK publication during the previous calendar year.
Titles are submitted by publishers. Founded 1985.

Artists' Residencies in Tuscany

Enquiries 31 Addison Avenue, London W11 4QS
email rmka101@ucl.ac.uk
website www.geocities.com/bgomperts/
Artists_in_Tuscany.html

Annual bursaries (value up to £2000) provide
board, lodging and studio facilities at the Centro
Verrocchio in Italy. Also, small grants to support
experimental projects on specified themes. Available
by competitive application. Open to artists aged
25–45 (UK only). Funded by the Juliet Gomperts
Memorial Trust. Closing date: end of January. Send
sae for further details.

The Arts Council/An Chomhairle Ealaíon, Ireland

Details The Arts Council/An Chomhairle Ealaíon,
70 Merrion Square, Dublin 2, Republic of Ireland
tel (01) 618 0200 *fax* (01) 676 1302
email info@artscouncil.ie
website www.artscouncil.ie

Publishes a guide for individuals and organisations
to Arts Council bursaries, awards and schemes. It is
also available online.

Arts Council England

Details The Literature Dept, Arts Council England,
14 Great Peter Street, London SW1P 3NQ
tel (0845) 300 6200 *textphone* 020-7973 6564
fax 020-7973 6590
email enquiries@artscouncil.org.uk
website www.artscouncil.org.uk

Arts Council England presents national prizes
rewarding creative talent in the arts. These are
awarded through the Council's flexible funds and
are not necessarily open to application: the
Children's Award, the David Cohen British
Literature Prize, the Independent Foreign Fiction

Prize, John Whiting Award, Meyer Whitworth
Award and the Raymond Williams Community
Publishing Prize. See the separate entries for details.

Arts Council England Writers' Awards

The Literature Dept, Arts Council England,
14 Great Peter Street, London SW1P 3NQ
tel 020-7973 6442
email info.literature@artscouncil.org.uk
website www.artscouncil.org.uk

The Arts Council England offers 15 awards annually
of £7000 each for writers who need finance for a
period of concentrated work on their next book.
These Awards are open to writers who have been
previously published in book form. Poetry, fiction,
autobiography, biography, drama intended for
publication, literature for young people, and other
creative works are eligible. At least one award will be
reserved specifically for a writer of Literature for
Young People and the Clarissa Luard Award will be
made to a fiction writer under 35 years of age. The
Award winners will be determined by a panel of
3 judges, who are themselves writers.

Arvon Foundation International Poetry Competition

Details Arvon Foundation Poetry Competition,
2nd Floor, 42A Buckingham Palace Road,
London SW1W 0RE
tel 020-7931 7611
email london@arvonfoundation.org

A biennial competition for previously unpublished
poems written in English. First prize £5000, plus at
least £5000 in other cash prizes. Next competition:
spring 2004. Founded 1980.

The Asham Award

Details The Administrator, Asham Literary
Endowment Trust, c/o Lewes House, 32 High Street,
Lewes, East Sussex BN7 2LX

A biennial national short story competition for
women writers over the age of 18 and currently
resident in the UK who have not previously had a
novel or anthology published. Winners receive a
cash prize and inclusion in an anthology published
by Bloomsbury. Next competition will be launched
in October 2004. Founded 1996.

Authors' Club Awards

Details Ann de La Grange, Secretary, Authors' Club,
40 Dover Street, London W1S 4NP
tel 020-7499 8581 *fax* 020-7409 0913

Best First Novel Award

An award of £1000 is presented at a dinner held in
the Club, to the author of the most promising first
novel published in the UK during each year. Entries
(one from each publisher's imprint) are accepted

during October and November and must be full-length novels – short stories are not eligible. Instituted by Lawrence Meynell in 1954.

Sir Banister Fletcher Award for Authors' Club

The late Sir Banister Fletcher, a former President of both the Authors' Club and the Royal Institute of British Architects instituted an annual prize 'for the book on architecture or the arts most deserving'. The award is made on the recommendation of the Professional Literature Committee of RIBA, to whom nominations for eligible titles (i.e. those written by British authors or those resident in the UK and published under a British imprint) should be submitted by the end of May of the year after publication. The prize of £1000 is awarded by the Authors' Club during September. First awarded in 1954.

The Authors' Foundation

The Society of Authors, 84 Drayton Gardens, London SW10 9SB
tel 020-7373 6642
email info@societyofauthors.org
website www.societyofauthors.org

Grants are available to novelists, poets and writers of non-fiction who are published authors working on their next book. The aim is to provide funding (in addition to a proper advance) for research, travel or other necessary expenditure. Closing dates: 30 April and 31 October. Send sae for an information sheet. Founded in 1984 to mark the centenary of the Society of Authors.

The Aventis Prizes for Science Books

Details The Royal Society, 6-9 Carlton House Terrace, London SW1Y 5AG
tel 020-7451 2513 *fax* 020-7451 2693
email scott.keir@royalsoc.ac.uk
website www.aventissciencebookprizes.com

These annual prizes reward books that make science more accessible to readers of all ages and backgrounds. Prizes of up to a total of £30,000 are awarded in 2 categories: General (£10,000) for a book with a general readership; and Junior (£10,000) for a book written for people aged under 14. Up to 5 shortlisted authors in each category receive £1000.

Eligible books should be written in English and their first publication in the UK must have been between 1 January and 31 December 2003. Seven copies of each entry should be supplied with a fully completed entry form. Publishers may submit any number of books for each prize. Entries may cover any aspect of science and technology but educational textbooks published for professional or specialist audiences are not eligible. The Prizes are managed by the Royal Society in cooperation with the sponsor, Aventis. Founded 1988.

BA/Book Data Author of the Year

Details The Booksellers Association of the UK and Ireland Ltd, 272 Vauxhall Bridge Road, London SW1V 1BA
tel 020-7802 0802 *fax* 020-7802 0803

This annual award of £1000 is judged by members of the Booksellers Association (3200 bookshops) in a postal ballot. Any living, British or Irish published writer is eligible and the award is given to the author judged to have had the most impact in the year. Founded 1993.

BAFTA (British Academy of Film and Television Arts) Awards

Chief Executive Amanda Berry, 195 Piccadilly, London W1J 9LN
tel 020-7734 0022 *fax* 020-7494 2759
email reception@bafta.org
website www.bafta.org

The pre-eminent organisation in the UK for film, TV and interactive, recognising and promoting the achievement and endeavour of industry practitioners. BAFTA Awards are awarded annually by members to their peers in recognition of their skills and expertise. Founded 1947.

The BBC Four Samuel Johnson Prize for Non-Fiction

Details Booksellers Association, Minster House, 272 Vauxhall Bridge Road, London SW1V 1BA
tel 020-7802 0802 *fax* 020-7802 0803
email sharon.down@booksellers.org.uk

A prize of £30,000 will be awarded to the winning writer of a non-fiction book in the areas of current affairs, history, politics, science, sport, travel, biography, autobiography and the arts. Each shortlisted author will receive £1000. Books must be published in English in the UK between 1 May 2003 and 30 April 2004, and authors must be alive when the books are submitted. Books must not be written by more than 2 authors. Both hardback and paperback originals are eligible. Founded 1998.

Besterman/McColvin Medals – see The CILIP/Whitaker Reference Awards

The Betty Trask Awards

Details Awards Secretary, The Society of Authors, 84 Drayton Gardens, London SW10 9SB
tel 020-7373 6642
email info@societyofauthors.org
website www.societyofauthors.org

These awards are for the benefit of young authors under the age of 35 and are given on the strength of a first novel (published or unpublished) of a romantic or traditional nature. It is expected that prizes totalling at least £25,000 will be presented each year. The winners are required to use the money for a period or periods of foreign travel. Send sae for entry form. Closing date: 31 January. Made possible through a generous bequest from Miss Betty Trask.

The Bisto Book of the Year Awards

Details The Administrator, Children's Books Ireland, 17 Lower Camden Street, Dublin 2, Republic of Ireland
tel (01) 872 5854 *fax* (01) 872 5854
email info@childrensbooksireland.com
bistoawards@childrensbooksireland.com

Annual awards open to authors and/or illustrators who were born in Ireland, or who were living in Ireland at the time of a book's publication.

The Bisto Book of the Year Award

An award of €3000 is presented to the overall winner (text and/or illustration).

Bisto Merit Awards

A prize fund of €2400 is divided between 3 authors and/or illustrators.

Bisto Eilís Dillon Award

An award of €1000 is presented to an author for a first children's book.

Closing date: 30 January 2004 for work published between 1 January and 31 December 2003. Founded 1990.

The Boardman Tasker Prize

Details Maggie Body, Pound House, Llangennith, Swansea SA3 1JQ
email margaretbody@lineone.net
website www.boardmantasker.co.uk

This annual prize of £2000 is given for a work of fiction, non-fiction or poetry, the central theme of which is concerned with the mountain environment. Authors of any nationality are eligible but the work must be published or distributed in the UK. Entries from publishers only. Founded 1983.

The Booker Prize – see The Man Booker Prize

The Booktrust Teenage Prize

Details Booktrust, Book House, 45 East Hill, London SW18 2QZ
tel 020-8516 2986 *fax* 020-8516 2978
email hannah@booktrust.org.uk
Contact Hannah Rutland

The first annual national book prize that aims to recognise and celebrate the best in young adult fiction. The author of the best book for teenagers receives £1500 and is chosen from a shortlist of 6. Eligible books must be fiction, aimed at teenagers between the ages of 13 and 16 and written in English by a citizen of the UK, or an author resident in the UK. The work must be published between 1 July and 30 June. Established 2003.

BP Portrait Award

Details National Portrait Gallery, St Martin's Place, London WC2H 0HE
tel 020-7306 0055 *fax* 020-7306 0056
website www.npg.org.uk

An annual award to encourage young artists (aged 18–40) to focus upon and develop the theme of portraiture within their work. 1st prize: £25,000 plus at the judges' discretion a commission worth £3000 to be agreed between the NPG and the artist; 2nd prize £8000; 3rd prize: £4000; 4th prize £4000. Closing date: March/April. A selection of entrants' work is exhibited at the National Portrait Gallery June–Oct. Founded 1978.

The Branford Boase Award

Details The Administrator, 8 Bolderwood Close, Bishopstoke, Eastleigh SO50 5PG
tel (01962) 826658 *fax* (01962) 856615
email anne@marleyhcl.freeserve.co.uk

An annual award is made to a first-time writer of a full-length children's novel (age 7+) published in the preceding year; the editor is also recognised. Its aim is to encourage new writers for children and to recognise the role of perceptive editors in developing new talent. The Award was set up in memory of the outstanding children's writer Henrietta Branford and the gifted editor and publisher Wendy Boase who both died in 1999. Closing date: 28 March 2004. Founded 2000.

The Bridport Prize

Details Bridport Arts Centre, South Street, Bridport, Dorset DT6 3NR
tel (01308) 459444 *fax* (01308) 459166
email info@bridport-arts.com
website www.bridportprize.org.uk

Annual prizes are awarded for poetry and short stories – 1st £3000, 2nd £1000, 3rd £500 in both categories. Entries should be in English, original work, typed or clearly written, and never published, read on radio/TV/stage. Winning stories are read by a leading London literary agent, without obligation, and an anthology of winning entries is published each autumn. Send sae for entry form or enter online. Closing date: 30 June each year.

The British Academy Book Prize

Details External Relations, The British Academy, 10 Carlton House Terrace, London SW1Y 5AH
tel 020-7969 5200 *fax* 020-7969 5413
email w.kaye@britac.ac.uk
website www.britac.ac.uk

Aims to increase the public appreciation of the humanities and social sciences by celebrating outstanding scholarly works that are accessible to the non-specialist. Eligible books must be published in English in the UK; the author may be of any nationality. The award is £2500. Applications from publishers only. Closing date: 20 February 2004. Founded 2001.

British Academy Medals and Prizes

The British Academy, 10 Carlton House Terrace, London SW1Y 5AH
tel 020-7969 5200 *fax* 020-7969 5300
email secretary@britac.ac.uk
website www.britac.ac.uk

A number of medals and prizes are awarded for outstanding work in various fields of the humanities on the recommendation of specialist committees: Burkitt Medal for Biblical Studies; Derek Allen Prize (made annually in turn for musicology, numismatics and Celtic studies); Sir Israel Gollancz Prize (for English studies); Grahame Clark Medal for Prehistoric Archaeology; Kenyon Medal for Classical Studies; Rose Mary Crawshay Prize (for English literature); Serena Medal for Italian Studies; Leverhulme Medal and Prize.

The British Academy Research Awards

Details/application form The British Academy, 10 Carlton House Terrace, London SW1Y 5AH
tel 020-7969 5200 *fax* 020-7969 5300
email secretary@britac.ac.uk
website www.britac.ac.uk

These awards are made quarterly to scholars conducting advanced academic research in the humanities and social sciences, and normally resident in the UK. Applications are accepted for travel and maintenance expenses in connection with an approved programme of research. There are also awards for attendance at scholarly conferences overseas; and for postdoctoral fellowships, research readerships and research professorships.

British Book Awards

Details Merric Davidson, PO Box 60, Cranbrook, Kent TN17 2ZR
tel (01580) 212041 *fax* (01580) 212041
email nibbies@mdla.co.uk
website www.britishbookawards.com

Presented annually, major categories include: Author of the Year, Publisher of the Year, Bookseller of the Year, Children's Book of the Year. Founded 1989.

British Council Grants to Artists Scheme

Details Grants to Artists Officer,
Visual Arts Dept, British Council,
10 Spring Gardens, London SW1A 2BN
tel 020-7389 3045 *fax* 020-7389 3101
website www.britishcouncil.org/arts/vad

The Visual Arts Department of the British Council is concerned with the promotion and presentation of UK art overseas. These awards (£100–£2000) are specifically aimed at UK visual artists who have been invited to exhibit their work abroad. It is there to help with the costs of the artists' travel and the transport and packaging of their work. Artists should submit a completed application form, CV, 6 slides of their work and a letter of invitation from the overseas venue before the deadline. The committee meets 3–4 weeks after this to decide on all the applications. Closing dates: 1 February, 1 May, 1 August, 1 November.

British Fantasy Awards

Details Robert Parkinson, Secretary,
The British Fantasy Society, 201 Reddish Road, South Reddish, Stockport SK5 7HR
email faliol@yahoo.com
website www.britishfantasysociety.org.uk

Members of the British Fantasy Society vote annually for the best novel, short fiction, artist, small press and anthology of the preceding year. A further award, the Committee Award, is decided separately. The awards take the form of a statuette. Closing date for nominations: end May each year. Founded 1972.

British Press Awards

Event Manager Angie Reid, Quantum Business Media, 19 Scarbrook Road, Croydon CR9 1LX
tel 020-8565 4392 *fax* 020-8565 4395
email angier@qpp.co.uk

Annual awards for British journalism judged by more than 80 respected, influential judges as well as representatives from all the national newspaper groups. Closing date: 9 January 2004.

Bryan MacMahon Short Story Award

Writers' Week, 24 The Square, Listowel, Co. Kerry, Republic of Ireland
tel (353) 6821074 *fax* (353) 6822893
email writersweek@eircom.net
website www.writersweek.ie

An annual award for the best short story (up to 3000 words) on any subject. Prize: €2000. Entry fee: €6.50. Closing date: 1 March. Founded 1971.

The Caine Prize for African Writing

Details Nick Elam, Administrator, 2 Drayson Mews, London W8 4LY
tel 020-7376 0440 *fax* 020-7938 3728
email caineprize@jftaylor.com

An annual award of $15,000 for a short story published in English (may be a translation into English) by an African writer in the 5 years before the closing date, and not previously submitted. Indicative length 3000–15,000 words. Submissions only by publishers. Closing date: 31 January each year. Founded 1999.

The Calvin and Rose G. Hoffman Memorial Prize for Distinguished Publication on Christopher Marlowe

Applications The Headmaster, The King's School, Canterbury, Kent CT1 2ES
tel (01227) 595501 *fax* (01227) 595595

This annual prize of around £5000 is awarded to the best unpublished work that examines the life and works of Christopher Marlowe and the relationship between the works of Marlowe and Shakespeare. Closing date: 1 September.

Cardiff International Poetry Competition

Details/entry form Cardiff International Poetry Competition, PO Box 438, Cardiff CF10 5YA
website www.academi.org

Eight prizes totalling £7000 are awarded annually for unpublished poetry written in English (prizes: 1st £5000; 2nd £700; 3rd £300; plus 5 prizes of £200). Entry forms may also be downloaded from the website. Closing date: 30 January 2004.

Carnegie Medal – see The CILIP Carnegie and Kate Greenaway Awards

Catherine Pakenham Award

Entry form Emma Gilbert-Harris,
Corporate Affairs Dept, The Sunday Telegraph,
1 Canada Square, Canary Wharf, London E14 5DT
email emma.gilbert-harris@telegraph.co.uk

This award is open to young women journalists aged 18–25 who may submit a non-fiction 750–2000-word article. The winner will receive £1000 and the chance to write for a *Telegraph* publication. Three runners-up each receive £200. Entry forms are available from February 2004. Closing date: 30 May 2004. Founded in 1970 in memory of Catherine Pakenham, who died in a car crash whilst working for the *Telegraph Magazine*.

'Charles Veillon' European Essay Prize

Details The Secretary, Charles Veillon Foundation, CH 1017 Lausanne, Switzerland
tel (021) 706 9029

A prize of 30,000 Swiss francs is awarded annually to a European writer or essayist for essays offering a critical look at modern society's way of life and ideology. Founded 1975.

The Children's Award

Details Literature Dept, Arts Council England, 14 Great Peter Street, London SW1P 3NQ
tel 020-7973 6431
email jemima.lee@artscouncil.org.uk

website www.artscouncil.org.uk

This award of £6000 is for playwrights who write plays of at least 45 minutes long for children up to the age of 12. Plays must have been professionally produced between 1 July 2002 and 30 June 2003.

The Children's Laureate

Details The Administrator, 19 Melrose Court, Calmore, Southampton SO40 2UZ
tel 023-8086 8562
email childrenslaureate@talkgas.net

A biennial award of £10,000 to honour a writer or illustrator of children's books for a lifetime's achievement. It highlights the importance of children's book creators in developing readers and illustrators of the future. Children's Laureates: Quentin Blake (1999–2001), Anne Fine (2001–3), Michael Morpurgo (2003–5). Founded 1998.

Cholmondeley Awards

Administered by The Society of Authors, 84 Drayton Gardens, London SW10 9SB

These honorary awards are to recognise the achievement and distinction of individual poets. Submissions are not accepted. Total value of awards about £8000. Established by the then Dowager Marchioness of Cholmondeley in 1965.

Christopher Ewart-Biggs Memorial Prize

Details The Secretary, Memorial Prize, Flat 3, 149 Hamilton Terrace, London NW8 9QS
fax 020-7328 0699

This prize of £5000 is awarded once every 2 years to the writer, of any nationality, whose work is judged to contribute most to:
• peace and understanding in Ireland;
• to closer ties between the peoples of Britain and Ireland;
• or to cooperation between the partners of the EU.
Eligible works must be published during the 2 years to 31 December 2004. Closing date: 31 December 2004.

The CILIP Carnegie and Kate Greenaway Awards

email marketing@cilip.org.uk
website www.ckg.org.uk

Recommendations for the following 2 awards are invited from members of CILIP (the Chartered Institute of Library and Information Professionals), who are asked to submit a preliminary list of not more than 2 titles for each award, accompanied by a 50-word appraisal justifying the recommendation of each book. The awards are selected by the Youth Libraries Group of CILIP.

Carnegie Medal

Awarded annually for an outstanding book for children (fiction or non-fiction) written in English and first published in the UK during the preceding year or co-published elsewhere within a 3-month time lapse.

Kate Greenaway Medal

Awarded annually for an outstanding illustrated book for children first published in the UK during the preceding year or co-published elsewhere within a 3-month time lapse. Books intended for older as well as younger children are included, and reproduction will be taken into account. The Colin Mears Award (£5000) is awarded annually to the winner of the Kate Greenaway Medal.

The CILIP/Whitaker Reference Awards
email marketing@cilip.org.uk
website www.cilip.org.uk

The Besterman/McColvin Medals

Awarded annually for outstanding works of reference published in the UK during the preceding year. There are 2 categories, one for electronic formats and one for printed works. Recommendations are invited from Members of CILIP (the Chartered Institute of Library and Information Professionals), publishers and others, who are asked to submit a preliminary list of not more than 3 titles via the website. Winners receive a cash prize of £500, a certificate and a prestigious golden medal.

The Walford Award

Awarded annually to an individual who has made a sustained and continued contribution to the science and art of British bibliography over a period of years. The bibliographer's work can encompass effort in the history, classification and description of printed, written, audiovisual and machine-readable materials. Recommendations may be made for the work of a living person or persons, or for an organisation. The award can be made to a British bibliographer or to a person or organisation working in the UK. The winner receives a cash prize of £500.

The Wheatley Medal

Awarded annually for an outstanding index published during the preceding year. Printed indexes to any type of publication may be submitted for consideration, providing that the whole work, including the index, or the index alone has originated in the UK. Recommendations for the award are invited from members of CILIP and the Society of Indexers, publishers and others; nominations should be made via the website. The final selection is made by a committee consisting of representatives of the CILIP Cataloguing and Indexing Group and the Society of Indexers.

The Citigroup Private Bank Photography Prize
Information The Photographers' Gallery, 5 Great Newport Street, London WC2H 7HY

tel 020-7831 1772 *fax* 020-7836 9704
website www.photonet.org.uk

An annual prize of £15,000 is awarded to the individual who is judged to have made the most significant contribution to the medium of photography over the previous year. Anyone who has exhibited or published a substantial body of work in the UK in the year prior to the award is eligible. Runners up are awarded £1500 each. Nominations deadline: July 2004 (provisional). Founded 1996.

Commonwealth Writers Prize
Details Booktrust, Book House, 45 East Hill, London SW18 2QZ
tel 020-8516 2973/2972 *fax* 020-8516 2978
email kate@booktrust.org.uk
tarryn@booktrust.org.uk
Contact Kate Mervyn-Jones, Tarryn McKay

This annual award is for the best work of fiction in English by a citizen of the Commonwealth published in the year prior to the award. A prize of £10,000 is awarded for overall best book and £3000 is awarded to the overall best first published book. The overall winners are selected from 8 regional winners who each receive £1000 for being regional winners. Sponsored by the Commonwealth Foundation. Established 1987.

CWA Awards
website www.thecwa.co.uk

Awards for crime writing: the Cartier Diamond Dagger; the Creasey Dagger; the Gold Dagger and Silver Dagger for Fiction; the Gold Dagger for Non-Fiction; the Short Story Dagger; the CWA Ellis Peters Historical Dagger; the Debut Dagger; the Ian Fleming Steel Dagger, the Dagger in the Library. See website for details.

The David Berry Prize
Council of the Royal Historical Society, University College London, Gower Street, London WC1E 6BT
tel 020-7387 7532 *fax* 020-7387 7532
email royalhistsoc@ucl.ac.uk
website www.rhs.ac.uk

Candidates may select any subject dealing with Scottish history. Value of prize: £250. Closing date: 31 October each year.

The David Cohen British Literature Prize
Details The Literature Dept, Arts Council England, 14 Great Peter Street, London SW1P 3NQ
tel 020-7973 6442
website www.artscouncil.org.uk

This prize marks a lifetime's literary achievement. The winner receives £30,000 plus an additional £10,000 to fund new work. For further information about the prize, including how members of the public can forward their choice of author to be considered for the judges, contact the Literature Dept.

The David St John Thomas Charitable Trust Competitions & Awards

The David St John Thomas Charitable Trust, PO Box 6055, Nairn IV12 4YB
tel (01667) 453351
Contact Lorna Edwardson (Competition & Awards Manager)

Programme of writing competitions and awards totalling £20,000–£30,000. Regular competitions are the annual ghost story and annual love story (each 1600–1800 words with £1000 1st prize) and the open poetry competition (up to 32 lines, total prize money £1000). Publication of winning entries is guaranteed, usually in *Writers' News/Writing Magazine* and/or an annual anthology. The Self-Publishing Awards are open to anyone who has self-published a book during the preceding calendar year, with 4 categories each with £250 prize. The overall winner is declared Self-Publisher of the Year with a total award of £1000. For full details of these and other awards, including an annual writers' groups anthology and letter-writer of the year send a large sae.

David T.K. Wong Fellowship

Details David T.K. Wong Fellowship, School of English & American Studies, University of East Anglia, Norwich NR4 7TJ
tel (01603) 592810 *fax* (01603) 507728
email v.striker@vea.ac.uk
website www.uea.ac.uk/eas/fellowships/wong/wongfell.htm

Founded by David Wong, retired senior civil servant, journalist and businessman, the annual Fellowship (worth £25,000) at the University of East Anglia will give writers of exceptional talent the chance to produce a work of fiction in English which deals seriously with some aspect of life in the Far East. Residential: Oct–June. Write for full details. Closing date: 31 October each year. Founded 1997.

The David T.K. Wong Prize for Short Fiction

tel 020-7253 4308 *fax* 020-7253 5711
email gvincent@dircon.co.uk
website www.internatpen.org

A biennial prize to promote literary excellence in the form of a short story (max. 6000 words) written in English. Unpublished stories are welcome from writers worldwide but entries must incorporate one or more of International PEN's ideals as set out in its charter. Entries should not be sent direct but should come from the applicant's local PEN Centre.

Closing date *circa* 30 September 2004 but check with local centre (see website for centres, charter and full details). Founded 2000.

David Watt Prize

Details/entry form The Administrator, The David Watt Prize, Rio Tinto plc, 6 St James's Square, London SW1Y 4LD
tel 020-7753 2316
email davidwattprize@riotinto.com
website www.riotinto.com

An annual award (£7500) initiated to commemorate the life and work of David Watt. Open to writers currently engaged in writing for English language newspapers and journals on international and national affairs. The winners are judged as having made 'outstanding contributions towards the greater understanding of national, international or global issues'. Entries must have been published during the year preceding the award. Final entry date: 31 March.

Dennis Potter Screenwriting Award

Details Jeremy Howe, BBC Broadcasting House, Whiteladies Road, Bristol BS8 2LR

Information about this award is obtainable from the above office. Founded 1994.

The Duff Cooper Prize

Details Artemis Cooper, 54 St Maur Road, London SW6 4DP
tel 020-7736 3729 *fax* 020-7731 7638

An annual prize for a literary work in the field of biography, history, politics or poetry published in English or French and submitted by a recognised publisher during the previous 12 months. The prize of £3000 comes from a Trust Fund established by the friends and admirers of Duff Cooper, 1st Viscount Norwich (1890–1954) after his death.

The Dundee Book Prize

Details Deborah Kennedy, Dundee City Council, Economic Development, 3 City Square, Dundee DD1 3BA
tel (01382) 434275 *fax* (01382) 434096
email deborah.kennedy@dundeecity.gov.uk
website www.dundeecity.gov.uk

A biennial prize (£6000 and the chance of publication by Polygon) awarded for an unpublished novel. Next award: 2004. Founded 1996.

E.C. Gregory Trust Fund

Details Awards Secretary, The Society of Authors, 84 Drayton Gardens, London SW10 9SB
tel 020-7373 6642
email info@societyofauthors.org
website www.societyofauthors.org

A number of substantial awards are made annually

for the encouragement of young poets who can show that they are likely to benefit from an opportunity to give more time to writing. An eligible candidate must:
• be a British subject by birth but not a national of Eire or any of the British dominions or colonies and be ordinarily resident in the UK or Northern Ireland;
• be under the age of 30 on 31 March in the year of the Award (i.e. the year following submission). Send sae for entry form. Closing date: 31 October.

E.M. Forster Award

The distinguished English author, E.M. Forster, bequeathed the American publication rights and royalties of his posthumous novel *Maurice* to Christopher Isherwood, who transferred them to the American Academy of Arts and Letters (633 West 155th Street, New York, NY 10032, USA), for the establishment of an E.M. Forster Award, currently $15,000, to be given annually to a British or Irish writer for a stay in the USA. Applications for this award are not accepted.

The Eleanor Farjeon Award

An annual prize of (minimum) £750 may be given to a librarian, teacher, author, artist, publisher, reviewer, TV producer or any other person working with or for children through books. Sponsored by Scholastic Ltd. Instituted in 1965 by the Children's Book Circle for distinguished services to children's books and named after the much-loved children's writer.

Encore Award

Details Awards Secretary, The Society of Authors, 84 Drayton Gardens, London SW10 9SB
tel 020-7373 6642
email info@societyofauthors.org
website www.societyofauthors.org

This annual award of £10,000 is for the best second novel of the year. The work submitted must be: a novel by one author who has had one (and only one) novel published previously, and in the English language, first published in the UK. Entries should be submitted by the publisher. Closing date: 30 November.

The Enid McLeod Literary Prize

Details Executive Secretary, Franco-British Society, Room 623, Linen Hall, 162-168 Regent Street, London W1R 5TB
tel 020-7734 0815 *fax* 020-7734 0815
email execsec@francobritishsociety.org.uk
website www.francobritishsociety.org.uk

This annual prize of £250 is given for a full-length work of literature which contributes most to Franco-British understanding. It must be first published in the UK between 1 January and

31 December, and written in English by a citizen of the UK, British Commonwealth, the Republic of Ireland, Pakistan, Bangladesh or South Africa. Closing date: 31 December.

European Jewish Publication Society Grants

Details Dr Colin Shindler, Editorial Director, European Jewish Publication Society, PO Box 19948, London N3 3ZJ
tel 020-8346 1668 *fax* 020-8346 1776
email cs@ejps.org.uk
website www.ejps.org.uk

Awards of up to £3000 are given to publishers to assist in the publication of books of Jewish interest, including fiction, non-fiction and poetry. Translations from other languages are considered eligible. Founded 1995.

European Publishers Award for Photography

Details Dewi Lewis Publishing, 8 Broomfield Road, Heaton Moor, Stockport SK4 4ND
tel 0161-442 9450 *fax* 0161-442 9450
email mail@dewilewispublishing.com
website www.dewilewispublishing.com

Annual competition for the best set of photographs suitable for publication as a book. All photographic material must be completed and unpublished in book form and be original. Projects conceived as anthologies are not acceptable. Copyright must belong to the photographer. Closing date: 31 January. Founded 1994.

Fallen Leaves Short Story Competition

Details Cork Campus Radio, Level 3, Áras na Mac Léinn, University College Cork, Cork City, Republic of Ireland
tel (021) 4902170 *fax* (021) 4903108
email radio@ucc.ie
Contact Sinéad O'Donnell, Station Manager

Fallen Leaves is a short story radio series devised to provide new and innovative Irish short story writers with an opportunity to write for radio. Stories should be 1800–2000 words long and unpublished. Fee: £4 for the first story and £2 for each subseqent story. Founded 1996.

The Felicia Hemans Prize for Lyrical Poetry

Submissions The Registrar, The University of Liverpool, PO Box 147, Liverpool L69 3BX
tel 0151-794 2458 *fax* 0151-794 3765
email wilderc@liv.ac.uk

This annual prize of books or money, open to past and present members and students of the University of Liverpool only, is awarded for a lyrical poem, the subject of which may be chosen by the competitor. Only one poem, either published or unpublished, may be submitted. The prize shall not be awarded more than once to the same competitor. Poems, endorsed 'Hemans Prize', must be sent on or before 1 May.

The Fidler Award
Administered by Scottish Book Trust, Sandeman House, 55 High Street, Edinburgh EH1 1SR
tel 0131-229 3663
email info@scottishbooktrust.com
website www.scottishbooktrust.com

An annual award for an unpublished novel for children aged 8–12 years, to encourage authors new to writing for this age group. The award is currently without a sponsor and entrants should contact Scottish Book Trust before submitting MSS.

The Fish Short Story Prize
Durrus, Bantry, Co. Cork, Republic of Ireland
tel (353) 27 61246
email info@fishpublishing.com
website www.fishpublishing.com
Contact Clem Cairns

An annual international award which aims to discover, encourage and publish exciting new literary talent. Previously unpublished stories of up to 5000 words are eligible. 1st prize: £1000 (€1500); 2nd prize: one week residence at Anam Cara Writers' and Artists' Retreat, West Cork. The best 15–20 stories are published in an anthology. Entry fee: £11 (€15) for the first, £8 (€10) for subsequent entries. Concession rate: £8 (€10). Closing date: 30 November. Critiques available all year for £35 (€45). Founded 1994.

Forward Poetry Prizes
Details Forward Poetry Prize Administrator, Colman Getty PR, Middlesex House, 34-42 Cleveland Street, London W1T 5JE
tel 020-7631 2666 *fax* 020-7631 2699
email pr@colmangettypr.co.uk

Three prizes are awarded annually:
• The Forward Prize for best collection of poetry published between 1 October and 30 September (£10,000);
• The Waterstones Prize for best first collection of poetry published between 1 October and 30 September (£5000); and
• The Tolman Cunard Prize for best individual poem, published but not as part of a collection between 1 May and 30 April (£1000).
All poems entered are also considered for inclusion in the *Forward Book of Poetry*, an annual anthology. Entries must be submitted by book publishers and editors of newspapers, periodicals and magazines in the UK and Eire. Entries from poets will not be accepted. Established 1992.

The Geoffrey Faber Memorial Prize
An annual prize of £1000 is awarded in alternate years for a volume of verse and for a volume of prose fiction, first published originally in the UK during the 2 years preceding the year in which the award is given which is, in the opinion of the judges, of the greatest literary merit. Eligible writers must be not more than 40 years old at the date of publication of the book and a citizen of the UK and Colonies, of any other Commonwealth state or of the Republic of Ireland. The 3 judges are reviewers of poetry or fiction who are nominated each year by the literary editors of newspapers and magazines which regularly publish such reviews. Faber and Faber invite nominations from reviewers and literary editors. No submissions for the prize are to be made. Established in 1963 by Faber and Faber Ltd, as a memorial to the founder and first Chairman of the firm.

George Orwell Memorial Prize
Details Simage Communications Ltd, Fulton House, Fulton Road, Wembley Park, Middlesex HA9 0TF
tel 020-8584 0444 *fax* 020-8584 0443
email orwell@simage-comms.co.uk
website www.simage-comms.co.uk
Contact Sue Dowsett

Two prizes of £1000 each are awarded in March/April each year – one for the best political book, and one for best political journalism – of the previous year, giving equal merit to content and good style accessible to the general public. Founded 1993.

The Gilchrist-Fisher Award
Contact Maria Morrow, Rebecca Hossack Gallery, 35 Windmill Street, London W1T 2JS

Biennial prize (approx. £3500) awarded to a young artist (aged under 30) for landscape painting. Award exhibition for finalists held at Rebecca Hossack Gallery, London W1. Founded 1987.

Gladstone History Book Prize
Submissions Executive Secretary, Royal Historical Society, University College London, Gower Street, London WC1E 6BT
email royalhistsoc@ucl.ac.uk

An annual award (value £1000) for a history book. The book must:
• be on any historical subject which is not primarily related to British history;
• be its author's first solely written history book;
• have been published in English during the calendar year of 2003 by a scholar normally resident in the UK;
• be an original and scholarly work of historical research.
Three non-returnable copies of an eligible book should be submitted before 31 December.

Glenfiddich Food & Drink Awards

Details The Glenfiddich Awards, 1 Bedford Avenue, London WC1B 3AU
tel 020-7255 1100 *fax* 020-7255 5454
website www.glenfiddich.com/foodanddrink

Awards are given annually to recognise excellence in writing, publishing and broadcasting relating to the subjects of food and drink. £1000 is given to each of 15 categories, together with a special bottling of Glenfiddich Single Malt Scotch whisky and an award. The overall winner receives the Glenfiddich Trophy and an additional £3000. Founded 1970.

Griffin Poetry Prize

Details The Griffin Trust for Excellence in Poetry, 6610 Edwards Boulevard, Mississauga, Ontario L5T 2V6, Canada
tel 905-565-5993 *fax* 905-564 3645
website www.griffinpoetryprize.com

Two annual prizes of C$40,000 will be awarded for collections of poetry published in English during the preceding year. One prize will go to a living Canadian poet, the other to a living poet from any country. Collections of poetry translated into English from other languages are also eligible and will be assessed for their literary quality in English. Submissions only from publishers. Closing date: 31 December. Founded 2000.

The Guardian Children's Fiction Prize

tel 020-7239 9694
email books@guardian.co.uk

The *Guardian's* annual prize of £1500 is for a work of children's fiction (for children over 8; no picture books) published by a British or Commonwealth writer. The winning book is chosen by the Children's Book Editor together with a team of 3–4 other authors of children's books.

The Guardian First Book Award

Contact Claire Armitstead
tel 020-7239 9694 *fax* 020-7713 4366
email books@guardian.co.uk
Submissions Literary Editor, The Guardian, 119 Farringdon Road, London EC1R 3ER

Open to first-time authors published in English in the UK across all genres of writing, the award will recognise and reward new writing by honouring an author's first book. The winner will receive £10,000 plus an advertising package within the *Guardian* and the *Observer*. Publishers may submit up to 3 titles per imprint with publication dates between January and December 2004. Closing date: late July.

The Hans Christian Andersen Medals

Details International Board on Books for Young People, Nonnenweg 12, Postfach, CH-4003 Basel, Switzerland
tel (61) 272 29 17 *fax* (61) 272 27 57
email ibby@eye.ch
website www.ibby.org

The Medals are awarded every 2 years to a living author and an illustrator who by the outstanding value of their work are judged to have made a lasting contribution to literature for children and young people.

The Hawthornden Prize

Details The Administrator, 42A Hays Mews, Berkeley Square, London W1J 5QA

This prize is awarded annually to the author of what, in the opinion of the Committee, is the best work of imaginative literature published during the preceding calendar year by a British author. Books do not have to be specially submitted.

Hawthornden Writers' Fellowships

Details The Administrator, Hawthornden Castle International Retreat for Writers, Hawthornden Castle, Lasswade, Midlothian EH18 1EG
tel 0131-440 2180

Applications are invited from novelists, poets, dramatists and other creative writers whose work has already been published. Four-week fellowships are offered to those working on a current project.

Heywood Hill Literary Prize

Administration Heywood Hill Booksellers, 10 Curzon Street, London W1J 5HH

An award of £12,000 is given annually to a person chosen for their lifetime's contribution to the enjoyment of books. No applications. Established 1995.

Hunting Art Prizes

Details Parker Harris Partnership, PO Box 279, Esher, Surrey KT10 8YZ
tel (01372) 462190 *fax* (01372) 460032
email hap@parkerharris.co.uk
website www.parkerharris.co.uk

An annual national art competition open to all artists resident in the UK. Total prize monies: £24,000. Entry fee is £10 (£4 students) per work and artists may submit up to 3 works. Closing date: November 2003. An exhibition will be held at the Royal College of Art in early 2004. Established 1980.

Images – The Best of British Illustration

Details Association of Illustrators, 81 Leonard Street, London EC2A 4QS
tel 020-7613 4328 *fax* 020-7613 4417
email info@a-o-illustrators.demon.co.uk
website www.theaoi.com
Contact Images Co-ordinator

Illustrators are invited to submit work for possible inclusion in the *Images Annual*, a jury-selected showcase of the best of contemporary British illustration. Selected work forms the Images exhibition, which tours the UK. UK illustrators or illustrators working for UK clients are all eligible. Send sae for entry form in the Spring. Founded 1976.

Independent Foreign Fiction Prize
Details The Literature Dept, Arts Council England, 14 Great Peter Street, London SW1P 3NQ
tel 020-7973 6442
website www.artscouncil.org.uk

In collaboration with the *Independent* newspaper and Champagne Taittinger, Arts Council England awards the £10,000 prize to honour a great work of fiction by a living author which has been translated into English from any other language and published in the UK. The prize is shared equally between the author and the translator.

Insight Guides Travel Photography Prize
Details APA Publications (UK) Ltd, 58 Borough High Street, London SE1 1XF
tel 020-7403 0284 *fax* 020-7403 0290
website www.insightguides.com

An annual competition open to amateur and professional photographers resident in the UK (theme to be announced). First prize is a commission to photograph for an Insight Guide worth £3000; 11 other prizes of equipment and film. Closing date: September 2003. Founded 2000.

International IMPAC Dublin Literary Award
Details International IMPAC Dublin Literary Award, Dublin City Library & Archive, 138-144 Pearse Street, Dublin 2, Republic of Ireland
tel (01) 674 4802 *fax* (01) 674 4879
email dubaward@iol.ie
website www.impacdublinaward.ie

An annual award of €100,000 is presented to the author of a work of fiction, written and published in the English language or written in a language other than English and published in English translation, which in the opinion of the judges is of high literary merit and constitutes a lasting contribution to world literature. Nominations are accepted from library systems of major cities from all over the world, regardless of national origin of the author or the place of publication. Founded 1995.

International Playwriting Festival
Details/entry form Festival Administrator, Warehouse Theatre, Dingwall Road, Croydon CR0 2NF
tel 020-8681 1257 *fax* 020-8688 6699
email info@warehousetheatre.co.uk
website www.warehousetheatre.co.uk

An annual competition for full-length unperformed plays. Selected plays are showcased during the festival weekend in November. Plays are also presented in Italy at the leading Italian playwriting festival Premio Candoni Arta Terme. Entries are welcome from all parts of the world. Send sae for further details or visit the website. Deadline for entries: 30 June. Founded 1985.

J.R. Ackerley Prize for Autobiography
Information PEN, Lancaster House, 33 Islington High Street, London N1 9LH
tel 020-020-7713 0023 *fax* 020-7713 0005
email enquiries@englishpen.org
website www.englishpen.org

An annual prize (£1000 and a silver Dupont pen) given for an outstanding work of literary autobiography written in English and published during the previous year by an author of British nationality or an author who has been a long-term resident in the UK. No submissions please – books are nominated by the judges only. First awarded in 1982.

The James Tait Black Memorial Prizes
Submissions Department of English Literature, David Hume Tower, George Square, Edinburgh EH8 9JX
tel 0131-650 3619 *fax* 0131-650 6898
website www.ed.ac.uk/englit/jtbinf.htm

Two prizes of £3000 are awarded annually: one for the best biography or work of that nature, the other for the best novel, published during the calendar year. The adjudicator is the Professor of English Literature in the University of Edinburgh. Eligible novels and biographies are those written in English and first published in Britain in the year of the award. Both prizes may go to the same author, but neither to the same author a second time.

   Publishers should submit a copy of any appropriate biography, or work of fiction, as early as possible with a note of the date of publication, marked 'James Tait Black Prize'. Closing date for submissions: 30 September. Founded in memory of a partner in the publishing house of A & C Black, these prizes were instituted in 1918.

Jerwood Painting Prize
PO Box 279, Esher, Surrey KT10 8YZ
tel (01372) 462190 *fax* (01372) 460032
email jpp@parkerharris.co.uk
website www.parkerharris.co.uk

An annual single prize of £30,000 is awarded to celebrate excellence and originality in contemporary painting in the UK. All professional artists are eligible. Closing date: February 2004. Founded 1993.

Jewish Quarterly Literary Prizes

Details The Administrator, Jewish Quarterly,
PO Box 35042, London NW1 7XH
tel 020-7284 1117

Prizes are awarded annually for a work of fiction
(£4000) and non-fiction (£4000) which best
stimulate an interest in and awareness of themes of
Jewish concern among a wider reading public.
Founded 1977.

The Jill Smythies Award

The Linnean Society of London, Burlington House,
Piccadilly, London W1J 0BF
tel 020-7434 4479 *fax* 020-7287 9364
email john@linnean.org
website www.linnean.org

Established in honour of Jill Smythies whose career
as a botanical artist was cut short by an accident to
her right hand. The rubic states that 'the Award, to
be made by Council usually annually consisting of a
silver medal and a purse (currently £1000) ... is for
published illustrations, such as drawings and
paintings, in aid of plant identification, with the
emphasis on botanical accuracy and the accurate
portrayal of diagnostic characteristics. Illustrations
of cultivars of garden origin are not eligible.'
Closing date for nominations: 30 September.
Founded 1988.

The John D. Criticos Prize

Coordinator Michael Moschos, The London Hellenic
Society, 11 Stormont Road, London N6 4NS
tel 020-7626 0006 *fax* 020-7626 0601

A prize of £10,000 will be awarded to an artist,
writer or researcher for an original work on
Hellenic culture. Areas of particular interest are
archaeology, art, art history, history and literature.
No application necessary: send 2 copies of book
plus covering letter. Closing date: 31 January.
Founded 1996.

The John Kobal Foundation Photographic Portrait Grants

Details The John Kobal Foundation,
Mount Pleasant Studios, 51-53 Mount Pleasant,
London WC1X 0AE
tel 020-7278 8482 *fax* 020-7278 8482

Portrait photography is defined here as 'photography
concerned with portraying people with the emphasis
on their identity as individuals' and applications for
grants towards portrait photographic projects are
accepted throughout the year.

John Moores Liverpool Exhibition

The Walker, William Brown Street,
Liverpool L3 8EL
tel 0151-478 4199 *fax* 0151-478 4190
email stephen.guy@nmgm.org

website www.nmgm.org.uk
Contact Stephen Guy

Biennial painting exhibition open to any artist
living or working in the UK. Cash prize of £25,000
plus acquisition (by gift) of prize-winning painting
by the Walker. Next exhibition Sept–Dec 2004 (tbc).
Founded 1957.

John Whiting Award

Details Literature Dept, Arts Council England,
14 Great Peter Street, London SW1P 3NQ
tel 020-7973 6431
email jemima.lee@artscouncil.org.uk
website www.artscouncil.org.uk

This prize of £6000 is to help further the careers
and enhance the reputations of British playwrights.
The play does not have to have been staged but
must have been written during 2002 or 2003.

Kate Greenaway Medal – see The CILIP Carnegie and Kate Greenaway Awards

The Kathleen Blundell Trust

Kathleen Blundell Trust, The Society of Authors,
84 Drayton Gardens, London SW10 9SB
tel 020-7373 6642
email info@societyofauthors.org
website www.societyofauthors.org

Awards are given to published writers under the age
of 40 to assist them with their next book. The
author's work must 'contribute to the greater
understanding of existing social and economic
organisation', but fiction is not excluded. Closing
dates: 30 April and 31 October. Send sae for an
information sheet.

Kent and Sussex Poetry Society Open Poetry Competition

Submissions The Organiser, 13 Ruscombe Close,
Southborough, Tunbridge Wells, Kent TN4 0SG

This competition is open to all unpublished poems,
no longer than 40 lines in length. Prizes: 1st £500,
2nd £200, 3rd £100, 4th 4 at £50. Closing date:
31 January. Entries should include an entry fee of
£3 per poem, the author's name and address and a
list of poems submitted. Founded 1985.

Kerry Group Irish Fiction Award

Details Writers' Week, 24 The Square,
Listowel, Co. Kerry, Republic of Ireland
tel (353) 6821074 *fax* (353) 6822893
email writersweek@eircom.net
website www.writersweek.ie

An annual award of €10,000 for a published work of
fiction by an Irish author. No entry fee. Closing
date: 1 March.

Kraszna-Krausz Awards

Details Andrea Livingstone, Administrator,
Kraszna-Krausz Foundation, 122 Fawnbrake Avenue,
London SE24 0BZ
tel 020-7738 6701 *fax* 020-7738 6701
email awards@k-k.org.uk
website www.k-k.org.uk

Awards totalling over £10,000 are made each year,
alternating annually between the best books on:
• still photography: art, culture and history; craft,
technology and scientific (2004).
• moving image (film, TV and video): culture and
history; business, techniques and technology (2005);

The prize in each category will be awarded to the
best book published in the preceding 2 years.
Closing date: 1 July. The Foundation is also open to
applications for grants (UK only) concerned with
the literature of photography and the moving
image. Instituted in 1985.

L. Ron Hubbard's Writers and Illustrators of the Future Contests

Administrator Andrea Grant-Webb, PO Box 218,
East Grinstead, West Sussex RH19 4GH

Aims to encourage new and aspiring writers and
illustrators of science fiction, fantasy and horror. In
addition to the quarterly prizes there is an annual
prize of £2500 for each contest. All 24 winners are
invited to the annual L. Ron Hubbard Achievement
Awards, which include a series of writers' and
illustrators' workshops, and their work is published
in an anthology. Write for an entry form.

Writers of the Future Contest

Entrants should submit a short story of up to
10,000 words or a novelette of less than 17,000
words. Prizes of £640 (1st), £480 (2nd) and £320
(3rd) are awarded each quarter. Founded 1984.

Illustrators of the Future Contest

Entrants should submit 3 b&w illustrations on
different themes. Three prizes of £320 are awarded
each quarter. Founded 1988.

The Lady Short Story Competition

The Lady, 39-40 Bedford Street, London WC2E 9ER

Open to anyone, details are published in an October
issue of *The Lady*. First prize is £1000. Subjects for
short stories change each year. Further information
in the relevant issue.

Leverhulme Research Fellowships

The Leverhulme Trust, 1 Pemberton Row,
London EC4A 3BG
tel 020-7822 6477 *fax* 020-7822 5084
email jcater@leverhulme.org.uk
website www.leverhulme.org.uk

The Leverhulme Trustees offer annually approximately 110 Fellowships to individuals in aid of
original research – not for study of any sort. These
awards are not available as replacement for past
support from other sources. Applications will be
considered in all subject areas. Total Fellowship
monies for 2003 was £20,000. Completed
application forms must be received by mid
November 2003 for 2004 awards. Founded 1933.

The Lionel Gelber Prize

Details Prize Manager, The Lionel Gelber Prize,
c/o Munk Center for International Studies,
1 Devonshire Place, Toronto, Ontario M5S 3K7,
Canada
tel 416-656-3722 *fax* 416-658-5205
email meisner@interlog.com

This international prize of $50,000 is awarded
annually in Canada to the author of the year's most
outstanding work of non-fiction in the field of
international relations. Submissions must be
published in English or in English translation
between 1 September and 31 August of the following
year. Submissions deadline: 31 May, i.e. 3 months
before the end of the period in question. Books must
be submitted by the publisher. Established 1989.

London Arts

Details Literature Administrator, London Arts,
2 Pear Tree Court, London EC1R 0DS
tel 020-7608 6100 *fax* 020-7608 4100
website www.arts.org.uk/londonarts

London Arts is the regional office for the Capital,
covering 32 boroughs and the City of London.
Grants are available to support a variety of
literature projects, focusing on 3 main areas:
• live literature, including storytelling;
• support for small presses and literary magazines in
the publishing of new or under-represented creative
writing;
• bursaries for writers who have published one book
and are working on their second work of fiction or
poetry.

There are 2 deadlines each year for applications.
Contact Literature Unit for more information and
an application form.

London Press Club Awards

Details The Hon. Secretary, London Press Club,
St Bride Institute, 14 Bride Lane, Fleet Street,
London EC4Y 8EQ
tel 020-7353 7086/7 *fax* 020-7353 7087
email lpressclub@aol.com

Business Journalist of the Year, New Media Journalist
of the Year and Broadcasting Journalist of the Year.

Scoop of the Year Award

Chosen by a panel of senior editors, this annual
award of a bronze statuette is given for the

reporting scoop of the year, appearing in either a newspaper or electronic media. Founded 1990.

Edgar Wallace Award

Chosen by a panel of senior editors, this annual award of a silver inkstand is given for outstanding writing or reporting by a journalist. Founded 1990.

London Writers Competition

Details Arts Office, Room 224A, Wandsworth Town Hall, High Street, London SW18 2PU
tel 020-8871 8711
email arts@wandsworth.gov.uk
website www.wandsworth.gov.uk

Open to writers who live, work or study in the Greater London Area. Awards are made annually in 4 classes (Poetry, Short Story, Fiction for Children and Play) and prizes total £1000 in each class. Entries must be previously unpublished work. Judging is under the chairmanship of Martyn Goff.

The McKitterick Prize

Details Awards Secretary, The Society of Authors, 84 Drayton Gardens, London SW10 9SB
tel 020-7373 6642
email info@societyofauthors.org
website www.societyofauthors.org

This annual award of £4000 is open to first published novels and unpublished typescripts by authors over the age of 40. Closing date: 20 December. Endowed by the late Tom McKitterick. Send sae for entry form.

The Macmillan Prize for Children's Picture Book Illustration

Applications Marketing Dept, Macmillan Children's Books, 20 New Wharf Road, London N1 9RR

Three prizes are awarded annually for unpublished children's book illustrations by art students in higher education establishments in the UK. Prizes: £1000 (1st), £500 (2nd) and £250 (3rd).

The Mail on Sunday/John Llewellyn Rhys Prize

Details Booktrust, Book House, 45 East Hill, London SW18 2QZ
tel 020-8516 2973/2972 *fax* 020-8516 2978
email kate@booktrust.org.uk
tarryn@booktrust.org.uk
Contact Kate Mervyn-Jones, Tarryn McKay

This annual prize of £5000 (plus £500 to each shortlisted author) is made to an author aged 35 or under for a work of literature (fiction, poetry, drama, non-fiction, etc) which has been published during the calendar year prior to the presentation (the 2003 prize will be awarded in 2004). The author must be a citizen of the UK or the Commonwealth. Inaugurated in memory of the writer John Llewellyn Rhys by his widow Jane Oliver. Established 1942.

The Man Booker Prize

Colman Getty PR, Middlesex House, 34-42 Cleveland Street, London W1T 4TE
tel 020-7631 2666 *fax* 020-7631 2699
email cathryn@colmangettypr.co.uk
website www.themanbookerprize.co.uk
Contact Cathryn Summerhayes

This annual prize for fiction of £65,000, including £2500 to each of 6 shortlisted authors, is awarded to the best novel published each year. It is open to novels written in English by citizens of the British Commonwealth and Republic of Ireland and published for the first time in the UK by a British publisher, although previous publication of a book outside the UK does not disqualify it. Entries only from UK publishers who may each submit not more than 2 novels with scheduled publication dates between 1 October of the previous year and 30 September of the current year, but the judges may also ask for other eligible novels to be submitted to them. In addition, publishers may submit eligible titles by authors who have been shortlisted or won the Booker Prize previously. Sponsored by the Man Group.

Marsh Award for Children's Literature in Translation

Administered by National Centre for Research in Children's Literature, Digby Stuart College, University of Surrey, Roehampton, Roehampton Lane, London SW15 5PU
tel 020-8392 3008
Contact Dr Gillian Lathey

This biennial award of £1000 is given to the translator of a book for children (aged 4–16) from a foreign language into English and published in the UK by a British publisher. Electronic books, and encyclopedias and other reference books, are not eligible. Next award: January 2005. Founded 1996.

Marsh Biography Award

Administered by The English-Speaking Union, Dartmouth House, 37 Charles Street, London W1J 5ED
tel 020-7529 1550 *fax* 020-7495 6108
email tim_rolph@esu.org

This major national biography prize of £4000 plus a trophy is presented every 2 years. Entries must be serious biographies written by British authors and published in the UK. Next award: October 2005. Founded 1985–6.

The Mathew Prichard Award for Short Story Writing

Details The Competition Secretary, The Mathew Prichard Award, 2 Rhododendron Close, Cyncoed, Cardiff CF23 7HS *website* www.samwaw.org.uk

Total prize money of £2000 is awarded annually in this open competition for original short stories in English of not more than 2500 words. Adjudication is organised in May each year by the South and Mid Wales Association of Writers. Send sae for entry form or download from website.

Meyer Whitworth Award

Details Literature Dept, Arts Council England, 14 Great Peter Street, London SW1P 3NQ
tel 020-7973 6431
email jemima.lee@artscouncil.org.uk
website www.artscouncil.org.uk

This award of £8000 is to help further the careers of UK playwrights who are not yet established.

Miles Franklin Literary Award

Details Permanent Trustee Company Ltd, 35 Clarence Street, Sydney, NSW 2001, Australia
email linda.ingalelo@permanentgroup.com.au

This annual award of $28,000 is for a novel or play first published in the preceding year, which presents Australian life in any of its phases. More than one entry may be submitted by each author, and collaborations between 2 or more authors are eligible. Biographies, collections of short stories or children's books are not eligible. Closing date: 15 December (tbc). Founded 1957.

Millfield Arts Projects

Atkinson Gallery, Millfield, Butleigh Road, Street, Somerset BA16 0YD
tel (01458) 442291 *fax* (01458) 447276
email lag@millfield.somerset.sch.uk
website www.millfield.somerset.sch.uk
Director of Art Len Green

'The mandate of the Millfield Arts Project programme is to search for, promote and support, primarily but not exclusively, young aspiring artists at local, regional, national and international levels.' In a professional art context MAP offers:
• Sculpture Commission. Artists work on campus for 8 weeks (£7500). Deadline for entries: mid January.
• Summer Show. An open exhibition. Application forms available: March.
• Six Gallery exhibitions selected by the Director of Art. Interested artists should send slides and CV to the Director of Art.

Mind Book of the Year

Details Anny Brackx, Information Department, Granta House, 15-19 Broadway, London E15 4BQ
tel 020-8519 2122 *fax* 020-8522 1725

This £1500 award is given to the author of any book (fiction or non-fiction) published in the UK in the current year which outstandingly furthers public understanding of the prevention, causes, treatment or experience of mental health problems. Entries by 31 December. Administered by Mind, the National Association for Mental Health. Inaugurated in memory of Sir Allen Lane in 1981.

National Poetry Competition

Contact Competition Organiser, The Poetry Society, 22 Betterton Street, London WC2H 9BX
tel 020-7420 9880 *fax* 020-7240 4818
email info@poetrysociety.org.uk
website www.poetrysociety.org.uk

One of Britain's major annual open poetry competitions. Poems on any theme, up to 40 lines. Prizes: 1st £5000, 2nd £1000, 3rd £500, plus 10 commendations of £50. All poems will be read by a team of poetry specialists before the final judging process. For rules and entry form send an sae. Entries also accepted via the website. Closing date: 31 October each year.

The Natural World Book Prize

(in partnership with The Wildlife Trusts)
Details/entry form Booktrust, Book House, 45 East Hill, London SW18 2QZ
tel 020-8516 2973/2972 *fax* 020-8516 2978
email kate@booktrust.org.uk
Contacts Kate Mervyn-Jones, Tarryn McKay

Awards of £5000 to the winner and £1000 to the runner up for an adult book which most imaginatively promotes the conservation of the natural environment and all its animals and plants. Books must have been published between 1 June and the following 31 May. An amalgamation of the BP Conservation Book Prize and the Natural World Book of the Year Award. Sponsored by BP and Subbuteo Books.

The Nestlé Smarties Book Prize

Details Booktrust, Book House, 45 East Hill, London SW18 2QZ
tel 020-8516 2973/2972 *fax* 020-8516 2978
email kate@booktrust.org.uk
tarryn@booktrust.org.uk
Contact Kate Mervyn-Jones, Tarryn McKay

Three prizes (Gold, Silver and Bronze) are awarded to the 3 shortlisted books in each category (5 and under, 6–8 and 9–11 years). The Gold Award winners each receive £2500, the Silver Award winners receive £1500, and the Bronze Award winners receive £500. Eligible books must be published in the UK in the 12 months ending 30 September of the year of presentation and be a work of fiction or poetry for children written in English by a citizen or resident of the UK. Closing date for entries: contact Administrator. Sponsored by Nestlé Smarties. Established in 1985.

New Millennial Science Essay Competition

Details The Wellcome Trust, 210 Euston Road,
London NW1 2BE
tel 020-7611 7221 *fax* 020-7611 8269
email r.birse@wellcome.ac.uk
website www.wellcome.ac.uk/ScienceEssay

Postgraduate students (in science, engineering or
technology) currently writing up their theses are
invited to write an entertaining essay on the
possible impact of their research on society of no
more than 700 words. The aim is to make the
research topic interesting and accessible to a wider
non-specialist audience. Applicants must be
registered at an internationally recognised
institution. The competition is open from mid
March to mid May each year. A collaboration
between the Wellcome Trust and *New Scientist*
magazine. Prizes: £1500 and publication in *New
Scientist* (1st), £750 (2nd), 2 prizes of £375 each
(3rd). All winners, including the next 10 best essays,
receive a one-year subscription to *New Scientist*.
Founded 1993.

The New Writer Prose and Poetry Prizes

Details The New Writer Poetry Prizes, PO Box 60,
Cranbrook, Kent TN17 2ZR
tel (01580) 212626 *fax* (01580) 212041
email editor@thenewwriter.com
website www.thenewwriter.com

Short stories up to 5000 words, novellas, essays and
articles; poets may submit either one or a collection
of 6–10 previously unpublished poems. Total prize
money £2500 as well as publication for the prize-
winners in the *New Writer* magazine. Entry fees: £3
per poem; £10 for a collection of 6–10 poems. Send
for an entry form or visit the website for information
about the short fiction and non-fiction sections.
Closing date: 30 November each year. Founded 1997.

Nielsen Gold and Platinum Book Awards

tel (01252) 742555 *fax* (01252) 742556
email gold&platinumawards@whitaker.co.uk

The awards are a recognition of sales purchases of a
book by the general public. Eligible books are those
priced at £4.99 or above that reach 500,000 unit
sales (Gold) or 1,000,000 unit sales (Platinum) as
measured by Nielsen BookScan within a 5-year
period. All qualifying titles receive an award, funded
for the author by their publisher. Founded 2001.

The Nobel Prize in Literature

Awarding authority Swedish Academy, Box 2118,
S-10313 Stockholm, Sweden
tel (08) 10-65-24 *fax* (08) 24-42-25
email sekretariat@svenskaakademien.se
website www.svenskaakademien.se

This is one of the awards stipulated in the will of
the late Alfred Nobel, the Swedish scientist who

invented dynamite. No direct application for a prize
will be taken into consideration. For authors
writing in English it was bestowed upon Rudyard
Kipling in 1907, W.B. Yeats in 1923, George Bernard
Shaw in 1925, Sinclair Lewis in 1930, John
Galsworthy in 1932, Eugene O'Neill in 1936, Pearl
Buck in 1938, T.S. Eliot in 1948, William Faulkner
in 1949, Bertrand Russell in 1950, Sir Winston
Churchill in 1953, Ernest Hemingway in 1954, John
Steinbeck in 1962, Samuel Beckett in 1969, Patrick
White in 1973, Saul Bellow in 1976, William
Golding in 1983, Wole Soyinka in 1986, Joseph
Brodsky in 1987, Nadine Gordimer in 1991, Derek
Walcott in 1992, Toni Morrison in 1993, Seamus
Heaney in 1995 and V.S. Naipaul in 2001.

Northern Rock Foundation Writer's Award

Details New Writing North, 7-8 Trinity Chare,
Quayside, Newcastle Upon Tyne NE1 3DF
tel 0191-232 9991 *fax* 0191-230 1883
email mail@newwritingnorth.com
website www.newwritingnorth.com
Contact Silvana Michelini

An annual award of £20,000 p.a. for a 3-year period
(i.e. £60,000) designed to release a writer from
commitments such as teaching to devote time to a
major work. Eligible are writers of poetry, prose,
children's books and biography with at least 2 books
published by a recognised publisher. Writers must
reside in Northumberland, Tyne & Wear, County
Durham or Teesside. Closing date: see website.
Founded 2002.

Northern Writers' Awards

Administered by New Writing North,
7-8 Trinity Chare, Quayside,
Newcastle upon Tyne NE1 3DF
tel 0191-232 9991 *fax* 0191-230 1883
email mail@newwritingnorth.com
website www.newwritingnorth.com
Contact Silvana Michelini

Awards (from £1000 to £5000) are aimed at
developing writers at different stages in their
careers. A panel of professional writers shortlists
and makes awards once a year. Applicants must be
resident in the Northern Arts region
(Northumberland, Tyne & Wear, Durham,
Teesside). See website for details. Deadline for
applications: usually November but check website
for up-to-date information.

The Observer Hodge Award/Exhibition

Details The Observer Hodge Award, The Observer,
119 Farringdon Road, London EC1R 3ER
tel 020-7886 9305
email hodge.award@observer.co.uk
website www.observer.co.uk/hodgeaward
Contact Ann Farragher

Set up in memory of David Hodge who died aged 29, this annual award is given to student and professional photographers under 30. First prize: £3000 plus an expenses-paid assignment for the *Observer*; best student prize: £1500. Next award to be launched March 2004; deadline: 27 June 2004. Founded 1986.

Orange Prize for Fiction

Details Booktrust, Book House, 45 East Hill, London SW18 2QZ
tel 020-8516 2973/2972 *fax* 020-8516 2978
email kate@booktrust.org.uk
tarryn@booktrust.org.uk
Contact Kate Mervyn-Jones, Tarryn McKay

This award of £30,000, and a statuette known as 'The Bessie', is for a full-length novel written in English by a woman of any nationality and first published in the UK between 1 April and 31 March. Sponsored by Orange PCS. Established 1996.

The Oscar Moore Screenwriting Prize

Details The Oscar Moore Foundation,
33-39 Bowling Green Lane, London EC1R 0DA
tel 020-7505 8080 *fax* 020-7505 8087
email annmarie.oconnor@media.emap.com
website www.screendaily.com

The Foundation works to build for a Europe-wide culture of screenwriting excellence and to this end makes this annual award (£10,000) to finance the first draft of a promising screenplay. A different genre is chosen for each year.

The Parker Romantic Novel of the Year Award

Details Mary de Laszlo, 57 Coniger Road,
London SW6 3TB
tel 020-7736 4968
website www.rna-uk.org

This annual award of £10,000 for the best romantic novel of the year is open to both members and non-members of the Romantic Novelists' Association, provided non-members are domiciled in the UK. Novels must be published between the previous 1 December and 30 November of the year of entry. Three copies of the novel are required. Send sae for entry form and details, available from July onwards.

New Writers' Award
Margaret James, 16 St Briac Way, Bystock,
Exmouth, Devon EX8 5RN
tel (01395) 279659
email margaret@jamesk.freeserve.co.uk

For writers previously unpublished in the adult novel field and who are probationary members of the Association. MSS can be submitted until the end of September under the New Writers' Scheme. All receive a critique. Any MSS which have passed through the Scheme and which are subsequently accepted for publication become eligible for the Award.

The Paul Hamlyn Foundation Awards to Artists

Details The Administrator, 18 Queen Anne's Gate, London SW1H 9AA
tel 020-7227 3500 *fax* 020-7222 0601
email information@phf.org.uk

Five awards of £30,000 spread over 3 years will be made to visual artists in 2004 to support the creative process. Strength of talent, promise and need, as well as achievement, are all assessed. Nominations are made by a nationwide panel of 20 artists and others. The scheme is not open to application. Founded 1993.

Peterloo Poets Open Poetry Competition

Details Peterloo Poets, The Old Chapel, Sand Lane, Calstock, Cornwall PL18 9QX

This annual competition offers a first prize of £2000 and 14 other prizes totalling £2100. There is also a 15–19 age group section with 5 prizes each of £100. Closing date: 1 March 2004. Founded 1986.

The Petra Kenney Poetry Competition

Details Morgan Kenney, Danny, Hurstpierpoint, East Sussex BN6 9BB
fax (01273) 831889
email morgan@petrapoetrycompetition.co.uk
website www.petrapoetrycompetition.co.uk

This annual competition is for unpublished poems on any theme and in any style, and is open to everyone. Poems should be no more than 80 lines. Prizes: £1000 (1st), £500 (2nd), £250 (3rd), 3 at £125; also an inscribed Royal Brierley crystal vase to each winner and publication in *Writers' Forum* magazine. Entry fee: £3 per poem. Closing date: 1 December each year. Founded 1995.

The Poetry Business Book & Pamphlet Competition

Competition Administrator The Poetry Business,
The Studio, Byram Arcade, Westgate,
Huddersfield HD1 1ND
tel (01484) 434840 *fax* (01484) 426566
email edit@poetrybusiness.co.uk
website www.poetrybusiness.co.uk
Directors Peter Sansom, Janet Fisher

An annual award is made for a poetry collection. The judges select up to 5 short collections for publication as pamphlets; on further submission of more poems, one of these will be selected for a full-length collection to be published under the Poetry Business's Smith/Doorstop imprint. All winners share a cash prize of £1000. Poets over the age of 18 writing in English from anywhere in the world are eligible. Closing date: 31 October. Founded 1986.

Poetry Life Open Poetry Competition

Details 1 Blue Ball Corner, Water Lane, Winchester, Hants SO23 0ER

email adrian.abishop@virgin.net
website http://freespace.virgin.net/poetry.life/
Competitions are held 3 times a year with a first
prize of £3000. Any style is acceptable with an
80-line limit on each poem. Poems must be
previously unpublished (in book form) and must
not have won a prize in another competition. All
winning poems are published in *Poetry Life*
magazine and on its website. Send sae for further
details. Founded 1994.

The Portico Prize
Details Miss Emma Marigliano, Librarian,
Portico Library, 57 Mosley Street,
Manchester M2 3HY
tel 0161-236 6785 *fax* 0161-236 6803
This biennial prize of £3000 is awarded for a
published work of fiction or non-fiction, of general
interest and literary merit set wholly or mainly in
the North-West of England (Lancashire,
Manchester, Liverpool, High Peak of Derbyshire,
Cheshire and Cumbria). Next award: 2004.
Founded 1985.

The Raymond Williams Community Publishing Prizes
Details The Literature Dept, Arts Council England,
14 Great Peter Street, London SW1P 3NQ
tel 020-7973 6442
website www.artscouncil.org.uk
This award commends published works of
outstanding creative and imaginative quality that
reflect the life, voices and experiences of the people
of particular communities. The winning entry will
be awarded £3000 and the runner-up £2000.

Real Writers Short Story Awards
(formerly The Real Writers Short Story Competition)
PO Box 170, Chesterfield, Derbyshire S40 1FE
tel (01246) 238492 *fax* (01246) 238492
email info@real-writers.com
website www.real-writers.com
First prize: £2500 plus 10 regional awards. Send sae
for entry form. Optional critiques. Entry fee: £5.
Closing date: 30 November. Founded 1994.

The Red House Children's Book Award
Details Marianne Adey, The Old Malt House,
Aldbourne, Marlborough, Wilts. SN8 2DW
tel (01672) 540629 *fax* (01672) 541280
email marianneadey@aol.com
This award is given annually to authors of works of
fiction for children published in the UK. Children
participate in the judging of the award. 'Pick of the
Year' booklist is published in conjunction with the
award. Founded in 1980 by the Federation of
Children's Book Groups.

Reginald Taylor and Lord Fletcher Essay Competition
Submissions Dr Martin Henig, Hon. Editor,
British Archaeological Association,
Institute of Archaeology, 36 Beaumont Street,
Oxford OX1 2PG
A prize of a medal and £300 is awarded biennially
for the best unpublished essay of high scholarly
standard, not exceeding 7500 words, which shows
original research on a subject of archaeological, art-
historical or antiquarian interest within the period
from the Roman era to AD 1830. The successful
competitor will be invited to read the essay before
the Association and the essay may be published in
the Association's *Journal*. Competitors should notify
the Hon. Editor in advance of the intended subject
of their work. Next award: autumn 2004. The essay
should be submitted not later than 1 June 2004,
enclosing an sae. Founded in memory of
E. Reginald Taylor FSA and Lord Fletcher FSA.

The Rhys Davies Trust
Details Prof Meic Stephens, The Secretary,
The Rhys Davies Trust, 10 Heol Don, Whitchurch,
Cardiff CF14 2AU
tel 029-2062 3359 *fax* 029-2052 9202
email meic@heoldon.fsnet.co.uk
The Trust aims to foster Welsh writing in English
and offers financial assistance to English-language
literary projects in Wales, directly or in association
with other bodies.

The Richard Imison Memorial Award
Details/entry form The Secretary,
The Broadcasting Committee,
The Society of Authors, 84 Drayton Gardens,
London SW10 9SB
tel 020-7373 6642
email info@societyofauthors.org
website www.societyofauthors.org
This annual prize of £1500 is awarded to any new
writer of radio drama first transmitted within the
UK during the period 1 January–31 December 2003
by a writer new to radio. Founded 1993.

The Rooney Prize for Irish Literature
Details J.A. Sherwin, Strathin,
Templecarrig, Delgany, Co. Wicklow,
Republic of Ireland
tel (01) 287 4769 *fax* (01) 287 2595
email rooneyprize@ireland.com
An annual prize of €8000 is awarded to encourage
young Irish writing talent. To be eligible individuals
must be Irish, published and under 40 years of age.
The prize is non-competitive and there is no
application procedure or entry form. Founded in
1976 by Daniel M. Rooney, Pittsburgh, Pennsylvania.

The Rose Mary Crawshay Prizes

The British Academy, 10 Carlton House Terrace,
London SW1Y 5AH
tel 020-7969 5200 *fax* 020-7969 5300
email secretary@britac.ac.uk
website www.britac.ac.uk

One or more prizes are awarded each year to
women of any nationality who, in the judgement of
the Council of the British Academy, have written or
published within the 3 calendar years immediately
preceding the date of the award an historical or
critical work of sufficient value on any subject
connected with English literature, preference being
given to a work regarding Byron, Shelley or Keats.
Founded 1888.

The Royal Society of Literature Award under the W.H. Heinemann Bequest

Details/Submissions The Secretary,
Royal Society of Literature, Somerset House,
Strand, London WC2R 1LA
tel 020-7845 4676 *fax* 020-7845 4679
email info@rslit.org

Serious works of non-fiction – biography, poetry,
history, criticism – may be submitted by publishers
for this award of £5000. Books must be written in
the English language and have been published in
the previous year. Translations are not eligible for
consideration, nor are single poems, nor collections
of pieces by more than one author, nor may
individuals put forward their own work. Entries
published during the current year should be
submitted between 1 October and 15 December.

The Royal Society of Literature Ondaatje Prize

Submissions The Royal Society of Literature,
Somerset House, Strand, London WC2R 1LA
tel 020-7845 4676 *fax* 020-7845 4679
email info@rslit.org

This annual prize replaces the Winifred Holtby
Memorial Prize. The value of the new prize is
£10,000 and is awarded to the book of the highest
literary merit (fiction or non-fiction) that evokes
the spirit of a place. The writer must be a citizen of
the UK, Commonwealth or Ireland, and must be
alive at the time of submission. Publishers and
imprints of publishers may submit 2 books for
entry. Poetry, children's books and translations are
not eligible. Entries must be published within the
current year and submitted between 1 September
and 1 December. Contact the Secretary for further
details.

RSPCA Young Photographer Awards

Details Publications Department, RSPCA,
Wilberforce Way, Southwater, Horsham,
West Sussex RH13 9RS

tel (0870) 7540455 *fax* (0870) 7530455
email publications@rspca.org.uk

Annual awards are made for animal photographs
taken by young people in 2 age categories: under 12
and 12–18. Prizes: overall winner (£250 cash, digital
camera), age group winners (£100 cash, camera).
Four runners-up in each age group receive a camera
and £50 cash. Sponsored by Olympus and Truprint.
Closing date for entries: 15 September 2003.
Founded 1990.

RTE New Playwrights Awards

RTE Radio Drama, Donnybrook, Dublin 4,
Republic of Ireland
tel (01) 2083111 *fax* (01) 2083248
Producer in Charge Michael Campion

An annual competition for a 30-minute original
radio play, open to unproduced writers born in or
living in Ireland. Prizes: €3000 (1st), €2000 (2nd),
€1000 (3rd). Closing date: tbc.

Runciman Award

Details The Administrator,
The Anglo-Hellenic League,
16-18 Paddington Street,
London W1U 5AS
tel 020-7486 9410 *fax* 020-7486 4254 (mark FAO
Anglo-Hellenic League)

An annual prize of not less than £5000 sponsored
by the National Bank of Greece and named after the
late Sir Steven Runciman, former Chairman of the
Anglo-Hellenic League, for a work wholly or mainly
about some aspect of Greece or the Hellenic scene.
The work must have been published in its first
English edition in the UK during the previous year
and listed in *Whitaker's Books in Print*. The Award
may be given for a work of fiction, poetry, drama or
non-fiction; concerned academically or non-
academically with the history of any period;
biography or autobiography; travel and topography;
the arts, architecture, archaeology and the environment; the social and political sciences and current
affairs; a guidebook or a translation from the Greek
of any period. Final entry date: 31 January; award
presented in May/June. Established 1985.

Sainsbury's Baby Book Award

Details Booktrust, Book House, 45 East Hill,
London SW18 2QZ
tel 020-8516 2973 *fax* 020-8516 2978
email kate@booktrust.org.uk
tarryn@booktrust.org.uk
Contact Kate Mervyn Jones, Tarryn McKay

An annual award of £2000 for the author and/or
illustrator of the best book for babies under one
year of age. Closing date: 2 June 2004. Sponsored by
Sainsbury's plc. Established 1999.

Scottish Arts Council

Contact Gavin Wallace, Head of Literature,
Scottish Arts Council, 12 Manor Place,
Edinburgh EH3 7DD
tel 0131-226 6051
email gavin.wallace@scottisharts.org.uk

A limited number of writers' bursaries – up to
£15,000 each – are offered to enable professional
writers based in Scotland, including writers for
children, to devote more time to writing. Priority is
given to writers of fiction and verse and playwrights,
but writers of literary non-fiction are also considered.
Applications may be discussed with Gavin Wallace.

Scottish Book Awards

Up to 7 awards ranging from £2000 to £10,000 are
made in the spring to new and established authors
of published books in recognition of high standards
of writing, for both adults and children. Preference
is given to literary fiction and poetry, but literary
non-fiction is also considered. Authors should be
Scottish, resident in Scotland or have published
books of Scottish interest. Entries from publishers
only. Guidelines available on request.

The Scottish Book of the Year and Scottish First Book

Details The Saltire Society, 9 Fountain Close,
22 High Street, Edinburgh EH1 1TF
tel 0131-556 1836 *fax* 0131-557 1675
email saltire@saltiresociety.org.uk
website www.saltiresociety.org.uk

These 2 annual awards (£5000 and £1500) are open
to any author of Scottish descent or living in
Scotland, or for a book by anyone which deals with
the work or life of a Scot or with a Scottish
problem, event or situation. Nominations are made
by literary editors of newspapers and periodicals.
Supported by the Royal Mail Group. Established in
1982 and 1988 respectively.

Shiva Naipaul Memorial Prize

Details The Spectator, 56 Doughty Street,
London WC1N 2LL

This annual prize of £3000 is given to an English
language writer of any nationality under the age of
35 for an essay of not more than 4000 words giving
the most acute and profound observation of a
culture alien to the writer. Founded 1985.

Singer & Friedlander/Sunday Times Watercolour Competition

Details Parker Harris Partnership, PO Box 279,
Esher, Surrey KT10 8YZ
tel (01372) 462190 *fax* (01372) 460032
email sf@parkerharris.co.uk
website www.parkerharris.co.uk

An annual competition 'to promote the continuance

of the British tradition of fine watercolour painting'.
Total prize money: £30,000. Open to artists born or
resident in the UK. Closing date: July 2004. Winning
entries will be exhibited in London and Manchester.
Launched 1987.

Society for Theatre Research Book Prize

Details The Society for Theatre Research,
c/o The Theatre Museum, 1E Tavistock Street,
London WC2E 7PR
email e.cottis@btinternet.com
website www.str.org.uk

An annual award (£400) is given to the author
whose book, in the opinion of the judges, is the best
original research into any aspect of the history and
technique of the British theatre. Books must have
been published in English in the preceding calendar
year. Founded 1997.

The Society of Authors and The Royal Society of Medicine Medical Book Awards

Details The Secretary, MWG, The Society of Authors,
84 Drayton Gardens, London SW10 9SB
tel 020-7373 6642
email info@societyofauthors.org
website www.societyofauthors.org

Entries should be submitted by the publisher.
Closing date for submissions of medical text books:
31 May. The Medical Writers Group of the Society
of Authors administers the prizes sponsored by the
Royal Society of Medicine.

The Somerset Maugham Awards

Details Awards Secretary, The Society of Authors,
84 Drayton Gardens, London SW10 9SB
tel 020-7373 6642
email info@societyofauthors.org
website www.societyofauthors.org

These annual awards, totalling about £12,000, are
for writers under the age of 35. Candidates must be
British subjects by birth, and ordinarily resident in
the UK or Northern Ireland. Poetry, fiction, non-
fiction, belles-lettres or philosophy, but not dramatic
works, are eligible. Entries should be submitted by
the publisher. Closing date: 20 December.

Sony Radio Academy Awards

Details Sony Radio Academy Awards Secretariat,
Zafer Associates, 47-48 Chagford Street,
London NW1 6EB
tel 020-7723 0106 *fax* 020-7724 6163
email secretariat@radioawards.org

'The Sony Radio Academy Awards celebrate
excellence in broadcast work. They reward creative
achievement through imagination, originality, wit
and integrity. The Awards offer an opportunity to
enter work in a range of categories which reflect
today's local, regional and national radio. The

Awards are for everyone regardless of resources – for stations big and small, for a team or for one person with a microphone.' Send for further information. Founded 1982.

The Spoken Word Awards
Contact The Spoken Word Publishing Association, c/o Zoe Howes, Macmillan Publishers Ltd, 20 New Wharf Road, London N1 9RR
tel 020-7014 6041 *fax* 020-7014 6141
email z.howes@macmillan.co.uk
website www.swpa.co.uk

Annual awards are made for excellence in the spoken word industry. There are over 40 judges from all areas of the industry including audiobook reviewers, radio broadcasters, producers, abridgers, etc. Closing date: tbc.

The Sunday Times Young Writer of the Year Award
Details The Society of Authors, 84 Drayton Gardens, London SW10 9SB
tel 020-7373 6642
email info@societyofauthors.org
website www.societyofauthors.org

Annual award to published fiction and non-fiction writers under the age of 35. The panel consists of *Sunday Times* journalists and critics. Entry by publishers. Closing date: 20 December. Established 1991.

The T.S. Eliot Prize
Applications Poetry Book Society, Book House, 45 East Hill, London SW18 2QZ
tel 020-8870 8403
email info@poetrybooks.co.uk
website www.poetrybooks.co.uk

An annual prize of £10,000 is awarded to the best collection of new poetry published in the UK or the Republic of Ireland during the year. Submissions are invited from publishers in the summer. Donated by Valerie Eliot. Founded 1993.

TAPS (Television Arts Performance Showcase)
Details Shepperton Studios, Studios Road, Shepperton, Middlesex TW17 0QD
tel (01932) 592151 *fax* (01932) 592233
email taps@tvarts.demon.co.uk

A national scheme to train and promote new writers for film and TV. TAPS workshop training courses are open to any British scriptwriter with less than 2 hours work broadcast on network TV. Will accept full-length drama (min. 60 mins), comedy (30 mins) or shorts (10 mins) as qualifying script submissions for appropriate course. Scripts selected from each course are showcased by professional actors, taped and screened to industry executives culminating in the annual Writer of the Year Awards.

The Thomas Cook Travel Book Award
Details Travel Book Award, Thomas Cook Publishing, 19-21 Coningsby Road, Peterborough PE3 8XX
tel (01733) 402009 *fax* (01733) 416688

This annual award (£10,000) is given to encourage the art of travel writing and to inspire the wish to travel. Travel narrative books (150pp minimum) written in English and published between 1 January and 31 December of the preceding year are eligible. Established in 1980.

Tir Na N-og Awards
Details Welsh Books Council, Castell Brychan, Aberystwyth, Ceredigion SY23 2JB
tel (01970) 624151 *fax* (01970) 625385
email menna.lloydwilliams@cllc.org.uk
website www.cllc.org.uk

There are 3 annual awards to children's authors and illustrators: best original Welsh fiction, including short stories and picture books; best original Welsh non-fiction book of the year; best English book with an authentic Welsh background. Total prize value is £3000. Founded 1976.

The Tom-Gallon Trust Award and the Olive Cook Prize
Details Awards Secretary, The Society of Authors, 84 Drayton Gardens, London SW10 9SB
tel 020-7373 6642
email info@societyofauthors.org
website www.societyofauthors.org

An award of £1000 is made on the basis of a submitted short story to fiction writers of limited means who have had at least one short story accepted for publication. Both awards are biennial and are awarded in alternate years. Send sae for entry form. Closing date: 20 September each year.

The Translators Association Awards
Details Dorothy Sym, The Translators Association, 84 Drayton Gardens, London SW10 9SB
tel 020-7373 6642
email info@societyofauthors.org
website www.societyofauthors.org

The Translators Association of the Society of Authors administers a number of prizes for published translations into English. They include prizes for translations of Dutch and Flemish, French, German, Greek, Italian, Japanese, Portuguese, Spanish and Swedish works. Entries should be submitted by the publisher.

The Travelling Scholarships
Administered by The Society of Authors, 84 Drayton Gardens, London SW10 9SB

These are honorary awards established in 1944 by an anonymous benefactor. Submissions are not accepted.

Trevor Reese Memorial Prize
Details Events and Publicity Officer, Institute of Commonwealth Studies, 28 Russell Square, London WC1B 5DS *tel* 020-7862 8825 *fax* 020-7862 8820 *email* robert.holland@sas.ac.uk *website* www.sas.ac.uk/ commonwealthstudies/

This prize of £1000 is awarded biennially, usually for a scholarly work by a single author in the field of Imperial and Commonwealth history. The next award (for a book published in 2002 or 2003) will be given in 2005.

The Trewithen Poetry Prize
Details The Competition Secretary, Chy-an-Dour, Trewithen Moor, Stithians, Truro, Cornwall TR3 7DU *website* www.trewithenpoetry.co.uk

A biennial prize to promote poetry with a rural theme. Poems can reflect contemporary rural living, environmental concerns, or any other aspect of nature or rural life in any country. Total prize money: £800. Entry fee: £3.50. Send sae for entry form or see website. Closing date: 31 October 2004.

The V&A Illustration Awards
Enquiries The Word & Image Department, Victoria and Albert Museum, London SW7 2RL *tel* 020-7942 2414 *website* www.nal.vam.ac.uk *Contact* Dr Leo De Freitas *tel/fax* (01295) 256110

These annual awards are given to practising book and magazine illustrators, for work first published in Great Britain in the 12 months preceding the judging of the awards. Book covers, illustrations of a purely technical nature and photographs together with works produced as limited editions are excluded. Cover illustrations to magazines are eligible.

The V.S. Pritchett Memorial Prize
Details The Royal Society of Literature, Somerset House, Strand, London WC2R 1LA *tel* 020-7845 4676 *fax* 020-7845 4679 *email* info@rslit.org *website* www.rslit.org

An annual prize of £1000 is awarded for a previously unpublished short story of up to 5000 words. Entry fee: £5 per story. For entry forms contact the Secretary. Founded 1999.

Ver Poets Open Competition
Organiser May Badman, Ver Poets, 61-63 Chiswell Green Lane, St Albans, Herts. AL2 3AL

tel (01727) 867005 *email* may.badman@virgin.net

A competition open to all for poems of up to 30 lines of any genre or subject matter, which must be unpublished work in English. Prizes: £500 (1st), £300 (2nd), 2 prizes of £100 (3rd). Entry fee: £3 per poem with 2 copies of each poem (each year a gift to charity is made); send sae for entry form. Closing date 30 April each year.

Verity Bargate Award
Details The Literary Officer, Soho Theatre and Writers' Centre, 21 Dean Street, London W1D 3NE *email* writers@sohotheatre.com *website* www.sohotheatre.com

A biennial award, set up in honour of the company's co-founder, is made to the writer of a new and previously unperformed full-length play. Writers with 3 or more professional productions to their credit are ineligible. The prize (£1500) represents an option to produce the play by Soho Theatre Company. Next award: 2004.

The Walford Award – see The CILIP/Whitaker Reference Awards

The Welsh National Literature Promotion Agency and Society for Writers
Mount Stuart House, Mount Stuart Square, Cardiff CF10 5FQ *tel* 029-2047 2266 *fax* 029-2049 2930 *email* post@academi.org *website* www.academi.org *Ceo* Peter Finch

Book of the Year Award

A £3000 prize is awarded to winners, in Welsh and English, and £1000 to 4 other short-listed authors for works of exceptional merit by Welsh authors (by birth, subject matter or residence) published during the previous calendar year in the categories of poetry, fiction and creative non-fiction.

Bursaries

Bursaries totalling about £100,000 are awarded annually to authors writing in both Welsh and English. Application forms are available or visit the website.

The Wheatley Medal – see The CILIP/Whitaker Reference Awards

Whitbread Book Awards
Details Nicola Tarling, The Booksellers Association, Minster House, 272 Vauxhall Bridge Road, London SW1V 1BA *tel* 020-7802 0816 *fax* 020-7802 0803 *email* denise.bayat@booksellers.co.uk

website www.whitbreadbookawards.co.uk

The awards celebrate and promote the most enjoyable contemporary British writing. Judged in 2 stages and offering a total of £50,000 prize money, the awards are open to 5 categories: Novel, First Novel, Biography, Poetry and Children's. They are judged by a panel of 3 judges and the winner in each category receives an award of £5000. Nine final judges then choose the Whitbread Book of the Year from the winners of all categories. The winner receives a cheque for £25,000. Writers must have lived in Great Britain or Ireland for 3 or more years. Submissions must be received from publishers. Closing date: early July.

The Whitfield Prize

Submissions Executive Secretary,
Royal Historical Society,
University College London,
Gower Street, London WC1E 6BT
tel 020-7387 7532 *fax* 020-7387 7532
email royalhistsoc@ucl.ac.uk
website www.rhs.ac.uk

The Prize (value £1000) is announced in July each year for the best work on a subject within a field of British history. It must be its author's first solely written history book, an original and scholarly work of historical research and have been published in the UK in the preceding calendar year. Three non-returnable copies of an eligible book should be submitted before 31 December to the Executive Secretary.

WHSmith 'People's Choice' Awards

Details WHSmith PLC, Nations House,
103 Wigmore Street, London W1U 1WH
tel 020-7514 9623 *fax* 020-7514 9635
email elizabeth.walker@group-whsmith.co.uk
website www.whsmith.co.uk
Contact Elizabeth Walker, Book Awards Manager

The awards celebrate good books from all genres of literature. There are 9 Award categories in total, and 8 are voted for by the public: Autobiography/Biography, Travel Writing, Business, General Knowledge, Fiction, New Talent, Home & Leisure and Children's. The 9th category, the long-standing Literary Award, is not put out to public vote but decided by a panel which includes 3 members of the public. Prize: £5000 to each winning author.

WHSmith Thumping Good Read Award

Details Award Administrator, WHSmith,
Greenbridge Road, Swindon, Wilts. SN3 3LD
tel (01793) 616161 *fax* (01793) 562590

An annual award of £5000 is presented to the best popular fiction author of the year. The award is judged by a panel of WHS customers. Founded 1992.

Wildlife Photographer of the Year

Details Wildlife Photographer of the Year,
The Natural History Museum, Cromwell Road,
London SW7 5BD
tel 020-7942 5015 *fax* 020-7942 5084
email wildphoto@nhm.ac.uk
website www.nhm.ac.uk/wildphoto

An annual award given to the photographer whose individual image is judged to be the most striking and memorable. The overall adult winner receives a trophy and £2000. The Young Wildlife Photographer of the Year receives a trophy of an ibis and £500, plus a day out with a photographer. Open to all ages. Closing date: April 2004.

William Hill Sports Book of the Year Award

Details Graham Sharpe, William Hill Organisation,
Greenside House, 50 Station Road, London N22 4TP
tel 020-8918 3731

This award is given annually in November for a book with a sporting theme (record books and listings excluded). The title must be in the English language, and published for the first time in the UK during the relevant calendar year. Total value of prize is £15,000, including £12,500 in cash. An award for the best cover design has total value of £1000. Founded 1989.

The Sir William Lyons Award

Details General Secretary, 30 The Cravens,
Smallfield, Surrey RH6 9QS
tel (01342) 843294 *fax* (01342) 844093
email sharon@scott-fairweather.freeserve.co.uk
website www.newspress.co.uk/guild

This annual award (trophy, £1000 and 2 years' probationary membership of the Guild of Motoring Writers) was set up to encourage young people in automotive journalism, including broadcasting, and to foster interest in motoring and the motor industry through these media. Open to any person of British nationality resident in the UK aged 17–23, it consists of writing 2 essays and an interview with the Award Committee.

Write A Story for Children Competition

Entry forms The Academy of Children's Writers,
PO Box 95, Huntingdon, Cambs. PE28 5RL
tel (01487) 832752
email per_ardua@lycos.co.uk

Three prizes (1st £1000, 2nd £200, 3rd £100) are awarded annually for a short story for children, maximum 1000 words, by an unpublished writer of children's fiction. Send sae for details. Founded 1984.

Writers' Forum Short Story Competition

Details Writers' International Ltd, PO Box 3229,
Bournemouth BH1 1ZS

tel (01202) 589828 *fax* (01202) 587758
email editorial@writers.forum.com
website www.writers.forum.com

Writers' Forum (10 p.a.) is an anthology of short stories from the winners of its competitions. Prizes range from £150 to £250 in each issue with an annual trophy and a cheque for £1000 for the best story of the year. Entry fee: £10 to non-subscribers of *Writers' Forum*; £6 to subscribers.

Writers' Week Poetry Competition

Details Writers' Week,
24 The Square,
Listowel, Co. Kerry,
Republic of Ireland
tel (353) 6821074 *fax* (353) 6822893
email writersweek@eircom.net
website www.writersweek.ie

Annual awards for a single poem (prize: €650; entry fee: €6.50) and for a collection of 6–12 poems (prize: €650 plus financial support towards publication of a slim volume; entry fee: €20).

Yorkshire Post Book of the Year

Submissions Margaret Brown, Yorkshire Post Literary Awards, Yorkshire Post Newspapers Ltd, PO Box 168, Wellington Street, Leeds LS1 1RF
tel (01423) 772217 *fax* (01423) 772217

An annual prize of £1200 for the Best Book, either fiction or non-fiction. Submissions are accepted only from publishers, and authors should be British or resident in the UK. Next closing date: 31 December.

Young Writers' Programme

Details Young Writers' Programme,
Royal Court Young Writers' Programme,
Sloane Square, London SW1W 8AS
tel 020-7565 5034 *fax* 020-7565 5001

Anyone aged 13–25 or under can submit a play on any subject. A selection of plays is professionally presented by the Royal Court Theatre with the writers fully involved in rehearsal and production. Pre-Festival Development Workshops are run by professional theatre practitioners and designed to help everyone attending to write a play.

Writers' & Artists' Yearbook 2004

Short Story Competition

For published and aspiring writers alike – enter the *Writers' & Artists' Yearbook* short story competition and you could win:

- a cash prize of £500 or £1000 of A & C Black books

- lunch with one of the top literary editors in the publishing industry

- publication of your entry on the A & C Black and Bloomsbury Publishing websites

For terms and conditions and further details, visit
www.acblack.com/shortstorycompetition

Literature festivals

There are hundreds of arts festivals held in the UK each year – too many to mention in this *Yearbook* and many of which are not applicable specifically to writers. We give here a selection of literature festivals and general arts festivals which include literature events. Space constraints and the nature of an annual publication together determine that only brief details are given; contact festival organisers for a full programme of events. The British Council will supply a list of forthcoming literature festivals on receipt of a large sae.

The Academi Ty Newydd Festival
3rd Floor, Mount Stuart House,
Mount Stuart Square, Cardiff CF10 5FQ
tel (02920) 472266 *fax* (02920) 492930
email post@academi.org
website www.academi.org
Contact Peter Finch, Chief Executive
Takes place April 2005 (biennial)

Events are centred on the writing centre at Llanystumdwy in Gwynedd and feature a mix of Welsh and English events including Poetry Stomps and guest readers. The Academi, the Welsh National Literature Promotion Agency and Ty Newydd work together to create this festival.

Aldeburgh Poetry Festival
Aldeburgh Poetry Trust, Goldings,
Goldings Lane, Leiston, Suffolk IP16 4EB
tel (01379) 668345
email info@aldeburghpoetryfestival.org
website www.aldeburghpoetryfestival.org
Festival Director Naomi Jaffa
Takes place First weekend in Nov

An annual contemporary poetry festival: readings, workshops, a public masterclass, a lecture and a children's event. Includes a substantial line-up of international and national poets as well as fringe events and a writer-in-residence. Aldeburgh Festival Prize is awarded for the year's best first collection.

Aspects Festival
North Down Heritage Centre, The Castle,
Bangor, Co. Down BT20 4BT
tel (028) 91 271200 *fax* (028) 91 271370
Festival Director Kenneth Irvine
Contact Gail Prentice, Arts Officer
Takes place last week of Sept 2003

An annual celebration of contemporary Irish writing with novelists, poets, playwrights and non-fiction writers. Includes readings, discussions, workshops and a children's day.

Ballymena Arts Festival
Ballymena Borough Council, Ardeevin,
80 Galgorm Road, Ballymena,
Co. Antrim BT42 1AB

tel (01266) 660300 *fax* (01266) 660400
Takes place Oct

Bath Literature Festival
Bath Festivals Trust, 5-6 Broad Street,
Bath BA1 5LJ
tel (01225) 462231 *fax* (01225) 445551
email info@bathfestivals.org.uk
website www.bathlitfest.org.uk
Director tba
Takes place 28 Feb–7 March 2004

An annual 9-day festival with leading guest writers. Includes readings, debates, discussions and workshops, and events for children and young people. Programme published in December.

Belfast Festival at Queen's
Festival House, 25 College Gardens,
Belfast BT9 6BS
tel 028-9066 7687 *fax* 028-9066 3733
email festival@qub.ac.uk
website www.belfastfestival.com
Director Stella Hall
Takes place 24 Oct–9 Nov 2003

The largest annual arts event in Ireland. Includes literature events. Programme available mid September.

Birmingham Book Festival
Unit 116, The Custard Factory, Gibb Street,
Birmingham B9 4AA
tel 0121-246 2770 *fax* 0121-246 2771
email jonathan@bookcommunications.co.uk
website www.lit-net.org/bbf
Programmer Jonathan Davidson
Takes place 9–24 Oct 2003, 7–22 Oct 2004

An annual festival which presents a range of events with all types of writers of both fiction and non-fiction.

Book Now!
Education, Arts & Leisure Department,
Orleans House Gallery, Riverside,
Twickenham TW1 3DJ
tel 020-8831 6000 *fax* 020-8744 0507
website www.richmond.gov.uk

Takes place Throughout Nov

An annual literature festival covering a broad range of subjects. Leading British and overseas guest writers and poets hold discussions, talks, debates and workshops and give readings. There are also exhibitions, storytelling sessions and a schools programme.

Brighton Festival

12A Pavilion Buildings, Castle Square,
Brighton BN1 1EE
tel (01273) 700747 *fax* (01273) 707505
email info@brighton-festival.org.uk
website www.brighton-festival.org.uk
Takes place May

An annual general arts festival with a large literature programme. Leading guest writers cover a broad range of subjects in a diverse programme of events. Programme published end of February.

Cambridge Conference of Contemporary Poetry

c/o Dr Rod Mengham, Jesus College,
Cambridge CB5 8BL
tel (01223) 339493
email r.mengham@jesus.cam.ac.uk
Kevin Nolan, 2 Bells Close, West Road,
Saffron Walden, Essex CB11 3DU
email k.nolan@virgin.net
website www.cccp-online.org
Takes place April

An annual weekend of poetry readings, discussion and performance of international poetry in the modernist tradition.

Canterbury Festival

Festival Office, Christ Church Gate,
The Precincts, Canterbury, Kent CT1 2EE
tel (01227) 452853 *fax* (01227) 781830
email info@canterburyfestival.co.uk
website www.canterburyfestival.co.uk
Takes place 11–25 Oct 2003

An annual general arts festival with a literature programme. Programme published in July.

Chaucer Festival

Chaucer Heritage Trust,
Chaucer Centre, 22 St Peter's Street,
Canterbury, Kent CT1 2BQ
tel 020-7229 0635 *fax* (01227) 761416
Director Martin Starkie,
Manager and Events Organiser Zoran Tesic
tel (01227) 470379
Takes place Spring, Summer and Autumn

An annual festival which includes commemoration services, theatre productions, exhibitions, readings, recitals, Chaucer site visits, medieval fairs, costumed cavalcades, educational programmes for schools. Takes place in London, Canterbury and the County

of Kent in the Spring (Easter Chaucer Pilgrimage), Summer (June–July), and Autumn (Oct).

Cheltenham Festival of Literature

Town Hall, Imperial Square, Cheltenham,
Glos. GL50 1QA
tel (01242) 227979 (box office), 237377 (brochure), 263494 (festival office) *fax* (01242) 256457
email sarahsm@cheltenham.gov.uk
website www.cheltenhamfestivals.co.uk
Festival Director Sarah Smyth
Takes place 8–17 Oct 2003

This annual festival is the largest of its kind in Europe. Events include talks and lectures, poetry readings, novelists in conversation, exhibitions, discussions, workshops and a large bookshop. *Book It!* is a festival for children within the main festival with an extensive programme of events and a multimedia room. Brochures are available in August.

Chester Literature Festival

8 Abbey Square, Chester CH1 2HU
tel (01244) 319985 *fax* (01244) 341200
email freda@chesterfestivals.co.uk
Festival Administrator Freda Hadwen
Takes place 4–6 Oct 2003

An annual festival with events including international, national and local writers and poets: a literary lunch, festival dinner and evenings staged at the Gateway Theatre; also a literary walk in Chester and Cheshire, workshops for adults and children and a poetry competition for children.

Chichester Festivities

Canon Gate House, South Street, Chichester,
West Sussex PO19 1PU
tel (01243) 785718 *fax* (01243) 528356
email info@chifest.org.uk
website www.chifest.org.uk
Takes place June/July

City of London Festival

Bishopsgate Hall, 230 Bishopsgate,
London EC2M 4HW
tel 020-7377 0540 *fax* 020-7377 1972
email admin@colf.org
website www.colf.org
Takes place 21 June–7 July 2004 (tbc)

An annual multi-arts festival with a programme of literary events. Programme published in April.

City Voice

Central Library, Calverley Street,
Leeds LS1 3AB
tel 0113-247 8421
website www.leeds.gov.uk/wordarena
Contact Festival Organiser

Takes place May/June

An annual 2-week celebration of the voices of the city – provides a platform for Leeds writers alongside established names.

The Cúirt International Festival of Literature

Galway Arts Centre, 47 Dominick Street,
Galway, Republic of Ireland
tel (091) 565886 *fax* (091) 568642
email gac@indigo.ie
website www.galwayartscentre.ie
Director Tomás Hardiman, *Coordinator and Progammer* Maura Kennedy
Takes place April

An annual week-long festival to celebrate writing, bringing together national and international writers to promote literary discussion. Events include readings, performances, workshops, seminars, lectures, poetry slams and talks. The festival is renowned for its convivial atmosphere ('cúirt' means a 'bardic court or gathering').

Dublin Writers' Festival

c/o Dublin City Council, Arts Office,
10 Cornmarket, Dublin 8,
Republic of Ireland
tel (01) 8722816 *fax* (01) 6773887
email dublinwritersfestival@eircom.net
website www.dublinwritersfestival.com
Programme Director Pat Boran
Takes place June

An annual festival with readings by major Irish and international poets and writers to celebrate the best in contemporary literature.

Durham Literature Festival 2004

c/o Durham City Arts Ltd, Byland Lodge,
Hawthorn Terrace, Durham DH1 4TD
tel 0191-301 8830 *fax* 0191-301 8821
email alison@durhamcityarts.demon.co.uk
Festival Coordinator Alison Lister
Takes place Sept–Oct

Dylan Thomas – 50th Anniversary 2003

The Dylan Thomas Centre, Somerset Place,
Swansea SA1 1RR
tel (01792) 463980 *fax* (01792) 463993
email dylanthomas.lit@swansea.gov.uk
websites www.dylanthomasfestival.com
www.dylanthomas.org
Events Manager David Woolley
Takes place 27 Oct–9 Nov 2003

An annual festival celebrating the life and work of Swansea's most famous son: performances, lectures, debates, poetry, music and film. Also, regular events throughout the summer including guided tours.

Edinburgh International Book Festival

Scottish Book Centre, 137 Dundee Street,
Fountainbridge, Edinburgh EH11 1BG
tel 0131-228 5444 *fax* 0131-228 4333
email admin@edbookfest.co.uk
website www.edbookfest.co.uk
Director Catherine Lockerbie
Takes place 7–23 Aug 2004 (tbc)

Now established as Europe's largest book event for the public. In addition to a unique independent bookselling operation, over 600 writers contribute to the programme of events. Programme details available in June.

Everybody's Reading

Leicester City Council, 12th Floor,
Block A, New Walk Centre, Welford Place,
Leicester LE1 6ZG
email libraries@leicester.gov.uk
Contact Sarah Butler
Takes place June

Exeter Festival

Festival Office, Civic Centre, Exeter EX1 1JJ
tel (01392) 265200 *fax* (01392) 265265
website www.exeter.gov.uk
Festival Manager Lesley Waters
Takes place July

An annual general arts festival which includes a programme of literary activities. Programme of events available in May.

Federation of Worker Writers and Community Publishers Festival of Writing

Burslem School of Art, Queen Street,
Stoke-on-Trent ST6 3EJ
tel/fax (01782) 822327
email thefwwcp@tiscali.co.uk
website www.thefwwcp.org.uk
Takes place April

Female Eye National Festival of Women's Writing

Female Eye, Watersmead, Norwood Green Hill,
Halifax, West Yorkshire HX3 8QX
tel/fax (01274) 670181
Takes place June

Festival at the Edge Storytelling Festival

c/o Rose Cottage, Church Road, Welshpool,
Powys SY21 7LN
tel (01939) 236626
email info@festivalattheedge.org
website www.festivalattheedge.org
Contact Ali Quarrell
Takes place Third full weekend of July in Much Wenlock, Shrops.

The Guardian Hay Festival

Festival Office, The Drill Hall, 25 Lion Street,
Hay-on-Wye HR3 5AD
tel (01497) 821217, (01497) 821299 (box office)
fax (01497) 821066
email admin@hayfestival.co.uk
website www.hayfestival.co.uk
Takes place May/June

This annual festival aims to celebrate the best in writing and performance from around the world, to commission new work, and to promote and encourage young writers of excellence and potential. Over 200 events in 10 days with leading guest writers. Programme published April.

Guildford Book Festival

c/o Tourist Information Office, 14 Tunsgate,
Guildford GU1 3QT
tel (01483) 225388
email book-festival-director@surrey.ac.uk
websites www.guildford.org.uk
www.guildfordbookfestival.co.uk
Festival Director Glenis Pycraft
Takes place 19 Oct–2 Nov 2003

An annual festival with a varied programme of over 60 events held at different venues in Guildford, including readings, discussions, literary lunches and teas, performance poetry, workshops, competitions. High-profile authors and many children's events. Its aim is to involve, instruct and entertain all who care about literature and to encourage in children a love of reading. Founded 1990.

Harrogate International Festival

1 Victoria Avenue, Harrogate,
North Yorkshire HG1 1EQ
tel (01423) 562303 *fax* (01423) 521264
email info@harrogate-festival.org.uk
crime@harrogate-festival.org.uk
website www.harrogate-festival.org.uk
Takes place July/Aug

An annual international multi-arts festival. Programme available in May.
Harrogate Crime Writing Festival (July). A weekend of events featuring the best of British and American crime writers.

Hastings International Poetry Festival

c/o The Snoring Cat, 16 Marianne Park,
Dudley Road, Hastings, East Sussex TN35 5PU
tel/fax (01424) 428855
email josephine-poetry@btopenworld
website www.josephineaustin.co.uk
Organiser and Editor of First Time Josephine Austin
Takes place 1–2 Nov 2003

Started in 1968, this national festival is now held in the Sussex Hall, White Rock Theatre. Includes the prize-giving of the *Hastings National Poetry*

Competition. Poems are invited for consideration for the bi-annual *First Time* poetry magazine. Please include sae.

Ilkley Literature Festival

The Manor House, Ilkley LS29 9DT
tel (01943) 601210 *fax* (01943) 817079
email admin@ilkleyliteraturefestival.org.uk
website www.ilkleyliteraturefestival.org.uk
Festival Director Rachel Feldberg
Takes place Oct

The north of England's oldest and largest literature festival organises a full programme of writing and reading events.

International Playwriting Festival

Warehouse Theatre, Dingwall Road,
Croydon CR0 2NF
tel 020-8681 1257 *fax* 020-8688 6699
email info@warehousetheatre.co.uk
website www.warehousetheatre.co.uk
Takes place Middle week of Nov

The weekend festival features: a showcase of the best selected work from the IPF competition (see page 504), and selected plays from the festival's international partners – the leading Italian playwriting festival, the Premio Candoni Arta Terme, and Theatro Ena, Cyprus.

King's Lynn Festival

5 Thoresby College, Queen Street, King's Lynn,
Norfolk PE30 1HX
tel (01553) 767557 *fax* (01553) 767688
website www.kl-festival.freeserve.co.uk
Administrator Joanne Rutterford
Takes place 18–31 July 2004

An annual general arts festival with literature events featuring leading guest writers.

King's Lynn Festivals

19 Tuesday Market Place, King's Lynn,
Norfolk PE30 1JW
tel (01553) 691661 *fax* (01553) 691779
Chairman Tony Ellis
Takes place Sept/March

Poetry Festival (26–28 Sept 2003, 27–29 Sept 2004). An annual festival which brings 8 published poets to King's Lynn for the weekend for readings and discussions. The King's Lynn Poetry Prize (value £1000) is awarded at the festival.
Fiction Festival (8–10 March 2004). An annual festival which brings 8 published novelists to King's Lynn for the weekend for readings and discussions.

Ledbury Poetry Festival

Town Council Offices, Church Street,
Ledbury HR8 1DH
tel (0845) 458 1743

email prog@poetry-festival.com
website www.poetry-festival.com
Festival Director Charles Bennett
Takes place 2–11 July 2004

An annual festival featuring top poets from around the world, together with a poet-in-residence programme, competitions (send sae for entry form), workshops and exhibitions. Full programme available in May.

Lincolnshire Literature Festival

Education and Cultural Services Directorate, Lincolnshire County Council, County Offices, Lincoln LN1 1YL
tel (01522) 552831 *fax* (01522) 552811
email david.lambert@lincolnshire.gov.uk
County Arts Development Officer David Lambert
County Literature Development Officer Paul Sutherland, PO Box 3, District Council Offices, Kesteven Street, Sleaford, Lincs. NG34 7EF
tel (01529) 414155
email paul_sutherland@n-kesteven.gov.uk
Takes place Throughout the year

A monthly series of varied literary events. Occasional festivals, tours, publications in Lincolnshire; work with East Midlands Arts.

Lit Up!

The Plough Arts Centre, 9-11 Fore Street, Torrington, Devon EX38 8HQ
tel (01805) 622552 *fax* (01805) 622113
Contact Richard Wolfenden-Brown
Takes place Throughout the year

An occasional literature programme including workshops, readings, performances and exhibitions, as part of a larger programme of arts work, including community and educational workshops, projects, residencies and performances.

Litfest

26 Castle Park, Lancaster, Lancs. LA1 1YQ
tel (01524) 62166
email all@litfest.org
website www.litfest.org
Contact Andrew Darby
Takes place mid Oct

Annual festival featuring readings, performances and workshops by contemporary writers for adults; includes performance of several new commissioned works each year. The Litfest also acts as a year-round literature development agency in Lancashire.

Manchester Poetry Festival

3rd Floor, 24 Lever Street, Manchester M1 1DZ
tel 0161-236 5725 *fax* 0161-236 5719
email manchesterpoetry@aol.com
website www.manchesterpoetry.co.uk
Festival Director Richard Michael

Takes place 9–14 Oct 2003

An annual festival catering for all ages, including readings, slams, workshops and live events. See website for details. Recent Regional Lottery Arts Programme funding now enables the Festival to take events out of the city centre and into districts of Greater Manchester and the Northwest for a year-round programme of events over 2003–4.

National Eisteddfod of Wales

40 Parc Ty Glas, Llanisien, Cardiff CF14 5WU
tel 029-2076 3777 *fax* 029-2076-3737
email elfedateisteddfod.org.uk
website www.eisteddfod.org.uk
Director Elfed Roberts
Takes place 30 July–8 Aug 2004

An annual festival attracting 160,000 visitors and over 6000 competitors. It is the largest popular festival of competitive music making and poetry writing in Europe.

Norfolk and Norwich Festival

42-58 St George's Street, Norwich NR3 1AB
tel (01603) 614921 *fax* (01603) 632303
email info@n-joy.org.uk
website www.n-joy.org.uk
Artistic Director/Chief Executive Peter Bolton
Takes place May

North East Lincolnshire Annual Literature Festival

Arts Development, Regeneration & Community Learning, King Edward Street, Grimsby, North East Lincolnshire DN31 3LU
tel (01472) 323007 *fax* (01472) 323377
email liz.bennet@nelincs.gov.uk
Contact Arts Development Unit
Takes place Oct/Nov

Reflecting the heritage and culture of the area, this annual festival aims to make literature accessible to all ages and abilities through a varied and unusual programme. Write or telephone for details.

Northern Children's Book Festival

22 Highbury, Jesmond, Newcastle Upon Tyne NE2 3DY
tel 0191-2813289
email annkey@waitrose.com
website www.ncbf.org.uk
Chairperson Ann Key
Takes place Second and third week in Nov

An annual festival to bring authors, illustrators, poets and performers to children in schools, libraries and community centres across the North East of England. About 36 authors visit the North East over the 2-week period for 2–8 days, organised by the 12 local authorities. The climax of the festival is a huge public event in a different part of the

North East each year when over 4000 children and their families visit to take part in author seminars, drama workshops, and to enjoy a variety of book-related activities.

Off the Shelf Literature Festival

c/o Central Library, Surrey Street,
Sheffield S1 1XZ
tel 0114-273 4716 *fax* 0114-273 5009
email off-the-shelf@pop3.poptel.org.uk
website www.offtheshelf.org.uk
Contacts Maria de Souza, Su Walker
Takes place 18 Oct–1 Nov 2003

The festival comprises a wide range of events for adults and children, including author visits, writing workshops, storytelling, competitions, theatre performances and exhibitions. Programme available in September.

Poetry International

Literature Department, Royal Festival Hall,
South Bank Centre, London SE1 8XX
tel 020-7921 0906 *fax* 020-7928 2049
email literature&talks@rfh.org.uk
website www.rfh.org.uk
Takes place 23–30 Oct 2004 (biennial)

The biggest poetry festival in the British Isles, bringing together a wide range of poets from around the world. Includes readings, workshops, discussions and events for children. The Literature Section also runs a year-round programme of readings, talks and debates.

Royal Court Young Writers' Festival

The Royal Court Young Writers' Programme,
Sloane Square, London SW1W 8AS
tel 020-7565 5050
Contact The Administrator
Takes place Biennially

A national festival which anyone aged 13–25 can enter. Promising plays which arise from the workshops are then developed and performed at the Royal Court's Theatre Upstairs (see page 517).

Royal National Eisteddfod of Wales

40 Parc Ty Glas, Llanishen,
Cardiff CF14 5WU
tel 029-2076 3777
email info@eisteddfod.org.uk
website www.eisteddfod.org.uk
Marketing Officer Betsan Williams
Takes place 31 July–7 Aug 2004

Wales' largest cultural festival, based on 800 years of tradition. Activities include competitions in all aspects of the arts, fringe performances and majestic ceremonies. In addition to activities held in the main pavilion, it houses over 300 trade stands along with a literary pavilion, a music studio, a movement and dance theatre, a rock pavilion and a purpose-built theatre. The event is set in a different location each year, and is set to visit Newport in August 2004.

Rye Festival

PO Box 33, Rye, East Sussex TN31 7YB
tel (01797) 224982 *fax* (01797) 224226
email hilary.brooke@virgin.net
website www.ryefestival.co.uk
Literary Events Manager Mrs Hilary Brooke
Takes place First 2 weeks of Sept (15 days); Winter Series held last weekend Jan and first weekend Feb (4 days)

An annual festival of 15 literary events featuring novelists, biographers, and political and scientific writers, with book signings and discussions. Runs concurrently with the Rye festival of music and visual arts.

Salisbury Festival

75 New Street, Salisbury, Wilts. SP1 2PH
tel (01722) 332241 *fax* (01722) 410552
Director Trevor Davies
Takes place May/June

An annual general multi-arts festival with a literature programme of events. Programme published in April.

Stratford-upon-Avon Poetry Festival

Shakespeare Centre, Henley Street,
Stratford-upon-Avon CV37 6QW
tel (01789) 204016 *fax* (01789) 296083
email info@shakespeare.org.uk
website www.shakespeare.org.uk
Director Roger Pringle
Takes place Usually Sunday evenings throughout July and Aug

An annual festival which aims to present poetry of many different ages and to provide opportunities for readings by established contemporary poets. Sponsored by the Shakespeare Birthplace Trust. Founded 1954.

The Sunday Times Oxford Literary Festival

301 Woodstock Road, Oxford OX2 7NY
tel (01865) 514149 *fax* (01865) 514804
email oxford.literary.festival@ntlworld.com
Festival Directors Angela Prysor-Jones, Sally Dunsmore
Takes place 2 weeks prior to Easter

An annual festival for both adults and children. Presents topical debates, fiction and non-fiction discussion panels, and adult and children's authors who have recently published books. Topics range from contemporary fiction to discussions on politics, history, science, gardening, food, poetry, philosophy, art and crime fiction.

Swindon Festival of Literature

Lower Shaw Farm, Shaw, Swindon, Wilts. SN5 5PJ
tel/fax (01793) 771080
email swindonlitfest@lsfarm.globalnet.co.uk
website www.swindonfestivalofliterature.co.uk
Festival Director Matt Holland
Takes place Starts at dawn on 1 May for 10–14 days

An annual celebration of literature – prose, poetry,
drama and storytelling – by readings, discussions,
performances, talks, etc, indoors and out.

Warwick Festival

Warwick Arts Society, Pageant House, 2 Jury Street,
Warwick CV34 4EW
tel (01926) 410747 *fax* (01926) 409050
email admin@warwickarts.org.uk
website www.warwickarts.org.uk
Festival Director Richard Phillips
Takes place First half of July

A music festival which includes some literature and
poetry events: readings, performances and
workshops.

Ways With Words Literature Festival

Droridge Farm, Dartington, Totnes,
Devon TQ9 6JQ
tel (01803) 867373 *fax* (01803) 863688
email admin@wayswithwords.co.uk
website www.wayswithwords.co.uk
Contact Kay Dunbar
Takes place 10 days in middle of July each year

200 speakers give readings, talks, interviews,
discussions, seminars, workshops with leading guest
writers. Also organises Words by the Water: a
Cumbrian literature festival (March) and Sole Bay
Literature Festival, Southwold (Nov), as well as
writing courses and writing and painting holidays
in Italy.

Wells Festival of Literature

25 Chamberlain Street, Wells, Somerset BA5 2PQ
tel (01749) 670929
website www.somersite.co.uk/wellsfest.htm
Takes place Late Oct

An annual festival which features leading guest
writers and poets. It also includes writing
workshops as well as short story and poetry
competitions. The main venue is the historic
Bishop's Palace, Wells.

Winter's Edge Storytelling Festival

c/o Rose Cottage, Church Road, Welshpool,
Powys SY21 7LN
tel (01939) 236626
email info@festivalattheedge.org
website www.festivalattheedge.org
Contact Ali Quarrell
Takes place 1–8 Feb 2004 in Much Wenlock, Shrops.

World Book Day

Colman Getty PR, Middlesex House,
34-42 Cleveland Street, London W1T 4JE
tel 020-7631 2666 *fax* 020-7631 2699
email pr@colmangettypr.co.uk
website www.worldbookday.com
Contact Truda Spruyt, Account Director
Takes place Early March

An annual celebration of books and reading aimed
at promoting their value and creating the readers of
the future. Every schoolchild in full-time education
receives a £1 book token. Events take place all over
the UK in schools, bookshops, libraries and arts
centres.

Writers' Week

24 The Square, Listowel, Co. Kerry,
Republic of Ireland
tel (068) 21074 *fax* (068) 22893
email writersweek@eircom.net
website www.writersweek.ie
Administrator Maria O'Connor
Takes place 26–30 May 2004

Aims to promote the work of Irish writers in both
the English and Irish language, and to provide a
platform for new and established writers to discuss
their works. Events include readings, seminars,
lectures and book launches.

Young Readers Birmingham

Children's Office, Central Library,
Chamberlain Square, Birmingham B3 3HQ
tel 0121-303 3368 *fax* 0121-464 1004
email patsy.heap@birmingham.gov.uk
website www.birmingham.gov.uk/youngreaders
Contact Patsy Heap
Takes place 17–31 May

An annual festival targeted at young people aged
0–19 and adults who care for or work with them. It
aims to motivate them to enjoy reading and
through this to encourage literacy; to provide
imaginative access to books, writers and storytellers;
to encourage families to share reading for pleasure;
to provide a national focus for the celebration of
books and reading for children and young people
and help raise the media profile of children's books
and writing. Approximately 150 events.

Writers and artists online

E-publishing

E-publishers offer a variety of services to authors and have no set standards of quality or provision. Jane Dorner looks at the electronic minefield facing authors.

All major UK publishers have websites on which they promote their books. Some are publishing electronic versions downloadable directly from the web. Some, like Random House, are sharing the revenue from e-titles 50–50 with their authors. This is still basically traditional publishing, and all the brand name expectations apply.

There's another, new, set of e-publishers which do not have an established track record – there has been no time for the investment in a brand (high standards, quality provision, peer review, integrity). Some are genuine publishers operating in the new environment and some come perilously close to vanity publishers eager to make money out of the unwary. Others offer useful services to self-publishers. And some call themselves publishers, but are effectively book showrooms. The boundaries can sometimes be so vague that it is difficult to be dogmatic about what value they provide.

For example, one e-publisher offers a core free service, but that is only if you throw a completely finished, edited file into a standard template; anything individual or quality-vetted costs £200 and upwards. Another charges £40 to act as an e-agent, showcasing a synopsis and first chapter and targeting agents and publishers with an email alerter. A third requires £99 to turn your book into an electronic format, plus minimal marketing, and charges a flat rate of nearly £5 a book of which £2 goes to the author. Some take anything they are offered (within the bounds of censorship) and others have strict filtering systems. Not many provide editing, design or quality control.

Until new reputations form, writers will have to look closely at the new e-publisher's websites, read carefully through submission statements, look for an online contract or terms and conditions and judge for themselves. Enter into an email dialogue and get as much information as you can before you submit anything.

The most obvious appeal is to writers who have unpublished works, out-of-print works whose rights have reverted to them, or previously published materials that could have a renewed life in a new format.

E-formats

The choice of formats is diverse, including:
- book-a-likes – book-sized electronic devices with screens of varying sizes designed for reading continuous texts – the texts displayed on them are e-books;
- personal organisers like the Palm Pilot, Sony Clié and others, also able to carry e-books;

- any platform using Adobe Portable Document Format (PDF), which is a universal standard for preserving the original appearance (fonts, formatting, colours and graphics) of any source document, regardless of the application and platform used to create it;
- notebook PCs using Microsoft Reader format – electronic reading software designed for easy screen reading;
- coded web pages (in HTML or XML, the coding used by software browsers);
- plain vanilla text (ASCII);
- tablet PCs – textbooks and notebooks rolled into one;
- new generation mobile phones.

All content can be downloaded into the reading devices from a website and can be paid for at that time. These formats are relatively cheap for a publisher to produce – but only assuming they do nothing to add to the editorial value. None of the electronic formats are secure from plagiarists, though some make a better attempt at security than others. At present, PDF files are the most secure (though hackable), with options ranging from preventing text selection (so users cannot cut and paste), disabling reading on screen (so only one print copy can be made), or, conversely, disabling printing, to password-protection. All these possibilities can form part of your email discussion.

The question here is whether yours is the sort of book that people will want to read from screens – small or large.

Print on Demand

E-publishers are also offering Print on Demand (POD) services for good quality paper copies in runs of 1 to 250. This has a double appeal to authors: for self-publishing and for bringing an out-of-print book back into circulation.

The self-publishing route is attractive. There's a set-up cost and a per title cost, but they're generally lower than the self-publishing options that have been available up to now. This option may well be of interest to authors who don't mind doing their own promotion. POD offers a potentially viable digital production model to the publishing industry as a whole. If the technology settles and origination costs come down a little lower than they are now, we could see certain types of book being ordered on the internet for collection an hour later at the local bookshop where it is bound and printed. Authors in some genres may be able to bypass publishers.

Out-of-print publishing is more complex. It is unlikely that the author will have a digital copy of a former work. Corrections, design and late changes to the latest version of either the author's or the editor's file is not the final version. This means a published copy must be scanned in and converted. To do this with acceptable accuracy requires a sophisticated scanner and two copies of the book with cut spines, merged and assembled in book order. There are two problems. With older books, the author may only have one precious copy and may not be willing to cut it up. With newer books, the chances are the rights have reverted, but the typographical right still belongs to the publisher for 25 years after publication. It's arguable that scanning violates that right.

Marketing

The listing below offers just some of the new e-publishers which are offering services to authors who would like to sell or resell their works in one of the formats described. Some market in the same way as traditional publishers. Many new e-publishers double as online booksellers, so they are not publishers in the sense we have been used to – although they also promote their best-selling authors more aggressively than the ones no one has heard of. The difference is that they can offer showcase capacity to any author, well known or not. Most guarantee visitors against pornography and real rubbish, but it's fairly rudimentary quality control. Showcasing is generally just that – a space on the bookshelf. And in this environment bookshelving is infinitely expandable. Most are sited in the US, but that doesn't matter since this is global exposure anyway.

Websites

Note, this is a fast-moving area and more online publishers will spring up and some of these will disappear. In all cases, authors should check all details of the contracts.

Writers' & Artists' Yearbook cannot be held responsible for any content on any of these sites. It came to our attention that in a previous edition one site led to a pornography page. This was because the original owner of the domain had not yet paid for a renewal and another party had instantly acquired it. They posted an offensive page and they effectively blackmailed the e-publisher to pay a large sum to get it back. Be aware that this can happen.

Artemis Press
www.artemispress.com/
Women's fiction, 40% royalty; contract and submission details online; exclusive rights requested.

Atlantic Bridge
www.atlanticbridge.net/
Seeks science fiction, horror, romance and mystery writers; non-exclusive contract and submission details online; 30–45% royalty.

Author's Studio
www.theauthorsstudio.org/
Community of small presses owned and operated by commercial authors.

Back-in-Print (UK)
www.backinprint.co.uk/
Out-of-print titles brought back into print in small print runs; sensible rights advice.

The Book & The Computer
www.honco.net/
International book culture. Pays contributors for articles.

Book4Publishing
www.book4publishing.com/
Shropshire-based e-agent which showcases synopsis and first chapter and then auto-targets publishers and agents; £49.95 fee.

BookLocker
www.booklocker.com/
E-book publisher offering 35–70% royalties to authors only requesting non-exclusive rights. Authors are free to list and sell their books elsewhere.

Book-on-Disk
www.book-on-disc.com/
Creates e-books in downloadable or disk format; pays royalties and appears to have been vetted by the American Guild of Writers; authors retain copyright. Not a vanity press.

Books on Line
www.books-on-line.com/
Public domain titles as well as opportunities to offer your own work.

Boson Books
www.cmonline.com/boson/

Electronic book imprint of C&M Online Media Inc.; eclectic list.

Centre House Press
www.centrehousepress.co.uk/

Publishes excerpts of literary works of all types, where the respective authors intend later full production in book form.

Crowsnest Books
www.computercrowsnest.com/

Science fiction, fantasy, horror, adventure, war, crime and thriller novels; some non-fiction.

Diskus Publishing
www.diskuspublishing.com/

Indiana-based romantic fiction niche publisher. Books for several e-reader formats can be downloaded for about £6.30 a book. Said to publish about 5% of submissions.

Domhan Books
www.domhanbooks.com/

Multicategory genre listing for publications in a variety of formats.

Eastgate
www.eastgate.com/

New hypertext technologies; publication of serious hypertext, fiction and non-fiction: serious, interactive writing. Good reputation.

eBook Palace
www.ebookpalace.com/

Visitor-submitted directory of e-books; authors can list their own.

eBookAd
www.ebookad.com/

A clearing house for all kinds of e-book information; appears to be pitched at publishers.

eBooks.com
www.ebooks.com/

Internet Digital Bookstore. Invites authors to let publisher or agent know about it; authors should check rights deals with their publishers.

EBooks on the Net
www.ebooksonthe.net/

Non-mainstream genres. Closes periodically to new submissions.

eBookWeb
http://12.108.175.91/ebookweb.org/

Central source for news and information on all aspects of electronic publishing.

Electronic Literature Organization
www.eliterature.org/

Promotes new media writing.

FictionWise
www.fictionwise.com/

Independent eBook publisher and distributor. Work must be previously published fiction works from established authors. Does not accept unsolicited material or work from new writers.

Fiction Works
www.fictionworks.com/

E-books and audio book opportunities; submissions in certain genres only.

1stBooks Library
www.1stbooks.com/

E-book distributor; offers books in PDF format; a 40% deal to established authors; motley collection.

Great Unpublished
www.greatunpublished.com/

Integrated community of writers, readers and professional editors, self-publishing venue and bookstore. Also provides a POD service. Operates a 2-tiered system: basic kit and special imprint program.

iUniverse
www.iuniverse.com/

A service for redeploying out-of-print books; check the author contract carefully.

KnowBetterCom
www.knowbetter.com/

Resource of information on the e-publishing scene, including the latest information on technology, industry news, tips, advice and reviews. Useful overview and discussion forums.

MediaVast
www.mediavast.com/

Digital everything marketplace and portal; opportunities for authors to sell directly.

Microsoft Reader
www.microsoft.com/reader/authors

The page about the Reader (e-books designed to be read on pocket PCs) aimed at authors; keep your eye on this one.

My Publish
www.mypublish.com/

Sales resource for digital content.

Neighborhood Press
www.neighborhoodpress.com/

All types of fiction, from political mysteries to western historical romances.

netLibrary
www.netlibrary.com/

Free and purchasable titles using the Knowledge Station software; expanding into hand-held computers; check the licensing agreements before signing up titles.

Netspace Publishing
www.netspace-publishing.co.uk/

Publishes electronic versions of texts not placed anywhere else. All books sold for £2.99; author gets £1.

New Concepts Publishing
www.newconceptspublishing.com/

Specialises in romance writers seeking publication; inexpensive for buyers; not obvious what the advantages to sellers are.

No Spine
www.nospine.com/

A UK self-publishing facilitator that takes 20% of whatever an author charges to cover e-commerce and web overheads. Quotes *Writers & Artists' Yearbook* profusely. Track record unknown.

Online Originals
www.onlineoriginals.com/

One of the higher-profile venues for new writers wanting to get published; UK based.

Open eBook initiative
www.openebook.org/

Format specifications, sponsored by the National Institute of Standards and Technology.

Overdrive Systems
www.overdrive.com/news/index.htm

How to publish with Microsoft Reader and other *soi-disant* e-publishing solutions.

Palm Digital Media
www.peanutpress.com/

E-books for hand-held computers; has published Palm versions of books by well-known authors.

Paperbackwriters
www.paperbackwriters.co.uk/

Showcase focusing exclusively on aspiring novelists in any genre looking for a publisher.

PublishingOnline
www.publishingonline.com/

An electronic publisher; no clear specialism; has a sample contract online.

Replica Books
www.replicabooks.com/

Would you like to see an out-of-print book back on the shelf? See what their terms are.

Rosetta Books
www.rosettabooks.com/

Sells and distributes books in various e-formats (Microsoft Reader and Adobe Acrobat).

Treeless Press
www.treelesspress.com/

Non-exclusive publishing deal with Rocket eBooks.

UK Children's Books
www.ukchildrensbooks.co.uk/

Listings of authors, illustrators and publishers.

Unlimited Publishing
www.unlimitedpublishing.com/

A POD system for new and out-of-print titles; will cost authors a minimum of $800 as long as they use Word or similar.

Virtual Bookworm
www.virtualbookworm.com/

POD and e-book supplier.

Virtual Volumes
www.virtualvolumes.com/

UK-based publisher offering a serious service for the 'manuscript in a drawer'.

Write Online
www.write-on-line.co.uk/

E-texts and traditional print works for the academic market. Aim to secure hard-copy contracts.

Writers Co-operative
www.books-4u-online.com/ www.rabbitbooks.com/

Mixed collection of UK self-publishing writers' work and its authors publishing venue.

Writers World
www.writersworld.co.uk/

A self-publishing resource for writers to publish their books by POD or e-books in both the USA and the UK. Huge resource database. Free newsletter and chatroom.

WritersServices.com
www.writersservices.com/

Offers editorial services and advice from well-known writers; pitched largely at unpublished authors.

Xlibris

www.xlibris.com/

Self-publishing centre; says it exists solely to serve and empower authors – at a price.

Zipped Books

www.zippedbooks.co.uk/

POD, quasi-vanity press. Author pays £20 for a single copy of their own book. 25% royalty on any copies sold.

Zoetrope Stories

www.all-story.com

Authors submit and critique each others' stories; seemingly no remuneration.

Setting up a website

Computer users who have email almost certainly have web space available to them. Jane Dorner explains the points for writers and artists to consider when setting up a personal website and how to best make it work for them.

This article assumes that readers are familiar with websites and have used the internet for research. To set up your own website the main investment you need to make is in time, perhaps more than you initially think. The process may have its frustrating moments, but it is ultimately creative.

Personal websites

A website can be a useful self-publicity medium for writers. It can be especially useful if you self-publish, but equally worthwhile for showing the world a portfolio of your artistic achievements and accomplishments. Many writers and artists are polymaths and the web shows up such diversity to advantage.

A personal website can be set up to demonstrate your writing or illustration style(s) and areas of interest with examples of work so that commissioning editors can see if they are choosing the right writer or artist for the job. You can include an outline of your skills and achievements, and list your publications – or you could even offer a personal syndication service for stories, articles, photographs or illustrations (if first or resale rights are yours).

You need to let people know that your website exists – there is no point having a wonderful site if no one visits it – for which old-fashioned marketing techniques are necessary. Posting your site on the web and registering hopefully with a few (or even a hundred) search engines is no substitute for careful targeting, although it is helpful once initial contact has been made. Refer potential clients to your website, and make sure it attracts them sufficiently to explore it.

Skills required

In order to create the website yourself, you will need to have:

- a capacity for logical thinking;
- secure language expertise;
- some technical understanding;
- good visual sense;

- patience; and
- familiarity with applicable law.

If you don't have (or can't acquire) these skills then it is worth thinking about asking someone else to build the site for you. Expect to pay for at least one day of a professional designer's time (between £250 and £450) to create a modest suite of individually tailored pages with some attention to what you want and need. Bear in mind that the less you pay, the more likely it is that your material is simply being poured into a standard template, as is the case with sites that offer five pages for £50.

Planning a website

Whether you get involved with the technological side or not, you will still have to plan and write the copy yourself. Writing for the web is a new art form that uses writerly skills: it is genuinely creative; requires writers, not programmers; and needs editors with an understanding of traditional editorial values.

Writing the text for a website is like any other writing project. The more effort that goes into the planning stage, the better the result. You need to identify who you are targeting and be clear about the purpose of the website. For instance, is it your calling card; a PR brochure; a sales outlet; an information resource; a literary club or part of a network; a designer's showcase; or a medium of self-expression? The website needs to be planned and created accordingly. For example, if you just want a simple calling card, then a single screen – called a splash page – might suffice. It would have your name, perhaps a photograph of you, a few lines about your specialist skills and interests, possibly some work you have had published, and your contact details. You can then be found by anyone who uses the internet; your personal front cover is on the world bookshelf.

Writing for screen reading

If you write for radio, you will have an advantage over other writers. Writing for the web is a bit like writing for broadcasting: the style has to compensate for the loss of the visual impact of words. It's a common mistake to cut and paste from documents created for print because the text will not read as well on a website.

The average adult spends eight hours a week reading as opposed to 27 hours watching television. And that's reading from paper – reading from a screen has so far proved less efficient than paper.

When writing the introductory text for a website, aim for the reluctant reader with a less than three-minute attention span and use easy words and short sentences. As readers delve deeper into a site, their acceptance of more discursive reading matter increases. Once they are committed to the subject material, you can write in your normal style and assume they will print out the text and read from paper. Take writing for radio or television as the paradigm and then make it even simpler. Here are a few pointers:

- **Use the tadpole or pyramid structure.** Hit your reader with the main points at the top of the page (people are reluctant to scroll). Use interior pages to unfold details.
- **Be concise.** The overall length of a radio or television piece is about a third of a print article; a web page should be even shorter. Cut every word that doesn't

contribute. A good web page length is under 200 words – it is better to divide anything longer than that into sub-topics.

- **Write short paragraphs.** Paragraph breaks refresh the eye: between two and five sentences is enough.
- **Write simple sentences.** Ideas are easier to digest in a simple subject-verb-object progression. Make subclauses into separate sentences. Use one idea per sentence. Make them under the 17-word print average.
- **Use the present or present perfect tense.** The web is here and now. Keep passives away.
- **Be consistent.** Use the same font, type size, alignment and background colour throughout your site. Or use different colour bands to denote different 'areas' (novels, poetry, teaching and so on). Remember that capital letters onscreen look like SHOUTING.
- **Consider navigation.** If a visitor makes Choice A here, what are the ramifications for Choice B there? Web writing is not static, but writing

Useful websites

Amazon Bookshop Associates Scheme
www.amazon.co.uk/associates/
For linking to sales of your own (or recommended) books.

Alert Box
www.useit.com/alertbox/
Web usability and readability analysis. Opinionated but pertinent.

The CGI Resource Index
www.cgi-resources.com/
Scripts that you can buy (some are free), e.g. automatic forms and page counters.

1st Site Free
www.1stsitefree.com/
Create a website in 7 easy steps. A good starting point; links to useful tools.

FTP Explorer
www.ftpx.com/
File transfer software for PCs.

The HTML Writers Guild
www.hwg.org/
Free membership and access to resources.

Netfinder
www.ozemail.com.au/~pli/netfinder/
File transfer software for Macs.

dynamically is something that most writers have not learned. It is, perhaps, something we will all have to discover as we progress into the web publishing age.

- **Links.** Don't link every prompt phrase that leads somewhere else. If you want readers to stay with you to absorb your point, put the link outside the main text area. Don't link just because you can.
- **Define the main areas of your site.** Consider synonyms for your top level labels (the four to six main areas of your site). How often have you got lost in a website simply because the way in which your mind works isn't the same as the mindset of the person who created it? Try to second guess what visitors to your site will want to see when they come to each page then find a single word that most unambiguously describes it.

Designing for screens

The first thing to remember about designing for screens is that you cannot control how the screen page will look as there are so many variables, such as screen resolution and type of web browser. You should therefore test your design on several platforms. Design depends on purpose, but here are a few good practice points:

● **Colour.** Have a white or pale cream background and black or very dark type (studies show that sharp contrasts aid readability). Use 'web-safe' colours (see box). There are 216 of them based on RGB, which simply stands for Red, Green, Blue – nature's three primary colours. Monitors and television sets transmit RGB – after all colour is light – so the only colours available are the ones that standard monitors can transmit.

● **Fonts.** How typefaces appear onscreen depends on which ones are on that particular system, not what you specify on yours. The ones you can rely on to look good on screens – and are universally available – are known as 'web-safe' fonts (see box).

● **Line length.** Put the text in invisible tables so that the line length is limited to about 10 words in standard browsers – this is an optimum reading line length. If you do not set a limit, the chances are that at high screen resolutions readers might get a line length of 25 words on the default reading typeface. This leads to what is known as 'regression pauses' while the reader struggles to make sense of the text.

● **Page size.** A reasonable rule of thumb is to make each page a maximum of 35k. People don't like watching a blank screen and research suggests that 10 seconds is as long as most people will wait for the screen to be filled. Standard dialup connections download at around 4–5k a second, so that means the first 20k or so need to be interesting enough to grab the viewer's attention. A short text page with three or four thumbnail-sized graphics will generally load fast.

● **Graphics.** Every graphic must speak: make sure its iconography is clear and unambiguous. Remember that when you insert a picture it is good form to give an explanatory note in the ALT (Alternative) command. This pops up as a little yellow box hovering over the image area and presents an opportunity to preview in words what the picture illustrates.

● **Artist's portfolio.** A gallery of small thumbnail illustrations is useful for showcasing an artist's range of work, with a click-link to larger pictures. Take care not to offer high-quality graphics that could be plagiarised: most internet graphics are in JPEG format, which is 72 dpi and not suitable for print reproduction. It's advisable to watermark all artwork.

- **Animation.** Bullet points or graphic elements help pick out key words but animations should be avoided. Studies show that the message is lost when television images fail to reinforce spoken words. The same is true of the web.
- **Frames.** Using frames can be an elegant solution to navigation problems, but for the user it's not ideal. Because the page name on the URL never varies, the visitor never knows where they are. They cannot bookmark a particular page, or find it again on a second visit and that can be very frustrating.

Going online

Once you have the planning, writing and graphics of your website organised, you need a little basic technical understanding to get it online. Your service provider will have a starter kit of instructions – although whether they make sense is another matter. You may well have to turn to other sources for instruction.

Websites for design

Art and the Zen of Web Sites
www.tlc-systems.com/webtips.shtml
Why the web is not a place to show off artistic skills.

Creating Graphics for the Web
www.widearea.co.uk/designer/
Information on GIFs, JPEGs, anti-aliasing and other design matters.

Killer Sites
www.killersites.com/
Website of *Creating Killer Web Sites* by David Siegal. Both book and site are full of information for designers.

VisiBone – Web-safe colours, style sheets and other resources
www.visibone.com/

Web-safe fonts
www.microsoft.com/truetype/fontpack/

The internet is chock-a-block with instructional material. Try 1st Site Free (see page 532), which outlines and expands on seven easy steps – plan, design, code, upload, test, promote and maintain.

An alternative is to use software that 'talks you through' setting up a small site with what are called 'wizards'. Wizards come in software programs such as FrontPage (part of Microsoft Office Premium) and its free look-a-like Site Aid. Both resemble word processors and keep the coding hidden from view. Hard core web designers will sneer at these programs, because programmers like to control the way the code works themselves. What they do not realise is that writers want to concentrate on the words, not the coding, and as long as it functions, the refinements of the underlying structure are of less importance. For artists who are more concerned with design, the best package is Dreamweaver (which is expensive and not easy to learn).

Once the pages are ready, the next step is to transmit them to the service provider's machines. The mechanics of this are frequently opaque even when you are offered a handy button that says 'Publish'. The chances are that your service provider will not have the extensions that make the 'Publish' button work and you will have to acquire a (free) File Transfer Protocol (ftp) program. If you are technophobe, this may seem frightening at first. However, it is really very simple and once you have successfully transferred (or uploaded) the pages from your computer to the web space on the remote server, you will wonder what the problem was. For this transfer process you will need to know the host name, your user ID and your password, information available from your provider.

HTML

If you want to learn HTML (HyperText Markup Language) – the code that tags elements such as text, links and graphics so that browser software will know how to display a document – then you need only a plain text program, like Notepad, and an HTML primer (there are plenty online as well as in printed form). Find some website pages which you like and look at their source code to see how they have been constructed (click the subsidiary button of the mouse, usually the right button, and select View Source). If the originators have used JavaScript or Cascading Style Sheets, this may well be more code than you want to know about so look at simple pages first.

Going a step further

You may wish to have a web address or URL that is short or memorable so that it is easier for people to find your website. You can choose this domain name yourself, and is now relatively cheap (see boxes on pages 532–3).

It is probably best to leave e-commerce (having a secure site that can handle credit card sales) till later. In the meantime, however, a simple way to boost your income is to become an Amazon Associate. If your book titles are linked to Amazon, you'll make 15% on a direct sale made from your site.

Websites for writers

The Internet: A Writer's Guide by Jane Dorner (www.internetwriter.co.uk) is published by A & C Black and has the full listing of over 1000 resources for writers from which the sites below have been selected.

New to the internet

BBC Web Wise
www.bbc.co.uk/education/webwise/
How to get started on the internet.

FAQ
www.faqs.org/
Frequently Asked Questions on just about anything to do with the internet.

Google
www.google.co.uk/
The current favourite amongst search engines.

How Stuff Works
www.howstuffworks.com/
Fairly technical explanations about how the internet works, and much more.

New to the Web
http://home.netscape.com/netcenter/newnet
A basic tutorial with a good glossary.

Fact finding online

Ananova (UK Press Association)
www.ananova.com/
Latest stories from the UK's top news and information websites; useful free daily round-up of news, sport and information by email.

Ask Oxford
www.askoxford.com/
Various bits from the language dictionaries; changing word news and word-based interest.

Bartlett's Familiar Quotations
www.bartleby.com/

Bibliomania
www.bibliomania.com/
Excellent full text with a good word or phrase retrieval; includes the wonderful Brewer's *Dictionary of Phrase & Fable* (which no author can do without).

Bookworks
www.bookworks.org.uk/
Text-related projects including internet and new media projects.

British Library
http://portico.bl.uk/
Free search for material held in the major Reference and Document Supply collections of the British Library.

CIA World Factbook
www.cia.gov/cia/publications/factbook/
Statistical data about countries and other useful data.

Crossref
www.crossref.org/
A collaborative reference linking service for researchers.

Encyclopaedia Britannica
www.britannica.com/
Full text and searching, together with a huge resource of information, grammar and reference links. Some free; premium subscription.

Free Pint
www.freepint.com/
Free bi-monthly email newsletter with tips and articles on finding reliable sites and searching more effectively. Written by information professionals.

Internet Public Library
www.ipl.org
Reference section containing subject overviews, biography, etc.

Response Source
http://sourcewire.com/
UK journalists can request business information in a single step from over 300 organisations.

Roget's Thesaurus
www.bartleby.com/62/
Third edition (1995).

WATCH – Writers, Artists and their Copyright Holders

Database of information on whom to contact for permission to publish in copyright text and images. A joint project of the University of Texas and the University of Reading.

WISDOM: Knowledge & Literature Search
http://thinkers.net/

Links to writing and literature sites under the headings Creativity, Literature, Authors, Thoughts, Publishing, Words, Languages.

Interactivity

Alt-X
www.altx.com/

Online publishing network – 'where the digerati meet the literati'.

Digital Arts
www.da2.org.uk

Eastgate Systems
www.eastgate.com

Many interesting works of serious hypertext offered for sale.

Electronic Poetry Center
http://wings.buffalo.edu/epc/

E-Zone
http://ezone.org

Literary site that includes an e-zine 'entryzone'; some permanent hypertext works.

Hyperizons: the Search for Hypertext Fiction
www.duke.edu/~mshumate/hyperfic.html

Plexus
www.plexus.org/

Interface to a flux of ideas contained in the writings and visual works of several artists and writers.

Writing communities

Author Zone
www.authorzone.com

Interactive author and writer community with free self-promotion opportunities and webspace.

AXIS
www.axisartists.org

Some writing installations.

Bloomsbury Magazine
www.bloomsburymagazine.com/writersarea/

Writers' area; advice and resources for authors.

Digital Literature Institute
www.digitallit.org/

E-Writers
http://e-writers.net

Community, competitions and advice – weekly online publishing newsletter.

Fiction Writer's Connection
www.fictionwriters.com

Provides help with novel writing and information on finding agents and editors and getting published; has a mailing list of 3000+.

For writers
www.forwriters.com

Self-help; links and professional markets.

HackWriters
www.hackwriters.com/

UK-based free internet magazine devoted to good writing on any subject. No fees; forum of exchange.

Hyperizons
www.duke.edu/~mshumate/hyperfic.html

Literary texts and criticism.

Literati Club
www.emeraldinsight.com/literaticlub

Site for journal authors.

Littoral
www.littoral.org.uk

Arts trust which aims to develop new arts projects.

Live Literature Network
www.liveliterature.net/

Database of writers offering live events in the UK.

National Association for Literature Development
www.literaturedevelopment.com/development/

Online Writing Community
http://trace.ntu.ac.uk

Centre of experimental writing in the UK; also has courses.

Pier Playwrights
www.pierplaywrights.co.uk/

Organisation for playwrights run by playwrights.

Reactive Writing
www.reactivewriting.co.uk/
Exploring writing on the Web.

StudioNotes
www.studionotes.com/
Service in entertainment industry to provide aspiring writers the opportunity to develop and market their material; costly.

Word Circuits
www.wordcircuits.com/
A community as well as a gallery of new fiction and poetry.

The Word Hoard
www.wordhoard.co.uk/
A cooperative of writers, visual artists, performers and musicians sited in Huddersfield. Has a text factory.

Writernet
www.writernet.org.uk/
British community, mostly for writers working in theatre, TV, radio, film, live art and performance poetry; a professional network.

Writers Net
www.writers.net
US-based forum for writers, editors, agents and publishers. Participants exchange ideas about the writing life and the business of writing.

Writelink
www.writelink.co.uk/
Resource site linking to paying markets, competitions, reference sites, software and so on.

Writers on the Net
www.writers.com
Busy community offering online (paid for) classes.

New media writing prizes

e-book Awards
www.digitalliteratureinstitute.org/
For e-books and digital stories self- or independently published.

Electronic Literature Awards
www.eliterature.org/
One for fiction and one for poetry.

Eppie Awards for E-books
www.epicauthors.org/
21 fiction and non-fiction categories.

Gutenberg-e
www.theaha.org/prizes/gutenberg/
A prize competition for the best history dissertations in fields where the traditional monograph has now become endangered.

Java Museum Online Awards
www.javamuseum.org/
For innovative art and new media installations.

Media Arts Plaza Awards
http://plaza.bunka.go.jp/english/

Nesta Awards for Art and Science
www.nesta.org.uk/
Up to £40,000 to spend a year developing a new creative idea; very competitive.

The Oscar Moore Screenwriting Prize
www.screendaily.com/html_files/APPFORM_02.doc
An annual prize of £10,000 is awarded to the best first draft screenplay in a specified genre, which changes each year.

The trAce/Alt-X International Hypertext Competition
http://trace.ntu.ac.uk/comp.cfm

Miscellany

Dying Words
www.corsinet.com/braincandy/dying.html
For the historical novelist.

Eponym
www.eponym.org/
Aimed at new parents and handy for finding a name for a character; names from just about everywhere in the world at different times in history.

Famous Birthdays
www.famousbirthdays.com/
Month-by-month and day-by-day listing of birth dates, historical and in the media.

Famous Firsts
www.corsinet.com/trivia/1-triv.html
People-who-did-something-first arranged in ascending date order.

iTools
www.itools.com/research-it
Little battery of dictionaries and acronym converters.

Literary Calendar: An Almanac of Literary Information
http://english.yasuda-u.ac.jp/lc
Significant literary events.

Lives
http://amillionlives.com/
Links to biographies, autobiographies, memoirs, diaries, letters, narratives and oral histories.

Perpetual Virtual Calendars
www.vpcalendar.net/
A historical or science fiction novelist's dream: verify any date or day of the week in the 20th and 21st centuries.

Rhyming dictionary
www.rhymezone.com

Time Zone Converter
www.timezoneconverter.com/
What time it is or will be anywhere in the world.

Who is or Was
www.biography.com/
Good for checking people's dates; incorporates the *Cambridge Dictionary of American Biography*.

World Wide Words
www.quinion.com/words/
Verbal cornucopia for anyone interested in words; circulates a newsletter.

Texts online

Bible Gateway
http://bible.gospelcom.net/bible

Electronic Text Center
http://etext.lib.virginia.edu/english.html
Collection of online English language texts; links to other texts online by subject or by author.

The English Server
http://eserver.org/
Large collection of interesting resources.

Etext Archives
www.etext.org
Archives of religious, political, legal and fanzine text.

Oxford Text Archive
www.ota.ahds.ac.uk/
Distributes more than 2500 resources in over 25 different languages for study purposes only.

Project Gutenberg
www.gutenberg.net/
The official sites (many mirrors all over the world); vast library of e-texts, mostly public domain; all in plain text format.

Shakespeare Resources
www.shakespeare.com/
Links to many other sites.

Writing tools
Screenwriting

Dramatica
www.dramatica.com/
Screenplay software; not free – compare it with ScreenForge below.

Final Draft
www.finaldraft.com/
Apparently the bees knees of scripting software – expensive (about £150), high functionality and cross-platform compatibility.

ScreenForge
www.apotheosispictures.com/
Almostfree Hollywood scriptwriting format bolt-on for Word.

Storyware

Alice
http://alice.cs.cmu.edu/
Software program for storyboard modelling; quite technical but interesting.

Blogger
www.blogger.com/
Free web-based tool for instantly publishing 'blogs' (web diaries).

Creativity Unleashed
www.cul.co.uk/
Software to stimulate creative thinking, originally intended for business.

KidPad
www.kidpad.org/
Collaborative story-writing tool for children being developed at the University of Maryland.

StoryBoard Quick
www.powerproduction.com/
Storyboard software for films, animation, games, etc.

Storycraft Writer's Software

www.writerspage.com/

Fiction-writing program that claims to turn ideas into complete novels, screenplays, plays or short stories.

Web Store for Writers and Creative Pros

www.masterfreelancer.com/

Plots Unlimited, Writer's Software Companion and other software aids.

Word-processing aids

Tricks and Trinkets

www.tricksandtrinkets.com/pk/

To make word processing easier, e.g. autotext for often-used phrases.

WordTips

www.VitalNews.com/wordtips/

How to get the best out of Microsoft Word; useful tips, many a real boon for writers.

Jane Dorner is the author of 21 books and represents authors' interests on the Boards of ALCS and CLA. She is author of *The Internet: A Writer's Guide* (A & C Black) (www.internetwriter.co.uk) which has the full listing of over 1000 resources for writers. The following genre areas have substantial listings: academic writing; business writing; children's writing; crime writing and mystery; fantasy; fiction; health writers; historical research; horror; interactive fiction and experimental forms; journalism; literature festivals; literature resources; mystery; poetry; prizes; residencies; romance; science fiction, fantasy and horror; specialist subjects; screen, TV and playwriting; translation; travel writing; STM writers; technical writing; women's and gender issues; writing courses and many other themes.

See also...

- *Setting up a website*, page 530
- *E-Publishing*, page 525

Websites for artists

In theory, the web should be an ideal way for artists to obtain support but in practice there are relatively few good information sites for visual artists. Ironically, most of the organisations that are involved in visual arts have not developed sites that are particularly useful to artists. They tend to have websites that are used more for marketing their own organisations than providing free information online. However, several of the regional arts offices sites are useful, as are some of the government sites, and some organisation sites provide links to places for further 'digging'. Alison Baverstock introduces some web addresses which will be useful as a starting point.

AN The Artists Information Company
www.anweb.co.uk

Sister sites www.workingwithartists.co.uk *and* www.artistscareers.co.uk

A very broad site, covering all aspects of being an artist from current events to developing and maintaining good business practice. Initial section headings are:

● Forum – an interactive space for artists to seek and exchange advice on practice, career, project and business issues
● Practice – practical information and examples on showing, selling, commissions, residencies, production and collaboration
● Career – information on developing a career as an artist: first steps, looking at yourself, skills, developing a career, portfolio careers
● Business – valuable know-how and tips on becoming and being self employed, accounts, tax, contracts, promotion and insurance
● Contacts – over 1000 links to visual arts organisations in the UK and internationally which offer email and web links
● Artists – artists tell the real story of practice: their approaches, achievements and setbacks
● Research – introducing research on visual arts and artists' practice.

AN publishes *AN Magazine*, which specifically caters for the needs of visual and applied artists.

Art Quest
www.artquest.com

This site directly connects buyers and sellers of art, helping artists and collectors eliminate the commissions and fees usually found in the process.

Art Train
www.arttrain.org.uk

A searchable database of courses and training providers in Scotland.

Artifact
www.artifact.ie

An online register representing work by over 1000 contemporary professional artists based in the Republic of Ireland and Northern Ireland.

The Arts Council England
www.artscouncil.org.uk

Offers useful information on public policy towards the arts and current funding (such as which areas of the arts each organisation handles). The 'news and information' section offers useful statistics on the arts in England as well as links to other sites.

The Arts Council of Northern Ireland
www.artscouncil-ni.org

Information on arts policy, funding schemes and contacts in Northern Ireland and the Republic.

The Arts Council of Wales
www.ccc-acw.org.uk

Information on arts policy, funding schemes and contacts in Wales.

AXIS
www.axisartists.org

The largest interactive database of contemporary British art on the internet.

Birkbeck College, University of London
www.bbk.ac.uk/lib/artlibgu/html

Offers details of art libraries in London.

Center for Safety in the Arts
http://artswire.org:70/1/csa

Based in the USA but includes excellent information on health and safety in the visual arts.

The Crafts Council
www.craftscouncil.org.uk

Offers services for both makers and members of the public interested in craft practice and purchase.

Cultural Enterprise – Menter Diwylliannol
www.cultural-enterprise.com

Information on business support for creative industries in Wales.

Cywaith Cymru – Artworks Wales
www.cywaithcymru.org

Listings of public art and residency projects in Wales.

Department for Culture, Media and Sport
www.culture.gov.uk

Holds the latest research reports on the creative industries.

Design and Artists Copyright Society
www.dacs.co.uk

Information on copyright and intellectual property.

The Gallery Channel UK
www.thegallerychannel.co.uk

An excellent and almost comprehensive exhibition listings website.

Inland Revenue
www.inlandrevenue.gov.uk

Useful information on tax, national insurance and self-assessment – particularly helpful if you are new to being self employed.

Institute of International Visual Arts (inIVA)
www.iniva.org

A contemporary visual arts organisation with a special interest in new technologies, commissioning site-specific artworks and international collaborations.

Intellectual Property
www.intellectual-property.gov.uk

The Government's information site on copyright and other intellectual property rights.

International Association of Residential Arts Centres
www.resartis.org

An online directory of residency centres worldwide.

International Cultural Desk
www.icd.org.uk

Offers international opportunities for Scottish artists.

Metier
www.metier.org.uk

The national training organisation for the arts and entertainment industries, representing 500,000 people involved in the arts (including visual arts and all aspects of arts management).

National Disability Arts Forum
www.ndaf.org

Offers disability arts news and information on opportunities and contacts.

National Statistics: the official UK statistics site
www.statistics.gov.uk

Publishes a range of general and specific statistics on the arts.

Public Art South West
www.publicartonline.org.uk

Offers information on contacts, opportunities and practical advice on public art.

The Scottish Arts Council
www.sac.org.uk

Information on arts policy, funding schemes and contacts in Scotland.

Trans Artists
www.transartists.nl

Netherlands-based site providing information on international artists-in-residence and exchange programmes, finances, cultural institutes (with links to their websites).

xrefer The web's reference engine
http://w1.xrefer.com

Free access online to over 50 reference titles including *The Bloomsbury Guide to Art*, *The Oxford Dictionary of Art* and the *Grove Concise Dictionary of Music*.

Your Creative Future
www.yourcreativefuture.org

A career-planning site for those involved in the arts.

After 10 years in publishing **Alison Baverstock** set up her own marketing consultancy, specialising in running campaigns for the book trade and training publishers to market more effectively. She is a well-established speaker on the book business and has written widely on how to market books. Her most recent title is *Marketing Your Book: An Author's Guide* (A & C Black 2001). She may be contacted at baverstockjam@cwcom.net

Resources for writers

The writer's toolkit

Sooner or later, whatever the nature of their work, all writers must do some research. When they confront the sheer volume of information currently available in printed and manuscript form, as well as on the internet, this can seem a daunting task. Ann Hoffmann looks at the skills involved and recommends a number of standard sources.

Throughout the centuries writers have relied for their research on their own curiosity and observation skills. They have also fed voraciously on the knowledge and output of others. The earliest storytellers gathered their material through a combination of oral enquiry and attentive listening, each one in turn 'embroidering' in varying degrees what they had learnt. These tales later came to be written down and laboriously copied again and again in manuscript form, with little or no regard for accuracy or spelling. A new dimension was added in the wake of Caxton: the newspaper and the printed book, so that by the mid-18th century Samuel Johnson would speak of a writer turning over 'half a library' to make one book. Clearly the great Doctor had in mind a private collection of a few hundred books – nothing like the vast libraries and databases available to us today.

We live in an age of 'information overload'. Books galore, websites, and internet 'newsgroups' are on offer on every subject under the sun. The skill no longer lies in *finding* the information, but in *finding it quickly* and, most importantly, *sorting out the authoritative from the inaccurate*. At the same time, because so few of us today maintain proper diaries, and most choose to telephone rather than write a personal letter, there is already a serious dearth of information at the disposal of biographers, social historians and writers of historical fiction, from the mid-20th century onwards. Thus the traditional skills of looking and listening have come back into their own. Today's researchers cannot safely rely only on books and manuscripts, or even on the web, but must look closely at video and film and – the novelist and the dramatist especially – listen to tape recordings and to the spoken word. They must also master the art of the interview.

Photocopying and microfilming techniques have relieved us of the laborious chore of copying by hand – with all the risks of error that that involved. Information technology (IT) enables us to obtain instantly, in the comfort of our own study, the most up-to-the-minute factual information on record, from anywhere in the world. Another bonus is that we can keep abreast of current research – new discoveries and theories which so often shed a different, if controversial, light on historical events and people, and which will be reflected in our creative work.

That said, writers should not regard the internet as a substitute for the library or archive centre, or original sources, but think of it rather as a springboard or first port of call. They should also be wary of using any material that does not come from an authoritative source.

Using the internet as a research tool

The internet is a global network of computers. Its most useful component for research is the World Wide Web (usually referred to as the 'web' or 'WWW'). This is the world's fastest-growing information research source. It is open 24 hours a day, 365 days a year.

To access the web, you must go online. Basic requirements are a personal computer, a telephone line and a modem. You then sign up with an Internet Service Provider (ISP), who supplies software to connect your computer with their own, through which you can access the worldwide network. If you are not yet online, you can gain access through your local library, university or college, or at one of the growing number of cybercafés.

The choice of ISP is wide open, and it is best to take the recommendation of a fellow writer. Some providers offer a 'free' service, in which case you incur telephone charges for every minute you spend online. Others quote a range of subscription rates, from the flat rate 'anytime' to 'off-peak', and/or a fixed number of hours online per month, with no additional charge for telephone calls. A 'broadband' subscription allows you to make and receive calls while online. The speed of connection and the time it takes for data to reach you are important factors, as is the facility of a 24-hour technical support service at a local call rate. Basically you get what you pay for, i.e. the fee-paying ISPs are usually the least complicated to use and may offer additional services. There is no difficulty about changing your ISP, should you wish to do so later.

The amount of information online is huge. It is accessed with the aid of 'web browser' software, such as Microsoft Internet Explorer or Netscape Navigator. When a web page address, known as a URL (Uniform Resource Locator) and starting usually with http://www., or simply www., is typed in, the required page appears on the screen. Most pages displayed contain useful 'links' and 'hyperlinks' (cross-references) to other web pages.

If you do not know the URL, or you are conducting a search by subject, you can use one or more of the 'search engines' on the web: when you type in a keyword or topic, all relevant sites found are displayed. As each search engine is different, a knowledge of how they operate is essential if you wish to speed up your research.

The secret of successful, economic researching on the web is to *be specific*. Refining searches down to the *precise* information required saves time and money, and also avoids the chore of having to wade through a mass of superfluous, irrelevant material. It is very important to keep a record of the path to your information, by using the 'Bookmark' or 'Favourite' facilities on the browser program. The maintenance of a personal website address book is also recommended.

There are two other internet resources of immense value to the writer: the 'Usenet' discussion or newsgroups, and email. Thousands of groups are listed on the Google Groups site. Messages 'posted' will be read by all members of the group,

Major UK sources

The British Library
96 Euston Road, London NW1 2DB
tel 020-7412 7676 (enquiries) fax 020-7412 7609
email reader-services-enquiries@bl.uk
reader-admissions@bl.uk
website www.bl.uk

The British Library Public Catalogue (BLPC)
website www.blpc.bl.uk

The British Library National Sound Archive
96 Euston Road, London NW1 2DB
tel 020-7412 7440 fax 020-7412 7441
email nsa@bl.uk
website www.bl.uk/nsa

The British Library Newspaper Library
Colindale Avenue, London NW9 5HE
tel 020-7412 7353 fax 020-7412 7379
email newspaper@bl.uk
website www.bl.uk/collections/newspapers

Family Records Centre
1 Myddleton Street, London EC1R 1UW
tel 020-8392 5300 (enquiries) fax 020-8392 5307
email enquiry@pro.gov.uk
website www.familyrecords.gov.uk

The National Archives: Public Record Office (PRO) and Historical Manuscripts Commission (HMC)
Ruskin Avenue, Kew, Richmond, Surrey TW9 4DU
tel 020-8876 3444 fax 020-8878 8905
email enquiry@pro.gov.uk
website www.pro.gov.uk

National Register of Archives
From autumn 2003 at the National Archives:
Historical Manuscripts Commission (see above).

and much information not available elsewhere may be forthcoming. Most groups produce a useful 'Frequently Asked Questions' (FAQ) information list. Email scarcely needs any recommendation here. It is fast, it is cheap, and it is indispensable.

Useful manuals catering specifically for the writer are: *The Internet: A Writer's Guide* by Jane Dorner (A & C Black, London, 2nd edn, 2001); *A Writer's Guide to the Internet* by Trevor Lockwood and Karen Scott (Allison & Busby, London, 2000); and *The Internet Writer's Handbook 2001–2002* by Karen Scott (Allison & Busby, London, 2001).

Using libraries and archive centres
Although much preparatory catalogue searching can be done online, the bulk of a writer's research is carried out in a library or archive centre. Nearly every country in the world has its national library and its national archives collection. Their catalogues – nowadays online – are among the most valuable of all research tools.

In the United Kingdom we have the British Library and the National Archives, a merger since April 2003 of the Public Record Office (PRO) and the Royal Commission on Historical Manuscripts (HMC). There are also six copyright libraries (The British Library, London; The Bodleian Library, Oxford; Cambridge University Library, Cambridge; The National Library of Wales, Aberystwyth; The National Library of Scotland, Edinburgh; Trinity College Library, Dublin), each of which has received one free copy of every book published here since the early 18th century. Among other major collections are the British Library Newspaper Library and the British Library National Sound Archive. We also have an excellent public library lending system which, if unable to meet a user's needs from its local stock, will obtain books on loan from other libraries or through the British Library Document Supply Service.

The advantage of using the local library, especially if it has a reference section, is that you have access to the stacks and can browse at will, whereas at the British Library and copyright libraries a limited number of books are on the open shelves: the rest have to be ordered, which means either entering author, title or keyword on the computer terminal or filling in a docket and waiting for the book to be delivered to the counter or to your desk.

To search official or genealogical records you may need to visit the National Archives at Kew, the Family Records Centre in London, or a local county record office or archives centre. The whereabouts of private papers can be ascertained by consulting the indexes at the National Register of Archives. A useful inexpensive publication, regularly updated, is the PRO/HMC *Record Repositories in Great Britain*.

Admission to the British Library and most of the sources mentioned above is free, with some exceptions, i.e. the Bodleian and Cambridge University Library, which currently make a modest charge, but you will need a reader's ticket (ask for details in advance). If you are a graduate you can use any university library. Professional bodies with specialist collections will usually grant bona fide researchers access on application. There are also a small number of private subscription libraries in London and the major cities.

There are few formalities at the Family Records Centre or county record offices, but you must book in advance to secure a seat, especially if you wish to use a computer or microfilm reader. Laptops are permitted in most libraries and archive centres, but you will almost certainly be restricted to note-taking in pencil and, if handling fragile documents, you may be issued with gloves.

The golden rule of research is *accuracy*. When transcribing or taking notes, you should check carefully all dates, figures and unusual names, and *keep a meticulous record of all sources*. Take full advantage of photocopying and filming facilities: the rule of thumb is that if copying by hand is likely to take more than 10 minutes, it is worth the expense. (A photocopy is an accurate copy!)

Selected titles for the bookshelf

Brewer's Dictionary of Phrase & Fable
The Cassell Dictionary of Slang (Jonathan Green)
Chambers Biographical Dictionary
Chronology of World History
The Companion to British History
  (C. Arnold-Baker)
Fowler's Modern English Usage
Mind the Gaffe: The Penguin Guide to Modern
  Errors in English (R.L. Trask)
The New Shell Book of Firsts (ed. P. Robertson)
The Oxford Companion to English Literature
  (ed. M. Drabble)
Oxford Style Manual
Pears Cyclopedia
Roget's Thesaurus (ed. B. Kirkpatrick)
The Statesman's Yearbook
The Times Atlas of the World (concise edition)
UK 2004 (formerly Britain: An Official
  Handbook) (annual)
Whitaker's Almanack
Who's Who
The Writers' & Artists' Yearbook
The Writer's Handbook

On CD-Rom

Encyclopedia Britannica
The Oxford Pop-up English Language
  Reference Shelf
Who Was Who 1897–2000

If you are very rich you may subscribe to The Oxford English Dictionary online; otherwise make do with the New Shorter OED or the Concise OED and consult the main version at the library. A third edition of the OED is due in 2010, and a new Dictionary of National Biography in 2004.

The Aslib Directory of Information Sources in the United Kingdom, published biennially, should be available in every reference library. *Walford's Guide to Reference Material* (3 vols) is a standard work, scheduled for major revision from 2004.

Indexes and bibliographies

A well-constructed index should lead the researcher directly to the subject matter required. A good bibliography suggests avenues of further search.

As well as indexes to individual books, the various indexes to newspapers and periodicals are useful tools. Outstanding among these are *The Times Index* (from 1906, with an unofficial earlier version from 1790) and *The British Humanities Index*, formerly the *Subject Index to Periodicals*, from 1915. There are of course subject indexes in many fields, too numerous to list here.

The British National Bibliography, known as the *BNB*, published since 1950, is also available online and on CD-Rom. One of the best international sources is *The World Bibliographical Series* launched in 1977 by Clio Press of Oxford.

The writer's bookshelf

Much reference material is now published in electronic as well as in printed form. Shelf space (and possibly also money!) may be saved by buying, say, your main encyclopedia, thesaurus and dictionary on CD-Rom; but it is wise to keep a concise edition (hardback or paperback) at your elbow for quick reference. From time to time the book clubs come up with excellent offers. Buying online (i.e. at www.amazon.co.uk) may also carry worthwhile discounts. Your minimum needs are:

- an up-to-date English dictionary;
- a thesaurus;
- a guide to English usage;
- an up-to-date atlas (also a historical atlas if you write about the past);
- a dictionary of quotations;
- a dictionary of dates;
- a concise world history and/or chronology;
- a biographical dictionary; and
- a current *Yearbook*.

Add to these according to your field of writing and your pocket: for the modern novelist perhaps a dictionary of slang; the historical novelist something on costume, the history of food, the cost of living in centuries past; and so on.

The easiest way to acquire an out-of-print title is to contact your local secondhand bookdealer or a major bookseller, i.e. Waterstone's, who operate a book-search service. Or you can try online at www.bibliofind.com, or use an independent searcher. Now that most bookfinders use the internet, obtaining out-of-print books is much faster – and cheaper – than it used to be.

Ann Hoffmann is a professional writer researcher of many years' standing and the author of five non-fiction books. Her *Research for Writers* (A & C Black, 7th edn 2003) includes chapters on research methods, online research, basic sources, research for modern and historical fiction writers, biographers, local and family historians, as well as an up-to-date listing by subject of major sources.

Digital imaging for writers

The way in which images are presented can sway an editor's decision to use an article. David Askham explains how to transfer images to a computer and suggests ways to arrange them for best effect.

An editor, who regularly commissioned me to produce profiles of small gardens, telephoned me as soon as he received one of my proposals. He said, "When I first read your letter, I was convinced that it would not be suitable for our British readers. Then I turned the page and said 'WOW!' Please go ahead with the feature."

So what tipped the scales? Admittedly the subject was a rather unusual one, in fact a so-called 'shade garden'. Furthermore, it was located far away in Australia! Because of this, I suspected that the proposal would fail if I sent words alone. I could have sent accompanying small colour prints to illustrate the potential of the article, but they would have lacked impact and risked becoming separated from my proposal. So I tried an experiment. I scanned a selection of photographs and compiled a simple but bold and colourful composite A4 sheet which formed part of my brief proposal. It worked and I have used variants of this idea with success ever since.

But the advantages of digital photography outlined above do not end there because once pictures are filed on a writer's personal computer they are available for a variety of useful purposes. They can serve as inspiration, providing quick recall of a scene or a person's facial features or attire. It is like revisiting a location or experiencing an unexpected reunion with an old friend. Digital images are quick visual references; they can jog a writer's memory and inspire. Let us look at the subject in a little more detail.

Technical aspects

Most writers will be familiar with cameras which use conventional film, either black and white or colour. These films produce negatives from which prints are produced; or transparencies which can be projected (for lecture purposes) or used by publishers to provide illustrations in print. In contrast, a new generation of cameras has arrived which do not use film, but instead record and store images digitally on special reusable memory. These digitally stored images must then be transferred to a personal computer so that they may be cropped, modified and integrated into the desired documents, such as a proposal. If the source is a digital camera it is relatively straightforward to transfer images using the computer software which came with the camera. Using the connecting cables supplied, images are 'down-loaded' into the computer or into special camera memory adapters which are inserted into a conventional floppy disk drive. The whole chain is digital which makes it so easy.

However, you do not necessarily need a digital camera to transfer images to your computer. You can work with prints which you already have – or could produce at will in the future. Or you can digitise your existing colour (or black and white) slides or negatives. For the latter operation your pictures need to be scanned and recorded on a CD, a process which has become increasingly available at most processing laboratories. Alternatively, with the right equipment, you can do the whole process yourself.

Possibly the easier and cheaper method is to buy a flatbed scanner which will produce digital files from your original colour or black and white prints. Flatbed scanners have tumbled in price over the past few years and are now often bundled with new computers. Alternatively, they can be bought for well under £100 although, like most consumer goods, it does not pay to buy the cheapest available. Take advice from a knowledgeable friend or trusted dealer.

If you wish to work from negatives or colour slides, you will need to buy a film scanner. These are more expensive (from £150 up to £1000 or more), but they give superior results particularly if you want to produce photo-realistic prints from a colour printer, say for promotional or exhibition purposes.

Initially, you can achieve commendable results by using your existing camera and having selected images scanned onto a CD by a processing laboratory. Then you can extract copies of the desired pictures from the CD and place them in your chosen document file. When you feel more confident and can justify the expense, you can then shop around for a suitable scanner to use at home.

Before moving on, I think a word is needed on the relative merits of using conventional film or digital cameras. The latter have developed rapidly over recent years. However, except for the top-priced models (£2000–£5000), results of consumer digital cameras are only just beginning to compare favourably with film and fall well short if big enlargements are needed in print. Like-for-like, they are also more expensive. However, the gap is already closing.

Using visual references

In addition to my example of the use of photographs in a book or article proposal, digital pictures are also a valuable aid to many forms of research and writing. For example, the value of tape-recorded research or interview notes is significantly enhanced if you add thumbnail pictures to enrich and augment the narrative information. Words and pictures which are integrated in this way have to be more reliable than unaided human memory when writing begins, particularly if there is a significant time interval between research and writing. But it is in the production of proposals, those all important selling documents, where digital imaging comes into its own.

However, I do not advocate using any old pictures. They have to be directly relevant to the subject being proposed and they must be of good quality. Therefore, it is worthwhile budgeting for your photography and providing high quality pictures using conventional cameras and films at the outset. You will then have confidence in being able to deliver high quality images to the editor.

Computing and software

Unless you are a computer buff, eyes can easily glaze when faced with yet more software to master. Unfortunately, some knowledge is essential but I will keep it simple. Most modern computers can handle graphics which includes digital photographs and drawings. Indeed most modern word processing software, such as WordPerfect, can integrate pictures directly into documents. Provided you know the filename of the required picture, or can find it by exploring the file listing hierarchy, you merely have to point to INSERT ... GRAPHICS ... FROM FILE and select the appropriate file. (The commands may be slightly different in other word processing programs.) The photograph then appears and you can adjust both its size and position within the document.

Ideally you will have made any cropping or other adjustments using the picture management software which may have been delivered with your digital camera or scanner. If the pictures supplied by your film processor were delivered on a CD, you may find a simple program included on the disk. Alternatively, you may choose to buy a picture processing program, such as Paint Shop Pro or Photoshop, which possess enormous capabilities for enhancing and transforming digital images, way beyond what you require initially. Photoshop is expensive, although a limited edition of the program is bundled with some scanners and is perfectly adequate for first-time users. Alternatively, Adobe Photoshop Elements is a lower cost option and could be a good investment. Consider buying one or two magazines which specialise in digital photography to study reviews and tables of available digital hardware and software. A study of analytical reports can be very helpful in short-listing potential solutions.

One last word on specialist software. Be prepared to invest plenty of time if you wish to explore digital image processing capabilities beyond basic cropping of your photographs. It can be very rewarding, but it takes time to learn and is beyond the scope of this article.

Adding visual elements

A simple example was given earlier of how you can add photographs to a text document. Sometimes it is better to devote an A4 page exclusively to the visual side of your proposals. Although this can be done using a word processor, a publishing program such as Microsoft Home Publishing or Serif PagePlus is more adept and flexible for designing layout and adding captions. However, you will soon find that you are straying into the realms of graphic design which appears to be much easier than it really is.

Working out the relative sizes of your pictures on the page and their positions can be extremely time consuming. It requires patience and discipline. My advice is to keep things as simple as possible before tackling more ambitious layouts. Avoid trying to include too many pictures on a page; six should be a maximum. Try to vary their individual sizes so that there is variety. Your aim should be to present just sufficient visual information to whet an editor's appetite with the whole effect being easy on the eye. There is no doubt that in a highly competitive world digital imaging can endow a writer with a competitive edge. Take heart and inspiration from my experience and see if your success rate improves.

David Askham is author of *Photo Libraries and Agencies* (BFP Books) and has been illustrating his written work for over 35 years. His photographs have been published worldwide in books, brochures, magazines and newspapers, many through international agencies.

Creative writing courses

Full details of courses are available on application to the institution. Anyone wishing to participate should first satisfy themselves as to content and quality. For day and evening courses consult your local Adult Education Centre.

Alston Hall Residential College for Adult Education
Alston Lane, Longridge, Preston PR3 3BP
tel (01772) 784661 *fax* (01772) 785835
email alston.hall@ed.lancscc.gov.uk
website www.alstonhall.u-net.com

Annual Writers' Conference
Chinook, Southdown Road, Winchester,
Hants SO21 2BY
tel (01962) 712307
email Writerconf@aol.com
website www.gmp.co.uk/writers/conference
Conference Director Barbara Large MBE, FRSA
Venue King Alfred's College, Winchester –
25–27 June 2004

Mini courses and workshops, lectures, seminars, one-to-one appointments with agents and commissioning editors, Bookfair, 15 writing competitions; followed by week-long workshops 30 June–4 July. Pitstop Refuelling Writers' Weekend Workshops planned for 19–21 March 2004 and 22–24 October 2004, and How to Self Publish Your Book day courses in May and October 2004.

The Arvon Foundation
Lumb Bank, Heptonstall, Hebden Bridge,
West Yorkshire HX7 6DF
tel/fax (01422) 843714
email l-bank@arvonfoundation.org
website www.arvonfoundation.org
Contact Ann Anderton
Moniack Mhor, Teavarran, Kiltarlity, Beauly,
Inverness-shire IV4 7HT
tel (01463) 741675 *fax* (01463) 741733
email m-mhor@arvonfoundation.org
Contact Chris Aldridge
The Arvon Foundation, Totleigh Barton,
Sheepwash, Beaworthy, Devon EX21 5NS
tel (01409) 231338 *fax* (01409) 231144
email t-barton@arvonfoundation.org
Contact Julia Wheadon

Belstead House Education & Conference Centre (Residential Courses)
Belstead, Ipswich, Suffolk IP8 3NA
tel (01473) 686321 *fax* (01473) 686664
email belstead.house@educ.suffolkcc.gov.uk

Burton Manor
Burton, Neston, Cheshire CH64 5SJ
tel 0151-336 5172 *fax* 0151-336 6586
email enquiry@burtonmanor.com
website www.burtonmanor.com
Principal Keith Chandler

Castle of Park
Cornhill, Aberdeenshire AB45 2AX
tel/fax (01466) 751111
email booking@castleofpark.net
website www.castleofpark.net
Proprietors Bill and Lois Breckon

Centerprise Literature Development Project
136 Kingsland High Street, London E8 2NS
tel 020-7249 6572 *fax* 020-7923 1951
email sharoncenterlit@care4free.net

See also page 454.

Creative in Calvados
1 Ormelie Terrace, Joppa, Edinburgh EH15 2EX
tel 0131-669 4025
email steveharvey@creativeincalvados.co.uk
website www.creativeincalvados.co.uk
Contact Stephen Harvey

Midweek and long weekend courses in poetry, songwriting/music, scriptwriting, drama and prose. Courses take place in Normandy. Founded 2001.

Dingle Writing Courses Ltd
Ballyneanig, Ballyferriter, Tralee, Co Kerry,
Republic of Ireland
tel 66 9154990 *fax* 66 9154992
email info@dinglewriting.com
website www.dinglewriting.com
Directors Abigail Joffe, Nicholas McLachlan

The Earnley Concourse
Earnley Trust Ltd, Earnley, Chichester,
West Sussex PO20 7JL
tel (01243) 670392 *fax* (01243) 670832
email info@earnley.co.uk
website www.earnley.co.uk

Far West
23 Chapel Street, Penzance, Cornwall TR18 4AP
tel (01736) 363146
email farwest@waitrose.com
website www.writing-courses-cornwall.com
Contact Angela Stoner

The Indian King Arts Centre
Fore Street, Camelford, Cornwall PL32 9PG
tel (01840) 212111
email info@indianking.co.uk
website www.indianking.co.uk

Knuston Hall
Irchester, Wellingborough, Northants. NN29 7EU
tel (01933) 312104 *fax* (01933) 357596
email enquiries@knustonhall.org.uk
website www.knustonhall.org.uk
Contact Daphne Brittin

Lancaster University
Dept of Continuing Education, Lonsdale College,
Lancaster University LA1 4YN
tel (01524) 592623/4 *fax* (01524) 592448
email Conted@lancaster.ac.uk
website www.lancs.ac.uk/users/conted/index.htm

Missenden Abbey
Great Missenden, Bucks HP16 0BN
tel (01494) 862904 *fax* (01494) 890087
email adultlearning@buckscc.gov.uk
website www.aredu.org.uk/missendenabbey

Open Studies – Part-time Courses for Adults: Office of Lifelong Learning
University of Edinburgh, 11 Buccleuch Place,
Edinburgh EH8 9LW
tel 0131-650 4400 *fax* 0131-667 6097
email oll@ed.ac.uk
website www.lifelong.ed.ac.uk

South and Mid Wales Association of Writers
c/o IMC Consulting Group, Denham House,
Lambourne Crescent, Cardiff CF14 5ZW
tel 029-2076 1170 *fax* 029-2076 1304
Contact Julian Rosser

Southern Writers' Conference
Stable House, Home Farm, Coldharbour Lane,
Dorking, Surrey RH4 3JG
Contact Lucia White
Venue The Earnley Concourse, Chichester
Caters for published and serious writers.

Summer Academy, Keynes College
The University, Canterbury, Kent CT2 7NP
tel (01227) 470402/823473 *fax* (01227) 784338
email summeracademy@ukc.ac.uk
website www.ukc.ac.uk/sa/index.html
Contact Andrea McDonnell

Swanwick, The Writers' Summer School
Contact Jean Sutton, The Secretary, 10 Stag Road,
Lake, Sandown, Isle of Wight PO36 8PE
website www.wss.org.uk

Ty Newydd
Ty Newydd, National Creative Writing
Centre of Wales, Llanystumdwy, Cricieth,
Gwynedd LL52 0LW
tel (01766) 522811 *fax* (01766) 523095
email tynewydd@dial.pipex.com
website www.tynewydd.org

University of Nottingham Study Tours
School of Continuing Education,
University of Nottingham, Jubilee Campus,
Wollaton Road, Nottingham NG8 1BB
tel 0115-951 6526 *fax* 0115-951 6556
email re-studytours@nottingham.ac.uk
Administrator Sylvia Stephens

Urchfont Manor College
Urchfont, Devizes, Wilts. SN10 4RG
tel (01380) 840495 *fax* (01380) 840005
email urchfont@wccyouth.org.uk

Wedgwood Memorial College
Station Road, Barlaston,
Stoke-on-Trent ST12 9DG
tel (01782) 372105/373427 *fax* (01782) 372393

Editorial, literary and production services

The following specialists offer a wide variety of services to writers (both new and established), publishers, journalists and others. Services include advice on manuscripts, editing and book production, indexing, translation, research and writing. See page 703 for a subject index.

'A Feature Factory' Editorial Services
4 St Andrews Court, Norwich NR7 0EW
tel (01603) 435229 mobile (07890) 182492
fax (01603) 435229
email editorial@fdsltd.com
Editors Dr Dennis Chaplin, Sara de Villeurbanne

Contract magazine/book publishing, editorial consultancy and troubleshooting, DTP (Quark/Photoshop), proofreading, sub-editing, legal copy checks, typesetting, advertisement design, copywriting, features, broadcast backgrounders, news releases, autobiography ghostwriting, novel/script editing, brochures, leaflets, research projects, tourist guides, editorial/journalism training. Researchers often needed (send CV and samples).

Aaron Editorial
19 Albemarle Road, Gorleston-on-Sea,
Norfolk NR31 7AR
tel/fax (01493) 444556
email aared@onetel.net.uk
Contact Eldo Barkhuizen

Onscreen editing, copy-editing, proofreading, Anglicising/Americanising. Psychology, philosophy, English literature, archaeology, business studies, theology, biblical studies, classical Hebrew, Hellenistic Greek, Jewish studies, self-help, diet/nutrition. Services supplied to publishers only. Advanced Member of SfEP. Established 1997.

Abbey Writing Services
Twitchen Cottage, Holcombe Rogus, Wellington,
Somerset TA21 0PT
tel/fax (01823) 672762
email john.mcilwain@virgin.net
Director John McIlwain

Comprehensive non-fiction writing, project management and editorial service. Educational consultants. Lexicography. Founded 1989.

Academic File
(in association with The Centre for Near East Afro-Asia Research – NEAR)
27 Wallorton Gardens, PO Box 13666,
London SW14 8WF
tel 020-8392 1122 fax 020-8392 1422
email afis@eapgroup.com
website www.eapgroup.com
Director Sajid Rizvi

Research, advisory and consultancy services related to politics, economics and societies of the Near and Middle East, Asia and North Africa and related issues in Europe. Risk analysis, editorial assessment, editing, contract publishing, design and production. Founded 1985.

Advice and Criticism Service
1 Beechwood Court, Syderstone,
Norfolk PE31 8TR
tel (01485) 578594 fax (01485) 578138
email hilary@hilaryjohnson.demon.co.uk
website www.hilaryjohnson.demon.co.uk
Contact Hilary Johnson

Authors' consultant: detailed and constructive assessment of typescripts/practical advice regarding publication. Former organiser of Romantic Novelists' Association's New Writers' Scheme, adjudicator of literary awards and publishers' reader. Specialities: crime/ thrillers/popular women's fiction. Advice also available on science fiction/fantasy, children's books, TV/radio/film scripts, poetry and non-fiction.

AFI Research (Richard M. Bennett Media)
The Ground Floor, 27 The Avenue,
Newton Abbot TQ12 2BZ
tel/fax (01626) 335040
email afi@supanet.com
Senior Associate Richard Bennett

Expert analysis, commentary and editorial consultancy for the news media, broadcasters and publishers worldwide. Specialists in defence, intelligence, wars and current affairs.

Amolibros
Loundshay Manor Cottage, Preston Bowyer,
Milverton, Somerset TA4 1QF
tel/fax (01823) 401527
email amolibros@aol.com
website www.amolibros.co.uk
Managing Consultant Jane Tatam

A self-publishing consultancy/packager. Also offers

copy-editing, proofreading, typesetting, advice on marketing and sales. Established 1992.

Anchor Editorial Services

Anchor House, 5 High Street, Dulverton,
Somerset TA22 9HB
tel/fax (01398) 324350
Editorial Director Leigh-Anne Perryman,
Photographic Director Martyn Collins

A complete editorial, research and photographic service for company brochures and magazines; guidebooks, publicity leaflets and tourism projects; press releases and newsletters. Established 1998.

Andrew Crofts

Westlands Grange, West Grinstead, Horsham,
West Sussex RH13 8LZ
tel (01403) 864518
email croftsa@aol.com
website www.andrewcrofts.com

Ghostwriting.

Angel Books

6 Lancaster Road, Harrogate,
North Yorkshire HG2 0EZ
tel (01423) 566804
Contact Angela Sibson BA, AFBPsS

Professional author (21 titles) and tutor in creative writing offers comprehensive, sympathetic assessment of fiction MSS. Revision suggested with a view to getting into print. Special interests: psychological suspense, crime, thrillers, women's, teenage. Established 1994.

Anne Barclay Enterprises

The Old Farmhouse, Hexworthy, Yelverton,
Devon PL20 6SD
tel/fax (01364) 631 405
email anne@theswiftgroup.co.uk
website www.theswiftgroup.co.uk

Typing MSS and audio transcription through to full editorial services – appraisal, editing, research, feature writing, co-writing and ghostwriting. Special interests: food, travel, crime, memoirs. Founded 1996.

Anton Rippon Press Services

Breedon House, 3 The Parker Centre,
Derby DE21 4SZ
tel (01332) 384235 *cellphone* (07702) 693864
fax (01332) 364063/521548
email anton@breedonpublishing.co.uk

General feature and sports writing for newspapers and magazines. Ghostwriting (preliminary letter essential). Radio and film documentary treatments and scripts. Complete book production service. Part of the Breedon Publishing Group.

Antony Hemans

Maranatha, 1 Nettles Terrace, Guildford,
Surrey GU1 4PA
tel (01483) 574511

Biographical and historical research, specialising in industrial archaeology – railways, canals and shipping, air, military and naval operations – genealogy and family history. Founded 1981.

Apple Pips Editing Services

18 Raglan Grove, Kenilworth,
Warwickshire CV8 2NH
tel (01926) 858864
email primrosecroft@hotmail.com
website www.applepipsediting.co.uk
Contact Ann Richards

Editing, copy-editing, proofreading, keying-in MSS (Word), research, book reviews. Special interests: history (especially Irish, social history of medicine, American – early colonial, Wild West, Tudor, Stuarts), educational books for schools, crime, fiction, biographies. Established 2001.

Arioma Editorial Services

PO Box 53, Aberystwyth, Ceredigion SY24 5WG
tel (01970) 871296 *fax* (01970) 871733
Proprietor Moira W. Smith

Research, co-writing, ghostwriting, DTP, complete book production service. Specialities: military, naval, aviation history and autobiography.

Arkst Publishing

1 Lindsey House, Lloyds's Place, London SE3 0QF
tel 020-8297 9997 *fax* 020-8318 4359
email jim@arkst.demon.co.uk
Director James H. Willis MA, FRCP (Edin.)

Independent appraisal of MSS – fiction and non-fiction. Founded 1995.

Authors' Advisory Service

24 Lyndale Avenue, Childs Hill, London NW2 2QA
tel 020-7794 3285

All typescripts professionally evaluated in depth by long-established publishers' reader specialising in constructive advice to new writers and with wide experience of current literary requirements. Founded 1972.

Authors' Aid

11 Orchard Street, Fearnhead, Warrington,
Cheshire WA2 0PL
tel (01925) 838431
email chris.sawyer@btinternet.com
website www.authorsaid.co.uk
Partners Chris Sawyer, Deborah Ramage

Appraisal and editorial services. Offers honest, constructive feedback and detailed guidance on style, presentation, characterisation, plot, construction, marketability, etc. A personalised service by a publishing professional with the clear aim of maximising the writer's chances of publication. Other services: rewriting, proofreading, ghostwriting, word processing, commissioned work. Write, phone or email before sending work. Established 1991.

Authors Appraisal Service

12 Hadleigh Gardens, Boyatt Wood, Eastleigh, Hants SO50 4NP
Literary consultant J. Evans

Professional writer offers critical appraisal of MSS – fiction only. Specialises in romantic and historical fiction. Competitive rates. Preliminary letter essential and sae for reply. Founded 1988.

AuthorsOnLine Ltd

15 Maidenhead Street, Hertford SG14 1DW
tel (01992) 586788 *fax* (01992) 586787
email theeditor@authorsonline.co.uk
website www.authorsonline.co.uk
Contact Richard Fitt (editor)

Publishes MSS (including short stories and poetry) on the AuthorsOnLine website. Offers full publishing facilities on a print-on-demand basis for authors of 'special interest' books. Authors retain control of editorial content and copyright, leaving them free to pursue hard copy contracts. Works closely with publishers and literary agents. New and established authors welcome. Fee for book-length MS: eformat £95; POD £550 including eformat. Founded 1997.

Authors' Research Services

32 Oak Village, London NW5 4QN
tel 020-7284 4316
email rmwindserv@aol.com
Contact Richard Wright

Offers comprehensive research service to writers, academics and business people worldwide, including fact checking, bibliographical references and document supply. Specialises in English history, social sciences, business. Founded 1966.

Barbara Cheney

9 St Johns Road, Lower Weston,
Bath BA1 3BN
tel (01225) 316376
email barscheney@aol.com

Copy-editing, proofreading, layout and design. Books (up to 768pp), directories, magazines, newsletters, annual reports, prospectuses, catalogues, leaflets. Clients include publishers, institutes and government departments. Freelance since 1987.

Bernard Hawton

6 Merdon Court, Merdon Avenue, Chandler's Ford, Hants SO53 1FP
tel 023-8026 7400
email bernardhawton@hotmail.com
Proofreading, copy-editing.

Beswick Writing Services

19 Haig Road, Stretford M32 0DS
tel 0161-865 1259
Contact Francis Beswick

Editing, research, information books. Special interests: religious, philosophical and educational. Expertise in correspondence courses and Open Learning materials. Founded 1988.

Black Ace Book Production

PO Box 6557, Forfar DD8 2YS
tel (01307) 465096 *fax* (01307) 465494
website www.blackacebooks.com
Directors Hunter Steele, Boo Wood

Book production and text processing, including text capture (or scanning), editing, proofing to camera-ready/film, printing and binding, jacket artwork and design. Delivery of finished books; can sometimes help with distribution. Founded 1990.

Blair Services

Blair Cottage, Aultgrishan, Melvaig, Gairloch, Wester Ross IV21 2DZ
tel/fax (01445) 771228
email BlairServices@aultgrisham.freeserve.co.uk
Director Ian Mertling-Blake MA, DPhil

Editing and revision: fiction and non-fiction (such as prospectus for schools and other educational purposes). Also specialist academic revision for books/articles on archaeology and associated subjects. Founded 1992.

Book Production Consultants plc

25-27 High Street, Chesterton, Cambridge CB4 1ND
tel (01223) 352790 *fax* (01223) 460718
email tl@bpccam.co.uk
website www.bpccam.co.uk
Directors A.P. Littlechild, C.S. Walsh

Complete publishing service: writing, editing, designing, illustrating, translating, indexing, photography; production management of printing and binding; specialised sales and distribution; advertising sales. For books, journals, manuals, brochures, magazines, catalogues, electronic media. Founded 1973.

Book-in-Hand Ltd

20 Shepherds Hill, London N6 5AH
tel/fax 020-8341 7650
Contact Ann Kritzinger

Production of cost-effective short-run books for small and self-publishers, from typescript (or disk) to bound copies (hardbacks or paperbacks, sewn or unsewn). Enquiries with sae, or by fax, please.

Brackley Proofreading Services
PO Box 5920, Brackley, Northants. NN13 6YB
tel/fax (01280) 703355
email brackleyproof@LineOne.net
Proofreading. Founded 2000.

Brooke Projects
21 Barnfield, Urmston, Manchester M41 9EW
tel 0161-746 8140 *fax* 0161-746 8132
email urmston@brooke.u-net.com
Research, editing and contract writing. Specialises in business, management, tourism, history, biography and social science.

C.N. Gilmore
27 Salisbury Street, Bedford MK41 7RE
tel (01234) 346142
email Intel_Thug@compuserve.com
Sub-editing, slush-pile reading, reviewing. Will also collaborate. Undertakes work in all scholarly and academic fields as well as fiction and practical writing. Specialises in editing translated works. Founded 1987.

Caroline White
78 Howard Road, London E17 4SQ
tel 020-8521 5791
email cwhite@bmjgroup.com
Print journalist specialising in health and medicine; also travel. Corporate literature and reports. Press and public relations. Written and spoken Italian, Spanish and French. Founded 1985.

Causeway Resources
8 The Causeway, Teddington, Middlesex TW11 0HE
tel/fax 020-8977 8797
email kskinner@causeway-dagonet.fsnet.co.uk
Director Keith Skinner
Biographical and historical research, specialising in Metropolitan Police history and true crime research. Founded 1989.

Chase Publishing Services
Mead, Fortescue, Sidmouth, Devon EX10 9QG
tel/fax (01395) 514709
email r.addicott@btinternet.com
Proprietor Ray Addicott
Coordinates a network of specialists in academic bookwork taking raw MSS through to finished books. Services include copy-editing and proofreading, design, typesetting, indexing and a full production service. Founded 1989.

Christine Foley Secretarial Services
Glyndedwydd, Login, Whitland, Carmarthenshire SA34 0TN
tel/fax (01994) 448414
Partners Christine Foley, Michael Foley
Word processing service: preparation of MSS from handwritten/typed notes and audio-transcription. Complete secretarial support. Founded 1991.

Christopher Pick
41 Chestnut Road, London SE27 9EZ
tel 020-8761 2585 *fax* 020-8761 6388
email cpick@netcomuk.co.uk
Publications consultancy, project management, writing and editing for companies and public-sector and voluntary-sector agencies: e.g. annual reports, brochures and booklets, information materials, websites, strategy documents, research reports, books, organisational histories. Extensive expertise and experience in presenting information clearly and concisely for non-specialist readers. Specialist in writing and producing corporate histories.

Combrógos
Prof Meic Stephens, 10 Heol Don, Whitchurch, Cardiff CF14 2AU
tel 029-2062 3359 *fax* 029-2052 9202
email meic@heoldon.fsnet.co.uk
Specialises in books (including fiction and poetry) about Wales or by Welsh authors, providing a full editorial service and undertaking arts and media research. Founded 1990.

Cornerstones & Kids' Corner Ltd
PO Box 22534, London W8 4GP
tel 020-7727 2478 *fax* 020-7727 6983
email helen@cornerstones.co.uk
kidscorner@cornerstones.co.uk
website www.cornerstones.co.uk
Proprietor Helen Corner
Specialist team of readers (authors and editors) provides literary guidance and constructive assessment of MSS for published or unpublished authors. Scouts for agents and publishers. Established 1998.
Kids' Corner (children's division)
All age ranges of children's fiction, from picture books to teenage.

D & N Publishing
Unit 3B, Lowesden Business Park, Lambourn Woodlands, Hungerford, Berks. RG17 7RU
tel/fax (01488) 73657
email dandnpub@aol.com
Partners David and Namrita Price-Goodfellow
Complete project management including some or all of the following: commissioning, editing, picture

research, illustration and design, page layout, proofreading, indexing, printing and repro. All stages managed in-house and produced on Apple Macs running the latest software. Founded 1991.

Mrs D. Buckmaster

51 Chatsworth Road, Torquay, Devon TQ1 3BJ
tel/fax (01803) 294663

General editing of non-fiction, with particular attention to clarity of expression and meaning, grammar, punctuation and flow. Experience in editing architecture, photography, financial, religious, natural health and human potential MSS. Founded 1966.

Dr David A. Cross

University College, The Castle, Durham DH1 3RW
tel 0191-374 4585

Research and information service; editing texts, specialising in art history, biography and genealogy; creative writing tutorials; lectures on artists and writers of the Lake District (especially George Romney and John Ruskin).

David L. Williams

7 Buckbury Heights, Newport,
Isle of Wight PO30 2LX
tel (01983) 528729 *fax* (01983) 822116
email davidw@genpix.fsnet.co.uk

Complete research and information service (pictures and text) specialising in transport – particularly maritime and aviation – history and genealogy. Established 1982.

David Price

Acupunctuation Ltd, 4 Harbidges Lane,
Long Buckby, Northampton NN6 7QL
tel/fax (01327) 844119
email dprice@macunlimited.net
website www.cancanplus.net

Copy-editing, proofreading, research, writing, rewriting. Special interests: fine art (particularly modern art), operetta and musicals, travel guides, modern European history (including the former Soviet Union), alternative health. Founded 1995.

David Wineman, Solicitors

Craven House, 121 Kingsway,
London WC2B 6NX
tel 020-7400 7800 *fax* 020-7400 7890
email law@davidwineman.co.uk
website www.davidwineman.co.uk
Contact Irving David

A broadly based media law firm. Offers legal advice to authors, illustrators, photographers, composers, songwriters and their agents on all forms of publishing agreement, including negotiation and review of commercial terms, where required, with

book and music publishers, film, TV and theatrical production companies, packagers and merchandisers. Founded 1981.

David Winpenny

33 St Marygate, Ripon,
North Yorkshire HG4 1LX
tel (01765) 608320 *fax* (01765) 607641
email david@dwpr.freeserve.co.uk

Writer and editor, including research and writing of features, news stories, brochures, speeches, advertising copy. Full public relations service. Special interest in country walks, architectural history, the arts, music, landscape, heritage, business and the North. Founded 1991.

Derek Wilde

59 Victoria Road, Woodbridge, Suffolk IP12 1EL
tel/fax (01394) 384557
email jill001@aol.com

Copy-editing, proofreading, indexing, research. Particular expertise in directories and reference books. Special interests: higher education, performing arts, travel and transport. Languages: French and Latin plus some knowledge of German and Italian. Established 1991.

Duncan McAra

28 Beresford Gardens, Edinburgh EH5 3ES
tel/fax 0131-552 1558
email duncanmcara@hotmail.com

Consultancy on all aspects of general trade publishing; editing; proof correction. Main subjects include art, architecture, archaeology, biography, military, Scottish and travel. See also page 354. Founded 1988.

E.J. Hunter

6 Dorset Road, London N22 7SL
tel 020-8889 0370

Editing, copy-editing, appraisal of MSS. Special interests: novels, short stories, drama, children's stories; primary education, complementary medicine, New Age.

Editorial Solutions

537 Antrim Road, Belfast BT15 3BU
tel 028-9077 2300 *fax* 028-9078 1356
email info@editorialsolutions.com
website www.editorialsolutions.com
Partners Sheelagh Hughes, Michael Johnston

Offers a comprehensive editorial and publications service, including news and feature writing, copywriting, editing and copy-editing, proofreading, publication design, page layout and complete publication management. Qualified journalists. Specialisms: business, public sector, education, web writing.

Editorial/Visual Research

21 Leamington Road Villas, London W11 1HS
tel 020-7727 4920 *mobile* (07973) 820020
Contact Angela Murphy

Comprehensive research service including historical, literary, film and picture research for writers, publishers, film and TV companies. Services also include copy-writing, editing, and travel and feature writing. Founded 1973.

Elizabeth Murray

3 Gower Mews Mansions, Gower Mews,
London WC1E 6HR
tel/fax 020-7636 3761
email MurraySearch@aol.com

Literary, biographical, historical, crime, military, cinema, genealogy research for authors, journalists, radio and TV from UK, European and USA sources. Founded 1975.

Felicity Trotman

Downside, Chicklade, Salisbury, Wilts. SP3 5SU
tel/fax (01747) 820503
email f.trotman@btinternet.com

For publishers only: editing, copy-editing, proofreading, writing, rewriting. Specialises in fiction and non-fiction for children, all ages. Established 1982.

Finers Stephens Innocent

179 Great Portland Street, London W1N 6LS
tel 020-7323 4000 *fax* 020-7344 5600
email nsolomon@fsilaw.co.uk
website www.fsilaw.co.uk
Contact Nicola Solomon, Partner

Services include: drafting and negotiating agency and publishing agreements; advice on copyright and moral rights, libel reading, defamation advice and insurance; breaches or termination of contract; errors in printing and failure or refusal to publish or delay in publishing; debt collection for payment of royalties, commission or fees, including suing or insolvency proceedings where necessary; injunctions; preparation of wills, administering artistic and literary estates; permissions, rights, copyright infringement and negligent misstatement; electronic rights and international sales. Solicitors to the Society of Authors, the Writers' Guild, the British Association of Picture Libraries and Agencies and the Association of Illustrators.

First Edition Translations Ltd

6 Wellington Court, Wellington Street,
Cambridge CB1 1HZ
tel (01223) 356733 *fax* (01223) 321488/316232
email info@firstedit.co.uk
website www.firstedit.co.uk
Directors Sheila Waller, Jeremy Waller

Translation, interpreting, voice-over recording, editing, proofreading, Americanisation, DTP; books, manuals, reports, journals and promotional material. Founded 1981.

FJN Associates

Little Theobald, Sandy Cross, Heathfield,
East Sussex TN21 8BT
tel (01435) 866653 *fax* (01435) 868998
email fred@nixonf.freeserve.co.uk
Partners Frederick J. Nixon, Brenda Mellen Nixon

Comprehensive DTP and editorial service including magazine and newsletter design and production; advice to authors, editing and preparation of MSS for submission to publishers/editors; proofreading. Founded 1990.

Freelance Market News

Sevendale House, 7 Dale Street, Manchester M1 1JB
tel 0161-228 2362 *fax* 0161-228 3533
email fmn@writersbureau.com
website www.writersbureau.com
Contact Angela Cox, Editor

A monthly market newsletter. A good rate of pay made for news of editorial requirements. Information on UK and overseas publications with editorial content, submission requirements and contact details. Founded 1968.

Freelance Services

41A Newal Road, Ballymoney, Co. Antrim BT53 6HB
tel 028-2766 2953
website www.joanshannon.co.uk
Contact Joan Shannon

Publishing services, photography and postcards. Commercial, industrial, scenic, fine art and natural light photography. Founded 1991.

Mrs Gene M. Spencer

63 Castle Street, Melbourne, Derbyshire DE73 1DY
tel (01332) 862133
email genespencer@supanet.com

Editing, copy-editing and proofreading; feature writing; theatrical profiles; book reviews; freelance writing. Founded 1970.

Geo Group & Associates

4 Christian Fields, London SW16 3JZ
tel 020-8764 6292 *fax* 0115-981 9418
email publishing@geo-group.co.uk
website www.geo-group.co.uk

Publishing services. From copy-editing and proofreading to complete package. Research and publishing consultancy. Low-cost, quality, short-run printing. Publishing imprint: Nyala Publishing. Two photo libraries (including aerial); photography commissioned. Special rates to author-publishers. Established 1968.

Geoffrey D. Palmer
47 Burton Fields Road, Stamford Bridge,
York YO41 1JJ
tel (01759) 372874
email gdp@lineone.net
website www.geoffreydpalmer.co.uk

Editorial and production services, including STM
and general copy-editing, on-screen editing,
artwork editing, proofreading and indexing.
Pre-press project management. Founded 1987.

Gill Shepherd
87 Elm Park Mansions, Park Walk,
London SW10 0AP
tel 020-7352 1770
email rgbshepherd@msn.com

Research, fact checking, rewriting for authors.
Specialises in history, politics, biography and
genealogy. Established 1985.

Gordon R. Wainwright
22 Hawes Court, Sunderland SR6 8NU
tel/fax 0191-548 9342
email gordon@gordonwainwright.co.uk
website www.gordonwainwright.co.uk

Criticism, advice and revision for non-fiction
authors; training seminars in business writing,
speed reading and other subjects; non-fiction
authors' publishing consultant. Established 1961.

Graham-Cameron Publishing
The Studio, 23 Holt Road, Sheringham,
Norfolk NR26 8NB
tel (01263) 821333 *fax* (01263) 821334
Partners Helen Graham-Cameron, Mike
Graham-Cameron

Complete editorial, including writing, editing,
illustration and production services. Absolutely no
unsolicited MSS. Founded 1984.

Hans Tasiemka Archives
80 Temple Fortune Lane, London NW11 7TU
tel 020-8455 2485 *fax* 020-8455 0231
Proprietor Mrs Edda Tasiemka

Comprehensive newspaper cuttings library from
1850s to the present day on all subjects for writers,
publishers, picture researchers, film and TV
companies. Founded 1950.

Hans Zell, Publishing Consultant
Glais Bheinn, Lochcarron, Ross-shire IV54 8YB
tel (01520) 722951 *fax* (01520) 722953
email hanszell@hanszell.co.uk
website www.hanszell.co.uk/

Consultancies, project evaluations, market
assessments, feasibility studies, research and surveys,
funding proposals, freelance editorial work,

commissioning, journals management, internet
training. Specialises in services to publishers and the
book community in Third World countries and
provides specific expertise in these areas. Also
mailing list services, and information resources
(pint/online) on African publishing and African
studies. Founded 1987.

Hurst Village Publishing
Henry and Elizabeth Farrar, High Chimneys,
Davis Street, Hurst, Reading RG10 0TH
tel 0118-9345211 *fax* 0118-9342073
email henry@heritagesites.eu.com

Offers design, photography, typesetting using the
latest desktop publishing programs, photographic
equipment and high resolution colour and laser
printers. Founded 1989.

Indexing Specialists (UK) Ltd
202 Church Road, Hove, East Sussex BN3 2DJ
tel (01273) 738299 *fax* (01273) 323309
email richardr@indexing.co.uk
website www.indexing.co.uk
Director Richard Raper BSc, DTA

Indexes for all types: books, journals and reference
publications on professional, scientific and general
subjects; copy-editing, proofreading services;
consultancy on indexing and electronic indexing.
Founded 1965.

The Information Bureau
(formerly Daily Telegraph Information Bureau)
51 The Business Centre, 103 Lavender Hill,
London SW11 5QL
tel 020-7924 4414 *fax* 020-7738 2513
email info@informationbureau.co.uk
website www.informationbureau.co.uk
Contact Jane Hall

Offers an on-demand research service on a variety
of subjects including current affairs, business,
marketing, history, the arts, media and politics.
Resources include range of cuttings amassed by the
bureau since 1948.

Ingrid Cranfield
16 Myddelton Gardens, London N21 2PA
tel/fax 020-8360 2433
email ingrid_cranfield@hotmail.com

Advisory and editorial services for authors,
publishers and media, including critical assessment,
rewriting, proofreading, copy-editing, indexing,
research, interviews, transcripts. Special interests:
geography, travel, exploration, adventure (own
archives), language, education, youth training, art
and architecture (including Japanese). Translations
from German and French. Not an employer or
agency. Founded 1972.

Janet McKerron
Apple Tree Cottage, Title Road, Middleton,
Saxmundham, Suffolk IP17 3NF
tel/fax (01728) 648973
email janet@janetmckerron.demon.co.uk

Indexing and proofreading books (up to 1000pp),
loose-leaf publications and academic journals.
Clients include publishers and NGOs. Specialist
subjects: civil law in England and Wales, European
law, the environment. Established 1996.

John Button – Editorial Services
Tower House, 6 Burnham Court, Martello Bay,
Clacton on Sea, Essex CO15 1RE
tel (01255) 470404 *fax* (01255) 470405
email johnbuttread@aol.com

Copy-editing and proofreading, specialising in
government committee of enquiry reports, legal,
financial, taxation, business education and
corporate identity publications; Legal Reference
Library series. Founded 1991.

John Vickers
27 Shorrolds Road, London SW6 7TR
tel 020-7385 5774

Archives of British Theatre photographs by John
Vickers, from 1938–74.

Johnathon Clifford
27 Mill Road, Fareham, Hants PO16 0TH
tel/fax (01329) 822218
website www.vanitypublishing.info

Offers a free, unbiased advice service for anyone
looking for a publisher or who has experienced
difficulties with a publishing house. Has extensive
knowledge of vanity publishing and acted as adviser
to the Advertising Standards Authority regarding
the wording of the 'Advice Note Vanity Publishing
July 1997'. See website for his report on the
government White Paper against rogue traders and
its effectiveness where authors are concerned. See
also page 247. Established 1994.

Josephine Curtis Editorial
Fairfield, Cade Street, Old Heathfield,
East Sussex TN21 9DA
tel (01435) 866637 *fax* (01435) 864746
email jcurtis002@aol.com

Editing – hard copy and onscreen, proofreading,
legal tabling. Established 1990.

Karyn Claridge Book Production
244 Bromham Road, Biddenham,
Bedford MK40 4AA
tel (01234) 347909
email kclaridge@eddisonsadd.co.uk

Complete book production management service

offered from MS to bound copies; graphic services
available; sourcing service for interactive book
projects. Founded 1989.

Keith Povey Editorial Services
Stoneleigh House, South Brentor, Tavistock,
Devon PL19 0NW
tel (01822) 810190 *fax* (01822) 810191
email Povedservs@aol.com

Copy-editing, indexing, proofreading, publisher/
author liaison. Partnership with T & A Typesetting
Services (*tel* 01706 861662) – specialist book typesetting to final output of any kind, graphic design.

Dr Kenneth Lysons
Lathom, Scotchbarn Lane, Whiston, Nr Prescot,
Merseyside L35 7JB
tel 0151-426 5513 *fax* 0151-430 6934
email lysons@literaryservices.co.uk
Contact Dr Kenneth Lysons MA, MEd, DPA, DMA, FCIS,
FInstPS, FBIM

Company and institutional histories, support
material for organisational management and
supervisory training, house journals, research and
reports service. Full secretarial support. Founded
1986.

Lewis Esson Publishing
45 Brewster Gardens, London W10 6AQ
tel 020-7854 0668 *fax* 020-8968 1623
email lewisesson@supanet.com

Project management of illustrated books in areas of
food, art and interior design; editing and writing of
food books; copywriting, especially in the area of
food packaging and FMCGs. Founded 1989.

Library Research Agency
Burberry, Devon Road, Salcombe, Devon TQ8 8HJ
tel (01548) 842769
Directors D.J. Langford MA, B. Langford

Research and information service for writers,
journalists, artists, businessmen from libraries,
archives, museums, record offices and newspapers
in UK, USA and Europe. Sources may be in English,
French, German, Russian, Serbo-Croat, Bulgarian,
and translations made if required. Founded 1974.

Lyn M. Taylor
(Eve-Line Editorial)
Anchorfield, 9 Gosford Road, Port Seton,
East Lothian EH32 0HE
tel (01875) 812315 *fax* (01875) 814126
email LynTaylor@compuserve.com

General comprehensive editorial service for
publishers: copy-editing (hard copy or onscreen)
and proofreading in all subjects. Specialises in
scientific and medical books, journals and reports
and wildlife publishing. Formatting, coding.

McText

Denmill, Tough, By Alford, Aberdeenshire AB33 8EP
tel/fax (019755) 62582
email d@mctext.com
website www.mctext.com
Partners K. and Duncan McArdle

Proofreading, copy-editing, website proofing.
Specialist interests: archaeology, equestrian, oil-related commerce. Founded 1986.

Manuscript Appraisals

Lanetrees, Simpson Cross, Haverfordwest,
Pembs. SA62 6AE
tel/fax (01437) 710534
email manuscript_app@hotmail.com
Proprietor Norman Price *Consultants* Ray Price,
Mary Hunt

Independent appraisal of authors' MSS (fiction and non-fiction, but no poetry) with full editorial guidance and advice. In-house editing, copy-editing, rewriting and camera-ready copy if required. Overseas enquiries welcome. Interested in the work of new writers. Founded 1984.

Marlinoak

22 Eve's Croft, Birmingham B32 3QL
tel/fax 0121-475 6139
Proprietor Hazel J. Billing JP, BA, DipEd

Preparation of scripts, plays, books, MSS service, proofreading; also audio-transcription, word processing. Founded 1984.

Meg Davies

31 Egerton Road, Ashton, Preston, Lancs. PR2 1AJ
tel (01772) 725120 *mobile* (07789) 433254
email megindex@aol.com

Indexing at general and postgraduate level in the arts and humanities. Also proofreading and copy-editing. Registered Indexer with Society of Indexers since 1971.

Murder Files

Dommett Hill Farm, Hare Lane, Buckland St Mary,
Chard, Somerset TA20 3JS
tel (01460) 234065
email enquiry@murderfiles.com
website www.murderfiles.com
Director Paul Williams

Crime writer and researcher specialising in UK murders. Holds information on thousands of well-known and less well-known murders dating from 1400 to the present day. Copies of press cuttings available from 1920 to date. Details of executions, particularly at the Tyburn and Newgate. Information on British Hangmen. Specialist in British police murders since 1700. Service available to general enquirers, writers, TV, radio, film, video, etc. Founded 1994.

My Word!

138 Railway Terrace, Rugby,
Warks. CV21 3HN
tel (01788) 571294 *fax* (01788) 550957
email enquiries@myword.co.uk
website www.myword.co.uk
Partners Roddie Grant, Janet Grant

Specialises in typesetting and website solutions. Produces materials for printing and websites, e.g. magazines, newsletters, books, brochures, leaflets, conference and sales literature. Founded 1994.

Nidaba Publishing Services

68 Bramblebury Road, London SE18 7TG
tel 020-8317 3767
email ali.glen@virgin.net
Contact Ali Glenny PhD Eng. Lit.

Copy-editing, proofreading and onscreen text correction (Word, Quark). Established 1997.

Nielsen BookData Ltd

Globe House, 1 Chertsey Road,
Twickenham TW1 1LR
tel 020-8843 8620 *fax* 020-8843 8744
email sales@bookdata.co.uk
websites www.bookdata.co.uk www.ehaus.co.uk
Woolmead House West, Bear Lane, Farnham,
Surrey GU9 7LG
tel (01252) 742500 *fax* (01252) 742501
email sales@whitaker.co.uk
website www.whitaker.co.uk
Contact Sales Department

Nielsen BookData is the leading supplier of high-quality, content-rich book information and other published media to the book industry. It takes its information from publishers and creates a unique title record which includes bibliographic details, text summaries, tables of contents, extensive subject-related information, market-rights details, jacket images and reviews. This bibliographic information is then made available through a variety of services worldwide. Data can be supplied as a direct feed, as a range of CD-Roms, DVDs or online: BookFind-Online, WhitakerWeb, LibWeb, PubWeb and print version. The company also offers order routing services through TeleOrdering and EDI.

e-haus creates websites for the industry and can provide a complete service – for web design, hosting and maintenance.

Northern Writers Advisory Services

77 Marford Crescent, Sale, Cheshire M33 4DN
tel 0161-969 1573
email grovesjill@aol.com
Proprietor Jill Groves

Offers typesetting to small publishers, societies and authors. Local history only. Founded 1986.

Oriental Languages Bureau

Lakshmi Building, Sir P. Mehta Road, Fort,
Bombay 400001, India
tel 22661258/22665640 *fax* 22664598
email icsolb@vsnl.net
Proprietor Rajan K. Shah

Undertakes translations, phototypesetting-DTP,
artwork and printing in all Indian languages and a
few foreign languages.

Ormrod Research Services

Weeping Birch, Burwash,
East Sussex TN19 7HG
tel/fax (01435) 882541

Comprehensive research service: literary, historical,
academic, biographical, commercial. Critical
reading with report (novels, theses, non-fiction),
editing, indexing, proofreading, ghostwriting.
Founded 1982.

OTS

29 Edge Avenue, Grimsby,
North East Lincolnshire DN33 2DD
tel/fax (01472) 237961
email pat.ots@virgin.net
Owner Pat Hewson

Video and audio transcription, verbatim and edited;
keying in/rekeying MSS, text and indexes;
proofreading. Specialises in research, social care,
crime (fiction and true) and finance; also general
reference/fiction. Not an employer or agency.
Founded 1995.

Oxford Designers & Illustrators

(formerly Oxford Illustrators and Oxprint Design)
Aristotle House, Aristotle Lane,
Oxford OX2 6TR
tel (01865) 512331 *fax* (01865) 512408
email name@odi-illustration.co.uk
website www.oxford-illustrators.co.uk
Directors Peter Lawrence, Richard Corfield,
Andrew King

Over 30 years' experience in the design, typesetting
and illustration of educational and general books.
In-house artists for all subjects including scientific
and technical, medical, natural history, cartoons,
maps and diagrams. Full project management and
repro service. Not an agency.

Pages Editorial & Publishing Services

Ballencrieff Cottage, Ballencrieff Toll, Bathgate,
West Lothian EH48 4LD
tel (01506) 632728
Director Susan Coon

Editorial and production service of magazines/
newspapers for companies or for commercial
distribution. Founded 1995.

Pagewise

2 Butlers Close, Amersham, Bucks. HP6 5PY
tel/fax (01494) 729760
email info@pagewise.co.uk
Director Monica Bratt

Specialist service for self publishers: design,
typesetting, editing and indexing, proofreading and
production services. Founded 1999.

Paul H. Niekirk

40 Rectory Avenue, High Wycombe,
Bucks. HP13 6HW
tel (01494) 527200

Text editing for works of reference and professional
and management publications, particularly texts on
law; freelance writing. Founded 1976.

Paul Nash

Munday House, Aberdalgie, Perth PH2 0QB
tel/fax (01738) 621584
email paulnash@zetnet.co.uk

Indexer specialising in sciences, engineering,
technology, environmental science. Registered with
the Society of Indexers. Winner of Library
Association Wheatley Medal (1992) for outstanding
index. Founded 1979.

Peter Nickol

50 St Leonards Road, Exeter EX2 4LS
tel/fax (01392) 255512
email pnickol@ninoakes.freeserve.co.uk

Editing and page layout; typesetting and music
engraving; copyright licensing; project management
including mixed media coordination, CD recording
and production. Specialises in music and music
education. Established 1987.

Phoenix 2

Lantern House, Lodge Drove, Woodfalls, Salisbury,
Wilts SP5 2NH
tel (01725) 512200 *fax* (01725) 511819
email enquiries@phoenix2.co.uk
Partners Bryan Walker, Amanda Walker

Writing, editing, sub-editing, typesetting and design
of magazines, newsletters, journals, brochures and
promotional literature. Specialist areas are business,
tourism, social affairs and education. Founded
1994.

Picture Research Agency

Jasmine Cottage, Spring Grove Road, Richmond,
Surrey TW10 6EH
tel/fax 020-8940 5986
email pat.hodgpix@virgin.net
Contact Pat Hodgson

Illustrations found for books, films and TV. Written
research also undertaken particularly on historical

subjects, including photographic and film history. Small picture library.

Picture Research Service – see Rich Research

Plum Communications
Fountain Head, Morchard Bishop, Crediton, Devon EX17 6NW
tel/fax (01363) 877463
email stephanie.plum@virgin.net
Contact Stephanie Walshe

Proofreading and copy-editing (hard copy and onscreen), copywriting, ghostwriting, rewriting, indexing, page layout, research, project management. Backlog reading, appraisal of fiction and non-fiction MSS with report (write, phone or email first), website authoring. Complete marketing service and production of all promotional material, training manuals, strategy documents, research reports and company histories. Founded 1990.

Reading and Righting (Robert Lambolle Services)
618B Finchley Road, London NW11 7RR
tel/fax 020-8455 4564
email ziph@macunlimited.net
website http://readingandrighting.netfirms.com

MSS/script advisory and evaluation service: fiction, non-fiction, stage plays and screenplays; editorial services; one-to-one tutorials, creative writing courses and lectures. Send sae for leaflet. Founded 1987.

Reginald Piggott
Decoy Lodge, Decoy Road, Potter Heigham, Norfolk NR29 5LX
tel (01692) 670384

Cartographer to the University Presses and academic publishers in Britain and overseas. Maps and diagrams for academic and educational books. Founded 1962.

Repertoire
21 Hindsleys Place, London SE23 2NF
tel 020-8244 5816
email parkerwrite@yahoo.co.uk
Contact John Parker

Ghostwriter for autobiographies, memoirs, fiction, etc. MSS typed, edited and rewritten for submission to publishers. Audio tapes transcribed. Humour and drama brought to stories and events. Tuition and advice on all personal writing projects. Free consultation. Established 1991.

Rich Research
One Bradby, 77 Carlton Hill, London NW8 9XE
tel/fax 020-7624 7755
Contact Diane Rich

Picture research service. Visuals found for all sectors of the media and publishing. Artwork and

photography commissioned. Rights and permissions negotiated. Founded 1978.

Richard A. Beck
49 Curzon Avenue, Stanmore, Middlesex HA7 2AL
tel 020-8933 9787 *fax* 020-8904 5182
email rbeck@bushinternet.com

Editing, proofreading, indexing, research, writing and rewriting. Reduced rates for new authors, senior citizens, the unemployed, etc. Founded 1991.

Richard M. Wright
32 Oak Village, London NW5 4QN
tel 020-7284 4316
email rmwindserv@aol.com

Indexing, copy-editing, specialising in politics, history, business, social sciences. Founded 1977.

Rita Winter Editorial Services
'Kilrubie', Eddleston, Peeblesshire EH45 8QP
tel/fax (01721) 730353
email rita@ednet.co.uk

On-screen editing, copy-editing and proofreading (English and Dutch). Academic and general material, books, dictionaries, company literature. Special interests: art, art history, exhibition catalogues, contemporary fiction.

Roger Palmer Ltd
Antonia House, 262 Holloway Road, London N7 6NE
tel 020-7609 4828 *fax* 020-7609 4878
email contracts@rogerpalmerltd.co.uk
Contact Peter Palmer

Drafts, advises on and negotiates all media contracts for publishers, packagers, agents, authors and others; operates complete outsourced contracts department functions for publishers; undertakes contractual audits and devises contracts and permissions systems; provides advice on copyright and related issues; provides training and seminars. Special terms for members of the Society of Authors and the Writers' Guild of Great Britain. Founded 1993.

Rosemary Dooley
Crag House, Witherslack, Grange-over-Sands, Cumbria LA11 6RW
tel (015395) 52286 *fax* (015395) 52013
email musicbks @rdooley.demon.co.uk
website www.booksonmusic.co.uk
Proprietor Rosemary Dooley

Collaborative publishers' exhibitions: music books. Founded 1985.

Rosemary Horstmann
122 Mayfield Court, 27 West Savile Terrace, Edinburgh EH9 3DR
tel 0131-667 1377

Broadcasting scripts evaluated; general consultancy on editorial and marketing matters.

S. Ribeiro, Literary Services

42 West Heath Court, North End Road,
London NW11 7RG
tel 020-8458 9082
email sribeiroeditor@aol.com
Contact S. Ribeiro

MSS reading and appraisal with detailed analysis and guidance in submission to agents and publishers. Sensitive editing to publication standard. Also rewriting, Americanisation, idiom for translations. Copywriting: synopses, reviews and book jackets. Creative writing tutor. Special experience: fiction and general non-fiction, memoirs, poetry. Published and new writers, including overseas, welcome. Guidance for self-publishing. Send sae or telephone for leaflet. Established 1986.

Sandhurst Editorial Consultants

36 Albion Road, Sandhurst, Berks. GU47 9BP
tel (01252) 877645 *fax* (01252) 890508
email mail@sand-con.demon.co.uk
website www.sand-con.demon.co.uk
Partners Lionel Browne, Janet Browne

Specialists in technical, professional and reference work. Project management, editorial development, writing, rewriting, copy-editing, proofreading, and general editorial consultancy. Founded 1991.

Sandton Literary Agency

PO Box 785799, Sandton 2146, South Africa
tel (011) 442-8624
Directors J. Victoria Canning, M. Sutherland

Evaluating, editing and/or indexing book MSS. Preparing reports, company histories, house journals, etc. Critical but constructive advice to writers. Lecture agents. Please write or phone first. Founded 1982.

SciText

18 Barton Close, Landrake, Saltash,
Cornwall PL12 5BA
tel/fax (01752) 851451
email bg@scitext.fsnet.co.uk
Contact Dr Brian Gee

Proofreading and editing in science, chemical and electrical engineering and the history of science and technology; IBM compatible PC. Founded 1988.

SfEP (Society for Editors and Proofreaders) – see page 478

Shelagh Furness

Hallgarth Farmhouse, The Hallgarth, Durham,
Co. Durham DH1 3BJ

tel 0191-384 3840
email sfurness543@aol.com

Research, editorial and information services. Experienced book and journal editor; online and library research; specialises in current affairs, geopolitics, environment and information systems. Founded 1992.

Small Print

The Old School House, 74 High Street, Swavesey,
Cambridge CB4 5QU
tel (01954) 231713 *fax* (01954) 205061
email info@smallprint.co.uk
website www.smallprint.co.uk
Proprietor Naomi Laredo

Editorial, design, page layout, project management, and audio production services for conventional or electronic publishing. Textbooks, manuals, travel guides, websites, newsletters. Translation from/to and editing in many European and Asian languages. Photography and picture research. Founded 1986.

Society of Indexers – see page 567

Special Edition Pre-press Services

Partners Romilly Hambling, 17 Almorah Road,
London N1 3ER
tel/fax 020-7226 5339
email mail@special-edition.co.uk
website www.special-edition.co.uk
and Corinne Orde, 2 Caledonian Wharf,
London E14 3EW
tel/fax 020-7987 9600

Integrated editing and page make-up for publishers of general and STM titles. Design and project management undertaken. See website for downloadable brochure. Established 1993.

SPREd (Society of Picture Researchers and Editors) – now the Picture Research Association, see page 471

StorytrackS

PO Box 3155, Glastonbury, Somerset BA16 0EJ
tel (01395) 279659
email storytracks@aol.com
website www.storytracks.net
Directors Marina Oliver, Margaret James, Chris Dukes

A team of widely published writers offer honest appraisals of MSS and comment on content and structure. Constructive guidance is based on extensive experience and sound market awareness. Fiction typescripts of publishable quality are guaranteed consideration by an appropriate editor or agent. Also offers ghostwriting services, advice on self-publishing and editorial assistance. Founded 2001.

Strand Editorial Services

16 Mitchley View, South Croydon, Surrey CR2 9HQ
tel 020-8657 1247 *fax* 020-8651 3525
Joint Principals Derek and Irene Bradley

Provide a comprehensive service to publishers, editorial departments, and public relations and advertising agencies. Proofreading and copy-editing a speciality. Founded 1974.

Success Writing Bureau

Thirsol House, Earby, Barnoldswick, Lancs BB18 6NE
tel/fax (01282) 842495
Contact John O'Toole

MSS appraisal with agency links where applicable. Home study courses in journalism/article writing, short story, radio, TV and novel writing. Speedy turnaround. John O'Toole tutorials since 1965; bureau founded 1980.

Tecmedia Ltd

Bruce House, 258 Bromham Road, Biddenham, Beds. MK40 4AA
tel (01234) 325223 *fax* (01234) 353524
email jojobaxter@cs.com
Managing Director J.D. Baxter

Specialists in the design, development and production of information packages, newsletters and promotional material. Founded 1972.

Teral Research Services

111 The Avenue, Bournemouth, Dorset BH9 2UX
tel (01202) 519220
45 Forest View Road, Bournemouth BH9 3BH
tel/fax (01202) 516834
Contact Alan C. Wood, Terry C. Treadwell

Research and consultancy on military aviation, army, navy, defence, space, weapons (new and antique), police, intelligence, medals, uniforms and armour. Founded 1980.

the Freelance Editorial Service

4 Cranston Drive, Cousland, Dalkeith, Midlothian EH22 2PP
tel 0131-663 1238
email williamhouston@amserve.com
Contact Bill Houston BSc, DipLib, MPhil

Editing, proofreading, indexing, abstracting, translations, bibliographies; particularly scientific and medical. Founded 1975.

The Literary Consultancy (TLC)

Diorama Arts Centre, 34 Osnaburgh Street, London NW1 3ND
tel/fax 020-7813 4330
email swifttlc@dircon.co.uk
website www.literaryconsultancy.co.uk
Director Rebecca Swift, *Administrator* Rebecca de Saintonge

Offers a detailed assessment of fiction, non-fiction and autobiography from a team of professional editors and writers. Fees based on length. Quick turnaround. Personal links with agents and publishers. Approved by the Arts Council England. Established 1996.

Thoughtbubble Ltd

58-60 Fitzroy Street, London W1T 5BU
tel 020-7387 8890 *fax* 020-7383 2220
email enquiries@thoughtbubble.com
website www.thoughtbubble.com
Contact James Maltby

Website design and development, database integration, Flash animation, audio/video editing and production, e-commerce, intranet design and development, software development, print design, CD-Rom design and production. Also presentation, training and website hosting. Founded 1997.

Vanessa Charles

38 Ham Common, Richmond, Surrey TW10 7JG
tel/fax 020-8940 9225
email 101361,1176@compuserve.com

Design and book production services. Founded 1975.

Victoria Ramsay

Abbots Rest, Chilbolton, Stockbridge, Hants SO20 6BE
tel (01264) 860251 *fax* (01264) 860026
email victoredit@supanet.com

Freelance editing, copy-editing and proofreading; non-fiction research and writing of promotional literature and pamphlets. Any non-scientific subject undertaken. Special interests: education, cookery, travel, Africa and Caribbean and works in translation. Established 1981.

WORDSmith

2 The Island, Thames Ditton, Surrey KT7 0SH
tel/fax 020-8339 0945
email ws@good-writing-matters.com
website www.good-writing-matters.com
Partners Michael Russell, Elaine Russell

Copy-editing on paper and onscreen: all areas including film scripts. Specialises in new writer fiction, rewriting and abridging. Also short-run publishing for new writing, as Riverside Press. No poetry. Founded 1984.

Wordwise

37 Elmthorpe Road, Wolvercote, Oxford OX2 8PA
tel (01865) 510098 *fax* (01865) 310556
email wordwise@mendes.demon.co.uk
Director Valerie Mendes

Specialises in creative writing projects for children and young adults. Founded 1990.

WordWise

66 Russell Road, Lee-on-the-Solent, Hants PO13 9HP
tel 023-9235 9960
email martyn@wordwise.co.uk
website www.wordwise.co.uk
Contact Martyn Yeo

For publishers only: typesetting, database maintenance, text processing, VBA programming. Specialist in directories and catalogues. Member of SfEP. Established 1984.

Write on...

62 Kiln Lane, Oxford OX3 8EY
tel/fax (01865) 744336
email Writeon1989@aol.com
Director Yvonne Newman

Non-fiction book planning workshops and one-to-one consultations. Send sae for details. Founded 1989.

The Writer's Helpline

tel (09061) 613005 (a premium rate service)
Director Jeff Kent

Offers professional guidance and advice to writers to help them perfect their writing, get into print and make money. An offshoot of Witan Books, established 1980.

The Writers' Exchange

14 Old School Mews, Bacup, Lancs. OL13 0QN
tel (01706) 877480
email writers'exchange@j-m-wright.freeserve.co.uk
website www.world-wide-words.co.uk
Secretary Mike Wright

Copywriting, ghostwriting, internet publishing and editorial services, including appraisal service for amateur writers preparing to submit material to literary agents/publishers. Offers 'constructive, objective evaluation service, particularly for those who cannot get past the standard rejection slip barrier, or who have had work rejected by publishers and need an impartial view of why it did not sell'. Novels, short stories, film, TV, radio and stage plays. Send sae for details. Founded 1977.

The Written Word

43 Green Lane, Beaumont, Lancaster LA1 2ES
tel/fax (01524) 35215
email steve@ashton01.freeserve.co.uk
Contact Steve Ashton

Script evaluation service (£45 articles, £120 for 3 chapters and synopsis of book). Editorial services by arrangement. Founded 1999.

Indexing

A good index is a joy to the user of a non-fiction book; a bad index will downgrade an otherwise good book. The function of indexes, together with the skills needed to compile them, are examined here.

An index is a detailed key to the contents of a document, in contrast to a contents list, which gives only the titles of the parts into which the document is divided (e.g. chapters). Precisely, an index is 'A systematic arrangement of entries designed to enable users to locate information in a document'. The document may be a book, a series of books, an issue of a periodical, a run of several volumes of a periodical, an audiotape, a map, a film, a picture, a CD-Rom, a website, an object, or any other information source in print or non-print form.

The objective of an index is to guide enquirers to information on given subjects in a document by providing the terms of their choice (single words, phrases, abbreviations, acronyms, dates, names, and so on) in an appropriately organised list which refers them to specific locations using page, column, section, frame, figure, table, paragraph, line or other appropriate numbers or hyperlinks.

An index differs from a catalogue, which is a record of the documents held in a particular collection, such as a library; though a catalogue may require an index, for example to guide searchers from subject words to class numbers.

A document may have separate indexes for different classes of heading, so that personal names are distinguished from subjects, for example, or a single index in which all classes of heading are interfiled.

The Society of Indexers

The Society of Indexers is a non-profit organisation founded in 1957 and is the only autonomous professional body for indexers in the UK. It is affiliated with the American Society of Indexers, the Australian Society of Indexers, the China Society of Indexers, the Indexing and Abstracting Society of Canada, and the Association of Southern African Indexers and Bibliographers, and has close ties with the Chartered Institute of Library and Information Professionals (CILIP) and the Society for Editors and Proofreaders (SfEP).

The main objectives of the Society are to promote all types of indexing standards and techniques and the role of indexers in the organisation of knowledge; to provide, promote and recognise facilities for both the initial and the further training of indexers; to establish criteria for assessing conformity to indexing standards; and to conduct research and publish guidance, ideas and information about indexing. It seeks to establish good relationships between indexers, librarians, publishers and authors, both to advance good indexing and to improve the role and wellbeing of indexers.

Services to indexers

The Society publishes a learned journal *The Indexer* (2 p.a.), a newsletter and *Occasional Papers in Indexing*. Local and special interest groups provide the chance for members to meet to discuss common interests, while email discussion lists have encouraged the development of a virtual community of indexers. A two-day conference is held every year. All levels of training are supported by regular workshops held at venues throughout the country.

Professional competence is recognised in two stages by the Society. Accredited Indexers who have completed the open-learning course qualification (see below) have shown

Further information

Society of Indexers
Blades Enterprise Centre, John Street,
Sheffield S2 4SU
tel 0114-292 2350 *fax* 0114-292 2351
email admin@indexers.org.uk
website www.indexers.org.uk
Administrator Wendy Burrow
Registrar Elizabeth Wallis *tel* 020-8940 4771
Membership £60 p.a. UK/Europe, £75 overseas;
£120 corporate

Contact the Administrator for further information.
Enquiries from publishers and authors seeking to
commission an indexer should be made to the
Registrar.

theoretical competence in indexing, while Registered Indexers have proved their experience and competence in practical indexing through a rigorous assessment procedure and admission to the Register of Indexers. The services of Registered Indexers are actively promoted by the Society while all trained and experienced members have the opportunity of an annual entry in *Indexers Available*, a directory published by the Society and distributed without charge to over 1000 publishers to help them find an indexer.

The Society sets annually recommended minimum rates for indexing (£16–£30 per hour; £1.20–£5 per page in 2003) and provides advice on the business side of indexing to its members.

Services to publishers and authors
Anyone who commissions indexes needs to be certain of engaging a professional indexer working to the highest standards and able to meet deadlines.

Indexers Available, now searchable on the Society's website, lists only qualified and experienced members of the Society and gives basic contact details, subject specialisms and indexing experience.

Advice on the selection of indexers is available from the Registrar, who may also be able to suggest names of professionals able to undertake related tasks such as thesaurus construction, terminology control or database indexing. The Registrar will also advise on relations with indexers.

The Society co-operates with CILIP in the award of the Wheatley Medal for an outstanding index.

Training in indexing
The Society's course (in printed and electronic format) is based on the principle of open learning with Units, tutorial support and formal tests all available separately so that individuals can learn in their own way and at their own pace. The Units cover four core subjects and contain practical exercises and self-administered tests. Members of the Society receive a substantial discount on the cost although anyone can purchase the Units. Only members of the Society can apply for the formal tests.

Further reading

British Standards Institution, *British Standard recommendations for examining documents, determining their subjects and selecting indexing terms,* (BS6529:1984)

International Standards Organisation, *Information and documentation – guidelines for the content, organization and presentation of indexes* (ISO 999:1996)

Correcting proofs

The following notes and table are extracted from BS 5261 Part 2: 1976 (1995) and are reproduced by permission of the British Standards Institution.

4 Marks for copy preparation and proof correction

4.1 The marks to be used for marking up copy for composition and for the correction of printers' proofs shall be as shown in Table 1 (see pages 571–80).

4.2 The marks in Table 1 are classified in three groups as follows:

(a) Group A: general.

(b) Group B: deletion, insertion and substitution.

(c) Group C: positioning and spacing.

Further information

British Standards Institution (BSI)
Technical Information Group,
389 Chiswick High Road, London W4 4AL
tel 020-8996 7111 *fax* 020-8996 7048
Customer Services tel 020-8996 9001
fax 020-8996 7001
email info@bsi.org.uk
website www.bsi.org.uk/

BSI is the independent national body responsible for preparing British Standards. It presents the UK view on standards in Europe and at the international level. It is incorporated by Royal Charter.

For a complete standard, contact Customer Services.

4.3 Each item in Table 1 is given a simple alpha-numeric serial number denoting the classification group to which it belongs and its position within the group.

4.4 The marks have been drawn keeping the shapes as simple as possible and using sizes which relate to normal practice. The shapes of the marks should be followed exactly by all who make use of them.

4.5 For each marking-up or proof correction instruction a distinct mark is to be made:

(a) in the text: to indicate the exact place to which the instruction refers;

(b) in the margin: to signify or amplify the meaning of the instruction.

It should be noted that some instructions have a combined textual and marginal mark.

4.6 Where a number of instructions occur in one line, the marginal marks are to be divided between the left and right margins where possible, the order being from left to right in both margins.

4.7 Specification details, comments and instructions may be written on the copy or proof to complement the textual and marginal marks. Such written matter is to be clearly distinguishable from the copy and from any corrections made to the proof. Normally this is done by encircling the matter and/or by the appropriate use of colour (see below).

4.8 Proof corrections shall be made in coloured ink thus:

(a) printer's literal errors marked by the printer for correction: green;

(b) printer's literal errors marked by the customer and his agents for correction: red;

(c) alterations and instructions made by the customer and his agents: black or dark blue.

5 Proofing procedure

5.1 The printer should supply the customer with proofs. The number of proofs required will depend upon the nature of the job and should be agreed between customer and printer.

5.2 One of the proofs to be supplied shall be the printer's marked proof on which he has marked literal errors and queries for the customer's attention. The printer should date and indicate the status of this proof, e.g. first galley proof, revised galley proof, page proof, etc.

5.3 The printer's marked proof shall be returned to the printer by the customer or his agent with all additional corrections marked on it, integrating those made by author, editor, designer, publisher, etc. It thus becomes a master reference for the next stage of the job.

5.4 The customer should keep a copy of the printer's marked proof, as returned to the printer, for his own reference.

5.5 Where the printer has drawn attention to any particular point on the printer's marked proof by means of a query (see Table 1, mark A4), it is essential that the appropriate authority should settle the query by writing a clear instruction on the proof or, if the matter is already correct, strike through the query.

5.6 The following additional information should be entered on the printer's marked proof before returning it:

(a) *Either* that a revised set of proofs is required (indicate whether these are to be supplied in galley/slip, page, imposed page or book form); *or* that the job is approved for press (indicate whether approval is subject to final corrections being made).

(b) The signature and status of the person who is returning the printer's marked proof.

(c) The date on which the printer's marked proof is returned to the printer; this clearly identifies the position of the proof in the production sequence.

Table 1. Classified list of marks

NOTE. The letters M and P in the notes column indicate marks for marking-up copy and for correcting proofs respectively.

Group A General

Number	Instruction	Textual mark	Marginal mark	Notes
A1	Correction is concluded	None	/	P Make after each correction
A2	Leave unchanged	‒ ‒ ‒ ‒ ‒ ‒ under characters to remain	Ⓙ	M P
A3	Remove extraneous marks	Encircle marks to be removed	✕	P e.g. film or paper edges visible between lines on bromide or diazo proofs
A3.1	Push down risen spacing material	Encircle blemish	⊥	P
A4	Refer to appropriate authority anything of doubtful accuracy	Encircle word(s) affected	(?)	P

Group B Deletion, insertion and substitution

B1	Insert in text the matter indicated in the margin	⋋	New matter followed by ⋋	M P Indentical to B2
B2	Insert additional matter identified by a letter in a diamond	⋋	⋋ Followed by for example ◈A	M P The relevant section of the copy should be supplied with the corresponding letter marked on it in a diamond e.g. ◈A
B3	Delete	/ through character(s) or ⊢———⊣ through words to be deleted	♪	M P
B4	Delete and close up	/ through character or ⊢———⊣ through characters e.g. charaᵃcter charaᵉᵉcter	♪	M P

Table 1 *(continued)*

Number	Instruction	Textual mark	Marginal mark	Notes
B5	Substitute character or substitute part of one or more word(s)	/ through character or ⊢——⊣ through word(s)	New character or new word(s)	M P
B6	Wrong fount. Replace by character(s) of correct fount	Encircle character(s) to be changed	⊗	P
B6.1	Change damaged character(s)	Encircle character(s) to be changed	✕	P This mark is identical to A3
B7	Set in or change to italic	——— under character(s) to be set or changed	⊔	M P Where space does not permit textual marks encircle the affected area instead
B8	Set in or change to capital letters	≡ under character(s) to be set or changed	≡	
B9	Set in or change to small capital letters	══ under character(s) to be set or changed	══	
B9.1	Set in or change to capital letters for initial letters and small capital letters for the rest of the words	≡ under initial letters and ══ under rest of the word(s)	≡	
B10	Set in or change to bold type	∿∿∿ under character(s) to be set or changed	∿	
B11	Set in or change to bold italic type	∿∿∿ under character(s) to be set or changed	⊔ ∿	
B12	Change capital letters to lower case letters	Encircle character(s) to be changed	≢	P For use when B5 is inappropriate

Table 1 *(continued)*

Number	Instruction	Textual mark	Marginal mark	Notes
B12.1	Change small capital letters to lower case letters	Encircle character(s) to be changed	≠	P For use when B5 is inappropriate
B13	Change italic to upright type	Encircle character(s) to be changed	⊔	P
B14	Invert type	Encircle character to be inverted	○	P
B15	Substitute or insert character in 'superior' position	/ through character or ∧ where required	˥ under character e.g. ˨	P
B16	Substitute or insert character in 'inferior' position	/ through character or ∧ where required	L over character e.g. L₂	P
B17	Substitute ligature e.g. ffi for separate letters	⊢———⊣ through characters affected	⌣ e.g. ffi	P
B17.1	Substitute separate letters for ligature	⊢———⊣	Write out separate letters	P
B18	Substitute or insert full stop or decimal point	/ through character or ∧ where required	⊙	M P
B18.1	Substitute or insert colon	/ through character or ∧ where required	⊙	M P
B18.2	Substitute or insert semi-colon	/ through character or ∧ where required	؛	M P

Table 1 *(continued)*

Number	Instruction	Textual mark		Marginal mark	Notes
B18.3	Substitute or insert comma	/	through character	,	M P
		or			
		⋏	where required		
B18.4	Substitute or insert apostrophe	/	through character	𝟋	M P
		or			
		⋏	where required		
B18.5	Substitute or insert single quotation marks	/	through character	and/or	M P
		or			
		⋏	where required		
B18.6	Substitute or insert double quotation marks	/	through character	and/or	M P
		or			
		⋏	where required		
B19	Substitute or insert ellipsis	/	through character	• • •	M P
		or			
		⋏	where required		
B20	Substitute or insert leader dots	/	through character	(• • •)	M P Give the measure of the leader when necessary
		or			
		⋏	where required		
B21	Substitute or insert hyphen	/	through character	⊢⊣	M P
		or			
		⋏	where required		
B22	Substitute or insert rule	/	through character	⊢—⊣	M P Give the size of the rule in the marginal mark e.g. ⊢1 em⊣ ⊢4 mm⊣
		⋏	where required		

Table 1 *(continued)*

Number	Instruction	Textual mark	Marginal mark	Notes
B23	Substitute or insert oblique	/ through character or ⅄ where required	⊘	M P

Group C Positioning and spacing

Number	Instruction	Textual mark	Marginal mark	Notes
C1	Start new paragraph			M P
C2	Run on (no new paragraph)			M P
C3	Transpose characters or words	between characters or words, numbered when necessary		M P
C4	Transpose a number of characters or words	**3 2 1** | | |	**1 2 3**	M P To be used when the sequence cannot be clearly indicated by the use of C3. The vertical strokes are made through the characters or words to be transposed and numbered in the correct sequence
C5	Transpose lines			M P
C6	Transpose a number of lines		——— 3 ——— 2 ——— 1	P To be used when the sequence cannot be clearly indicated by C5. Rules extend from the margin into the text with each line to be transposed numbered in the correct sequence
C7	Centre	⌈enclosing matter⌉ ⌊to be centred⌋	[ ]	M P
C8	Indent			P Give the amount of the indent in the marginal mark

Table 1 (continued)

Number	Instruction	Textual mark	Marginal mark	Notes
C9	Cancel indent			P
C10	Set line justified to specified measure	and/or		P Give the exact dimensions when necessary
C11	Set column justified to specified measure			M P Give the exact dimensions when necessary
C12	Move matter specified distance to the right	enclosing matter to be moved to the right		P Give the exact dimensions when necessary
C13	Move matter specified distance to the left	enclosing matter to be moved to the left		P Give the exact dimensions when necessary
C14	Take over character(s), word(s) or line to next line, column or page			P The textual mark surrounds the matter to be taken over and extends into the margin
C15	Take back character(s), word(s), or line to previous line, column or page			P The textual mark surrounds the matter to be taken back and extends into the margin
C16	Raise matter	over matter to be raised under matter to be raised		P Give the exact dimensions when necessary. (Use C28 for insertion of space between lines or paragraphs in text)
C17	Lower matter	over matter to be lowered under matter to be lowered		P Give the exact dimensions when necessary. (Use C29 for reduction of space between lines or paragraphs in text)
C18	Move matter to position indicated	Enclose matter to be moved and indicate new position		P Give the exact dimensions when necessary

Table 1 *(continued)*

Number	Instruction	Textual mark	Marginal mark	Notes
C19	Correct vertical alignment			P
C20	Correct horizontal alignment	Single line above and below misaligned matter e.g. mi$_s$align$_e$d		P The marginal mark is placed level with the head and foot of the relevant line
C21	Close up. Delete space between characters or words	linking ⌣ characters	⌣	M P
C22	Insert space between characters	between characters affected	Y	M P Give the size of the space to be inserted when necessary
C23	Insert space between words	between words affected	Y	M P Give the size of the space to be inserted when necessary
C24	Reduce space between characters	between characters affected	⋔	M P Give the amount by which the space is to be reduced when necessary
C25	Reduce space between words	between words affected	⋔	M P Give amount by which the space is to be reduced when necessary
C26	Make space appear equal between characters or words	between characters or words affected	Ⴋ	M P
C27	Close up to normal interline spacing	(each side of column linking lines)		M P The textual marks extend into the margin

Marked galley proof of text

At the sign of the red pale

The Life and Work of William Caxton, by H W Larken

[An Extract]

Few people, even in the field of printing, have any clear conception of what William Caxton did or, indeed, of what he was. Much of this lack of knowledge is due to the absence of information that can be counted as factual and the consequent tendency to vague generalization.

Though it is well known that Caxton was born in the county of Kent, there is no information as to the precise place. In his prologue to the *History of Troy*, William Caxton wrote 'for in France I was never and was born and learned my English in Kent in the Weald where I doubt not is spoken as broad and rude English as in any place of England.' During the fifteenth century there were a great number of Flemish cloth weavers in Kent; most of them had come to England at the instigation of Edward III with the object of teaching their craft to the English. So successful was this venture that the English cloth trade flourished and the agents who sold the cloth (the mercers) became very wealthy people. There have been many speculations concerning the origin of the Caxton family and much research has been carried out. It is assumed often that Caxton's family must have been connected with the wool trade in order to have secured his apprenticeship to an influential merchant.

W. Blyth Crotch (Prologues and Epilogues of William Caxton) suggests that the origin of the name Caxton (of which there are several variations in spelling) may be traced to Cambridgeshire but notes that many writers have suggested that Caxton was connected with a family at Hadlow or alternatively a family in Canterbury.

Of the Canterbury connection a William Caxton became freeman of the City in 1431 and William Pratt, a mercer who was the printer's friend, was born there. H. R. Plomer suggests that Pratt and Caxton might possibly have been schoolboys together, perhaps at the school St. Alphege. In this parish there lived a John Caxton who used as his mark three cakes over a barrel (or tun) and who is mentioned in an inscription on a monument in the church of St. Alphege.

In 1941, Alan Keen (an authority on manuscripts) secured some documents concerning Caxton; these are now in the British Museum. Discovered in the library of Earl Winterton at Shillinglee Park by Richard Holworthy, the documents cover the period 1420 to 1467. One of Winterton's ancestors purchased the manor of West Wratting from a family named Caxton, the property being situated in the Weald of Kent.

There is also record of a property mentioning Philip Caxton and his wife Dennis who had two sons, Philip (born in 1413) and William.

Particularly interesting in these documents is one recording that Philip Caxton junior sold the manor of Little Wratting to John Christemasse of London in 1436, the deed having been witnessed by two aldermen, one of whom was Robert Large, the printer's employer. Further, in 1439 the other son, William Caxton, conveyed Wratting to John Christemasse, and an indenture of 1457 concerning this property mentions one William Caxton conveyed his rights in the manor Bluntes Hall at Little alias Causton. It is an interesting coincidence to note that the lord of the manor of Little Wratting was the father of Margaret, Duchess of Burgundy.

In 1420, a Thomas Caxton of Tenterden witnessed the will of a fellow townsman; he owned property in Kent and appears to have been a person of some importance.

¹ See 'William Caxton'.

Ⓐ *attached to Christchurch Monastery in the parish of*

AT THE SIGN OF THE RED PALE

The Life and Work of William Caxton, *by H W Larken*

An Extract

FEW PEOPLE, even in the field of printing, have any clear conception of what William Caxton did or, indeed, of what he was. Much of this lack of knowledge is due to the absence of information that can be counted as factual and the consequent tendency to vague generalisation.

Though it is well known that Caxton was born in the county of Kent, there is no information as to the precise place. In his prologue to the *History of Troy*, William Caxton wrote '. . . for in France I was never and was born and learned my English in Kent in the Weald where I doubt not is spoken as broad and rude English as in any place of England.'

During the fifteenth century there were a great number of Flemish cloth weavers in Kent; most of them had come to England at the instigation of Edward III with the object of teaching their craft to the English. So successful was this venture that the English cloth trade flourished and the agents who sold the cloth (the mercers) became very wealthy people.

There have been many speculations concerning the origin of the Caxton family and much research has been carried out. It is often assumed that Caxton's family must have been connected with the wool trade in order to have secured his apprenticeship to an influential merchant.

W. Blyth Crotch (*Prologues and Epilogues of William Caxton*) suggests that the origin of the name Caxton (of which there are several variations in spelling) may be traced to Cambridgeshire but notes that many writers have suggested that Caxton was connected with a family at Hadlow or alternatively a family in Canterbury.

Of the Canterbury connection: a William Caxton became freeman of the City in 1431 and William Pratt, a mercer who was the printer's friend, was born there. H. R. Plomer[1] suggests that Pratt and Caxton might possibly have been schoolboys together, perhaps at the school attached to Christchurch Monastery in the parish of St. Alphege. In this parish there lived a John Caxton who used as his mark three cakes over a barrel (or tun) and who is mentioned in an inscription on a monument in the church of St. Alphege.

In 1941, Alan Keen (an authority on manuscripts) secured some documents concerning Caxton; these are now in the British Museum. Discovered in the library of Earl Winterton at Shillinglee Park by Richard Holworthy, the documents cover the period 1420 to 1467. One of Winterton's ancestors purchased the manor of West Wratting from a family named Caxton, the property being situated in the Weald of Kent. There is also record of a property mentioning Philip Caxton and his wife Dennis who had two sons, Philip (born in 1413) and William.

Particularly interesting in these documents is one recording that Philip Caxton junior sold the manor of Little Wratting to John Christemasse of London in 1436—the deed having been witnessed by two aldermen, one of whom was Robert Large, the printer's employer. Further, in 1439, the other son, William Caxton, conveyed his rights in the manor Bluntes Hall at Little Wratting to John Christemasse, and an indenture of 1457 concerning this property mentions one William Caxton alias Causton. It is an interesting coincidence to note that the lord of the manor of Little Wratting was the father of Margaret, Duchess of Burgundy.

In 1420, a Thomas Caxton of Tenterden witnessed the will of a fellow townsman; he owned property in Kent and appears to have been a person of some importance.

[1] See 'William Caxton'.

Table 1 *(continued)*

Number	Instruction	Textual mark	Marginal mark	Notes
C28	Insert space between lines or paragraphs	or		M P The marginal mark extends between the lines of text. Give the size of the space to be inserted when necessary
C29	Reduce space between lines or paragraphs	or		M P The marginal mark extends between the lines of text. Give the amount by which the space is to be reduced when necessary

Government offices and public services

Enquiries to any of the following bodies should be sent to the Public Relations Officer, accompanied by a sae. The names and addresses of many other public bodies can be found in *Whitaker's Almanack*.

Advertising Standards Authority
2 Torrington Place, London WC1E 7HW
tel 020-7580 5555 *fax* 020-7631 3051
email enquiries@asa.org.uk
website www.asa.org.uk

American Embassy
24 Grosvenor Square, London W1A 1AE
tel 020-7499 9000
website www.usembassy.org.uk

Apsley House, The Wellington Museum
Hyde Park Corner, London W1J 7NT
tel 020-7499 5676 *fax* 020-7493 6576
website www.apsleyhouse.org.uk

Open Tues–Sun, 11am–5pm.

Arts Council England – see page 444

Arts Council of Northern Ireland – see page 445

Arts Council of Wales – see page 445

Australian High Commission
Australia House, Strand, London WC2B 4LA
tel 020-7379 4334 *fax* 020-7240 5333
website www.australia.org.uk

Austrian Embassy
18 Belgrave Mews West, London SW1X 8HU
tel 020-7235 3731 *fax* 020-7344 0292
email embassy@austria.org.uk
website www.austria.org.uk
Austrian Cultural Forum, 28 Rutland Gate, London SW7 1PQ
tel 020-7584 8653 *fax* 020-7225 0470
email culture@austria.org.uk

The Bank of England
Threadneedle Street, London EC2R 8AH
tel 020-7601 4444 *fax* 020-7601 4771
website www.bankofengland.co.uk

Belgian Embassy
103 Eaton Square, London SW1W 9AB
tel 020-7470 3700 *fax* 020-7259 6213
email info@belgium-embassy.co.uk
website www.belgium-embassy.co.uk

Bodleian Library
Oxford OX1 3BG
tel (01865) 277000 *fax* (01865) 277182
email enquiries@bodley.ox.ac.uk
website www.bodley.ox.ac.uk

British Board of Film Classification
3 Soho Square, London W1D 3HD
tel 020-7440 1570 *fax* 020-7287 0141
email webmaster@bbfc.co.uk
website www.bbfc.co.uk
Director Robin Duval

British Broadcasting Corporation
Broadcasting House, London W1A 1AA
tel 020-7580 4468
website www.bbc.co.uk

The British Council – see page 450

British Film Commission
10 Little Portland Street, London W1W 7JG
tel 020-7861 7860 *fax* 020-7861 7864
email info@bfc.co.uk
website www.bfc.co.uk

British Film Institute – see page 450

The British Library
96 Euston Road, London NW1 2DB
tel 020-7412 7332 *fax* 020-7412 7340
website www.bl.uk

British Library Document Supply
Boston Spa, Wetherby, West Yorkshire LS23 7BQ
tel (01937) 546060 *fax* (01937) 546333
email dsc-customer-services@bl.uk
website www.bl.uk

British Library Newspaper Library
Colindale Avenue, London NW9 5HE
tel 020-7412 7353 *fax* 020-7412 7379
email newspaper@bl.uk
website www.bl.uk/collections/newspaper/

British Museum
Great Russell Street, London WC1B 3DG
tel 020-7323 8000
email information@thebritishmuseum.ac.uk
website www.thebritishmuseum.ac.uk

British Railways Board – see Strategic Rail Authority

British Standards Institution
Technical Information Group,
389 Chiswick High Road, London W4 4AL
tel 020-8996 7111 *fax* 020-8996 7048
email info@bsi.org.uk
website www.bsi.org.uk/

British Tourist Authority
Thames Tower, Black's Road, London W6 9EL
tel 020-8846 9000 *fax* 020-8563 0302
websites www.visitbritain.com
www.britishtouristauthority.org

Broadcasting Standards Commission – see The Office of Communications

The Cabinet Office
70 Whitehall, London SW1A 2AS
tel 020-7276 1234
website www.cabinet-office.gov.uk

Cadw: Welsh Historic Monuments
Crown Building, Cathays Park, Cardiff CF10 3NQ
tel 029-2050 0200 *fax* 029-2082 6375
email cadw@wales.gsi.gov.uk
website www.cadw.wales.gov.uk

Canadian High Commission
Cultural Affairs Section, Canada House,
Trafalgar Square, London SW1Y 5BJ
tel 020-7258 6412 *fax* 020-7258 6434
Contact Literature Officer

Central Office of Information – see COI Communications

Centre for Information on Language Teaching and Research (CILT)
20 Bedfordbury, London WC2N 4LB
tel 020-7379 5101 *fax* 020-7379 5082
email library@cilt.org.uk
website www.cilt.org.uk

Charity Commission
Harmsworth House, 13-15 Bouverie Street,
London EC4Y 8DP
tel (0870) 3330123, *minicom* (0870) 3330125
fax 020-7674 2300
email feedback@charitycommission.gsi.gov.uk
website www.charitycommission.gsi.gov.uk
2nd Floor, 20 King's Parade, Queen's Dock,
Liverpool L3 4DQ
tel (0870) 3330123 *fax* 0151-703 1555
Woodfield House, Tangier, Taunton TA1 4BL
tel (0870) 3330123 *fax* (01823) 345003

The Coal Authority
200 Lichfield Lane, Mansfield, Notts. NG18 4RG
tel (01623) 427162 *fax* (01623) 622072
email thecoalauthority@coal.gov.uk
website www.coal.gov.uk

COI Communications
Hercules House, Hercules Road, London SE1 7DU
tel 020-7928 2345

College of Arms (or Heralds' College)
Queen Victoria Street, London EC4V 4BT
tel 020-7248 2762 *fax* 020-7248 6448
email enquiries@college-of-arms.gov.uk
website www.college-of-arms.gov.uk

Commission for Architecture and the Built Environment (CABE)

The Tower Building, 11 York Road,
London SE1 7NX
tel 020-7960 2400 *fax* 020-7960 2444
email enquiries@cabe.org.uk
website www.cabe.org.uk

Commission for Racial Equality

St Dunstan's House, 201 Borough High Street,
London SE1 1GZ
tel 020-7939 0000 *fax* 020-7939 0004
website www.cre.gov.uk

Committee on Standards in Public Life

35 Great Smith Street, London SW1P 3BQ
tel 020-7276 2595 *fax* 020-7276 2585
email nigel.wicks@gtnet.gov.uk
website www.public-standards.gov.uk

Commonwealth Secretariat

Marlborough House, Pall Mall, London SW1Y 5HX
tel 020-7747 6200 *fax* 020-7930 6128
email info@commonwealth.int
website www.thecommonwealth.org

Competition Commission

(formerly Monopolies and Mergers Commission)
New Court, 48 Carey Street,
London WC2A 2JT
tel 020-7271 0243 *fax* 020-7271 0367
email info@competition-commission.org.uk
website www.competition-commission.org.uk

Contributions Agency, International Services (InS) – see The Inland Revenue

Copyright Directorate – see Patent Office

Copyright Tribunal

Room 1/8, Harmsworth House,
13-15 Bouverie Street, London EC4Y 8DP
tel 020-7596 6510 *textphone* (08459) 222250
fax 020-7596 6526
email copyright.tribunal@patent.gov.uk
website www.patent.gov.uk/copy/tribunal/index.htm

Corporation of London Records Office

Guildhall, London EC2P 2EJ
tel 020-7332 1251 *fax* 020-7710 8682
email CLRO@corpoflondon.gov.uk
website www.cityoflondon.gov.uk/archives/clro

Corporation of Trinity House

Tower Hill, London EC3N 4DH
tel 020-7481 6900 *fax* 020-7480 7662
email howard.cooper@thls.org
website www.trinityhouse.co.uk

Countryside Agency

John Dower House, Crescent Place, Cheltenham,
Glos. GL50 3RA
tel (01242) 521381 *fax* (01242) 584270
website www.countryside.gov.uk

Court of the Lord Lyon

HM New Register House, Edinburgh EH1 3YT
tel 0131-556 7255 *fax* 0131-557 2148

Crafts Council

Resource Centre, 44A Pentonville Road,
London N1 9BY
tel 020-7806 2501 *fax* 020-7833 4479
email reference@craftscouncil.org.uk
website www.craftscouncil.org.uk

Cyprus High Commission

93 Park Street, London W1K 7ET
tel 020-7499 8272 *fax* 020-7491 0691
email cyphclondon@dial.pipex.com
presscounsellor@chclondon.org.uk (press office)
website www.cyprus.gov.cy

DEFRA (Department for Environment, Food and Rural Affairs)

3-8 Whitehall Place, London SW1A 2HH
tel 020-7270 8000 *Helpline* (0845) 9335577
fax 020-7270 8419
website www.defra.gov.uk

Department for Culture, Media and Sport

2-4 Cockspur Street, London SW1Y 5DH
tel 020-7211 6200
email enquiries@culture.gov.uk
website www.culture.gov.uk

Department for Education and Skills

Sanctuary Buildings, Great Smith Street,
London SW1P 3BT
tel (0870) 000 2288 *minicom* (01928) 794274
fax (01928) 794248
email info@dfes.gsi.gov.uk
website www.dfes.gov.uk

Department of Health

Richmond House, 79 Whitehall, London SW1A 2NS
tel 020-7210 3000
website www.doh.gov.uk

Department of Social Security – see DWP (Department for Work and Pensions)

Design Council

34 Bow Street, London WC2E 7DL
tel 020-7420 5200 *fax* 020-7420 5300
email info@designcouncil.org.uk
website www.designcouncil.org.uk

DFID (Department for International Development)

1 Palace Street, London SW1E 5HE
tel 020-7023 0000
email enquiry@dfid.gov.uk
website www.dfid.gov.uk
Abercrombie House, Eaglesham Road,
East Kilbride, Glasgow G75 8EA
tel (01355) 844000
Public Enquiry Point tel (0845) 300 4100 (local rate)
tel (01355) 843132 (for enquiries from overseas)

DTI (Department of Trade and Industry)

1 Victoria Street, London SW1H 0ET
tel 020-7215 5000 (general enquiries)
minicom/textphone 020-7215 6740 *fax* 020-7215 0105
website www.dti.gov.uk

DTLR (Department of Transport, Local Government and the Regions)

Eland House, Bressenden Place, London SW1E 5DU
Great Minster House, 76 Marsham Street,
London SW1P 4DR
Ashdown House, 123 Victoria Street,
London SW1E 6DE
tel 020-7944 3000
website www.dtlr.gov.uk

DWP (Department for Work and Pensions)

Richmond House, 79 Whitehall, London SW1A 2NS
tel 020-7238 0800

Economic and Social Research Council

Polaris House, North Star Avenue, Swindon,
Wilts. SN2 1UJ
tel (01793) 413000 *fax* (01793) 413130
email exrel@esrc.ac.uk
website www.esrc.ac.uk

Embassy of Bosnia and Herzegovina

5-7 Lexham Gardens, London W8 5JJ
tel 020-7373 0867 *fax* 020-7373 0871

Embassy of Finland

38 Chesham Place, London SW1X 8HW
tel 020-7838 6200 *fax* 020-7235 3680 (general)
020-7259 5602 (press and information office)
website www.finemb.org.uk

Embassy of Greece

Press and Information Office, 1A Holland Park,
London W11 3TP
tel 020-7727 3071 *fax* 020-7727 8960
email pressoffice@greekembassy.org.uk

Embassy of Ireland

17 Grosvenor Place, London SW1X 7HR
tel 020-7235 2171 *fax* 020-7245 6961

Passport and Visa Office Montpelier House,
106 Brompton Road, London SW3 1JJ
tel 020-7225 7700 *fax* 020-7225 7777/8

Embassy of Israel

2 Palace Green, London W8 4QB
tel 020-7957 9500 *fax* 020-7957 9555
email info-assist@london.mfa.gov.il
website www.israel-embassy.org.uk

Embassy of Japan

101-104 Piccadilly, London W1J 7JT
tel 020-7465 6500 *fax* 020-7491 9348 (information)
020-7491 9348 (visa section)
email info@embjapan.org.uk
website www.uk.emb-japan.go.jp

Embassy of Luxembourg

27 Wilton Crescent, London SW1X 8SD
tel 020-7235 6961 *fax* 020-7235 9734

Embassy of Romania

4 Palace Green, London W8 4QD
tel 020-7937 9666 *fax* 020-7937 8069
email romania@roemb.demon.uk.co

Embassy of Serbia and Montenegro

28 Belgrave Square, London SW1X 8QB
tel 020-7235 9049 *fax* 020-7235 7092
email londre@jugisek.demon.co.uk
website www.yugoslavembassy.org.uk

Embassy of Slovenia

10 Little College Street, London SW1P 3SH
tel 020-7222 5400 *fax* 020-7222 5277
email vlo@mzz-dkp.gov.si

Embassy of Sweden

11 Montagu Place, London W1H 2AL
tel 020-7917 6400 *fax* 020-7917 6477
email embassy@swednet.org.uk
website www.swedish-embassy.org.uk

Embassy of the Czech Republic

26 Kensington Palace Gardens, London W8 4QY
tel 020-7243 1115 *fax* 020-7727 9654
email london@embassy.mzv.cz
website www.czechembassy.org.uk

Embassy of the Republic of Bulgaria

186-188 Queen's Gate, London SW7 5HL
tel 020-7584 9400/9433, 020-7581 3144 (5 lines)
fax 020-7584 4948
email bgembasy@globalnet.co.uk

Embassy of the Republic of Croatia

21 Conway Street, London W1T 6BN
tel 020-7387 1790 *fax* 020-7387 3289

Embassy of the Republic of Hungary
35 Eaton Place, London SW1X 8BY
tel 020-7235 5218 *fax* 020-7823 1348
email office@huemblon.org.uk
website www.huemblon.org.uk

Embassy of the Republic of Poland
47 Portland Place, London W1B 1JH
tel (0870) 774 2700 *fax* 020-7291 3575
email polishembassy@polishembassy.org.uk
website www.home.btclick.com/polishembassy/
index.htm
Polish Cultural Institute, 34 Portland Place,
London W1B 1HQ
tel (0870) 7742 900 *fax* 020-7637 2190
email pci@polishculture.org.uk
website www.polishculture.org.uk

Embassy of the Russian Federation
13 Kensington Palace Gardens,
London W8 4QX
tel 020-7229 2666 *fax* 020-7727 8625
email office@rusemblon.org
website www.great-britain.mid.ru

Embassy of the Slovak Republic
25 Kensington Palace Gardens,
London W8 4QY
tel 020-7313 6470 *fax* 020-7313 6481
email mail@slovakembassy.co.uk

Engineering and Physical Sciences Research Council
Polaris House, North Star Avenue, Swindon,
Wilts. SN2 1ET
tel (01793) 444000
email infoline@epsrc.ac.uk
website www.epsrc.ac.uk
Press Officer Jane Reck *tel* (01793) 444312
email jane.reck@epsrc.ac.uk

English Heritage
23 Savile Row, London W1S 2ET
tel 020-7973 3000 *fax* 020-7973 3001
website www.english-heritage.org.uk

The Environment Agency
Head Office Rio House, Waterside Drive,
Aztec West, Almondsbury, Bristol BS32 4UD
tel (01454) 624400 *fax* (01454) 624409
website www.environment-agency.gov.uk

Equal Opportunities Commission
Arndale House, Arndale Centre,
Manchester M4 3EQ
tel (0845) 601 5901 *fax* 0161-838 8303
email info@eoc.org.uk
website www.eoc.org.uk

The European Commission
8 Storey's Gate, London SW1P 3AT
tel 020-7973 1992 *fax* 020-7973 1900
email eu-uk-press@cec.eu.int
website www.cec.org.uk

European Parliament
UK Office 2 Queen Anne's Gate,
London SW1H 9AA
tel 020-7227 4300 *fax* 020-7227 4302
library fax 020-7227 4301
email eplondon@europarl.eu.int
website www.europarl.org.uk

European Parliament Office in Scotland
The Tun, 4 Jackson's Entry, Holyrood Road,
Edinburgh EH8 8PJ
tel 0131-557 7866 *fax* 0131-557 4977
email epedinburgh@europarl.eu.int

Foreign and Commonwealth Office
King Charles Street, London SW1A 2AH
tel 020-7270 3000
website www.fco.gov.uk

Forestry Commission
Silvan House, 231 Corstorphine Road,
Edinburgh EH12 7AT
tel 0131-334 0303 *fax* 0131-334 4473
email info@forestry.gov.uk
website www.forestry.gov.uk

French Embassy
58 Knightsbridge, London SW1X 7JT
tel 020-7073 1000
email box.office@ambafrance.org.uk
website www.institut-francais.org.uk
Cultural Department 23 Cromwell Road,
London SW7 2EL
tel 020-7073 1300

German Embassy
23 Belgrave Square, London SW1X 8PZ
tel 020-7824 1300 *fax* 020-7824 1435
email mail@german-embassy.org.uk
website www.german-embassy.org.uk

Hayward Gallery
Belvedere Road, London SE1 8XZ
tel 020-7960 5226 *fax* 020-7401 2664
website www.hayward.org.uk

Health and Safety Executive Infoline
Caerphilly Business Park, Caerphilly CF83 3GG
tel (08701) 545500 *minicom* (02920) 808537
fax (02920) 859260
email hseinformationservices@natbrit.com
website www.hse.gov.uk

High Commission of India, Press & Information Wing

India House, Aldwych, London WC2B 4NA
tel 020-7836 8484 ext 147, 286, 327
fax 020-7836 2632
email 106167.1470@compuserve.com

High Commission of the Democratic Socialist Republic of Sri Lanka

13 Hyde Park Gardens, London W2 2LU
tel 020-7262 1841 *fax* 020-7262 7970

Historic Scotland

Longmore House, Salisbury Place,
Edinburgh EH9 1SH
tel 0131-668 8600 *fax* 0131-668 8699
website www.historic-scotland.gov.uk

Historical Manuscripts Commission – see the National Archives

HM Land Registry

Lincoln's Inn Fields, London WC2A 3PH
tel 020-7917 8894 *fax* 020-7917 5934
email michele.bennett@landreg.gsi.gov.uk
website www.landreg.gov.uk
Head of Communications Mrs M. Bennett

HM Treasury

Parliament Street, London SW1P 3AG
tel 020-7270 5000 *Press Office tel* 020-7270 5238
fax 020-7270 5244
website www.hm-treasury.gov.uk

HMSO Books – see The Stationery Office

Home Office

Queen Anne's Gate, London SW1H 9AT
tel 020-7273 3757
Director, Communication B. Butler

Housing Corporation

Maple House, 149 Tottenham Court Road,
London W1T 7BN
tel 020-7393 2000 *fax* 020-7393 2111
email enquiries@housingcorp.gsx.gov.uk
website www.housingcorp.gov.uk

Information Commissioner's Office

(formerly Office of the Data Protection
Commissioner)
Wycliffe House, Water Lane, Wilmslow,
Cheshire SK9 5AF
tel (01625) 545745 (enquiries),
(01625) 545700 (switchboard) *fax* (01625) 524510
email data@dataprotection.gov.uk
website www.informationcommissioner.gov.uk

The Inland Revenue

Visitors Centre, Ground Floor, SW Wing,
Bush House, Strand, London WC2B 4RD
tel 020-7438 6420/5
website www.inlandrevenue.gov.uk
Inland Revenue, Centre for Non-Residents
(Newcastle), Benton Park View, Longbenton,
Newcastle upon Tyne NE98 1ZZ
tel 0191-225 4811 *fax* 0191-225 0067
email internationalservices.ir.sbg@ir.gsi.gov.uk
Contact Inland Revenue, Centre for Non-Residents
(Newcastle) for queries about working abroad and
paying National Insurance contributions.

International Pension Centre

Tyneview Park, Whitley Road,
Newcastle upon Tyne NE98 1BA
tel 0191-218 7878
email tvp-customer-care@dwp.gsi.gov.uk

Italian Embassy

14 Three Kings Yard, Davies Street,
London W1K 4EH
tel 020-7312 2200 *fax* 020-7312 2230
email emblondon@embitaly.org.uk
website www.embitaly.org.uk

Law Commission

Conquest House, 37-38 John Street,
Theobalds Road, London WC1N 2BQ
tel 020-7453 1220 *fax* 020-7453 1297
email secretary@lawcommission.gsi.gov.uk
website www.lawcom.gov.uk
Covers England and Wales.

The Legal Deposit Office

The British Library, Boston Spa, Wetherby,
West Yorkshire LS23 7BY
tel (01937) 546267/546268 *fax* (01937) 546176

Legal Services Commission

(formerly Legal Aid Board)
85 Gray's Inn Road, London WC1X 8TX
tel 020-7759 0000
website www.legalservices.gov.uk

Malta High Commission

Malta House, 36-38 Piccadilly,
London W1J 0LE
tel 020-7292 4800 *fax* 020-7734 1831
website www.foreign.gov.mt/london

Medical Research Council

20 Park Crescent, London W1B 1AL
tel 020-7636 5422 *fax* 020-7436 6179
email firstname.surname@headoffice.mrc.ac.uk
website www.mrc.ac.uk

Millennium Commission
Portland House, Stag Place, London SW1E 5EZ
tel 020-7880 2001 *fax* 020-7880 2000
email info@millennium.gov.uk
website www.millennium.gov.uk

Ministry of Agriculture, Fisheries and Food – see DEFRA (Department for Environment, Food and Rural Affairs)

Ministry of Defence
Northumberland House, Northumberland Avenue,
London WC2N 5BP
tel 020-7218 9000
website www.mod.uk/

Monopolies and Mergers Commission – now Competition Commission

Museum of London
London Wall, London EC2Y 5HN
tel 020-7600 3699 *fax* 020-7600 1058
email info@museumoflondon.org
website www.museumoflondon.org

The National Archives
Ruskin Avenue, Kew, Richmond, Surrey TW9 4DU
tel 020-8876 3444 *fax* 020-8878 8905
email enquiry@nationalarchives.gov.uk
website www.nationalarchives.gov.uk

The National Archives of Scotland
HM General Register House, Edinburgh EH1 3YY
tel 0131-535 1314 *fax* 0131-535 1360
email enquiries@nas.gov.uk
website www.nas.gov.uk

National Assembly for Wales
Public Information and Education Services,
Cardiff Bay, Cardiff CF99 1NA
tel 029-2089 8200
email Assembly.Info@wales.gsi.gov.uk
website www.wales.gov.uk

National Audit Office
157-197 Buckingham Palace Road,
London SW1W 9SP
tel 020-7798 7000 *fax* 020-7798 7070
email enquiries@nao.gsi.gov.uk
Audit House, 23-24 Park Place, Cardiff CF1 3BA
tel 029-2037 8661 *fax* 029-2067 8501

National Consumer Council
20 Grosvenor Gardens, London SW1W 0DH
tel 020-7730 3469 *fax* 020-7730 0191
email info@ncc.org.uk
website www.ncc.org.uk

National Council for Vocational Qualifications (NCVQ) – see Qualifications and Curriculum Authority

National Galleries of Scotland
National Gallery of Scotland
The Mound, Edinburgh EH2 2EL
Scottish National Portrait Gallery
1 Queen Street, Edinburgh EH2 1JD
Scottish National Gallery of Modern Art
Belford Road, Edinburgh EH4 3DR
The Dean Gallery Belford Road,
Edinburgh EH4 3DS
tel 0131-624 6200, 0131-624 6332 (press office)
fax 0131-343 3250 (press office)
email pressinfo@nationalgalleries.org
website www.nationalgalleries.org

National Gallery
Trafalgar Square, London WC2N 5DN
tel 020-7747 2885 *fax* 020-7747 2423
email information@ng-london.org.uk
website www.nationalgallery.org.uk

National Library of Scotland
George IV Bridge, Edinburgh EH1 1EW
tel 0131-226 4531 *fax* 0131-622 4803
email enquiries@nls.uk
website www.nls.uk

The National Library of Wales
Aberystwyth, Ceredigion SY23 3BU
email holi@llgc.org.uk
website www.llgc.org.uk

National Lottery Commission
101 Wigmore Street, London W1U 1QU
tel 020-7016 3400 *fax* 020-7016 3464
email publicaffairs@natlotcomm.gov.uk
website www.natlotcomm.gov.uk

National Maritime Museum
Greenwich, London SE10 9NF
tel 020-8858 4422 *fax* 020-8312 6632
websites www.nmm.ac.uk www.port.nmm.ac.uk
(gateway site for maritime information)
www.rog.nmm.ac.uk (for astronomy information)

The National Monuments Record
English Heritage, National Monuments Record
Centre, Kemble Drive, Swindon, Wilts. SN2 2GZ
tel (01793) 414600 *fax* (01793) 414606
email nmrinfo@english-heritage.org.uk
website www.english-heritage.org.uk

Natural Environment Research Council
Polaris House, North Star Avenue, Swindon,
Wilts. SN2 1EU
tel (01793) 411500 *fax* (01793) 411501

email requests@nerc.ac.uk
website www.nerc.ac.uk

The Natural History Museum
Cromwell Road, London SW7 5BD
tel 020-7942 5000

New Zealand High Commission
New Zealand House, Haymarket,
London SW1Y 4TQ
tel 020-7930 8422 *fax* 020-7839 4580
website www.nzembassy.com/uk

Northern Ireland Assembly
Parliament Buildings, Belfast BT4 3XX
tel 028-9052 1333

Northern Ireland Authority for Energy Regulation
Brookmount Buildings, 42 Fountain Street,
Belfast BT1 5EE
tel 028-9031 1575 *fax* 028-9031 1740
email ofreg@nics.gov.uk
website http://ofreg.nics.gov.uk/

Northern Ireland Office
11 Millbank, London SW1P 4PN
tel 020-7210 3000
Castle Buildings, Belfast BT4 3ST
tel 028-9052 0700
website www.nio.gov.uk

Northern Ireland Tourist Board
59 North Street, Belfast, Northern Ireland BT1 1NB
tel 028-9023 1221 *fax* 028-9024 0960
email info@nitb.com
website www.discovernorthernireland.com

Office for Standards in Education (OFSTED)
Alexandra House, 33 Kingsway, London WC2B 6SE
tel 020-7421 6800 *fax* 020-7421 6707

The Office of Communications (Ofcom)
Riverside House, 2A Southwark Bridge Road,
London SE1 9HA
tel 020-7981 3000 *fax* 020-7981 3333
email wwwenq@ofcom.org.uk
website www.ofcom.org.uk

Office of Fair Trading
Fleetbank House, 2-6 Salisbury Square,
London EC4Y 8JX
tel 020-7211 8000 *fax* 020-7211 8800
email enquiries@oft.gov.uk
website www.oft.gov.uk

Office of Gas and Electricity Markets (OFGEM)
Head Office 9 Millbank, London SW1P 3GE
tel 020-7901 7000
website www.ofgem.gov.uk

OFGEM Scotland Regents Court,
70 West Regent Street, Glasgow G2 2QZ
tel 0141-331 2777

Office of Telecommunications
50 Ludgate Hill, London EC4M 7JJ
tel 020-7634 8700 *fax* 020-7634 8943
email infocent@oftel.gov.uk
website www.oftel.gov.uk

Office of the Data Protection Commissioner – see Information Commissioner's Office

Office of the Legal Services Ombudsman
3rd Floor, Sunlight House, Quay Street,
Manchester M3 3JZ
tel 0161-839 7262, *Lo call* 0845-6010794 (charged at local rate) *fax* 0161-832 5446
email lso@olso.gsi.gov.uk
website www.olso.org

Office of Water Services (OFWAT)
Centre City Tower, 7 Hill Street,
Birmingham B5 4UA
tel 0121-625 1300 *fax* 0121-625 1400
email enquiries@ofwat.gsi.gov.uk
website www.ofwat.gov.uk

Oftel (Office of Telecommunications) – see The Office of Communications

OFWAT – see Office of Water Services

Ordnance Survey
Romsey Road, Southampton SO16 4GU
Press Office tel 023-8079 2265, *Customer Contact Centre* (08456) 050505 *fax* 023-8079 2615
email enquiries@ordsvy.gov.uk
website www.ordnancesurvey.co.uk

Particle Physics and Astronomy Research Council (PPARC)
Polaris House, North Star Avenue, Swindon,
Wilts. SN2 1SZ
tel (01793) 442000 *fax* (01793) 442002
email pr.pus@pparc.ac.uk
website www.pparc.ac.uk

Patent Office
General enquiries (designs, patents, trade marks),
Concept House, Cardiff Road, Newport,
South Wales NP10 8QQ
tel (0645) 500505 *text phone* (0645) 222250
email enquiries@patent.gov.uk
website www.patent.gov.uk
Copyright enquiries Copyright Directorate,
The Patent Office, Room 1/10, Harmsworth House,
13-15 Bouverie Street, London EC4Y 8DP

tel 020-7596 6566 *textphone* (0645) 222250
fax 020-7596 6526
email copyright@patent.gov.uk
website www.patent.gov.uk
www.intellectual-property.gov.uk

The Pensions Ombudsman
11 Belgrave Road, London SW1V 1RB
tel 020-7834 9144 *fax* 020-7821 0065
email enquiries@pensions-ombudsman.org.uk
website www.pensions-ombudsman.org.uk
Ombudsman David Laverick

Pensions and Overseas Benefits Directorate (POD) – see DWP (Department for Work and Pensions)

PLR Office – see page 602

Police Complaints Authority
10 Great George Street, London SW1P 3AE
tel 020-7273 6450 *fax* 020-7273 6401
website www.pca.gov.uk

Portuguese Embassy
11 Belgrave Square, London SW1X 8PP
tel 020-7235 5331 *fax* 020-7245 1287, 020-7235 0739
email Portembassy-London@dialin.net

Post Office Headquarters – see Royal Mail Headquarters

Privy Council Office
2 Carlton Gardens, London SW1Y 5AA
tel 020-7210 1033 *fax* 020-7210 1071
email jackie.lindsay@pco.x.gsi.gov.uk
website www.privy-council.gov.uk

Public Guardianship Office
Archway Tower, 2 Junction Road, London N19 5SZ
tel 020-7664 7000 *fax* 020-7664 7705
website www.guardianship.gov.uk

Public Record Office – see The National Archives

Qualifications and Curriculum Authority (QCA)
83 Piccadilly, London W1J 8QA
tel 020-7509 5555 *fax* 020-7509 6666
email info@qca.org.uk
website www.qca.org.uk
Chairman Sir Anthony Greener, *Chief Executive* Dr Ken Boston

The Radio Authority – see The Office of Communications

Resource: The Council for Museums, Archives and Libraries
16 Queen Anne's Gate, London SW1H 9AA

tel 020-7273 1444 *fax* 020-7273 1404
website www.resource.gov.uk

Royal Commission on the Ancient and Historical Monuments of Scotland
(with National Monuments Record of Scotland)
John Sinclair House, 16 Bernard Terrace, Edinburgh EH8 9NX
tel 0131-662 1456 *fax* 0131-662 1477/1499
email postmaster@rcahms.gov.uk
website www.rcahms.gov.uk

Royal Commission on the Ancient and Historical Monuments of Wales
(with National Monuments Record of Wales)
Crown Building, Plas Crug, Aberystwyth, Ceredigion SY23 1NJ
tel (01970) 621200 *fax* (01970) 627701
email nmr.wales@rcahmw.org.uk
website www.rcahmw.org.uk

Royal Commission on the Historical Monuments of England – merged with English Heritage

Royal Danish Embassy
55 Sloane Street, London SW1X 9SR
tel 020-7333 0200 *fax* 020-7333 0270
email lonamb@um.dk
website www.denmark.org.uk

Royal Fine Art Commission for Scotland
Bakehouse Close, 146 Canongate, Edinburgh EH8 8DD
tel 0131-556 6699 *fax* 0131-556 6633
email plan@RoyfinartcomforSco.gov.uk
website www.RoyfinartcomforSco.gov.uk

Royal Mail Headquarters
5th Floor, 148 Old Street, London EC1V 9HQ
tel 020-7490 2888
websites www.royalmail.com www.postoffice.co.uk

Royal Mint
Llantrisant, Pontyclun CF72 8YT
tel (01443) 222111
email victoria.francis@royalmint.gov.uk
website www.royalmint.com

Royal National Theatre Board
South Bank, London SE1 9PX
tel 020-7452 3333 *fax* 020-7452 3344
website www.nationaltheatre.org.uk
Chairman Sir Christopher Hogg, *Director* Trevor Nunn CBE

Royal Netherlands Embassy
38 Hyde Park Gate, London SW7 5DP
tel 020-7590 3200 *fax* 020-7581 0053

email cultural@netherlands-embassy.org.uk
website www.netherlands-embassy.org.uk

Royal Norwegian Embassy
25 Belgrave Square, London SW1X 8QD
tel 020-7591 5500 *fax* 020-7245 6993
email emb.london@mfa.no
website www.norway.org.uk/

Royal Observatory of Greenwich – see National Maritime Museum

Science Museum
Exhibition Road, London SW7 2DD
tel (0870) 870 4868
email sciencemuseum@nmsi.ac.uk
website www.sciencemuseum.org.uk

The Scotland Office
Dover House, Whitehall, London SW1A 2AU
tel 020-7270 6828
website www.scottishsecretary.gov.uk

Scottish Arts Council
12 Manor Place, Edinburgh EH3 7DD
tel 0131-226 6051, *Help Desk tel* 0131-240 2443/2444
fax 0131-225 9833
email help.desk@scottisharts.org.uk
website www.scottisharts.org.uk

The Scottish Executive
St Andrew's House, Regent Road,
Edinburgh EH1 1DG
tel 0131-556 8400
website www.scotland.gov.uk

Scottish Law Commission
140 Causewayside, Edinburgh EH9 1PR
tel 0131-668 2131 *fax* 0131-662 4900
email info@scotlawcom.gov.uk
website www.scotlawcom.gov.uk

Scottish Legal Aid Board
44 Drumsheugh Gardens, Edinburgh EH3 7SW
tel 0131-226 7061 *fax* 0131-220 4878
website www.slab.org.uk

Scottish Natural Heritage
12 Hope Terrace, Edinburgh EH9 2AS
tel 0131-447 4784 *fax* 0131-446 2279 (press office)
website www.snh.org.uk

The Scottish Office – see The Scotland Office

The Scottish Parliament
Edinburgh EH99 1SP
tel 0131-348 5000 *fax* 0131-348 5601
email sp.info@scottish.parliament.uk
website www.scottish parliament.uk

Serpentine Gallery
Kensington Gardens, London W2 3XA
tel 020-7402 6075, *Public information* 020-7298 1501
fax 020-7402 4103

Singapore High Commission
9 Wilton Crescent, London SW1X 8SP
tel 020-7235 8315 *fax* 020-7245 6583
email info@singaporehc.org.uk
consular@singaporehc.org.uk
website www.mfa.gov.sg/london

South Africa High Commission
South Africa House, Trafalgar Square,
London WC2N 5DP
tel 020-7451 7299 *fax* 020-7451 7283/7284
email general@southafricahouse.com
website www.southafricahouse.com

Spanish Embassy
39 Chesham Place, London SW1X 8SB
tel 020-7235 5555 *fax* 020-7259 5392

Sport England
16 Upper Woburn Place, London WC1H 0QP
tel 020-7273 1500 *fax* 020-7383 5740
email info@sportengland.org
website www.sportengland.org

The Stationery Office (TSO)
PO Box 291, Norwich NR3 1GN
tel (0870) 600 5522
website www.clickkso.com

Strategic Rail Authority
55 Victoria Street, London SW1H 0EU
tel 020-7654 6000 *fax* 020-7654 6010
website www.sra.gov.uk

Swiss Embassy Cultural Section
16-18 Montagu Place, London W1H 2BQ
tel 020-7616 6000 *fax* 020-7723 6949
email swissembassy@lon.rep.admin.ch
website www.swissembassy.org.uk

Tate
Tate Britain
Millbank, London SW1P 4RG
tel 020-7887 8008, 020-7887 8000 (admin)
email information@tate.org.uk
website www.tate.org.uk
Tate Modern, Bankside, London SE1 9TG
tel 020-7887 8008
Tate Liverpool, Albert Dock, Liverpool L3 4BB
tel 0151-702 7400
Tate St Ives, Porthmeor Beach, St Ives,
Cornwall TR26 1TG
tel (01736) 796226

Theatre Museum – see page 433

Transport for London (TfL)
Windsor House, 42-50 Victoria Street,
London SW1H 0TL
tel 020-7941 4500
website www.tfl.gov.uk

Turkish Embassy
43 Belgrave Square, London SW1X 8PA
tel 020-7393 0202 *fax* 020-7393 0066
email info@turkishembassy.co.uk

UK Film Council
10 Little Portland Street, London W1W 7JG
tel 020-7861 7861 *fax* 020-7861 7862

Victoria and Albert Museum
South Kensington, London SW7 2RL
tel 020-7942 2000
website www.vam.ac.uk

Visiting Arts
Bloomsbury House, 74-77 Great Russell Street,
London WC1B 3DA
tel 020-7291 1600 *fax* 020-7291 1616
email information@visitingarts.org.uk
website www.visitingarts.org.uk
Director T. Sandell OBE

VisitScotland
23 Ravelston Terrace, Edinburgh EH4 3TP
tel 0131-332 2433 *fax* 0131-343 1513
email info@visitscotland.com
website www.visitscotland.com

The Wales Office
Gwydyr House, Whitehall, London SW1A 2ER
tel 020-7270 0549 *fax* 020-7270 0568
website www.walesoffice.gov.uk

Wales Tourist Board
Brunel House, 2 Fitzalan Road, Cardiff CF24 0UY
tel 029-2047 5214 *fax* 029-2048 2436
email info@tourism.wales.gov.uk
website www.visitwales.com

Women's National Commission
Cabinet Office, 1st Floor, 35 Great Smith Street,
London SW1P 3BQ
tel 020-7276 2555 *fax* 020-7276 2563
website www.thewnc.org.uk

Publishing practice

Publishing agreements

Publisher's agreements are not a standard form. Before signing one, the author must check it carefully, taking nothing for granted. Michael Legat navigates the reader through this complex document.

Any author, presented with so complex a document as a publisher's agreement, should read it carefully before signing, making sure that every clause is understood, and not taking anything for granted. Bear in mind that there is no such thing as a standard form. A given publisher's 'standard' contract may not only differ substantially from those of other publishers, but will often vary from author to author and from book to book. Don't be fooled into believing that it is a standard form because it appears to have been printed – most agreements are individually produced on a word processor to give exactly that effect.

A fair and reasonable agreement

You should be able to rely on your agent, if you have one, to check the agreement for you, or – if you are a member – you can get it vetted by the Society of Authors or the Writers' Guild of Great Britain. But if you are on your own, you must either go to one of the solicitors who specialise in publishing business (probably expensive) or Do It Yourself. In the latter case it will help to compare the contract you have been offered, clause by clause, with a typical Minimum Terms Agreement such as those printed in my own books, *An Author's Guide to Publishing* and *Understanding Publishers' Contracts*.

Minimum Terms Agreement

The Minimum Terms Agreement (MTA), developed jointly by the Society of Authors and the Writers' Guild, is signed by a publisher on the one hand and the Society and the Guild on the other. It is not an agreement between a publisher and an individual author. It commits the publisher to offering his or her authors terms which are at least as good as those in the MTA. The intention is that only members of the Society and the Guild should be eligible for this special treatment, but in practice publishers who sign the agreement tend to offer its terms to all their authors. There is no standard MTA, and most signatory publishers have insisted on certain variations in the agreement; nevertheless, the more important basic principles have always been accepted. It must be pointed out that the MTA does not usually apply to:

● books in which illustrations take up 40% or more of the space;
● specialist works on the visual arts in which illustrations fill 25% or more of the space;
● books involving three or more participants in royalties; or
● technical books, manuals and reference books.

Since its origins in 1980, comparatively few publishers have signed a Minimum Terms Agreement, although the signatories include several major publishing houses. Some publishers have refused, claiming to treat their authors quite well enough already, while others say that each author and each book is so different that standard terms cannot be laid down. Nonetheless, the MTA has been a resounding success. Almost all non-signatory publishers have adopted some or all of its provisions, and even in the case of the excluded books mentioned above, the terms have tended to improve. All authors can now argue, from a position of some strength, that their own agreements should meet the MTA's standards.

The provisions of the MTA

The MTA is a royalty agreement (usually the most satisfactory form for an author), and it lays down the minimum acceptable royalties on sales, and the levels at which the rate should rise. These royalties are expressed as percentages of the book's retail price but can easily be adjusted to apply to royalties based on price received, a system to which a number of publishers are changing, increasing the percentages so that the author's earnings are not adversely affected. The MTA also covers the size of the advance (calculated in accordance with the expected initial print quantity and retail price), and recommended splits between publisher and author of moneys from the sale of subsidiary rights (including US and translation rights).

However, the MTA is not by any means concerned solely with money, but with fairness to the author in all clauses of a publishing agreement, special attention being paid to provisions designed to make the author/publisher relationship more of a partnership than it has often been in the past. While recognising the publisher's right to take final decisions on such matters as print quantity, publication date, retail price, jacket or cover design, wording of the blurb, promotion and publicity, and remaindering, the MTA insists that the author has a right to consultation (which should not be an empty formality but should mean that serious consideration is given to his or her views), in all such cases. Also the author's approval must be sought for the sale of any subsidiary rights.

Some essential clauses

Any publisher's agreement you sign should contain, in addition to acceptable financial terms, clauses covering:

● **Rights licensed.** A clear definition of which rights you are licensing to the publisher. The publisher will normally require volume rights but the agreement must specify whether such rights will apply in all languages (or perhaps only in English) and throughout the world (or only in an agreed list of territories). The duration of the publisher's licence should be spelt out; commonly this is for the period of copyright (currently the author's lifetime plus 70 years), although some publishers now accept a shorter term. A list of those subsidiary rights of which control is granted to the publisher must be included (make sure that the splits of moneys earned from these rights are in accordance with, or approximate reasonably to, those in the MTA, especially in the currently growing area of merchandising).

• **Publication date.** Commitment by the publisher to publication of the book by a specific date (usually within a year or 18 months from the delivery of the typescript). Avoid signing an agreement which is vague on this point, saying, for instance, only that the book will be published 'within a reasonable period'.

• **Copyright.** Confirmation that in all copies of the book the publisher will print a copyright notice in the author's name and a statement that the author has asserted his or her 'Right of Paternity' (the right to be identified as the author in future exploitation of the material in any form), and that a similar commitment will be required from any subsidiary licensee.

• **Fees and permissions.** Clarification, if the book is to include a professionally prepared index or material the copyright of which does not belong to the author, of whether the author or the publisher will be responsible for the fees (or if costs are to be shared, in what proportions) and the clearance of permissions.

• **Acceptable accounting procedures.** Most publishers divide the year into two six-month periods, accounting to the author, and paying any sums due, three months after the end of each period. Look askance at any less frequent accounting or longer delay after the royalty period. The publisher should also agree to pay the author the due share of any subsidiary moneys promptly on receipt, provided that the advance on the book has been earned.

• **Termination.** A clear definition of the various conditions under which the agreement shall be terminated, with reversion of rights to the author.

Clauses to question

You can question anything in a publisher's agreement before you sign it. Provided that you do so politely and are not just being difficult, the publisher should be prepared to answer every query, to explain, and where possible to meet your objections. Most publishing contracts are not designed to exploit the author unfairly, but you should watch out for:

• **Rights assigned elsewhere.** It is unwise to accept a clause which allows the publisher to assign the rights in your book to another firm or person without your approval.

• **Non-publication.** The contract for a commissioned book often includes wording which alludes to the publisher's acceptance of the work, implying that there is no obligation to publish it if he or she deems it unacceptable. It may be understandable that the publisher wants an escape route in case the author turns in an inferior work, but he or she should be obliged to justify the rejection, and to give the author an opportunity to revise the work to bring it up to standard. If, having accepted the book, the publisher then wishes to cancel the contract prior to publication, the author can usually expect to receive financial compensation, which should be non-returnable even if the book is subsequently placed with another publisher. However, this point is not normally covered in a publishing agreement.

• **Sole publisher.** Some agreements prohibit the author from writing similar material for any other publisher. This may clearly affect the author's earning ability.

- **Editing consultation.** Don't agree to the publisher's right to edit your work without any requirement for him or her to obtain your approval of any changes made.
- **Royalty rate.** While it is normal practice for an agreement to allow the publisher to pay a lower royalty on books which are sold at high trade discounts, such sales are more frequently made nowadays than in the past, and it is essential to make sure the royalty rate on high discount sales is not unfairly low.
- **Future books.** The Society of Authors and the Writers' Guild are both generally opposed to clauses giving the publisher the right to publish the author's next work, feeling that this privilege should be earned by the publisher's handling of the earlier book. If you accept an option clause, at least make sure that it leaves all terms for a future book to be agreed.

Electronic and other multimedia rights

The importance of electronic, digital and other multimedia rights, which already require a carefully worded clause in a contract, is likely to increase in years to come, when the only form of publication for a book may be on the internet or whatever may replace it as technology develops. In the meantime publishers, on the one hand, and literary agents and authors' organisations on the other, are in dispute about these rights, including other rights as yet unknown.

The two main issues are concerned with control of the rights and with royalties. Should these rights remain in the direct control of the author (possibly negotiating through an agent) or, as publishers maintain, be regarded as a part of volume rights, and therefore licensed to the publisher? If the publisher controls the rights, should the author receive a royalty of 15% or thereabouts on the publisher's receipts from sales of these rights, or at least 50% of the income, as the Society of Authors and the Association of Authors' Agents insist is fair? Until some agreement has been reached on these and other matters, it is advisable for authors to seek advice on suitable wording of the relevant clause from a literary agent or the Society of Authors or any other established body representing writers.

Joint and multiple authorship

In the case of joint authorship (a work so written that the individual contributions of the authors cannot be readily separated), the first written agreement should be between the authors themselves, setting out the proportions in which any moneys earned by the book will be split, specifying how the authors' responsibilities are to be shared, and especially laying down the procedure to be adopted should the authors ever find themselves in dispute. The terms of any publishing agreement which they sign (each author having an identical copy) should reflect their joint understanding. The total earnings should not be less than would be paid were the book by a single author, and the authors should have normal rights of consultation.

In the case of multiple authorship (when the work of each contributor can be clearly separated), each author is likely to have an individual contract, and may not be aware of what terms are offered to the others involved. Because of the possibility of disagreement between the authors, the publisher will probably offer little in the way of consultation. All the individual author can do is to ensure that the agreement appears to be fair in relation to the amount of work contributed, and that the author's responsibilities indicated by the contract refer only to his or her work.

Outright sale

As a general rule no author should agree to surrender his or her copyright to the publisher, although this may be unavoidable in the case of a book with many contributors, such as an encyclopedia. Even then, give up your copyright with great reluctance and only after an adequate explanation from the publisher of why you should (and probably a substantial financial inducement, including, if possible, provision for the payment of a further fee each time the book is reprinted). The agreement itself will probably be no more than a brief and unequivocal letter.

Subsidies and vanity publishing

Few commercial publishers will be interested in publishing your book on a subsidy basis (i.e. with a contribution from you towards costs), unless perhaps it is of a serious, highly specialised nature, such as an academic monograph, when a publisher who is well established within that particular field will certainly behave with probity and offer a fair contract. Vanity publishers, on the other hand, will accept your book with enthusiasm, ask for 'a small contribution to production costs' (which turns out to be a very substantial sum, not a penny of which you are likely to see again), and will fail to achieve any sales for your book apart from the copies which you yourself buy. If you want to put your own money into the publication of your book, try self-publishing (see page 234) – you will be far better off than going to a vanity house. How do you tell which are the vanity publishers? That's easy – they're the ones who put advertisements in the papers saying things like, 'Authors Wanted!'. Regular publishers don't need to do that.

Michael Legat became a full-time writer after a long and successful publishing career. He is the author of a number of highly regarded books on publishing and writing.

Further reading

Clark, Charles (ed.), *Publishing Agreements: A Book of Precedents*, Tolley, 6th edn, 2002

Flint, Michael F., *A User's Guide to Copyright*, Butterworths, 5th edn, 2000

Legat, Michael, *An Author's Guide to Publishing*, Robert Hale, 3rd edn revised, 1998

Legat, Michael, *Understanding Publishers' Contracts*, Robert Hale, 2nd edn revised, 2002

Unwin, Sir Stanley, *The Truth About Publishing*, Unwin Hyman, 8th edn, 1976, o.p.

FAQs about ISBNs

The Standard Book Numbering Agency receives a large number of enquiries about the ISBN system. The most frequently asked questions are answered here.

What is an ISBN?

An ISBN (International Standard Book Number) is a 10-digit product number used by publishers, booksellers and libraries for ordering, listing and stock control purposes. It enables them to identify a specific edition of a specific title in a specific format from a particular publisher. The 10 digits are always divided into four parts, separated by spaces or hyphens. The four parts can be of varying length and are as follows:

- Group Identifier – Identifies a national, geographic or language grouping of publishers. It tells you which of these groupings the publisher belongs to (not the language of the book).
- Publisher Prefix – Identifies a specific publisher or imprint.
- Title Number – Identifies a specific edition of a specific title in a specific format.
- Check Digit – This is always and only the final digit which mathematically validates the rest of the number. It is calculated using a Modulus 11 system with weights 10–2.

Do all books need to have an ISBN?

There is no legal requirement for an ISBN and it conveys no form of legal or copyright protection. It is a product number.

What can be gained from using an ISBN?

If you wish to sell your publication through major bookselling chains, or internet booksellers, they will require you to have an ISBN to assist their internal processing and ordering systems. The ISBN also provides access to Bibliographic Databases such as Whitaker BookBank, which are organised using ISBNs as references. These databases are used by the book trade and libraries to provide information for customers. The ISBN therefore provides access to additional marketing tools which could help sales of your product.

Where can we get an ISBN?

ISBN prefixes are assigned to publishers in the country in which the publisher is based by the national agency for that country. In the UK and Republic of Ireland this agency is the Standard Book Numbering Agency Ltd which is a wholly owned subsidiary of J. Whitaker & Sons Ltd. The Agency introduces new publishers to the system, assigns prefixes to new and existing publishers and deals with any queries or problems in using the system. The Standard Book Numbering Agency Ltd was the first ISBN Agency in the world. Publishers based elsewhere will not be able to get numbers from the UK Agency but should contact them for details of the relevant Agency.

Who is eligible for ISBNs?
Any publisher which is publishing a qualifying product for general sale or distribution to the market is eligible (see 'Which products do not qualify for ISBNs?').

What is a publisher?
It is sometimes difficult to decide who the publisher is and who their agent may be, but the publisher is generally the person or body which takes the financial risk in making a product available. For example, if a product went on sale and sold no copies at all, the publisher is usually the person or body which loses money. If you get paid anyway, you are likely to be a designer, printer, author or consultant of some kind.

How long does it take to get an ISBN?
In the UK the Standard service time is 10 working days. There is also a Fast Track service, which is a three-working day processing period.

How much does it cost to get an ISBN?
In the UK there is a registration fee which is payable by all new publishers. The fees are £60 plus VAT for the Standard service and £96 plus VAT for the Fast Track service. A publisher prefix unique to you will be provided and allows for 10 ISBNs. Larger allocations are available where appropriate.

ISBNs are only available in blocks. The smallest block is 10 numbers. It is not possible to obtain a single ISBN.

Which products do not qualify for ISBNs?
Calendars; diaries; greetings cards, videos for entertainment; documentaries on video/ CD-Rom; computer games; computer application programs; items which are available to a restricted group of people, e.g. a history of a golf club which is only for sale to members, or an educational course book only available to those registered as students on the course.

Can I turn my ISBN into a barcode?
Where a product carries a barcode and an ISBN, the barcode is derived from the ISBN and includes the Bookland Prefix (978). The barcode also contains a check digit which is derived by a different calculation method from that used for ISBNs. Further information about barcoding for books is available on the Book Industry Communication website (www.bic.org.uk).

Contact details

ISBN Agency
Woolmead House West, Bear Lane, Farnham,
Surrey GU9 7LG
tel (01252) 742590 *fax* (01252) 742526
email isbn@whitaker.co.uk
website www.whitaker.co.uk/isbn.htm

What is an ISSN?
An International Standard Serial Number is the numbering system for journals, magazines, periodicals, newspapers and newsletters. It is administered by the British Library (*tel* (01937) 546959).

Public Lending Right

Under the PLR system, payment is made from public funds to authors (writers, translators, illustrators and some editors/compilers) whose books are lent out from public libraries. Payment is made once a year, and the amount authors receive is proportionate to the number of times (established from a sample) that their books were borrowed during the previous year (July to June).

The legislation

PLR was created, and its principles established, by the Public Lending Right Act 1979 (HMSO, 30p). The Act required the rules for the administration of PLR to be laid down by a scheme. That was done in the Public Lending Right Scheme 1982 (HMSO, £2.95), which includes details of transfer (assignment), transmission after death, renunciation, trusteeship, bankruptcy, etc. Amending orders made in 1983, 1984, 1988, 1989 and 1990 were consolidated in December 1990 (SI 2360, £3.90). Some further amendments affecting author eligibility came into effect in December 1991 (SI 2618, £1), July 1997 (SI 1576, £1.10), December 1999 (SI 420, £1) and July 2000 (SI 933, £1.50).

How the system works

From the applications he receives, the Registrar of PLR compiles a register of authors and books which is held on computer. A representative sample of book issues is recorded, consisting of all loans from selected public libraries. This is then multiplied in proportion to total library lending to produce, for each book, an estimate of its total annual loans throughout the country. Each year the computer compares the register with the estimated loans to discover how many loans are credited to each registered book for the calculation of PLR payments. The computer does this using code numbers – in most cases the ISBN printed in the book.

Parliament allocates a sum each year (£7,000,000 for 2002–3) for PLR. This Fund pays the administrative costs of PLR and reimburses local authorities for recording loans in the sample libraries. The remaining money is then divided by the total registered loan figure in order to work out how much can be paid for each estimated loan of a registered book.

Limits on payments

Bottom limit. If all the registered interests in an author's books score so few loans that they would earn less than £5 in a year, no payment is due.

Top limit. If the books of one registered author score so high that the author's PLR earnings for the year would exceed £6000, then only £6000 is paid. No author can earn more than £6000 in PLR in any one year.

Money that is not paid out because of these limits belongs to the Fund and increases the amounts paid that year to other authors.

The sample

The basic sample represents only public libraries (no academic, school, private or commercial libraries are included) and only loans made over the counter (not

Summary of the 20th year's results

Registration: authors. When registration closed for the 20th year (30 June 2002) the number of shares in books registered was 350,396 for 35,078 authors.

Eligible loans. Of the 406 million estimated loans from UK libraries, 184 million belong to books on the PLR register. The loans credited to registered books – 45% of all library borrowings – qualify for payment. The remaining 55% of loans relate to books that are ineligible for various reasons, to books written by dead or foreign authors, and to books that have simply not been applied for.

Money and payments. PLR's administrative costs are deducted from the fund allocated to the Registrar annually by Parliament. Operating the Scheme this year cost £817,000, representing some 11.7% of the PLR fund. The Rate per Loan for 2002–3 increased to 4.21 pence and was calculated to distribute all the £6,200,000 available. The total of PLR distribution and costs is therefore the full £7 million which the Government provided in 2002–3.

The numbers of authors in various payment categories are as follows:

*320	payments at	£5000–6000
340	payments between	£2500–4999.99
759	payments between	£1000–2499.99
894	payments between	£500–999.99
3,952	payments between	£100–499.99
12,799	payments between	£5–99.99
19,064	TOTAL	

* includes 251 authors where the maximum threshold applied.

consultations of books on library premises). It follows that only those books which are loaned from public libraries can earn PLR and make an application worthwhile.

The sample consists of the entire loans records for a year from libraries in 30 public library authorities spread through England, Scotland, Wales and Northern Ireland. Sample loans represent at least 10% of the national total. Several computerised sampling points in an authority contribute loans data ('multi-site' sampling). This change has been introduced gradually, and began in July 1991. The aim has been to increase the sample without any significant increase in costs. In order to counteract sampling error, libraries in the sample change every two to three years. Loans are totalled every 12 months for the period 1 July to 30 June.

An author's entitlement to PLR depends, under the 1979 Act, on the loans accrued by his or her books in the sample. This figure is averaged up to produce first regional and then finally national estimated loans.

ISBNs

PLR depends on the use of code numbers to identify books lent and to correlate loans with entries on the register so that payment can be made. The system uses the International Standard Book Number (ISBN), which is required for all new registrations. Different editions (e.g. 1st, 2nd, hardcover, paperback, large print) of the same book have different ISBNs.

Authorship

In the PLR system the author of a book is the writer, illustrator, translator, compiler, editor or reviser. Authors must be named on the book's title page, or be able to prove authorship by some other means (e.g. receipt of royalties). The ownership of copyright has no bearing on PLR eligibility.

Co-authorship/illustrators. In the PLR system the authors of a book are those writers, translators, editors, compilers and illustrators as defined above. Authors must apply for registration before their books can earn PLR. There is no restriction on the number of authors who can register shares in any one book as long as they satisfy the eligibility criteria.

Writers and/or illustrators. At least one must be eligible and they must jointly agree what share of PLR each will take. This agreement is necessary even if one or two are ineligible or do not wish to register for PLR. Share sizes should be based on contribution. The eligible authors will receive the share(s) specified in the application. PLR can be any whole percentage. Detailed advice is available from the PLR office.

Translators. Translators may apply, without reference to other authors, for a 30% fixed share (to be divided equally between joint translators).

Editors and compilers. An editor or compiler may apply, either with others or without reference to them, to register a 20% share. Unless in receipt of royalties an editor must have written at least 10% of the book's content or more than 10 pages of text in addition to normal editorial work. The share of joint editors/compilers is 20% in total to be divided equally. An application from an editor or compiler to register a greater percentage share must be accompanied by supporting documentary evidence of actual contribution.

Dead or missing co-authors. Where it is impossible to agree shares with a co-author because that person is dead or untraceable, then the surviving co-author or co-authors may submit an application without the dead or missing co-author but must name the co-author and provide supporting evidence as to why that co-author has not agreed shares. The living co-author(s) will then be able to register a share in the book which will be 20% for the illustrator (or illustrators) and the residual percentage for the writer (or writers). If this percentage is to be divided between more than one writer or illustrator, then this will be in equal shares

Most borrowed children's authors

1. Jacqueline Wilson
2. R.L. Stine
3. Mick Inkpen
4. Janet & Allan Ahlberg
5. Lucy Daniels
6. Roald Dahl
7. Enid Blyton
8. Nick Butterworth
9. Dick King-Smith
10. Eric Hill
11. Joan Jonker
12. Martin Waddell
13. Terry Deary
14. John Cunliffe
15. J.K. Rowling
16. Colin & Jacqui Hawkins
17. Jenny Dale
18. Shirley Hughes
19. David McKee
20. Sally Grindley

These two lists are of the most borrowed authors in UK public libraries. They are based on PLR sample loans in the period July 2001–June 2002. They include all writers, both registered and unregistered, but not illustrators where the book has a separate writer. Writing names are used; pseudonyms have not been combined.

Most borrowed authors (adult fiction)

1. Catherine Cookson
2. Danielle Steel
3. Josephine Cox
4. Dick Francis
5. Agatha Christie
6. Jack Higgins
7. Audrey Howard
8. Patricia Cornwell
9. Ruth Rendell
10. Emma Blair
11. Bernard Cornwell
12. John Grisham
13. Mary Higgins Clark
14. Lyn Andrews
15. Maeve Binchy
16. Ian Rankin
17. Barbara Taylor Bradford
18. Virginia Andrews
19. Wilbur Smith
20. Mary Jane Staples

unless some other apportionment is requested and agreed by the Registrar.

The PLR Office keeps a file of missing authors (mostly illustrators) to help locate co-authors. Help is also available from publishers, the writers' organisations, and the Association of Illustrators.

Life and death. Authors can only be registered for PLR during their lifetime. However, for authors so registered, books can later be registered if first published within one year before their death or 10 years afterwards. New versions of titles registered by the author can be registered posthumously.

Residential qualifications. With effect from 1 July 2000, PLR is open to authors living in the European Economic Area (i.e. EU member states plus Norway, Liechtenstein and Iceland). A resident in these countries (for PLR purposes) has his or her only or principal home there. The United Kingdom does not include the Channel Islands or the Isle of Man.

Eligible books

In the PLR system each separate edition of a book is registered and treated as a separate book. A book is eligible for PLR registration provided that:

- it has an eligible author (or co-author);
- it is printed and bound (paperbacks counting as bound);
- copies of it have been put on sale (i.e. it is not a free handout and it has already been published);
- it is not a newspaper, magazine, journal or periodical;
- the authorship is personal (i.e. not a company or association) and the book is not crown copyright;
- it is not wholly or mainly a musical score;
- it has an ISBN.

Notification and payment

Every registered author receives from the Registrar an annual statement of estimated loans for each book and the PLR due.

Sampling arrangements

To help minimise the unfairnesses that arise inevitably from a sampling system, the Scheme specifies the eight regions within which authorities and sampling points have to be designated and includes libraries of varying size. Part of the sample drops out by rotation each year to allow fresh libraries to be included. The following library authorities have been designated for the year beginning 1 July 2003 (all are multi-site authorities):

- London – Harrow, Kingston upon Thames, Bexley, Brent;
- Metropolitan Boroughs – Stockport, North Tyneside, Coventry, The Wirral, Leeds;
- Counties: Northern – Durham, Lancashire, Northumberland;
- Counties: South West – Southampton, Somerset, Devon, Stoke on Trent;
- Counties: South East – Bedfordshire/Luton, Kent, Milton Keynes/Bucks, Northamptonshire, Hertfordshire;
- Scotland – Orkney, Dundee, South Lanarkshire, Fife;
- Northern Ireland – Belfast, North-Eastern Education & Library Board (NEELB);
- Wales – Carmarthenshire, Pembrokeshire, Cardiff.

Participating local authorities are reimbursed on an actual cost basis for additional expenditure incurred in providing loans data to the PLR Office. The extra PLR work mostly consists of modifications to computer programs to accumulate loans data in the local authority computer and to transmit the data to the PLR Office at Stockton-on-Tees.

Reciprocal arrangements

In 1981–2 reciprocal arrangements with West Germany were sought by British writers to help ensure that they did not lose the German PLR payments they had enjoyed since 1974 under international copyright law. The German Scheme, although loan based, is very different in most other respects and operates under German copyright law. Reciprocity was brought into effect in January 1985. Authors can apply for German PLR through the Authors' Licensing and Collecting Society. (Further information on PLR schemes internationally and recent developments within the EC towards wider recognition of PLR is available from the PLR Office or on the international website.)

Further information

Public Lending Right

PLR Office, Richard House, Sorbonne Close, Stockton-on-Tees TS17 6DA
tel (01642) 604699 *fax* (01642) 615641
websites www.plr.uk.com www.plrinternational.com
Contact The Registrar

Application forms, information, publications and a copy of its *Annual Report* are all obtainable from the PLR Office. See website for further information on eligibility for PLR, loans statistics and forthcoming developments.

PLR Advisory Committee

Advises the Secretary of State for Culture, Media and Sport and the Registrar on the operation of the PLR scheme.

Copyright and libel
Copyright questions

Copyright is a vital part of any writer's assets, and should never be assigned or sold without due consideration and the advice of a competent authority, such as the Society of Authors, the Writers' Guild of Great Britain, or the National Union of Journalists. Michael Legat answers some of the most commonly asked questions about copyright.

Is there a period of time after which the copyright expires?
Copyright in the European Union lasts for the lifetime of the author and for a further 70 years from the end of the year of death, or, if the work is first published posthumously, for 70 years from the end of the year of publication. In most other countries of the world copyright exists similarly for the lifetime and for either 50 years or 70 years after death or posthumous publication.

If I want to include an extract from a book, poem or article, do I have to seek copyright? How much may be used without permission? What happens if I apply for copyright permission but do not get a reply?
It is essential to seek permission to quote from another author's work, unless that author has been dead for 70 years or more, or 70 years or more has passed from the date of publication of a work published posthumously. Only if you are quoting for purposes of criticism or review are you allowed to do so without obtaining permission, and even then the Copyright, Designs and Patents Act of 1988 restricts you to 400 words of prose in a single extract from a copyright work, or a series of extracts of up to 300 words each, totalling no more than 800 words, or up to 40 lines of poetry, which must not be more than 25% of the poem. However, a quotation of no more than, say, half a dozen words may usually be used without permission since it will probably not extend beyond a brief and familiar reference, as, for example, Rider Haggard's well-known phrase, 'she who must be obeyed'. If in doubt, always check. If you do not get a reply when you ask for permission to quote, insert a notice in your work saying that you have tried without success to contact the copyright owner, and would be pleased to hear from him or her so that the matter could be cleared up – and keep a copy of all the relevant correspondence, in order to back up your claim of having tried to get in touch.

If a newspaper pays for an article and I then want to sell the story to a magazine, am I free under the copyright law to do so?
Yes, provided that you have not granted copyright or exclusive use to the newspaper. When selling your work to newspapers or magazines make it clear, in writing, that you are selling only First or Second Serial Rights, not your copyright.

If I agree to have an article published for no payment do I retain any rights over how it appears?

Whether or not you are paid for the work has no bearing on the legal situation. However, the Moral Rights which apply to books, plays, television and radio scripts, do not cover you against a failure to acknowledge you as the author of an article, nor against the mutilation of your text, when it is published in a newspaper or magazine.

I want to publish a photograph that was taken in 1950. I am not sure how to contact the photographer or even if he is still alive. Am I allowed to go ahead and publish it?

The Copyright, Designs and Patents Act of 1988 works retrospectively, so a photograph taken in 1950 is bound to be in copyright until at least 2020, and the copyright will be owned by the photographer, even though, when it was taken, the copyright would have belonged to the person who commissioned it, according to the laws then in place. You should therefore make every effort to contact the photographer, keeping copies of any relevant correspondence, and in case of failure take the same course of action as described above in relation to a textual extract the copyright owner of which you have been unable to trace.

I recently read an article on the same subject as one I have written. It contained many identical facts. Did this writer breach my copyright? What if I send ideas for an article to a magazine editor and those ideas are used despite the fact that I was not commissioned? May I sue the magazine?

Facts are normally in the public domain and may be used by anyone. However, if your article contains a fact which you have discovered and no one else has published, there could be an infringement of copyright if the author who uses it fails to attribute it to you. There is no copyright in ideas, so you cannot sue a writer or a journal for using ideas that you have put forward; in any case you would find it very difficult to prove that the idea belonged to you and to no one else. There is also no copyright in titles.

Does being paid a kill fee affect my copyright in a given piece?

No, provided that you have not sold the magazine or newspaper your copyright.

Do I need to copyright a piece of writing physically – whether an essay or a novel – or is it copyrighted automatically? Does it have to carry the © symbol?

Anything that you write is your copyright, assuming that it is not copied from the work of someone else, as soon as you have written it on paper or recorded it on the disk of a computer or on tape, or broadcast it. It is not essential for the work to carry the © symbol, although its inclusion may act as a warning and help to stop another writer from plagiarising it.

Am I legally required to inform an interviewee that our conversation is being recorded?

The interviewee owns the copyright of any words that he or she speaks as soon as they are recorded on your tape. Unless you have received permission to use those words in direct quotation, you could be liable to an action for infringement of copyright. You should therefore certainly inform the interviewee that the conversation is being recorded and seek permission to quote what is said directly.

More and more newspapers and magazines have versions both in print and on the internet. How can I ensure that my work is not published on the internet without my permission?
Make sure that any clause granting electronic rights to anyone in any agreement that you sign in respect of your work specifies not only the proportion of any fees received which you will get, but that your agreement must be sought before the rights are sold. Copyright extends to electronic rights, and therefore to publication on the internet, in just the same way as to other uses of the material.

I commissioned a designer to design a business card for me, and I paid her well. Does the design belong to me or to her?
Copyright would belong to the designer, and not to the person who commissioned it (as is also true in the case of a photograph, copyright in which belongs to the photographer). However, copyright in the business card might be transferred to you if a court considered you to have gained beneficially from the card.

Michael Legat became a full-time writer after a long and successful publishing career. He is the author of a number of highly regarded books on publishing and writing.

UK copyright law

Amanda Michaels describes the main types of work which may qualify for copyright protection, or related protection as a design, together with some of the main problems which may be faced by readers of this Yearbook in terms of protecting their own works or avoiding infringement of existing works in the UK. This is a technical area of the law, and one which is constantly developing; in an article of this length, it is not possible to deal fully with all the complexities of the law. It must also be emphasised that copyright is national in scope, and whilst works of UK authors will be protected in many other countries of the world, foreign laws may deal differently with questions of subsistence, ownership and infringement.

Copyright is a creation of statute, now shaped and influenced significantly by EU harmonisation measures. On 1 August 1989, the Copyright, Designs & Patents Act 1988 ('the Act') replaced the Copyright Act 1956, which in turn replaced the Copyright Act 1911. All three Acts are still relevant to copyright today. Whilst the Act to a large degree restated the existing law, it was also innovative, in particular in the creation of a new 'design right' offering protection (generally speaking in lieu of copyright) for many industrial or commercial designs, and in the wider protection of moral rights.

The law has changed further since 1989, largely as a result of EU directives. Perhaps the most important change occurred on 1 January 1996, when the duration of copyright protection in respect of most works (see below) was extended from 'life of the author' plus 50 years to life plus 70 years. Further changes came into force on 1 January 1998, when a new 'database right' was created. New Community design rights were brought into effect in 2003 (see below).

Continuing relevance of old law
In this article, I discuss the law as it currently stands, but where a work was created prior to 1 August 1989 it will always be necessary to consider the law in force at the time of creation (or possibly first publication) in order to assess the existence or scope of any rights. Particular difficulties may arise with foreign works, which may qualify for protection in the UK as a matter of international obligation. Each Act has contained transitional provisions and these, as well as the substantive provisions of any relevant earlier Act, will need to be considered where, for instance, you wish to use an earlier work and it is necessary to decide whether permission is needed and if so, who may grant it. Publishing or licence agreements designed for use under older Acts and prior to the development of modern technologies may be unsuitable for current use.

Copyright protection of works
Copyright protects the particular form in which an author's idea has been expressed, not the idea itself. Generally speaking, plots or artistic ideas are not protected by copyright, but what is protected is the particular manner in which the idea is presented. See *Designers Guild Limited* v. *Russell Williams (Textiles) Limited* [2001] FSR 113 in which a fairly simple fabric design was found to be

original and to have been copied. Of course, if someone has written an outline, script or screenplay for a television show, film, etc and that idea is confidential, then dual protection may arise in the confidential idea embodied in the documents and in the literary (and sometimes artistic) works in which the idea has taken material form. But, if the idea is used, but not the form, this might give rise to an action for breach of confidence, but not for infringement of copyright. Copyright prevents the copying of the *material form* in which the idea has been presented, or of a substantial part of it, measured in terms of quality, not quantity.

S.1 of the Act sets out a number of different categories of works which can be the subject of copyright protection. These are:

- original literary, dramatic, musical or artistic works,
- sound recordings, films, broadcasts or cable programmes, and
- typographical arrangements of published editions.

These works are further defined in ss.3–8 (see box for examples).

However, no work of any description enjoys copyright protection until it has been reduced into or recorded in a tangible form, as s.3(2) provides that no copyright shall subsist in a literary, musical or artistic work until it has been recorded in writing or otherwise.

On the other hand, all that is required to achieve copyright protection is to record the original work in an appropriate medium. Once that has been done, copyright will subsist in the work (assuming that the qualifying features set out below are present) without any formality of registration or otherwise. There is, for instance, no need to publish a work to protect it. Please note, however, that the law of the United States does differ on this – see page 625.

Nonetheless, there can be a real benefit in keeping a proper record of the creation of a work. Drafts or preliminary sketches should be kept and dated, so as to be able to show the development of a work. It may also be beneficial (especially where works are to be submitted to potential publishers or purchasers) to take a complete copy of the documents and send them to oneself or lodge them with a responsible third party, sealed and dated, so as to be able to provide cogent evidence of the form or content of the work at that date. Such evidence may help prove one's independent title either as claimant or defendant in a copyright infringement (or indeed breach of confidence) action.

Originality

In order to gain copyright protection, literary, dramatic, artistic and musical works must be original. Sound recordings or films which are copies of pre-existing sound recordings or films, broadcasts which infringe rights in another broadcast or cable programmes which consist of immediate retransmissions of broadcasts are not protected by copyright.

Just as the law protects the form, rather than the idea, originality relates to the 'expression of the thought', rather than to the thought itself. A work need not be original in the sense of showing innovative artistic, literary or cultural merit, but only to have been the product of skill and labour on the part of the author. This can be seen for instance in the definition of certain artistic works, and in the fact that copyright protects works such as compilations (like football pools coupons or directories) and tables (including mathematical tables).

There may be considerable difficulty, at times, in deciding whether a work is of sufficient originality, or has original features, where there is a series of similar designs or amendments of existing works. See *L.A. Gear Inc.* [1992] FSR 121 and *Biotrading* [1998] FSR 109. A new edition or an adaptation of an existing work may obtain a new copyright depending upon the scope of the changes to the work; this will not affect the earlier copyright protection. See *Cala Homes* [1995] FSR 818. What is clear, though, is that merely making a 'slavish copy' of a work will not create an original work: see *Interlego AG* [1989] AC 217. On the other hand, if

> ### Definitions under the Act
>
> **Literary work** is defined as: 'any work, other than a dramatic or musical work, which is written, spoken or sung, and accordingly includes: (a) a table or compilation other than a database, (b) a computer program, (c) preparatory design material for a computer program and (d) a database.'
>
> **A musical work** means: 'a work consisting of music, exclusive of any words or action intended to be sung, spoken or performed with the music.'
>
> **An artistic work** means: '(a) a graphic work, photograph, sculpture or collage, irrespective of artistic quality, (b) a work of architecture being a building or model for a building, or (c) a work of artistic craftsmanship.'
>
> These categories of work are not mutually exclusive, e.g. a film may be protected both as a film and as a dramatic work. See *Norowzian* v. *Arks* [2000] FSR 363.

the work gives particular expression to a commonplace idea or an old tale, copyright may subsist in it (see *Christoffer* v. *Poseidon Film Distributors Limited* (6/10/99) in which it was held that a script for an animated film of a story from Homer's *Odyssey* was an original literary work). Copyright protection will be limited to the original features of the work, or those features created or chosen by the author's input of skill and labour.

'Works' such as the titles of books or periodicals, or advertising slogans, which may have required a good deal of original thought, generally are not accorded copyright protection, because they are too short to be deemed literary works.

Qualification

The Act is limited in its effects to the UK (and to colonies to which it may be extended by Order). It is aimed primarily at protecting the works of British citizens, or works which were first published here. However, in line with the requirements of various international conventions, copyright protection in the UK is also accorded to the works of nationals of many foreign states, as well as to works first published in those states, on a reciprocal basis.

As for works of nationals of other member states of the European Union, there is a principle of equal treatment, so that protection must be offered to such works here: see *Phil Collins* [1993] 3 CMLR 773.

The importance of these rules mainly arises when one is trying to find out whether a foreign work is protected by copyright here, for instance, if one wishes to make a film based upon a foreign novel.

Ownership

The general rule is that the copyright in a work will first be owned by its author, the author being the creator of the work. In most cases this is self-explanatory, but the definition of 'author' in relation to films and sound recordings has changed over the years; currently, the author of a sound recording is its producer, and the authors of a film are the producer and principal director.

One important exception to the general rule is that the copyright in a work made by an employee in the course of his or her employment will belong to their employer, subject to any agreement to the contrary. However, this rule does not apply to freelance designers, journalists, etc, and not even to nominally self-employed company directors. This obviously may lead to problems if the question of copyright ownership is not dealt with when an agreement is made to create, purchase or use a work (see box, page 611).

Where a work is produced by several people who collaborate in such a way that each one's contribution is not distinct from that of the other(s), then they will be joint authors of the work. Where two people collaborate to write a song, one producing the lyrics and the other the music, there will be two separate copyright works, the copyright of which will be owned by each of the authors separately. But where two people write a play, each rewriting what the other produces, there will be a joint work.

The importance of knowing whether the work is joint or not arises:

● in working out the duration of the copyright, and
● from the fact that joint works can only be exploited with the agreement of all the joint authors, so that all of them have to join in any licence, although each of them can sue for infringement without joining the other(s) as a claimant in the proceedings.

Duration of copyright

As a result of amendments brought into effect on 1 January 1996, copyright in literary, dramatic, musical or artistic works expires at the end of the period of 70 years from the end of the calendar year in which the author dies (s.12(1)). Where there are joint authors, then the 70 years runs from the death of the last of them to die. If the author is unknown, there will be 70 years protection from the date the work was first made or (where applicable) first made available to the public. Previously, the protection was for 'life plus 50'.

The extended 70-year term also applies to films, and runs from the end of the calendar year in which the death occurs of the last to die of the principal director, the author of the screenplay, the dialogue or the composer of any music created for the film (s.13B). This obviously may be a nightmare to establish, and there are certain presumptions in s.66A which may help someone wishing to use material from an old film.

However, sound recordings are still protected by copyright only for 50 years from the year of making or release (s.13A); similarly, broadcasts, cable programmes and computer-generated works still get only 50 years protection.

The new longer term applies without difficulty to works created after

1 January 1996 and to works in copyright on 31 December 1995. The owner of that extended copyright will be the person who owned it on 31 December 1995, unless that person had only a limited term of ownership, in which case the extra 20 years will be added on to the reversionary term.

Where copyright had expired here, but the author died between 50 and 70 years ago, the position is more complicated. EC Directive 93/98 provided that if a work was protected

Licensing

A licence is granted to another to exploit the right whilst the licensor retains overall ownership.

Licences do not need to take any form in particular, and may indeed be granted orally. However, an exclusive licence (i.e. one which excludes even the copyright owner himself from exploiting the work) must be in writing, if the licensee is to enjoy rights in respect of infringements concurrent with those of the copyright owner.

by copyright anywhere in the European Union on 1 July 1995, copyright revives for it in any other state until the end of the same 70-year period. Differences in national laws may make it necessary to look at the position in the states offering a longer term of protection, namely Germany, France and Spain.

Ownership of the revived term of copyright will belong to the person who was the owner of the copyright when the initial term expired, save that if that person died (or a company, etc, ceased to exist) before 1 January 1996, then the revived term will vest in the author's personal representatives, and in the case of a film, in the principal director's personal representatives.

Any licence affecting a copyright work which subsisted on 31 December 1995 and was then for the full term of the copyright, continues to have effect during any extended term of copyright, subject to any agreement to the contrary (paragraph 21 of the Regulations).

The increased term offered to works of other EU nationals as a result of the Term Directive is not offered automatically to the nationals of other states, but will only apply where an equally long term is offered in their state of origin.

Where acts are carried out in relation to such revived copyright works, pursuant to things done whilst they were in the public domain, protection from infringement is available. A licence as of right may also be available, on giving notice to the copyright owner and paying a royalty.

Dealing with copyright works

Ownership of the copyright in a work confers upon the owner the exclusive right to deal with the work in a number of ways, and essentially stops all unauthorised exploitation of the work. Ownership of the copyright is capable of being separated from ownership of the material form in which the work is embodied, depending upon the terms of any agreement or the circumstances. Even buying an original piece of artwork will not in general carry with it the copyright, as an effective assignment must be in writing signed by the assignor.

Copyright works can be exploited by their owners in two ways:

- Assignment: rights in a work may be sold, with the owner retaining no interest in it (except, possibly, for payment by way of royalties or some

Assignments

In an assignment, rights in the work are sold, with the owner retaining no interest in it (except, possibly, for payment by way of royalties).

An assignment must be in writing, signed by or on behalf of the assignor, but no other formality is required. One can make an assignment of future copyright (under s.91). Where the author of a projected work agrees in writing that he will assign the rights in a future work to another, the copyright vests in the assignee immediately upon the creation of the work, without further formalities.

These rules do not affect the common law as to beneficial interests in copyright. One possibility may be that a court will, in the right circumstances, find or infer an agreement to assign the copyright in a work, e.g. where a sole trader had title to the copyright used in his business later incorporated his business and allowed the company to exploit the software as if it were its own, an agreement to assign was inferred (see *Lakeview Computers plc* 26/11/99). Alternatively, if the court finds that a work was commissioned to be made, and that there was a common intention that the purchaser should own the copyright, the court may order the author to assign the copyright to him. 'Commission' in this context means only to order a particular piece of work to be done: see *Apple Corps Ltd* v. *Cooper* [1993] FSR 286 (on the 1956 Act).

reversionary rights in certain agreed circumstances) – see box; or

- Licensing: the owner may grant a licence to another to exploit the right, whilst retaining overall ownership (see box).

Agreements dealing with copyright should make it clear whether an assignment or a licence is being granted. There may be significant advantages in granting a licence rather than an assignment, for where an assignee sells the rights to a third party, or perhaps the rights of an insolvent assignee are sold, as one cannot normally enforce the original agreement to pay royalties, etc against a purchaser (*Barker* v. *Stickney* [1919] 1 KB 121). If the agreement is unclear, the Court is likely to find that the grantee took the minimum rights necessary for his intended use of the work (*Ray* v. *Classic FM plc* [1998] FSR 622). The question of moral rights (see below) will also have to be considered by parties negotiating an assignment or licence.

Both assignments and licences can, and frequently do, split up the various rights contained within the copyright. So, for instance, a licence might be granted to one person to publish a novel in book form, another person might be granted the film, television and video rights, and yet another the right to translate the novel into other languages.

Assignments and licences may also confer rights according to territory, dividing the USA from the EU or different EU countries one from the other. Any such agreement should take into account divergences between different national copyright laws. Furthermore, when seeking to divide rights between different territories of the EU there is a danger of infringing the competition rules of the EU. Professional advice should be taken, as breach of these rules may attract a fine and can render the agreement void in whole or in part.

Licences can, of course, be of varying lengths. There is no need for a licence to be granted for the whole term of copyright. Well-drafted licences will provide for termination on breach, including the failure of the licensee to exploit the work, and on the insolvency of the licensee and will specify whether the rights may be assigned or sub-licensed.

Copyright may be assigned by will. A bequest of an original document, etc embodying an unpublished copyright work will carry the copyright.

Infringement

The main type of infringement is what is commonly thought of as plagiarism, that is, copying the work. In fact, copyright confers on the owner the exclusive right to do a number of specified acts, so that anyone doing those acts without his permission will infringe. It is important to note that it is not necessary to copy a work exactly or use all of it; it is sufficient if a substantial part is used. That question is to be judged on a qualitative not a quantitative basis, bearing in mind that it is the skill and labour of the author which is to be protected (see *Ravenscroft* v. *Herbert* [1980] RPC 193 and *Designers Guild*).

The form of infringement common to all forms of copyright works is that of copying. This means reproducing the work in any material form. It is important to note that primary infringement, such as copying, can be done innocently of any intention to infringe.

Infringement may occur where an existing work provides the inspiration for a later one, if copying results, for example by including edited extracts from a history book in a novel (*Ravenscroft*), using a photograph as the inspiration for a painting (*Baumann* v. *Fussell* [1978] RPC 485), or words from a verse of one song for another (*Ludlow Music* v. *Williams* [2001] FSR 271). Infringement will not necessarily be prevented merely by the application of significant new skill and labour by the infringer, nor by a change of medium.

In the case of a two-dimensional artistic work, reproduction can mean making a copy in three dimensions, and vice versa. However, s.51 of the Act provides that in the case of a 'design document or model' (for definition, see page 614) for something which is not *itself* an artistic work, it is no infringement to make an article to that design. This means that whilst it would be an infringement of copyright to make an article from a design drawing for, say, a sculpture, it will not be an infringement of copyright to make a handbag from a copy of the design drawing for it, or from a handbag which one has purchased. Instead, such designs are generally protected by design right or as registered designs (for both see below).

Copying a film, broadcast or cable programme can include making a copy of the whole or a substantial part of any image from it (see s.17(4)). This means that copying one frame of the film will be an infringement. It is not an infringement of copyright in a film to reshoot the film (*Norowzian*) (though there would doubtless be an infringement of the copyright in underlying works such as the literary copyright in the screenplay).

Copying is generally proved by showing substantial similarities between the original and the alleged copy, plus an opportunity to copy. Surprisingly often, minor errors in the original are reproduced by an infringer.

Copying need not be direct, so that, for instance, where the copyright is in a fabric design, copying the material without ever having seen the original drawing will still be an infringement, as will 'reverse engineering' of industrial designs for

'Secondary' infringements

Secondary infringements consist not of making infringing copies, but of dealing with them in some way. It is an infringement to import an infringing copy into the UK, and to possess in the course of business, or to sell, hire, offer for sale or hire, or distribute in the course of trade an infringing copy. However, none of these acts will be an infringement unless the alleged infringer knew or had reason to believe that the articles were infringing copies. What is sufficient knowledge will depend upon the facts of each case (see *LA Gear Inc.* [1992] FSR 121, *ZYX Records* v. *King* [1997] 2 All ER 132 and *Pensher Security* [2000] RPC 249). Merely putting someone on notice of a dispute as to ownership of copyright may not suffice to give him or her reason to believe in infringement for this purpose: *Hutchison* [1995] FSR 365.

Other secondary infringements consist of permitting a place to be used for a public performance in which copyright is infringed and supplying apparatus to be used for infringing public performance, again, in each case, with safeguards for innocent acts.

example to make unlicensed spare parts (*British Leyland* [1986] AC 577; *Mars* v. *Teknowledge* [2000] FSR 138).

Issuing copies of a work to the public when they have not previously been put into circulation in the UK is also an infringement of all types of work.

Other acts which may amount to an infringement depend upon the nature of the work. It will be an infringement of the copyright in a literary, dramatic or musical work to perform it in public, whether by live performance or by playing recordings. Similarly, it is an infringement of the copyright in a sound recording, film, broadcast or cable programme to play or show it in public. Many copyright works will also be infringed by the rental or lending of copies of the work.

One rather different form of infringement is to make an adaptation of a literary, dramatic or musical work. An adaptation includes, in the case of a literary work, a translation, in the case of a non-dramatic work, making a dramatic work of it, and vice versa. A transcription or arrangement of a musical work is an adaptation of it.

There are also a number of 'secondary' infringements – see box.

Exceptions to infringement

The Act provides a large number of exceptions to the rules on infringement. They are far too numerous to be dealt with here in full, but they include:

• fair dealing with literary, dramatic, musical or artistic works for the purpose of research or private study;
• fair dealing for the purpose of criticism or review or reporting current events, as to which see for example *Pro Sieben Media* [1999] FSR 610; *Hyde Park* v. *Yelland* [2001] Ch. 143; *NLA* v. *Marks & Spencer Plc* [2002] RPC 4);
• incidental inclusion of a work in an artistic work, sound recording, film, broadcast or cable programme;
• educational exceptions (see ss.32–36);
• exceptions for libraries (see ss.37–44) and public administration (see ss.45–50);
• backing-up, or converting a computer program or accessing a licensed database (see s.50A–D);

- dealing with a work where the author cannot be identified and the work seems likely to be out of copyright;
- public recitation, if accompanied by a sufficient acknowledgement;
- various e-commerce, transient use, etc exceptions based upon Directive 2001/29/EC (which should be brought into effect in the UK soon).

The effect of the Human Rights Act on copyright in relation to the right to free speech seems likely to be limited, as sufficient protection is to be found in the fair dealing provisions: *Ashdown* v. *Telegraph Group Limited* [2002] Ch. 149. There is no defence of parody.

Remedies for infringements

The copyright owner will usually want to prevent the repetition or continuation of the infringement and he will want compensation.

In almost all cases an injunction will be sought to stop the infringement. The Courts have useful powers to grant an injunction at an early stage, indeed, even before any infringement takes place, if a real threat of damage can be shown. Such an interim injunction can be applied for on three days notice (or without notice in appropriate cases), but will not be granted unless the claimant has a reasonably good case and can show that he would suffer 'unquantifiable' damage if the defendant's activities continue pending trial. Delay in bringing an interim application may be fatal to its success. An injunction may not be granted where the claimant clearly only wants financial compensation (*Ludlow Music*).

Financial compensation may be sought in one of two forms. Firstly, damages. These will usually be calculated upon evidence of the loss caused to the claimant, sometimes based upon loss of business, at others upon the basis of what would have been a proper licence fee for the defendant's acts. Additional damages may be awarded in rare cases for flagrant infringements. See for example *Notts. Healthcare* v. *News Group Newspapers* [2002] RPC 49.

Damages will not be awarded for infringement where the infringer did not know, and had no reason to believe, that copyright subsisted in the work. This exception is of limited use to a defendant, though, in the usual situation where the work was of such a nature that he should have known that copyright would subsist in it.

The alternative to damages is an account of profits, that is, the net profits made by the infringer by virtue of his illicit exploitation of the copyright. Where an account of profits is sought, no award of flagrant damages can be made. See *Redrow Homes Limited* [1999] 1 AC 197.

A copyright owner may also apply for delivery up of infringing copies.

Finally, there are various criminal offences relating to the making, importation, possession, sale, hire, distribution, etc of infringing copies.

Design right

Many industrial designs are excluded from copyright protection, by s.51. Alternatively, the term of copyright protection is limited to 25 years from first industrial exploitation, by s.52. However, they may instead be protected by the 'design right' created by ss.213–64. Like copyright, design right does not depend upon registration, but upon the creation of a suitable design by a qualified person.

Design right is granted to original designs consisting of the shape or configuration (internal or external) of the whole or part of an article, not being merely 'surface decoration'. A design is not original if it was commonplace in the design field in question at the time of its creation. In *Farmers Build* [1999] RPC 461, 'commonplace' was defined as meaning a design of a type which would excite no 'peculiar attention' amongst those in the trade, or one which amounts to a run-of-the-mill combination of well-known features. Designs are not protected if they consist of a method or principle of construction, or are dictated by the shape, etc of an article to which the new article is to be connected or of which it is to form part, the so-called 'must-fit' and 'must-match' exclusions. In *Ocular Sciences* [1997] RPC 289, these exclusions had a devastating effect upon numerous design rights claimed for contact lens designs.

Design right subsists in designs made by or for qualifying persons (see, broadly, 'Qualification' on page 608) or first marketed in the UK or EU or any other country to which the provision may be extended by Order.

Design right lasts only 15 years from the end of the year in which it was first recorded or an article made to the design, or (if shorter) 10 years from the end of the year in which articles made according to the design were first sold or hired out. During the last five years of the term of protection, a licence to use the design can be obtained 'as of right' but against payment of a proper licence fee. Hence, design right may give only five years 'absolute' protection, as opposed to the 'life plus 70' of copyright.

The designer will be the owner of the right, unless it was commissioned, in which case the commissioner will be the first owner. An employee's designs made in the course of employment will belong to the employer.

The right given to the owner of a design right is the exclusive right to reproduce the design for commercial purposes. The rules as to assignments, licensing and infringement, both primary and secondary, are substantially similar to those described above in relation to copyright, as are the remedies available.

There have recently been significant changes to the law on registered designs, which coexist with the right given by the unregistered design right discussed above. The Registered Design Act 1949 has been amended (and expanded) in line with EU legislation, and now permits the registration of designs consisting of the appearance of the whole or any part of a product resulting from features of the product itself, such as shape, materials, etc or from the ornamentation of the product. It covers industrial or handicraft items, their packaging or get-up, etc. Designs must be novel and not solely dictated by function. The range of designs which may be registered is wider than under the old law, and designs need not necessarily have 'eye appeal'. Such designs provide a monopoly right renewable for up to 25 years. For further explanation see the useful guidance on the Patent Office website.

EU Regulation 6/2002 has created two new Community design regimes, one for registered and one for unregistered designs. It is not possible in the space available here to describe these new regimes in detail but the regulation is available online at http://europa.ue.int/eur-lex. In brief, such designs (which are *very* broadly defined in Article 3) for example must be 'new' and have 'individual character'. The registered right, available from April 2003, may be enjoyed for up to 25 years in five-year tranches, but an unregistered Community design right lasts only three years. The unregistered right protects the design from copying, but the registered right gives 'absolute' exclusivity, in that it may be infringed without copying.

Moral rights

The Act also provides for the protection of certain 'moral rights'.

The right of 'paternity' is for the author of a copyright literary, dramatic, musical or artistic work, or the director of a copyright film, to be identified as the author/ director, largely whenever the work is commercially exploited (s.77).

However, the right does not arise unless it has been 'asserted' by appropriate words in writing, or in the case of an artistic work by ensuring that the artist's name appears on the frame, etc (see end). There are exceptions to the right, in particular where first ownership of the copyright vested in the author's or director's employer.

The right of 'integrity' protects work from 'derogatory treatment', meaning an addition to, deletion from, alteration or adaptation of a work which amounts to distortion or mutilation of the work or is otherwise prejudicial to the honour or reputation of the author/director.

Again, infringement of the right takes place when the maltreated work is published commercially or performed or exhibited in public. There are various exceptions set out in s.81 of the Act, in particular where the publication is in a newspaper, etc, and the work was made for inclusion in it or made available with the author's consent.

Where the copyright in the work vested first in the author's or director's employer, he or she has no right to 'integrity' unless identified at the time of the relevant act or on published copies of the work.

These rights subsist for as long as the copyright in the work subsists.

A third moral right conferred by the Act is not to have a literary, dramatic, musical or artistic work falsely attributed to one as author, or to have a film falsely attributed to one as director, again where the work in question is published, etc. This right subsists until 20 years after a person's death.

None of these rights can be assigned during the person's lifetime, but all of them either pass on the person's death as directed by his or her will or fall into his residuary estate.

A fourth but rather different moral right is conferred by s.85. It gives a person who has commissioned the taking of photographs for private purposes a right to prevent copies of the work being issued to the public, etc.

The remedies for breach of these moral rights again include damages and an injunction, although s.103(2) specifically foresees the granting of an injunction qualified by a right to the defendant to do the acts complained of, if subject to a suitable disclaimer.

Moral rights are exercisable in relation to works in which the copyright has revived subject to any waiver or assertion of the right made before 1 January 1996 (see details as to who may exercise rights in paragraph 22 of the Regulations).

NOTICE

AMANDA LOUISE MICHAELS hereby asserts and gives notice of her right under s.77 of the Copyright, Designs & Patents Act 1988 to be identified as the author of the foregoing article.

AMANDA MICHAELS

Amanda L. Michaels is a barrister in private practice in London, and specialises in copyright, designs, trade marks, and similar intellectual property and 'media' work. She is author of *A Practical Guide to Trade Mark Law* (Sweet & Maxwell, 3rd edn 2001).

Further reading

Garnett, Rayner James and Davies, *Copinger and Skone James on Copyright*, Sweet & Maxwell, 14th edn, 1999 and Supplement 2002

Laddie, Prescott and Vitoria, *The Modern Law of Copyright*, Butterworths, 3rd edn, 2000

Flint, *A User's Guide to Copyright*, Butterworths, 5th edn, 2000

Bainbridge, David, *Intellectual Property*, Pearson Education, 5th edn, 2002

Copyright Acts

Copyright, Designs and Patents Act 1998

The Duration of Copyright and Rights in Performances Regulations 1995 (SI 1995 No 3297)

see also Numerous Orders in Council

The Copyright Licensing Agency Ltd

The Copyright Licensing Agency (CLA) collects and distributes money on behalf of artists, writers and publishers for the photocopying of their work. CLA operates on a non-profit basis, and issues licences to schools, further and higher education, business and government bodies so that such organisations can access the copyright material in books, journals, law reports, magazines and periodicals.

Why was CLA established?

CLA was established in 1982 by its members, the Authors' Licensing and Collecting Society (ALCS) and the Publishers Licensing Society (PLS) to promote and enforce the intellectual property rights of British rightsholders both at home and abroad. CLA also has close ties with the Design and Artists Copyright Society (DACS), which represents artists and illustrators.

ALCS has two corporate members – the Society of Authors and the Writers' Guild of Great Britain. It also has a large number of individual authors as members and affiliations with the National Union of Journalists and the Chartered Institute of Journalists. PLS members are the Publishers Association, the Periodical Publishers Association and the Association of Learned and Professional Society Publishers.

How CLA helps artists and writers

CLA allows licensed users access to over 16 million titles worldwide. In return CLA ensures artists and writers, along with publishers, are fairly recompensed by the licence fees, which CLA collects and forwards to its members for onward distribution to artists, writers and publishers.

The collective management of licensing schemes means that CLA can provide users with the simplest and most cost-effective means of obtaining authorisation for photocopying, while copy limits ensure fair recompense is maintained for rightsholders.

CLA is currently developing licences which will enable digitisation of existing print material. The licence will enable users to scan and electronically send extracts from copyright works. Scanning and email distribution is only available for UK works at present.

Licence to copy

CLA's licensees fall into three main categories:
- education (schools, further and higher education);
- government (central, local, public bodies); and
- business (business, industry, professionals).

CLA develops licences to meet the specific needs of each sector and groupings within each sector. Depending on the requirement, there are both blanket and transactional licences available. Every licence allows the photocopying of most books, journals, magazines and periodicals published in the UK.

An international dimension

Many countries have established equivalents to CLA and the number of such agencies is set to grow. Nearly all these agencies, including CLA, are members of the International Federation of Reproduction Rights Organisations (IFRRO).

Through reciprocal arrangements with these organisations, any CLA licence also allows copying from an expanding list of publications in other countries. Currently these countries are: Australia, Canada (including Quebec), Denmark, Finland, France, Germany, Greece, Iceland, Ireland, The Netherlands, New Zealand, Norway, South Africa, Spain, Sweden, Switzerland and the USA.

CLA receives monies from these organisations for the copying of UK material abroad and forwards it to rightsholders.

Further information

The Copyright Licensing Agency Ltd
90 Tottenham Court Road, London W1T 4LP
tel 020-7631 5555 *fax* 020-7631 5500
email cla@cla.co.uk
website www.cla.co.uk
CBC House, 24 Canning Street,
Edinburgh EH3 8E9
tel 0131-272 2711 *fax* 0131-272 2811
email clascotland@cla.co.uk

Distribution

The fees collected from licensees are forwarded to artists, authors and publishers via ALCS, DACS and PLS respectively, and are based on statistical surveys and records of copying activity. For the year ending 31 March 2002 in excess of £25 million was returned to rightsholders.

Respecting copyright

CLA also believes it is important to raise awareness of the copyright in published material and the need to protect the creativity of artists, authors and publishers. To this end, CLA organises a range of activities such as copyright workshops in schools, seminars for businesses and institutions and an extensive exhibition programme. A comprehensive website is regularly updated and a bi-annual newsletter, Clarion, is posted to all licensees and to those individuals and groups concerned with copyright.

Protecting creativity

CLA believes in working together with all sectors to take into account their differing needs, meaning legal action is rare. However, organisations – especially in the business sector – need to be made aware that copyright is a legally enforceable right enshrined in statute law, not a voluntary option. CLA's recently restructured compliance division aims to continue the education programme. However, as a last resort it has the power to take legal proceedings on behalf of rightsholders.

Authors' Licensing and Collecting Society

The Authors' Licensing and Collecting Society (ALCS) represents the interests of all UK writers and ensures that they are fairly compensated for any works that are copied, broadcast or recorded.

The Authors' Licensing and Collecting Society (ALCS) is the UK rights management society for writers. Established in 1977, the Society represents the interests of all UK writers and ensures that they are fairly compensated for any works that are copied, broadcast or recorded.

A non-profit company, ALCS was set up in the wake of the campaign to establish a Public Lending Right to help writers protect and exploit their collective rights. Today, it is the largest writers' organisation in the UK with a membership of over 42,000 and an annual distribution of more than £11 million in secondary royalties to writers.

The Society is committed to ensuring that the rights of writers, both legal and moral, are fully respected and fairly rewarded. It represents all types of writers, fiction and non-fiction; including educational, research and academic authors drawn from the professions; scriptwriters, adaptors, playwrights, poets, editors and freelance journalists, across the print and broadcast media.

Internationally recognised as a leading authority on copyright matters and authors' interests, ALCS is committed to fostering an awareness of Intellectual Property issues among the writing community. It maintains a close watching brief on all matters affecting copyright both in the UK and abroad and makes regular represen-tations to the UK government and the EU.

ALCS works closely with the Writers' Guild of Great Britain (see page 490), the Society of Authors (see page 487) and by reciprocal agreement with over 50 collecting societies overseas. Owned and controlled by writers, it is governed by a non-executive 12-Member Council of Management, all of whom are working writers. Four are

Membership

Authors' Licensing and Collecting Society Ltd
14-18 Holborn, London EC1N 2LE
Tel 020-7395 0600 *Fax* 020-7395 0660
Email alcs@alcs.co.uk
Website www.alcs.co.uk

ALCS membership is open to all writers and successors to their estates at a current annual subscription fee of £10 for Ordinary members. Members of the Society of Authors and the Writers' Guild of Great Britain have free Ordinary membership of ALCS. Free Associate membership is given to members of:

● National Union of Journalists
● Chartered Institute of Journalists
● British Association of Journalists
● British Comedy Writers' Association.

You may also register direct with ALCS for free Associate membership.

ALCS is primarily funded through a commission levied on distributions and membership fees. The commission on funds generated for Ordinary members is currently 11%. Writers do not have to be Ordinary members of ALCS to receive funds due to them for the reproduction of their works; however, such funds are subject to a levy of 14%. Most writers find that this, together with a number of other membership benefits, provides excellent value to membership.

nominated by the Writers' Guild and four by the Society of Authors. A further four independent members are elected directly by ALCS Ordinary members.

The Society collects fees that are difficult, time-consuming or legally impossible for writers and their representatives to claim on an individual basis, money that is nonetheless due to them. To date, it has distributed over £80 million in secondary royalties to writers.

Over the years, ALCS has developed highly specialised knowledge and sophisticated systems that can track writers and their works against any secondary use for which they are due payment. A network of international contacts and reciprocal agreements with foreign collecting societies also ensures that British writers are compensated for any similar use overseas.

Its primary sources of fees due to writers are secondary royalties from the following:

Photocopying

The single largest source of income, this is administered by the Copyright Licensing Agency (CLA; see page 618). Created in 1982 by ALCS and the Publishers Licensing Society (PLS), the CLA grants licences to users for the copying of books, periodicals and journals. This includes schools, colleges, universities, central and local government departments as well as the British Library, businesses and other institutions. Licence fees are based on the number of people who benefit and the number of copies made. The revenue from this is then split between the rightsholders: authors, publishers and artists. Money due to authors is transferred to ALCS for distribution. ALCS also receives photocopying payments from foreign sources.

Digitisation

In 1999, the CLA also launched its licensing scheme for the digitisation of printed texts. It offers licences to organisations for storing and using digital versions of authors' printed works, which have been scanned into a computer. Again, the fees are split between authors and publishers.

Foreign Public Lending Right

The Public Lending Right (PLR) system pays authors whose books are borrowed from public libraries. Through reciprocal agreement with VG Wort (the German collecting society), ALCS members receive payment whenever their books are borrowed from German libraries. A similar agreement is planned with the Netherlands too. (Please note that ALCS does not administer the UK Public Lending Right; this is managed directly by the UK PLR Office. See page 598.)

ALCS also receives other payments from Germany. These cover the loan of academic, scientific and technical titles from academic libraries; extracts of authors' works in textbooks and the press, together with other one-off fees.

Simultaneous cable retransmission

This involves the simultaneous showing of one country's television signals in another country, via a cable network. Cable companies pay a central collecting organisation a percentage of their subscription fees, which must be collectively administered. This sum is then divided by the rightsholders. ALCS receives the writers' share for British programmes containing literary and dramatic material and distributes this to them.

BBC Prime
ALCS licenses BBC Worldwide Ltd for the inclusion of material within the ALCS repertoire. The licence covers the direct reception and cable retransmission of BBC Prime, an entertainment satellite channel, in Europe and Africa.

Educational recording
ALCS, together with the main broadcasters and rightsholders, set up the Educational Recording Agency (ERA) in 1989 to offer licences to educational establishments. ERA collects fees from the licensees and pays ALCS the amount due to writers for their literary works.

Other sources of income include a blank tape levy and small, miscellaneous literary rights.

Unclaimed monies
ALCS is dedicated to protecting and promoting authors' rights and enabling authors to maximise their income. It is committed to ensuring that secondary royalties due to writers are efficiently collected and speedily distributed to them. One of its greatest challenges is finding some of the writers for whom it holds funds and ensuring that they claim their money.

Any published author or broadcast writer may well have some funds held by ALCS for them. It may be a nominal sum or it could run in to several thousand pounds. Such authors should call or visit the ALCS website. It is helpful for all concerned if they register with ALCS as an Associate member (free) and spread the word...

The Design and Artists Copyright Society Ltd

The Design and Artists Copyright Society Ltd (DACS) is the copyright and collecting society for visual artists in the UK. It is an independent, non-profit-making society open to all artists and photographers.

About DACS

Founded in 1983, DACS works to create a fair working environment for visual creators by administering and protecting copyright on behalf of its members, and by lobbying for all artists at both national and international levels on rights-related issues. It is the only organisation working for artists and photographers in the UK that deals solely with copyright and artists' rights. DACS is part of a national framework of UK artists' and photographers' professional associations and trade unions, which ensures a consistent approach to all copyright and rights-related issues in the UK. Any individual or business based in the UK that wishes to reproduce an artistic work by a member must apply to DACS for permission to do so.

Copyright

Copyright is a right granted to creators under law. Copyright in all artistic works is established from the moment of creation – the only qualification required is that the work must be original. DACS' activities complement those of other UK collecting societies, such as the Performing Rights Society (PRS) and the Authors' Licensing and Copyright Society (ALCS).

DACS administers copyright in the UK on behalf of its members. This principally involves providing users of visual works (such as a publisher) with licences for inclusion of works of art in various products, such as books and posters. Permission to reproduce a work is normally granted in return for a fee. DACS charges fees calculated according to published tariffs or via negotiation for merchandising and advertising uses. Each licence granted to a publisher, film producer, or any other user is legally binding.

Often professional and commercial artists create their works as a result of a commission, and they may directly administer and control their primary rights in these works. However, individual creators are often unable to control their secondary rights, and a system of Collective Administration has been established, so that these rights are administered on behalf of many creators by one collecting society. In the UK, DACS is the collecting society for visual artists' secondary rights. The Payback campaign seeks to unite artists with monies collected in this manner. It is not necessary to be a member of DACS to benefit from Payback since DACS represents the entire visual artists' repertoire in the UK.

Worldwide protection

DACS represents 40,000 artists through reciprocal representation agreements with visual arts collecting societies throughout Europe and internationally. In the UK, DACS represents the copyright interests of artists from all over the world and in turn societies abroad represent DACS' members there. Artists and photographers therefore benefit from a global network of societies that provides administration and copyright protection.

Artists' rights

DACS is currently working towards the successful implementation of *droit de suite*, or the Artist's Resale Right.

Membership

The Design and Artists Copyright Society Ltd (DACS)
Parchment House, 13 Northburgh Street, London EC1V 0JP
tel 020-7336 8811 *fax* 020-7336 8822
email info@dacs.org.uk
website www.dacs.org.uk

Membership is open to any visual artist of any discipline who is resident in the UK or the Republic of Ireland. Currently DACS represents artists from a wide variety of disciplines: fine art, photography, sculpture, illustration, textiles, glass and ceramics, to name but a few. Contact DACS for a membership application pack.

This right ensures that artists receive a percentage of the revenue each time a work is sold after the first sale, a right enjoyed by artists across Europe.

As new issues and technologies affecting copyright and artists' rights arise, such as the internet, DACS and its sister societies develop systems to protect their members' interests while encouraging creativity. As part of an international network, DACS can keep abreast of the global issues affecting artists and ensure that artists are represented at all levels, and on every major area of concern.

Structure

DACS is governed by a Council of Management, which consists of elected members of the Society. The Council is responsible for making all major policy and financial decisions at DACS. The day-to-day running of the Society is carried out by the Chief Executive in conjunction with a specialised staff experienced in copyright matters.

As a non-profit-making society, DACS is financed primarily by commission deducted from the fees and royalties that it collects. Other income is derived from membership fees.

US copyright law

Gavin McFarlane, barrister, introduces US copyright law and points out the differences, and similarities, of British copyright law.

International copyright
International copyright conventions

No general principle of international copyright provides a uniform code for the protection of right owners throughout the world. There are, however, two major international copyright conventions which lay down certain minimum standards for member states, in particular requiring member states to accord to right owners of other member states the same protection which is granted to their own nationals. One is the higher standard Berne Convention of 1886, the most recent revision of which was signed in Paris in 1971. The other is the Universal Copyright Convention signed in 1952 with lower minimum standards, and sponsored by Unesco. This also was most recently revised in Paris in 1971, jointly with the Berne Convention. To this latter Convention the United States has belonged since 1955. On 16 November 1988, the Government of the United States deposited its instrument of accession to the Paris Revision of the Berne Convention. The Convention entered into force as regards the United States on 1 March 1989. Together with certain new statutory provisions made in consequence of accession to Berne, this advances substantially the process of overhaul and modernisation of US copyright law which was begun in the 1970s.

Effect on British copyright owners

The copyright statute of the United States having been brought into line with the requirements of the Berne Convention, compliance with the formalities required by American law has been largely removed. The Berne Convention Implementation Act of 1988 makes statutory amendments to the way foreign works are now treated in US law. These are now inserted in the US codified law as Title 17 – The Copyright Act. 'Foreign works' are works having a country of origin other than the United States. The formalities which were for so long a considerable handicap for foreign copyright owners in the American system have now become optional, though not removed altogether. The new system provides incentives to encourage foreign right owners to continue to comply with formalities on a voluntary basis, in particular notice, renewal and registration.

US copyright law – summary
Introduction of new law

The Copyright Statute of the United States was passed on 19 October 1976. The greater part of its relevant provisions came into force on 1 January 1978. It has extended the range of copyright protection, and further eased the requirements whereby British authors can obtain copyright protection in America. New Public Law 100–568 of 31 October 1988 has made further amendments to the

Copyright Statute which were necessary to enable ratification of the Berne Convention to take place. The Universal Copyright Convention is now for all practical purposes moribund. The problems which derived from the old system of common law copyright no longer exist.

The rights of a copyright owner

(1) To reproduce the copyrighted work in copies or phonorecords.

(2) To prepare derivative works based upon the copyrighted work.

(3) To distribute copies or phonorecords of the copyrighted work to the public by sale or other transfer of ownership, or by rental, lease or lending.

(4) In the case of literary, musical, dramatic and choreographic works, pantomimes, and motion pictures and other audiovisual works, but not sound recordings, to perform the copyrighted work publicly. However, in 1995 Congress granted a limited performance right to sound recordings in digital format in an interactive medium.

Works protected in American law

Works of authorship include:
- Literary works. Note: Computer programs are classified as literary works for the purposes of United States copyright. In *Whelan Associates Inc.* v. *Jaslow Dental Laboratory Inc.* (1987) FSR1, it was held that the copyright of a computer program could be infringed even in the absence of copying of the literal code if the structure was part of the expression of the idea behind a program rather than the idea itself.
- Musical works, including any accompanying words.
- Dramatic works, including any accompanying music.
- Pantomimes and choreographic works.
- Pictorial, graphic and sculptural works.
- Motion pictures and other audiovisual works. Note: copyright in certain motion pictures has been extended by the North American Free Trade Agreement Information Act 1993.
- Sound recordings, but copyright in sound recordings is not to include a right of public performance.
- Architectural works: the design of a building as embodied in any tangible medium of expression, including a building, architectural plans or drawings. The Architectural Works Copyright Protections Act applies this protection to works created on or after 1 December 1990.

(5) In the case of literary, musical, dramatic, and choreographic works, pantomimes, and pictorial, graphic, or sculptural works, including the individual images of a motion picture or other audiovisual work, to display the copyrighted work publicly.

(6) By the Record Rental Amendment Act 1984, s.109 of the Copyright Statute is amended. Now, unless authorised by the owners of copyright in the sound recording and the musical works thereon, the owner of a phonorecord may not, for direct or indirect commercial advantage, rent, lease or lend the phonorecord. A compulsory licence under s.115(c) includes the right of a maker of a phonorecord of non-dramatic musical work to distribute or authorise the distribution of the phonorecord by rental, lease, or lending, and an additional royalty is payable in respect of that. This modifies the 'first sale doctrine', which otherwise permits someone buying a copyright work to hire or sell a lawfully purchased copy to third parties without compensating the copyright owners, and without his or her consent.

(7) A further exception to the 'first sale doctrine' and s.109 of the Copyright Act is made by the Computer Software Rental Amendments Act. A similar restriction has been placed on the unauthorised rental, lease or lending of software, subject to certain limited exceptions. Both the phonorecord and software exceptions to the first sale doctrine terminated, and were extended by Congress on 1 October 1997.

(8) The Semiconductor Chip Protection Act 1984 adds to the Copyright Statute a new chapter on the protection of semiconductor chip products.

(9) The Visual Artists Rights Act 1990 has added moral rights to the various economic rights listed above. These moral rights are the right of integrity, and the right of attribution or paternity. A new category of 'work of visual art' is defined broadly as paintings, drawings, prints and sculptures, with an upper limit of 200 copies. Works generally exploited in mass market copies such as books, newspapers, motion pictures and electronic information services are specifically excluded from these moral rights provisions. Where they apply, they do so only in respect of works created on or after 1 June 1991, and to certain works previously created where title has not already been transferred by the author.

Manufacturing requirements

With effect from 1 July 1986, these ceased to have effect. Prior to 1 July 1986, the importation into or public distribution in the United States of a work consisting preponderantly of non-dramatic literary material in the English language and protected under American law was prohibited unless the portions consisting of such material had been manufactured in the United States or Canada. This provision did not apply where, on the date when importation was sought or public distribution in the United States was made, the author of any substantial part of such material was not a national of the United States or, if a national, had been domiciled outside the United States for a continuous period of at least one year immediately preceding that date.

Since 1 July 1986, there is no manufacturing requirement in respect of works of British authors. With American ratification of the Berne Convention, the formalities previously required in relation to copyright notice, deposit and registration have been greatly modified.

Formalities

Notice of copyright. Whenever a work protected by the American Copyright Statute is published in the United States or elsewhere by authority of the copyright owner, a notice of copyright should be placed on all publicly distributed copies. This should consist of:

- either the symbol © or the word 'Copyright' or the abbreviation 'Copr.' plus
- the year of first publication of the work, plus
- the name of the copyright owner.

Since the Berne Amendments, both US and works of foreign origin which were first published in the US after 1 March 1989 without having notice of copyright placed on them will no longer be unprotected. In general, authors are advised to place copyright notices on their works, as this is a considerable deterrent to plagiarism. Damages may well be lower in a case where no notice of copyright was placed on the work.

Deposit. The owner of copyright or the exclusive right of publication in a work published with notice of copyright in the United States must within three months of such publication deposit in the Copyright Office for the use or disposition of the Library of Congress two complete copies of the best edition of the work (or two records, if the work is a sound recording). Failure to comply with the deposit requirements does not result in the loss of copyright, but a court could assess fines and issue an injunction.

Registration. Registration for copyright in the United States is optional. However, any owner of copyright in a work first published outside the United States may register a work by making application to the Copyright Office with the appropriate fee, and by depositing one complete copy of the work. This requirement of deposit may be satisfied by using copies deposited for the Library of Congress. Whilst registration is still a requirement for works of US origin and from non-Berne countries as a precondition to filing an infringement action, it is no longer necessary for foreign works from Berne countries. But as a matter of practice there are procedural advantages in any litigation where there has been registration. The United States has interpreted the Berne Convention as allowing formalities which are not in themselves conditions for obtaining copyright protection, but which lead to improved protection. The law allows statutory damages and attorneys' fees only if the work was registered prior to the infringement.

Restoration of copyright

Works by non-US authors which lost copyright protection in the United States because of failure to comply with any of these formalities may have had protection automatically restored in certain circumstances. Works claiming restoration must still be in copyright in their country of origin. If a work succeeds in having copyright restored, it will last for the remainder of the period to which it would originally have been entitled in the United States.

Duration of copyright

Copyright in a work created on or after 1 January 1978 endures for a term of the life of the author, and a period of 50 years after the author's death. The further amendments made by Public Law 100–568 of 31 October 1988 have enabled the government to ratify the higher standard Berne Convention. Copyright in a work created before 1 January 1978, but not published or copyrighted before then, subsists from 1 January 1978, and lasts for the life of the author and a post-mortem period of 50 years.

Any copyright, the first term of which under the previous law was still subsisting on 1 January 1978, shall endure for 28 years from the date when it was originally secured, and the copyright proprietor or his or her representative may apply for a further term of 47 years within one year prior to the expiry of the original term. Until 1992, application for renewal and extension was required.

Copyright: criminal proceedings

- Anyone who infringes a copyright wilfully and for purposes of commercial advantage and private financial gain shall be fined not more than $10,000 or imprisoned for not more than 3 years, or both. However, if the infringement relates to copyright in a sound recording or a film, the infringer is liable to a fine of not more than $250,000 or imprisonment for not more than 5 years or both on a first offence, which can be increased to a fine of up to $250,000 or imprisonment for not more than 10 years or both for a subsequent offence.
- Following a conviction for criminal infringement a court may in addition to these penalties order the forfeiture and destruction of all infringing copies and records, together with implements and equipment used in their manufacture.
- It is an offence knowingly and with fraudulent intent to place on any article a notice of copyright or words of the same purport, or to import or distribute such copies. A fine is provided for this offence of not more than $2500. The fraudulent removal of a copyright notice attracts the same maximum fine, as does the false representation of a material particular on an application for copyright representation.

Failure to do so produced disastrous results with some material of great merit passing into the public domain in error. By Public Law 102–307 enacted on 26 June 1992, there is no longer necessity to make a renewal registration in order to obtain the longer period of protection. Now renewal copyright vests automatically in the person entitled to renewal at the end of the 28th year of the original term of copyright.

The duration of any copyright, the renewal term of which was subsisting at any time between 31 December 1976 and 31 December 1977, or for which renewal registration was made between those dates, is extended to endure for a term of 75 years from the date copyright was originally secured.

All terms of copyright provided for by the sections referred to above run to the end of the calendar year in which they would otherwise expire.

Public performance

Under the previous American law provisions relating to performance in public were less generous to right owners than those existing in United Kingdom copyright law. In particular, performance of a musical work was formerly only an infringement if it was 'for profit'. Moreover, the considerable American coin-operated record-playing machine industry (juke boxes) had obtained an exemption from being regarded as instruments of profit, and accordingly their owners did not have to pay royalties for the use of copyright musical works.

Now by the new law one of the exclusive rights of the copyright owner is, in the case of literary, musical, dramatic and choreographic works, pantomimes, and motion pictures and other audiovisual works, to perform the work publicly, without any requirement of such performance being 'for profit'. By s.114 however, the exclusive rights of the owner of copyright in a sound recording are specifically stated not to include any right of public performance, although this provision was modified in 1995.

The position of coin-operated record players (juke boxes) is governed by the new s.116A, inserted by Public Law 100–568 of 31 October 1988. It covers the position of negotiated licences. Limitations are placed on the exclusive right if licences are not negotiated.

Mechanical right

Where sound recordings of a non-dramatic musical work have been distributed to the public in the United States with the authority of the copyright owner, any other person may obtain a compulsory licence to make and distribute sound recordings of the work. This right is known in the United Kingdom as 'the mechanical right'. Notice must be served on the copyright owner, who is entitled to a royalty in respect of each of his or her works recorded of either two and three fourths cents or one half of one cent per minute of playing time or fraction thereof, whichever amount is the larger. These rates are adjusted periodically by the Copyright Arbitration Royalty Panels (CARP). Failure to serve or file the required notice forecloses the possibility of a compulsory licence and, in the absence of a negotiated licence, renders the making and distribution of such records actionable as acts of infringement.

Transfer of copyright

Under the previous American law copyright was regarded as indivisible, which meant that on the transfer of copyright, where it was intended that only film rights or some other such limited right be transferred, the entire copyright nevertheless had to be passed. This led to a cumbersome procedure whereby the author would assign the whole copyright to his or her publisher, who would return to the author by means of an exclusive licence those rights which it was not meant to transfer.

Now it is provided by s.201(d) of the Copyright Statute that (1) the ownership of a copyright may be transferred in whole or in part by any means of conveyance or by operation of law, and may be bequeathed by will or pass as personal property by the applicable laws of intestate succession, and (2) any of the exclusive rights comprised in a copyright (including any subdivision of any of the rights set out in 'The rights of a copyright owner' above) may be transferred as provided in (1) above and owned separately. The owner of any particular exclusive right is entitled, to the extent of that right, to all the protection and remedies accorded to the copyright owner by that Statute. This removes the difficulties which existed under the previous law, and brings the position much closer to that existing in the copyright law of the United Kingdom. All transfers and assignments of copyright must be recorded in the US Copyright Office to have legal effect.

Copyright Arbitration Royalty Panels

In 1993, the Copyright Royalty Tribunal which had been established by the Copyright Act was eliminated by Congress. In its place a new administrative mechanism was established in the Copyright Office with the purpose of making adjustments of reasonable copyright royalty rates in respect of the exercise of certain rights, mainly affecting the musical interests. The Copyright Arbitration Royalty Panels are constituted on an ad hoc basis and perform in the United States a function similar to the Copyright Tribunal in the United Kingdom.

The American law spells out the economic objectives which the CARP is to apply in calculating the relevant rates. These are:
- to maximise the availability of creative works to the public;

- to afford the copyright owner a fair return for his or her creative work and the copyright user a fair income under existing economic conditions;
- to reflect the relative roles of the copyright owner and the copyright user in the product made available to the public with respect to relative creative contribution, technological contribution, capital investment, cost, risk, and contribution to the opening of new markets for creative expression and media for their communication;
- to minimise any disruptive impact on the structure of the industries involved and on generally prevailing industry practices.

Every final determination of the CARP shall be published in the Federal Register. It shall state in detail the criteria that the CARP determined to be applicable to the particular proceeding, the facts that it found relevant to its determination in that proceeding, and the reasons for its determination. Any final decision of the CARP may be appealed to the United States Court of Appeals within 30 days after its publication in the Federal Register.

Fair use

One of the most controversial factors which held up the revision of the American copyright law for at least a decade was the extent to which a balance should be struck between the desire of copyright owners to benefit from their works by extending copyright protection as far as possible, and the pressure from users of copyright to obtain access to copyright material as cheaply as possible – if not completely freely.

The new law provides by s.107 that the fair use of a copyright work, including such use by reproduction of excerpts, for purposes such as criticism, comment, news reporting, teaching (including multiple copies for classroom use), scholarship or research is not an infringement of copyright. In determining whether the use made of a work is a fair use, the factors to be considered include:

- the purpose and character of the use, including whether such use is of a commercial nature or is for non-profit educational purposes;
- the nature of the copyrighted work;
- the amount and substantiality of the portion used in relation to the copyrighted work as a whole; and
- the effect of the use upon the potential market for or value of the copyrighted work.

It is not an infringement of copyright for a library or archive, or any of its employees acting within the scope of their employment, to reproduce or distribute no more than one copy of a work, if:

- the reproduction or distribution is made without any purpose of direct or indirect commercial advantage;
- the collections of the library or archive are either open to the public or available not only to researchers affiliated with the library or archive or with the institution of which it is a part, but also to other persons doing research in a specialised field; and
- the reproduction or distribution of the work includes a notice of copyright.

It is not generally an infringement of copyright if a performance or display of a work is given by instructors or pupils in the course of face-to-face teaching activities of a non-profit educational institution, in a classroom or similar place devoted to instruction.

Nor is it an infringement of copyright to give a performance of a non-dramatic literary or musical work or a dramatico-musical work of a religious nature in the course of services at a place of worship or other religious assembly.

It is also not an infringement of copyright to give a performance of a non-dramatic literary or musical work other than in a transmission to the public, without any purpose of direct or indirect commercial advantage and without payment of any fee for the performance to any of the performing artists, promoters or organisers if either:

- there is no direct or indirect admission charge; or
- the proceeds, after deducting the reasonable costs of producing the performance, are used exclusively for educational, religious or charitable purposes and not for private financial gain.

In this case the copyright owner has the right to serve notice of objection to the performance in a prescribed form.

Note the important decision of the Supreme Court in *Sony Corporation of America* v. *Universal City Studios* (No. 81–1687, 52 USLW 4090). This decided that the sale of video recorders to the public for the purpose of recording a copyrighted programme from a broadcast signal for private use for time-switching purposes alone (not for archiving or 'librarying') does not amount to contributory infringement of the rights in films which are copied as a result of television broadcasts of them. In 2001 the World Trade Organisation upheld a complaint by the EU that s.110(5)(B) of the US Copyright Act infringes WTO agreements. The US must now abolish its present exemption from public performance royalties for bars, shops and restaurants.

Remedies for copyright owners
Infringement of copyright
Copyright is infringed by anyone who violates any of the exclusive rights referred to in 'The rights of a copyright owner' (page 626), or who imports copies or records into the United States in violation of the law. The owner of copyright is entitled to institute an action for infringement so long as that infringement is committed while he or she is the owner of the right infringed. Previously, no action for infringement of copyright could be instituted until registration of the copyright claim had been made, but this requirement has been modified now that the United States has ratified the Berne Convention. Under the new provision, US authors must register, or attempt to register, but non-US Berne authors are exempt from this requirement.

Injunctions
Any court having civil jurisdiction under the copyright law may grant interim and final injunctions on such terms as it may deem reasonable to prevent or restrain infringement of copyright. Such injunction may be served anywhere in

the United States on the person named. An injunction is operative throughout the whole of the United States, and can be enforced by proceedings in contempt or otherwise by any American court which has jurisdiction over the infringer.

Impounding and disposition

While a copyright action under American law is pending, the court may order the impounding on such terms as it considers reasonable of all copies or records claimed to have been made or used in violation of the copyright owner's exclusive rights; it may also order the impounding of all VCRs, tape recorders, plates, moulds, matrices, masters, tapes, film negatives or other articles by means of which infringing copies or records may be reproduced. A court may order as part of a final judgement or decree the destruction or other disposition of all copies or records found to have been made or used in violation of the copyright owner's exclusive rights. It also has the power to order the destruction of all articles by means of which infringing copies or records were reproduced.

Damages and profits

An infringer of copyright is generally liable either for the copyright owner's actual damage and any additional profits made by the infringer, or for statutory damages.

- The copyright owner is entitled to recover the actual damages suffered by him or her as a result of the infringement, and in addition any profits of the infringer which are attributed to the infringement and are not taken into account in computing the actual damages. In establishing the infringer's profits, the copyright owner is only required to present proof of the infringer's gross revenue; it is for the infringer to prove his or her deductible expenses and the elements of profit attributable to factors other than the copyright work.
- Except where the copyright owner has persuaded the court that the infringement was committed wilfully, the copyright owner may elect, at any time before final judgement is given, to recover, instead of actual damages and profits, an award of statutory damages for all infringements involved in the action in respect of any one work, which may be between $750 and $30,000 according to what the court considers justified.
- Where the copyright owner satisfies the court that the infringement was committed wilfully, the court has the discretion to increase the award of statutory damages to not more than $150,000. Where the infringer succeeds in proving that he or she was not aware and had no reason to believe that his or her acts constituted an infringement of copyright, the court has the discretion to reduce the award of statutory damages to not less than $200.

Costs: time limits

In any civil proceedings under American copyright law, the court may allow the recovery of full costs by or against any party except the Government of the United States. It may also award a reasonable sum in respect of an attorney's fee. No civil or criminal proceedings in respect of copyright law shall be permitted unless begun within three years after the claim or cause of action arose.

Counterfeiting
By the Piracy and Counterfeiting Amendment Act 1982, pirates and counterfeiters of sound recordings and of motion pictures now face maximum penalties of up to five years imprisonment or fines of up to $250,000.

Colouring films
The United States Copyright Office has decided that adding colour to a black and white film may qualify for copyright protection whenever it amounts to more than a trivial change.

Satellite home viewers
The position of satellite home viewers is controlled by the Satellite Home Viewer Act of 1988. (Title II of Public Law 100– 667 of 16 November 1988.) The Copyright Remedy Clarification Act has created s.511 of the Copyright Act, in order to rectify a situation which had developed in case law. By this, the component States of the Union, their agencies and employees are placed in the same position as private individuals and entities in relation to their liability for copyright infringement.

Digital Millennium Copyright Act
The US Congress in 1998 passed new legislation to make clear that copyright law applies to all works transmitted, or simply made available to, users over the internet.

This measure is unique in that for the first time it gives its copyright owner the right to control access to the digital work, which is so crucial to security on the internet. To allow the United States to ratify two new WIPO (World Intellectual Property Organisation) treaties – the WIPO Copyright Treaty and the WIPO Performance and Phonograms Treaty, negotiated in 1996 – the Digital Millennium Copyright Act (DMCA) makes two changes in US law. First, it outlaws, with substantial criminal and civil penalties, any tampering with copyright management information – the invisible digital coding embedded on sound recordings, software, motion pictures, and databases that identify the owner of the work and stipulate the price and conditions of use. This encoding will help promote e-commerce and curtail internet piracy.

Second, the DMCA prohibits anyone from disabling anti-copying circuitry in a machine or signal. It also bans the manufacture, sale, and importation of electronic devices that would permit the disabling of that circuitry. The DMCA specifies stiff civil and criminal penalties for acts of circumvention and for the manufacture or sale of the devices.

With the DMCA passed, the United States quickly joined the two new WIPO treaties in the hope that its action would serve as an example to other countries.

General observations
The copyright law of the United States was improved as a result of the statute passed by Congress on 19 October 1976. (Title 17, United States Code.) Apart from lifting the general standards of protection for copyright owners to a higher level than that which previously existed, it has on the whole shifted the

balance of copyright protection in favour of the copyright owner and away from the copyright user in many of the areas where controversy existed. But most important for British and other non-American authors and publishers, it has gone a long way towards bringing American copyright law up to the same standards of international protection for non-national copyright proprietors which have long been offered by the United Kingdom and the other major countries, both in Europe and elsewhere in the English-speaking world. The ratification by the United States of the Berne Convention with effect from 1 March 1989 was an action which at that time put American copyright law on par with the protection offered by other major countries.

Gavin McFarlane LLM, PhD is a barrister at Temple Chambers, Cardiff. He specialises in international trade law, and is particularly interested in the involvement of the World Trade Organisation in intellectual property matters.

Libel

Any writer should be aware of the law of libel. Antony Whitaker gives an outline of the main principles, concentrating on points which are most frequently misunderstood. But this article is no more than that, and specific legal advice should be taken when practical problems arise.

The law discussed is the law of England and Wales. Scotland has its own, albeit somewhat similar, rules. A summary of the main differences between the two systems appears in the box (below). The Defamation Act 1996, designed mainly to streamline and simplify libel litigation, became fully effective in February 2000.

Libel: liability to pay damages

English law draws a distinction between defamation published in permanent form and that which is not. The former is libel, the latter slander. 'Permanent form' includes writing, printing, drawings and photographs and radio and television broadcasts. It follows that it is the law of libel rather than slander which most concerns writers and artists professionally, and the slightly differing rules applicable to slander will not be mentioned in this article.

Publication of a libel can result in a civil action for damages, an injunction to prevent repetition and/or in certain cases a criminal prosecution against those responsible, who include the author (or artist or photographer), the publishers and the editor, if any, of the publication in which the libel appeared. 'Innocent disseminators', such as printers, distributors, broadcasters, internet service providers and retailers, who can show they took reasonable care and had no reason to believe what they were handling contained a libel, are protected under the 1996 Act. Prosecutions are rare. Certain special rules apply to them and these will be explained below after a discussion of the question of civil liability, which in practice arises much more frequently.

Libel claims do not qualify for legal aid, although the closely analagous remedy of malicious falsehood does. Most libel cases are usually heard by a judge and jury, and it is the jury which decides the amount of any award, which is tax-free. It is not necessary for the plaintiff to prove that he or she has actually suffered any loss, because the law presumes damage. While the main purpose of a libel claim is to compensate the plaintiff for the injury to his or her reputation, a jury may give additional sums either as 'aggravated' damages, if it appears a defendant has behaved malevolently or spitefully, or as 'exemplary', or 'punitive', damages where a defendant hopes the economic advantages of publication will outweigh any sum awarded. Damages can also be 'nominal' if the libel complained of is trivial. It is generally very difficult to forecast the amounts juries are likely to award, though awards against newspapers disclose a tendency towards considerable generosity. The Court of Appeal has power to reduce excessive awards of damages.

In an action for damages for libel, it is for the plaintiff to establish that the matter he or she complains of has been published by the defendant; refers to the plaintiff, is defamatory. If this is done, the plaintiff establishes a prima facie case. However, the defendant will escape liability if he or she can show he has a good defence. There are five defences to a libel action. They are: Justification; Fair Comment; Privilege; Offer of Amends: ss.2–4 of the Defamation Act, 1996; Apology, etc, under the Libel Acts, 1843 and 1845. A libel claim can also become barred under the Limitation Acts, as explained below. These matters must now be examined in detail.

The plaintiff's case

The meaning of 'published'

'Published' in the legal sense means communicated to a person other than the plaintiff. Thus the legal sense is wider than the lay sense but includes it. It follows that the content of a book is published in the legal sense when the manuscript is first sent to the publishing firm just as much as it is when the book is later placed on sale to the public. Subject to the 'innocent dissemination' defence referred to above, both types of publication are sufficient for the purpose of establishing liability for libel, but the law differentiates between them, since the scope of publication can properly be taken into account by the jury in considering the actual amount of damages to award. Material placed on the internet is unquestionably 'published' there, and the extent of publication can be judged by the number of visits made to the relevant website. It should be noted that Internet Service Providers can compel website operators to identify the authors of defamatory material anonymously posted to their discussion boards.

Establishing identity

The plaintiff must also establish that the matter complained of refers to him or her. It is of course by no means necessary to mention a person's name before it is clear that he or she is referred to. Nicknames by which he or she is known or corruptions of his name are just two ways in which his or her identity can be indicated. There are more subtle methods. The sole question is whether the plaintiff is indicated to those who read the matter complained of. In some cases he or she will not be unless it is read in the light of facts known to the reader from other sources, but this is sufficient for the plaintiff's purpose. The test is purely objective and does not depend at all on whether the writer intended to refer to the plaintiff.

It is because it is impossible to establish reference to any individual that generalisations, broadly speaking,

English and Scottish law

Much of the terminology of the Scots law of defamation differs from that of English law, and in certain minor respects the law itself is different. North of the border, libel and slander are virtually indistinguishable, both as to the nature of the wrongs and their consequences; and Scots law does not recognise the offence of criminal libel. Where individual English litigants enjoy absolute privilege for what they say in court, their Scottish counterparts have only qualified privilege. 'Exemplary', or 'punitive', damages are not awarded by the Scottish courts. Until recently, libel cases in Scotland were for the most part heard by judges sitting alone, but there is now a marked trend towards trial by jury, which has been accompanied by a significant increase in the levels of damages awarded.

are not successfully actionable. To say boldly 'All lawyers are crooks' does not give any single lawyer a cause of action, because the statement does not point a finger at any individual. However, if anyone is named in conjunction with a generalisation, then it may lose its general character and become particular from the context. Again, if one says 'One of the X Committee has been convicted of murder' and the X Committee consists of, say, four persons, it cannot be said that the statement is not actionable because no individual is indicated and it could be referring to any of the committee. This is precisely why it is actionable at the suit of each of them as suspicion has been cast on all.

Determining what is defamatory

It is for the plaintiff to show that the matter complained of is defamatory. What is defamatory is decided by the jury except in the extreme cases where the judge rules that the words cannot bear a defamatory meaning. Various tests have been laid down for determining this. It is sufficient that any one test is satisfied. The basic tests are:

- Does the matter complained of tend to lower the plaintiff in the estimation of society?
- Does it tend to bring him or her into hatred, ridicule, contempt, dislike or disesteem with society?
- Does it tend to make him shunned or avoided or cut off from society? The mere fact that what is published is inaccurate is not enough to involve liability; it is the adverse impact on the plaintiff's reputation that matters. For example, merely to overstate a person's income is not defamatory; but it will be if the context implies he has not fully declared it to the tax authorities.

'Society' means right-thinking members of society generally. It is by reference to such people that the above tests must be applied. A libel action against a newspaper which had stated that the police had taken a statement from the plaintiff failed, notwithstanding that the plaintiff gave evidence that his apparent assistance to the police (which he denied) had brought him into grave disrepute with the underworld. It was not by their wrongheaded standards that the matter fell to be judged.

Further, it is not necessary to imply that the plaintiff is at fault in some way in order to defame him. To say of a woman that she has been raped or of someone that he is insane imputes to them no degree of blame, but nonetheless both statements are defamatory. Lawyers disagree over whether the claim that an individual is 'ugly' is, or could be, defamatory.

Sometimes a defamatory meaning is conveyed by words which on the face of them have no such meaning. 'But Brutus is an honourable man' is an example. If a jury finds that words are meant ironically they will consider this ironical sense when determining whether the words are defamatory. In deciding, therefore, whether or not the words are defamatory, the jury seeks to discover what, without straining the words or putting a perverse construction on them, they will be understood to mean. In some cases this may differ substantially from their literal meaning.

Matter may also be defamatory by innuendo. Strictly so called, an innuendo is a meaning that words acquire by virtue of facts known to the reader but not stated in the passage complained of. Words, quite innocent on the face of them, may acquire a defamatory meaning when read in the light of these facts. For example, where a newspaper published a photograph of a man and a woman, with the caption that they had just announced their engagement, it was held to be defamatory of the man's wife since those who knew that she had cohabited with him were led to the belief that she had done so only as his mistress. The newspaper was unaware that the man was already married, but some of its readers were not. In general, however, imputations of unchastity against members of either sex would today be regarded as far less defamatory than they were in 1929 when this case was decided.

Defences to a libel action
Quite apart from the provisions concerning statutory apologies mentioned below, a swift and well publicised apology will always go some way towards assuaging injured feelings and help reduce an award of damages.

Justification
English law does not protect the reputation that a person either does not or should not possess. Stating the truth therefore does not incur liability, and the plea of justification – namely, that what is complained of is true in substance and in fact – is a complete answer to an action for damages. However, this defence is by no means to be undertaken lightly. For instance, to prove one instance of using bad language will be insufficient to justify the allegation that a person is 'foulmouthed'. It would be necessary to prove several instances, and the defendant is obliged in most cases to particularise in his pleadings giving details, dates and places. However, the requirement that the truth of every allegation must be proved is not absolute, and is qualified by the 'multiple charge – no worse off' defence. This applies where two or more distinct charges are levelled against a plaintiff, and some of what is said turns out to be inaccurate. If his or her reputation in the light of what is shown to be true is made no worse by the unprovable defamatory allegations – for example, mistaken accusations that a convicted pickpocket and car thief is also a shoplifter – the publisher will be safe. This is the extent of the law's recognition that some individuals are so disreputable as to be beyond redemption by awards of damages regardless of what is said about them. Subject to this, however, it is for the defendant to prove that what he or she has published is true, not for the plaintiff to disprove it, though if he can do so, so much the better for him.

One point requires special mention. It is insufficient for the defendant to prove that he or she has accurately repeated what a third person has written or said or that such statements have gone uncontradicted when made on occasions in the past. If X writes 'Y told me that Z is a liar', it is no defence to an action against X merely to prove that Y did say that. X has given currency to a defamatory statement concerning Z and has so made it his own. His only defence is to prove that Z is a liar by establishing a number of instances of Z's untruthfulness. Nor does it help a defence of justification to prove that the defendant genuinely believed what he or she published to be true. This may, however, form part of a qualified privilege defence (see below), and might well be a complete answer in an action, other than a libel action, based on a false but non-defamatory statement. For such statements do not incur liability in the absence of fraud or malice which, in this context, means a dishonest or otherwise improper motive. Bona fide belief, however, may be relevant to the assessment of damages, even in a libel action.

Special care should be taken in relation to references to a person's convictions, however accurately described. Since the Rehabilitation of Offenders Act, 1974, a person's less serious convictions may become 'spent' and thereafter it may involve liability to refer to them. Reference to the Act and orders thereunder must be made in order to determine the position in any particular case.

Fair comment

It is a defence to prove that what is complained of is fair comment made in good faith and without malice on a matter of public interest. 'Fair' in this context means 'honest'. 'Fair comment' means therefore the expression of the writer's genuinely held opinion. It does not necessarily mean opinion with which the jury agree. Comment may therefore be quite extreme and still be 'fair' in the legal sense. However, if it is utterly perverse the jury may be led to think that no one could have genuinely held such views. In such a case the defence would fail, for the comment could not be honest. 'Malice' here covers any dishonest or improper motive but, in contrast to its application in the context of qualified privilege (see below), it does not include actuation by spite or animosity, even if this is the dominant or sole motive. Care should, however, be taken since evidence of such motivation could also be seen as a lack of genuine belief in the view expressed.

The defence only applies when what is complained of is comment as distinct from a statement of fact. The line between comment and fact is notoriously difficult to draw in some cases. Comment means a statement of opinion. The facts on which comment is made must be stated together with the comment or be sufficiently indicated with it. This is merely another way of saying that it must be clear that the defamatory statement is one of opinion and not of fact, for which the only defence would be the onerous one of justification. The exact extent to which the facts commented on must be stated or referred to is a difficult question, but some help may be derived in answering it by considering the purpose of the rule, which is to enable the reader to exercise his own judgement and to agree or disagree with the comment. It is quite plain that it is not necessary to state every single detail of the facts. In one case it was sufficient merely to mention the name of one of the Press lords in an article about a newspaper though not one owned by him. He was so well known that to mention his name indicated the substratum of fact commented upon, namely his control of his group of newspapers. No universal rule can be laid down, except that, in general, the fuller the facts set out or referred to with the comment, the better. All these facts must be proved to be true subject, however, to the flexibility of the 'proportionate truth' rule. This means that the defence remains available even if, for example, only three out of five factual claims can be proved true, provided that these three are by themselves sufficient to sustain, and are proportionate to, the fairness of the comment. The impact of the two unproven claims would probably fall to be assessed in accordance with the 'multiple charge – no worse off' rule in justification, set out above.

The defence only applies where the matters commented on are of public interest, i.e. of legitimate concern to the public or a substantial section of it. Thus the conduct of national and local government, international affairs, the administration of justice, etc, are all matters of public interest, whereas other people's private affairs may very well not be, although they undoubtedly interest the public, or provoke curiosity.

In addition, matters of which criticism has been expressly or impliedly invited, such as publicly performed plays and published books, are a legitimate subject of comment. Criticism need not be confined merely to their artistic merit but equally may deal with the attitudes to life and the opinions therein expressed.

It is sometimes said that a man's moral character is never a proper subject of comment for the purpose of this defence. This is certainly true where it is a private individual who is concerned, and some authorities say it is the same in the case of a public figure even though his or her character may be relevant to his or her public life. Again, it may in some cases be exceeding the bounds of fair comment to impute a dishonourable motive to a person, as is frequently done by way of inference from facts. In general, the imputation is a dangerous and potentially expensive practice.

Privilege

Privilege in the law of libel is either 'absolute' or 'qualified', and denotes the two levels of protection from liability afforded, in the public interest, to defamatory statements made on certain occasions. Absolute privilege – where the individual defamed has no remedy whatever – has applied to Parliamentary papers published by the direction of either House, or full republications thereof, since early in the 19th century. Following the implementation of section 14 of the 1996 Defamation Act, this privilege also applies to fair, accurate and contemporaneous reports of public judicial proceedings in the United Kingdom, the European Courts of Justice and Human Rights, and any international criminal tribunal established by the Security Council.

Qualified privilege confers protection provided publication is made only for the reason that the privilege is given and not for some wrongful or indirect motive. In October 1999 the House of Lords extended the defence to protect publications where a defamatory mistake on a matter of public concern has been made by a writer who can show he did his best to uncover the truth. He must show he acted responsibly both in checking his sources and, where appropriate, seeking the potential plaintiff's comments. The precise limits of this defence are not clear, and will only become so as other cases are decided in the future.

The defence also applies, under section 15 of the Act, to fair and accurate reports of public proceedings before a legislature, a court, a government inquiry and an international organisation or conference anywhere in the world, and of certain documents, or extracts from such documents, issued by those bodies. While there is no requirement to correct or publish explanations concerning these reports, such an obligation does arise under section 15 in respect of a separate category of reports of notices issued by various bodies within the European Community and of proceedings of certain bodies or organisations within the United Kingdom. Apart from the Act, such privilege also attaches to extracts from Parliamentary papers and fair and accurate reports of Parliamentary proceedings.

This list of privileged occasions is by no means exhaustive, and the second category may now be expanded by an order of the Lord Chancellor. The privilege defence is extended to the media generally, rather than being restricted, as it was hitherto, simply to newspapers.

Offers of Amends under the 1996 Act

Sections 2, 3 and 4 of the 1996 Act offer a flexible method of nipping in the bud potential libel actions by those who have been unintentionally defamed. The range of libel meanings for which this defence caters is much wider than that previously available. It envisages the payment of damages as well as costs, together with the offer of a correction and apology, and the damages figure will be fixed by a judge if the parties cannot agree. He or she will do this bearing in mind the generosity of the correction and apology, and the extent of its publication. While recourse to this defence excludes reliance on the defences of justification, privilege and fair comment, it offers a considerable incentive to settle complaints and will save substantially on costs.

Apology under 1843 and 1845 Acts

This defence is rarely utilised, since if any condition of it is not fulfilled, the plaintiff must succeed and the only question is the actual amount of damages. It only applies to actions in respect of libels in newspapers and periodicals. The defendant pleads that the libel was inserted without actual malice and without gross negligence and that before the action commenced or as soon afterwards as possible he inserted a full apology in the same newspaper, etc, or had offered to publish it in a newspaper, etc, of the plaintiff's choice, where the original newspaper is published at intervals greater than a week. Further a sum must be paid into court with this defence to compensate the plaintiff.

'Fast-track disposal' procedure

In its recognition of the generally cumbersome nature of libel litigation, the 1996 Act provides a simplified mechanism for dealing with less serious complaints. Sections 8, 9 and 10 enable a judge alone to dismiss unrealistic claims at the outset; and he will also be able to dispose 'summarily' of relatively minor, but well-founded, claims, on the basis of an award of up to £10,000, a declaration that the publication was libellous, an order for an apology and an order forbidding repetition.

Limitation and death

The 1996 Act has reduced from three years to one the period within which a libel action must generally be started if it is not to become 'statute-barred' through lapse of time. But successive and subsequent publications, such as the issue of later editions of the same book, or the sale of surplus copies of an old newspaper, or the failure to remove libellous material from the internet, can give rise to fresh claims.

Civil claims for libel cannot be brought on behalf of the dead. If an individual living plaintiff or defendant in a libel case dies before the jury gives their verdict, the action 'abates', i.e. comes to an end, so far as their involvement is concerned, and no rights arising out of it survive either for or against their personal representatives.

Insurance

For an author, the importance of at least an awareness of this branch of law lies first, in the fact that most book contracts contain a clause enabling the publisher to look to him should any libel claims result; and second, in the increasingly large awards of damages. It is therefore advisable to check what libel insurance a publisher carries, and whether it also covers the author who, if he or she is to have the benefit of it, should always alert the publisher to any potential risk. One company which offers libel insurance for authors is Royal Sun Alliance, Professional and Financial Risks, 4th Floor, Leadenhall Court, Leadenhall Street, London EC3V 1PP (tel 020-7283 9000). Premiums start at £1000, and can be substantially higher if the book is tendentious or likely to be controversial. The company generally insists on the author obtaining, and paying for, a legal opinion first. Indemnity limits vary between £50,000 and £1 million, and the author is required to bear at least the first £5000 of any loss. It is worth remembering that 'losses' include legal costs as well as damages, which they can often exceed. Libel insurance can also be obtained through a Lloyds broker.

Criminal liability in libel

Whereas the object of a civil action is to obtain compensation for the wrong done or to prevent repetition, the object of criminal proceedings is to punish the wrongdoer by fine or imprisonment or both. There are four main types of writing which may provoke a prosecution: defamatory libel; obscene publications; sedition and incitement to racial hatred; blasphemous libel.

Defamatory libel

The publication of defamatory matter is in certain circumstances a crime as well as a civil wrong. But whereas the principal object of civil proceedings will normally be to obtain compensation, the principal object of a criminal prosecution will be to secure punishment of the accused, for example by way of a fine. Prosecutions are not frequent, but there have been signs of late of a revival of interest. There are important differences between the rules applicable to criminal libel and its civil counterpart. For example, a criminal libel may be 'published' even though only communicated to the person defamed and may be found to have occurred even where the person defamed is dead, or where only a group of persons but no particular individual has been maligned. During election campaigns, it is an 'illegal practice' to publish false statements about the personal character or conduct of a candidate irrespective of whether they are also defamatory.

Obscene publications

It is an offence to publish obscene matter. By the Obscene Publications Act, 1959, matter is obscene if its effect is such as to tend to deprave and corrupt persons who are likely, having regard to all relevant circumstances, to read, see or hear it. 'To deprave and corrupt' is to be distinguished from 'to shock and disgust'. It is a defence to a prosecution to prove that publication of the matter in question is justified as being for the public good, on the ground that it is in the interests of science, literature, art or learning, or of other objects of general concern. Expert evidence may be given as to its literary, artistic, scientific or other merits. Playwrights, directors and producers should note that the Theatres Act, 1968, though designed to afford similar protection to stage productions, does not necessarily prevent prosecutions for indecency under other statutes.

Sedition/incitement to racial hatred

Writings which tend to destroy the peace of the realm may be prosecuted as being seditious or as amounting to incitement to racial hatred. Seditious writings include those which advocate reform by unconstitutional or violent means or incite contempt or hatred for the monarch or Parliament. These institutions may be criticised stringently, but not in a manner which is likely to lead to insurrection or civil commotion or indeed any physical force. Prosecutions are a rarity, but it should be remembered that writers of matter contemptuous of the House of Commons, though not prosecuted for seditious libel are, from time to time, punished by that House for breach of its privileges, although, if a full apology is made, it is often an end of the matter. The Public Order Act 1986 makes it an offence, irrespective of the author's or publisher's intention, to publish, or put on plays containing, threatening, abusive or insulting matter if hatred is likely to be stirred up against any racial group in Great Britain.

Blasphemous libel

Blasphemous libel consists in the vilification of the Christian religion or its ceremonies. Other religions are not protected. The offence lies essentially in the impact of what is said concerning, for instance, God, Christ, the Bible, the Book of Common Prayer, etc; it is irrelevant that the publisher does not intend to shock or arouse resentment. While temperate and sober writings on religious topics however anti-Christian in sentiment will not involve liability, if the discussion is 'so scurrilous and offensive as to pass the limit of decent controversy and to outrage any Christian feeling', it will.

Antony **Whitaker** OBE is a barrister and an independent media legal adviser; *email* blairwhitaker@lineone.net

Finance for writers and artists

FAQs for writers

Peter Vaines, a chartered accountant and barrister, addresses some questions
frequently asked by writers.

What can a working writer claim against tax?
A working writer is carrying on a business and can therefore claim all the
expenses which are incurred wholly and exclusively for the purposes of that
business. A list showing most of the usual expenses is contained on page 651–2
of this *Yearbook* but there will be other expenses which can be allowed in special
circumstances.

Strictly, only expenses which are incurred for the sole purpose of the business
can be claimed; there must be no 'duality of purpose' so an item of expenditure
cannot be divided into private and business parts. However, the Inland Revenue
is usually quite flexible and is prepared to allow all reasonable expenses
(including apportioned sums) where the amounts can be commercially justified.

Allowances can also be claimed for the cost of business assets such as a motor
car, personal computers, fax, copying machines and all other equipment
(including books) which may be used by the writer. An allowance of 25% of the
cost can be claimed on the reducing balance each year and for most assets
(except cars) an allowance of 40% can be claimed in the first year of purchase.
Some expenditure on information technology now benefits from a special 100%
allowance. Further details of the deductions available in respect of capital
expenditure may be found on page 652.

Can I request interest on fees owed to me beyond 30 days of my invoice?
Yes. A writer is like any other person carrying on a business and is entitled to
charge interest at a rate of 8% over bank base rate on any debt outstanding for
more than 30 days – although the period of credit can be varied by agreement
between the parties. It is not compulsory to claim the interest; it is up to you to
decide whether to enforce the right.

What can I do about bad debts?
A writer is in exactly the same position as anybody else carrying on a business over
the payment of his or her invoices. It is generally not commercially sensible to
insist on payment in advance but where the work involved is substantial (which
will normally be the case with a book), it is usual to receive one third of the fee on
signature, one third of the fee on delivery of the manuscript and the remaining one
third on publication. On other assignments, perhaps not as substantial as a book,
it could be worthwhile seeking 50% of the fee on signature and the other 50% on
delivery. This would provide a degree of protection in case of cancellation of the
assignment because of changes of policy or personnel at the publisher.

What financial disputes can I take to the Small Claims Court?
If somebody owes you money you can take them to the Small Claims Section of your local County Court, which deals with financial disputes up to £5000. The procedure is much less formal than normal court proceedings and involves little expense. It is not necessary to have a solicitor. You fill in a number of forms, turn up on the day and explain the background to why you are owed the money. Full details of the procedure can be found on: www.courtservice.gov.uk.

If I receive an advance, can I divide it between two tax years?
Yes. There used to be a system known as 'spreading' but in 2001 a new system called 'averaging' was introduced. This enables writers (and others engaged in the creation of literary, dramatic works or designs) to average the profits of two or more consecutive years if the profits for one year are less than 75% of the profits for the highest year. This relief will apply even if the work takes less than 12 months to create. Both the spreading relief and the averaging relief allow the writer to avoid the higher rates of tax which might arise if the income in respect of a number of years' work were all to be concentrated in a single year.

How do I make sure I am taxed as a self-employed person so that tax and National Insurance Contributions are not deducted at source?
To be taxed as a self-employed person under Schedule D you have to make sure that the contract for the writing cannot be regarded as a contract of employment. This is unlikely to be the case with a professional author. The subject is highly complex but the most important feature is that the publisher must not be in a position to direct or control the author's work. Where any doubt exists, the author might find the publisher deducting tax and National Insurance Contributions as a precaution and that would clearly be highly disadvantageous. The author would be well advised to discuss the position with the publisher before the contract is signed to agree that he or she should be treated as self employed and that no tax or National Insurance Contributions will be deducted from any payments. If such agreement cannot be reached, professional advice should immediately be sought so that the detailed technical position can be explained to the publisher.

Is it a good idea to operate through a limited company?
It can be a good idea for a self-employed writer to operate through a company but generally only where the income is quite large. The costs of operating a company can outweigh any benefit if the writer is paying tax only at the basic rate. Where the writer is paying tax at the higher rate of 40%, being able to retain some of the income in a company at a tax rate of only 19% is obviously attractive. However, this will be entirely ineffective if the writer's contract with the publisher would otherwise be an employment. The whole subject of operating through a company is complex and professional advice is essential.

When does it become necessary to register for VAT?
Where the writer's self-employed income (from all sources, not only writing) exceeds £56,000 in the previous 12 months or is expected to do so in the next

30 days, he or she must register for VAT and add VAT to all his/her fees. The publisher will pay the VAT to the writer, who must pay the VAT over to the Customs and Excise each quarter. Any VAT the writer has paid on business expenses and on the purchase of business assets can be deducted. It will be possible for some authors to take advantage of the simplified system for VAT payments which applies to small businesses. This involves a flat rate payment of VAT without any need to keep records of VAT on expenses.

If I make a loss from my writing can I get any tax back?
Where a writer makes a loss, the Inland Revenue may suggest that the writing is only a hobby and not a professional activity thereby denying any relief or tax deduction for the loss. However, providing the writing is carried out on a sensible commercial basis with an expectation of profits, any resulting loss can be offset against any other income the writer may have for the same or the previous year.

Income tax

Despite attempts by successive Governments to simplify our taxation system, the subject has become increasingly complicated. Peter Vaines, a chartered accountant and barrister, gives a broad outline of taxation from the point of view of writers and other creative professionals. The proposals in the April 2003 Budget are broadly reflected in this article.

How income is taxed
Generally
Authors are usually treated for tax purposes as carrying on a profession and are taxed in a similar fashion to other professionals, i.e. as self-employed persons assessable under Schedule D. This article is directed to self-employed persons only, because if a writer is employed he or she will be subject to the much less advantageous rules which apply to employment income.

Attempts are often made by employed persons to shake off the status of 'employee' and to attain 'freelance' status so as to qualify for the advantages of Schedule D, such attempts meeting with varying degrees of success. The problems involved in making this transition are considerable and space does not permit a detailed explanation to be made here – individual advice is necessary if difficulties are to be avoided.

Particular attention has been paid by the Inland Revenue to journalists and to those engaged in the entertainment industry with a view to reclassifying them as employees so that PAYE is deducted from their earnings. This blanket treatment has been extended to other areas and, although it is obviously open to challenge by individual taxpayers, it is always difficult to persuade the Inland Revenue to change its views.

There is no reason why employed people cannot carry on a freelance business in their spare time. Indeed, aspiring authors, painters, musicians, etc, often derive so little income from their craft that the financial security of an employment, perhaps in a different sphere of activity, is necessary. The existence of the employment is irrelevant to the taxation of the freelance earnings although it is most important not to confuse the income or expenditure of the employment with the income or expenditure of the self-employed activity. The Inland Revenue is aware of the advantages which can be derived by an individual having 'freelance' income from an organisation of which he or she is also an employee, and where such circumstances are contrived, it can be extremely difficult to convince an Inspector of Taxes that a genuine freelance activity is being carried on. Where the individual operates through a company or partnership providing services personally to a particular client, and would be regarded as an employee if the services were supplied directly by the individual, additional problems arise from the notorious IR35 legislation and professional advice is essential.

For those starting in business or commencing work on a freelance basis the Inland Revenue produces a very useful booklet, *Starting in Business (IR28)*, which is available from any tax office.

Arts Council category A awards

- Direct or indirect musical, design or choreographic commissions and direct or indirect commission of sculpture and paintings for public sites.
- The Royalty Supplement Guarantee Scheme.
- The contract writers' scheme.
- Jazz bursaries.
- Translators' grants.
- Photographic awards and bursaries.
- Film and video awards and bursaries.
- Performance Art Awards.
- Art Publishing Grants.
- Grants to assist with a specific project or projects (such as the writing of a book) or to meet specific professional expenses such as a contribution towards copying expenses made to a composer or to an artist's studio expenses.

Income

For income to be taxable it need not be substantial, nor even the author's only source of income; earnings from casual writing are also taxable but this can be an advantage, because occasional writers do not often make a profit from their writing. The expenses incurred in connection with writing may well exceed any income receivable and the resultant loss may then be used to reclaim tax paid on other income. There may be deducted from the income certain allowable expenses and capital allowances which are set out in more detail below. The possibility of a loss being used as a basis for a tax repayment is fully appreciated by the Inland Revenue, which sometimes attempts to treat casual writing as a hobby so that any losses incurred cannot be used to reclaim tax; of course by the same token any income receivable would not be chargeable to tax. This treatment may sound attractive but it should be resisted vigorously because the Inland Revenue does not hesitate to change its mind when profits begin to arise. In the case of exceptional or non-recurring writing, such as the autobiography of a sports personality or the memoirs of a politician, it could be better to be treated as pursuing a hobby and not as a professional author. Sales of copyright cannot

Arts Council category B awards

- Bursaries to trainee directors.
- Bursaries for associate directors.
- Bursaries to people attending full-time courses in arts administration (the practical training course).
- In-service bursaries to theatre designers and bursaries to trainees on the theatre designers' scheme.
- In-service bursaries for administrators.
- Bursaries for actors and actresses.
- Bursaries for technicians and stage managers.
- Bursaries made to students attending the City University Arts Administration courses.
- Awards, known as the Buying Time Awards, made not to assist with a specific project or professional expenses but to maintain the recipient to enable him or her to take time off to develop his personal talents. These at present include the awards and bursaries known as the Theatre Writing Bursaries, awards and bursaries to composers, awards and bursaries to painters, sculptures and print makers, literature awards and bursaries.

be charged to income tax unless the recipient is a professional author. However, the proceeds of sale of copyright may be charged to capital gains tax, even by an individual who is not a professional author.

Royalties

Where the recipient is a professional author, a series of cases has laid down a clear principle that sales of copyright are taxable as income and not as capital receipts. Similarly, lump sums on account of, or in advance of royalties are also taxable as income in the year of receipt, subject to a claim for spreading relief (see below).

Copyright royalties are generally paid without deduction of income tax. However, if royalties are paid to a person who normally lives abroad, tax will be deducted by the payer or his agent at the time the payment is made unless arrangements are made with the Inland Revenue for payments to be made gross under the terms of a Double Taxation Agreement with the other country.

Arts Council grants

Persons in receipt of grants from the Arts Council or similar bodies will be concerned whether or not such grants are liable to income tax. The Inland Revenue has issued a Statement of Practice after detailed discussions with the Arts Council regarding the tax treatment of such awards. Grants and other receipts of a similar nature have now been divided into two categories (see boxes) – those which are to be treated by the Inland Revenue as chargeable to tax and those which are not. Category A awards are considered to be taxable; awards made under category B are not chargeable to tax.

This Statement of Practice has no legal force and is used merely to ease the administration of the tax system. It is open to anyone in receipt of a grant or award to disregard the agreed statement and challenge the Inland Revenue view on the merits of their particular case. However, it must be recognised that the Inland Revenue does not issue such statements lightly and any challenge to their view would almost certainly involve a lengthy and expensive action through the Courts.

The tax position of persons in receipt of literary prizes will generally follow a decision by the Special Commissioners in connection with the Whitbread Literary Award. In that case it was decided that the prize was not part of the author's professional income and accordingly not chargeable to tax. The precise details are not available because decisions of the Special Commissioners were not, at that time, reported unless an appeal was made to the High Court; the Inland Revenue chose not to appeal against this decision. Details of the many literary awards which are given each year start on page 493, and this decision is of considerable significance to the winners of each of these prizes. It would be unwise to assume that all such awards will be free of tax as the precise facts which were present in the case of the Whitbread award may not be repeated in another case; however it is clear that an author winning a prize has some very powerful arguments in his or her favour, should the Inland Revenue seek to charge tax on the award.

Allowable expenses

To qualify as an allowable business expense, expenditure has to be laid out wholly and exclusively for business purposes. Strictly there must be no 'duality of purpose', which means that expenditure cannot be apportioned to reflect the private and business usage, e.g. food, clothing, telephone, travelling expenses, etc. However, the Inland Revenue does not usually interpret this principle strictly and is prepared to allow all reasonable expenses (including apportioned sums) where the amounts can be commercially justified.

It should be noted carefully that the expenditure does not have to be 'necessary', it merely has to be incurred 'wholly and exclusively' for business purposes. Naturally, however, expenditure of an outrageous and wholly unnecessary character might well give rise to a presumption that it was not really for business purposes. As with all things, some expenses are unquestionably allowable and some expenses are equally unquestionably not allowable – it is the grey area in between which gives rise to all the difficulties and the outcome invariably depends on negotiation with the Inland Revenue.

Great care should be taken when claiming a deduction for items where there is a 'duality of purpose' and negotiations should be conducted with more than usual care and courtesy – if provoked the Inspector of Taxes may well choose to allow nothing. An appeal is always possible although unlikely to succeed as a string of cases in the Courts has clearly demonstrated. An example is the case of *Caillebotte* v. *Quinn* where the taxpayer (who normally had lunch at home) sought to claim the excess cost of meals incurred because he was working a long way from his home. The taxpayer's arguments failed because he did not eat only in order to work, one of the reasons for his eating was in order to sustain his life; a duality of purpose therefore existed and no tax relief was due.

Other cases have shown that expenditure on clothing can also be disallowed if it is the kind of clothing which is in everyday use, because clothing is worn not only to assist the pursuit of one's profession but also to accord with public decency. This duality of purpose may be sufficient to deny relief – even where the particular type of clothing is of a kind not otherwise worn by the taxpayer. In the case of *Mallalieu* v. *Drummond* a lady barrister failed to obtain a tax deduction for items of sombre clothing purchased specifically for wearing in Court. The House of Lords decided that a duality of purpose existed because clothing represented part of her needs as a human being.

Allowances

Despite the above, Inspectors of Taxes are not usually inflexible and the following list of expenses are among those generally allowed.

(a) Cost of all materials used up in the course of preparation of the work.

(b) Cost of typewriting and secretarial assistance, etc; if this or other help is obtained from one's spouse then it is entirely proper for a deduction to be claimed for the amounts paid for the work. The amounts claimed must actually be paid to the spouse and should be at the market rate although some uplift can be made for unsocial hours, etc. Payments to a wife (or husband) are of course taxable in her (or his) hands and should therefore be most carefully considered. The wife's earnings may also be liable for National Insurance contributions and it is important to take care because otherwise you may find that these contributions may outweigh the tax savings. The impact of the National Minimum Wage should also be considered.

(c) All expenditure on normal business items such as postage, stationery, telephone, email, fax and answering machines, agent's fees, accountancy charges, photography, subscriptions, periodicals, magazines, etc, may be claimed. The cost of daily papers should not be overlooked if these form part of research material. Visits to theatres, cinemas, etc, for research purposes may also be permissible (but not the cost relating to guests). Unfortunately, expenditure on all types of business entertaining is specifically denied tax relief.

(d) If work is conducted at home, a deduction for 'use of home' is usually allowed providing the amount claimed is reasonable. If the claim is based on an appropriate proportion of the total costs of rent, light and heat, cleaning and maintenance, insurance, etc (but not the Council Tax), care should be taken to ensure that no single room is used 'exclusively' for business purposes, because this may result in the Capital Gains Tax exemption on the house as the only or main residence being partially forfeited. However, it would be a strange household where one room was in fact used exclusively for business purposes and for no other purpose whatsoever (e.g. storing personal bank statements and other private papers); the usual formula is to claim a deduction on the basis that most or all of the rooms in the house are used at one time or another for business purposes, thereby avoiding any suggestion that any part was used exclusively for business purposes.

(e) The appropriate business proportion of motor running expenses may also be claimed although what is the appropriate proportion will naturally depend on the particular circumstances of each case; it should be mentioned that the well-known scale benefits, whereby one is taxed according to the size and cost of the car, do not apply to self-employed persons.

(f) It has been long established that the cost of travelling from home to work (whether employed or self-employed) is not an allowable expense. However, if home is one's place of work then no expenditure under this heading is likely to be incurred and difficulties are unlikely to arise.

(g) Travelling and hotel expenses incurred for business purposes will normally be allowed but if any part could be construed as disguised holiday or pleasure expenditure, considerable thought would need to be given to the commercial reasons for the journey in order to justify the claim. The principle of 'duality of purpose' will always be a difficult hurdle in this connection – although not insurmountable.

(h) If a separate business bank account is maintained, any overdraft interest thereon will be an allowable expense. This is the only circumstance in which overdraft interest is allowed for tax purposes and care should be taken to avoid overdrafts in all other circumstances.

(i) Where capital allowances (see below) are claimed for a personal computer, fax, modem, television, video, CD or tape player, etc, used for business purposes the costs of maintenance and repair of the equipment may also be claimed.

Clearly many other allowable items may be claimed in addition to those listed. Wherever there is any reasonable business motive for some expenditure it should be claimed as a deduction although it is necessary to preserve all records relating to the expense. It is sensible to avoid an excess of imagination as this would naturally cause the Inspector of Taxes to doubt the genuineness of other expenses claimed.

The question is often raised whether the whole amount of an expense may be deducted or whether the VAT content must be excluded. Where VAT is reclaimed from the Customs and Excise (on the quarterly returns made by a registered person), the VAT element of the expense cannot be treated as an allowable deduction. Where the VAT is not reclaimed, the whole expense (inclusive of VAT) is allowable for income tax purposes.

Capital allowances
Allowances
Where expenditure of a capital nature is incurred, it cannot be deducted from income as an expense – a separate and sometimes more valuable capital allowance being available instead. Capital allowances are given for many different types of expenditure, but authors and similar professional people are likely to claim only for 'plant and machinery'; this is a very wide expression which may include motor cars, personal computers, fax and photocopying machines, modems, televisions, CD, video and cassette players used for business purposes. Plant and machinery generally qualify for a 40% allowance in the year of purchase and 25% of the reducing balance in subsequent years. Expenditure on information technology for the purposes of the business now benefits from a special 100% allowance in the year of purchase. Where the useful life of an asset is expected to be short, it is possible to claim special treatment as a 'short life asset' enabling the allowances to be accelerated.

The reason these allowances can be more valuable than allowable expenses is that they may be wholly or partly disclaimed in any year that full benefit cannot be obtained – ordinary business expenses cannot be similarly disclaimed. Where, for example, the income of an author does not exceed his personal allowances, he would not be liable to tax and a claim for capital allowances would be wasted. If the capital allowances were to be disclaimed their benefit would be carried forward for use in subsequent years. Careful planning with claims for capital allowances is therefore essential if maximum benefit is to be obtained.

As an alternative to capital allowances, claims can be made on the 'renewals' basis whereby all renewals are treated as allowable deductions in the year; no allowance is obtained for the initial purchase, but the cost of replacement (excluding any improvement element) is allowed in full. This basis is no longer widely used, as it is considerably less advantageous than claiming capital allowances as described above.

Leasing is a popular method of acquiring fixed assets, and where cash is not available to enable an outright purchase to be made, assets may be leased over a period of time. Whilst leasing may have financial benefits in certain circumstances, in normal cases there is likely to be no tax advantage in leasing an asset where the alternative of outright purchase is available. Indeed, leasing can be a positive disadvantage in the case of motor cars with a new retail price of more than £12,000. If such a car is leased, only a proportion of the leasing charges will be tax deductible.

Books

The question of whether the cost of books is eligible for tax relief has long been a source of difficulty. The annual cost of replacing books used for the purposes of one's professional activities (e.g. the cost of a new *Writers' & Artists' Yearbook* each year) has always been an allowable expense; the difficulty arose because the initial cost of reference books, etc (e.g. when commencing one's profession) was treated as capital expenditure but no allowances were due as the books were not considered to be 'plant'. However, the matter was clarified by the case of *Munby* v. *Furlong* in which the Court of Appeal decided that the initial cost of law books purchased by a barrister was expenditure on 'plant' and eligible for capital allowances. This is clearly a most important decision, particularly relevant to any person who uses expensive books in the course of exercising his or her profession.

Pension contributions

Personal pensions

Where a self-employed person pays annual premiums under an approved personal pension policy, tax relief may now be obtained each year for the following amounts:

Age at 6/4/2003	Maximum %
35 and under	17.5% (max) £17,325
36 – 45	20% (max) £19,800
46 – 50	25% (max) £24,750
51 – 55	30% (max) £29,700
56 – 60	35% (max) £34,650
61 – 74	40% (max) £39,600

These figures do not apply to existing retirement annuity policies; these remain subject to the old limits which are unchanged.

These arrangements can be extremely advantageous in providing for a pension as premiums are usually paid when the income is high (and the tax relief is also high) and the pension (taxed as earned income when received) usually arises when the income is low and little tax is payable. There is also the opportunity to take part of the pension entitlement as a tax-free lump sum. It is necessary to take into account the possibility that the tax advantages could go into reverse. When the pension is paid it could, if rates rise again, be taxed at a higher rate than the rate of tax relief at the moment. One would be deferring income in order to pay more tax on it later. However, this involves a large element of guesswork, and many people will be content simply with the long-term pension benefits.

From 6 April 2001 the Stakeholder pension rules came into force allowing payment of up to £3600 to be paid into a Stakeholder pension without the need for any earnings.

Class 4 National Insurance contributions
Allied to pensions is the payment of Class 4 National Insurance contributions, although no pension or other benefit is obtained by the contributions; the Class 4 contributions are designed solely to extract additional amounts from self-employed persons and are payable in addition to the normal Class 2 (self-employed) contributions. The rates are changed each year and for 2003/04 self-employed persons will be obliged to contribute 8% of their profits between the range £4615–£30,940 per annum. This amount is collected in conjunction with the Schedule D income tax liability.

From 6 April 2003 the rate of NIC went up to 8% and there will be a further 1% charge on the earnings above the £30,940 limit to correspond with the increase in employees' contributions.

Spreading relief
Relief for copyright payments
For many years special provisions have enabled authors and similar persons engaged on a literary, dramatic, musical or artistic work for a period of more than 12 months, to spread certain amounts received over two or three years depending on the time spent in preparing the work. If the author was engaged on the work for a period exceeding 12 months, the receipt may be spread backwards over two years; if the author was engaged on the work for more than 24 months, the receipt may be spread backwards over three years. (Analogous provisions applied to sums received for the sale of a painting, sculpture or other work of art.) The relief applied to:

- lump sums received on the assignment of copyright, in whole or in part;
- sums received on the grant of any interest in the copyright by licence;
- non-returnable advances on account of royalties;
- any receipts of or on account of royalties or any periodical sums received within two years of first publication.

A claim for spreading relief had to be made within eight years from 5 April following the date of first publication.

Where copyright was assigned (or a licence in it was granted) more than 10 years after the first publication of the work, then the amounts received could qualify for a different spreading relief. The assignment (or licence) must have been for a period of more than two years and the receipt was spread forward over the number of years for which the assignment (or licence) was granted – but with a maximum of six years. The relief was terminated by death, but there were provisions enabling the deceased author's personal representatives to re-spread the amounts if it was to the beneficiaries' advantage.

The above rules were arbitrary and cumbersome, only providing a limited measure of relief in special circumstances. The provisions could sometimes be helpful to repair matters when consideration of the tax position had been neglected.

This system was replaced on 6 April 2001 by a new system of averaging which is simpler. Under these new rules, professional authors and artists engaged in the creation of literary, dramatic works or designs will be able to make a claim to average the profits of two or more consecutive years if the profits for one year are less than 75% of the profits for the highest year. This new relief will apply even if the work took less than 12 months to create and will be available to people who create works in partnership with others.

The purpose of the relief (and of the previous spreading relief) is to enable the creative artist to utilise his allowances fully and to avoid the higher rates of tax which might apply if all the income were to arise in a single year.

Collection of tax
Self-assessment
In 1997, the system of sending in a tax return showing all your income and the Inland Revenue raising an assessment to collect the tax was abolished. So was the idea that you pay tax on your profits for the preceding year. Now, when you send in your tax return you have to work out your own tax liability and send a cheque; this is called 'self-assessment'. If you get it wrong, or if you are late with your tax return or the payment of tax, interest and penalties will be charged.

Under this new system, the Inland Revenue will rarely issue assessments; they are no longer necessary because the idea is that you assess yourself. A new colour-coded tax return is issued, designed to help individuals meet their new tax obligations. This is a daunting task but the term 'self-assessment' is not intended to imply that individuals have to do it themselves; they can (and often will) engage professional help. The term is only intended to convey that it is the taxpayer, and not the Inland Revenue, who is responsible for getting the tax liability right and for it to be paid on time.

The deadline for sending in the tax return is 31 January following the end of the tax year; so for the tax year 2003/04, the tax return has to be submitted to the Inland Revenue by 31 January 2005. If for some reason you are unwilling or unable to calculate the tax payable, you can ask the Inland Revenue to do it for you, in which case it is necessary to send in your tax return by 30 September 2004.

Income tax on self-employed earnings remains payable in two instalments but the payment dates have been moved to 31 January and 31 July each year.

Because the accurate figures may not necessarily be known, these payments in January and July will therefore be only payments on account based on the previous year's liability. The final balancing figure will be paid the following 31 January together with the first instalment of the liability for the following year.

When the Inland Revenue receives the self-assessment tax return, it is checked to see if there is anything obviously wrong; if there is, a letter will be sent to you immediately. Otherwise, the Inland Revenue has 12 months from the filing date of 31 January in which to make further enquiries; if it doesn't, it will have no further opportunity to do so and your tax liabilities are final – unless there is something seriously wrong such as the omission of income or capital gains. In that event, the Inland Revenue will raise an assessment later to collect any extra tax together with appropriate penalties. It is essential for the operation of the new system that all records relevant to your tax returns are retained for at least 12 months in case they are needed by the Inland Revenue. For the self-employed, the record-keeping requirement is much more onerous because the records need to be kept for nearly six years. One important change in the rules is that if you claim a tax deduction for an expense, it will be necessary to have a receipt or other document proving that the expenditure has been made. Because the existence of the underlying records is so important to the operation of self-assessment, the Inland Revenue treats them very seriously and there is a penalty of £3000 for any failure to keep adequate records.

Interest

Interest is chargeable on overdue tax at a variable rate, which at the time of writing is 4.75% per annum. It does not rank for any tax relief, which can make the Inland Revenue an expensive source of credit.

However, the Inland Revenue can also be obliged to pay interest (known as repayment supplement) tax-free where repayments are delayed. The rules relating to repayment supplement are less beneficial and even more complicated than the rules for interest payable but they do exist and can be very welcome if a large repayment has been delayed for a long time. Unfortunately, the rate of repayment supplement is only 2.5%, much lower than the rate of interest on unpaid tax.

Value added tax

The activities of writers, painters, composers, etc, are all 'taxable supplies' within the scope of VAT and chargeable at the standard rate. (Zero rating which applies to publishers, booksellers, etc on the supply of books does not extend to the work performed by writers.) Accordingly, authors are obliged to register for VAT if their income for the past 12 months exceeds £56,000 or if their income for the coming month will exceed that figure.

Delay in registering can be a most serious matter because if registration is not effected at the proper time, the Customs and Excise can (and invariably do) claim VAT from all the income received since the date on which registration should have been made. As no VAT would have been included in the amounts received during this period the amount claimed by the Customs and Excise must inevitably come straight from the pocket of the author.

The author may be entitled to seek reimbursement of the VAT from those whom he or she ought to have charged VAT but this is obviously a matter of some difficulty and may indeed damage his commercial relationships. Apart from these disadvantages there is also a penalty for late registration. The rules are extremely harsh and are imposed automatically even in cases of innocent error. It is therefore extremely important to monitor the income very carefully because if in any period of 12 months the income exceeds the £56,000 limit, the Customs and Excise must be notified within 30 days of the end of the period. Failure to do so will give rise to an automatic penalty. It should be emphasised that this is a penalty for failing to submit a form and has nothing to do with any real or potential loss of tax. Furthermore, whether the failure was innocent or deliberate will not matter. Only the existence of a 'reasonable excuse' will be a defence to the penalty. However, a reasonable excuse does not include ignorance, error, a lack of funds or reliance on any third party.

However, it is possible to regard VAT registration as a privilege and not a penalty, because only VAT registered persons can reclaim VAT paid on their expenses such as stationery, telephone, professional fees, etc, and even typewriters and other plant and machinery (excluding cars). However, many find that the administrative inconvenience – the cost of maintaining the necessary records and completing the necessary forms – more than outweighs the benefits to be gained from registration and prefer to stay outside the scope of VAT for as long as possible.

Overseas matters

The general observation may be made that self-employed persons resident and domiciled in the United Kingdom are not well treated with regard to their overseas work, being taxable on their worldwide income. It is important to emphasise that if fees are earned abroad, no tax saving can be achieved merely by keeping the money outside the country. Although exchange control regulations no longer exist to require repatriation of foreign earnings, such income remains taxable in the UK and must be disclosed to the Inland Revenue; the same applies to interest or other income arising on any investment of these earnings overseas. Accordingly, whenever foreign earnings are likely to become substantial, prompt and effective action is required to limit the impact of UK and foreign taxation. In the case of non-resident authors it is important that arrangements concerning writing for publication in the UK, e.g. in newspapers, are undertaken with great care. A case concerning the wife of one of the great train robbers who provided detailed information for a series of articles in a Sunday newspaper is most instructive. Although she was acknowledged to be resident in Canada for all the relevant years, the income from the articles was treated as arising in this country and fully chargeable to UK tax.

The United Kingdom has double taxation agreements with many other countries and these agreements are designed to ensure that income arising in a foreign country is taxed either in that country or in the UK. Where a withholding tax is deducted from payments received from another country (or where tax is paid in full in the absence of a double taxation agreement), the amount of foreign tax paid can usually be set off against the related UK tax liability. Many successful authors can be found living in Eire because of the complete exemption from tax which attaches to works of cultural or artistic merit by persons who are resident there. However, such a step should only be contemplated having careful regard to all the other domestic and commercial considerations and specialist advice is essential if the exemption is to be obtained and kept; a careless breach of the conditions could cause the exemption to be withdrawn with catastrophic consequences.

Further information concerning the precise conditions to be satisfied for exemption for tax in Eire can be obtained from the Revenue Commissioners, Blocks 3–10, Dublin Castle, Dublin 2, or from their website (www.revenue.ie).

Companies

When an author becomes successful the prospect of paying tax at the higher rate may drive him or her to take hasty action such as the formation of companies, etc, which may not always be to his advantage. Indeed some authors seeing the exodus into tax exile of their more successful colleagues even form companies in low tax areas in the naive expectation of saving large amounts of tax. The Inland Revenue is fully aware of the opportunities and have extensive powers to charge tax and combat avoidance. Accordingly, such action is just as likely to increase tax liabilities and generate other costs and should never be contemplated without expert advice; some very expensive mistakes are often made in this area which are not always able to be remedied.

To conduct one's business through the medium of a company can be a most effective method of mitigating tax liabilities, and providing it is done at the right time and under the right circumstances very substantial advantages can be derived. However, if done without due care and attention the intended advantages will simply evaporate. At the very least it is essential to ensure that the company's business is genuine and conducted properly with regard to the realities of the situation. If the author continues his or her activities unchanged, simply paying all the receipts from his work into a company's bank account, he cannot expect to persuade the Inland Revenue that it is the company and not himself who is entitled to, and should be assessed to tax on, that income.

It must be strongly emphasised that many pitfalls exist which can easily eliminate all the tax benefits expected to arise by the formation of the company. For example, company directors are employees of the company and will be liable to pay much higher National Insurance contributions; the company must also pay the employer's proportion of the contribution and a total liability of over 23% of gross salary may arise. This compares most unfavourably with the position of a self-employed person. Moreover, on the commencement of the company's business the individual's profession will cease and the possibility of revisions being made by the Inland Revenue to earlier tax liabilities means that the timing of a change has to be considered very carefully.

The tax return

No mention has been made above of personal reliefs and allowances; this is because these allowances and the rates of tax are subject to constant change and are always set out in detail in the explanatory notes which accompany the Tax Return. The annual Tax Return is an important document and should be completed promptly with extreme care, particularly since the introduction of self-assessment. If filling in the Return is a source of difficulty or anxiety, comfort may be found in the Consumer Association's publication *Money Which?* – *Tax Saving Guide*; this is published in March of each year and includes much which is likely to be of interest and assistance.

Peter Vaines FCA, ATII, barrister, is a partner in the international law firm of Haarmann Hemmelrath and writes and speaks widely on tax matters. He is Managing Editor of *Personal Tax Planning Review*, on the Editorial Board of *Taxation*, and tax columnist of *Accountancy* and *New Law Journal*.

Social security contributions

In general, every individual who works in Great Britain either as an employee or as a self-employed person is liable to pay social security contributions. The law governing this subject is complicated and Peter Arrowsmith FCA gives here a summary of the position. This article should be regarded as a general guide only.

All contributions are payable in respect of years ending on 5 April. See box (below) for the classes of contributions.

Employed or self-employed?

The question as to whether a person is employed under a contract *of* service and is thereby an employee liable to Class 1 contributions, or performs services (either solely or in partnership) under a contract *for* service and is thereby self-employed liable to Class 2 and Class 4 contributions, often has to be decided in practice. One of the best guides can be found in the case of *Market Investigations Ltd* v. *Minister of Social Security* (1969 2 WLR 1) when Cooke J. remarked:

'… the fundamental test to be applied is this: "Is the person who has engaged himself to perform these services performing them as a person in business on his own account?" If the answer to that question is "yes", then the contract is a contract for services. If the answer is "no", then the contract is a contract of service. No exhaustive list has been compiled and perhaps no exhaustive list can be compiled of the considerations which are relevant in determining that question, nor can strict rules be laid down as to the relative weight which the various considerations should carry in particular cases. The most that can be said is that control will no doubt always have to be considered, although it can no longer be regarded as the sole determining factor; and that factors which may be of importance are such matters as:

- whether the man performing the services provides his own equipment,
- whether he hires his own helpers,
- what degree of financial risk he takes,
- what degree of responsibility for investment and management he has, and
- whether and how far he has an opportunity of profiting from sound management in the performance of his task.'

Classes of contributions

Class 1 These are payable by employees (primary contributions) and their employers (secondary contributions) and are based on earnings.

Class 1A Payable only by employers in respect of all taxable benefits in kind (cars and fuel only prior to 6 April 2000).

Class 1B Payable only by employers in respect of PAYE Settlement Agreements entered into by them.

Class 2 These are weekly flat rate contributions, payable by the self-employed.

Class 3 These are weekly flat rate contributions, payable on a voluntary basis in order to provide, or make up entitlement to, certain social security benefits.

Class 4 These are payable by the self-employed in respect of their trading or professional income and are based on earnings.

The above case has often been considered subsequently – notably in November 1993 by the Court of Appeal in the case of *Hall* v. *Lorimer*. In this case a vision mixer with around 20 clients and undertaking around 120–150 separate engagements per annum was held to be self-employed. This follows the, perhaps surprising, contention of the Inland Revenue that the taxpayer was an employee.

Further guidance

There have been three cases dealing with musicians, in relatively recent times, which provide further guidance on the question as to whether an individual is employed or self-employed.

- *Midland Sinfonia Concert Society Ltd* v. *Secretary of State for Social Services* (1981 ICR 454). A musician, employed to play in an orchestra by separate invitation at irregular intervals and remunerated solely in respect of each occasion upon which he plays, is employed under a contract for services. He is therefore self-employed, not an employed earner, for the purposes of the Social Security Contributions and Benefits Act 1992, and the orchestra which engages him is not liable to pay National Insurance contributions in respect of his earnings.

- *Addison* v. *London Philharmonic Orchestra Ltd* (1981 ICR 261). This was an appeal to determine whether certain individuals were employees for the purposes of section 11(1) of the Employment Protection (Consolidation) Act 1978.

  The Employment Appeal Tribunal upheld the decision of an industrial tribunal that an associate player and three additional or extra players of the London Philharmonic Orchestra were not employees under a contract of service, but were essentially freelance musicians carrying on their own business. The facts found by the industrial tribunal showed that, when playing for the orchestra, each appellant remained essentially a freelance musician, pursuing his or her own profession as an instrumentalist, with an individual reputation, and carrying on his or her own business, and they contributed their own skills and interpretative powers to the orchestra's performances as independent contractors.

- *Winfield* v. *London Philharmonic Orchestra Ltd* (1979 ICR 726). This case dealt with the question as to whether an individual was an employee within the meaning of section 30 of the Trade Union and Labour Relations Act 1974. The following remarks by the appeal tribunal are of interest in relation to the status of musicians:

  "… making music is an art, and the co-operation required for a performance of Berlioz's *Requiem* is dissimilar to that required between the manufacturer of concrete and the truck driver who takes the concrete where it is needed … It took the view, as we think it was entitled on the material before it to do, that the company was simply machinery through which the members of the orchestra managed and controlled the orchestra's operation … In deciding whether you are in the presence of a contract of service or not, you look at the whole of the picture. This picture looks to us, as it looked to the industrial tribunal, like a co-operative of distinguished musicians running themselves with self and mutual discipline, and in no sense like a boss and his musician employees."

Other recent cases have concerned a professional dancer and holiday camp entertainers (all of whom were regarded as employees). In two recent cases income from part-time lecturing was held to be from an employment.

Accordingly, if a person is regarded as an employee under the above rules, he or she will be liable to pay contributions even if his employment is casual, part-time or temporary. Furthermore, if a person is an employee and also carries on a trade or profession either solely or in partnership, there will be a liability to more than one class of contributions (subject to certain maxima – see below).

Exceptions
There are certain exceptions to the above rules, those most relevant to artists and writers being:
● The employment of a wife by her husband, or vice versa, is disregarded for social security purposes unless it is for the purposes of a trade or profession (e.g. the employment of his wife by an author would not be disregarded and would result in a liability for contributions if her salary reached the minimum levels).
● The employment of certain relatives in a private dwelling house in which both employee and employer reside is disregarded for social security purposes provided the employment is not for the purposes of a trade or business carried on at those premises by the employer. This would cover the employment of a relative (as defined) as a housekeeper in a private residence.
● In general, lecturers, teachers and instructors engaged by an educational establishment to teach on at least four days in three consecutive months are regarded as employees, although this rule does not apply to fees received by persons giving public lectures.

Freelance film workers
There is a list of grades in the film industry in respect of which PAYE need not be deducted and who are regarded as self-employed for tax purposes.

Further information can be obtained from the Summer 2000 edition of the Inland Revenue guidance notes on the application of PAYE to casual and freelance staff in the film industry. In view of the Inland Revenue announcement that the same status will apply for PAYE and National Insurance contributions purposes, no liability for employee's and employer's contributions should arise in the case of any of the grades mentioned above.

However, in the film and television industry this general rule was not always followed in practice. In December 1992, after a long review, the DSS agreed that individuals working behind the camera and who have jobs on the Inland Revenue Schedule D list are self-employed for social security purposes.

There are special rules for, *inter alia*, personnel appearing before the camera, short engagements, payments to limited companies and payments to overseas personalities.

Artistes, performers/non-performers
The status of artistes and performers for tax purposes will depend on the individual circumstances but for social security new regulations which took

effect on 17 July 1998 require most actors, musicians or similar performers to be treated as employees for social security purposes, whether or not this status applies under general and/or tax law. It also applies whether or not the individual is supplied through an agency.

Personal service companies
From 6 April 2000, those who have control of their own 'one-man service companies' are subject to special rules. If the work that the owner of the company does for the company's customers would – but for the one-man company – fall to be considered as an employment of that individual (i.e. rather than self-employment), a deemed salary may arise. If it does, then some or all of the income of the company will be treated as salary liable to PAYE and National Insurance contributions. This will be the case whether or not such salary is actually paid by the company. The same situation may arise where the worker owns as little as 5% of a company's share capital.

The calculations required by the Inland Revenue are complicated and have to be done very quickly at the end of each tax year (even if the company's year-end is different). It is essential that affected businesses seek detailed professional advice about these rules which may also, in certain circumstances, apply to partnerships.

Class 1 contributions
As mentioned above, these are related to earnings, the amount payable depending upon whether the employer has applied for his employees to be 'contracted-out' of the State earnings-related pension scheme; such application can be made where the employer's own pension scheme provides a requisite level of benefits for his or her employees and their dependants or, in the case of a money purchase scheme (COMPS) certain minimum safeguards are covered. Employers with employees contributing to 'stakeholder pension plans' continue to pay the full not contracted-out rate. Such employees have their contracting out arrangements handled separately by government authorities.

Contributions are payable by employees and employers on earnings that exceed the earnings threshold. Contributions are normally collected via the PAYE tax deduction machinery, and there are penalties for late submission of returns and for errors therein. From 19 April 1993, interest is charged automatically on unpaid PAYE and social security contributions.

Employees liable to pay
Contributions are payable by any employee who is aged 16 years and over (even though he or she may still be at school) and who is paid an amount equal to, or exceeding, the earnings threshold. Nationality is irrelevant for contribution purposes and, subject to special rules covering employees not normally resident in Great Britain, Northern Ireland or the Isle of Man, or resident in EEA countries or those with which there are reciprocal agreements, contributions must be paid whether the employee concerned is a British subject or not provided he is gainfully employed in Great Britain.

Employees exempt from liability to pay

Persons over pensionable age (65 for men; 60 – until 2010 – for women) are exempt from liability to pay primary contributions, even if they have not retired. However, the fact that an employee may be exempt from liability does not relieve an employer from liability to pay secondary contributions in respect of that employee.

Employees' (primary) contributions

From 6 April 2003, the rate of employees' contributions on earnings from the earnings threshold to the upper earnings limit is 11% (9.4% for contracted-out employments). Certain married women who made appropriate elections before 12 May 1977 may be entitled to pay a reduced rate of 4.85%. However, they will have no entitlement to benefits in respect of these contributions.

From April 2003, earnings above the upper earnings limit attract an employee contribution liability of 1% – previously, there was no such liability.

Employers' (secondary) contributions

All employers are liable to pay contributions on the gross earnings of employees. As mentioned above, an employer's liability is not reduced as a result of employees being exempted from contributions, or being liable to pay only the reduced rate (4.85%) of contributions.

For earnings paid on or after 6 April 2003 employers are liable at a rate of 12.8% on earnings paid above the earnings threshold (without any upper earnings limit), 9.3% where the employment is contracted out (salary related) or 11.8% (money purchase). In addition, special rebates apply in respect of earnings falling between the lower earnings limit and the earnings threshold. This provides, effectively, a negative rate of contribution in that small band of earnings. It should be noted that the contracted-out rates of 9.3% and 11.8% apply only up to the upper earnings limit. Thereafter, the not contracted-out rate of 12.8% is applicable.

The employer is responsible for the payment of both employees' and employer's contributions, but is entitled to deduct the employees' contributions from the earnings on which they are calculated. Effectively, therefore, the employee suffers a deduction in respect of his or her social security contributions in arriving at his weekly or monthly wage or salary. Special rules apply to company directors and persons employed through agencies.

Rates of Class 1 contributions and earnings limits from 6 April 2003				
	Rates payable on earnings in each band			
Earnings per week	Not contracted-out		Contracted-out	
	Employee	Employer	Employee	Employer
£	%	%	%	%
Below 77.00	—	—	—	—
77.00 – 88.99	—	—	— (*)	— (*)
89.00 – 595.00	11	12.8	9.4	9.3 or 11.8
Over £595.00	1	12.8	1	12.8

* Special rebates deductible in respect of this band of earnings.

Items included in, or excluded from, earnings

Contributions are calculated on the basis of a person's gross earnings from his or her employment. This will normally be the figure shown on the deduction working sheet, except where the employee pays superannuation contributions and, from 6 April 1987, charitable gifts under payroll giving – these must be added back for the purposes of calculating Class 1 liability.

Earnings include salary, wages, overtime pay, commissions, bonuses, holiday pay, payments made while the employee is sick or absent from work, payments to cover travel between home and office, and payments under the statutory sick pay, statutory maternity pay, statutory paternity pay and statutory adoption pay schemes.

However, certain payments, some of which may be regarded as taxable income for income tax purposes, are ignored for Class 1 purposes. These include:

- certain gratuities paid other than by the employer,
- redundancy payments and some payments in lieu of notice,
- certain payments in kind,
- reimbursement of specific expenses incurred in the carrying out of the employment,
- benefits given on an individual basis for personal reasons (e.g. wedding and birthday presents),
- compensation for loss of office.

IR Booklet CWG 2 (2003 edition) gives a list of items to include in or exclude from earnings for Class 1 contribution purposes. Some such items may, however, be liable to Class 1A contributions.

Miscellaneous rules

There are detailed rules covering a person with two or more employments; where a person receives a bonus or commission in addition to a regular wage or salary; and where a person is in receipt of holiday pay. From 6 April 1991 employers' social security contributions arise under Class 1A in respect of the private use of a company car, and of fuel provided for private use therein. From 6 April 2000, this charge was extended to cover most benefits in kind. The rate is now 12.8%. From 6 April 1999, Class 1B contributions are payable by employers using PAYE Settlement Agreements in respect of small and/or irregular expense payments and benefits, etc. This rate is also currently 12.8%.

Class 2 contributions

Class 2 contributions are payable at the weekly rate of £2.00 as from 6 April 2000 and remains at that rate for 2003/04. Exemptions from Class 2 liability are:

- A man over 65 or a woman over 60.
- A person who has not attained the age of 16.
- A married woman or, in certain cases, a widow who elected prior to 12 May 1977 not to pay Class 2 contributions.
- Persons with small earnings (see below).
- Persons not ordinarily self-employed (see below).

Small earnings
Application for a certificate of exception from Class 2 contributions may be made by any person who can show that his or her net self-employed earnings per his profit and loss account (as opposed to taxable profits):

● for the year of application are expected to be less than a specified limit (£4095 in the 2003/04 tax year); or
● for the year preceding the application were less than the limit specified for that year (£4025 for 2002/03) and there has been no material change of circumstances.

Certificates of exception must be renewed in accordance with the instructions stated thereon. At the Inland Revenue's discretion the certificate may commence up to 13 weeks before the date on which the application is made. Despite a certificate of exception being in force, a person who is self-employed is still entitled to pay Class 2 contributions if they wish, in order to maintain entitlement to social security benefits.

Persons not ordinarily self-employed
Part-time self-employed activities (including as a writer or artist) are disregarded for contribution purposes if the person concerned is not ordinarily employed in such activities and has a full-time job as an employee. There is no definition of 'ordinarily employed' for this purpose but a person who has a regular job and whose earnings from spare-time occupation are not expected to be more than £1300 per annum may fall within this category. Persons qualifying for this relief do not require certificates of exception but may be well advised to apply for one nonetheless.

Method of payment
From April 1993, Class 2 contributions may be paid by monthly direct debit in arrears or, alternatively, by cheque, bank giro, etc following receipt of a quarterly (in arrears) bill.

Overpaid contributions
If, following the payment of Class 2 contributions, it is found that the earnings are below the exception limit (e.g. the relevant accounts are prepared late), the Class 2 contributions that have been overpaid can be reclaimed, provided a claim is made between 6 April and 31 December immediately following the end of the tax year.

Class 3 contributions
Class 3 contributions are payable voluntarily, at the weekly rate of £6.95 per week from 6 April 2003, by persons aged 16 or over with a view to enabling them to qualify for a limited range of benefits if their contribution record is not otherwise sufficient. In general, Class 3 contributions can be paid by employees, the self-employed and the non employed.

Broadly speaking, no more than 52 Class 3 contributions are payable for any one tax year, and contributions are not payable after the end of the tax year in which the individual concerned reaches the age of 64 (59 for women).

Class 3 contributions may be paid in the same manner as Class 2 (see above) or by annual cheque in arrears.

Class 4 contributions
In addition to Class 2 contributions, self-employed persons are liable to pay Class 4 contributions. These are calculated at the rate of 8% on the amount of profits or gains chargeable to income tax under Schedule D Case I or II which exceed £4615 per annum but which do not exceed £30,940 per annum for 2003/04. For the first time from 6 April 2003, profits above the upper limit of £30,940 attract a Class 4 charge at the rate of 1%.

The income tax profit on which Class 4 contributions are calculated is after deducting capital allowances and losses, but before deducting personal tax allowances or retirement annuity or personal pension or stakeholder pension plan premiums.

Class 4 contributions produce no additional benefits, but were introduced to ensure that self-employed persons as a whole pay a fair share of the cost of pensions and other social security benefits yet without those who make only small profits having to pay excessively high flat rate contributions.

Payment of contributions
In general, contributions are now self-assessed and paid to the Inland Revenue together with the income tax under Schedule D Case I or II, and accordingly the contributions are due and payable at the same time as the income tax liability on the relevant profits. Under self-assessment, interim payments of Class 4 contributions are payable at the same time as interim payments of tax.

Class 4 exemptions
The following persons are exempt from Class 4 contributions:
● Men over 65 and women over 60 at the commencement of the year of assessment (i.e. on 6 April).
● An individual not resident in the United Kingdom for income tax purposes in the year of assessment.
● Persons whose earnings are not 'immediately derived' from carrying on a trade, profession or vocation (e.g. sleeping partners and, possibly, limited partners).
● A child under 16 on 6 April of the year of assessment.
● Persons not ordinarily self-employed.

Married persons and partnerships
Under independent taxation of husband and wife from 1990/91 onwards, each spouse is responsible for his or her Class 4 liability.

In partnerships, each partner's liability is calculated separately. If a partner also carries on another trade or profession, the profits of all such businesses are aggregated for the purposes of calculating his or her Class 4 liability.

When an assessment has become final and conclusive for the purposes of income tax, it is also final and conclusive for the purposes of calculating Class 4 liability.

Maximum contributions
There is a form of limit to the total liability for social security contributions payable by a person who is employed in more than one employment, or is also self-employed or a partner.

Where only not contracted-out Class 1 contributions, or not contracted-out Class 1 and Class 2 contributions, are payable, the maximum contribution payable at the main rates (11%, 9.4% or 4.85% as the case may be) is limited to 53 primary Class 1 contributions at the maximum weekly not contracted-out standard rate. For 2003/04 this 'maximum' will thus be £2949.98 (amounts paid at only 1% are to be excluded in making this comparison).

However, where contracted-out Class 1 contributions are payable, the maximum primary Class 1 contributions payable for 2003/04 where all employments are contracted out are £2520.89.

Where Class 4 contributions are payable in addition to Class 1 and/or Class 2 contributions, the Class 4 contributions payable at the full 8% rate are restricted so that they shall not exceed the excess of £2212.00 (i.e. 53 Class 2 contributions plus maximum Class 4 contributions) over the aggregate of the Class 1 and Class 2 contributions.

Transfer to Inland Revenue

The administrative functions of the former Contributions Agency transferred to the Inland Revenue from 1 April 1999. Responsibility for National Insurance contribution policy matters was also transferred from DSS Ministers to the Inland Revenue and Treasury Ministers on the same date. The DSS is now known as the Department for Work and Pensions (DWP).

Peter Arrowsmith FCA is a sole practitioner specialising in National Insurance matters. He is chairman of the Employer Issues Committee of the Institute of Chartered Accountants in England and Wales and Consulting Editor to *Tolley's National Insurance Contributions 2003/04*.

Further information

Further information can be obtained from the many booklets published by the Inland Revenue, available from local Inland Revenue Enquiry Centres.

National Insurance Contributions Office, International Services
Newcastle upon Tyne NE98 1ZZ
tel (08459) 154811 (local call rates apply)
Address for enquiries for individuals resident abroad.

Social security benefits

There are many leaflets produced by the Department for Work and Pensions. However, due to the nature of the subject social security benefits can be quite difficult to understand. In this article, K.D. Bartlett FCA has summarised some of the more usual benefits that are available under the Social Security Acts.

This article deliberately does not cover every aspect of the legislation but the references given should enable the relevant information to be easily traced. These references are to the leaflets issued by the Department for Work and Pensions.

It is usual for only one periodical benefit to be payable at any one time. If the contribution conditions are satisfied for more than one benefit it is the larger benefit that is payable. Benefit rates shown below were those payable from the week commencing 6 April 2003.

Self-employed persons (Class 2 and Class 4 contributors) are covered for all benefits except earnings-related supplements, unemployment benefit, widow's and invalidity pensions, widowed mother's allowance and industrial injury benefits. Most authors are self employed.

Family benefits

Child benefit (Leaflet CH 1) is payable for all children who are either under 16 or under 19 and receiving full-time education at a recognised educational establishment. The rate is £16.05 for the first or eldest child and £10.75 a week for each subsequent child. It is payable to the person who is responsible for the child but excludes foster parents or people exempt from UK tax. Furthermore, one-parent families receive £17.55 per week for the eldest child.

Those with little money may apply for a maternity loan or grant from the social fund. Those claiming Working Families Tax Credit or Disabled Persons Tax Credit can apply for a Sure Start Maternity Grant of £300 for each baby expected, born, adopted or subject to a parental order. Any savings over £500 are taken into account. This grant will only be paid on the provision of a relevant certificate from a doctor, midwife or health visitor.

A guardian's allowance (Leaflet NI 14) is paid at the rate of £9.70 a week. For each subsequent child the rate of benefit is £11.55 a week to people who have taken orphans into their own family. Usually both of the child's parents must be dead and at least one of them must have satisfied a residence condition.

The allowance can only be paid to the person who is entitled to child benefit for the child (or to that person's spouse). It is not necessary to be the legal guardian. The claim should be made within three months of the date of entitlement.

Disability living allowance

Disability living allowance has replaced attendance allowance for disabled people before they reach the age of 65. It has also replaced mobility allowance.

Those who are disabled after reaching 65 may be able to claim attendance allowance. The attendance allowance board decide whether, and for how long, a person is eligible for this allowance. Attendance allowance is not taxable. The care component is divided into three rates whereas the mobility allowance has two rates. The rate of benefit from 6 April 2003 is as follows:

	Per week
Care component	
Higher rate (day and night, or terminally ill)	£57.20
Middle rate (day or night)	£38.30
Lower rate (if need some help during day, or over 16 and need help preparing a meal)	£15.15
Mobility component	
Higher rate (unable or virtually unable to walk)	£39.95
Lower rate (can walk but needs help when outside)	£15.15

Benefits for the ill

Incapacity benefit (Leaflet DS 700) replaced sickness benefit and invalidity benefit. The contribution conditions haven't changed but a new medical test has been brought in which includes a comprehensive questionnaire. The rates from 8 April 2003 are:

Long-term incapacity benefit	£72.15
Short-term incapacity benefit	£54.40
Increase of long-term incapacity benefit for age:	
Higher rate	£15.15
Lower rate	£7.60

Carers allowance, formerly invalid care allowance, is a taxable benefit paid to people of working age who cannot take a job because they have to stay at home to look after a severely disabled person. The basic allowance is £43.15 per week. An extra £9.70 is paid for the first dependent child and £11.55 for each subsequent child.

Pensions and widow's benefits

The state pension (Leaflets NP 23, NP 35, NP 31) is divided into two parts – the basic pension, presently £77.45 per week for a single person or £123.80 per week for a married couple.

Women paying standard rate contributions into the scheme are eligible for the same amount of pension as men but five years earlier, from age 60. The Pensions Act 1995 incorporated the provision for an equal state pension age of 65 for men and women to be phased in over a 10-year period beginning 6 April 2010. If a woman stays at home to bring up her children or to look after a person receiving attendance allowance she can have her basic pension rights protected without paying contributions.

The widow's pension and widowed mother's allowance also consists of a basic pension and an additional earnings-related pension. The full amount of the additional pension applies only if the husband has contributed to the new scheme for at least 20 years.

Widow's benefits

From 11 April 1988 there are three main widow's benefits:

Widow's payment, which has replaced the widow's allowance, is currently a lump sum payment of £2000 payable to widows who were bereaved on or after 11 April 1988. It is payable immediately on the death of the husband. Entitlement to this benefit is based on the late husband's contribution record but no payment will be made if the widow is living with another man as husband and wife at the date of death. The late husband must have actually paid contributions on earnings of at least 25 times the weekly or lower earnings limit for a given tax year in any tax year ending before his death (or ending before he reached pensionable age if he was over 65 when he died). The equivalent number of Class 2 or voluntary Class 3 contributions will be sufficient.

When claiming, the widow should complete the form on the back of the death certificate and send it to the local social security office. On receipt of this information the DSS will send the claimant a more detailed form (BD8) which, once completed, has to go back to the social security office. It is important to claim the benefit within 12 months of the husband's death.

Widowed mother's allowance (Leaflet NP 45). Those widowed before 9 April 2001 left with children to look after, are entitled to a widowed mother's allowance provided that her late husband had paid sufficient National Insurance contributions. These contributions are:

● 25 Class 1, 2 or 3 contributions before age 65 and before 6 April 1975; or
● contributions in any one tax year after 6 April 1975 on earnings of at least 25 times the weekly lower earnings limit for that year.

It is important that the widow is looking after either her own child or her husband's child and that the child is under 16 or, if between the age of 16 and 19, is continuing in full-time education.

The allowance stops immediately if the widow remarries and will be suspended if she lives with a man as his wife. From April 2003 the basic allowance is £77.45 with £11.35 increase for each child. Where a husband's contributions only satisfied the first test above, the basic allowance may be payable at a reduced rate. This reduction does not alter the rate of an increase for a child.

Widow's pension (Leaflet NP 45). A widow who is widowed before 9 April 2001 and who is over the age of 45 when her husband dies may be eligible for a widow's pension unless she is eligible for the widowed mother's allowance. In this situation the widow's pension becomes payable when the widowed mother's allowance ends, provided she is still under the age of 65. However, where a woman had been receiving the widowed mother's allowance, she becomes entitled to a widow's pension if she is between the ages of 45 and 65 when the allowance ends, no matter what her age may have been when her husband died. Before 11 April 1988 a widow aged 40 or over could qualify for a widow's pension.

Qualification conditions
- The contributions conditions must be satisfied and these conditions are the same as those for the widowed mother's allowance above.
- The widow must not be receiving the widowed mother's allowance.
- When her husband died she was aged between 45 and 65 or she was entitled to widowed mother's allowance and is aged between 45 and 65 when her widowed mother's allowance finished.

Cessation of widow's pension
- Entitlement finishes if the widowed mother's allowance stops because she has remarried.
- Widow's pension must not be claimed when the payment of the widowed mother's allowance has been suspended because the widow is in pension or is living with a man as his wife.

From 11 April 1988 both the basic and additional pension are paid at a reduced rate if the widow was aged under 55:
- when her husband died, if she did not subsequently become entitled to widowed mother's allowance; or
- when her widowed mother's allowance ceased to be paid. The relevant rates from April 2003 are as follows:

Age related	£	%
Basic	77.45	100
Age 54 (49)	72.03	93
53 (48)	66.61	86
52 (47)	61.19	79
51 (46)	55.76	72
50 (45)	50.34	65
49 (44)	44.92	58
48 (43)	39.50	51
47 (42)	34.08	44
46 (41)	28.66	37
45 (40)	23.24	30

(The ages given in parentheses apply to women for whom widow's pension was payable before 11 April 1988.)

Bereavement payment and benefits
From 9 April 2001 bereavement benefits are payable to both widows and widowers but the benefits are only paid to those without children. Benefits are based on the National Insurance contributions of the deceased. No benefit is payable if the couple were divorced at the date of death or if either of the survivors remarries or cohabits.

Widows and widowers bereaved on or after 9 April 2001 are entitled to a tax-free bereavement payment of £2000.

The death grant to cover funeral expenses was abolished from 6 April 1987. It has been replaced by a funeral payment from the social fund where the claimant is in receipt of income support, income-based Jobseekers' Allowance, Disabled Persons' Tax Credit, Working Families' Tax Credit or housing benefit. The full cost of a reasonable funeral is paid, reduced by any savings of over £500 held by the claimant or his or her family (£1000 for couples over 60).

Tax credit changes from April 2003

In April 2003 Working Families' Tax Credit (WFTC), Disabled Person's Tax Credit (DPTC) and Children's Tax Credit were replaced by two new tax credits called Child Tax Credit and Working Tax Credit. These new tax credits provide support to a wider range of people through a single framework.

To receive these tax credits you need to claim either by filling in the new tax credit form (the TC600) or by visiting the website and claiming online. You can claim for either or both of the new tax credits on one claim form.

If you are an existing WFTC or DPTC user, you will likely qualify for the next tax credits. You will receive a claim form through the post in late summer 2003. On receiving the form you should either complete it and return it straight away, or go to the Inland Revenue website to claim online. If you receive a renewal claim form for WFTC or DPTC, complete it as usual.

The amount of tax credit you receive is based on your income for the year 2001/02, If you are an employee, you will probably find the easiest way of obtaining your income details is from your P60 End of Year Certificate. You will receive this certificate from your employer and you will need to keep this for your tax credit claim. If you are self-employed, you need to know the income figure that you put on your tax return for 2001/02.

Claimants have been able to claim the new tax credits from August 2002 and payments started in April 2003. However, the Inland Revenue have suffered administrative problems and have received many complaints. If you are eligible but haven't received payment then you should apply in writing and keep copies of any correspondence.

Working Tax Credit

This is a tax credit for people who are in paid work. You may be eligible if:
- you are a single person, or
- you are a man and woman living together as if you are married, and
- you are in paid work (including working as a self-employed person) for the required number of hours.

Table 1 Non-working people with children

Child Tax Credit only

Child element	Maximum credit* per week	Maximum income to get some credit per week	per year
1 child	£27.75	£327	£17,097
2 children	£55.50	£402	£21,019
3 children	£83.25	£477	£24,940
Family element	£10.45	£1,105	£57,776
Baby element	£20.90	£1,261	£65,932

* To get the maximum child element, income must be no more than £13,230 a year or £254 a week.
To get the maximum family or baby element, income must be no more than £50,000 a year.

Table 2 Working people without children

Working Tax Credit only

Aged 25–49	Maximum credit* per week	Maximum income to get some credit per week	per year
Work 30 hours or more	£41	£206	£10,771
Disabled work 16–29 hours	£68	£279	£14,588
Disabled work 30 hours or more	£80	£312	£16,313
Over 50** work 30 hours or more	£71	£287	£15,006
Over 50 16–29 hours and disabled	£88	£334	£17,463
Over 50 30 hours or more and disabled	£110	£393	£20,548

* NB To get the maximum tax credit, gross income must be less than £5,060 a year or around £97 a week, which at minimum wage is around 23 hours' work.
** Over 50 rates last for one year only.

The amount you receive will depend on your annual income and you must be 16 years of age or over to apply for the tax credits.

Child Tax Credit

This was introduced in April 2003 and replaces children's tax credit. The Child Tax Credit will be paid direct to the main carer in a family. All families with total household incomes under £59,000 will be eligible for some help. Families with a household income of £25,000–£50,000 will receive the Child Tax Credit at a flat rate of £10.45 regardless of how many children there are. Child Tax Credit payments can be paid into the mother's bank account in the same way as child benefit, but payments will be kept separate.

In the first year of a child's life, in recognition of the cost of a newborn baby, the Baby Tax Credit pays another £10.45 a week, increasing the total to £20.90 a week. You can calculate whether you qualify by using the Inland Revenue's calculator at www.taxcredits.inlandrevenue.gov.uk

Disabled Persons' Tax Credits

Disabled Persons' Tax Credits (DPTC) is a tax credit payable to people with an illness or disability who are in work, depending on their circumstances which:
- has replaced Disability Working Allowance;
- includes the Fast Track Gateway to help those who become disabled while working to keep their job;
- is administered by the Inland Revenue;
- was replaced in April 2003 by the two new tax credits, Child Tax Credit and Working Tax Credit.

Working Tax Credit

Working Tax Credit (WTC) is for people in low-paid work – or in low-paid self-employment – and for the first time can be paid to people

Further information

Further information can be obtained from the local office of the Department of Social Security or from Accountants Digest No. 439 published by the Institute of Chartered Accountants in England and Wales. Readers resident abroad who have queries should write to the Department's Overseas Branch, Newcastle upon Tyne NE98 1BA.

without children. It replaces WFTC and DPTC. To get it you must normally be 25 or over and work for at least 30 hours a week. But people who are disabled or who have children can be as young as 16 and only have to work for 16 hours a week. People aged over 50 or over who have just returned to work can get extra WTC for a year and need only work for 16 hours a week or more.

Arithmetic

Tax credit arithmetic is very strange. The annual amounts are generally the ones set by law. The Inland Revenue reckons there are not 52 weeks but 366 days divided by seven in the leap tax year 2003/04. So weekly amounts are approximate and all figures have been rounded.

K.D. Bartlett FCA qualified as a Chartered Accountant in 1969 and became a partner in a predecessor firm of Horwath Clark Whitehill in 1972.

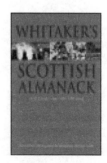

Subject indexes

Magazines by subject area

These lists can be only a broad classification. They should be regarded as a pointer to possible markets and be used with discrimination. Addresses for magazines start on page 21.

Fiction (see also Literary)
Active Life
Ambit
Aquila
The Australian Women's Weekly
Bella
Best
Brownie
Cencrastus: Scottish &
   International Literature, Arts
   and Affairs
Chapman
Chat
Critical Quarterly
Cyphers
The Dalhousie Review (Can.)
Day by Day
Diva
The Edge
The Erotic Review
The Fiddlehead (Can.)
Fly-Fishing & Fly-Tying
For Women
Granta
Interzone
Ireland's Own
The Jewish Quarterly
Junior Magazine
Kent Life
The Lady
Leviathan Quarterly
The London Magazine: A Review
   of Literature and the Arts
Lothian Life
The Malahat Review (Can.)
More!
Mslexia
My Weekly
My Weekly Story Collection
New Impact
The New Writer
New Zealand Woman's Day
New Zealand Woman's Weekly
The Newspaper
Overland (Aus.)
Peninsular Magazine
People's Friend

People's Friend Story Collection
Planet
Pride Magazine
Prospect
Quadrant (Aus.)
Queen's Quarterly (Can.)
QWF
The Scots Magazine
Scuba Diver (Aus.)
SHERLOCK
Springboard
Stand Magazine
Staple
Starburst
Takahe (NZ)
Take a Break
that's life!
The Third Alternative
Time Out
The Times Literary Supplement
Wascana Review of
   Contemporary Poetry & Short
   Fiction (Can.)
The Weekly News
Woman and Home
Woman's Day (Aus.)
Woman's Own
Woman's Value (SA)
Woman's Way
Woman's Weekly
Woman's Weekly Fiction Special
Writers' Forum
Young Writer
Your Cat Magazine
Yours

Letters to the Editor
Architecture Today
The Australian Women's Weekly
Bella
Best
The Big Issue
Bizarre
Caledonia
Caravan Magazine
Chat
Choice
Classics

Dolly (Aus.)
The Economist
Electrical Times
Executive PA
Femina Magazine (SA)
FHM (For Him Magazine)
Flora International
The Furrow
H&E Naturist
Here's Health
Modern Painters
Moneywise
Mother & Baby
My Weekly
New Law Journal
New Zealand Woman's Day
Now
Nursery Education
NW Magazine (Aus.)
People's Friend
PN Review
Practical Householder
Practical Parenting
The Practising Midwife
Prima
Racing Post
Retail Week
Saga Magazine
Scuba World
Ski and Board
Television
that's life!
Third Way
TV Quick
The Weekly News
What's on TV
Woman's Day (Aus.)
Woman's Value (SA)
Woman's Weekly
Woman's Way
Yours

Gossip paragraphs
Australian Bookseller & Publisher
The Big Issue
Broadcast
Buses
Campaign

Brief filler paragraphs

Puzzles and quizzes

The following take puzzles and/or quizzes on an occasional or, in some cases, regular basis. Ideas must be tailored to suit each publication: approach in writing in the first instance.

The Woodworker
The Word
World Soccer
Your Dog Magazine
Your Family (SA)

UK ethnic weekly newspapers

Asian Times
Caribbean Times
Eastern Eye
The Voice

Women's interest magazines (see also Health and home)

The Australian Women's Weekly
B
Bella
Best
Black Beauty & Hair
Bliss!
Bona (SA)
Chat
Chatelaine (Can.)
Company
Cosmopolitan
Diva
Elle (UK)
Essentials
Executive PA
Executive Woman
Femina Magazine (SA)
For Women
Girl About Town Magazine
Glamour
Good Housekeeping
Hairflair
Harpers & Queen
Harper's Bazaar (Aus.)
Hello!
Home
HQ Magazine (Aus.)
In Style
Irish Tatler
Junior Magazine
The Lady
Living and Loving (SA)
Marie Claire
Modern Woman Nationwide
More!
Mother & Baby
Ms London
Mslexia
My Weekly
My Weekly Story Collection
New Woman (Aus.)
New Woman

New Zealand Woman's Day
New Zealand Woman's Weekly
19
Now
Nursery World
Office Secretary (OS Magazine)
OK! Magazine
People's Friend
The Pink Paper
Pride Magazine
Prima
Prima Baby
Real
Red
She (NZ)
She
Take a Break
Tatler
that's life!
U magazine
Vanity Fair
Vive (Aus.)
Vogue
Vogue Australia (Aus.)
Wedding and Home
WI Home and Country
Woman
Woman Alive
Woman and Home
Woman's Day (Aus.)
Woman's Own
Woman's Value (SA)
Woman's Way
Woman's Weekly
Woman's Weekly Fiction Special
Women's Health
World's Children
You & Your Wedding
Your Family (SA)

Men's interest magazines

Arena
Attitude
Country
Esquire
FHM (For Him Magazine)
Gay Times
GQ
Jack Magazine
Loaded
Maxim
Men Only
Men's Health
The Pink Paper

Children's and young adult magazines

Animals and You
Aquila
The Beano
Brownie
Commando
Cosmogirl
The Dandy
Dolly (Aus.)
Football Picture Story Library
Hot Press
i-D Magazine
J–17
Mizz
The Newspaper
Pony Magazine
Scouting Magazine
Shoot
Shout
Smash Hits
Young Writer

Subject articles

Advertising, design, printing and publishing
(see also Literary)

Australian Bookseller & Publisher
British Journalism Review
Campaign
The Face
Freelance Market News
Greetings Today
Irish Printer
Media Week
PR Week
Press Gazette
Printing World
Publishing News

Agriculture, farming and horticulture

Country Life
Country Smallholding
The Countryman
Dairy Farmer
Farmers Weekly
Farmer's Weekly (SA)
The Field
The Grower
Horticulture Week
Irish Farmers Journal
Pig Farming
Poultry World
The Scottish Farmer
Smallholder
Straight Furrow (NZ)

Architecture and building

The Architects' Journal
Architectural Design
The Architectural Review
Architecture Today
Blueprint
Building
Building Design
Built Environment
Country Homes and Interiors
Country Life
Education Journal
Homes and Gardens
Housebuilder

Art and collecting

AN Magazine
Antiques & Art Independent
Antiques and Collectables
Apollo
Art Business Today
Art Monthly
Art Monthly Australia
The Art Newspaper
Art Review
The Artist
Artists and Illustrators
The Book Collector
Book and Magazine Collector
Burlington Magazine
C international contemporary art
 (Can.)
Coin News
Contemporary
Country Life
Eastern Art Report
Embroidery
Gibbons Stamp Monthly
The Illustrated London News
Inuit Art Quarterly (Can.)
Leisure Painter
Medal News
Modern Painters
RA Magazine
Stamp Lover
Stamp Magazine
TATE

Aviation

Aeroplane Monthly
Air International
Air Pictorial International
Australian Flying (Aus.)
Flight International
Pilot
Today's Pilot
World Airnews (SA)

Business, industry and management

Business Life
Business Scotland
Chartered Secretary
Communicate
Cosmetic World News
Director
European Chemical News
Executive PA
Executive Woman
Fasttrack
Fire
Fishing News
Land & Liberty
Management Magazine (NZ)
Management Today
New Impact
Office Secretary (OS Magazine)
People Management
Restaurant Magazine
Ulster Business
The Woodworker

Cinema and films

Campaign
The Edge
Empire
Film Review
Hotdog
Screen International
Sight and Sound
Studio Sound
Total DVD
Total Film

Computers

Computer Weekly
Computing
Internet
MacUser
Macworld
.net The Internet Magazine
PC Advisor
PC Answers
Personal Computer World
Scientific Computing World
Total DVD
What Laptop & Handheld PC

Economics, accountancy and finance

Accountancy
Accountancy Age
Accounting & Business
Active Life
Africa Confidential
African Business
The Australian Financial Review

The Banker
Business Scotland
Contemporary Review
Economica
The Economist
Financial Adviser
The Grower
Insurance Age
Insurance Brokers' Monthly
Investors Chronicle
Land & Liberty
MoneyMarketing
Moneywise
Pensions World
Personal Finance
Post Magazine & Insurance Week

Education

Aquila
Carousel – The Guide to
 Children's Books
Child Education
Education Journal
Infant Projects
Junior Education
Junior Focus
The Linguist
Modern Language Review
Music Teacher
New Impact
Nursery Education
Nursery World
Practical Parenting
Reality
Report
Right Start
Safety Education
The School Librarian
The Teacher
The Times Educational
 Supplement
Times Educational Supplement
 Scotland
Times Higher Education
 Supplement
Under Five Contact
World's Children
Young People Now

Engineering and mechanics (see also Architecture, Aviation, Business, Motor transport, Nautical, Radio, Sciences)

Car Mechanics
EA Today Magazine (Aus.)
EE Times
Electrical Review

Electrical Times
The Engineer
Engineering
Everyday Practical Electronics
Fire
Model Engineer
Practical Woodworking
Rail
Railway Gazette International
Railway Magazine

Gardening

Amateur Gardening
Country
Country Life
Country Smallholding
The English Garden
Essential Water Garden
The Field
The Garden
Garden and Home (SA)
Garden Answers
Garden News
Homestyle
Hortus
House & Garden
Kitchen Garden
NZ House & Garden
Organic Gardening
Water Gardener

Health and home (See also Women's interest magazines)

Active Life
Australian Home Beautiful (Aus.)
Australian House and Garden
Black Beauty & Hair
British Deaf News
Choice
Classic Stitches
Country Homes and Interiors
Country Living
Garden and Home (SA)
H&E Naturist
Health & Fitness
Here's Health
Home
Homes and Gardens
Homestyle
House & Garden
House Beautiful
Ideal Home
In Balance Health & Lifestyle
   Magazine
Inspirations For Your Home
Junior Magazine
Kids Out

NZ House & Garden
Perfect Home
Period Living & Traditional
   Homes
Practical Householder
Practical Parenting
Prediction
Prima Baby
Running Fitness
Safety Education
Saga Magazine
Sainsbury's Magazine
Scottish Home and Country
Slimmer, Healthier, Fitter
Slimming Magazine
The Vegan
Weight Watchers Magazine
Woman's Value (SA)
Women's Health
The World of Interiors
Your Family (SA)
Your Home and Garden (NZ)
Yours
Zest

History and archaeology

Best of British
Coin News
Geographical Magazine
History Today
The Illustrated London News
In Britain
The National Trust Magazine
Picture Postcard Monthly
Scottish Memories

Hotel, catering and leisure

Caterer & Hotelkeeper
Health Club Management
Hotel and Catering Review
The Leisure Manager

Humour and satire

Private Eye
Viz Comic

Inflight magazines

Business Life

Legal and police

Family Law
Justice of the Peace
The Lawyer
Legal Week
New Law Journal
Police Journal
Police Review
Solicitors Journal

Leisure interests, pets (see also Nautical, Sports)

Astronomy Now
Bird Watching
Birdwatch
British Philatelic Bulletin
Camping Magazine
Canal & Riverboat
Caravan Magazine
Classic Stitches
Classics
Climber
Country Walking
Decanter
Dogs Today
Family Tree Magazine
The Field
Flora International
Folio
Gibbons Stamp Monthly
Guiding Magazine
The List
Military Modelling
Mixmag
Model Boats
Motor Caravan Magazine
Motorcaravan Motorhome
   Monthly (MMM)
Needlecraft
Our Dogs
Park Home & Holiday Caravan
Popular Crafts
Practical Caravan
Practical Fishkeeping
Radio Control Models and
   Electronics
The Rambler
Scottish Field
Scouting Magazine
Scuba World
Sewing World
The Spark Magazine
Stamp Lover
Stamp Magazine
Swimming Magazine
TGO (The Great Outdoors)
   Magazine
Time Out
Venue
Wine
The Woodworker
Workbox Magazine
Your Cat Magazine
Your Dog Magazine
Your Horse

Literary (see also Poetry)

American Markets Newsletter
Australian Bookseller & Publisher

Nautical and marine

Australian Powerboat (Aus.)
Canal & Riverboat
Classic Boat & The Boatman
Diver
Motor Boat and Yachting
Motor Boats Monthly
Nautical Magazine
Practical Boat Owner
Sea Breezes
Ships Monthly
Waterways World
Yachting Monthly
Yachting World
Yachts and Yachting

Photography

Amateur Photographer
Australian Camera
Australian Photography
The British Journal of
    Photography
Camcorder User
Freelance Photographer
Market Newsletter
Photo Life (Can.)
Practical Photography
Professional Photographer
What Camcorder

Poetry

*Magazines that only take the
occasional poem: check with the
Editor before submitting*
Acumen
Agenda
Ambit
Best of British*
Brownie*
Cencrastus: Scottish &
    International Literature, Arts
    and Affairs
Chapman
Contemporary Review*
The Countryman*
Critical Quarterly
Cumbria and Lake District
    Magazine
Cyphers
Dalesman*
The Dalhousie Review (Can.)
Dance Today!*
Day by Day*
Dolly* (Aus.)
East Lothian Life*
Edinburgh Review
Envoi
The Erotic Review*
Evergreen*

The Fiddlehead (Can.)
Fortnight – An Independent
    Review of Politics and the Arts*
Home Words*
HQ Poetry Magazine
The Jewish Quarterly*
The Lady*
Leviathan Quarterly
The Literary Review
The London Magazine: A Review
    of Literature and the Arts
London Review of Books
The Malahat Review (Can.)
Meanjin (Aus.)
Mslexia*
New Humanist*
New Welsh Review
The New Writer*
Orbis
Other Poetry
Outposts Poetry Quarterly
Overland (Aus.)
Oxford Poetry
Peninsular Magazine
People's Friend*
Planet
PN Review
Poetry Ireland Review/Éigse
    Éireann
Poetry London
Poetry Nottingham International
Poetry Review
Poetry Wales
Pride Magazine
Quadrant (Aus.)
Queen's Quarterly (Can.)
The Rialto
The Scots Magazine*
Scuba Diver* (Aus.)
The Shop: A Magazine of Poetry
The Sign*
The Spectator*
Springboard
Stand Magazine
Staple
Takahe (NZ)
Third Way*
This England*
The Times Literary Supplement*
Traveller*
Tribune*
Wascana Review of
    Contemporary Poetry & Short
    Fiction (Can.)
WI Home and Country*
Writers' Forum*
Young Writer*
Yours*

Politics

Africa Confidential
Australian Journal of
    International Affairs
Australian Journal of Politics and
    History
The China Quarterly
Christian Herald
Contemporary Review
Fortnight – An Independent
    Review of Politics and the Arts
Green Futures
The Illustrated London News
International Affairs
Justice of the Peace
New Internationalist
New Statesman
Peace News
The Political Quarterly
Prospect
Red Pepper
Studies, An Irish quarterly review
Tribune
The World Today

Radio, TV and video

Broadcast
Cable Guide
Campaign
EA Today Magazine (Aus.)
Empire
Film Review
Hi-Fi News
InterMedia
Opera Now
Practical Wireless
Radio Times
Satellite Times
The Short Wave Magazine
The Stage
Studio Sound
Television
Total DVD
TV Quick
TVTimes Magazine
What's on TV

Religion, philosophy and New Age

Africa: St Patrick's Missions
Baptist Times
The Catholic Herald
Catholic Pictorial
Catholic Times
Christian Herald
Church of England Newspaper
Church Times
Contemporary Review
Day by Day

Fortean Times
The Friend
The Furrow
Home and Family
Home Words
Jewish Chronicle
The Jewish Quarterly
Jewish Telegraph
Kids Alive! (The Young Soldier)
Life & Work: Magazine of the
    Church of Scotland
Methodist Recorder
New Humanist
Priests & People
Reality
Reform
The Sign
Southern Cross (SA)
Studies, An Irish quarterly review
The Tablet
Third Way
The Universe
The War Cry
Woman Alive
The Word

Rural life and country
(see also Natural history)
Buckinghamshire Countryside
Cambridgeshire Journal
Country
Country Life
Country Quest
The Countryman
Cumbria and Lake District
    Magazine
Dalesman
Derbyshire Life and Countryside
Dorset Life – The Dorset
    Magazine
East Lothian Life
Essex Life & Countryside
Essex Magazine and East Anglian
    Life
Evergreen
The Field
Hampshire – The County
    Magazine
Hertfordshire Countryside
In Britain
Kent Life
Lancashire Magazine
Lincolnshire Life
Lothian Life
The National Trust Magazine
The Rambler

The Scots Magazine
Scottish Field
Scottish Home and Country
Shooting Times and Country
    Magazine
The Shropshire Magazine
Somerset Magazine
Staffordshire Life Magazine
This England
Yorkshire Ridings Magazine

Sciences
Equinox (Can.)
Focus
Geological Magazine
Nature
New Scientist
Science Progress
Scientific Computing World
Technology Ireland

Sports and games (see also Leisure interests, Motor transport, Nautical)
Ace Tennis Magazine
Angler's Mail
Angling Times
Athletics Weekly
Australian Powerboat
Boards
Bowls International
Cycle Sport
Darts World
Descent
Eventing
The Field
Fly-Fishing & Fly-Tying
FourFourTwo
Golf Monthly
Golf Weekly
Golf World
Horse & Hound
Horse and Rider
Our Dogs
Racing Post
Rock (Aus.)
Rugby World
Runner's World
Running Fitness
Scuba Diver (Aus.)
Scuba World
Sea Angler
Shoot
Shooting Times and Country
    Magazine

Ski and Board
The Skier and The Snowboarder
    Magazine
Snooker Scene
Sport First
The Squash Player
Swimming Magazine
Tennis World
TGO (The Great Outdoors)
    Magazine
Today's Golfer
Trail
Trout and Salmon
The Wisden Cricketer
The Word
World Fishing
World Soccer

Theatre, drama and dancing (see also Cinema, Music)
Amateur Stage
Canadian Theatre Review (CTR)
Dance Australia
Dance Today!
Dancing Times
The Illustrated London News
In Britain
New Theatre Quarterly
Performing Arts & Entertainment
    in Canada (PA&E)
Radio Times
The Stage
Tribune
TVTimes Magazine

Travel and geography
Australian Geographic
Caledonia
Caravan Magazine
The China Quarterly
Condé Nast Traveller
Equinox (Can.)
FRANCE Magazine
Geo Australasia
Geographical Journal
Geographical Magazine
The Illustrated London News
In Britain
In Dublin
Ireland of the Welcomes
Natal Witness (SA)
Traveller
Wanderlust
Wild (Aus.)

Publishers of fiction

Addresses for *Book publishers UK and Ireland* start on page 127.

Adventure/thrillers

Bantam
Bantam Press
Black Ace Books
Black Swan
Blackstaff Press Ltd
Bloomsbury Publishing Plc
Chatto & Windus
Constable & Robinson Ltd
Faber & Faber Ltd
Gairm Publications
The Gay Men's Press
Harlequin Mills & Boon Ltd
Headline Book Publishing Ltd
Hodder Headline Ltd
Honno Ltd (Welsh Women's Press)
John Murray (Publishers) Ltd
Macmillan Publishers Ltd
Mentor Books
The Orion Publishing Group Ltd
Penguin Group (UK)
Piatkus Books
Random House Group Ltd
Robert Hale Ltd
Seafarer Books
Time Warner Books UK
TownHouse, Dublin
Transworld Publishers
Vintage
Virago
Warner
The X Press

Crime/mystery/suspense

Allison & Busby Ltd
Arcadia Books Ltd
Arrow Books Ltd
Bantam
Bantam Press
Black Ace Books
Black Swan
BlackAmber Books Ltd
Blackstaff Press Ltd
Bloomsbury Publishing Plc
Breese Books Ltd
Constable & Robinson Ltd
Corgi
Coronet
Everyman's Library
Faber & Faber Ltd
Flambard Press
Gairm Publications
The Gay Men's Press

Hamish Hamilton
HarperCollins Publishers
Headline Book Publishing Ltd
Hodder & Stoughton
Hodder Headline Ltd
Honno Ltd (Welsh Women's Press)
Hutchinson
Macmillan Publishers Ltd
Mentor Books
Michael Joseph
Michael O'Mara Books Ltd
New English Library
Oldcastle Books Ltd
The Orion Publishing Group Ltd
Pan
Penguin Group (UK)
Piatkus Books
Polygon
Random House Group Ltd
Robert Hale Ltd
Sceptre
Seren
Serpent's Tail
Severn House Publishers
Time Warner Books UK
TownHouse, Dublin
Transworld Publishers
Viking
Vintage
Virago
William Heinemann
The Women's Press
The X Press

Gay/lesbian

Arcadia Books Ltd
Bantam
Black Swan
Chapman Publishing
Corgi
The Gay Men's Press
Hamish Hamilton
HarperCollins Publishers
Honno Ltd (Welsh Women's Press)
Libris Ltd
Macmillan Publishers Ltd
Marion Boyars Publishers Ltd
Michael O'Mara Books Ltd
MQ Publications Ltd
Onlywomen Press Ltd
Penguin Group (UK)
Polygon
Sceptre

Serpent's Tail
Time Warner Books UK
Vintage
Virago
The Women's Press

General

Abacus
Allison & Busby Ltd
Arcadia Books Ltd
Bantam
Bantam Press
Black Ace Books
Black Swan
BlackAmber Books Ltd
Blackstaff Press Ltd
Bloomsbury Publishing Plc
Calder Publications Ltd
Canongate Books Ltd
Century
Chapman Publishing
Chatto & Windus
Cló Iar-Chonnachta Teo.
Corgi
Crescent Moon Publishing
Doubleday (UK)
Faber & Faber Ltd
Gairm Publications
The Gallery Press
Garnet Publishing Ltd
Hamish Hamilton
Harlequin Mills & Boon Ltd
HarperCollins Publishers
Headline Book Publishing Ltd
Hodder & Stoughton
Honno Ltd (Welsh Women's Press)
Hutchinson
John Hunt Publishing Ltd
Jonathan Cape
Karnak House
Libris Ltd
Macmillan Publishers Ltd
Marion Boyars Publishers Ltd
Mentor Books
The Mercat Press
Methuen Publishing Ltd
Michael Joseph
Michael O'Mara Books Ltd
MQ Publications Ltd
New English Library
New Island Books
The Oleander Press
Onlywomen Press Ltd

Severn House Publishers
Silhouette®
Time Warner Books UK
Transworld Publishers
Warner
William Heinemann

Science fiction/fantasy

Arrow Books Ltd
Bantam
Bantam Press
Black Swan
Corgi
Coronet
Gollancz
HarperCollins Publishers
Headline Book Publishing Ltd
Hodder & Stoughton
Hodder Headline Ltd
Honno Ltd (Welsh Women's Press)
Macmillan Publishers Ltd
New English Library
Orbit
The Orion Publishing Group Ltd
Pan
Penguin Group (UK)
Pipers' Ash Ltd
Random House Group Ltd
Simon & Schuster
Time Warner Books UK
Transworld Publishers
Victor Gollancz Ltd
Voyager
The Women's Press

Short stories

Chapman Publishing
Chatto & Windus
Cló Iar-Chonnachta Teo.
Everyman's Library
Faber & Faber Ltd
Flambard Press
Gairm Publications
Granta Publications
Hamish Hamilton
Hodder & Stoughton
Honno Ltd (Welsh Women's Press)
Jonathan Cape
Karnak House
The Lilliput Press Ltd
Macmillan Publishers Ltd
Methuen Publishing Ltd
The Octagon Press Ltd
Pan
Penguin Group (UK)
Pipers' Ash Ltd
Polygon
Random House Group Ltd
SCP Publishers Ltd

Secker and Warburg
Seren
TownHouse, Dublin
Transworld Publishers
William Heinemann
The Women's Press
Y Lolfa Cyf.

Other

Ethnic

Allison & Busby Ltd
Arcadia Books Ltd
Chapman Publishing
Honno Ltd (Welsh Women's Press)
MQ Publications Ltd
Skoob Russell Square
The Women's Press
The X Press

Erotic

Black Lace
Honno Ltd (Welsh Women's Press)
Nexus
The Women's Press
X Libris

Graphic

Knockabout Comics
Titan Books

Horror

Black Ace Books
Mentor Books
Titan Books
Warner

Humour

Allison & Busby Ltd
Black Swan
Breese Books Ltd
Corgi
Everyman's Library
Methuen Publishing Ltd
Michael O'Mara Books Ltd
The Oleander Press
The Orion Publishing Group Ltd
Paternoster
Piccadilly Press
Time Warner Books UK
Transworld Publishers
Victor Gollancz Ltd
Warner
The Women's Press

New/experimental

Calder Publications Ltd
Canongate Books Ltd
Chapman Publishing
Crescent Moon Publishing

Faber & Faber Ltd
Flambard Press
Honno Ltd (Welsh Women's Press)
Polygon
Quartet Books Ltd
Seren
Serpent's Tail
Stride Publications

Teenage fiction

Andersen Press Ltd
Bantam Children's
HarperCollins Publishers
Livewire
Mantra
The O'Brien Press Ltd
Piccadilly Press
Walker Books Ltd

Translations

Arcadia Books Ltd
Calder Publications Ltd
Canongate Books Ltd
Chapman Publishing
Cló Iar-Chonnachta Teo.
Dedalus Ltd
Enitharmon Press
Everyman's Library
Faber & Faber Ltd
Flambard Press
Gomer Press
The Harvill Press
Honno Ltd (Welsh Women's Press)
Libris Ltd
The Oleander Press
The Orion Publishing Group Ltd
Peter Halban Publishers Ltd
Pipers' Ash Ltd
Pushkin Press
Seren
Serpent's Tail
Skoob Russell Square
The Women's Press

War

Calder Publications Ltd
Libris Ltd
The Orion Publishing Group Ltd
Pipers' Ash Ltd
Severn House Publishers
Time Warner Books UK
Transworld Publishers
Ulric Publishing

Westerns

Robert Hale Ltd

Children's book publishers and packagers

Listings for *Book publishers UK and Ireland* start on page 127 and listings for *Book packagers* start on page 187.

Teenage fiction
Book publishers
Andersen Press Ltd
Bantam Children's
HarperCollins Publishers
Livewire
Mantra
The O'Brien Press Ltd
Piccadilly Press
Walker Books Ltd

Children's fiction
Book publishers
A & C Black Publishers Ltd
Andersen Press Ltd
Anvil Books/The Children's Press
Bantam Children's
Barefoot Books Ltd
Bloomsbury Publishing Plc
Bodley Head Children's Books
Child's Play (International) Ltd
Cló Iar-Chonnachta Teo.
D.C. Thomson & Co. Ltd –
    Publications
David Fickling Books
Dref Wen
Egmont Books
Evans Brothers Ltd
Everyman's Library
Faber & Faber Ltd
Floris Books
Frances Lincoln Ltd
Gairm Publications
Gomer Press
HarperCollins Publishers
Hippo
Hodder Children's Books
Honno Ltd (Welsh Women's Press)
Hutchinson Children's Books
John Hunt Publishing Ltd
Jonathan Cape Children's Books
Kevin Mayhew Ltd
Kingfisher Publications plc
Ladybird
Lion Publishing plc
Lutterworth Press
Macmillan Children's Books Ltd
Mantra
Mentor Books

The O'Brien Press Ltd
Orchard Books
The Orion Publishing Group Ltd
Oxford University Press
Patrick Hardy Books
Piccadilly Press
Pipers' Ash Ltd
Point
Puffin
Ragged Bears Publishing Ltd
Random House Children's Books
Ransom Publishing Ltd
Red Fox Children's Books
Robinson
Saint Andrew Press
Scholastic Press
Scottish Children's Press
Scripture Union
Simon & Schuster
Tamarind Ltd
Usborne Publishing
Walker Books Ltd
The Watts Publishing Group Ltd
The Women's Press
Y Lolfa Cyf.
Zero to Ten Ltd

Book packagers
Graham-Cameron Publishing &
    Illustration
Mathew Price Ltd
Quarto Children's Books Ltd
Working Partners Ltd

Non-fiction
Book publishers
A & C Black Publishers Ltd
Aladdin/Watts
Anness Publishing
Apple Press
Atlantic Europe Publishing Co. Ltd
Award Publications Ltd
Bantam Children's
Child's Play (International) Ltd
Chrysalis Children's Books
Dref Wen
Egmont Books
Encyclopaedia Britannica (UK) Ltd
Evans Brothers Ltd

Faber & Faber Ltd
First and Best in Education Ltd
Folens Ltd
Frances Lincoln Ltd
Geddes & Grosset
Gomer Press
HarperCollins Publishers
Hippo
Hodder Children's Books
Hopscotch Educational
    Publishing Ltd
John Hunt Publishing Ltd
Kingfisher Publications plc
Ladybird
Lion Publishing plc
Lutterworth Press
Macmillan Children's Books Ltd
Mantra
Mentor Books
The National Trust
Neate Publishing
NMSI
The O'Brien Press Ltd
The Orion Publishing Group Ltd
Oxford University Press
Piccadilly Press
Pipers' Ash Ltd
Portland Press Ltd
Puffin
Random House Children's Books
Ransom Publishing Ltd
Saint Andrew Press
Salariya Book Company Ltd
Schofield & Sims Ltd
Scottish Children's Press
Scripture Union
Simon & Schuster
Tamarind Ltd
Tango Books
Usborne Publishing
Walker Books Ltd
Warne
The Watts Publishing Group Ltd
The Women's Press
Y Lolfa Cyf.
Zero to Ten Ltd
Zoë Books Ltd

Book packagers
Aladdin Books Ltd
Andromeda Oxford Ltd
Bender Richardson White
BLA Publishing Ltd
Breslich & Foss Ltd
The Brown Reference Group Plc
Brown Wells & Jacobs Ltd
Cambridge Publishing
    Management Ltd
Design Eye Ltd
Graham-Cameron Publishing &
    Illustration
Hart McLeod Ltd
John Brown Junior
Marshall Editions Ltd
Mathew Price Ltd
Monkey Puzzle Media Ltd
Orpheus Books Ltd
Quarto Children's Books Ltd
Roger Coote Publishing
Toucan Books Ltd
Tucker Slingsby Ltd
Wordwright Books

Picture books
Book publishers
Andersen Press Ltd
Award Publications Ltd
Bantam Children's
Barefoot Books Ltd
Bloomsbury Publishing Plc
Bodley Head Children's Books
Buster Books
Child's Play (International) Ltd
Chrysalis Children's Books
Cló Iar-Chonnachta Teo.
David Fickling Books
Dref Wen
Egmont Books
Evans Brothers Ltd
Everyman's Library
Faber & Faber Ltd
Floris Books
Frances Lincoln Ltd
Gairm Publications
Geddes & Grosset
Gomer Press
Gullane Children's Books
HarperCollins Publishers
Hippo
Hodder Children's Books
Hutchinson Children's Books
John Hunt Publishing Ltd
Jonathan Cape Children's Books
Kingfisher Publications plc
Ladybird
Lion Publishing plc
Lutterworth Press

Macmillan Children's Books Ltd
Magi Publications
Mantra
The O'Brien Press Ltd
Orchard Books
The Orion Publishing Group Ltd
Oxford University Press
Piccadilly Press
Puffin
Ragged Bears Publishing Ltd
Red Fox Children's Books
Schofield & Sims Ltd
Scholastic Children's Books
Scottish Children's Press
Scripture Union
Tamarind Ltd
Usborne Publishing
Walker Books Ltd
Warne
The Watts Publishing Group Ltd
Zero to Ten Ltd

Book packagers
Aladdin Books Ltd
Albion Press Ltd
Angus Hudson Ltd
Breslich & Foss Ltd
Brown Wells & Jacobs Ltd
Graham-Cameron Publishing &
    Illustration
John Brown Junior
Marshall Editions Ltd
Mathew Price Ltd
Tangerine Designs Ltd
The Templar Company plc
Tucker Slingsby Ltd
Ventura Publishing Ltd

Other
Activity and novelty
Book publishers
A & C Black Publishers Ltd
Apple Press
Award Publications Ltd
Bloomsbury Publishing Plc
Buster Books
Child's Play (International) Ltd
Chrysalis Children's Books
Dref Wen
Egmont Books
First and Best in Education Ltd
Floris Books
Frances Lincoln Ltd
Geddes & Grosset
Gullane Children's Books
Hippo
Hodder Children's Books
John Hunt Publishing Ltd
Kevin Mayhew Ltd

Kingfisher Publications plc
Ladybird
Lion Publishing plc
Lutterworth Press
Macmillan Children's Books Ltd
Magi Publications
Mentor Books
Orchard Books
Oxford University Press
Puffin
Ransom Publishing Ltd
Robinson
Scottish Children's Press
Scripture Union
Tango Books
Tarquin Publications
Treehouse Children's Books
Usborne Publishing
Walker Books Ltd
Warne
The Watts Publishing Group Ltd

Book packagers
Aladdin Books Ltd
Andromeda Oxford Ltd
Angus Hudson Ltd
Breslich & Foss Ltd
Brown Wells & Jacobs Ltd
Cowley Robinson Ltd
Design Eye Ltd
John Brown Junior
Marshall Cavendish Partworks Ltd
Mathew Price Ltd
Pinwheel Ltd
Playne Books Ltd
The Puzzle House
Quarto Children's Books Ltd
Sadie Fields Productions Ltd
Tangerine Designs Ltd
The Templar Company plc
Tucker Slingsby Ltd

Audiobooks
Book publishers
Barefoot Books Ltd
BBC Audiobooks Ltd
Child's Play (International) Ltd
Dref Wen
HarperCollins Audio
Hodder Children's Books
Ladybird
Mantra
Naxos AudioBooks
The Orion Publishing Group Ltd
Random House Children's Books
St Pauls
Scripture Union
The Watts Publishing Group Ltd

Multimedia
Book publishers
Atlantic Europe Publishing Co. Ltd
Ginn & Co.
HarperCollins Publishers
Heinemann Educational
Macmillan Children's Books Ltd
Mantra
Nelson Thornes Ltd
Oxford University Press
Puffin
Random House Group Ltd
Ransom Publishing Ltd
St Pauls
Warne

Book packagers
Andromeda Oxford Ltd
John Brown Junior

Poetry
Book publishers
A & C Black Publishers Ltd
Anvil Press Poetry
Bantam Children's
Bloomsbury Publishing Plc
Bodley Head Children's Books
Dref Wen
Evans Brothers Ltd
Everyman's Library
Faber & Faber Ltd

Frances Lincoln Ltd
Gairm Publications
Gomer Press
HarperCollins Publishers
Hutchinson Children's Books
Jonathan Cape Children's Books
Kingfisher Publications plc
Lutterworth Press
Macmillan Children's Books Ltd
Orchard Books
Puffin
Red Fox Children's Books
Saint Andrew Press
Scholastic Children's Books
Scottish Children's Press
Walker Books Ltd
The Watts Publishing Group Ltd

Book packagers
Albion Press Ltd

Religion
Book publishers
A & C Black Publishers Ltd
Atlantic Europe Publishing Co. Ltd
Canterbury Press Norwich
Catholic Truth Society
Christian Education
Dref Wen
Frances Lincoln Ltd
George Ronald

Gresham Books Ltd
HarperCollins Publishers
Hodder & Stoughton
The Islamic Foundation
John Hunt Publishing Ltd
Kevin Mayhew Ltd
Kingfisher Publications plc
Lion Publishing plc
Lutterworth Press
Mantra
Marshall Pickering
Oxford University Press
Paternoster
Religious and Moral Education
    Press
Saint Andrew Press
St Pauls
Scripture Union
Society for Promoting Christian
    Knowledge
Stacey International
Usborne Publishing
Veritas Publications
The Watts Publishing Group Ltd

Book packagers
Albion Press Ltd
Angus Hudson Ltd
Tucker Slingsby Ltd

Publishers of audiobooks

Addresses for *Book publishers UK and Ireland* start on page 127.

BBC Audiobooks Ltd
Cló Iar-Chonnachta Teo.
HarperCollins Audio
Hodder Headline Ltd
Macmillan Publishers Ltd
Mantra
Naxos AudioBooks

The Orion Publishing Group Ltd
Random House Group Ltd
Royal National Institute of the
 Blind
Simon & Schuster Audioworks
Walker Books Ltd

Publishers of plays

Playwrights are reminded that it is unusual for a publisher of trade editions of plays to publish plays which have not had at least reasonably successful, usually professional, productions on stage first. See listings beginning on page 127 for addresses.

Amber Lane Press Ltd
Brown, Son & Ferguson, Ltd
Calder Publications Ltd
Chapman Publishing
Cló Iar-Chonnachta Teo.
Colin Smythe Ltd
Cressrelles Publishing Co. Ltd
Dublar Scripts
Everyman's Library
Faber & Faber Ltd
The Gallery Press

J. Garnet Miller
Josef Weinberger Plays Ltd
Kenyon-Deane
Kevin Mayhew Ltd
The Lilliput Press Ltd
Methuen Publishing Ltd
New Playwrights' Network
New Theatre Publications/The
 Playwright Co-operative
Nick Hern Books Ltd
Oberon Books

The Oleander Press
Pipers' Ash Ltd
The Playwrights Publishing
 Company
Samuel French Ltd
SCP Publishers Ltd
Seren
Skoob Russell Square
Ward Lock Educational Co. Ltd

Publishers of poetry

Addresses for *Book publishers UK and Ireland* start on page 127.

Anvil Press Poetry
Arc Publications
Blackstaff Press Ltd
Bloodaxe Books Ltd
Calder Publications Ltd
Carcanet Press Ltd
Chapman Publishing
Chatto & Windus
Cló Iar-Chonnachta Teo.
Crescent Moon Publishing
diehard
Enitharmon Press
Everyman Publishers plc
Faber & Faber Ltd
Flambard Press

Gairm Publications
The Gallery Press
The Goldsmith Press
Gomer Press
Headland Publications
Hippopotamus Press
Honno Ltd (Welsh Women's Press)
Jonathan Cape
Libris Ltd
The Lilliput Press Ltd
Liverpool University Press
MQ Publications Ltd
New Beacon Books
New Island Books
The Oleander Press

Onlywomen Press Ltd
Payback Press
Penguin Group (UK)
Peterloo Poets
Pipers' Ash Ltd
Polygon
Random House Group Ltd
Rivelin Grapheme Press
Saint Andrew Press
SCP Publishers Ltd
Seren
Skoob Russell Square
Stride Publications
TownHouse, Dublin

Literary agents for children's books

The following literary agents will consider work suitable for children's books, from both authors and illustrators. Listings start on page 348. See also *Writing and the children's book market* on page 226 and *Art agents and commercial art studios* on page 388.

Literary agents for television, film, radio and theatre

Listings for these and other literary agents start on page 348.
*US literary agents

Newspapers and magazines which accept cartoons

Listed below are newspapers and magazines which take cartoons – either occasionally, or on a regular basis. Approach in writing in the first instance (see listings starting on pages 3, 11 and 21 for addresses) to ascertain the Editor's requirements.

Newspapers and colour supplements

(Adelaide) Advertiser
(Brisbane) The Sunday Mail
(Christchurch) The Press
Daily Dispatch
Daily Mirror
Evening Gazette
Express & Echo
The Independent
Independent Newspapers (South Africa) Ltd
Independent Newspapers Gauteng
Independent Newspapers Kwa-Zulu Natal Ltd
Independent on Sunday
(Invercargill) The Southland Times
Ireland on Sunday
The Leicester Mercury
Mail on Sunday
(Melbourne) Herald Sun
Morning Star
(New Plymouth) The Daily News
The Southern Daily Echo
The Star
The Sun
The Sun
Sunday Independent
The Sunday Sun
The Sunday Times Scotland
The Sunday Tribune
(Sydney) The Sunday Telegraph
The Times
(Wellington) The Dominion Post
The Western Mail
Yorkshire Evening Post

Consumer and special interest magazines

Active Life
Aeroplane Monthly
African Business
Aquila
Art Business Today
The Author
Back Street Heroes
Bella
Best of British
The Big Issue Australia
Boards
Bowls International
British Philatelic Bulletin
Canal & Riverboat
Car
The Catholic Herald
Chapman
Christian Herald
Church of England Newspaper
Classic Cars
Computer Weekly
Computing
The Countryman
Cycle Sport
Cycling Weekly
Dance Australia
The Dandy
Dirt Bike Rider
Disability Now
Dogs Today
Dolly
EA Today Magazine
East Lothian Life
The Erotic Review
Flora International
Football Picture Story Library
Fortean Times
Garden News
Gay Times
Golf Monthly
Golf World
GQ
H&E Naturist
Index on Censorship
Ireland of the Welcomes
Ireland's Own
Jewish Telegraph
Kids Alive! (The Young Soldier)
Life & Work: Magazine of the Church of Scotland
Lothian Life
Men Only
Modern Woman Nationwide
More!
Motor Caravan Magazine
Mslexia
Musical Opinion
New Internationalist
New Musical Express
New Scientist
New Statesman
The Oldie
Opera Now
Organic Gardening
Overland
Park Home & Holiday Caravan
Picture Postcard Monthly
Planet
Poetry Review
Pony Magazine
Pride Magazine
Private Eye
The Rambler
Red Pepper
Reform
Rugby World
Running Fitness
Scottish Home and Country
Scouting Magazine
Sight and Sound
Ski and Board
Smallholder
The Spectator
The Squash Player
Staple
The Strad
Suffolk Norfolk Life
The Tablet
that's life!
Time Out
Tribune
Trout and Salmon
The Universe
The Vegan
Viz Comic
The Voice
The War Cry
The Weekly News
Weight Watchers Magazine
What's on TV
WI Home and Country
The Word

Writers' Forum
Yachting Monthly
Yachting World
Young Writer
Yours

**Business and
professional magazines**
Accountancy
BMA News

Broadcast
Education Journal
EE Times
Electrical Review
Electrical Times
Hospital Doctor
Hotel and Catering Review
Housebuilder
Irish Medical Times
Nursing Times

PCS View
Pilot
Police Review
Post Magazine & Insurance Week
Printing World
Therapy Weekly
Truck & Driver

Picture agencies and libraries by subject area

This index gives the major subject area(s) only of each entry in the main listing which begins on page 407, and should be used with discrimination.

Aerial photography
Aerofilms
Aviation Picture Library (Austin
   J. Brown)
Geo Aerial Photography
Jason Hawkes Library
Sealand Aerial Photography Ltd
Skyscan Photolibrary
Sue Cunningham Photographic

Africa
Academic File News Photos
AMIS
Ancient Egypt Picture Library
Andes Press Agency
Animal Photography
C.M. Dixon
Geoslides
Images of Africa Photobank
Link Picture Library
Sue Cunningham Photographic
Tibet Pictures
Yemen Pictures

Agriculture and farming
The Anthony Blake Photo
   Library
Dennis Davis Photography
Ecoscene
Frank Lane Picture Agency Ltd
Heritage & Natural History
   Photography
Holt Studios
Stephen Benson Slide Bureau
Sutcliffe Gallery

Aircraft and aviation
Air Photo Supply
Dr Alan Beaumont
Aviation Picture Library (Austin
   J. Brown)
Photo Link
The Picture Company
Skyscan Photolibrary
TRH Pictures

Archaeology, antiquities, ancient monuments and heritage
A.A. & A. Ancient Art &
   Architecture Collection
AKG London
Ancient Egypt Picture Library
C.M. Dixon
Country Collections Photolibrary
English Heritage Photo Library
Fortean Picture Library
Heritage & Natural History
   Photography
Rev. J. Catling Allen
John Glover Photography
Kilmartin House Trust
Lesley and Roy Adkins Picture
   Library
Mick Sharp Photography
Photo Resources
Ritmeyer Archaeological Design
Sarah Boait Photography and
   Picture Library
Sites, Sights and Cities

Stephen Benson Slide Bureau
Travel Photo International
Werner Forman Archive
Woodmansterne Publications Ltd
York Archaeological Trust Picture
   Library

Architecture, houses and interiors
A.A. & A. Ancient Art &
   Architecture Collection
Abode Interiors Picture Library
Arcaid Architectural Photography
   and Picture Library
BookArt & Architecture Picture
   Library
Dennis Davis Photography
English Heritage Photo Library
Houses & Interiors Photographic
   Features Agency
Rev. J. Catling Allen
Mick Sharp Photography
Stephen Benson Slide Bureau
Sylvia Cordaiy Photo Library
Venice Picture Library
Werner Forman Archive
Woodmansterne Publications Ltd

Art, sculpture and crafts
AKG London
Allied Artists
Ann and Bury Peerless
Bodleian Library
BookArt & Architecture Picture
   Library

The Bridgeman Art Library
Crafts Council Photostore®
Fine Art Photographic Library
National Galleries of Scotland
Picture Library
National Portrait Gallery Picture
Library
Photo Resources
Retrograph Nostalgia Archive
Royal Collection
Sotheby's Picture Library
V&A Images
Venice Picture Library
Werner Forman Archive

Asia

Academic File News Photos
Andes Press Agency
Andrew N. Gagg's Photo Flora
Ann and Bury Peerless
Australia Pictures
C.M. Dixon
Das Photo
Douglas Dickins Photo Library
Geoslides
Imagefinder Pte Ltd
Japan Archive
Link Picture Library
The Royal Society for Asian Affairs
Society for Anglo-Chinese
Understanding
Tibet Pictures
Travel Ink Photo & Feature Library
World Religions Photo Library
Yemen Pictures

Australia and New Zealand

Australia Pictures
Frontline Photo Press Agency
George A. Dey
Geoslides
Yemen Pictures

Britain (see also Ireland, Scotland, Wales)

Air Photo Supply
Bill Meadows Picture Library
Britain on View
COI Photo Library
Collections
David Broadbent/Peak District
Pictures
English Heritage Photo Library
Isle of Wight Pictures
Rev. J. Catling Allen
Jason Hawkes Library
John Birdsall Social Issues Photo
Library

Lakeland Life Picture Library
Merseyside Photo Library
Photofusion
Roy J. Westlake ARPS
S. & O. Mathews
Sarah Boait Photography and
Picture Library
Simon Warner
Skyscan Photolibrary
Tim Woodcock
True North Picture Source
Westcountry Pictures
Woodmansterne Publications Ltd
York Archaeological Trust Picture
Library
Yorkshire Now!

Business, industry and commerce

Ace Stock Ltd
Christopher Ware Photography
Financial Times Pictures
Fotoccompli – The Picture
Library
Horizon International
Photolibrary.com

Children and people (see also Social issues)

Angela Hampton – Family Life
Picture Library
Barnardo's Photographic Archive
Barry Davies
Das Photo

Cities and towns (see also London)

Bill Meadows Picture Library
Financial Times Pictures
Lesley and Roy Adkins Picture
Library
Sites, Sights and Cities
Skyscan Photolibrary

Civilisations, cultures and way of life

A.A. & A. Ancient Art &
Architecture Collection
Andalucía Slide Library
Angela Hampton – Family Life
Picture Library
Australia Pictures
Bryan and Cherry Alexander
Photography
Country Collections Photolibrary
Dee Conway Ballet & Dance
Picture Library
The Irish Image Collection

Peter Sanders Photography Ltd
Photo Resources
Royal Geographical Society
Picture Library
STILL PICTURES The Whole
Earth Photo Library
Tibet Pictures
Werner Forman Archive
World Religions Photo Library

Countryside and rural life (see also Landscapes)

Dr Alan Beaumont
Andalucía Slide Library
Forest Life Picture Library
National Museums & Galleries of
Northern Ireland, Ulster Folk
& Transport Museum
Wildlife Matters Photographic
Library

Developing countries

Exile Images
Geoslides
Nature Picture Library
Panos Pictures
STILL PICTURES The Whole
Earth Photo Library
Tropix Photo Library
World Religions Photo Library

Environment, conservation, ecology and habitats

Arctic Camera
Brian Gadsby Picture Library
Chris Mattison
Colin Varndell Natural History
Photography
Ecoscene
Environmental Investigation
Agency
Fogden Wildlife Photographs
Forest Life Picture Library
Frank Lane Picture Agency Ltd
GeoScience Features
Harper Horticultural Slide
Library
Heather Angel/Natural Visions
Holt Studios
Horizon International
Martin and Dorothy Grace
Natural Image
Nature Picture Library
NHPA Ltd
OSF Ltd, Photo Library
Panos Pictures
Premaphotos Wildlife

STILL PICTURES The Whole
  Earth Photo Library
Sylvia Cordaiy Photo Library
Tropix Photo Library
Wildlife Matters Photographic
  Library

Europe and Eastern Europe (excluding UK and Ireland)

Andalucía Slide Library
Andes Press Agency
C.M. Dixon
Charles Tait Photo Library
Das Photo
David Williams Picture Library
John Birdsall Social Issues Photo
  Library
John Massey Stewart Picture
  Library
Just Europe
Medimage
Panos Pictures
Russia and Eastern Images
Skishoot – Offshoot
Sue Cunningham Photographic
Venice Picture Library
Vidocq Photo Library
The Weimar Archive

Fashion and lifestyle

Joefilmbase.com
V&A Images

Food and drink

The Anthony Blake Photo
  Library
Cephas Picture Library
Retrograph Nostalgia Archive

Gardens, gardening and horticulture (see also Plant life)

A-Z Botanical Collection Ltd
Arcaid Architectural Photography
  and Picture Library
Dennis Davis Photography
Forest Life Picture Library
Garden Matters Photographic
  Library
Garden World Images
Harper Horticultural Slide Library
Holt Studios
Hortipix/PSP Image Library
Houses & Interiors Photographic
  Features Agency
John Glover Photography
Natural Image

S. & O. Mathews
Tim Woodcock

General and stock libraries

Ace Stock Ltd
Barry Davies
Bruce Coleman Inc.
C.M. Dixon
Chandra S. Perera Cinetra
Chrysalis Images
Corbis
Dawn Runnals Photographic
  Library
Fotoccompli – The Picture Library
Freelance Focus
Frontline Photo Press Agency
GeoScience Features
Geoslides
Getty Images
Greg Evans International Photo
  Library
Horizon International
Huntley Film Archive
Hutchison Picture Library
Image Diggers
Imagefinder Pte Ltd
ImageState Pictor Ltd
Joefilmbase.com
The MacQuitty International
  Collection
Photofusion
Photolibrary.com
Popperfoto (Paul Popper Ltd)
Raleigh International Picture
  Library
Retna Pictures Ltd
Robert Harding Picture Library
S & G Press Agency Ltd
Spectrum Colour Library
Stephen Benson Slide Bureau
Topham Picturepoint
Universal Pictorial Press &
  Agency (UPPA)
Woodmansterne Publications Ltd

Geography, biogeography and topography

Arctic Camera
B. & B. Photographs
GeoScience Features
Geoslides
John Massey Stewart Picture
  Library
Mick Sharp Photography
Royal Geographical Society
  Picture Library

Glamour, moods and nudes

Murray Wren Picture Library
Scope Features

Health and medicine

Angela Hampton – Family Life
  Picture Library
Education Photos
Science Photo Library
Science & Society Picture Library
Shout Picture Library
Wellcome Photo Library

High-tech, high-speed, macro/micro, special effects and step-by-step

Earth Images Picture Library
GeoScience Features
Houses & Interiors Photographic
  Features Agency
Microscopix
The Nature and Landscape File
NHPA Ltd
OSF Ltd, Photo Library

History

AKG London
American History Picture Library
Ann Ronan Picture Library
The Associated Press Ltd
Barnaby's Picture Library
The Billie Love Historical
  Collection
Bodleian Library
British Library Picture Library
Chrysalis Images
Dave Lewis Nostalgia Collection
Elizabeth Linley Collection
Heritage & Natural History
  Photography
John Frost Newspapers
Katz Pictures Ltd
London Metropolitan Archives
Mary Evans Picture Library
Museum of London
The National Archives Image
  Library
National Museums & Galleries of
  Northern Ireland, Ulster Folk
  & Transport Museum
Pat Hodgson Library & Picture
  Research Agency
Peter Newark Picture Library
Pixfeatures
Retrograph Nostalgia Archive
Rex Features Ltd
The Royal Photographic Society

The Royal Society for Asian
Affairs
Royal Society of Chemistry
Library and Information
Centre
SCR Photo Library
Sylvia Pitcher Photo Library
The Tank Museum Archive &
Reference Library
Topham Picturepoint
The Weimar Archive

Illustrations, prints, engravings, lithographs and cartoons

Allied Artists
American History Picture Library
Ann Ronan Picture Library
Barnaby's Picture Library
The Billie Love Historical
Collection
Bodleian Library
British Library Picture Library
CartoonStock
Elizabeth Linley Collection
Fotomas Index
The Illustrated London News
Picture Library
Katz Pictures Ltd
Mary Evans Picture Library
The National Archives Image
Library
National Portrait Gallery Picture
Library
Pat Hodgson Library & Picture
Research Agency
Peter Newark Picture Library
Punch Cartoon Library &
Archive
Retrograph Nostalgia Archive
Royal Society of Chemistry
Library and Information
Centre
V&A Images
Western Americana Picture
Library
Zoological Society of London

Ireland

Collections
Heritage & Natural History
Photography
The Irish Image Collection
National Museums & Galleries of
Northern Ireland, Ulster Folk
& Transport Museum
The Weimar Archive

Landscapes and scenics

The Allan Wright Photo Library
Andalucía Slide Library
Ardea Wildlife & Pets
Barry Davies
Bill Meadows Picture Library
BookArt & Architecture Picture
Library
Bruce Coleman The Natural
World
Charles Tait Photo Library
George A. Dey
Hortipix/PSP Image Library
Isle of Wight Pictures
John Glover Photography
Lesley and Roy Adkins Picture
Library
Medimage
The Nature and Landscape File
The Photolibrary Wales
Railways – Milepost 92¹/₂
Raleigh International Picture
Library
Richard Welsby Photography
Roy J. Westlake ARPS
S. & O. Mathews
Simon Warner
Windrush Photos

Latin America

Andes Press Agency
Das Photo
Sue Cunningham Photographic

London

The Illustrated London News
Picture Library
Jason Hawkes Library
London Metropolitan Archives
Museum of London

Middle East

Academic File News Photos
Ancient Egypt Picture Library
Ann and Bury Peerless
Australia Pictures
Barry Davies
Das Photo
Link Picture Library
Stephen Benson Slide Bureau
World Religions Photo Library
Yemen Pictures

Military and armed forces

Air Photo Supply
Chrysalis Images
Imperial War Museum
Military History Picture Library
The National Archives Image
Library
The Tank Museum Archive &
Reference Library

Mountains

AMIS
Chris Bonington Picture Library
Hamish Brown, Scottish
Photographic
Mountain Dynamics
Mountain Visions and Faces
Royal Geographical Society
Picture Library
Wilderness Photographic Library

Natural history (see also Environment, Plant life)

A-Z Botanical Collection Ltd
Dr Alan Beaumont
Animal Photography
Ardea Wildlife & Pets
B. & B. Photographs
Barry Davies
Bird Images
Brian Gadsby Picture Library
Bruce Coleman Inc.
Bruce Coleman The Natural
World
Chris Mattison
Christine Foord
Colin Varndell Natural History
Photography
David Broadbent/Peak District
Pictures
David Hosking FRPS
Ecoscene
Environmental Investigation
Agency
Fogden Wildlife Photographs
Forest Life Picture Library
Frank Lane Picture Agency Ltd
GeoScience Features
Heather Angel/Natural Visions
Heritage & Natural History
Photography
Hortipix/PSP Image Library
Image Diggers
Martin and Dorothy Grace
Michael Leach
Natural Image
The Nature and Landscape File

Royalty

Camera Press Ltd
J.S. Library International
Mirrorpix
Monitor Picture Library
Pixfeatures
Tim Graham Picture Library
V&A Images

Russia

C.M. Dixon
John Massey Stewart Picture
Library
Russia and Eastern Images
SCR Photo Library

Science, technology and meteorology

Ace Stock Ltd
Ann Ronan Picture Library
Earth Images Picture Library
Frank Lane Picture Agency Ltd
GeoScience Features
Horizon International
Microscopix
OSF Ltd, Photo Library
Royal Society of Chemistry
Library and Information
Centre
Science Photo Library
Science & Society Picture Library

Scotland

The Allan Wright Photo Library
Charles Tait Photo Library
David Williams Picture Library
Edinburgh Photographic Library
George A. Dey
Gordon Wright Scottish Photo
Library
Hamish Brown, Scottish
Photographic
Kilmartin House Trust
Richard Welsby Photography
Scotland in Focus Picture Library
Simon Warner
The Still Moving Picture
Company

Social issues and social history

Ann Ronan Picture Library
Barnardo's Photographic Archive
COI Photo Library
Education Photos
Elizabeth Linley Collection
Exile Images
FirePix International
Getty Images

The Illustrated London News
Picture Library
Imperial War Museum
John Birdsall Social Issues Photo
Library
London Metropolitan Archives
Mary Evans Picture Library
Photofusion
RSPCA Photolibrary
Science & Society Picture Library
Shout Picture Library
Stockwave
Welfare History Picture Library
Wellcome Photo Library

South America

Animal Photography
Australia Pictures
Das Photo
David Hosking FRPS
Stephen Benson Slide Bureau

Space and astronomy

Bruce Coleman The Natural
World
Earth Images Picture Library
Galaxy Picture Library
Genesis Space Photo Library
National Maritime Museum
Picture Library
OSF Ltd, Photo Library
Science Photo Library
TRH Pictures

Sport and leisure

Action Plus
The Associated Press Ltd
B.M. Totterdell Photography
Boxing Picture Library
Eyeline Photography
Fotosports International
Frontline Photo Press Agency
George A. Dey
Getty Images
Isle of Wight Pictures
Ludvigsen Library
Michael Cole Camerawork
Mirrorpix
Mountain Visions and Faces
PA Photos
Peter Dazeley
Popperfoto (Paul Popper Ltd)
Skishoot – Offshoot
Skyscan Photolibrary
Snookerimages (Eric Whitehead
Photography)
Sporting Pictures (UK) Ltd
The Still Moving Picture
Company

Sylvia Cordaiy Photo Library
Tim Woodcock
Universal Pictorial Press &
Agency (UPPA)
Visions in Golf
Waterways Photo Library
World Pictures

Strange phenomena, occult and mystical

Fortean Picture Library
Image Diggers
Sites, Sights and Cities

Transport (cars and motoring, railways)

Christopher Ware Photography
Das Photo
George A. Dey
Ludvigsen Library
Motorcycles Unlimited
Motoring Picture Library
National Museums & Galleries of
Northern Ireland, Ulster Folk
& Transport Museum
Railways – Milepost 92¹/₂
Science & Society Picture Library
TRH Pictures

Travel and tourism

Ace Stock Ltd
Andrew N. Gagg's Photo Flora
Arcaid Architectural Photography
and Picture Library
Aviation Picture Library (Austin
J. Brown)
Brian Gadsby Picture Library
Britain on View
Bruce Coleman Inc.
C.M. Dixon
Charles Tait Photo Library
Douglas Dickins Photo Library
Ecoscene
Getty Images
Greg Evans International Photo
Library
Hutchison Picture Library
The Illustrated London News
Picture Library
J.S. Library International
James Davis Travel Photography
Just Europe
Lonely Planet Images
Mountain Visions and Faces
Papilio Natural History & Travel
Library
Peter Cumberlidge Photo Library
Photolibrary.com
The Picture Company

Prizes and awards by subject area

This index gives the major subject area(s) only of each entry in the main listing which begins on page 493, and should be used with discrimination.

The Somerset Maugham Awards
The Sunday Times Young Writer of the Year Award
Whitbread Book Awards
WHSmith 'People's Choice' Awards
Yorkshire Post Book of the Year

Fine art – see Visual art

Grants, bursaries and fellowships

Alfred Bradley Bursary Award
The Arts Council/An Chomhairle Ealaíon, Ireland
Arts Council England
The Authors' Foundation
The British Academy Research Awards
David T.K. Wong Fellowship
E.C. Gregory Trust Fund
E.M. Forster Award
European Jewish Publication Society Grants
Hawthornden Writers' Fellowships
The Kathleen Blundell Trust
Leverhulme Research Fellowships
London Arts
Northern Writers' Awards
The Rhys Davies Trust
Scottish Arts Council
The Travelling Scholarships
The Welsh National Literature Promotion Agency and Society for Writers

Illustration

The Bisto Book of the Year Awards
British Fantasy Awards
The Eleanor Farjeon Award
The Hans Christian Andersen Medals
Images – The Best of British Illustration
The Jill Smythies Award
L. Ron Hubbard's Writers and Illustrators of the Future Contests
The Macmillan Prize for Children's Picture Book Illustration
Sainsbury's Baby Book Award
Tir Na N-og Awards
The V&A Illustration Awards

Journalism

ABSW/Glaxo Science Writers Awards
British Press Awards
Catherine Pakenham Award
George Orwell Memorial Prize
London Press Club Awards

Non-fiction

The Alexander Prize
The André Simon Memorial Fund Book Awards
Authors' Club Awards
The Aventis Prizes for Science Books
The BBC Four Samuel Johnson Prize for Non-Fiction
The British Academy Book Prize
British Academy Medals and Prizes
The Calvin and Rose G. Hoffman Memorial Prize for Distinguished Publication on Christopher Marlowe
Christopher Ewart-Biggs Memorial Prize
The CILIP/Whitaker Reference Awards
CWA Awards
The David Berry Prize
David Watt Prize
The Duff Cooper Prize
The Enid McLeod Literary Prize
Gladstone History Book Prize
Glenfiddich Food & Drink Awards
Jewish Quarterly Literary Prizes
The John D. Criticos Prize
Kraszna-Krausz Awards
The Mail on Sunday/John Llewellyn Rhys Prize
Mind Book of the Year
The Natural World Book Prize
Northern Rock Foundation Writer's Award
The Portico Prize
The Rose Mary Crawshay Prizes
The Royal Society of Literature Award under the W.H. Heinemann Bequest
Runciman Award
Scottish Arts Council
Society for Theatre Research Book Prize
The Society of Authors and The Royal Society of Medicine Medical Book Awards
The Somerset Maugham Awards
The Sunday Times Young Writer of the Year Award

The Thomas Cook Travel Book Award
Trevor Reese Memorial Prize
The Whitfield Prize
WHSmith 'People's Choice' Awards
Yorkshire Post Book of the Year

Photography – see Visual art

Poetry

The Arts Council/An Chomhairle Ealaíon, Ireland
Arts Council England
Arvon Foundation International Poetry Competition
The Bridport Prize
Cardiff International Poetry Competition
Cholmondeley Awards
The David Cohen British Literature Prize
The David St John Thomas Charitable Trust Competitions & Awards
The Felicia Hemans Prize for Lyrical Poetry
Forward Poetry Prizes
The Geoffrey Faber Memorial Prize
Kent and Sussex Poetry Society Open Poetry Competition
London Arts
London Writers Competition
National Poetry Competition
The Nestlé Smarties Book Prize
The New Writer Prose and Poetry Prizes
Northern Rock Foundation Writer's Award
Peterloo Poets Open Poetry Competition
The Petra Kenney Poetry Competition
The Poetry Business Book & Pamphlet Competition
Poetry Life Open Poetry Competition
The Royal Society of Literature Award under the W.H. Heinemann Bequest
Runciman Award
Scottish Arts Council
The Somerset Maugham Awards
The T.S. Eliot Prize
The Trewithen Poetry Prize
Ver Poets Open Competition
The Welsh National Literature

Editorial, literary and production services by specialisation

Addresses for editorial, literary and production services start on page 553.

Complete editorial, literary and book production services

'A Feature Factory' Editorial Services
Academic File
Anchor Editorial Services
Anton Rippon Press Services
Book Production Consultants plc
Chase Publishing Services
D & N Publishing
Editorial Solutions
Geo Group & Associates
Graham-Cameron Publishing
Karyn Claridge Book Production
Keith Povey Editorial Services
Oxford Designers & Illustrators
Pages Editorial & Publishing Services
Pagewise
WordWise

Advisory and consultancy services, critical assessments, reports

Academic File
Advice and Criticism Service
Amolibros
Angel Books
Arkst Publishing
Authors' Advisory Service
Authors' Aid
Authors Appraisal Service
C.N. Gilmore
Christopher Pick
Cornerstones & Kids' Corner Ltd
Duncan McAra
E.J. Hunter
Felicity Trotman
FJN Associates
Geo Group & Associates
Gordon R. Wainwright
Hans Zell, Publishing Consultant
Indexing Specialists (UK) Ltd
Ingrid Cranfield
Johnathon Clifford
Manuscript Appraisals

Ormrod Research Services
Reading and Righting (Robert Lambolle Services)
Rosemary Horstmann
S. Ribeiro, Literary Services
Sandhurst Editorial Consultants
Sandton Literary Agency
StorytrackS
Success Writing Bureau
Teral Research Services
The Literary Consultancy (TLC)
Wordwise
Write on...
The Writer's Helpline
The Writers' Exchange

Editing, copy-editing, proofreading

Aaron Editorial
Abbey Writing Services
Amolibros
Apple Pips Editing Services
Arkst Publishing
Authors' Aid
Barbara Cheney
Bernard Hawton
Beswick Writing Services
Black Ace Book Production
Blair Services
Brooke Projects
C.N. Gilmore
Christopher Pick
Combrógos
Mrs D. Buckmaster
Dr David A. Cross
David Price
David Winpenny
Derek Wilde
Duncan McAra
E.J. Hunter
Editorial Solutions
Editorial/Visual Research
Felicity Trotman
First Edition Translations Ltd
FJN Associates
Freelance Services
Mrs Gene M. Spencer
Geoffrey D. Palmer
Hans Zell, Publishing Consultant

Indexing Specialists (UK) Ltd
Ingrid Cranfield
John Button – Editorial Services
Josephine Curtis Editorial
Keith Povey Editorial Services
Lewis Esson Publishing
Lyn M. Taylor
McText
Manuscript Appraisals
Marlinoak
Meg Davies
My Word!
Nidaba Publishing Services
Northern Writers Advisory Services
Ormrod Research Services
OTS
Paul H. Niekirk
Peter Nickol
Phoenix 2
Plum Communications
Reading and Righting (Robert Lambolle Services)
Richard A. Beck
Richard M. Wright
Rita Winter Editorial Services
S. Ribeiro, Literary Services
Sandhurst Editorial Consultants
Sandton Literary Agency
SciText
Small Print
Strand Editorial Services
the Freelance Editorial Service
Victoria Ramsay
The Writer's Helpline
The Writers' Exchange

Design, typing, word processing, DTP, book production

'A Feature Factory' Editorial Services
Arioma Editorial Services
Authors' Aid
Barbara Cheney
Black Ace Book Production
Book-in-Hand Ltd
Christine Foley Secretarial Services

Editorial Solutions
First Edition Translations Ltd
FJN Associates
Freelance Services
Hurst Village Publishing
Marlinoak
My Word!
Nidaba Publishing Services
Northern Writers Advisory
  Services
Oriental Languages Bureau
Peter Nickol
Phoenix 2
Shelagh Furness
Small Print
Special Edition Pre-press Services
Tecmedia Ltd
Vanessa Charles
The Writer's Helpline
The Writers' Exchange

Research and/or writing, rewriting, picture research

'A Feature Factory' Editorial
  Services
Aaron Editorial
Abbey Writing Services
Academic File
AFI Research (Richard M.
  Bennett Media)
Anton Rippon Press Services
Antony Hemans
Arioma Editorial Services
Authors' Research Services
Beswick Writing Services
Blair Services
Brooke Projects
Caroline White
Causeway Resources
Christopher Pick
Combrógos
Dr David A. Cross
David L. Williams
David Price
David Winpenny
Editorial Solutions
Editorial/Visual Research
Elizabeth Murray
Felicity Trotman
Freelance Services
Mrs Gene M. Spencer
Geo Group & Associates
Gill Shepherd

Gordon R. Wainwright
Hans Zell, Publishing Consultant
The Information Bureau
Ingrid Cranfield
Dr Kenneth Lysons
Lewis Esson Publishing
Library Research Agency
Manuscript Appraisals
Murder Files
Ormrod Research Services
Paul H. Niekirk
Phoenix 2
Picture Research Agency
Plum Communications
Repertoire
Rich Research
Richard A. Beck
S. Ribeiro, Literary Services
Sandhurst Editorial Consultants
Sandton Literary Agency
Shelagh Furness
Small Print
Teral Research Services
Victoria Ramsay
Wordwise
The Writers' Exchange

Indexing

David L. Williams
Geoffrey D. Palmer
Indexing Specialists (UK) Ltd
Ingrid Cranfield
Janet McKerron
Keith Povey Editorial Services
Meg Davies
Ormrod Research Services
Paul Nash
Richard A. Beck
Richard M. Wright
Sandton Literary Agency
Society of Indexers
the Freelance Editorial Service
WordWise

Translations

First Edition Translations Ltd
Ingrid Cranfield
Oriental Languages Bureau
Small Print
the Freelance Editorial Service

Specialist services

Archives

Hans Tasiemka Archives
The Information Bureau
John Vickers
Murder Files
Nielsen BookData Ltd

Cartography

Reginald Piggott

Cassettes, visual aids

OTS
Repertoire
Small Print

Contracts and copyright services

Geoffrey D. Palmer
Peter Nickol

Interpreting

First Edition Translations Ltd

Legal services

David Wineman, Solicitors
Finers Stephens Innocent

Media and publicity services

Freelance Market News
Nielsen BookData Ltd
Plum Communications
Rosemary Dooley

Multimedia/websites/ internet/database services

AuthorsOnLine Ltd
Editorial Solutions
Hans Zell, Publishing Consultant
McText
My Word!
Nielsen BookData Ltd
Peter Nickol
Thoughtbubble Ltd
WordWise

Index